Microsoft® Office Word 2010

A Lesson Approach, Complete

Microsoft® Office Word 2010

A Lesson Approach, Complete

Deborah Hinkle

The McGraw-Hill Companies

MICROSOFT® OFFICE WORD 2010: A LESSON APPROACH, COMPLETE

Published by McGraw-Hill, a business unit of The McGraw-Hill Companies, Inc., 1221 Avenue of the Americas, New York, NY, 10020.

This book is printed on acid-free paper.

3 4 5 6 7 8 9 0 RMN/RMN 1 0 9 8 7 6 5 4 3 2

ISBN 978-0-07-351929-6
MHID 0-07-351929-4

Vice president/Editor in chief: *Elizabeth Haefele*
Vice president/Director of marketing: *John E. Biernat*
Executive editor: *Scott Davidson*
Developmental editor: *Alan Palmer*
Marketing manager: *Tiffany Wendt*
Lead digital product manager: *Damian Moshak*
Digital development editor: *Kevin White*
Director, Editing/Design/Production: *Jess Ann Kosic*
Lead project manager: *Rick Hecker*
Buyer II: *Sherry L. Kane*
Senior designer: *Marianna Kinigakis*
Media project manager: *Cathy L. Tepper*
Interior design: *Kay Lieberherr*
Typeface: *10.5/13 New Aster*
Compositor: *Aptara®, Inc.*
Printer: *R. R. Donnelley*

Library of Congress Cataloging-in-Publication Data

Hinkle, Deborah A.
Microsoft Office Word 2010 : a lesson approach, complete / Deborah Hinkle.
p. cm.
Includes index.
ISBN-13: 978-0-07-351929-6 (spiral-bound : acid-free paper)
ISBN-10: 0-07-351929-4 (spiral-bound : acid-free paper)
1. Microsoft Word. 2. Word processing. I. Title.
Z52.5.M52H564 2011
005.52—dc22

2010015017

www.mhhe.com

CONTENTS

WORD

Unit 1 *Basic Skills*

UNIT 2 *Paragraph Formatting, Tabs, and Advanced Editing*

UNIT 3 *Page Formatting*

UNIT 5 *Graphics and Charts*

UNIT 6 *Advanced Topics*

UNIT 7 *Long Documents and Document Sharing*

PREFACE

Microsoft Word 2010: A Lesson Approach is written to help you master Microsoft Word. The text guides you step by step through the Word features that you are likely to use in both your personal and business life.

Case Study

Learning the features of Word is one component of the text, and applying what you learn is another component. A case study was created to offer the opportunity to learn Word in a realistic business context. Take the time to read the case study about Campbell's Confections, a fictional business located in Grove City, Pennsylvania. All the documents for this course relate to Campbell's Confections.

Organization of the Text

The text includes seven units, and each unit is divided into lessons. There are twenty-four lessons, each self-contained but building on previously learned procedures. This building-block approach, together with the case study and the following features, enables you to maximize the learning process.

Features of the Text

- Objectives are listed for each lesson.
- The estimated time required to complete each lesson up to the Summary section is stated.
- Within a lesson, each heading corresponds to an objective.
- Easy-to-follow exercises emphasize learning by doing.
- Key terms are italicized and defined as they are encountered.
- Extensive graphics display screen contents.
- Ribbon commands and keyboard keys are shown in the text when used.
- Lessons contain important notes, useful tips, and helpful reviews.
- The Lesson Summary reviews the important concepts taught in the lesson.
- The Command Summary lists the commands taught in the lesson.
- Concepts Review includes true-false, short answer, and critical thinking questions that focus on lesson content.
- Skills Review provides skill reinforcement for each lesson.
- Lesson Applications apply your skills in a more challenging way.
- On Your Own exercises apply your skills creatively.
- Unit Applications give you the opportunity to practice the skills you learn throughout a unit.
- The appendixes include "Proofreaders' Marks" and "Standard Forms for Business Documents." Also included are a glossary and an index. An Appendix of Microsoft's Certification standards is also available on the OLC at www.mhhe.com/lessonapproach2010.

Lesson Approach Web Site

Visit the Lesson Approach Web site at www.mhhe.com/lessonapproach2010 to access a wealth of additional materials.

Conventions Used in the Text

This text uses a number of conventions to help you learn the program and save your work.

- Text to be keyed appears either in **red** or as a separate figure.
- File names appear in **boldface**.
- Options that you choose from tabs and dialog boxes, but that aren't buttons, appear in **green**; for example, "Choose **Print** from the File tab."
- You are asked to save each document with your initials followed by the exercise name. For example, an exercise might end with this instruction: "Save the document as ***[your initials]*****4-12**." Documents are saved in folders for each lesson.

If You Are Unfamiliar with Windows

If you are not familiar with Windows, review the next section "Windows Tutorial" before beginning Lesson 1. This tutorial provides a basic overview of Microsoft's operating system and shows you how to use the mouse. You might also want to review "File Management" on the Lesson Approach Web site to get more comfortable with files and folders.

Screen Differences

As you practice each concept, illustrations of the screens help you follow the instructions. Don't worry if your screen is different from the illustration. These differences are due to variations in system and computer configurations.

You will need Microsoft Word 2010 to work through this textbook. Word 2010 needs to be installed on the computer's hard drive or on a network.

WINDOWS TUTORIAL

If you are not familiar with Windows, review this "Windows Tutorial" carefully. You will learn how to:

- Use a mouse.
- Start Windows and explore window features.
- Use the taskbar, menus, Ribbon, dialog boxes, and other important aspects of Windows.
- Practice using Search and Help.
- End a computer session.

If you are familiar with Windows but need help navigating Windows files and folders, refer to the "File Management" tutorial. There you will find information on how Windows stores information and how to use Windows Explorer, a tool for managing files and folders.

Computers differ in the ways they can be configured. In most cases, when you turn on your computer, Windows loads automatically and the Windows log-on screen appears. When you see the Windows log-on screen, you need to log on and key a password. In order to log on, you need to know how to use the mouse.

Using the Mouse

A *mouse* is a pointing device and is your access to the computer screen, allowing you to accomplish specific tasks. A mouse typically has two buttons—one on the left (primary) and one on the right (secondary). A mouse might also have a center button or a wheel. To use a mouse, place your right index finger over the left mouse button. Place your thumb on the left side of the mouse. (Left-handed users can switch mouse button functions by using the Control Panel.)

NOTE

Laptop computers typically use a touch pad to select or move objects rather than a mouse.

The mouse operates through a pointer, a screen object you use to point to objects on the computer screen. The normal shape for the mouse pointer is an arrow . To move the pointer arrow on the screen, you roll the mouse on any flat object, or on a mouse pad, which has a smooth surface designed for easy mouse rolling. Although you can use the keyboard with Windows, you will probably find yourself using the mouse most of the time.

To use the mouse to point to an object on the computer screen:

1. Turn on the computer (if it is not on already). Windows loads, and the log-on screen appears. The screen includes at least one log-on name and picture. If the computer has multiple users, you will see several names and pictures.

To log on, you need to move the mouse pointer to the log-on name that was assigned to you when your user account was created. The pointer on the computer screen mirrors the actions made by the mouse when you roll it. Place your hand over the mouse and roll it to the left. The pointer on the screen moves to the left.

NOTE

All examples in this tutorial refer specifically to Windows 7 using the Aero desktop feature. If you are using any other version of Windows, your screen might differ slightly from the images shown in this tutorial. However, because most basic features are common to all versions of Windows, this tutorial should be helpful to you no matter which version of Windows you use.

2. Roll the mouse to the right, and watch the pointer on the screen move to the right.
3. Practice rolling the mouse in all directions.
4. Roll your mouse to the edge of the pad, and then lift it up and place it back in the middle of the pad. When you feel that you can control the mouse position on the screen, roll the mouse to the name you have been assigned.

To log on, you will need to click the name to select it. Mouse clicks are covered in the next section; instructions for logging on to Windows 7 are covered in succeeding sections.

Clicks and Double-Clicks

Pointing is a mouse action used to position the mouse pointer at a specific screen location. The tip of the mouse pointer should be touching the object on the screen. You may see a ScreenTip when you point to an object. A *ScreenTip* identifies or describes the object or command.

Figure 1
ScreenTip

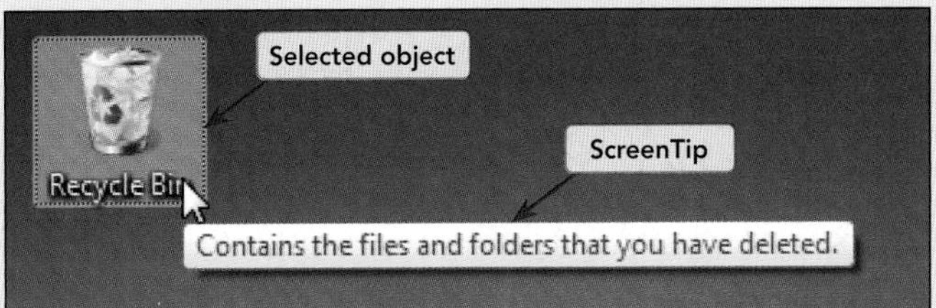

Single-click actions with the mouse are used to select objects or commands. To practice a single click:

1. Roll the mouse around on the mouse pad until the pointer on the screen is over the Recycle Bin icon. Remember that the direction in which you move the mouse on the pad represents the pointer's movement on the screen.
2. Press and release the left mouse button once. Pressing and releasing the mouse button is referred to as a *click*. The computer tells you that the action has been performed when the object you click is *highlighted* (typically, the color of the selected object changes) to indicate to you that it has been *selected*. In Windows, you often need to select an object before you can perform an action. For example, you usually need to select an object before you can copy it. Click a blank area of the computer screen to deselect the Recycle Bin icon.

Pressing and releasing the mouse button twice is referred to as a *double-click*. When you double-click an object on the screen, it is selected—the object is highlighted—and an action is performed. For example:

When you double-click a folder, it is highlighted and opens to a window showing the items the folder contains.

When you double-click a word in a text file, it is selected for a future action. In a text file, the pointer becomes an I-beam for selecting text in the document.

1. Point to and double-click the Recycle Bin icon. The Recycle Bin window displays.

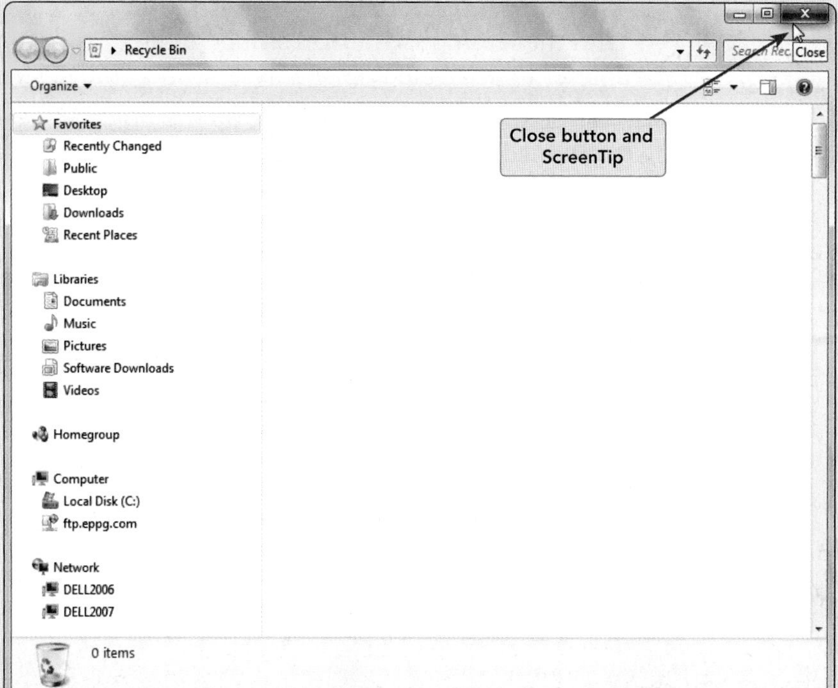

Figure 2
Recycle Bin window

2. Locate and point to the red button in the upper-right corner of the Recycle Bin window. A ScreenTip identifies the Close button.
3. Click the Close button one time to close the Recycle Bin window.

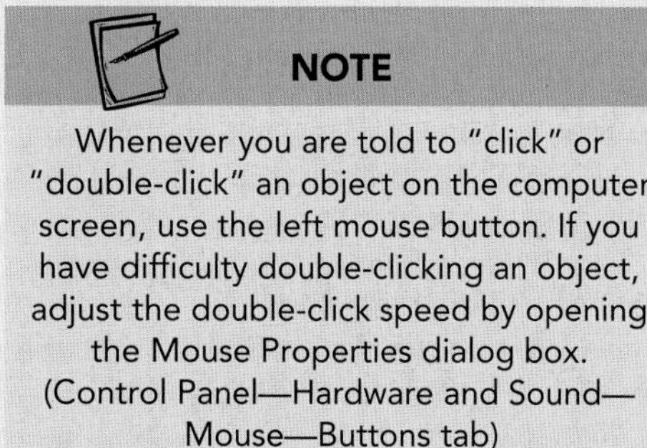

NOTE
Whenever you are told to "click" or "double-click" an object on the computer screen, use the left mouse button. If you have difficulty double-clicking an object, adjust the double-click speed by opening the Mouse Properties dialog box. (Control Panel—Hardware and Sound—Mouse—Buttons tab)

Selecting and Highlighting

You can also select a larger object such as a picture or a block of text by using the mouse. Position the pointer on one side of the object, and hold down the left mouse button. Roll the mouse until the pointer reaches the other side of the object. Release the mouse button. The selected object is highlighted.

Drag and Drop—Moving an Object Using the Mouse

You can use the mouse to move an object on the screen to another screen location. In this operation, you select an object and drag the mouse to move the selected object, such as an icon. The operation is known as *drag and drop.* Follow the steps listed below to drag and drop objects.

1. Using the mouse, move the pointer over the object you want to drag.
2. Press the left mouse button but keep it pressed down. The selected object will be highlighted.
3. With the left mouse button still depressed, roll the mouse until the pointer and selected object are placed at the desired new location.
4. Release the mouse button to drop the object. The object is now positioned at the new location.

Using the Right Mouse Button

Pressing and quickly releasing the right mouse button is referred to as a *right-click*. Although the right mouse button is used less frequently, using it can be a real time-saver. When you right-click an icon, a *shortcut menu* appears with a list of commands. The list of commands displayed varies for each icon or object.

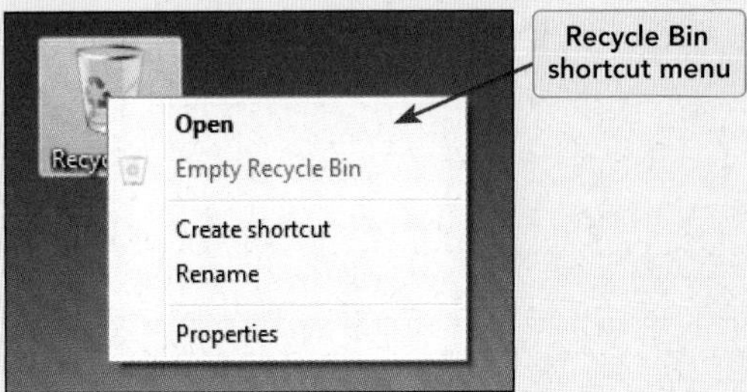

Figure 3 Shortcut menu

As you progress in this tutorial, you will become familiar with the terms in Table 1, describing the actions you can take with a mouse.

TABLE 1 Mouse Terms

TERM	DESCRIPTION
Point	Roll the mouse until the tip of the pointer is touching the desired object on the computer screen.
Click	Quickly press and release the left mouse button. Single-clicking selects objects.
Double-click	Quickly press and release the left mouse button twice. Double-clicking selects an object and performs an action such as opening a folder.
Drag	Point to an object on-screen, hold down the left mouse button, and roll the mouse until the pointer is in position. Then release the mouse button (drag and drop).
Right-click	Quickly press and release the right mouse button. A shortcut menu appears.
Select	When working in Windows, you must first select an object in order to work with it. Many objects are selected with a single click. However, depending on the size and type of object to be selected, you may need to roll the mouse to include an entire area: Holding down the left mouse button, roll the mouse so that the pointer moves from one side of an object to another. Then release the mouse button.

Pointer Shapes

As you perform actions on screen using the mouse, the mouse pointer changes its shape, depending on where it is located and what operation you are performing. Table 2 shows the most common types of mouse pointers.

TABLE 2 Frequently Used Mouse Pointers

SHAPE	NAME	DESCRIPTION
	Pointer	Used to point to objects.
	I-Beam	Used in keying text, inserting text, and selecting text.
	Two-headed arrow	Used to change the size of objects or windows.
	Four-headed arrow	Used to move objects.
	Busy	Indicates the computer is processing a command. While the busy or working in background pointer is displayed, it is best to wait rather than try to continue working. Note: Some of the working in background actions will not allow you to perform other procedures until processing is completed.
	Working in background	
	Link Select	Used to select a *link* in Windows' Help or other programs.

Starting Windows: The Log-on Screen

The Windows 7 log-on screen allows several people to use the same computer at different times. Each person is assigned a user account that determines which files and folders can be accessed and personal preferences, such as your desktop background. Each person's files are hidden from other users. However, users may share selected files using the Public folder. The log-on screen lists each user allocated to the computer by name.

If the administrator has added your name to a given computer, the log-on screen will include your name. If the computers are not assigned to specific individuals, you may find a box for Guest or for a generic user. If your computer is on a network, your instructor might need to provide you with special start-up instructions.

After you have logged on to Windows 7, the *desktop* is the first screen you will see. It is your on-screen work area. All the elements you need to start working with Windows appear on the desktop.

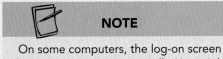

NOTE

On some computers, the log-on screen does not appear automatically. You might have to press the following keys, all at once, and then quickly release them: Ctrl+Alt+Delete.

1. If you have not already turned on the computer, do so now to begin the Windows 7 loading process. The Windows log-on screen appears.
2. Click your name to select it. The Password box appears with an I-beam in position ready for you to key your password.
3. Key your password.
4. Click the arrow icon to the right of the box. If you have entered the password correctly, the Windows desktop appears. If you made an error, the Password box returns for you to key the correct password.

The Windows Desktop

The Windows Desktop includes the Start button, taskbar, and Notification area. You may also see icons on the desktop that represent folders, programs, or other objects. You can add and delete icons from the desktop as well as change the desktop background. The Start button is your entry into Windows 7 functions.

Figure 4
Windows 7 Desktop

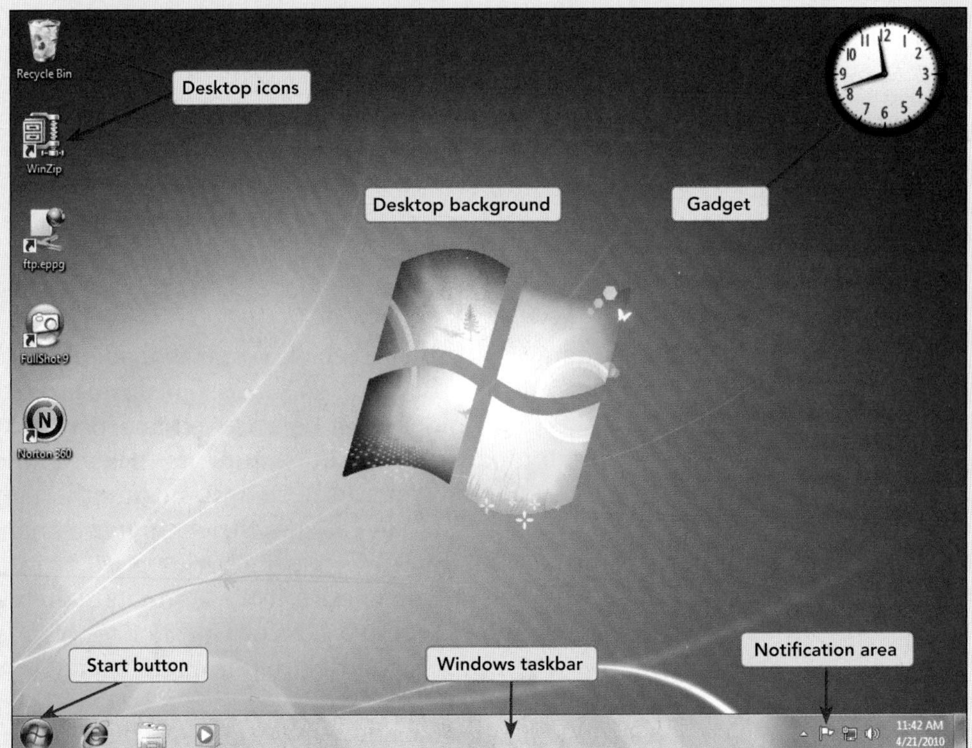

Using the Start Menu

Click the Start button on the Windows taskbar to open the Start menu. You can also press the Windows logo key on the keyboard or press Ctrl+Esc to open the Start menu. Use the Start menu to launch programs, adjust computer settings, search for files and folders, and turn off the computer. If this is a computer assigned to you for log-on, your Start menu may contain items that differ from those of another user assigned to the same computer

1. To open and learn about the Start menu, first click the Start button on the Windows taskbar. The Start menu appears.

Figure 5
Start menu

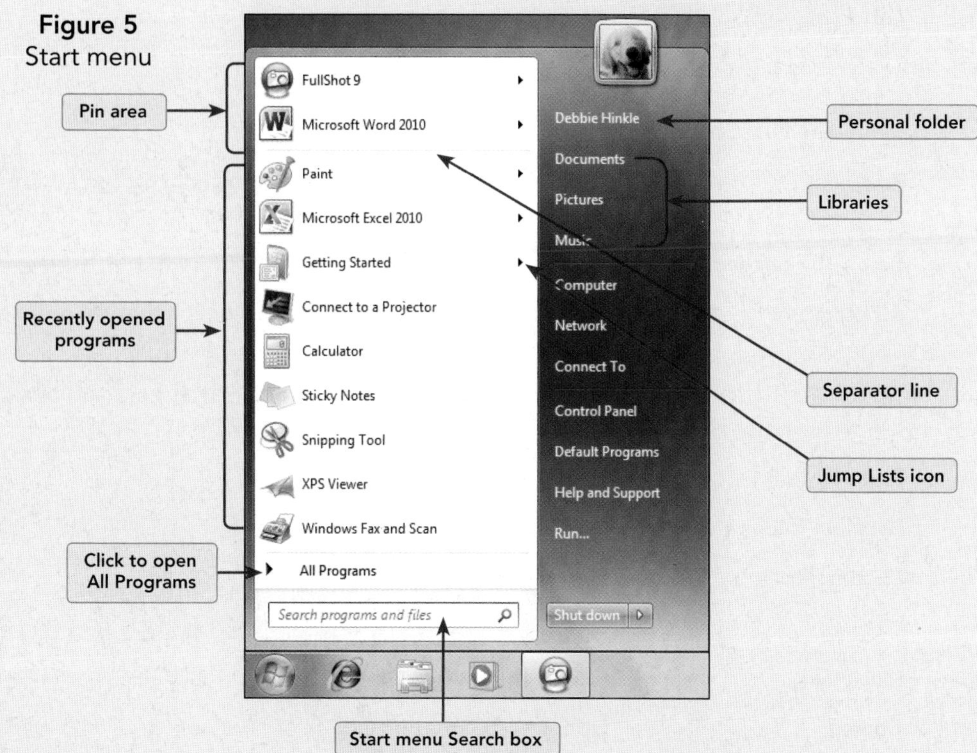

The left pane consists of three sections divided by separator lines. The top section, called the *pin area*, lists programs that are always available for you to open. These programs can include your Internet browser, e-mail program, your word processor, and so forth. You can remove programs you do not want listed, rearrange them, and add those you prefer.

Below the separator line are shortcuts to programs you use most often, placed there automatically by Windows. You can remove programs you do not want listed, rearrange them, but not add any manually. The Recently opened programs list displays up to ten programs. Use the Jump Lists icon ▸ for quick access to documents, files, or tasks. Simply click the Jump Lists icon ▸, and a submenu appears to the right of the Start menu program. *All Programs* displays a list of programs on your computer and is used to launch programs not listed on the Start menu.

> **NOTE**
>
> The list of programs in your Start menu is dynamic. Installing new programs adds new items to the Start menu. Frequently used programs are placed in the left pane of the Start menu automatically.

Below the left pane is the *Search box,* which is used to locate programs and files on your computer.

The right pane is also divided into three sections. It is used to select folders, files, and commands and to change settings. Use the Shut down button at the bottom of the right pane to end the computer session.

2. Close the Start menu by clicking a blank area of the desktop.

Table 3 describes the typical components of the Start menu.

TABLE 3 Typical Components of the Start Menu

COMMAND	USE
Left Pane	
Pin area	Lists programs that are always available. You can add and delete items to the pin area.
Below the First Separator Line	
Programs	Lists programs that you use most often. You can add to and rearrange the programs listed.
Below the Second Separator Line	
All Programs	Click to display a list of programs in alphabetical order and a list of folders. Click to open a program.
Search	Use to search programs and folders. Key text and results appear.
Right Pane	
Personal folder	Opens the User folder.
Documents	Opens the Documents library.
Pictures	Opens the Pictures library.
Music	Opens the Music library.
Games	Opens the Games library.
Computer	Opens a window where you can access disk drives and other hardware devices.
Network	Opens the Network window where you can access computers and other devices on your network.
Connect To	Displays networks and other connections that you can access.
Control Panel	Opens the Control Panel.
Devices and Printers	Opens a window where you can view devices installed on your computer.
Default Programs	Opens the Default Programs window where you can define default programs and settings.
Help and Support	Opens the Windows Help and Support window. Help offers instructions on how to perform tasks in the Windows environment.
Run	Opens a program, folder, document, or Web site.
Shut down button	Turns off the computer.

Using the All Programs Command

Most programs on your computer can be started from the All Programs command on the Start menu. This is the easiest way to open a program not listed directly on the Start menu.

1. To open the All Programs menu, click the Start button. The Start menu appears.
2. Click **All Programs** or the triangle to the left near the bottom of the left pane. The All Programs menu appears, listing the programs installed on your computer. Every computer has a different list of programs. Notice that some menu entries have an icon to the left of the name and others display a folder. Click a folder, and a list of programs stored in that folder appears. Point to a program to see a short description of the program. Click a program to open it.

Figure 6
All Programs

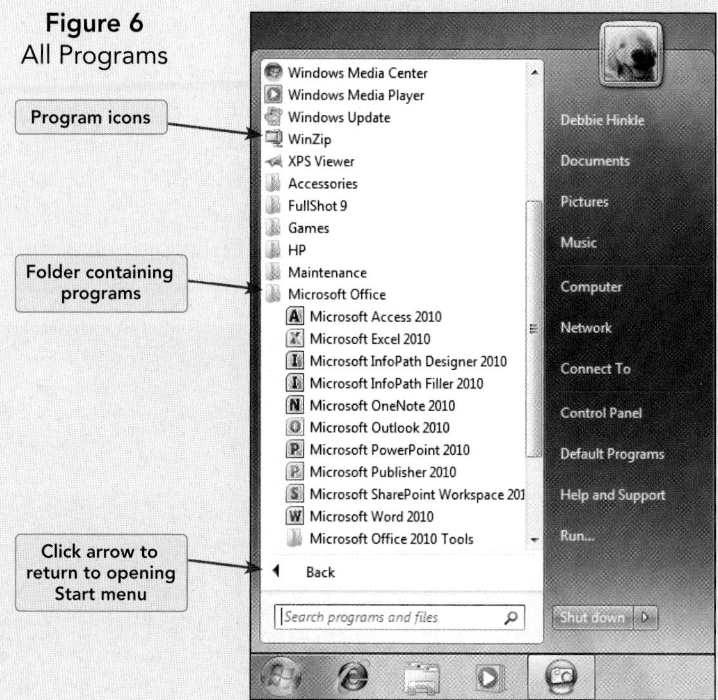

3. Click **Microsoft Office** to open a list of programs in the Microsoft Office folder. Click **Microsoft Word 2010**. (See Figure 6.) In a few seconds, the Word program you selected loads and the Word window appears. Notice that a button for the Word program appears on the taskbar. Press Alt+F4 to close the window.

Customizing the Start Menu

Both the Start menu and the desktop can be customized. You can add shortcuts to the desktop if you prefer, and you can add and delete items from the Start menu. However, if your computer is used by others, the administrator may limit some customization functions.

To add a program to the pin area of the Start menu:

1. Point to the program you want to add to the pin list from the All Programs menu, and right-click it. A shortcut menu appears.
2. Click **Pin To Start Menu** on the shortcut menu. The program will be added to the pin list in the left pane above the first separator line.

To remove a program from the pin area of the Start menu:

1. Point to the program you want to remove from the pin list, and right-click. A shortcut menu appears.
2. Click **Unpin From Start Menu**. The program will be removed from the pin list.

To change the order in which programs are listed in the pin area:

1. Point to the program icon.
2. Drag the icon to the desired position.

Using the Taskbar

The taskbar at the bottom of your screen is one of the most important features in Windows 7. The taskbar is divided into several segments, each dedicated to a different use. The taskbar displays a button for launching Internet Explorer, Windows Explorer, and Windows Media Player, and each of these buttons is pinned to the taskbar. Point to each button to display a ScreenTip. The taskbar shows programs that are running, and you can use the taskbar to switch between open programs and between open documents within a program. A thumbnail preview appears when you move the mouse over a button on the taskbar.

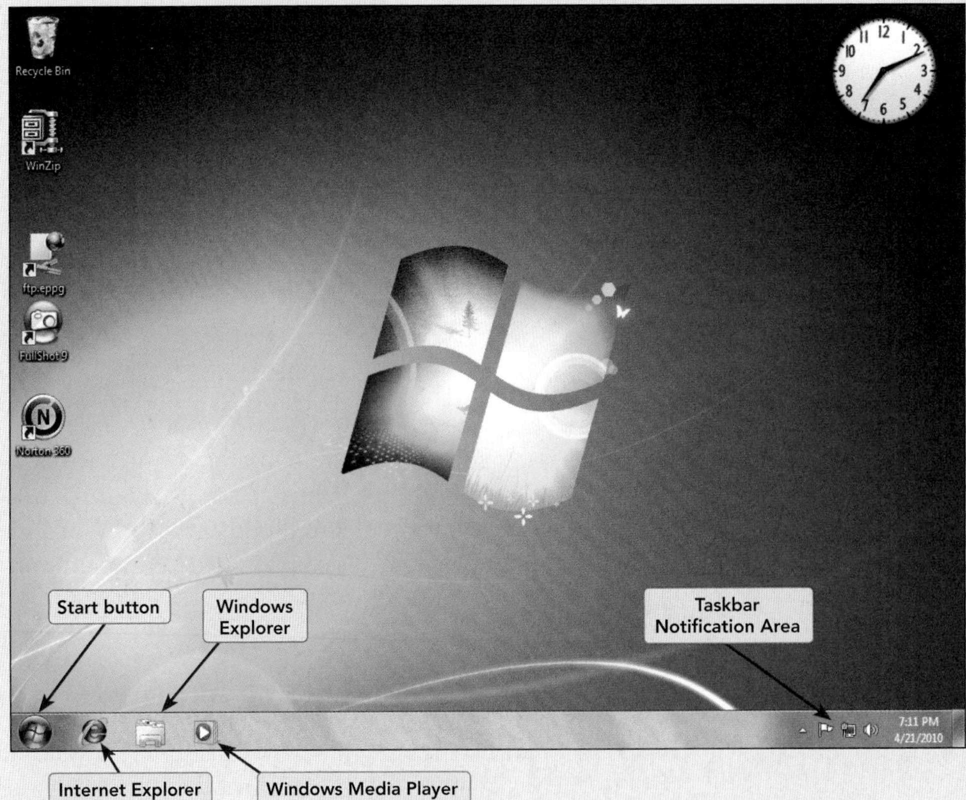

Figure 7 The desktop and the taskbar

Taskbar Notification Area

The *notification area* is on the right side of the taskbar, where the current time is usually displayed. Along with displaying the time, tiny icons notify you as to the status of your browser connection, virus protection, and so forth. In the interest of removing clutter, the notification area hides most of the icons. Clicking the Show Hidden Icons button "hides" or "unhides" the icons in the notification area. Point to an icon to see a ScreenTip. Click an icon to open the control or program.

The Taskbar Notification area also includes the Show Desktop button. The Show Desktop button appears at the right side of the taskbar. When you point to the Show Desktop button, the open program windows become transparent, and the desktop displays. The Show Desktop button is a toggle button. Click the Show Desktop button one time to minimize all open programs. Click again to display the programs. The *minimize* command temporarily removes a window from the desktop.

Figure 8
Taskbar Notification area

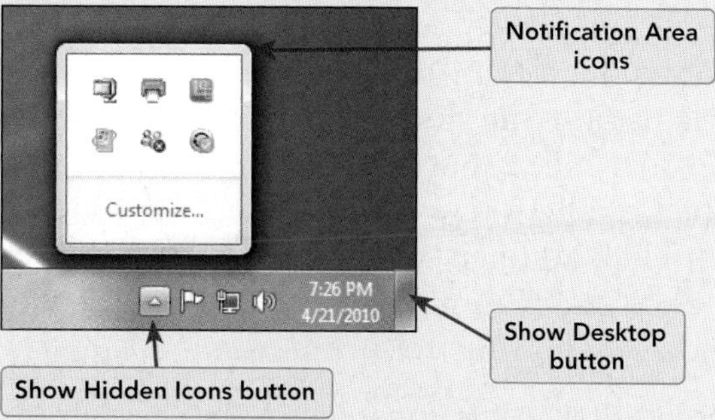

The Active Window

The window in which you are working is called the *active window*. The title bar for the active window is highlighted, and its taskbar button is also highlighted.

1. Click the **Start** button and then click **All Programs**, **Microsoft Office**, **Microsoft Word 2010** from the Start menu. The Word window displays.
2. Click the **Start** button and then click **All Programs, Microsoft Office, Microsoft Excel 2010** from the Start menu. The Excel window displays. Notice how the Excel window covers the Word window, indicating that the window containing Excel is now active. Notice, too, that a new button for Excel has been added to the taskbar.

Figure 9
Excel (the active window) covering the Word window

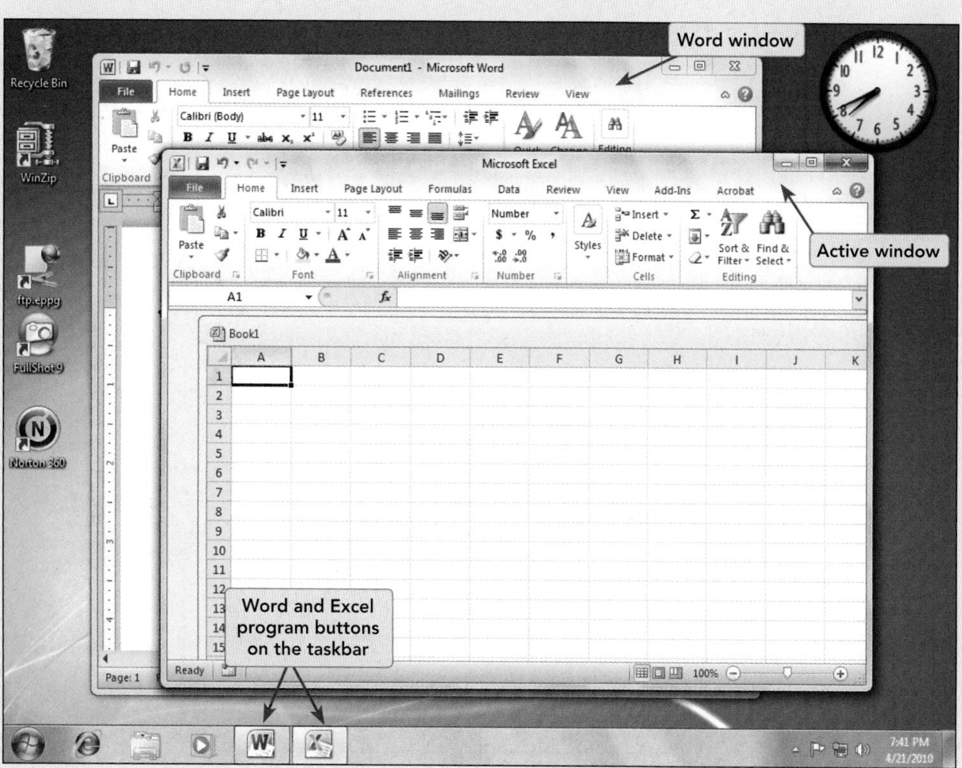

3. Click the button on the taskbar for Word, the first program you opened. Word reappears in front of Excel. Notice the change in the appearance of the title bar for each program.
4. Click the button on the taskbar for Excel. Notice that you switch back to Excel.
5. Click the Word button on the taskbar to return to Word.

Changing the Size of the Taskbar

You can change the size of the taskbar using your mouse if your toolbar is crowded. It is usually not necessary, because of the multiple document style buttons and other hide/unhide arrows on the taskbar. Before you can change the size of the taskbar, it may be necessary for you to unlock it. To unlock the taskbar, right-click an open area of the taskbar and click **Lock the Taskbar** to remove the checkmark. A checkmark is a toggle command. Click to turn it off, and click a second time to turn it on.

1. Move the pointer to the top edge of the taskbar until it changes from a pointer to a two-headed arrow ⇕. Using the two-headed arrow, you can change the size of the taskbar.
2. With the pointer displayed as a two-headed arrow, hold down the left mouse button and move the arrow up until the taskbar enlarges upward.
3. Move the pointer to the top edge of the taskbar once again until the two-headed arrow displays. Hold down the left mouse button, and move the arrow down to the bottom of the screen. The taskbar is restored to its original size.
4. Close the Word and Excel programs by clicking the Close button X for each program.

Parts of a Windows

Windows 7 displays programs and files in windows. When multiple windows display on the desktop, you will notice several common features in their appearance. Study the following windows and notice the similarities.

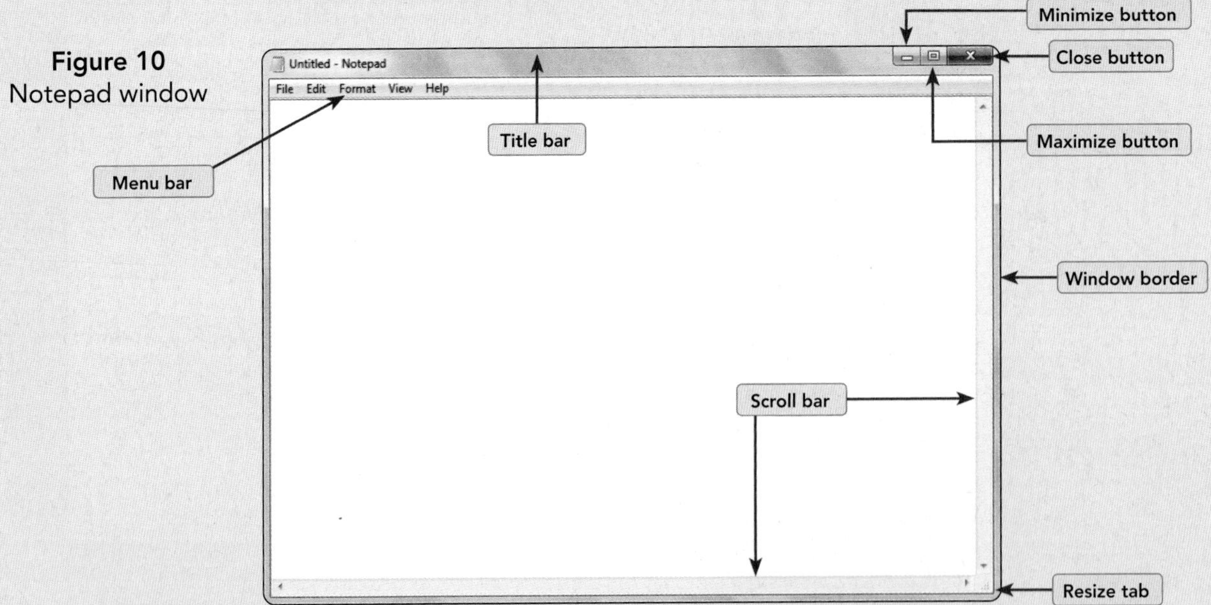

Figure 10
Notepad window

Figure 11 Microsoft Word window

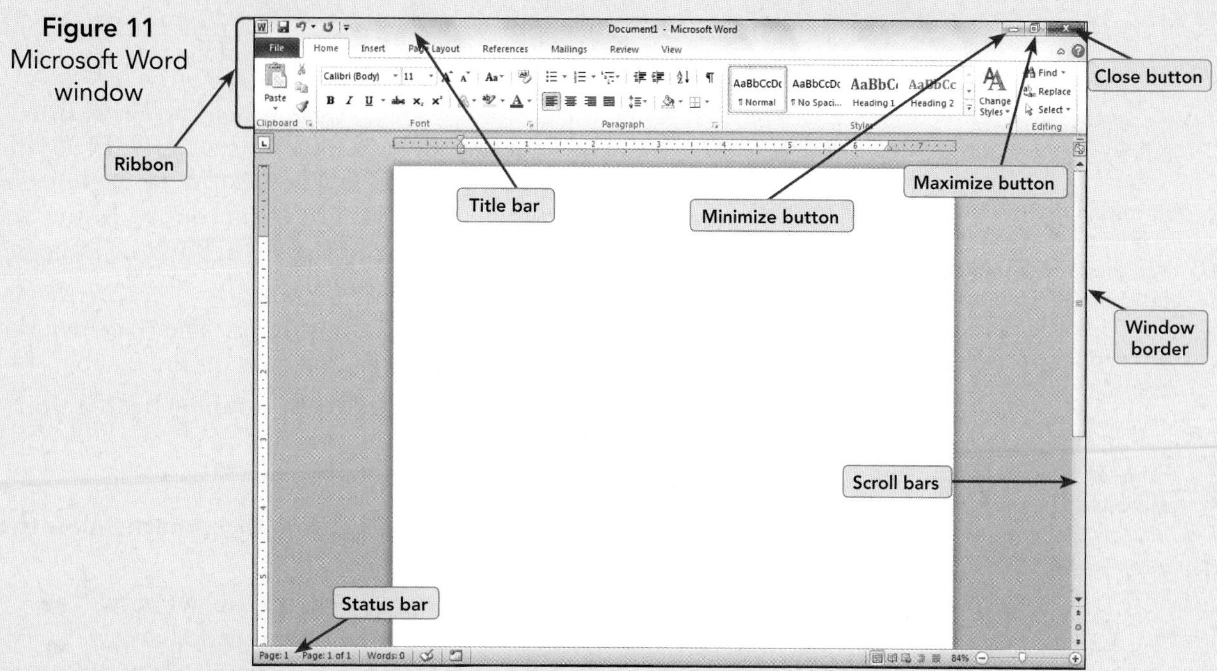

NOTE

Notice that the window occupies the entire desktop, and the Maximize button has changed to a Restore Down button. This type of function is known as a toggle: When a button representing one state (Maximize) is clicked, an action is performed, the button toggles to the alternate state, and the other button (Restore Down) appears. A number of actions in Windows operate this way.

Changing the Size of a Window

You can change the size of any window using either the mouse or the sizing buttons. Sizing buttons are the small buttons on the right side of the title bar that allow you to minimize or maximize the window (see Figures 10 and 11). This can be especially useful when you would like to display several open windows on your desktop and see them simultaneously.

1. Open the Word and Excel programs if necessary. Click the Maximize button on the Excel title bar if the Excel window does not fill the entire desktop.

Table 4 describes the sizing buttons.

TABLE 4 Sizing Buttons

BUTTON	USE
Minimize	Reduces the window to a button on the taskbar.
Maximize	Enlarges the window to fill the entire desktop (appears only when a window is reduced).
Restore Down	Returns the window to its previous size and desktop position (appears only when a window is maximized).

To practice changing the size of a window using the sizing buttons, follow these steps:

NOTE

You can double-click a window title bar to maximize or restore the window or right-click the program button on the taskbar and choose minimize, maximize, restore, or close. You can also use the *Shake* command to minimize every open window except the window you are "shaking." To use the shake feature, drag the title bar back and forth with your mouse until the other windows are minimized. You can also use the *Snap* feature to maximize a window. Point to the window's title bar and drag the window to the top of the screen. When the window's outline fills the screen, release the mouse.

2. Click the **Restore Down** button on the Excel title bar. The Excel window reduces in size, and the Word window appears behind it. The Restore Down button has now changed to a Maximize button. Notice that the highlighted title bar of the Excel window indicates it is the active window.
3. Click the Excel **Minimize** button. The Excel window disappears, and its button appears on the taskbar.
4. Maximize the Word window by double-clicking the title bar. Double-click the title bar again to restore the window.

To practice resizing a window using the mouse, follow these steps:

5. Point to the lower right corner of the window. The mouse pointer changes to a two-headed arrow. Drag the window border toward the center of the screen. Drag the window border down and to the right to enlarge the window.

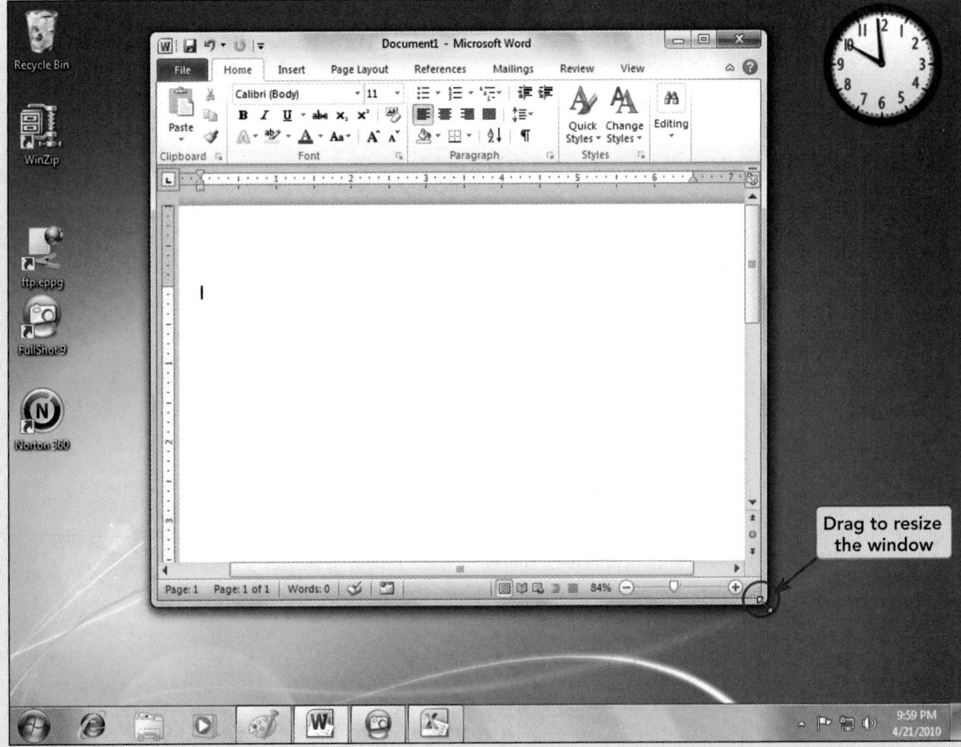

Figure 12 Sizing a window using the mouse

6. Point to the top border of the window. Drag the border down to reduce the height of the window.
7. Point to the right border of the window. Drag the border to the left to reduce the width of the window.
8. Drag the window to the top of the screen. When the window outline expands to fill the screen, release the mouse.

NOTE

You can place the pointer on any part of the window border to change its size. To change both the height and width of the window, move the pointer to the bottom right corner of the window. The double-headed arrow changes its orientation to a 45-degree angle (see Figure 12). Dragging this arrow resizes a window vertically and horizontally. Dragging a window border (top, bottom, left, or right) changes the vertical or horizontal size of the window. Sometimes the borders of a window can move off the computer screen. If you are having trouble with one border of a window, try another border or drag the entire window onto the screen by using the title bar.

Moving a Window

To move a window, point to the title bar and drag the window to a new location. You cannot move a maximized window.

1. Click the Word Restore Down button if necessary, and point to the Word title bar.
2. Drag the window to the lower left corner of the screen. Release the mouse.

Switch between Windows

When more than one program is open, you can switch between windows by using the sizing buttons or the taskbar. You can also press Alt+Tab to switch to the previous window.

1. If necessary, open Word and Excel, and maximize both windows.
2. Minimize the Excel window. The Word window displays.
3. Point to the Excel button on the taskbar. A thumbnail preview of the Excel window displays. If you point to the thumbnail, the thumbnail enlarges so that you can preview the window. This feature is called *Aero Peek*.

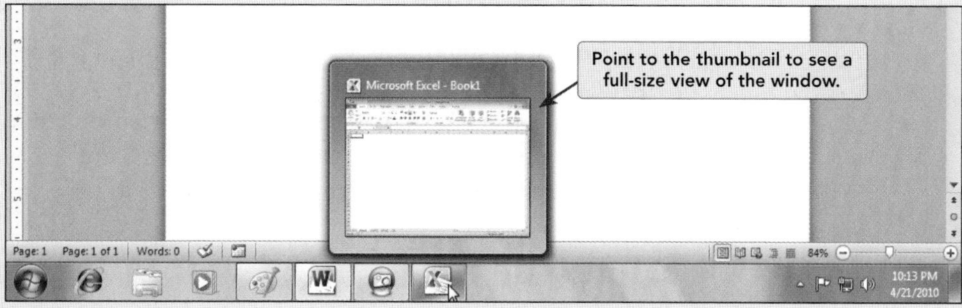

Figure 13
Taskbar buttons and thumbnail preview

4. Click the Excel button to display the Excel window and to make it the active window.
5. Press Alt+Tab to switch to Word. You can switch to the previous window by pressing this shortcut, or you can continue to press Tab to switch to an open window on the desktop.

NOTE

To display thumbnail preview, your computer must support the Windows Aero feature.

Display Two Program Windows Simultaneously

When multiple programs are open, you can arrange the windows using the following commands from the taskbar. You can also use the *Snap* feature to display two windows side by side on the desktop. To position two windows side by side, drag the title bar of one window to the left side of the screen until the window snaps to the left side. Release the mouse. Drag the second window to the right side of the screen until it snaps into place.

- Cascade windows
- Show windows stacked
- Show windows side-by-side
- Show the desktop

1. Open the Start menu, and display Excel and Word if necessary.
2. Right-click the taskbar, and click **Show windows side by side**. The windows display vertically.
3. Right-click the taskbar, and click **Cascade windows**. The windows display on top of each other. The title bar for each window is visible.
4. Click the Show Desktop button located on the right side of the taskbar to see the desktop. The Word and Excel programs are minimized.
5. Click the Show Desktop button again to restore the programs.
6. Right-click the taskbar, and click **Show windows stacked**. The windows are stacked vertically.
7. Click the **Close** button on the title bars of each of the two program windows to close them and to show the desktop.

Using Menus

When you open a window you may see a row of descriptive names just below the title bar. A menu bar contains a list of options for working with programs and documents. These operations are either mouse or keyboard driven. They are called commands because they "command" the computer to perform functions needed to complete the task you, the user, initiate at the menu level.

Executing a Command from a Menu

You open a menu by clicking the menu name listed in the menu bar. When a menu is opened, a list of command options appears. To execute a particular command from an open menu, press the left mouse button and then drag down and release the mouse (click and drag). You can also click the command once the menu is open.

Other Menu Symbols

Three dots following a menu option (an ellipsis . . .) indicate that a dialog box is displayed when that menu option is chosen. (Dialog boxes, discussed later, are small windows requesting and receiving input from a user.) Menus may also include a triangular arrow. Clicking the arrow displays a submenu with additional choices. If a menu command has a keyboard shortcut, the key or the combination of keys you press to activate the option appear on the right side of the menu. Commands that appear gray or dimmed are currently not available.

Figure 14
Notepad menu bar

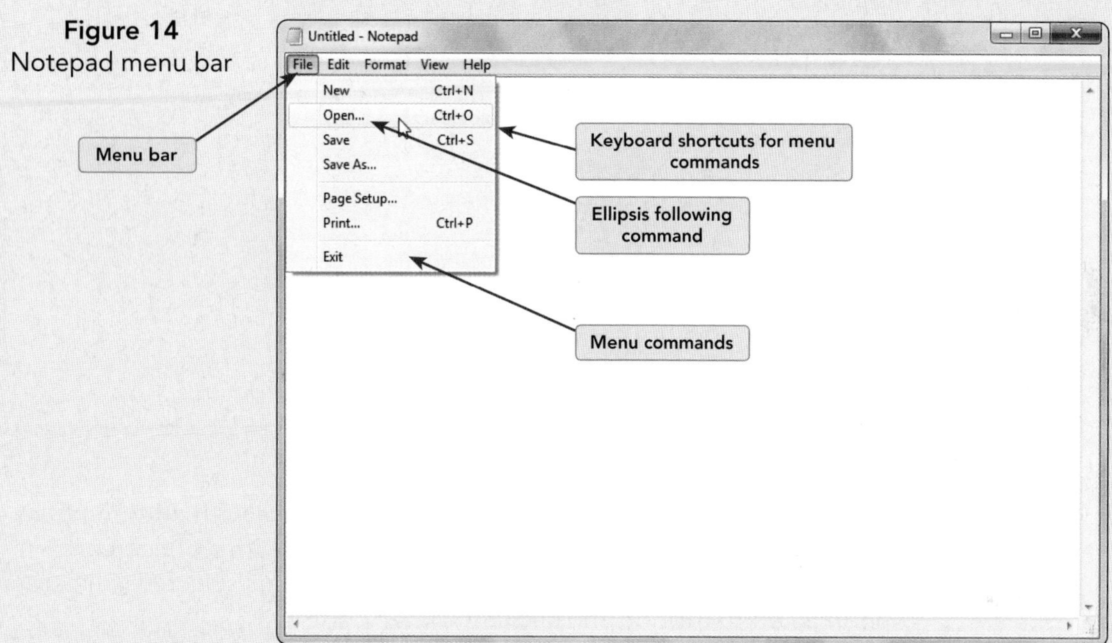

Perform the following steps for using menus:

1. Open the **Start menu**, click **All Programs**, and click the **Accessories** folder. Click **Notepad**. The Notepad program opens, and a button appears on the Windows taskbar.
2. Locate the menu bar, and click **File**. The File menu displays. Notice the keyboard shortcuts listed on the right side of the menu.
3. Locate the **Open** command and notice that three dots follow the command. Click the Open command. The Open dialog box displays. Click **Cancel** to close the Open dialog box.
4. Click **File** on the menu bar. Click **Exit** to close the Notepad window.
5. Click the Windows Explorer button on the taskbar. The Windows Explorer window displays.
6. Locate the Organize command Organize ▾, and click the button. A menu of options appears below the command button.

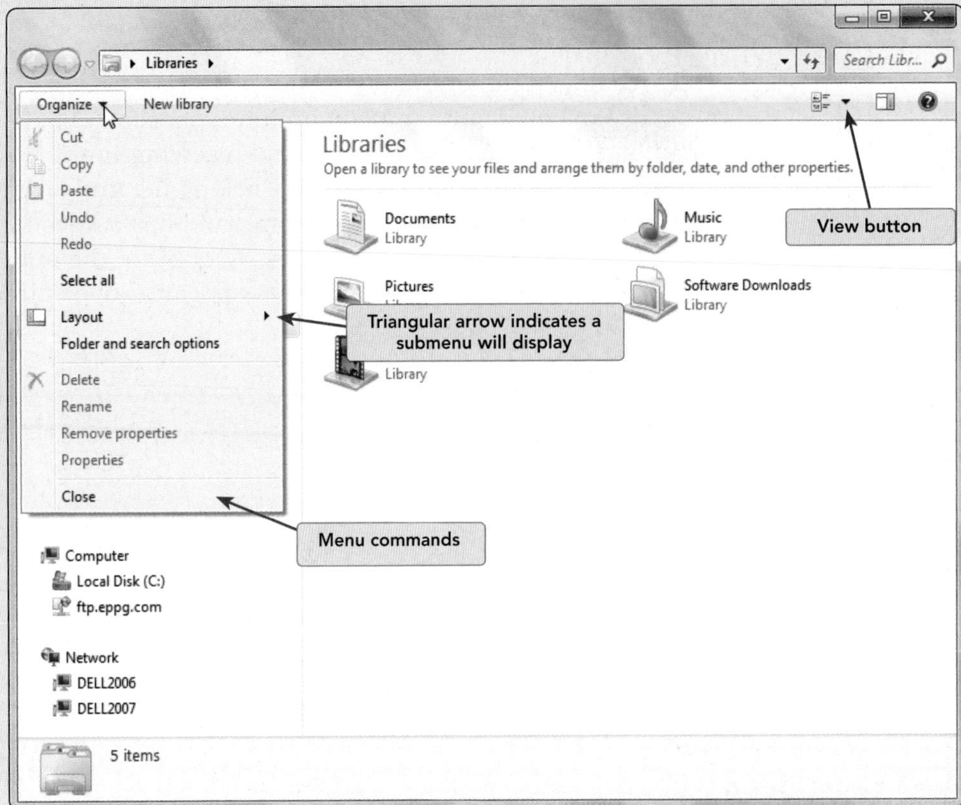

Figure 15 Windows Explorer window

7. Click the **Layout** command, and a submenu displays with additional options. Notice that several of the options appear with a checkmark. The checkmark option ✓ indicates that the option is selected. Click the option again to turn off the checkmark.
8. Locate the View button, and click the arrow beside the button. Drag the slider to **Medium Icons** and notice the change in the appearance of the icons in the Windows Explorer window.
9. Press the Alt key, and a traditional-looking menu bar appears. Press Alt again to hide the menu bar.
10. Press Alt+F4 to close the Windows Explorer window.

Displaying a Shortcut Menu

When the mouse pointer is on an object or an area of the Windows desktop and you right-click, a shortcut menu appears. A shortcut menu typically contains commands that are useful in working with the object or area of the desktop to which you are currently pointing.

1. Position the mouse pointer on a blank area of the desktop, and right-click. A shortcut menu appears with commands that relate to the desktop, including view and sort options.
2. Click outside the shortcut menu to close it.
3. Right-click the time in the bottom right corner of the taskbar. A shortcut menu appears.

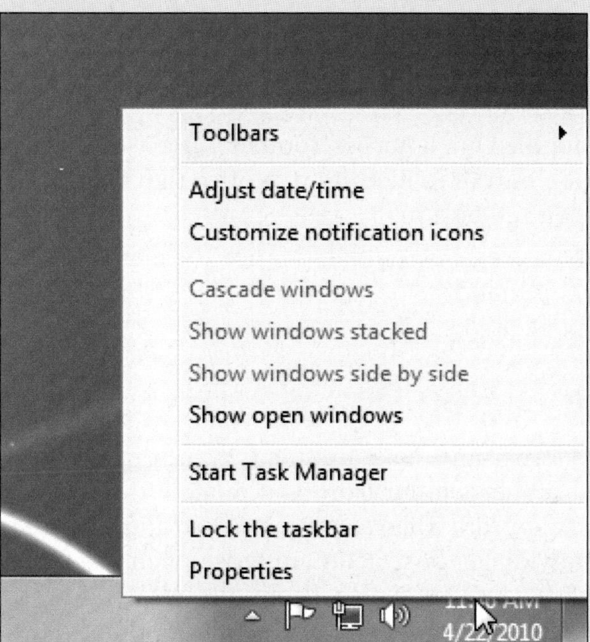

Figure 16
Time shortcut menu

4. Click **Adjust date/time** on the shortcut menu. The Date and Time dialog box appears. You can use this dialog box to adjust your computer's date and time.
5. Click **Cancel**.
6. Right-click an icon on the desktop to display its shortcut menu, and then close the shortcut menu.

Using the Ribbon and Quick Access Toolbar

Microsoft Office 2010 applications include a Quick Access Toolbar and a Ribbon to access commands. The *Quick Access Toolbar* contains frequently used commands and is positioned above the Ribbon. The *Ribbon* consists of tabs, and each tab contains a group of related commands. The number of commands for each tab varies. A command can be one of several formats. The most popular formats include buttons and drop-down lists. The *File tab* displays a menu which lists the commands to create, open, save, and print a document.

1. Open the Word program. The Quick Access Toolbar arrow should point to the Save button.

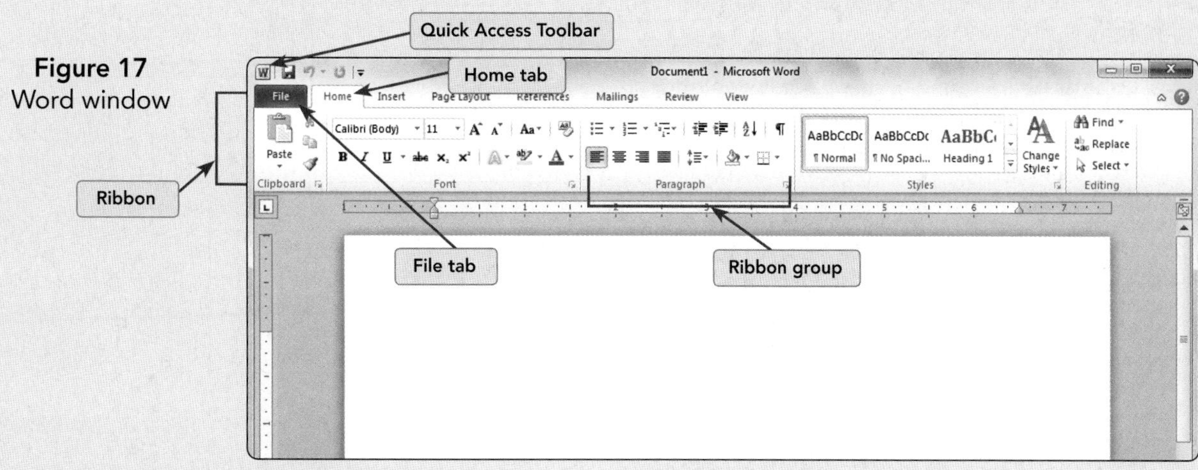

Figure 17
Word window

2. Point to and click the **File** tab. Notice the commands in the left pane.
3. Click the **Home** tab, and locate the groups of commands on the Home tab (Clipboard, Font, Paragraph, Styles, and Editing).
4. Locate the Quick Access Toolbar above the Ribbon. Point to each button to identify it. Notice that a keyboard shortcut displays beside each button.
5. Click the **Page Layout** tab. Notice the change in the number of groups and commands.
6. Click the **Home** tab.

Using Dialog Boxes

Windows programs make frequent use of dialog boxes. A *dialog box* is a window that requests input from you related to a command you have chosen. A dialog box appears when a command listed in a menu is followed by an ellipsis (. . .). Many dialog boxes contain tabs which resemble file folder tabs. Click a tab to select it and to display its options. All Windows programs use a common dialog box structure. Table 5 lists several options you will see in dialog boxes.

TABLE 5 Dialog Box Options

Description	Example
Check boxes are square in shape. Click a box to turn on (check) or turn off (uncheck) the option. You can select as many check box options as needed.	Small caps All caps Hidden
A *Combo* or *List box* displays a list of choices. Use the scroll bar to display hidden choices. Use scroll arrows to move up or down in small increments. Drag the scroll box up or down to move quickly through the list of options. Click an item to select it, or key information in the text box.	Font: +Body +Body +Headings Agency FB Aharoni Albertus
Command buttons are rectangles with rounded corners, and they initiate an immediate action. If followed by an ellipsis (. . .) another dialog box opens.	OK Cancel Text Effects...
A *Drop-down list box* is rectangular in shape and displays the current selection in the rectangle. Click the arrow at the right of the box for a list of available options.	Font color:
Option buttons are round in shape. Only one option may be selected from within a group of options. If selected, the option contains a dot.	Alignment Left Center Right Decimal Bar
A *Slider* represents a range of values for a particular setting. Drag the slider left or right or click an arrow to change the current setting.	Brightness and Contrast Presets: Brightness: 14% Contrast: -34%

(continues)

TABLE 5 Dialog Box Options (*continued*)

Spin Box/Spinner **includes two arrows. Click the up arrow to increase value. Click the down arrow to decrease value. Changes usually occur in an increment of one. You can also select the current value, and key a new number.**	Margins Top: 1" Left: 1" Gutter: 0"
Text boxes **are rectangular in shape and are used to enter data. An insertion point appears at the left side of the box, and text will be entered at the position of the insertion point. Press Delete or Backspace to delete or edit existing text. Double-click or drag over existing text to select it. Use the Home, End, or arrow keys to move the insertion point.**	File name:

Practice using dialog box options by completing the following instructions.

1. Open Word, if necessary, and click the **Home** tab.
2. Locate the **Font** group, and notice the arrow in the lower right corner. Click the arrow (Font Dialog Box Launcher), and the Font dialog box displays.

Figure 18
Font dialog box

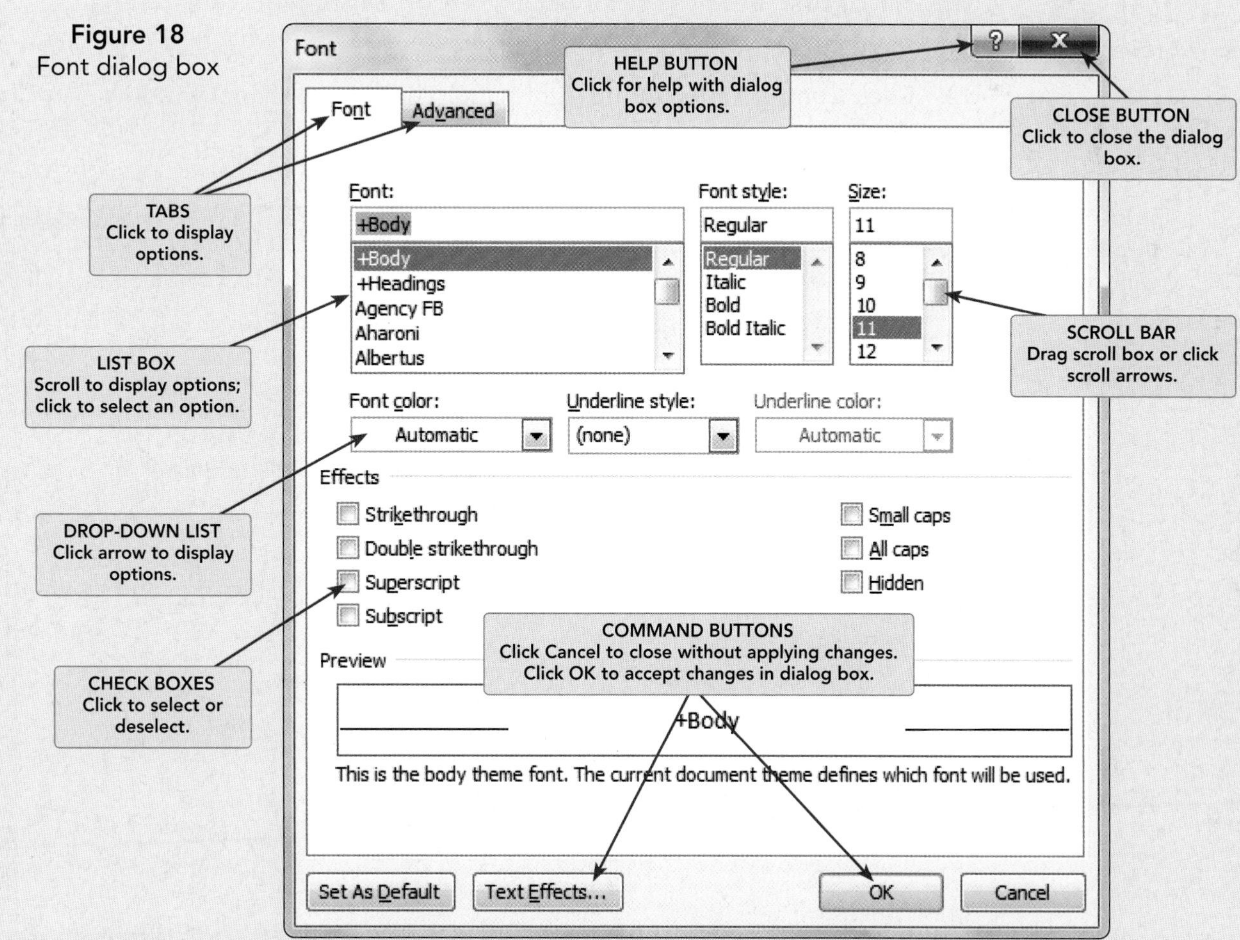

3. Click the **Advanced** tab, and notice the options in the dialog box. Click the **Font** tab.
4. Locate the **Font** group. The Font group displays a list box with several fonts available for formatting a document. Drag the scroll box to the bottom to view a list of available fonts. Click to select the **Tahoma** font. You can also click the up or down arrows to locate a font.
5. Locate the **Font color** group, and click the down arrow to the right of the box. Locate the **Standard Colors**, and point to the colors to view a ScreenTip. Click **Blue**. Notice the change in the Font color drop-down list.
6. Locate the **Effects** section. Click to select the check box for **Small caps**. A checkmark appears in the box.
7. Locate the command buttons at the bottom of the dialog box. Click **Cancel** Cancel.
8. Close the Word program by clicking the Close button.

Changing the Desktop

Use the Control Panel to change the way Windows looks and works. Because your computer in school is used by other students, you should be very careful when changing settings. Others might expect Windows to look and work the standard way. Having Windows look or work in a nonstandard way could easily confuse other users. (Table 6 describes how to access other settings.) To change the appearance of your computer, follow these steps. Talk to your instructor first, however, before changing any settings on your computer.

1. Click the **Start** button on the taskbar.
2. Click **Control Panel** on the right pane. The Control Panel window displays.

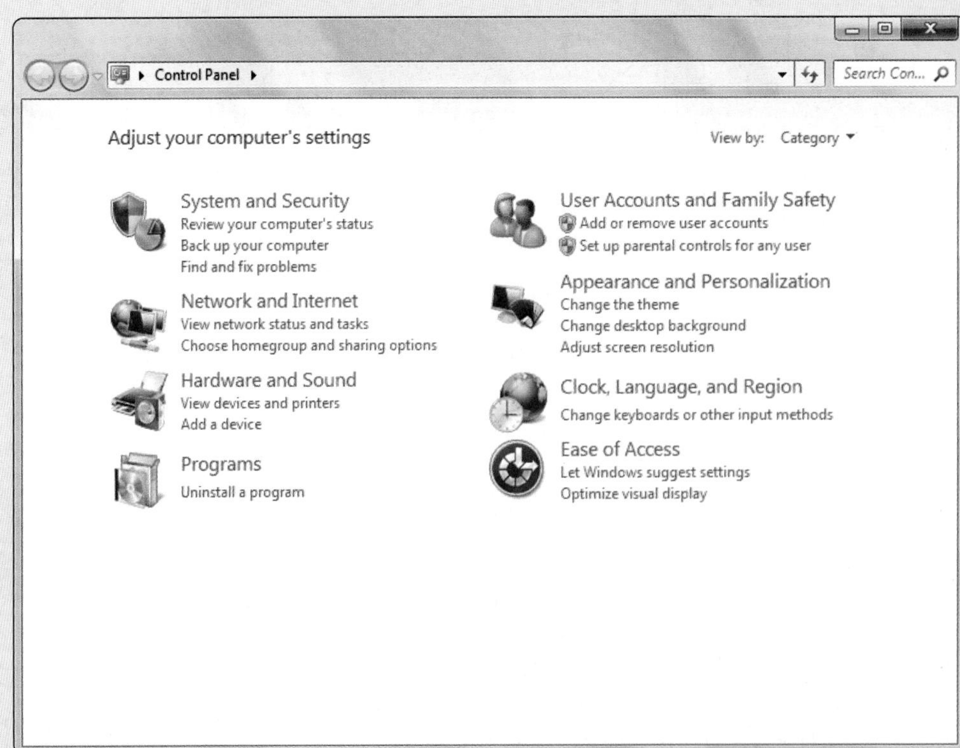

Figure 19 Control Panel window

3. Click the **Appearance and Personalization** link. The Appearance and Personalization window displays.
4. Click **Personalization** and click the **Window Color** icon near the bottom of the window. Click a color from the color palette.
5. Click **Save Changes**.
6. Click the **Desktop Background** icon at the bottom of the Personalization window. Scroll through the list of pictures, and click to select a picture. Click **Save Changes**.
7. Close the **Personalization** window.

TABLE 6 Settings Options

OPTION	USE
Control Panel	Displays the Control Panel window, which lets you change background color, add or remove programs, change the date and time, and change other settings for your hardware and software. The items listed below are accessed from the Control Panel.
Network and Internet	Includes options to view the network status, connect to a network, set up file sharing, change Internet options, and so on.
Hardware and Sound	Includes options to add a printer, change default settings for AutoPlay, sound, mouse settings, keyboard, and so on.
Appearance and Personalization	Includes options to change the desktop background, adjust screen resolution, customize the Start menu and icons on the taskbar, and change sidebar properties.

Using the Search Command

If you do not know where a file or folder is located, you can use the Search command on the Start menu to help you find and open it. You can also use the Search box in Windows Explorer to locate an item.

1. Click the **Start** button on the taskbar. Notice the blinking insertion point in the Start Search box. You can start keying the name of a program, folder, or file immediately.
2. Key **calculator**. The Start menu is replaced with a list of options including programs, Control Panel items, files, and documents containing the characters you keyed in the Search box.
3. Click the **Calculator** option. The Calculator window displays.
4. **Close** the Calculator window.
5. Click the Windows Explorer button on the taskbar. The Windows Explorer window displays.

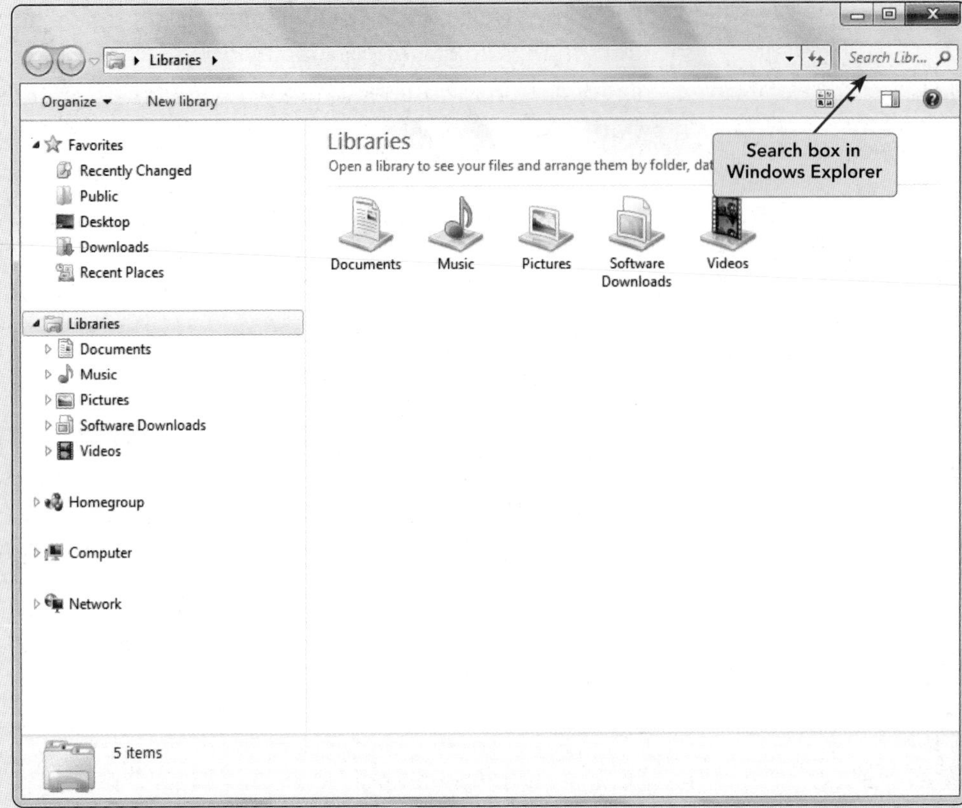

Figure 20
Windows Explorer window

6. Locate the **Search** box in the upper right corner of the Windows Explorer window.
7. Click in the Search box, and key **penguins**. A picture of penguins appears in the window.
8. Close the Windows Explorer window.

Using the Run Command

Windows allows you to start a program by using the Run command and keying the program name. This command is often employed to run a "setup" or "install" program that installs a new program on your computer. It is best to use this command after you have become more familiar with Windows 7.

1. Click the **Start** button on the taskbar.
2. Click **All Programs**, and click the **Accessories** folder.
3. Click **Run**.

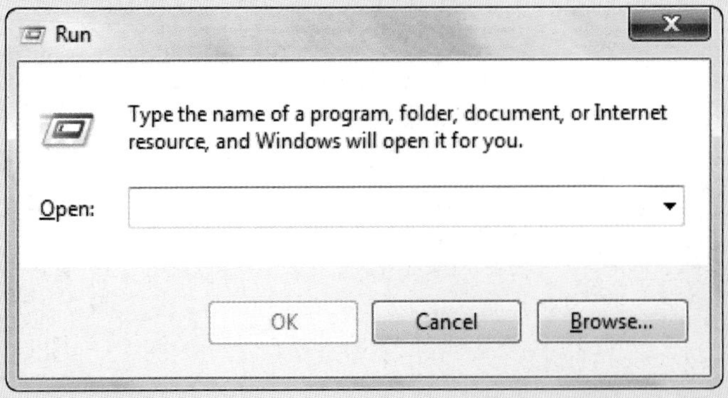

Figure 21
Run dialog box

Run

Type the name of a program, folder, document, or Internet resource, and Windows will open it for you.

Open:

OK Cancel Browse...

4. If you know the name of a program you want to run, type the name in the **Open** text box. Often you will need to click **Browse** to open a drop-down list of the disk drives, folders, and files available to you.
5. Click **Cancel** to close the Run dialog box.

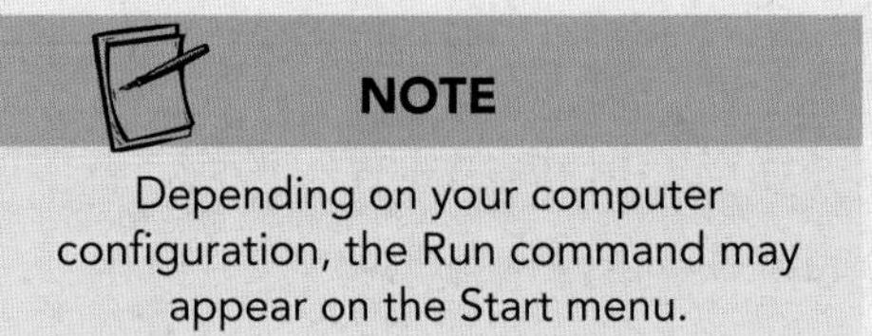

NOTE
Depending on your computer configuration, the Run command may appear on the Start menu.

6. Open the **Start** menu, and locate the **Start Search** box.
7. Key **run**, and notice that the Run program displays under **Programs**.
8. Click the program name, and the Run dialog box displays.
9. Close the Run dialog box.

Deleting Files Using the Recycle Bin

The *Recycle Bin* is the trash can icon on your desktop. To delete a file, click the file icon, and drag it to the Recycle Bin.

1. Double-click the **Recycle Bin** icon on the desktop. A window opens listing files you have deleted.

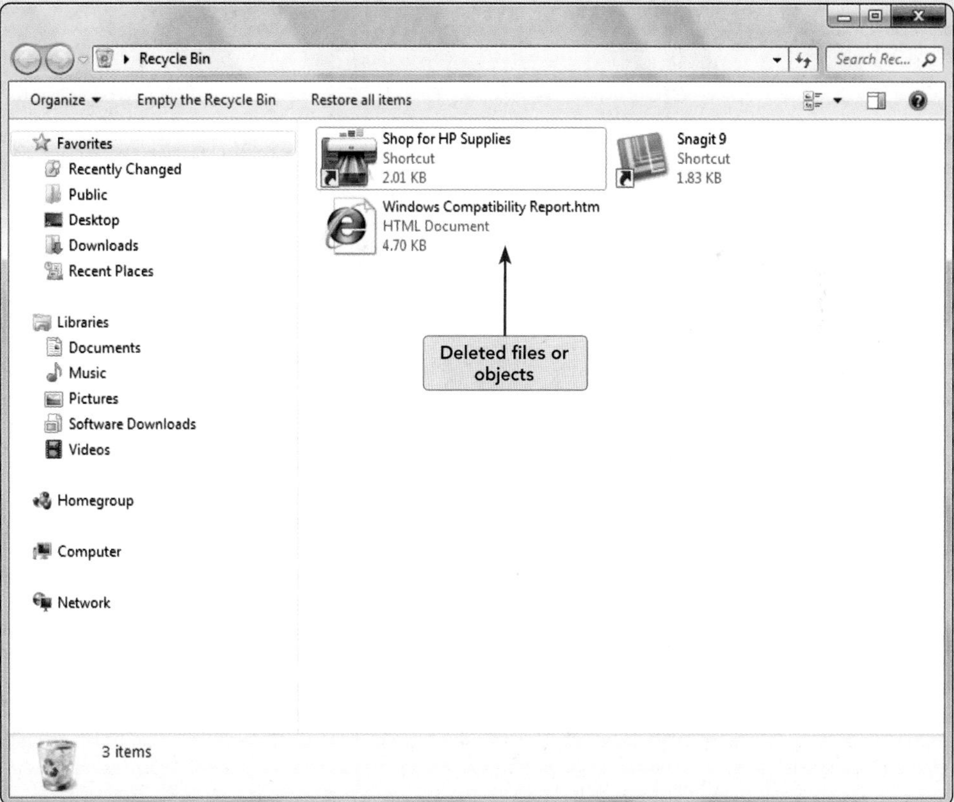

Figure 22
Recycle Bin window

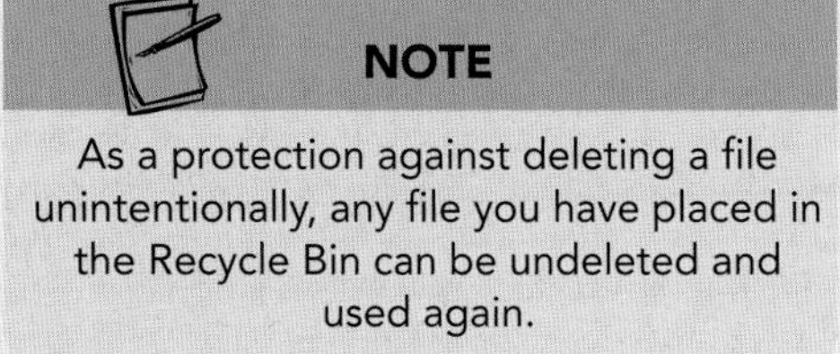

NOTE
As a protection against deleting a file unintentionally, any file you have placed in the Recycle Bin can be undeleted and used again.

2. To undelete a file, merely drag it out of the Recycle Bin window and place it on the desktop or right-click the file and click Restore.
3. To empty the Recycle Bin and permanently delete files, click **Empty the Recycle Bin** in the Recycle Bin window, or right-click the Recycle Bin icon on the desktop. The shortcut menu appears. Click **Empty Recycle Bin**.

Help and Support

Windows Help and Support is available to you as you work. Use the Help feature to answer questions, to provide instructions on how to do a procedure, or to troubleshoot problems you are experiencing.

1. Press the Windows logo key on the keyboard or click the Start button to display the Start menu.
2. Locate the **Help and Support** feature on the right side of the Start menu, and click to open the Windows Help and Support window.

Figure 23 Windows Help and Support Window

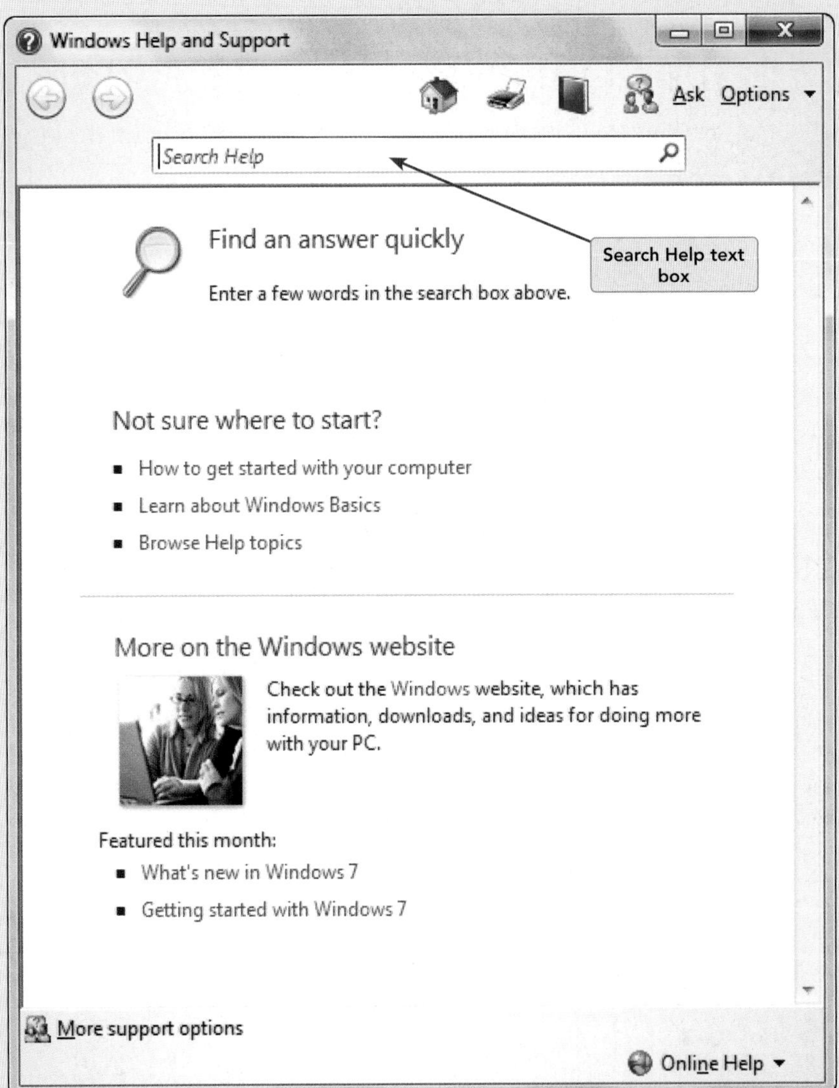

3. Key **gadget** in the Search Help text box, and press Enter. A list of results for gadget appears in the Windows Help and Support window.

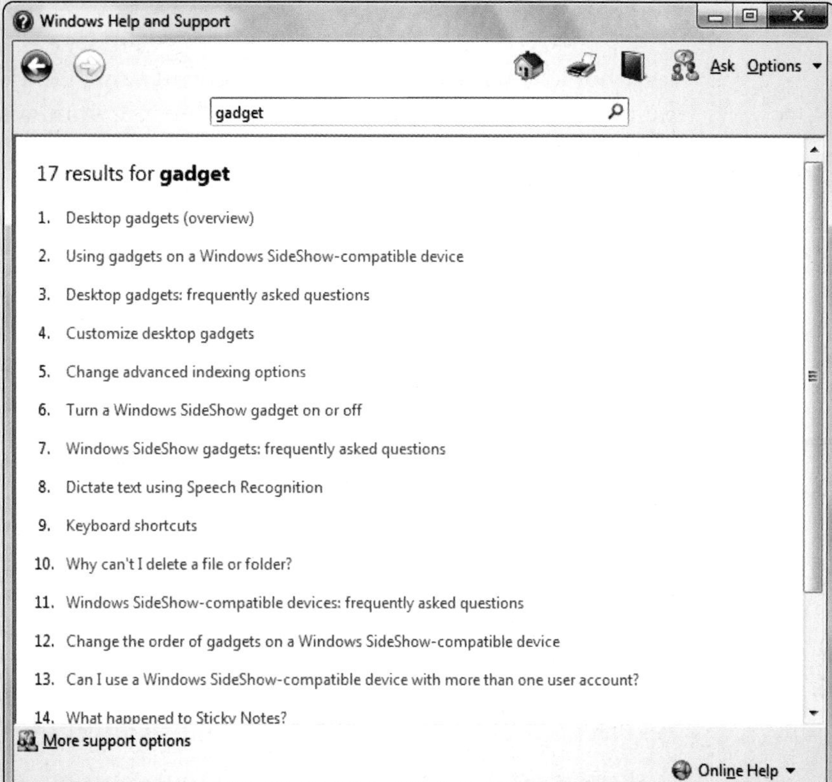

Figure 24
Search results for gadget

4. Point to the topic entitled "**Desktop gadgets (overview)**." Notice the shape of the mouse pointer. Click the topic, and the Windows Help and Support window displays information about gadgets. Read the information on Desktop gadgets.
5. Click the Back button located in the upper left corner. You return to the list of gadget topics. Notice that the "Desktop gadgets (overview)" topic is a different color. When you visit a topic, the color of the topic (link) changes.
6. Click the topic entitled "**Desktop gadgets: frequently asked questions**."
7. Locate the **Show all** link in the upper right corner of the window. Click **Show all** to expand the text.
8. Key the text **keyboard shortcuts** in the Search text box, and press Enter. Click the link **Keyboard shortcuts**, then click the link **Windows logo key keyboard shortcuts**. Review the list. (You may want to print this list for future reference.)
9. Click the Browse Help button at the top of the Windows Help and Support window. Click the **All Help** link. A list of subject headings displays. Click a heading to view related categories.
10. Locate the Help button on the taskbar. Right-click the button, and choose **Close window**.

Exiting Windows

You should always exit any open programs and Windows before turning off the computer. This is the best way to be sure your work is saved. Windows also performs other "housekeeping" routines that ensure everything is ready for you when you next turn on your computer. Failure to shut down properly will often force Windows to perform time-consuming system checks the next time it is loaded. You can either log off the computer to make it available for another user, or shut it down entirely.

To Log Off

1. Click the **Start** button on the taskbar.
2. Click the arrow to the right of the Shut down button Shut down ▷, and click **Log Off.**

To Shut Down

To exit Windows, use the Shut down command on the Start menu.

This command has two important shut-down options which are accessed by clicking the arrow beside the Shut down button.

- *Restart:* Restarts the computer without shutting off the power. This is sometimes necessary when you add new software.
- *Sleep:* Puts the computer in a low-activity state. It appears to be turned off but will restart when the mouse is moved. Press the computer power button to resume work.

To shut down completely, click the Shut down button Shut down ▷. *Shut down* closes all open programs and makes it safe to turn off the computer. Some computers will turn off the power automatically.

1. Click the **Start** button on the taskbar.
2. Click the Shut down button Shut down ▷.
3. Windows prompts you to save changes in any open documents. It then prepares the computer to be shut down.

There is more to learning a word processing program like Microsoft Word than simply pressing keys. You need to know how to use Word in a real-world situation. That is why all the lessons in this book relate to everyday business tasks.

As you work through the lessons, imagine yourself working as an intern for Campbell's Confections, a fictional candy store and chocolate factory located in Grove City, Pennsylvania.

Campbell's Confections

It was 1950. Harry Truman was president. Shopping malls and supermarkets were appearing in suburban areas. And Campbell's Confections began doing business.

Based in Grove City, Pennsylvania, Campbell's Confections started as a small family-owned business. Originally, Campbell's Confections was a candy store, with a few display cases in the front of the building and a kitchen in the back to create chocolates and to try new recipes. The store was an immediate success, with word traveling quickly about the rich, smooth, creamy chocolates made by Campbell's Confections. Today, the store includes several display cases for chocolates and hard candies and special displays for greeting cards and gifts. The factory is now located in a separate building on Monroe Street and offers tours for visitors.

Within a few years of opening the first store, the company expanded its business by opening Campbell's Confections candy stores in Mercer, New Castle, and Meadville. Today there are 24 stores in 3 states—Pennsylvania, Ohio, and West Virginia.

The goal of Campbell's Confections is to offer "quality chocolate," and the company has grown from its retail base to include wholesale and fund-raising divisions. E-commerce has been the latest venture with Internet sales increasing monthly.

Currently, Thomas Campbell is the president-owner, and Lynn Tanguay is the vice president.

To understand the organization of Campbell's Confections, take a look at Figure CS-1. Notice each of the specialty areas and management divisions.

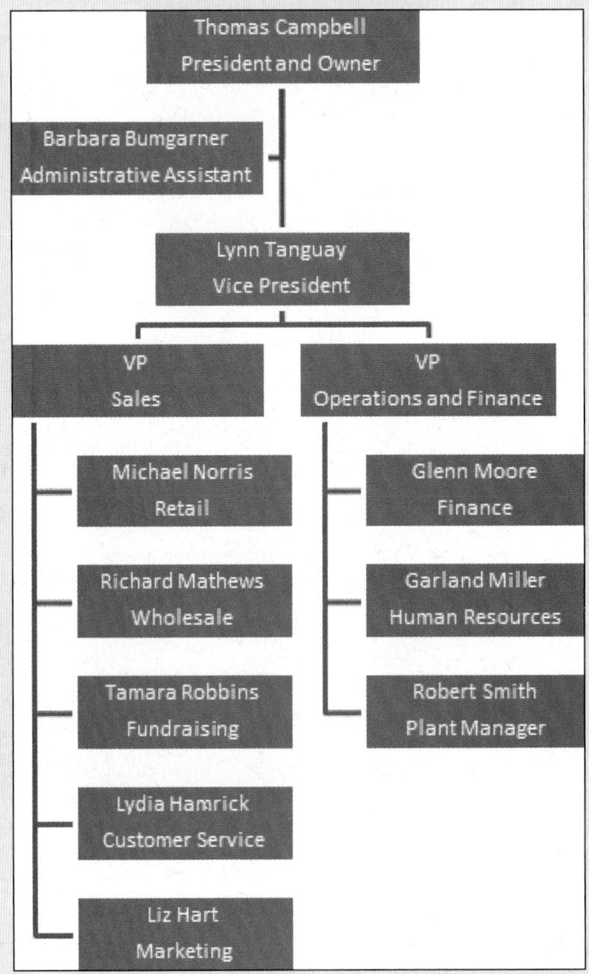

All the documents you will use in this text relate to Campbell's Confections. As you work through the documents in the text, take the time to notice the following:

- How the employees interact, and how they respond to customers' queries.
- The format and tone of the business correspondence (if you are unfamiliar with the standard formats for business documents, refer to Appendix B).
- References to the *Gregg Reference Manual,* a standard reference manual for business writing and correspondence.
- The content of the correspondence (and its relation to Campbell's Confections).

As you use this text and become experienced with Microsoft Word, you will also gain experience in creating, editing, and formatting the type of documents that are generated in a real-life business environment.

Unit 1

BASIC SKILLS

Lesson 1

Creating and Editing a Document

OBJECTIVES ***After completing this lesson, you will be able to:***

1. Start Word and identify parts of the Word screen.
2. Key and edit text.
3. Name and save a document.
4. Open an existing document.
5. Move within a document.
6. Select text.
7. Print a document.
8. Close a document and exit Word.

Estimated Time: 1½ hours

Microsoft Word is a versatile, easy-to-use word processing program that helps you create letters, memos, reports, and other types of documents. This lesson begins with an overview of the Word screen. Then you learn how to create, edit, name, save, print, and close a document. The documents you create for this unit will provide an overview of Campbell's Confections, its products, and the process of making chocolate.

Starting Word and Identifying Parts of the Word Screen

There are several ways to start Word, depending on your system setup and personal preferences. For example, you can use the Start button on the Windows taskbar or double-click a Word shortcut icon that might be on your desktop.

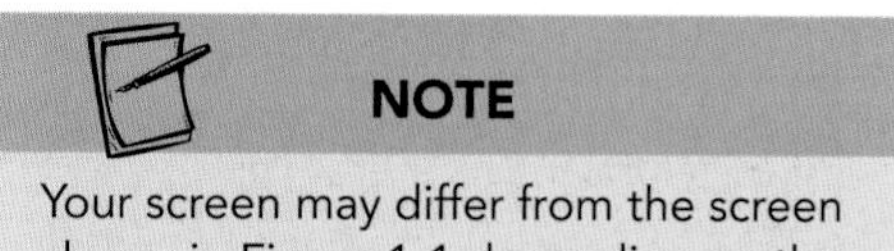

NOTE

Your screen may differ from the screen shown in Figure 1-1 depending on the programs installed on your computer.

Exercise 1-1 START WORD

1. Click the Start button on the Windows taskbar, and point to **All Programs**.
2. On the All Programs menu, click **Microsoft Office**, and then click **Microsoft Word 2010**. In a few seconds, the program loads, and the Word screen appears.

Figure 1-1
Start menu

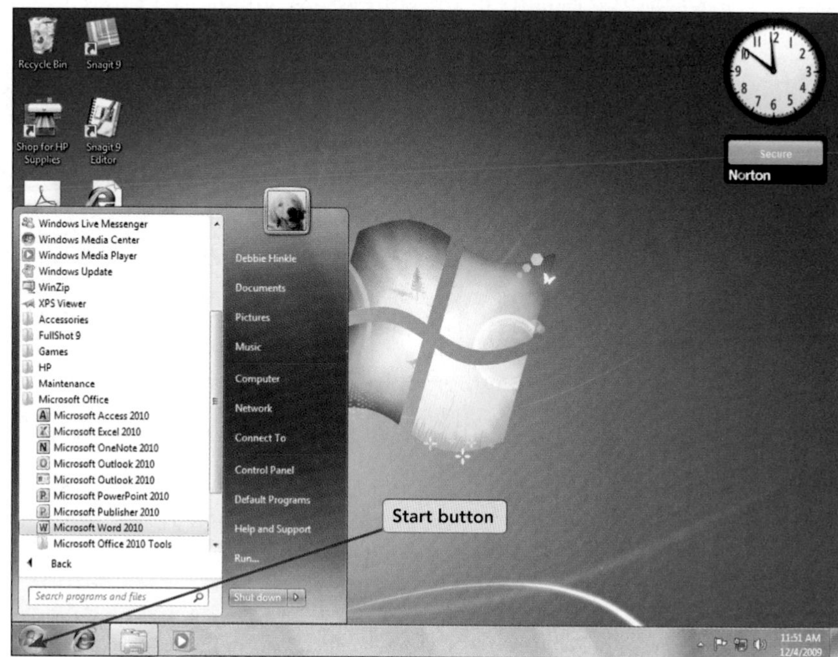

Figure 1-2
Word screen

Quick Access Toolbar
Title bar
Ribbon
File tab
Rulers
Ribbon tabs
Group
Vertical scroll bar
Text area
Status bar
View buttons
Zoom level controls

TABLE 1-1 Parts of the Word Screen

Part of Screen	Purpose
Quick Access Toolbar	The Quick Access Toolbar is located at the top of the Word window, and its commands are available for all tabs on the Ribbon. By default, it displays icons for save, undo, and repeat. The Quick Access Toolbar can be customized to include commands that you use frequently.
Title bar	Displays the name of the current document. The opening Word screen is always named "Document1."
Ribbon	Displays contextual tabs. Each tab contains groups, and each group includes related commands. Commands can be buttons, menus, or drop-down list boxes.
File tab	Displays the Backstage view with options to create, save, open, and close documents. You can also display recently opened documents.
Ruler	The horizontal and vertical rulers display in Print Layout view. The horizontal ruler shows the placement of margins, indents, and tabs. Use the View Ruler button to show or hide the rulers.
Text area	Displays the text and graphics in the document.
Scroll bars	Used with the mouse to move right or left and up or down within a document.
Status bar	Displays the page number and page count of the document, the document view buttons, and the zoom control. It also displays the current mode of operation. The status bar can be customized.
View buttons	Used to switch from one document view to another. Available views include Print Layout, Full Screen Reading, Web Layout, Outline, and Draft View.

Exercise 1-2 IDENTIFY THE RIBBON AND THE QUICK ACCESS TOOLBAR

To become familiar with Word, start by identifying the parts of the screen you will work with extensively, such as the Ribbon and the Quick Access Toolbar. As you practice using Word commands, you will see *ScreenTips* to help you identify screen elements such as buttons. A ScreenTip appears when you point to a command on the Ribbon. It includes the name of the command and a brief description. ScreenTips also appear to help you identify parts of the Word screen.

When you start Word, the Ribbon appears with the Home tab selected. The Ribbon consists of eight tabs by default. Each tab contains a group of related commands, and the number of commands for each tab varies. A command can be one of several formats. The most popular formats include buttons and drop-down lists.

The *Quick Access Toolbar* contains frequently used commands and is positioned above the Ribbon by default. You can minimize the Ribbon so that only the names of the tabs display, or you can place the Quick Access Toolbar below the Ribbon. The commands on the Quick Access Toolbar are available for all tabs on the Ribbon, and you can customize the Quick Access Toolbar to include the commands you frequently use.

1. Move the mouse pointer to the **File** tab on the Ribbon. Click the left mouse button to open the Backstage view. The Backstage view replaces the Microsoft Office Button and the File menu from earlier versions of Microsoft Word. It lists commands to create, open, save, and print documents. The Navigation Pane appears on the left side of Backstage view and includes a list of the Quick commands. Click the **Info** command to view information about your document. When a document is open, the Info tab displays the document properties such as size, number of pages, and number of words. You can also see when your document was last modified.

Figure 1-3
Backstage view

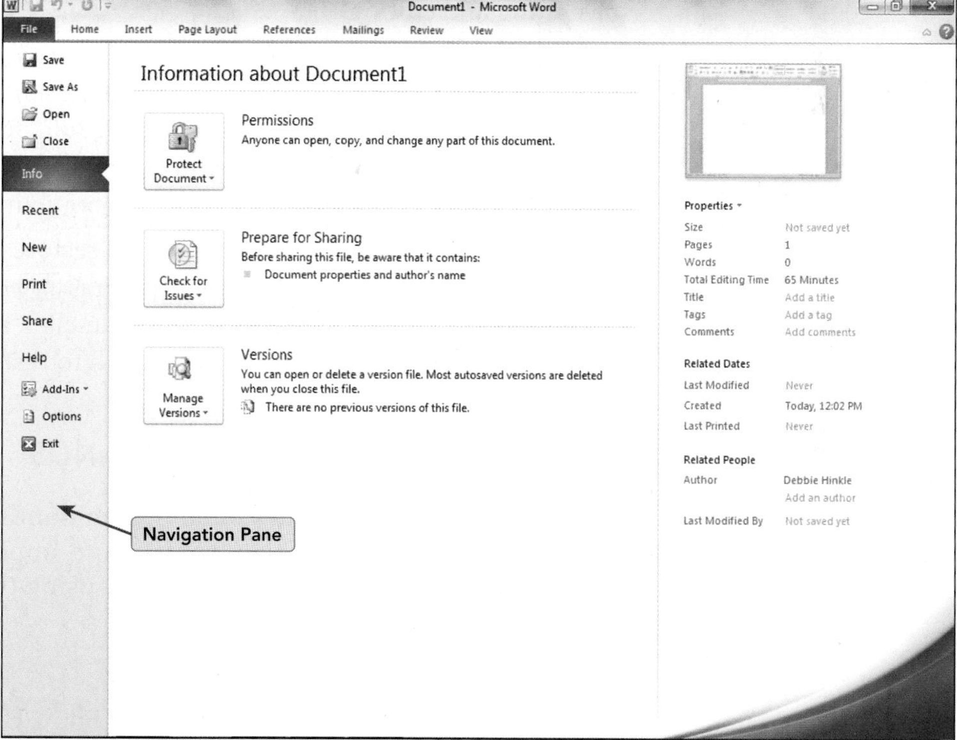

TIP

Commands may appear in more than one location. For example, you can save a document by choosing Save from the File tab, by clicking the Save command on the Quick Access Toolbar, or by pressing Ctrl+S.

2. Click the **File** tab to close Backstage view. You can also close the Backstage view by pressing Esc or clicking another tab on the Ribbon.
3. Move the mouse pointer above the File tab to the Quick Access Toolbar, and point to the Save button. A ScreenTip and a keyboard shortcut to save a document display.

NOTE

The width of the application window affects the size and shape of the Ribbon commands.

NOTE

Any Ribbon command with a light gray icon is currently not available. However, you can still identify the button by pointing to it with the mouse.

4. Point to the commands to the right of the Save command. Notice each command includes descriptive text and a keyboard shortcut. The Save, Undo, and Repeat commands are located on the Quick Access Toolbar by default.
5. Move the mouse pointer to the **Insert** tab on the Ribbon, and click **Insert**. Notice the change in the number and types of groups displayed. When you point to a Ribbon tab, the name of the tab is outlined but not active. Click the Ribbon tab to display the commands.
6. Click the **Page Layout** tab. There are five groups of commands on the Page Layout tab. Point to the **Margins** command. Read the ScreenTip.
7. Click the **Home** tab. Notice the groups and buttons available for formatting and editing.
8. Move the mouse pointer to the right of the last tab on the Ribbon, and locate the caret symbol (^). This symbol represents a button and is used to minimize the Ribbon. Click the Minimize the Ribbon button, and notice that only the Ribbon tabs and ruler display. The Minimize the Ribbon button changes to Expand the Ribbon button.
9. Click the Expand the Ribbon button to restore the Ribbon. The keyboard shortcut to minimize the Ribbon is Ctrl+F1. To restore the Ribbon, press Ctrl+F1. You can also double-click any tab on the Ribbon to minimize the Ribbon. Double-click a tab to restore the Ribbon.

Exercise 1-3 IDENTIFY COMMANDS

Use the Ribbon to locate and execute commands to format and edit your document. Commands also control the appearance of the Word screen. You can access Ribbon commands by using the mouse or keyboard Access Keys.

1. Activate the **Home** tab.
2. Locate the **Paragraph** group, and click the Show/Hide ¶ button ¶. This button shows or hides formatting marks on the screen. Formatting marks display for spaces, paragraph marks, and tab characters. The command toggles between show and hide.

3. Press the Alt key. Small lettered or numbered squares, called *Key Tips,* appear on the File tab, Quick Access Toolbar, and Ribbon to access or execute a command.

Figure 1-4
Key Tips

4. Press the letter P on the keyboard to select the **Page Layout** tab.
5. Press the letter M on the keyboard to display the **Margins** gallery. Press Esc to close the gallery. Press Esc twice to turn off the Key Tips.

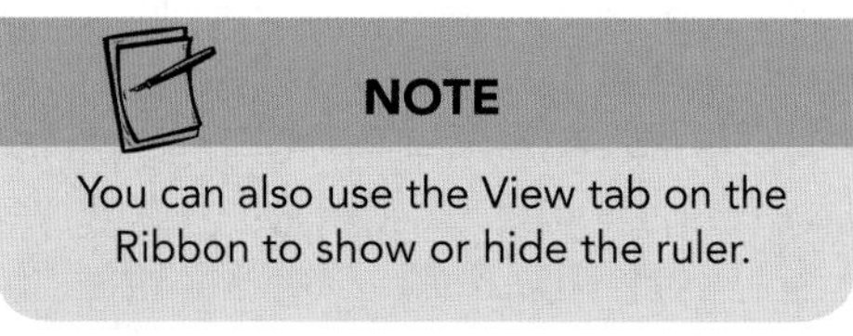

NOTE

You can also use the View tab on the Ribbon to show or hide the ruler.

NOTE

Drag the Zoom slider to the right to zoom in, and drag the Zoom slider to the left to zoom out. You can also use Ctrl+the wheel on your mouse to zoom in and zoom out. The View tab on the Ribbon contains Zoom commands.

6. Locate the vertical scroll bar, and click the View Ruler button. Notice the rulers disappear from the Word screen. Click the View Ruler button again to display the rulers.
7. Locate the Zoom button 100% on the status bar.
8. Click the Zoom button to open the Zoom dialog box, and click **200%**. Click **OK**. The text area is magnified, and you see a portion of the page.
9. Point to and click the Zoom Out button. The document magnification changes to 190%. Click the Zoom In button twice to change the magnification to 210%. Drag the Zoom slider to 100%. The document returns to normal display.

Keying and Editing Text

When keying text, you will notice various shapes and symbols in the text area. For example:

- The *insertion point* | is the vertical blinking line that marks the position of the next character to be entered.
- The mouse pointer takes the shape of an *I-beam* I when it is in the text area. It changes into an arrow when you point to a command on the Quick Access Toolbar or the Ribbon.
- The *paragraph mark* ¶ indicates the end of a paragraph. The paragraph mark displays when the Show/Hide ¶ button ¶ is selected.

Exercise 1-4 KEY TEXT AND MOVE THE INSERTION POINT

1. Before you begin, make sure the Show/Hide ¶ button ¶ on the **Home** tab, **Paragraph** group is selected. When this feature is "turned on," you can see paragraph marks and spacing between words and sentences more easily.
2. Key the words **Campbell's Confections** (don't worry about keying mistakes now—you can correct them later). Notice how the insertion point and the paragraph mark move as you key text. Notice also how a space between words is indicated by a dot.

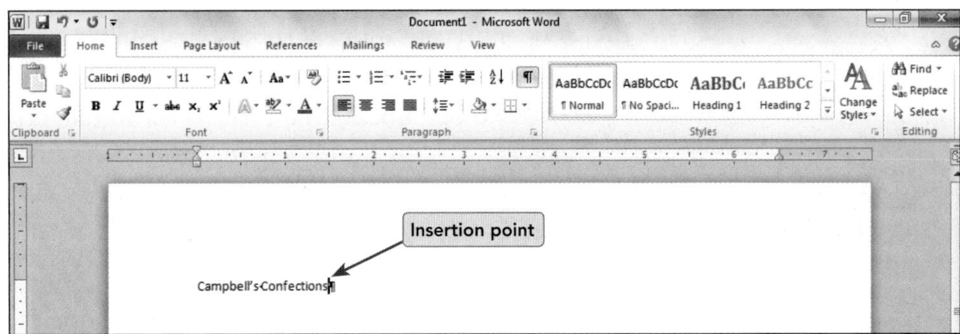

Figure 1-5
The insertion point marks the place where you begin keying

> **NOTE**
>
> The documents you create in this course relate to the case study about Campbell's Confections, a fictional candy store and chocolate factory (see the Case Study in the front matter).

3. Move the insertion point to the left of the word "Campbell's" by positioning the I-beam and clicking the left mouse button.
4. Move the insertion point back to the right of "Confections" to continue keying.

Exercise 1-5 WRAP TEXT AND CORRECT SPELLING

As you key additional text, you will notice Word performs several tasks automatically. For example, Word does the following by default:

- Wraps text from the end of one line to the beginning of the next line.
- Alerts you to spelling and grammatical errors.
- Corrects common misspellings, such as "teh" for "the" and "adn" for "and."
- Suggests the completed word when you key the current date, day, or month.

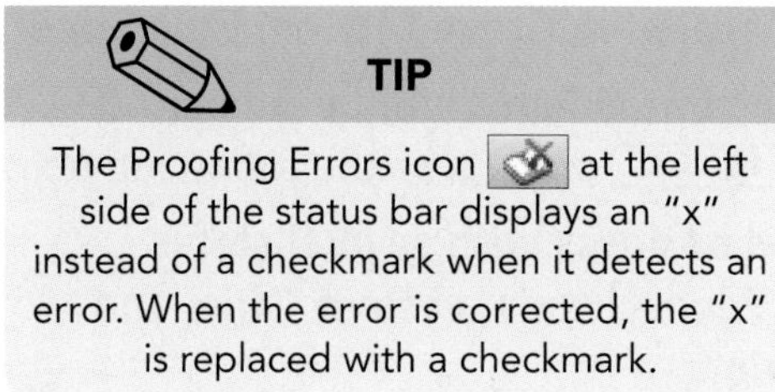

TIP

The Proofing Errors icon at the left side of the status bar displays an "x" instead of a checkmark when it detects an error. When the error is corrected, the "x" is replaced with a checkmark.

1. Continue the sentence you started in Exercise 1-4, this time keying a misspelled word. Press Spacebar, and then key **is western Pennsylvania's leeding candy maker** (don't key a period). Word recognizes that "leeding" is misspelled and applies a red, wavy underline to the word. The status bar displays a Proofing Errors icon to indicate an error exists in the document.
2. To correct the misspelling, use the mouse to position the I-beam anywhere on top of the red, underlined word and click the *right* mouse button. A shortcut menu appears with suggested spellings. Click "leading" with the *left* mouse button. The misspelled word is corrected. Notice the change in the icon that displays in the status bar. The Proofing Errors icon changes to a No Proofing Errors icon on the status bar.

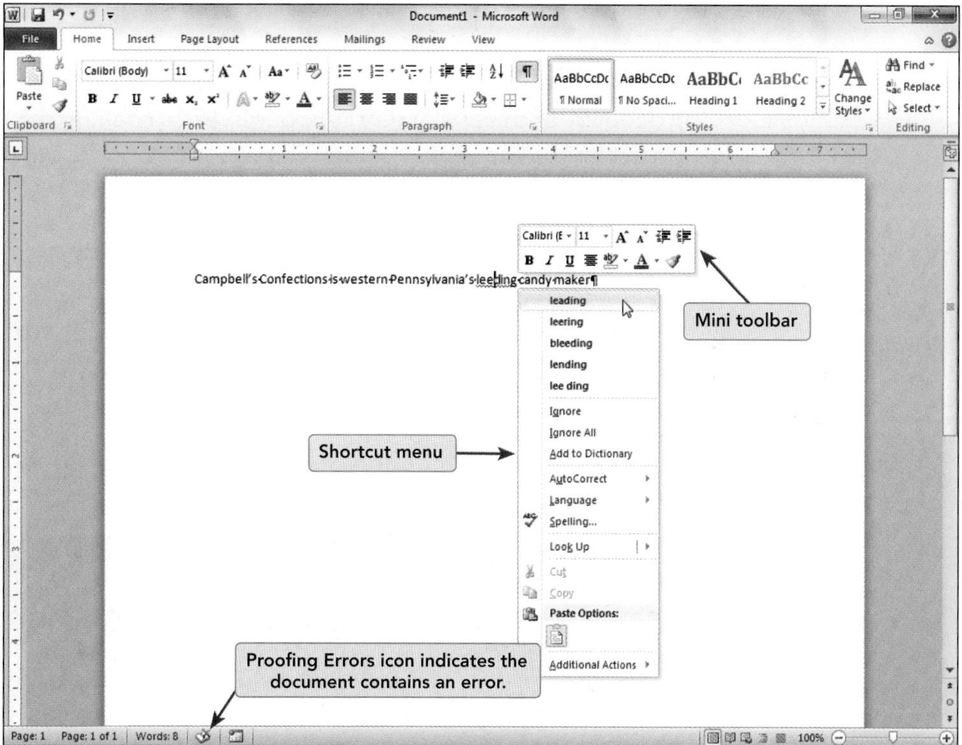

Figure 1-6
Choose the correct spelling from the shortcut menu

3. Move the insertion point to the right of "maker," and press Spacebar. Continue the sentence with another misspelled word by keying **adn**, and press Spacebar. Notice that "adn" is automatically corrected to "and" when you press Spacebar.

4. Complete the sentence by keying **is located in Grove City on Main Street.**
5. Verify that the insertion point is to the immediate right of the period following Street, and then press the [Spacebar] once. Key the following text:

   It is a family-owned business with several stores located in western Pennsylvania, eastern Ohio, and northern West Virginia.

   Notice how the text automatically wraps from the end of the line to the beginning of the next line.

NOTE

Throughout this text, one space is used after a period to separate sentences. This is the standard format for word processing and desktop publishing.

NOTE

When Word suggests a completed word as you key text, you can ignore the suggested word and continue keying or insert it by pressing [Enter].

6. Press [Enter] once to start a new paragraph.
7. Key the second paragraph shown in Figure 1-7. When you key the first four letters of "Monday" in the first sentence, Word suggests the completed word in a small box. Press [Enter] to insert the suggested word, and then press [Spacebar] before you key the next word. Follow the same procedure for "Saturday."

Figure 1-7

```
For more information about Campbell's Confections, visit one
of our stores Monday through Saturday, or visit our Web site
anytime. Our sales associates will be happy to assist you.
```

Exercise 1-6 DELETE TEXT

The keyboard offers many options for basic text editing. For example, you can press [Backspace] to delete a single character to the left of the insertion point or press [Ctrl]+[Delete] to delete an entire word.

TABLE 1-2 Basic Text Editing

Key	Result
[Backspace]	Deletes the character to the left of the insertion point.
[Ctrl]+[Backspace]	Deletes the word to the left of the insertion point.
[Delete]	Deletes the character to the right of the insertion point.
[Ctrl]+[Delete]	Deletes the word to the right of the insertion point.

1. Move the insertion point to the right of the word "It" in the second sentence of the first paragraph. (Use the mouse to position the I-beam, and click the left mouse button.)
2. Press Backspace twice to delete both characters, and key **Campbell's Confections**.
3. Move the insertion point to the left of "one" in the second paragraph.
4. Press Delete three times and key **any**.
5. Move the insertion point to the left of the word "information" in the second paragraph.
6. Hold down Ctrl and press Backspace. The word "more" is deleted.
7. Move the insertion point to the right of "Grove City" in the first sentence of the first paragraph.
8. Hold down Ctrl and press Delete to delete the word "on." Press Ctrl+Delete two more times to delete the words "Main Street."

NOTE

When keyboard combinations (such as Ctrl+Backspace) are shown in this text, hold down the first key as you press the second key. Release the second key, and then release the first key. An example of the entire sequence is this: Hold down Ctrl, press Backspace, release Backspace, and release Ctrl. With practice, this sequence becomes easy.

Exercise 1-7 INSERT TEXT

When editing a document, you can insert text or key over existing text. When you insert text, Word is in regular *Insert mode,* and you simply click to position the insertion point and key the text to be inserted. To key over existing text, you switch to *Overtype mode.* The Overtype feature is turned off by default.

1. In the first sentence of the first paragraph, move the insertion point to the left of the "G" in "Grove City." Key **downtown**, and press Spacebar once to leave a space between the two words.
2. Move the insertion point to the beginning of the document, to the left of "Campbell's."
3. Click the **File** tab, and click the **Options** command.
4. Click **Advanced** in the Navigation Pane of the Word Options dialog box. Locate **Editing options**, and click to select **Use overtype mode**. Click **OK**.
5. Press Caps Lock. When you key text in Caps Lock mode, the keyed text appears in all uppercase letters.
6. Key **campbell's confections** over the existing text.

7. Move the mouse pointer to the status bar, and press the right button on the mouse. Locate **Overtype** in the shortcut menu, and click the left mouse button to select the option. Click in the text area to hide the shortcut menu. Notice that the Overtype mode indicator appears in the status bar.
8. Position the insertion point to the left of "Campbell's Confections" in the second sentence of the first paragraph. Verify that Caps Lock is still active, and key **campbell's confections**.
9. Click the Overtype mode indicator Overtype to turn off Overtype.

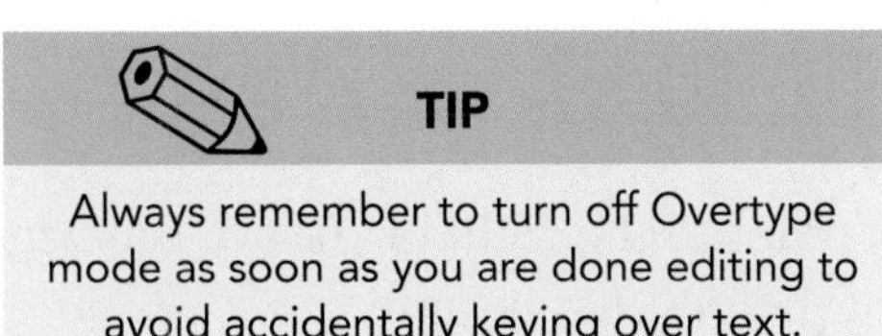

TIP

Always remember to turn off Overtype mode as soon as you are done editing to avoid accidentally keying over text.

10. Press Caps Lock to turn off Caps Lock mode. Click the **File** tab, and click the **Options** command. Click **Advanced**, locate **Editing options**, and verify that the **Use overtype mode** is deselected. Click **OK**.
11. Right-click the status bar, and deselect **Overtype**. Click in the text area to close the shortcut menu.

Exercise 1-8 COMBINE AND SPLIT PARAGRAPHS

1. At the end of the first paragraph, position the insertion point to the left of the paragraph mark (after the period following "West Virginia").
2. Press Delete once. The two paragraphs are now combined, or merged, into one.
3. Press Spacebar once to insert a space between the sentences.
4. With the insertion point to the left of "For" in the combined paragraph, press Enter once to split the paragraph.

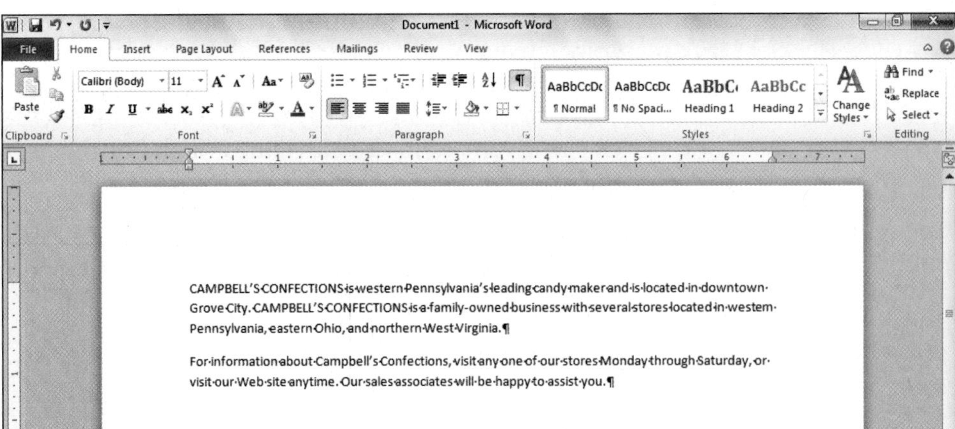

Figure 1-8
Edited document

Naming and Saving a Document

Your document, called "Document1," is stored in your computer's temporary memory. Until you name and save the document, the data can be lost if you have a power failure or a computer hardware problem. It is always good practice to save your work frequently.

The first step in saving a document for future use is to assign a *file name.* Study the following rules about naming documents:

- File names can contain up to 260 characters, including the drive letter, the folder name, and extension. The following characters cannot be used in a file name:

  / \ > < * ? " : |

- File names can include uppercase letters, lowercase letters, or a combination of both. They can also include spaces. For example, a file can be named "Business Plan."
- Throughout this course, document file names will consist of [your initials] (which might be your initials or the identifier your instructor asks you to use, such as **rst**), followed by the number of the exercise, such as **1-12**. The file name would, therefore, be **rst1-12**.

You can use either the Save command or the Save As command to save a document. Here are some guidelines about saving documents:

- Use Save As when you name and save a document the first time.
- Use Save As when you save an existing document under a new name. Save As creates an entirely new file and leaves the original document unchanged.
- Use Save to update an existing document.

NOTE

Your instructor will advise you on the proper drive and folder to use for this course.

Before you save a new document, decide where you want to save it. Word saves documents in the current drive and folder unless you specify otherwise. For example, to save a document to a removable storage device, you need to change the drive to F:, or whichever is appropriate for your computer.

Document files are typically stored in folders that are part of a hierarchal structure similar to a family tree. At the top of the tree is a disk drive letter (such as C:) that represents your computer, network, removable storage device, or CD/DVD drive. Under the disk drive letter, you can create folders to organize your files. These folders can also contain additional folders.

For this course, you will create a new folder for each lesson and store your completed exercise documents in these folders.

Exercise 1-9 NAME AND SAVE A DOCUMENT

1. Click the **File** tab to open the Backstage view, and click **Save As**. The Save As dialog box appears. The appearance of the Save As dialog box is determined by the operating system. The Save As dialog box in Windows 7 is different from the Save As dialog box shown in Windows XP.

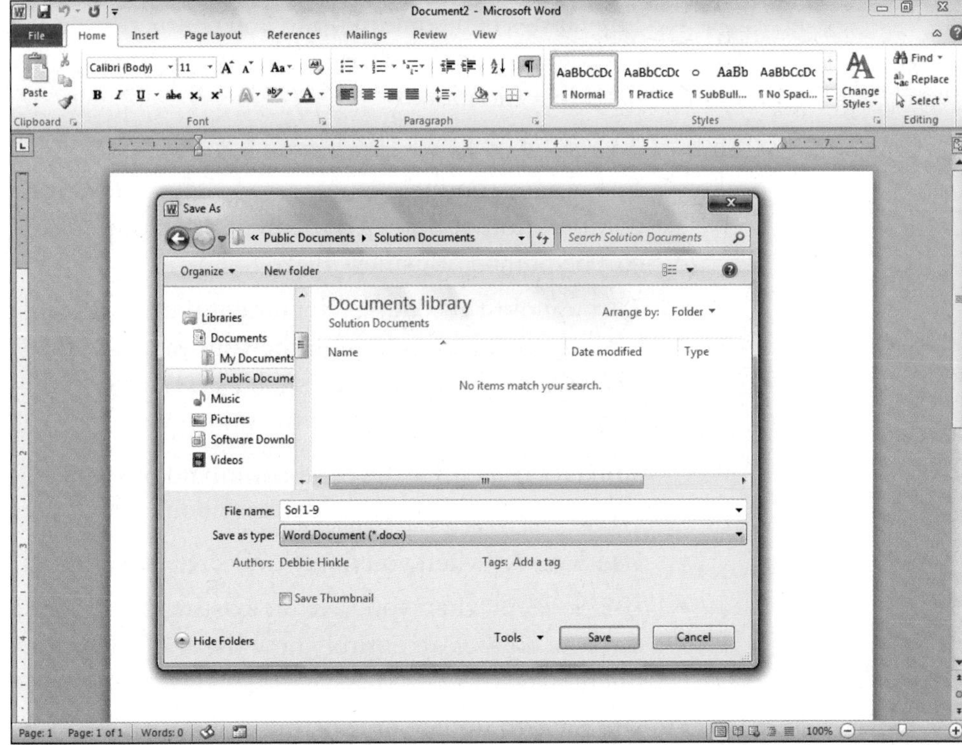

Figure 1-9
Save As dialog box using Windows 7

NOTE

To save a document as a PDF file, open the Save As dialog box, choose the appropriate drive and folder for saving the document, key the file name, open the Save as type drop-down list, and choose PDF (*.pdf). Click Save.

2. Locate the **File name** text box. A suggested file name is highlighted. Replace this file name by keying ***[your initials]*** **1-9**.
3. Drag the scroll box in the Navigation Pane, and choose the appropriate drive for your removable storage device—Removable Disk (F:), for example.

NOTE

When no document is open, the document window displays a shaded background. If you want to create a new document, click the File tab, click New, click Blank document, and click Create. The keyboard shortcut to start a new document is Ctrl+N.

4. Click the New Folder button New folder. A New Folder icon appears in the File list section. Key the folder name ***[your initials]*** **Lesson1**, and press Enter. The folder name appears in the Address bar and in the Navigation Pane. Word is ready to save the file in the new folder.
5. Click the Save button Save. Your document is named and saved for future use.
6. Open the File tab and click Close. The Close command in Backstage view closes the current document but does not exit the Word program. If you click the Close button located on the title bar and no other documents are open, you exit Word.

Opening an Existing Document

Instead of creating a new document for this exercise, you start this exercise by opening an existing document. There are several ways to open a document:

- Choose Open from the File tab.
- Press Ctrl+O.
- Use the document links in the Recent Documents file listing.

The Open command displays the Open dialog box. The commands and features listed in the Open dialog box resemble the commands and features you studied in the Save As dialog box. Remember the operating system determines the appearance of the Open dialog box.

TIP

The keyboard shortcut to open the File tab is Alt+F.

NOTE

The push pin icon that appears to the right of files listed under Recent Documents is used to pin a document to the list so that it does not disappear from view. Click the pinned icon to unpin the document from the list.

Exercise 1-10 OPEN AN EXISTING FILE

1. Click the File tab to open the Backstage view. Click the Recent command. The file names listed under Recent Documents are files opened from this computer. If the file you want is listed, click its name to open it. The Recent Documents section displays up to 22 documents by default.
2. Click Open to display the Open dialog box. You are going to open a student file named **Campbell-1**.

3. Locate the appropriate drive and folder according to your instructor's directions.

Figure 1-10
Files listed in the Open dialog box using Windows 7

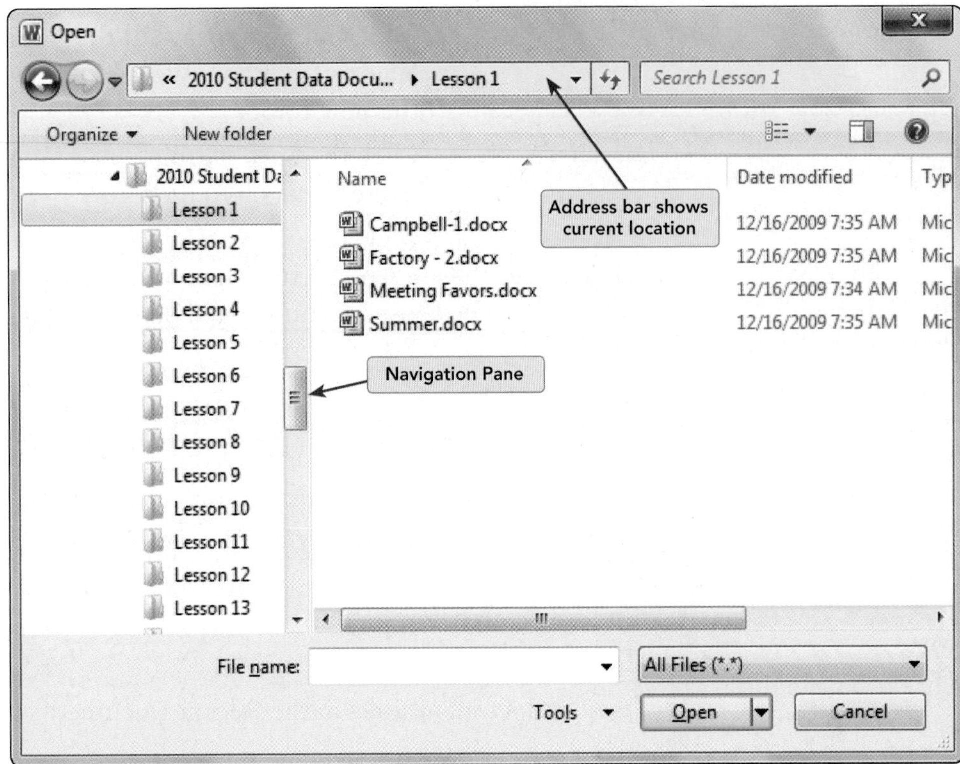

TABLE 1-3 Open Dialog Box Buttons

Button	Name	Purpose
« Public Docume... ▸ Student Data Files	Address bar	Navigates to a different folder.
	Back button	Works with the Address bar, and returns to previous location.
	Forward button	Works with the Address bar, and returns to location already opened.
Search Documents	Search box	Looks for a file or subfolder.
Organize	Organize	Opens a menu of file functions, such as cutting a file, copying a file, pasting a file, deleting a file, or renaming a file. Includes the Layout option to display the Navigation Pane, Details Pane, and the Preview Pane.
New folder	New Folder	Creates a new folder to organize files.
	View	Displays a menu of view options for displaying drives, folders, files, and their icons.

4. After you locate the student files, click the arrow next to the View button in the Open dialog box to display a list of view options.
5. Choose **List** to list the files by file name.

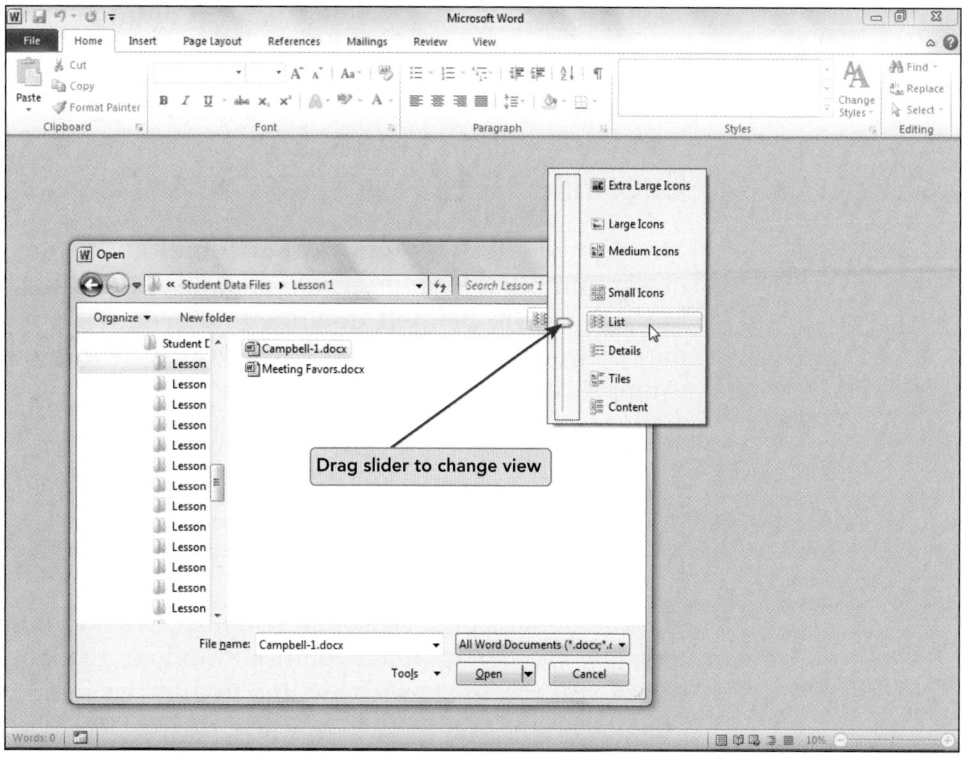

Figure 1-11
View menu in the Open dialog box

TIP

You can also double-click a file name to open a file.

6. From the list of file names, locate **Campbell-1** and click it once to select it.
7. Click **Open**.

NOTE

Documents created in earlier versions of Word display Compatibility Mode in the Title bar when opened. Compatibility Mode enables you to open, edit, and save documents that were created using earlier versions of Word. New features in Microsoft Word 2010 are not available in Compatibility Mode. To check for features not supported by earlier versions of the Word program, click the File tab, and click the Info command. Click the Check for Issues button. Click Check Compatibility. To convert a document created in an earlier version of Word to Microsoft Word 2010, click the Info command, and click Convert. Click OK.

8. Click the File tab, and choose Save As. You are going to save **Campbell-1** under a new file name.
9. Use the Navigation Pane to locate the appropriate drive and the folder you created for Lesson 1.
10. Verify that the file's original name (**Campbell-1**) is selected. If it is not selected, double-click it.
11. Key the file name ***[your initials]*****1-10**, and click Save.

Exercise 1-11 ENTER FORMATTING CHARACTERS

The Show/Hide ¶ button on the Home tab displays or hides paragraph marks and other *formatting marks*. These characters appear on the screen, but not in the printed document. Formatting marks are included as part of words, sentences, and paragraphs in a document. Here are some examples:

- A word includes the space character that follows it.
- A sentence includes the end-of-sentence punctuation and at least one space.
- A paragraph is any amount of text followed by a paragraph mark.

The document you opened contains two additional formatting characters: *tab characters,* which you use to indent text, and *line-break characters,* which you use to start a new line within the same paragraph. Line-break characters are useful when you want to create a paragraph of short lines, such as an address, and keep the lines together as a single paragraph.

Another formatting character is a *nonbreaking space,* which you use to prevent two words from being divided between two lines. For example, you can insert a nonbreaking space between "Mr." and "Smith" to keep the name "Mr. Smith" undivided on one line.

TABLE 1-4 Formatting Characters

Character	To Insert, Press
Tab (→)	Tab
Space (·)	Spacebar
Nonbreaking space (°)	Ctrl+Shift+Spacebar
Paragraph mark (¶)	Enter
Line-break character (↵)	Shift+Enter

1. Click the Show/Hide ¶ button [¶] if the formatting characters in the document are hidden.
2. Move the insertion point to the end of the document (after "family recipes.").
3. Press [Enter] to begin a new paragraph, and key **Campbell's Confections has been a member in good standing of the NCA for over 50** (do not press [Spacebar]).
4. Insert a nonbreaking space after "50" by pressing [Ctrl]+[Shift]+[Spacebar]. Then key **years.** (including the period). Word now treats "50 years" as a single unit.

Figure 1-12 Formatting characters

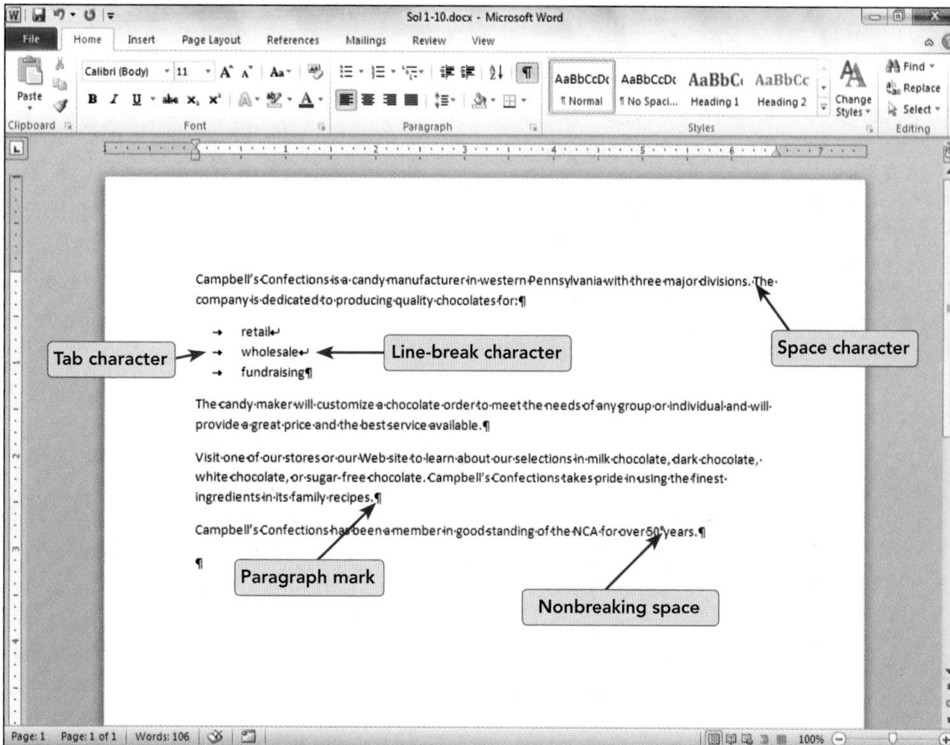

5. Press [Enter] and key the following text as one paragraph at the end of the document, pressing [Shift]+[Enter] at the end of the first and second lines instead of [Enter].

   Campbell's Confections
   25 Main Street
   Grove City, PA 16127

6. Click the Show/Hide ¶ button [¶] to hide the formatting characters, and click it again to redisplay them.

Moving within a Document

You already know how to move around a short document by positioning the I-beam pointer with the mouse and clicking. This is the easiest way to move around a document that displays in the document window. If a document is too long or too wide to view in the window, you need to use different methods to navigate within a document.

Word offers two additional methods for moving within a document:

- *Using the keyboard:* You can press certain keys on the keyboard to move the insertion point. The arrow keys, for example, move the insertion point up or down one line or to the left or right one character. Key combinations quickly move the insertion point to specified locations in the document.
- *Using the scroll bars:* Use the vertical scroll bar at the right edge of the document window to move through a document. The position of the scroll box indicates your approximate location in the document, which is particularly helpful in long documents. To view and move through a document that is wider than the document window, use the horizontal scroll bar at the bottom of the document window.

NOTE

Scrolling through a document does not move the insertion point. It moves only the portion of the document you are viewing in the document window. When you use the keyboard to move within a document, the insertion point always moves to the new location.

Exercise 1-12 USE THE KEYBOARD TO MOVE THE INSERTION POINT

1. Press Ctrl+Home to move to the beginning of the document. Press End to move to the end of the first line.
2. Press Ctrl+↓ several times to move the insertion point down one paragraph at a time. Notice how the text with the line-break characters is treated as a single paragraph.

TIP

Word remembers the last three locations in the document where you edited or keyed text. You can press Shift+F5 to return the insertion point to these locations. For example, when you open a document you worked on earlier, press Shift+F5 to return to the place where you were last working before you saved and closed the document.

3. When you reach the end of the document, press PageUp until you return to the beginning of the document.

TABLE 1-5 Keys to Move the Insertion Point

To Move	Press
One word to the left	Ctrl+←
One word to the right	Ctrl+→
Beginning of the line	Home
End of the line	End
One paragraph up	Ctrl+↑
One paragraph down	Ctrl+↓
Previous page	Ctrl+PageUp
Next page	Ctrl+PageDown
Up one window	PageUp
Down one window	PageDown
Top of the window	Alt+Ctrl+PageUp
Bottom of the window	Alt+Ctrl+PageDown
Beginning of the document	Ctrl+Home
End of the document	Ctrl+End

NOTE

The horizontal scroll bar does not display if the document window is wide enough to display the document text. To display the horizontal bar, resize the window.

Exercise 1-13 SCROLL THROUGH A DOCUMENT

Using the mouse and the scroll bars, you can scroll up, down, left, and right. You can also set the Previous and Next buttons on the vertical scroll bar to scroll through a document by a specific object, such as tables or headings. For example, use these buttons to jump from one heading to the next, going forward or backward.

1. Locate the vertical scroll bar, and click below the scroll box to move down one window.

Figure 1-13
Using the scroll bars

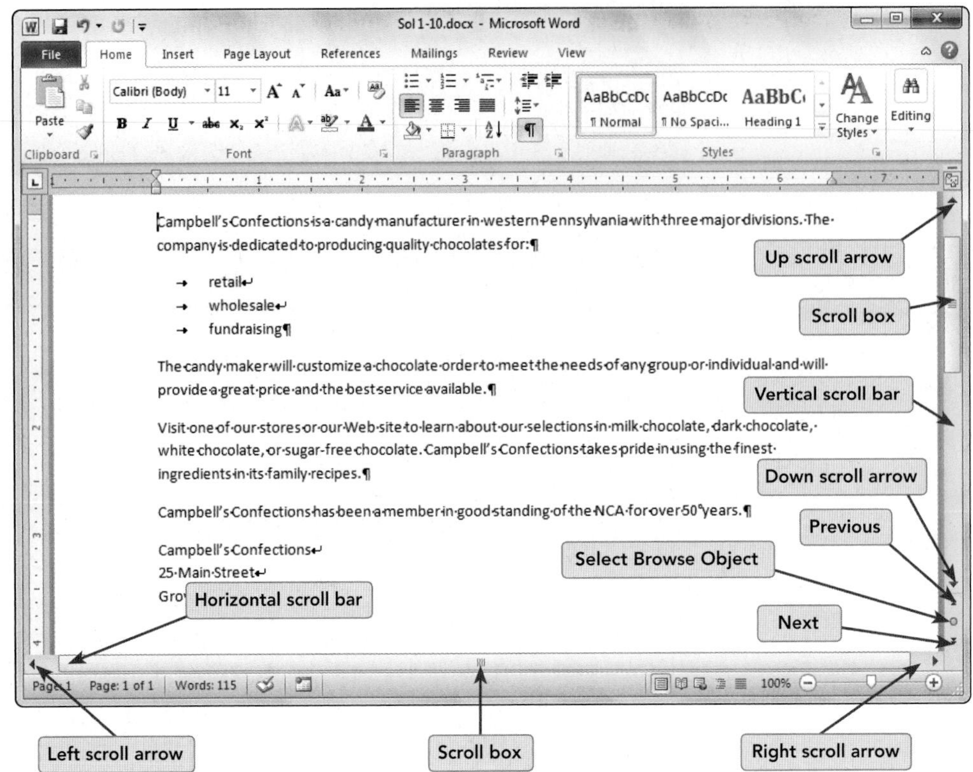

TIP

The keyboard shortcut to display the Select Browse Object menu is Ctrl+Alt+Home.

TIP

If you are using a mouse with a wheel, additional navigating options are available. For example, you can roll the wheel forward or backward instead of using the vertical scroll bars, hold down the wheel and drag in any direction to pan the document, or hold down Ctrl as you roll the wheel to change the magnification.

2. Drag the scroll box to the top of the scroll bar.
3. Click the down scroll arrow on the scroll bar three times. The document moves three lines.
4. Click the up scroll arrow on the vertical scroll bar three times to bring the document back into full view.

   Notice that as you scroll through the document, the insertion point remains at the top of the document.
5. Click the Select Browse Object button, located toward the bottom of the vertical scroll bar. A palette of icons appears.
6. Move the pointer over each icon to identify it. These browse options become significant as your documents become more complex. Click the Browse by Page icon.

TABLE 1-6 Scrolling through a Document

To Move	Do This
Up one line	Click the up scroll arrow.
Down one line	Click the down scroll arrow.
Up one window	Click the scroll bar above the scroll box.
Down one window	Click the scroll bar below the scroll box.
To any relative position	Drag the scroll box up or down.
To the right	Click the right scroll arrow.
To the left	Click the left scroll arrow.
Into the left margin	Hold down Shift and click the left scroll arrow.
Up or down one page	Click Select Browse Object, click Browse by Page, and then click Next or Previous.

Selecting Text

Selecting text is a basic technique that makes revising documents easy. When you select text, that area of the document is called the *selection,* and it appears as a highlighted block of text. A selection can be a character, group of characters, word, sentence, or paragraph or the whole document. In this lesson, you delete and replace selected text. Future lessons show you how to format, move, copy, delete, and print selected text.

You can select text several ways, depending on the size of the area you want to select.

TABLE 1-7 Mouse Selection

To	Use the Mouse to Select
A series of characters	Click and drag, or click one end of the text block, and then hold down Shift and click the other end.
A word	Double-click the word.
A sentence	Press Ctrl and click anywhere in the sentence.
A line of text	Move the pointer to the left of the line until it changes to a right-pointing arrow, and then click. To select multiple lines, drag up or down.
A paragraph	Move the pointer to the left of the paragraph and double-click. To select multiple paragraphs, drag up or down. You can also triple-click a paragraph to select it.
The entire document	Move the pointer to the left of any document text until it changes to a right-pointing arrow, and then triple-click (or hold down Ctrl and click).

Exercise 1-14 SELECT TEXT WITH THE MOUSE

1. Select the first word of the document by double-clicking it. Notice that the space following the word is also selected. When text is selected, a Mini toolbar appears with formatting options.

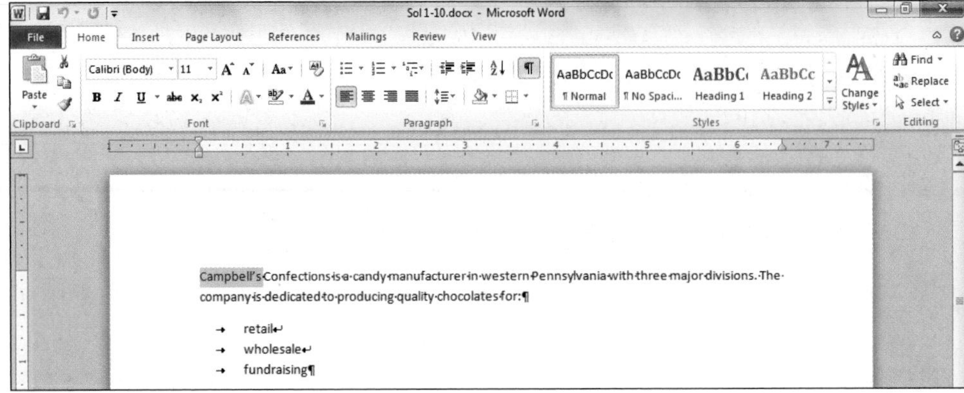

Figure 1-14
Selecting a word

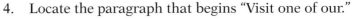

2. Cancel the selection by clicking anywhere in the document. Selected text remains highlighted until you cancel the selection.
3. Select the first sentence by holding down Ctrl and clicking anywhere within the sentence. Notice that the period and space following the sentence are part of the selection. Cancel the selection.
4. Locate the paragraph that begins "Visit one of our."
5. To select the text "milk chocolate," click to the left of "milk." Hold down the left mouse button and slowly drag through the text, including the comma and space after "chocolate." Release the mouse button. Cancel the selection.
6. To select the entire paragraph by dragging the mouse, click to position the insertion point to the left of "Visit." Hold down the mouse button, and then drag across and down until all the text and the paragraph mark are selected. Cancel the selection.
7. Select the same paragraph by moving the pointer into the blank area to the left of the text "Visit." (This is the margin area.) When the I-beam pointer changes to a right-pointing arrow, double-click. Notice that the first click selects the first line and the second click selects the paragraph, including the paragraph mark. Cancel the selection.

TIP

When selecting more than one word, you can click anywhere within the first word and then drag to select additional text. Word "smart-selects" the entire first word.

TIP

You can also triple-click within a paragraph to select it.

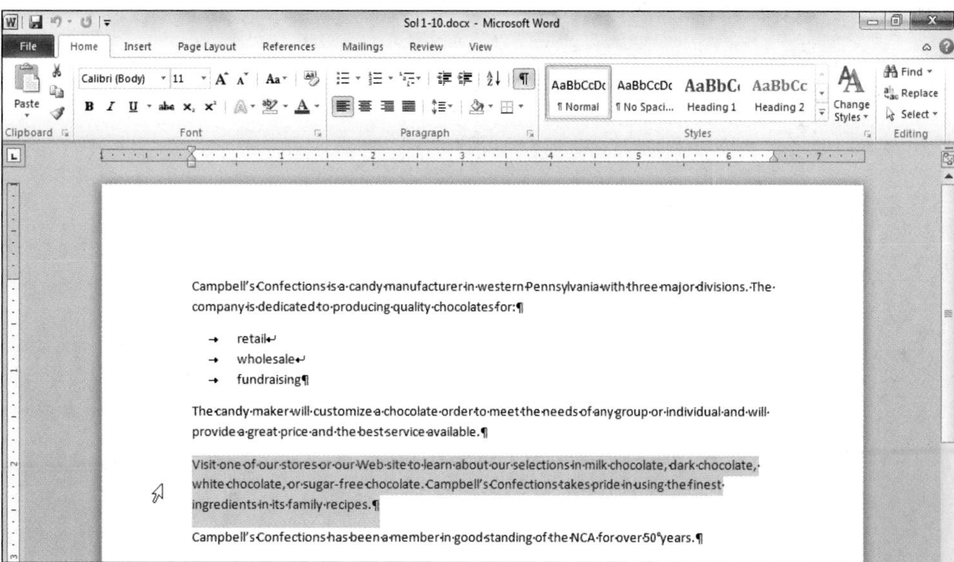

Figure 1-15
Selecting text

Exercise 1-15 SELECT NONCONTIGUOUS TEXT

In the previous exercise, you learned how to select *contiguous text,* where the selected characters, words, sentences, or paragraphs follow one another. But sometimes you would like to select *noncontiguous text,* such as the first and last items in a list or the third and fifth word in a paragraph. In Word, you can select noncontiguous text by using Ctrl and the mouse.

1. Select the first line of the list ("retail").
2. Press Ctrl and select the third line of the list ("fundraising"). With these two separate lines selected, you can delete, format, or move them without affecting the rest of the list.
3. Cancel the selection, and go to the paragraph that begins "Visit one of our."
4. In the paragraph that begins "Visit one of our," double-click the word "our" before "Web site." With the word now selected, hold down Ctrl as you double-click the word "selections" in the same sentence and "finest" in the next sentence. (See Figure 1-16.) All three words are highlighted.

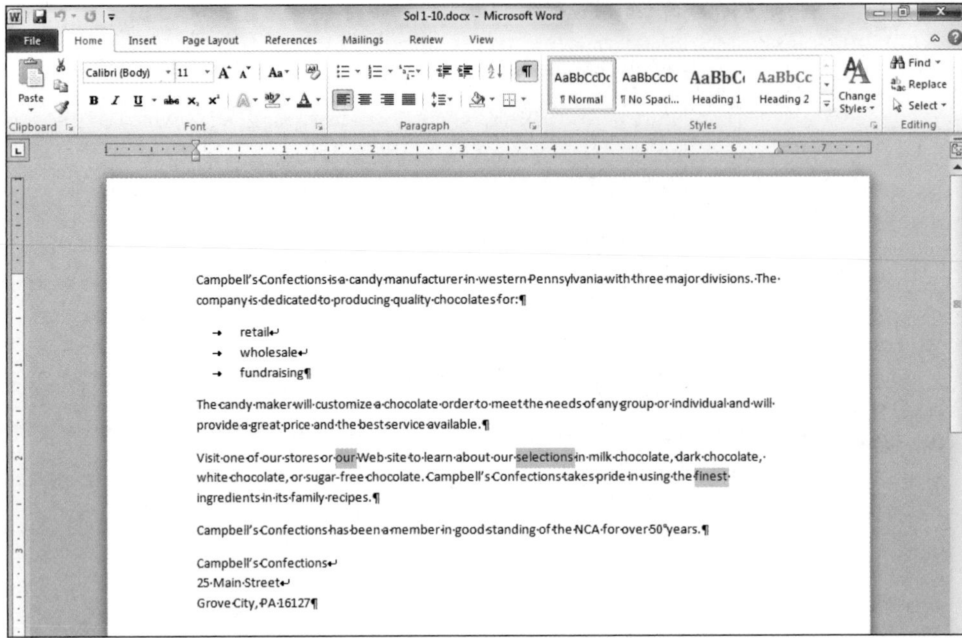

Figure 1-16 Selecting noncontiguous words

5. Cancel the selection.

Exercise 1-16 ADJUST A SELECTION USING THE MOUSE AND THE KEYBOARD

NOTE

Another way to extend a text selection is to turn on Selection mode by pressing F8. In Selection mode, you can press F8 to select a word, press it again to select a sentence, press it again to select a paragraph, and press it again to select the entire document. Press Shift+F8 to shorten the selection. Press Esc to turn off Selection mode. Right-click the status bar, and click Selection Mode to turn on or turn off the status bar indicator.

1. Select the paragraph beginning "Visit one of our."
2. Hold down Shift and press ← until the last sentence is no longer highlighted. Release Shift.
3. Increase the selection to include the last sentence by holding down Shift and pressing End and then pressing ↓. Release Shift.
4. Increase the selection to include all the text below it by holding down Shift and clicking at the end of the document (after the ZIP Code).
5. Select the entire document by pressing Ctrl+A. Cancel the selection.

TABLE 1-8 Keyboard Selection

To Select	Press
One character to the right	Shift+→
One character to the left	Shift+←
One word to the right	Ctrl+Shift+→
One word to the left	Ctrl+Shift+←
To the end of a line	Shift+End
To the beginning of a line	Shift+Home
One line up	Shift+↑
One line down	Shift+↓
One window down	Shift+PageDown
One window up	Shift+PageUp
To the end of a document	Ctrl+Shift+End
To the beginning of a document	Ctrl+Shift+Home
An entire document	Ctrl+A

Exercise 1-17 EDIT TEXT BY REPLACING A SELECTION

You can edit a document by selecting text and deleting or replacing the selection.

NOTE

Although keying over selected text is an excellent editing feature, it sometimes leads to accidental deletions. Remember, when text is selected in a document (or even in a dialog box) and you begin keying text, Word deletes all the selected text with your first keystroke. If you key text without realizing a portion of the document is selected, use the Undo command to restore the text.

1. Locate the paragraph that begins "Visit one of our," and select the word "our" in the first sentence that follows the word "about."
2. Key **the variety of** to replace the selected text.
3. Locate the paragraph that begins "Campbell's Confections has been," and select "NCA." Key **National Confectioners Association**. Notice that, unlike using Overtype mode, when you key over selected text, the new text can be longer or shorter than the selection.

Exercise 1-18 UNDO AND REDO ACTIONS

Word remembers the changes you make in a document and lets you undo or redo these changes. For example, if you accidentally delete text, you can use the Undo command to reverse the action and restore the text. If you change your mind and decide to keep the deletion, you can use the Redo command to reverse the canceled action.

NOTE

The Redo button is also identified as the Repeat button. Use the Repeat command to repeat the last action performed.

There are two ways to undo or redo an action:

- Click the Undo button or the Redo button on the Quick Access Toolbar.
- Press Ctrl+Z to undo or Ctrl+Y to redo.

1. Delete the first word in the document, "Campbell's," by moving the insertion point to the right of the space after the word and pressing Ctrl+Backspace. (Remember that a word includes the space that follows it.)
2. Click the Undo button to restore the word.
3. Move the insertion point to the left of the word "candy" in the first line of the first paragraph.
4. Key **midsize** and press Spacebar once. The text now reads "midsize candy manufacturer."
5. Press Ctrl+Z. The word "midsize" is deleted.
6. Click the Redo button to restore the word "mid-size."
7. Click the down arrow to the right of the Undo button. Word displays a drop-down list of the last few actions, with the most recent action at the top. You can use this feature to choose several actions to undo rather than just the last action. Click **Cancel** to close the list.
8. Click the Undo button.

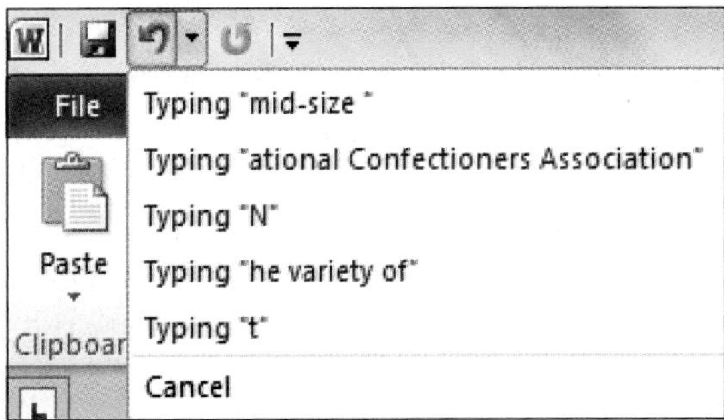

Figure 1-17
Undo drop-down list

Exercise 1-19 REPEAT ACTIONS

Suppose you key text you want to add to other areas of a document. Instead of rekeying the same text, you can use the Repeat command to duplicate the text.

To use the Repeat command, press either:

- Ctrl+Y
- F4

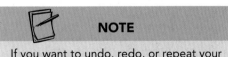

NOTE

If you want to undo, redo, or repeat your last action, do so before you press another key.

1. In the first paragraph position the insertion point to the left of the word "candy."
2. Key **popular** and press Spacebar once. The sentence now begins "Campbell's Confections is a popular candy."

3. Move the insertion point to the left of the word "selections" in the paragraph that begins "Visit one of our."
4. Press F4 and the word "popular" is repeated.

Printing a Document

After you create a document, printing it is easy. You can use any of the following methods:

- Choose Print from the File tab.
- Press Ctrl+P.

The Print command in Backstage view and the keyboard shortcut to print display the Print tab, where you can select printing options and preview the document. Clicking the Print button sends the document directly to the printer, using Word's default settings.

Exercise 1-20 PRINT A DOCUMENT

1. Click the **File** tab to open the Backstage view. Click the **Print** command. The Print tab displays Word's default print settings and a preview of the document.

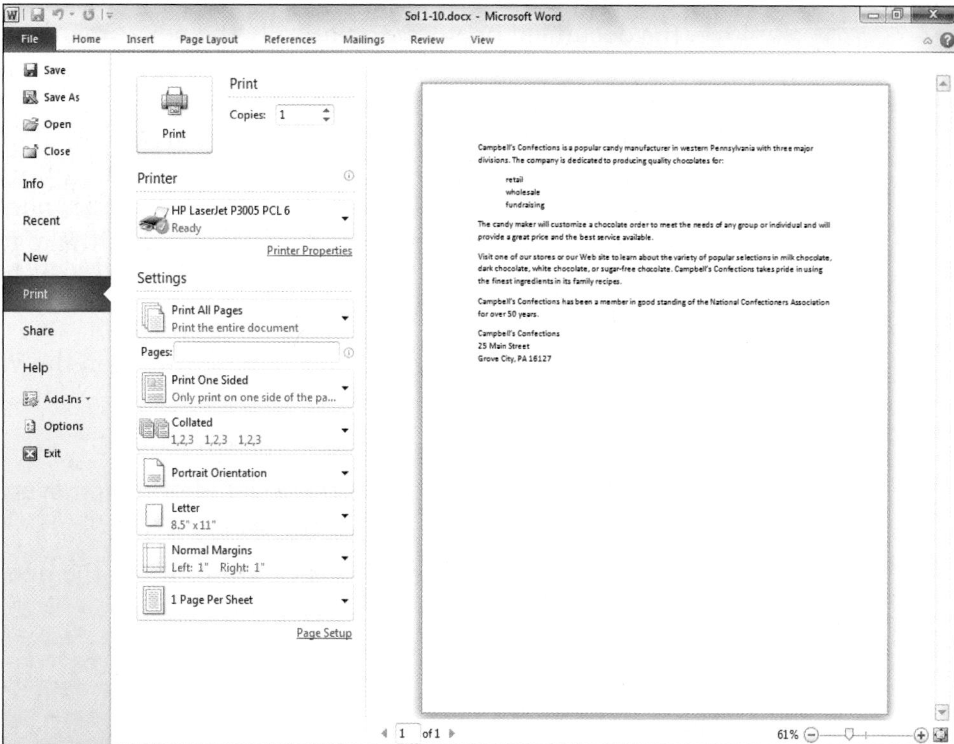

Figure 1-18
Print tab

2. Click the Print button to accept the default print settings.

Closing a Document and Exiting Word

NOTE

If you wanted to save the current document with a different file name, you would use the Save As command.

Exercise 1-21 SAVE A REVISED DOCUMENT

You have already used the Save As command to rename the document you opened earlier in this lesson. Now that you have made additional revisions, you can save a final version of the document by using the Save command. The document is saved with all the changes, replacing the old file with the revised file.

1. Click the Save button on the Quick Access Toolbar. This action saves the changes to the document. Since the document was saved earlier in the lesson, the Save As dialog box does not display.

Exercise 1-22 CHECK WORD'S AUTORECOVER SETTINGS

Word's *AutoRecover* feature can automatically save open documents at an interval you specify. However, this is not the same as saving a file yourself, as you did in the preceding exercise. AutoRecover's purpose is to save open documents "in the background," so a recently saved version is always on disk. Then if the power fails or your system crashes, the AutoRecover version of the document opens automatically the next time you launch Word. In other words, AutoRecover ensures you always have a recently saved version of your document.

Even with AutoRecover working, you need to manually save a document (by using the Save command) before closing it. AutoRecover documents are not always available. If you save and close your file normally, the AutoRecover version is deleted when you exit Word. Still, it is a good idea to make sure AutoRecover is working on your system and to set it to save recovery files frequently.

1. Open the **File** tab, and click **Options** to open the Word Options dialog box.
2. Click the **Save** command in the left pane.
3. Make sure the **Save AutoRecover information every** box is checked. If it is not checked, click the box.
4. Click the up or down arrow buttons to set the **minutes** to 5. Click **OK**.

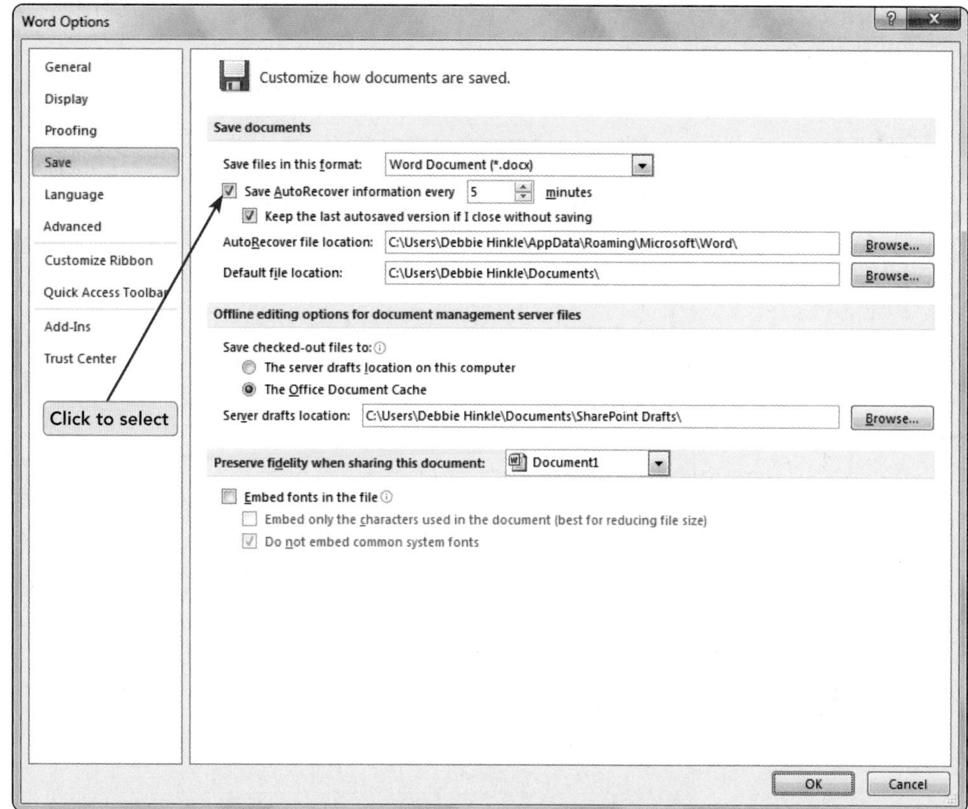

Figure 1-19
Setting AutoRecover options

Exercise 1-23 REVIEW AND EDIT DOCUMENT PROPERTIES

Information that describes your document is called a *property*. Word automatically saves your document with certain properties, such as the file name, the date created, and the file size. You can add other properties to a document, such as the title, subject, author's name, and keywords. This information can help you organize and identify documents.

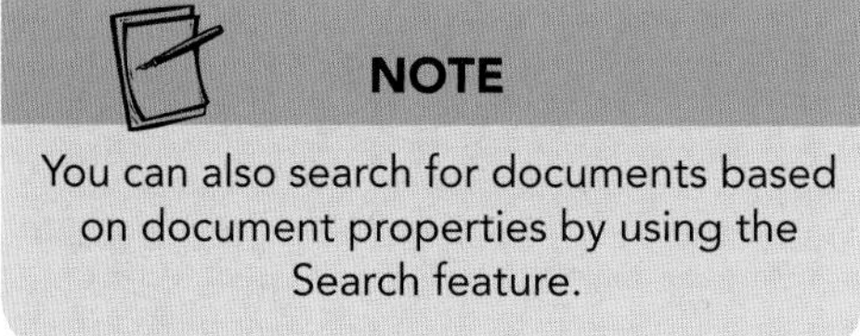
NOTE

You can also search for documents based on document properties by using the Search feature.

1. With the file ***[your initials]*****1-10** still open, click the **File** tab and click the **Info** command. Locate the Properties button Properties under the document preview. Click the down arrow, and click **Advanced Properties**. The Document Properties dialog box displays.

Figure 1-20
Entering Summary information

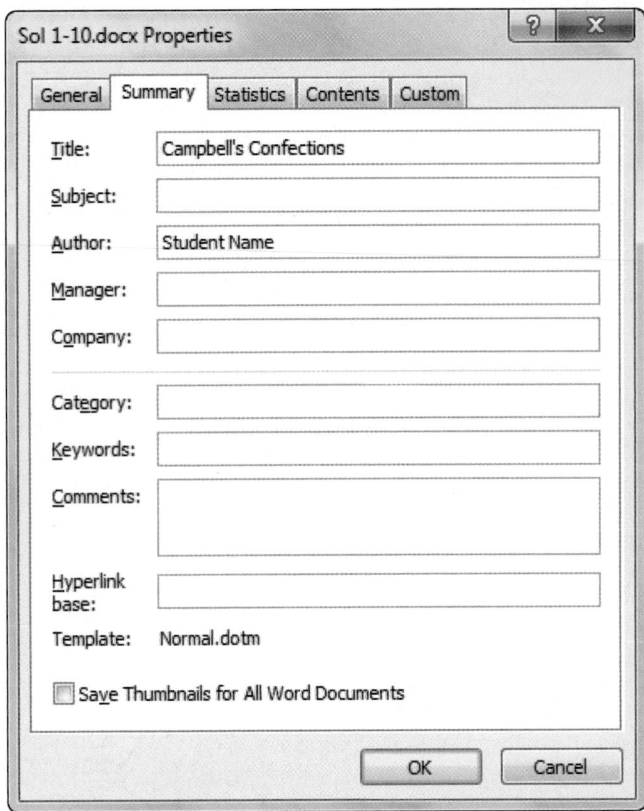

2. Click the **General** tab. This tab displays basic information about the file, such as file name, file type, location, size, and creation date.
3. Click the **Statistics** tab. This tab shows the exact breakdown of the document in number of paragraphs, lines, words, and characters.
4. Click the **Summary** tab. Here you can enter specific document property information or change existing information.
5. Key or edit the title to read **Campbell's Confections**, and key *[your name]* as the author. Click **OK**.
6. Save the document, and submit your work.

Exercise 1-24 CLOSE A DOCUMENT AND EXIT WORD

When you finish working on a document and save it, you can close it and open another document, or you can exit Word.

The easiest ways to close a document and exit Word include using the following:

- The Close button in the upper right corner of the Word window.
- The Close command from the File tab.
- Keyboard shortcuts:

  Ctrl+W closes a document.

  Alt+F4 exits Word.

NOTE

When no document is open, the document window is gray. If you want to create a new document, choose New from the File tab, click Blank Document, and click the Create button. The keyboard shortcut to create a new document is Ctrl+N.

1. Click the **File** tab, and choose **Close** from the Backstage view Navigation Pane.
2. Click the Close button in the upper right corner of the screen to exit Word and to display the Windows desktop.

Using Online Help

Online Help is available to you as you work in Word. Click the Help button or press F1 to open the Word Help window. You can click a Word Help link or key a word or phrase in the Search box.

FIND OUT MORE ABOUT USING HELP

1. Start Word.
2. Locate the Help button in the upper right corner of the screen. Click the button to open the Word Help window.
3. Locate and click the link **Getting started with Word 2010**.

Figure 1-21
Using the Word Help window

4. Review the list of topics.
5. Click the topic "What's new in Microsoft Word," and review the information.
6. Click the Back button to return to the list of categories.
7. Close Help by clicking the Word Help window's Close button.

Lesson 1 Summary

- To start Microsoft Word, click the Start button on the Windows taskbar, point to All Programs, click Microsoft Office, and click Microsoft Word 2010.
- The File tab is located to the left of the Home tab on the Ribbon. Click the tab to open the Backstage view.
- The title bar is at the top of the Word screen and displays the current document name.
- The Quick Access Toolbar displays icons for Save, Undo, and Repeat.
- The Ribbon contains tabs which include groups of related commands. Commands can be buttons, menus, or drop-down list boxes.
- Click a tab name to display related groups of commands. The number of groups and commands varies for each tab.
- Identify a command by name by pointing to it with the mouse. Word displays a ScreenTip with the command name.
- The horizontal ruler appears below the Ribbon.
- Scroll bars appear as shaded bars to the right and bottom of the text area. They are used to view different portions of a document.
- The status bar is located at the bottom of the Word screen. It displays the page number and page count of the document, the document view buttons, and the zoom control. It also displays the current mode of operation. Right-click the status bar to customize it.
- Use the Zoom feature to change the magnification of the text area.
- The blinking vertical line in the text area is called the insertion point. It marks the position of the next character to be keyed.
- The mouse pointer displays as an I-beam when it is in the text area and as an arrow when you point to a command outside the text area.
- When the Show/Hide ¶ button is turned on, a paragraph mark symbol appears at the end of every paragraph. A dot between words represents a space.
- Word automatically wraps text to the next line as you key text. Press Enter to start a new paragraph or to insert a blank line.
- Word flags spelling errors as you key text by inserting a red, wavy line under the misspelled word. To correct the spelling, point to the underlined word, click the right mouse button, and choose the correct spelling.
- Word automatically corrects commonly misspelled words for you as you key text. Word can automatically complete a word for you, such as the name of a month or day. Word suggests the completed word, and you press Enter to insert it.
- Delete a single character by using Backspace or Delete. Ctrl+Backspace deletes the word to the left of the insertion point. Ctrl+Delete deletes the word to the right of the insertion point.
- To insert text, click to position the insertion point, and key the text.
- To key text over existing text, turn on Overtype mode.

- Insert one space between words and between sentences.
- Document names, or file names, can contain 260 characters, including the drive letter, folder name, and extensions. The file name can contain spaces. The following characters cannot be used in a file name: **/ \ > < * ? " : |**
- Save a new document by using the Save As command and giving the document a file name. Use the Save command to update an existing document.
- Create folders to organize your files. You can do this in the Save As dialog box, using the New Folder button. Rename folders by locating and selecting the folder. Right-click the folder name, and choose Rename from the shortcut menu
- To start a new blank document, press Ctrl+N, or click the File tab. Click New, click Blank document, and click Create.
- Use the Open dialog box to open an existing file. Use the Views button in the dialog box to change the way files are listed.
- Formatting characters—such as blank spaces or paragraph marks—appear on-screen, but not in the printed document. Insert a line-break character to start a new line within the same paragraph. Insert a nonbreaking space between two words to make sure they appear on the same line.
- When a document is larger than the document window, use the keyboard or the scroll bars to view different parts of the document. Keyboard methods for moving within a document also move the insertion point.
- Keyboard techniques for moving within a document include single keys (such as PageUp and Home) and keyboard combinations (such as Ctrl+↑). See Table 1-5.
- Scrolling techniques for moving within a document include clicking the up or down scroll arrows on the vertical scroll bar or dragging the scroll box. Scrolling does not move the insertion point. See Table 1-6.
- Selecting text is a basic technique for revising documents. A selection is a highlighted block of text you can format, move, copy, delete, or print.
- There are many different techniques for selecting text, using the mouse, the keyboard, or a combination of both. Mouse techniques involve dragging or clicking. See Table 1-7. Keyboard techniques are listed in Table 1-8.
- You can select any amount of contiguous text (characters, words, sentences, or paragraphs that follow one another) or noncontiguous text (such as words that appear in different parts of a document). Use Ctrl along with the mouse to select noncontiguous blocks of text.
- When text is selected, Word replaces it with any new text you key, or it deletes the selection if you press Delete.
- If you make a change in a document that you want to reverse, use the Undo command. Use the Redo command to reverse the results of an Undo command.
- If you perform an action, such as keying text in a document, and you want to repeat that action elsewhere in the document, use the Repeat command.
- Choose Print from the File tab, or press Ctrl+P to print a document.

- Use the Save command to save any revisions you make to a document.
- Word's AutoRecover feature periodically saves open documents in the background so you can recover a file in the event of a power failure or system crash.

NOTE

Word provides many ways to accomplish a particular task. As you become more familiar with Word, you will find the methods you prefer.

- Document properties are details about a file that help identify it. Properties include the file name, file size, and date created, which Word updates automatically. Other properties you can add or change include title, subject, author's name, and keywords. View or add properties for an open document by clicking the File tab and clicking Info.
- To use Word Help, click the Help button or press F1.

LESSON		Command Summary	
Feature	**Button**	**Command**	**Keyboard**
Close a document	X	File tab, Close	Ctrl+W or Ctrl+F4
Document Properties	Properties ▾	File tab, Info command	
Exit Word	X	File tab, Exit	Alt+F4
Help	?		F1
Open		File tab, Open	Ctrl+O or Ctrl+F12
Print		File tab, Print	Ctrl+P
Redo		Quick Access Toolbar	Ctrl+Y or Alt+Shift+Backspace
Repeat		Quick Access Toolbar	Ctrl+Y or F4
Save		Quick Access Toolbar	Ctrl+S or Shift+F12
Save As		File tab, Save As	F12
Select entire document		Home tab, Editing group, Select All	Ctrl+A
Undo		Quick Access Toolbar	Ctrl+Z or Alt+Backspace

Concepts Review

True/False Questions

Each of the following statements is either true or false. Indicate your choice by circling T or F.

T F 1. A line-break character is used to begin a new paragraph.

T F 2. The Overtype mode indicator appears on the status bar by default.

T F 3. You can view more than one Ribbon tab at a time.

T F 4. To select a sentence, you can double-click anywhere within the sentence.

T F 5. Noncontiguous text is text that does not appear consecutively in a Word document.

T F 6. Pressing Delete deletes characters to the left of the insertion point.

T F 7. Ctrl+Delete deletes the word to the right of the insertion point.

T F 8. You can save a document by choosing Save from the File tab.

Short Answer Questions

Write the correct answer in the space provided.

1. What is the keyboard shortcut to print a document?

____

2. Which formatting character would you insert between two words to keep them together in a sentence?

____

3. If you begin keying a word such as “January” or “Thursday,” how can you have Word complete the word for you automatically?

____

4. Which area of the Word screen shows the number of pages in the document and displays indicators that show the current mode of operation?

____

5. What is the keyboard shortcut to move the insertion point to the beginning of a document?

____

6. What is the shape of the mouse pointer when it appears in the text area of the screen?

____

7. Which command is used to save a document under a different file name?

____

8. What is the keyboard shortcut for Help?

____

Critical Thinking

Answer these questions on a separate page. There are no right or wrong answers. Support your answers with examples from your own experience, if possible.

1. You can use the Show/Hide ¶ button to hide paragraph marks and space characters. When might it be useful to show these characters? When would you want to hide them?
2. Word allows great flexibility when naming files. Many businesses and individuals establish their own rules for naming files. What kinds of rules would you recommend for naming files in a business? For personal use?

Skills Review

Exercise 1-25

Key, edit, and save a document.

1. Press Ctrl+N to create a new document.
2. Key the text shown in Figure 1-22. (Use default formatting.)

Figure 1-22

```
Campbell's Confections recently celebrated another
anniversary in the candy business. The company manufactures
over 600 candy creations and produces over 1 million pounds
of chocolate each year. Caramel Pecanettes and Cordial
Cherries are the most popular candy creations. Campbell's
Confections has been at its current location for all of its
57 years.
```

3. Correct any spelling mistakes Word locates.
4. Delete the text "all of its" in the last sentence by following these steps:
   a. Move the insertion point to the right of the word "for" by positioning the I-beam and clicking the left mouse button.
   b. Hold down Ctrl and press Delete three times to delete the words "all of its."
5. Insert text after the word "Pecanettes" in the third sentence by following these steps:
   a. Move the insertion point to the immediate right of the word "Pecanettes," and key a comma and a space.
   b. Key **Melt-a-ways** followed by a comma.
6. Split the paragraph by following these steps:
   a. Move the insertion point to the immediate left of the word "Campbell's" in the last sentence.
   b. Press Enter.
7. Select the first word of the second sentence in the first paragraph "The," and key **Our**. Locate the phrase "the most popular" in the last sentence of the first paragraph, and change "the" to **our**.
8. Save the document as ***[your initials]*1-25** in your Lesson 1 folder.
9. Close the document.

Exercise 1-26

Key, edit, save, and print a document.

1. Start a new blank document by pressing Ctrl+N.
2. Key the text shown in Figure 1-23. Correct spelling mistakes as you key.

Figure 1-23

```
When you visit our inaugural store, take advantage of our
factory tour where you can see each of the steps in candy
making. You will follow the chocolate manufacturing line
beginning with melting the chocolate, preparing the rich
cream centers, and dipping the candy with two coats of
chocolate. All of our chocolates are hand decorated and
carefully packaged.
```

3. Move the insertion point to the left of the word "inaugural" in the first line of the paragraph.
4. Open the **File** tab. Click **Options**, and click **Advanced** in the left pane. Under Editing options, click **Use overtype mode** to turn on Overtype mode. Click **OK**.

5. Key **flagship** over the word "inaugural." Be sure to delete the extra character.
6. Turn off Overtype mode by clicking the **File** tab and clicking **Options**. Click **Advanced** in the left pane, and click **Use overtype mode** to turn off Overtype mode. Click **OK**.
7. Double-click to select the word "manufacturing" and key **production** to replace it.
8. Check the spacing before and after the replacement text.
9. Save the document as ***[your initials]*1-26** in your Lesson 1 folder.
10. Press Ctrl+P to display the Print tab. Click the Print button to print the document.
11. Close the document by pressing Ctrl+W.

Exercise 1-27

Open a document, undo, redo, and repeat editing actions.

1. Open the file **Meeting Favors**.
2. Position the insertion point after the heading "Meeting Favors" and press [Enter]. Click the Undo button to undo the insertion.
3. Move the insertion point to the left of "flavors" in the first sentence of the second paragraph. Key **chocolate** to create the phrase "chocolate flavors."
4. In the same paragraph, move the insertion point to the left of "favor shapes." Press F4 to create the phrase "chocolate favor shapes."
5. In the first sentence of the first paragraph, move the insertion point to the left of "for." Key **favors** and press Spacebar.
6. Locate "premier chocolate" in the last paragraph, and use the **Repeat** command to insert "favors" to the left of "for your."
7. Click the Undo button to undo the text. Then click the Redo button to redo the text.
8. In the last sentence of the last paragraph, replace the sentence by following these steps:
   a. Select the last sentence by pressing Ctrl and clicking anywhere in the sentence.
   b. Key **Visit www.campbellsconfections.biz for additional information.**
9. Save the document as ***[your initials]*1-27** in your Lesson 1 folder.
10. Submit your work, and close the document.

Exercise 1-28

Select text, save a revised document, and enter summary information.

1. Press Ctrl+N to start a new document. Key the text shown in Figure 1-24.

Figure 1-24

```
Campbell's Confections' chocolate factory tour and candy
store is one of Butler County's major attractions. The
factory tour enables visitors to watch the entire process of
candy making from melting the bulk chocolate to packing the
individual pieces in airtight containers. The information
provided by the tour guide is informative and educational.

If you are planning a family trip to Mercer County, be sure
to research other attractions in the area. You are miles
away from museums, antique shops, a forge that creates
aluminum, bronze, and other metal gifts, and many outdoor
activities. There are opportunities for camping, hiking,
biking, boating, and fishing. Winter activities include
sledding, ice fishing, ice skating, cross-country skiing,
and snowmobile trails. Contact us for brochures and other
information on area attractions.
```

2. Save the document as ***[your initials]*1-28** in your Lesson 1 folder.
3. Select and replace a word by following these steps:
   a. Place the insertion point in the word "Butler" in the first sentence of the first paragraph.
   b. Double-click the word to select it and key **Mercer** to replace it.
4. Select and replace text in the second paragraph by following these steps:
   a. Double-click "us" in the last line of the second paragraph.
   b. Key **the Chamber of Commerce** in place of the selected text.
5. Select "miles" in the second paragraph, and key **minutes** to replace the text.
6. Select a sentence by following these steps:
   a. Position the I-beam pointer over any sentence.
   b. Hold down Ctrl and click the mouse button. Release Ctrl.
   c. Deselect the sentence.
7. Select the first paragraph by following these steps:
   a. Move the pointer to the left of the paragraph until it changes to a right-pointing arrow.
   b. Double-click the mouse button.

8. Extend the current selection by following these steps:
   a. Hold down Shift and press ↓ twice to extend the selection two lines.
   b. Continue holding down Shift and press End to select the entire line.
   c. Continue holding down Shift and press PageDown to select the rest of the document. Release Shift.
9. Click anywhere to cancel the selection.
10. Select noncontiguous text by following these steps:
    a. Double-click the document's first word ("Campbell's").
    b. Move the pointer to the left of the paragraph's third line until the pointer changes to a right-pointing arrow. Hold down Ctrl and click to select the line.
    c. Hold down Ctrl and select the second paragraph by dragging the pointer from the beginning of the paragraph to the end.
11. Click anywhere to cancel the selection.
12. Review the document properties, and enter summary information by following these steps:
    a. Click the **File** tab and choose **Info**.
    b. Click the down arrow beside **Properties** in the right pane, and click **Advanced Properties**.
    c. Review the data on the General tab and the Statistics tab, and click the **Summary** tab.
    d. Click in the **Title** text box, and key **Mercer County**.
    e. Key ***[your name]*** in the Author text box.
    f. Click **OK**. Click the **File** tab to return to the document.
13. Click the Save button to save the revised document.
14. Submit your work, and close the document.

Lesson Applications

Exercise 1-29

Key, edit, and print a document.

1. Start a new document. Turn on Caps Lock mode and key **TO SALES ASSOCIATES:**
2. Turn off Caps Lock, and press Enter to start a new paragraph.
3. Key the text shown in Figure 1-25, including the corrections. Refer to Appendix A, "Proofreaders' Marks," if necessary. *Proofreaders' marks* are handwritten corrections to text, often using specialized symbols.

TIP

When Word suggests the completed word for "September," you can press Enter to insert the word. Remember to press Spacebar after the completed word.

Figure 1-25

```
Campbell's Confections' shipping policy changes will take
                    Formerly
effect immediately.^Chocolate was shipped to warmer
                  September        May
climates between June 1 and August 15 only. The new
                                                       during
policy includes year-round shipping with Campbell's  extremely
                                                   hot conditions
confections reserving the right to postpone shipments^.
Chocolate shipped to warm climates (temperatures over
             are
70 degrees) will be surrounded with ice packs. A chart
                      to all store managers
has been distributed^listing the statistical average high
temperature for each state by month. Next-day delivery is
recommended for warm weather destinations. Use sealed
moisture-proof containers to prevent damage caused by
high humidity.
Remember: Fine chocolates are perishable.
```

4. Edit the last two sentences of the first paragraph to read: Next-day delivery and sealed moisture-proof containers are recommended for warm weather destination.
5. Insert a comma at the end of the last sentence in the last paragraph, and key the following text: **and our customers expect their packages to arrive in perfect condition.**
6. In the second paragraph, delete "Fine" after "Remember" and key **Quality** before "chocolates."

7. Save the document as ***[your initials]*1-29** in your Lesson 1 folder.
8. Print the document, and then close it.

Exercise 1-30

Key, edit, and print a document.

1. Start a new document, and key the two paragraphs shown in Figure 1-26, including the corrections. Refer to Appendix A, "Proofreaders' Marks," if necessary.

Figure 1-26

```
Campbell's Confections offer[s] group tours from September
to June. Tours include watching a video on the history of
Campbell's Confections as well as the history of
chocolate. After the video, a tour thru the factory is
conducted by the plant manager. [At the end of the tour, each person receives a candy sample.]

Group tours [arranged/are] for families visiting the area,
school[s] or any group with an interest in ~~learning about~~
chocolate.
```

2. Correct the spelling of "thru" in the third sentence to **through**.
3. In the last sentence of the last paragraph, key **type of** after "or any." Delete "families visiting the area" and key **tourists** in its place.
4. Add the following text to the end of the second paragraph:

   Reservations are required two weeks in advance with a minimum of ten members in the tour. To schedule a tour or for more information, call 1-800-555-2025 or visit www.campbells.confections.biz.

5. Save the document as ***[your initials]*1-30** in your Lesson 1 folder.
6. Print, and then close the document

Exercise 1-31

Select and edit text, and insert a nonbreaking space.

1. Open the file **Factory - 2**.
2. Split the first paragraph at the sentence that begins "The chocolate factory."
3. Merge the second paragraph with the third paragraph. Be sure to insert a space between sentences.

4. Spell out "sq." and "ft." Replace "all of its" with **the**.
5. At the end of the last paragraph, key this sentence:
   Educational materials are available for elementary and middle school teachers.
6. Add a nonbreaking space between "June" and "30."
7. Insert the following sentence at the end of the first paragraph.
   The factory hosts special events throughout the year such as Candy Making 101 and Secrets of Dipping Strawberries. Each year Campbell's Confections sponsors an expert chocolatier to demonstrate the art of making chocolate.
8. Save the document as ***[your initials]*1-31** in your Lesson 1 folder.
9. Submit and close the document.

Exercise 1-32 ◆ Challenge Yourself

Select and edit text, use formatting characters, and enter summary information.

1. Open the file **Summer**.
2. Revise the document as shown in Figure 1-27.

Figure 1-27

```
Summer is a great time to visit Grove City. In June, the
Grove City Area Chamber of Commerce hosts the annual
                                        in June  Visitors can
Strawberry Days Art & Music Festival. Enjoy free working
exhibitions, live entertainment, and wonderful ethnic food.
  Fourth of
The July 4 patriotic celebration and fireworks are a
                     fantastic
special treat. Dozens of aerial displays and fantastic
ground displays are all part of the Fireworks Spectacular
at Memorial Park.

In August, the Chamber of Commerce hosts Art in the Park.
This annual event features more than 100 artisans with a
wide variety of fine art and handcrafted treasures.
```

3. Add the following sentence after "Music Festival in June" in the first paragraph:
   The festival features more than 75 craftspeople and artists.
4. In the last sentence of the first paragraph, replace "wonderful" with **a wide variety of**.

5. Change the last paragraph so it becomes three lines of text, as follows (use line breaks to start new lines):

   Coming in August:
   Art in the Park
   Fine art and handcrafted treasures

6. Select the three-line paragraph you just created.
7. Press Delete, and then undo the deletion.
8. At the end of the first paragraph, change "food" to **foods**.
9. Save the document named ***[your initials]*1-32** in your Lesson 1 folder.
10. Open the **Properties** dialog box, and click the **Summary** tab. Key **Summer in Grove City** as the title, key your name as the author, and key **Summer tourist attractions** in the Comments box. Click **OK**.
11. Save the document and submit your work.

On Your Own

In these exercises you work on your own, as you would in a real-life business environment. Use the skills you've learned to accomplish the task—and be creative.

Exercise 1-33

Browse the various tabs on the Ribbon until you find a command that looks intriguing. Use the Help feature to learn more about the feature. In a new blank document, write a few paragraphs about your findings. Save the document as ***[your initials]*1-33** and submit it.

Exercise 1-34

Locate a novel or historical text written before the twentieth century. Create a new document, and key approximately one-half page of text using the historical reference you located. Save the document as ***[your initials]*1-34a**. Edit the document to change the language to a contemporary writing style. On the Summary tab of the Document Properties dialog box, key the name of the original author in the Author text box. In the Comments box, key **Modified by *[your name]***. Use the Save As command, and save the document as ***[your initials]*1-34b** and submit it.

Exercise 1-35

Write a one-page summary about a local family-owned business. Include information about the company, number of employees, and products or services provided. Switch to Overtype mode, turn on Caps Lock, and then select headings or key terms to emphasize in the document. Save the document as ***[your initials]*1-35** and submit it.

Lesson 2
Formatting Characters

OBJECTIVES ***After completing this lesson, you will be able to:***

1. Work with fonts.
2. Apply basic character formatting.
3. Work with the Font dialog box.
4. Repeat and copy character formats.
5. Change case and highlight text.
6. Apply special effects

Estimated Time: 1 hour

Every document is based on a theme. A *theme* is a set of formatting instructions for the entire document and includes fonts, colors, and object effects. The default theme is Office, and you can easily change the theme by selecting an option from the Themes gallery.

Character formatting is used to emphasize text. You can change character formatting by applying bold or italic format, for example, or by changing the style of the type. Word also provides special features to copy formats, highlight text, and apply text effects for visual emphasis.

Working with Fonts

A *font* is a type design applied to an entire set of characters, including all letters of the alphabet, numerals, punctuation marks, and other keyboard symbols. Every theme defines two fonts—one for headings and one for body text.

Figure 2-1
Examples of fonts

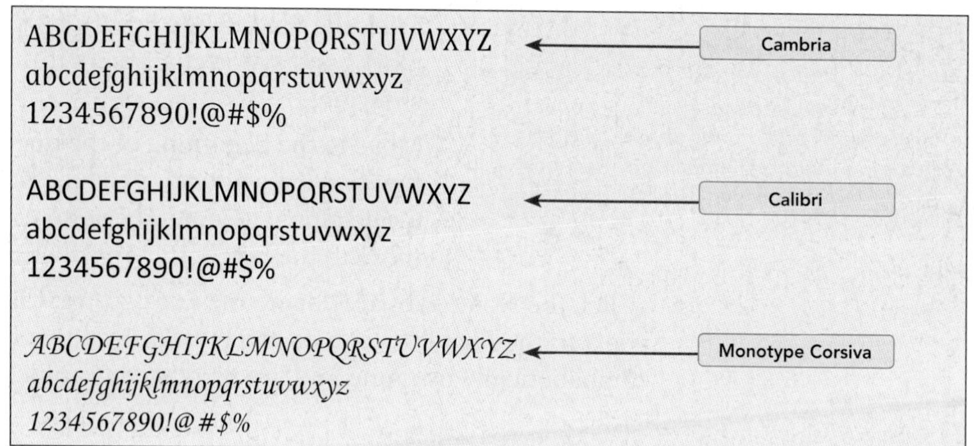

The Office theme includes a Heading font and a Body font. Calibri is the default Body font, and it is an example of a plain font. Cambria is more ornate, and it is the default Heading font. Monotype Corsiva is an example of a script font. Calibri is a *sans serif* font because it has no decorative lines, or serifs, projecting from its characters. Cambria is a *serif* font because it has decorative lines. Fonts are available in a variety of sizes and are measured in *points*. There are 72 points to an inch. Like other character formatting, you can use different fonts and font sizes in the same document.

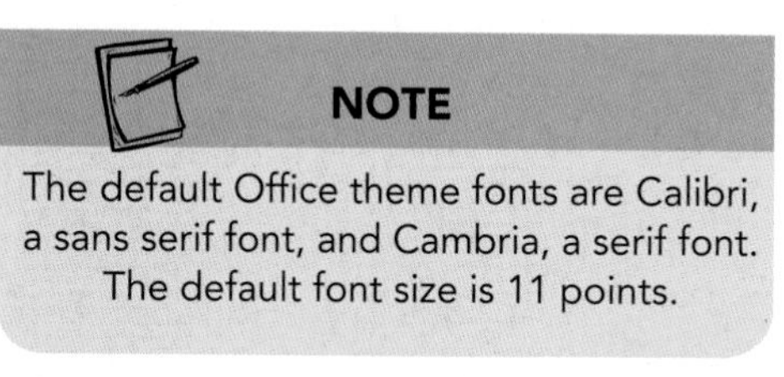

NOTE

The default Office theme fonts are Calibri, a sans serif font, and Cambria, a serif font. The default font size is 11 points.

Figure 2-2
Examples of different point sizes

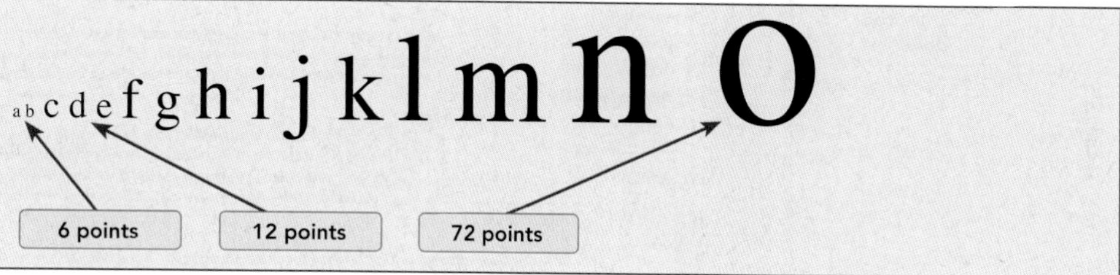

Exercise 2-1 CHANGE FONTS AND FONT SIZES USING THE RIBBON

The easiest way to choose fonts and font sizes is to use the Ribbon. The Home tab includes the Font group that contains frequently used character formatting commands.

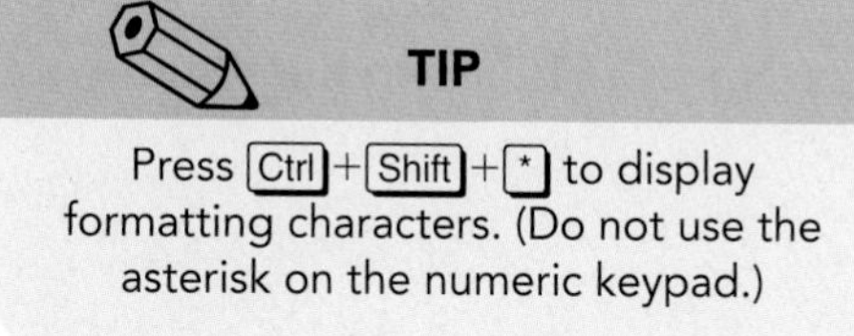

TIP

Press Ctrl+Shift+* to display formatting characters. (Do not use the asterisk on the numeric keypad.)

1. Open the file **Festival**. This document is a text document that will be used to practice character formatting and to create a flyer for the Chocolate Festival.

NOTE

The fonts you used most recently appear below the Theme Fonts. Shaded divider lines separate the Theme Fonts, Recently Used Fonts, and the list of All Fonts.

2. Click the Show/Hide ¶ button [¶] to display paragraph marks and space characters if they are not already showing.
3. Move to the beginning of the document, and select the first two lines of text, which begins "Campbell's Confections." (Remember, you can press Ctrl+Home to move to the beginning of a document.)
4. Click the **Home** tab, and locate the **Font** group. Click the down arrow next to the **Font** box to open the Font drop-down list. Fonts are listed alphabetically by name and are displayed graphically.

Figure 2-3
Choosing a font

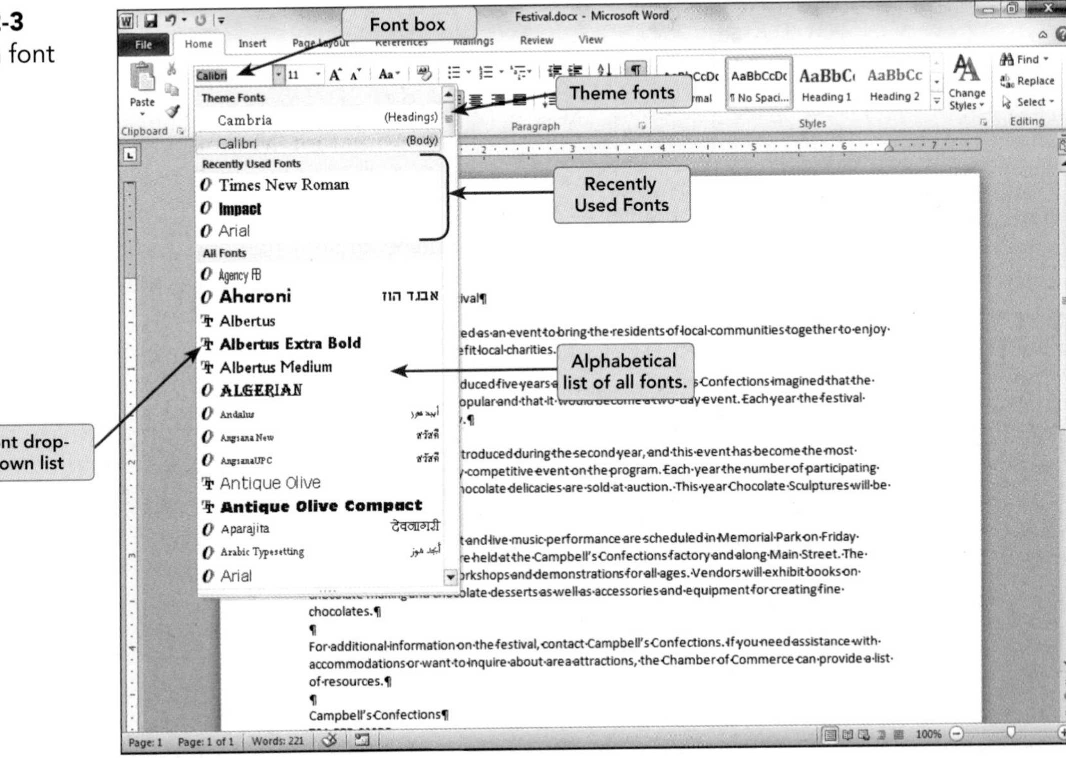

NOTE

As you scroll the list of fonts and font sizes, the Live Preview feature enables you to preview the change in the document before you select an option.

5. Use the ↓ on the keyboard or the scroll box on the font list's scroll bar and choose **Arial**.
6. Click the down arrow button to open the **Font Size** drop-down list, and choose 16 points. When you point to 16 in the drop-down list, the selected text previews the change in format. Now the first two lines stand out as a headline.

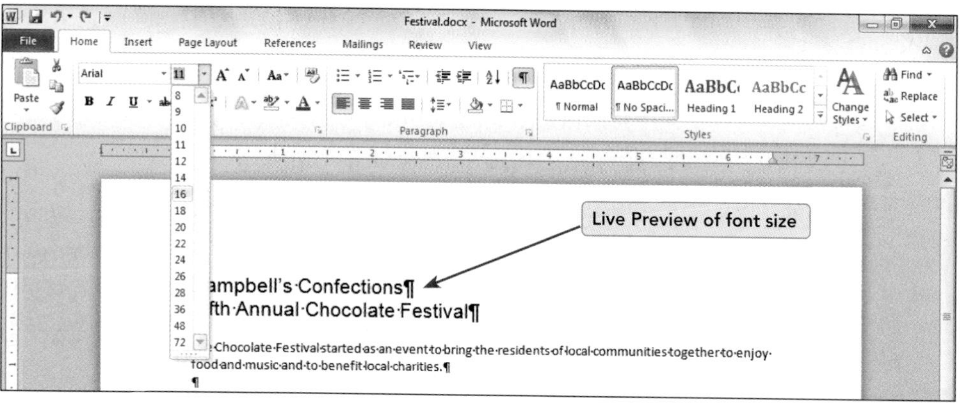

Figure 2-4
Choosing a font size

Exercise 2-2 CHANGE FONT SIZE USING KEYBOARD SHORTCUTS

If you prefer keyboard shortcuts, you can press Ctrl+Shift+> to increase the font size or Ctrl+Shift+< to decrease the font size. You can also press Ctrl+] to increase the font size by one point, or press Ctrl+[to decrease the font size by one point.

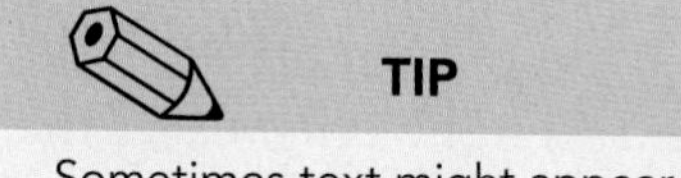

TIP

Sometimes text might appear bold on your screen when it is simply a larger font size.

1. Move the insertion point to the end of the document, and press Enter to start a new paragraph.
2. Press Ctrl+Shift+>, and key **Save the Date!**. The new text appears in 12-point type.
3. Press Enter to begin another paragraph. Press Ctrl+Shift+< to reduce the font size to 11 points, and key **September 26, 20--**.

Basic Character Formatting

The basic font styles or character formats are bold, italic, and underline. Text can have one or more character formats.

NOTE

The underline feature is rarely used for emphasis because it affects the readability of text. Use bold or italic for emphasis.

TABLE 2-1 Character Formatting

Attribute	Example
Normal	This is a sample.
Bold	**This is a sample.**
Italic	*This is a sample.*
Underline	This is a sample.
Bold and italic	***This is a sample.***

The simplest ways to apply basic character formatting are to use:

- Commands on the Ribbon, Home tab, Font group
- Keyboard shortcuts
- Commands on the Mini toolbar

You can apply character formatting to existing text, including text that is noncontiguous. You can also turn on a character format before you key new text and turn it off after you enter the text. For example, you can click the Bold button **B**, key a few words in bold, click the button again to turn off the format, and continue keying regular text.

Exercise 2-3 APPLY BASIC CHARACTER FORMATTING USING THE RIBBON

1. Select "Chocolate Festival" in the first paragraph below the heading.
2. Click the Bold button **B** on the Ribbon to format the text bold. (The Bold command is located in the Font group.)
3. With the text still selected, click the Italic button *I* on the Ribbon to format the text bold and italic.
4. Click the Bold button **B** again to turn off the bold format and to leave the text as italic only. Click the Bold button **B** again to restore the bold-italic formatting.

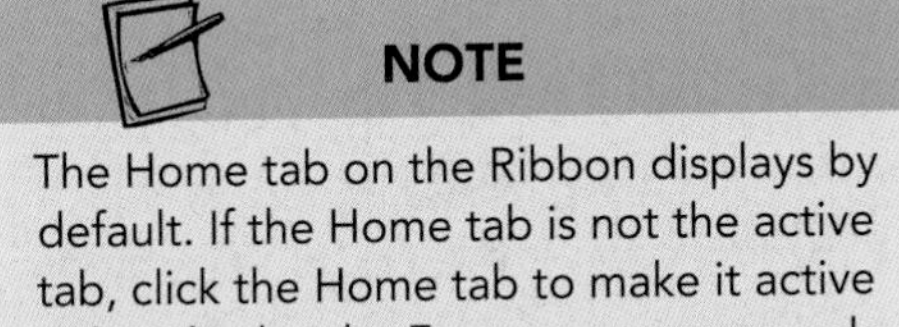

NOTE

The Home tab on the Ribbon displays by default. If the Home tab is not the active tab, click the Home tab to make it active and to display the Font group commands.

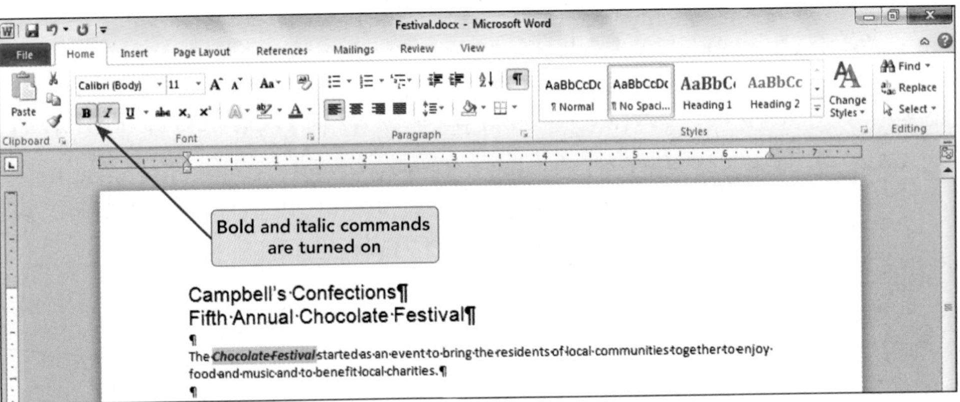

Figure 2-5
Using the Ribbon to apply character formatting

5. Move the insertion point to the end of the same paragraph, and press the Spacebar once.

6. Click the Bold button [B] and the Italic button [I], and key **Visitors to the festival will be able to sample and purchase chocolate creations as well as listen to area musicians throughout the festival celebration.** in bold italic.
7. Click both buttons to turn off the formatting.
8. Select the bold-italic text "Chocolate Festival."
9. Press Ctrl, and select the bold-italic sentence that begins "Visitors to the festival" as well.
10. Click the Underline button [U] on the Ribbon to underline the noncontiguous selections.
11. Click the Undo button to remove the underline.
12. Select the first line in the document.
13. Click the Change Case button [Aa], and click UPPERCASE.

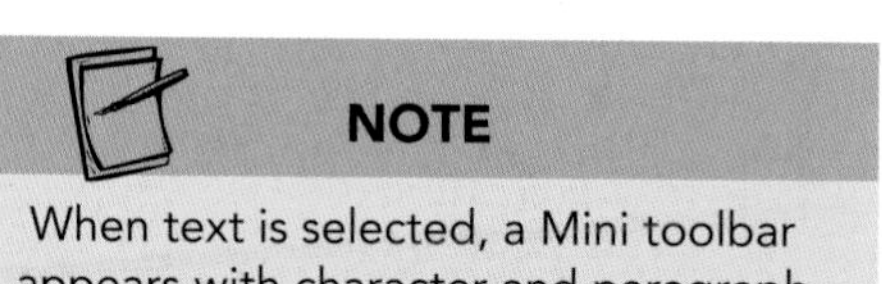

NOTE

When text is selected, a Mini toolbar appears with character and paragraph formatting commands.

Exercise 2-4 APPLY AND REMOVE BASIC CHARACTER FORMATTING USING KEYBOARD SHORTCUTS

If you prefer to keep your hands on the keyboard instead of using the mouse, you can use keyboard shortcuts to turn basic character formatting on and off. You can press Ctrl+B for bold, Ctrl+I for italic, and Ctrl+U for underline. To remove character formatting from selected text, press Ctrl+Spacebar.

1. Select the text "Chamber of Commerce" near the end of the document.
2. Press Ctrl+B to apply bold format to the selected text, and press Ctrl+I to add italic format.
3. Move the insertion point to the end of the document, and press Enter to start a new paragraph.
4. Press Ctrl+B to turn on the bold option, and key **Visit our Web site for a list of events.**
5. Select the bold-italic text "Chocolate Festival" in the first paragraph, and press Ctrl+Spacebar to remove the formatting.
6. Click the Undo button to restore the bold-italic formatting.

Exercise 2-5 APPLY AND REMOVE BASIC CHARACTER FORMATTING USING THE MINI TOOLBAR

The Mini toolbar appears when you select text in a document. You can click any of the buttons on the toolbar to apply or remove character formatting from the selected text.

1. Select the first line of text. Notice the Mini toolbar displays.

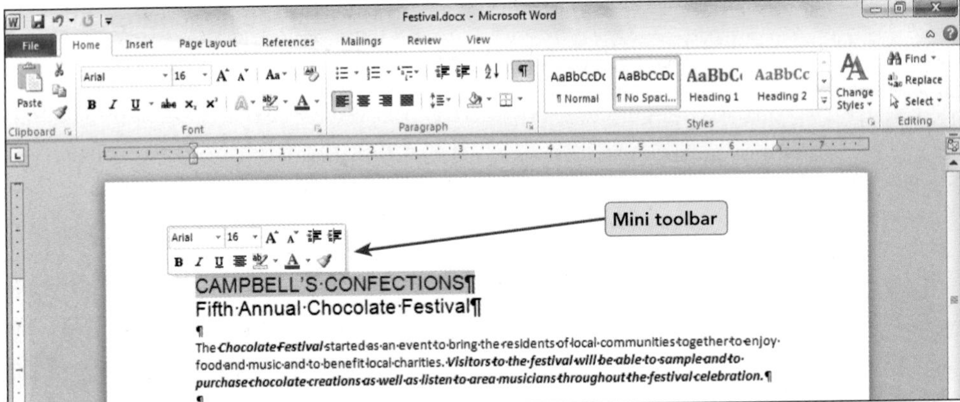

Figure 2-6
Mini toolbar

2. Click the drop-down arrow beside the Font Color button [A]. Locate Standard Colors in the palette, and click **Blue**.
3. Click the Grow Font button [A] two times, and notice the change in the font size. Click the Shrink Font button [A] one time.

Using the Font Dialog Box

The Font dialog box offers a wider variety of options than those available on the Ribbon, and you can conveniently choose several options at one time.

There are several ways to open the Font dialog box:

- Click the Font Dialog Box Launcher.
- Right-click (use the right mouse button) selected text to display a *shortcut menu,* and then choose Font. A shortcut menu shows a list of commands relevant to a particular item you click.
- Use keyboard shortcuts.

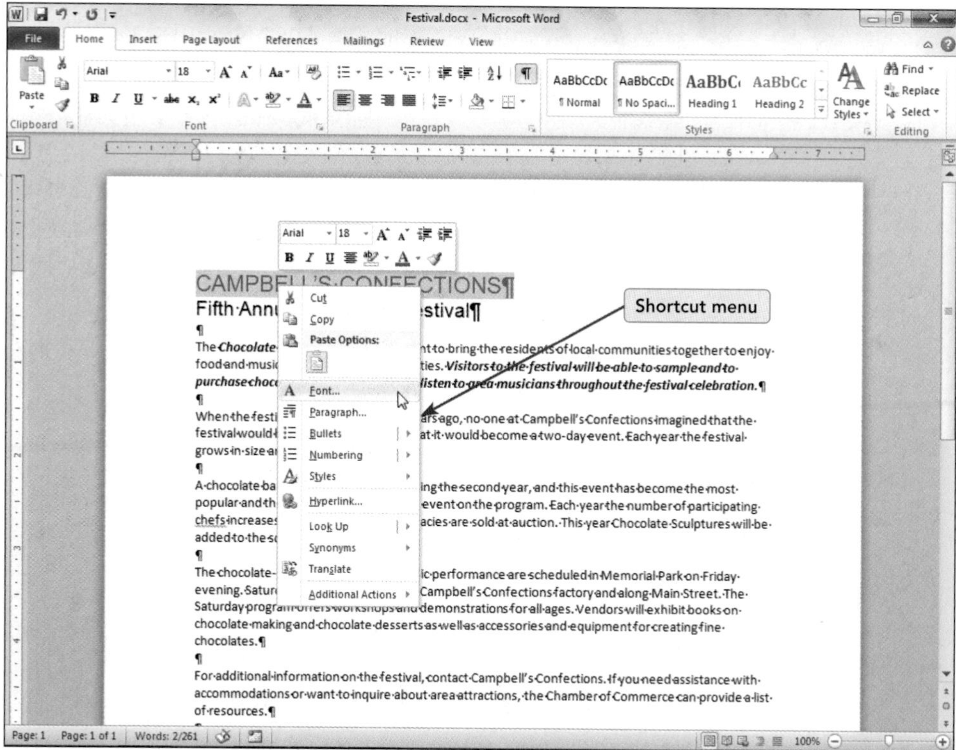

Figure 2-7
Shortcut menu

Exercise 2-6 CHOOSE FONTS AND FONT STYLES USING THE FONT DIALOG BOX

1. Select the first line of text, which is currently 18-point Arial and blue.
2. Click the Font Dialog Box Launcher in the lower right corner of the Font group on the Ribbon. The Font dialog box displays.

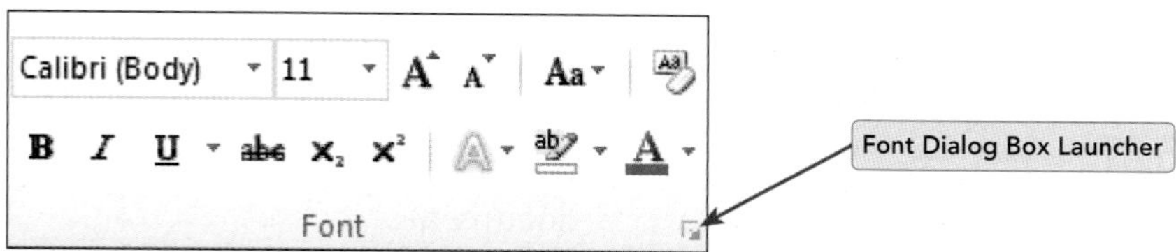

Figure 2-8
Font Dialog Box Launcher

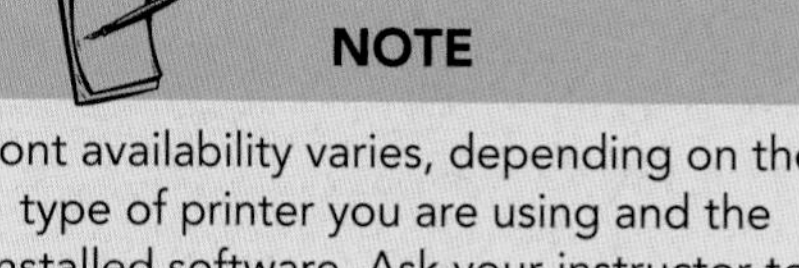

NOTE

Font availability varies, depending on the type of printer you are using and the installed software. Ask your instructor to recommend a substitute font if the specified one is unavailable.

3. Choose **ITC Bookman Demi** from the **Font** list, **Italic** from the **Font style** list, and **20** from the **Size** list. Look at your choices in the **Preview** box, and click **OK**.

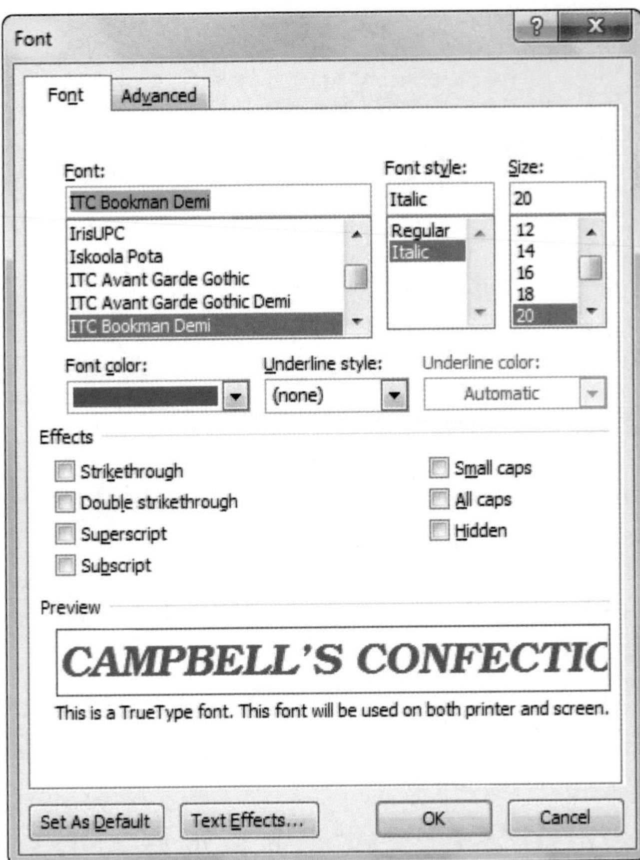

Figure 2-9
Using the Font dialog box

TIP

The Reveal Formatting task pane allows you to see the formatting that is applied to selected text without having to navigate to individual formatting dialog boxes. To display the Reveal Formatting task pane, press Shift+F1. To open the Font dialog box, move the mouse pointer over **Font** under the Font section. When the mouse pointer becomes a hand pointer , click to open the Font dialog box.

Exercise 2-7 APPLY UNDERLINE OPTIONS AND CHARACTER EFFECTS

In addition to choosing font, font size, and font style, you can choose font color, a variety of underlining options, and special character effects from the Font dialog box.

1. Select the text "Save the Date!" near the end of the document.
2. Press Ctrl+D to open the Font dialog box.

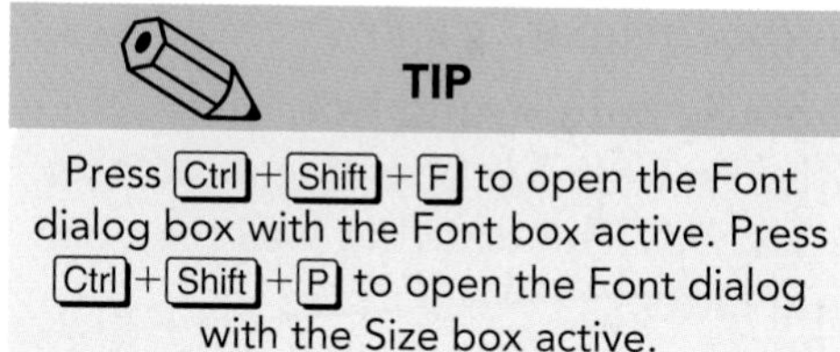

TIP

Press Ctrl+Shift+F to open the Font dialog box with the Font box active. Press Ctrl+Shift+P to open the Font dialog with the Size box active.

3. Click the down arrow ▾ to open the **Underline style** drop-down list. Drag the scroll box down to see all the available underline styles. Choose one of the dotted-line styles.
4. Click the down arrow ▾ next to the Font color box, and choose Green in the Standard Colors palette. (Each color is identified by name when you point to it.)

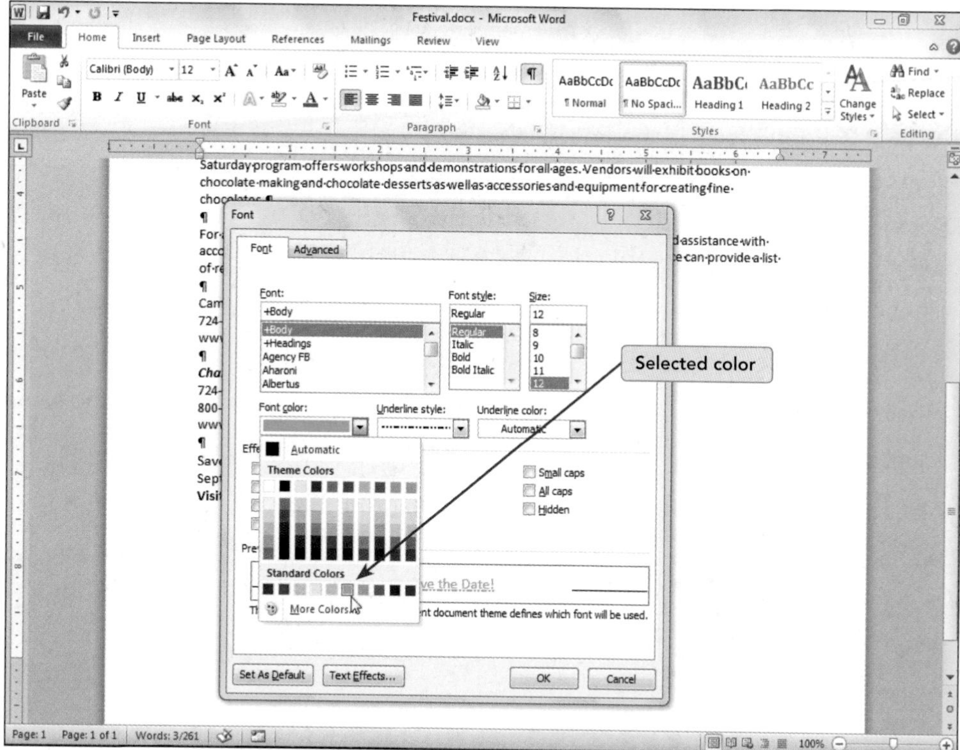

Figure 2-10
Font color options in the Font dialog box

5. Click the down arrow next to the **Underline color** box, and choose Red.
6. Click **OK**. The text is green with a red dotted underline.

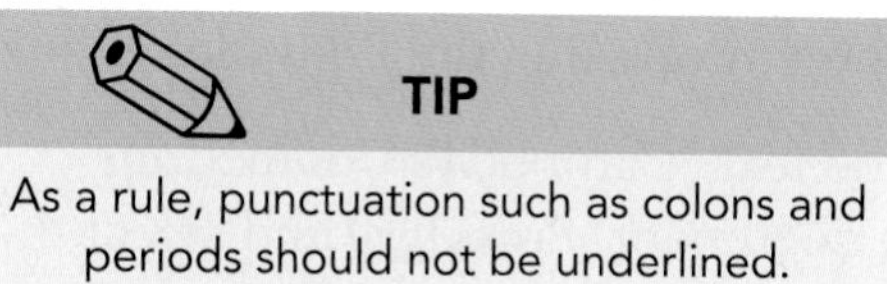

TIP

As a rule, punctuation such as colons and periods should not be underlined.

7. Select the sentence in the first paragraph below the heading that begins "Visitors to the festival."
8. Move the mouse pointer to the Ribbon, and click the Clear Formatting button.

9. Select the text “Chocolate Festival” in the first paragraph.
10. Click the selected text with the right mouse button, and from the shortcut menu, choose **Font** to open the Font dialog box. Locate **Effects**, click the **Small caps** check box, and click **OK**. The text that was formerly lowercase now appears in small capital letters.
11. Select the text “Save the Date.”
12. Click the Strikethrough button [abc] on the Ribbon. The text appears with a horizontal line running through it.
13. Click the Undo button [↶] to undo the strikethrough effect.

TABLE 2-2 Font Effects in the Font Dialog Box

Effect	Description and Example
Strikethrough	Applies ~~a horizontal line~~.
Double strikethrough	Applies a ~~double horizontal line~~.
Superscript	Raises text above other characters on the same line.
Subscript	Places text below other characters on the same line.
Small Caps	Makes lowercase text SMALL CAPS.
All Caps	Makes all text UPPERCASE.
Hidden	Hidden text does not print and appears on-screen only if Word’s Display options are set to display hidden text. See File tab, Options.

Exercise 2-8 USE KEYBOARD SHORTCUTS FOR UNDERLINE OPTIONS AND FONT EFFECTS

Word provides keyboard shortcuts for some underlining options and font effects as an alternative to using the Ribbon or opening the Font dialog box.

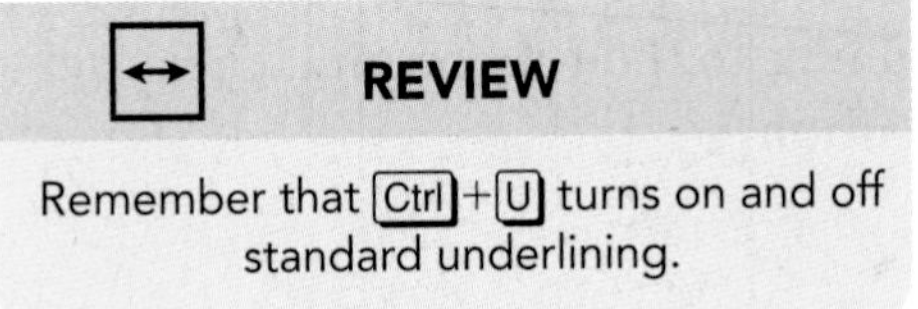

REVIEW

Remember that Ctrl+U turns on and off standard underlining.

1. Locate and select the text “Campbell’s Confections” near the end of the document. Press Ctrl and select the text “Chamber of Commerce.”
2. Press Ctrl+Shift+K to apply small caps to the selected text.
3. Select the text “chocolate bake-off” in the third paragraph that begins “A chocolate bake-off.”
4. Press Ctrl+Shift+D to apply double underlining, and press Ctrl+Shift+K to apply small caps format.

TABLE 2-3 Keyboard Shortcuts for Underlining and Character Effects

Keyboard Shortcut	Action
Ctrl+Shift+W	Turn on or off words-only underlining.
Ctrl+Shift+D	Turn on or off double underlining.
Ctrl+Shift+=	Turn on or off superscript.
Ctrl+=	Turn on or off subscript.
Ctrl+Shift+K	Turn on or off small capitals.
Ctrl+Shift+A	Turn on or off all capitals.
Ctrl+Shift+H	Turn on or off hidden text.

Exercise 2-9 CHANGE CHARACTER SPACING

The Character Spacing tab in the Font dialog box offers options for changing the space between characters or the position of text in relation to the baseline. Character spacing can be expanded or condensed horizontally, as well as raised or lowered vertically.

1. Select the first line of text, which begins "Campbell's Confections."
2. Open the **Font** dialog box, and click the **Advanced** tab.
3. Click the down arrow to open the **Scale** drop-down list. Click **150%**, and notice the change in the **Preview** box. Change the scale back to **100%**.

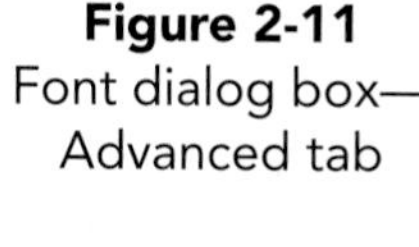

Figure 2-11
Font dialog box—
Advanced tab

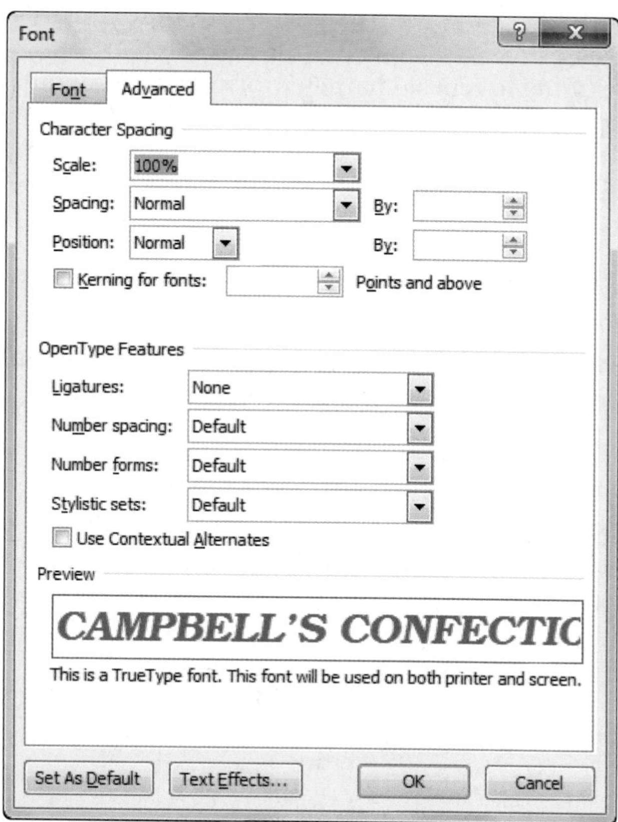

TIP

You can increase the space between characters even more by increasing the number in the By box (click the arrows or key a specific number). Experiment with the Spacing and Scale options on your own to see how they change the appearance of text.

4. Click the down arrow to display the **Spacing** options. Click **Expanded**, and then click **OK**. The text appears with more space between each character. When you expand or condense text spacing, you change the spacing between all the selected characters.
5. Select the first line if necessary, and use the Mini toolbar to change the font to **Arial**.
6. Open the **Save As** dialog box, create a new folder for your Lesson 2 files, and save the document as ***[your initials]*2-9**.

NOTE

Remember to use this folder for all the exercise documents you create in this lesson.

Repeating and Copying Formatting

You can use F4 or Ctrl+Y to repeat character formatting. You can also copy character formatting with a special tool on the Ribbon—the Format Painter button.

Exercise 2-10 REPEAT CHARACTER FORMATTING

Before trying to repeat character formatting, keep in mind that you must use the Repeat command immediately after applying the format. In addition, the Repeat command repeats only the last character format applied. (If you apply multiple character formats from the Font dialog box, the Repeat command applies all formatting.)

1. Select "chocolate tasting event" in the fourth paragraph, and click the Italic button to italicize the text.
2. Select "chocolate delicacies" in the third paragraph, and press F4 to repeat your last action (turning on italic format).
3. Select the text "Save the Date!"
4. Open the **Font** dialog box. Click the **Font** tab, if it is not already displayed, and choose another font, such as Impact. Select the font size **14** points, and change the font color to Red. Click **OK**. The text appears with the new formatting.

5. Select the text “September 26, 20--” and press F4. Word repeats all the formatting you chose in the Font dialog box. If you apply each character format separately, using the Ribbon, the Repeat command applies only the last format you chose.

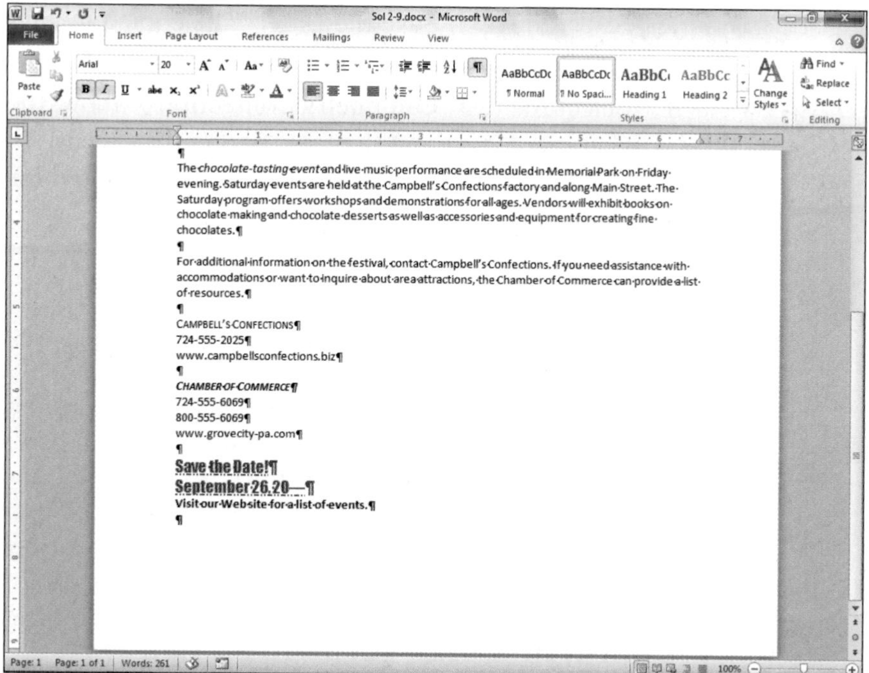

Figure 2-12
Repeating character formatting

Exercise 2-11 COPY CHARACTER FORMATTING

The Format Painter button makes it easy to copy a character format. This is particularly helpful when you copy text with multiple formats, such as bold-italic small caps.

To use Format Painter to copy character formatting, first select the text with the formatting you want to copy, and then click the Format Painter button. The mouse pointer changes to a paintbrush with an I-beam pointer. Use this pointer to select the text to which you want to apply the copied formatting.

1. In the paragraph that begins “When the,” select “festival” and click the Font color button. Change the font color to Dark Blue. Apply bold and italic format to the selected text.
2. With the text still selected, locate the **Clipboard** group on the **Home** tab, and click the Format Painter button. When you move the pointer back into the text area, notice the new shape of the pointer.
3. Use the paintbrush pointer to select “festival” in the next sentence. This copies the font color, bold, and italic format to the selected text, and the pointer returns to its normal shape.

4. Select the text "*CHAMBER OF COMMERCE*" near the end of the document.
5. Press Ctrl+D to open the **Font** dialog box. Change the **Font color** to Blue, and change the **Size** to 12. Click **OK**. Do not deselect the text.
6. Double-click the Format Painter button. You double-click the Format Painter button to copy formatting repeatedly.
7. Select the text "Save the Date!" The copied formatting is applied to the text, and the pointer remains the paintbrush pointer.
8. Select the text "Campbell's Confections" above the Chamber of Commerce text and the text "September 26, 20--." The paintbrush pointer copies the new formatting over the old formatting.
9. Press Esc or click the Format Painter to stop copying and to restore the normal pointer.

Changing Case and Highlighting Text

You have used Caps Lock to change case, and you have seen the Small Caps and All Caps options in the Font dialog box. You can also change the case of characters by using keyboard shortcuts and the Change Case command on the Ribbon. The Change Case command includes options for Sentence case, lowercase, UPPERCASE, Capitalize Each Word, and tOGGLE cASE.

Exercise 2-12 CHANGE CASE

1. Locate the paragraph that begins "For additional," and select the text "Campbell's Confections." Press Shift+F3. This keyboard shortcut changes case. Now the text appears in all uppercase letters.
2. With the text still selected, press Shift+F3 again. Now the sentence appears in all lowercase letters.
3. Press Shift+F3 again, and the original capitalization is restored.
4. Select the first line of the document, and click the Change Case button **Aa** on the Ribbon.
5. Click **tOGGLE cASE**. This option changes the text to lowercase. Click the Change Case button **Aa**, and click **UPPERCASE**.
6. Click anywhere in the document to deselect the text.

Exercise 2-13 HIGHLIGHT TEXT

To emphasize parts of a document, you can mark text with a color highlighter by using the Highlight button on the Ribbon, Home tab, Font group. As with the Format Painter button, when you click the Highlight button, the pointer changes shape. You then use the highlight pointer to select the text you want to highlight. In addition, you can choose from several highlighting colors.

1. Make sure no text is selected. On the Ribbon, click the down arrow next to the Highlight button to display the color choices. Click **Yellow** to choose it as the highlight color. This turns on the Highlight button, and the color indicator box on the button is now yellow.

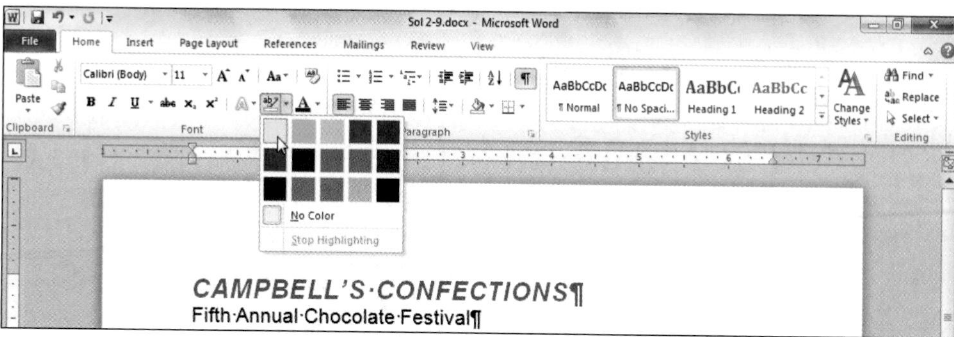

Figure 2-13
Choosing a highlight color

2. Move the highlight pointer into the text area.
3. Drag the pointer over the telephone numbers below "Chamber of Commerce."
4. Press Esc to turn off the highlighter and restore the normal pointer.
5. Select the first line of text in the document.
6. Click the Highlight button to highlight the selection. This is another way to use the highlighter—by selecting the text and then clicking the Highlight button.
7. Select the first line of text again. Remove the highlight by clicking the down arrow to display the highlight color choices and choosing **No Color**.
8. Select the remaining highlighted text, and click the Highlight button. Because "No Color" was last chosen (as shown in the color indicator box on the button), this action removes the highlight from the selected text.

NOTE

You can use highlighting to mark text as you work on a document or to point out text for others opening the same document later. It might not work as well for printed documents because the colors might print too dark. You can use the shading feature to emphasize text in a printed document.

Applying Special Effects

One way to call attention to a paragraph is to use a dropped capital letter, or a *drop cap*. A drop cap is a large letter that appears below the text baseline. It is usually applied to the first letter in the first word of a paragraph.

A second way to add visual emphasis to your text is to use the Text Effects feature. Text Effects include the following features: Outline, Shadow, Reflection, Glow, and Bevel. Each of these features includes special options for a variety of effects.

Exercise 2-14 CREATE A DROP CAP

1. Place the insertion point at the beginning of the first paragraph that begins "The Chocolate Festival."
2. Click the **Insert** tab on the Ribbon, and click the Drop Cap button. Click **In margin**.
3. Undo the drop cap.
4. Click the Drop Cap button, and click **Drop Cap Options**. The Drop Cap dialog box opens.

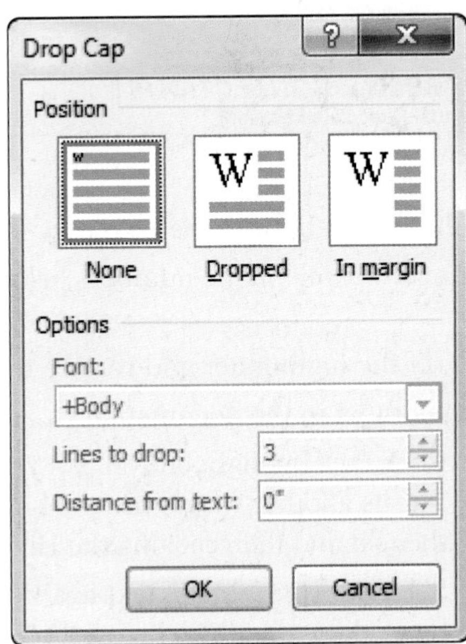

Figure 2-14
Drop Cap dialog box

5. Under **Position**, click **Dropped**. This option is used to wrap the paragraph around the letter.
6. Change the **Distance from text** to **.1**, and click **OK**. Click within the document to deselect the "T." Notice the appearance of "The" and that it is dropped three lines.

Exercise 2-15 APPLY TEXT EFFECTS

1. Select the second line of text in the document that begins "Fifth Annual."
2. Click the Home tab, and click the Text Effects button to display a gallery of options. Click the fourth option in the third row **Gradient Fill–Blue, Accent 1**.

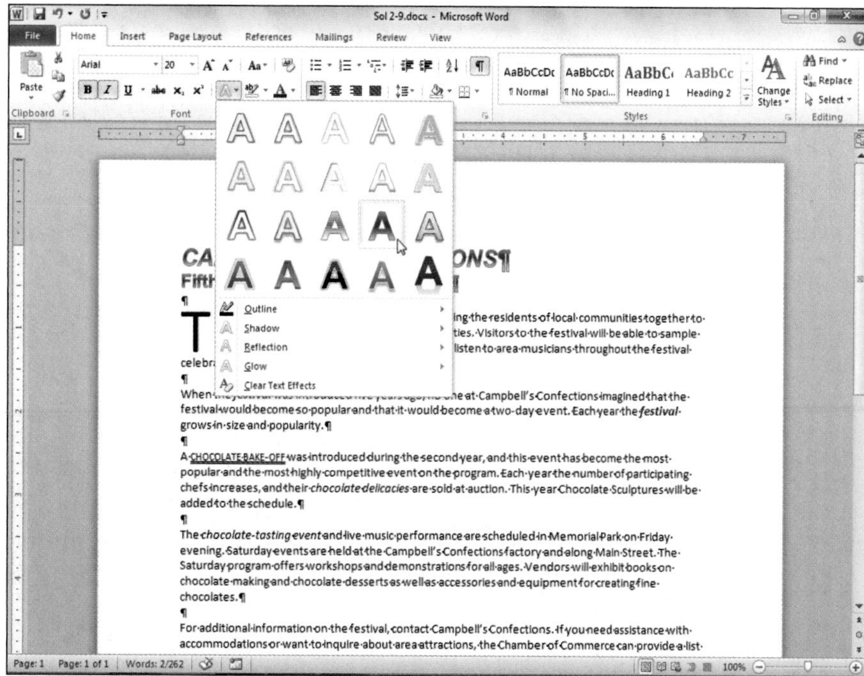

Figure 2-15
Text Effects gallery

3. Select the first line of text in the document, and display the Text Effects gallery.
4. Click **Shadow**, and click an option in the **Outer** group.
5. Click the Text Effects button, point to **Shadow**, and click **Shadow Options**. The Format Text Effects dialog box displays with the Shadow option selected.
6. Click the Color button, and select a color. Drag the **Transparency** slider to **65** percent. Drag the **Blur** slider to **6** points, and drag the **Distance** slider to **5** points. Change the **Angle** option to **180** degrees. Click **Close** to return to the document.
7. Save the document as ***[your initials]*2-15** in your Lesson 2 folder.
8. Submit your work, and close the document.

NOTE

An alternative to dragging the slider is to use the increment arrows to move the value up or down one percent, one point, or one degree, or to key a value in the text box.

NOTE

Each of the text effects listed in the Text Effects gallery has additional options for changing the appearance of the text.

Lesson 2 Summary

- A font is a type design applied to an entire set of characters, including all the letters of the alphabet, numerals, punctuation marks, and other keyboard symbols.
- A font can be serif (with decorative lines) or sans serif (with no decorative lines).
- Fonts are available in a variety of sizes, which are measured in points. There are 72 points to an inch.
- You can use the Ribbon to change fonts and font sizes.
- Keyboard shortcuts can also be used to change font sizes: Ctrl+Shift+> increases the text size and Ctrl+Shift+< decreases the text size.
- Use the Ribbon, Home tab, Font group to apply basic character formatting (for example, bold, italic, and/or underline) to selected contiguous (text that is together) or noncontiguous text (text that is not together).
- Use keyboard shortcuts to apply and remove basic character formatting.
- Use the Mini toolbar to apply character formatting to selected text.
- The Font dialog box can be used to change fonts, font sizes, and font styles. The Font dialog box also has settings for underline styles, font and underline colors, effects such as small caps (see Table 2-2), and character spacing.
- A hyperlink often appears as blue underlined text you click to open a software feature (such as a dialog box or a Help topic) or to go to an e-mail or a Web address.
- Keyboard shortcuts are available for some underline styles and font effects (see Table 2-3).
- A shortcut menu shows a list of commands relevant to a particular item. To display a shortcut menu, point to the item and right-click the mouse.
- Use F4 or Ctrl+Y to repeat character formatting.
- Use Format Painter to copy character formatting. Double-click the Format Painter button to apply formatting to more than one selection.
- To change the case of selected characters, use the keyboard shortcut Shift+F3 or the Change Case command on the Ribbon, Home tab.
- Use the Highlight button to apply a color highlight to selected text you want to emphasize on-screen.
- Use Drop Cap from the Insert tab to create a dropped cap. A drop cap is a large letter that appears below the text baseline. It is usually applied to the first letter in the first word of a paragraph.
- Text Effects add visual emphasis to your text. Choose an Outline, Shadow, Reflection, Glow, or Bevel effect.

LESSON 2		Command Summary	
Feature	**Button**	**Command**	**Keyboard**
Bold	B	Home tab, Font group	Ctrl+B
Change case	Aa	Home tab, Font group	Shift+F3
Decrease font size	A	Home tab, Font group	Ctrl+Shift+<
Drop Cap		Insert tab, Text group	
Font color	A	Home tab, Font group	
Format Painter		Home tab, Clipboard group	
Highlight text		Home tab, Font group	
Increase font size	A	Home tab, Font group	Ctrl+Shift+>
Italic	I	Home tab, Font group	Ctrl+I
Remove character formatting		Home tab, Font group	Ctrl+Spacebar
Text effects	A	Home tab, Font group	
Underline	U	Home tab, Font group	Ctrl+U

Concepts Review

True/False Questions

Each of the following statements is either true or false. Indicate your choice by circling T or F.

T F 1. Underline styles are only available in the Font dialog box.

T F 2. To remove character formatting, press Ctrl+Delete.

T F 3. The Home tab on the Ribbon is used to insert a drop cap.

T F 4. Times New Roman is an example of a sans serif font.

T F 5. You can use F4 to repeat text or to repeat character formatting.

T F 6. After clicking the Format Painter button, you can press Esc to restore the normal pointer.

T F 7. You can use the Font dialog box to change character spacing.

T F 8. The superscript text effect places text below the baseline.

Short Answer Questions

Write the correct answer in the space provided.

1. Which Ribbon tab contains a command to highlight text?

____

2. Which dialog box do you use to choose bold-italic style?

____

3. What unit of measurement is used to measure fonts?

____

4. What keyboard shortcut increases the font size of selected text?

____

5. What character effect places a horizontal line through text?

____

6. Which command do you use to copy character formatting?

____

7. What keyboard shortcut do you use to change the case of selected text?

8. What character spacing setting inserts additional space between characters?

Critical Thinking

Answer these questions on a separate page. There are no right or wrong answers. Support your answers with examples from your own experience, if possible.

1. Select three examples of effective character formatting in magazine advertisements, articles, or other publications. Describe why you think the character formatting was particularly effective for each example.
2. Using a large font size, key **Fonts & styles** 10 times on 10 separate lines. (You can use the Repeat Typing command.) Apply a different font to each line. Describe the differences you see among the fonts.

Skills Review

Exercise 2-16

Apply basic character formatting. Change font and font size.

1. Open the file **Candy - 1**. Click the Show/Hide ¶ button ¶ if necessary.
2. At the top of the document, press Enter. Move to the paragraph mark, and key **Fine Chocolates**.
3. Change the font for the entire document by following these steps:
   a. Select the entire document by pressing Ctrl+A.
   b. Select the Home tab. Open the **Font** drop-down list by clicking the down arrow.
   c. Locate and click **Arial**.
4. Change the first line heading to 16-point bold by following these steps:
   a. Select the text by moving the pointer to the left of the text. When the arrow points to the text, click the left mouse button.
   b. Choose 16 from the Font Size drop-down list on the Ribbon.
   c. Click the Bold button **B** on the Ribbon.
5. Apply italic formatting to noncontiguous text by following these steps:
   a. Move to the end of the document, and press Enter.
   b. Key **Call our toll-free number: 800-555-2025.**
   c. Select the sentence you just keyed.

d. Press and hold Ctrl, and select the text "Campbell's Confections" in the first line of the previous paragraph.

e. Click the Italic button *I*.

6. Key new bold text by following these steps:

   a. Move to the end of the document, and place the insertion point to the immediate left of the period.

   b. Click the Italic button *I* to turn off italic.

   c. Click the Bold button **B** to turn on bold. Press the Spacebar, and key **or visit our Web site at www.campbellsconfections.biz.**

   d. Turn off bold.

7. Save the document as ***[your initials]*2-16** in your Lesson 2 folder.

8. Submit and close the document.

Exercise 2-17

Apply formatting options using the Font dialog box and using repeat character formatting.

1. Open the file **Cocoa Beans**.

2. Apply character formatting to the first line. Use the Font dialog box, and follow these steps:

   a. Select the first line. Click the selected text with the right mouse button, and choose Font from the shortcut menu.

   b. Click the Font tab, if it is not already displayed. For font, font style, and font size, choose Arial, Bold, and 14 points.

   c. Apply the effect Small caps by clicking the check box.

   d. View your options in the Preview box, and click OK.

3. Apply and repeat character formatting by following these steps:

   a. Select the text "chocolate-covered cocoa beans" in the second line, and press Ctrl+D to open the Font dialog box.

   b. Choose the font style Bold Italic.

   c. Open the Font color drop-down list, and choose Blue. Click to select Small Caps in the Effects section. Click OK.

   d. Select the text "chocolate-covered cocoa beans" in the fourth line, and press F4. Repeat the formatting for each occurrence of "chocolate-covered cocoa beans:"

4. Apply the Superscript effect from the Font dialog box by following these steps:

   a. Position the insertion point after the period following "chocolate-covered beans" in the second sentence.

   b. Key an asterisk (*) after the period. Select the asterisk.

   c. Locate and click the Font Dialog Box Launcher on the Ribbon.

d. Click the Superscript check box.

e. Click OK. Notice the superscript effect.

f. Click the Show/Hide ¶ button ¶ to hide the text and formatting characters.

5. Move to the end of the document, press Enter, and key ***Cacao bean is the original spelling, but cocoa bean is the popular spelling.**

6. Select the asterisk, and apply the superscript format by clicking the Superscript button x^2 in the Font group on the Ribbon.

7. Save the document as ***[your initials]*2-17** in your Lesson 2 folder.

8. Submit your work.

Exercise 2-18

Copy character formatting and change case.

1. Open the file **WV Stores**.

2. Change the first line to read **Campbell's Confections—West Virginia Retail Stores.**

3. At the end of the first line, press Enter, and key **premiere chocolates and specialty items.**

4. Select the first two lines of text, and format them 14-point bold.

5. Use a keyboard shortcut to change the case of the first line to all uppercase by following these steps:

   a. Select the first line of text.

   b. Press Shift+F3.

6. Change the case of the second line using the Change Case command by following these steps:

   a. Select the second line of text.

   b. Click the Change Case button Aa on the Ribbon.

   c. Click Capitalize Each Word.

7. Use the Font dialog box to format the first store name, "Campbell's Confections," as bold-italic small caps.

8. Copy the character formatting to the other store names by following these steps:

   a. With the formatted text selected, double-click the Format Painter button.

   b. Drag the pointer over the next store name, "Campbell's Confections."

   c. Continue copying the formatting to the other store names. Use the scroll bar as needed. When you finish copying, click the Format Painter button to restore the normal pointer.

9. In the second line, change "And" to lowercase.
10. Save the document as ***[your initials]*2-18** in your Lesson 2 folder.
11. Submit your work, and close the document.

Exercise 2-19

Highlight text, apply text effects, and create a dropped capital letter.

1. Start a new document by keying the text shown in Figure 2-16. Use 12-point Arial type.

Figure 2-16

```
Bittersweet chocolate also known as semi-sweet chocolate
is the darkest eating chocolate. It also has the highest
percentage of chocolate liquor (unsweetened chocolate).
Bittersweet chocolate usually consists of 50 percent
chocolate liquor, and semi-sweet chocolate typically
consists of 35 to 45 percent chocolate liquor. Both have
a rich, smooth taste and are used for chocolate chips and
baking.
```

2. Highlight part of the document by following these steps:
   a. Click the down arrow next to the Highlight button, and click the yellow highlight.
   b. Use the highlight pointer to select the text "50 percent."
   c. Press Esc to restore the normal pointer.
3. Create a dropped capital letter by following these steps:
   a. Position the insertion point at the beginning of the document.
   b. Click the **Insert** tab, and click **Drop Cap**.
   c. Click **Dropped**.
4. Remove the highlight by following these steps:
   a. Select the highlighted text "50 percent."
   b. Click the **Home** tab. Click the down arrow next to the Highlight button and choose **No Color**.
5. Format the first two words after the drop cap (beginning with "i") as 14-point bold. Do not deselect the text.
6. Add text effects to the selected text by following these steps:
   a. Click the Text Effects button, and click **Outline**. Click **More Outline Colors**, and click the **Standard** tab in the Colors dialog box.
   b. Click a brown color, and click **OK**.
7. Save the document as ***[your initials]*2-19** in your Lesson 2 folder.
8. Submit and close the document.

Lesson Applications

Exercise 2-20

Apply and copy character formatting. Change font size.

1. Open the file **Milk Chocolate**.
2. Format the first line ("Milk Chocolate") to 14 points, and change the font to Impact. (If Impact is not available, choose another bold-looking font from the Font drop-down list.)
3. Select the text "10 percent" and format the text as italic. Change the font color to blue.
4. Use the Format Painter button to apply the formatting of "10 percent" to "12 percent."
5. Apply small caps effects to the first line, and add a text effect. Change the character spacing to expanded 1 pt to improve readability.
6. Select "Milk chocolate" at the beginning of the descriptive paragraph under the heading. Use the Ribbon to bold the text and apply italic formatting.
7. Position the insertion point before the word "best." Press F4 to repeat the last selected character formatting (italic), key **very**, and press Spacebar.
8. Press Ctrl+End to go to the end of the document. Press Enter and key **Enjoy!**
9. Select the last line, and change the text to 12-point Times New Roman. Add red double underlining to the line, except the exclamation point.
10. Save the document as ***[your initials]*2-20** in your Lesson 2 folder.
11. Submit your work, and close the document.

Exercise 2-21

Apply and copy character formatting. Change font size, case, and character spacing.

1. Start a new document by keying the text shown in Figure 2-17, including the corrections. Use 12-point Arial type. Click the Change Styles button [A], and click **Style Set**. Choose **Word 2010**.

Figure 2-17

```
A chocolate glossary is helpful to understand the
differences and similarities among chocolate ingredients.
           (unsweetened chocolate)           (nibs)
Chocolate liquor^is the ground up center^of the roasted
                                                and
cocoa bean. It is the basic ingredient of chocolate^cocoa
products. Cocao butter is the vegetable fat extracted
                                         (stet)
during the refining process. ~~It is the base of white
chocolate~~. Cocao powder is made by removing most of the
cocoa butter from the chocolate liquor. The remaining
solids are ground to produce unsweetened cocoa powder.
There are two types of cocoa powder: Dutch-processed
and natural unsweetened cocoa powder.
```

2. In the first line, change the case of the text "chocolate glossary" to all capitals.
3. Copy or repeat the all-capitals formatting to the following words in the paragraph: "Chocolate liquor," "Cocoa butter," and "Cocoa powder."
4. Create a new paragraph for each term, beginning with "CHOCOLATE LIQUOR." (You should have four paragraphs in the document.)
5. At the beginning of the document, insert one blank line (press Enter once). Key the title **Guide to Chocolate Terminology** at the paragraph mark.
6. Format the text you just keyed to bold, dark blue, small caps, and 16-point type.
7. Format the text "nibs" as italic. Repeat the italic formatting to "Dutch-processed" and "natural unsweetened cocoa powder."
8. Select all the paragraphs below the heading, and change the font size to 11 points.

9. Use the Ctrl key to select noncontiguous text, and select "CHOCOLATE GLOSSARY," "CHOCOLATE LIQUOR," "COCOA BUTTER," AND "COCOA POWDER." Change the font color to light blue.
10. Save the document named ***[your initials]*2-21** in your Lesson 2 folder.
11. Submit your work, and close the document.

Exercise 2-22

Apply and copy character formatting, highlight text, and create a dropped capital letter.

1. Open the file **Favors - 2**.
2. Key the text shown in Figure 2-18 at the end of the document. The text should be the last sentence of the last paragraph.

Figure 2-18

```
For more information, call our toll-free number 800-555-2025
or visit our Web site www.campbellsconfections.biz.
```

3. Format the "C" of "Campbell's" in the first paragraph as a dropped capital letter.
4. Highlight the second paragraph (which begins "Our chocolate") in yellow.
5. Format the list of items from "wedding bells" through "other assorted shapes" as 11-point Arial italic small caps.
6. Copy the formatting to the second list (from "solid milk chocolate" to "dark chocolate with mint filling").
7. Split the last paragraph so "For more information" starts a new paragraph.
8. Copy the formatting from one of the lists to the new last paragraph.
9. Format the phone number in the last paragraph as red, bold, and a dotted underline.
10. Remove the highlight from the second paragraph.
11. Select the first line of the document, format the text with 24 points, and apply a text effects option from the gallery. Experiment with the options available for the text effect.
12. Save the document as ***[your initials]*2-22** in your Lesson 2 folder.
13. Submit your work, and close the document.

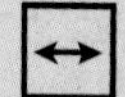

REVIEW

You need select only one, or a portion of, the formatted words, click the Format Painter button, and then select the new paragraph.

Exercise 2-23 ◆ Challenge Yourself

Apply character formatting, change case, and apply text effects.

1. Open the file **Club**.
2. Locate "Chocolate Club" in the first sentence of the first paragraph. Select the text, and apply bold, small caps format.
3. Copy the bold and small caps format to all occurrences of "Chocolate Club" in the document.
4. Select "Campbell's Confections" in the first paragraph. Format the selected text as blue, bold, 12 points, and small caps. Copy the format to all occurrences of "Campbell's Confections."
5. Move to the beginning of the document, and key **Chocolate Club**. Press Enter. Select the title, and change the font size to 24 points. Use the Text Effects button to format the title attractively. Experiment with the text effects options.
6. Select "$36." Use the Ribbon to format the text with a blue, dotted underline.
7. Copy the format applied to "$36" to "$360."
8. Save the document as ***[your initials]*2-23** in your Lesson 2 folder.
9. Submit your work, and close the document.

On Your Own

In these exercises you work on your own, as you would in a real-life business environment. Use the skills you've learned to accomplish the task—and be creative.

Exercise 2-24

Create a list of three companies in the United States that manufacture chocolate. Include the companies' addresses, a brief history of each company, and a description of the types of chocolate they manufacture. Apply interesting text effects to the first company name. Copy and repeat the formatting to the other companies in the list. Apply character format to headings and text you want to emphasize. Save the document as ***[your initials]*2-24** and submit it.

Exercise 2-25

Use the Internet to research the format to follow when creating an itinerary. Create an itinerary for a trip to visit Hershey, Pennsylvania. (Be imaginative! This could be a real trip or a fantasy trip.) To make the itinerary interesting, use several of the character formatting features you learned in this lesson. Remember, though, the itinerary must be readable. Save the document as ***[your initials]*****2-25** and submit it.

Exercise 2-26

Log onto the Internet, and locate two different sources for guidelines on type design. Create a document describing the guidelines one should follow to create a document that looks professional and follows the recommended procedures for character formatting. Save the document as ***[your initials]*****2-26** and submit it.

Lesson 3

Writing Tools

OBJECTIVES ***After completing this lesson, you will be able to:***

1. Use AutoComplete, AutoCorrect, and Actions.
2. Work with Building Blocks.
3. Insert the date and time as a field.
4. Check spelling and grammar.
5. Use the thesaurus and Research task pane.

Estimated Time: 1 hour

Word provides several automated features that save you time when keying frequently used text and correcting common keying errors. Word also provides important writing and research tools: a spelling and grammar checker, a thesaurus, and access to research services. These tools help you create professional-looking documents.

Using AutoComplete and AutoCorrect

By now, you might be familiar with three of Word's automatic features, though you might not know their formal names:

- *AutoComplete* suggests the completed word when you key the first four or more letters of a day, month, or date. If you key "Janu," for example, Word displays a ScreenTip suggesting the word "January," which you can insert by pressing Enter. Continue keying if you do not want the word inserted.

- *AutoCorrect* corrects commonly misspelled words as you key text. If you key "teh" instead of "the," for example, Word automatically changes the spelling to "the." You can create AutoCorrect entries for text you frequently use, and you can control AutoCorrect options.
- *Actions* help you save time by pressing the right mouse button for certain words or phrases and displaying a shortcut menu of actions. Word recognizes names, dates, addresses, and telephone numbers, as well as user-defined data types.

Exercise 3-1 PRACTICE AUTOCOMPLETE AND AUTOCORRECT

1. Open a new document. Click the **File** tab, and click **Options**. Click **Proofing**, and click **AutoCorrect Options** to open the AutoCorrect dialog box. Notice the available AutoCorrect options.
2. Scroll down the list of entries, and notice the words that Word corrects automatically (assuming the **Replace text as you type** option is checked).

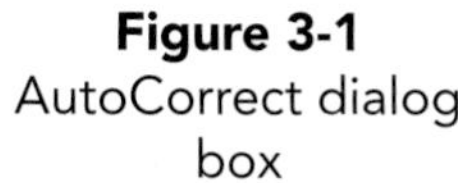

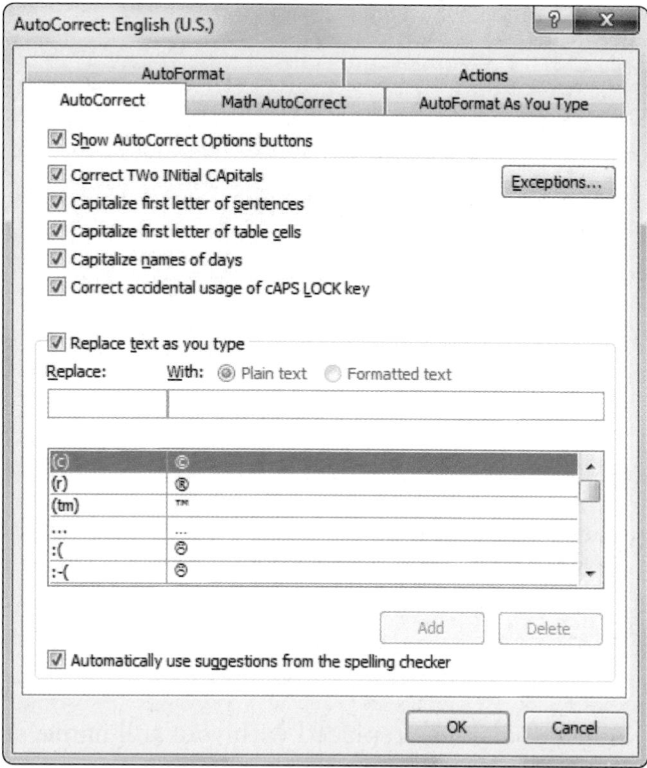

Figure 3-1 AutoCorrect dialog box

3. Click **Cancel** to close the dialog box. Click **Cancel** to close the Word Options dialog box.
4. Key **i am testing teh AutoCorrect feature.** Press Enter. Word corrects the "i" and "teh" automatically.

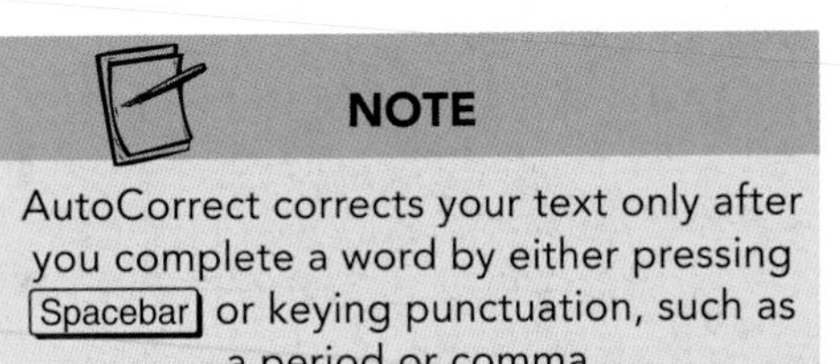

NOTE

AutoCorrect corrects your text only after you complete a word by either pressing Spacebar or keying punctuation, such as a period or comma.

5. Try keying another incorrect sentence. Using the exact spelling and case as shown, key **TOdya is.** AutoCorrect corrects the spelling and capitalization of "Today."
6. Key today's date, beginning with the month, and then press Spacebar. When you see the AutoComplete ScreenTip that suggests the current date, press Enter.
7. Key a period at the end of the sentence.

TABLE 3-1 AutoCorrect Options

Options	Description
Correct TWo INitial Capitals	Corrects words keyed accidentally with two initial capital letters, such as "WOrd" or "THis."
Capitalize first letter of sentences	Corrects any word at the beginning of a sentence that is not keyed with a capital letter.
Capitalize first letter of table cells	Corrects any word at the beginning of a table cell that is not keyed with a capital letter.
Capitalize names of days	Corrects a day spelled without an initial capital letter.
Correct accidental usage of cAPS LOCK key	If you press Caps Lock accidentally and then key "tODAY," AutoCorrect changes the word to "Today" and turns off Caps Lock.
Replace text as you type	Makes all corrections automatically.

Exercise 3-2 CREATE AN AUTOCORRECT ENTRY

You can create AutoCorrect entries for words you often misspell. You can also use AutoCorrect to create shortcuts for text you use repeatedly, such as names or phrases. Here are some examples of these types of AutoCorrect entries:

- "asap" for "as soon as possible"
- Your initials to be replaced with your full name, such as "**jh**" for "**Janet Holcomb**"
- "cc" for "Campbell's Confections"

1. Click the **File** tab, and click **Options**. Click **Proofing**.
2. Click **AutoCorrect Options** to open the AutoCorrect dialog box. Click the **AutoCorrect** tab if necessary. In the **Replace** box, key **fyi.**
3. Press Tab, and key **For your information** in the **With** box.
4. Click the **Add** button to move the entry into the alphabetized list. Click **OK** to close the AutoCorrect dialog box. Click **OK** to close the Word Options dialog box.
5. Start a new paragraph in the current document, and key **fyi, this really works.** Word spells out the entry, just as you specified in the AutoCorrect dialog box. It is not necessary to capitalize text keyed in the Replace text box.

Exercise 3-3 CONTROL AUTOCORRECT OPTIONS

Sometimes you might not want text to be corrected. You can undo a correction or turn AutoCorrect options on or off by clicking the AutoCorrect Options button and making a selection.

1. Move the I-beam over the word "For" until a small blue box appears beneath it.

Figure 3-2
Controlling AutoCorrect options

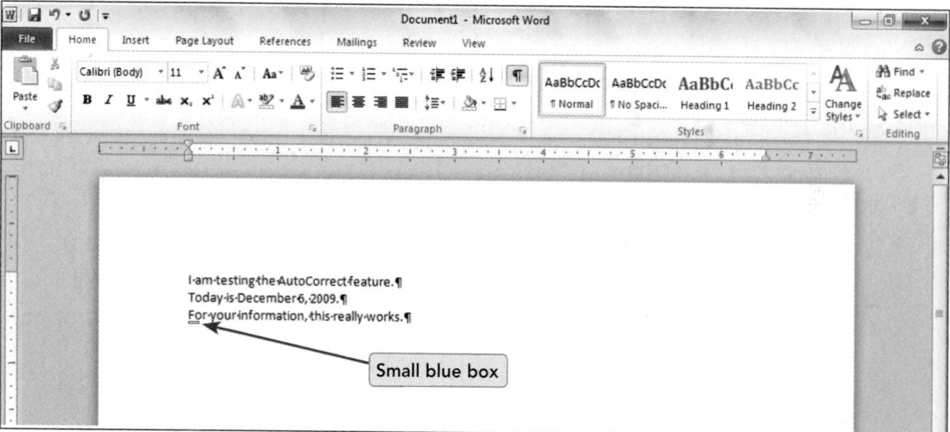

2. Drag the I-beam down over the small blue box until your mouse becomes a pointer and the box turns into the AutoCorrect Options button.
3. Click the button, and choose **Change back to "fyi"** from the menu list.

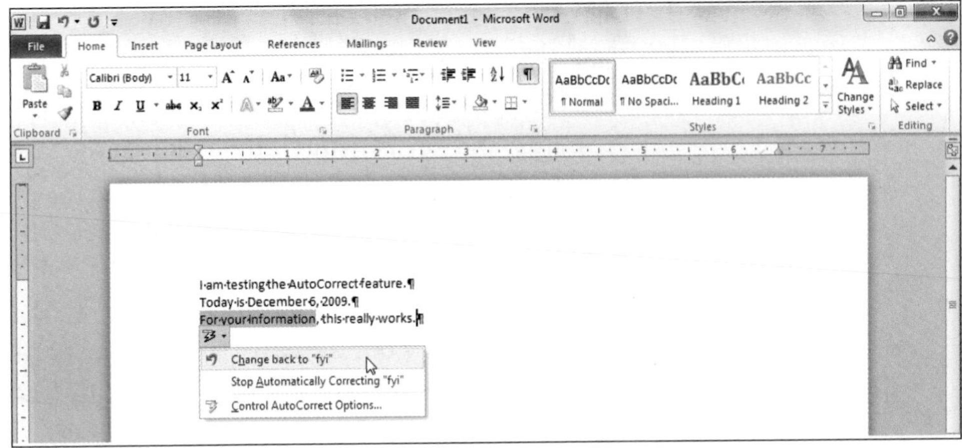

Figure 3-3
Undoing Automatic corrections

4. Click the AutoCorrect Options button again, and choose **Redo AutoCorrect** from the list. The words "For your information" are restored.
5. Click the button again, and choose **Control AutoCorrect Options**. The AutoCorrect dialog box opens.
6. Position the insertion point in the Replace text box, and key **fyi**. The AutoCorrect entry displays and is highlighted. Click **Delete**, and then click **OK**.

Exercise 3-4 CREATE AN AUTOCORRECT EXCEPTION

Another way to keep Word from correcting text you do not want corrected is to create an AutoCorrect exception. For example, you might have a company name that uses nonstandard capitalization such as "tuesday's bookstore." In such a case, you can use the AutoCorrect Exceptions dialog box to prevent Word from making automatic changes.

1. In a new paragraph, key the following on two separate lines:

   The ABCs of chocolate:
   ABsolute

   Press the Spacebar. Notice that AutoCorrect automatically changes the "B" in "ABsolute" to lowercase.

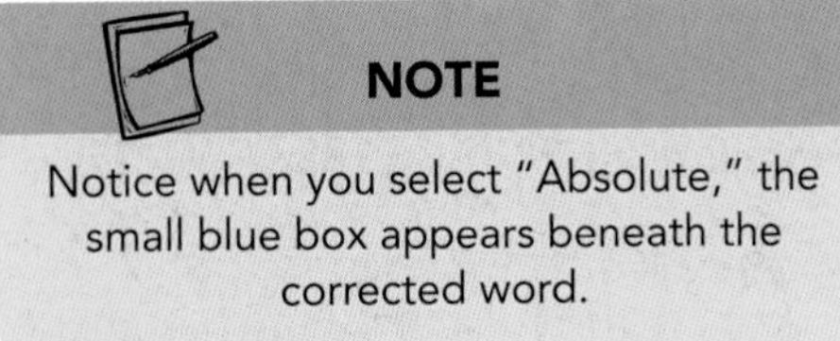

NOTE

Notice when you select "Absolute," the small blue box appears beneath the corrected word.

2. Open the AutoCorrect dialog box by moving the mouse over the word "Absolute" and clicking the AutoCorrect Options button. Click **Control AutoCorrect Options**. Click **Exceptions**. The AutoCorrect Exceptions dialog box displays.

3. Click the **INitial CAps** tab.
4. Key the exception **ABsolute** in the **Don't Correct** text box. Click **Add**. The entry is now in the list of exceptions.

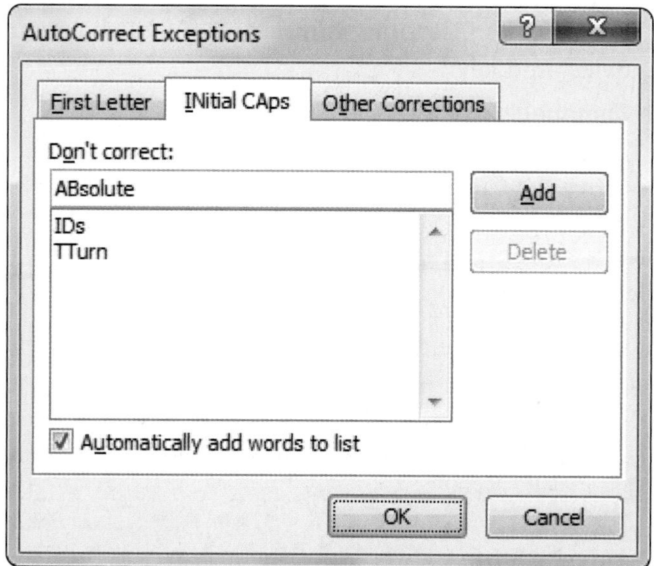

Figure 3-4
AutoCorrect Exceptions dialog box

TIP

Another good example of an AutoCorrect exception is the use of lowercase initials, which are sometimes entered at the bottom of a business letter as reference initials (see Appendix B, "Standard Forms for Business Documents"). In this case, you would not want Word to capitalize the first letter. To add your initials to AutoCorrect Exceptions, click the First Letter tab, and key your initials (lowercase) in the Don't capitalize after text box. Click OK twice.

5. Click **OK**, to close the AutoCorrect Exceptions dialog box, and then click **OK** again to close the AutoCorrect dialog box.
6. Select "Absolute" and then key **ABsolute storage temperature is a must.**
7. Right-click "Absolute," and choose **AutoCorrect** from the shortcut menu. Click **AutoCorrect Options** from the submenu, and click **Exceptions**. Select "ABsolute" from the list, and click **Delete**. Click **OK** to close the AutoCorrect Exceptions dialog box, and click **OK** to close the AutoCorrect dialog box.

Exercise 3-5 DEFINE ACTIONS

Just as Word recognizes an e-mail or Web address and automatically creates a hyperlink, it also recognizes names, dates, addresses, telephone numbers, and user-defined data types. You can right-click a word or phrase, and perform actions in Word for which you would normally open other programs, such as Microsoft Outlook. For instance, you can add a contact, schedule a meeting, or display your calendar.

1. Open the **File** tab, and click **Options**. Click **Proofing**, and click **AutoCorrect Options**.
2. Click the **Actions** tab, and click the **Enable additional actions in the right-click menu** check box if it is not selected.

3. Locate the heading **Available Actions**, and select **Address (English)** and **Date (XML)**. Deselect all other options.
4. Click **OK** to close the AutoCorrect dialog box. Click **OK** to close the Word Options dialog box.
5. Position the insertion point at the end of the document, press Enter twice, and key:

   Campbell's Confections
   25 Main Street
   Grove City, PA 16127

6. Select the address, and click the right-mouse button. Choose **Additional Actions**, and click **Add to Contact**. Microsoft Outlook launches, and an Untitled-Contact dialog box opens. You can add contact information including name, business, e-mail address, and telephone numbers. You can also search for directions using the Map It link.

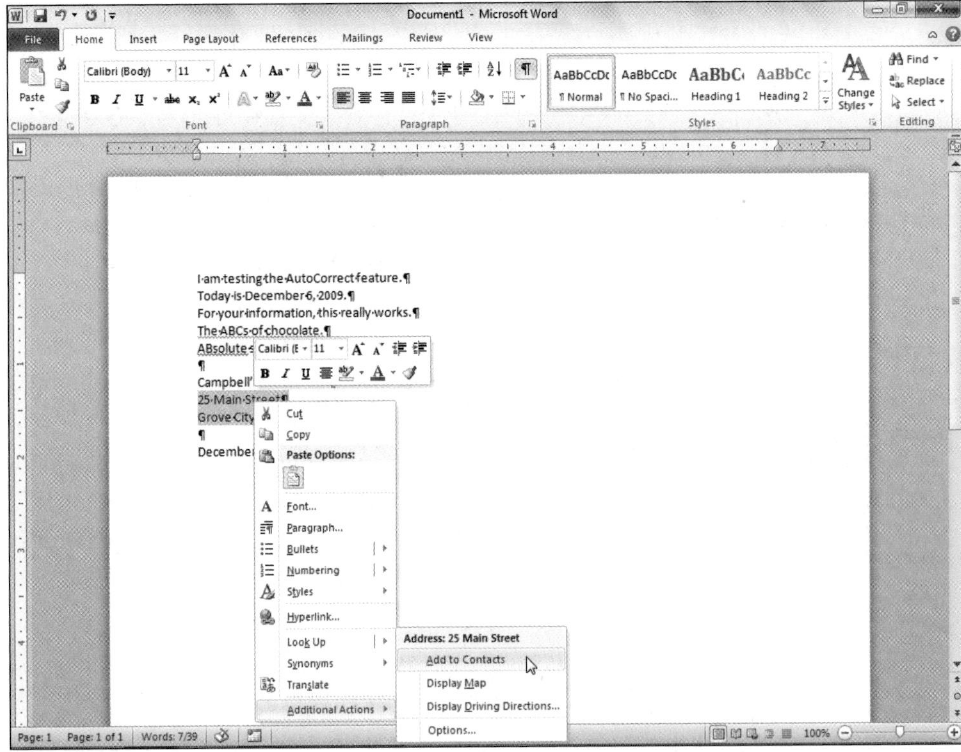

Figure 3-5
List of actions

NOTE

Microsoft Outlook is a program included in the Microsoft Office suite. If it is not set up on your machine, just close the dialog box when it asks you to configure it, or ask your instructor for help. If Outlook does launch, the Add to Contacts option lets you record information about individuals and businesses.

7. Close the Contact window without saving.
8. Select the date near the top of the document. Right-click to display the shortcut menu, and click **Additional Actions.** Choose **Show my Calendar**. Microsoft Outlook Calendar launches. Study the calendar features, and then close the Calendar window.
9. Close the document without saving.

Working with AutoText and Building Blocks

AutoText is another feature you can use to insert text automatically. This feature is extremely versatile. You can use it to create AutoText entries for text you use repeatedly (the AutoText entry can even include the text formatting). The text for which you create an AutoText entry can be a phrase, a sentence, paragraphs, logos, and so on.

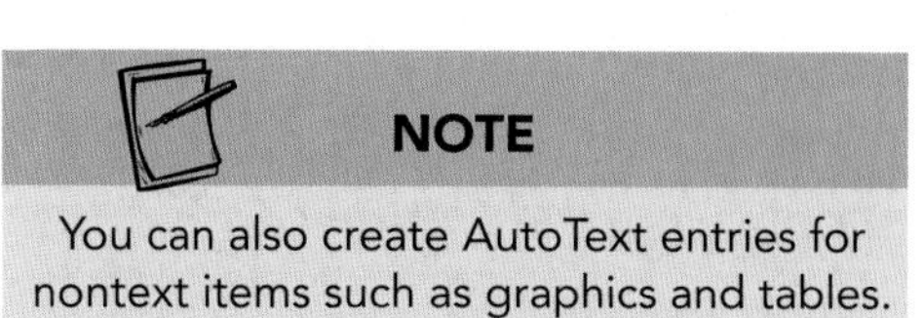

NOTE

You can also create AutoText entries for nontext items such as graphics and tables.

After you create an entry, you can insert it with just a few keystrokes.

Exercise 3-6 CREATE AN AUTOTEXT ENTRY

To create an AutoText entry, you key the text that you want to save and select it, or you select text that already exists in a document. When you select the text to be used for an AutoText entry, be sure to include the appropriate spaces, blank lines, and paragraph marks.

1. Open the file **Letter - 1**.
2. Press Ctrl+A to select the document.
3. Click the **Insert** tab on the Ribbon.
4. Locate the Text group, and click **Quick Parts**. Click **AutoText**, and an AutoText gallery displays. Click **Save selection to AutoText gallery**. The Create New Building Block dialog box displays.

Figure 3-6
Quick Parts menu

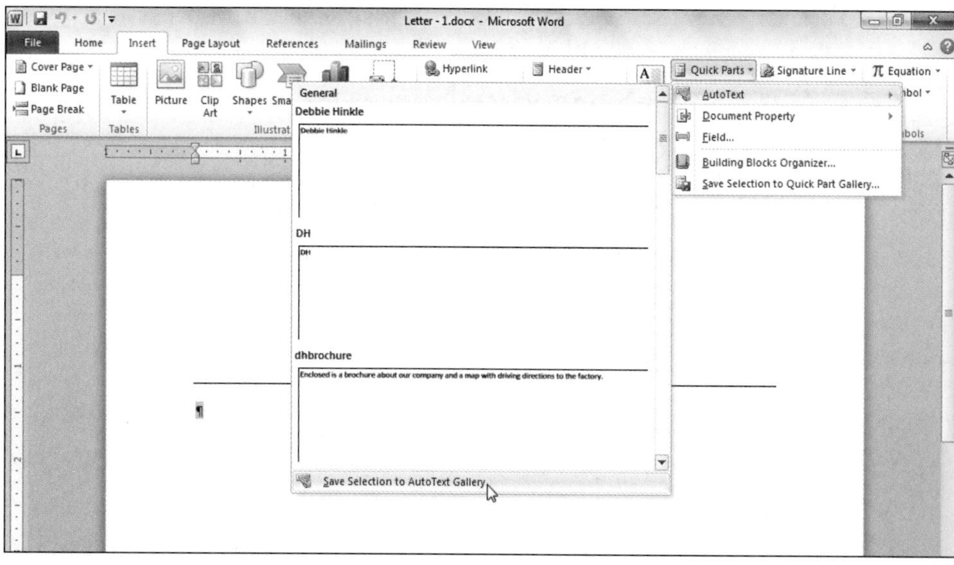

5. Key ***[your initials]*****Letterhead** in the **Name** box. Each AutoText entry must have a unique name.
6. Select **AutoText** from the **Gallery** drop-down list box if necessary.
7. Verify that **General** is selected in the **Category** drop-down list box.
8. Key **Grove City Letterhead** in the **Description** text box.
9. Select **Normal.dotm** from the **Save in** drop-down list.
10. Select **Insert content only** from the **Options** drop-down list. Click **OK**.
11. Press Ctrl+End to move to the end of the document. Key the text in Figure 3-7.

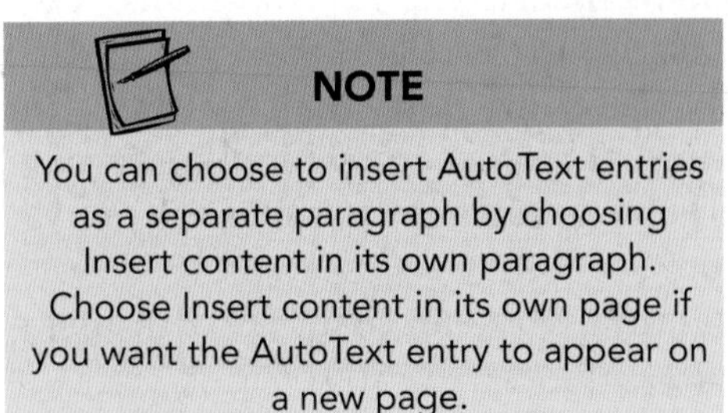

NOTE

You can choose to insert AutoText entries as a separate paragraph by choosing Insert content in its own paragraph. Choose Insert content in its own page if you want the AutoText entry to appear on a new page.

Figure 3-7

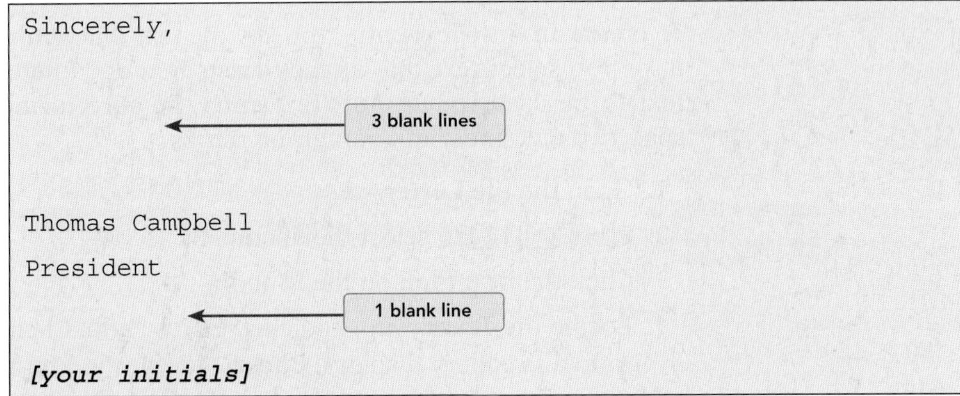

12. Select the text you just keyed, and press Alt+F3 to open the Create New Building Block dialog box.
13. Key or select the following information in the Create New Building Block dialog box.

Name:	***[your initials]*****Closing**
Gallery:	**AutoText**
Category:	**General**
Description:	**Closing**
Save in:	**Normal.dotm**
Options:	**Insert content only**

14. Click **OK** to close the Create New Building Block dialog box.
15. Close the document, and do not save the changes.

Exercise 3-7 INSERT AUTOTEXT ENTRIES

There are several ways to insert an AutoText entry. If the AutoText entry is stored in the Normal.dotm, key the first four letters of the entry, and an AutoComplete box displays. Press Enter or Tab to insert the text. If you have an AutoText entry that is unique or short, you can key the first few letters of the entry name and press F3 to insert the entry. A third method is to click the Insert tab, click Quick Parts, click AutoText, and click the AutoText entry from the AutoText gallery. To insert an AutoText entry using the Building Blocks Organizer, position the insertion point and open the Building Blocks Organizer. When the Building Blocks Organizer dialog box opens, click one of the column headings to sort the entries. Click the Name heading to sort the text alphabetically by name. Click the Gallery heading to display the entries by gallery type. AutoText entries appear at the top of the Gallery listing. Select the entry, and click the Insert button.

1. Create a new document.
2. Click the **Insert** tab, and locate the Text group. Click **Quick Parts**, and click **Building Blocks Organizer**. The Building Blocks Organizer dialog box displays.

Figure 3-8
Building Blocks Organizer dialog box

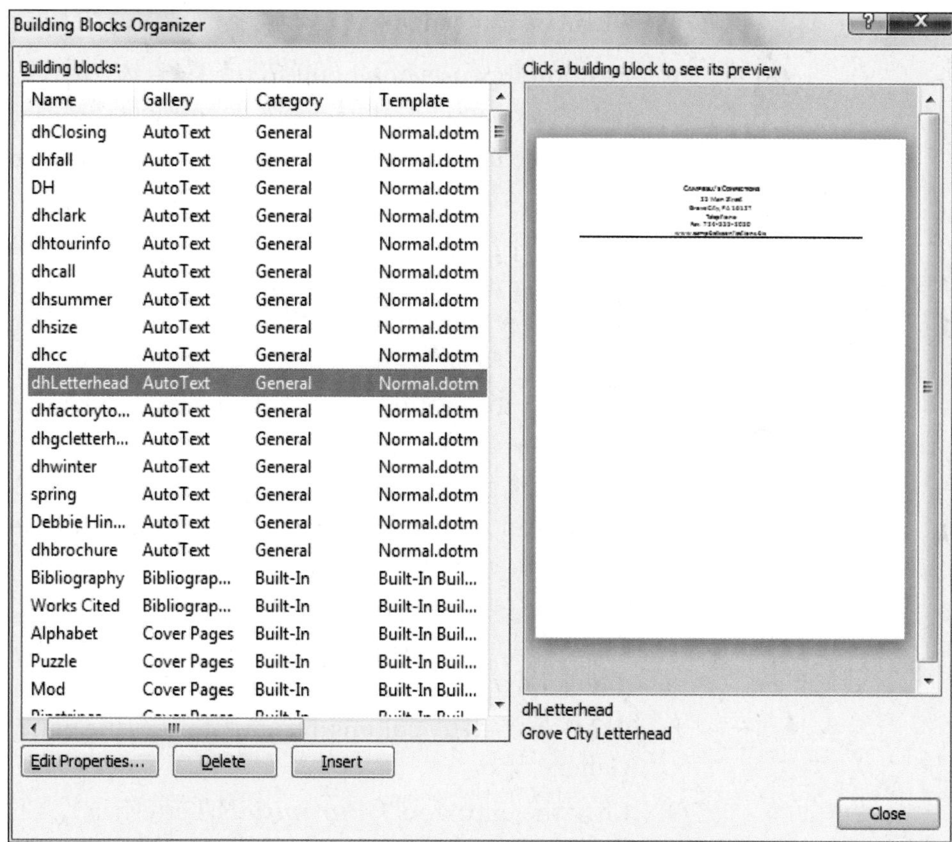

3. Click the **Gallery** heading, and the list sorts by gallery type.
4. Click the **Name** heading, and the list is sorted alphabetically by name.

5. Click the Gallery heading, and locate the "*[your initials]*Letterhead" AutoText entry.
6. Click the *[your initials]*Letterhead entry, and click Insert. The letterhead information is automatically inserted.
7. Click the Undo button to remove the AutoText entry.
8. Key ***[your initials]*Letterhead**, and press Enter to insert the Autotext entry when the AutoComplete box displays.
9. Begin keying *[your initials]*Closing, and press the Enter key when the AutoComplete box displays.

TIP

Check Appendix B, "Standard Forms for Business Documents," to double-check that your letter has the correct number of blank lines between items.

Exercise 3-8 EDIT AND DELETE AUTOTEXT ENTRIES

After you create an AutoText entry, it may need to be edited. If you no longer use an entry, you can delete it.

1. Position the insertion point to the right of "Telephone:" in the letterhead, and key the telephone number **724-555-2025**.
2. Select the letterhead text beginning with "Campbell's Confections" and ending with the left-aligned paragraph mark.
3. Press Alt+F3 to open the Create New Building Block dialog box.
4. Key ***[your initials]*Letterhead** in the Name box, and select AutoText from the Gallery drop-down list. Select Normal.dotm from the Save in drop-down list. Click OK.
5. Click Yes to redefine the AutoText entry. The entry now includes the telephone number.
6. To test the change, delete all the document text. Key ***[your initials]*Letterhead**, and press Enter to insert the letterhead AutoText.
7. Click the Insert tab on the Ribbon, and click the Quick Parts command. Click Building Blocks Organizer to open the Building Blocks Organizer dialog box.
8. Click the Gallery column heading to sort the entries in the list by Gallery type.
9. Click the entry for "*[your initials]*Letterhead." Click Delete to remove the AutoText entry from the Gallery. Click No to prevent the deletion of the AutoText entry. Click Close to return to your document.

Inserting the Date and Time

You have seen that when you begin keying a month, AutoComplete displays the suggested date, and you press Enter to insert the date as regular text. You can also insert the date or time in a document as a field. A *field* is a hidden code that tells Word to insert specific text that might need to be updated automatically, such as a date or page number. If you insert the date or time in a document as a field, Word automatically updates it each time you print the document.

There are two ways to insert the date or time as a field:

- Click the Insert tab on the Ribbon, and click the Date and Time command. Select the desired format from the Date and Time dialog box.
- Press Alt+Shift+D to insert the date and Alt+Shift+T to insert the time.

Exercise 3-9 INSERT THE DATE AND TIME

You can enter date and time fields that can be updated automatically. You can also choose not to update these fields automatically.

1. Move the insertion point to the end of the current document.
2. Press Alt+Shift+D to enter the default date field.
3. Press Ctrl+Z to undo the date insertion.
4. Click the **Insert** tab on the Ribbon, and click the **Date and Time** command to open the Date and Time dialog box.

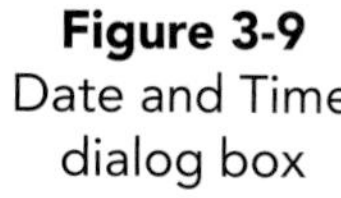

Figure 3-9
Date and Time dialog box

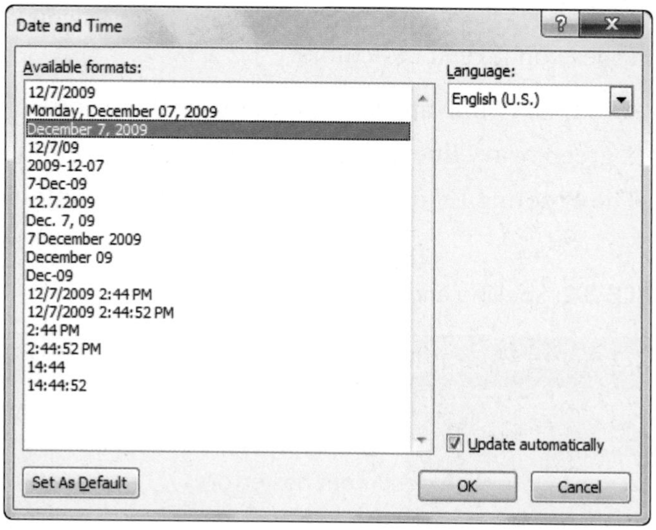

NOTE

You can also use the Date and Time dialog box to insert the date and time in a particular text format without inserting it as an updatable field.

TIP

Although printing updates a field, you can also update a field on-screen by clicking the field and pressing F9. To change the date or time format, right-click the field, and choose Edit Field.

5. Scroll the list of available time and date formats, and choose the third format in the list (the standard date format for business documents).
6. Check the **Update automatically** check box so the date is automatically updated each time you print the document. Click **OK**.
7. Move the insertion point after the date field, and press Spacebar twice.
8. Press Alt+Shift+T to insert the time as a field.
9. Save the document as ***[your initials]*3-9** in your Lesson 3 folder.
10. Submit your work, and close the document.

TIP

Remember that the Update Automatically option will change the date in your document. If you are sending correspondence, do not choose this option because the date in the letter will then always reflect the current date, not the date on which you wrote the letter.

Checking Spelling and Grammar

Correct spelling and grammar are essential to good writing. As you have seen, Word checks your spelling and grammar as you key text and flags errors with these on-screen indicators:

- A red, wavy line appears under misspelled words.
- A green, wavy line appears under possible grammatical errors.
- The Proofing Errors icon on the status bar contains an "X."

TABLE 3-2 Spelling and Grammar Status

Icon	Indicates
	Word is checking for errors as you key text.
	The document has errors.
	The document has no errors.

Exercise 3-10 SPELL- AND GRAMMAR-CHECK ERRORS INDIVIDUALLY

NOTE

If no green, wavy lines appear in your document, open the File tab, and click Options. Click Proofing in the left pane. Click the Check grammar with spelling check box, and click OK.

TIP

Word's spelling and grammar tools are not foolproof. For example, it cannot correct a word that is correctly spelled but incorrectly keyed, such as "sue" instead of "use." It might also apply a green, wavy line to a type of grammatical usage, such as the passive voice, which might not be preferred, but is not incorrect.

You can right-click text marked as either a spelling or a grammar error and choose a suggested correction from a shortcut menu.

1. Open the file **Milk Chocolate - 2**. This document has several errors, indicated by the red and green wavy lines.
2. At the top of the document, press Enter and move the insertion point to the blank paragraph mark. Notice that the Proofing Errors indicator on the status bar contains an "X."
3. Using 14-point bold type, key a misspelled word by keying the title **Mlk Chocolate**. When you finish, "Mlk" is marked as misspelled.
4. Right-click the misspelled word, and choose "Milk" from the spelling shortcut menu.
5. Right-click the grammatical error "It contain" in the second sentence. Choose "contains" from the shortcut menu.

Exercise 3-11 SPELL- AND GRAMMAR-CHECK AN ENTIRE DOCUMENT

Instead of checking words or sentences individually, you can check an entire document. This is the best way to correct spelling and grammar errors in a long document. Use one of these methods:

- Click the Spelling and Grammar button on the Review tab of the Ribbon.
- Press F7.

1. Position the insertion point at the beginning of the document, and click the **Review** tab. Click the Spelling & Grammar button. Word locates the first misspelling, "choclate."

Figure 3-10
Checking spelling and grammar

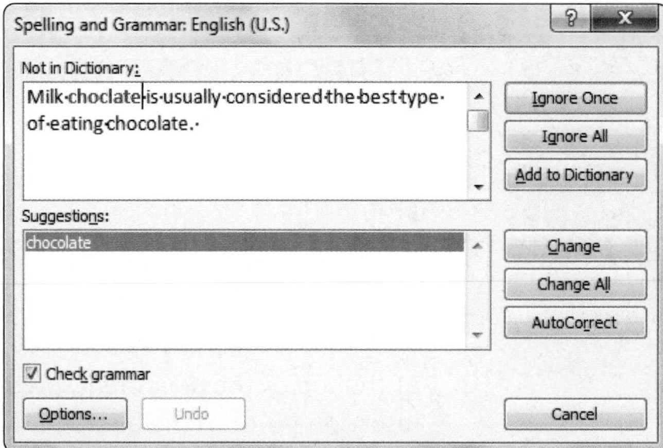

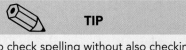

TIP

To check spelling without also checking grammar, click the Check grammar check box to clear it.

2. Click **Change** to correct the spelling to the first suggested spelling, "chocolate." Next, Word finds a word choice error, "hole."
3. Click **Change** to correct the word choice. Next, Word finds two words that should be separated by a space.
4. Click **Change** to correct the spacing. Next Word finds a repeated word, "of."
5. Click **Delete** to delete the repeated word. Next Word finds a grammatical error—"it" is not capitalized.
6. Click **Change** to correct the capitalization in the document.
7. Click **OK** when the check is complete. Notice there are no more wavy lines in the document, and the Proofing Errors indicator shows a checkmark.
8. Read the paragraph, and check for errors that were not found by the Spelling and Grammar checker.
9. Locate "10 per cent" in the second sentence. Delete the space between "per" and "cent."
10. Locate the sentence that begins "It is mild," and change "type" to "**types**."
11. Locate the sentence that begins "It used," and change it to read "**It is used**."

NOTE

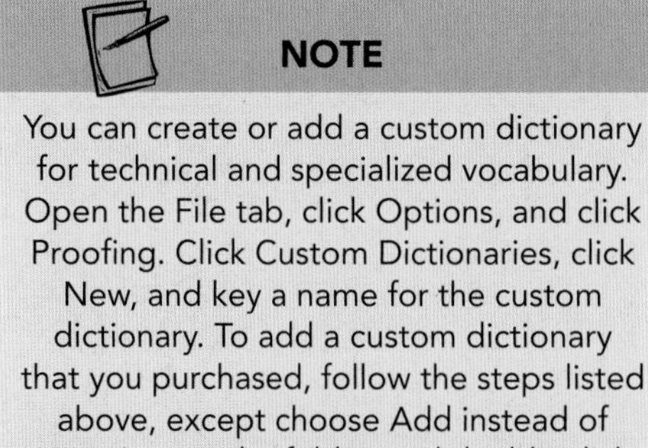

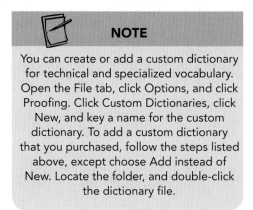

You can create or add a custom dictionary for technical and specialized vocabulary. Open the File tab, click Options, and click Proofing. Click Custom Dictionaries, click New, and key a name for the custom dictionary. To add a custom dictionary that you purchased, follow the steps listed above, except choose Add instead of New. Locate the folder, and double-click the dictionary file.

TABLE 3-3 Dialog Box Options When Checking Spelling and Grammar

Option	Description
Ignore Once	Skips the word.
Ignore All	Skips all occurrences of the word in the document.
Add to Dictionary	Adds the word to the default dictionary file in Word. You can also create your own dictionary and add words to it.
Change	Changes the word to the entry in the Change To box or to the word you chose from the Suggestions list.
Change All	Same as Change, but changes the word throughout the document.
AutoCorrect	Adds the word to the list of corrections Word makes automatically.
Options	Lets you change the Spelling and Grammar options in Word.
Undo	Changes back the most recent correction made.
Cancel	Discontinues the checking operation.

Using the Thesaurus and Research Task Pane

The *thesaurus* is a tool that can improve your writing. Use the thesaurus to look up a *synonym* (a word with a similar meaning) for a selected word to add variety or interest to a document. You can look up synonyms for any of the synonym recommendations to get additional word choices. The thesaurus sometimes displays *antonyms* (words with the opposite meaning) and related words.

After selecting a word to change, you can start the thesaurus in one of three ways:

- Click the Review tab, and click Thesaurus.
- Press Shift+F7.
- Right-click the word, and choose Synonyms from the shortcut menu.

Exercise 3-12 USE THE THESAURUS

1. Select the word "best" in the first sentence, or place the insertion point in the word.
2. Press Shift+F7. The Research task pane appears with a list of synonyms for "best."

Figure 3-11
Using the thesaurus

NOTE

You can also look up a synonym by clicking the word with the right mouse button and choosing Synonyms from the shortcut menu.

3. Point to the word "finest," and click the drop-down arrow. Click **Look Up**. A list of additional synonyms appears for "finest" in the task pane.
4. Go back to the word "finest" by clicking the Previous search button Back.
5. Point to "finest," click the down arrow, and choose **Insert**. Word replaces "best" with "finest" and returns to the document.
6. Save the document as ***[your initials]*3-12** in your Lesson 3 folder.
7. Submit the document, but do not close it.

TIP

Click the Translation button on the Ribbon for additional options, including Translate Document, Translate Selected Text, Mini Translator, or Choose Translation Language.

Exercise 3-13 USE REFERENCES

If you are connected to the Internet, you can access several research sources, such as a dictionary, an encyclopedia, and research sites such as Factiva iWorks, HighBeam Research, and Live Search. From the Review tab on the Ribbon, you can click the Research button; right-click a word and click Look Up in the shortcut menu; or press Alt and click a word to open the Research task pane.

1. Press Alt and click the word "chocolate" in the first sentence.

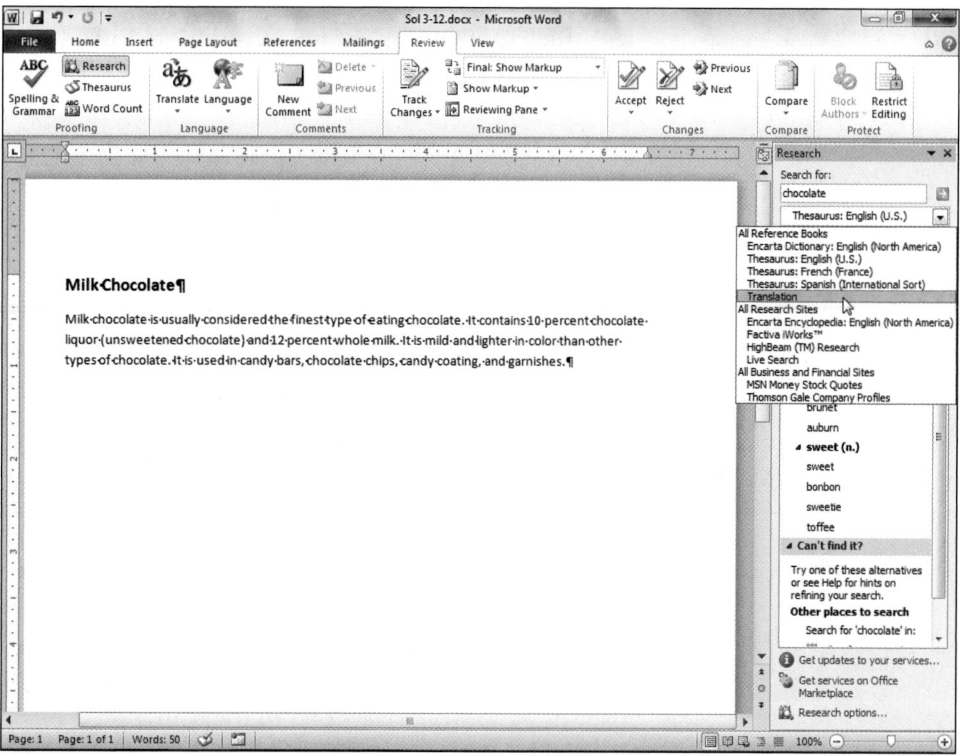

Figure 3-12
Using references

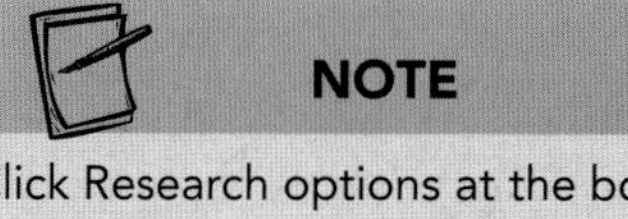

NOTE

Click Research options at the bottom of the Research task pane to open the Research Options dialog box for additional research options.

2. Click the drop-down arrow beside the **All Reference Books** box, and choose **Encarta Dictionary**. The task pane indicates the part of speech, syllabication, and several definitions for "chocolate."
3. Click the drop-down arrow beside the All Reference Books box, and choose **Translation**.
4. Choose **English** in the **From** box and **French (France)** in the **To** box. The bilingual dictionary displays the French word for chocolate—*chocolat*.
5. Close the document.

Lesson 3 Summary

- The AutoComplete feature suggests the completed word when you key the first four or more letters of a day, month, or date.
- The AutoCorrect feature corrects some misspelled words and capitalization errors for you automatically as you key text.

- Use the AutoCorrect dialog box to create entries for words you often misspell and the AutoCorrect Options button to control AutoCorrect options.
- Use the AutoCorrect Exceptions dialog box to create an AutoCorrect exception so Word will not correct it.
- Use Actions to perform Microsoft Outlook functions, such as creating entries in Outlook's contact list.
- AutoText is another versatile feature you can use to insert text automatically. You create AutoText entries for text you use repeatedly, including text formatting.
- Use the Building Blocks Organizer to edit and delete AutoText entries.
- Insert the date and time in a document as an automatically updated field, which is a hidden code that tells Word to insert specific information—in this case, the date and/or time. Use the Date and Time dialog box to choose different date and time formats.
- Use the spelling and grammar checker to correct misspelled words in your document as well as poor grammar usage. Check errors individually or throughout your entire document.
- Use the thesaurus to look up synonyms (words with similar meaning) or sometimes antonyms (words with the opposite meaning) for a selected word to add variety and interest to your document.
- Use the Research task pane to look up words or phrases in a dictionary, to research topics in an encyclopedia, or to access bilingual dictionaries for translations. You can also access research sites such as Live Search.

LESSON 3 — Command Summary

Feature	Button	Command	Keyboard
Check spelling and grammar		Review tab, Proofing group, Spelling & Grammar	F7
Create AutoText entry		Insert tab, Text group, Quick Parts, AutoText	Alt+F3
Insert Date		Insert tab, Text group, Date & Time	Alt+Shift+D
Insert Time		Insert tab, Text group, Date & Time	Alt+Shift+T
Research		Review tab, Proofing group, Research	Alt+Click
Thesaurus		Review tab, Proofing group, Thesaurus	Shift+F7
Translate		Review tab, Language group, Translate	

Concepts Review

True/False Questions

Each of the following statements is either true or false. Indicate your choice by circling T or F.

T F 1. AutoCorrect automatically changes "THis" to "This" and "monday" to "Monday."

T F 2. You can edit an AutoText entry by redefining an existing AutoText entry.

T F 3. The Grammar button is located on the Home tab.

T F 4. To start the thesaurus, press F7.

T F 5. The thesaurus finds synonyms for words.

T F 6. AutoComplete suggests a complete word or phrase for a date or an AutoText entry.

T F 7. You can choose to check only the spelling of a document, without checking the grammar.

T F 8. You can insert a date automatically by pressing Ctrl+D.

Short Answer Questions

Write the correct answer in the space provided.

1. Which function key starts a spell check?

____

2. Which option in the Spelling and Grammar dialog box skips over an incorrectly spelled word?

____

3. Which dialog box is used to display and delete AutoText entries?

____

4. When the Building Blocks Organizer dialog box is open, what is the easiest way to display the entries in a gallery in alphabetical order?

____

5. Which tab on the Ribbon lists the Date and Time command?

____

6. Which Word feature corrects accidental usage of Caps Lock?

____

7. Which task pane is used to access references such as dictionaries and encyclopedias?

____

8. What must you do to a word before using the thesaurus?

____

Critical Thinking

Answer these questions on a separate page. There are no right or wrong answers. Support your answers with examples from your own experience, if possible.

1. Some educators believe the spell-checking feature in word processing programs will lead to decreased spelling skills in future generations. Do you think students' spelling skills will deteriorate? Explain your answer.
2. Review several Word documents that you recently created. Study the content of the documents, and determine if there is any repetitive content. Would it be time effective to create AutoText entries for this text? Why or why not?

Skills Review

Exercise 3-14

Use AutoCorrect and AutoComplete.

1. Start a new document.
2. Key the following sentences (including the errors):

   CAmpbell's Confections is a candy manufacturer in western pennsylvania with three major divisions. quality chocolates are produced for retail, wholesale, and fundraising.

3. Press Caps Lock, and key the following sentence as shown.

   there are 24 campbell's confections retail stores located in three states.

4. Continue the paragraph by keying the following sentence in all lowercase letters, letting AutoCorrect capitalize the first letter of each sentence. When you see the AutoComplete tip for the months, press Enter and continue keying.

   from january through december, you can visit any of our stores or Web site to find sales promotions for our boxed chocolate candy, chocolate favors, or novelty items.

5. Start a new paragraph. Key the following sentence (including the errors in the first two words)

   thisyear, consider a visit to Campbell's Confections and tour our factory.

6. Save the document as ***[your initials]*3-14** in your Lesson 3 folder.
7. Submit your work, and close the document.

Exercise 3-15

Use AutoText.

1. Open the file **Letter - 2**. Replace [Date] with the current date.
2. Change the formatting for the entire letterhead to small caps and dark blue. Select the first line of the letterhead, and change the font size to 14.
3. At the second blank paragraph mark below "Dear Mr. Matthews," key the following sentence,

   Thank you for your interest in Campbell's Confections, western Pennsylvania's most popular chocolate factory and candy store.

4. Using the text you just keyed, create an AutoText entry by following these steps:
   a. Select the text "Campbell's Confections." Do not select the comma at the end of the text.
   b. Click the **Insert** tab on the Ribbon, and click **Quick Parts**.
   c. Click **AutoText**, and click **Save Selection to AutoText Gallery**.
   d. Key the AutoText entry name ***[your initials]*****cc** (Example: dhcc).
   e. Select **AutoText** in the **Gallery** drop-down list. Select **Normal.dotm** in the **Save in** drop-down list.
   f. Click **OK**.
5. Press Enter twice at the end of the first paragraph to start a new paragraph.
6. Click the **Insert** tab on the Ribbon. Click **Quick Parts**, and click **Building Blocks Organizer**.
7. Click the **Gallery** column heading to sort the list. Locate and click ***[your initials]*****cc** to select the AutoText entry. Click **Insert**.
8. Complete the sentence by pressing the Spacebar and keying the following text:

   is your full-service candy store, offering the greatest selections of milk, dark, white, and sugar-free chocolates. We also create specialty chocolates with logos, monograms, or custom artwork.

9. Start a new paragraph, and key the following text. When you key "***[your initials]***cc," an AutoComplete box displays. Press Enter when the AutoComplete box appears to accept the text insertion.

   The enclosed brochures will provide more information about *[your initials]* cc. We look forward to helping you place your next order.

10. Press Enter twice, and key **Sincerely yours,**.

NOTE

An alternative method to insert the AutoText entry is to click the Insert tab, and click Quick Parts. Point to AutoText, and a list of AutoText entries displays. Click to select the AutoText entry.

11. Press Enter four times, and key the following information:

    Lydia Hamrick
    Customer Service

12. Press Enter twice, key ***[your initials]*** in lowercase, and press Enter.

13. Control the AutoCorrect function with the AutoCorrect Options button by following these steps:
    a. Move the I-beam over your first initial until you see the small blue box.
    b. Move the pointer to the small blue box until the AutoCorrect Options button appears.
    c. Click the button icon and choose **Undo Automatic Capitalization**.

14. On the line below your initials, key **Enclosures (2)**.

15. Delete the AutoText entry by following these steps:
    a. Click the **Insert** tab on the Ribbon, and click **Quick Parts**. Click **Building Blocks Organizer**.
    b. Select the AutoText entry, ***[your initials]*cc**, from the list.
    c. Click **Delete** and click **Yes**. Click **Close**.

16. Work with Actions by following these steps:
    a. Move the I-beam over the street address "Main Street," and then press the right mouse button to display a shortcut menu.
    b. Choose **Additional Actions**.
    c. Click **Add to Contacts**.
    d. Review the content of the Contact tab, and close the window.
    e. Click **No** when you are asked if you want to save the changes.

17. Save the document as ***[your initials]*3-15** in your Lesson 3 folder.

18. Submit and close the document.

Exercise 3-16

Spell-check and grammar-check a document.

1. Open the file **Favors - 3**.

2. Spell-check and grammar-check the document by following these steps:
    a. Click the **Review** tab on the Ribbon.
    b. Click the Spelling Grammar button.
    c. When Word locates the first misspelled word, choose **Campbell's** from the Suggestions list and click **Change**. Next Word finds a misspelling, "ocasions." Click **Change**.
    d. When Word locates "sugarfree" as an error, click in the "Not in Dictionary" section, and key a hyphen after the "r" and click **Change**.

e. Correct the spelling of "wraped," "ribon," and "minature." When Word locates "ment" as an error, click in the "Not in Dictionary" section, and press Backspace to delete the extra space and to form the word "assortment." Click **Change**.

f. When Word locates "carmel" as an error, edit the text to read "caramel." Click **Change**.

g. Continue checking the document, changing spelling, deleting words, or correcting grammar as appropriate.

3. Select the title, and change the font size to 14 and the font color to dark blue.

4. Save the document as ***[your initials]*3-16** in your Lesson 3 folder.

5. Submit and close the document.

Exercise 3-17

Use the thesaurus.

1. Open the file **Summer**.

2. Use the thesaurus to find another word for "wonderful" by following these steps:

   a. Select "wonderful" in the last sentence of the first paragraph.

   b. Press Shift+F7.

   c. Point to a synonym, and click the drop-down arrow to the right of the word.

   d. Choose **Insert** from the drop-down list.

   e. Close the Research task pane by clicking the Research task pane Close button.

3. Start a new paragraph at the end of the document and key **Come and enjoy the fun!**

4. Select the word "fun."

5. Click the **Review** tab on the Ribbon. Click the Thesaurus button.

6. Replace "fun" with a noun listed in the Research task pane. Remember to click the down arrow and choose **Insert**. Close the Research task pane.

7. Save the document as ***[your initials]*3-17** in your Lesson 3 folder.

8. Use the Research task pane to define a word by following these steps:

   a. Press Alt and click "ethnic" in the first paragraph.

   b. Choose **Encarta Dictionary** from the All Reference Books drop-down list.

   c. Read the definition.

   d. Close the task pane.

9. Submit your work, and close the document.

Lesson Applications

Exercise 3-18

Create an AutoText entry, and check grammar and spelling.

1. Create a new document, and key the text **Campbell's Confections** and press Enter.
2. Select the text and the paragraph marks, and format them as 12-point Cambria.
3. Select the text "Campbell's Confections" (excluding the paragraph marks), and create an AutoText entry named ***[your initials]*cc**.
4. Go to the end of the document, and key the text shown in Figure 3-13. Include the corrections. Wherever "***[your initials]***cc" appears, key the name of the AutoText entry you just created, pressing Enter or F3 to expand the entry.

Figure 3-13

```
The best hand made chocolate candy inWestern Pennsylvania
is made by [your initials]cc. The family owned business
opened its first store in 1957 on Main ST in grove city
Pennsylvania.

                                          milk and dark
[your initials]cc specialize in assorted chocolate-covered
nuts, creams, melt-a-ways, and truffles. Additional
candy
selections include chocolate-covered prezels, peppermint
       cordial     caramel
patties, cherries, pecanettes, croquettes, and peanut
butter cups. You can also buy several varieties of hard
and soft candies. [your initials]cc takes pride inusing
the finest ingredients in its recipes.

Visit one of [your initials]cc candy stores to make your
candy selections. The candy stores are open 6 days a week.
                                        retail
In addition to buying your candy at the stores, you can
call our toll-free number at 800-555-2025 or visit our Web
site at www.campbellsconfections.biz.
```

REVIEW

Use the Repeat command F4 to format the name.

5. Spell-check and grammar-check the document.
6. Format the title as 16-point bold, small caps, and add a text effect.
7. Format "Campbell's Confections" in small caps throughout the document.
8. Delete the AutoText entry you created.
9. Save the document as ***[your initials]*****3-18** in your Lesson 3 folder.
10. Submit your work, and close the document.

Exercise 3-19

Spell-check and grammar-check a document, and use the Research task pane.

1. Open the file **Fountain - 2**.
2. Spell-check and grammar-check the document, making the appropriate corrections.
3. Proofread the document to ensure the document does not contain errors.
4. Use the thesaurus to look up the word "finest" in the second sentence of the paragraph that begins "Campbell's Confections."
5. Capitalize each word in the first line of the document.
6. Format the title as 14-point bold, small caps with expanded character spacing.
7. Save the document as ***[your initials]*****3-19** in your Lesson 3 folder.
8. Submit and close the document.

Exercise 3-20

Format a document as a letter, check spelling and grammar, and use the thesaurus.

1. Open the document **Letter - 3**.
2. Position the insertion point on the second blank paragraph mark after the letterhead text.
3. Click the **Insert** tab, and click the **Date and Time** command. Click the third format in the Date and Time dialog box.
4. Press Enter four times, and key the text in Figure 3-15. Include one blank line after the address and the salutation. (Refer to Appendix B, "Standard Forms for Business Documents," for correct letter format.)

Figure 3-15

```
Mr. George Henderson
3850 Fifth Avenue
Altoona, PA 16602

Dear Mr. Henderson:
```

5. At the end of the last paragraph, press Enter twice. Key the closing **Sincerely**, and press Enter four times. Key **Lydia Hamrick**, and press Enter. On the next line, key **Customer Service**. Press Enter twice, and key your initials in lowercase. Press Enter and key **Enclosure**.
6. Use the AutoCorrect Options button to undo the capitalization of your first initial.
7. Check the spelling and grammar of the document, making the appropriate corrections.
8. Use the thesaurus to find a synonym for "delighted" in the first sentence of the document.
9. Save the document as ***[your initials]*****3-20** in your Lesson 3 folder.
10. Submit and close the document.

Exercise 3-21 ◆ Challenge Yourself

Create an AutoText entry, and check the grammar and spelling of a document.

1. Open the file **WV Stores**.
2. Select the complete address and contact information for the Clarksburg store, and create an AutoText entry named ***[your initials]*****clark**. Be sure to store the AutoText entry in the Normal.dotm.
3. Close the document and open the file **Refer**.
4. Place the insertion point on the second paragraph mark after the letterhead text, and insert the date using the Ribbon. Use appropriate format for a business letter.
5. Press Enter four times and key the inside address listed in Figure 3-16.

Figure 3-16

```
Ms. Jill Gresh
360 Lincoln Street
Grafton, WV 26354
```

6. Press Enter twice, and key **Dear Ms. Gresh:**.
7. Verify that there is one blank line between the inside address and the salutation and one blank line between the salutation and the first paragraph.
8. Position the insertion point at the beginning of the paragraph that begins "Please let."
9. Insert the AutoText entry ***[your initials]*****clark**. Press Enter if necessary to insert a blank line.

10. Spell- and grammar-check from the beginning of the document.
11. Delete the AutoText entry "***[your initials]***clark."
12. Save the document as ***[your initials]*3-21** in your Lesson 3 folder.
13. Submit your work, and close the document.

On Your Own

In these exercises you work on your own, as you would in a real-life business environment. Use the skills you've learned to accomplish the task—and be creative.

Exercise 3-22

Write a summary about a book you have recently read, but before you start the summary, create an AutoCorrect entry for a word you know you often misspell. Next create an AutoText entry for a phrase you use frequently. Use these stored items in the summary as often as you can. Delete the entries when you have finished. Spell- and grammar-check your document. Format the document, save it as ***[your initials]*3-22**, and submit it.

Exercise 3-23

Create a new document, and create an AutoText entry to be used as a salutation in a letter. Create an AutoText entry to include a complimentary closing and signature line. Delete the text keyed for the AutoText entries from the document, and write a letter to a local government official. Insert the date using the Date and Time feature on the Insert tab of the Ribbon. Key the inside address, and insert the AutoText entry you created for the salutation. Key the body of the letter, and insert the AutoText entry you created for the closing. Delete the AutoText entries when you have finished. Spell- and grammar-check your document. Format the document using correct business letter format. Save the document as ***[your initials]*3-23**, and submit your work.

Exercise 3-24

Locate a Web site about one of your hobbies or interests. Summarize the information from the site in a Word document. Add a title to the document, and apply character formatting. Use the thesaurus to insert synonyms. Spell- and grammar-check the document. Proofread the document. Save the document as ***[your initials]*3-24**, and submit your work.

Unit 1 Applications

Applications 1-1

Edit, spell-check, use the thesaurus, and apply formatting to a document.

1. Open the file **Chocolate**.
2. Format the entire document as 12-point Times New Roman.
3. Merge the first and second paragraphs.
4. Move to the top of the document, and key **Types of Chocolate.** Press Enter.
5. Format the title as 14-point bold, small caps, and font color brown.
6. Format the first paragraph with a dropped capital letter that drops three lines and is .1 inch from the text.
7. Spell-check and grammar-check the document. Ignore proper names.
8. In the first paragraph, use the thesaurus to choose a synonym for the word "type" in the last sentence.
9. Use noncontiguous text selection to format the names "Milk chocolate" in the second paragraph and "white chocolate" in the fifth paragraph as follows:
   - Small caps
   - Bold
   - Italic
   - Expanded character spacing
10. Copy the formatting applied in the previous step to the remaining chocolate names: "Bittersweet chocolate" in the third paragraph, "semi-sweet chocolate" in the third paragraph, "Sweet or dark chocolate" in the fourth paragraph, and "Baking chocolate" in the last paragraph.
11. Save the document as ***[your initials]*u1-1** in a new Unit 1 Applications folder.
12. Submit and close the document.

Unit Application 1-2

Create AutoText entries, use AutoComplete format, spell-check, and grammar-check a document.

1. Open the file **Form Letter Paragraphs**.
2. Select the letterhead information and one blank line below it, and create an AutoText entry named ***[your initials]*gcletterhead.**

3. Select the first paragraph, and create an AutoText entry named ***[your initials]*factorytour**.

4. Select each of the remaining paragraphs and create an AutoText entry using the naming pattern listed below.

Second paragraph beginning "Factory tours"	***[your initials]*tourinfo**
Third paragraph beginning "We welcome"	***[your initials]*size**
Fourth paragraph beginning "Call us"	***[your initials]*call**
Fifth paragraph beginning "Enclosed"	***[your initials]*brochure**
Sixth paragraph ending with "summer"	***[your initials]*summer**
Seventh paragraph ending with "fall"	***[your initials]*fall**
Eighth paragraph ending with "spring"	***[your initials]*spring**
Ninth paragraph ending with "winter"	***[your initials]*winter**
Remainder of document (closing)	***[your initials]*closing**

5. Close the document without saving.

6. Start a new document. Click the Home tab if necessary, and locate the Styles group. Click the No Spacing button. Insert the AutoText entry "***[your initials]***gcletterhead."

7. Insert the date using the Date and Time dialog box and selecting the third format. Press Enter four times.

8. Address the letter as shown in Figure U1-1.

Figure U1-1

```
Ms. Margo Taylor
1660 North 13 Street
Reading, PA 19604

Dear Ms. Taylor:
```

9. For the body of the letter, insert the following AutoText entries. Insert in the order listed.
   - ***[your initials]***Factorytour
   - ***[your initials]***Tourinfo
   - ***[your initials]***Brochure
   - ***[your initials]***Spring
   - ***[your initials]***Closing

10. Key your reference initials at the end of the document. Press Enter and key **Enclosure**. Control the capitalization of the first initial of your reference initials by using AutoCorrect Options.

11. Refer to Appendix B, "Standard Forms for Business Documents," to check your line spacing.

12. Insert nonbreaking spaces wherever a number appears at the end of a line.
13. Spell-check and grammar-check the document.
14. Delete the AutoText entries you created.
15. Save the document as ***[your initials]*****u1-2** in your Unit 1 Applications folder.
16. Submit and close the document.

Unit Application 1-3

Compose a document, apply formatting, and check grammar and spelling.

1. Start a new document.
2. Refer to Figure U1-2 to create a document describing the items listed in the table. Include a title for each item in the description column, and create a paragraph for each of the products described in the table.
3. Format the title attractively using a text effect.
4. Select an appropriate font, font size, and font effects for the body text.

Figure U1-2

Campbell's Confections–Product Listing			
Description	Choices	Weight	Price
Chocolate-covered nuts	Almond, Brazil, cashew, filbert, pecan	1 lb. box 2 lb. box	$12.95 $25.90
Chocolate-covered creams	Vanilla, chocolate, strawberry, butter, cherry, coconut, coffee, maple, orange, pineapple, raspberry, strawberry	1 lb. 2 lb.	$10.50 $21.00
Turtles	Pecan, cashew, peanut	1 lb. 2 lb.	$12.95 $25.90
Assortment–Chocolate-covered nuts and creams	See choices listed above.	1 lb. 2 lb.	$11.75 $23.50

5. Insert nonbreaking spaces in the document, if they are needed.
6. Grammar-check and spell-check the document.
7. Save the document as ***[your initials]*****u1-3** in your Unit 1 Applications folder.
8. Submit and close the document.

Unit Application 1-4

Use the Internet, apply character formatting, use AutoFormat features, and check grammar and spelling.

1. Using the Internet, create a list of five organizations. Be creative. The organizations could be:
   - Companies where you would like to work
   - Schools you would be interested in attending
   - Associations related to your hobbies or interests
2. Include the organization's name and its Web site address.
3. Include an e-mail address, the physical address, and the telephone and fax numbers.
4. Allow AutoFormat to format the Web addresses and e-mail addresses as hyperlinks.
5. Create a title for the document, followed by a paragraph that describes the content of the list.
6. Apply appropriate formatting.
7. Check spelling and grammar, watching carefully as Word's spelling and grammar checker moves through the addresses.
8. Save the document named ***[your initials]*****u1-4** in your Unit 1 Applications folder.

Unit 2

PARAGRAPH FORMATTING, TABS, AND ADVANCED EDITING

Lesson 4

Formatting Paragraphs

OBJECTIVES ***After completing this lesson, you will be able to:***

1. Align paragraphs.
2. Change line spacing.
3. Change paragraph spacing.
4. Set paragraph indents.
5. Apply borders and shading.
6. Repeat and copy paragraph formats.
7. Create bulleted and numbered lists.
8. Insert symbols and special characters.

Estimated Time: 1½ hours

In Microsoft Word, a *paragraph* is a unique block of information. Paragraph formatting controls the appearance of individual paragraphs within a document. For example, you can change the space between paragraphs or change the space between lines. For emphasis, you can indent paragraphs, number them, or add borders and shading.

A paragraph is always followed by a *paragraph mark*. All the formatting for a paragraph is stored in the paragraph mark. Each time you press Enter, you copy the formatting instructions in the current paragraph to a new paragraph. You can copy paragraph formats from one paragraph to another and view paragraph formats in the Reveal Formatting task pane.

Paragraph Alignment

Paragraph alignment determines how the edges of a paragraph appear horizontally. There are four ways to align text in a paragraph, as shown in Figure 4-1.

Figure 4-1
Paragraph alignment options

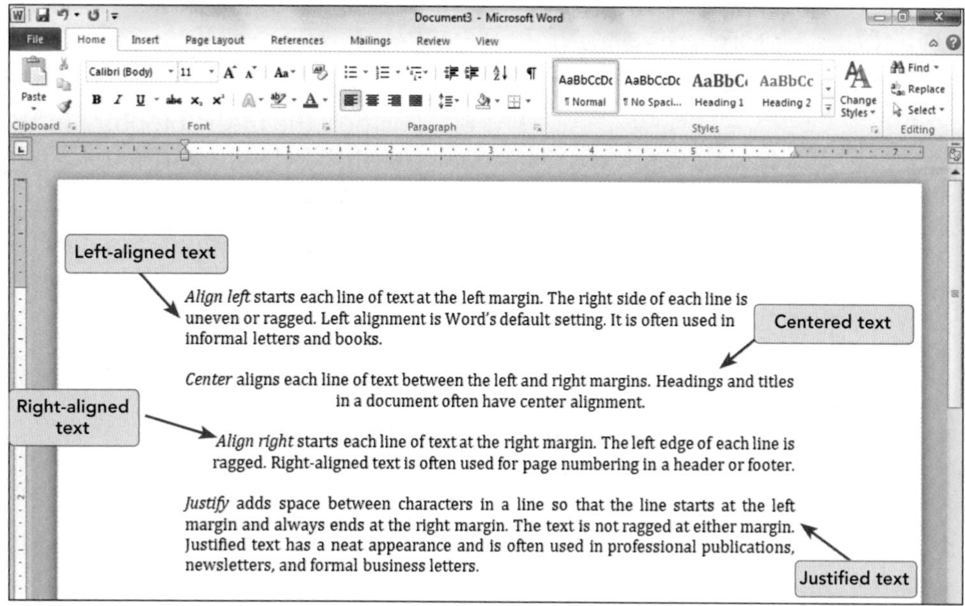

Exercise 4-1 CHANGE PARAGRAPH ALIGNMENT

The easiest way to change paragraph alignment is to use the alignment buttons on the Ribbon, Home tab, Paragraph group. You can also use keyboard shortcuts: left align, Ctrl+L; center, Ctrl+E; right align, Ctrl+R; and justify, Ctrl+J. To change the alignment of one paragraph, position the insertion point in the paragraph. To change the alignment of multiple paragraphs, select the paragraphs and then apply the alignment format.

Figure 4-2
Alignment buttons on the Ribbon

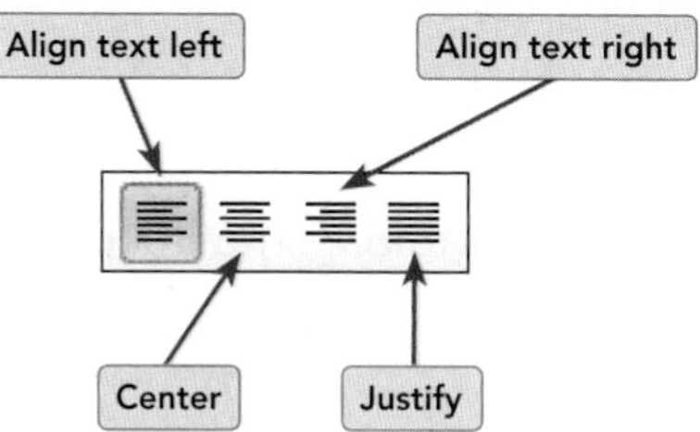

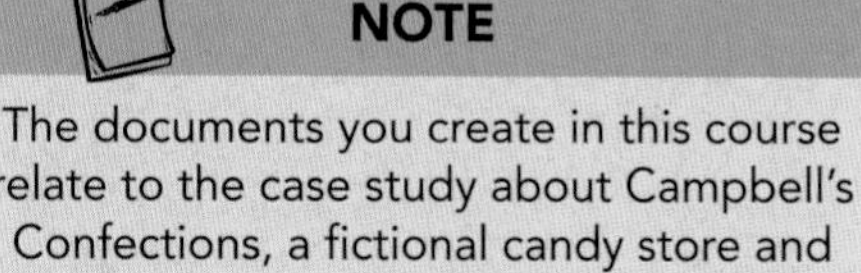

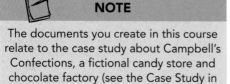

The documents you create in this course relate to the case study about Campbell's Confections, a fictional candy store and chocolate factory (see the Case Study in the front matter).

1. Open the file **Corporate Gifts**. Click the Show/Hide ¶ button ¶ to display paragraph marks if they are turned off.

2. Position the insertion point anywhere in the first paragraph.
3. Click the Center button on the Ribbon (Home tab, Paragraph group) to center the paragraph.
4. Continue to change the paragraph's formatting by clicking the Align Right button, the Justify button, and the Align Left button. Notice how the lines of text are repositioned with each change.
5. Position the insertion point in the second paragraph, and press Ctrl+E to center the paragraph.
6. Position the insertion point in the third paragraph. Use the keyboard shortcut Ctrl+R to right-align the third paragraph.
7. Position the insertion point in the fourth paragraph, and press Ctrl+J to justify the fourth paragraph.

NOTE

When applying paragraph formatting, you do not have to select the paragraph—you just need to have the insertion point within the paragraph or just before the paragraph mark.

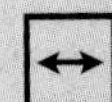

REVIEW

If you do not see one of the alignment buttons, check the Ribbon to verify that the Home tab is active.

Exercise 4-2 USE CLICK AND TYPE TO INSERT TEXT

You can use *Click and Type* to insert text or graphics in any blank area of a document. This feature enables you to position the insertion point anywhere in the document without pressing Enter repeatedly. Word automatically inserts the paragraph marks before that point and also inserts a tab.

1. Open the file **Factory**, and leave the Corporate Gifts document open.
2. Click the File tab, and click Options. Click Advanced in the left pane, and locate the Editing options group. Click Enable click and type if it is not already selected. Click OK.
3. Press Ctrl+End to move to the end of the document.
4. Position the I-beam about five lines below the last line of text, in the center of the page. The I-beam is now the Click and Type pointer, which includes tiny lines that show left, right, or center alignment.

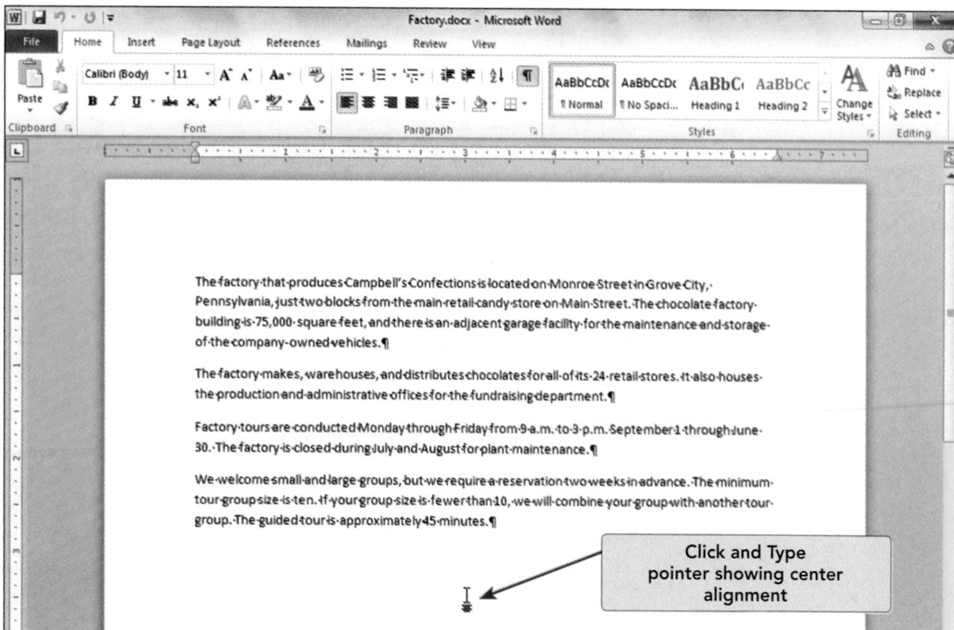

Figure 4-3
Using Click and Type

5. Move the I-beam back and forth until it shows center alignment. Double-click, and key **Visit us at www.campbellsconfections.biz.** The text is centered, and paragraph marks are inserted before the new line.
6. Save the document as ***[your initials]*4-2** in your Lesson 4 folder.
7. Submit your work, and close the document.

Line Spacing

Line space is the amount of vertical space between lines of text in a paragraph. Line spacing is typically based on the height of the characters, but you can change it to a specific value. For example, some paragraphs might be single-spaced and some double-spaced. The default line spacing is Multiple 1.15.

Exercise 4-3 CHANGE LINE SPACING

You can apply the most common types of line spacing by using keyboard shortcuts: single space, Ctrl+1; 1.5-line space, Ctrl+5; and double space, Ctrl+2. Additional spacing options, as well as other paragraph formatting options, are available in the Paragraph dialog box or from the Line and Paragraph Spacing button.

1. Position the insertion point in the first paragraph.
2. Press Ctrl+2 to double-space the paragraph.

3. With the insertion point in the same paragraph, press Ctrl+5 to change the spacing to 1.5 lines. Press Ctrl+1 to change the paragraph format to single spacing.
4. With the insertion point in the same paragraph, click the down arrow to the right of the Line and Paragraph Spacing button on the Ribbon, Home tab, Paragraph group, and choose **2.0** to change the line spacing to double. Click the down arrow again, and choose **1.0** to restore the paragraph to single spacing.
5. Right-click the first paragraph, and choose **Paragraph** from the shortcut menu. (You can also open the Paragraph dialog box by clicking the Dialog Box Launcher in the right corner of the Paragraph group.)
6. Click the down arrow to open the **Line spacing** drop-down list, and choose **Double**. The change is reflected in the **Preview** box.

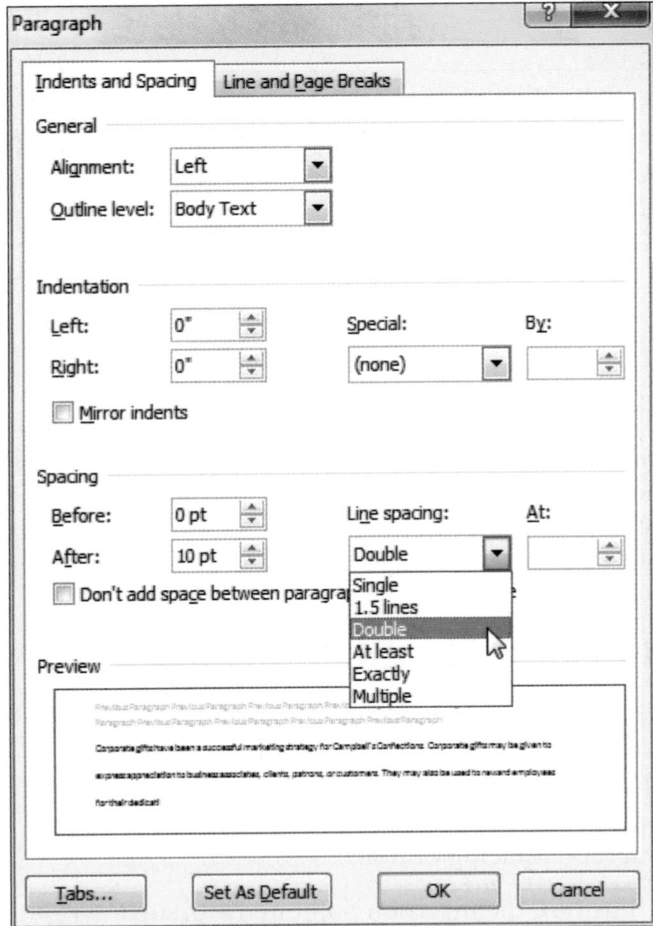

Figure 4-4
Line-spacing options in the Paragraph dialog box

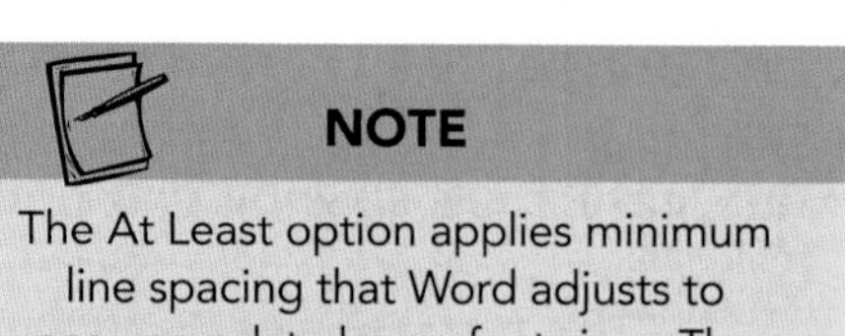

NOTE

The At Least option applies minimum line spacing that Word adjusts to accommodate larger font sizes. The Exactly option applies fixed line spacing that Word does not adjust. This option makes all lines evenly spaced. The Multiple option increases or decreases line spacing by the percentage you specify. For example, setting line spacing to a multiple of 1.25 increases the space by 25 percent, and setting line spacing to a multiple of 0.8 decreases the space by 20 percent.

7. With the dialog box still open, choose **Single** from the Line spacing drop-down list. The **Preview** box shows the change.
8. Choose **Multiple** from the Line spacing drop-down list. In the **At** box, key **1.25**. (Select the text that appears in the box and key over it.) Press Tab to see the change displayed in the **Preview** box.
9. Click **OK**. Word adds an extra quarter-line space between lines in the paragraph.

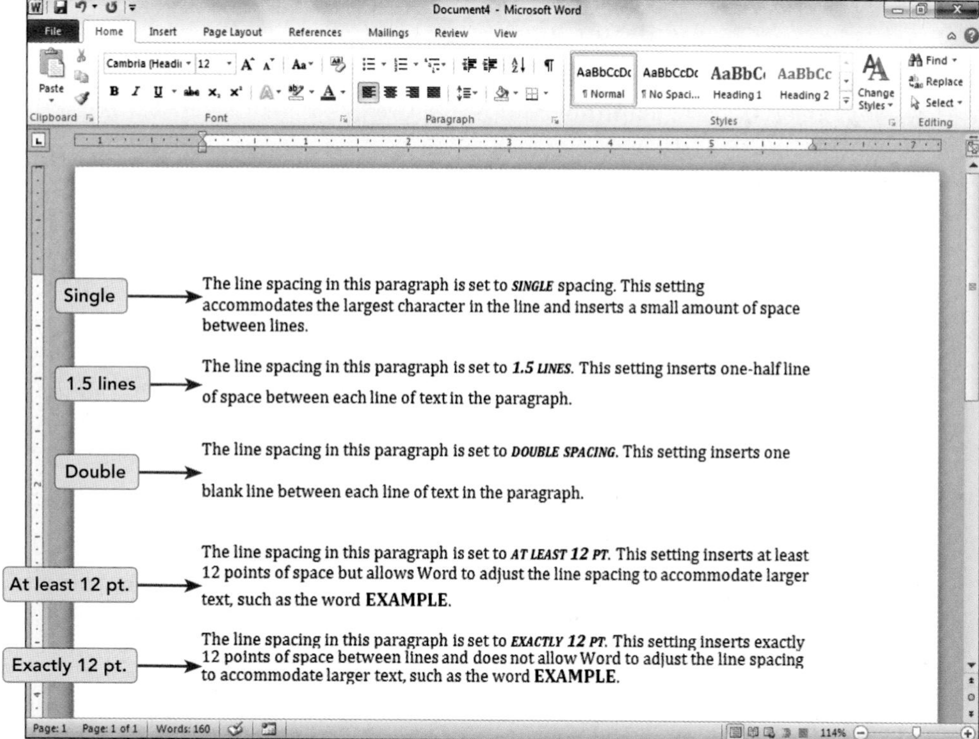

Figure 4-5
Examples of line spacing

Paragraph Spacing

In addition to changing spacing between lines of text, you can change *paragraph space*. Paragraph space is the amount of space above or below a paragraph. Instead of pressing Enter multiple times to increase space between paragraphs, you can use the Ribbon or the Paragraph dialog box to set a specific amount of space before or after paragraphs.

Paragraph spacing is set in points. If a document has 12-point text, one line space equals 12 points. Likewise, one-half line space equals 6 points, and two line spaces equal 24 points. By default, paragraph spacing is 0 points before and 10 points after.

Exercise 4-4 CHANGE THE SPACE BETWEEN PARAGRAPHS

1. Press Ctrl+Home to move the insertion point to the beginning of the document. Select the whole document by pressing Ctrl+A. Press Ctrl+L to left-align all paragraphs.
2. Use the keyboard shortcut Ctrl+1 to change the entire document to single spacing.
3. Deselect the text, and position the insertion point at the beginning of the document.
4. Click the Bold button **B** to turn on bold, key **CORPORATE GIFTS** in all capitals, and press Enter.
5. Move the insertion point into the heading you just keyed. Although this heading includes only two words, it is considered a paragraph. Any text followed by a paragraph mark is a paragraph.
6. Open the Paragraph dialog box by clicking the Paragraph Dialog Box Launcher. You use the text boxes labeled **Before** and **After** to choose an amount of space for Word to insert before or after a paragraph.
7. Set the **Before** text box to 72 points (select the "0" and key **72**). Because 72 points equal 1 inch, this adds to the existing 1-inch top margin and places the title 2 inches from the top of the page.
8. Press Tab, set the **After** text box to **24** points, and click **OK**. The heading now starts 2 inches from the top of the page and is followed by two line spaces.
9. Right-click the **status bar** and click **Vertical Page Position**. Deselect the shortcut menu. The status bar displays **At 2″** on the left side.
10. Click the Center button to center the heading.

NOTE

Many business documents start 2 inches from the top of the page. You can set this standard by using paragraph formatting, as done here, or by changing margin settings.

TIP

The keyboard shortcut to add or remove 12 points of spacing before a paragraph is Ctrl+0. Ctrl+Shift+N removes all paragraph and character formatting, restoring the text to default formatting. The Line Spacing button on the Ribbon includes an option to add or remove space before paragraph and an option to add or remove space after paragraph. The default is to add 12 points before or after the paragraph.

Paragraph Indents

An *indent* increases the distance between the sides of a paragraph and the two side margins. Indented paragraphs appear to have different margin settings. Word provides a variety of indents to emphasize paragraphs in a document, as shown in Figure 4-6.

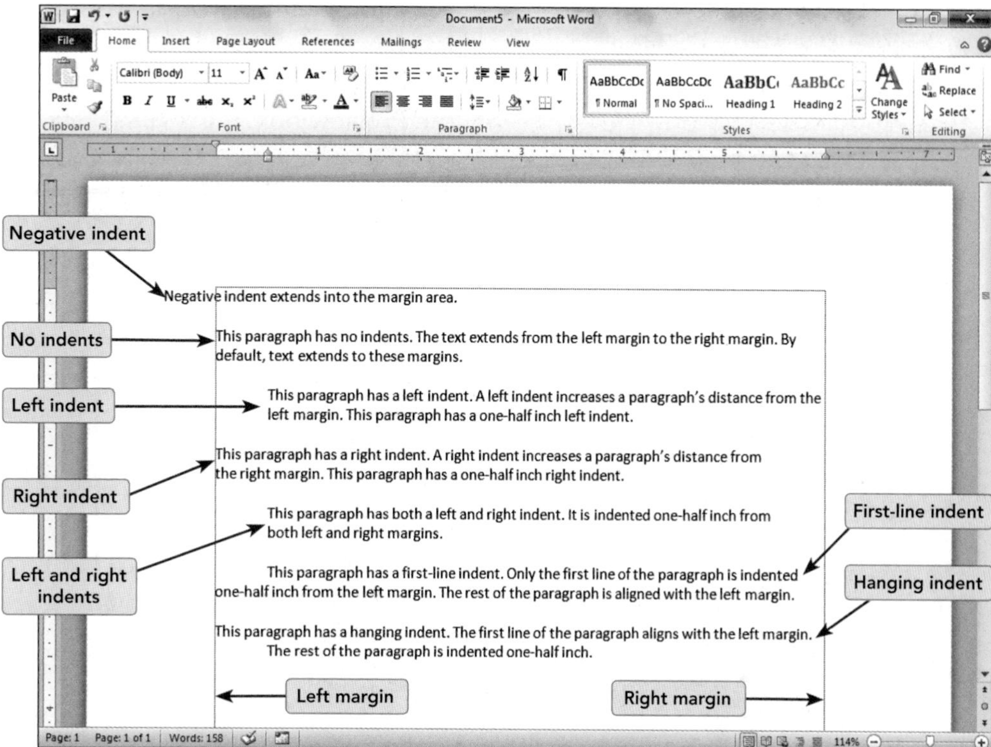

Negative indent
Negative indent extends into the margin area.
No indents
This paragraph has no indents. The text extends from the left margin to the right margin. By default, text extends to these margins.
Left indent
This paragraph has a left indent. A left indent increases a paragraph's distance from the left margin. This paragraph has a one-half inch left indent.
This paragraph has a right indent. A right indent increases a paragraph's distance from the right margin. This paragraph has a one-half inch right indent.
Right indent
This paragraph has both a left and right indent. It is indented one-half inch from both left and right margins.
First-line indent
Left and right indents
This paragraph has a first-line indent. Only the first line of the paragraph is indented one-half inch from the left margin. The rest of the paragraph is aligned with the left margin.
Hanging indent
This paragraph has a hanging indent. The first line of the paragraph aligns with the left margin. The rest of the paragraph is indented one-half inch.
Left margin
Right margin

Figure 4-6
Types of paragraph indents

To set paragraph indents, you can use one of these methods:

- Indent buttons on the Ribbon, Home tab, Paragraph group
- Paragraph dialog box
- Keyboard shortcuts
- Ruler

Exercise 4-5 SET INDENTS BY USING INDENT BUTTONS AND THE PARAGRAPH DIALOG BOX

1. Select the paragraph that begins "Our line" through the end of the document.
2. Click the Increase Indent button on the Ribbon. The selected text is indented 0.5 inch from the left side.
3. Click the Increase Indent button again. Now the text is indented 1 inch.

4. Click the Decrease Indent button twice to return the text to the left margin.

NOTE

To set a *negative indent*, which extends a paragraph into the left or right margin areas, enter a negative number in the Left or Right text boxes. Any indent that occurs between the left and right margins is known as a *positive indent*.

5. With the text still selected, open the Paragraph dialog box by clicking the Paragraph Dialog Box Launcher.
6. Under **Indentation**, change the **Left** setting to **0.75** inch and the **Right** setting to **0.75** inch.
7. Click to open the **Special** drop-down list in the Paragraph dialog box, and choose **First line**. Word sets the **By** box to 0.5 inch by default. Notice the change in the Preview box.

Figure 4-7
Setting indents

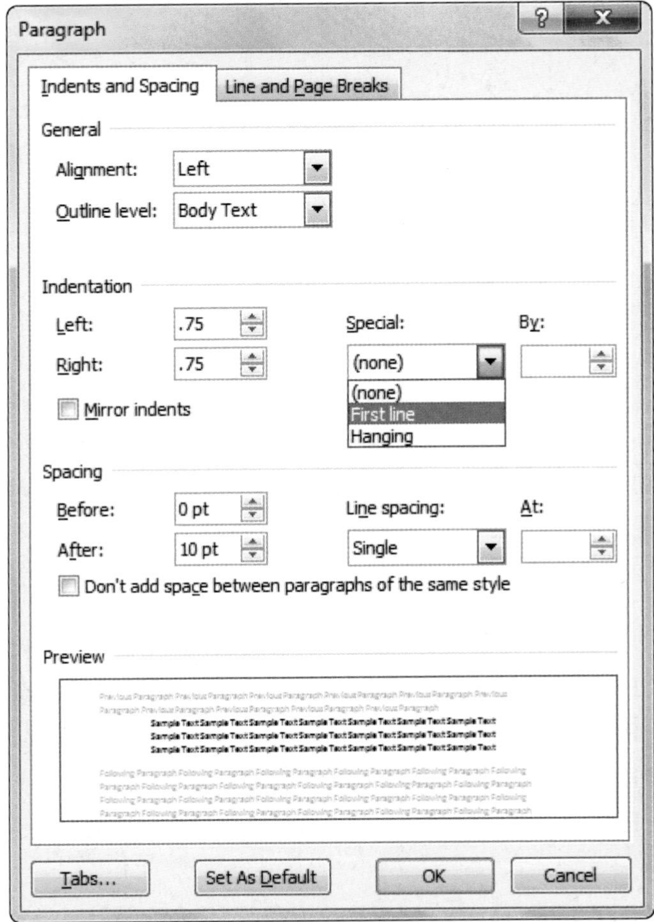

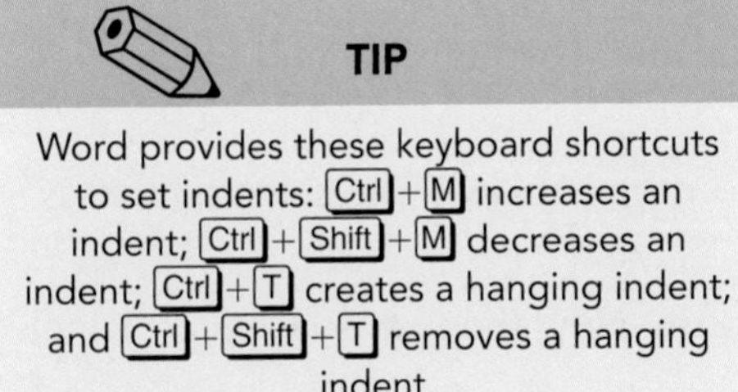

TIP

Word provides these keyboard shortcuts to set indents: Ctrl+M increases an indent; Ctrl+Shift+M decreases an indent; Ctrl+T creates a hanging indent; and Ctrl+Shift+T removes a hanging indent.

8. Click **OK**. Now each paragraph is indented from the left and right margins by 0.75 inch, and the first line of each paragraph is indented another 0.5 inch.

Exercise 4-6 SET INDENTS BY USING THE RULER

You can set indents by dragging the *indent markers* that appear at the left and right of the horizontal ruler. There are four indent markers:

- The *first-line indent marker* is the top triangle on the left side of the ruler. Drag it to the right to indent the first line of a paragraph.
- The *hanging indent marker* is the bottom triangle. Drag it to the right to indent the remaining lines in a paragraph.
- The *left indent marker* is the small rectangle. Drag it to move the first-line indent marker and the hanging indent marker at the same time.
- The *right indent marker* is the triangle at the right side of the ruler, at the right margin. Drag it to the left to create a right indent.

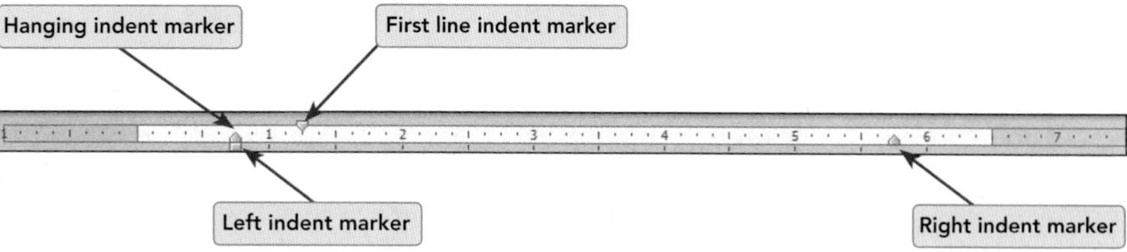

Figure 4-8 Indent markers on the ruler

1. Make sure the horizontal ruler is displayed. If it is not, click the View Ruler button, or click the **View** tab, and click **Ruler** in the Show group.
2. Position the insertion point in the first paragraph below the title.
3. Point to the first-line indent marker on the ruler. A ScreenTip appears when you are pointing to the correct marker.
4. Drag the first-line indent marker 0.5 inch to the right. The first line of the paragraph is indented by 0.5 inch.
5. Press Shift+F1 to display the **Reveal Formatting** task pane. Locate the **Paragraph** section, and notice the settings under **Indentation**.
6. Drag the first-line indent marker back to the zero position. Point to the hanging indent marker, and drag it 0.5 inch to the right. The lines below the first line are indented 0.5 inch, creating a hanging indent.
7. Drag the hanging indent marker back to the zero position. Drag the left indent marker (the small rectangle) 1 inch to the right. The entire paragraph is indented by 1 inch.

NOTE

To make sure you are pointing to the correct indent marker, check the ScreenTip identifier before you drag the marker.

8. Select the first two paragraphs below the title, and press Ctrl+Shift+N to remove all formatting from the paragraphs. Notice that the line spacing and spacing after format return to the default settings.
9. Position the insertion point in the second paragraph, which begins "Our line," and re-create the indents by using the ruler:
   - Drag the left indent marker 0.75 inch to the right to indent the entire paragraph.
   - Drag the first-line indent marker to the 1.25-inch mark on the ruler.
   - Drag the right indent marker 0.75 inch to the left (to the 5.75-inch mark on the ruler). Now the paragraph is indented like the paragraphs below it.
10. Select all the indented paragraphs, and drag the first-line indent marker to the 1-inch mark on the ruler. Now the opening line of each paragraph is indented only 0.25 inch.

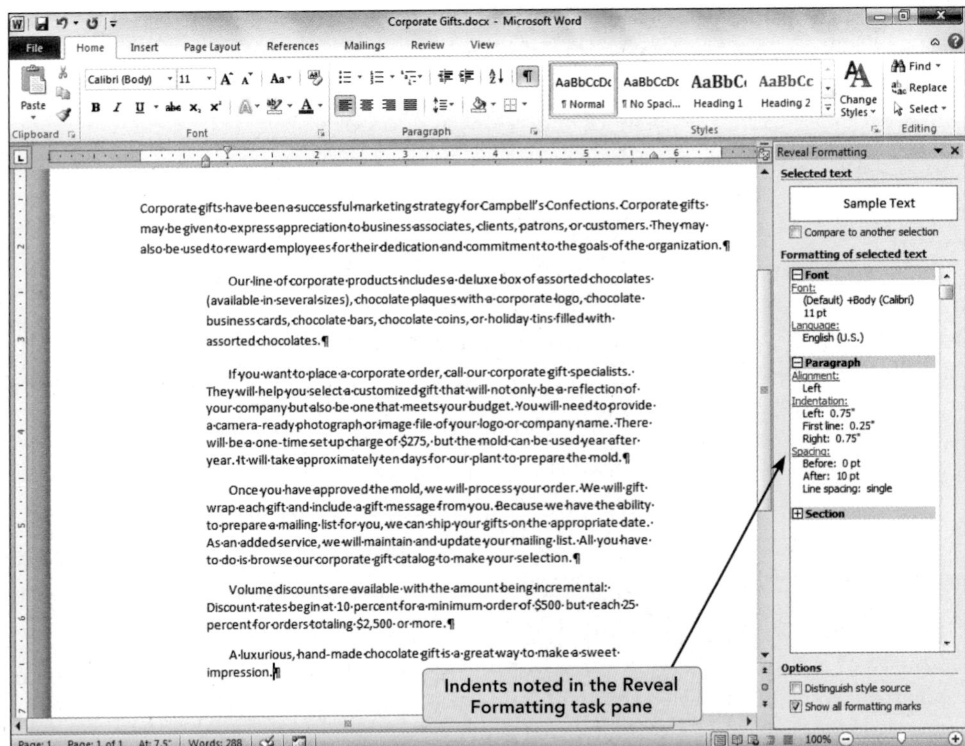

Figure 4-9
Document with indented text

11. Close the Reveal Formatting task pane.
12. Save the document as ***[your initials]*4-6** in a new folder for Lesson 4.
13. Submit the document, but do not close it.

Borders and Shading

To add visual interest to paragraphs or to an entire page, you can add a *border*—a line, box, or pattern—around text, a graphic, or a page. In addition, you can use *shading* to fill in the background behind the text of a paragraph. Shading can appear as a shade of gray, as a pattern, or as a color. Borders can appear in a variety of line styles and colors.

This lesson explains how to use the Borders and Shading dialog box to set border and shading options, and how to use the Borders button on the Ribbon (which applies the most recently selected border style). The Borders button ScreenTip will change to display the most recently selected border style.

Exercise 4-7 ADD BORDERS TO PARAGRAPHS

1. With the file ***[your initials]*4-6** open, go to the end of the document. Press Enter to start a new paragraph, and press Ctrl+Q to remove the paragraph formatting carried over from the previous paragraph.
2. Key the text shown in Figure 4-10.

Figure 4-10

```
Let Campbell's Confections help you with your marketing
strategy and your employees' recognition plan! We can
provide you with a unique and personalized gift that will
create a lasting impression. Call us today at 724-555-2025
for more information.
```

3. Make sure the insertion point is to the left of the current paragraph mark or within the paragraph.

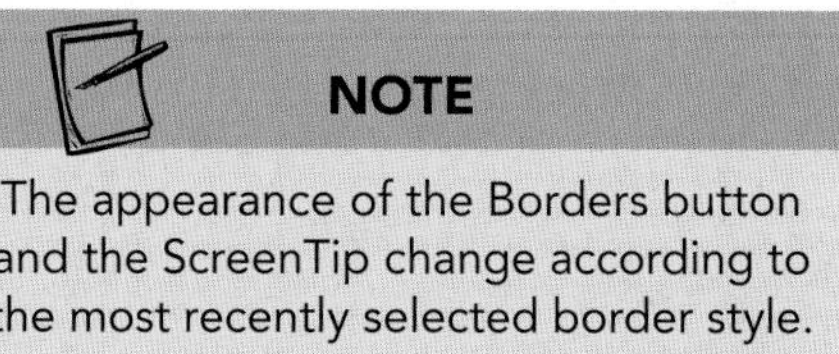

The appearance of the Borders button and the ScreenTip change according to the most recently selected border style.

4. Click the down arrow beside the Borders button and click **Borders and Shading** at the bottom of the drop-down list. The Borders and Shading dialog box appears. Click the **Borders** tab if it is not displayed.
5. Under **Setting**, click the **Box** option. The **Preview** box shows the Box setting. Each button around the Preview box indicates a selected border.
6. Scroll to view the options in the **Style** box. Choose the first border style (the solid line).
7. Open the **Color** drop-down list, and choose Green in the Standard Colors section. (ScreenTips identify colors by name.)
8. Open the **Width** drop-down list and choose **2¼ pt**.

9. Click the top line of the box border in the **Preview** box. The top line is deleted, and the corresponding button is no longer selected. Click the Top Border button or the top border area in the diagram to restore the top line border.

Figure 4-11
Borders and Shading dialog box

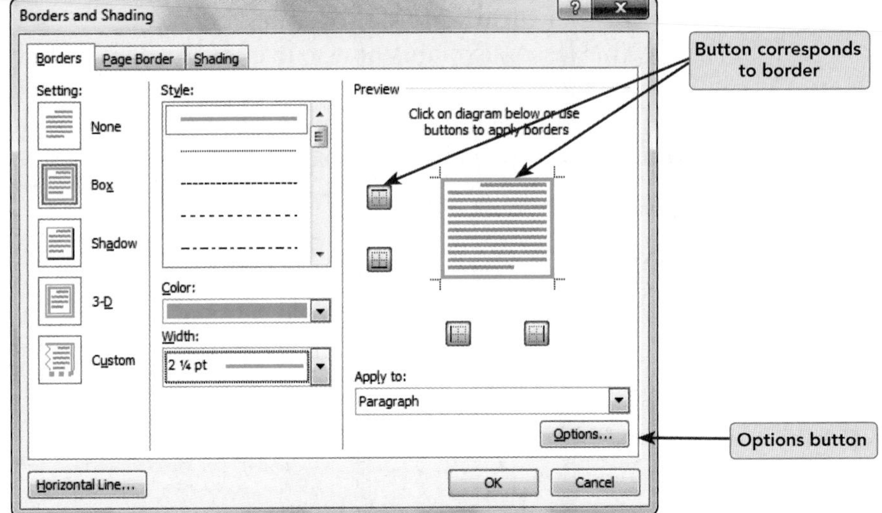

10. Click the **Options** button. In the Border and Shading Options dialog box, change the **Top** setting to 5 pt, press Tab, and change the **Bottom** setting to 5 pt. Press Tab, and change the **Left** and **Right** settings to 5 pt to increase the space between the text and the border. Click **OK**.
11. Change the **Setting** from Box to **Shadow**. This setting applies a black shadow to the green border. Notice that the **Apply to** box is set to **Paragraph**. Click **OK**. The shadow border is applied to the paragraph.
12. Click anywhere within the title "CORPORATE GIFTS."
13. Click the down arrow next to the Borders button on the Ribbon. A drop-down menu of border options appears.

Figure 4-12
Border options on the Ribbon

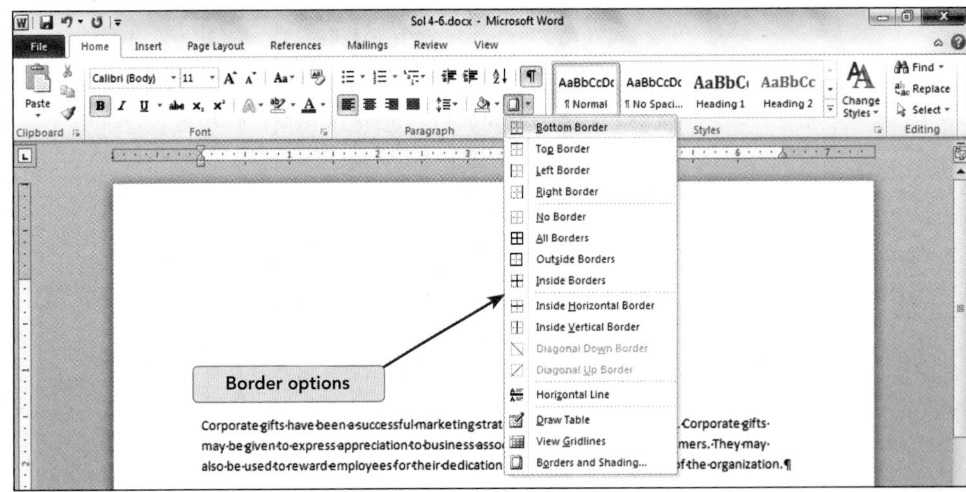

14. Click **Bottom Border**. A bottom border with the options previously set in the Borders and Shading dialog box is applied to the title.
15. Click the down arrow next to the Borders button. Click the No Border button to delete the border.

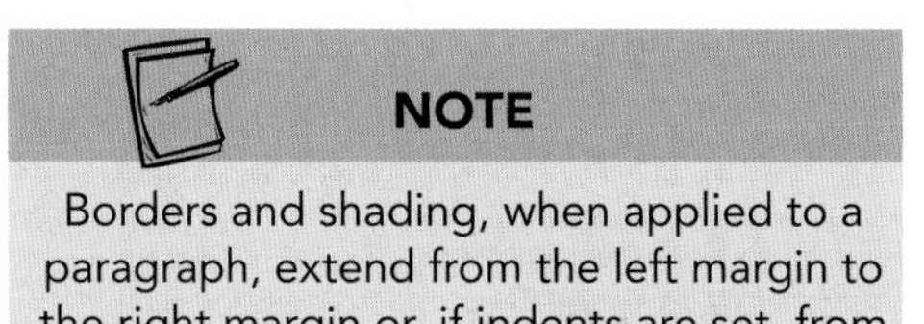

NOTE

Borders and shading, when applied to a paragraph, extend from the left margin to the right margin or, if indents are set, from the left indent to the right indent.

16. Reapply the bottom border, and click the Top Border button to add a top border as well.
17. Open the **Paragraph** dialog box, and change the left and right indents to **.5 inch**. Click **OK**, to close the Paragraph dialog box. Notice the border is indented from the left and right margins.

Exercise 4-8 APPLY BORDERS TO SELECTED TEXT AND A PAGE

In addition to paragraphs, you can apply borders to selected text or to an entire page. When you apply a border to a page, you can choose whether to place the border on every page, the current page, the first page, or all but the first page in a document.

1. In the third paragraph below the title (which begins "If you"), select the text "$275." Open the **Borders and Shading** dialog box.
2. From the **Style** box, scroll to the fifth line style from the bottom. Word automatically applies this style as the **Box** setting.
3. Change the **Color** to Blue. Notice that the **Apply to** box indicates **Text**.

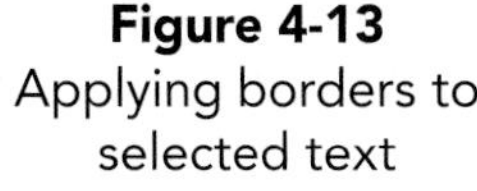

Figure 4-13
Applying borders to selected text

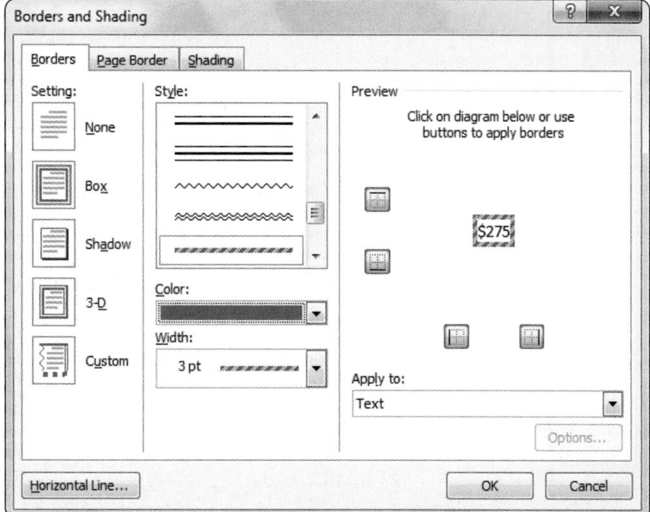

4. Click the **Page Border** tab. Choose the third-to-last line style (a band of three shades of gray), and click the **3-D** setting. The width should be **3 pt**.
5. Click **OK**. Notice the text border added to "$275" and the page border. Deselect the text so you can see the border color.

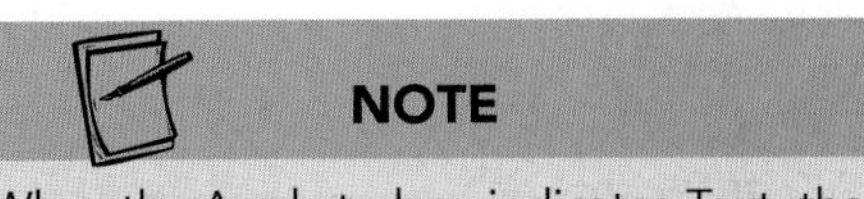

NOTE

When the Apply to box indicates Text, the borders are applied only to the selected text and not to the paragraph. If you include a paragraph mark in your selection, the borders are applied to all lines of the paragraph unless you change the Apply to setting to Text. It is important to notice the Apply to setting when applying borders and shading, or you might not get the results you intended.

Figure 4-14
Document with border formatting

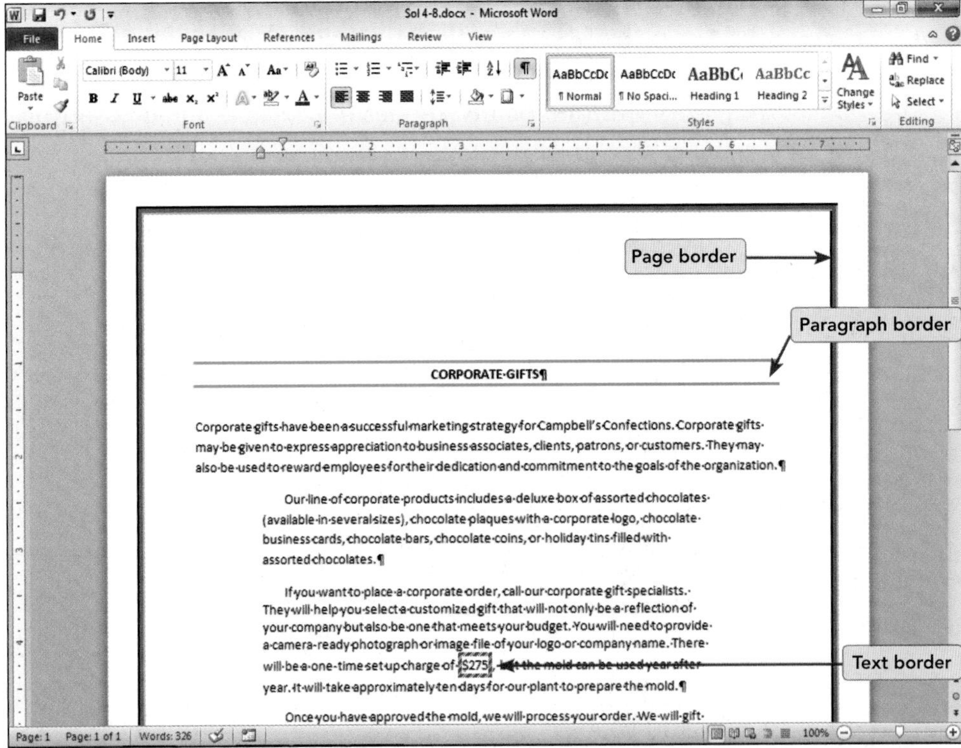

6. Save the document as ***[your initials]*4-8** in your Lesson 4 folder. Submit the document. Leave it open.

Exercise 4-9 ADD A HORIZONTAL LINE

Word includes special horizontal lines to divide or decorate a page. These lines are actually picture files (or "clips") in the shape of horizontal lines that are normally used when creating Web pages.

NOTE

The Borders button drop-down list includes an option to insert a horizontal line. If you choose this option, the horizontal line inserted is based on the last horizontal line or border definition. Choose Horizontal Line from the Borders and Shading dialog box to select a style from the gallery.

1. Position the insertion point anywhere in the last paragraph, and click the down arrow beside the Borders button . Click the **No Border** option.
2. Position the insertion point at the beginning of the last paragraph.
3. Open the **Borders and Shading** dialog box. Click **Horizontal Line** at the bottom of the dialog box.

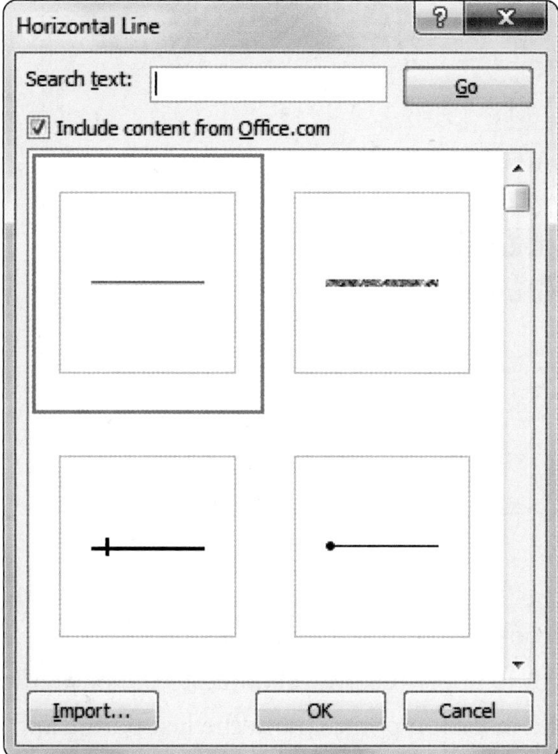

Figure 4-15
Inserting a horizontal line

NOTE

Available horizontal line clips might vary, depending on which files are installed on your computer. Check with your instructor if the specified line is not available.

4. In the Horizontal Line dialog box, click the first box in the third row. Click **OK**. The line is inserted in the document.

Exercise 4-10 APPLY SHADING TO A PARAGRAPH

The Shading feature adds color and contrast to your document. You can apply shading to a single paragraph or to a group of paragraphs by using the Borders and Shading dialog box or the Shading button on the Ribbon. Shading can affect the readability of text, especially when you use dark colors or patterns. It is a good idea to choose a larger type size and bold text when you use the shading feature.

1. Click anywhere in the last paragraph, and open the **Borders and Shading** dialog box.
2. Click the **Shading** tab.
3. Click the down arrow in the **Fill** box. Notice that you can apply theme colors or standard colors or select another color. Click a gray color in the first column.

Figure 4-16
Shading options in the Borders and Shading dialog box

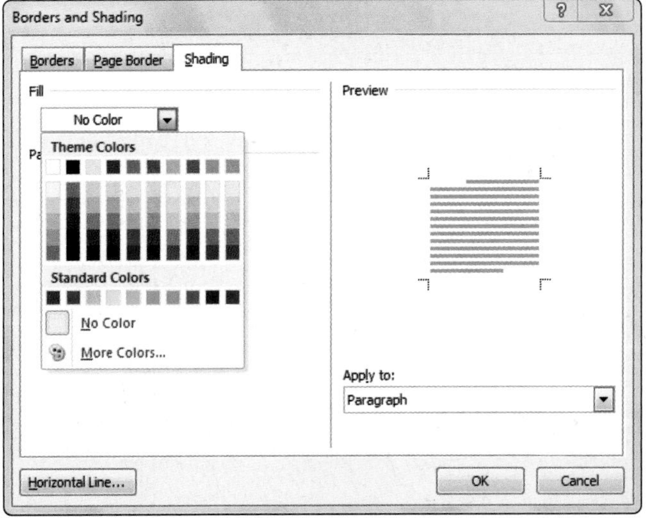

4. Open the **Style** drop-down list to view other shading options. Close the **Style** drop-down list without choosing a style.
5. Click **OK** to apply the gray shading to the paragraph.
6. With the insertion point still in the last paragraph, remove the gray shading by clicking the Shading button on the Ribbon. Click **No Color**.
7. Click the Undo button to restore the shading.

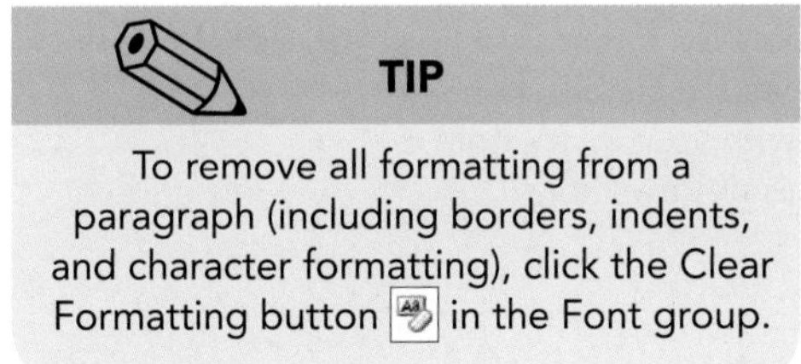

TIP

To remove all formatting from a paragraph (including borders, indents, and character formatting), click the Clear Formatting button in the Font group.

Exercise 4-11 APPLY BORDERS AUTOMATICALLY

Word provides an AutoFormat feature to apply bottom borders. Instead of using the Borders button or the Borders and Shading dialog box, you can key a series of characters and Word automatically applies a border.

1. Press Ctrl+N to create a new document and leave the current document open.
2. Key --- (three consecutive hyphens) and press Enter. Word applies a bottom border. Press Enter two times.
3. Key === (three consecutive equal signs) and press Enter. Word applies a double-line bottom border. Press Enter two times.
4. Key ___ (three consecutive underscores) and press Enter. Word applies a thick bottom border.
5. Close the document without saving.

TIP

If you do not want to format borders automatically, click the AutoCorrect Options button displayed after you key a series of characters and choose Stop Automatically Creating Border Lines.

TABLE 4-1 Auto Formatting Borders

You Key	Word Applies
Three or more underscores (_) and press Enter	A thick bottom border
Three or more hyphens (-) and press Enter	A thin bottom border
Three or more equal signs (=) and press Enter	A double-line bottom border

Repeating and Copying Formats

You can quickly repeat, copy, or remove paragraph formatting. For example, press F4 or Ctrl+Y to repeat paragraph formatting and click the Format Painter button to copy paragraph formatting.

Exercise 4-12 REPEAT, COPY, AND REMOVE PARAGRAPH FORMATS

1. Click anywhere in the first paragraph under the title (which begins "Corporate Gifts"), and change the paragraph alignment to justified.
2. Select the rest of the indented paragraphs, starting with the paragraph that begins "Our line" through the paragraph that begins "A luxurious." Press F4 to repeat the formatting.

NOTE

You can click in a paragraph when repeating, copying, or removing formatting. You do not have to select the entire paragraph.

3. Click anywhere in the last paragraph (with the shading).
4. Click the Format Painter button; then click within the paragraph above the shaded paragraph to copy the formatting.
5. Click the Undo button to undo the paragraph formatting.
6. Click anywhere in the shaded paragraph. Click the Clear Formatting button on the Ribbon to remove the formatting.
7. Click the Undo button to restore the formatting.
8. Click just before the paragraph mark for the horizontal line you inserted above the last paragraph. Open the **Paragraph** dialog box, add 24 points of spacing before the paragraph, and click **OK**.
9. Save the document as ***[your initials]*4-12** in your Lesson 4 folder.
10. Submit and close the document.

Bulleted and Numbered Lists

Bulleted lists and *numbered lists* are types of hanging indents you can use to organize important details in a document. In a bulleted list, a bullet (•) precedes each paragraph. In a numbered list, a sequential number or letter precedes each paragraph. When you add or delete an item in a numbered list, Word automatically renumbers the list.

To create bulleted lists or numbered lists, use the Bullets button or the Numbering button on the Ribbon (which apply the most recently selected bullet or numbering style).

Exercise 4-13 CREATE A BULLETED LIST

1. Open the file **Memo - 1**. This document is a one-page memo. Key the current date in the memo date line.
2. Locate and select the four lines of text beginning with "Monday" and ending with "Thursday."
3. Click the Bullets button on the Ribbon, Home tab, Paragraph group. Word applies the bullet style that was most recently chosen in the Bullets list.

Figure 4-17
Bulleted list

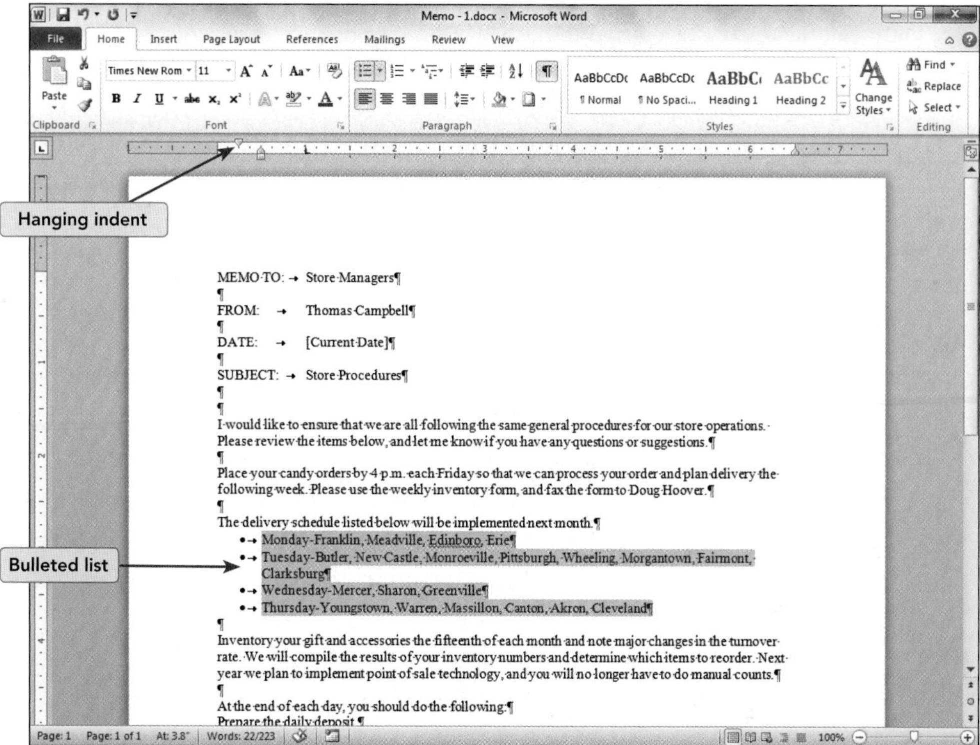

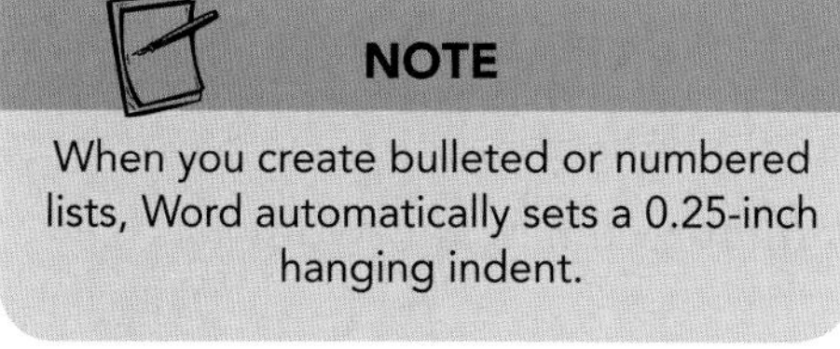

NOTE
When you create bulleted or numbered lists, Word automatically sets a 0.25-inch hanging indent.

4. With the list still selected, click the down arrow beside the Bullets button, and click one of the bullet shapes listed in the **Bullet Library**. The list is formatted with a different bullet shape. Deselect the list.

Figure 4-18
Bullet options

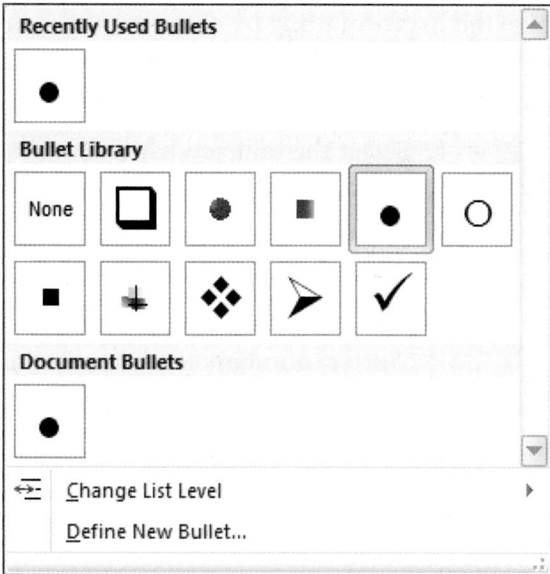

5. Click the first bullet in the bulleted list you just created to select all bullets.
6. Right-click the selected bullets, and click **Adjust List Indents** from the shortcut menu.
7. Change the **Bullet position** text box value to **.4**. Change the **Text indent** to **.65**. Click **OK**.

Exercise 4-14 CREATE A NUMBERED LIST

1. Select the last four paragraphs in the document, from "First Quarter" to "Fourth Quarter."
2. Click the Numbering button to format the list with the style that was most recently chosen from the Numbering list.
3. With the list still selected, click the down arrow beside the Numbering button. Click the roman numeral format. Word reformats the list with roman numerals.

Exercise 4-15 CHANGE A BULLETED OR NUMBERED LIST

Word's bulleting and numbering feature is very flexible. When a list is bulleted or numbered, you can change it in several ways. You can:

- Convert bullets to numbers or numbers to bullets in a list.
- Add or remove items in a bulleted or numbered list, and Word renumbers the list automatically.
- Interrupt a bulleted or numbered list to create several shorter lists.
- Customize the list formatting by changing the symbol used for bullets or changing the alignment and spacing of the bullets and numbers.
- Turn off bullets or numbering for part of a list or the entire list.

NOTE

When you select a bulleted or numbered list by dragging over the text, the list is highlighted but the bullets or numbers are not. You can select a list by clicking a bullet or number.

1. Select the bulleted list that starts with "Monday."
2. Click the down arrow beside the Numbering button.
3. Choose a numbered format that starts with "1" to convert the bullets to numbers.
4. Select and delete the line that begins "Wednesday." Word renumbers the list automatically.
5. Press Ctrl+Z to undo.
6. Place the insertion point at the end of the last item in the numbered list, after "Cleveland."
7. Press Enter and key **Friday-Emergency deliveries**. The formatting is carried to the new line.
8. Place the insertion point at the end of the fourth item (after "Cleveland.") and press Enter.
9. Key in italic ***When absolutely necessary:***

TIP

To change the shape, size, and color of a bullet, click the down arrow on the Bullets button and click Define New Bullet. Click the Symbol button to choose a new shape. Click the Font button to change size and color. Click the drop-down arrow of the Alignment box to change the bullet alignment. If you click the Picture button, you can insert a picture bullet—a decorative bullet often used in Web pages. You can format numbers or bullets of a list in a format different from the text of the list.

NOTE

After you format a list with bullets or numbering, each time you press Enter the format carries forward to the next paragraph. Pressing Enter twice turns off the format.

10. Click within the italic text, and click the Numbering button on the Ribbon to turn off numbering for this item. The list continues with the following paragraph.
11. Select and right-click the numbered text below the italic text (the numbered item that begins "Friday").
12. Choose **Restart at 1**. The new list starts with "1."
13. Insert a blank line above the italic text (click to the left of "*When*" and press Enter).
14. Select the list beginning with "At the" through "Check and organize."
15. Click the down arrow beside the Bullets button, and click **Define New Bullet**.
16. Click **Symbol**, and change the **Font** to **Wingdings**. Scroll to locate and select the small, solid black square (■). Click **OK** to close the Symbol dialog box, and click **OK** to close the Define New Bullet dialog box.

Exercise 4-16 CREATE LISTS AUTOMATICALLY

Word provides an AutoFormat feature to create bulleted and numbered lists as you key text. When this feature is selected, you can enter a few keystrokes, key your list, and Word inserts the numbers and bullets automatically.

1. Press Ctrl+End to move to the end of the document.
2. Key the following: **Create a list of all equipment and fixtures in the store. Provide the following:**
3. Press Enter. Key * and press Spacebar.
4. Key **Description/Model number** and press Enter. Word automatically formats your text as a bulleted list.
5. Key the following text to complete the list, pressing Enter at the end of each line except the last line:

   Serial number
   Date acquired
   Purchase price
   Location
   Inventory number

TABLE 4-2 AutoFormatting Numbered and Bulleted Lists

You Key	Word Creates
A number; a period, closing parenthesis, or hyphen; a space or tab; and text. Press Enter. Example, **1.**, **1)**, or **1-**	A numbered list
An asterisk (*) or hyphen (-); a space or tab; and text. Press Enter.	A bulleted list

Exercise 4-17 CREATE A MULTILEVEL LIST

A *multilevel list* has indented subparagraphs. For example, your list can start with item number "1)," followed by another level of indented items numbered "a)," "b)," and "c)." An outline numbered list can have up to nine levels and is often used for technical or legal documents. The Multilevel List button is located on the Ribbon, Home tab, Paragraph group.

1. Go to the end of the document and press Enter four times.
2. Click the arrow beside the Multilevel List button. Notice the outline numbering styles available in the List Library.

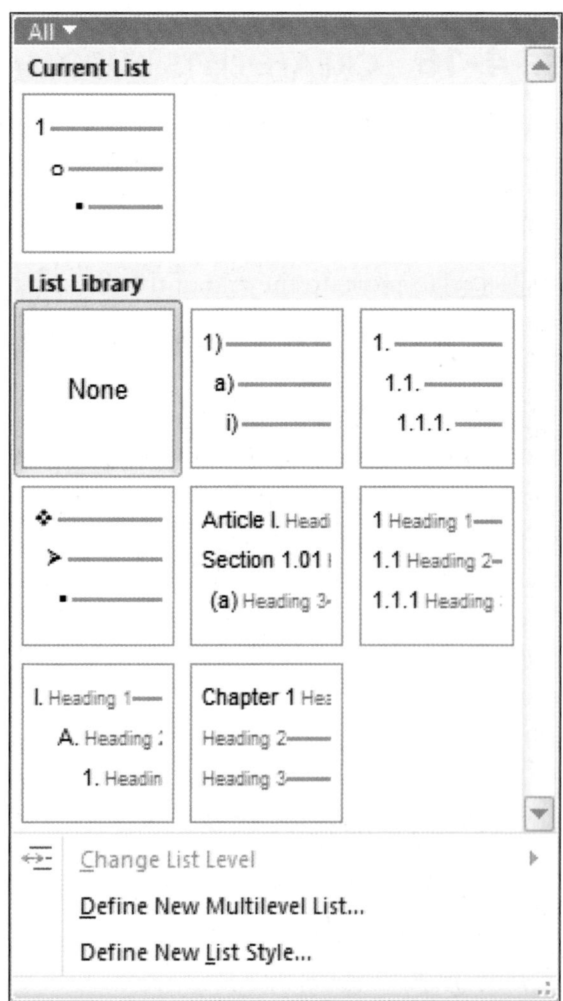

Figure 4-19
Multilevel List Library

3. Click the outline numbering style that begins with "I." Notice the uppercase roman numeral in the text. Click the **View** tab, and click to select the **Navigation Pane** check box. The Navigation Pane displays on the left and is used to move quickly from one heading to another.
4. Key **January** and press Enter. Word automatically formats the text with bold, 14 point text. The text may also appear in another font color.
5. Click the Increase Indent button (or press Tab), and key **A.** Spacebar **Prepare memo to employees regarding changes to W-4 forms.**
6. Press Enter and key **B.** Spacebar **Prepare and mail W-2 forms to employees.** The numbered list now has two indented subparagraphs. Press Enter. Key **C.** Spacebar **Prepare and mail 1099 forms.** Press Enter.
7. Position the insertion point at the left margin. (If necessary, click the Decrease Indent button. You can now add a second first-level paragraph to your list.
8. Key **II. February**.
9. Review the Navigation Pane. Notice that the headings in the multilevel list appear in the Navigation Pane. Click the January heading in the Navigation Pane to move the heading to the top of the screen. Click the February heading to move it to the top of the screen.
10. Close the Navigation Pane by clicking the Navigation Pane Close button.

NOTE

You can create and define a multilevel list style and add it to the List Library. Click the arrow beside the Multilevel List button, and click Define New Multilevel List. Enter the text and format for each level. Click OK.

Symbols and Special Characters

The fonts you use with Word include *special characters* that do not appear on your keyboard, such as those used in foreign languages (for example, ç, Ö, and Ω). There are additional fonts, such as *Wingdings* and *Symbol* that consist entirely of special characters.

To insert symbols and special characters in your documents, click the Insert tab on the Ribbon, locate the Symbols group, and click the Symbol command.

Exercise 4-18 INSERT SYMBOLS

1. Scroll toward the beginning of the document. Position the insertion point to the immediate left of the paragraph that begins "*When absolutely*."
2. Click the **Insert** tab. Locate the **Symbols** group, and click the Symbol button Ω Symbol. Click **More Symbols**. The Symbol dialog box appears.
3. Make sure the **Symbols** tab is displayed, and choose **(normal text)** from the **Font** drop-down list box.

4. Scroll through the grid of available symbol characters for normal text, and notice that the grid contains diacritical marks that you can use for foreign languages. You will also see the symbol for cents (¢) and degrees (°).

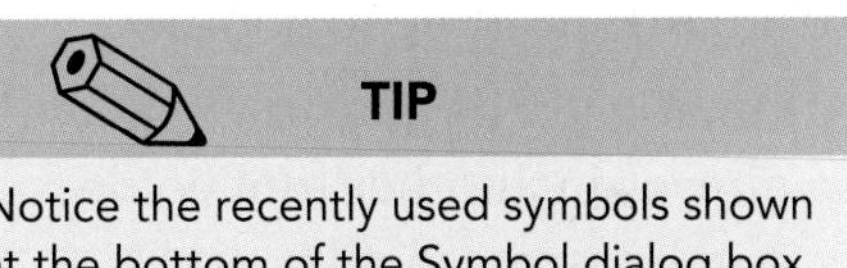

TIP

Notice the recently used symbols shown at the bottom of the Symbol dialog box. Word displays the 16 most recently used symbols.

5. Click the arrow to open the **Font** drop-down list box and choose **Symbol**. Review the available symbol characters.
6. Change the font to **Wingdings**. The characters included in the Wingdings font appear in the grid.

Figure 4-20
Symbol dialog box

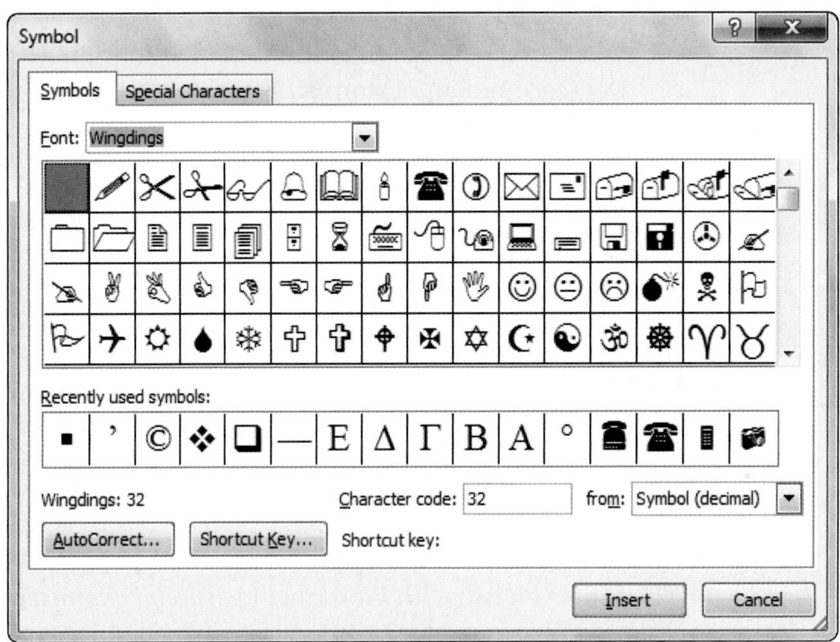

TIP

You can assign shortcut keys or AutoText to a symbol by clicking Shortcut Key or AutoCorrect in the Symbol dialog box. You can also press Alt and key the numeric code (using the numeric keypad, if you have one) for a character. For example, if you change the font of the document to Wingdings and press Alt+0040, you will insert the character for a Wingdings telephone. Remember to change the Wingdings font back to your normal font after inserting a special character.

7. Scroll down several rows until you see symbols similar to an asterisk (*). Click one of the symbols.
8. Click **Insert**, and then click **Close**. The symbol appears in the document.
9. Select the list with roman numerals beginning with "I. First Quarter" through "IV. Fourth Quarter."
10. Click the **Home** tab, and click the arrow beside the Bullets button.
11. Click **Define New Bullet** and click **Picture**. Click one of the picture bullets, and click **OK**, and then click **OK** again. The roman numerals are replaced with your chosen picture bullet.

Exercise 4-19 INSERT SPECIAL CHARACTERS

You can use the Symbol dialog box and shortcut keys to insert characters such as an en dash, an em dash, or smart quotes. An *en dash* (–) is a dash slightly wider than a hyphen. An *em dash* (—), which is twice as wide as an en dash, is used in sentences where you would normally insert two hyphens. *Smart quotes* are quotation marks that open a quote curled in one direction (“) and close a quote curled in the opposite direction (”).

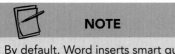

NOTE

By default, Word inserts smart quotes automatically.

1. Make sure nonprinting characters are displayed in the document. If they are not, click the Show/Hide ¶ button ¶.
2. On page 1, locate the paragraph that begins “1. Monday.” Position the insertion point to the immediate right of “Monday.” Press Delete to remove the hyphen.
3. Click the **Insert** tab, and click the Symbol button Ω Symbol. Click **More Symbols**, and click the **Special Characters** tab.
4. Choose **Em Dash** from the list of characters. (Notice the keyboard shortcut listed for the character.) Click **Insert**, and then click **Close**. The em dash replaces the hyphen.
5. Select the hyphen immediately following “Tuesday.” Press Alt+Ctrl+− (the minus sign on the numeric keypad). An em dash is inserted. (If you don’t have a numeric keypad, press F4 to repeat the character.)
6. Insert em dashes after “Wednesday,” “Thursday,” and “Friday.”

Exercise 4-20 CREATE SYMBOLS AUTOMATICALLY

You can use Word’s AutoCorrect feature to create symbols as you type. Just enter a few keystrokes, and Word converts them into a symbol.

1. Scroll to the “SUBJECT” line, and click to the left of “Store.”
2. Key < = = and notice that Word automatically creates an arrow (←).

NOTE

To review the symbols AutoCorrect can enter automatically, open the Word Options dialog box, and click Proofing. Click AutoCorrect Options, and click the AutoCorrect tab.

3. Position the insertion point to the right of “Procedures.” Key = = >. Word creates another arrow pointing to the right.
4. Format the first line of the memo with 72 points of paragraph spacing before it. This starts the first line two inches from the top of the page. (See Appendix B, “Standard Forms for Business Documents.”)
5. Save the document as ***[your initials]*4-20** in your Lesson 4 folder.
6. Submit and close the document.

Lesson 4 Summary

- A paragraph is any amount of text followed by a paragraph mark.
- Paragraph alignment determines how the edges of a paragraph appear horizontally. Paragraphs can be left-aligned, centered, right-aligned, or justified.
- The Click and Type feature enables you to insert text in any blank area of a document by simply positioning the insertion point and double-clicking.
- Line space is the amount of vertical space between lines of text in a paragraph. Lines can be single-spaced, 1.5-line-spaced, double-spaced, or set to a specific value.
- Paragraph space is the amount of space above or below a paragraph. Paragraph space is set in points—12 points of space equals one line space for 12-point text. Change the space between paragraphs by using the Before and After options in the Paragraph dialog box or by using the Ctrl+0 keyboard shortcut to add or remove 12 points before a paragraph.
- A left indent or right indent increases a paragraph's distance from the left or right margin. A first-line indent indents only the first line of a paragraph. A hanging indent indents the second and subsequent lines of a paragraph.
- To set indents by using the horizontal ruler, drag the left indent marker (small rectangle), the first-line indent marker (top triangle), or the hanging indent marker (bottom triangle), which are all on the left end of the ruler, or drag the right indent marker (triangle) on the right end of the ruler.
- A border is a line or box added to selected text, a paragraph, or a page. Shading fills in the background of selected text or paragraphs. Borders and shading can appear in a variety of styles and colors.
- In addition to regular borders, Word provides special decorative horizontal lines that are available from the Borders and Shading dialog box.
- The AutoFormat feature enables you to create a border automatically. Key three or more hyphens -, underscores _, or equal signs =, and press Enter. See Table 4-1.

- Repeat paragraph formats by pressing F4 or Ctrl+Y. Copy paragraph formats by using the Format Painter button. Remove paragraph formats by pressing Ctrl+Q or choosing Clear Formatting from the Font group.
- Format a list of items as a bulleted or numbered list. In a bulleted list, each item is indented and preceded by a bullet character or other symbol. In a numbered list, each item is indented and preceded by a sequential number or letter.
- Remove a bullet or number from an item in a list by clicking the Bullets button or the Numbering button on the Ribbon. Press Enter in the middle of the list to add another bulleted or numbered item automatically. Press Enter twice in a list to turn off bullets or numbering. Change the bullet symbol or the numbering type by clicking the arrow beside the Bullets button to display the Bullet Library or the arrow beside the Numbering button to open the Numbering Library.
- The AutoFormat feature enables you to create a bulleted or numbered list automatically. See Table 4-2.
- Create a multilevel list by clicking the Multilevel List button. A multilevel list has indented subparagraphs, such as paragraph "1)" followed by indented paragraph "a)" followed by indented paragraph "i)." To increase the level of numbering for each line item, click the Increase Indent button or press Tab. To decrease the level of numbering, click the Decrease Indent button or press Shift+Tab.
- Insert symbols, such as foreign characters, by clicking the Insert tab and clicking the Symbol command. Wingdings is an example of a font that contains only symbols.
- Insert special characters, such as an em dash (—), by using the Special Characters tab in the Symbol dialog box.
- Create symbols automatically as you type by keying AutoCorrect shortcuts, such as keying :) to produce the ☺ symbol.

LESSON 4		Command Summary	
Feature	**Button**	**Command**	**Keyboard**
1.5-line space		Home tab, Paragraph group	Ctrl+F5
Borders		Home tab, Paragraph group	
Bulleted list		Home tab, Paragraph group	
Center text		Home tab, Paragraph group	Ctrl+E
Decrease indent		Home tab, Paragraph group	Ctrl+Shift+M
Double space		Home tab, Paragraph group	Ctrl+2
Hanging indent		Home tab, Paragraph group	Ctrl+T
Increase indent		Home tab, Paragraph group	Ctrl+M
Justify text		Home tab, Paragraph group	Ctrl+J
Left-align text		Home tab, Paragraph group	Ctrl+L
Multilevel List		Home tab, Paragraph group	
Numbered list		Home tab, Paragraph group	
Remove paragraph formatting		Home tab, Paragraph group	Ctrl+Q
Restore text to Normal formatting		Home tab, Font group	Ctrl+Shift+N
Right-align text		Home tab, Paragraph group	Ctrl+R
Shading		Home tab, Paragraph group	
Single space		Home tab, Paragraph group	Ctrl+1
Symbols and special characters	Ω Symbol	Insert tab, Symbols group	

Concepts Review

True/False Questions

Each of the following statements is either true or false. Indicate your choice by circling T or F.

T F 1. You can use the Ribbon, Home tab, Font group to right-align paragraphs.

T F 2. Text that is left-aligned has a ragged left edge.

T F 3. You can open the Paragraph dialog box from the shortcut menu.

T F 4. The keyboard shortcut Ctrl+F5 changes line spacing to 1.5 lines.

T F 5. You can use Word's AutoCorrect feature to create symbols as you type by using certain keyboard combinations.

T F 6. To apply a page border to a document, click the Borders tab in the Borders and Shading dialog box.

T F 7. Ctrl+Q removes all paragraph formatting.

T F 8. A hanging indent indents all lines in a paragraph except the first line.

Short Answer Questions

Write the correct answer in the space provided.

1. Which type of paragraph alignment adjusts spacing between words?

____

2. What is the keyboard shortcut for centering text?

____

3. Single, 1.5, and double are examples of what type of spacing?

____

4. If you click [icon] once, what happens to selected text?

____

5. With an outline numbered list, instead of clicking [icon], what key can you press to achieve the same result?

____

6. Which keystrokes apply a double-line border automatically?

____

7. What is the procedure to display the Reveal Formatting task pane?

____

8. Which indent marker is the top triangle on the left side of the ruler?

____

Critical Thinking

Answer these questions on a separate page. There are no right or wrong answers. Support your answers with examples from your own experience, if possible.

1. You can use keyboard shortcuts to change paragraph alignment, or you can use the alignment buttons on the Formatting toolbar. Which method do you prefer? Why? When might you use the other method?
2. Many people use bulleted lists and numbered lists interchangeably. Are there times when it would be more appropriate to use a bulleted list than a numbered list and vice versa? Explain your answer.

Skills Review

Exercise 4-21

Change paragraph alignment and line spacing.

1. Start a new document.
2. Change the character formatting and paragraph alignment for the first paragraph by following these steps:
   a. Select the paragraph mark and set the font to 12-point Cambria.
   b. Click the Center button on the Ribbon, Home tab, Paragraph group, to center the text you are about to key.
   c. Key the first two lines shown in Figure 4-21 in all capitals. Use a line break (press Shift+Enter) after the first line to make the two lines one paragraph.

Figure 4-21

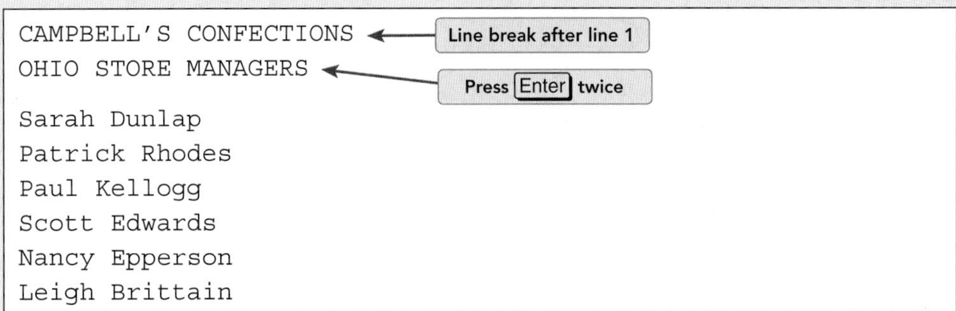

CAMPBELL'S CONFECTIONS
Line break after line 1
OHIO STORE MANAGERS
Press Enter twice
Sarah Dunlap
Patrick Rhodes
Paul Kellogg
Scott Edwards
Nancy Epperson
Leigh Brittain

3. At the end of this paragraph, press Enter twice, turn off Caps Lock, and key the six names shown in Figure 4-21. Again, use a line break after each name to make the names all one paragraph.

4. Change the alignment of each paragraph by following these steps:
   a. Move the insertion point into the first paragraph, and click the Align Right button [≡] on the Ribbon, Home tab, to right-align the first two lines.
   b. Move the insertion point into the paragraph containing the six names, and press Ctrl+L to left-align the names.
   c. Select the entire document, and click the Center button [≡] to center all the text.
5. Change line spacing by following these steps:
   a. Click within the second paragraph.
   b. Press Ctrl+5 to change the line spacing to 1.5 lines.
6. Save the document as ***[your initials]*4-21** in your Lesson 4 folder.
7. Submit and close the document.

Exercise 4-22

Change paragraph spacing and set indents.

1. Open the file **Club**. (Make sure the Show/Hide ¶ button [¶] is turned on.)
2. Change spacing between paragraphs by following these steps:
   a. Select the entire document, click the right mouse button, and choose **Paragraph** from the shortcut menu.
   b. Click the **Indents and Spacing** tab if it is not displayed.
   c. Click the up arrow to the right of **After** to set the spacing after paragraphs to 12 points. Click **OK**.
3. Press Ctrl+Home to move to the top of the document. Key in bold uppercase letters **CAMPBELL'S CONFECTIONS' CHOCOLATE CLUB**.
4. Press Enter once. Click within the new title and open the **Paragraph** dialog box. Change spacing to 72 points before and 24 points after. Change the **Alignment** setting to **Centered** and click **OK**.
5. Apply a first-line indent to the paragraphs by following these steps:
   a. Select all the paragraphs below the title.
   b. Make sure the horizontal ruler is displayed. Point to the first-line indent marker [▽] on the ruler. When a ScreenTip identifies it, drag it 0.5 inch to the right.
6. Change the indentation of the last paragraph by following these steps:
   a. Deselect the paragraphs.
   b. Right-click the last paragraph and open the **Paragraph** dialog box.
   c. Set the Left and Right indentation text boxes to 1 inch.
   d. Remove the first-line indent by choosing **(none)** from the **Special** drop-down list. Click **OK**.
7. Key **Note:** and press Spacebar at the beginning of the newly indented paragraph. Format "Note" in bold and small caps.

8. Justify four paragraphs below the title beginning with the paragraph that begins "The marketing department" and ending with the paragraph that begins "Gift announcements."
9. Save the document as ***[your initials]*4-22** in your Lesson 4 folder.
10. Submit and close the document.

Exercise 4-23

Apply borders and shading; repeat and copy formatting.

1. Open the file **Retail Stores**.
2. At the end of the document, key the following text as a separate paragraph. Use bold text.

   To learn more about our stores and products, call Campbell's Confections at 800-555-2025 or visit our Web site at www.campbellsconfections.biz.
3. Apply borders and shading to the new paragraph by following these steps:
   a. Place the insertion point in the paragraph.
   b. Click the arrow beside the Borders button on the Ribbon, Paragraph group. Click **Borders and Shading**, and click the **Borders** tab if it is not displayed.
   c. Use the first line style, and change the line **Color** to **Blue**.
   d. Change the **Width** to **1½ pt**.
   e. In the Preview box, click the Top Border button and the Bottom Border button.
   f. Click the **Shading** tab. Click the down arrow beside the **Fill** box. From the **Theme Colors** palette, click the third box in the first column (**White, Background 1, Darker 15%**). Click **OK**.
4. Repeat the formatting by clicking within the first paragraph and pressing F4.
5. Click the Undo button to undo the formatting in the first paragraph.
6. Apply a border to text automatically by following these steps:
   a. Key the following title at the top of the document: **Campbell's Confections**.
   b. Press Enter two times.
   c. Click in front of the blank paragraph mark. Key = = = and press Enter to automatically insert a double-line border under the title. Delete the blank paragraph mark.
7. Copy formatting from one paragraph to another by following these steps:
   a. Click in the last paragraph.
   b. Click the Format Painter button.
   c. Click in the title paragraph.

8. Change the font size of the title to 14 points, and apply bold and a text effect to the title. Verify that the title text is easy to read after applying the text effect. Choose another effect if necessary.
9. Add 72 points of spacing before and 24 points after the paragraph and center the title.
10. Save the document as ***[your initials]*4-23** in your Lesson 4 folder.
11. Submit and close the document.

Exercise 4-24

Align paragraphs, change paragraph spacing, create bulleted lists, and insert symbols and special characters.

1. Open the file **Designs**.
2. Format the title as bold, all caps, and centered. Set the paragraph spacing to 72 points before and 24 points after. Delete the blank paragraph mark after the title.
3. Create a bulleted list by following these steps:
   a. Select the text beginning with "Milk chocolate" and ending with "White chocolate."
   b. Click the arrow beside the Bullets button [Bullets].
   c. Choose a bullet option.
4. Insert symbols by following these steps:
   a. Position the insertion point to the right of "Computer."
   b. Click the Insert tab on the Ribbon. Click the Symbol button [Ω Symbol]. Click More Symbols.
   c. Change the Font to Wingdings. Double-click the computer symbol in the second row.
   d. Click Close.
5. Click to the right of "Camera," and open the Symbol dialog box. Change the Font to Webdings, and scroll to the tenth row to locate the camera symbol. Click Insert. Click Close.
6. Click to the right of "Cell phone," and open the Symbol dialog box. Change the Font to Webdings, and scroll to the eleventh row to locate the cell phone symbol. Click Insert. Click Close.
7. Insert an em dash by following these steps:
   a. Position the insertion point in front of the computer symbol.
   b. Press Alt+Ctrl+- (the minus key on the numeric keypad). Or click the Insert tab on the Ribbon, click the arrow beside Symbol, click More Symbols, and click the Special Characters tab to select the em dash.
8. Insert an em dash before the camera symbol and the cell phone symbol. Select each symbol, and change the font size to 14.
9. Save the document as ***[your initials]*4-24** in your Lesson 4 folder.
10. Submit and close the document.

Lesson Applications

Exercise 4-25

Change alignment, line spacing, and paragraph spacing and apply shading.

1. Start a new document.
2. Key the text shown in Figure 4-22, including the corrections. Use Times New Roman, single spacing, and 0 points spacing before and 0 points spacing after paragraphs. Use line breaks (Shift+Enter) to format the text as two paragraphs.

Figure 4-22

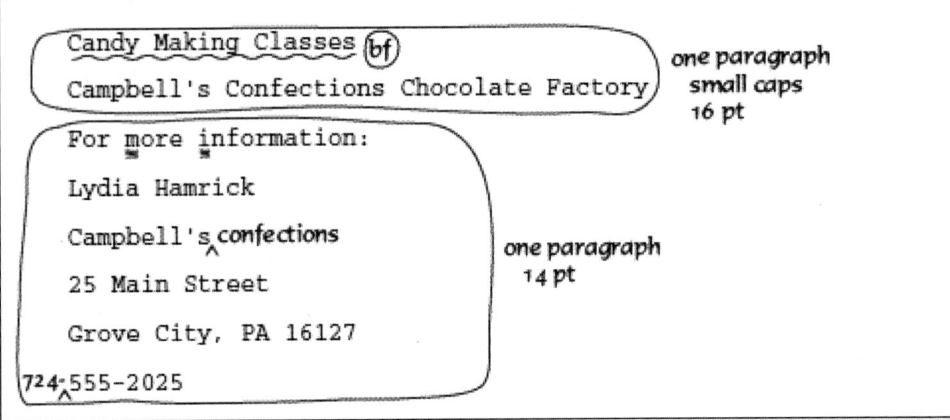

Candy Making Classes
Campbell's Confections Chocolate Factory
For more information:
Lydia Hamrick
Campbell's confections
25 Main Street
Grove City, PA 16127
724-555-2025

3. Center all text in the document.
4. Change the line spacing in only the second paragraph to 1.5 lines.
5. Change the paragraph spacing for only the first paragraph to 72 points before and 36 points after.
6. Add 10 percent gray shading to the first paragraph. (Open the Borders and Shading dialog box. Click the Shading tab and display the drop-down list for Style.)
7. Add a page border, using the box setting and the double-wavy line style.
8. Save the document as ***[your initials]*4-25** in your Lesson 4 folder.
9. Submit and close the document.

Exercise 4-26

Change alignment, line spacing, and paragraph spacing; add a border; repeat formatting; and add symbols.

1. Open the file **WV Stores**.
2. Change the title to "Campbell's Confections—West Virginia Stores." There should be one blank line below the title and a blank line after each of the remaining office locations.
3. Format all lines of the first office location with 1.5-line spacing.
4. Repeat the formatting for the remaining locations.
5. Change the title to 20-point bold and small caps with paragraph spacing of 72 points before and 24 points after. Delete the blank paragraph mark after the title.
6. Add a ¾-point double-line bottom border to the title.
7. Center the second and third office location text, and right-align the last office location text.
8. Replace the text "Telephone:" throughout the document with the telephone symbol from the Wingdings font (first row, eighth symbol). Leave the space between the symbol and the telephone number.
9. Replace the text "Fax:" throughout the document with a fax symbol from the Webdings font (eleventh row, tenth symbol).
10. Save the document as ***[your initials]*4-26** in your Lesson 4 folder.
11. Submit and close the document.

Exercise 4-27

Indent paragraphs, create bulleted and numbered lists, and change paragraph spacing.

1. Open the file **Favors - 2**.
2. Select the title and apply 14-point bold formatting. Add a text effect to the title. Change the paragraph spacing to 72 points before and 24 points after. Center the title.
3. Select the text from "wedding bells" to "other assorted shapes." Format the selected text as a bullet list using the standard round bullet.
4. Select the text from "solid milk chocolate" to "dark chocolate with mint filling." Format the selected text as a bullet list using a picture bullet.
5. Set 0.25-inch first-line indents for all paragraphs except the title, the bulleted lists, and the final paragraph.
6. Format the final paragraph with 0.75-inch left and right indents.

7. Add gray shading to the final paragraph.
8. Save the document as ***[your initials]*****4-27** in your Lesson 4 folder.
9. Submit and close the document.

Exercise 4-28 ◆ Challenge Yourself

Indent and align paragraphs, change paragraph spacing, apply a border, and create bulleted lists.

1. Open the file **Fundraising**.
2. Key the heading **Fundraising** at the top of the document. Format the heading in bold, uppercase letters with a negative left indent of –0.25 inch and 12 points of spacing before the paragraph and 24 points of spacing after the paragraph.
3. Format the paragraphs from "Solid milk chocolate" to "Milk chocolate with double chocolate filling" as a bulleted list, using a bullet style of your choice.
4. Format the paragraphs from "Sales Department" to "555-2025" with a 0.75-inch left indent and with 6 points of spacing after paragraphs.

NOTE

If horizontal line clips are not available, use a border.

5. Add one blank paragraph mark above "Specialty fundraising." Position the insertion point at the blank paragraph mark. Open the **Borders and Shading** dialog box, and click **Horizontal Line**. Add a horizontal line of your choice.
6. Justify all paragraphs in the document except the title and bulleted lists.
7. Add a page border to the document, using a line style of your choice, 3-point width, and the 3-D setting.
8. Save the document as ***[your initials]*****4-28** in your Lesson 4 folder.
9. Submit and close the document.

On Your Own

In these exercises you work on your own, as you would in a real-life business environment. Use the skills you've learned to accomplish the task—and be creative.

Exercise 4-29

Create a flyer for Campbell's Confections. Use a variety of paragraph alignment settings, line spacing, and paragraph spacing. Add shading to one or more paragraphs and a page border using the Art option. Include a bulleted list. Use the Text Effects feature if appropriate. Save the document as ***[your initials]*4-29**. Submit the document.

Exercise 4-30

Create a set of instructions for accessing Campbell's Confections using a mobile device. Use a numbered list to describe the step-by-step instructions. Use a bulleted list for the advantages of using Campbell's Confections Mobile Web site. Use borders or shading for emphasis or for paragraphs containing special notes or tips. Save the document as ***[your initials]*4-30** and submit it.

Exercise 4-31

Review the foreign-language characters in the Symbols dialog box (normal text). Use a foreign-language dictionary (such as an online dictionary on the Internet) to find a few foreign words you can key in a document by inserting the appropriate foreign-language characters. Include the English translations. Display the Research task pane to help you define and translate vocabulary, or use the Mini Translator. Save the document as ***[your initials]*4-31** and submit it.

Lesson 5

Tabs and Tabbed Columns

OBJECTIVES

After completing this lesson, you will be able to:

1. Set tabs.
2. Set leader tabs.
3. Clear tabs.
4. Adjust tab settings.
5. Create tabbed columns.
6. Sort paragraphs and tabbed columns.

Estimated Time: 1 hour

A *tab* is a paragraph-formatting feature used to align text. When you press Tab, Word inserts a tab character and moves the insertion point to the position of the tab setting, called the *tab stop*. You can set custom tabs or use Word's default tab settings.

As with other paragraph-formatting features, tab settings are stored in the paragraph mark at the end of a paragraph. Each time you press Enter, the tab settings are copied to the next paragraph. You can set tabs before you key text or set tabs for existing text.

In this lesson you will create documents with tabbed columns by setting tabs. Use the tab feature to create documents requiring an open table format and less complex layout. Use the table feature to create documents with tabbed columns requiring advanced formatting and design layout.

Lesson 5 introduces the memo format that is used for internal business communication. The printed memo format is not as popular today as it was a few years ago due to the increased use of e-mail. Use the memo format for documents that require a permanent record of the document content. When the document content does not require a permanent record, such as scheduling a meeting, create an e-mail message. The heading information for both a memo and an e-mail message include the name(s) of the recipient(s), the current date, and the subject of the message.

Setting Tabs

Word's default tabs are left-aligned and set every half-inch from the left margin. These tabs are indicated at the bottom of the horizontal ruler by tiny tick marks.

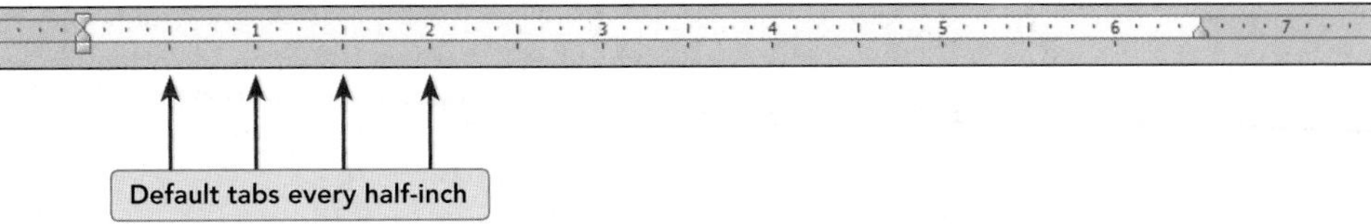

Figure 5-1
Default tabs

If you don't want to use the half-inch default tab settings, you have two choices:

- Change the distance between the default tab stops.
- Create custom tabs.

The four most common types of custom tabs are left-aligned, centered, right-aligned, and decimal-aligned. Custom tab settings are indicated by *tab markers* on the horizontal ruler. Additional custom tab options, such as leader tabs and bar tabs, are discussed later in the lesson.

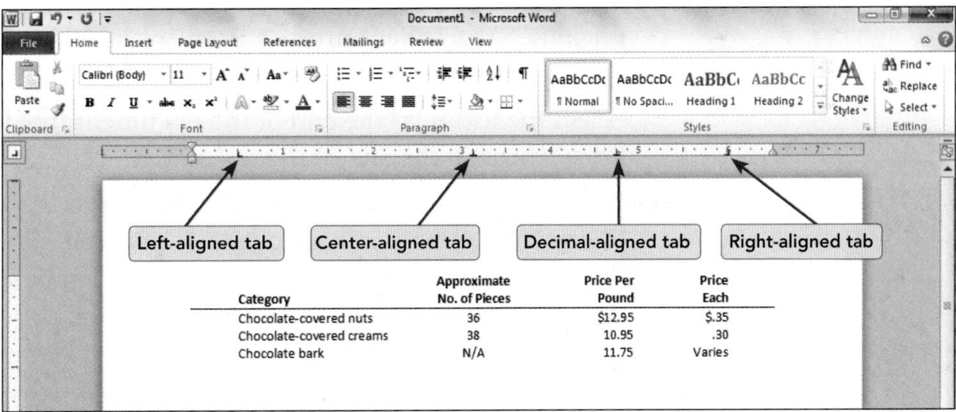

Figure 5-2
Types of tabs

TABLE 5-1 Types of Tabs

Ruler Symbol	Type of Tab	Description
	Left-aligned	The left edge of the text aligns with the tab stop.
	Centered	The text is centered at the tab stop.
	Right-aligned	The right edge of the text aligns with the tab stop.
	Decimal-aligned	The decimal point aligns with the tab stop. Use this option for columns of numbers.
	Bar	Inserts a vertical line at the tab stop. Use this option to create a divider line between columns.

There are two ways to set tabs:

- Use the Tabs dialog box.
- Use the ruler.

Exercise 5-1 SET TABS BY USING THE TABS DIALOG BOX

1. Open the file **Memo - 2**.
2. Click the View Ruler button to display the horizontal ruler, if necessary.
3. Select the text near the end of the document that begins "Item New Price" through the end of the document.
4. Click the **Home** tab, and locate the **Paragraph** group. Click the Paragraph Dialog Box Launcher. Click the **Tabs** button Tabs... at the bottom of the dialog box. The Tabs dialog box appears. Notice that the **Default tab stops** text box is set to 0.5 inch.

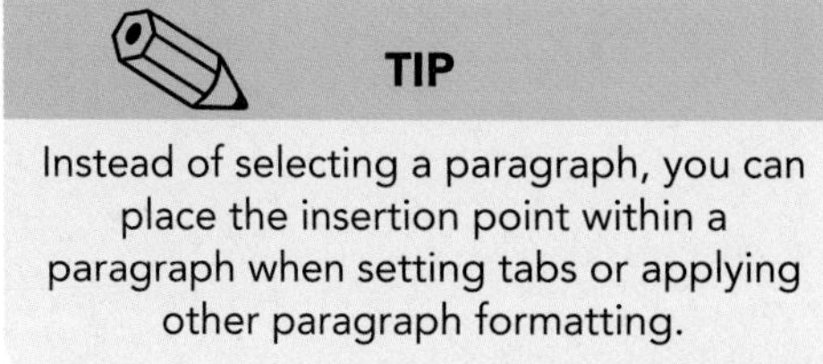

TIP
Instead of selecting a paragraph, you can place the insertion point within a paragraph when setting tabs or applying other paragraph formatting.

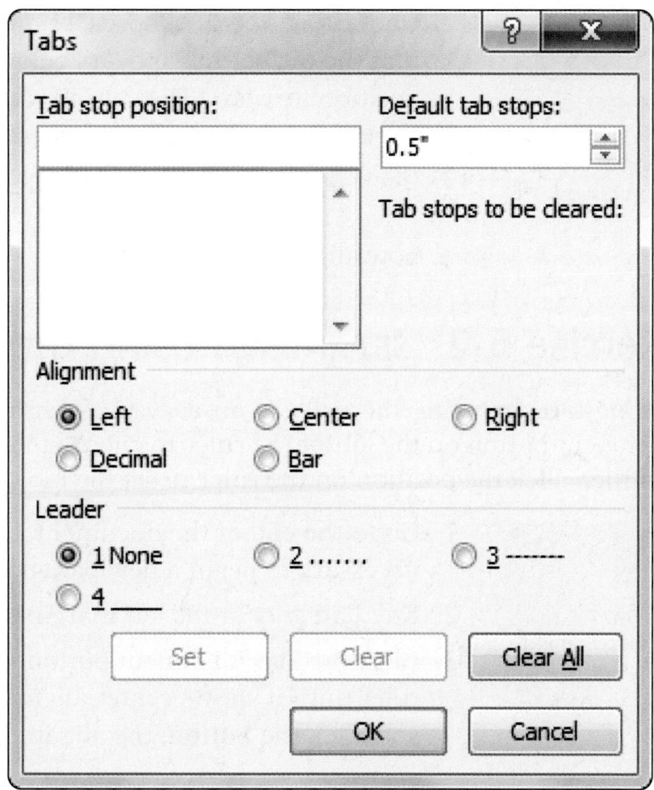

Figure 5-3
Tabs dialog box

5. Key **.25** in the **Tab stop position** text box. The alignment is already set to left, by default.
6. Click **OK**. The ruler displays a left tab marker, the symbol used to indicate the type and location of a tab stop on the ruler.
7. Move the insertion point to the left of the first word on the first line of the selected text, "Item."
8. Press Tab. The first line of the group is now indented 0.25 inch. This produces the same effect as creating a first-line indent.
9. Press Tab at the beginning of each of the lines that you formatted with the 0.25-inch left tab ("1.25 oz.," "1 lb.," "1 lb.," "4 oz.," and "4 oz.").
10. Select the same six lines of text ("Item" through "2.25") at the end of the document. Notice that there are tab characters between some of the words and that the text is crowded and difficult to read. The text is aligned at the default tab settings (every 0.5 inch).
11. Open the **Tabs** dialog box by double clicking the tab marker at 0.25 on the ruler. Key **3.0** in the **Tab stop position** text box.

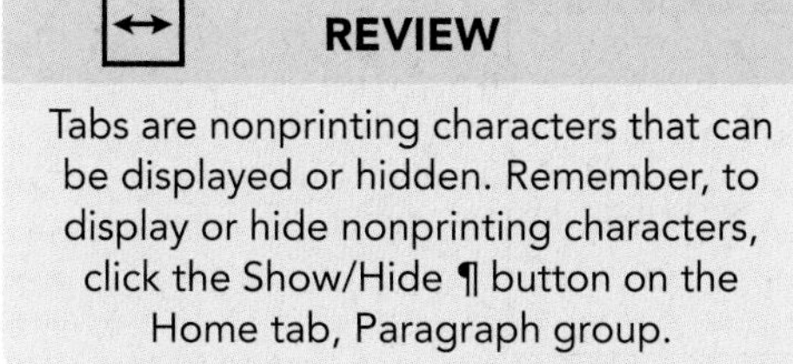

REVIEW

Tabs are nonprinting characters that can be displayed or hidden. Remember, to display or hide nonprinting characters, click the Show/Hide ¶ button on the Home tab, Paragraph group.

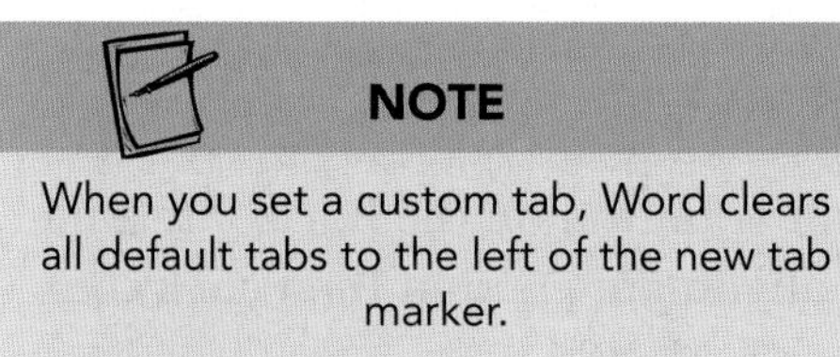

NOTE

When you set a custom tab, Word clears all default tabs to the left of the new tab marker.

NOTE

The column heading "New Price" does not contain a decimal, but is aligned at the decimal point. You will adjust the tab for this heading later in this lesson.

12. Under **Alignment**, choose **Decimal**. Click **Set**. Notice that the tab setting appears below the Tab stop position text box. The setting is automatically selected so that another tab setting can be keyed.
13. Click **OK**. The column headings "Item" and "New Price," along with the text below the headings, are now aligned at the tab stops.

Exercise 5-2 SET TABS BY USING THE RULER

Setting tabs by using the ruler is an easy two-step process: Click the Tab Alignment button on the left of the ruler to choose the type of tab alignment, and then click the position on the ruler to set the tab.

TIP

When choosing tab settings for information in a document, keep in mind that left-aligned text and right- or decimal-aligned numbers are easier to read.

1. Go to the end of the document, and press [Enter] if necessary to begin a new paragraph.
2. Key **Category** at the left margin.
3. Click the Tab Alignment button on the horizontal ruler until it shows center alignment. Each time you click the button, the alignment changes.

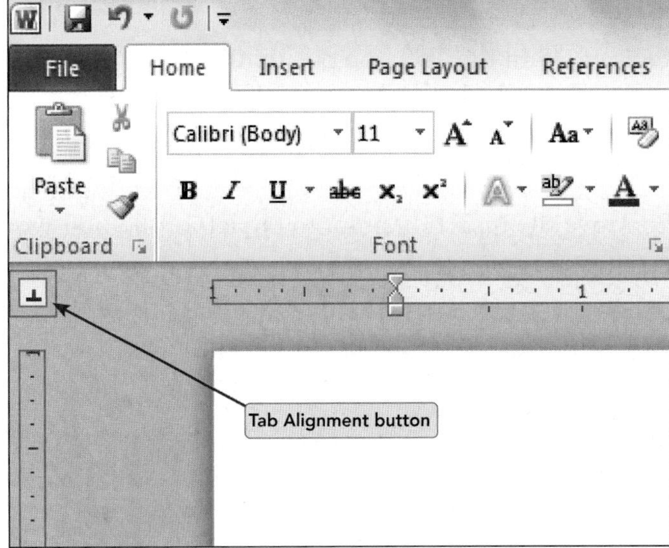

Figure 5-4 Tab Alignment button on the ruler

TIP

As you toggle through the Tab Alignment button symbols, notice the appearance of the first-line indent symbol and the hanging indent symbol. You can display one of these symbols, and then just click the ruler to the desired indent position instead of using the point-and-drag method.

4. Click the ruler at 3.25, and a center tab marker displays.
5. Press [Tab], and key **No. of Pieces**.
6. Click the **Tab Alignment** button on the horizontal ruler until it shows right alignment, and then click the ruler at 5.5.
7. Press [Tab], and key **Price/Pound**.

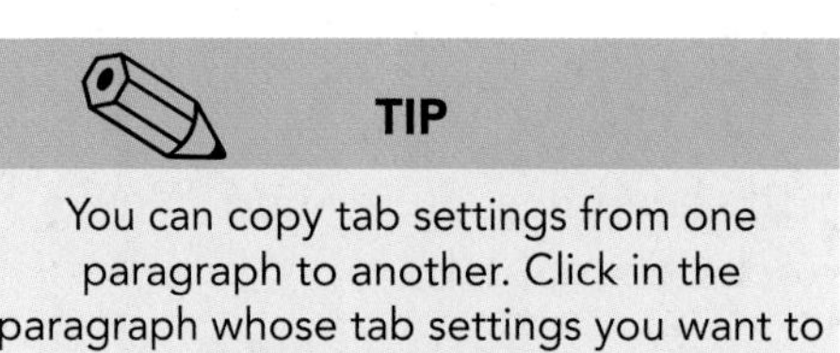

TIP

You can copy tab settings from one paragraph to another. Click in the paragraph whose tab settings you want to copy. Click the Format Painter button. Click in the paragraph to which you are copying the tab settings.

8. Press Enter to start a new line. The tab settings will carry forward to the new line.
9. Key **Chocolate-covered nuts**, press Tab, key **36**, press Tab, and key **$12.95**.
10. Press Enter and key **Chocolate-covered creams**, press Tab, key **38**, press Tab, and key **10.95**. Press Enter.

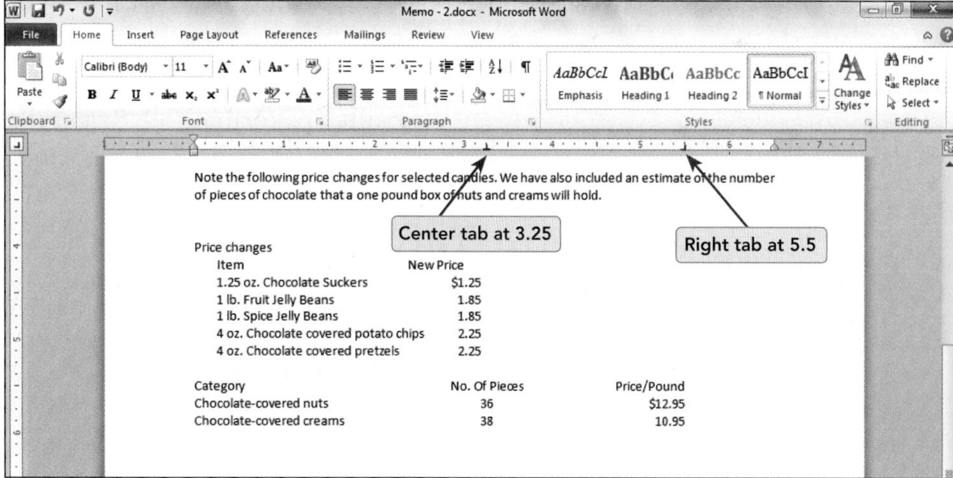

Figure 5-5
Document with tabbed text

Setting Leader Tabs

You can set tabs with *leader characters,* patterns of dots or dashes that lead the reader's eye from one tabbed column to the next. Leaders may be found in a table of contents, in which dotted lines fill the space between the headings on the left and the page numbers on the right.

Word offers three leader patterns: dotted line, dashed line, and solid line.

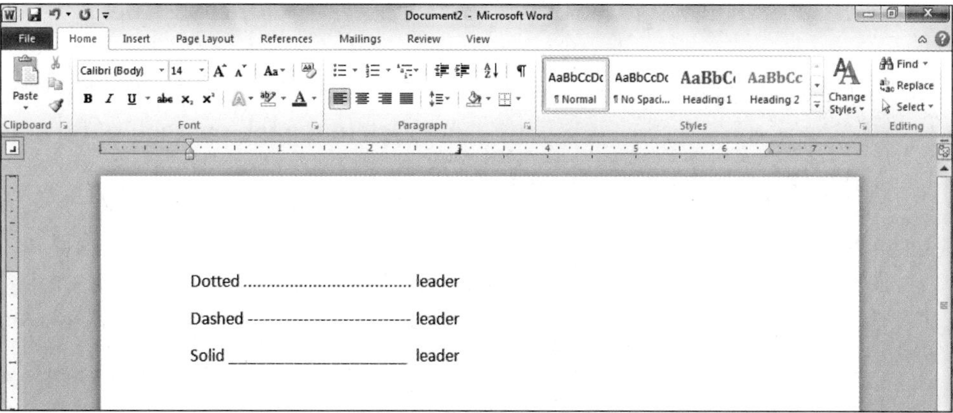

Figure 5-6
Leader patterns

Exercise 5-3 SET LEADER TABS

1. Select the two columns of text under the headings "Item" and "New Price." The prices are aligned at a 3-inch decimal tab.
2. Open the Tabs dialog box. The tab settings for the selected text are displayed in the Tab stop position text box with the 0.25-inch tab highlighted.
3. Click to select 3", and under Leader, click the second leader pattern (the dotted line).
4. Click Set and click OK. A dotted-line leader fills the space to the left of the 3-inch tab setting.
5. Select the heading "Price Changes" and apply bold, small caps formatting. Select the headings "Item" and "New Price" and apply bold and italic.

NOTE

Leader patterns always fill the space to the left of a leader tab setting.

Clearing Tabs

You can clear custom tabs all at once or individually. When you clear custom tabs, Word restores the default tab stops to the left of the custom tab stop.

There are three ways to clear a tab:

- Use the Tabs dialog box.
- Use the ruler.
- Press Ctrl+Q.

Exercise 5-4 CLEAR A TAB BY USING THE TABS DIALOG BOX AND THE KEYBOARD

1. Select the six lines of text under the heading "Price Changes."
2. Open the Tabs dialog box. The 0.25-inch tab is highlighted in the Tab stop position text box.
3. Click Clear and click OK. Word clears the 0.25-inch custom tab, and the text moves to the right to align at the tab stop at 3.0. (The text moves because each line is preceded by a tab character (→).
4. Delete the tab character (→) at the beginning of each line. The text in the first column moves to the left margin, and the text in the second column is aligned at the tab setting.
5. Select the six lines of text under the heading "Price Changes" once again. Press Ctrl+Q. The remaining tab setting is deleted, and the text is no longer aligned.
6. Click the Undo button to restore the 3-inch custom tab.
7. Save the document as ***[your initials]*5-4** in your Lesson 5 folder.

NOTE

Remember, to remove tabs from text, you must delete the tab characters.

Exercise 5-5 CLEAR A TAB BY USING THE RULER

1. Position the insertion point at the beginning of the line of text with the heading "Category."
2. Position the pointer on the 5.5-inch right-aligned tab marker on the ruler.
3. When the ScreenTip "Right Tab" appears, drag the tab marker down and off the ruler. The custom tab is cleared, and the heading "Price/Pound" moves to a default tab stop.
4. Undo the last action to restore the tab setting.
5. Select the headings "Category," "No. of Pieces," and "Price/Pound," and apply bold, small caps formatting.

NOTE

When clearing or adjusting tabs by using the ruler, watch for the ScreenTip to correctly identify the item to which you are pointing. If no ScreenTip appears, you might inadvertently add another tab marker.

Adjusting Tab Settings

You can adjust tabs inserted in a document by using either the Tabs dialog box or the ruler. Tabs can be adjusted only after you select the text to which they have been applied.

Exercise 5-6 ADJUST TAB SETTINGS

1. Select the line with the headings "Item" and "New Price." The second heading is not aligned with the text below.
2. Point to the tab marker at 3 inches on the ruler.
3. Drag the tab marker to the right until the heading aligns with the text below.
4. Select the last three lines of text in the document ("Category" through "10.95").
5. Open the **Tabs** dialog box.
6. Click to select the tab setting **5.5** in the **Tab stop position** text box.
7. Change the tab alignment setting by clicking **Left**. Click **OK**. Notice the change in the alignment of the heading and the text below.
8. Click the Undo button.

NOTE

When you change tab settings with the ruler, be careful to drag the tab marker only to the right or to the left. If you drag the tab marker up or down, you might clear it from the ruler. If you inadvertently clear a tab marker, undo your action to restore the tab.

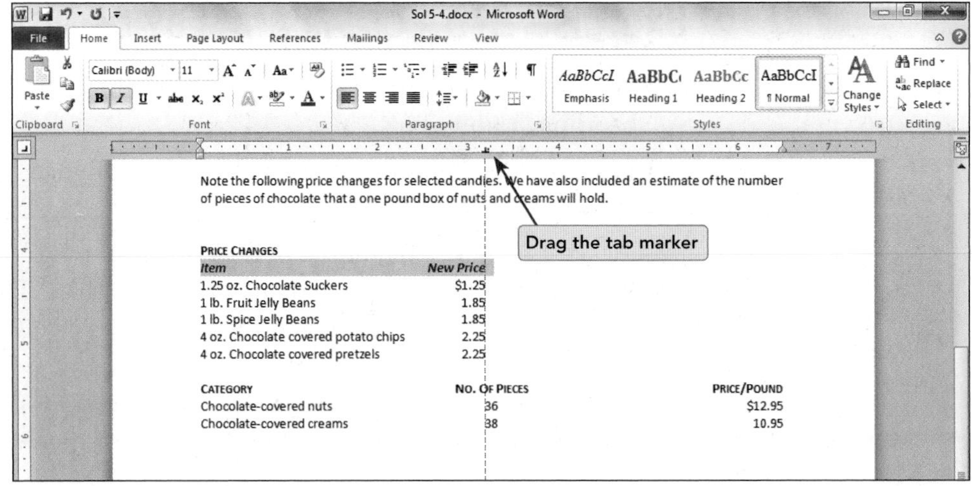

Figure 5-7
Using the ruler to adjust a tab setting

9. With the text still selected, drag the 5.5-inch tab marker to 6.5 inches on the ruler. The text is now aligned at the right margin.

Creating Tabbed Columns

As you have seen in these practice documents, you can use tabs to present information in columns.

When you format a table using tabbed columns, follow these rules for existing text or text to be keyed.

- The table should be centered horizontally within the margins.
- Columns within the table should be between 6 and 10 spaces apart.
- The width of the table should not exceed the width of the document's body text.
- At least one blank line should separate the top and bottom of the table from the body text of the document.

Exercise 5-7 SET TABBED COLUMNS

1. Position the insertion point at the end of the document, and press Enter twice.
2. Press Ctrl+Q to remove the tab settings from the paragraph mark; then key the text shown in Figure 5-8. Use single spacing.

Figure 5-8

```
The following stores offer a complete line of gifts and
accessories in addition to our fine chocolates. Other
stores offer a limited selection of gifts and accessories
due to space limitations.
```

3. Press Enter twice.

4. Study Figure 5-9 to determine the longest item in each column. (Pennsylvania is the longest item in the first column. Youngstown is the longest item in the second column, and West Virginia is the longest item in the third column.)

Figure 5-9

Pennsylvania	Ohio	West Virginia
Grove City	Akron	Clarksburg
Pittsburgh	Canton	Fairmont
Erie	Cleveland	Morgantown
Monroeville	Youngstown	Wheeling

5. Create a guide line that contains the longest item in each column by keying the following with 10 spaces between each group of words:

   Pennsylvania   Youngstown   West Virginia

6. Click the Center button on the Ribbon to center the line.
7. Change the Tab Alignment button to left alignment. Using the I-beam as a guide, click the ruler to set a left-aligned tab at the beginning of each group of words.

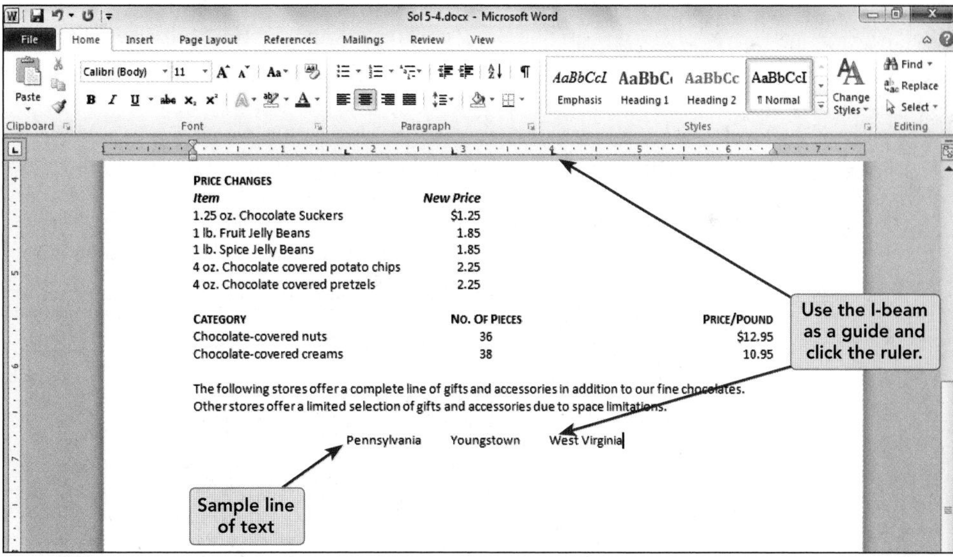

Figure 5-10
Guide line for centering tabbed columns

8. Delete the text in the guide line up to the paragraph mark. Do not delete the paragraph mark, which is now storing your left-aligned tab settings.
9. Click the Align Left button to left-align the insertion point.
10. Key the table text as shown in Figure 5-9, pressing Tab before each item and single-spacing each line. Underline each column heading.
11. Select the text near the top of the document beginning with "Item No." and ending with the line that begins "BC32."
12. Change the Tab Alignment button to left alignment, and click the ruler at 2.5.

13. Change the Tab Alignment button to right alignment, and click the ruler at 5.5.
14. Select the text if necessary, and click the Increase Indent button two times to move the text away from the left margin.

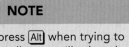

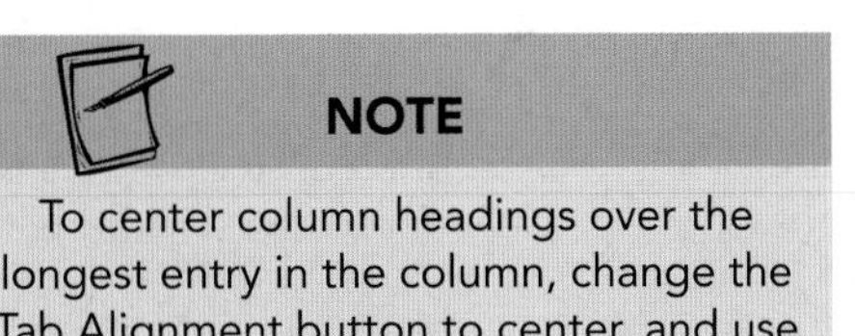

NOTE

To center column headings over the longest entry in the column, change the Tab Alignment button to center, and use the I-beam as a guide to set a center tab on the ruler.

15. Drag the left tab marker (right or left) to position the middle column an equal distance from the first and third columns.
16. Bold and center the heading "Standard-Size Boxes." Format the title with all caps and 12 points spacing after. Apply bold and italic formatting to the column headings.

Exercise 5-8 SELECT A TABBED COLUMN

After text is formatted in tabbed columns, you can select columns individually by selecting a vertical block of text. Selecting tabbed text can be helpful for formatting or deleting text. You use Alt to select a vertical block of text.

NOTE

If you do not press Alt when trying to select text vertically, you will select the entire first line of text, rather than just the column header for the column you are selecting.

1. Scroll to the end of the document. Hold down Alt and position the I-beam to the immediate left of "Ohio."
2. Drag across the heading, and then down until the heading and all four cities are selected.

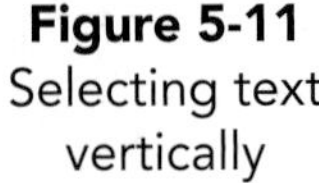

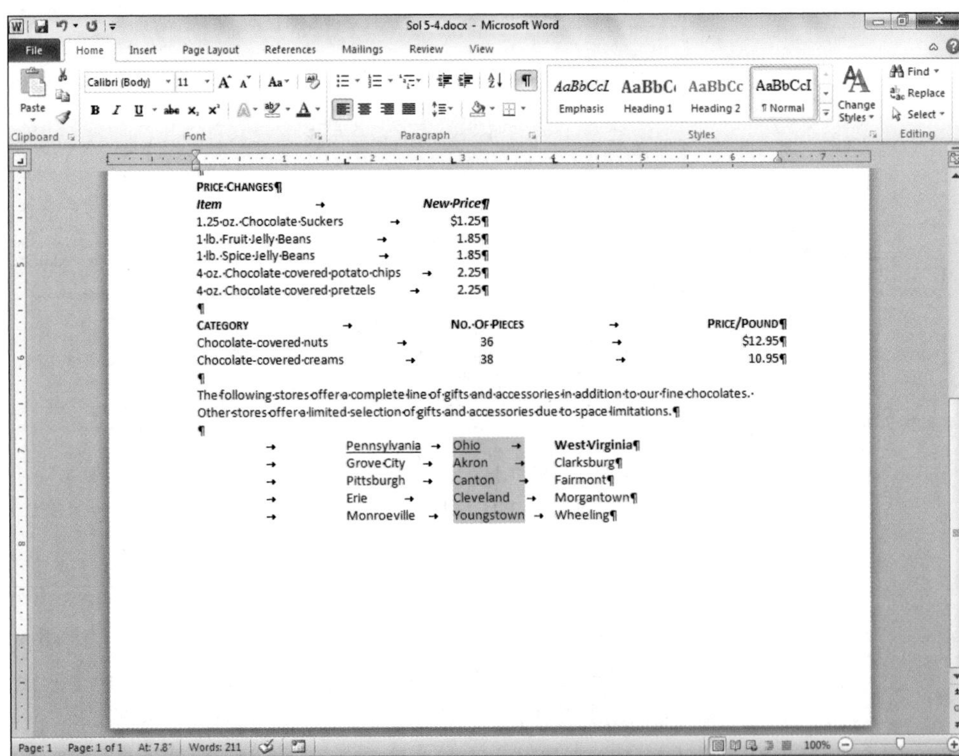

Figure 5-11 Selecting text vertically

3. Press [Delete] to delete the column.
4. Undo the deletion.
5. Select the column again, this time selecting only the names under the column heading "Ohio."
6. Click the Italic button [*I*] to format the text.

Exercise 5-9 INSERT BAR TABS

Bar tabs are used to make tabbed columns look more like a table with gridlines. A bar tab inserts a vertical line at a fixed position, creating a border between columns. You can set bar tabs by using the ruler or the Tabs dialog box.

1. At the bottom of the document, select the four lines of tabbed text below the headings "Pennsylvania," "Ohio," and "West Virginia."
2. Open the **Tabs** dialog box. Key **2.5** in the text box, click **Bar**, and click **OK**. The vertical bar is placed between the first and second columns. Do not deselect the tabbed text.
3. To set bar tabs by using the ruler, click the Tab Alignment button until it changes to a bar tab. Click the ruler at 3.75 inches. The bar tab markers appear as short vertical lines on the ruler.
4. Adjust the bar tab markers on the ruler to make them more evenly spaced, as needed.
5. Deselect the tabbed text. Click the Show/Hide ¶ button [¶] to view the document without nonprinting characters. The bar tabs act as dividing borders between the columns.

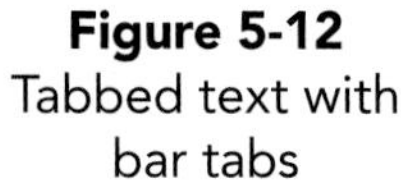

Figure 5-12 Tabbed text with bar tabs

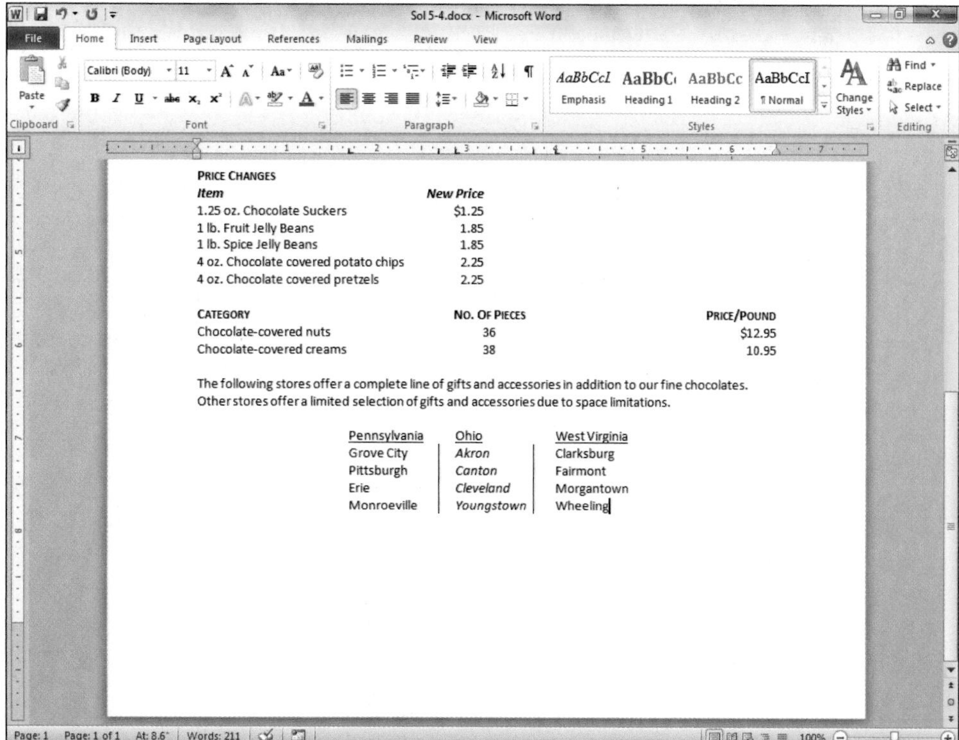

6. Position the insertion point in the line that contains "Grove City."
7. Point to the 3.75-inch bar tab on the ruler, and drag it off the ruler. The vertical line in the table disappears.
8. Undo the deletion to restore the bar tab.
9. Save the document as ***[your initials]*****5-9** in your Lesson 5 folder.
10. Submit the document.

Sorting Paragraphs and Tabbed Columns

Sorting is the process of reordering text alphabetically or numerically. You can sort to rearrange text in ascending order (from lowest to highest, such as 0–9 or A–Z) or descending order (from highest to lowest, such as 9–0 or Z–A).

You can sort any group of paragraphs, from a single-column list to a multiple-column table, such as one created by tabbed columns. When sorting a tabbed table, you can sort by any of the columns.

Figure 5-13
Sorting paragraphs and tables

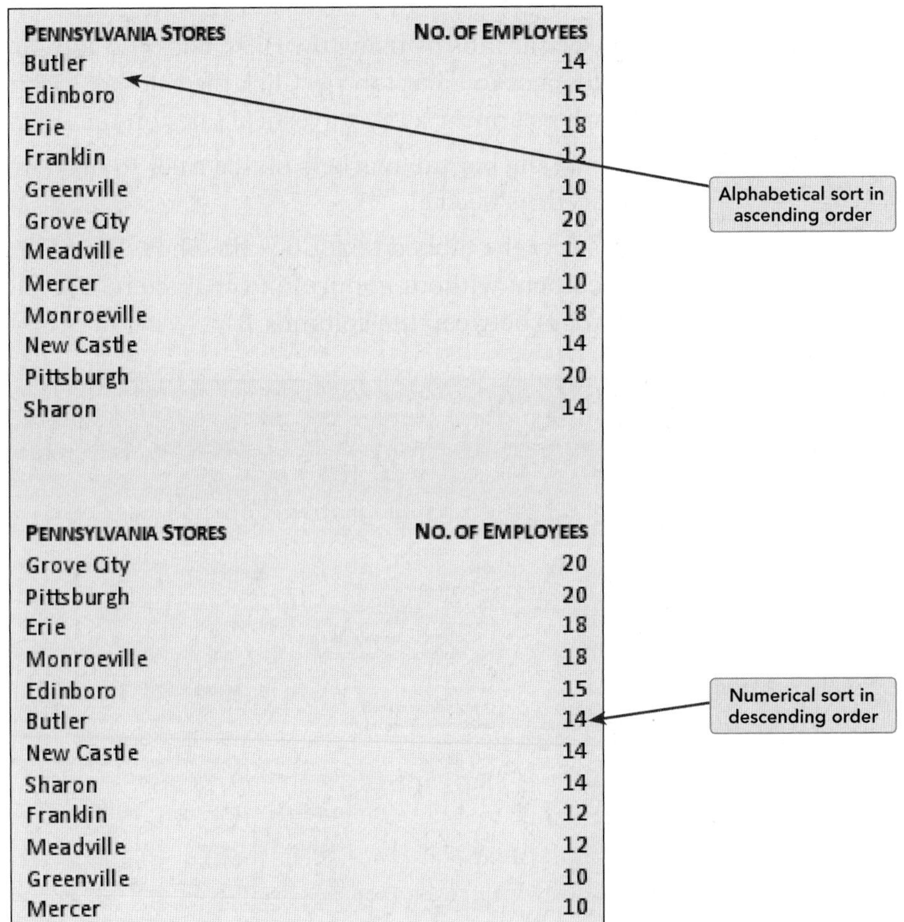

Exercise 5-10 SORT TABBED TABLES

1. Select the headings "Pennsylvania," "Ohio," and "West Virginia" and the four lines of text below the headings.
2. Click the Sort button on the Ribbon, Paragraph group.
3. Open the **Sort by** drop-down list to view the other sort options. Field numbers represent each of the columns. Open the **Type** drop-down list. Notice that the type options include **Text**, **Number**, and **Date**.
4. Click **Descending** to change the sort order, and click the **Header row** option to select it. Click **OK**. The text in the first column is sorted alphabetically in descending order.
5. Press Ctrl+Z to undo the sort. Do not deselect the text.
6. Click the Sort button to open the Sort Text dialog box.
7. Click **Header row** at the bottom of the dialog box. This option indicates that the selection includes column headings, which should not be sorted with the text.
8. Open the **Sort by** drop-down list. Now you can sort by the table's column headings instead of by field numbers.
9. Choose **Ohio** from the drop-down list. Click **Descending** and click **OK**.

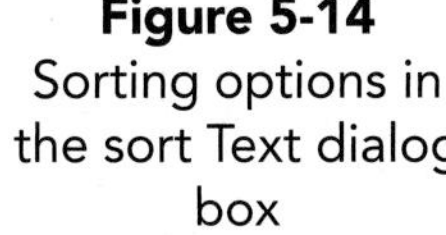

Figure 5-14
Sorting options in the sort Text dialog box

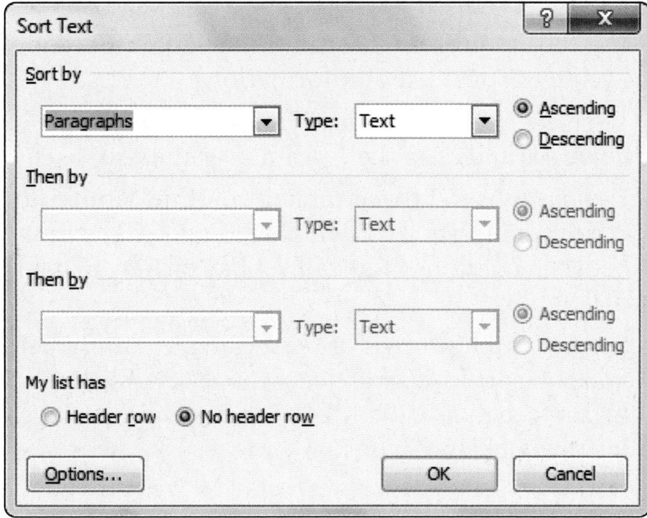

10. Save the document as ***[your initials]*5-10** in your Lesson 5 folder.
11. Submit and close the document.

Lesson 5 Summary

- Tabs are a paragraph-formatting feature used to align text. When you press Tab, Word inserts a tab character and moves the insertion position to the tab setting, called the tab stop.
- Word's default tabs are left-aligned and set every half-inch from the left margin, as indicated at the bottom of the horizontal ruler.
- The four most common types of custom tabs are left-aligned, centered, right-aligned, and decimal-aligned. Custom tab settings are indicated on the horizontal ruler by tab markers.
- Set tabs by using the Tabs dialog box or the ruler. To use the ruler, click the Tab Alignment button on the left of the ruler to select the type of tab alignment, and then click the position on the ruler to set the tab. See Table 5-1.
- A leader tab uses a series of dots, dashes, or solid underlines to fill the empty space to the left of a tab stop. Use the Tabs dialog box to set a leader tab.
- Clear custom tabs all at once or individually. To clear a tab, use the Tabs dialog box, the ruler, or press Ctrl+Q.
- To adjust tab settings, position the insertion point in the tabbed text (or select the text), and then either open the Tabs dialog box or drag the tab markers on the ruler.
- Use tabs to present information in columns. Tabbed columns are a side-by-side vertical list of information.
- To select a tabbed column (for formatting or deleting the text), hold down Alt and drag the I-beam over the text.
- Use bar tabs to format tabbed columns similar to a table with gridlines. A bar tab inserts a vertical line at a fixed position, creating a border between columns. You can set bar tabs by using the ruler or the Tabs dialog box.
- Sorting is the process of reordering text alphabetically or numerically. You can sort to rearrange text in ascending order (from lowest to highest, such as 0–9 or A–Z) or descending order (from highest to lowest, such as 9–0 or Z–A).

LESSON 5	**Command Summary**		
Feature	**Button**	**Command**	**Keyboard**
Bar tab		Home tab, Paragraph group	
Center tab		Home tab, Paragraph group	
Clear tabs		Home tab, Paragraph group	Ctrl+Q
Decimal tab		Home tab, Paragraph group	
Leader tabs		Home tab, Paragraph group	
Left tab		Home tab, Paragraph group	
Right tab		Home tab, Paragraph group	
Sort text		Home tab, Paragraph group	

Concepts Review

True/False Questions

Each of the following statements is either true or false. Indicate your choice by circling T or F.

T F 1. In Word, you can use Spacebar to precisely align text.

T F 2. When you set a custom tab, Word clears all default tabs to the left of the tab stop.

T F 3. You cannot set tabs for existing text.

T F 4. You can either select a paragraph or place the insertion point within the paragraph when setting tabs for the paragraph.

T F 5. When custom tabs are cleared, you must reestablish default tabs, or you will have no tabs at all.

T F 6. Tabs inserted in a document cannot be adjusted after they are set.

T F 7. The symbol for a bar tab marker is a short vertical line.

T F 8. You can use the ruler to set a leader tab.

Short Answer Questions

Write the correct answer in the space provided.

1. What are the two ways to set tabs?

____

2. What are the five types of tabs you can set when using the Tab Alignment button?

____

3. Which dialog box is used to set a leader tab?

____

4. What type of tab do you use [button] to create?

____

5. What interval does Word use for default tabs?

____

6. How do you clear a tab by using the ruler?

____

7. Which key is used to select a tabbed column?

8. Which Ribbon tab and group contains the Sort feature?

Critical Thinking

Answer these questions on a separate page. There are no right or wrong answers. Support your answers with examples from your own experience, if possible.

1. Books and magazines may use leader tabs in the table of contents and index. Based on representative books and magazines, create a few general guidelines on when to use leader tabs. Support your view with examples.
2. Do you find it easier to read text that is centered in a column or text that is left-aligned? What about numbers that are centered or right-aligned? Create samples to support your position.

Skills Review

Exercise 5-11

Set tabs and create a business memo.

1. Start a new document, and set a 1-inch left-aligned tab by following these steps:
   a. Make sure the Tab Alignment button on the horizontal ruler shows left alignment [L].
   b. Click the ruler at the 1-inch mark.
2. Select the paragraph mark and open the Paragraph dialog box. Change the **Spacing After** to 0 and change the **Line spacing** to **Single**. Click **OK** to close the Paragraph dialog box.
3. Key the text in Figure 5-15, using the spacing shown. Press Tab after each colon. Refer to Appendix B, “Standard Forms for Business Documents.”

Figure 5-15

```
      MEMO TO:          Store Managers
one   FROM:             Thomas Campbell
blank
line  DATE:             <Current Date>

      SUBJECT:          Monroeville Store
two →                              tele                            412
blank The Monroeville store has added a second ^phone line. The number is 8̸1̸4-555-8228.
lines
      Please record the number and update the company directory.
```

4. In the date line, key today's date.
5. Select the first line of the memo heading and open the Paragraph dialog box. Change the **Spacing Before** to **72** points.
6. Add your reference initials at the end of the document.
7. Spell-check the document.
8. Save the document as ***[your initials]*****5-11** in your Lesson 5 folder.
9. Submit and close the document.

Exercise 5-12

Set leader tabs.

1. Start a new document. Format the paragraph mark as 14 points Arial Narrow. Change the **Spacing After** to **24 pt** and change the **Line spacing** to **Single**.
2. Key the first line in Figure 5-16.
3. Before keying the remaining text, set a solid leader tab that extends to the right margin by following these steps:
   a. Click the **Paragraph Dialog Box Launcher** to open the Paragraph dialog box. Click **Tabs**.
   b. In the **Tab stop position** box, key **6.5**. (The right margin setting.)
   c. Under **Alignment**, click **Right**.
   d. Choose the fourth leader option, click **Set**, and click **OK**.

Figure 5-16

```
Enter a drawing for a free pound of chocolate-covered nuts.
Complete the form below.

Name ______________________________________________________

Address ___________________________________________________

City/State/ZIP ____________________________________________

Telephone _________________________________________________
```

4. Key the remaining information, beginning with "Name." Press Tab to move to the 6.5-inch right-aligned tab setting, and then press Enter. Continue keying the text in the figure.
5. Format the text with the solid-line leaders as small caps.
6. Save the document as ***[your initials]*5-12** in your Lesson 5 folder.
7. Submit and close the document.

Exercise 5-13

Set, adjust, and clear tab settings.

1. Open the file **Price Change**.
2. Position the insertion point at the top of the document, and locate the Tab Alignment button. If necessary, change the alignment to left, and click the ruler at the 1-inch mark.
3. Key the memo heading text listed below. Press Tab after each colon. A blank line should follow the first three lines of the heading. Two blank lines should follow the subject line.

   MEMO TO: Store Managers
   FROM: Lynn Tanguay
   DATE: August 10, 20--
   SUBJECT: Price Change

4. Add 72 points spacing before the first line of the memo heading. Add your reference initials 1 blank line below the last line of the memo.
5. Use the ruler to adjust the tab settings for the column headings by following these steps:
   a. Position the insertion point in the column heading line.
   b. Point to and drag the tab marker positioned at 3.75 on the ruler to 4.5 on the ruler.
   c. Point to and drag the tab marker positioned at 2.8 on the ruler to 3.5 on the ruler.
6. Select the six lines of tabbed text below the column headings. Point to the tab marker at 2.8, and drag it down and off the ruler. Drag the tab marker positioned at 3.75 off the ruler.
7. Change the Tab Alignment button to a right tab, and click the ruler at 3.8 and 5.0. The text is centered below the headings, and the numbers are right-aligned.
8. Select the column headings, and apply bold, small caps formatting. Change the line spacing for all tabbed text (including the column headings) to 1.15 spacing.
9. Save the document as ***[your initials]*5-13** in your Lesson 5 folder.
10. Submit and close the document.

Exercise 5-14

Create tabbed columns and sort text.

1. Start a new document. Key **MOST POPULAR HOLIDAY CHOCOLATES** in uppercase bold. Center the text and press Enter.
2. Left-align the paragraph mark and turn off bold and uppercase. Change the **Spacing After** to **12 pt**, and change the **Line spacing** to **Single**.
3. Create a table with single-spaced, tabbed columns that are horizontally centered between the left and right margins by following these steps:
   a. Key a guide line containing the longest text from each column in Figure 5-17, with 10 spaces between columns. (Include the column headings when determining the longest item in each column.)
   b. Center the text.
   c. Using the I-beam for guidance, set a left-aligned tab for each of the columns.
   d. Delete the guide line up to the paragraph mark. Left-align the paragraph mark.
   e. Key the text shown in Figure 5-17, pressing Tab before each item in each column.

Figure 5-17

Holiday	Pennsylvania	Ohio	West Virginia
Valentine's Day	1 lb. chocolate nuts	1 lb. assorted	1 lb. turtles
Easter	1 lb. chocolate basket	8 oz. solid rabbit	8 oz. chocolate nut egg
Halloween	chocolate suckers	chocolate suckers	chocolate suckers

4. Bold the column headings. Format the first line of the document with 72 points spacing before and 24 points spacing after.
5. Sort the table alphabetically by holiday by following these steps:
   a. Select the entire table, including the column headings.
   b. Click the Sort button in the Paragraph group.
   c. Click **Header row** to display the column headings in the **Sort by** drop-down list.
   d. Choose **Holiday** from the **Sort by** drop-down list.
   e. Choose **Text** from the **Type** list, and choose **Ascending**. Click **OK**.
6. Save the document as ***[your initials]*5-14** in your Lesson 5 folder.
7. Submit and close the document.

Lesson Applications

Exercise 5-15

Set tabs for a memo.

1. Start a new document. Open the **Paragraph** dialog box, and change the **Line spacing** to **Single**, and change the **Spacing After** to **0** points.
2. Set a 1-inch left tab and key the text for a memo heading.
3. The memo is to **Lydia Hamrick** from **Thomas Campbell**. The subject is **Renovation**. Remember to include today's date, and insert a blank line between lines in the memo heading.
4. Press Enter three times after the subject line, and key the text shown in Figure 5-18, including the corrections. Use single spacing and insert a blank line between paragraphs.

Figure 5-18

, Pennsylvania
Renovation work is almost complete at Campbell's Confections in Erie. The Erie store is
our
the newest acquisition, and its modern up to date interior provides a spacious area for retail
a -controlled
sales, large temperature storage area, and a private office for the store manager.

tourists is
The Erie store is close ~~enough~~ to the Peninsula to attract ~~visitors~~, two blocks from the
and is from
hospital, conveniently located in a plaza with easy access to and the parking lot for local
residents.

d ①
The store renovation will be features in the Erie Times this weekend.

5. Change the font for the entire document to Arial.
6. Change the font for the memo guide words ("MEMO TO:," "FROM:," "DATE:," and "SUBJECT:") to Arial Black.
7. Move to the beginning of the document, and change the spacing before to 72 points for the first line of the memo.
8. Spell-check the document.
9. Add your reference initials to the document.
10. Save the document as ***[your initials]*5-15** in your Lesson 5 folder.
11. Submit and close the document.

Exercise 5-16

Set leader tabs and sort paragraphs.

1. Open the file **Chocolate Glossary**.
2. Select the title, and change the spacing before to 72 points and the spacing after to 24 points.
3. Format the title to 14-point small caps, and center the text.
4. Position the insertion point at the beginning of the first line under the title, and key the paragraph shown in Figure 5-19. Use single spacing. Include one blank line below the paragraph.

Figure 5-19

```
The following list represents popular and commonly used
phrases in chocolate making. Refer to the list to help you
become familiar with the terms.
```

5. Select the list of terms and definitions. Drag the left tab marker off the ruler.
6. Set a dotted leader tab that right-aligns the glossary definitions at the right margin. (The right margin for this document is 6.5 inches as shown on the ruler.)
7. Sort each paragraph in the glossary alphabetically, from A to Z.
8. Change the spacing for each glossary definition to 6 points after paragraphs.
9. Apply a page border, using the box setting and a triple-line style. Change the border color.
10. Spell-check the document.
11. Save the document as ***[your initials]*****5-16** in your Lesson 5 folder.
12. Submit and close the document.

Exercise 5-17

Set and adjust tab settings.

1. Start a new document.
2. Key the title in Figure 5-20. Format the title as 12-point Arial bold, uppercase, and centered.
3. Insert two blank lines below the title, and key the paragraph that begins "Even." Use left alignment, single spacing, 11 points, and Arial no bold. Change the spacing after to 0 points.

Figure 5-20

CHOCOLATE CONSUMPTION

Even though Americans consume over 3 billion pounds of chocolate a year, the United States is not ranked in the top five countries for worldwide consumption of chocolate. Americans consume an average of 12 pounds of chocolate per person per year. The following countries are listed as the top five chocolate-consuming nations according to the *World Atlas of Chocolate*.

Country	Pounds/Year
Switzerland	22.36
Austria	20.13
Ireland	19.47
Germany	18.04
Norway	17.93

4. Key the remaining text in the figure, beginning with "Country," using a 1.5-inch left indent and an appropriate right tab setting for the second column. The text should be evenly spaced between the left and right margins, as shown in the figure. (Hint: Subtract 1.5 from the right margin to calculate the tab setting.)
5. Format the paragraph that begins with "Even" with justified alignment and a dropped capital letter (use the default drop cap settings). There should be one blank line between this paragraph and the table below it.
6. Adjust the tab setting for the table text, so it includes a dotted leader. The column headings for the table should not include the dot leader format.
7. Change the line spacing for the entire table to 1.5 lines.
8. Increase the font size of the title to 16 points and change the spacing before to 72 points. Change the spacing after to 24 points and delete the blank paragraph marks. Apply bold and small caps to "Country" and "Pounds/Year."
9. Spell-check the document.
10. Save the document as ***[your initials]*****5-17** in your Lesson 5 folder.
11. Submit and close the document.

Exercise 5-18 ◆ Challenge Yourself

Create a memo with tabbed columns, sort the text, and add bar tabs.

1. Start a new document. Using the proper line and a 1-inch left tab setting, create a memo to **Thomas Campbell** from **Lydia Hamrick**. The subject is **Weekend Hours for the Ohio Stores**.
2. For the body of the memo, key the text in Figure 5-21. Use single spacing. For the tabbed columns, create a guide line to set the tabs. Align the tabbed columns as indicated. Insert a blank line above and below the tabbed columns.

Figure 5-21

As you requested, the following is a list of the hours of operation for the Ohio stores.

Store	Weekdays	Saturday	Sunday
Akron	9 to 5	9 to 3	Closed
Cleveland	10 to 6	9 to 4	1 to 6
Massillon	9 to 5	9 to 4	Closed
Warren	9 to 6	9 to 5	Closed
Youngstown	9 to 6	9 to 5	Closed
Canton	9 to 6	9 to 4	Closed

Let me know if you need additional information.

3. Apply a ¾-point box border around the entire memo heading (excluding the blank lines below "SUBJECT:"). Add 10 percent gray shading to the memo heading. Click in the first line and apply 72 points spacing before.
4. Adjust the tab setting for the memo heading to 1.25 inches, and set a 1-inch bar tab to create a vertical dividing line.
5. Select the first column of the memo heading (which begins "MEMO TO:") and apply bold formatting.
6. Sort the tabbed table by store in ascending order.
7. Select the tabbed table (including the column headings), and apply 1.5 line spacing.
8. Add your reference initials to the bottom of the memo.
9. Spell-check the document.
10. Save the document as ***[your initials]*5-18** in your Lesson 5 folder.
11. Submit and close the document.

On Your Own

In these exercises, you work on your own, as you would in a real-life business environment. Use the skills you've learned to accomplish the task—and be creative.

Exercise 5-19

Use the Internet to investigate the advantages and disadvantages of flextime. Create a business memo from you to a co-worker. Describe the benefits of flextime and how it could be implemented in your department. Use the correct spacing and tab settings for the memo heading. Save the document as ***[your initials]*5-19** and submit it.

Exercise 5-20

Create a list of your monthly expenses in the form of a tabbed table. Set and adjust the tabs using the ruler. The tabbed text should be positioned attractively on the page. Sort the table. Save the document as ***[your initials]*5-20** and submit it.

Exercise 5-21

Log onto the Internet, and find a chocolate store you would like to visit. Create a tabbed table containing the names of your favorite chocolates, a brief description, and the price. Use leaders and sort the information. Save the document as ***[your initials]*5-21** and submit it.

Lesson 6

Moving and Copying Text

OBJECTIVES ***After completing this lesson, you will be able to:***

1. Use the Office Clipboard.
2. Move text by using cut and paste.
3. Move text by dragging.
4. Copy text by using copy and paste.
5. Copy text by dragging.
6. Work with multiple document windows.
7. Move and copy text among windows.

Estimated Time: 1 hour

One of the most useful features of word processing is the capability to move or copy a block of text from one part of a document to another or from one document window to another, without rekeying the text. In Word, you can move and copy text quickly by using the Cut, Copy, and Paste commands or the drag-and-drop editing feature.

Using the Office Clipboard

Perhaps the most important tool for moving and copying text is the *Clipboard,* which is a temporary storage area. Here is how it works: Cut or copy text from your document, and store it on the Clipboard. Then move to a different location in your document, and insert the Clipboard's contents using the Paste command.

There are two types of clipboards:

- The system Clipboard stores one item at a time. Each time you store a new item on this Clipboard, it replaces the previous item. This Clipboard is available to many software applications on your system.
- The Office Clipboard can store 24 items, which are displayed on the Clipboard task pane. The Office Clipboard collects multiple items without erasing previous items. You can store items from all Office applications.

Exercise 6-1 DISPLAY THE CLIPBOARD TASK PANE

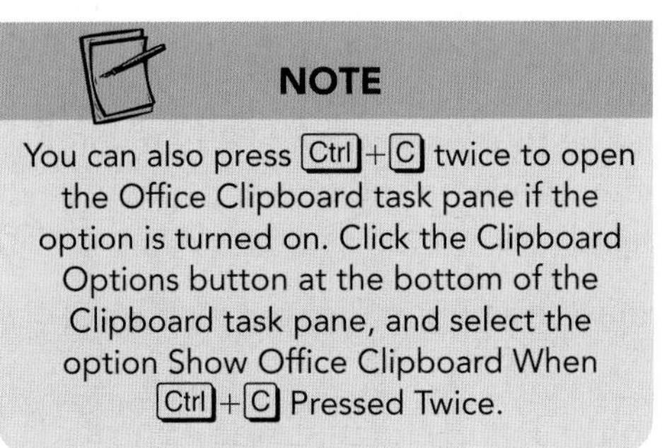

NOTE

You can also press Ctrl+C twice to open the Office Clipboard task pane if the option is turned on. Click the Clipboard Options button at the bottom of the Clipboard task pane, and select the option Show Office Clipboard When Ctrl+C Pressed Twice.

1. Click the **Home** tab. The first group is the **Clipboard** group, and it contains a Dialog Box Launcher to open the Clipboard task pane.
2. Click the **Clipboard Dialog Box Launcher**. The Clipboard task pane opens. At the top of the task pane, notice the Paste All [Paste All] and Clear All [Clear All] buttons. At the bottom of the screen, at the right end of the taskbar in the Notification Area, notice the Clipboard icon, indicating that the Office Clipboard is in use.

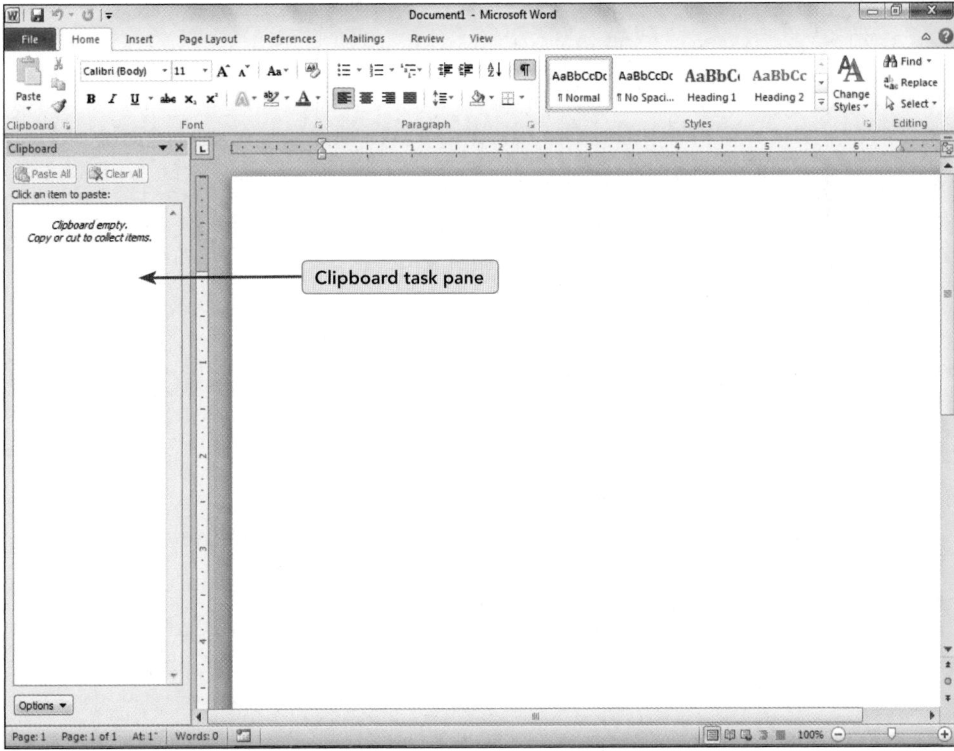

Figure 6-1
Clipboard task pane

NOTE

If the option Show Office Clipboard Automatically is selected, the Clipboard task pane will open automatically when you copy twice in a row without pasting.

3. If the Office Clipboard contains items from previous use, click the Clear All button [Clear All] to empty the Clipboard.
4. Click the **Options** button at the bottom of the task pane. Notice the options available for using the Office Clipboard.
5. Click outside the task pane, making sure not to choose any of the options in the list.

Moving Text by Using Cut and Paste

To move text by using the *cut-and-paste* method, start by highlighting the text you want to move and using the Cut command. Then move to the location where you want to place the text, and use the Paste command. When you use cut and paste to move paragraphs, you can preserve the correct spacing between paragraphs by following these rules:

- Include the blank line below the paragraph you are moving as part of the selection.
- When you paste the selection, click to the left of the first line of text following the place where your paragraph will go—not on the blank line above it.

There are multiple ways to cut and paste text. The most commonly used methods are:

- Use the Cut and Paste buttons on the Ribbon, Home tab.
- Use the shortcut menu.
- Use the keyboard shortcuts Ctrl+X to cut and Ctrl+V to paste.
- Use the Clipboard task pane.

Exercise 6-2 USE THE RIBBON TO CUT AND PASTE

1. Open the file **Festival Memo**.
2. Key the current year in the date line of the memo heading.
3. Select the text “Strawberry Days” in the subject line of the memo.
4. Click the **Home** tab, and click the Cut button to remove the text from the document and place it on the Clipboard. Notice the Clipboard item in the task pane.

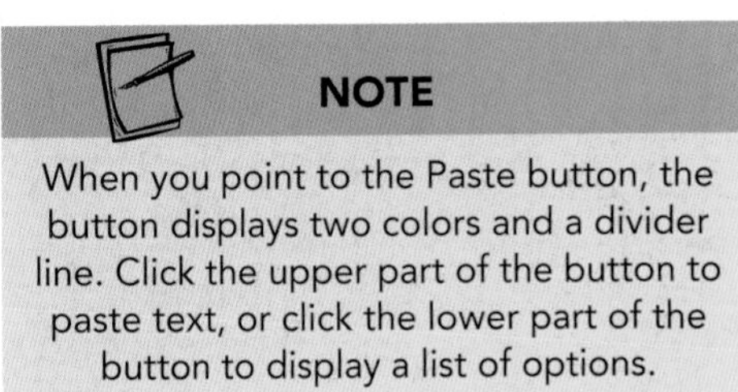

NOTE

When you point to the Paste button, the button displays two colors and a divider line. Click the upper part of the button to paste text, or click the lower part of the button to display a list of options.

5. Position the insertion point to the left of "Art" in the subject line to indicate where you want to insert the text.
6. Click the Paste button to insert "Strawberry Days" in its new location. The Paste Options button (Ctrl) appears below the pasted text, and the Clipboard item remains in the task pane. The Paste Options button is available to make sure the text you paste has the type of formatting you want.
7. Move the I-beam over the Paste Options button (Ctrl). (The I-beam will change to an arrow when it passes over the Paste Options button.) Click the button's drop-down arrow to view the Paste Options gallery. A ScreenTip displays when you point to the gallery icons. Click in the document window to close the gallery.

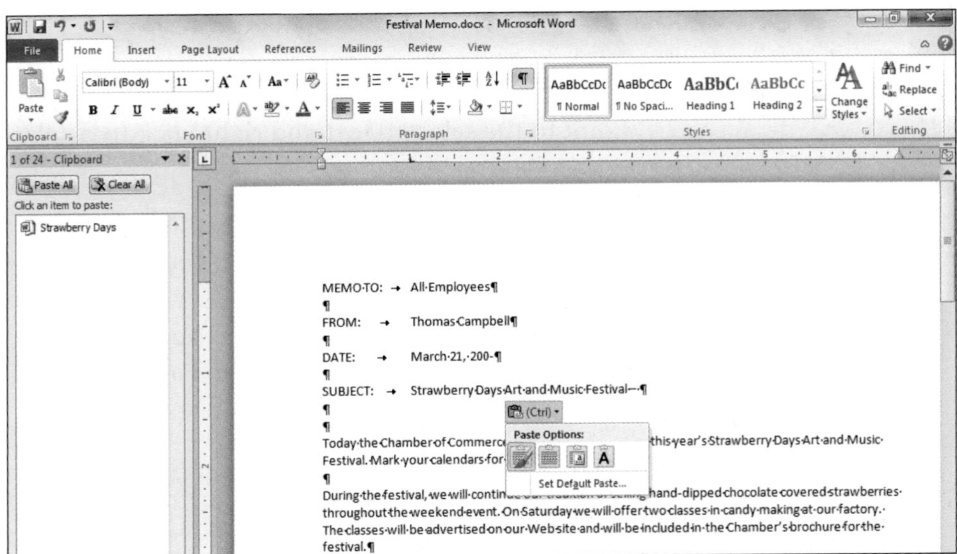

Figure 6-2
Paste options

8. Delete the em dash and extra spaces at the end of the subject line.

Exercise 6-3 USE THE SHORTCUT MENU TO CUT AND PASTE

1. Select the paragraph near the bottom of the document that begins "All hotels are." Include the paragraph mark on the blank line following the paragraph.

Figure 6-3
Using the shortcut menu to cut

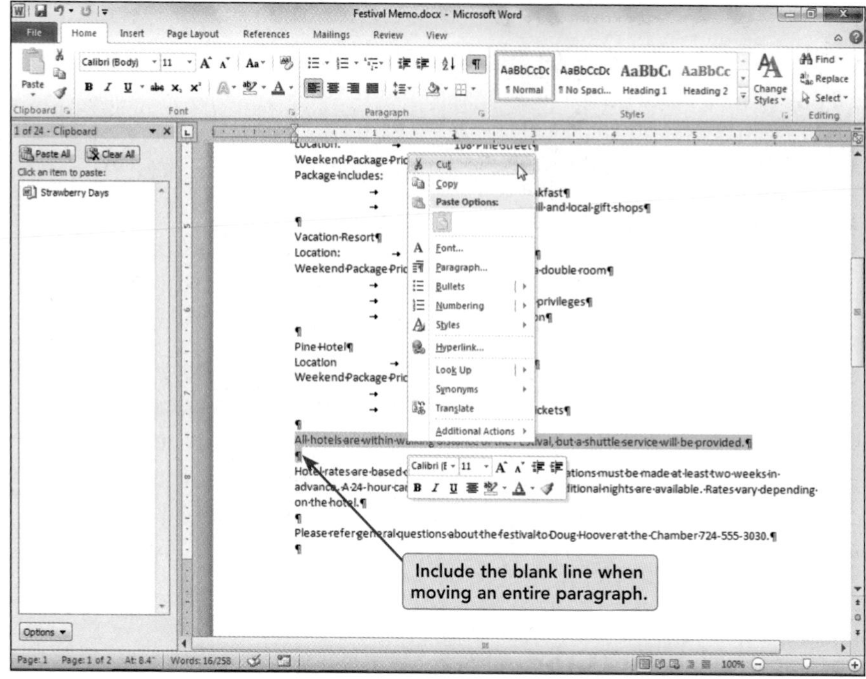

2. Point to the selected text and right-click to display the shortcut menu.
3. Click **Cut**. The item is added to the Clipboard task pane.

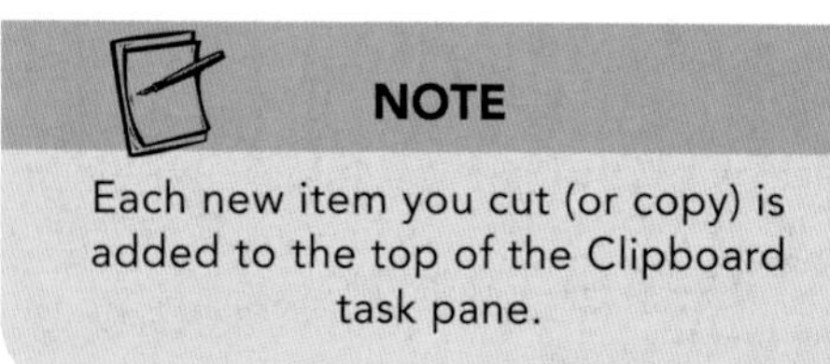

NOTE

Each new item you cut (or copy) is added to the top of the Clipboard task pane.

4. Position the I-beam to the left of the paragraph that begins "Several special." Right-click and click the first Paste Option—(Keep Source Formatting)—from the shortcut menu. The paragraph moves to its new location, and the Paste Options button (Ctrl) appears below the pasted text.

Figure 6-4
Using the shortcut menu to paste

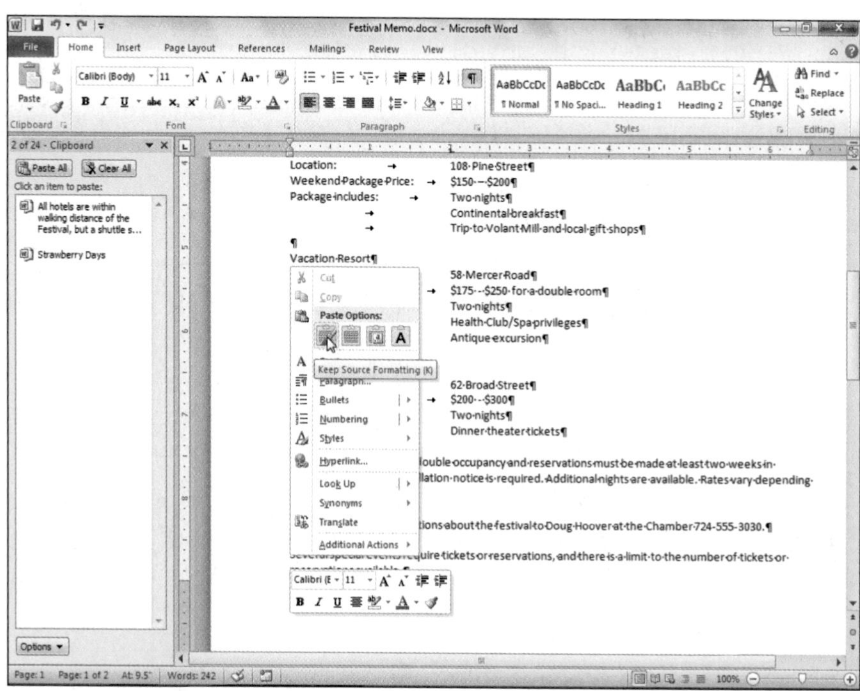

Exercise 6-4 USE KEYBOARD SHORTCUTS TO CUT AND PASTE

If you prefer using the keyboard, you can press Ctrl+X to cut text and Ctrl+V to paste text. You can also use Ctrl+Z to undo an action. The location of these shortcut keys is designed to make it easy for you to move your mouse with your right hand while you press command keys with your left hand.

1. Select the paragraph that begins "Several special" and the blank line that follows the paragraph. Press Ctrl+X to cut the text. A new item appears in the task pane.
2. Position the insertion point just before the paragraph that begins "Please refer." Press Ctrl+V to paste the text.
3. Press Ctrl+Z to undo the paste. Press Ctrl+Y to redo the paste. (Remember, you can also click the Undo button to undo actions.) Notice that the Clipboard item remains in the task pane.

Exercise 6-5 USE THE OFFICE CLIPBOARD TO PASTE

Each time you cut text in the previous exercises, a new item was added to the Office Clipboard. You can paste that item directly from the task pane.

1. Select all the information that goes with the "Pine Hotel," including the title "Pine Hotel" and the blank line that follows the hotel information.
2. Cut this text, using the Cut button on the Ribbon. The text is stored as a new item at the top of the Clipboard task pane.
3. Position the insertion point to the left of the paragraph that begins "Wolf Creek Hotel."
4. Click the task pane item for the Pine Hotel text that you just cut. (Do not click the drop-down arrow.) The text is pasted at the location of the insertion point.
5. Press Ctrl+Z to undo the paste. Press Ctrl+Z again to undo the cut. The Clipboard item remains in the task pane.
6. Point to this Clipboard item in the task pane, and click the drop-down arrow that appears to its right.
7. Choose **Delete** from the list to delete the item from the Clipboard.

NOTE

Choosing the Paste option from the drop-down list pastes that item, just like clicking directly on the item. The Paste All button  on the Clipboard task pane is used to copy all Office Clipboard items to the location of the insertion point.

Moving Text by Dragging

You can also move selected text to a new location by using the *drag-and-drop* method. Text is not transferred to the Clipboard when you use drag and drop.

Exercise 6-6 USE DRAG AND DROP TO MOVE TEXT

1. Select all the information related to "Vacation Resort," including the title "Vacation Resort" and the blank line below the information.
2. Point to the selected text. Notice that the I-beam changes to a left-pointing arrow.
3. Click and hold down the left mouse button. The pointer changes to the drag-and-drop pointer. Notice the dotted insertion point near the tip of the arrow and the dotted box at the base of the arrow.
4. Drag the pointer until the dotted insertion point is positioned to the left of the line beginning "Wolf Creek Hotel." Release the mouse button. The paragraph moves to its new location, and the Paste Options button (Ctrl) appears.

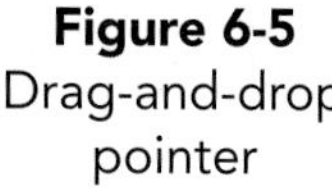

TIP

Use cut and paste to move text over long distances—for example, onto another page. Use drag and drop to move text short distances where you can see both the selected text and the destination on the screen at the same time.

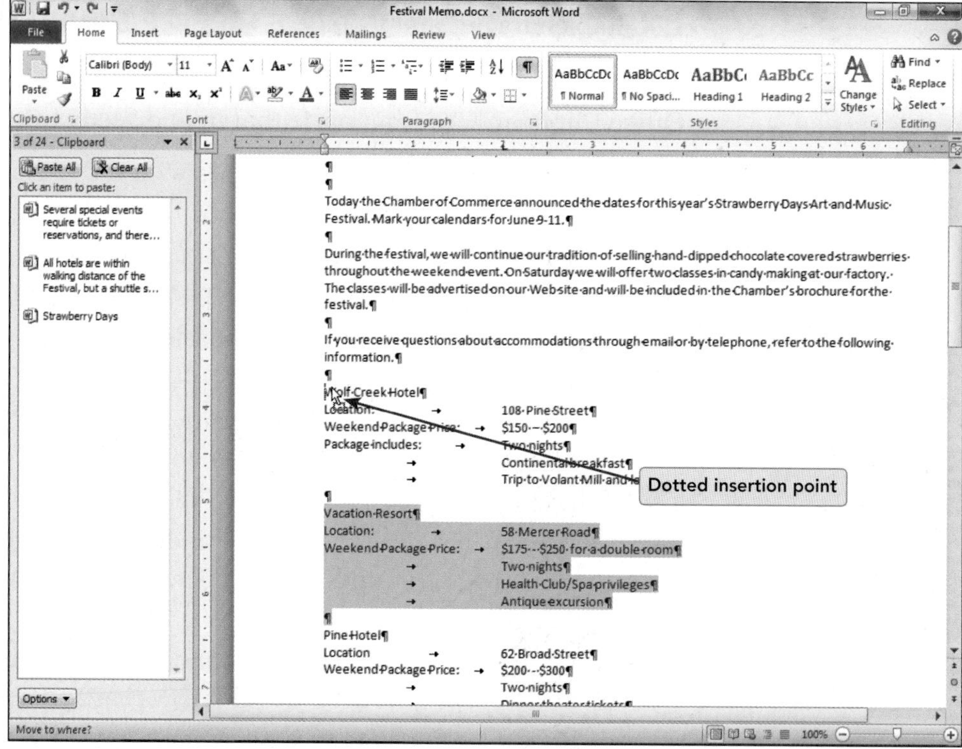

Figure 6-5
Drag-and-drop pointer

Copying Text by Using Copy and Paste

Copying and pasting text is similar to cutting and pasting text. Instead of removing the text from the document and storing it on the Clipboard, you place a copy of the text on the Clipboard.

There are several ways to copy and paste text. The most common methods are:

- Use the Copy and Paste buttons on the Ribbon, Home tab.
- Use the shortcut menu.
- Use keyboard shortcuts Ctrl+C to copy and Ctrl+V to paste.
- Use the Clipboard task pane.

Exercise 6-7 USE COPY AND PASTE

1. Under "Wolf Creek Hotel," select the entire line that contains the text "Continental breakfast." Include the tab character to the left of the text and the paragraph mark to the right of the text. If necessary, click the Show/Hide ¶ button ¶ to display formatting characters. (The selected text should begin at the left margin and end with the paragraph mark.)
2. Click the Copy button on the Ribbon to transfer a copy of the text to the Clipboard. Notice that the selected text remains in its original position in the document.
3. Position the insertion point to the left of the paragraph that begins with a tab character and includes "Health Club/Spa privileges" in the text under "Vacation Resort."
4. Click the Paste button. A copy of the paragraph is added to the "Vacation Resort" package description, and the Paste Options button (Ctrl) appears.
5. Point to the Paste Options button (Ctrl). When you see the down arrow, click the button. Notice that the same options are available when you copy and paste text. Click in the document window to close the list of options and keep the source formatting.
6. Position the insertion point to the left of the paragraph that begins "Dinner theater tickets." Press Ctrl+V to paste the text into the "Pine Hotel" package description.

Exercise 6-8 USE THE OFFICE CLIPBOARD TO PASTE COPIED TEXT

A new item is added to the Office Clipboard each time you copy text. You can click this item to paste the text into the document.

NOTE

You can store up to 24 cut or copied items on the Office Clipboard. When the Clipboard is full and you cut or copy text, the bottom Clipboard item is deleted and the new item is added to the top of the task pane.

1. Under "Vacation Resort," select the text "for a double room." Include the space character to the left of the text.
2. Press Ctrl+C to copy this text.
3. Position the insertion point to the right of the text that begins "$150–$200" in the Wolf Creek Hotel information.
4. Click the Clipboard that contains the text "for a double room." The Clipboard content is pasted into the document at the location of the insertion point.

Copying Text by Dragging

To copy text by using the drag-and-drop method, press Ctrl while dragging the text. Remember, drag and drop does not store text on the Clipboard.

Exercise 6-9 USE DRAG AND DROP TO COPY TEXT

NOTE

You may already have noticed that when you delete, cut, move, or paste text, Word automatically adjusts the spacing between words. For example, if you cut a word at the end of a sentence, Word automatically deletes the leftover space. If you paste a word between two other words, Word automatically adds the needed space as part of its Smart Cut-and-Paste feature. The Smart Cut-and Paste feature is turned on by default.

1. Scroll until you can see the text under "Wolf Creek Hotel" and "Pine Hotel."
2. Select the text under the Wolf Creek Hotel beginning with "for a double room."
3. While pressing Ctrl, drag the selected text to the immediate right of the text "$200–$300" in the "Pine Hotel" section. The plus (+) sign attached to the drag-and-drop pointer indicates the text is being copied rather than moved.
4. The text is copied, and a space is automatically inserted between "$300" and "for."

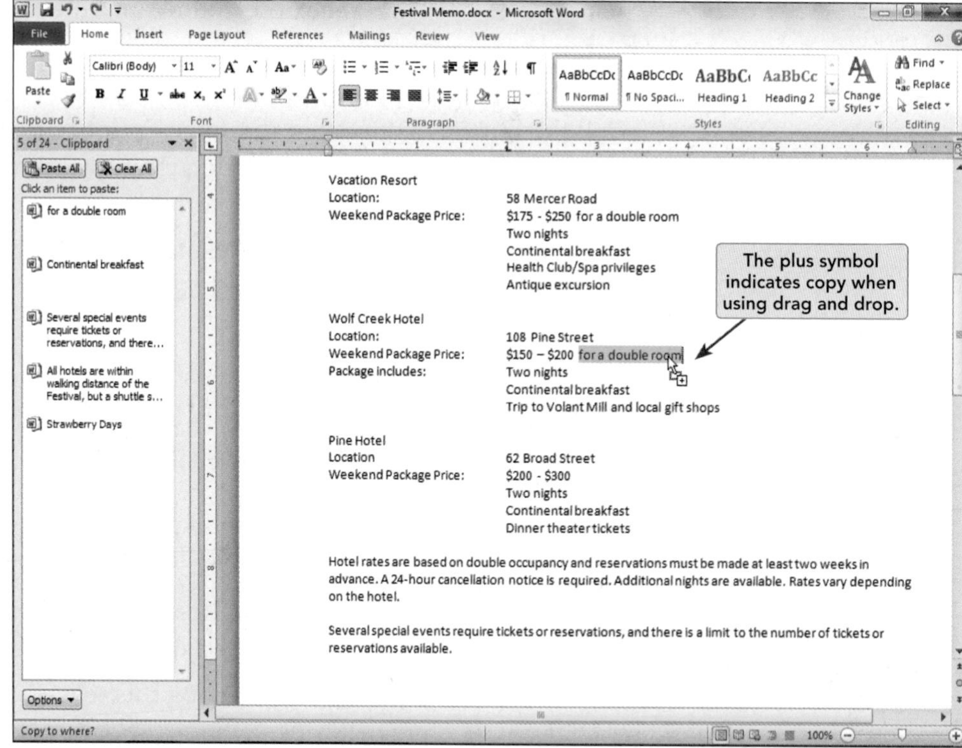

Figure 6-6
Copying with the drag-and-drop pointer

5. Move to the top of the document, and change the spacing before to 72 points, and insert your reference initials at the end of the document.

TIP

Dragging is not effective over long distances within a document. Try these alternative methods: To cut, select the text, hold down Ctrl, scroll as needed, and right-click where you want to paste the text. To copy, select the text, hold down Ctrl and Shift, scroll as needed, and right-click where you want to paste the text.

6. Open the File tab, and click Print. The Print tab displays. Drag the Zoom slider in the lower right corner to approximately 25% to see both pages of the document.
7. Save the document as ***[your initials]*6-9** in a new folder for Lesson 6.
8. Click the Clear All button Clear All on the Office Clipboard to clear all items. Click the Close button on the task pane to close the Office Clipboard.
9. Submit and close the document.

Working with Multiple Document Windows

In Word, you can work with several open document windows. Working with multiple windows makes it easy to compare different parts of the same document or to move or copy text from one document to another.

Exercise 6-10 SPLIT A DOCUMENT INTO PANES

Splitting a document divides it into two areas separated by a horizontal line called the *split bar.* Each of the resulting two areas, called *panes,* has its own scroll bar.

To split a screen, click the View tab and click the Split button or use the split box at the top of the vertical scroll bar.

1. Open the file **Fund2**.
2. Click the View tab and click the Split button. A gray bar appears along with the split pointer.
3. Move your mouse up or down (without clicking) until the gray bar is just below the second paragraph of the letter.

Figure 6-7
Splitting a document into two panes

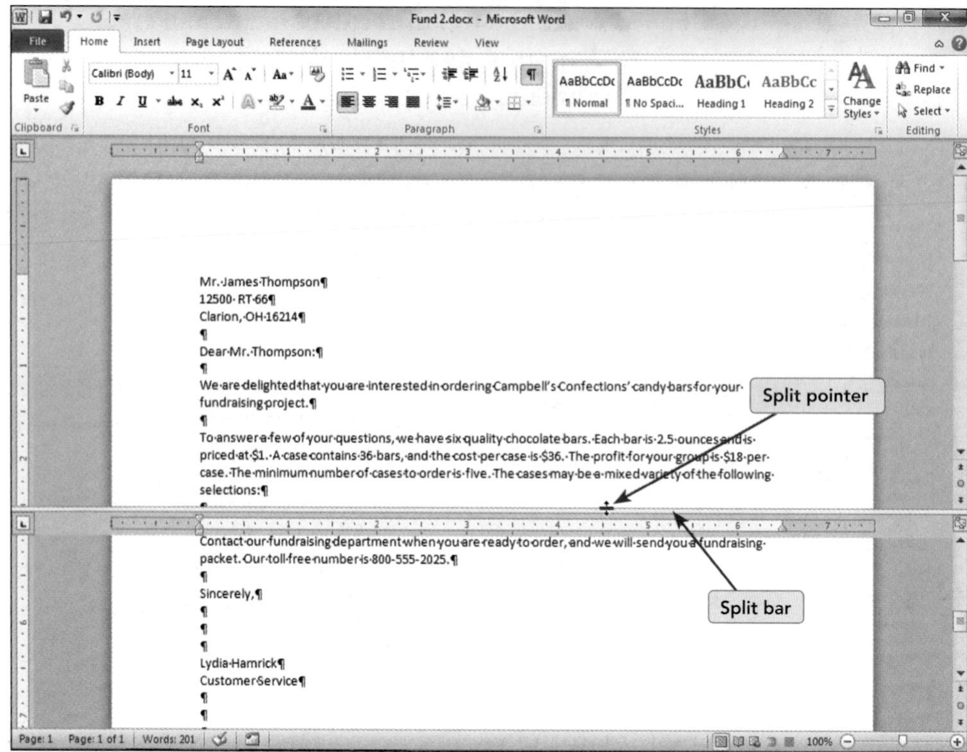

TIP

To see more of each document, you can hide the rulers by clicking the View Ruler button on the vertical scroll bar.

4. Click the left mouse button to set the split. The document divides into two panes, each with its own ruler and scroll bar.
5. To change the split position, move the mouse pointer over the split bar (between the top and bottom panes) until you see the split pointer and a ScreenTip that says "Resize." Then drag the bar above the list.
6. To remove the split bar, move the mouse pointer over it. When you see the split pointer, double-click. The split bar is removed.
7. Position the pointer over the *split box*—the thin gray rectangle at the top of the vertical scroll bar.
8. When you see the split pointer, double-click. Once again the document is split into two panes. (You can also remove the split bar by choosing Remove Split from the View tab.)

Figure 6-8
Double-clicking the split box to create two window panes

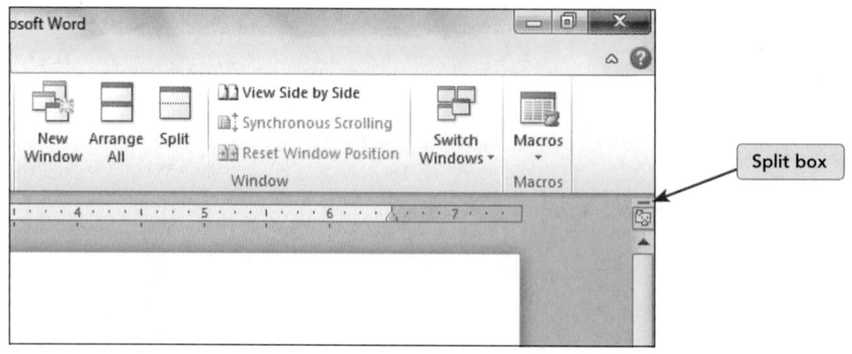

Exercise 6-11 MOVE BETWEEN PANES TO EDIT TEXT

After you split a document, you can scroll each pane separately and easily move from pane to pane to edit separate areas of the document. To switch panes, click the insertion point in the pane you want to edit.

1. Click in the top pane.
2. With the insertion point in the top pane, click the insertion point in the bottom pane.
3. Use the scroll bar in the bottom pane to scroll to the top of the document. Both panes should now show the inside address.
4. In the bottom pane, change the street address to **12575 Route 66** and the state to **PA**. Notice that the changes also appear in the top pane.
5. In the bottom pane, scroll until the paragraph beginning "Specialty fundraising" is displayed. Click within the top pane, and scroll until the paragraphs beginning "Specialty fundraising" and "There are no" are both displayed.
6. Go back to the bottom pane. Select the paragraph beginning "Specialty fundraising," and click the Cut button on the Home tab. (Remember to include the blank line after the paragraph when selecting it.)
7. Move to the top pane, position the insertion point to the left of "There are no," and click the Paste button. The paragraph is moved from one part of the document to another.
8. Drag the split bar to the top of the screen. This is another way to remove the split bar. The document is again displayed in one pane.
9. Apply the correct letter formatting to the document by adding the date and your reference initials. Use the correct spacing between all letter elements, and place 72 points spacing before the date.
10. Save the document as ***[your initials]*6-11** in your Lesson 6 folder.
11. Submit and close the document.

NOTE

Editing in a pane is the same as editing in a single window. It is important to understand that the changes you make to one pane affect the entire document.

TIP

See Appendix B, "Standard Forms for Business Documents," for standard business letter formatting.

Exercise 6-12 OPEN MULTIPLE DOCUMENTS

In addition to working with window panes, you can work with more than one document file at the same time. This is useful if you keyed text in one document that you want to use in a second document.

NOTE

Noncontiguous files are files that are not listed consecutively. You can open several noncontiguous files at the same time if you keep Ctrl pressed while selecting additional files.

1. Display the **Open** dialog box. Simultaneously open the noncontiguous files **Bittersweet** and **Milk Chocolate**. To do this, click **Bittersweet** once, press Ctrl, and click **Milk Chocolate** once. With both files selected, click **Open**.
2. Click the **View** tab. Click the Switch Windows button, and notice that the two open files are listed at the bottom of the list. The active file has a check next to it. Switch documents by clicking the file that is not active.
3. Press Ctrl+F6 to switch back.
4. Point to the Word button in the Windows taskbar. The button expands to display thumbnails for each open document. Move the mouse from one thumbnail to another to preview the documents and to change the active document. Click the **Bittersweet** button to activate that document.

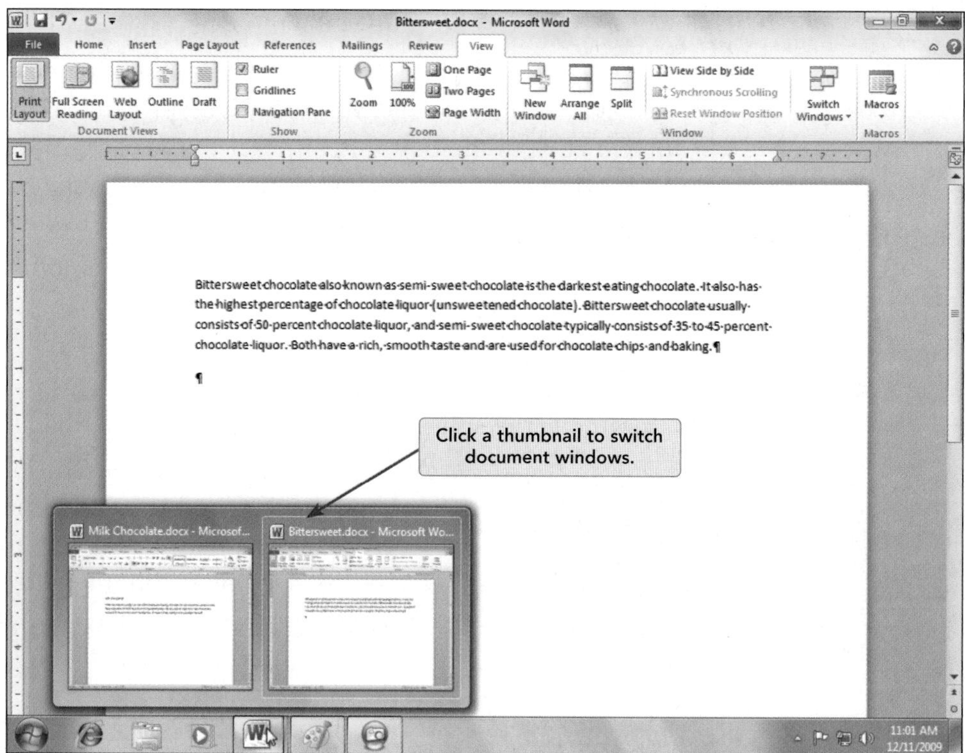

Figure 6-9
Switching document windows using the taskbar

NOTE

Your screen may display separate buttons for each document in the task bar.

5. Click the **View** tab, if necessary. Click the Arrange All button to view both documents at the same time. The two documents appear one below the other.

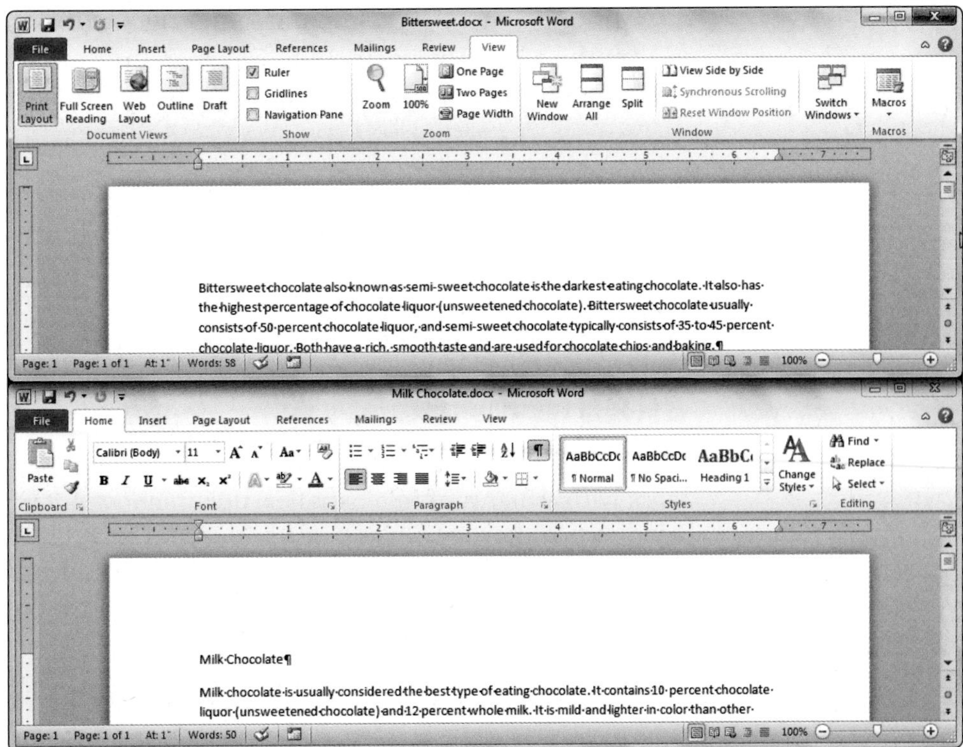

Figure 6-10
Two documents displayed on one screen

6. Press Ctrl+F6 to switch between documents. Press Ctrl+F6 again. Notice that the active window—the one containing the insertion point—has a highlighted title bar.
7. Close the **Bittersweet** and **Milk Chocolate** documents.
8. Start Word if necessary, or click the Maximize button to maximize the Word window.
9. Simultaneously open three files, **Bittersweet**, **Chocolate - 2**, and **Milk Chocolate**, by accessing the Open dialog box. Select the first file, **Bittersweet**, and then press Ctrl and select the other two files. Click Open.
10. Choose Arrange All from the View tab to display all three documents simultaneously.

Exercise 6-13 REARRANGE AND RESIZE DOCUMENT WINDOWS

You can rearrange the open documents in Word by using basic Windows techniques for minimizing, maximizing, restoring, and sizing windows.

1. Click the **Bittersweet** title bar, and drag this document's window toward the top of the screen. Click the Close button for **Chocolate - 2**. Click the Maximize button for **Milk Chocolate**.

2. Minimize the **Milk Chocolate** window by clicking its Minimize button. The document disappears from view. The **Milk Chocolate** button is on the taskbar, indicating that Word is still running.
3. Restore the **Milk Chocolate** document for viewing by clicking its taskbar button.
4. Click the Close button for **Milk Chocolate**. Close the **Bittersweet** document.

Moving and Copying Text among Windows

When you want to copy or move text from one document to another, you can work with either multiple (smaller) document windows or full-size document windows. Either way, you can use cut and paste or copy and paste. If you work with multiple windows, you can also use drag and drop. To use this technique, you must display both documents at the same time.

Exercise 6-14 COPY TEXT FROM ONE DOCUMENT TO ANOTHER BY USING COPY AND PASTE

When moving or copying text from one document into another, the paste default is to paste text in the format of the document from which it was cut or copied. To control the formatting of pasted text, you can use the Paste Options gallery or the Paste Special function. In this exercise, you will use the Paste Options gallery to paste text without formatting.

1. Open the files **Bittersweet**, **Chocolate - 2**, and **Milk Chocolate**. Click the **Bittersweet** button on the taskbar to make it the active document. Maximize the window if necessary.
2. In the **Bittersweet** document, select the entire document and change the font to 12-point Arial. Click the Copy button.
3. Switch to the **Chocolate - 2** document. Maximize the window if necessary.
4. Click the insertion point at the beginning of the paragraph that begins "Sweet or." Press Ctrl+V to insert the text copied from **Bittersweet**. Notice the format of the new text does not match the format of the current document.
5. Click the Paste Options button (Ctrl), or press Ctrl to display the Paste Options gallery.
6. Point to the first option in the gallery. The Keep Source Formatting button previews the pasted text, and the text retains the 12-point Arial format.

TIP

You can insert an entire file into the current document by using the Insert tab. Move the insertion point to the place in the document where you want to insert the file. Then from the Insert tab, click the Object button. Click Text from File and double-click the file name. The text from the entire file is inserted at the insertion point.

7. Point to the second option in the Paste Options gallery. The Merge Formatting button previews the pasted text, and the text matches the destination document format.
8. Point to the fourth option in the Paste Options gallery. The Keep Text Only button previews the text with no format. The format from the destination document (12-point Arial) is removed from the text.
9. Choose the second option, Merge Formatting.

TABLE 6-1 Paste Options

Paste Gallery Icon	Option	Description
	Keep Source Formatting (K)	Text retains format from the source (original) document.
	Merge Formatting (M)	Format for copied text matches the destination document format.
	Use Destination Theme (H)	Format for copied text matches the destination styles format.
A	Keep Text Only (T)	The formatting from the source (original) document is removed, and the pasted text displays as plain, unformatted text.
Set Default Paste...	Set Default Paste	Use this feature to control the default settings. When pasting within the same document, pasting between documents, or pasting from other programs, the default setting is to keep source formatting.

10. Click the **View** tab, and click the Switch Windows button to activate **Bittersweet** again. Close this document without saving it.

Exercise 6-15 MOVE TEXT FROM ONE DOCUMENT TO ANOTHER BY USING DRAG AND DROP

1. Arrange the two open documents (**Milk Chocolate** and **Chocolate - 2**), so they are both displayed.
2. Switch to the **Milk Chocolate** document, and select the paragraph below the title.
3. Drag the selected paragraph to the **Chocolate - 2** document, and position the insertion point in front of the paragraph that begins "Sweet or."

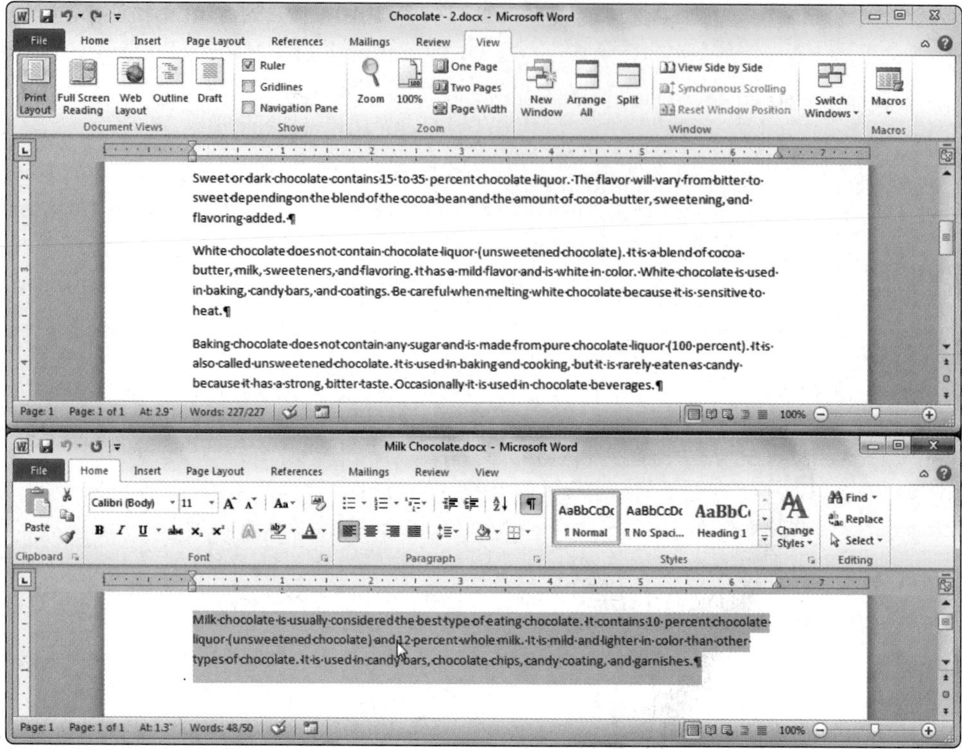

Figure 6-11
Dragging a paragraph between document windows

4. Close the **Milk Chocolate** document without saving.
5. Maximize the **Chocolate - 2** document. Correct the spacing between paragraphs (if you have extra paragraph marks, for example).
6. At the top of the document, add the title **TYPES OF CHOCOLATE**, formatted as 14-point bold and centered. Add 72 points spacing before and 24 points spacing after the title.
7. Save the document as ***[your initials]*6-15** in your Lesson 6 folder; then submit and close it.

Lesson 6 Summary

- The most important tool for moving and copying text is the Clipboard, which is a temporary storage space.
- When you display the Clipboard task pane, you are activating the Office Clipboard, which can store up to 24 cut or copied items. With the Clipboard task pane open, cut or copied text appears as a new item in the task pane.
- You move text by cutting and pasting—cut the text from one location and paste it to another.
- Copy and paste is similar to cut and paste, but instead of removing the text from the document, you place a copy of it on the Clipboard.

- There are many methods for cutting, copying, and pasting text. Use buttons on the Ribbon, keyboard shortcuts, or the shortcut menu. Use the Clipboard task pane to paste stored text items.
- Use the Paste Options button to control the formatting of pasted text.
- You can use the drag-and-drop method to copy or move text from one location to another in a document or between documents.
- Split a document into panes to compare different parts of the document or to cut or copy text from one part of the document to another. Use the View tab or the split box above the vertical scroll bar to split a document.
- Open multiple documents and arrange them to fit on one screen to move or copy text from one document to another.

LESSON 6		**Command Summary**	
Feature	**Button**	**Command**	**Keyboard**
Arrange multiple windows		View tab, Window group	
Copy		Home tab, Clipboard group	Ctrl+C
Cut		Home tab, Clipboard group	Ctrl+X
Insert file	Object	Insert tab, Text group	
Next window		View tab, Window group, Switch Windows, <*file name*>	Ctrl+F6
Open Office Clipboard		Home tab, Clipboard group	Ctrl+C twice
Paste		Home tab, Clipboard group	Ctrl+V
Previous window		View tab, Window group, Switch Windows, <*file name*>	Ctrl+Shift+F6
Split a document		View tab, Window group	

Concepts Review

True/False Questions

Each of the following statements is either true or false. Indicate your choice by circling T or F.

T F 1. Drag and drop stores text on the clipboard.

T F 2. The content of the Office Clipboard is replaced each time you copy or cut text.

T F 3. The keyboard shortcut for cut is Ctrl+C.

T F 4. You can drag text between two documents when both windows are maximized.

T F 5. The Cut, Copy, and Paste commands are all available from the shortcut menu.

T F 6. The only difference between cut and copy is that selected text remains in the document after copying.

T F 7. When you move a paragraph, you should select the blank line following it to preserve proper line spacing.

T F 8. When a document is split into panes, you can remove the split by double-clicking the split bar.

Short Answer Questions

Write the correct answer in the space provided.

1. How can you copy text without using the Clipboard?

___

2. Which buttons on the Ribbon, Home tab, do you use to move text?

___

3. What is the keyboard shortcut for moving between two documents?

___

4. For which command is Ctrl+V the keyboard shortcut?

___

5. Which command displays all open documents at the same time?

___

6. What is the keyboard shortcut to undo?

___

7. What is different about the drag-and-drop pointer when you are copying, as opposed to moving, text?

---

8. Where is the split box located?

Critical Thinking

Answer these questions on a separate page. There are no right or wrong answers. Support your answers with examples from your own experience, if possible.

1. Many people once wrote first-draft documents by hand or by using a typewriter. In either case, people would then literally cut and paste pieces of their document together and type a final draft. Some people say that word processing—specifically moving and copying text—has caused a basic change in the way people write. What do you think? Explain your answer.
2. You have learned different methods for moving text by using cut and paste. You also learned the drag-and-drop method of moving text. Which method do you prefer? Why? Include advantages and disadvantages.

Skills Review

Exercise 6-16

Move text to a new location by using cut and paste and by dragging.

1. Open the file **Property**.
2. Display the Office Clipboard by following these steps:
   a. Click the Home tab, and click the Clipboard Dialog Box Launcher.
   b. Click Clear All [Clear All] if there are any items in the task pane.
3. Use keyboard shortcuts to move text by following these steps:
   a. Click the insertion point at the beginning of the line that starts "Equipment – office." Press and hold [Shift]. Click at the end of the line beginning "Key employees."
   b. Press [Ctrl]+[X] to cut the text.
   c. Position the insertion point to the left of the line that begins "Types of coverage."
   d. Press [Ctrl]+[V] to paste the text. Press [Enter] to add a line space between the paragraphs.

4. Drag text by following these steps:
   a. Select the text "All employees" through "Customers."
   b. Point to the selected text. Press and hold down the left mouse button to display the drag-and-drop pointer and the dotted insertion point.
   c. Drag the dotted insertion point to the left of the word "Research," and release the mouse button.
   d. Press Enter after "Customers."
5. Use the Ribbon to cut and paste text by following these steps:
   a. Select the text "Fire" through "Loss of income."
   b. Click the Cut button.
   c. Position the insertion point at the beginning of the line that starts "Who to cover."
   d. Click the Paste button.
   e. Press Enter.
6. Select "Types of insurance." Press Ctrl and select "Types of coverage," "Who to cover," and "Research."
7. Apply 12-point bold, small caps format to the selected text. A blank line should precede each heading.
8. Clear and close the Office Clipboard by following these steps:
   a. Click Clear All Clear All to remove all Clipboard items.
   b. Click the task pane's Close button.
9. Select the title of the document, and change it to 14-point bold uppercase, and apply 72 points spacing before and 24 points spacing after.
10. Save the document as ***[your initials]*****6-16** in your Lesson 6 folder.
11. Submit and close the document.

Exercise 6-17

Copy text by using copy and paste and by dragging.

1. Open the file **Stores - 2**.
2. Display the Office Clipboard, and clear the Office Clipboard if it contains any items.
3. Select text in the document beginning with "Pennsylvania" through the end of the document.
4. Set a left tab at 2 inches on the ruler.
5. Position the insertion point to the right of "Grove City," and press Tab. Key **Carole Walters**.

6. Use the Office Clipboard to copy text by following these steps:
   a. Select the tab character (→) and "Carole Walters." (Do not select the paragraph mark at the end of the line.)
   b. Click the Copy button to copy the text to a Clipboard.
   c. Position the insertion point to the right of "Meadville."
   d. Paste the text by clicking the Clipboard.
7. Position the insertion point to the right of "Clarksburg" and press Tab. Key **Rebecca Surrena**.
8. Select the tab character and "Rebecca Surrena," and press Ctrl+C to place the selected text on a clipboard.
9. Position the insertion point to the right of "Fairmont," and press Ctrl+V.
10. Use the drag-and-drop method to copy "Carole Walters" by following these steps:
    a. Select the tab character and the text "Carole Walters."
    b. Point to the text. Press and hold down Ctrl; then click and hold down the left mouse button.
    c. Drag the dotted insertion point to the right of the word "Mercer," and release both the mouse button and Ctrl.
11. Click to the right of "Butler," press Tab, and key **Cynthia Rhodes**. Select the tab character and the text you just keyed, and copy it to the clipboard.
12. Click to the right of "Akron," press Tab, and key **Jane Daniels**. Select the tab character and the text you just keyed and copy it to the clipboard. The clipboard should contain four names. Paste the text "Jane Daniels" to all cities listed under Ohio.
13. Use the Clipboard task pane to paste the text "Carole Walters" to the following cities: Edinboro, Erie, Sharon, Greenville, and Franklin.
14. Use the Clipboard task pane to paste the text "Rebecca Surrena" to Morgantown and Wheeling.
15. Use the Clipboard task pane to paste the text "Cynthia Rhodes" to New Castle, Pittsburgh, and Monroeville.
16. Bold and center the two lines at the top of the document. Format the first line in all caps and 16 points and 72 points spacing before. Format the second line in small caps and 14 points.
17. Format each of the state names as bold, italic, and small caps.
18. Select the text from "Pennsylvania" through the end of the document, and format the selected text with a 1-inch left indent. Drag the left tab marker on the ruler to 4 inches.
19. Clear and close the Office Clipboard.
20. Save the document as ***[your initials]*6-17** in your Lesson 6 folder.
21. Submit and close the document.

Exercise 6-18

Split a document into panes.

1. Open the file **Favors - 2**
2. Split the document into two panes by double-clicking the split box above the View Ruler button and the vertical scroll bar.
3. In the top pane, use the scroll bar to display the list beginning with "wedding bells" through "other assorted shapes." Format the selected text as a bulleted list.
4. In the bottom pane, scroll to the list that begins with "solid milk chocolate." Sort the list alphabetically.
5. In the bottom pane, format the list of chocolate squares as a bulleted list.
6. Remove the split by double-clicking the split bar.
7. Scroll through the document to view the changes.
8. Apply bold formatting to the title and change the spacing before to 72 points and the spacing after to 24 points.
9. Place the insertion point in the title line and apply a bottom border.
10. Save the document as ***[your initials]*6-18** in your Lesson 6 folder.
11. Submit and close the document.

REVIEW

Click the Sort button in the Paragraph group on the Home tab.

Exercise 6-19

Arrange windows to move and copy text.

1. Start a new document. Key the text shown in Figure 6-12, and format it as a standard business memo. Use single spacing and 0 points spacing after for the body of the memo, and include today's date. Format the first line of the heading to include 72 points spacing before.

Figure 6-12

```
Memo to Robert Smith from Pete Barnes

Subject is Vehicle Reports

Please review the following, and let me know if the
information provided is compatible with the new fleet
management software.

Mileage numbers will be provided the first of each month.
```

2. Save the document as ***[your initials]*6-19** in your Lesson 6 folder.
3. Simultaneously open the files **Vehicle** and **Maintenance**.
4. Arrange the documents by following these steps:
   a. Switch to **Maintenance** if necessary, and minimize it by clicking the Minimize button.
   b. Display the other two documents at the same time by clicking the **View** tab and clicking **Arrange All**.
5. Drag a paragraph between documents by following these steps:
   a. In the ***[your initials]*6-19** window, scroll to display the sentence beginning "Mileage numbers."
   b. In the **Vehicle** window, select the entire document by pressing Ctrl+A.
   c. Holding down Ctrl to copy, drag the paragraph to the ***[your initials]*6-19** window until it precedes the paragraph beginning "Mileage." Select the copied text and change the line spacing to single and the spacing after to 0 if necessary.
6. Close the **Vehicle** document and restore the **Maintenance** document by clicking its taskbar button.
7. Use **View tab**, **Arrange All** to display ***[your initials]*6-19** and **Maintenance** at the same time, if necessary.
8. In **Maintenance**, select the text beginning "Scheduled Maintenance Guide" through the blank line preceding "10,000 miles." Copy and paste this text to the end of ***[your initials]*6-19**. If necessary, add a blank line before "Scheduled Maintenance Guide." If necessary, change the line spacing to single and the spacing after to 0.
9. Close the **Maintenance** document without saving it. Maximize ***[your initials]*6-19**. Format the entire document in 12-point Cambria. Insert your reference initials at the bottom of the memo.
10. Select "Vehicle Listing" and "Scheduled Maintenance Guide," and format each heading with 14-point bold and small caps. Format the column headings of the tabbed text to bold, small caps, and underlined.
11. Save the document again.
12. Submit and close the document.

Lesson Applications

Exercise 6-20

Move and copy text.

1. Open the file **OH Stores - 2**.
2. Move the address text for the Cleveland store to follow the address text for the Canton store.
3. Click on the blank line following the Akron address, and key the following text on two lines. Press Enter after each line.

   Telephone:
   Fax:

4. Select "Telephone:" and "Fax:" and copy the text to the Clipboard.
5. Paste the copied text at the end of each address using F4 to repeat the past action.
6. Format the document heading as uppercase, bold, and 14 points with 72 points of spacing before and 24 points of spacing after. Delete the blank paragraph mark below the heading.
7. Apply bold-italic and small caps formatting to each store name. (Hint: Use Format Painter or select each store name before applying the character format.)
8. Save the document as ***[your initials]*6-20** in your Lesson 6 folder.
9. Submit and close the document.

Exercise 6-21

Copy and move text in a memo.

1. Open the file **Walk**.
2. At the top of the document, insert a memo heading to the staff from you, using today's date.
3. Move the first line in the document (which begins "Getting ready") to the subject line, and apply italic formatting. In the subject line, replace "walk" with a copy of the words "Chamber of Commerce Walk-a-Thon" found in the paragraph that begins "Here is." Apply the appropriate capitalization to the subject line.
4. Delete the punctuation at the end of the subject line and extra blank lines below the subject line.

5. In the paragraph that begins "Once again," move the last sentence (beginning with "We are") to the end of the document as a separate paragraph.
6. At the top of the document, combine the paragraphs that begin "Once again" and "Here is."
7. In the paragraph that begins "We need," delete the words "We need a volunteer to" and capitalize the next word "check."
8. Format the three action paragraphs, beginning "Arrange," "Check," and "Contact," as a numbered list.
9. Format the two uppercase and blue headings as uppercase, bold, black, and with 6 points of spacing after them.
10. Save the document as ***[your initials]*6-21** in your Lesson 6 folder.
11. Submit and close the document.

REVIEW

Remember to add your reference initials to the memo.

Exercise 6-22

Copy text from multiple documents into an existing document.

1. Open the file **Holtz**. Copy the inside address and salutation. Close the document without saving.
2. Create a new document. Click the **Home** tab. Locate the Styles group, and click the No Spacing button in the Styles gallery.
3. Insert the date using the Insert tab on the Ribbon. (Use appropriate format for a business letter.) Press Enter four times, and paste the copied text. Format the date with 72 points spacing before.
4. For the first paragraph of the new letter, key the text shown in Figure 6-13.

Figure 6-13

```
I am looking forward to your visit to Grove City in June.
You will be staying at the Wolf Creek Hotel as our guest.
```

5. From the file **Wolf Creek**, copy the second paragraph, beginning "The hotel has 200 rooms," and paste it at the end of the paragraph you keyed in step 4. Delete the last sentence in the paragraph.
6. Start a new paragraph by keying **When you arrive, the Strawberry Days Arts and Music Festival will be in full swing.**
7. From the file **Summer**, copy the last sentence of the first paragraph, and paste it at the end of the sentence you just keyed. Edit the beginning of the sentence to "You can enjoy."

8. Key the text shown in Figure 6-14 as a closing paragraph.

Figure 6-14

```
Jack, I am delighted that you are coming to Grove City! I
know you are going to have a great time at the Festival
and touring our facilities.
```

9. Add an appropriate closing. The letter is from Thomas Campbell, President.
10. Check for correct spacing, and spell-check the document.
11. Save the document as ***[your initials]*6-22** in your Lesson 6 folder. Submit and close the document.
12. Close all other open documents without saving them.

Exercise 6-23 ◆ Challenge Yourself

Copy text from multiple documents to create a new document.

1. Start a new document. Key the title **WEST VIRGINIA CONTACT INFORMATION** in 12-point Arial. Center the title and apply bold formatting.
2. Insert two blank lines after the title.
3. Save the document as ***[your initials]*6-23** in your Lesson 6 folder. Keep the document open.
4. Open the files **Stores - 3**, **WV Managers**, and **WV Stores**.
5. Refer to the three open documents to create a new document that includes the name and complete address for each store, the telephone and fax numbers for each store, the name of the store manager, and the name of the account executive.
6. Use tabs to arrange the text attractively.
7. Format document headings to include character and paragraph formatting.
8. Add 72 points of spacing before the first line in the document (the title). Increase the size of the title to 14 points.
9. Save the document again.
10. Submit and close the document.

On Your Own

In these exercises, you work on your own, as you would in a real-life business environment. Use the skills you've learned to accomplish the task—and be creative.

Exercise 6-24

Write a short proposal for implementing a change in your city, neighborhood, or school. Make the proposal at least three paragraphs long. At the end of the document, create a bulleted summary of the proposal, copying and pasting text from the proposal for the bulleted items. Save the document as ***[your initials]*6-24** and submit it.

Exercise 6-25

Copy text from the Internet about a person (present day or historical) you admire. Use Paste Options to paste the text, without formatting, into a new document. Apply your own character and paragraph formatting. Save the document as ***[your initials]*6-25** and submit it.

Exercise 6-26

Write a summary about a TV show or video you have recently seen. Save it as ***[your initials]*6-26a**. Keep this document open, and start a new document. Begin a letter to a friend, telling him or her about the TV show or video. Copy and paste or drag and drop text from the summary document into the letter. Save the document as ***[your initials]*6-26b** and submit both documents.

Lesson 7

Find and Replace

OBJECTIVES ***After completing this lesson, you will be able to:***

1. Find text.
2. Find and replace text.
3. Find and replace special characters.
4. Find and replace formatting.

Estimated Time: 1¼ hours

When you create documents, especially long documents, you often need to review or change text. In Word, you can do this quickly by using the Find and Replace commands.

The *Find* command locates specified text and formatting in a document. The *Replace* command finds the text and formatting and replaces it automatically with a specified alternative.

Finding Text

Instead of scrolling through a document, you can use the Find command to locate text or to move quickly to a specific document location.

Two ways to use find are:

- Ribbon, Home tab, Editing group, Find command.
- Press Ctrl+F.

You can use the Find command to locate whole words, words that sound alike, font and paragraph formatting, and special characters. You can search an entire document or only selected text and specify the direction of the search. In the following exercise, you use find to locate all occurrences of the word "Campbell."

Exercise 7-1 FIND TEXT

1. Open the file **Stevenson - 1**.
2. Click the **Home** tab, and locate the **Editing** group. Click the Find button to open the Navigation Pane.

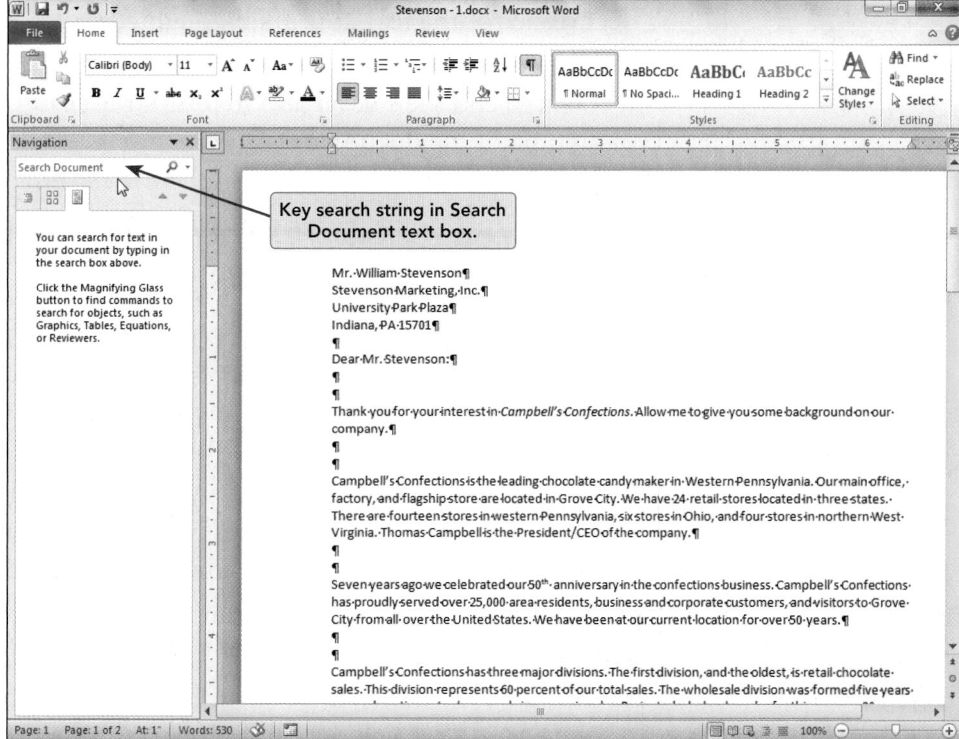

Figure 7-1
Navigation Pane

3. Delete any text in the **Search Document** text box, and key **Campbell**.
4. Notice that each occurrence of Campbell appears highlighted in the document and that 10 matches were located. The Campbell text string was located as a whole word and within a word such as "Campbell's."
5. Click the Next Search Result button to move to the first occurrence of Campbell. A box displays around the first entry in the Navigation Pane, and the first occurrence in the document appears highlighted. Notice that the search text "Campbell" is embedded within "Campbell's" and includes italic formatting.
6. Click the Next Search Result button two more times. Each time you click the Next Search Result button the next block of text appears highlighted in the Navigation Pane.
7. Click the Previous Search Result button two times to return to the first occurrence of "Campbell."
8. Click the Browse the pages button to display document pages in the Navigation Pane. Click the thumbnail for page 2 of the document. The second page of the document displays in the document window. Click the thumbnail for page 1.

9. Click the Browse the results button to display the search results in the Navigation Pane.
10. Click the Navigation Pane Close button to close the Navigation Pane.
11. Place the insertion point at the beginning of the paragraph that begins "Thank you." Press Ctrl+F to open the Navigation Pane.
12. Key **Campbell's Confections** in the **Search Document** text box. Every occurrence of the text appears highlighted.
13. Click the End Search button to the right of the Search Document text box to end the search and to return the insertion point to the first paragraph of the document.

Exercise 7-2 FIND TEXT BY USING THE MATCH CASE OPTION

The Find command includes options for locating words or phrases that meet certain criteria. One of these options is Match case, which locates text that matches the case of text keyed in the Search text box. The next exercise demonstrates how the Match case option narrows the search when using the Find command.

1. Move to the end of the document by pressing Ctrl+End. Position the insertion point to the right of "Hamrick" in the closing.
2. Delete any text in the **Search Document** text box, and key **confections**. Eight matches appear highlighted in the document.
3. Click the End Search button to end the search.
4. Click the down arrow to the right of the **Search Document** text box, and click **Options** to open the **Find Options** dialog box.

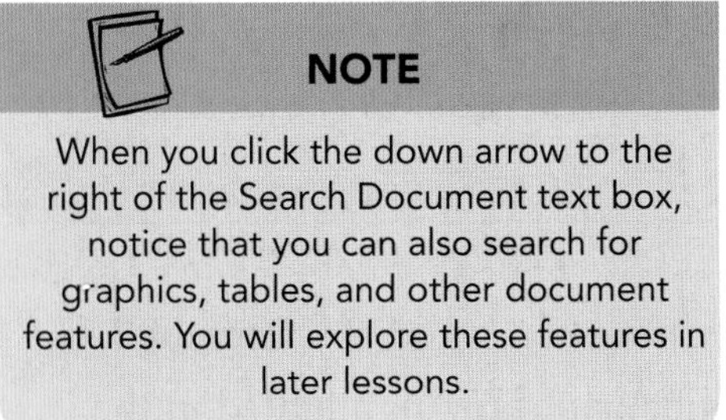

NOTE

When you click the down arrow to the right of the Search Document text box, notice that you can also search for graphics, tables, and other document features. You will explore these features in later lessons.

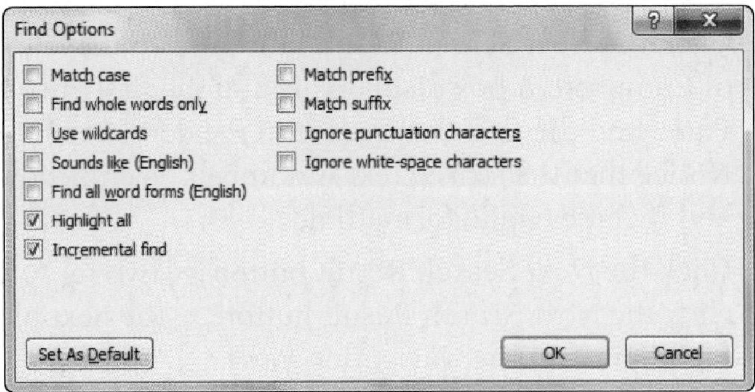

Figure 7-2
Find Options dialog box

5. Click the **Match case** check box to select this option. Click **OK** to close the Find Options dialog box.

6. Key **confections** in the **Search Document** text box, and notice that only one occurrence appears highlighted.
7. Close the Navigation Pane.

Exercise 7-3 FIND TEXT BY USING THE FIND WHOLE WORDS ONLY OPTION

The Find whole words only option is another way to narrow the search criteria. Word locates separate words but not characters embedded in other words.

1. Move the insertion point to the beginning of the document. Press Ctrl+F to open the Navigation Pane.
2. Key **or** in the Search Document text box. Forty-nine matches appear highlighted. Notice that almost every occurrence appears as embedded text within a word.
3. Click × to clear the Search text box.
4. Click the down arrow to the right of the **Search Document** text box, and click **Options** to open the Find Options dialog box.
5. Click the **Find whole words only** check box to select the option, click to deselect the **Match case** option, and click **OK** to close the Find Options dialog box.
6. Key **or** in the Search Document text box. Only two matches appear highlighted as a result of narrowing the search to whole words.
7. Open the **Find Options** dialog box, and clear the **Find whole words only** option. Close the Navigation Pane.

NOTE

When you select Match case, Find whole words only, or other options in the Find Options dialog box, the options are selected until you deselect them. When you finish a search, the selected options are not deselected automatically. You must open the Find Options dialog box to deselect the options.

Exercise 7-4 FIND TEXT BY USING THE WILDCARD OPTION

You can use the wildcard option to search for text strings using special search operators. A *wildcard* is a symbol that stands for missing or unknown text. For example, the Any Character wildcard "?" finds any character. Using the "?" wildcard, a search for "b?te" would find both "bite" and "byte." The question mark is replaced by a character that follows "b" and precedes "te."

Search options are available in the Find Options dialog box and the Find and Replace dialog box. The Find and Replace dialog box includes options to find formatting and special characters.

TABLE 7-1 Search Options in the Find and Replace Dialog Box

Option	Description
Sounds like	Word locates words that have a similar pronunciation to the keyed text. Example: In the practice document, key "ur" in the Find what text box, and study the results.
Find all word forms (English)	Use this feature to find noun or adjective forms or verb tenses. Example: In the practice document, key "are" in the Find what text box.
Match prefix	Select this feature to locate text that appears at the beginning of a word.
Match suffix	Select this feature to locate text that appears at the end of a word.
Ignore punctuation characters	Select this feature to ignore punctuation in the search.
Ignore white-space characters	Select this feature to ignore space between words.

1. Position the insertion point at the beginning of the document, and click the down arrow ▾ to the right of the Find command in the Editing group on the Home tab. Click **Advanced Find** to open the **Find and Replace** dialog box with the **Find** tab displayed.

Figure 7-3
Find and Replace dialog box

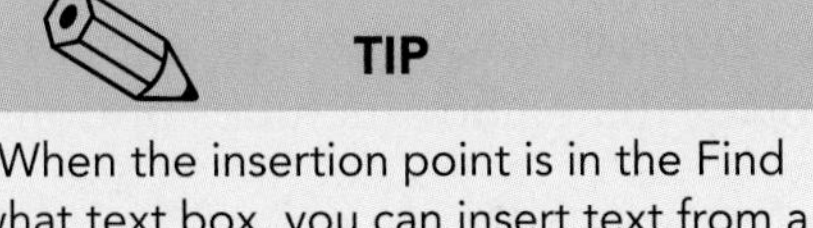

TIP

When the insertion point is in the Find what text box, you can insert text from a previous search by clicking the down arrow to the right of the Find what text box and choosing the appropriate option. The drop-down list includes the last seven search strings.

2. Click the More button [More >>] to display the expanded dialog box and click **Use wildcards** to select this option.
3. Select and delete text in the **Find what** text box, and key **ca**.
4. Click the Special button [Special ▾], and choose **Any Character** from the list. The "^?" is inserted.

Figure 7-4
Choosing a special search operator

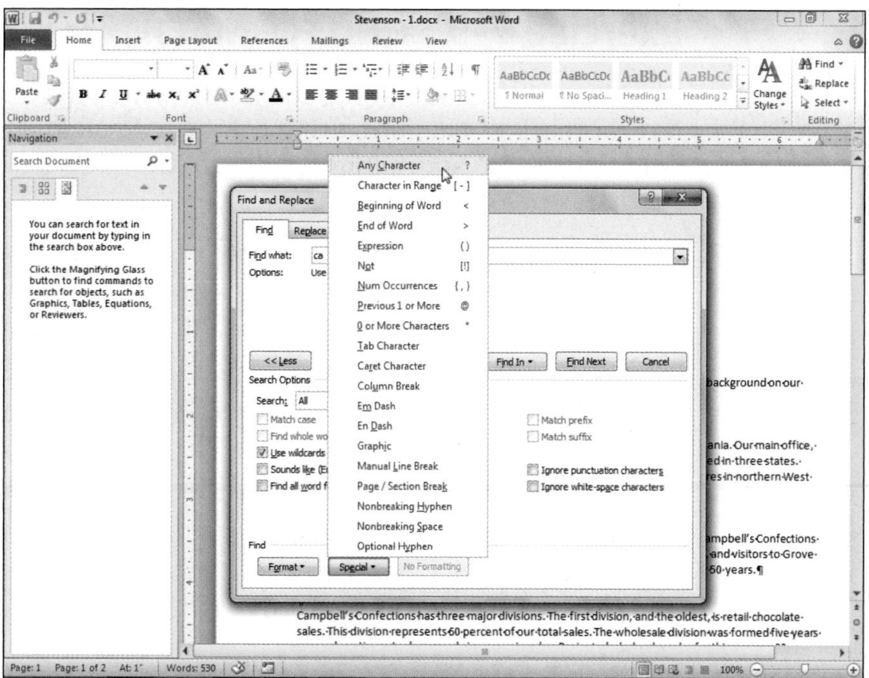

TIP

Press Esc to cancel a search. You can also interrupt a search by clicking outside the Find and Replace dialog box, editing the document text, and then clicking the dialog box to reactivate it.

TIP

After you initiate a find by using the Find and Replace dialog box, you can close the dialog box and use the Next Find/Go To button and Previous Find/Go To button located at the bottom of the vertical scroll bar to continue the search without having the dialog box in your way. (See Figure 7-5.)

5. Choose **All** from the **Search** direction drop-down list, if it is not already selected. Then click **Less** to collapse the dialog box.
6. Click **Find Next**. The first occurrence appears highlighted.
7. Continue clicking **Find Next** and notice all the occurrences of "ca^?" in the document. Both lowercase and uppercase words are highlighted in the search for "ca^?"
8. Click **OK** in the dialog box that says Word finished searching the document.
9. Click **Cancel** to close the Find and Replace dialog box.

Figure 7-5
Finding text without the Find and Replace dialog box

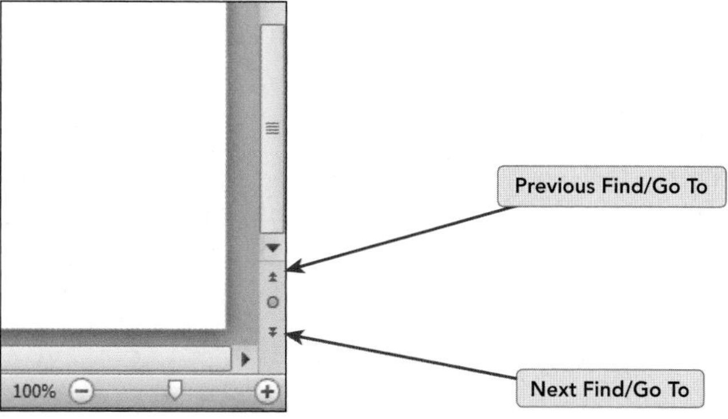

Exercise 7-5 FIND FORMATTED TEXT

In addition to locating words and phrases, the Find command can search for text formatting. The formatting can include character formatting, such as bold and italic, and paragraph formatting, such as alignment and line spacing.

1. Position the insertion point at the beginning of the document. Open the **Find and Replace** dialog box by clicking the down arrow to the right of the Find command on the Home tab and choosing **Advanced Find**.
2. Key **Campbell's Confections** in the **Find what** text box. Click **More** to expand the dialog box, and choose **All** from the **Search** direction drop-down list. Click any checked search options to clear them.
3. Click the Format button [Format ▾], and choose **Font**.

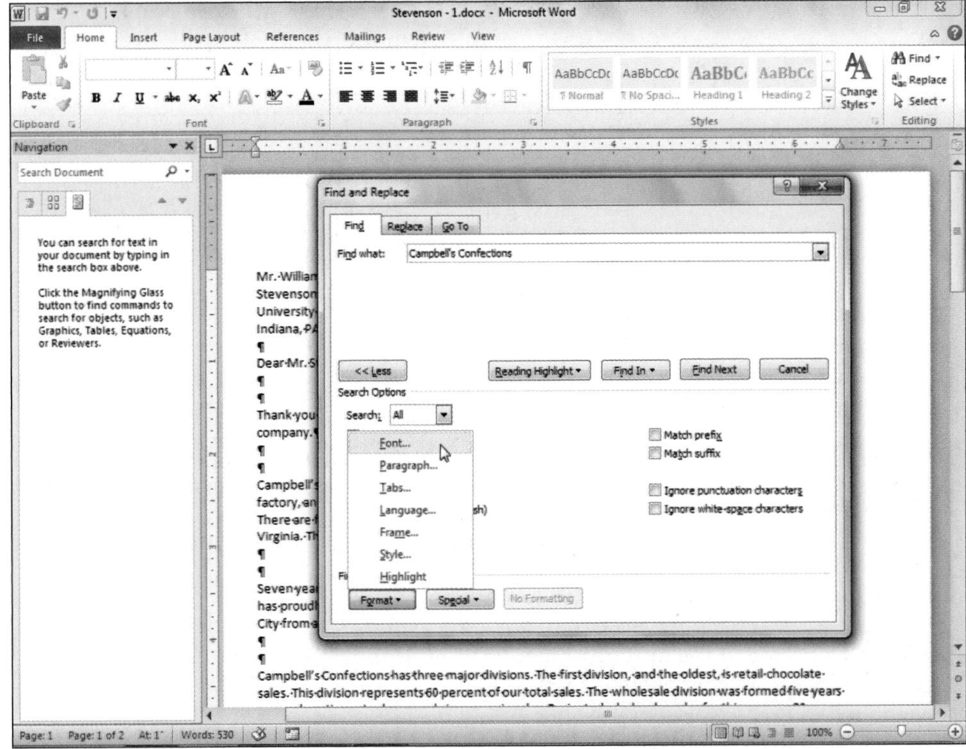

Figure 7-6
Format options

4. In the Find Font dialog box, choose **Italic** from the **Font style** list and click **OK**. The italic format now appears below the **Find what** text box.
5. Click **Less**, and then click **Find Next**. Word locates *"Campbell's Confections."*
6. Click **Cancel** to close the Find and Replace dialog box.

Finding and Replacing Text

The Replace command searches for specific text or formatting and replaces it with your specified alternative. You can replace all instances of text or formatting at once, or you can find and confirm each replacement.

Two ways to replace text are:

- Ribbon, Home tab, Editing group, Replace command.
- Press Ctrl+H.

Exercise 7-6 REPLACE TEXT BY USING FIND NEXT

1. Position the insertion point at the beginning of the document, locate the **Editing** group, and click the Replace button. The Find and Replace dialog box displays with the **Replace** tab selected.
2. Key **traveler** in the Find what text box. Expand the dialog box, and click the No Formatting button [No Formatting] to remove formatting from previous searches. Make sure no options under **Search Options** are selected.
3. Press Tab to move to the **Replace with** text box, and key **visitor**. Click the No Formatting button [No Formatting] if it is active.

Figure 7-7
Replacing text

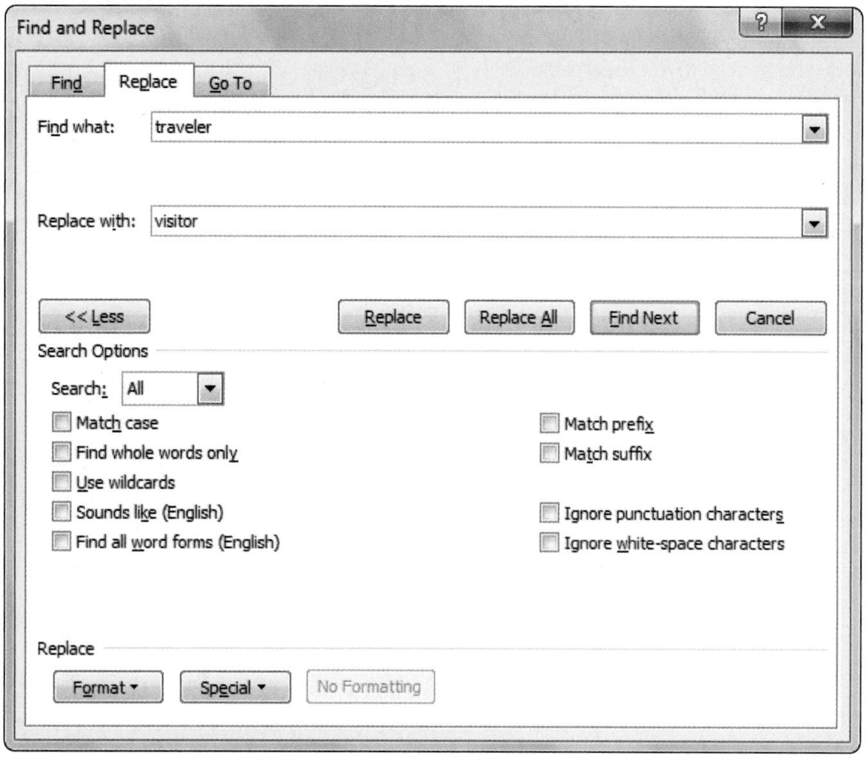

NOTE

Remember, pressing Tab in a dialog box moves the insertion point from one text box to another and highlights existing text, or pressing Tab moves from one option or command to the next option or command in the dialog box. Pressing Enter executes the dialog box command.

4. Adjust the position and size (click **Less** to reduce the size, and drag the title bar to move the dialog box) of the dialog box so you can see the document text. Click **Find Next**. Click **Replace** to replace the first occurrence of "traveler" with "visitor."
5. Continue to click **Replace** until Word reaches the end of the document.
6. Click **OK** when Word finishes searching the document.
7. Close the Find and Replace dialog box.

Exercise 7-7 REPLACE TEXT BY USING REPLACE ALL

The Replace All option replaces all occurrences of text or formatting in a document without confirmation.

1. Move the insertion point to the beginning of the document, and press Ctrl+H to open the Find and Replace dialog box with the **Replace** tab selected.
2. Key **Campbell's Confections** in the **Find what** text box. Press Tab and key **CAMPBELL'S CONFECTIONS** in the **Replace with** text box.

NOTE

After replacing text or formatting, you can always undo the action. If you used replace all, all changes are reversed at once. If you used replace, only the last change is reversed, but you can undo the last several changes individually by selecting them from the Undo drop-down list.

3. Expand the dialog box, clear the **Match case** check box if necessary, and click **Replace All**. Word will indicate the number of replacements made.
4. Click **OK**, and close the Find and Replace dialog box. "Campbell's Confections" now appears as "CAMPBELL'S CONFECTIONS" throughout the document.
5. Click the Undo button to undo the Replace All command.

Exercise 7-8 DELETE TEXT WITH REPLACE

You can also use the Replace command to delete text automatically. Key the text to be deleted in the Find what text box and leave the Replace with text box blank. You can find and delete text with confirmation by using the Find Next option or without confirmation by using the Replace All option. When keying text in the Find what text box, be sure to key the text exactly as it appears in the document including blank spaces and punctuation. You may need to include a blank space after the text to ensure correct spacing between words.

1. Position the insertion point at the beginning of the document, and open the **Find and Replace** dialog box with the Replace tab selected.
2. Key **Campbell's** in the **Find what** text box, and press Spacebar once. The space character is not visible in the text box.

3. Press Tab to move to the **Replace with** text box, and press Delete to remove the previous entry.
4. Click the Replace All button Replace All.
5. Click **OK** and close the dialog box. The word "Campbell's" followed by a space is deleted from the company name throughout the document. If the word "Campbell's" was followed by a punctuation mark, the word would not be deleted.
6. Click the Undo button.
7. Save the document as ***[your initials]*****7-8** in a new folder for Lesson 7. Leave the document open for the next exercise.

TIP

Another option in the Find and Replace dialog box is Find all word forms. Use this option to find different forms of words and replace the various word forms with comparable forms.

Finding and Replacing Special Characters

The Find and Replace features can search for characters other than ordinary text. Special characters include paragraph marks and tab characters. Special characters are represented by codes that you can key or choose from the Special drop-down list.

Exercise 7-9 FIND AND REPLACE SPECIAL CHARACTERS

1. Click the Show/Hide ¶ button ¶ to display special characters in the document if they are not showing.
2. Position the insertion point at the top of the document. Open the **Find and Replace** dialog box with the **Replace** tab selected. Expand the dialog box, if necessary. Delete the text that appears in the **Find what** text box.
3. Click the **Special** button and choose **Paragraph Mark**. A code (^p) is inserted in the **Find what** text box. Add two additional paragraph mark codes in the **Find what** text box to search for three consecutive paragraph marks in the document. (Use the **Special** drop-down list or key **^p^p**.)
4. Move to the **Replace with** text box, and insert two paragraph mark codes.

NOTE

The dialog box that appears when you end the search process is determined by the search direction and the position of the insertion point when you begin the search. When Word searches through the entire document, the dialog box tells you Word is finished searching, and the insertion point returns to its original position. When you search from a point other than the top or bottom of the document and choose up or down as your search direction, Word asks if you want to continue the search. If you choose not to continue, the insertion point remains at the last occurrence found.

5. Clear any **Search Options** check boxes and click **Less**.
6. Click **Find Next**. Word locates the extra paragraph mark after the salutation of the letter.

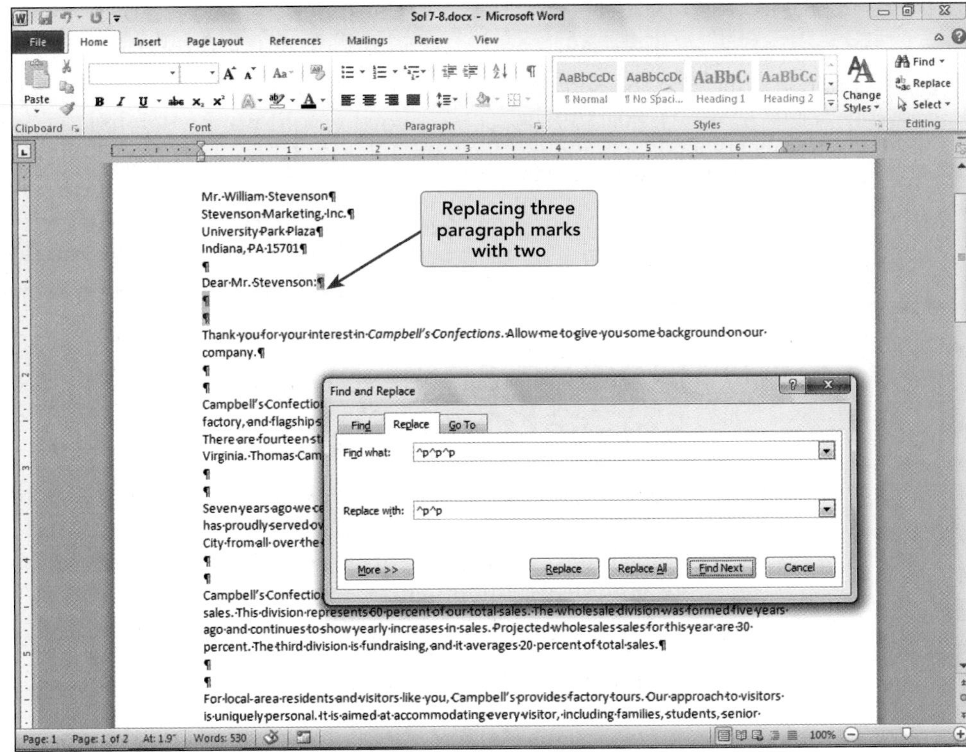

Figure 7-8 Replacing special characters

7. Click **Replace**. Notice the elimination of the extra paragraph mark. Continue to click **Replace** for each paragraph mark until you reach the paragraph marks after "Sincerely."
8. Close the Find and Replace dialog box. The document paragraphs are now correctly spaced.

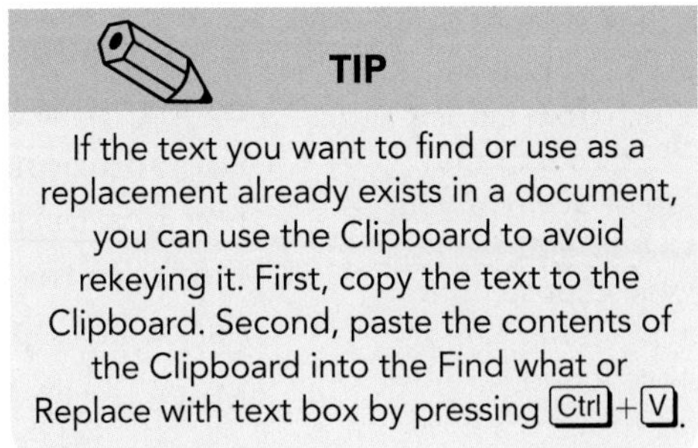

TIP
If the text you want to find or use as a replacement already exists in a document, you can use the Clipboard to avoid rekeying it. First, copy the text to the Clipboard. Second, paste the contents of the Clipboard into the Find what or Replace with text box by pressing Ctrl+V.

TABLE 7-2 Find and Replace Special Characters

Find or Replace	Special Character Code to Key
Paragraph mark (¶)	^p (must be lowercase)
Tab character (→)	^t (must be lowercase)
Any character (find only)	^?
Any digit (find only)	^#
Any letter (find only)	^$
Column break	^n
Clipboard contents (replace only)	^c
Em dash	^+
En dash	^=
Field (find only)	^d
Footnote mark (find only)	^f
Graphic (find only)	^g
Manual line break	^l
Manual page break	^m
Nonbreaking hyphen	^~
Nonbreaking space	^s
Section break (find only)	^b
White space (find only)	^w

Finding and Replacing Formatting

Word can search for and replace both character and paragraph formatting. You can specify character or paragraph formatting by clicking the Format button in the Find and Replace dialog box or using keyboard shortcuts.

Exercise 7-10 FIND AND REPLACE CHARACTER FORMATTING

1. Position the insertion point at the top of the document, and open the **Find and Replace** dialog box with the **Replace** tab selected. Expand the dialog box.

2. Key **Campbell's Confections** in the **Find what** text box. Press Tab and delete the text in the **Replace with** text box.
3. Click the **Format** button and choose **Font**. Choose **Bold** and **Small caps**. Click **OK**.
4. Click **Replace All**.
5. Click **OK** when Word finishes searching the document, and close the dialog box. "Campbell's Confections" appears bold and in small caps throughout the document.
6. Reopen the **Find and Replace** dialog box with the **Replace** tab selected. Expand the dialog box.
7. Highlight the text in the **Find what** text box, if it is not already. Click the **Format** button and choose **Font**. Choose **Bold** and **Small caps** and click **OK**.
8. Press Tab to move the insertion point to the **Replace with** text box. Click the No Formatting button [No Formatting] to clear existing formatting.
9. Click the Format button [Format] and choose **Font**. Choose the **Not Bold** style, deselect **Small caps**, and click **OK**.
10. Press Ctrl+I (the keyboard shortcut for italic text). Now the format for the **Replace with** text box is "Not Bold, Not Small caps, Not All caps, Italic."
11. Click **Replace All**.
12. Click **OK** and close the Find and Replace dialog box. "Campbell's Confections" is now italic, and not bold, small caps, throughout the document.

TIP

You can use keyboard shortcut keys to apply or remove formatting in the Find what or Repace with text boxes. To apply bold, press Ctrl+B, and Font: Bold displays below the Find what text box. To remove bold, press Ctrl+B twice, and you will see Font: Not Bold below the Find what or Replace with text box.

Exercise 7-11 FIND AND REPLACE PARAGRAPH FORMATTING

1. Position the insertion point at the beginning of the second paragraph that begins "Campbell's Confections." Open the Find and Replace dialog box with the Replace tab selected.
2. In the **Find what** text box, insert two paragraph mark special characters (use the **Special** list or key **^p^p**). Clear existing formatting.
3. Move to the **Replace with** text box, enter two paragraph mark special characters, and clear existing formatting.

4. Click the **Format** button and choose **Paragraph**. Click the **Indents and Spacing** tab if it is not active. Deselect **Mirror indents** if necessary.
5. Choose **First Line** from the **Special** drop-down list. If "0.5" is not the measurement displayed in the **By** text box, select the text in the **By** box and key **0.5**. Click **OK**.

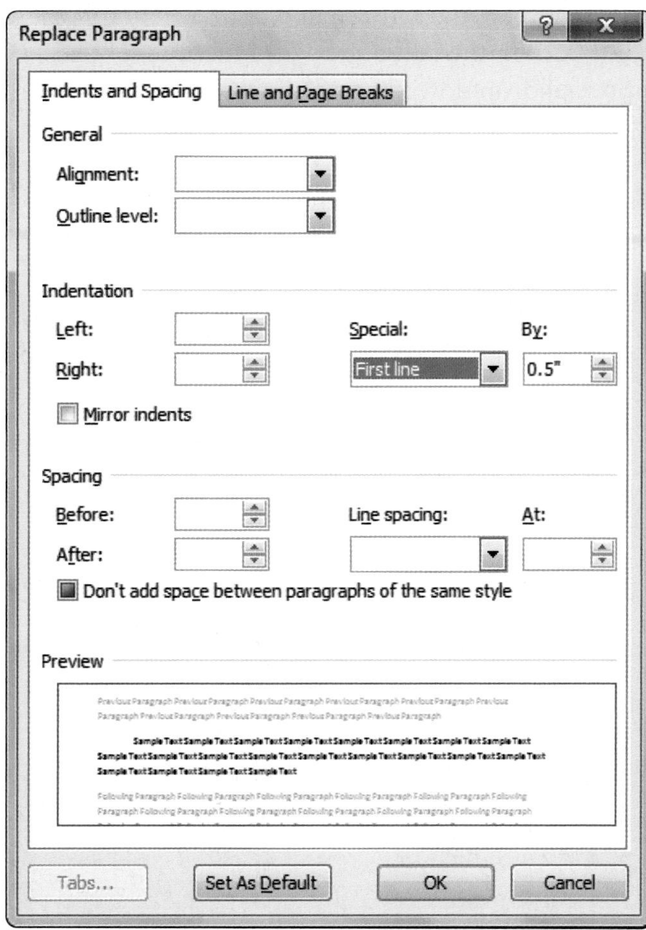

Figure 7-9
Defining paragraph formatting

6. Click **Find Next** and Word highlights the paragraph marks after "company." Click **Replace** to format that paragraph.
7. Click **Replace** seven more times (through the paragraph ending "enclosed brochure").
8. Close the Find and Replace dialog box. Scroll through the document to view the paragraph formatting changes. The paragraphs should now have a 0.5-inch first-line indent.

9. Position the insertion point at the top of the document. Open the Find and Replace dialog box with the Replace tab selected.
10. Delete the text in the **Find what** text box, and set the text box to look for a 0.5-inch first-line indent. Deselect **Mirror indents** if necessary. Close the Paragraph dialog box.
11. Delete the text in the **Replace with** text box, and clear the formatting. Click the **Format** button, and click **Paragraph**. Deselect **Mirror indents**, key **0.25** in the **Left** and **Right** indent text boxes. Choose **(none)** from the **Special** drop-down list. Click **OK**.

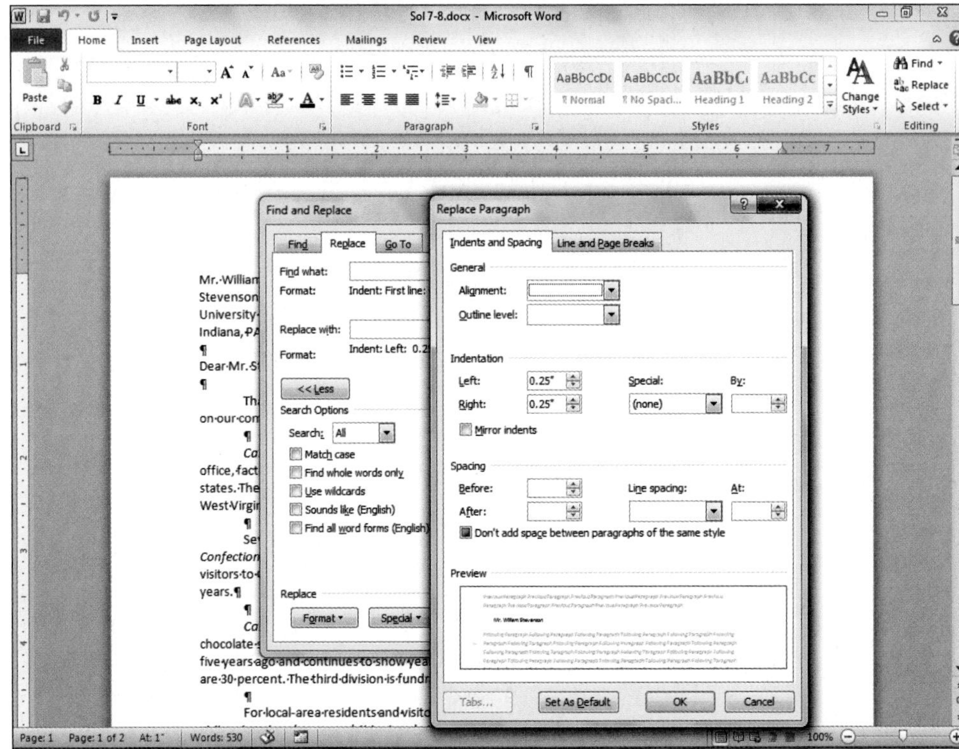

Figure 7-10
Replacing paragraph formatting

12. Click **Replace All** and click **OK**. Close the Find and Replace dialog box.
13. Scroll through the document to observe the replacement of first-line indented paragraphs with 0.25-inch left- and right-indented paragraphs.
14. Enter the date at the top of the document, with 72 points spacing before and three blank lines after it. Replace "xx" with your reference initials. Add an enclosure notation.
15. Save the document as ***[your initials]*7-11** in your Lesson 7 folder.
16. Submit and close the document.

TABLE 7-3 Find and Replace Formatting Guidelines

Guideline	Procedure
Find specific text with specific formatting.	Key the text in the Find what text box and specify its formatting (choose Font or Paragraph from the Format drop-down list or use a keyboard shortcut).
Find specific formatting.	Delete text in the Find what text box, and specify formatting.
Replace specific text but not its formatting.	Key the text in the Find what text box. Click the No Formatting button to clear existing formatting. Key the replacement text in the Replace with text box, and clear existing formatting.
Replace specific text and its formatting.	Key the text in the Find what text box, and specify its formatting. Delete any text in the Replace with text box, key the replacement text, and specify the replacement formatting.
Replace only formatting for specific text.	Key the text in the Find what text box, and specify its formatting. Delete any text in the Replace with text box, and specify the replacement formatting.
Replace only formatting.	Delete any text in the Find what text box, and specify formatting. Delete any text in the Replace with text box, and specify the replacement formatting.

Lesson 7 Summary

- The Find command locates specified text and formatting in a document. The Replace command finds text and formatting and replaces it automatically with specified alternatives.
- Use the Find command to locate whole words, words that sound alike, font and paragraph formatting, and special characters. Using the Find command, you can search an entire document or selected text. You can also specify the direction of the search.
- Use the Match case option to locate text that matches the case of document text. Example: When searching for "Confections," Word would not find "confections."
- When you want to locate whole words and not parts of a word, use the Find whole words only option. Example: When searching for the whole word "can," Word would find only "can," but not "candy" or "candidate."
- Use the Use wildcards option to search for text strings by using special search operators. A wildcard is a symbol that stands for missing or unknown text. Example: A search for "b^?yte" would find "bite" and "byte." See Table 7-2.
- Use the Sounds like option to find a word that sounds similar to the search text but spelled differently or to find a word you do not know how to spell. When you find the word, you can stop the search process and edit your document.

- Use the Find command to search for formatted text. The formatting can include character formatting, such as bold and italic, and paragraph formatting, such as alignment and line spacing. Use the Replace command to replace the formatting. See Table 7-3.
- Use the Replace command to search for all instances of text or formatting at once or to find and confirm each replacement.
- Use the Replace command to delete text automatically. Key the text to be deleted in the Find what text box, and leave the Replace with text box blank.

LESSON 7		Command Summary	
Feature	**Button**	**Command**	**Keyboard**
Find		Home tab, Editing group	Ctrl+F
Replace		Home tab, Editing group	Ctrl+H

Concepts Review

True/False Questions

Each of the following statements is either true or false. Indicate your choice by circling T or F.

T F 1. You can use keyboard shortcuts to specify formatting in the Find and Replace dialog box.

T F 2. To find text or formatting, you must have the insertion point at the beginning of the document.

T F 3. Line spacing and indents are two examples of paragraph formatting that you can specify in the Find what or Replace with text boxes.

T F 4. The question mark represents a special character code used to search for any character.

T F 5. You use the Match case option to specify only uppercase when finding or replacing text.

T F 6. The keyboard command to find text is Ctrl+H.

T F 7. The Undo command undoes all replacements made if you used the Replace All option.

T F 8. You can use the Find command to search either selected text or an entire document.

Short Answer Questions

Write the correct answer in the space provided.

1. What is the special character code for a paragraph mark?

____

2. Which button can you use to continue a find operation when the Find and Replace dialog box is closed?

____

3. With the insertion point in the Find what text box, how do you move to, and automatically highlight the contents of, the Replace with text box?

____

4. Which Find option do you use to locate a specific word rather than all occurrences of the text string?

____

5. If the insertion point is in the Find what text box, what is the shortcut to insert text for which you previously searched?

____

6. How do you clear previous formatting when it appears below the text boxes in the Find and Replace dialog box?

____

7. Which button expands the Find and Replace dialog box to show more options, and which button reduces the dialog box to make it smaller?

____

8. Which option, Replace or Replace All, allows for selective replacement of text?

____

Critical Thinking

Answer these questions on a separate page. There are no right or wrong answers. Support your answers with examples from your own experience, if possible.

1. Click the Start button, and click the link for Windows **Help and Support**. In the Search Help text box, key **find files** and press Enter. Read the information about finding files and folders. Create a document to summarize the facts. Be sure to include the instructions for finding a file that contains specific text as well as files created on a particular date.
2. The Replace All option can be very useful. It can also lead to occasional problems if you have not thought through a specific replace all operation. After you experiment with the feature, describe some precautions you would suggest for the use of replace all.

Skills Review

Exercise 7-12

Find and replace text.

1. Open the file **Walk - 2**.
2. Use the Find command to locate the text "8 a.m." by following these steps:
   a. Position the insertion point at the beginning of the document, and click the **Home** tab. Click the Find button.
   b. Key **8 a.m.** in the **Search Document** text box. The document highlights the search string, and the sentence containing the highlighted text appears in the Navigation Pane. If the text does not appear highlighted in the document, click the button that resembles a magnifier if necessary to begin the search.
   c. Edit the found text to read **8:30 a.m.** Close the Navigation Pane.

3. Change the text "walk-a-thon" to "Walk-a-Thon," using the Replace command, by following these steps:
   a. Move the insertion point to the beginning of the document. Click the Home tab, and click the Replace button.
   b. Key **walk-a-thon** in the Find what text box, press Tab, and key **Walk-a-Thon** in the Replace with text box.
   c. Expand the dialog box by clicking More. Click No Formatting if necessary.
   d. Click Less to reduce the size of the dialog box, and drag the dialog box to the bottom of the screen.
   e. Click Find Next, and then click Replace. Click Replace until Word reaches the end of the document. Click OK, and close the dialog box.
4. Change the date, using the Replace command, by following these steps:
   a. Position the insertion point at the beginning of the document, and press Ctrl+H.
   b. Key **May 1** in the Find what text box.
   c. Press Tab and key **April 25** in the Replace with text box.
   d. Click More to expand the dialog box, and click any checked search options to deselect them.
   e. Click Replace All. Click OK and close the dialog box.
5. Replace the text "Education Fund" with "Outreach Program."
6. Move to the top of the document, and format the first line with 72 points spacing before. Edit the text to read "**Put on your walking shoes—Become a Friend of the Library Outreach Program!**."

REVIEW

To format "Campbell's Confections," select the formatted text, click the Format Painter button 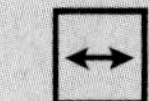, and then select "Chamber of Commerce."

7. Format the first line of text as 14-point bold and small caps.
8. Move to the end of the document, and format "Campbell's Confections" as bold italic. Copy the formatting to the text "Chamber of Commerce" located below the address.
9. Spell-check the document.
10. Save the document as ***[your initials]*7-12** in your Lesson 7 folder.
11. Submit and close the document.

Exercise 7-13

Replace special characters and delete text.

1. Start a new document.
2. Key the text shown in Figure 7-11 on the next page, using single spacing and 0 points spacing after. When keying the hyphens, do not insert space characters before or after the hyphen.

Figure 7-11

```
Campbell's Confections
Chocolate Factory Hours
September, April, May, June
Monday-Saturday
9 a.m.-4 p.m.
Winter Schedule
October 1 through March 31
Monday-Friday
9 a.m.-3 p.m.
For more information, call 724-555-2025
```

3. Center the entire document horizontally, and change the font to Arial.
4. Change the first line to 16-point bold and the last line to bold italic. Apply bold and small caps format to the second line.
5. Replace special characters by following these steps:
   a. Position the insertion point at the end of the document, click the **Home** tab, and click the Replace button. Click **More** to expand the dialog box, if it is not already expanded.
   b. Key a hyphen in the **Find what** text box.
   c. Press Tab to move to the **Replace with** text box.
   d. Click the **Special** button and choose **En Dash**.
   e. Choose **Up** from the **Search** drop-down list, and clear any search options that are selected.
   f. Click **Less**, and then click **Find Next**. Do not replace the hyphens in the telephone number.
   g. Click **Find Next** and click **Replace** to replace the hyphen in the time.
   h. Continue replacing hyphens until you reach the beginning of the document.
   i. Click **OK** and close the dialog box when the search is complete.
6. Use the Replace feature to delete text by following these steps:
   a. Position the insertion point at the top of the document, and press Ctrl+H.
   b. Key **Winter Schedule** in the **Find what** dialog box.
   c. Expand the dialog box and clear any formatting.
   d. Delete any text or formatting in the **Replace with** text box.
   e. Select **All** for the **Search** direction.
   f. Click **Replace All** to delete the text. Click **OK** and close the dialog box.
7. Undo the replacement by clicking the Undo button on the Quick Access Toolbar.
8. Change the spacing after to 12 points for the entire document. Change the spacing before for the first line to 72 points.

9. Spell-check the document.
10. Save the document as ***[your initials]*7-13** in your Lesson 7 folder.
11. Submit and close the document.

Exercise 7-14

Delete special characters, replace text, and replace formatting.

1. Open the file **OH Hours**.
2. Use the Replace command to delete all tabs by following these steps:
   a. Position the insertion point at the beginning of the document, and click the Replace button.
   b. Key **^t** (the code for a tab character) in the **Find what** text box, and clear existing formatting.
   c. Delete any text in the **Replace with** text box, and clear existing formatting and search options. Change the **Search** direction to **All**.
   d. Click **Replace All**, click **OK**, and click **Close**. Notice the change in the tabbed columns.
3. Undo the replacement.
4. Replace the em dash (—) with the word "to," by following these steps:
   a. Press Ctrl+H.
   b. Delete text or formatting that appears in the **Find what** text box. Click **More** to expand the dialog box. Click the Special button Special, and click **Em Dash**.
   c. In the **Replace with** text box, press Spacebar, key **to**, and press Spacebar.
   d. Click **Replace All**. Click **OK** and click **Close**.
5. Replace the underline format with bold format by following these steps:
   a. Press Ctrl+H.
   b. Delete text or formatting that appears in the **Find what** text box. Click **More** to expand the dialog box. Press Ctrl+U. "Underline" should display under the Find what text box.
   c. Tab to the **Replace with** text box, delete text or formatting, click the Format button Format, and click **Font**. Click the down arrow for the Underline Style drop-down list, and click **(none)**. Select **Bold** and **Small caps** formatting. Click **OK**.
   d. Click **Replace All**. Click **OK** and click **Close**.
6. Change the heading of the document to 14 points with 72 points spacing before. Change the line spacing for all the tabbed text, including the tabbed heading, to double spacing.
7. Save the document as ***[your initials]*7-14** in your Lesson 7 folder.
8. Submit and close the document.

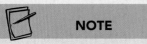

NOTE

If you do not change the Underline style to "(none)," Word will keep the underline style when it replaces the formatting.

Exercise 7-15

Replace character and paragraph formatting.

1. Open the file **Homecoming**.
2. Format the first page of the document as a memo. Key the memo heading information as shown in Figure 7-12. Add your reference initials and an attachment notation

Figure 7-12

```
MEMO TO: Robert Smith
FROM: Thomas Campbell
DATE: May 30, 20--
SUBJECT: Homecoming Dates
```

3. Find and replace special characters by following these steps:
   a. Position the insertion point at the top of page 2, and open the Find and Replace dialog box with the **Replace** tab selected.
   b. Delete existing text in the **Find what** text box, and clear all search options and formatting. Expand the dialog box, and click the Special button [Special ▾] and click **Manual Line Break**.
   c. Tab to the **Replace with** text box, and delete all text and formatting. Click the Special button [Special ▾] and click **Paragraph Mark**. (Notice that "^p" should appear in the Replace with text box.)
   d. Change the search direction to **Down** and click **Replace All**. When Word reaches the end of the document, click **No** to end the task. Close the Find and Replace dialog box.
4. Find and replace character formatting by following these steps:
   a. Position the insertion point at the top of page 2, and open the Find and Replace dialog box with the **Replace** tab selected.
   b. Delete existing text in the **Find what** text box, and clear all search options and formatting. Press Ctrl+U to specify underline formatting.
   c. Tab to the **Replace with** text box, and delete all text. Click the **Format** button and choose **Font**.
   d. In the Replace Font dialog box, choose **Bold Italic** and set the **Underline style** to **(none)**. Click **OK**.
   e. Change the search direction to **Down** and click **Replace All**. When Word reaches the end of the document, click **No** to end the task. Close the Find and Replace dialog box.

5. Find and replace paragraph formats by following these steps:
   a. Place the insertion point before the text "***Allegheny College***" on page 2, and open the Find and Replace dialog box with the **Replace** tab selected.
   b. In the **Find what** text box, enter two paragraph mark codes by keying **^p^p** or by using the **Special** button. Clear all search options and formatting.
   c. In the **Replace with** text box, clear any text, formatting, and search options. Enter one paragraph mark code (^p).
   d. Click the **Format** button and choose **Paragraph**. Set **Spacing After** to 6 points (**6 pt**) and click **OK**.
   e. Click **Less** and then click **Find Next**. Replace the formatting on page 2 only. Close the dialog box.
6. Format the title on page 2 ("Homecoming Events") as 14-point bold, uppercase, and centered. Change the spacing after to 24 points and delete the blank paragraph mark below the title. Format all the text below the title with a 2.25-inch left indent.
7. Spell-check the memo portion of the document.
8. Save the document as ***[your initials]*****7-15** in your Lesson 7 folder.
9. Submit and close the document.

Lesson Applications

Exercise 7-16

Replace text and character formatting.

1. Open the file **Chocolate - 3**.

REVIEW

Remember to remove all formatting from previous search and replace actions.

TIP

The Small caps check box and all the other check boxes in the Find and Replace Font dialog boxes initially appear shaded. Click the Small caps check box once to select it.

2. Format the document as a memo to "Store Managers" from Thomas Campbell. Use today's date. The subject is "Chocolate Terms."
3. Replace the text "cocoa bean" with **cacao bean** throughout the document.
4. Replace the italic formatting of the chocolate terms with bold, small caps formatting. Check the format options under the Replace with text box. (It should read "Bold, Not Italic, Small caps, Not All caps." Press Ctrl+I to turn off italic format if necessary.) Make sure no search options are checked before you begin replacing.
5. Add your reference initials to the document.
6. Save the document as ***[your initials]*7-16** in your Lesson 7 folder.
7. Submit and close the document.

Exercise 7-17

Find and replace text, special characters, and formatting.

1. Open the file **Holiday**. Format the document as a memo to "Store Managers" from Thomas Campbell. Use the current date, and the subject is "Holiday Sales."
2. Key the text in Figure 7-13 below the subject line.

Figure 7-13

```
                             popular       during
The table below lists the most ^ items sold for our busiest
                                         results
holidays by state. We compiled the numbers using sales
                                               ¶
from the (3)-week period preceding each holiday. If you
would like a breakdown by individual stores, let me know.
We will use these figures to determine our production
          for next year
schedules ^. If you have any comments regarding this
information, please call me.
```

3. Replace the text "chocolate suckers" with **Halloween favors**.
4. Replace the 3 points spacing after paragraph formatting with double spacing.
5. Replace all bold formatting with blue underline, small caps, and blue font color formatting.
6. Format the first line of text in the document with 72 points of spacing before the paragraph.
7. Add your reference initials, and spell-check the document.
8. Save the document as ***[your initials]*****7-17** in your Lesson 7 folder.
9. Submit and close the document.

Exercise 7-18

Find and replace text and formatting.

1. Open the file **Club - 2**.
2. Alphabetize the list that begins "milk chocolate–covered nuts" through "three-tier."
3. Copy the text "CC Chocolate Club" and paste the text at the beginning of the document. Press Enter.
4. Replace the text "CC Chocolate Club" with "Campbell's Confections' Chocolate Club."
5. Replace the single-spaced paragraph format with 12 points spacing after (12 pt) and .25 first-line indent.
6. Replace all hyphens with an en dash.
7. Format the list beginning with "caramel" through "truffles" as a bulleted list.
8. Format the first line of the document as a title—uppercase, bold, 14 points, center alignment, and no indent. Apply 72 points spacing before and 24 points spacing after.
9. Add a page border to the document. (Open the Borders and Shading dialog box, and click the Page Border tab. Click Box under setting, and choose a geometric pattern located near the bottom of the Art drop-down list. Select an appropriate width and color.)
10. Spell-check the document.
11. Save the document as ***[your initials]*****7-18** in your Lesson 7 folder.
12. Submit and close the document.

Exercise 7-19 ◆ Challenge Yourself

Find and replace text, special characters, and formatting.

1. Open the file **Agenda**.
2. Replace each single paragraph mark with 12 points spacing after (**12 pt**).
3. Find the text "PM" and replace it with **p.m.** Include the Match case option.
4. Find the text "AM" and replace it with **a.m.**
5. Replace italic formatting with 12-point bold and small caps formatting.
6. Replace each hyphen (-) with an em dash.
7. Use the Replace command to format all session numbers (Session 1, Session 2, etc.) with italic format by using the wildcard "?"
8. Center the three-line title, and apply 16-point bold and small caps formatting. Add 48 points of spacing before the first line and 24 points of spacing after the third line of the heading. Apply a bottom border to the third line of the title.
9. Format "Agenda" with center alignment, 14 points, bold, and small caps.
10. Save the document as ***[your initials]*7-19** in your Lesson 7 folder.
11. Submit and close the document.

TIP

Click in the Find what text box. Key "Session"; press Spacebar; click Special; and choose Any Character, that is, "Session ^?".

On Your Own

In these exercises, you work on your own, as you would in a real-life business environment. Use the skills you have learned to accomplish the task—and be creative.

Exercise 7-20

Key a song lyric you know, preferably one with a repetitive chorus. Copy the lyric, and paste it below the original. In the copy of the lyric, find an important word that is used repeatedly in the lyric and replace it with its opposite. Save the document as ***[your initials]*7-20** and submit it.

Exercise 7-21

Write a summary about a book you recently read using paragraph default settings. Replace the 10-point spacing after paragraph setting with 12-point spacing after. Replace the 1.15 line spacing with single spacing. Replace any occurrence of two spaces with one space. Save the document as ***[your initials]*7-21**. Submit the document.

Exercise 7-22

Use the Help feature to explore additional Find and Replace features. Create a document to explain the following Search options:

- Find all word forms
- Match prefix
- Match suffix
- Ignore punctuation characters
- Ignore white-space characters

Provide examples for each option. Save the document as ***[your initials]*7-22** and submit it.

Unit 2 Applications

Unit Application 2-1

Apply paragraph spacing, indent text, set tabs, add borders and shading, replace text.

1. Open the file **Customer Service**.
2. Format the document as a memo to "Customer Service Account Executives" from Thomas Campbell. Use today's date, and the subject is brochure information.
3. Select the first line of the memo heading ("MEMO TO"), and apply 72 points spacing before.
4. Below the memo heading, key the text shown in Figure U2-1. Include the corrections. Use single spacing.

Figure U2-1

```
The         department              company
                                         u
^marketing^ is revising our^ brochre and updating the

information on our web site. Please review the following

paragraphs, and let me know your suggestions or
                                           #
recommendations. If you would like tomeet to discuss your
proposed
^changes, let me know.
```

5. Format the paragraph heading ("Customer Service") as 14-point bold and small caps.
6. Format the "Customer Service" heading and the paragraph that follows the heading using a 0.5-inch left and right indent and Calibri font.
7. Select the "SUBJECT" line, and apply a thin, single-line bottom border.
8. Apply a box border and light gray shading to the "Customer Service" paragraphs.
9. Replace each hyphen with an en dash.
10. Save the document as ***[your initials]*****u2-1** in a new folder for Unit 2 Applications.
11. Submit and close the document.

Unit Application 2-2

Apply paragraph spacing and change alignment; create a bulleted list; create tabbed text; find and replace text; copy and paste text.

1. Open the file **Ordering**. Change the font size of the document to 11 points.
2. Format the title in the first line of the document as 14-point uppercase, centered, with 72 points spacing before and 24 points spacing after.
3. Insert the following tabbed text near the end of the document so that it follows the paragraph that begins "Orders shipped." A blank line should precede and follow the tabbed text. Right-align the text in the second and third columns.

Figure U2-2

Amount	Standard	Rush
$0 to $20.00	$5.95	$18.95
20.01 to 40.00	8.95	21.95
40.01 to 60.00	11.95	24.95
60.01 to 80.00	14.95	27.95
80.01 to 100.00	17.95	30.95
100.01 to 125.00	20.95	33.95
125.01 to 150.00	23.95	36.95
150.01 to 200.00	26.95	39.95
Over $200.00	10% of Total	18% of Total

4. Key the text **Delivery Chart** as a heading above the tabbed text.
5. Format "Delivery Chart" as 14-point bold, centered, and small caps. Format the column headings for the tabbed text to be bold and underlined.
6. Select the paragraph headings ("Online," "Telephone," etc.), and format the headings as a bulleted list, using the small square-shaped bullet (■).
7. Indent the text below the bulleted paragraphs so the paragraph text aligns with the text that follows the bullet.
8. Remove the bullet format from the paragraphs that begin "Note." Indent the "Note" paragraphs to match the other paragraphs.
9. Use the Find and Replace commands to format the text "Note:" as bold, italic, and small caps.
10. Find the text "April through September," and key the following sentence after "September" but before the period: **or when temperatures reach 72**. Add the degree symbol to follow "72" (°).

11. Spell-check the document.
12. Save the document as ***[your initials]*****u2-2** in your Unit 2 Applications folder.
13. Submit and close the document.

Unit Application 2-3

Apply and change bulleted lists, create tabbed columns, apply indents, and sort text.

1. Start a new document, and change the left and right indents to 0.5 inch.
2. Key the text shown in Figure U2-3, using 12-point Arial. Use leader tabs to create the lines under "Task Completed." The leaders should extend to the right indent setting.

Figure U2-3

```
Before you go on vacation, use this handy checklist to make
sure you have not forgotten any details.

                                                Task Completed

Change your voice mail recording                ______________
Create an out-of-office message                 ______________
Meet with supervisor                            ______________
Back up important files                         ______________
Create a checklist for the temp                 ______________
Check calendar                                  ______________
File/archive papers and data files              ______________
```

TIP

You need to set two tabs—a left tab to begin the second column and a right tab for the solid-line leader.

3. Right-align the text "Task Completed," and insert one blank line above it. Apply bold and small caps format to "Task completed."
4. Apply bullets to the list, using the checkmark bullet.
5. Format the opening paragraph as bold italic.
6. Select the list with the checkmark bullets, and change the bullet to the 3-D box (❑) Wingding character.
7. Customize the 3-D box bullet format by increasing the bullet size to 14 points and changing the bullet color to blue. Drag the hanging indent marker to 1.25 on the ruler.
8. Apply a 3-D page border, using the fourth-to-last line style. Change the color to blue.

9. Select the bulleted list, and sort the text in ascending order. Change the line spacing for the bulleted list to 3.0.
10. Save the document as ***[your initials]*****u2-3** in your Unit 2 Applications folder.
11. Submit and close the document.

Unit Application 2-4

Using the Internet, work with a variety of paragraph formatting features, move and copy text, and find and replace text.

1. Locate three or more Web sites that contain information on your favorite hobby or on a topic that interests you.
2. Copy text from each site, and paste it into a new Word document.
3. Use the **Keep Text Only** option from the Paste Options button to remove Web formatting.
4. Create a formatted title for the document.
5. Use paragraph and character formatting features to format the document attractively.
6. Use the Find and Replace features to locate selected text, and apply formatting for emphasis.
7. Check spelling and grammar (Web sites may contain misspelled words or poor grammar).
8. Save the document as ***[your initials]*****u2-4** in your Unit 2 Applications folder.
9. Submit and close the document.

Unit 3

PAGE FORMATTING

Lesson 8

Margins and Printing Options

OBJECTIVES ***After completing this lesson, you will be able to:***

1. Change margins.
2. Preview a document.
3. Change paper size and orientation.
4. Print envelopes and labels.
5. Choose print options.

Estimated Time: 1½ hours

In a Word document, text is keyed and printed within the boundaries of the document's margins. *Margins* are the spaces between the edges of the text and the edges of the paper. Adjusting the margins can significantly change the appearance of a document.

Word offers many useful printing features: changing the orientation (the direction, either horizontal or vertical, in which a document is printed), selecting paper size, and printing envelopes and labels.

Changing Margins

By default, a document's margin settings are:

- Top margin: 1 inch
- Bottom margin: 1 inch
- Left margin: 1 inch
- Right margin: 1 inch

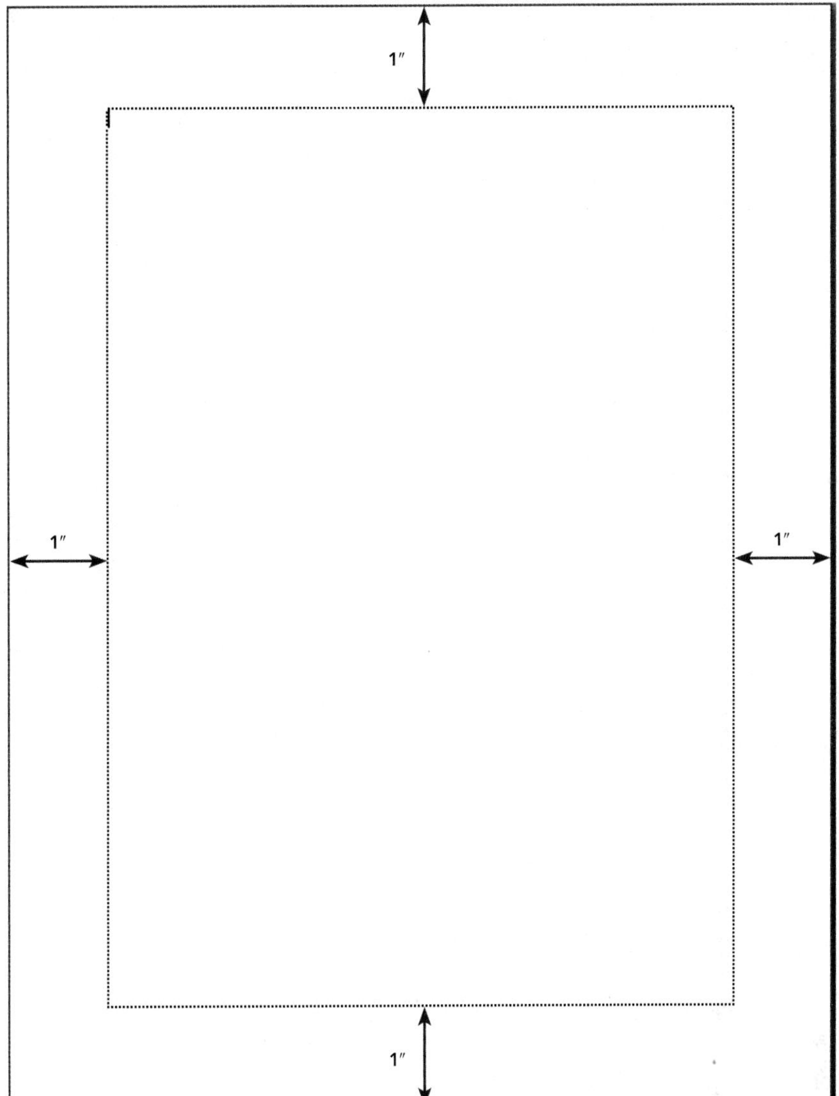

Figure 8-1
Default margin settings

Using standard-size paper (8.5 by 11 inches) and Word's default margin settings, you have 6.5 by 9 inches on the page for your text. To increase or decrease this workspace, you can change margins by using the Page Setup dialog box or the rulers or the Print tab.

To set margins, you can use one of these methods:

- Choose a preset margin setting from the Margin command list.
- Change settings in the Page Setup dialog box.
- Drag margins using the horizontal and vertical rulers.
- Change settings when previewing the document using the Print tab.

Figure 8-2
Actual workspace using default margin settings and standard-size paper

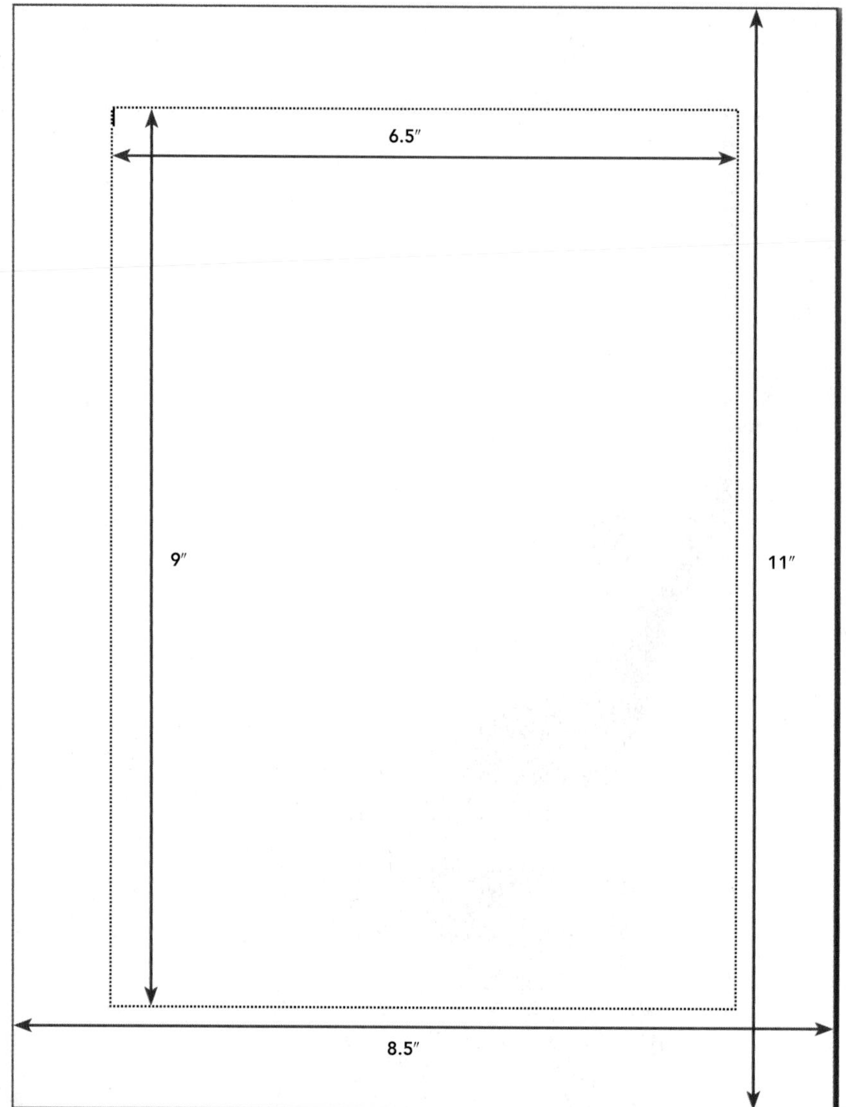

Exercise 8-1 CHANGE MARGINS FOR A DOCUMENT USING THE PAGE SETUP DIALOG BOX

NOTE

The documents you create in this course relate to the case study about Campbell's Confections, a fictional candy store and chocolate factory (see the Case Study in the front matter).

TIP

You can view page margins by opening the Word Options dialog box. Click Advanced, scroll to Show document content, and click Show text boundaries.

One way to change margins for a document is to use the Page Setup dialog box. You can change margins for an entire document or selected text. You can open the Page Setup dialog by clicking the Margins button on the Page Layout tab, clicking the Page Setup Dialog Box Launcher, or double clicking the vertical or horizontal ruler.

1. Open the file **Corporate Gifts**. (Make sure no text is selected.)
2. Click the Page Layout tab and click the Margins button. Locate the Normal option, and notice that it displays the default margin settings.
3. Click Custom Margins at the bottom of the Margins gallery, and click the Margins tab, if it is not active. The dialog box shows the default margin settings.

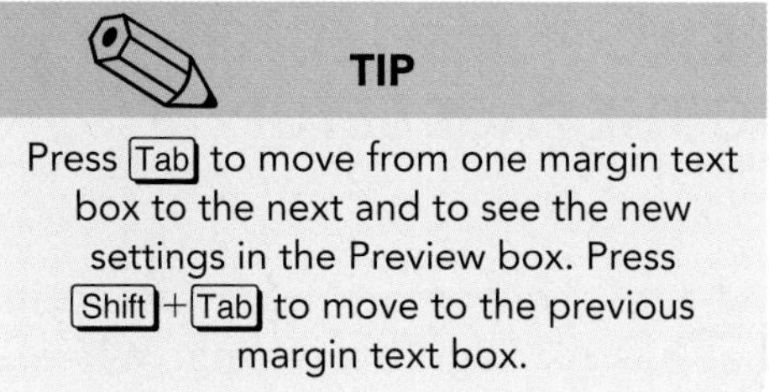

TIP

Press Tab to move from one margin text box to the next and to see the new settings in the Preview box. Press Shift+Tab to move to the previous margin text box.

4. Edit the margin text settings so they have the following values (or click the arrow to change the settings). As you do so, notice the changes in the **Preview** box.

Top	**1.5**
Bottom	**1.5**
Left	**2**
Right	**2**

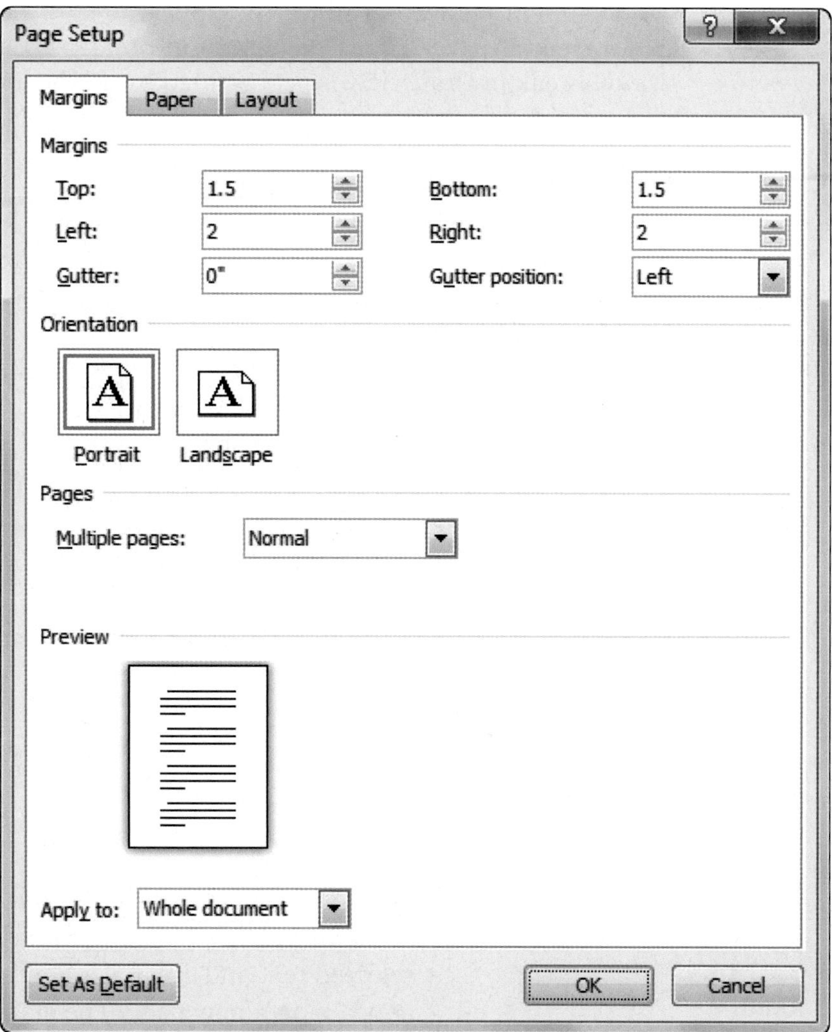

Figure 8-3
Changing margins in the Page Setup dialog box

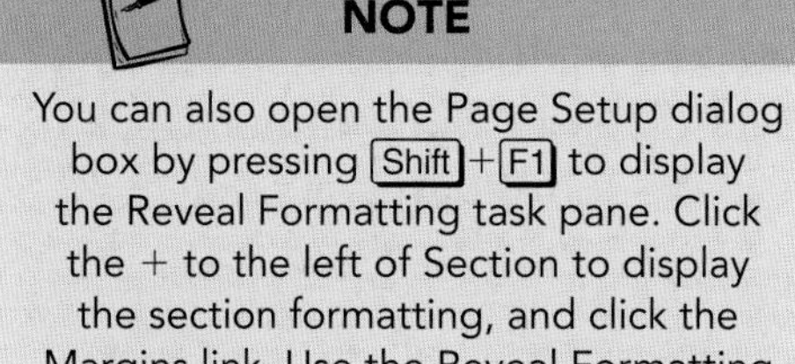

NOTE

You can also open the Page Setup dialog box by pressing Shift+F1 to display the Reveal Formatting task pane. Click the + to the left of Section to display the section formatting, and click the Margins link. Use the Reveal Formatting task pane to verify margin settings.

5. Click the down arrow to open the **Apply to** drop-down list. Notice that you can choose either **Whole document** or **This point forward** (from the insertion point forward). Choose **Whole document** and click **OK** to change the margins of the entire document.

Exercise 8-2 CHANGE MARGINS FOR SELECTED TEXT BY USING THE PAGE SETUP DIALOG BOX

When you change margins for selected text, you create a new section. A *section* is a portion of a document that has its own formatting. When a document contains more than one section, *section breaks* indicate the beginning and end of a section. When you insert a next page section break, the document view determines the appearance of the section break. Print layout view displays a next page section break as a new page. A next page section break in Draft view is represented by double-dotted lines.

1. Select the text from the second paragraph to the end of the document.
2. Click the **Page Layout** tab. Click the **Page Setup Dialog Box Launcher** (see Figure 8-4) to display the Page Setup dialog box.

Figure 8-4
Page Setup Dialog Box Launcher

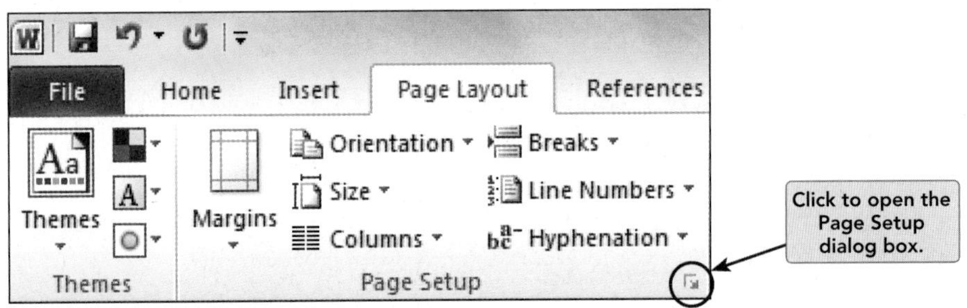

3. Change the margins to the following settings:

   Top 2
   Bottom 2
   Left 1.5
   Right 1.5

4. Choose **Selected text** from the **Apply to** box. Click **OK**.
5. Deselect the text, and scroll to the beginning of the selection. Word applied the margin changes to the selected text and created a new section. The section appears on a new page. The status bar displays section numbers and page numbers to help you identify the position of the insertion point in the document. To display section numbers and page numbers in the status bar, right-click the status bar, and click to select Section and Page Number. Click in the document to close the shortcut menu.

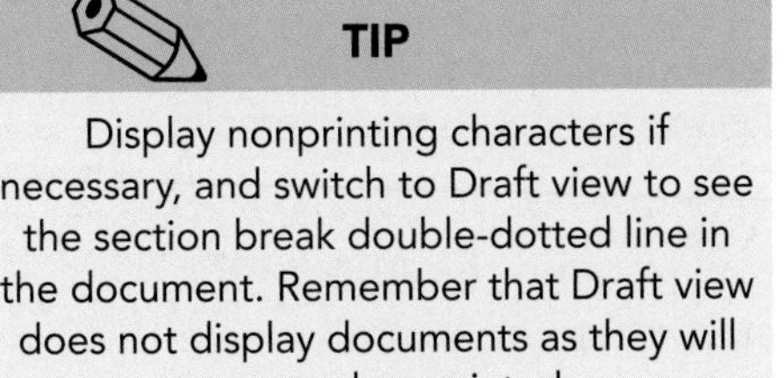

TIP

Display nonprinting characters if necessary, and switch to Draft view to see the section break double-dotted line in the document. Remember that Draft view does not display documents as they will appear when printed.

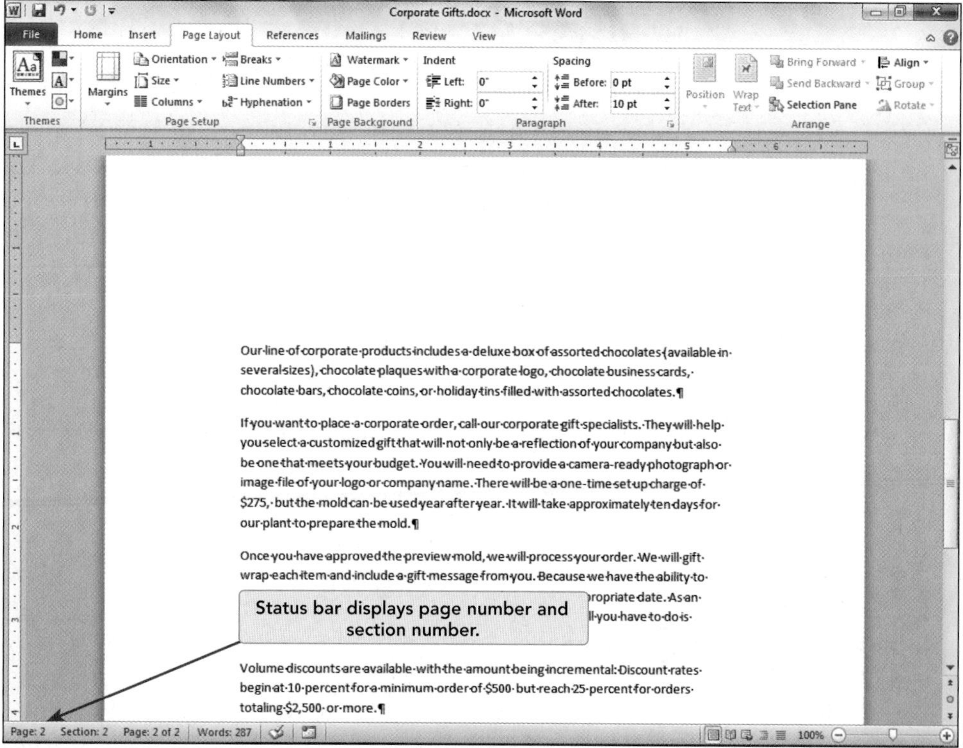

Figure 8-5
Creating a new section by changing margins for selected text

Exercise 8-3 CHANGE MARGINS FOR A SECTION BY USING THE PAGE SETUP DIALOG BOX

After a section is created, you can change the margins for just the section (not the entire document) by using the Page Setup dialog box. To help you know which section you are formatting, customize the status bar to display section numbers.

1. Move the insertion point anywhere in the new section (section 2), and right-click the status bar. Click **Section** to select the display option, and click in the document to close the shortcut menu. Open the **Page Setup dialog box**.
2. Change the left and right margin settings to **1.25** inches.
3. Open the **Apply to** drop-down list to view the options. Notice that you can apply the new margin settings to the current section, to the whole document, or from the insertion point forward.
4. Choose **This section** and click **OK** to apply the settings to the new section.

Exercise 8-4 CHANGE MARGINS USING THE RULERS

To change margins using the rulers, use Print Layout view. The status bar includes five buttons for changing document views. This lesson discusses two of the document views. The default view for Word documents is Print Layout, which displays text as it will appear on the printed page. Use Print Layout view to display headers, footers, and other page elements. Draft view displays the main text of the document. It does not display headers, footers, multicolumn layout, or graphics.

There are two ways to switch document views:

- Click a view button on the right side of the status bar.
- Click the View tab, and click a view button.

Figure 8-6 View buttons on the status bar and the View tab

Status Bar View Buttons

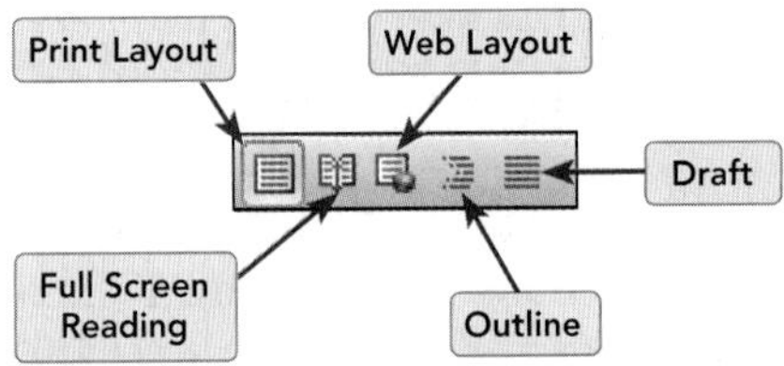

View Tab Buttons

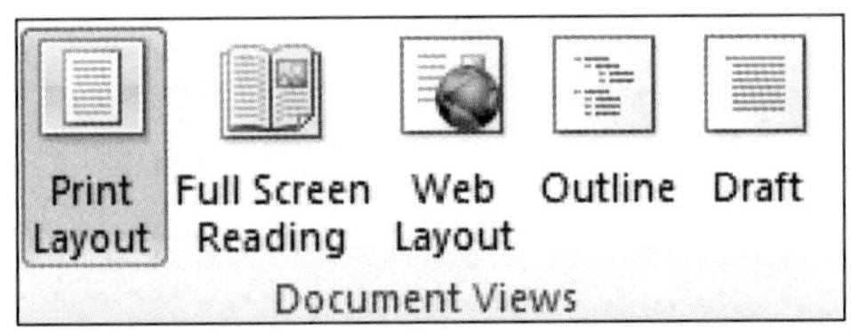

1. Place the insertion point at the beginning of the document (Ctrl+Home). In bold uppercase letters, key **CORPORATE GIFTS**, and then press Enter. Center the title and add 24 points spacing after. The Page Layout tab includes a Paragraph group and an option to change paragraph spacing.
2. Click the View Ruler button at the top of the vertical scroll bar if necessary to display the rulers.
3. Click in the new section (page 2). The status bar shows that the document contains two pages and two sections. Notice the extra space at the top of the page. The new section has a large top margin (2 inches).

NOTE

You can also use the View tab to change the Zoom level. Click the One Page option to view the entire page. Click the Zoom button to display the Zoom dialog box, and click the 100% button to return the zoom level to 100% of the normal size. The Page Width button changes the zoom level so that the width of the page matches the width of the document window.

4. To see more of the page, including the margin areas, click the Zoom button on the status bar 100%, and then choose **Whole page**. Click **OK**. Review the document then drag the Zoom slider to 100%.
5. Move the insertion point to the top of the document (the first section). The shaded area at the top of the vertical ruler represents the 1.5-inch top margin. The shaded area on the left and right side of the horizontal ruler represents the 2-inch left and right margins. The white area between the shaded areas on the horizontal ruler shows the text area, which is a line length of 4.5 inches. (See Figure 8-7.)

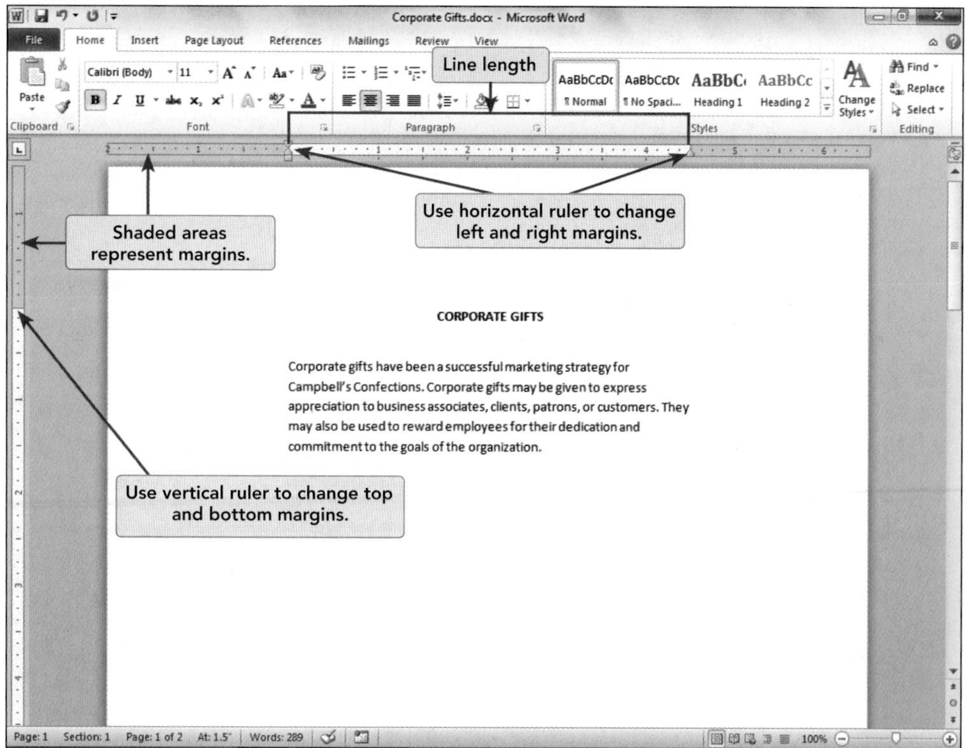

Figure 8-7
Rulers in Print Layout view

6. To change the top margin, position the pointer over the top margin boundary on the vertical ruler. The top margin boundary is the line between the shaded area and the white area on the ruler. The pointer changes to a two-headed vertical arrow and a ScreenTip displays the words "Top Margin."
7. Press and hold down the left mouse button. The margin boundary appears as a dotted horizontal line.
8. Drag the margin boundary slightly up, and release the mouse button. The text at the top of the document moves up to align with the new top margin.
9. Click the Undo button to restore the 1.5-inch top margin.
10. Hold down the Alt key, and drag the top margin boundary down until it is at 2 inches on the ruler. Release Alt and the mouse button. Holding down the Alt key as you drag shows the exact margin and text area measurements.
11. To change the left margin, position the pointer over the left margin boundary on the horizontal ruler. The left margin boundary is between the shaded area and the white area on the ruler. Move the mouse to the point where the first-line indent marker meets the hanging indent marker. The pointer changes to a two-headed horizontal arrow, and a ScreenTip displays the words "Left Margin."

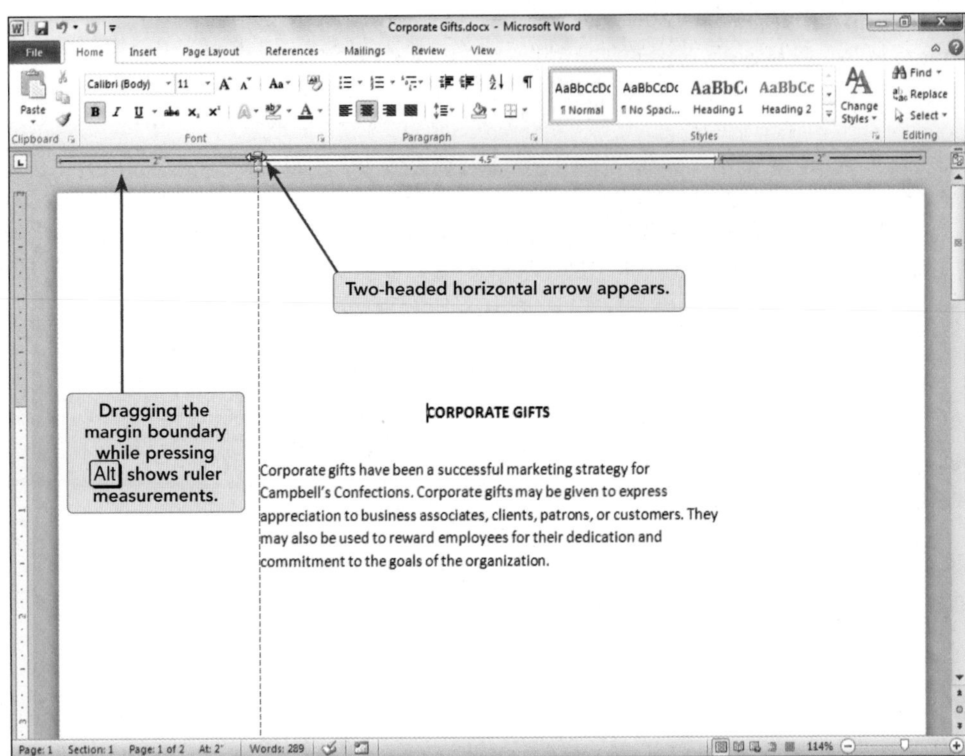

Figure 8-8
Adjusting the left margin

NOTE

You might have to fine-tune the pointer position to place it directly on the left margin boundary. Move the pointer slowly until you see the two-headed arrow and the "Left Margin" ScreenTip.

12. Hold down the Alt key, and drag the margin boundary to the left to create a 1.75-inch left margin.
13. Using the same procedure, drag the right margin boundary until it is located 1.75 inches from the right. Be sure to watch for the two-headed arrow before dragging. The first section now has 1.75-inch left and right margins and a 2-inch top margin.
14. Scroll to the next page (section 2). Click within the text to activate this section's ruler. Change the top margin to 1.75 inches.
15. Click the **File** tab, and click the **Options** command. Click **Advanced** in the left pane and scroll to **Show document content**. Click **Show text boundaries**, and click **OK**. Dotted lines mark the page margins.
16. Remove the page margins from view by clicking the **File** tab, clicking the **Options** command, clicking **Advanced**, scrolling to **Show document content**, and deselecting **Show text boundaries**. Click **OK**.
17. Save the document as ***[your initials]*8-4** in a new Lesson 8 folder, and close the document.

NOTE

If you move the pointer to the top edge of the page in Print Layout view, you will see the Hide White Space button. Double-click the button to hide the white space (the margin area) at the top and bottom of each page and the shaded space between pages so you can see more document text. Point to the top of the page, and double-click the Show White Space button to restore the space.

Exercise 8-5 SET FACING PAGES WITH GUTTER MARGINS

If your document is going to be bound—put together like a book, with printing on both sides of the paper—you will want to use mirror margins and gutter margins. *Mirror margins* are inside and outside margins on facing pages that mirror one another. *Gutter margins* add extra space to the inside or top margins to allow for binding.

Figure 8-9
Mirror margins

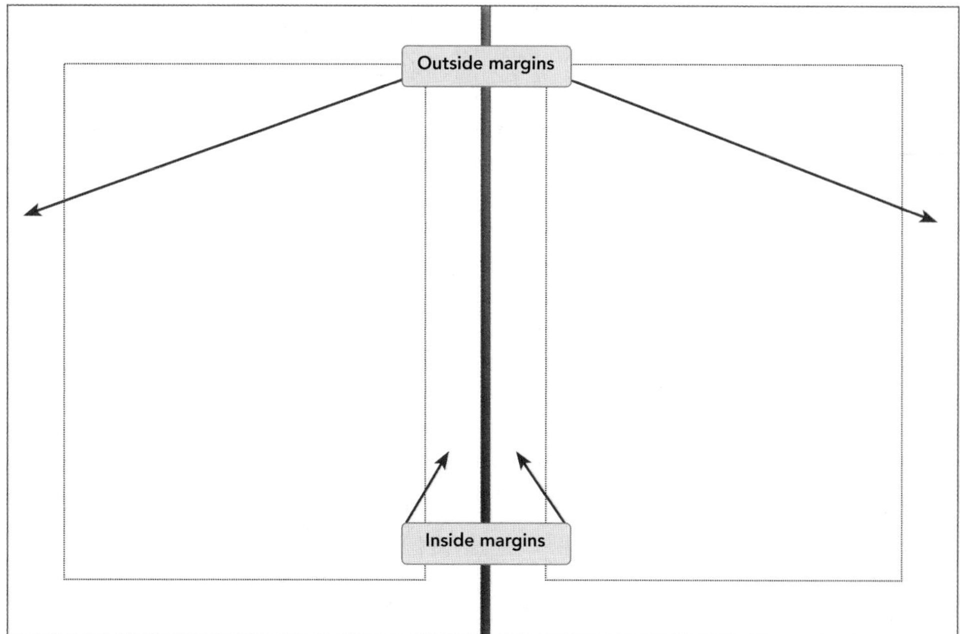

1. Open the file **Festival Planning**. Position the insertion point at the top of the document. Open the Page Setup dialog box, and click the down arrow to display the Multiple pages drop-down list. Choose Mirror margins. Notice that the Preview box now displays two pages. The left and right margin text boxes are now labeled inside and outside margins.
2. Change the Inside margin setting to **1.25** inches and the Outside margin setting to **1** inch.

TIP

Visualize the document as double-sided, facing pages in a book by placing the back of page 2 against the back of page 1 and placing page 3 beside page 2. The gutter margin of page 1 is on the left. The gutter margin on the right of page 2 and on the left of page 3 allows space for the binding and represents facing pages. *Facing pages* appear as a two-page spread with odd-numbered right pages and even-numbered left pages.

3. Set the Gutter margin to **1** inch, and press Tab to reflect the change in the Preview box. Click OK. A 1-inch gutter margin is added to the document. (Make sure you use at least 1-inch gutter margins to allow room for binding and to prevent the inside margin text from disappearing into the document binding.)
4. Click the Zoom button 100% on the status bar, and click the Many pages button. Move the mouse over the grid of pages that displays, and select three pages in the first row. Click OK. Notice that the first page and the third page have wide margins on the left side of the page (outside margins). The second page has a wide right (inside) margin.

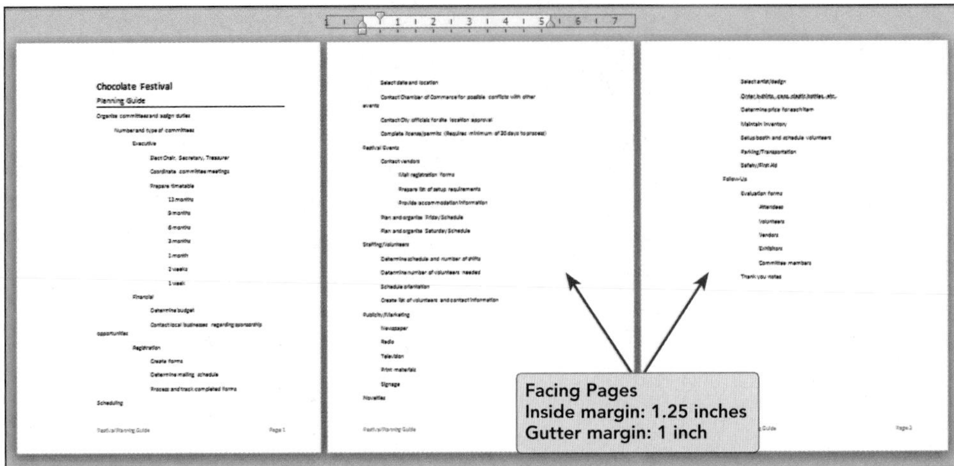

Figure 8-10
Facing pages and gutter margins

5. Drag the Zoom slider to 100%, and position the insertion point at the top of the document.
6. Open the Page Setup dialog box, and open the Multiple pages drop-down list. Choose Normal. Change the Gutter setting to **0.75**, and change the Gutter position to Top. Click OK. The document is ready for top binding.
7. Drag the Zoom slider to 35% to see the changes in the document. Notice the additional space at the top of the document to allow for binding. Change the zoom level to 100%.
8. Open the Page Setup dialog box. Change the Left and Right margins to **1** inch, change the Gutter setting to **0** inch, and change the Gutter position to Left. Click OK.
9. Save the document as ***[your initials]*8-5** in your Lesson 8 folder.
10. Submit the document, and leave it open for the next exercise.

Previewing a Document

Use the Print tab to preview a document and to check how the document will look when you print it. You can view multiple pages at a time, adjust margins, and change page orientation using the Print tab.

To preview a document, click the File tab, and click the Print command to display the Print tab. The keyboard shortcut to preview a document is Alt+Ctrl+I or Ctrl+F2.

Exercise 8-6 VIEW A DOCUMENT IN PRINT PREVIEW

The Print tab displays a document in reduced size. You can view one page of a document or multiple pages. The Print tab includes buttons to navigate from one page to another and to change the zoom level of a document.

1. Move the insertion point to the beginning of the document.
2. Click the **File** tab, and click the **Print** command. The Navigation Pane displays on the left. The Print tab displays print settings and a preview of the document.

Figure 8-11
Print tab

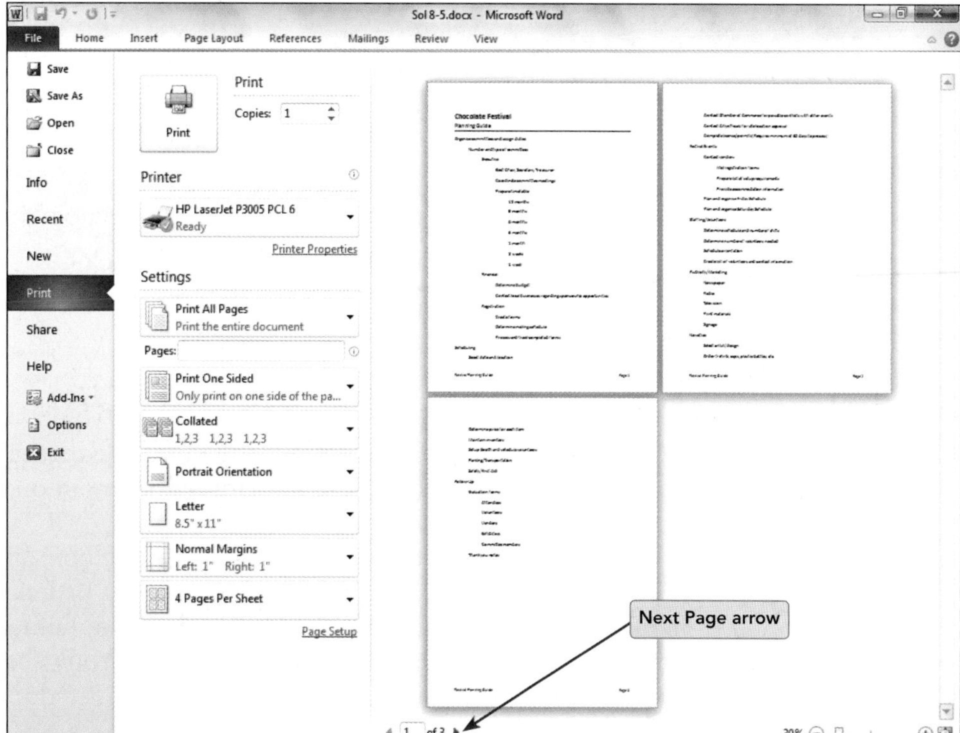

3. Change the zoom level to 60%. To move to page 2, click the Next Page arrow ▶.
4. Drag the **Zoom slider** to 25% to view all the pages of the document.
5. Drag the **Zoom slider** to 100%, and click the **Home** tab to return to Print Layout view.

TIP

You use the Zoom slider or the Zoom button to view multiple pages of your document. Click the Zoom button on the status bar. Click the Many Pages button, and a grid appears to choose the number of pages you want to view and how they are configured in the window. If you drag the pointer as you move across the grid, you can expand the grid to display additional rows and pages, which is useful in a long document. Drag the Zoom slider to 100% to return to a one-page view.

Exercise 8-7 CHANGE MARGINS USING THE PRINT TAB

The Print tab displays a preview of the active document and includes print and page formatting settings. Once you have had a chance to study the preview of your document, it is easy to make changes to the margin settings.

1. Move the insertion point to the beginning of the document (page 1, section 1).
2. Click the **File** tab, and click the **Print** command.
3. Locate the **Settings** gallery, and click the down-arrow for **Margins**. Click **Custom Margins** to open the Page Setup dialog box.
4. Change the top margin to **2** inches and click **OK**.
5. Save the document as ***[your initials]*8-7**.

Paper Size and Orientation

When you open a new document, the default paper size is 8.5 by 11 inches. You can change the paper size to print a document on legal paper (8.5 by 14) or define a custom-size paper.

The Page Layout tab, the Page Setup dialog box, and the Print tab display options to choose orientation settings: portrait or landscape. A *portrait* page is taller than it is wide. This orientation is the default in new Word documents. A *landscape* page is wider than it is tall. You can apply page-orientation changes to sections of a document or to the entire document.

Exercise 8-8 CHANGE PAPER SIZE AND PAGE ORIENTATION

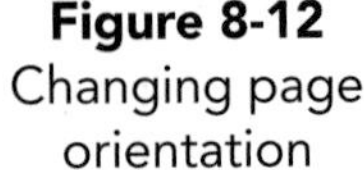

Figure 8-12 Changing page orientation

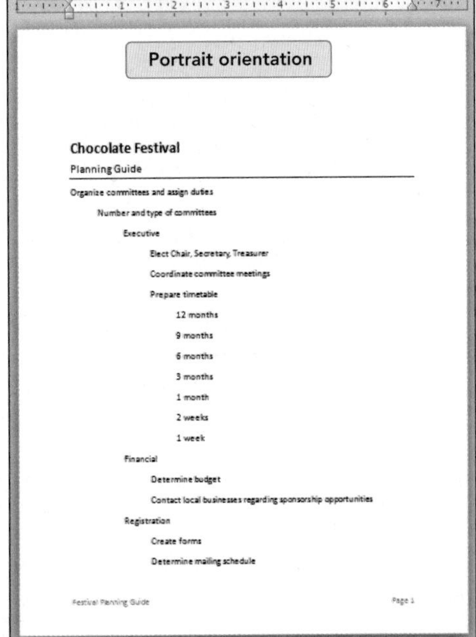

Landscape orientation

Chocolate Festival

Planning Guide

1. Display the Page Layout tab.
2. Locate the Page Setup group, and click the Orientation command.
3. Click Landscape, and drag the Zoom slider to 65% to view the change. Change the zoom level to 100%.
4. Click the Size command in the Page Setup group. Notice the default paper size for letter paper.
5. Click the More Paper Sizes option, and choose Legal from the Paper size drop-down list. Click the Margins tab, and choose Portrait. Click OK. Notice how the orientation and paper size changed.
6. Press Ctrl+Z twice to undo the changes to paper size and orientation.
7. Display the Print tab, and locate the Settings gallery.
8. Click the Orientation command, and click Landscape Orientation.
9. Save the document as ***[your initials]*8-8**.
10. Submit and close the document.

NOTE

You can change orientation for an entire document or from the insertion point forward by choosing an option from the Apply to drop-down list in the Page Setup dialog box. When you choose This point forward, a new section is created with the orientation you choose. When selected text is formatted with a different orientation, a section break is automatically inserted before and after the selected text.

Printing Envelopes and Labels

Word provides a tool to print different-size envelopes and labels. Using the Envelopes and Labels command, you can:

- Print a single envelope without saving it, or attach the envelope to a document for future printing. The envelope displays at the beginning of the document as a separate section.
- Print labels without saving them, or create a new document that contains the label text. You can print a single label or a full page of the same label.

Exercise 8-9 PRINT AN ENVELOPE

Printing envelopes often requires that you manually feed the envelope to your printer. If you print labels on paper that is a different size than 8.5- by 11-inch sheets, you might need to feed the labels manually. Your printer will display a code and not print until you feed an envelope or label sheet manually.

1. Open the file **Matthews**. This document is a one-page business letter.
2. Click the Mailings tab, and locate the Create group. Click the Envelopes button.
3. Click the Envelopes tab if it is not active. Notice that Word detected the inside address in the document and placed this text in the Delivery address text box. You can edit this text as needed.

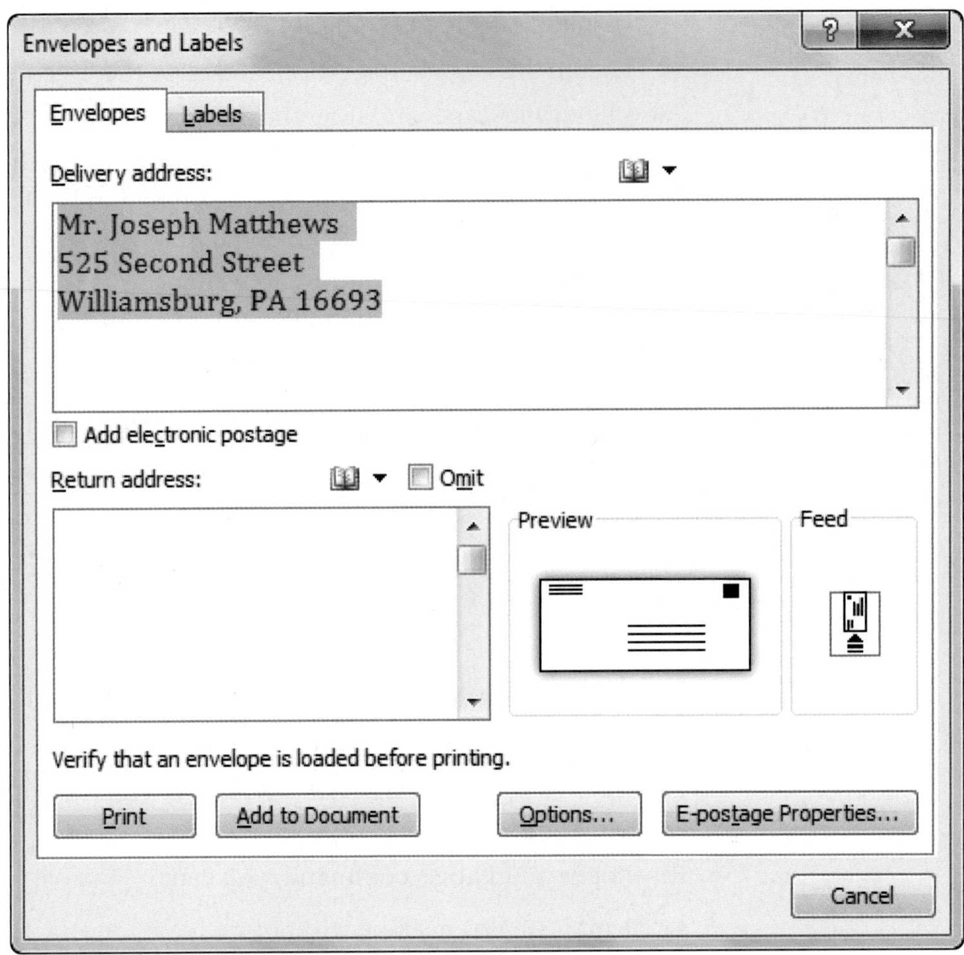

Figure 8-13 Envelopes and Labels dialog box

4. In the **Delivery address** text box, enter the full ZIP+4 Code by keying **-1129** after "16693."
5. Make sure the **Omit** box is not checked. Select and delete any text in the **Return address** text box, and then key the following return address, starting with your name:

   [your name]
   Campbell's Confections
   25 Main Street
   Grove City, PA 16127-0025

6. Place a standard business-size envelope in your printer. The **Feed** box illustrates the feeding method accepted by your printer. Before proceeding with the next step, check with your instructor for guidelines for printing envelopes.

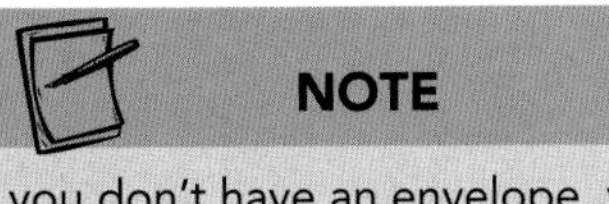

NOTE

If you don't have an envelope, you can use a blank sheet of paper to test the placement of the addresses. Ask your instructor how to proceed. You might have to feed the envelope or blank sheet manually.

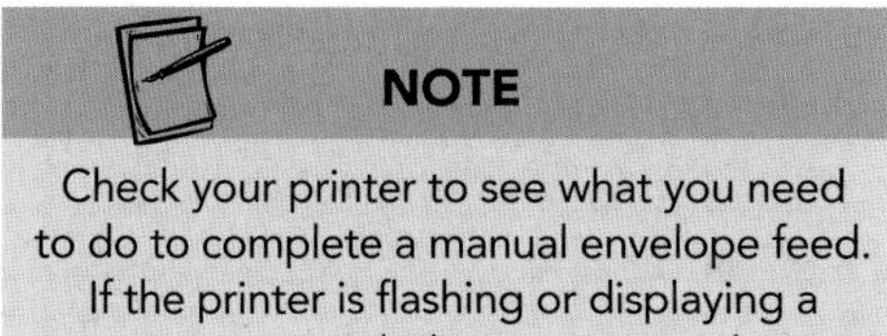

NOTE

Check your printer to see what you need to do to complete a manual envelope feed. If the printer is flashing or displaying a message, you might have to press a button.

7. Click **Print**. When Word asks if you want to save the return address as the default return address, click **No**. Word prints the envelope with the default font and text placement settings. If the envelope does not print, check with your instructor. Do not create a second envelope.

Exercise 8-10 CHOOSE ENVELOPE OPTIONS

Before printing an envelope, you can choose additional envelope options. For example, you can add the envelope content to the document for future use. You can also click the Options button in the Envelopes and Labels dialog box to:

- Change the envelope size. The default size is Size 10, which is a standard business envelope.
- Change the font and other character formatting of the delivery address or return address.
- Verify printing options.

1. Open the **Envelopes and Labels** dialog box again.
2. Key your name and address in the **Return address** box.
3. Click the **Options** button in the Envelopes and Labels dialog box to open the Envelope Options dialog box. Click the **Envelope Options** tab if it is not active.
4. Under **Envelope size**, click the down arrow to look at the different-size options. Click the arrow again to close the list.

Figure 8-14 Envelope Options dialog box

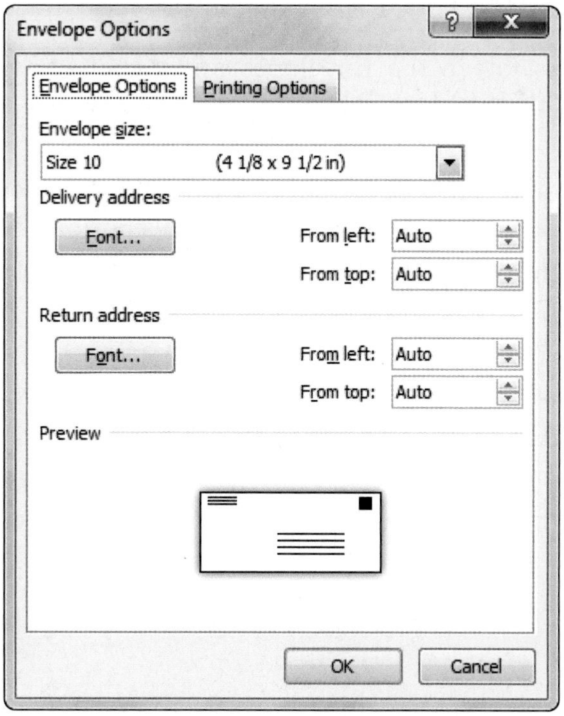

5. Click the Font button [Font...] for the **Delivery address**. The Envelope Address dialog box for the delivery address opens.
6. Format the text as bold and all caps, and change the font size to 10. Click **OK** to close the Envelope Address dialog box. Click **OK** to close the Envelope Options dialog box.
7. Delete the punctuation from the delivery address, and add **-1129** to the ZIP Code.
8. Click **Add to Document** to add the envelope information to the top of the document as a separate section. Do not save the return address as the default address. Once the envelope is added to the document, you can also format or edit the envelope text just as you would any document text. The default font for envelope addresses is Cambria.

NOTE

The delivery address format preferred by the U.S. Postal Service is all caps with no punctuation.

NOTE

If you are asked to feed the envelope manually, you might be asked to feed the letter manually as well.

9. Replace "[Today's date]" with the current date. Correct any spacing between the elements of the letter. Add your reference initials followed by **Enclosures (2)**. To make sure the letter follows the correct format, see Appendix B, "Standard Forms for Business Documents."
10. Preview the letter and envelope using the Print tab.
11. Save the document as ***[your initials]*8-10** in your Lesson 8 folder.
12. Submit the document.
13. Leave the document open for use in the next exercise.

Exercise 8-11 PRINT LABELS

The Labels tab in the Envelopes and Labels dialog box makes it easy to print different-size labels for either a return address or a delivery address.

1. Position the insertion point in the envelope section of the document. Click the **Mailings** tab. Click the Labels button.
2. Click the **Use return address** check box to create labels for the letter sender.
3. Select the address text, and press Ctrl+Shift+A to turn on all caps. Delete the comma after the city.
4. Click the option **Full page of the same label**, if it is not active, to create an entire page of return address labels.
5. Click the Options button [Options...] to choose a label size.

Figure 8-15
Label Options dialog box

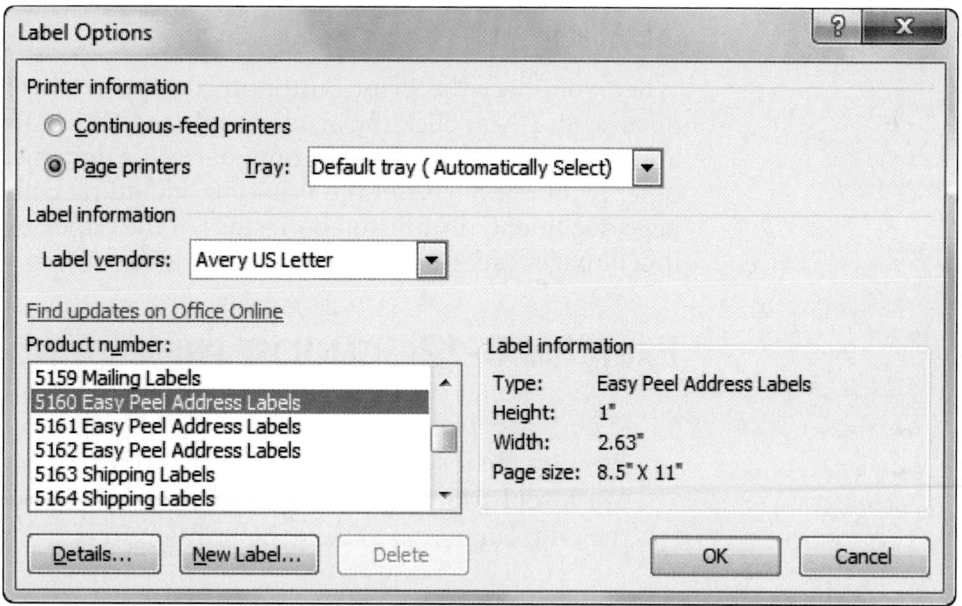

NOTE

Be sure to verify the options selected in the Printer information and Label information sections.

NOTE

When you select a product number in the Label Options dialog box, the Label information section displays the type of label, the height and width of the label, and the page size. There are several types of labels available including address labels, identification labels, media labels, file folder labels, and shipping labels. Labels are available for laser and ink jet printers. Read the label description, size information, and printer type before purchasing labels.

6. Verify that **Page printers** is selected under **Printer information** and that **Avery US Letter** is listed in the **Label vendors** list box.
7. Scroll the **Product number** list to see the various label options, and choose **5160**, the product number for a standard Avery address label.
8. Click **OK**, and then click **New Document** to save the labels as a separate document. (If you click Print, you can print the labels without saving them.) Do not save the return address.
9. Select all text in the new document, and reduce the font size to 11 points.
10. Save the document as ***[your initials]*8-11** in your Lesson 8 folder.
11. Change the zoom level to view the labels on the page.
12. Submit the document, or prepare the printer for a sheet of 5160-size labels, or feed a blank sheet of paper into the printer, and then print the labels.
13. Close the document containing the full sheet of labels.

Setting Print Options

When you click the Print button on the Print tab, Word prints the entire document. If you click the arrow beside the Print All Pages command, however, you can choose to print only part of a document. You can also select other print options from the Print tab, including collating copies of a multipage document, printing on both sides of the paper, or printing multiple document pages on one sheet of paper.

Exercise 8-12 CHOOSE PRINT OPTIONS FROM THE PRINT TAB

1. Position the insertion point to the left of the date in the letter to Mr. Joseph Matthews (***[your initials]*8-10**). Click the **File** tab, and click the **Print** command to view the print options.

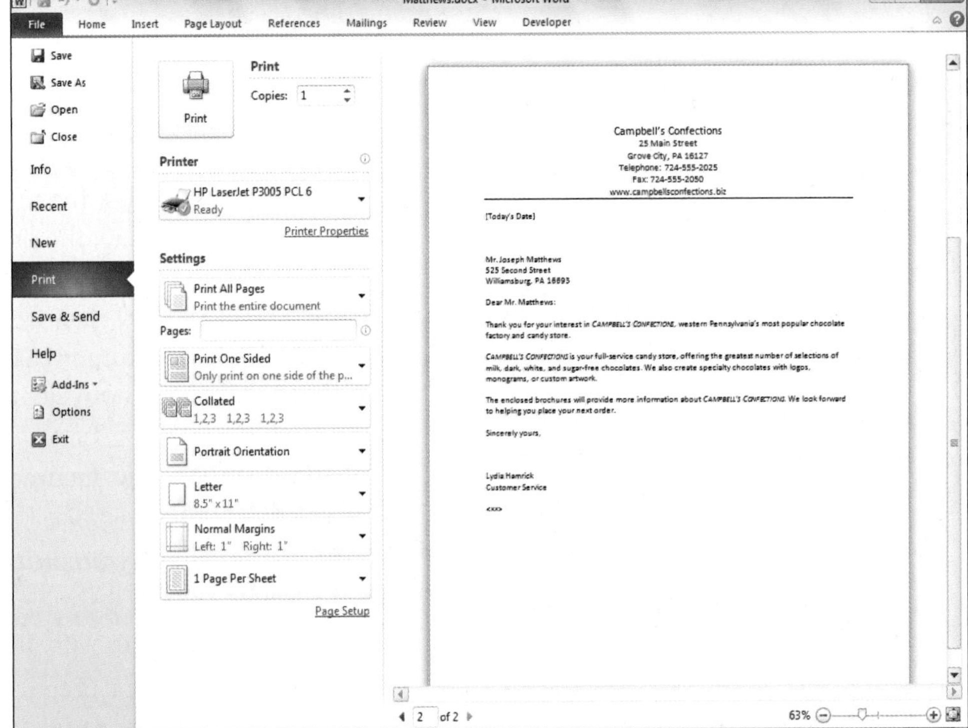

Figure 8-16
Print tab

2. Click the down arrow of the **Print All Pages** option, and choose **Print Current Page**. Click **Print**. Word prints the business letter.
3. Open the **Print** tab again. Key **1-2** in the **Pages** text box. You can enter specific page numbers or page ranges.
4. In the **Copies** text box, use the up arrow to change the number of copies to **2**.
5. Click the down arrow beside the **Collated** option, and verify that **Collated** is selected. Click the **Uncollated** option. Word will print two copies of page 1 and then two copies of page 2.

NOTE

Each time you select an option in the Print tab, the name of the setting changes. For example, when you open the Print tab, the first print setting is identified as Print All Pages. If you choose the Print Current Page option, the print setting name changes to Print Current Page. The settings remain in effect until you make the next change.

6. Change the number of copies back to 1.
7. Click the down arrow to open the **Print Current Page** drop-down list. It shows the various elements you can print in addition to the entire document. Click again to close the list.
8. Click the down arrow to open the **1 Page Per Sheet** drop-down list, which gives you the option to print your selection over a specified number of sheets. Choose the **2 Pages Per Sheet** setting. This option prints two pages on one sheet of 8.5- by 11-inch paper, with each page reduced to fit on the sheet.
9. Click the down arrow to open the **2 Pages Per Sheet** list, and locate the **Scale to Paper Size** option. Point to the Scale to Paper Size command to view the option to print on a different paper or envelope size (Word adjusts the scaling of the fonts, tables, and other elements to fit the new size). Click **No Scaling** to close the list.

TABLE 8-1 Print Tab Settings

Button	Description	Function
Print	Print	Print the document in the Print Preview window.
Copies: 1	Number of copies	Prints one or multiple copies of document.
HP LaserJet P3005 PCL 6 Ready	Printer	Select printer to use.
Print All Pages Print the entire document	Print All Pages	Options include the entire document, selected text, current page, specific pages, document properties, odd and even pages.
Pages:	Pages	Specify print range. Example: Key 1-4, 6 to print pages 1 through 4 and page 6.
Print One Sided Only print on one side of the p...	Print One Sided	Use the option to print on both sides of the paper.
Collated 1,2,3 1,2,3 1,2,3	Collated	Choose to collate or not to collate a document. In a three-page document, uncollated prints all first-page copies before printing copies of the second page or the third page. The collated option prints one set of pages 1 through 3 and then prints the second set.
Portrait Orientation	Portrait Orientation	Switch between portrait and landscape orientation.
Letter 8.5" x 11"	Paper Size	Choose a paper size for the document or the current active section.
Normal Margins Left: 1" Right: 1"	Margins	Change margin settings.
1 Page Per Sheet	Pages Per Sheet	Choose the number of pages to print per sheet of paper, or choose an option to scale the document to a different paper size.

10. Click the Print button [Print icon]. Word prints reduced versions of pages 1 and 2 on one sheet of paper.
11. Close the document without saving.

Lesson 8 Summary

- In a Word document, text is keyed and printed within the boundaries of the document's margins. Margins are the spaces between the edges of the text and the edges of the paper.
- Change the actual space for text on a page by changing margins (left, right, top, and bottom). You can key new margin settings in the Page Setup dialog box.
- Changing margins for selected text results in a new section for the selected text. A section is a portion of a document that has its own formatting. When a document contains more than one section, you see double-dotted lines, or section breaks, between sections to indicate the beginning and end of a section.
- Print Layout view shows the position of text on the printed page. Use the View buttons on the right of the status bar to switch between Print Layout view and Draft view.
- The Print tab shows how an entire document looks before printing. Use the navigation buttons, Zoom slider, and the scroll bar to view all or part of the document. Change the zoom level as needed.
- Change margins in Print Layout view by positioning the pointer over a margin boundary on the ruler and dragging. Press Alt to see the exact ruler measurement as you drag.
- For bound documents, use mirror margins and gutter margins. Mirror margins are inside and outside margins on facing pages that mirror one another. Gutter margins add extra space to allow for top or inside binding.
- A document can print in either portrait (8.5- by 11-inch) or landscape (11- by 8.5-inch) orientation. Choose an orientation using the Orientation command on the Page Layout tab, in the Page Setup dialog box, Margins tab, or using the Print tab.
- Scale a document to fit a particular paper size. Choose paper size options by clicking the Pages Per Sheet down arrow, and choosing Scale to Paper Size.
- Use Word to print different-size envelopes. You can change address formatting and make the envelope part of the document for future printing. Use Word to print different-size address labels—either a single label or a sheet of the same label.
- Choose print options such as printing only the current page, specified pages, selected text, collated copies of pages, and reduced pages by opening the Print tab.

LESSON 8		Command Summary	
Feature	**Button**	**Command**	**Keyboard**
Choose print options		File tab, Print	Ctrl+P
Margins		Page Layout tab, Page Setup group	
Print envelopes or labels		Mailings tab, Envelopes or Mailings tab, Labels command	
Print Layout view		View tab, Print Layout command	Alt+Ctrl+P
Print Preview		File tab, Print	Ctrl+F2 or Alt+Ctrl+I

Concepts Review

True/False Questions

Each of the following statements is either true or false. Indicate your choice by circling T or F.

T F 1. Word has default settings for margins that are automatically set for each new document.

T F 2. You can change margins in Print Layout view by using the ruler.

T F 3. The default page length is 8.5 inches.

T F 4. Switch to Draft view to see the page as it will appear when printed.

T F 5. The only way to change margins for the entire document is to use the Page Setup dialog box.

T F 6. Gutter margins are outside margins on a bound document.

T F 7. To view two pages of a document, increase the zoom level to 150%.

T F 8. Landscape is the default page orientation.

Short Answer Questions

Write the correct answer in the space provided.

1. Which document view displays vertical and horizontal rulers and special document elements such as headers and footers?

___

2. What does the pointer look like when it is located over the margin boundary on the vertical ruler in Print Layout view?

___

3. What is created when you change margins for selected text?

___

4. Which kind of document needs gutter margins?

___

5. Which tab displays the Orientation command?

___

6. What is the procedure to display the Print tab?

___

7. Which key to you press to show the exact margin and text area measurements when using the ruler to change margins?

8. What is the term for pages that appear as a two-page spread with odd-numbered right pages and even-numbered left pages?

Critical Thinking

Answer these questions on a separate page. There are no right or wrong answers. Support your answers with examples from your own experience, if possible.

1. Collect samples of printed documents with interesting treatments of margins (such as books, advertisements, or reports). Pay particular attention to mirror margins and gutter margins. How does the margin treatment contribute to the overall feeling of the document?

2. Use Microsoft Word Help (F1) or practice on your own to explore the Book fold feature that is located in the Page Setup dialog box, Multiple Pages section. What type of document would you create to use this feature? Is the feature helpful?

Skills Review

Exercise 8-13

Set margins for an entire document and for selected text by using the Page Setup dialog box.

1. Open the file **Gresh**.
2. Change the margins for the entire document by following these steps:
   a. Click the Page Layout tab, and click the Margins button.
   b. Click Custom Margins, and set the Top margin to **2** inches, the Bottom margin to **0.75** inch, and the Left and Right margins to **1.25** inches. Click OK.
3. Change the margins, and create a new section for selected text by following these steps:
   a. Select the address text within the body of the letter that begins "Campbell's Confections" through "Fax: 304-555-6660."
   b. Open the Page Setup dialog box.
   c. Set the left and right margins to **2** inches.
   d. Choose Selected text from the Apply to drop-down list, and click OK. The address appears by itself on a new page.

4. Position the insertion point in the new section (section 2) if necessary, and open the Page Setup dialog box.
5. Click the Layout tab, and locate the Section start list box. Choose Continuous, and click OK. The first and second sections appear on page 1 of the document.
6. Position the insertion point in section 3, and follow the procedure listed in the previous step to change the section layout to continuous. All sections appear on one page.
7. Key the text **Matthew Garrett, Manager** as a separate line before "Campbell's Confections" in the address information below the second paragraph.
8. Move to the top of the document, and change the top margin for section 1 to 0.75 inch.
9. Save the document as ***[your initials]*8-13** in your Lesson 8 folder.
10. Submit and close the document.

Exercise 8-14

Set margins in Print Layout view and the Print tab and change orientation.

1. Open the file **Chocolate**.
2. Change the left and right margins in Print Layout view by following these steps:
   a. Click the Print Layout View button located on the right of the status bar if necessary.
   b. If the rulers are not visible, click the View Ruler button.
   c. Using the horizontal ruler, position the pointer on the left-margin boundary until it becomes a two-headed horizontal arrow (and the ScreenTip "Left Margin" appears).
   d. Hold down Alt and drag the margin boundary until the left margin measures 1.5 inches.
   e. Position the pointer on the right margin boundary, and use the same method to drag it to 1.5 inches. The ruler displays a line length of 5.5 inches.
3. Change the top margin using the Print tab by following these steps:
   a. Click the File tab. Click Print to display the Print tab.
   b. Locate the section entitled Settings, and click the Custom Margins option.
   c. Click Custom Margins. . . at the bottom of the list, and change the Top margin to 2 inches. Click OK, and preview the document. Click the Home tab to return to Print Layout view.

4. Add a bold, centered, and uppercase title **TYPES OF CHOCOLATE** to the top of the document, with 24 points spacing after.
5. Change the orientation to landscape by following these steps:
   a. Select the **Page Layout** tab.
   b. Click the Orientation button, and choose **Landscape**.
6. Change the top margin to **2** inches, change the bottom margin to **1** inch, and change the left and right margins to **1.25** inches. Click **OK** to close the Page Setup dialog box.
7. Save the document as ***[your initials]*8-14** in your Lesson 8 folder.
8. Submit and close the document.

Exercise 8-15

Set mirror and gutter margins.

1. Open the file **Corporate Gifts - 2**.
2. Use the Page Setup dialog box to set mirror and gutter margins by following these steps:
   a. Open the **Page Setup** dialog box.
   b. Choose **Mirror margins** from the **Multiple pages** drop-down list.
   c. Change the inside and outside margins to **1.5** inches.
   d. Set the **Gutter margin** to **0.5** inch.
   e. Click **OK**.
3. Scroll through the document in Print Layout view to see the new margin settings.
4. Click the Zoom button 100%.
5. Click the Many Pages button, and drag to select two pages. Click **OK**. Notice the change in the margins. Drag the Zoom slider to 100%.
6. Save the document as ***[your initials]*8-15** in your Lesson 8 folder.
7. Print the document two pages per sheet, by following these steps:
   a. Click the **File** tab.
   b. Click **Print** to open the Print tab.
   c. Click the **1 Page Per Sheet** option, and choose **2 Pages Per Sheet**.
   d. Click **Print**.
8. Close the document

Exercise 8-16

Set print options, print an envelope, and print labels.

1. Open the file **WV Stores**. Select the title and apply 16-point, bold, all caps formatting.
2. Print a portion of the document by following these steps:
   a. Select the text for the "Wheeling, WV" store—from "Campbell's Confections" through the fax number.
   b. Press Ctrl+P to open the Print tab.
   c. Locate the **Print All Pages** option, and click the drop-down arrow.
   d. Choose **Print Selection**, and click **Print**.
3. Insert the date by following these steps:
   a. Go to the end of the document, and press Enter four times. Key the text **Updated** and press Spacebar.
   b. Click the **Insert** tab, and click the Date and Time button.
   c. Choose the fourth date format, make sure **Update automatically** is not checked, and click **OK**.
   d. Insert a blank line after the date.
4. Prepare an envelope addressed to the Morgantown store by following these steps:
   a. Select the name and address lines for the Morgantown store. Do not select the telephone and fax numbers.
   b. Click the **Mailings** tab. Click the Envelopes button. Click the **Envelopes** tab.
   c. In the **Delivery address** box, delete the comma in the address, and key **-3301** at the end of the ZIP Code.
   d. In the **Return address** box, key your name, followed by the office address:

      Campbell's Confections
      25 Main Street
      Grove City, PA 16127

TIP

Because this document contains many addresses, you need to select the text you want to appear in the Delivery address box of the Envelopes and Labels dialog box.

5. Choose additional envelope options, and add the envelope to the document by following these steps:
   a. Click the **Options** button, and choose the **Envelope Options** tab, if it is not already displayed.
   b. Make sure the envelope size is **Size 10**.
   c. Click the **Font** button Font... for the delivery address. Change the format to bold and all caps, and click **OK**.
   d. Click **OK** in the Envelope Options dialog box. Click **Add to Document** in the Envelopes and Labels dialog box. Do not save the return address as the default.

6. Prepare the printer for a standard business envelope (or feed a blank sheet of paper into the printer). Print the document (envelope included), or submit the document.

7. Save the document as ***[your initials]*****8-16a** in your Lesson 8 folder.

8. Create and print a page of return address labels by following these steps:

   a. With the insertion point in section 1 (the envelope), open the Envelopes and Labels dialog box and click the **Labels** tab.

   b. Locate the **Use return address** box, and click to select. (Word recognizes the return address you previously entered for the envelope.)

   c. Choose the option **Full page of the same label**.

   d. Click **Options**. Verify that the **Page Printers** option is selected, and choose **Avery US Letter** in the **Label vendors** list box. Set the **Product number** to **5160**, and click **OK**.

   e. Click **New Document** to save the labels as a separate document. Do not save the return address as the default.

   f. Save the labels as ***[your initials]*****8-16b** in your Lesson 8 folder.

   g. Print the labels on a blank sheet of paper, or submit the document.

9. Close both documents.

Lesson Applications

Exercise 8-17

Set margins for a document and for selected text.

1. Open the file **PA Stores**.
2. At the beginning of the document, key the text shown in Figure 8-17. Use single spacing, and insert one blank line between paragraphs.

Figure 8-17

```
Thank you for choosing Campbell's Confections to provide
your company with our boxed chocolates. Our candy
creations include chocolate-covered nuts, creams, and
melt-a-ways as well as our popular cordial cherries and
caramel pecanettes.

You can order our candy by calling our toll-free number,
accessing our Web site, or visiting one of our retail
stores. We have 14 stores in Pennsylvania, and the store
addresses and telephone numbers are listed on the
following pages.
```

3. At the top of the document, key the title **Pennsylvania Stores** in 14-point bold small caps as a separate line. Center the title, and add 24 points spacing after. Copy the title, and paste it to the left of the first store.
4. Open the Page Setup dialog box, and set the top margin to 2 inches and the left and right margins to 1.25 inches.
5. Select the text beginning with the second title "Pennsylvania Stores" through the end of the document. Use the Page Setup dialog box to change the left and right margins for *only* the selected text to 3 inches.
6. Change the top margin of the new section to 1.5 inches.
7. Use the Replace command to format all occurrences of "Campbell's Confections" in the second section as bold italic.
8. Save the document as ***[your initials]*8-17** in your Lesson 8 folder.
9. Print the document using the 2 Pages per sheet option in the Print tab. Close the document.

Exercise 8-18

Set margins for a document and for selected text, change page orientation, and set print options.

1. Open the file **Memo - 3**.
2. Insert today's date in the date line.
3. In the opening paragraph of the memo, replace the text "items below" with **following information**.
4. Change the top margin to 2 inches and the left and right margins to 1.25 inches.
5. Select the text from "Beginning next quarter" through the end of the document. Open the Page Setup dialog box, and change the orientation to landscape for the selected text.
6. Format the new section as follows: Change the top margin to 1.5 inches, change the bottom margin to 1 inch, and change the left and right margins to 1 inch.
7. Place a blank line above "Description/Model number." Delete the paragraph mark after "Model Number," and insert a tab character. Delete the paragraph mark after "Serial Number," and insert a tab character. Continue this procedure until the line includes all items. Adjust the tab settings to distribute the text evenly between the margins. Change the font of the headings to Arial Narrow, and apply bold and small caps formatting. Apply a bottom border to the headings.
8. Save the document as ***[your initials]*8-18** in your Lesson 8 folder.
9. Print the document two pages per sheet. Close the document.

Exercise 8-19

Set margins, mirror margins, and gutter margins.

1. Open the file **Holiday Confections**.
2. Change the left and right margins to 0.75 inch, and change the paper size to 5.5 by 8.5 inches.
3. Set mirror margins and a 0.5-inch gutter margin.
4. Format the title as 20-point bold with a text effect and expanded spacing.
5. Justify all text below the title.
6. Format each side heading using 12-point, bold, small caps.
7. Position the insertion point at the beginning of the "Chocolate-Covered Pretzel" heading, and press Ctrl+Enter to insert a page break.

8. Change the zoom level to view both pages of the document. Add a page border to the document.
9. Save the document as ***[your initials]*8-19** in your Lesson 8 folder.
10. Submit and close the document.

Exercise 8-20 ◆ Challenge Yourself

Create labels.

1. Open the file **Haas**.
2. Format the document as a standard business letter. (Refer to Appendix B, "Standard Forms for Business Documents," for margin and spacing requirements.) Enter the date as an automatically updated field. The letter is from you with the title **Sales Associate** and to the following person:

   Mr. Mark Haas
   215 Lake Street
   Girard, PA 16417

3. Key the text shown in Figure 8-18 as the closing paragraphs.

Figure 8-18

```
Call our corporate gift specialists for assistance in
selecting your customized gifts, maintaining your mailing
list, and for information on volume discounts. The
enclosed brochure explains the procedure for ordering.

We look forward to doing business with you.
```

4. Add an enclosure notation to the letter.
5. Add an envelope to the document, and key your name in the Return addresss box. Preview the letter.
6. Save the document as ***[your initials]*8-20a** in your Lesson 8 folder.
7. Create a sheet of labels (Avery Standard 5160) of Mr. Haas's address as a new document. Use all caps and no punctuation in the address.
8. Save the labels as ***[your initials]*8-20b** in your Lesson 8 folder.
9. Submit both documents and close them.

On Your Own

In these exercises you work on your own, as you would in a real-life business environment. Use the skills you have learned to accomplish the task—and be creative.

Exercise 8-21

Write a summary about a book you have recently read. Change the margins for the document, and change the margins of one of the sections of the summary that you want to highlight. Save the document as ***[your initials]*8-21** and submit it.

Exercise 8-22

Create a document, and use the Page Layout tab to create a custom paper size. Change the width to 5 inches and the height to 3 inches. Change all margins to 0.4 inch, and change the orientation to landscape. Key a favorite recipe and format the text attractively. Save the document as ***[your initials]*8-22** and submit it.

Exercise 8-23

Log on to the Internet, and find five Web sites about today's current political topic. Create a document summarizing the topic with a pro and con approach. Format the document using landscape orientation. Save the document as ***[your initials]*8-23** and submit it.

Lesson 9

Page and Section Breaks

OBJECTIVES ***After completing this lesson, you will be able to:***

1. Use soft and hard page breaks.
2. Control line and page breaks.
3. Control section breaks.
4. Format sections.
5. Use the Go To feature.

Estimated Time: 1 hour

In Word, text flows automatically from the bottom of one page to the top of the next page. This is similar to how text wraps automatically from the end of one line to the beginning of the next line. You can control and customize how and when text flows from the bottom of one page to the top of the next. This process is called *pagination*.

Sections are a common feature of long documents and have a significant impact on pagination. This lesson describes how to insert and manage sections.

Using Soft and Hard Page Breaks

As you work on a document, Word is constantly calculating the amount of space available on the page. Page length is determined by the size of the paper and the top and bottom margin settings. For example, using standard-size paper and default margins, page length is 9 inches. When a document exceeds this length, Word creates a *soft page break*. Word adjusts this automatic page break as you add or delete text. A soft page break appears as a horizontal dotted line on the screen in Draft view. In Print Layout view, you see the actual page break—the bottom of one page and the top of the next. Draft view is frequently used to edit and format text. It does not show the page layout as it appears on a printed page, nor does it show special elements of a page such as columns, headers, or footers.

Exercise 9-1 ADJUST A SOFT PAGE BREAK AUTOMATICALLY

NOTE

When you format and edit long documents, check the status bar settings to make sure section and page numbers display. To verify the settings, right-click the status bar, and click to select the options.

NOTE

The page breaks described in this lesson might appear in slightly different locations on your screen.

1. Open the file **History**. Switch to Draft view by clicking the Draft view button on the status bar. Change the zoom level to 100% if necessary. Click the Show/Hide button if necessary to turn on the display of formatting characters.
2. Scroll to the bottom of page 3. Notice the soft page break separating the heading "Gourmet Chocolate" from the paragraph below it.
3. Locate the paragraph just above the heading "Gourmet Chocolate" (it begins "In 2001"). Move the insertion point to the left of "The Web site has proven" in the middle of the paragraph, and press Enter to split the paragraph. Notice the adjustment of the soft page break. Press Ctrl+Z to undo the paragraph split.

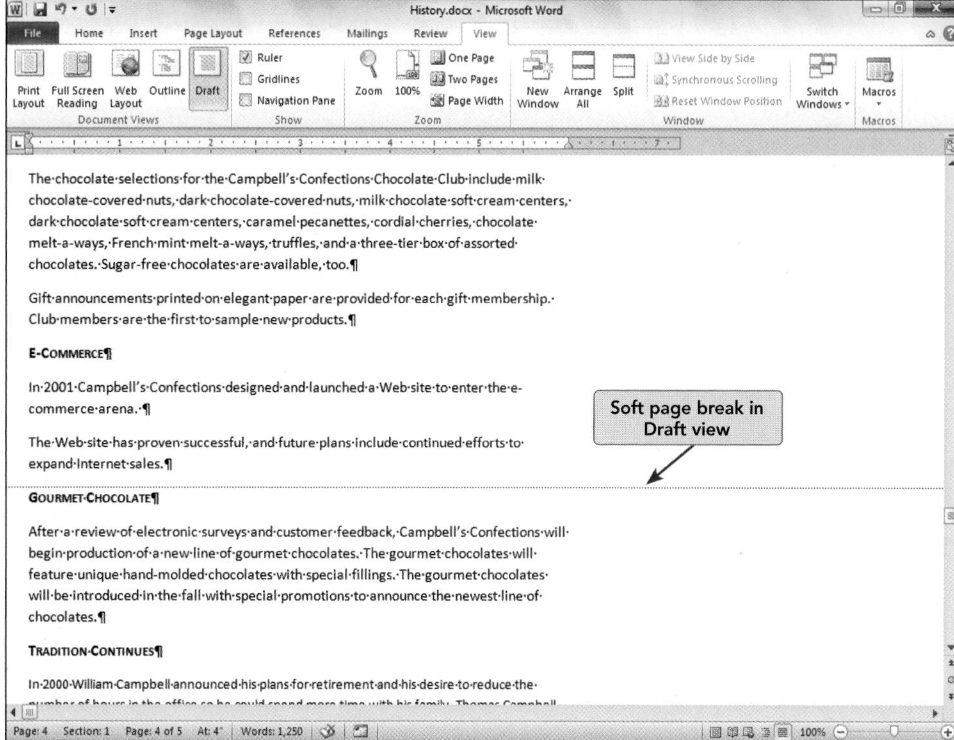

Figure 9-1
Adjusting the position of a soft page break

TIP

Remember the various methods for moving within a long document. For example, you can drag the scroll box on the vertical scroll bar and use the scroll arrows to adjust the view. You can also use keyboard shortcuts: Ctrl+↑ or Ctrl+↓ to move up or down one paragraph, PageUp or PageDown to move up or down one window, and Ctrl+Home or Ctrl+End to move to the beginning or end of a document.

Exercise 9-2 INSERT A HARD PAGE BREAK

When you want a page break to occur at a specific point, you can insert a *hard page break*. In Draft view, a hard page break appears on the screen as a dotted line with the words "Page Break." In Print Layout view you see the actual page break.

There are three ways to insert a hard page break:

- Use the keyboard shortcut Ctrl+Enter.
- Click the Insert tab, and click the Page Break button.
- Click the Page Layout tab, and click the Breaks button.

1. Move the insertion point to the bottom of page 2, to the beginning of the paragraph that starts "The most popular."
2. Press Ctrl+Enter. Word inserts a hard page break so the paragraph and bulleted text are not divided between two pages.
3. Move to the middle of page 4, and place the insertion point to the left of the heading text that begins "Chronology."
4. Click the **Insert** tab, and click the Page Break button to insert a page break. Word inserts a hard page break and adjusts pagination in the document from this point forward.

TIP

You can also insert a page break by clicking the Page Layout tab, clicking the Breaks button, and clicking Page.

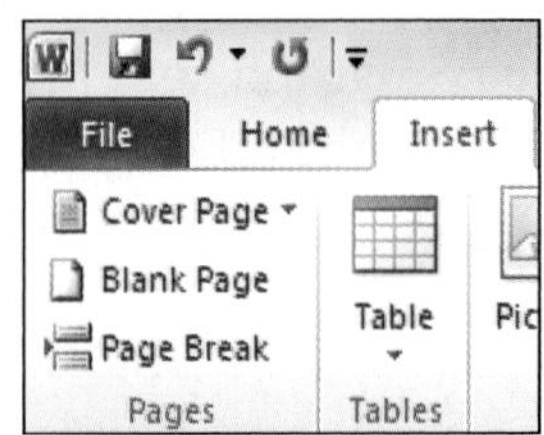

Figure 9-2
Insert tab, pages group

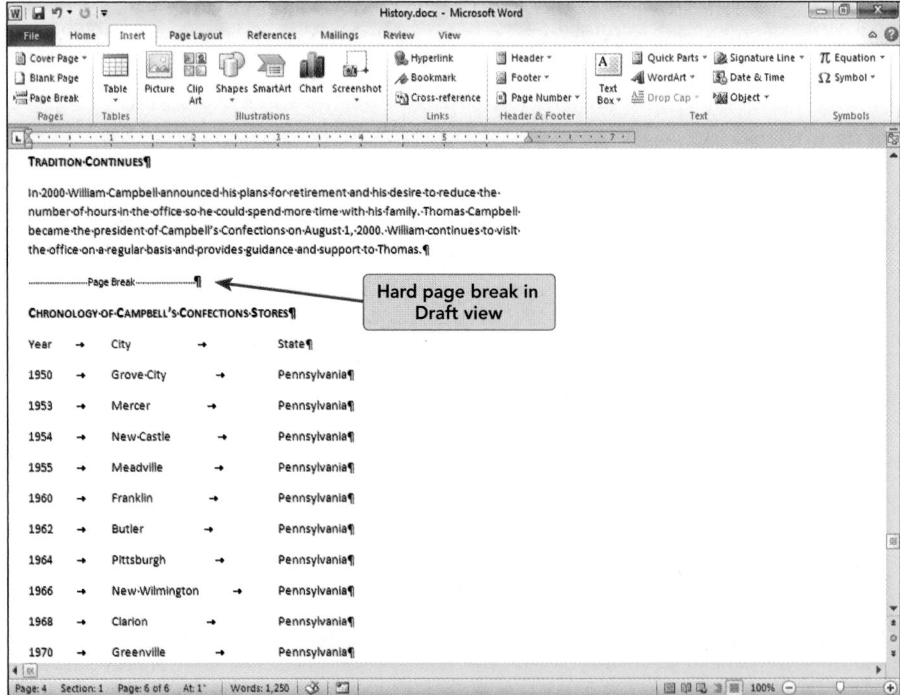

Figure 9-3
Inserting a hard page break

Exercise 9-3 DELETE A HARD PAGE BREAK

You cannot delete a soft page break, but you can delete a hard page break by clicking the page break and pressing Backspace or Delete.

1. Select the page break you just inserted by dragging the I-beam over the page break. Be sure to select the paragraph mark.
2. Press Delete to delete the page break.
3. Scroll back to the hard page break you inserted at the top of page 3. Position the insertion point to the left of "The most popular" and press Backspace two times (one time to delete the paragraph mark and one time to delete the page break). The page break is deleted, and Word adjusts the pagination.

Controlling Line and Page Breaks

To control the way Word breaks paragraphs, choose one of four line and page break options from the Paragraph dialog box:

- *Widow/orphan control:* A *widow* is the last line of a paragraph and appears by itself at the top of a page. An *orphan* is the first line of a paragraph and appears at the bottom of a page. By default, this option is turned on to prevent widows and orphans. Word moves an orphan forward to the next page and moves a widow back to the previous page.
- *Keep lines together:* This option keeps all lines of a paragraph together on the same page rather than splitting the paragraphs between two pages.
- *Keep with next:* If two or more paragraphs need to appear on the same page no matter where page breaks occur, use this option. This option is most commonly applied to titles that should not be separated from the first paragraph following the title.
- *Page break before:* Use this option to place a paragraph at the top of a new page.

Exercise 9-4 APPLY LINE AND PAGE BREAK OPTIONS TO PARAGRAPHS

TIP

To reopen the file quickly, click the File tab and click Recent. Click the file name **History** under Recent Documents.

1. Close **History** without saving; then reopen the document. Switch to Draft view.
2. At the bottom of page 3, click within the heading "Gourmet Chocolate." You are going to format this heading so it will not be separated from its related paragraph.

3. Click the **Home** tab, and click the **Paragraph Dialog Box Launcher** to open the Paragraph dialog box. Click the **Line and Page Breaks** tab.

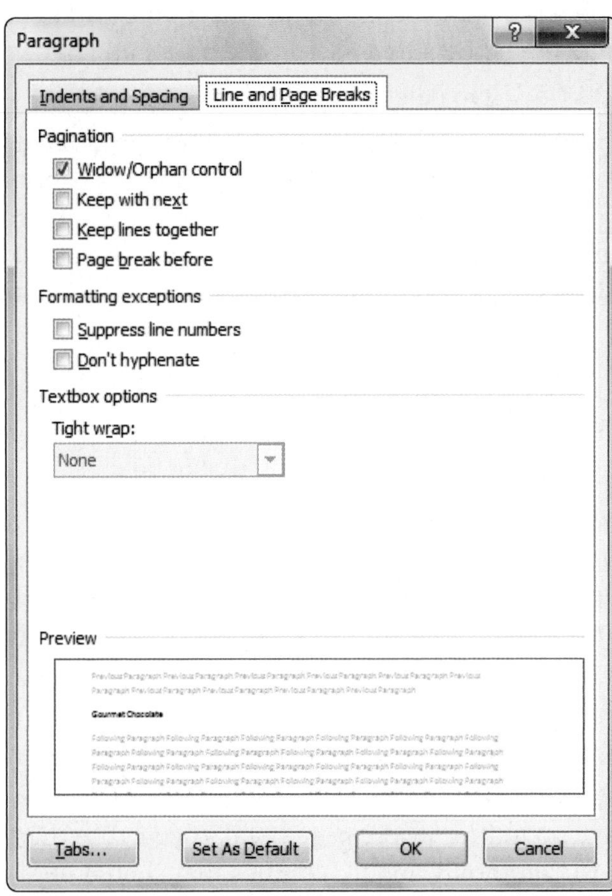

Figure 9-4 Line and Page Breaks tab in the Paragraph dialog box

4. Click **Keep with next** to select it, and click **OK**. Word moves the soft page break, keeping the two paragraphs together.

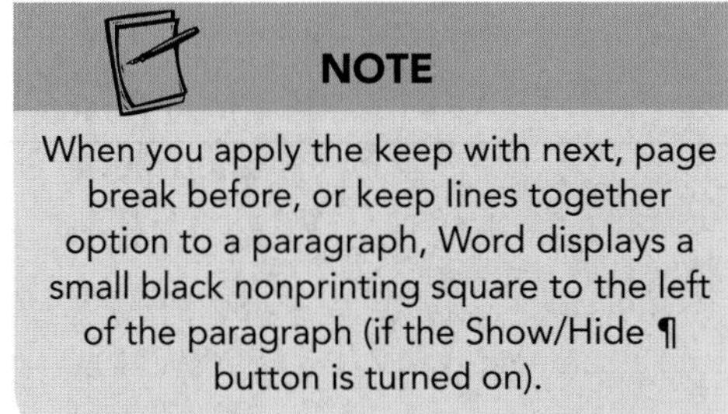

NOTE

When you apply the keep with next, page break before, or keep lines together option to a paragraph, Word displays a small black nonprinting square to the left of the paragraph (if the Show/Hide ¶ button is turned on).

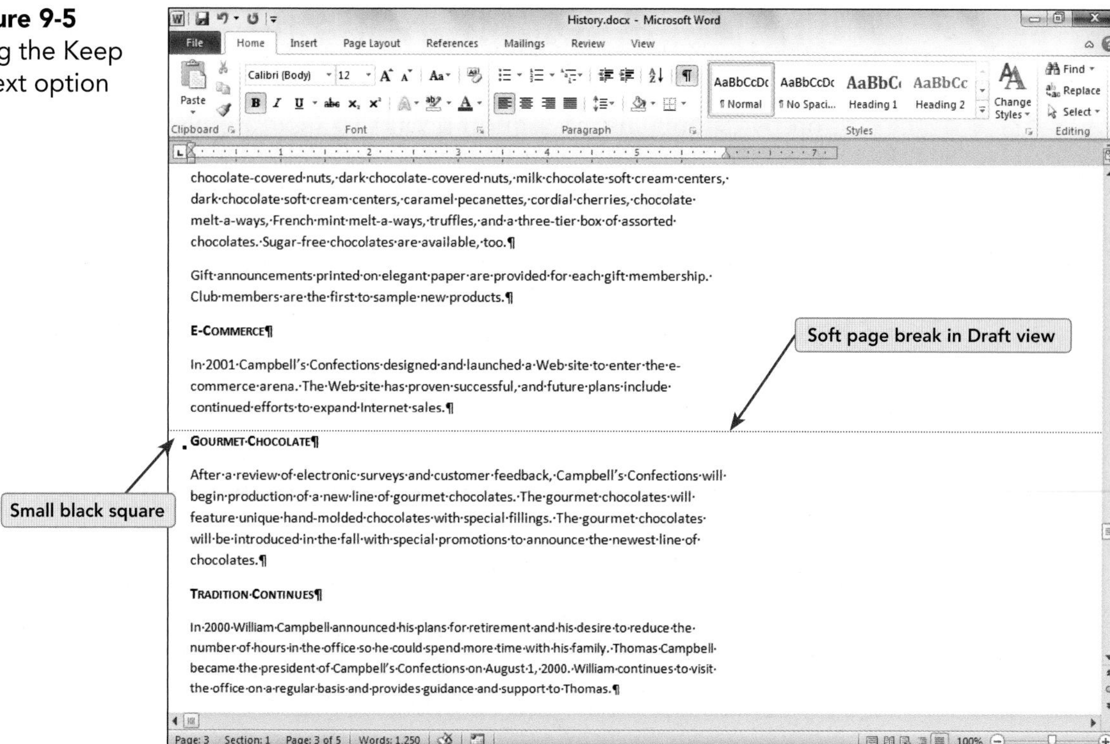

Figure 9-5
Applying the Keep with next option

5. Press Ctrl+Home to go to the top of the document. Select the title, and apply 48 points spacing before.
6. Locate the text at the bottom of page 1 that begins "By 1980." The paragraph is divided by a soft page break.
7. Right-click the paragraph to open the shortcut menu. Click **Paragraph**. Click the **Line and Page Breaks** tab if necessary.
8. Choose **Keep lines together** and click **OK**. The soft page break moves above the paragraphs to keep the lines of text together.
9. Move to page 4, and place the insertion point in the paragraph that begins "Chronology." You will format this paragraph so it begins at the top of the page.
10. Open the **Paragraph** dialog box, click **Page break before**, and click **OK**. Word starts the paragraph at the top of page 5 with a soft page break.
11. Press Shift+F1 to open the **Reveal Formatting** task pane. Click the plus symbol ⊞ to the left of **Paragraph** to display the paragraph formatting. Notice the link for Line and Page Breaks. When you click the link, the Paragraph dialog box opens. Close the Paragraph dialog box and the Reveal Formatting task pane.
12. Save the document as ***[your initials]*9-4** in a new folder for Lesson 9. Leave it open for the next exercise.

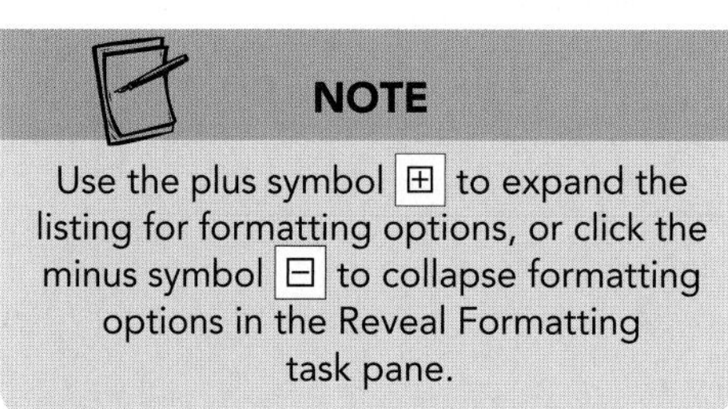

NOTE

Use the plus symbol ⊞ to expand the listing for formatting options, or click the minus symbol ⊟ to collapse formatting options in the Reveal Formatting task pane.

Controlling Section Breaks

When you create a new document, the document is formatted with one section by default. Insert section breaks to separate parts of a document that have formatting different from the rest of the document. For example, you may want to insert a section at the beginning of a document to include a title page with special formatting and centered vertically. When you change the left and right margins of selected text, a separate section is created.

For better control in creating section breaks, you can insert a section break directly into a document at a specific location by using the Break dialog box. You can also specify the type of section break you want to insert. Insert a *next page* section break to start a section on a new page. Insert a *continuous* section break to start a new section on the same page. Switch to Draft view to see the double-dotted section break lines.

TABLE 9-1 Types of Section Breaks

Type	Description
Next page	Section starts on a new page.
Continuous	Section follows the text before it without a page break.
Even page or odd page	Section starts on the next even- or odd-numbered page. Useful for reports in which chapters must begin on either odd- or even-numbered pages.

Exercise 9-5 INSERT SECTION BREAKS BY USING THE BREAK COMMAND

1. Place the insertion point to the left of the paragraph at the top of page 5 that begins "Chronology."
2. Press Ctrl+Q. This clears the formatting for the paragraph, removing the soft page break you applied earlier.
3. Click the **Page Layout** tab, and click the Breaks button. Under **Section Breaks**, click **Continuous**. Word begins a new section on the same page, at the position of the insertion point.
4. Click above and below the section mark. Notice that the section number changes on the status bar but the page number stays the same.

Figure 9-6
Inserting a continuous section break

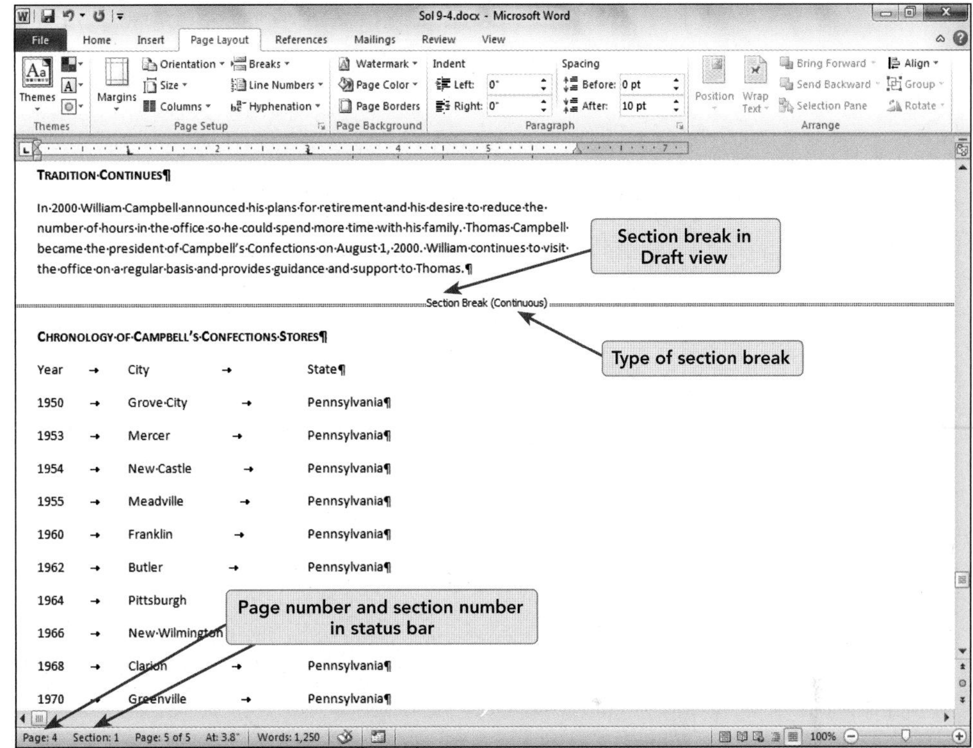

Formatting Sections

After you create a new section, you can change its formatting, or you can specify the section break to be a different type of section break. This is often useful for long documents, which sometimes contain many sections that require different page formatting, such as different margin settings or page orientation. For example, you can change a next page section break to a continuous section break, or you can change the page orientation of a section, without affecting the rest of the document.

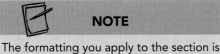

NOTE

The formatting you apply to the section is stored in the section break. If you delete a section break, you also delete the formatting for the text above the section break. For example, if you have a two-section document and you delete the section break at the end of section 1, the document becomes one section with the formatting of section 2.

Exercise 9-6 APPLY FORMATTING TO SECTIONS

1. Position the insertion point before the text "Wholesale" on page 2. Use the **Page Layout** tab, Breaks button to insert a **Next page** section break.
2. With the insertion point in the new section (section 2), open the **Page Setup** dialog box by clicking the **Page Setup Dialog Box Launcher**.

3. Click the **Layout** tab, and click to open the **Section start** drop-down list. From this list you can change the section break from New page to another type.
4. Choose **Continuous** so the section does not start on a new page.

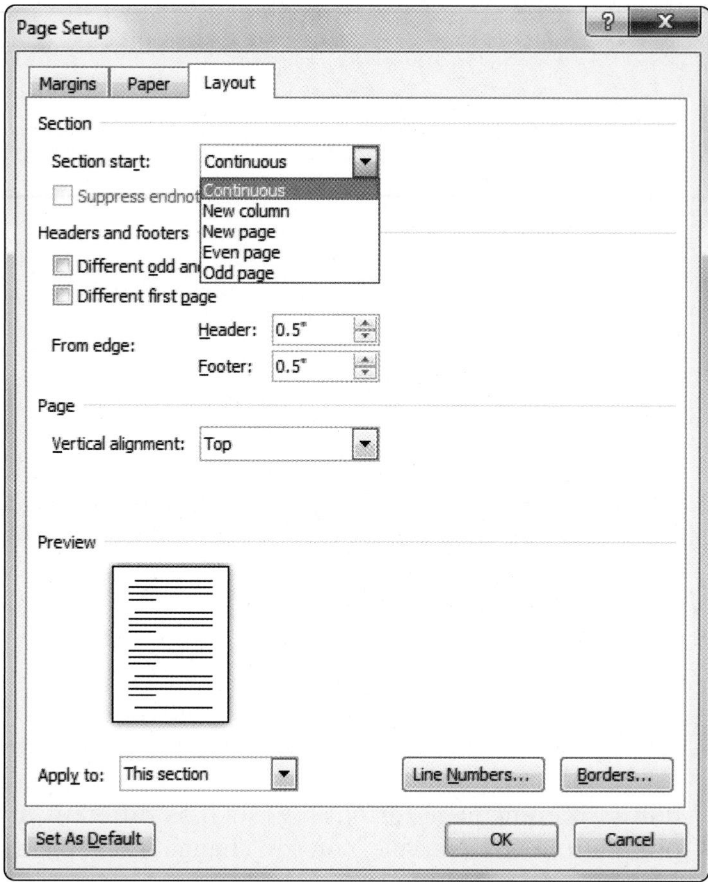

Figure 9-7
Using the Page Setup dialog box to modify the section

5. Click the **Margins** tab.
6. Set 1.5-inch left and right margins. Make sure **This section** appears in the **Apply to** box, and click **OK**. Section 2 of the document now has new margin settings. Click the Print Layout button on the status bar to view the change.

Exercise 9-7 CHANGE THE VERTICAL ALIGNMENT OF A SECTION

Another way to format a section is to specify the vertical alignment of the section on the page. For example, you can align a title page so the text is centered between the top and bottom margins. Vertical alignment is a layout option available in the Page Setup dialog box.

1. Move the insertion point to the last section of the document (which begins "Chronology"). Notice that the section type is continuous. Because this section does not start on a new page, a page break interrupts the list of stores.
2. Open the **Page Setup** dialog box, and click the **Layout** tab.
3. Use the **Section start** drop-down list to change the section from **Continuous** to **New page**.
4. Open the **Vertical alignment** drop-down list and choose **Center**. Click **OK**.

TABLE 9-2 Vertical Alignment Options

Options	Description
Top	Aligns the top line of the page with the top margin (default setting).
Center	Centers the page between the top and bottom margins with equal space above and below the text.
Justified	Aligns the top line of the page with the top margin and the bottom line with the bottom margin, with equal spacing between the lines of text (similar in principle to the way Word justifies text between the left and right margins).
Bottom	Aligns the bottom line of a partial page along the bottom margin.

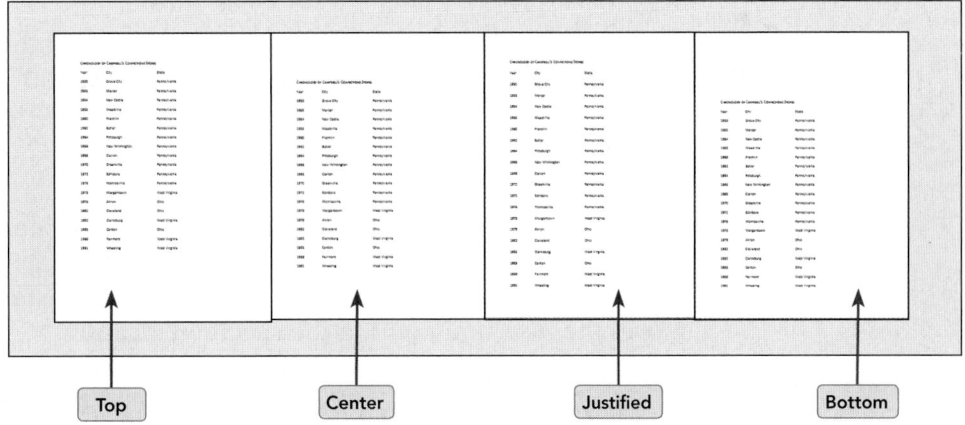

Figure 9-8 Vertical alignment options

Exercise 9-8 CHECK PAGINATION USING THE PRINT TAB OR PAGE LAYOUT VIEW

After you apply page breaks, section breaks, or section formatting, use Print Preview on the Print tab or Print Layout view to check the document. Viewing the pages in relation to one another provides ideas for improvement before printing.

Remember, you can change the page formatting of a document using Print Layout view or the Print tab.

1. Click the **File** tab, and click **Print**. Notice that the text is centered between the top and bottom margins. Notice also that viewing a document using the Print tab does not show the dotted lines of the section breaks, but it does show how the page will look when you print it.
2. While still displaying the document using the Print tab, click the **Margins Setting** option, and choose **Custom Margins** at the bottom of the list. Click the **Layout** tab, and change the vertical alignment to **Justified**. Click **OK**. Word justifies the last page of the document so the text extends from the top margin to the bottom margin.

NOTE

The appearance of the buttons in the Settings section will vary depending on the last formatting option selected.

3. Click the Previous Page button [◄] to scroll back, page by page, to page 2, section 1, of the document.
4. Drag the Zoom slider to 50%. You cannot see the continuous section break before "Wholesale," but you can check the formatting and see how the document will look when printed.
5. Click the **Home** tab, and switch to Print Layout view.
6. Scroll to page 2, section 1. Notice that in Print Layout view, page breaks are indicated by the actual layout of each page as it will look when printed.
7. Click the Zoom button [100%] on the status bar to open the Zoom dialog box. Click the **Many Pages** button, and click on the grid to display **1 × 2** (one row, two pages). Click **OK**. This reduces the document display so you can see two pages at the same time.
8. Scroll to the end of the document. Click the Draft View button [ ] to switch to Draft view. Drag the **Zoom slider** to **100%** if necessary.

Using the Go To Feature

You use the Go To feature to move through a document quickly. For example, you can go to a specific section, page number, comment, or bookmark. *Go To* is a convenient feature for long documents—it is faster than scrolling, and it moves the insertion point to the specified location.

There are three ways to initiate the Go To command:

- Click the Home tab, and click the drop-down arrow beside the Find [ ] command, and choose Go To or click the Replace button [ ] to open the Find and Replace dialog box. Click the Go To tab.
- Double-click on the status bar (anywhere to the left of "Words").
- Press Ctrl+G or press F5.

Exercise 9-9 GO TO A SPECIFIC PAGE OR SECTION

1. With the document in Draft view, press F5. Word displays the **Go To** tab, located in the Find and Replace dialog box.

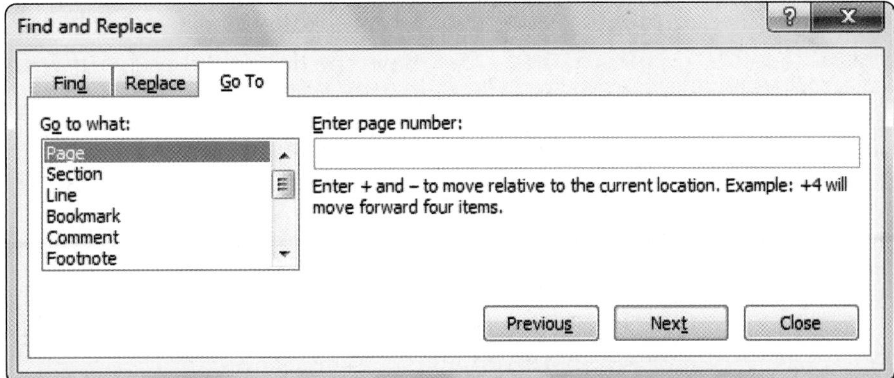

Figure 9-9
Using the Go To feature

2. Scroll through the **Go to what** list to review the options. Choose **Section** from the list, and click **Previous** until you reach the beginning of the document.
3. Click **Next** until the insertion point is located at the beginning of the last section, which is section 3.
4. Choose **Page** from the **Go to what** list and click **Previous**. The insertion point moves to the top of the previous page.
5. Key **2** in the **Enter page number** text box, and click **Go To**. The insertion point moves to the top of page 2.
6. Close the dialog box.

Exercise 9-10 GO TO A RELATIVE DESTINATION

You can use the Go To command to move to a location relative to the insertion point. For example, with Page selected in the Go to what list, you can enter "+2" in the text box to move forward two pages from the insertion point. You can move in increments of pages, lines, sections, and so on. Another option is to move by a certain percentage within the document, such as 50%—the document's midpoint.

1. Double-click the word "Page" on the status bar to open the Find and Replace dialog box with the Go To tab active.
2. Choose **Line** from the **Go to what** list, and key **4** in the text box. Click **Go To**. The insertion point moves to the fourth line in the document.
3. Key **+35** in the text box, and click **Go To**. The insertion point moves forward 35 lines from the previous location.

NOTE

You must select Page in the Go to what list to use a percentage.

TIP

You can use the Go To feature to delete a single page of content. Position the insertion point, and open the Find and Replace dialog box. Click the Go To tab, and key \page in the text box. Click Go To. Click Close (the text will be highlighted), and press Delete.

4. Key **-35** in the text box, and click **Go To**. The insertion point moves back to the previous location.
5. Click **Page** in the **Go to what** list, key **50%** in the text box, and click **Go To**. The insertion point moves to the midpoint of the document.
6. Close the dialog box.
7. Save the document as ***[your initials]*9-10** in the Lesson 9 folder.
8. Open the **Print** tab, and choose **4 Pages Per Sheet** in the **1 Page Per Sheet** list box. Click **Print**.
9. Close the document.

Lesson 9 Summary

- Pagination is the Word process of flowing text from line to line and from page to page. Word creates a soft page break at the end of each page. When you edit text, you adjust line and page breaks. You can adjust the way a page breaks by manually inserting a hard page break (Ctrl+Enter).
- Delete a hard page break by selecting it and pressing Delete or Backspace.
- The Paragraph dialog box contains line and page break options to control pagination. To prevent lines of a paragraph from displaying on two pages, click in the paragraph and apply the Keep lines together option. To keep two paragraphs together on the same page, click in the first paragraph and apply the Keep with next option. To insert a page break before a paragraph, click in the paragraph and choose the Page break before option.
- Use section breaks to separate parts of a document that have different formatting. Apply a next page section break to start a section on a new page or a continuous section break to continue the new section on the same page. Apply an even page or odd page section break to start a section on the next even- or odd-numbered page.
- Change the vertical alignment of a section by clicking within the section and opening the Page Setup dialog box. On the Layout tab, under Vertical alignment, choose an alignment option (top, center, justified, or bottom).

- Check pagination using the Print tab or Print Layout view. Scroll through the document or change the zoom to display a different view.
- Use the Go To command to go to a specific page or section in a document. You can also go to a relative destination, such as the midpoint of the document or the 50th line.

LESSON 9		Command Summary	
Feature	**Button**	**Command**	**Keyboard**
Formatting sections		Page Layout tab, Page Setup group, Page Setup dialog box	
Go To	or	Home tab, Editing group, Find or Replace command, Go To tab	Ctrl+G or F5
Hard page break		Insert tab, Pages group, Page Break	Ctrl+Enter
Line and page break options		Home tab, Paragraph group, Paragraph dialog box, Line and Page Breaks tab	
Section breaks		Page Layout tab, Page Setup group, Breaks command	

Concepts Review

True/False Questions

Each of the following statements is either true or false. Indicate your choice by circling T or F.

T F 1. You can delete a hard or soft page break by pressing Delete.

T F 2. To insert a section break, press Ctrl+Enter.

T F 3. One way to insert a page break is to choose Page Break from the Insert tab.

T F 4. Page break before is a paragraph-formatting option that starts a paragraph at the top of a new page.

T F 5. A nonprinting character appears to the left of any paragraph to which you apply the Keep with next option.

T F 6. Section breaks appear in the Print tab preview as double-dotted lines.

T F 7. Page breaks appear in Print Layout view as single-dotted lines.

T F 8. You can use the Go To feature to move the insertion point from one section to another.

Short Answer Questions

Write the correct answer in the space provided.

1. Which type of page break is automatically adjusted as you key text?

____

2. Which type of section break does not start on a new page?

____

3. What is the term for the last line of a paragraph that appears alone at the top of a page?

____

4. Which option would you apply to a paragraph so it is not divided by a page break?

____

5. Which dialog box and tab would you display to change the vertical alignment of a section?

____

6. Which type of vertical alignment spaces text so the top line aligns with the top margin and the bottom line aligns with the bottom margin?

____

7. In Print Layout view, which feature do you use to view two pages at the same time?

____

8. Describe the appearance of the nonprinting character Word displays next to a paragraph when you apply certain line and page break options.

____

Critical Thinking

Answer these questions on a separate page. There are no right or wrong answers. Support your answers with examples from your own experience, if possible.

1. In a long document that requires extensive editing, why would it be most efficient to perform all your edits before inserting hard page breaks?
2. Describe a situation where you would use a continuous section break.

Skills Review

Exercise 9-11

Adjust soft page breaks and insert hard page breaks.

1. Open the file **Terms**. Position the insertion point in the first line of the memo, and change the spacing before to 72 points.
2. Scroll to the bottom of page 1 to see where the soft page break occurs.
3. Change the font size for the entire document to 11 points. Notice how the change affects the soft page break.
4. Insert a page break before the text "Chocolate Terms" by following these steps:

   a. Place the insertion point to the left of the text.

   b. Press Ctrl+Enter.
5. Change the last line on page 1 to read **is listed on the next page**. Change the font size of the title on page 2 to 14 points, and apply 24 points spacing after. Center the title.
6. Key today's date in the memo heading, and key your reference initials at the bottom of page 1.

7. Display the Print tab, and preview the document.
8. Change the zoom level to 40% to view two pages at once. Return to a one-page view by clicking the Zoom to Page button to the right of the Zoom slider, and click the Home tab.
9. Select the text for the subject line ("Chocolate Terms"), and apply italic formatting using the keyboard shortcut Ctrl+I.
10. Save the document as ***[your initials]*9-11** in your Lesson 9 folder.
11. Submit and close the document.

Exercise 9-12

Apply line and page break options to paragraphs.

1. Open the file **Directory**.
2. Change the left and right margins to 1.25 inches.
3. Format the first line of the title as 14-point bold, uppercase. Add 36 points of spacing before. Format the second line as 12-point bold, small caps.
4. Key the current date.
5. Apply paragraph formatting to the heading "Ohio Stores" so it begins on a new page by following these steps:
   a. Move the insertion point within the heading.
   b. Click the **Home** tab, and click the **Paragraph Dialog Box Launcher**.
   c. Click the **Line and Page Breaks** tab.
   d. Choose **Page break before** and click **OK**.
6. Click within the heading "West Virginia Stores," and press F4 to repeat the format. Repeat the formatting to the heading "Pennsylvania Stores" if necessary.
7. Scroll through the document to verify that the stores are listed by state on a new page. The document should be four pages.
8. Save the document as ***[your initials]*9-12** in your Lesson 9 folder.
9. Submit and close the document.

Exercise 9-13

Specify section breaks by type, and change the margin settings in sections.

1. Open the file **Homecoming - 2**.
2. Insert a next page section break on page 1 before the heading "Homecoming Events" by following these steps:
   a. Place the insertion point to the left of the heading.
   b. Click the **Page Layout** tab, and click the Breaks button. Click **Next Page**.

3. Move the insertion point to section 1. Change the top margin to 2 inches, and change the left and right margins to 1.25 inches. Be sure to apply the format to the section and not the whole document.
4. Position the insertion point in section 2. Use the Page Setup dialog box to format section 2 with 1.5-inch left and right margins. Make sure This section appears in the Apply to box.
5. Select the list of colleges, and change the left indent to 1.5 inches. Add a blank line after the Homecoming Events title.
6. Change the vertical alignment for section 2 to centered by following these steps:
   a. Place the insertion point in the second section.
   b. Open the Page Setup dialog box, and click the Layout tab. Select Center from the Vertical alignment drop-down list. Click OK.
7. Format page 2 (section 2) with a page border using the Box setting and a 3-point double line. Be sure to apply the border to "This Section." (Hint: Use the Page Borders command on the Page Layout tab.)
8. Save the document as ***[your initials]*9-13** in your Lesson 9 folder.
9. Submit and close the document.

Exercise 9-14

Vertically align a section, and move around a document by using the Go To feature.

1. Open the file **Leadership**.
2. Insert Next page section breaks at "*Please join us*" on page 1 and at "Possible Agenda Topics" near the end of the document.
3. Vertically align the text in section 2 by following these steps:
   a. With the insertion point in section 2, click the Page Layout tab, and click the Page Setup Dialog Box Launcher. Click the Layout tab.
   b. Choose Center from the Vertical alignment drop-down list.
   c. Make sure This section appears in the Apply to box, and click OK.
4. Display the Print tab, and view only the second page (section 2).
5. From the Print tab, open the Page Setup dialog box again, and change the vertical alignment to Justified.
6. Click the Home tab.
7. Select all the text in section 2, and center the text horizontally.
8. Use the Go To feature to move within the document by following these steps:
   a. Press F5.
   b. Choose Section from the Go to what list, and key **3** in the text box.
   c. Click Go To and close the dialog box.

9. Select the first line of section 3, and change the font to 14-point bold and small caps. Select the second line through the end of the document, and apply a bullet format.
10. Use the zoom level to view three pages at one time by following these steps:
    a. Click the Zoom button 100% on the status bar.
    b. Click the Many Pages button, and drag across the first row to highlight three pages.
    c. Click **OK**.
11. Drag the Zoom slider to **100%**. Add 72 points of spacing before the first line on page 1. Add your reference initials to the bottom of page 1.
12. Save the document as ***[your initials]*****9-14** in your Lesson 9 folder.
13. Submit and close the document.

Lesson Applications

Exercise 9-15

Insert page breaks, apply line and page break options, and format text as a new section.

1. Open the file **Staff - 2**.
2. Key the text in Figure 9-10 at the beginning of the document. Use 12-point Calibri, no bold, no small caps for the paragraph below the title.

Figure 9-10

```
Corporate Staff—Brief Biographies        [format 14 points-bold-small caps]

                                      significant      financial
Campbell's Confections has experienced ^growth and ^success
since William Campbell started the company in 19[05]. One
                 the
explanation for this success of this company is the
                 t
continued commiement to people—both customers and
employees. merge
                                                       retain
Campbell's Confections has been able to attract and hold
employees and is proud of the fact that the average length
                                  15
of service for employees is 51 years. William Campbell
believed in the importance of demonstrating care for
       es       Thomas
employe^, and Tom Campbell continues this philosophy.

[12 pt Calibri]
```

3. Use the Find feature or scroll to locate “Tamara Robbins.” Use the Keep with next feature to place the heading “Tamara Robbins” with the descriptive paragraph.
4. Place the insertion point to the left of “Corporate Staff.” And insert a next page section break.
5. Change the top margin for section 1 to 2 inches and the left and right margins to 1.5 inches.
6. Locate the text “Cynthia Parker,” and insert a page break at the beginning of the line.
7. Increase the font size of the title in section 1 to 20 points, and apply a text effect. Change the font size of the title in section 2 to 20 points, and apply bold, small caps, and a text effect.

8. Add a 3-D page border to all pages of the document. Select a double-line style, dark blue color, and 3-point width.
9. In section 2, center the text vertically.
10. Preview the document.
11. Save the document as ***[your initials]*****9-15** in your Lesson 9 folder.
12. Print the document four sheets per page, and then close it.

Exercise 9-16

Add and format sections.

1. Open the file **Forman**.
2. Set a 2-inch top margin, and change the left and right margins to 1.25 inches. Key the current date at the top of the document, and include an enclosures notation.
3. Position the insertion point at the end of the document on a blank line below the enclosure notation. Click the **Insert** tab, and click the arrow beside the Object button Object. Click **Text from file**. Locate the file **Retail Stores - 2**, and click **Insert**.
4. Position the insertion point at the end of the document on a blank line, and follow the same procedure to insert the file **Store Directory**.
5. Locate the text "There are 24" and insert a next page section break. In the new section, key the title **CAMPBELL'S CONFECTIONS' RETAIL STORES** using bold uppercase text. Center the title, and increase the font size to 14 points. Add 24 points of spacing after.
6. Insert a next page section break before the text "Pennsylvania Stores."
7. Format section 2 so it is vertically centered and in landscape orientation. Set 1.5-inch left and right margins. Change the top and bottom margins to 1 inch. Select all paragraphs below the title, and change the spacing after to 12 points.
8. Go to section 3, and insert a page break before "Ohio Stores" and a page break before "West Virginia Stores."
9. Change the top margin for section 3 to 1.5 inches, and change the left and right margins to 1 inch.
10. Save the document as ***[your initials]*****9-16** in your Lesson 9 folder.
11. Submit and close the document.

Exercise 9-17

Apply line and page break options, add and format sections, and use the Go To feature.

1. Open the file **Price Change**.
2. Add a continuous section break before the line "Standard-size" and another at the bottom of the list (before the paragraph that begins "Price changes").
3. Format section 2 with a 1.5-inch left margin, and double-space all lines in this section. Adjust the tab settings to space the columns evenly between the margins. The third column should be formatted with a right tab at 5 inches. Bold and underline the column headings. Center, bold, and apply 14-point small caps to the title. Change the title paragraph spacing before to 24 points.
4. Go to section 1, and key a memo heading to "Store Managers" from Thomas Campbell. Use the current date, and the subject is "Price changes." Align memo heading information with a left tab. Add your reference initials at the end of section 1 with an attachment reference. Change the top margin to 2 inches and the bottom margin to 0.5 inch.
5. Copy the formatting from the title in section 2 to the title in section 3.
6. Change the double-spaced text in section 2 to 1.5-line spacing.
7. Change the section layout for section 3 from a continuous section break to a section break that starts on a new page using the Page Setup dialog box.
8. Change the left and right margins for section 3 to 1 inch. Select the tabbed text in section 3, and change the left indent to 1 inch. Set a right dotted-leader tab at 5.5 inches. Bold and underline the column headings, and format the tabbed text with 1.5-line spacing. Remove the dotted leaders from the column headings. Format the title with 24 points spacing before and 12 points spacing after.
9. Change the alignment in section 3 so it is centered vertically.
10. Preview the document, and save it as ***[your initials]*9-17** in your Lesson 9 folder.
11. Submit and close the document.

Exercise 9-18 ◆ Challenge Yourself

Add and delete page breaks, and add and format a new section.

1. Create a standard business memo from you to store managers. Use single spacing and change the spacing after to 0. Key **September 1** for the date. The subject is "Candy Bar Wrapper Contest." Key the body text shown in Figure 9-11.

Figure 9-11

```
Thank you for sending your comments regarding our first
candy bar wrapper contest. We want our first contest to be
a success, and we hope to use one of the winning designs
for one of our fundraising candy bar wrappers.

Please review the following list, and provide your comments
no later than Wednesday. We want to send the rules and
guidelines to the graphic artist for layout and printing.
When we receive the flyer, we will e-mail it to you for
printing and distribution to high schools in your service
area.

Your comments regarding possible awards were enlightening.
Because Campbell's Confections' stores are located in the
tri-state area, it has taken great effort to work with
three state treasurers to establish our scholarship awards
program.
```

2. At the end of the memo, add an attachment reference. After the reference, create a new section that starts on a new page.

TIP

To insert a file, place the insertion point in the new section, click the Insert tab, and click the arrow beside Object. Click Text from File. Locate the file and click Insert.

3. In the new section, insert the file **Wrapper**.
4. Format the two-line title as 14-point bold, all caps, and centered. Change the spacing after for the second line to 24 points. Delete the blank line that follows the title.
5. Select all lines below the title and format with 12 points spacing after.
6. Select "Rules/Guidelines" and "Prizes" and apply bold, italic, and small caps formatting. Select the text below each side heading, and format it as a bulleted list.
7. Use the Replace feature to replace all occurrences of "contest" with **competition**.
8. Add a page border to section 2. Select a geometric-pattern border from the Art drop-down list. Select an appropriate width and color.
9. If you have not already done so, format section 1 with a 2-inch top margin. Make sure section 2 has the regular 1-inch top margin and is centered vertically.
10. Spell-check section 1 only.
11. Save the document as ***[your initials]*9-18** in your Lesson 9 folder.
12. Submit and close the document.

On Your Own

In these exercises you work on your own, as you would in a real-life business environment. Use the skills you've learned to accomplish the task—and be creative.

Exercise 9-19

Write a short report about your 10 favorite television shows or movies. Include a document title. Each show or movie should be a separate paragraph with its own heading. Adjust page breaks as needed to keep headings with their related paragraphs. Save the document as ***[your initials]*****9-19** and submit it.

Exercise 9-20

Create a document that includes three poems by three different poets. Use headings to identify each poet and title. Use page breaks to start each poem on a separate page. Save the document as ***[your initials]*****9-20** and submit it.

Exercise 9-21

Create a document that lists three different categories of restaurants in your area. Include descriptions of three restaurants per category. Format each category as a separate section, and apply a different page, paragraph, and character format to each. Save the document as ***[your initials]*****9-21** and submit it.

Lesson 10

Page Numbers, Headers, and Footers

OBJECTIVES ***After completing this lesson, you will be able to:***

1. Add page numbers.
2. Change the starting page number.
3. Add headers and footers.
4. Add headers and footers within sections.
5. Link section headers and footers.
6. Create continuation page headers.
7. Create alternate headers and footers.

Estimated Time: 1½ hours

Page numbers, headers, and footers are useful additions to multiple-page documents. Page numbers can appear in either the top or bottom margin of a page. The text in the top margin of a page is a *header;* text in the bottom margin of a page is a *footer*. Headers and footers can also contain descriptive information about a document, such as the date, title, and author's name.

Adding Page Numbers

Word automatically keeps track of page numbers and indicates on the left side of the status bar the current page and the total number of pages in a document. Each time you add, delete, or format text or sections, Word adjusts page breaks and page numbers. This process, called *background repagination,* occurs automatically when you pause while working on a document. Right-click the status bar to select formatted page number, section, and page number options when working with long documents.

Figure 10-1 Status bar indicators for a multiple-page document

Exercise 10-1 ADD AND PREVIEW PAGE NUMBERS

Page numbers do not appear on a printed document unless you specify that they do. The simplest way to add page numbers is to click the Insert tab and click Page Number.

1. Open the file **History**.
2. With the insertion point at the top of the document, click the **Insert** tab and click the Page Number button. Word displays a list of options for placing your page number in the document. Notice that you can choose top of page, bottom of page, or page margins. Once you choose a position for the page number, you select a design from the gallery. A *gallery* is a list of design options for modifying elements of a page.

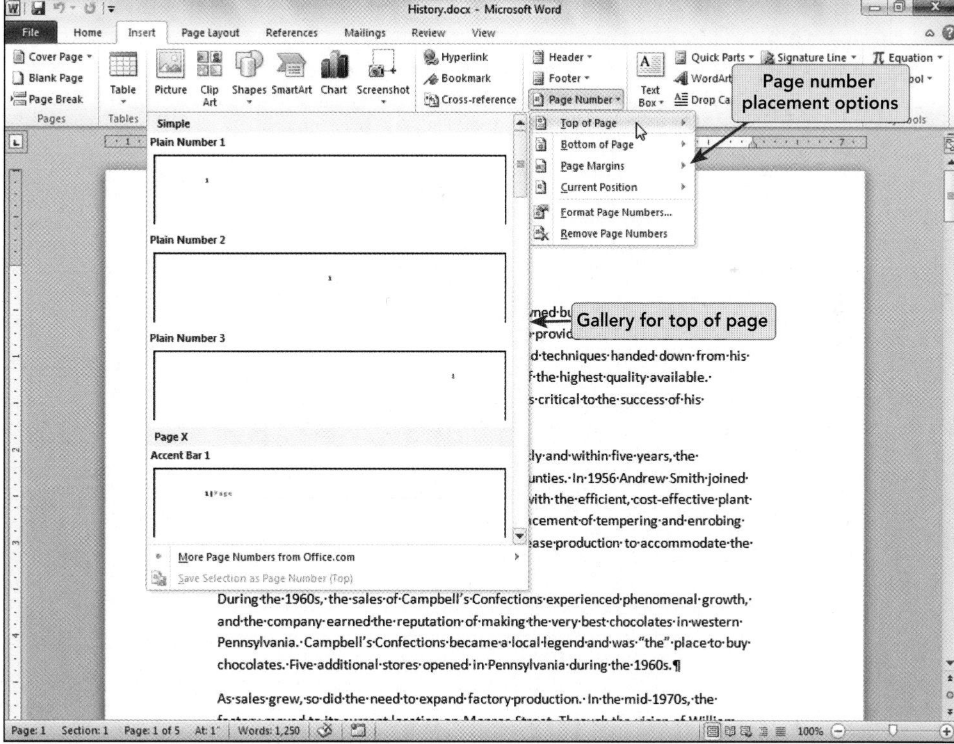

Figure 10-2 Page number options

NOTE

If you key the number 2 in the header or footer pane, the document will print the number 2 on every page of the document instead of the page number. Remember to use the Insert Page Number button to add page numbers to a document.

3. Click **Top of Page** to display the gallery for placing numbers at the top of the page. Click **Plain Number 3** to place a page number in the upper right corner of the document.
4. Scroll through the document to view the page numbers. By default Word places page numbers on every page. Notice the divider line that separates the header pane from the document text.
5. Notice that the **Ribbon** adds a new tab when page numbers have been added to a document. The **Header & Footer Tools Design** tab includes additional options for formatting the document.
6. Click the Close Header and Footer button.

NOTE

You can see page numbers when Print Layout view is the selected view, when the Print tab is displayed, or on the printed page.

7. Click the **Insert** tab, and click the Page Number button. Click **Bottom of Page**, and scroll to the bottom of the gallery. Click **Triangle 2**. A page number appears at the bottom right corner of each page.
8. Click the Zoom button 100%, and choose **Whole page**. Click **OK**. Notice that page numbers appear in the header and footer of the page.

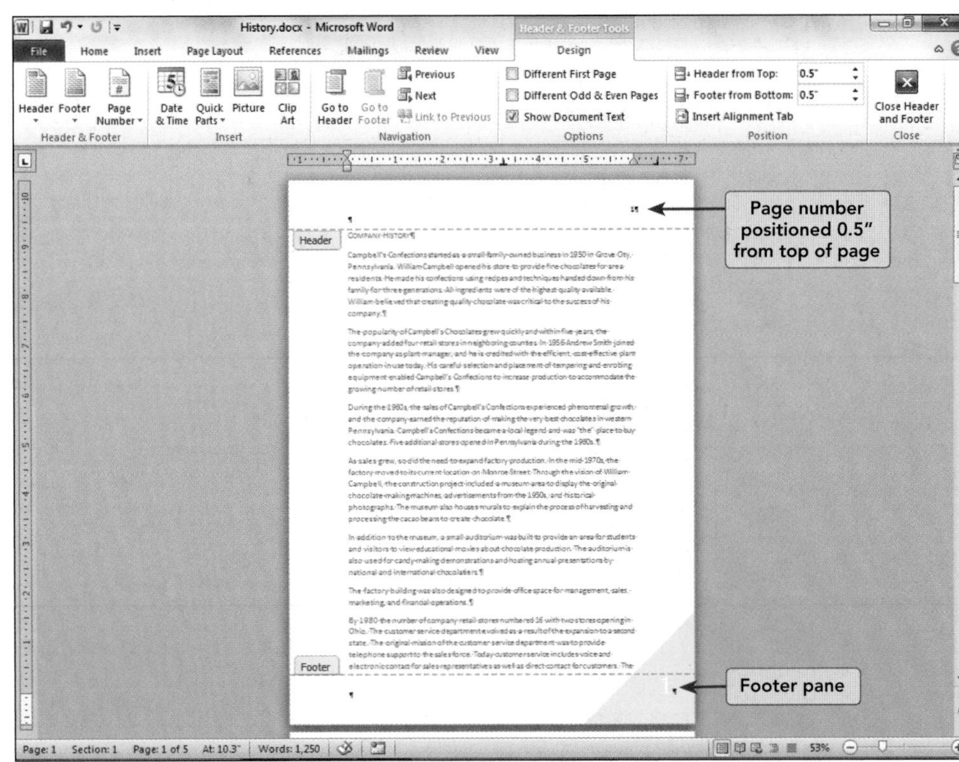

Figure 10-3 Viewing page numbers

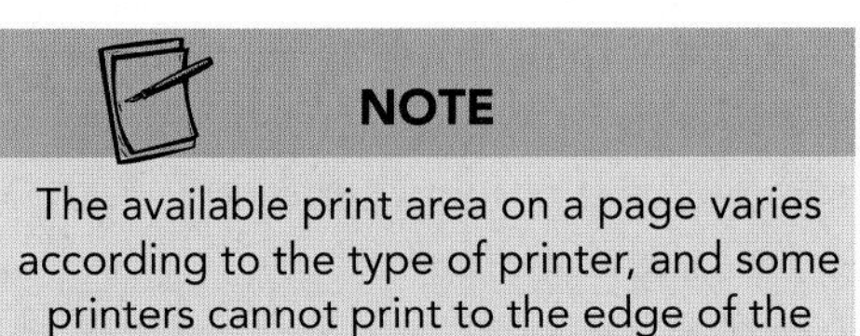

The available print area on a page varies according to the type of printer, and some printers cannot print to the edge of the paper. If your footer is not completely visible, ask your instructor about changing the footer position from 0.5 inch to 0.6 inch from the bottom edge of the page.

9. Change the zoom level to 100%, and scroll to view the first page of the document. The page number appears within the 1-inch top margin and is positioned 0.5 inch from the top edge of the page at the right margin.
10. Click the Undo button to remove the page number in the footer.

Exercise 10-2 CHANGE THE POSITION AND FORMAT OF PAGE NUMBERS

Not only can you change the placement of page numbers and decide if you want to number the first page or not, but you can also change the format of page numbers. For example, instead of using traditional numerals such as 1, 2, and 3, you can use roman numerals (i, ii, iii) or letters (a, b, c). You can also start page numbering of a section with a different value. For instance, you could number the first page ii, B, or 2.

1. Double-click the header on page 1. This activates the header pane (the area at the top of the page that contains the page number), displays the Header & Footer Tools Design tab, and dims the document text.
2. Select the page number, and change the format of the number to italic using the Mini toolbar. Press Ctrl+E to center the number. Press Ctrl+Z to undo the center alignment.

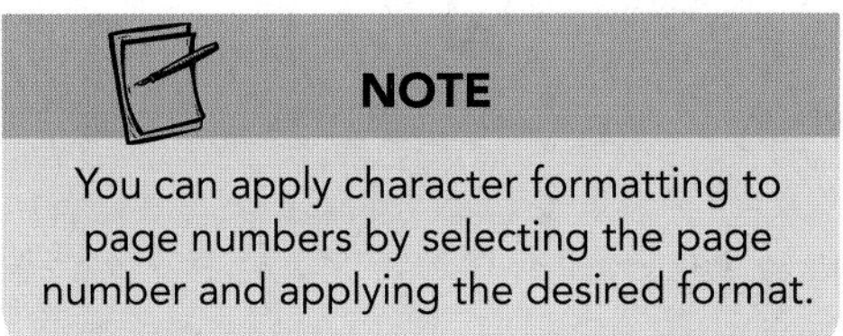

You can apply character formatting to page numbers by selecting the page number and applying the desired format.

3. Locate the **Header and Footer** group on the Header & Footer Tools Design tab. Click the Page Number button and click **Format Page Numbers**.
4. Open the **Number format** drop-down list, and choose uppercase roman numerals (I, II, III). Click **OK**.

Figure 10-4
Page Number Format dialog box

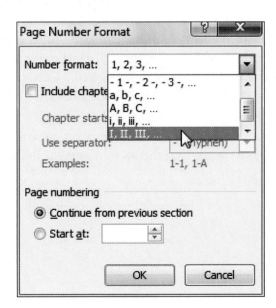

Page Number Format
Number format: 1, 2, 3, ...
- 1 -, - 2 -, - 3 -, ...
a, b, c, ...
A, B, C, ...
i, ii, iii, ...
I, II, III, ...
Include chapte
Chapter starts
Use separator: - (hyphen)
Examples: 1-1, 1-A
Page numbering
Continue from previous section
Start at:
OK Cancel

5. Locate the **Options** group on the Header & Footer Tools Design tab, and click **Different First Page**. Selecting the Different First Page option creates a separate header for the first page of the document and removes the page number from page 1 of the document.
6. Locate the **Navigation** group on the Header & Footer Tools Design tab, and click the Previous button. Scroll to the top of page 1, and notice that the page number does not display on the first page of the document. Click the Next button to return to page 2 of the document. Click the Close Header and Footer button.
7. View the document using the Print tab, and note that page 1 does not display a page number. Click the Next Page button to display page 2. The header page numbering format is now italic, starting with roman numeral II on page 2.
8. Click the **Home** tab to return to the document.

Changing the Starting Page Number

In addition to formatting page numbers and changing the page number placement, you can change the starting page numbering. You can format a document to include a cover page and change the page number options to display no page number on page 1 and to display page number 1 on the actual page 2 of the document.

To add a cover page, click the Insert tab and click the Cover Page button. Select a design from the gallery, and the cover page automatically appears at the beginning of the document. You can also insert a blank page by clicking the Blank Page button on the Insert tab.

Exercise 10-3 ADD A COVER PAGE

1. Position the insertion point at the beginning of the document. Click the **Insert** tab, and click the Cover Page button. Click the **Sideline** design from the gallery. Click the placeholder "[Type the document title]," and key **History**. Click the placeholder for "[Type the company name]," and key **Campbell's Confections**. Key your name in the Author section. Click the Pick the Date control, and select today's date.
2. Notice that the cover page is not numbered. Scroll to page 2 of the document, and notice that the second page of the document is numbered page I.

3. Position the insertion point at the top of the second page of the document. Click the **Insert** tab, and click the Page Number button. Click **Format Page Numbers**. Click the option **Continue from previous section**. Click **OK** to close the dialog box. The second page of the document is now numbered page II.

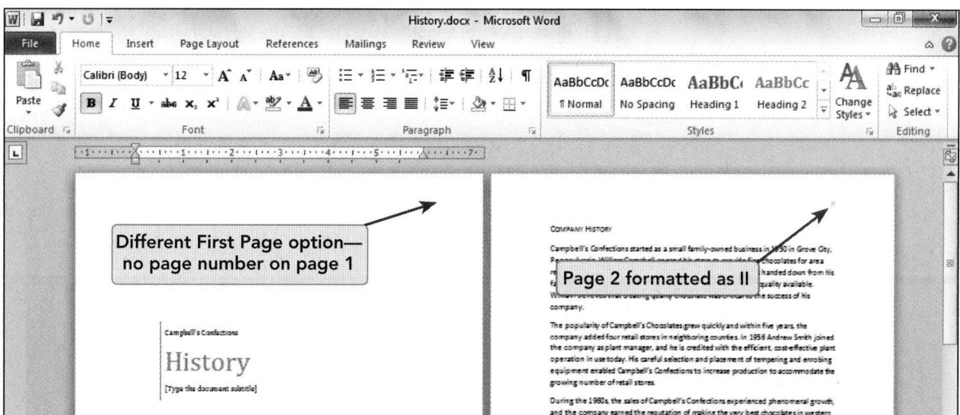

Figure 10-5
Preview page numbers

4. Click the Zoom button 100%, and click the Many Pages button. Drag to select three pages on the first row. Click **OK**. Notice that the cover page is not numbered and that page numbering starts with page 2. Return the zoom level to 100%.
5. Double-click the page number of page 2 of the document. Position the insertion point to the immediate left of the page number. Key **Page** and press Spacebar once.
6. Scroll to the header pane on page 3 to view the revised header text.
7. Close the Header and Footer pane.
8. Save the document as ***[your initials]*10-3** in your Lesson 10 folder.

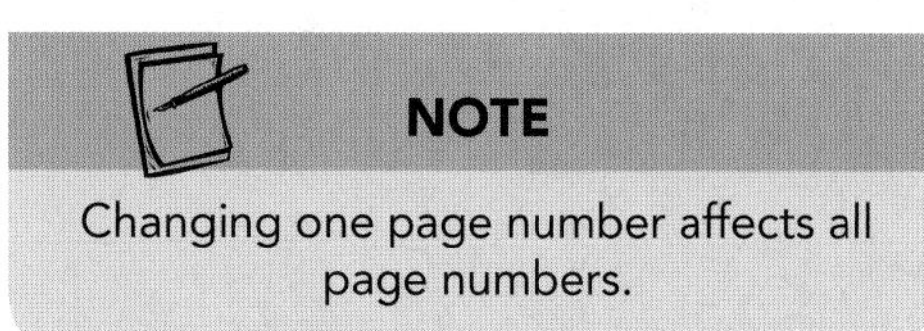

NOTE

Changing one page number affects all page numbers.

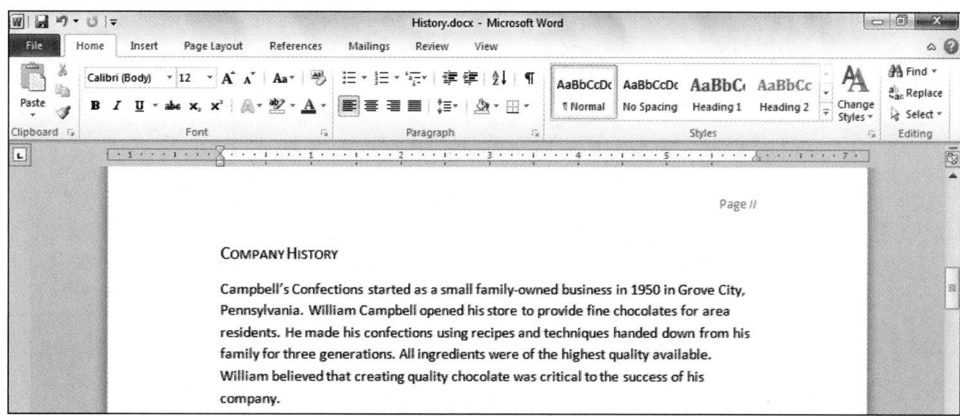

Figure 10-6
Formatted page number with "Page" added

Exercise 10-4 REMOVE PAGE NUMBERS

To remove page numbers, delete the text in the header or footer area or click the Remove Page Numbers button.

1. Click the **Insert** tab, and click the Page Number button. Click **Remove Page Numbers**.
2. Scroll through the document, and notice that the page number has been deleted from all pages.
3. Click the Cover Page button, and click **Remove Current Cover Page**.
4. Close the document without saving it.

Adding Headers and Footers

Headers and footers are typically used in multiple-page documents to display descriptive information. In addition to page numbers, a header or footer can contain:

- The document name
- The date and/or the time you created or revised the document
- An author's name
- A graphic, such as a company logo
- A draft or revision number

This descriptive information can appear in many different combinations. For example, the second page of a business letter typically contains a header with the name of the addressee, the page number, and the date. A report footer could include the report name and a header with the page number and chapter name. A newsletter might contain a header with a title and logo on the first page and a footer with the title and page number on the pages that follow.

Figure 10-7
Examples of headers and footers

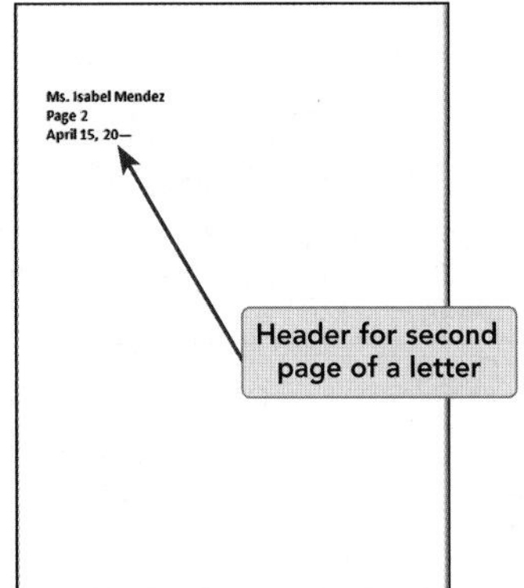

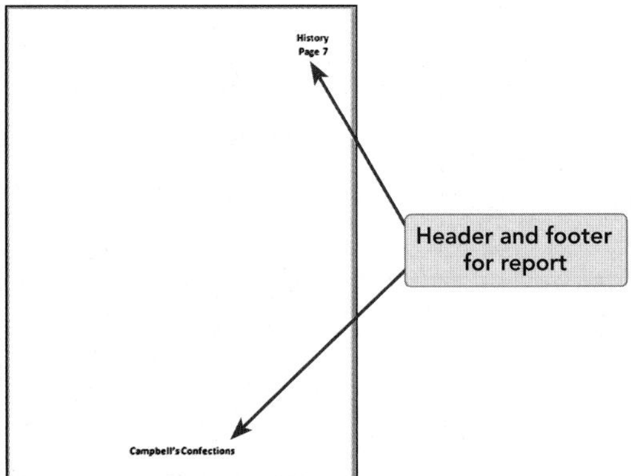

Exercise 10-5 ADD A HEADER TO A DOCUMENT

1. Open the file **History - 2**. This file is a six-page document with a title page. You will add a header and footer to pages 2 through 6.
2. Click the **Insert** tab, and click the Header button. Click the **Blank** design at the top of the Header gallery. Word displays the Header & Footer Tools Design tab and the blank header pane.
3. Locate the **Options** group on the Header & Footer Tools Design tab, and click the **Different First Page** check box. This enables you to give the document two different headers—a header for the title page (the first page), which you will leave blank, and a header for the rest of the document, which will contain identifying text. Notice that this header pane is labeled "First Page Header."
4. Click the Next button. Notice that this header pane is labeled "Header." The Previous button and the Next button are useful when you move between different headers and footers within sections of a document.
5. Key **Campbell's Confections History** in the page 2 header pane. This text now appears on every page of the document except the first page.

NOTE

These preset tab settings in the header and footer pane are default settings for a document with the default 1-inch left and right margins. In such a document, the 3.25-inch tab centers text and the 6.5-inch tab right-aligns text. This document, however, has 1.25-inch left and right margins, so it is best to adjust the tabs.

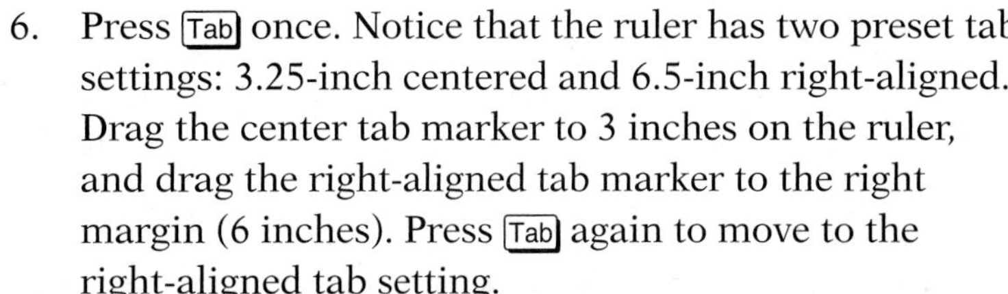

6. Press Tab once. Notice that the ruler has two preset tab settings: 3.25-inch centered and 6.5-inch right-aligned. Drag the center tab marker to 3 inches on the ruler, and drag the right-aligned tab marker to the right margin (6 inches). Press Tab again to move to the right-aligned tab setting.

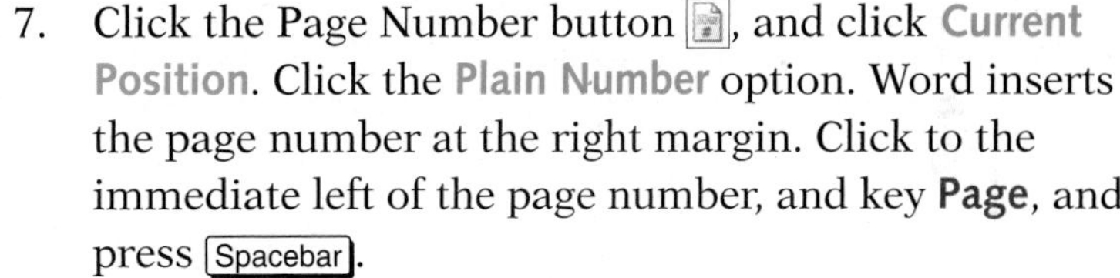

7. Click the Page Number button, and click **Current Position**. Click the **Plain Number** option. Word inserts the page number at the right margin. Click to the immediate left of the page number, and key **Page**, and press Spacebar.
8. Click the Previous button, and notice that the first-page header pane is still blank. Click the Next button to return to the header you created on page 2.

TABLE 10-1 Header and Footer Tools Design Tab

Button	Name	Purpose
	Header	Edit the document header.
	Footer	Edit the document footer.
	Insert Page Number	Insert page numbers.
	Date and Time	Insert the current date or time.
	Quick Parts	Insert common header or footer items, such as running total page numbers (for example, page 1 of 10) or document properties.
	Picture	Insert a picture from a file.
	Clip Art	Insert clip art.
	Go to Header	Activates header for editing.
	Go to Footer	Activates footer for editing.
	Previous	Show the header or footer of the previous section.
	Next	Show the header or footer of the next section.
Link to Previous	Link to Previous	Link or unlink the header or footer in one section to or from the header or footer in the previous section.
Different First Page	Different First Page	Create a header and footer for the first page of the document.
Different Odd & Even Pages	Different Odd and Even Pages	Specify a header or footer for odd-numbered pages and a different header or footer for even-numbered pages.
Show Document Text	Show Document Text	Display or hide the document text.
	Header from Top	Specify height of header area.
	Footer from Bottom	Specify height of footer area.
	Insert Alignment Tab	Insert a tab stop.

Exercise 10-6 ADD A FOOTER TO A DOCUMENT

1. With the header on page 2 displayed, click the Go to Footer button to display the footer pane.
2. Key your name and press Tab.
3. Save the document as ***[your initials]*10-6** in your Lesson 10 folder.
4. With the insertion point at the center of the footer, click the Date & Time button on the Header & Footer Tools Design tab.
5. Click the third option in the **Available formats** list. Remove the check from the **Update automatically** check box. Click **OK**. The current date is inserted in the footer.
6. Press Tab to move to the right margin, and click the Quick Parts button. Click **Field** and scroll the list of **Field names** to locate **FileName**. Click **FileName**, and notice that a list of **Field properties** appears in the middle of the dialog box. Click **First capital**. Click **OK**.

Figure 10-8
Inserting fields

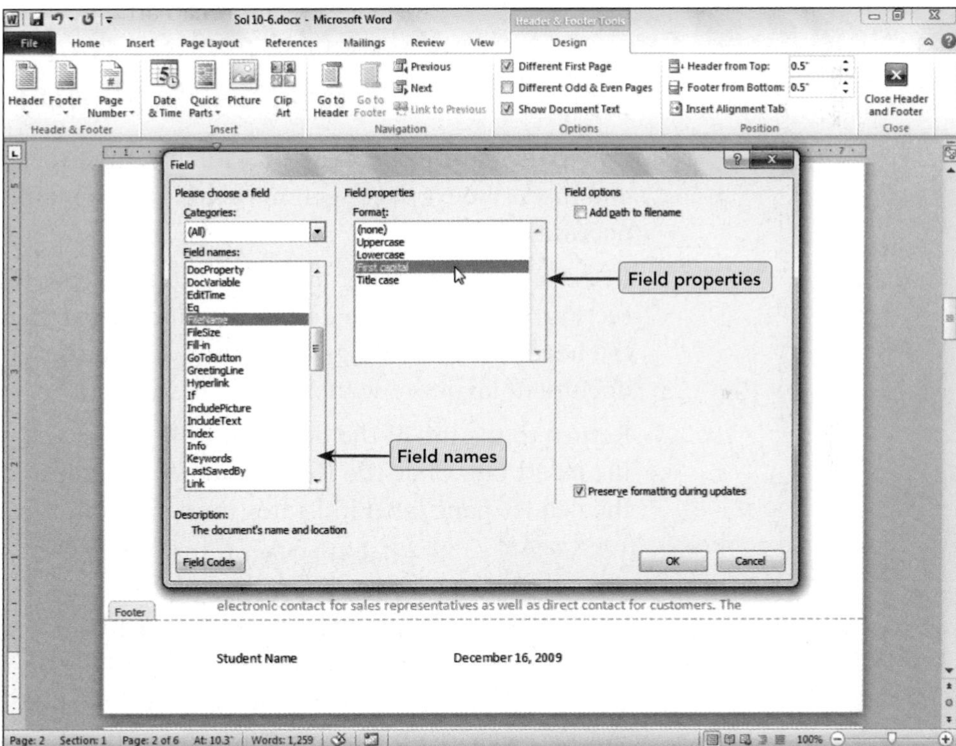

7. View the footer text. The document's file name is inserted at the right margin. This footer information prints at the bottom of each page except the first.
8. Improve the footer tab positions by dragging the center tab marker to 3 inches and the right tab marker to 6 inches. (Remember, this document has 1.25-inch left and right margins, not the default 1-inch margins.)

9. Click the Close Header and Footer button to return to the document.
10. Switch to the Print tab. Check that no header or footer appears on the title page. Click the Next Page button to move through each page of the document and to view the header and footer.
11. Return to Page Layout view and save the document. Leave it open for the next exercise.

Adding Headers and Footers within Sections

Section breaks have an impact on page numbers, headers, and footers. For example, you can number each section differently or add different headers and footers for each section.

When you add page numbers to a document, it is best to add the page numbers first and then add the section breaks. Otherwise, you have to apply page numbering to each individual section.

Exercise 10-7 ADD SECTIONS TO A DOCUMENT WITH HEADERS AND FOOTERS

1. Delete the hard page break that follows the title page of the document, and insert a next page section break. Delete blank paragraph marks if necessary.
2. Insert a next page section break before the heading "Fundraising" in section 2 (page 3 of the document) and a next page section break before the heading "Chronology" in section 3 (page 5 of the document). The document layout now includes four sections.
3. Return to the top of the document (by pressing Ctrl+Home), and click the **Insert** tab. Click the Header button. Click **Edit Header**. Notice that the header pane label indicates the section number.

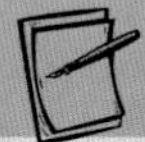

NOTE

If a document has two sections, there are multiple variations for headers and footers. For example, section 1 can display a header and section 2 can display a different header. If the Different First Page option is selected, the document could have four different headers or footers. Section 1 would include a header for the first page and a header for the remaining pages in the section. Section 2 would include a header for the first page and a header for the remaining pages in section 2. To avoid confusion, read carefully the label for each header and footer pane.

4. Click the Next button to move to the header, in section 2. Notice that this header is also blank, and it is labeled "First Page Header – Section 2." Earlier in the lesson you selected the Page Setup option **Different First Page**, and the option was applied to the entire document. This means the first page of each section can be formatted separately from the other pages in the section. It can include the same text and format as the other pages in the section, or it can contain different text and formatting.
5. Click the Next button again to move to Header – Section 2. The header and footer text begin on page 3.

6. Click the Next button to move to section 3. Because the **Different First Page** option applies to the entire document, the first page of this section contains no header or footer.
7. Turn off the Different First Page option for section 3 by clicking the **Different First Page** option on the Header & Tools Design tab to clear the check box. Page 1 of section 3 displays the document header and footer text. Turning off this option applies only to this section, as you will see in the next step.

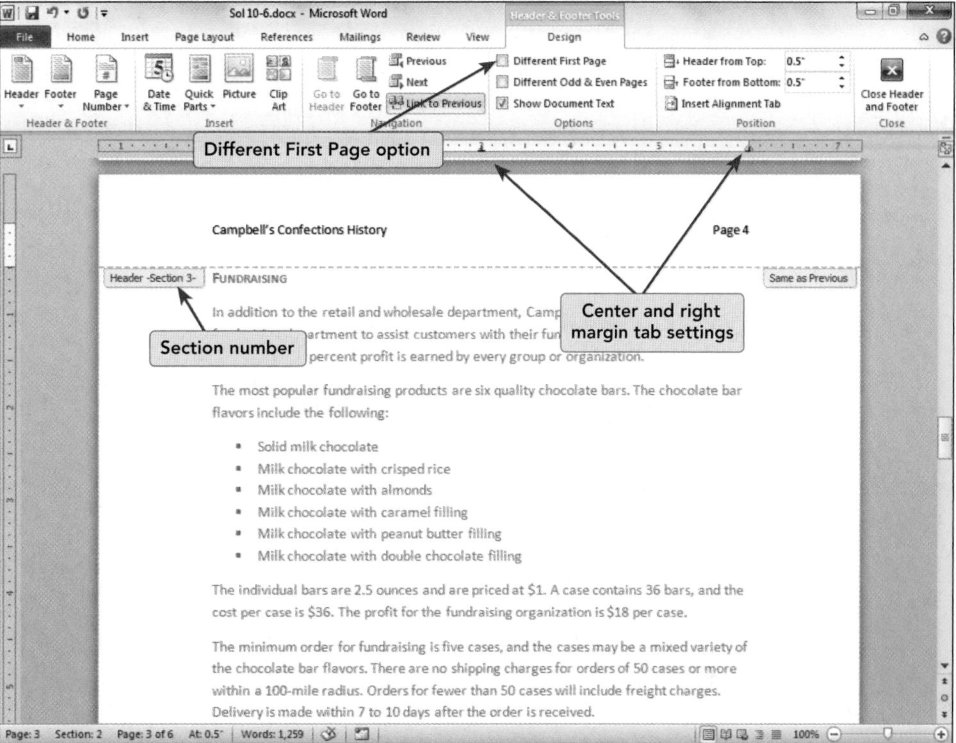

Figure 10-9
The header text for section 3

8. Click the Previous button twice to move to the header on page 1 of section 2. The header pane should read **First Page Header–Section 2**. Notice that the header pane is still blank because the **Different First Page** option is still checked for this section.
9. Click to deselect the **Different First Page** option for this section. Now the header and footer display for page 1 of section 2.
10. Click the Next button two times to move to the first-page header of section 4. Click to deselect the **Different First Page** option. The header appears on page 1 of section 4.
11. View each header in the document by dragging the scroll box (on the vertical scroll bar) up one page at a time. As you display each page's header, notice the page numbering. Also notice that the text "Same as Previous" appears on the header panes. Same as previous means the header or footer is linked to the header or footer in the previous section.

Linking Section Headers and Footers

By default, the Link to Previous button [Link to Previous] is "on" when you work in a header or footer pane. As a result, the text you key in the header (or the footer) is the same from section to section. Any change you make in one section header or footer is reflected in all other sections. You can use the Link to Previous button to break the link between header or footer text from one section to another section. Breaking the link enables you to key different header or footer text for each section.

NOTE

Breaking the link for the header does not break the link for the footer. You must unlink them separately.

Exercise 10-8 LINK AND UNLINK SECTION HEADERS AND FOOTERS

1. Scroll to the header for section 3, and select the text "Campbell's Confections History" and apply italic formatting.
2. Click the Previous button to move to the header in section 2. The header text is italic, demonstrating the link that exists between the headers.
3. Click the Next button to return to section 3. Click the Link to Previous button [Link to Previous] to turn off this option. Now sections 2 and 3 are unlinked, and you can create a different header for section 3.
4. Delete all the text in the header for section 3, including the page number.
5. Press Tab to move to the center tab setting and key **Supplement**. Press Tab again and click the Date & Time button. Select the first number format, and click **OK**. Drag the center tab marker to 3 inches and the right tab marker to 6 inches.
6. Click the Go to Footer button to switch to the footer for section 3. The footer text between sections 2 and 3 is still linked, so click the Link to Previous button [Link to Previous] to break the link.
7. Delete all the footer text in section 3 except your name. Click the Previous button to view the footer text in section 2. The footer text has not been affected. Click the Next button to return to the footer in section 3.
8. Click the Link to Previous button [Link to Previous] to restore the link between section footers. When Word asks if you want to delete the current text and connect to the text from the previous section, click **Yes**.

TIP

To select text in a header or footer, you can point and click from the area to the immediate left of the header or footer pane.

NOTE

By default, page numbering continues from the previous section.

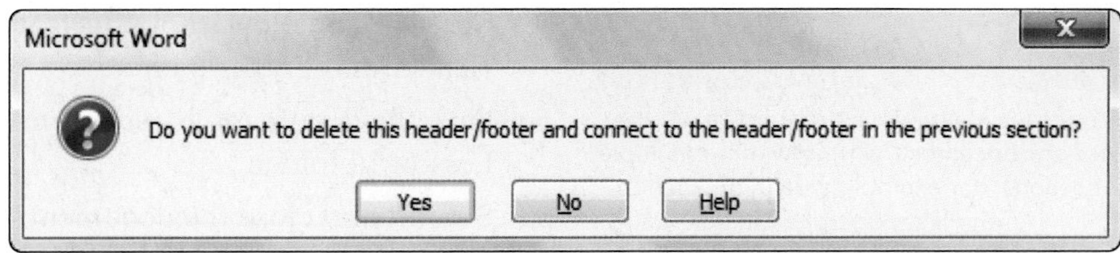

Figure 10-10 Restoring the link between section footers

9. Move to the header pane by clicking the Go to Header button. Click the Next button to move to section 4.
10. Click the Link to Previous button to disconnect the section 4 header from the section 3 header.
11. Move to the header for section 3, and click the Link to Previous button, and click **Yes** to connect the section 3 header to the header in section 2.
12. Click the Close Header and Footer button.
13. Format the title page attractively. Adjust page breaks throughout the document as needed.
14. Save the document as ***[your initials]*10-8**. Submit the document.

Exercise 10-9 CHANGE THE STARTING PAGE NUMBER

So far, you have seen page numbering start either with 1 on page 1 or 2 on page 2. When documents have multiple sections, you might need to change the starting page number. For example, in the current document, section 1 is the title page and the header on section 2 begins numbering with page 2. You can change this format so that section 2 starts with page 1.

1. Double-click the page number in section 2, page 1, to display the header pane.
2. Click the Page Number button, and click **Format Page Numbers** to open the Page Number Format dialog box.
3. Click to select the **Start at** option, and key **1** in the text box.

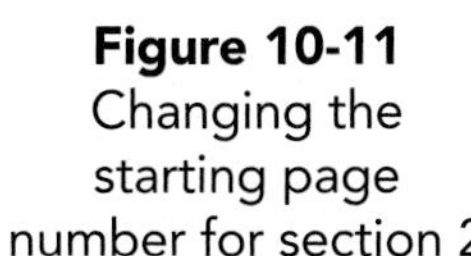

Figure 10-11 Changing the starting page number for section 2

NOTE

You can change the starting page number for any document, with or without multiple sections. For example, you might want to number the first page of a multiple-page document "Page 2" if you plan to print a cover page as a separate file.

4. Click **OK**. Section 2 now starts with page 1. Close the Header and Footer pane.
5. Save the document as ***[your initials]*10-9** in your Lesson 10 folder.
6. Submit and close the document.

Creating Continuation Page Headers

It is customary to use a header on the second page of a business letter or memo. A continuation page header for a letter or memo is typically a three-line block of text that includes the addressee's name, the page number, and the date.

There are three rules for letters and memos with continuation page headers:

- Page 1 must have a 2-inch top margin.
- Continuation pages must have a 1-inch top margin.
- Two blank lines must appear between the header and the continuation page text.

Exercise 10-10 ADD A CONTINUATION PAGE HEADER TO A LETTER

The easiest way to create a continuation page header using the proper business format is to apply these settings to your document:

- Top margin: 2 inches.
- Header position: 1 inch from edge of page.
- Page Setup layout for headers and footers: Different first page.
- Additional spacing: Add two blank lines to the end of the header.

By default, headers and footers are positioned 0.5 inch from the top or bottom edge of the page. When you change the position of a continuation page header to 1 inch, the continuation page appears to have a 1-inch top margin, beginning with the header text. The document text begins at the page's 2-inch margin, and the two additional blank lines in the continuation header ensure correct spacing between the header text and the document text.

1. Open the file **Mendez**.
2. Add the date to the top of the letter, followed by three blank lines.

3. Open the **Page Setup** dialog box, and display the **Layout** tab. Check **Different First Page** under **Headers and Footers**. Locate the section **From edge**, and set the **Header** to 1 inch from the edge.

TIP

Letters and memos should use the spelled-out date format (for example, December 12, 2012), and the date should not be a field that updates each time you open the document. To insert the date as text, with the correct format, click the Date and Time button and clear the Update automatically check box.

4. Click the **Margins** tab, and set a 2-inch top margin and 1.25-inch left and right margins. Click **OK**.
5. Click the **Insert** tab, and click the Header button. Click **Edit Header** to display a blank header pane.
6. Click the Next button to move to the header pane on page 2.
7. Create the header in Figure 10-12, inserting the information as shown. Press Enter twice after the last line. Use appropriate format for the page number and date.

Figure 10-12

```
Ms. Isabel Mendez

Page [Click Page Number, Current Position, Plain Number
for the page number.]

Date [Click Date & Time, and choose the third format to
insert the current date.]
```

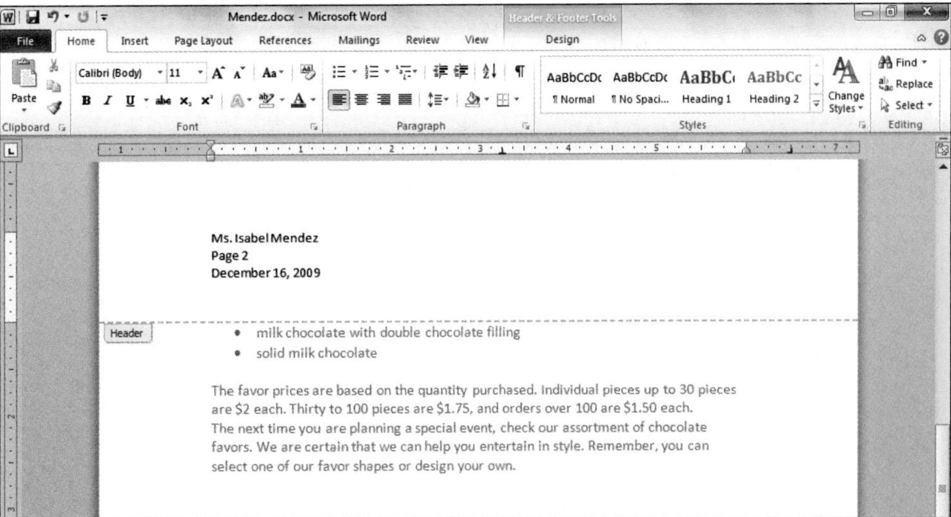

Figure 10-13 Continuation page header for a letter

8. Close the header pane, and change the zoom level to view both pages. Return the zoom level to 100%.
9. Add a complimentary closing, and key **Lydia Hamrick** and the title **Customer Service** at the end of the letter, followed by your reference initials.
10. Save the document as ***[your initials]*10-10** in your Lesson 10 folder.
11. Submit, and close the document.

Creating Alternate Headers and Footers

In addition to customizing headers and footers for different sections of a document, you can also change them for odd and even pages throughout a section or document. For example, this textbook displays the unit name for even pages and displays the lesson name for odd pages.

Exercise 10-11 CREATE ALTERNATE FOOTERS IN A DOCUMENT

To create alternate headers or footers in a document, you use the Different odd and even check box and then create a header or footer for both even and odd pages.

1. Open the file **History - 2**. Delete the page break on page 1, and insert a next page section break. Delete blank paragraph marks if necessary.
2. Position the insertion point in section 1, click the **Insert** tab, and click the Footer button.
3. Click **Edit Footer**, and click the **Different Odd and Even Pages** option. Click the **Different First Page** option so the first page does not display a footer.
4. Click the Next button, and verify that the insertion point is in the Even Page Footer pane for section 2.
5. Click the Footer button, and scroll through the gallery. Select **Contrast (Even Page)**. Click the Pick the Date control, and choose today's date. The footer displays on page 2.

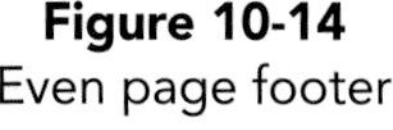

Figure 10-14
Even page footer

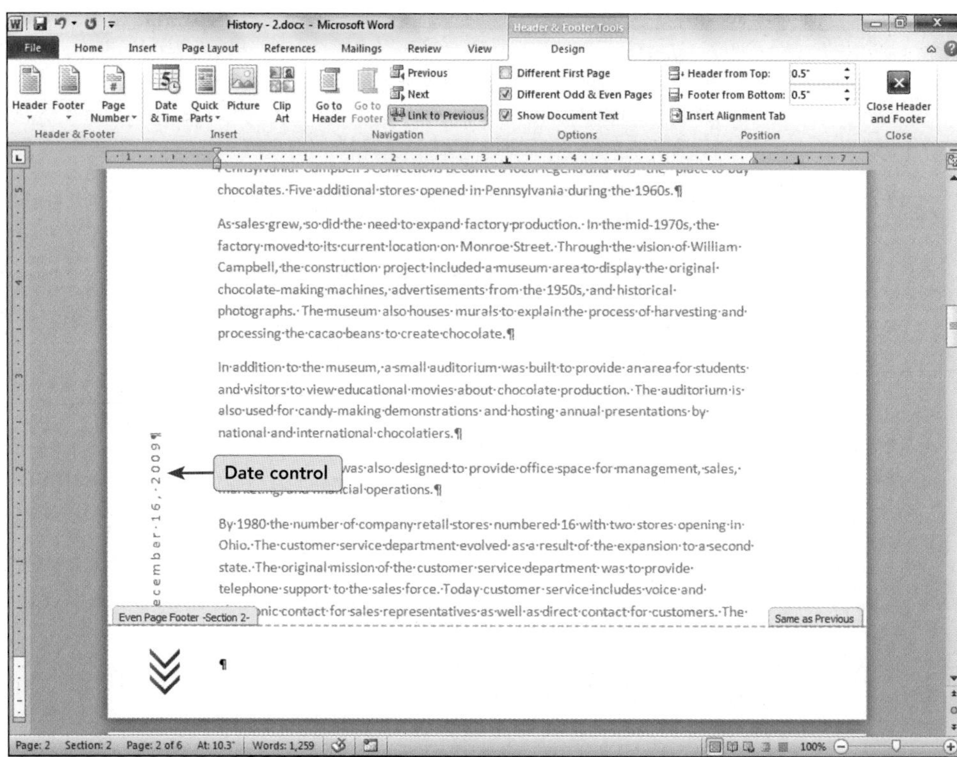

6. Click the Next button to move to the footer on page 3. The footer pane is labeled "Odd Page Footer–Section 2" and is blank.
7. Click the Footer button, and scroll through the gallery. Select **Contrast (Odd Page)**. The footer displays on page 3.
8. Click the Close Header and Footer button.
9. Click the Zoom button 100%, and click the Many Pages button. Drag over the grid to select six pages. Click **OK**. View each page of the document. Notice the position of the page number on the odd and even pages.
10. Change the zoom level to 100%. Add 72 points of paragraph space before the title on page 1, and center the text on page 1 horizontally. Apply a page border to section 1. Adjust page breaks throughout the document as needed.
11. Save the document as ***[your initials]*10-11** in your Lesson 10 folder.
12. Print the document four pages per sheet, or submit the document, and then close it.

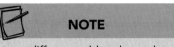

NOTE

To create different odd and even headers or footers within a section, you must first break the link between that section's header or footer and the previous section's header or footer.

Lesson 10 Summary

- A header is text that appears in the top margin of the printed page; a footer is text that appears in the bottom margin. These text areas are used for page numbers, document titles, the date, and other information.
- Always add page numbers to long documents. You can choose the position of page numbers (for example, bottom centered or top right) and the format (for example, 1, 2, 3 or A, B, C). You can also choose to number the first page or begin numbering on the second page.
- Check page numbers using the Print tab or Print Layout view (page numbers are not visible in Draft view). In Print Layout view, you can activate the header or footer pane that contains the page number by double-clicking the text and then modifying the page number text (for example, apply bold format or add the word "Page" before the number).
- To remove page numbers, activate the header or footer pane that contains the numbering, select the text, and then delete it. You can also click the Page Number button and choose Remove Page Numbers.
- To add header or footer text to a document, click the Insert tab, and click Header or Footer. Select a design from the gallery. Use the Header & Footer Tools Design tab buttons to insert the date and time or to insert Quick Parts for the file name, author, print date, or other information. See Table 10-1.

- Adjust the tab marker positions in the header or footer pane as needed to match the width of the text area.
- A document can have a header or footer on the first page different from the rest of the pages. Apply the Different First Page option in the Page Setup dialog box (Layout tab), or use the Different First Page button on the Header & Footer Tools Design tab.
- Header and footer text is repeated from section to section because headers and footers are linked by default. To unlink section headers and footers, click the Link to Previous button. To relink the header or footer, click the button again.
- Sections can have different starting page numbers. Click the Page Number button to open the Page Number Format dialog box, and then set the starting page number.
- Memos or letters that are two pages or longer should have a continuation page header—a three-line block containing the addressee's name, page number, and date. Set the header to 1 inch from the edge, add two blank lines below the header, and use a 2-inch top margin. Apply the Different First Page option, and leave the first-page header blank.
- Use the Header & Footer Tools Design Tab or the Page Setup dialog box to change the position of the header or footer text from the edge of the page. The default position is 0.5 inch.
- A document can have different headers and footers on odd and even pages. Apply the Different odd and even option.

LESSON 10		Command Summary	
Feature	**Button**	**Command**	**Keyboard**
Add or edit footer		Insert tab, Footer	
Add or edit header		Insert tab, Header	
Add page numbers		Insert tab, Page Number	
Change layout settings		Page Layout tab, Page Setup dialog box, or Header & Footer Tools Design tab	
Change page number format		Insert tab, Page Number, Format Page Numbers	

Concepts Review

True/False Questions

Each of the following statements is either true or false. Indicate your choice by circling T or F.

T F 1. The simplest way to add page numbers is to choose Page Numbers from the Page Layout tab.

T F 2. You can position a page number in a header or a footer.

T F 3. You can change the number format (for example, from numbers to roman numerals) by using the Page Number Format dialog box.

T F 4. You can apply character formatting to headers and footers in Draft view.

T F 5. A gallery displays designs for page numbers, headers, and footers.

T F 6. Deselect the Link to Previous option on the Header & Footer Tools Design tab to unlink a header in one section to the header in the previous section.

T F 7. Use Quick Parts to insert fields and document properties.

T F 8. The only way to create alternate page headers or footers is to use the Page Setup dialog box.

Short Answer Questions

Write the correct answer in the space provided.

1. What is the name of the process in which Word automatically adjusts page numbers and page breaks when you edit a document?

___

2. In addition to numbering such as 1, 2, 3 and roman numerals such as I, II, III, what other page number formatting can you use?

___

3. Which option do you use to leave the first page of a document blank and begin a header or footer on the second page?

___

4. Which Ribbon tab displays the Header and Footer buttons?

___

5. is used for what purpose?

___

6. What three items are included in a continuation page header for a letter?

____

7. By default, how far from the edge of the page does Word print headers and footers?

____

8. If you create different odd and even pages in a document, how is the header pane on page 1 labeled?

____

Critical Thinking

Answer these questions on a separate page. There are no right or wrong answers. Support your answers with examples from your own experience, if possible.

1. What information do you think most businesses would include in the header or footer for a business report? Does the information included in a business report header or footer differ from the information found in a business letter header or footer?
2. Where do you prefer to place the page number in a business report? In a business letter? Explain your answer.

Skills Review

Exercise 10-12

Add and modify page numbers and add a header.

1. Open the file **Chronology - 2**.
2. Add page numbers to the bottom of each page by following these steps:
   a. Click the Insert tab, and click the Page Number button.
   b. Click Bottom of Page, scroll through the gallery, and click to select Two Bars 1. Close the Header & Footer Tools Design tab.
3. Modify the page number in Print Layout view by following these steps:
   a. Scroll to the bottom of page 1 to see the page number.
   b. Double-click the page number to activate the footer pane.
   c. Drag the I-beam over the page number, and apply bold, italic format. change the Font Size to 14.
   d. Close the Header & Footer Tools Design tab.

4. Add 72 points of spacing before the title on page 1.
5. View the document using the Print tab; then display it in Print Layout view.
6. Add a header to the document by following these steps:
   a. Click the **Insert** tab, and click the Header button. Click the **Blank** design at the top of the gallery.
   b. Press Tab twice to position the insertion point at the right-aligned tab setting.
   c. Key your name, followed by a comma and space.
   d. Click the Quick Parts button and click **Field**. Drag the scroll box in the **Field Names** list, and click **FileName**. Click **First Capital** in the **Format** list box. Click **OK**.
   e. Close the Header & Footer Tools Design tab.
7. Save the document as ***[your initials]*10-12** in your Lesson 10 folder.
8. Submit and close the document.

NOTE

The file name **Chronology - 2** will change to the file name you assign the document after you close and reopen the document, print the document, or update the field.

Exercise 10-13

Add a footer to a document with sections, unlink the header, and change the starting page number.

1. Open the file **Wrapper - 2**.
2. Insert a **Next page** section break at the heading "CAMPBELL'S CONFECTIONS."
3. Go to section 2, and change the vertical alignment to justified.
4. Create a footer for section 2 that is not linked to section 1 by following these steps:
   a. Move the insertion point to section 2, and click the **Insert** tab. Click the Footer button, and select the **Blank** option in the Footer gallery.
   b. Click the Link to Previous button to unlink the section 2 footer from the section 1 footer (to keep the section 1 footer blank) and key ***Instructions for the design of the wrapper are on the application form.**
   c. Press Tab and key **Page**. Insert a space, click the Page Number button, click **Current Position**, and click **Plain Number**.
   d. Click the Previous button to show the footer for section 1, which should be blank.

5. Change the starting page number of section 2 to page 1 by following these steps:
   a. Click the Next button to go back to section 2.
   b. Click the Page Number button, and click **Format Page Numbers**.
   c. Click **Start at**, and make sure the number 1 appears in the text box. Click **OK**, and then close the Header & Footer Tools Design tab.
6. Change the top margin in section 1 to 2 inches.
7. Save the document as ***[your initials]*10-13** in your Lesson 10 folder.
8. Print the document two pages per sheet, or submit the document, and then close it.

Exercise 10-14

Create a continuation page header for a memo.

1. Open the file **Bio Memo**. Delete the page break on page 1, and insert a **Next Page** section break.
2. Key the current date in the memo heading.
3. Open the **Page Setup** dialog box, and change the top margin to 2 inches. Change the left and right margins to 1.25 inches. Click the **Layout** tab, and click to select **Different First Page**. Click **OK**.
4. Add a continuation page header to page 2 of the memo by following these steps:
   a. Click the **Insert** tab, and click the Header button. Click **Edit Header**.
   b. Click the Next button to move to the header on page 2.
   c. Change the **Header from Top** setting to 1 inch. (**Header & Footer Tools Design** tab, **Position** group.)
   d. Key the text in Figure 10-15, inserting the information as shown.

Figure 10-15

```
Staff
Page [Click Page Number, Current Position, Plain Number.]
[Current date]
```

   e. To insert the current date in the correct format, click the Date & Time button, and select the third format. Be sure to clear the **Update automatically** box so the memo date does not change.
   f. Press Enter twice after the date, and verify that there are two blank lines following the date.
5. Click the Previous button to check that no header appears on page 1, and close the Header & Footer Tools Design tab.

6. Adjust line and page breaks if necessary.
7. Save the document as ***[your initials]*10-14** in your Lesson 10 folder.
8. Submit and close the document.

Exercise 10-15

Add alternate footers to a document, and add a different first-page footer.

1. Open the file **Guidelines - 2**.
2. Add a page break before the bold heading "Identification Numbers."
3. Move the insertion point to the top of the document (page 1).
4. Create a footer that appears only on even pages by following these steps:
   a. Click the **Insert** tab, and click the Footer button. Click **Blank** at the top of the gallery.
   b. Click the Different First Page button [Different First Page] and the Different Odd and Even Pages button [Different Odd & Even Pages].
   c. Click the Next button to move to the even page footer.
   d. Key **Guidelines—New Store Owners**. Press Tab twice to move to the right margin.
   e. Key **Page** and press Spacebar. Click the Page Number button, click **Current Position**, and click **Plain Number**.
   f. Select the footer text, and use the Mini toolbar to apply italic formatting.
5. Create and format a footer that appears only on odd pages by following these steps:
   a. Click the Next button to move to the odd page footer pane on page 3.
   b. Click the Date & Time button. Click the third format, and click **OK**.
6. Close the Header & Footer Tools Design tab.
7. On page 1, format the two-line title in bold, 14 points, and all caps. Apply bold and small caps formatting to "Campbell's Confections." Apply italic formatting to "Preliminary Draft." Vertically center the text on the first page, and apply a page border to section 1.
8. View the document in Print Preview. Check the odd and even footers, and make sure the first-page footer is blank. Adjust page breaks if necessary.
9. Save the document as ***[your initials]*10-15** in your Lesson 10 folder.
10. Submit and close the document.

Lesson Applications

Exercise 10-16

Add page numbers, change the page number font, and adjust the starting page number.

1. Open the file **Directory - 2**.
2. Position the insertion point at the beginning of the document, and click the **Insert** tab. Click **Blank Page**.
3. Format page 1 as a memo. The memo is to the staff from Barbara Bumgarner. Use today's date, and the subject is "Updated Directory." Key the text in Figure 10-16.

Figure 10-16

```
Attached is an updated directory for the corporate office
          Confections                               the
and Campbell's^ stores in (PA), (OH), and (WV). A few^ of area
codes have changed so you may need to update your files.

                           #
Our goal is to have toll free numbers for all stores by
  December
the end of the year. We will update the directory on an
on going basis, and changes will be e-mailed to you.

If information pertaining to your department changes,
please notify me. immediately.
```

4. Replace the page break after page 1 with a **Next Page** section break. Go to page 2, and insert a **Next Page** section break immediately preceding the bold heading "Pennsylvania." Insert a page break preceding the bold headings "Ohio" and "West Virginia."
5. Position the insertion point in section 2, and click the Insert tab. Click the Footer button, and choose the Edit Footer option. Deselect Link to Previous [Link to Previous]. Click the Page Number button, and choose Bottom of Page. Select the **Thick Line** design from the gallery to position the number at the bottom center of the section. Change the start number to 1.

6. In the footer of section 3, select the page number and change the format to 10-point Arial.
7. View the page numbers in Print Preview.
8. Format the memo on page 1 with a 2-inch top margin. Change the spacing after for the subject line to 24 points. Format the first three lines of section 2, and key today's date.
9. Spell-check the document.
10. Save the document as ***[your initials]*****10-16** in your Lesson 10 folder.
11. Print the document six pages per sheet, or submit the document, and then close it.

Exercise 10-17

Create and unlink headers and footers within sections.

1. Open the file **Orders - 2**.
2. Insert a Next Page section break at the bold heading "How to Place an Order." Select the text on page 1, and format the text with a box border, using a double-line style, dark blue color, and width of 2¼ points. On the title page, center the boxed title vertically and horizontally on the page, and reduce the width of the border by formatting the text in the box with 1-inch left and right indents.
3. Position the insertion point in section 1, and deselect any text that may be highlighted. Open the Borders and Shading dialog box, and click the Page Border tab. For the box setting, select the double-rule style used in the previous step, with dark blue color and 1½ points wide. Apply the border to this section.
4. Format the tabbed text on page 2 (which starts with the text "Delivery Chart") as a separate section by placing a Next Page section break before it. Format this new section (section 3) with a 2-inch top margin.
5. Create a footer that starts on the first page of section 2 and is not linked to section 1. Key **Campbell's Confections** at the left margin. Move to the right margin, and key **Page** followed by a space and the page number. Press Spacebar after the page number, and key **of** followed by a space. Open the Field dialog box, and click the NumPages field name and the 1, 2, 3 format. Click OK.
6. Italicize the footer text, and format the footer with a single-line, 1½-point top border.
7. Change the top margin for section 2 to 1.5 inches.
8. View the document in Print Preview.

9. Save the document as ***[your initials]*10-17** in your Lesson 10 folder.
10. Submit and close the document.

Exercise 10-18

Create a continuation page header for a business letter.

1. Open the file **Yang**.
2. Format the document as a business letter. Use the address shown in Figure 10-17. The letter will be from Tamara Robbins, Fundraising Coordinator.

Figure 10-17

```
Ms. Emiko Yang
7 South Diamond Street
Greenville, PA 16125
```

3. Adjust page setup options for a continuation page header by choosing the **Different First Page** option, changing the header to 1 inch from the edge, and setting a 2-inch top margin and 1.25-inch left and right margins.
4. Insert a page break at the beginning of the paragraph that begins "Specialty."
5. Create a three-line continuation page header that prints on page 2. (Use the correct date format.)
6. Switch to Print Preview to view the document.
7. Add your reference initials, and spell-check the document.
8. Save the document as ***[your initials]*10-18** in your Lesson 10 folder.
9. Submit and close the document.

Exercise 10-19 ◆ Challenge Yourself

Create alternate footers, unlink and format section footers, change starting page numbers, and change page formats.

1. Open the file **Company**.
2. Replace the page break after page 1 with a next page section break. On page 2, insert a next page section break at the bold heading "Pennsylvania." Insert next page section breaks at the bold heading "Services" and one at the bold heading "Customer Service."

3. Insert page breaks at the bold headings "Ohio Stores," "West Virginia Stores," "Chocolate Club," "Corporate Gifts," "Favors," "Chocolate Fountains," "Fundraising," "Wholesale," and "Customer Service Account Executives."
4. Go to section 5 ("Customer Service" heading on page 13), and insert a blank footer. Deselect the Different First Page option and select the Different Odd and Even Pages option. Click the Link to Previous button [Link to Previous] to break the link for the odd page footer in Section 5.
5. Click the Next button, and break the link for the even page footer for section 5.
6. Click the Previous button. Key **Customer Service** in the odd page footer for section 5, and apply italic formatting. Center the footer text. Copy the text to the even page footer for section 5. Close the Header and Footer pane.
7. Change the bottom margin for section 5 to 0.5 inch, and change the font size for text beginning with "Pennsylvania" through the end of the document to 11 points. Verify that only section 5 has footer text.
8. Open the footer pane, and go to the first-page footer for section 4. Unlink the first-page footer from the previous section. Key **Campbell's Confections** at the left margin in the first-page footer for section 4.
9. Click the Next button, and verify that the odd page footer for section 4 displays. Key **Page** followed by a space and page number. Change the start number to **1**. Go to the even page footer for section 4, and tab to the right margin. Key **Page** followed by a space and page number.
10. Go to the first-page footer of section 3, and unlink the first-page footer from the previous section. Unlink the even page and odd page footers for section 3.
11. Key **Store Directory** at the left margin in the first-page footer pane of section 3. Press Tab twice to move to the right margin, and key **Page** followed by a page number. Change the starting number for this section to **1**.
12. Go to section 2, and break the link from the previous section. Delete any text in the footer pane.
13. Go to section 1, and verify that the footer is blank. Close the Header and Footer tab. Add a page border to this section.

14. Go to section 5, and insert a blank header. Starting at section 5 and moving to the beginning of the document, break the link for all headers in the document. Go to the first-page header of section 2, and click the header button to open the header gallery. Select the Annual design. Click the Company placeholder, and key **Campbell's Confections**. Key the current year.
15. Preview the document; then save it as ***[your initials]*10-19** in your Lesson 10 folder.
16. Print the document four pages per sheet, or submit the document, and then close it.

On Your Own

In these exercises you work on your own, as you would in a real-life business environment. Use the skills you've learned to accomplish the task—and be creative.

Exercise 10-20

Write a two-page letter. Create your letterhead in the first-page header pane, and create a continuation header in the second-page header pane. Use correct business letter format. Save the document as ***[your initials]*10-20** and submit it.

Exercise 10-21

Write a two-page report on a current event. Check pagination. Add appropriate headers and footers, and include page numbering. Create a title page as a separate section without a header or footer. Save the document as ***[your initials]*10-21** and submit it.

Exercise 10-22

Write a short report about 10 places you would like to visit. Each place should be a separate paragraph with its own heading. Include a title page. Adjust page breaks as needed. Format the document for odd and even headers and footers, and then insert different identifying information in the headers or footers. Save the document as ***[your initials]*10-22** and submit it.

Lesson 11

Styles and Themes

OBJECTIVES

After completing this lesson, you will be able to:

1. Apply styles.
2. Create new styles.
3. Redefine, modify, and rename styles.
4. Use style options.
5. Apply and customize a theme.

Estimated Time: 1¼ hours

A *style* is a set of formatting instructions you can apply to text. Styles make it easier to apply formatting and ensure consistency throughout a document. You can apply styles, modify them, or create your own.

In every document, Word maintains *style sets*—a list of style names and their formatting specifications. A style set, which is stored with a document, includes standard styles for body text and headings. Word includes several built-in styles, and a few of the built-in styles appear in the Quick Style Gallery on the Home tab. When you point to a style in the Quick Style Gallery, you can see a preview of the style formatting.

A *theme* is a set of formatting instructions for the entire document. A theme includes style sets, theme colors, theme fonts, and theme effects. Themes can be customized and are shared across Office programs.

Applying Styles

The default style for text is called the *Normal* style. Unless you change your system's default style, the Normal style is a paragraph style with the following formatting specifications: 11-point Calibri, English language, left-aligned, 1.15-line spacing, 10 points spacing after, and widow/orphan control.

To change the appearance of text in a document, you can apply five types of styles:

- A *character style* is formatting applied to selected text, such as font, font size, and font style.
- A *paragraph style* is formatting applied to an entire paragraph, such as alignment, line and paragraph spacing, indents, tab settings, borders and shading, and character formatting.
- A *linked style* formats a single paragraph with two styles. It is typically used to assign a heading style to the first few words of a paragraph.
- A *table style* is formatting applied to a table, such as borders, shading, alignment, and fonts.
- A *list style* is formatting applied to a list, such as numbers or bullet characters, alignment, and fonts.

Exercise 11-1 APPLY STYLES

There are two ways to apply styles:

NOTE

Define a style set before you apply formatting to ensure you are using the appropriate styles.

- Open the Styles task pane and select a style to apply. To open the Styles task pane, click the Styles Dialog Box Launcher or press Alt+Ctrl+Shift+S. The Styles task pane includes the built-in styles featured in the Quick Style Gallery plus all available styles.
- Click the Home tab, and click a Quick Style.

1. Open the file **Volume 1**.
2. Click the **Home** tab, and click the **Styles Dialog Box Launcher** to open the Styles task pane. The task pane lists formatting currently used in the document and includes some of Word's built-in heading styles. Each style has a drop-down list of options to help you manage the styles.
3. Activate the **Home** tab, and click the Change Styles button. Click **Style Set**, and click **Word 2010**. The style set defines the built-in styles for the document.
4. Click in the line "Choc Talk," and place the mouse pointer (without clicking) over the Heading 1 style in the task pane. A ScreenTip displays the style's attributes.
5. Click the **Heading 1** style in the Styles task pane. The text is formatted with 14-point bold Cambria, blue, 24 points spacing before, and 1.15-line spacing.

NOTE

To apply a style to a paragraph, you can simply click anywhere in the paragraph without selecting the text. Remember, this is also true for applying a paragraph format (such as line spacing or alignment) to a paragraph.

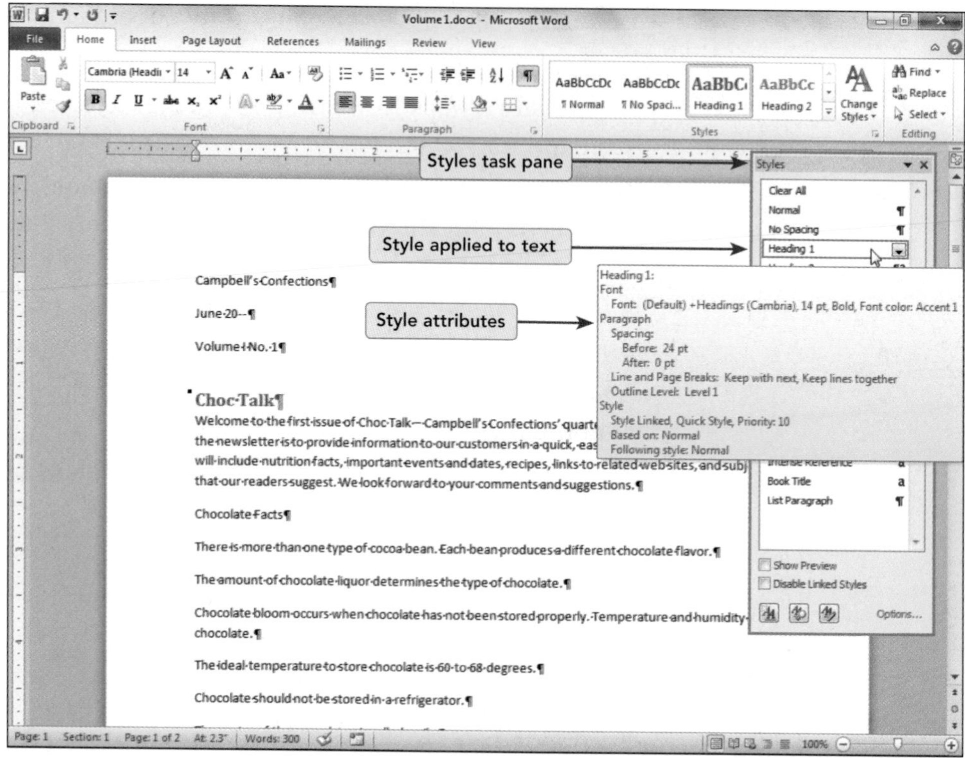

Figure 11-1 Using the Styles task pane to apply a style

6. Close the Styles task pane by clicking the Styles task pane Close button.
7. Position the insertion point in the text "Chocolate Facts."

TIP

Style sets may only show those styles already used in the document. To see all styles available, click **Options** in the Styles task pane, and click the arrow beside Select styles to Show. Select All styles.

8. Click the **Home** tab, and locate the **Styles** group. The Styles group includes a gallery of styles that provides a quick and convenient way to apply styles. One row of the styles gallery displays by default. Click the More arrow to display all the styles in the Quick Style Gallery. Move the mouse pointer over each of the quick styles to preview the format.
9. Choose **Heading 2**. Notice the applied formatting.

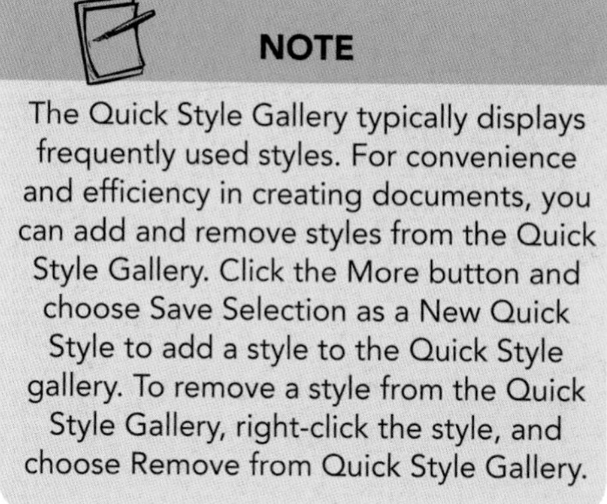

NOTE

The Quick Style Gallery typically displays frequently used styles. For convenience and efficiency in creating documents, you can add and remove styles from the Quick Style Gallery. Click the More button and choose Save Selection as a New Quick Style to add a style to the Quick Style gallery. To remove a style from the Quick Style Gallery, right-click the style, and choose Remove from Quick Style Gallery.

Figure 11-2
Using the Quick Style Gallery

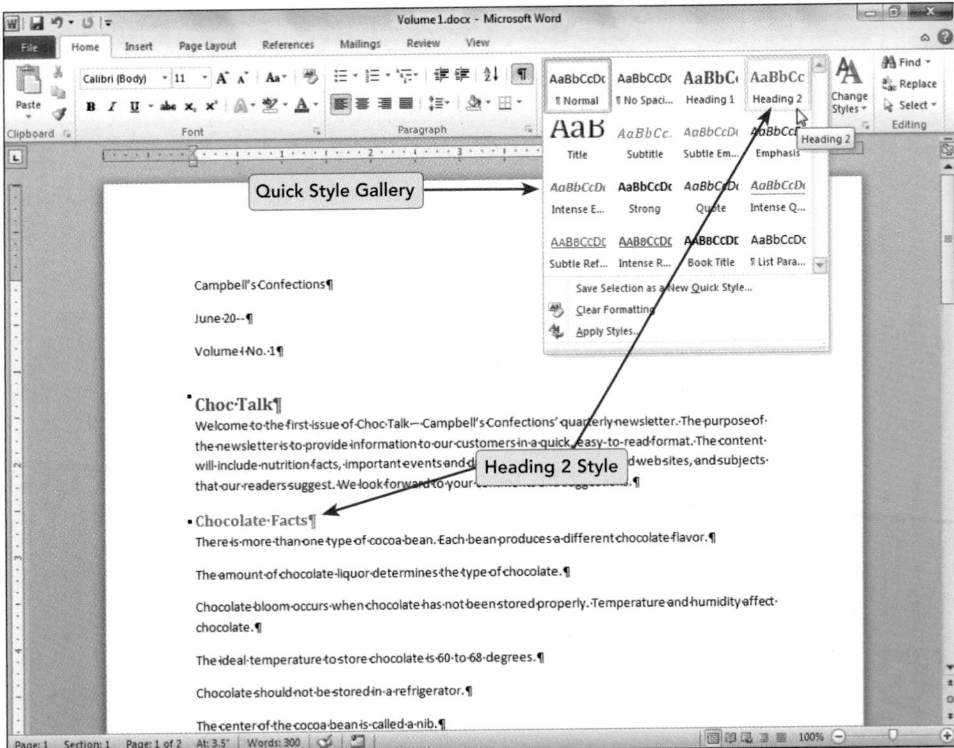

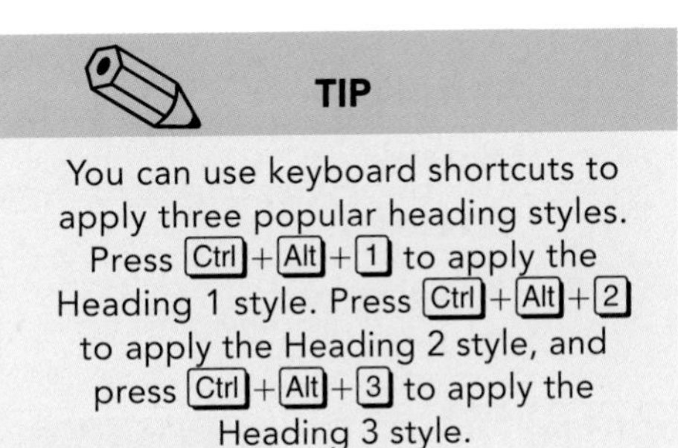

TIP

You can use keyboard shortcuts to apply three popular heading styles. Press Ctrl+Alt+1 to apply the Heading 1 style. Press Ctrl+Alt+2 to apply the Heading 2 style, and press Ctrl+Alt+3 to apply the Heading 3 style.

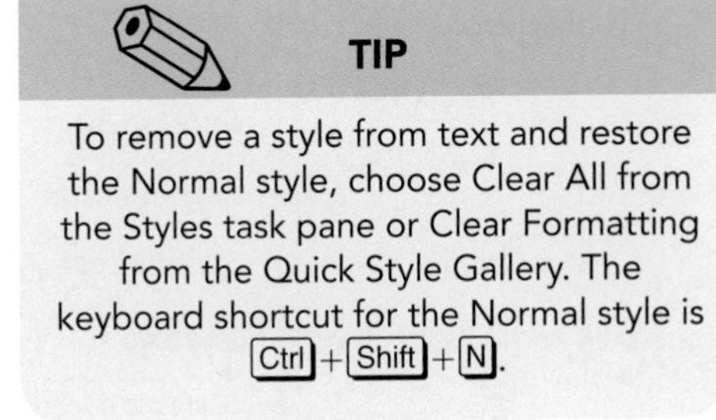

TIP

To remove a style from text and restore the Normal style, choose Clear All from the Styles task pane or Clear Formatting from the Quick Style Gallery. The keyboard shortcut for the Normal style is Ctrl+Shift+N.

10. Position the insertion point in the heading "Nutrition." Press F4 to repeat the Heading 2 style.

Creating New Styles

Creating styles is as easy as formatting text and then giving the set of formatting instructions a style name. Each new style name must be different from the other style names already in the document.

Word saves the styles you create for a document when you save the document.

Exercise 11-2 CREATE A PARAGRAPH STYLE

There are two ways to create a new paragraph style:

- Use the Quick Style Gallery.
- Click the New Style button in the Styles task pane.

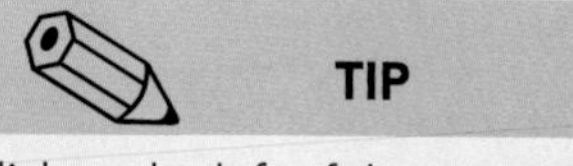

TIP

Click to the left of the text to select the entire paragraph. (Be sure your mouse is in the margin area and the mouse pointer changes to a white arrow.)

NOTE

Click to select the Show Preview check box in the Styles task pane to display style names with formatting.

1. Reopen the Styles task pane by clicking the **Styles Dialog Box Launcher**.
2. Select the heading "Chocolate Facts."
3. Increase the font size to 14 points, and press Ctrl+Shift+K to apply small caps.
4. Click the New Style button at the bottom of the Styles task pane. The Create New Style from Formatting dialog box opens.
5. Key **Side Heading** in the **Name** box. Verify that **Paragraph** is the **Style type**.

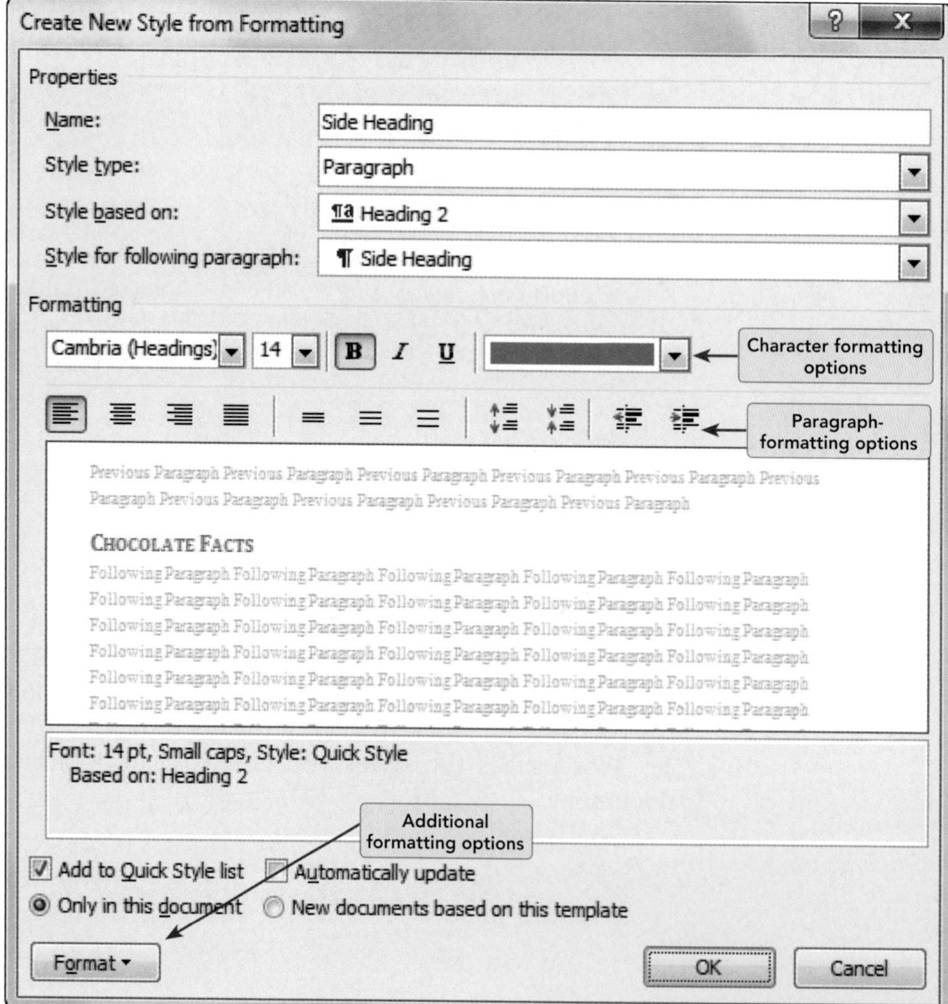

Figure 11-3 Create New Style from Formatting dialog box

NOTE

If you key a style name that already exists in the Style box, you apply the existing style; you do not create a new one.

TIP

Use the formatting buttons in the Create New Style from Formatting dialog box to apply basic font and paragraph formatting. For more formatting options, click the Format button, and choose Font, Paragraph, Tabs, Border, or Numbering to open the corresponding dialog boxes.

6. Notice the two rows of buttons under **Formatting**. The first row applies character formatting, and the second row applies paragraph formatting.
7. Click **OK**. The style appears in the Quick Style Gallery and in the Styles task pane.
8. Locate the heading "Nutrition." Click in the paragraph, and click the **Side Heading** style in the task pane. The new style is applied.
9. Repeat the formatting to the side headings "Pets and Chocolate" and "Important Chocolate Dates."
10. Select the text "June 20—" at the top of the document, and change the font size to 12.
11. Right-click the selected text, and click **Styles** in the shortcut menu. The Styles Gallery displays as well as options to update the Normal style to match the selected text or to save the selection as a new style. Click **Save Selection as a New Quick Style**.

Figure 11-4
Creating a new style

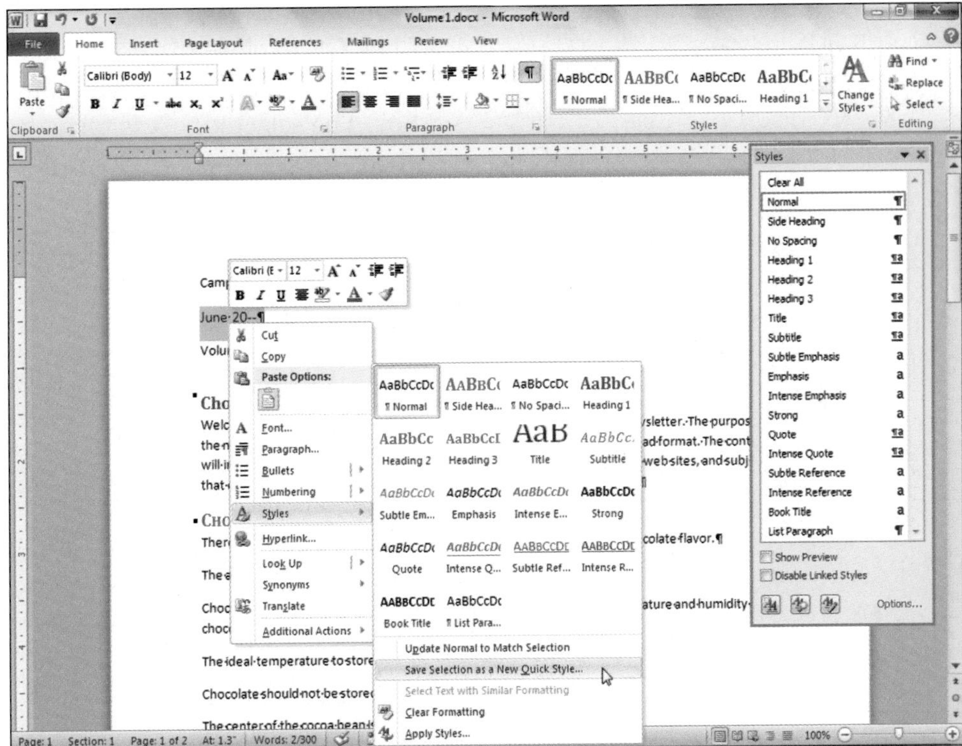

NOTE

Press Shift+F1 to display the Reveal Formatting task pane. The Reveal Formatting task pane displays formatting of selected text. Expand or collapse the information in the task pane by clicking the plus or minus symbols. Click an underlined link to open a dialog box.

12. Key **Issue Date** in the **Name** text box, and click **OK**.
13. Notice that the Side Heading style and the Issue Date style appear in the Styles task pane and the Quick Style Gallery.

Exercise 11-3 CREATE A CHARACTER STYLE

A character style is applied to selected text and only contains character formatting.

NOTE

When you change the style type to character, the paragraph format buttons in the Create New Style from Formatting dialog box dim. Paragraph, Tabs, and Numbering options in the Format button menu are also unavailable for character styles.

NOTE

In a list of styles, paragraph styles display a paragraph symbol (¶) and character styles display a text symbol (a) to the right of the style name. Linked styles display both a paragraph symbol (¶) and a text symbol (a).

1. Select the text "Choc Talk" in the first paragraph under the heading "Choc Talk." Open the Create New Style from Formatting dialog box by clicking the New Style button, and key **Accent** in the **Name** text box.
2. Choose **Character** from the **Style type** drop-down list box. Once the style type is defined as a character style, paragraph-formatting options are not available.
3. Click the **Format** button, choose **Font**, and set the formatting to 11-point Calibri and italic.
4. Click **OK** to close the Font dialog box. Click **OK** to close the Create New Style from Formatting dialog box. The selected text is formatted, and the Accent style appears in the Styles task pane and the Quick Style Gallery.
5. Note that a character style is applied to selected text, not the entire paragraph.

TIP

At the bottom of the Styles task pane, you can click the Options link to choose which types of styles are displayed. The default setting, "Recommended," lists styles and unnamed formats available to the current document. "In use" lists styles and unnamed formats applied in the current document. "In current document" lists styles and unnamed formats available in the current document. "All styles" lists styles in the current document and all of Word's built-in styles. You can also specify how the styles are sorted: alphabetical, as recommended, font, based on, and by type.

Figure 11-5
Applying the character style

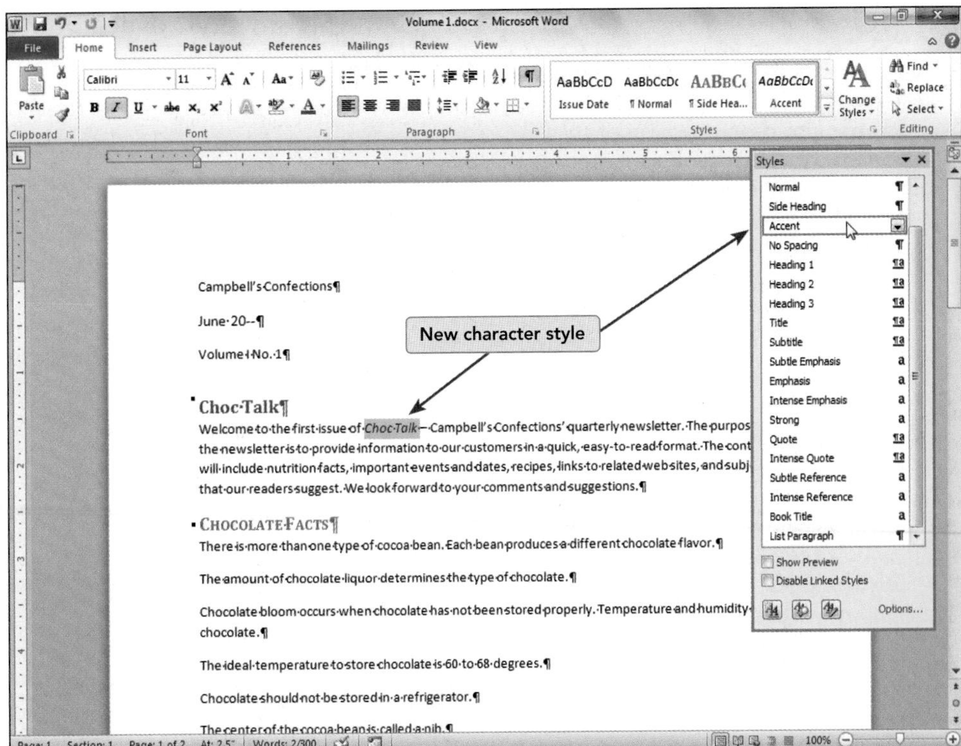

6. Save the document as ***[your initials]*****11-3** in a new folder for Lesson 11. Do not print the document; leave it open for the next exercise.

Modifying and Renaming Styles

After creating a style, you can modify it by changing the formatting specifications or renaming the style. When you modify a style, the changes you make affect each instance of that style. You can quickly replace one style with another by using the Replace dialog box, the Styles task pane, or the shortcut menu.

Exercise 11-4 MODIFY AND RENAME STYLES

To modify a style, right-click the style in the Styles task pane and then choose Modify. Or select the styled text, modify the formatting, right-click the style name in the Styles task pane, and choose Update to Match Selection. You can also select and modify text formatting. Right-click the selected text, choose Styles, and click Update to Match Selection.

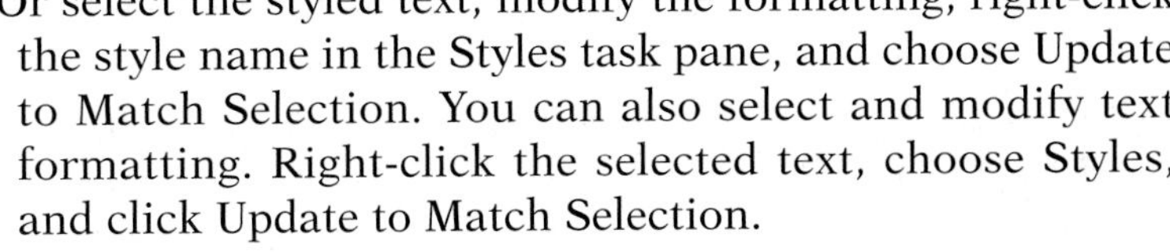

NOTE

You can modify any of Word's built-in styles as well as your own styles. However, you cannot rename Word's standard heading styles.

1. In the Styles task pane, right-click the style name **Heading 1**. Choose **Modify** from the shortcut menu.

TIP

Instead of using the right mouse button to open this drop-down list of style options, you can use the left mouse button to click the down arrow next to a style name. Remember, if you click a style name (not its down arrow) with the left mouse button, you will apply the style to the text containing the insertion point.

2. In the Modify Style dialog box, change the point size to 18, and click **OK** to update the style.
3. Select the text "June 20—" and open the **Paragraph** dialog box. Change the **Spacing After** to 0 points and click **OK**. Right-click the selected text "June 20—." Choose **Styles**, then choose **Update Issue Date to Match Selection**. The style is updated to match the selected text formatting.

TIP

You can also click the Select All Instances option in the Styles task pane to select all instances of a style.

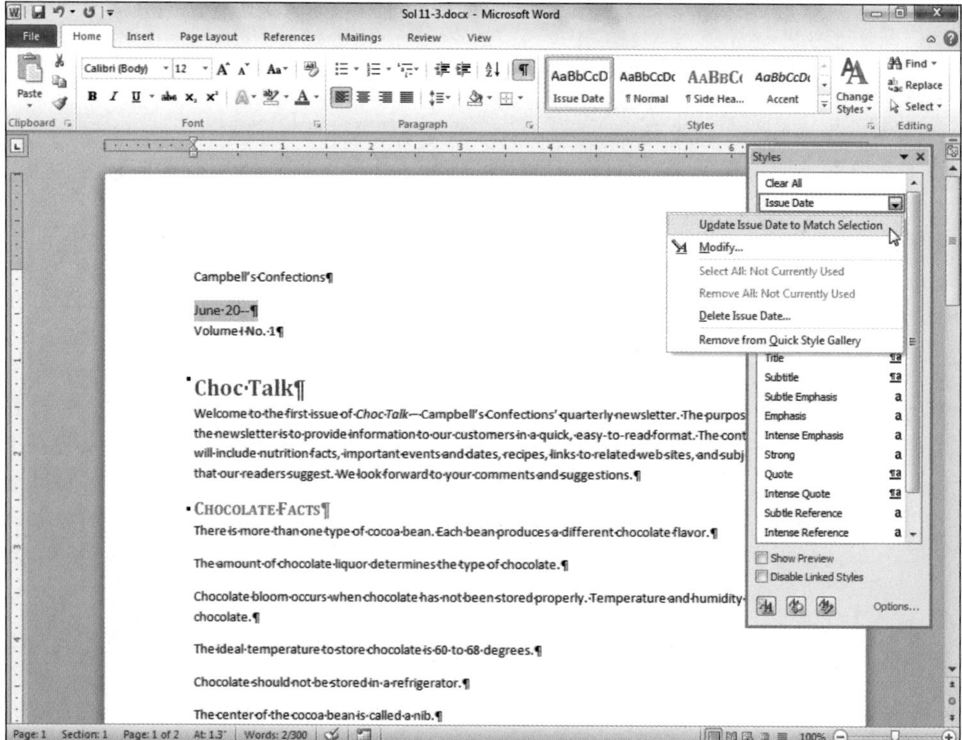

Figure 11-6
Modifying a style by updating

NOTE

After modifying or renaming a style, you can undo your action (for example, click Undo from the Quick Access Toolbar).

4. Position the insertion point in the text "June 20—." Right-click the **Issue Date** style in the task pane, and choose **Modify**.
5. Rename the Issue Date style by keying **Pub Date** in the **Name** text box. Click **OK**. The style Pub Date appears in the task pane, replacing the style name Issue Date.

Exercise 11-5 REPLACE A STYLE

1. Click the **Home** tab, and locate the **Editing** group. Click the Replace button. Click the **More** button More >>, if needed, to expand the dialog box. Clear any text or formatting from a previous search.
2. Click the **Format** button and choose **Style**. The Find Style dialog box displays.
3. Click **Side Heading** from the **Find what style** list, and click **OK**.

Figure 11-7
Find Style dialog box

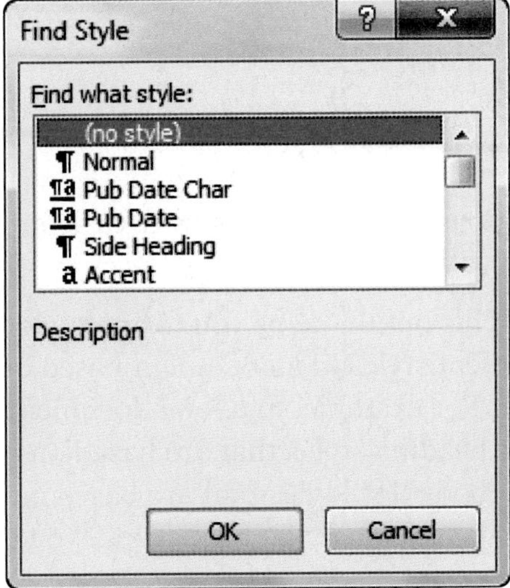

TIP

You can also use the Styles task pane to replace one style with another style: Right-click a style name in the task pane, choose Select All Instances, and then click another style name in the Styles task pane. An alternative method is to right click the styled text, choose Styles from the shortcut menu, choose Select text with Similar Formatting, and then click another style name in the Styles task pane.

4. Tab to the **Replace with** text box, click **Format**, and choose **Style**.
5. Choose **Heading 3** from the **Replace With Style** list, and click **OK**.
6. Click **Replace All**. Click **OK**. Word replaces all occurrences of the Side Heading style with the Heading 3 style. Close the Find and Replace dialog box. Notice the change in the format. Click the Undo button.

Exercise 11-6 DELETE A STYLE

1. Click the Manage Styles button at the bottom of the Styles task pane. Click the **Edit** tab. Select the **Pub Date** style in the **Select a style to edit** list box. Click **Delete**.
2. Click **Yes** when prompted to verify the deletion. Click **OK**. The Pub Date style is deleted, and the paragraph returns to Normal, the default style.
3. Click the Undo button to reverse the style deletion.

4. Right-click the Pub Date style in the Styles task pane. Choose **Delete Pub Date** from the drop-down list. Click **Yes** to verify the deletion. The Pub Date style is deleted, and the paragraph returns to the Normal style.

NOTE

When you delete a style from the style sheet, any paragraph that contained the formatting for the style returns to the Normal style. You cannot delete the standard styles (Word's built-in styles) from the style sheet.

NOTE

When you right-click a style in the Quick Style Gallery, and choose Remove from Quick Style Gallery, the style is removed from the Style Gallery but not deleted from the Styles task pane.

Using Style Options

Word offers two options in the Create New Style from Formatting dialog box to make formatting with styles easier:

- *Style based on:* This option helps you format a document consistently by creating different styles in a document based on the same underlying style. For example, in a long document, you can create several different heading styles that are based on one heading style and several different body text styles that are based on one body text style. Then if you decide to change the formatting, you can do so quickly and easily by changing just the base styles.
- *Style for following paragraph:* This option helps you automate the formatting of your document by applying a style to a paragraph and then specifying the style that should follow immediately after the paragraph. For example, you can create a style for a heading and specify a body text style for the next paragraph. After you key the heading and apply the heading style, press Enter, and the style changes to the body text style.

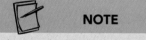

NOTE

The standard styles available with each new Word document are all based on the Normal style.

Exercise 11-7 USE THE STYLE FOR FOLLOWING PARAGRAPH OPTION

1. Go to the end of the document, and position the insertion point in the blank paragraph above "Copyright."
2. Click the **New Style** button in the Styles task pane.
3. Key **StaffName** in the **Name** text box.
4. Click **Format** and choose **Font**. Set the font to 11-point Cambria, and click **OK** to close the Font dialog box. Click **OK** to close the Create New Style from Formatting dialog box.

5. Click the New Style button in the Styles task pane. Key **StaffTitle** in the **Name** text box. The **Style type** is **Paragraph**. Change the **Style based on** to **Normal**. Click **Format** and choose **Font**. Set the font to 11-point Calibri, with bold and small caps, and click **OK**.
6. Check that the Align Left button is selected. Click **Format**, and choose **Paragraph**. Change the **Spacing After** to 0 points, and change the **Line spacing** to single. Click **OK**. Click the down arrow for **Style for following paragraph**, and select **StaffName**. Click **OK**.

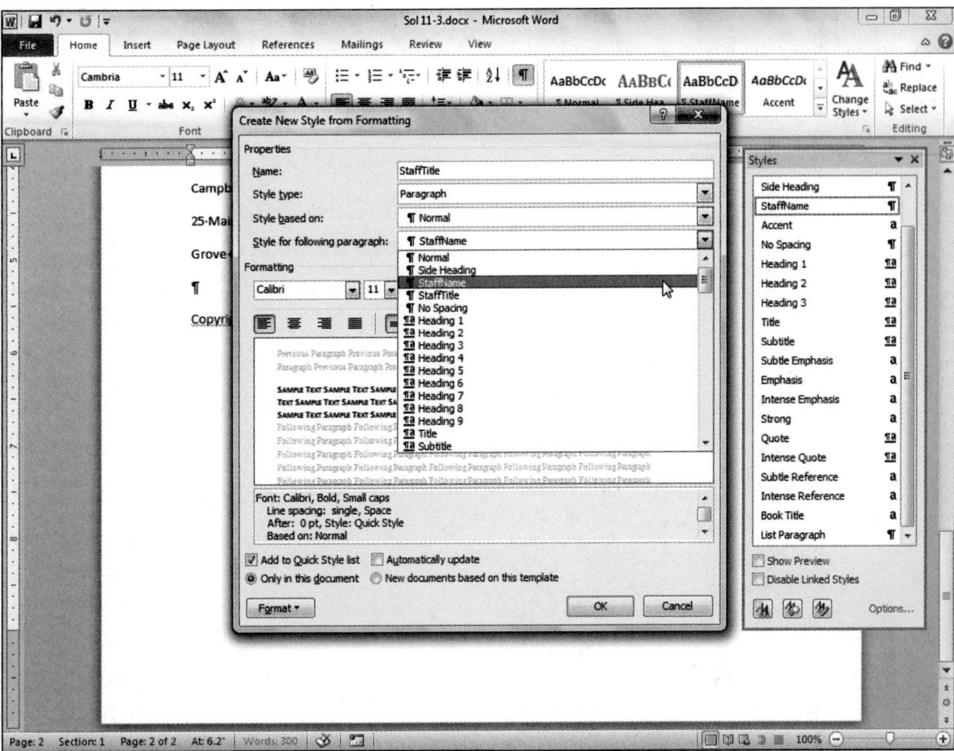

Figure 11-8 Choosing a style for the following paragraph

7. Key **President** on the blank line above "Copyright," and apply the **StaffTitle** style. Notice the format of the text. Press Enter. Key **Thomas Campbell**.
8. Note that the style automatically changes from StaffTitle to StaffName, which was the style indicated as the style for the following paragraph.
9. Key the text shown in Figure 11-9. Apply the appropriate styles.

Figure 11-9

```
Vice President     ← StaffTitle, Enter StaffName
Lynn Tanguay
Editor             ← StaffTitle, Enter StaffName
Margo Razzano
```

Exercise 11-8 USE THE BASED ON OPTION

1. Select the text near the bottom of page 2, from "Choc Talk" to "16127." Click the New Style button on the Styles task pane. Key **BaseBody** in the **Name** box. Verify that **Paragraph** is selected for the **Style type**, and **Normal** is selected for **Style based on**.
2. Change the font to Times New Roman, 12 points. Change the paragraph formatting to 0 points spacing after and single spacing. Click **OK** to close the Create New Style from Formatting dialog box.
3. Click the New Style button in the task pane.
4. Key **Body2** as the name of the new style. Click the Italic button in the Create New Style from Formatting dialog box to change the font to italic. Check that **Basebody** appears in the **Style based on** list box. Click **OK**.
5. Notice that the selected paragraph(s) are formatted with the Body2 style. Apply the BaseBody text to the text that was formatted by the new style. Deselect the text, and press Enter after the ZIP Code.
6. Place the mouse pointer over (without clicking) the Body2 style in the task pane. The ScreenTip indicates that the Body2 style is based on the Basebody style.
7. Click the New Style button in the task pane to create another style.
8. Key **Body3** as the name of the new style. Choose **Basebody** from the **Style based on** list, if it is not already selected. Change the font size to 10 points. Click **OK**. Apply the BaseBody style to any text or paragraph that was formatted by the new style.
9. Move to the top of the document. Select the text from "June 20—" to "Volume 1 No. 1." Apply the Body2 style. Deselect the text.
10. Right-click the style **Basebody** in the task pane, and choose **Modify**.
11. Change the font to Calibri. Click **OK**. All the text using or based on the Basebody style changes to the Calibri font.

TIP

When you want to use an existing style as the based on style, select the text with that style before opening the New Style dialog box. The style will automatically appear in the Style based on box.

TIP

An alternative to using the Quick Style Gallery or the Styles task pane to apply styles is to use the Apply Styles window. To display the Apply Styles window, choose Apply Styles from the Quick Style Gallery drop-down list or press Ctrl+Shift+S. You can choose a style from the list or key the first few letters of the style name.

Exercise 11-9 DISPLAY AND PRINT STYLES

To make working with styles easier, you can display a document's styles on the screen and print the style sheet. To see the styles, switch to Draft view.

1. Switch to Draft view. Open the Word Options dialog box, and click **Advanced** in the left pane. Scroll to the **Display** group of options.

2. Set the **Style area pane width** box to **0.5** inch and click **OK**. The style area appears in the left margin.

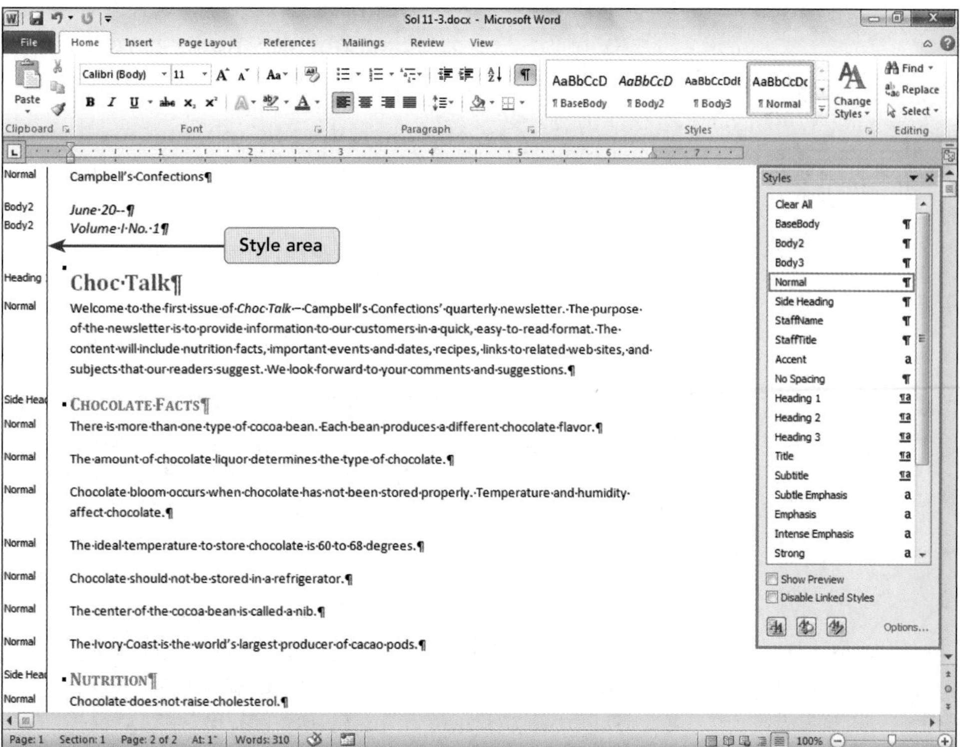

Figure 11-10
Styles shown in Style area

3. Right-click the **Normal** style in the Styles task pane. Click **Select All Instance(s)**. Click the **Basebody** style in the Styles task pane. Text previously formatted with the Normal style is now formatted with the Basebody style.

NOTE

The style area is intended for on-screen purposes in Draft view only (it is not available in Print Layout view). If you open the Print tab and preview the document, this area does not display or appear on the printed document. Additionally, when you display the Style area, it will be displayed for any document you open unless you reduce the view to 0 inches. The default Style area pane width is 0 inches.

4. Select the text under "Chocolate Facts" beginning with "There is" through "cacao pods." Format the list as a bulleted list using a small square bullet.
5. Select the bulleted list you just formatted if necessary. Right-click the selected bulleted list, and select **Styles** from the shortcut menu. Select **Save Selection as a New Quick Style**. Name the style **BaseBullet**, and click **Modify**. Set the **Style based on** setting to Basebody. Click **OK** to close the dialog box.
6. Apply the BaseBullet style to the text under the headings "Nutrition," "Pets and Chocolate," and "Important Chocolate Dates."
7. Modify the Heading 2 style so it is based on Basebody. Apply the Heading 2 style to the first line of the document "Campbell's Confections." Move to the last page of the document, and repeat the Heading 2 format for the "Choc Talk" line.

NOTE

You can assign a shortcut key to a style you use frequently. In the Styles task pane, right-click the style to which you want to assign a shortcut key. Choose Modify. Click Format and then click Shortcut key. In the Customize Keyboard dialog box, press an unassigned keyboard combination, such as Alt+B, for a body text style. The shortcut key is saved with the document.

8. Open the Word Options dialog box, and click **Advanced**. Scroll to the **Display** section, set the **Style area pane width** box to **0** inch, and click **OK**. Switch to Print Layout view.
9. Save the document as ***[your initials]*11-9** in your Lesson 11 folder.
10. Click the File tab, and open the **Print** tab. Choose **Styles** from the **Print All Pages** drop-down list, and click **Print**. Word prints the styles for your active document.
11. Submit the document.

Exercise 11-10 CHANGE STYLE SET

Word provides several style sets to format your document. The number and types of styles available varies for each style set. You can choose Word 2010 as the style set or try Elegant, Fancy, Formal, or other style sets. Each style set affects the format of your document.

1. Position the insertion point at the top of the document. Click the Change Styles button, and click **Style Set**. The default style set is currently selected. Click **Fancy**, and scroll through the document to notice the changes in format.
2. Save the document as ***[your initials]*11-10**.
3. Submit and close the document.

Apply and Customize a Document Theme

You can use document themes to format an entire document quickly. A gallery of theme designs is available to format your document, or you can go to Microsoft Online for additional theme selections. Themes can also be customized and saved. Themes define the fonts used for body text and the fonts used for headings. For example, the default theme is Office, and Calibri is the default font for body text, and Cambri is the default font for headings. Themes affect the styles of a document.

Exercise 11-11 APPLY A THEME

1. Reopen the file **Volume 1**. Make sure the Styles task pane displays.
2. Click the **Page Layout** tab, and click the Themes button. The design gallery for themes displays.

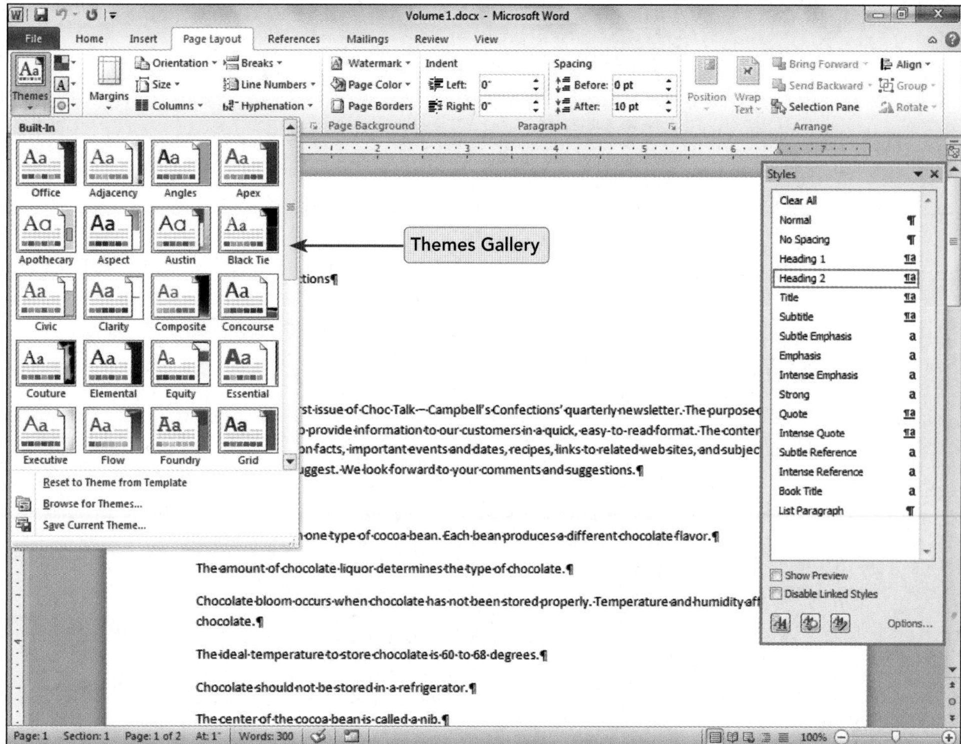

Figure 11-11
Themes Gallery

3. Move your mouse over each of the theme designs, and preview the changes in your document. Click the **Technic** theme.
4. Scroll through the document, and notice the changes made. The default body text font is 11-point Arial, and the default heading font is Franklin Gothic Book.
5. View the style names in the Styles task pane. When you change a document theme, styles are updated to match the new theme.
6. Using the new styles, change the text "Campbell's Confections" at the beginning of the document to the Heading 2 style, and change "Choc Talk" to the Heading 1 style.

Exercise 11-12 CUSTOMIZE A THEME

Theme colors include text and background colors, accent colors, and hyperlink colors. The Theme Colors button displays the text and background colors for the selected theme.

1. Click the **Page Layout** tab, and locate the **Themes** group. Click the Theme Colors button. The design gallery for theme colors displays with the current theme colors selected.

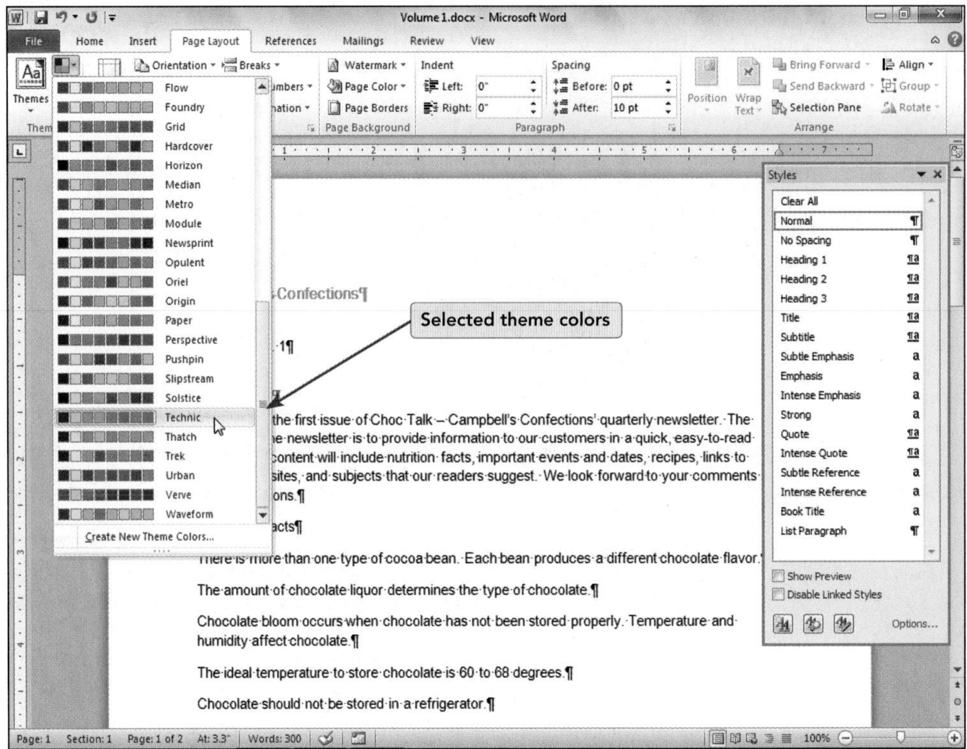

Figure 11-12
Theme colors

2. Click **Create New Theme Colors**. Notice that there is a button for each element of the theme. Click the down arrow beside the Accent 1 button, and notice that the first color in the fifth row of Theme Colors is selected. Click the last color in the fifth row, **Aqua, Accent 1, Darker 50%**. Key **Custom Accent 1** in the **Name** box. Click **Save**. The accent color for the heading text in the document changes.

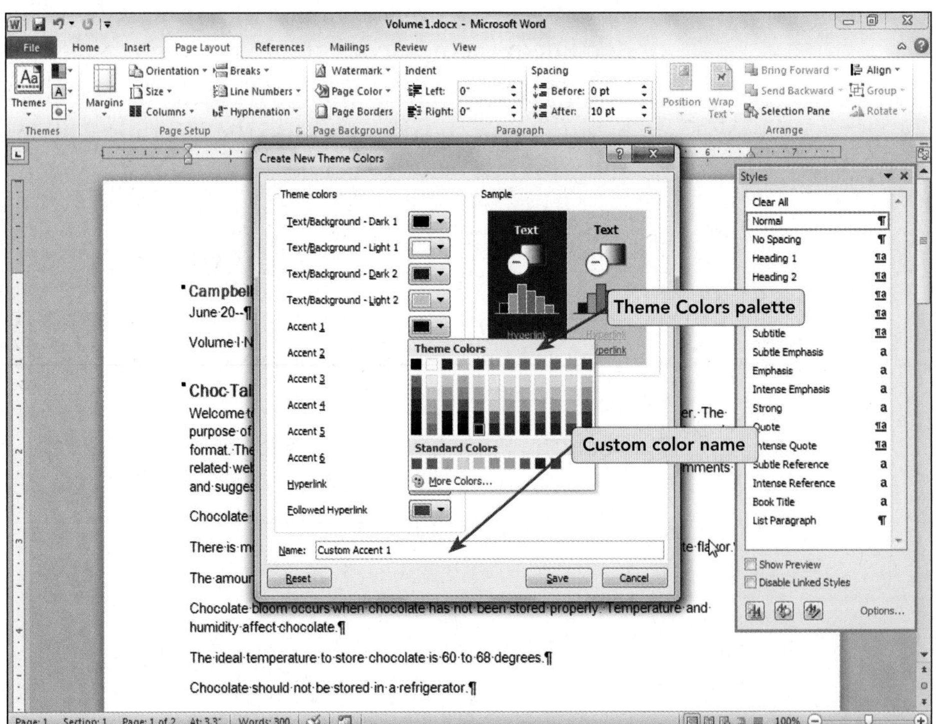

Figure 11-13
Create New Theme Colors dialog box

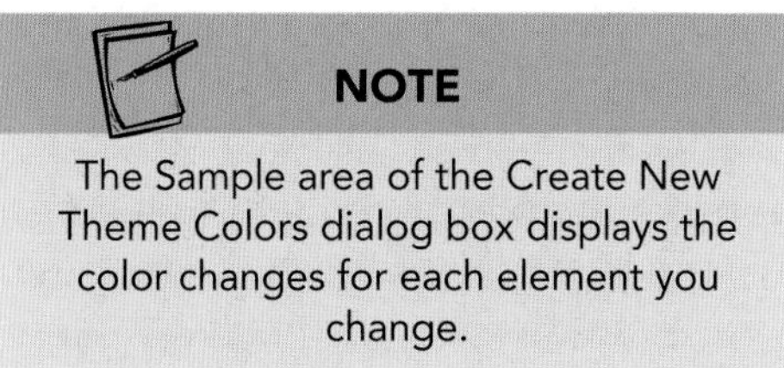

NOTE

The Sample area of the Create New Theme Colors dialog box displays the color changes for each element you change.

3. Click the Theme Colors button on the Page Layout tab, and notice that the Custom Accent 1 theme color appears at the top of the list. Right-click the Custom Accent 1 color, and click **Delete**. Click **No**.
4. Click the **Page Layout** tab, and click the Theme Fonts button. The heading and body text font for each theme displays.
5. Click the option to **Create New Theme Fonts**. The current heading font and body font are selected in the Create New Theme Fonts dialog box.

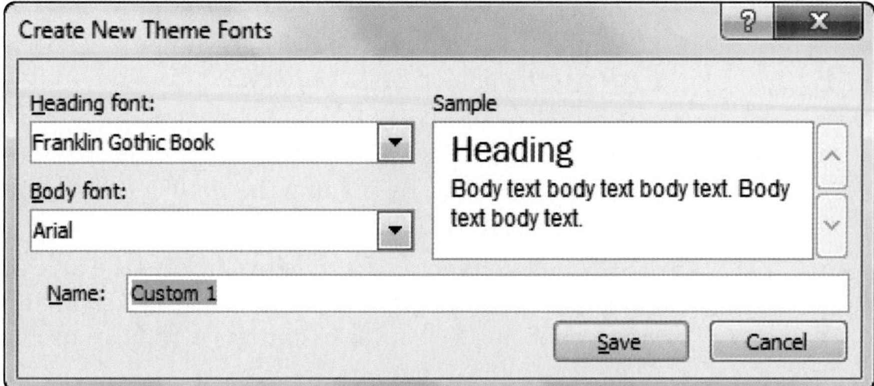

Figure 11-14
Create New Theme Fonts dialog box

6. Change the **Heading font** to **Footlight MT Light**, and change the **Body font** to **Arial Narrow**. Key **Custom Font** in the **Name** box. Click **Save**.
7. Click the Theme Fonts button, and notice that "Custom Font" appears at the top of the list. Right-click **Custom Font**, and click **Edit**. Change the **Heading font** to **Eras Medium ITC**, and change the **Body font** to **Footlight MT Light**. Click **Save**.
8. Select the headings "Chocolate Facts," "Nutrition," "Pets and Chocolate," and "Important Chocolate Dates," and apply the Heading 3 style.
9. Apply the Heading 4 style to the line that begins "Volume." Apply the Heading 5 style to the second line "June 20—."
10. Select the lines of text under each of the headings formatted with the Heading 3 style, and format the lines as a bulleted list.
11. At the end of the document, delete the text that begins "Choc Talk" through the end of the document.
12. Click the **Page Layout** tab, and click the Themes button. Click **Save Current Theme**. Key **Custom Theme** in the File name box. Click **Save**.
13. Click the Themes button, and notice that the design gallery displays built in designs and custom designs. Right-click the **Custom Theme** at the top of the gallery, and click **Delete**. Click **Yes** to delete the theme.
14. Save the document as ***[your initials]*11-12** in your Lesson 11 folder.
15. Submit and close the document.

Lesson 11 Summary

- A style is a set of formatting instructions you can apply to text to give your document a unified look. The five types of styles are character, paragraph, linked, table, and list.
- Word's default style for text is called the Normal style. The default settings for body text are 11-point Calibri, left-aligned, 1.15-line spacing, 10 points spacing after, with widow/orphan control. Word provides nine built-in heading styles (for example, Heading 1, Heading 2). The default font for heading text is Cambria.
- To apply a style, select the text you want to style (or click in a paragraph to apply a paragraph style). Then choose the style from the Styles task pane or the Quick Style Gallery.
- View the attributes of a style by placing the mouse pointer over the style name in the Styles task pane and reading the text in the ScreenTip. Preview the style by placing the mouse pointer over the style name in the Quick Style Gallery.
- Select all instances of a style by clicking the arrow for the style name in the Styles task pane or by right-clicking a style name in the task pane and choosing Select All Instance(s). You can use the Quick Style Gallery to select all instances too.
- To create a new paragraph style: Select text, modify the text, right-click the text, select Styles from the shortcut menu, select Save Selection as a New Quick Style, key a new style name, and click OK. Or click the New Style button in the Styles task pane, and set the style's attributes in the Create New Style from Formatting dialog box.
- To create a character style, select the text and apply the font formatting. Click the New Style button in the Styles task pane, and key the style name. Change the Style type to Character, and click OK. An alternative is to select text, modify the text, right-click the text, select Styles from the shortcut menu, choose Save Selection as a New Quick Style, key a new style name, and click Modify. Change the Style type to character, and click OK.
- To modify or rename a style, right-click the style name in the Styles task pane (or point to the style name and click the down arrow), choose Modify, and then change the attributes. Or select text that uses the style, change the format, right-click the style name in the task pane, and choose Update to Match Selection.
- After applying a style throughout a document, you can replace it with another style. Click the Replace command on the Home tab (in the dialog box, click Format, choose Style, and select the style name in both the Find what and Replace with boxes).
- You can also replace styles by using the Styles task pane (select all instances of a style and then choose another style).

- To delete a style, right-click the style name in the Styles task pane, and choose Delete. Click Yes to delete the style. You can also click the Manage Styles button in the Styles task pane, select the style, and click Delete. Click Yes to delete the style, and click OK.
- When creating new styles, you can specify that they be based on an existing style. You can also specify that one style follows another style automatically. Both these options are offered in the Create New Style from Formatting dialog box.
- Display styles along the left margin of a document in Draft view by opening the Word Options dialog box, clicking Advanced, and scrolling to the Display group. Change the Style area width box to 0.5 inch. Do the reverse to stop displaying styles.
- Print a style sheet by choosing Print from the File tab and choosing Styles from the Print All Pages drop-down list.
- The theme feature formats an entire document using design elements. Themes include theme colors, theme fonts, and theme effects.

LESSON 11		Command Summary	
Feature	**Button**	**Command**	**Keyboard**
Apply styles		Home tab, Styles group	
Create styles		Home tab, Styles group, Styles task pane	
Styles task pane		Home tab, Styles group, Styles Dialog Box Launcher	Shift+Ctrl+Alt+S
Theme colors		Page Layout tab, Themes group	
Theme fonts		Page Layout tab, Themes group	
Themes		Page Layout tab, Themes group	
View style area		Word Options, Advanced, Display	

Concepts Review

True/False Questions

Each of the following statements is either true or false. Indicate your choice by circling T or F.

T F 1. Paragraph styles can include both paragraph- and character-formatting instructions.

T F 2. You can apply character styles to selected text within a paragraph.

T F 3. You can use either the Styles task pane or the Quick Style Gallery to apply a paragraph style.

T F 4. If you select only part of a paragraph to change the paragraph style, only the selected portion is reformatted.

T F 5. You can create a paragraph style by changing the formatting of selected text, right-click the selection, and select Styles.

T F 6. A style named and created for a specific document cannot be modified for that document.

T F 7. When you delete a style from the style sheet, any paragraph or text containing that style returns to the Normal style.

T F 8. You save the styles created for a document by saving the document.

Short Answer Questions

Write the correct answer in the space provided.

1. In the list of styles, which symbol designates a paragraph style?

___

2. In the list of styles, which symbol designates a character style?

___

3. How do you print a list of a document's styles?

___

4. What is the purpose of a theme?

___

5. How do you display style names in the left margin of a document?

___

6. How do you open the Create New Style from Formatting dialog box?

___

7. What are the five types of styles?

____

8. On which style are all standard styles based?

____

Critical Thinking

Answer these questions on a separate page. There are no right or wrong answers. Support your answers with examples from your own experience, if possible.

1. The Based on option is often used to create a group of heading styles based on one style and a group of body text styles based on another style. Why aren't heading styles and body text styles typically based on the same style?
2. Create complementary styles for a heading and for body text, using two different fonts. Describe the formatting for each style, and provide a sample of the styles used together. Describe the type of document for which this combination would be suited.

Skills Review

Exercise 11-13

Apply styles and create new styles.

1. Open the file **Agenda - 1**.
2. Use the Quick Style Gallery to apply a style to the document title by following these steps:
   a. Position the insertion point in the title (the first line).
   b. Click the More Arrow button to open the Quick Style Gallery.
   c. Click **Title**.
3. Use the Styles task pane to apply a style by following these steps:
   a. Click the **Home** tab, and click the **Styles Dialog Box Launcher** to display the Styles task pane.
   b. Position the insertion point in the next heading, "Sponsored by."
   c. Click **Subtitle** in the Styles task pane.
4. Apply the Heading 1 style to the heading "Agenda."
5. Create a new paragraph style for a heading by following these steps:
   a. Select the heading "Thursday, February 10."
   b. Click the New Style button, and key **Day** in the **Name** text box.
   c. Change the font formatting to 14-point bold and small caps.

d. Change the paragraph formatting to 12 points spacing before and 6 points spacing after. Click **OK** to close the Create New Style from Formatting dialog box.

e. Apply the Day style to the line beginning "Friday."

6. Use the Create New Style from Formatting dialog box to create a new style for the agenda text by following these steps:

   a. Position the insertion point at the beginning of the line that begins "12 Noon." Click the New Style button in the task pane.

   b. Key **Agenda Items** in the **Name** text box.

   c. Change the font size to 12.

   d. Click **Format** and choose **Paragraph**.

   e. Change the left indent to 0.25 inch, and change the spacing after to 3 points. Click **OK**.

   f. Click **OK** in the Create New Style from Formatting dialog box.

7. Select all the agenda text under the headings "Thursday" and "Friday." Choose the **Agenda Items** style from the Styles task pane.

8. Apply the Heading 2 style to the line that begins "Grove City College."

9. Change the document title to small caps and add 72 points of spacing before the paragraph.

10. Save the document as ***[your initials]*11-13** in your Lesson 11 folder.

11. Submit and close the document.

Exercise 11-14

Create, redefine, modify, and rename styles.

1. Open the file **OH Stores**. Display the Styles task pane.

2. Select the document title, and apply 14-point Times New Roman, bold italic format. Create and apply a paragraph style by right-clicking the selected text, and choosing Styles. Choose **Save Selection as a New Quick Style**, and name the style **Office Heading**.

3. For the text "Campbell's Confections," create and apply a paragraph style named **Subhead** with the formatting 12-point Arial, bold italic and with 12 points spacing before and 3 points spacing after paragraphs.

4. Position the insertion point in each line of text that contains a Campbell's Confections' store name, and apply the Subhead style (press F4 to repeat the style).

5. Redefine the Subhead style by following these steps:

   a. Select the first occurrence of "Campbell's Confections," and remove the italic format by clicking the italic button *I*.

   b. Right-click the **Subhead** style in the task pane. Choose **Update Subhead to Match Selection**.

6. Create a new character style for the word "Fax" by following these steps:
   a. Position the insertion point at the beginning of the second telephone number for the Akron Office. Click the **New Style** button in the task pane.
   b. Key **Fax Num** in the **Name** text box.
   c. Choose **Character** from the **Style type** drop-down list.
   d. Click the **Font Color** down arrow to display the color palette, and change the color to dark blue.
   e. Click **Format**, choose **Font**, and choose **Small caps**. Click **OK**. Click **OK** again.
7. Key the word **Fax:** followed by a space at the beginning of the second telephone number for the Akron office. Repeat for the other five offices.
8. Select the word "Fax" the first time it occurs, and apply the **Fax Num** style from the task pane. Apply the same style to each occurrence of "Fax" by selecting the word and pressing F4.
9. Rename the Fax Num style by following these steps:
   a. Right-click the **Fax Num** style in the task pane, and choose **Modify**.
   b. In the **Name** text box, edit the text to "Fax" and click **OK**.
10. Delete the Office Heading style by following these steps:
    a. Right-click the **Office Heading** style in the task pane.
    b. Choose **Delete Office Heading**. Click **Yes**.
11. Apply the Title style to the document title. Modify the style to include small caps. Delete the blank paragraph after the title.
12. Change the top margin to 1.5 inches and the bottom margin to 0.5 inch.
13. Key **Telephone:** followed by a space to the left of each telephone number for all offices. (The telephone number is the first number listed.) Apply the Fax style to the "Telephone:" text.
14. Save the document as ***[your initials]*11-14** in your Lesson 11 folder.
15. Submit and close the document.

Exercise 11-15

Create styles, use style options, and display and print styles.

1. Open the file **Health Fair**. Display the Styles task pane. Change the date in the memo heading to today's date. Change the date in the third paragraph below the memo heading to a date two weeks from today's date. Delete the instruction text.
2. Select the text "Board Room No. 1," and create and apply a new paragraph style named **Room** with the formatting 12-point Arial, with bold italic and with 3 points spacing after.
3. Apply the new Room style to "Board Room No. 2" and "Board Room No. 3."

4. Create a new paragraph style named "Session" that is based on the Room style by following these steps:
   a. Position the insertion point after "Board Room No. 1" and press Enter. Key **30-Minute Sessions**. Click the New Style button on the Styles task pane.
   b. Key **Session** in the **Name** text box.
   c. Check that **Style based on** is set to the **Room** style.
   d. Using the Formatting buttons in the Create New Style from Formatting dialog box, change the font formatting to 11 points and turn off bold and italic.
   e. Click **OK**.
5. Click at the beginning of the paragraph that starts with the word "Topics." Create a new paragraph style named **Info** that is based on the Normal style. Use the formatting 11-point Arial, with 3 points of spacing after paragraphs.
6. Assign Session as the following paragraph style for Room, and assign Info as the following paragraph style for Session by following these steps:
   a. Right-click the **Room** style in the task pane.
   b. Choose **Modify**.
   c. Choose **Session** from the **Style for following paragraph** drop-down list.
   d. Click **OK**. Repeat the procedure to assign Info as the following paragraph style for Session.
7. Position the insertion point at the end of the heading "Board Room No. 2," press Enter to apply the Session style, and key **45-Minute Sessions**.
8. Press Enter to apply the Info style and key **Topics:**.
9. At the end of "Board Room No. 3," press Enter, and key the following two lines of text:

   30-Minute Sessions
   Topics:
10. Select the text from "CPR" to "First Aid," and format the text as a bulleted list using a small square bullet (▪). Right-click the selected text, and choose **Styles** from the shortcut menu. Click **Save Selection as a New Quick Style**. Name the style **Content**, and click **OK**.
11. Select the two lines of text that follow "Topics for Board Room No. 2," and apply the Content style. Repeat the style for the three lines of text under "Topics for Board Room No. 3."
12. Modify the Normal style to be Arial, with single spacing.
13. Display the style area for the document by following these steps:
    a. Open the **Word Options** dialog box, and click **Advanced**. Scroll to the **Display** group.
    b. Set the **Style area width** to 0.5 inch and click **OK**. Switch to Draft view.
14. Format the memo with the correct spacing at the top of the page, and remember to include your reference initials at the end of the document. Change the bottom margin to 0.5 inch.

15. Restore the style area width to zero. Switch to Print Layout view.
16. Print the document style sheet by following these steps:
    a. Open the Print tab.
    b. Choose Styles from the Print All Pages drop-down list, and click OK.
17. Spell-check the document, and save it as ***[your initials]*11-15** in your Lesson 11 folder.
18. Submit and close the document.

Exercise 11-16

Apply and customize document themes.

1. Open the file **Health Fair - 2**. Display the Styles task pane.
2. Change the document theme by following these steps:
    a. Click the Page Layout tab, and click the Themes button.
    b. Click the Median design from the Themes Gallery.
3. Change the theme font by following these steps:
    a. Click the Theme Fonts button.
    b. Click Create New Theme Fonts.
    c. Change the heading font to Tahoma, and change the body font to Tahoma.
    d. Key **Custom Font** in the Name text box. Click Save.
4. Modify the Normal style by changing the font size to 12.
5. Apply the style Heading 1 to the first line of the document. Apply the Heading 2 style to the text that begins "Saturday."
6. Apply the Heading 3 style to the headings "Employee's Full Name," "Store Location," and "Preferred Sessions." Modify the Heading 3 style to 24 points spacing before and 3 points spacing after.
7. Click the Page Layout tab if necessary, and click the Theme Colors button. Click Create New Theme Colors. Change the Accent 1 color to the last color in the fifth column, Ice Blue, Accent 1, Darker 50%. Key **Custom Color** in the Name text box, and click Save.
8. Format the document with a 1.5-inch top margin.
9. Spell-check the document.
10. Save the document as ***[your initials]*11-16** in your Lesson 11 folder.
11. Submit and close the document.

Lesson Applications

Exercise 11-17

Create, apply, and modify styles; print styles.

1. Start a new document. Key the text shown in Figure 11-15. Create the styles as indicated for the first two lines.

Figure 11-15

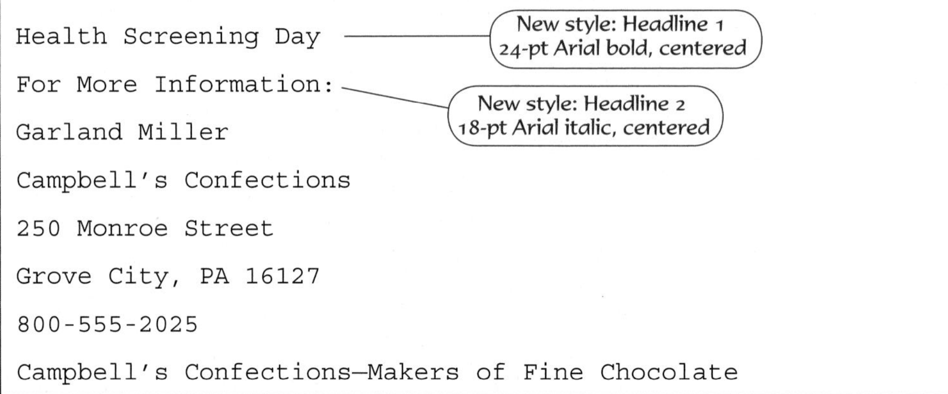

Health Screening Day
New style: Headline 1
24-pt Arial bold, centered
For More Information:
New style: Headline 2
18-pt Arial italic, centered
Garland Miller
Campbell's Confections
250 Monroe Street
Grove City, PA 16127
800-555-2025
Campbell's Confections—Makers of Fine Chocolate

2. Apply the Headline 2 style to the last line of text. Modify the style to include 18 points of paragraph spacing before and after.
3. Create a style called **Body 1** (based on the Normal style) for the remainder of the text; the style should be 12-point Arial, centered, with 1.5-line spacing.
4. Center the document vertically on the page.
5. Click the Change Styles button on the Home tab, and change the style set to Traditional.
6. Add a page border to the document.
7. Spell-check the document.
8. Save the document as ***[your initials]*11-17** in your Lesson 11 folder.
9. Submit the document and the style sheet, and close the document.

Exercise 11-18

Create, modify, and rename styles; print styles.

1. Open the file **Screening**.
2. Create a character style named **Memo Heading** using Arial Black, 12 points.

3. Select "Memo To:" and apply the Memo Heading style. Repeat the style formatting for "From:," "Date:," and "Subject:."
4. Select the four lines in the memo heading, and adjust the tab setting to 1.25 inches.
5. Modify the Normal style to include 12-point Times New Roman and 12 points spacing after.
6. Select the text beginning "Height and weight" through "Asthma screening," and format the text using a picture bullet.
7. Rename the style Memo Heading with the name **Memo Head**.
8. Position the insertion point in the subject line of the memo heading, and change the spacing after to 24 points. Add a bottom border to the subject line.
9. Change the top margin to 2 inches and the bottom margin to 0.5 inch.
10. Add your reference initials to the document.
11. Save the document as ***[your initials]*****11-18** in your Lesson 11 folder.
12. Submit and close the document.

Exercise 11-19

Modify styles, use style options, and print styles.

1. Open the file **Property - 2**.
2. Format the document as a letter to the name and address shown below, from Lynn Tanguay, vice president. Remember to use the correct top margin and spacing and to include your reference initials. Change the bottom margin to 0.5 inch.

   Dr. James Wenner
   West College
   PO Box 1000
   New Wilmington, PA 16172
3. Edit the first line of the letter to read:

   Thank you for agreeing to present a seminar on property insurance for Campbell's Confections' store owners/managers. Please discuss the following topics.
4. Select the text "Types of insurance," and create a style named **Topic** with 12-point bold and small caps formatting.
5. Position the insertion point at the end of the document, and create a new style named **Subjects** with 12-point formatting.
6. Modify the Topic style by changing the style for following paragraph to Subjects.
7. Position the insertion point at the end of the line "Types of Insurance." Press Enter and key the text shown in Figure 11-16.

Figure 11-16

```
Equipment
Inventory
Buildings
Land
Liability
Business Interruption
Key Employees
```

8. Apply the Topic style to the text "Types of Coverage," press Enter, and key the following items. Place each on a separate line, and omit the commas.

   Fire, Theft, Catastrophes, Accidents, Loss of Income

9. Press Enter twice after keying "Loss of income," and apply the Normal style.
10. Key the following closing paragraph.

    If time permits, you may want to include comments on how to select an insurance agent. We look forward to your presentation next month.

11. Key the closing lines of the letter.
12. Modify the font size of the Normal style to 12 points.
13. Spell-check the document.
14. Save the document as ***[your initials]*****11-19** in your Lesson 11 folder.
15. Print the style sheet and the document, and close the document.

Exercise 11-20 ◆ Challenge Yourself

Create, apply, and modify styles; apply themes.

1. Open the file **Ordering**. Display the Styles task pane.
2. Apply the Opulent theme to the document.
3. Apply the Title style to the first line of the document.
4. Position the insertion point in the "Online" paragraph. Create a style called **Side Heading** using 14-point bold and small caps formatting.
5. Apply the Side Heading style to each of the document side headings. (There are seven side headings.)
6. Position the insertion point in the paragraph that begins "Note," and create a new style named **Special Note** using 11 points and 0.25-inch left indent.
7. Apply the Special Note style to each "Note" paragraph and the paragraph that follows "Note."

8. Modify the style of the Normal font to 11 points.
9. Modify the Title style to small caps.
10. Create a left-aligned header for page 2 to include the following text. Place two blank paragraphs after the second line of the header.

    Place an Order
    Page *[Number]*
11. Add a bottom border to the page number paragraph in the header.
12. Add your reference initials to the bottom of the document.
13. Save the document as ***[your initials]*11-20** in your Lesson 11 folder.
14. Print the document and the style sheet, and close the document.

On Your Own

In these exercises you work on your own, as you would in a real-life business environment. Use the skills you've learned to accomplish the task—and be creative.

Exercise 11-21

Create a one-page newsletter with three or four articles. Create and use styles for the different newsletter elements, such as the title, date line, body text, and publisher information. Save the document as ***[your initials]*11-21**. Submit the document and the styles.

Exercise 11-22

Assume you have been on a job interview. Write a follow-up letter for the interview. If necessary, use the Internet to locate guidelines for appropriate content. Compare the document appearance by applying three different themes. Select an appropriate theme and document styles for your letter. Save the document as ***[your initials]*11-22**. Submit the document and the styles.

Exercise 11-23

Create a document that includes your five favorite songs. Each song should appear as a three-line description—song title, songwriter, and performer—with each line using a different style. The songwriter and performer styles should be based on the song title style. Specify the songwriter style as the style following the title style, and the performer style as the style following the songwriter style. Create the styles first; then key the text. Modify the styles as desired. Save the document as ***[your initials]*11-23**. Submit the document and the styles.

Lesson 12

Templates

OBJECTIVES ***After completing this lesson, you will be able to:***

1. Use Word templates.
2. Create new templates.
3. Attach templates to documents.
4. Modify templates.
5. Use the Organizer.

Estimated Time: 1½ hours

If you often create the same types of documents, such as reports or letters, you can save time by using templates. Word provides a variety of sample templates and templates online that contain built-in styles to help you produce professional-looking documents. You can also create your own templates and reuse them as often as you like.

Using Word's Templates

A *template* is a file that contains formatting information, styles, and sometimes text for a particular type of document. For instance, a company letterhead could be created and stored as a template. The template would include the company name and address, corporate logo, and telephone and fax numbers. The template would also include the margins, font, and font size for the letter. The letterhead template provides a reusable model for all documents requiring the company letterhead.

The following features can be included in templates:

- Formatting features, such as margins, columns, and page orientation.
- Standard text that is repeated in all documents of the same type, such as a company name and address in a letter template.

- Character and paragraph formatting that is saved within styles.
- Macros (automated procedures).

Templates also include *placeholder text* that is formatted and replaced with your own information when you create a new document.

Every Word document is based on a template. The default template file in Word is called *Normal.* New documents that you create in Word are based on the Normal template and contain all the formatting features assigned to this template, such as the default font, type size, paragraph alignment, margins, and page orientation. The Normal template differs from other templates because it stores settings that are available globally. In other words, you can use these settings in every new document even if it is based on a different template. The file extension for template files is .dotx or .dotm. (A .dotm file is used to enable macros in the file.)

Exercise 12-1 USE A WORD TEMPLATE TO CREATE A NEW DOCUMENT

TIP

Pressing Ctrl+N or clicking the New button opens a new document window but does not display the available templates. You can customize the Quick Access Toolbar to include a New button.

Starting Word opens a new blank document that is based on the Normal template.

1. Click the **File** tab, and click **New**.

Opens new document based on Normal template.

Opens new document based on templates you create.

Templates available at Office.com

Figure 12-1
Available templates

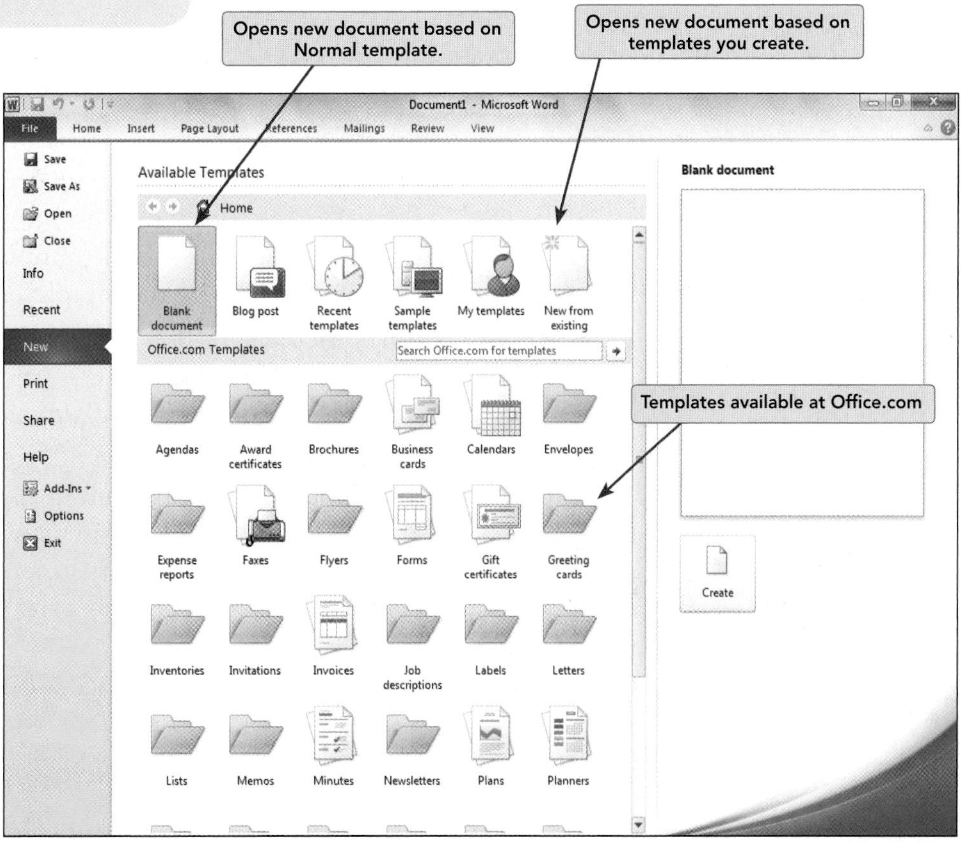

NOTE

Some templates might not be installed on your computer. Check with your instructor for instructions on locating the template.

2. Under **Available Templates**, click **Sample Templates**.
3. Click the **Equity Fax** sample template. Notice the design of the template in the **Preview** pane.

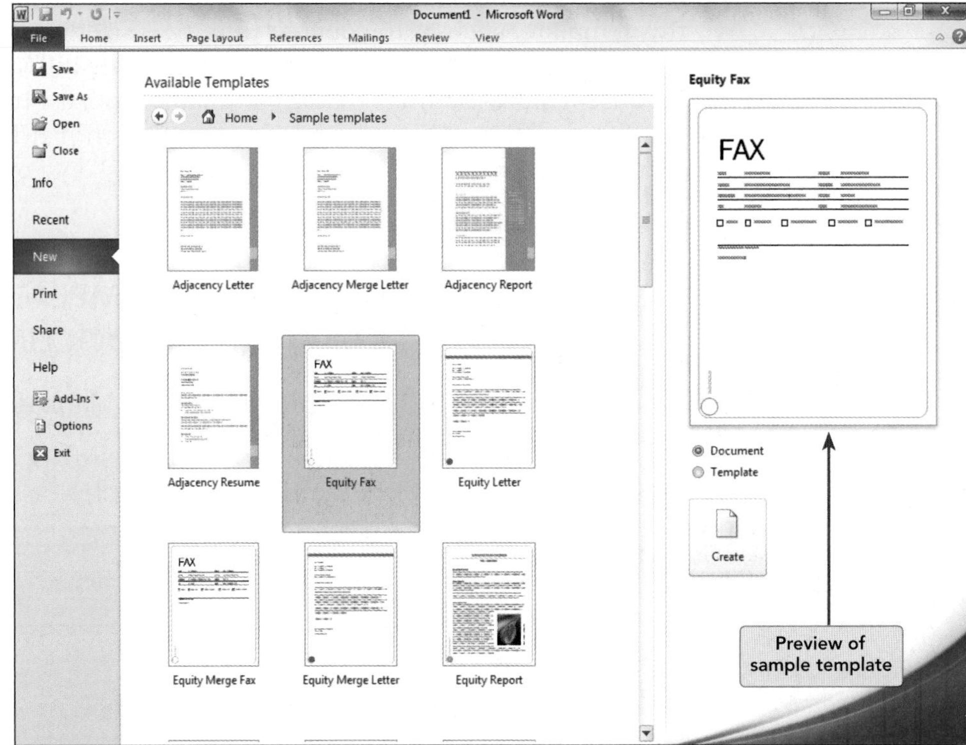

Figure 12-2
Sample templates

4. Scroll through the sample templates, and click the thumbnails to view the templates in the Preview pane.
5. Click the Back button to return to the Available Templates Home page.
6. Locate the **Office.Com Templates** section, and click the **Letters** icon. Click the **Business** folder, and click the folder named **Sales letters**. Click **Follow-up to exhibit booth visitors** to preview the letter. Click the Download button. The document displays in a new window.

NOTE

The formatting stored in templates is often complex and highly stylized and does not necessarily conform to the traditional formatting for business documents as described in *The Gregg Reference Manual.*

Figure 12-3
Creating a document from the downloaded template

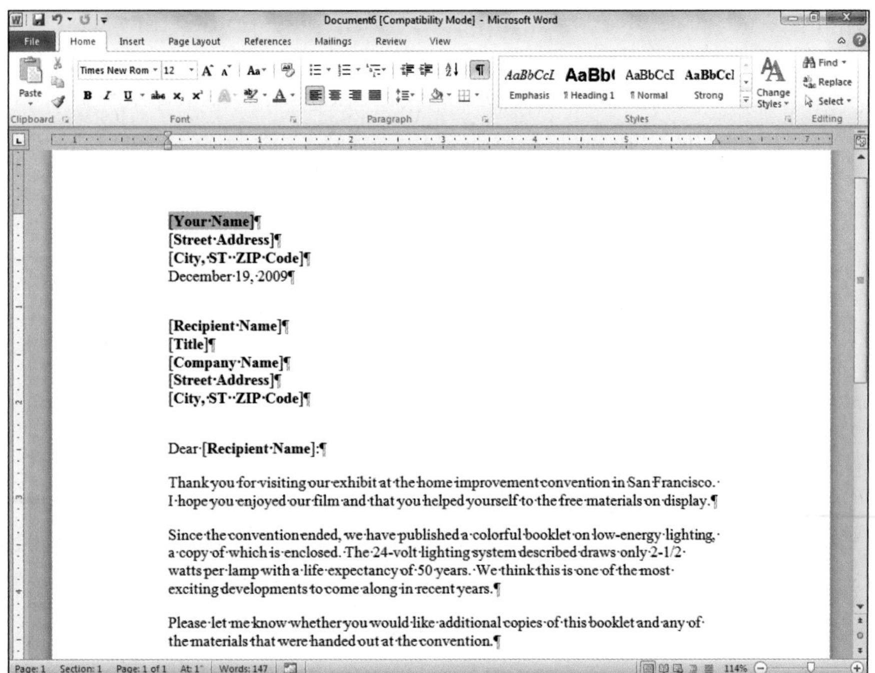

[Your Name]
[Street Address]
[City, ST ZIP Code]
December 19, 2009

[Recipient Name]
[Title]
[Company Name]
[Street Address]
[City, ST ZIP Code]

Dear [Recipient Name]:

Thank you for visiting our exhibit at the home improvement convention in San Francisco. I hope you enjoyed our film and that you helped yourself to the free materials on display.

Since the convention ended, we have published a colorful booklet on low-energy lighting, a copy of which is enclosed. The 24-volt lighting system described draws only 2-1/2 watts per lamp with a life expectancy of 50 years. We think this is one of the most exciting developments to come along in recent years.

Please let me know whether you would like additional copies of this booklet and any of the materials that were handed out at the convention.

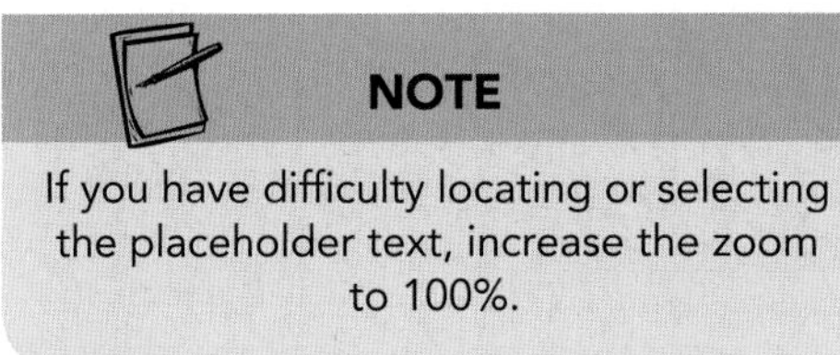

NOTE

If you have difficulty locating or selecting the placeholder text, increase the zoom to 100%.

7. Select the first line of the return address, "[Your Name]," and key **Campbell's Confections**. Click to select the placeholder text that reads "[Street Address]." Key **25 Main Street**. Click to select the placeholder that reads "[City, ST ZIP Code]," and key **Grove City, PA 16127**.
8. Click each of the placeholders for the inside address, and key the following replacement text.

   Mr. Paul Sakkal
   President
   Wholesale Nut Company
   1000 Millington Court
   Cincinnati, OH 45242
9. Click the placeholder in the salutation, and key **Mr. Sakkal**.
10. Edit the first paragraph that begins "Thank you for" as shown in Figure 12-4.

Figure 12-4

> Thank you for visiting our exhibit at the **National Confections Association Conference** in **Chicago**. I hope you enjoyed our **video** and that you helped yourself to the free materials on display.

11. Change the second paragraph to read as follows:

    Since the convention ended, we have published a colorful booklet on **our complete line of candy**, a copy of which is enclosed. **Our most popular selections include cordial cherries, caramel pecanettes, and chocolate melt-a-ways.**

12. Key **Lynn Tanguay** in the placeholder for [Your Name] and **Vice President** in the [Title] placeholder. Key your initials at the end of the document before the enclosure notation.
13. Format the first line of the return address (Campbell's Confections) using 14-point bold and small caps.
14. Save the document as ***[your initials]*12-1** in a new Lesson 12 folder. Click **OK**, if a message box appears.
15. Submit and close the document.

Creating New Templates

You can create your own templates for different types of documents by using one of three methods:

- Create a blank template file by using the default template, and define the formatting information, styles, and text according to your specifications.
- Open an existing template, modify it, and save it with a new name.
- Open an existing document, modify it, and save it as a new template.

Exercise 12-2 CREATE A NEW TEMPLATE

1. Click the **File** tab, click **New**, and click **My Templates**. Click the **Blank Document** icon.

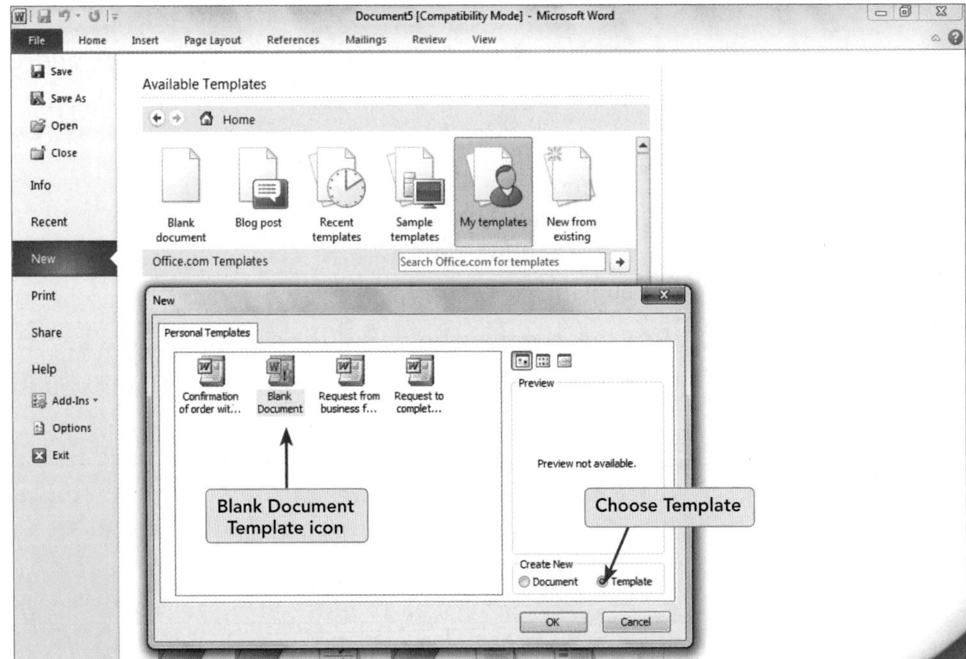

Figure 12-5
New dialog box showing personal templates

NOTE

If you select Blank Document or Recent Templates, you open a document window which can be saved as a template. If you select My Templates, you can choose to open a document or template window.

2. In the lower right corner of the dialog box, under **Create New**, click **Template** and then click **OK**. A new template file opens with the default name Template1.
3. Change the top margin to 0.5 inch.
4. Key the text shown in Figure 12-6.

Figure 12-6

```
Campbell's Confections

25 Main Street

Grove City, PA 16127

Telephone: 724-555-2025

Fax: 724-555-2050

www.campbellsconfections.biz
```

5. Select the letterhead information, and center the text horizontally. Select the first line, and apply 14-point bold and small caps formatting.
6. Modify the Normal style to 0 points spacing after and single spacing. Press Enter three times to insert blank lines after the Web address, and change the paragraph alignment to left.
7. Insert the date as a field at the third blank paragraph mark after the letterhead by clicking the **Insert** tab, and clicking **Date and Time**. Use the third date format in the **Available formats** list in the Date and Time dialog box. Check **Update automatically** so the date field is updated each time the document is printed. Click **OK**.
8. Press Enter four times.
9. Click the last line of the letterhead text, and apply a bottom border. If necessary, right-click the Web address, and remove the hyperlink format.
10. Click the **File** tab, and click **Save As**. A folder named "Templates" appears in the address bar of the Save As dialog box, and "Word Template" should appear in the Save as type list box.

NOTE

By default, Word saves new templates in a User template folder on your hard disk. The specific location is C:\Users\ *[Username]*\AppData\Roaming\Microsoft\ Templates (or a similar location in your computer). Before proceeding, ask your instructor where you should save your templates. If you use the default location, you can create new documents from your templates by using the New tab. If you use your Lesson 12 folder, you create new documents from your templates by using Windows Explorer or Computer.

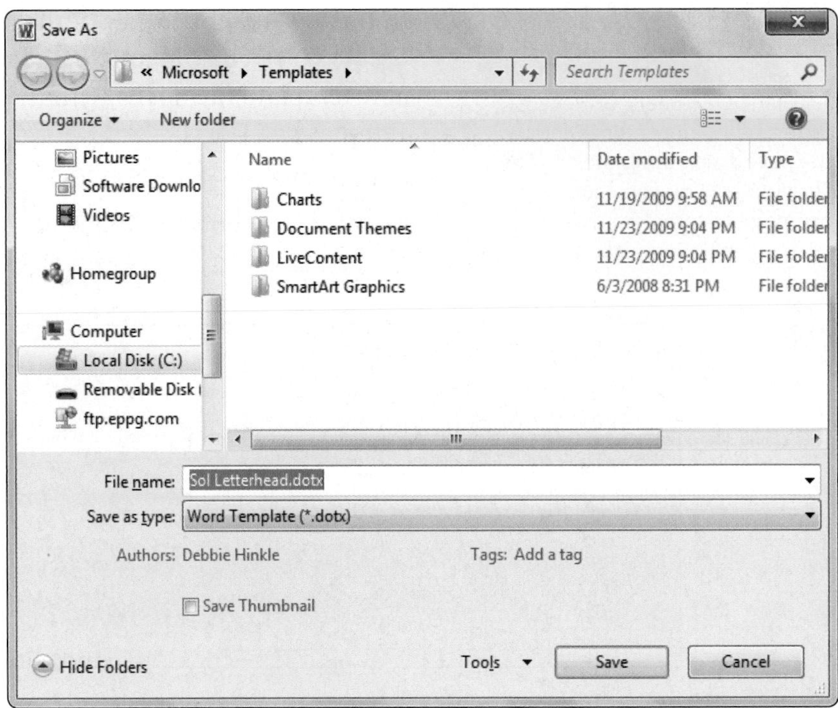

Figure 12-7
Save As dialog box

11. Save the template with the file name ***[your initials]*Letterhead** in your Lesson 12 folder (unless your instructor advises you to save in the default Templates folder).
12. Close the template.

Exercise 12-3 CREATE A NEW TEMPLATE BY USING AN EXISTING DOCUMENT

1. Reopen the New tab by choosing New from the File tab. Click New from Existing.
2. Locate and click to select the student data file **Memo - 1**. Click the Create New button [Create New ▾]. Word opens a copy of the document.
3. Change the top margin to 2 inches. Select the document, and change the font size to 12 points.
4. Delete all text to the right of each tab character in the memo heading.
5. Insert the date as a field; use the third date format. Check Update automatically so the date field is updated each time the document is printed.
6. Delete all the document paragraphs, but include the blank paragraph marks after the subject line.
7. Open the File tab, click Save As. Change the Save as type drop-down list box to display Word Template (*.dotx).

8. Save the file as ***[your initials]*****Memo** in your Lesson 12 folder (unless your instructor advises you to save in the default Templates folder).
9. Close the template.

Attaching Templates to Documents

All existing documents have an assigned template—either Normal or another template that was assigned when the document was created. You can change the template assigned to an existing document by *attaching* a different template to the document. When you attach a template, that template's formatting and elements are applied to the document, and all the template styles become available in the document.

Exercise 12-4 ATTACH A TEMPLATE TO A DOCUMENT

1. Open the New tab. Click the Memos icon in the Office.com Templates section.
2. Click Credit memo (Blue Gradient design), and click the Download button. You may see a dialog box that indicates that downloading a template is only available for machines with genuine Microsoft Office software.
3. Save the credit memo as a template file named ***[your initials]*****CreditMemo** in your Lesson 12 folder (unless your instructor advises you to save in the default Templates folder). Click OK if necessary, and close the template.
4. Open the student data file **Memo - 4**.
5. Open the Word Options dialog box, and click Customize Ribbon in the left pane. Locate the section entitled Customize the Ribbon on the right side of the dialog box. Click to select Developer under Main Tabs. Click OK.
6. Click to select the Developer tab on the Ribbon. Click the Document Template button. The Templates and Add-ins dialog box shows that the document is currently based on the Normal template.

NOTE

If you do not see a list of Word documents, check that All Word Documents displays in the Files of type box.

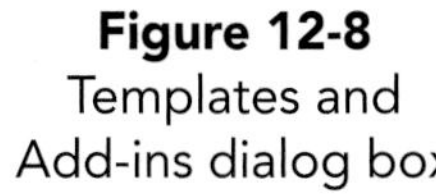

Figure 12-8
Templates and Add-ins dialog box

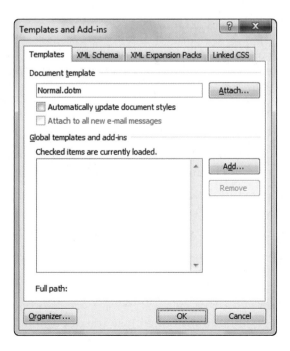

7. Click **Attach**. The Attach Template dialog box opens, displaying available templates and folders in the current folder.
8. Locate your Lesson 12 folder, and display **All Word Templates** in the **Files of type** box.

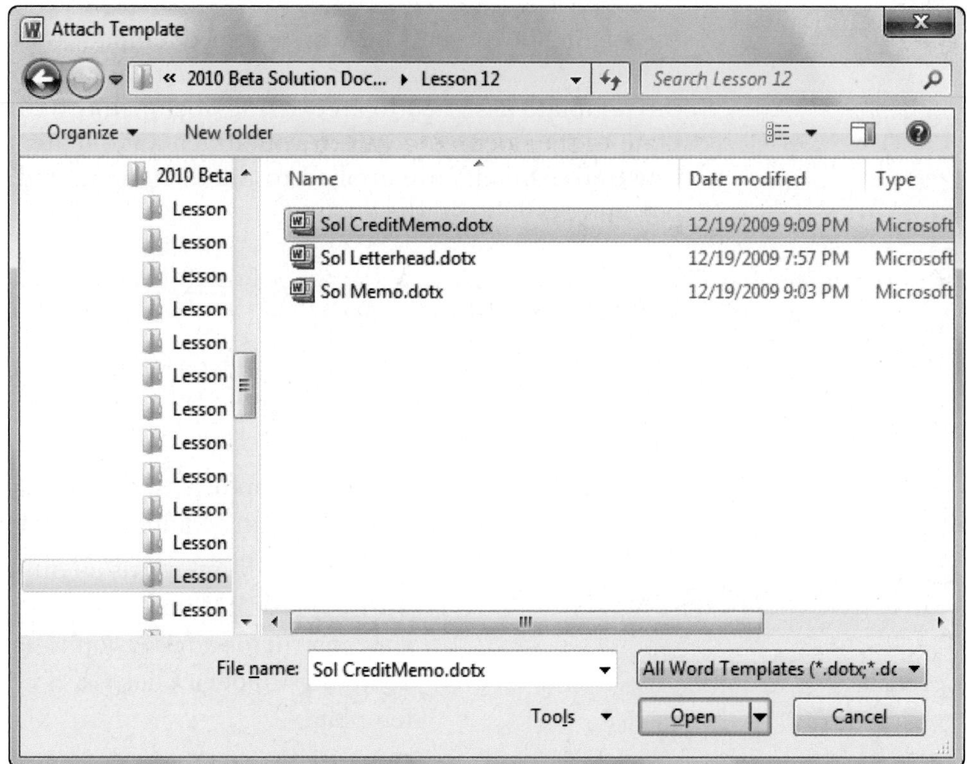

Figure 12-9
Attach template dialog box

9. Double-click the template ***[your initials]*****CreditMemo**.
10. Click the **Automatically update document styles** check box, and click **OK**. Formatting from the ***[your initials]*****Credit Memo** template is applied to this document, and you can now apply any of the Credit Memo styles.
11. Display the Styles task pane.
12. Right-click the **Normal style**, and click **Modify**. Change the spacing after to 12 points, and change the line spacing to single.
13. Delete the text in the date line, and key today's date. Select the subject line, and change the spacing after to 24 points.
14. Set a 2-inch top margin.
15. Add your reference initials.
16. Save the document as ***[your initials]*****12-4** in your Lesson 12 folder.
17. Submit and close the document.

NOTE

Attaching a template replaces the template that is currently attached to the document.

Modifying Templates

After you create a template, you can change its formatting and redefine its styles. You can also create new templates by modifying existing templates and saving them with a new name.

NOTE

Any changes you make to the formatting or text in a template affect future documents based on that template. The changes do not affect documents that were created from the template before you modified it.

TIP

You can point to a file name to check its file type.

Exercise 12-5 MODIFY TEMPLATE FORMATTING

1. Click the **File** tab, and click **Open**. From the **Files of type** drop-down list, choose **All Word Templates**.
2. Locate the folder you used to save your templates (for example, the Templates folder on your hard disk under either C:\Users*[Username]*\AppData\Roaming\Microsoft or your Lesson 12 folder).
3. Locate the file ***[your initials]*Letterhead**.
4. Double-click the file ***[your initials]*Letterhead** to open it. Display the Styles task pane.
5. Click the **Page Layout** tab, and click the Themes button. Change the document theme to **Flow**.
6. Modify the Normal style font size to 12 points.
7. Click the Save button to save the changes. The earlier version of the template is overwritten by the new version.
8. Close the template.

TIP

Opening a template through the Open dialog box opens the actual template. Double-clicking a template in Windows Explorer, Computer, or the Templates dialog box opens a new document based on the template. Changes that you make to the new document do not affect the template.

NOTE

To create a new template based on an existing template, modify the existing template as desired and then save the template with a new name.

Using the Organizer

Instead of modifying template styles, you can copy individual styles from another document or template into the current document or template by using the Organizer. The copied styles are added to the style sheet of the current document or template. When you copy styles, remember these rules:

- Copied styles replace styles with the same style names.
- Style names are case sensitive—if you copy a style named "HEAD" into a template or document that contains a style named "head," the copied style is added to the style sheet and does not replace the existing style.

You can also copy styles by using the Organizer. To open the Organizer, display and activate the Developer tab if necessary. Click the Document Template button. Click the Organizer button; then select the Styles tab.

Exercise 12-6 COPY STYLES TO ANOTHER TEMPLATE

1. Open the **New** tab, and click **Sample Templates**. Click to select the **Equity Lettter** template, click **Template**, and click **Create**.
2. Save the document as a template named ***[your initials]*EquityLetter** in your Lesson 12 folder. Display the Styles task panel, and notice the list of styles. Close the document.
3. Open the template ***[your initials]*Letterhead** revised in Exercise 12-5.
4. Click the **Developer** tab, and click the Document Template button. Click the **Organizer** button Organizer....
5. Click the **Styles** tab in the Organizer dialog box. On the left side of the dialog box, the Organizer lists the template and styles currently in use. You use the right side of the dialog box to copy styles to or from another template.
6. Click the **Close File** button Close File on the right side of the dialog box. The Normal template closes, and the **Close File** button changes to **Open File**.
7. Click the Open File button Open File.... In the Open dialog box, make sure **All Word Templates** appears in the **Files of type** box.
8. Locate the folder that contains the ***[your initials]*EquityLetter** template.
9. Double-click the ***[your initials]*EquityLetter** template. You can now choose styles from this template to copy into your letterhead template.

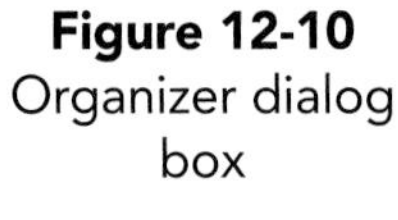

Figure 12-10 Organizer dialog box

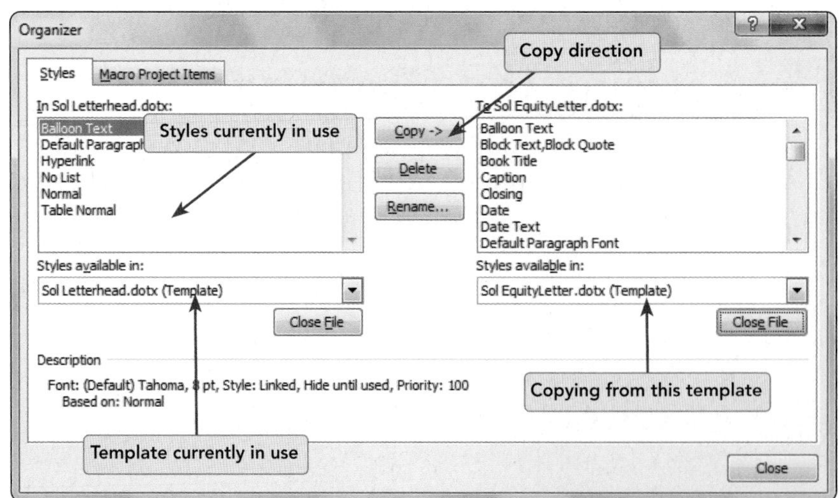

10. Scroll down the list of styles in the Equity Letter template. Click **Date Text** and click **Copy**.
11. Choose the **Normal** style from the Equity Letter style list. Notice the style description.
12. Click **Copy** and then click **Yes** to overwrite the existing style Normal.
13. Close the Organizer dialog box. The styles you chose from the Equity Letter template are copied to the current template. Notice that the Normal style from the Equity Letter template replaced the previous Normal style, so the text is formatted in Constantia 11 point with 8 points spacing after.
14. Click the Options link at the bottom of the Styles task pane. Click the down arrow for **Select styles to show** and select **All styles**. Click **OK**.
15. Apply the newly copied style Date Text to the date line. Modify the Normal style by changing the spacing after to 0 and changing the line spacing to single.
16. Close the template without saving changes.

Lesson 12 Summary

- A template is a reusable model for a particular type of document. Templates can contain formatting, text, and other elements. By default, all new documents are based on the Normal template.
- Word provides a variety of templates upon which you can base a new document or a new template. You can modify an existing template and save it with a new name. You can also modify an existing document and save it as a new template.
- Every document is based on a template. You can change the template assigned to an existing document by attaching a different template to the document, thereby making the new template's styles available in the document.
- To modify a template you created, open the Open dialog box and choose All Word Templates from the Files of type drop-down list. Locate and open the file.
- Instead of modifying template styles, use the Organizer to copy individual styles from one document or template to another.

LESSON 12		Command Summary	
Feature	**Button**	**Command**	**Keyboard**
Attach template		Developer tab, Templates group, Document Template	
Copy styles		Developer tab, Templates group, Document Template, Organizer	
Use a template		File tab, New	

Concepts Review

True/False Questions

Each of the following statements is either true or false. Indicate your choice by circling T or F.

T F 1. The file extension for a Word template is .tmp.

T F 2. You can open the New tab by pressing Ctrl+N.

T F 3. After a template is assigned to a document, it cannot be changed.

T F 4. A Word template can contain placeholder text that you replace with your own information.

T F 5. When styles are copied to a template, if the style names do not match the existing styles, they are added to the style sheet.

T F 6. Existing templates cannot be modified.

T F 7. If you do not specify a template when you create a new document, the document is created without one.

T F 8. You can use the Organizer to copy styles between templates or documents.

Short Answer Questions

Write the correct answer in the space provided.

1. What is the file extension assigned to a template file name?

____

2. When you choose New from the File tab, what happens?

____

3. Which commands would you use to open the dialog box to attach a different template to a document?

____

4. How can you create a new template by using an existing document?

____

5. How can you change the styles in a template to match the styles in another template or document?

____

6. What is the procedure to download a template from Office.com?

7. What is the procedure to save a template?

8. How do you change a template theme?

Critical Thinking

Answer these questions on a separate page. There are no right or wrong answers. Support your answers with examples from your own experience, if possible.

1. Review Word's templates for letters and reports. How do they compare with the standard business format for these documents as described in *The Gregg Reference Manual* (or a similar handbook)?
2. Many businesses create templates that are used by all employees for internal and external correspondence. Why would a business take this approach? What advantages does it offer to a business?

Skills Review

Exercise 12-7

Use an existing Word template to create a letter.

1. Create a letter based on a template from Office.com by following these steps:
   a. Click the **File** tab, and click **New**.
   b. Click the **Letters** icon under Office.com Templates, and click the **Business** folder. Click the **Announcements** folder, and click the **Announcement of extended store hours** template. Click **Download**.
2. At the top of the document, click the placeholder text for [Your Name] and key **Campbell's Confections**. Key the following address in the appropriate placeholders.

   25 Main Street
   Grove City, PA 16127
3. Display the Styles task pane. Modify the Sender Address style to 14-point bold and small caps.

4. Replace or edit the placeholder text in the document with the text shown in Figure 12-11. Click or select each placeholder before entering the appropriate text. You might want to increase the zoom when keying the last two lines.

Figure 12-11

```
Ms. Ann Foster

Vice President

Foster Travel

600 Maple Street

Slippery Rock, PA 16057

Dear Ms. Foster:

[First Paragraph Changes]

We have extended the hours for our store in Grove City in
order to accommodate our customers during the holiday
season. We are now open from 9 a.m. to 7 p.m. Monday
through Friday, 9 a.m. to 6 p.m. on Saturday, and 1 p.m. to
6 p.m. on Sunday.

Lynn Tanguay

Vice President
```

5. Add your reference initials.
6. Modify the Normal style to the font Cambria. (This changes all the styles used below the company name, which are based on the Normal style.)
7. Change the paragraph spacing for the Date style to 24 points before and 36 points after.
8. Save the document as ***[your initials]*****12-7** in your Lesson 12 folder.
9. Submit and close the document.

Exercise 12-8

Create a new template, attach it to another document, and modify a template.

1. Create a new template by following these steps:
   a. Open the File tab, and click New.
   b. Click My templates, and click the icon for the Blank Document template.
   c. Under Create New, click Template and click OK.

2. Modify the Normal style to be 11-point Arial.
3. Modify the Heading 1 style so the paragraph formatting is center-aligned and the font size is 18 points.
4. Modify the Heading 2 style so the paragraph formatting is center-aligned with bold and italic formatting.
5. Modify the Heading 3 style to include small caps format. (If necessary click **Options** at the bottom of the Styles task pane and click the arrow for **Select styles to show** and select **All styles**.)
6. Save the template as ***[your initials]*Agenda** in your Lesson 12 folder or in the default Templates folder on the hard disk, whichever your instructor told you to use. Close the template.
7. Start a new document based on the Normal template by clicking the **File** tab, and clicking **New**. Click the **Blank Document** icon, and click **Create**.
8. Key the text shown in Figure 12-12. Use single spacing. Apply the heading styles to the paragraphs indicated.

Figure 12-12

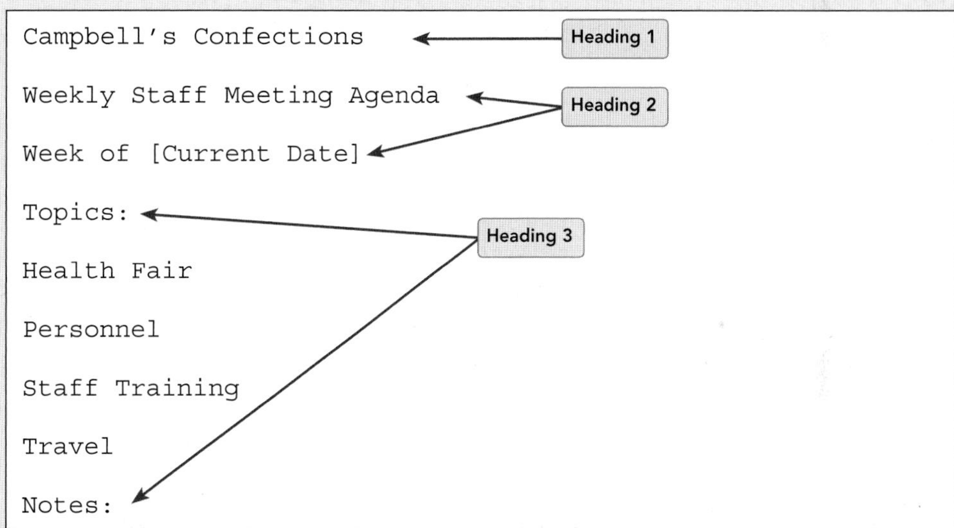

9. Attach the template you created, and automatically update the styles by following these steps:
   a. Click the **Developer** tab, and click the Document Template button.
   b. Click **Attach**.
   c. Locate ***[your initials]*Agenda,** and click **Open**.
   d. Check the **Automatically update document styles** check box, and click **OK**.
10. Save the document as ***[your initials]*12-8** in your Lesson 12 folder.
11. Submit and close the document.

Exercise 12-9

Use the Organizer to copy styles.

1. Open the New tab, and click Sample Templates. Locate and click the icon for Equity Report. Click Template and click Create.
2. Save the document template as ***[your initials]*EquityReport** in your Lesson 12 folder. Close the template.
3. Open the file **Company - 2**.
4. Apply the Heading 1 style to the first line (the company name). Apply the Heading 2 style to the bold side headings.
5. Display all styles by following these steps:
   a. Click Options in the Styles task pane.
   b. Click the arrow to display the drop-down list for Select styles to show.
   c. Click All styles. Click OK.
6. Use the Organizer to copy styles from another template by following these steps:
   a. Click the Developer tab, and click the Document Template button. Click Organizer.
   b. Click the Styles tab. Click the Close File button Close File on the right side of the dialog box (under Normal.dotm).
   c. Click the Open File button Open File... on the right side of the dialog box.
   d. Locate the folder that contains the ***[your initials]*EquityReport** template, and click Open.
   e. Click Normal in the list on the right side of the dialog box (under EquityReport), and then click Copy. Click Yes to overwrite the existing style entry.
   f. Repeat the previous step to copy the Footer, Heading 1, Heading 2, and Heading 3 styles from the Equity Report template on the right to the **Company - 2** document on the left. To copy the styles simultaneously, hold down Ctrl while selecting each of the styles to copy. When prompted, overwrite the existing style entries in the **Company - 2** document.
   g. Click the Close button to close the Organizer dialog box.
7. Insert page numbers at the bottom right of the document, starting with 2 on page 2.
8. Modify the paragraph spacing for the Heading 1 style to 72 points before and 24 points after.
9. Save the document as ***[your initials]*12-9** in your Lesson 12 folder.
10. Submit and close the document.

Exercise 12-10

Use an online template to create a new template.

1. Open the **New** tab, and click **Agendas** under **Office.com Templates**.
2. Click **Agenda (Capsules design)**, and download the template. Save the document as a template named ***[your initials]*MeetingAgenda** in your Lesson 12 folder. Close the template, and create a new document based on the Meeting Agenda template.
3. Select the text in the **[Meeting Name]** placeholder, and key **Quarterly Meeting**.
4. Select "Date" and key today's date. Select "Time" and key **1 p.m.** Select "Place of Meeting" and key **Conference Room**.
5. Locate "Monthly status" and change the text to **Quarterly status**. Select "Dues Update," and key **Managers' Reports**. Select the first item under "Old Business," and change the text to **Fitness Membership Plan**. Select the second item under "Old Business," and change the text to **Employee Recognition Banquet**.
6. Locate "New Business," and change the text for the first item to **Holiday Confections**. Change the text for the second item to **Chocolate Festival**.
7. Save the document as ***[your initials]*12-10**.
8. Submit and close the document.

Lesson Applications

Exercise 12-11

Use a template to create a document.

1. Create a document based on the **Letterhead** template located in the Lesson 12 student data folder.
2. Key the following information for the inside address:

   Ms. Barbara Scott
   National Fitness Center
   1237 West Main Street
   Grove City, PA 16127

3. Key **Dear Ms. Scott:** for the salutation.
4. Open the file **Fitness**. Copy all the text and paste it into the letter.
5. Add as a closing paragraph.

   Thank you for your assistance. I will call for an appointment to discuss a formal agreement.

6. Key an appropriate complimentary closing and the following signature name and title:

   Garland Miller
   Human Resources

7. On the next line, key your reference initials followed by an enclosure notation.
8. Modify the Normal style by changing the font to Cambria.
9. Spell-check the document, and save it as ***[your initials]*****12-11** in your Lesson 12 folder.
10. Submit the document. Close both open documents.

Exercise 12-12

Use a template and copy styles by using the Organizer.

1. Start a new document based on the template **Memo.dotx**.
2. The memo is to "All Employees" from Garland Miller. The subject is "Fitness Center Membership."
3. Two blank lines below the subject line, key the text from Figure 12-13.

Figure 12-13

```
Campbell's Confections is contacting area fitness centers
to negotiate a contract to provide lower membership fees
for our employees.

Please complete the attached survey so that we can
determine which programs you prefer as well as your
preferences for hours of operation, types of membership,
and payment plans.

Please return the completed survey by Friday.
```

4. Open the Organizer dialog box by displaying the Developer tab and clicking the Document Template button. Click Organizer. On the right side of the dialog box, close the Normal template file and open the **CreditMemo** template.
5. Copy the Normal style to the current document, replacing the Normal style entry when prompted. Close the Organizer dialog box.
6. Insert a blank paragraph mark above the "To:" line. At the new paragraph mark, key **Campbell's Confections** and apply the Heading 1 style.
7. Modify the Heading 1 style by changing the font size to 24 points and adding 24 points spacing after. Change the line spacing to At least 12 pt. Change the top margin to 1 inch. Add a bottom border to the Heading 1 style.
8. Key your reference initials at the end of the document.
9. Modify the Normal style by increasing the font size to 12 points.
10. Save the document as ***[your initials]*12-12** in your Lesson 12 folder.
11. Submit and close the document.

Exercise 12-13

Modify a template and attach a template.

1. Open the template **Letterhead.dotx**. (Use the Open dialog box—do not create a document based on this template.)
2. Modify the Normal style to a 12-point font of your choice.
3. Save the template as ***[your initials]*Letterhead2** in the folder where you saved the other templates. Close the template.
4. Open the file **Hernandez**.
5. Attach the template ***[your initials]*Letterhead2**, updating document styles automatically.

6. Key the date at the top of the document followed by three blank lines.
7. Add your reference initials and an enclosure notation.
8. Set a 2-inch top margin. Add blank lines between paragraphs to format the document as a business letter.
9. Save the document as ***[your initials]*12-13** in your Lesson 12 folder.
10. Submit and close the document.

Exercise 12-14 ◆ Challenge Yourself

Copy and apply styles.

1. Open the sample template file **Equity Fax** by changing to the folder that contains the installed Word Templates (Program Files\Microsoft Office\Templates\1033\Fax). Save the template as ***[your initials]* EquityFax** in your Lesson 12 folder.
2. Use the Organizer dialog box to copy all styles from the Origin Fax sample template to the Equity Fax template. (Remember: To select all styles, click the first file, scroll to the last file, press Shift, and click.)
3. Click Yes to overwrite the styles, and close the dialog box.
4. Open the Styles task pane.
5. Select "To:" in the heading, and apply the Message Header style. If necessary, display all styles in the Styles task pane.
6. Apply the Message Header style to all headings in the Equity Fax template.
7. Save the template as ***[your initials]*12-14** in your Lesson 12 folder.
8. Submit and close the document.

NOTE

To locate the Origin Fax template, change to the folder that contains the installed Word Templates (Program Files\Microsoft Office\Templates\1033\Fax).

On Your Own

In these exercises you work on your own, as you would in a real-life business environment. Use the skills you've learned to accomplish the task—and be creative.

Exercise 12-15

Use a résumé template to create your résumé. Include as much detail about yourself as possible. Modify the formatting as needed. Save the document as ***[your initials]*****12-15** and submit it.

Exercise 12-16

Create a cover letter for your résumé, using a matching template style. Address the cover letter to a prospective employer. Create an envelope for the letter. Save the document as ***[your initials]*****12-16** and submit it.

Exercise 12-17

Using the New tab, go to Office.com and choose a template from any category. Preview and download the template. Format and edit the template using your own information to create a document. Save the document as ***[your initials]*****12-17** and submit it.

Unit 3 Applications

Unit Application 3-1

Create a cover letter for a document as a separate section; insert a page break and a continuation page header.

1. Open the file **Assortment**.
2. Add a blank page to the beginning of the document (use a section break to separate the blank page from the **Assortment** document). Key the text shown in Figure U3-1 on page 1 of the document including the corrections. Use 12-point Cambria for the font. Remove bold and small caps formatting if necessary. Open the Paragraph dialog box and change the spacing after to 0 points, and change the line spacing to single. Format the document using the standard letter format. The letter is from Richard Matthews, Wholesale Sales Division. Include your reference initials and an enclosure notation.

Figure U3-1

Mr. Patrick O'Reilly

Village Center

226 Pierce Avenue

Sharpsville, PA 16150

Dear Mr. O'Reilly:

~~As~~ you requested enclosed is the information about our wholesale division.

Campbell's Confections entered the wholesale market during the mid-1990s. Contracts were negotiated with a large hotel chain and the Pittsburgh airport to provide ^boxed^ chocolates for gift stores.

Wholesale contracts are only negotiated with business^es^ that can provide ^multiple^ locations for ^selling^ our chocolates. Wholesale prices are based on a minimum order of $570. the wholesale agreements also stipulate the proper conditions for storing and displaying Campbell's Chocolates.

Initial chocolate offerings for the wholesale market include^d^ assorted chocolate^-^covered nuts (milk and dark chocolate), assorted chocolate^-^covered creams (milk and dark chocolate), and assorted melt-a-ways (milk and dark chocolate). Sugar-free chocolates and chocolate bars are also available.

Let me know if you have any questions. I look forward to speaking with you soon.

3. Change the top margin for section 1 to 2 inches.
4. Create a right-aligned footer for section 2. The text should include the text **Updated** followed by today's date inserted as a field that is automatically updated.
5. In section 2, delete blank paragraphs, and center the text vertically.
6. Select the bulleted list for each category on the page, and sort the text alphabetically.
7. Spell-check the document.
8. Change the first heading in section 2 to all caps, and center the heading. Change the spacing after to 24 points.
9. Save the document as ***[your initials]*****u3-1** in a new folder for Unit 3 Applications.
10. Submit and close the document.

Unit Application 3-2

Create a memo; change page orientation; apply section formatting.

1. Open the file **Emboss**. Format the document as a memo to "Store Managers" from Robert Smith. Use the current date, and the subject is "New Products."
2. Add a next page section break at the end of the document, and key the text shown in Figure U3-2. Set a left-aligned tab for the text in each column under "Sample Letters." Use the Symbol dialog box (Symbol font) to insert the Greek letters.

Figure U3-2

```
Campbell's Confections
announces
Chocolate Embossing:
Greek Alphabet
Mascots
Sample Letters:
Alpha       Α
Beta        Β
Gamma       Γ
Delta       Δ
Epsilon     Ε
```

3. Change the top margin for section 1 to 2 inches. Key your reference initials and an attachment notation at the end of section 1.
4. Format section 2 with landscape orientation and centered vertically. Center the first six lines.
5. Open the Styles task pane, and modify the Heading 1 style for center alignment, 18 points, and small caps. Modify Heading 2 style for center alignment, 16 points spacing after, and 14-point small caps.
6. Select "Chocolate Embossing:" through "Sample Letters:" and apply 14-point bold and italic formatting.
7. Apply the Heading 1 style to the first line of section 2, and apply the Heading 2 style to the second line of section 2.
8. Format "Sample Letters:" to have 24 points spacing before, 18 points spacing after, and small caps formatting.
9. Select the text from "Sample Letters:" through "E," and apply 1-inch left and right indents, and 18-point font size. Adjust the tab settings for the text below "Sample Letters:." Add a 2¼-point box border with 10% gray shading to the text beginning with "Sample Letters:" through "E."
10. Add a double-line page border to section 2.
11. Preview the document, and then save it as ***[your initials]*****u3-2** in your Unit 3 Applications folder.
12. Submit and close the document.

Unit Application 3-3

Create a new template, create and apply paragraph and character styles, modify styles, and use style options.

1. Open the file **HolidayUpdate**. Change the left and right margins to 1.25 inches.
2. Center the first line of the document, and change the font size to 20 points and apply small caps. Add 3 points spacing after.
3. Create a paragraph style named **Subhead** that is 14-point Arial, all caps, and centered. Add a single-line 1-point bottom border to the style by clicking the Format button and choosing Border. Apply the style to the second line of text.
4. Create and apply a paragraph style for the "Chocolate Events" paragraph based on the Normal style and named **UpdateHead**. Use 12-point Arial bold with all caps and 3 points spacing after.
5. Save the document as a template named ***[your initials]*****Update** in your Unit 3 Applications folder or in the default Templates folder on the hard disk, whichever your instructor tells you to use. Close the template.
6. Start a new document based on the template ***[your initials]*****Update**.

7. Replace the words "CHOCOLATE EVENTS" with the current year.
8. Select the Akron, OH, paragraph. Create and apply a paragraph style named **CityName** using 12-point Arial bold with a 3-inch left tab setting.
9. Click in the paragraph that begins "National Chocolate." Create a paragraph style named **IndentedPara** based on the CityName style, using 12-point Arial regular, with 12 points spacing after paragraphs and a 3-inch left indent.
10. Assign Indentedpara as the style for the paragraph following CityName.
11. Assign CityName as the style for the paragraph following Indentedpara.
12. Select the text "January 3," and create a character style named **EventDate** using 11-point Arial bold and italic.
13. Press Enter after "Chocolate-Covered Cherry Day," and key the text shown in Figure U3-3. Press Tab before each date.

Figure U3-3

```
Clarksburg, WV          February 19
                        Chocolate Mint Day

Grove City, PA          March—Third Week
                        American Chocolate Week

Canton, OH              April 21
                        National Chocolate-Covered Cashews Day

Morgantown, WV          May 15
                        National Chocolate Chip Day

Monroeville, PA         June
                        National Candy Month

Youngstown, OH          July 7
                        Chocolate Day

Fairmont, WV            September 22
                        National White Chocolate Day

Butler, PA              October 28
                        National Chocolate Day
```

14. Apply the EventDate style to all the date text.
15. Modify the CityName style to 11 points, and change the font to Lucida Sans. Modify the Subhead style to include 12 points spacing after, and change the font to Lucida Sans. Modify the EventDate style by changing the font to Lucida Sans.
16. Center the document vertically on the page.
17. Spell-check the document, and save it as ***[your initials]*****u3-3** in your folder for Unit 3 Applications.
18. Submit and close the document.

Unit Application 3-4

Use the Internet, and work with sections, page numbers, and headers and footers.

1. Using the Internet, research the history of chocolate.
2. Create a three- to five-page report, and organize the document into sections.
3. Include the following topics and create sections for each topic:
   - A timeline of the history of chocolate—include a brief description of major events for each century.
   - Mention Columbus, Aztecs, Mayas, and European influence.
   - Major producers of cacao pods.
4. Include the following formats in your document:
   - Create and apply styles.
   - Create a title page for the document as a separate section.
   - Title each subsequent section of the document.
   - Check pagination, and apply line and page break options where needed.
   - Include appropriate headers, footers, and page numbering on all pages except the title page.
5. Save the document as ***[your initials]*u3-4** in your Unit 3 Applications folder, and submit it.

Unit 4

TABLES AND COLUMNS

Lesson 13

Tables

OBJECTIVES ***After completing this lesson, you will be able to:***

1. Insert a table.
2. Key and edit text in tables.
3. Select cells, rows, and columns.
4. Edit table structures.
5. Format tables and cell contents.
6. Convert tables and text.

Estimated Time: 1½ hours

A *table* is a grid of rows and columns that intersect to form *cells*. The lines that mark the cell boundaries are called *gridlines*. It is often easier to read or present information in table format than in paragraph format. Using Word's table feature, you can create a table and insert text, pictures, and other types of data into the table's cells.

Inserting a Table

There are several ways to insert a table:

- Insert a table by using the Insert Table menu.
- Insert a table by using the Insert Table command.
- Insert a table by using a table template.

You can also create a table by drawing rows and columns or converting text to tables. These methods are discussed later in the lesson.

Figure 13-1
Columns, rows, and cells in a table

WEST VIRGINIA STORES		
STORE	MANAGER	ACCOUNT EXECUTIVE
Clarksburg	Matthew Garrett	Rebecca Surrena
Fairmont	Marianne Bentley	Rebecca Surrena
Morgantown	Ethan Myers	Rebecca Surrena
Wheeling	Jackson Sigmon	Rebecca Surrena

NOTE

You can apply formatting options, such as borders and shading, to tables. You can also display tables without gridlines.

Exercise 13-1 INSERT A TABLE

Use the Insert Table menu or the Insert Table command to create a table with the number of rows and columns you specify.

- Use the Table button on the Ribbon, Insert tab, to display an adjustable grid.
- Use the Insert Table dialog box, which is accessed by clicking the Table button on the Ribbon, Insert group.

1. Open the file **Shipping**. Enter today's date in the memo date line.
2. Position the insertion point at the end of the document.
3. Click the **Insert** tab, and click the Table button. A grid containing columns and rows appears below the button.
4. Position the pointer in the upper left cell of the grid. Drag the pointer across to highlight four columns, and then drag the pointer down the grid to highlight five rows. The table dimensions are highlighted in the grid, and a table displays in the document.

NOTE

The documents you create in this course relate to the case study about Campbell's Confections, a fictional candy store and chocolate factory. (See the Case Study in the front matter).

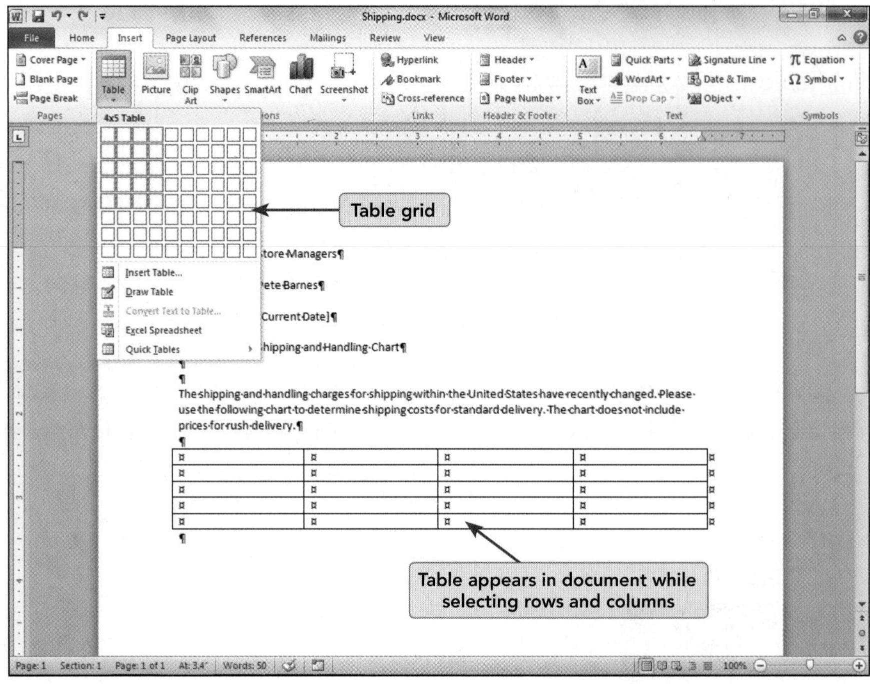

Figure 13-2
Specifying table dimensions with the table grid

NOTE

When you create a table, each gridline automatically has a 0.5-point black border that is printed. You can remove borders by clicking the arrow beside the Borders button on the Table Tools Design tab and choosing No Border. You can also open the Borders and Shading dialog box, display the Borders tab, and choose None under Setting. Gray table gridlines appear on-screen only and not in the printed document.

5. Release the mouse button. A 5-row by 4-column table appears with the insertion point in the first cell. Each column is the same width, and the table extends from the left to the right margin. Notice the markers on the ruler that indicate the column widths.
6. Click the Undo button to undo the table. You will now try a second method for inserting a table.
7. Click the **Insert** tab, and then click the Table button. Click the **Insert Table** command that appears below the grid. The Insert Table dialog box appears.

Figure 13-3
Insert Table dialog box

Insert Table

Table size

Number of columns: 5

Number of rows: 2

AutoFit behavior

Fixed column width: Auto

AutoFit to contents

AutoFit to window

Remember dimensions for new tables

OK Cancel

8. Key **4** in the **Number of columns** text box and **5** in the **Number of rows** text box. You can also click the up or down arrows to the right of these boxes.
9. In the **Fixed column width** text box, change the default (Auto) setting to **1.5"**, and click **OK**. Word inserts a 4 × 5 table with 1.5-inch columns. The insertion point is positioned in the first cell, and the table is left-aligned.

Exercise 13-2 DRAW A TABLE

You can draw a table in your document by using the Draw Table command, which is located on the Table menu and the Table Tools Design tab on the Ribbon. When you create a table, the Ribbon displays two Table Tools tabs when the insertion point is located in a table: Design and Layout.

TABLE 13-1 Table Tools: Design Tab

Button	PURPOSE Table Style Options Group
Header Row	Displays formatting for the first row of the table
Total Row	Displays formatting for the last row of the table
Banded Rows	Displays formatting for even and odd rows
First Column	Displays formatting for the first column of the table
Last Column	Displays formatting for the last column of the table
Banded Columns	Displays formatting for even and odd columns
	Table Styles Group
	Displays built-in styles for tables
Shading	Displays shading colors for cell background
Borders	Displays border options
	Draw Borders Group
	Changes the line style
1 pt	Changes the weight (width) of a border
Pen Color	Changes the pen color
	Draws a freehand table
	Erases the borders of a table

1. Click the **Insert** tab, and click the Table button. Click the **Draw Table** command, which is listed below the grid. The pointer changes to a pencil shape.

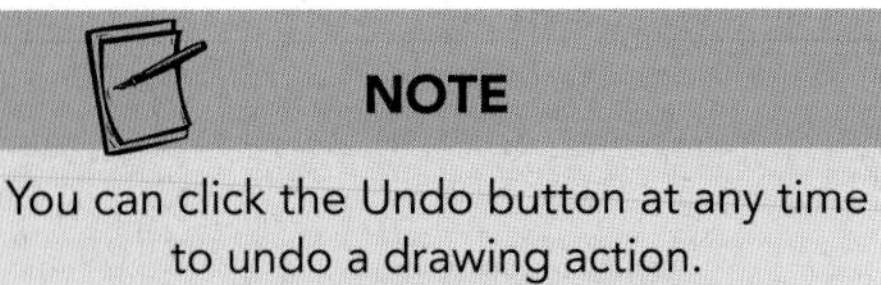

NOTE

You can click the Undo button at any time to undo a drawing action.

2. Position the pencil pointer at the last paragraph mark below the current table. Drag diagonally down and to the right to draw a rectangle about the same size as the current table. As you drag, the pointer creates a dotted rectangle. Release the mouse button.
3. After drawing the outside border of the table, draw three vertical lines in the table to create four columns (just as in the other table).

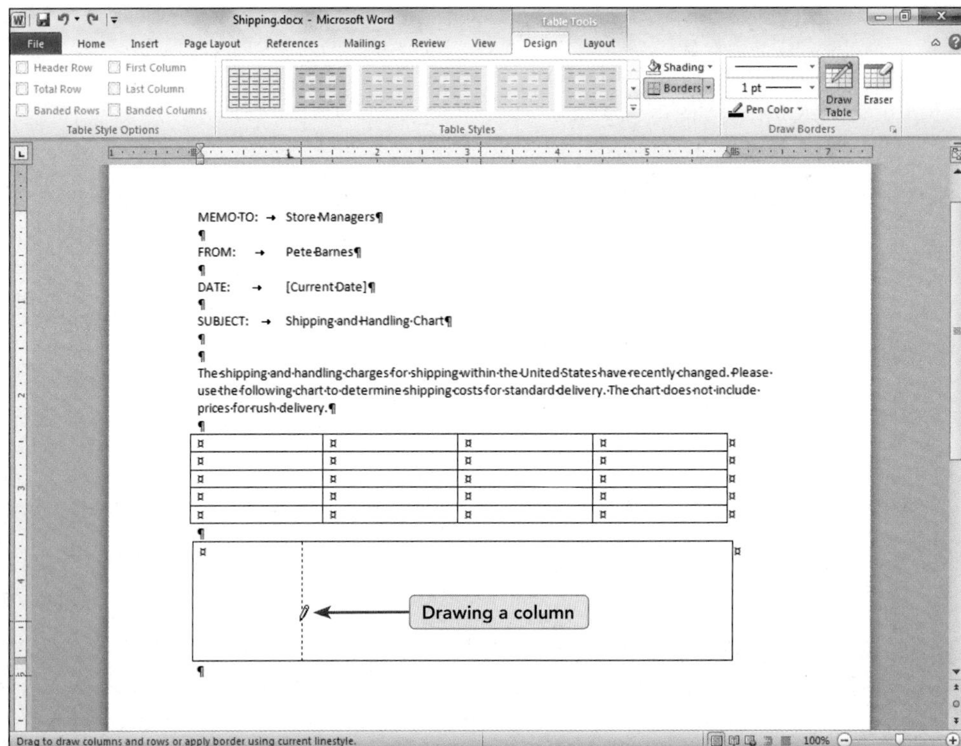

Figure 13-4
Drawing a table

4. Draw four horizontal lines, creating five rows. Don't worry about creating perfectly spaced rows or columns—you will space them evenly later in the lesson. Press Esc to restore the normal pointer.

Figure 13-5
Adding rows

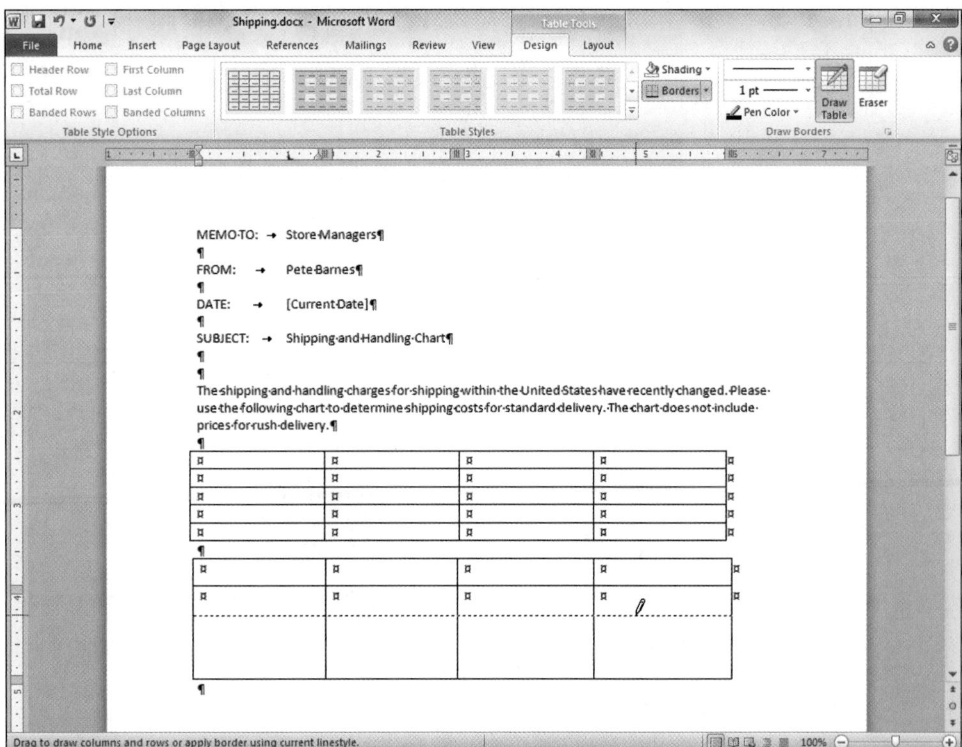

5. Click the Eraser button on the Table Tools Design tab, and drag the eraser pointer across one of the row lines you drew. Release the mouse button. The line is removed, and the height of one row of the table is adjusted.
6. Click the Undo button to restore the line.
7. Press Esc or click the Eraser button to restore the normal pointer.

Exercise 13-3 INSERT A TABLE USING A TABLE TEMPLATE

You can insert a preformatted table by selecting a design from the Built-In Table gallery. Each of the designs contains sample data that you replace with your own text.

1. Press Ctrl+N to start a new document. Do not close the Shipping document.
2. Click the **Insert** tab, and click the Table button. Click the **Quick Tables** command in the Table menu to display the Built-In Table designs.
3. Click the **Calendar 4** design.

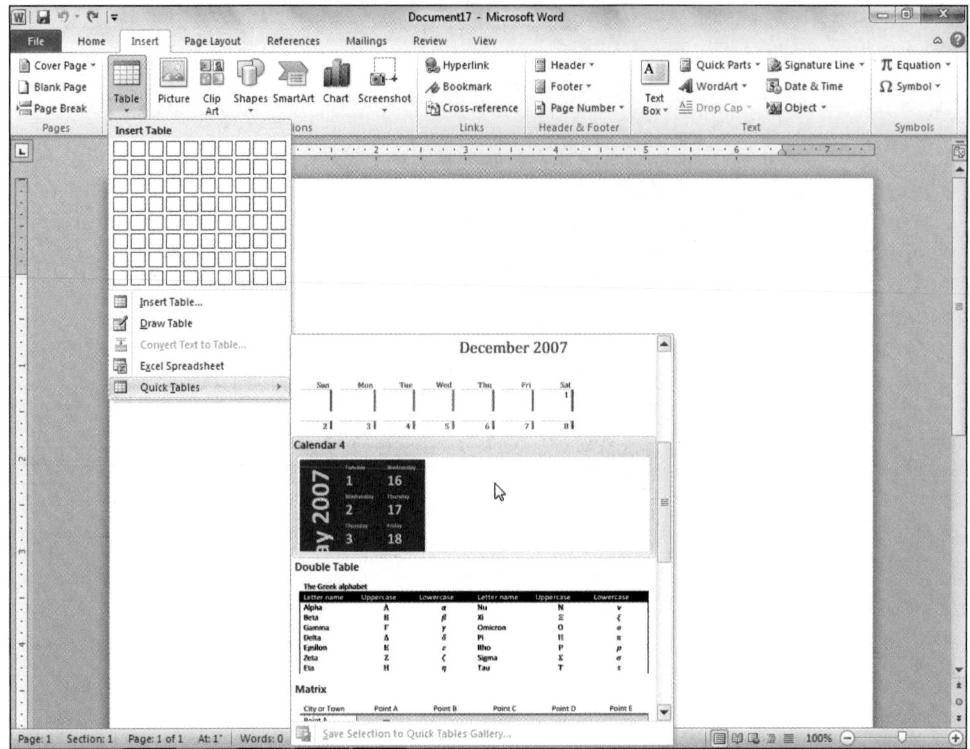

Figure 13-6 Quick Tables

4. Notice the layout and format of the design. The font, font size, and other elements can be customized.
5. Close the document without saving it.

Keying and Editing Text in Tables

Keying and editing text in tables is similar to working with text in paragraphs. But if you key text in a cell and press Enter, a new paragraph is created within the same cell.

To move the insertion point to different cells in a table, use the mouse, the arrow keys, or the keyboard shortcuts in Table 13-2.

TABLE 13-2 Shortcuts for Moving between Cells

Movement	Press
Next cell	Tab
Previous cell	Shift + Tab
First cell in the current row	Alt + Home
Last cell in the current row	Alt + End
Top cell in the current column	Alt + PageUp
Last cell in the current column	Alt + PageDown

Exercise 13-4 KEY AND EDIT TEXT IN A TABLE

1. In the first table, position the insertion point in the first cell and key **Up to 1 pound**.

NOTE

Many tables include a *header row*. The header row is the first row of a table (or the second row, if the table has a title row), in which each cell contains a heading for the column of text beneath it.

2. Press Tab and key **$7.25** in the next cell. Press Tab and key **Up to 1 pound**. Press Tab and key **$12.00**.
3. Press Tab to go to the first cell of the second row, and key **2 pounds**.
4. Press Tab or → to go to the next cell, and key **7.90**. Go to the next cell, key **2 pounds**, press Tab, and key **12.40**.
5. Key the text shown in Figure 13-7 in the remaining rows of the table, inserting each word or number into a different cell. Remember not to press Enter.

Figure 13-7

3 pounds	8.25	3 pounds	12.75
4 pounds	8.75	4 pounds	12.75
5 pounds	9.00	5 pounds	13.75

6. Press Alt+Home to move to the first cell in the last row, and press Shift+Tab to move to the fourth cell in the previous row. Change "12.75" to **13.25**.

Selecting Cells, Rows, and Columns

There are several ways to select the contents of cells, rows, and columns. Once you select cells, rows, or columns, you can delete, copy, or move the contents or change the format of the selected cells, rows, or columns.

To help with selection, *end-of-cell markers* ¤ indicate the end of each cell. In addition, *end-of-row markers* ¤ to the right of the gridline of each row indicate the end of each row.

Exercise 13-5 SELECT CELLS

1. Click the Show/Hide ¶ button ¶ to display your end-of-cell markers if nonprinting characters are not visible.
2. To select the first cell in the first table, position the pointer just inside the left edge of the cell (between the cell's left border and the letter "U"). When the pointer becomes a solid black, right-pointing arrow, click to select the cell.

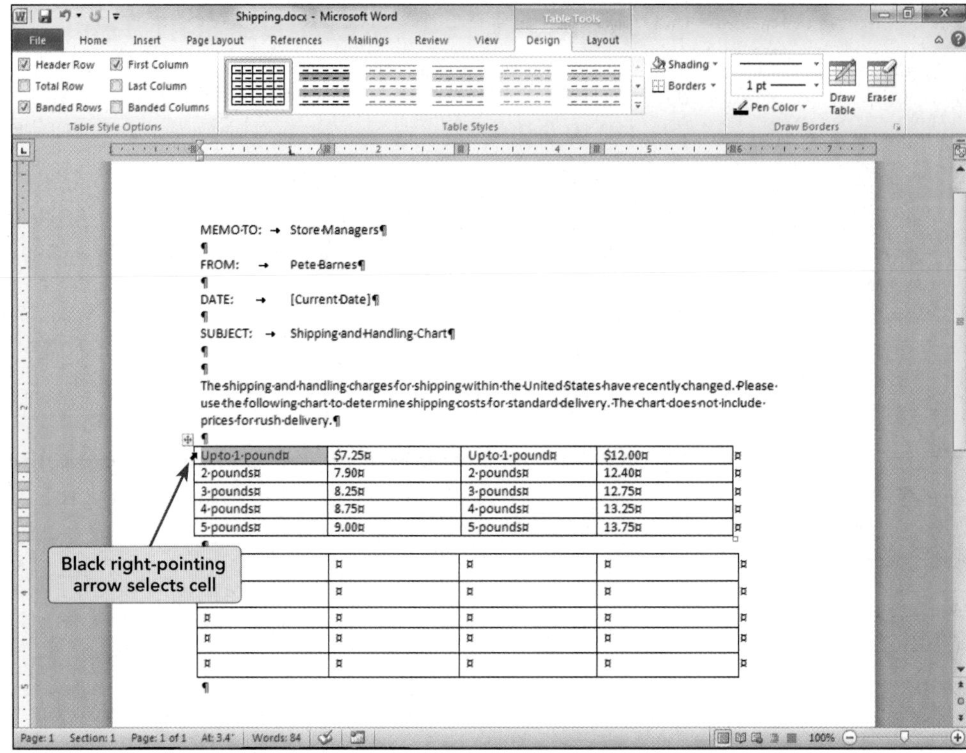

Figure 13-8
Selecting a cell

3. Next, using the I-beam pointer, drag over the text "12.75" in the third row. Notice that the text is highlighted but the end-of-cell marker is not.
4. Press Tab to move to the next cell. Again, the text in the cell is highlighted, but the end-of-cell marker is not.
5. Using the I-beam pointer, triple-click within any cell to select the entire cell.

Exercise 13-6 SELECT ROWS, COLUMNS, AND TABLES

1. In the first table, point to the left of the fourth row. When you see the white right-pointing arrow, click to select the row.

Figure 13-9
Selecting a row

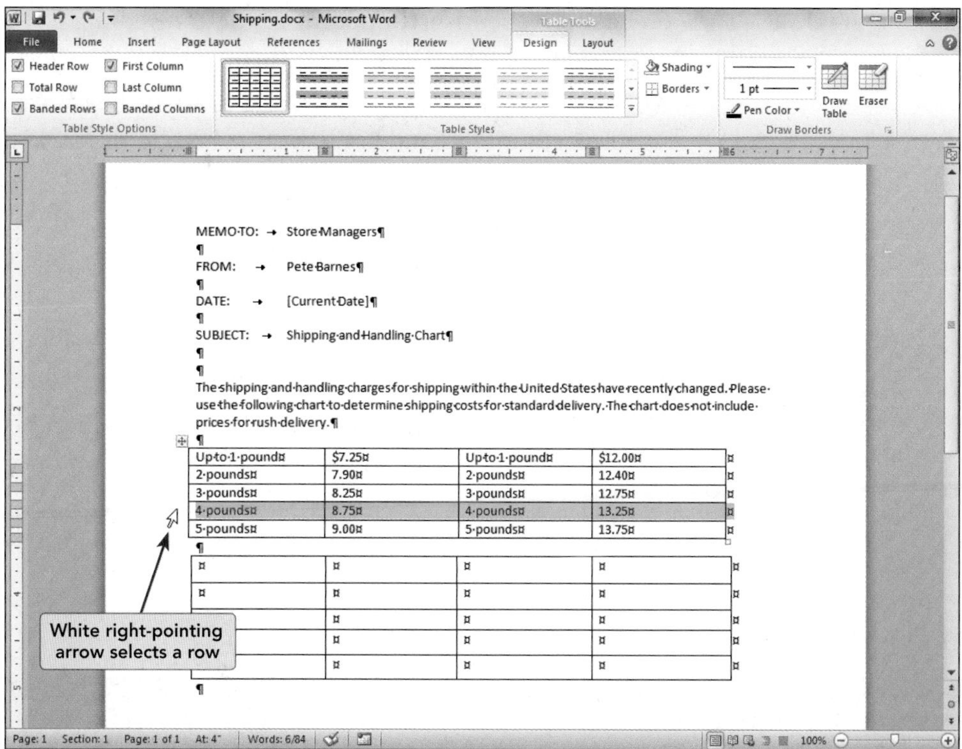

2. Point just inside the left border of any cell in the previous row, and double-click. That row is selected.
3. Position the insertion point anywhere within "4 pounds" in the fourth row. Click the **Table Tools Layout** tab, and click the Select button. Click **Select Row**. The fourth row is selected again.
4. Point to the left of the third row, and drag the pointer down one row to select both the third and fourth rows.
5. Point to the top border of the third column. When the pointer changes to a solid black down arrow, click to select the column.

Figure 13-10
Selecting a column

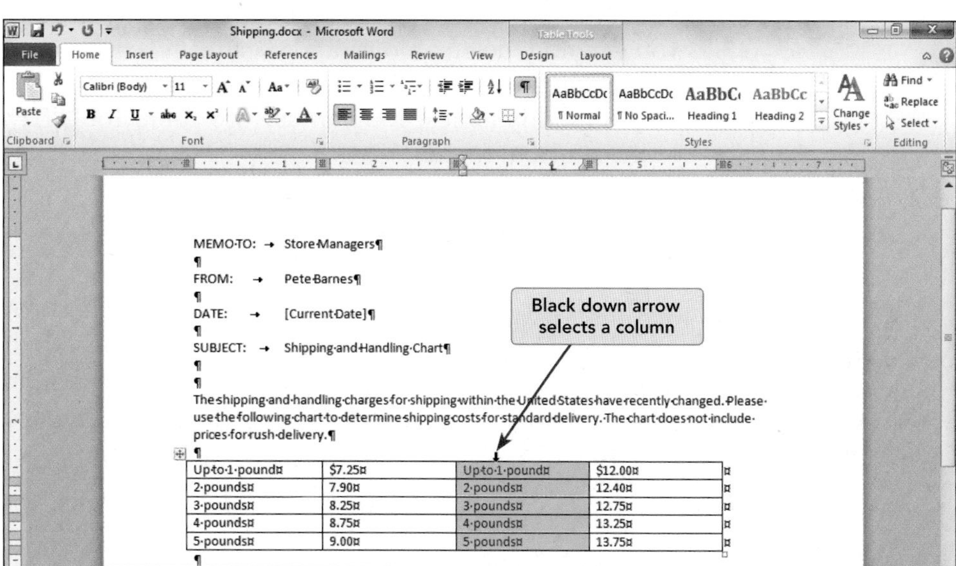

6. Position the insertion point to the immediate left of "$7.25" in the second column. Drag down through "9.00" to select column 2.
7. Point to the top of column 2, and drag the black arrow pointer across to select columns 2 and 3. Click anywhere in the table to deselect the columns.
8. With the insertion point anywhere in the table, click the **Table Tools Layout** tab. Click the Select button [Select], and then choose **Select Table** from the drop-down list to select the entire table. Click anywhere in the table to deselect it.

NOTE

Another way to select a table is to position the insertion point anywhere in the table, make sure Num Lock is turned off, and press Alt+5 on the numeric keypad.

9. Move the I-beam over the table until the table move handle appears at the top left of the table.
10. Move the I-beam over the handle. When the I-beam changes to a four-headed arrow pointer, click to select the table.
11. Click anywhere in the table to deselect it.

TABLE 13-3 Selecting Table Elements

Selection	Mouse	Command	Keyboard
Cell	Click the left inside edge of the cell.	Table Tools, Layout tab, Select	Shift+End
Row	Click to the left of the row, *or* double-click the left inside edge of a cell.	Table Tools, Layout tab, Select	
Column	Click the column's top border.	Table Tools, Layout tab, Select	
Table	Click the table move handle in Print Layout view.	Table Tools, Layout tab, Select	Num Lock Off Alt+5 (Numeric keypad)

Editing Table Structures

In addition to editing the contents of a table, you can edit a table's structure. You can add, delete, move, and copy cells, rows, and columns. You can also merge and split cells or change a table's position or dimensions.

To modify tables, you can use the Table Tools Layout tab on the Ribbon or the shortcut menu.

Exercise 13-7 INSERT CELLS, ROWS, AND COLUMNS

NOTE

To insert cells, position the insertion point in a cell that is to the right of or below where you want to insert a cell.

1. Select the first cell in the first row of the first table. Notice that the Table Tools tab displays above the Ribbon and that the Design and Layout tabs display on the Ribbon. Click the **Layout** tab on the Ribbon.
2. Click the **Rows and Columns Dialog Box Launcher**. The Insert Cells dialog box opens.

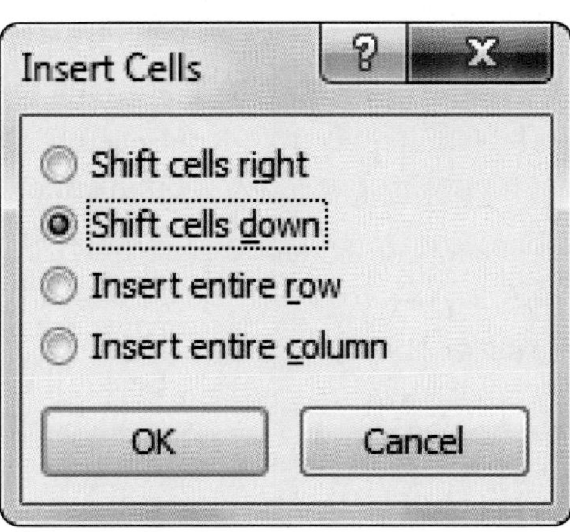

Figure 13-11
Insert Cells dialog box

3. Click **Shift cells right** and click **OK**. Word inserts a new cell and shifts the other cells in row 1 to the right.
4. Press Ctrl+Z to undo.
5. Drag the mouse pointer from "Up to 1 pound" in the first cell through "7.90" in the second column of the second row. Click the **Rows and Columns Dialog Box Launcher**.
6. Click **Shift cells down** if it is not already selected. Click **OK**. Four new cells appear above the selected cells. Deselect the text.
7. Select the first row of the first table. Click the Insert Above button on the Table Tools Layout tab. A new row appears at the top of the table.
8. Select the second row. Click the Insert Below button. A new row appears below the selected row.
9. Press Ctrl+Z to undo.
10. Select the second column of the first table by pointing to the top border of the first cell in the column and clicking the left mouse button. Click the Insert Left button on the Table Tools Layout tab. The new column appears to the left of the selected column.
11. Select the third column. Click the Insert Right button on the Table Tools Layout tab. A new column appears to the right of the selected column.
12. Press Ctrl+Z to undo.

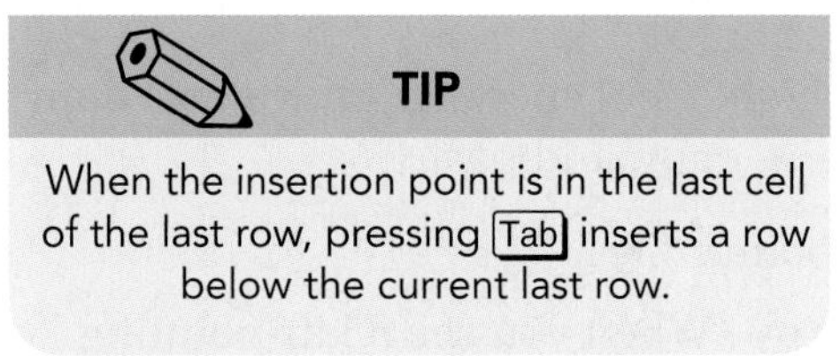

TIP

When the insertion point is in the last cell of the last row, pressing Tab inserts a row below the current last row.

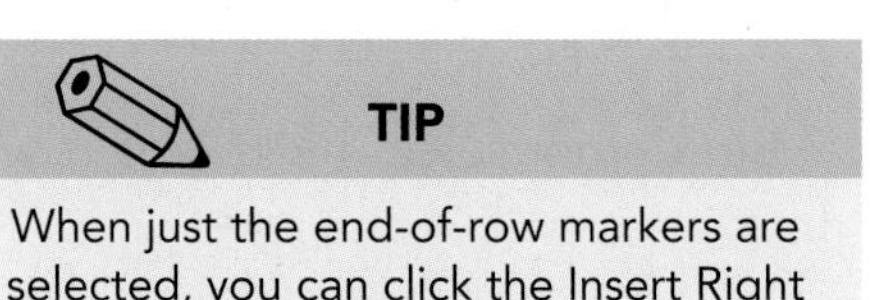

TIP

When just the end-of-row markers are selected, you can click the Insert Right button from the Table Tools Layout tab to extend the table to the right.

Exercise 13-8 DELETE CELLS, ROWS, AND COLUMNS

Deleting cells, rows, and columns is different from deleting text (selecting text and pressing Delete). You must first select the table structure you wish to delete and then choose Delete from the Table Tools Layout tab. You can also right-click the selection, and choose Delete Rows or Delete Columns from the shortcut menu.

1. In the first table, select the blank cells in the second and third rows. Locate the **Rows & Columns** group, and click the Delete button. Click **Delete Cells**. The Delete Cells dialog box opens.

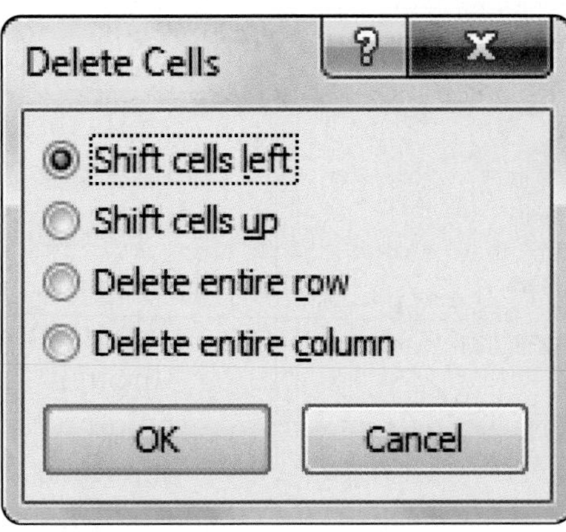

Figure 13-12 Delete Cells dialog box

2. Click **Shift cells up**. Click **OK**, and the blank cells disappear.
3. Select the blank rows at the bottom of the first table. Click the Delete button, and then choose **Delete Rows**. The blank rows are deleted.
4. Select the second column (which is blank). Right-click the column, and choose **Delete Columns** from the shortcut menu. Only the top row of your table is now blank.

Exercise 13-9 MOVE AND COPY CELLS, ROWS, AND COLUMNS

In addition to using the Ribbon and the shortcut menu to move and copy, you can also use keyboard shortcuts to cut, copy, and paste.

1. Select the row that begins "Up to 1 pound."
2. Point to the first selected cell in the row. When you see a left-pointing arrow, drag and drop the selection into the empty row above. The text now appears in the first row.
3. Select the row that begins "2 pounds," but do not select its end-of-row marker.
4. Click the **Home** tab, and click the Cut button. The text is deleted, but the empty row remains.
5. Position the insertion point in the first cell of the second row. Press Ctrl+V to paste the text.
6. Select the bottom three cells in the fourth column, and copy them to the Clipboard.
7. Click within the cell containing "8.25," and paste the text. The pasted cells overwrite the previous text.
8. Undo the Paste command.
9. Select the blank row and right-click. Click **Delete Rows**.

NOTE

If you paste text somewhere on the table where there is not enough room for all the cells, Word adds additional columns or rows to accommodate the text.

Exercise 13-10 MERGE AND SPLIT CELLS

1. Select the first two rows of the table. Click the **Table Tools Layout** tab, and click Insert Above. Two rows are added to the table. The number of cells, rows, or columns selected determines the number of cells, rows, or columns inserted in the table.

2. Select the first row of blank cells in the table. Click the Merge Cells button on the Table Tools Layout tab. The cells in the first row merge into a single cell.
3. Key the table title **Shipping and Handling Weight Chart** in the first row.
4. Select the second row of blank cells, and click the Merge Cells button. The cells in the row merge into a single cell. Once you merge a row of cells, you can undo the merge or use the Split Cells command.

Figure 13-13
Split Cells dialog box

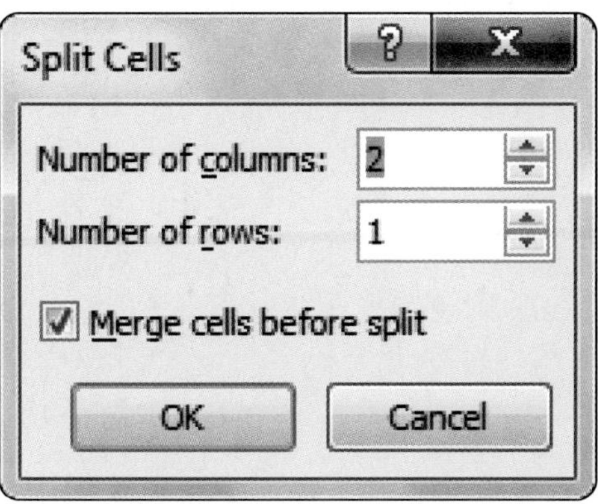

5. Select the second row, which is now one cell, and click the Split Cells button. The Split Cells dialog box displays.
6. Key **2** in the **Number of columns** text box, and verify that "1" appears in the **Number of rows** text box. Click **OK**. The row is split into two cells.
7. Key the title **Without Ice Pack** in the first cell, and key **With Ice Pack** in the second cell.

Exercise 13-11 CHANGE TABLE DIMENSIONS AND POSITION TABLES

You can adjust and position a table in the following ways:

- Change the width of columns, the space between columns, and the height of rows.
- Use AutoFit to change the width of a column to fit the longest text.
- Indent a table or center it horizontally on the page.

NOTE

You can also select a table by positioning the insertion point in any cell and clicking Select from the Table Tools Layout tab or by positioning the insertion point in any cell and pressing Alt+5 on the numeric keypad with Num Lock turned off.

1. Select the second table by clicking the table move handle.
2. Click the **Table Tools Layout** tab if necessary, and click the Properties button. Click the **Column** tab in the Table Properties dialog box.

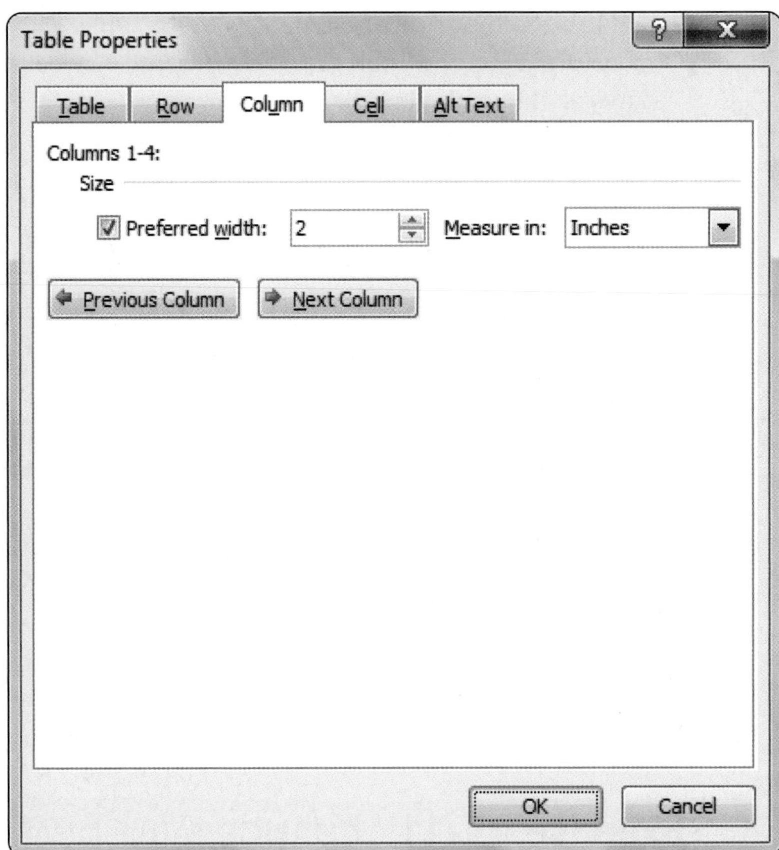

Figure 13-14 Table Properties dialog box

3. Click **Preferred width** and key **2** in the text box. Click **OK**. The columns are now 2 inches wide.
4. Press Ctrl+Z to undo.
5. With the second table selected and using the Table Tools Layout tab, click the Distribute Rows button. Then click the Distribute Columns button. The hand-drawn rows and columns are now evenly spaced.
6. Select the first table. Click the **Table Tools Layout** tab if necessary, and click the Properties button. Click the **Row** tab.
7. Click **Specify height**, and key **0.4** in the text box. Choose **At least** from the **Row height is** drop-down list if it is not already selected.
8. Click the **Table** tab in the Table Properties dialog box. Under **Alignment**, choose **Center** and click **OK**. The table is centered horizontally on the page, and the height of each row has increased.
9. Deselect the table, and position the pointer on the right border of the last column until it changes to a vertical double bar for resizing.

NOTE

Like column width, row height is expressed in inches, not points. You can also change the column width and row height by keying the measurements in the Table Column Width text box and Table Row Height text box in the Cell Size group on the Table Tools Layout tab.

TIP

When a table appears on a page by itself, center it vertically and horizontally. Use the Layout tab in the Page Setup dialog box to choose vertical alignment options.

Figure 13-15
Dragging a table border

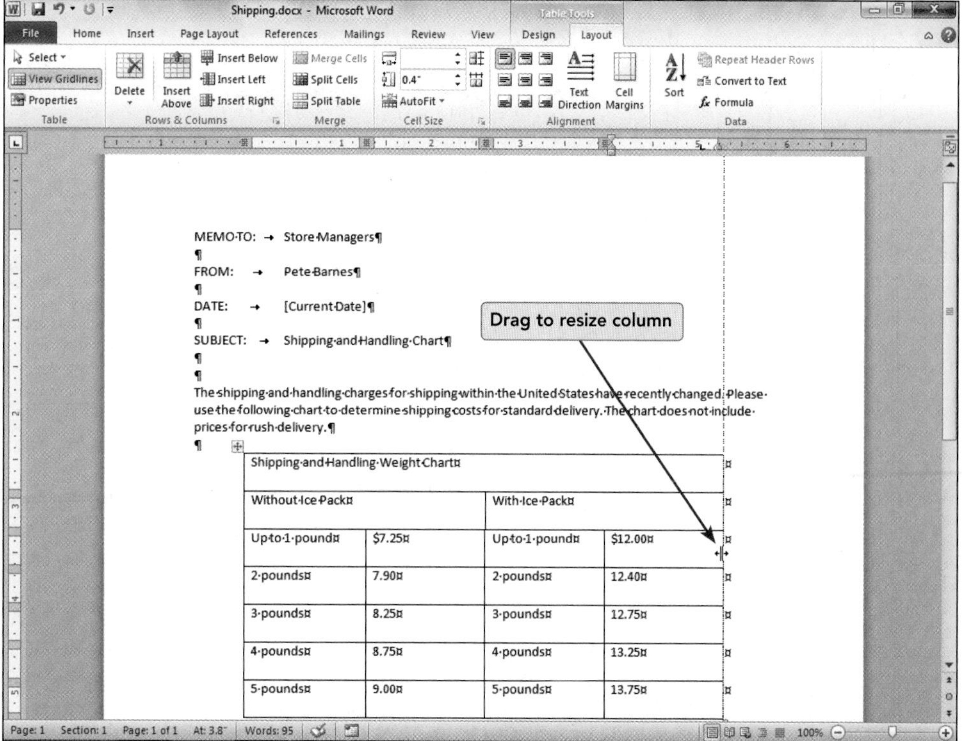

NOTE

As long as the cell is not selected, dragging the right border adjusts the entire column width, not just the cell width.

TIP

You can simultaneously adjust all the columns to fit the width of each column's widest cell entry by clicking the AutoFit down arrow and then choosing AutoFit Contents from the Table Tools Layout tab.

NOTE

This technique is similar to dragging margin borders in Print Layout view.

10. Drag the border 0.5 inch to the right to widen the column. (Hold down Alt as you drag to see the exact ruler measurements.)
11. Click the Undo button, and position the pointer on the right border of the cell containing "8.25." Drag 0.5 inch to the right. The second column is wider, but the third column is now narrower.
12. Press Ctrl+Z to undo. Hold down Shift and drag the second column border 0.5 inch to the right again. The second column is now wider, and the third column remains the same width. Press Ctrl+Z to undo.
13. Double-click the right border of the second column. The column is adjusted to the width of the widest cell entry.
14. Click anywhere in rows 3 through 5 of the first table.
15. On the ruler, point to the right column marker for the second column. When you see the ScreenTip "Move Table Column," drag the marker a short distance to the right and then release the mouse button.
16. Hold down Alt and drag the marker until the ruler measurement for the second column is 1.2 inches.

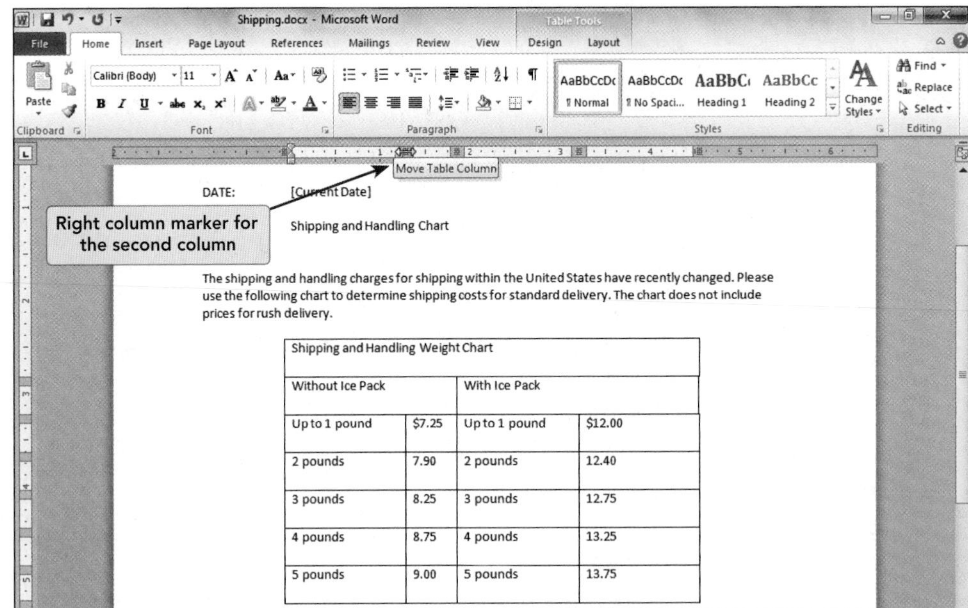

Figure 13-16
Dragging a column marker

TIP

The ruler measures column width by the actual space for text within the cells. The Table Properties dialog box (Column tab, Preferred width text box) includes the left and right cell margins, each of which is 0.08 inch by default. This means columns that are 1 inch wide when set by using the ruler will appear as 1.16 inches wide in the dialog box.

17. Use the same technique to adjust the other column widths to 1.2 inches. Each table column is now 1.2 inches wide, and the merged row adjusts to the new table width.

Exercise 13-12 RESIZE A TABLE PROPORTIONATELY

The table resize handle in the lower right corner of a table provides a convenient way to resize a table proportionately. When you drag the handle to the left, each column becomes proportionately narrower. When you drag the handle to the right, each column becomes proportionately wider. If needed, word wrapping will occur to fit a cell's contents into a narrower column.

1. Click anywhere inside the second table, and let the mouse pointer rest on the table. The table resize handle appears below the lower right corner of the table.
2. Point to the table resize handle. The mouse pointer changes to a two-headed diagonal arrow. Drag the table resize handle to the left until the dotted box's right border is even with the 4.5-inch marker on the horizontal ruler. Release the mouse button. The table columns are now narrower.

Figure 13-17
Resizing a table

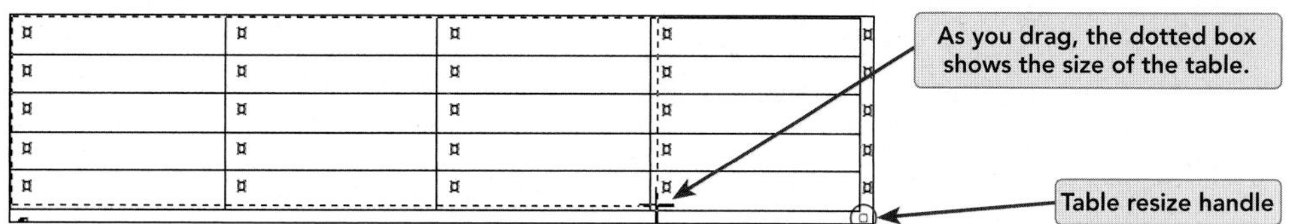
As you drag, the dotted box shows the size of the table.
Table resize handle

Formatting Tables and Cell Contents

There are many ways to make a table more attractive and easier to read. For example, you can:

- Format table text.
- Align text horizontally within columns.
- Align text vertically within cells or rows.
- Apply borders and shading.
- Use the Table Styles feature to apply a predesigned table style.
- Rotate the direction of text from horizontal to vertical.
- Sort table text.

Exercise 13-13 FORMAT TABLE TEXT

TIP

The default alignment for text in a table cell is top left. Text can be positioned vertically at the top, center, or bottom of the cell. Text can be positioned horizontally at the left, center, or right of the cell.

1. Select the table title in the first row of the first table, and format it as centered, bold, 14 points, and small caps.
2. Select row 2 and apply bold formatting. With the second row selected, click the **Table Tools Layout** tab, and locate the **Alignment** group. Click the Align Center button to align the text horizontally and vertically in the cell.
3. Select "Up to 1 pound" in the first column and the cells below it. Click the Align Center Left button on the Ribbon to left-align the text horizontally and center the text vertically.
4. Select "Up to 1 pound" in the third column and the cells below it, and format the text using the Align Center Left button.
5. Click within the title in the first row, and then click the Align Center button on the Ribbon to center the text vertically and horizontally.

TIP

When a column contains all text, it should be left-aligned. When it contains all numbers, it should be right-aligned.

TIP

To change the vertical alignment of a large group of cells without affecting the horizontal alignments in each cell (left, right, or center), choose Properties from the Table Tools Layout tab. Click the Cell tab. Under Vertical alignment, click Center to vertically center the text in every cell.

6. Select "$7.25" and the cells below it. Click the Align Center Right button to right-align the text and vertically center the text within the selected cells.
7. Select "$12.00" and the cells below it. Click the Align Center Right button to right-align the text and vertically center the text within the selected cells.
8. Format the second row as italic.

Exercise 13-14 SORT TABLE TEXT

You can sort a table by any of its columns. Sorting means arranging items in a particular order. When you sort items in a table, you select a sort order in either ascending (A to Z or 0 to 9) or descending (Z to A or 9 to 0) order. When sorting a table, you do not need to select the entire table. The contents of an entire row always sort together unless you specifically choose to sort only one column. If the beginning row or rows of a table have been defined as header rows, they automatically stay at the top of the table after sorting.

1. Select row 3 (the text below the header row) through row 7 of the first table.

NOTE

Select only the cells you want sorted when using the Sort command.

2. From the **Table Tools Layout** tab, click the Sort button. Choose **Column 1** from the **Sort by** drop-down list, choose **Text** from the **Type** drop-down list, and click **Descending**.
3. Click **OK** to sort the rows alphabetically in descending order.
4. Press Ctrl+Z to undo the sort.

Exercise 13-15 APPLY BORDERS AND SHADING

You can increase the attractiveness of your table by changing border line styles and line weight and applying shading to selected cells. It is important to choose appropriate line color, line style, and shading options to ensure that text is easy to read and the document is attractive.

NOTE

Selecting black shading creates reverse text. *Reverse text* displays white text on a black background, which is the opposite of black type on a white background.

1. Select the first row in the first table (the title). Click the **Table Tools Design** tab, click the arrow next to the Shading button Shading, and click **Black** on the palette (the first color in the second column).
2. Select the entire table.
3. Click the Line Style button, and select a double-line border. Click the Line Weight button 1 pt, and click 1½-point weight.
4. Click the arrow beside the Borders button Borders, and click **Outside Borders**. Click within the table to deselect the table and view the borders.

5. Click the arrow beside the Pen Color button [Pen Color], and choose a dark blue color from the palette.
6. Click the Draw Table button to activate the pencil pointer, and drag the pencil over each outside border of the second table, one border at a time, and then over the bottom border of the first row.

Figure 13-18
Drawing a border

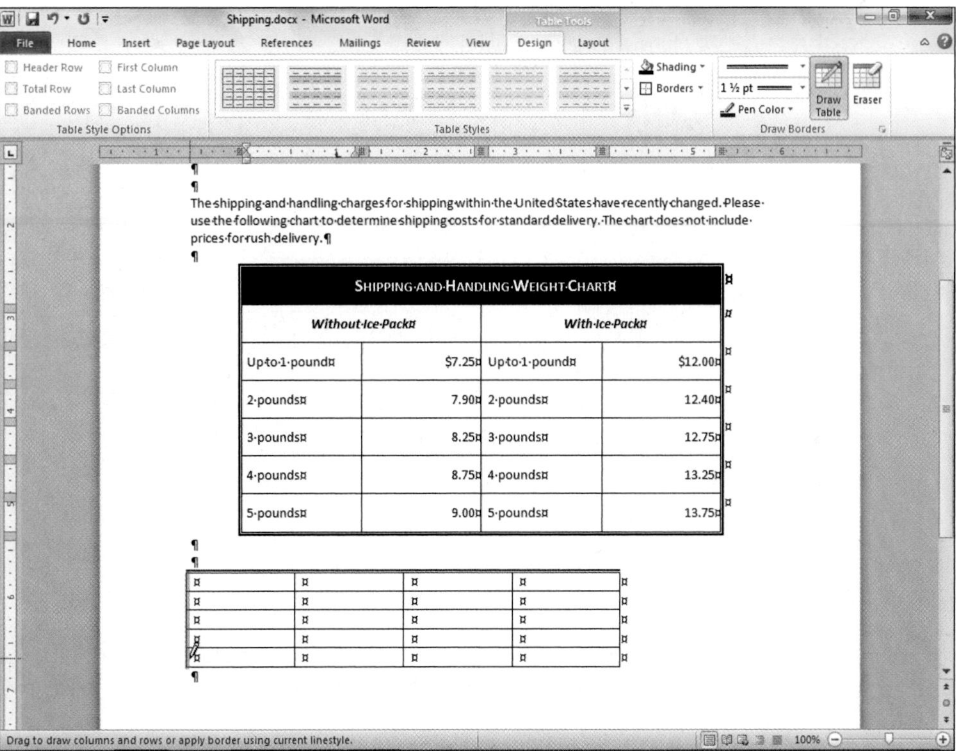

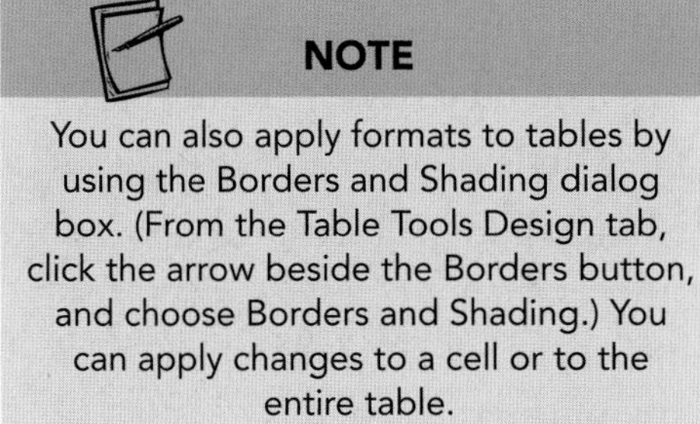

NOTE

You can also apply formats to tables by using the Borders and Shading dialog box. (From the Table Tools Design tab, click the arrow beside the Borders button, and choose Borders and Shading.) You can apply changes to a cell or to the entire table.

7. Click the Draw Table button or press Esc to restore the normal pointer.

Exercise 13-16 USE TABLE STYLES TO FORMAT A TABLE

Word can format your table automatically and attractively when you use table styles.

1. Select the text in rows 3 through 7 (from "Up to 1 pound" to "13.75") but not the end-of-row markers. Copy the selected text to the Clipboard.
2. Click the first cell in the blank table, and paste the copied text.

3. Click the first cell of the second table. Click the **Table Tools Design** tab. Move the pointer over each table style in the **Table Styles** group to preview each table style.
4. Click the More arrow in the Table Styles group to view additional styles.

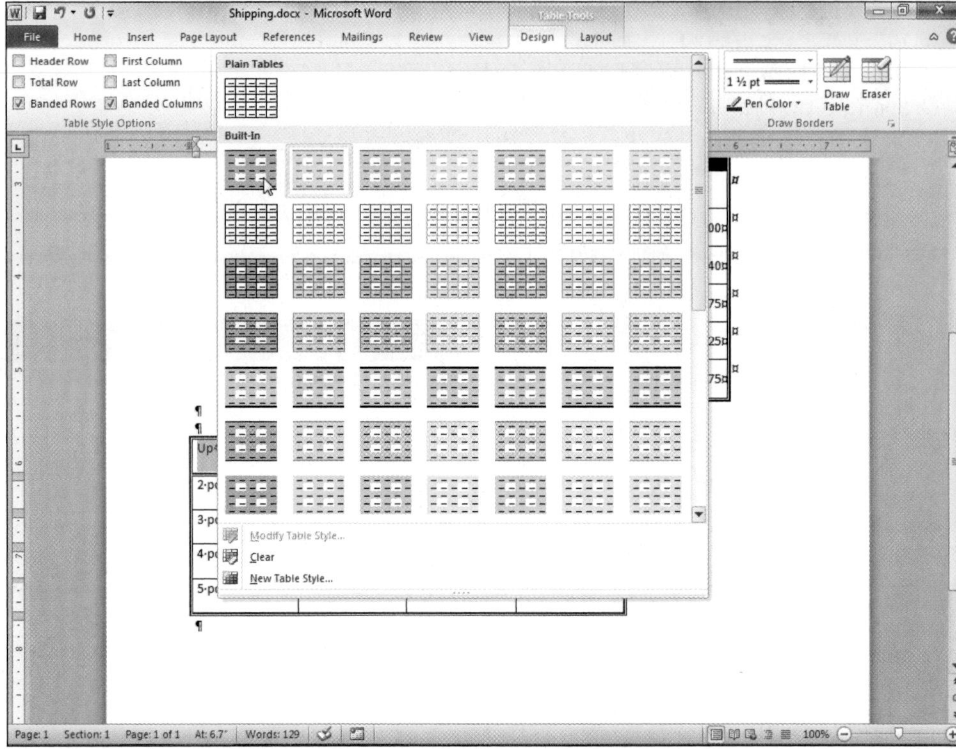

Figure 13-19
Selecting a table style

5. Click a style with gray shading.
6. Locate the **Table Style Options** group on the **Table Tools Design** tab, and clear the check box for **First Column** if necessary.
7. Click the More arrow and click **Clear**. The table style is removed.
8. Select the second table, and apply a table style of your choice.
9. Select the second table, including the blank paragraph marks above and below it, and press Delete.
10. Add an extra paragraph mark above the table, and add your reference initials below the table. Change the top margin to 2 inches.
11. Save the document as ***[your initials]*13-16** in a new Lesson 13 folder.
12. Submit and close the document.

Exercise 13-17 ROTATE TEXT

1. Start a new document.
2. Click the **Insert** tab, and click the Table button. Click **Insert Table** on the Table menu.
3. In the Insert Table dialog box, set the **Number of columns** to **2** and the **Number of rows** to **8**. Click **OK**.

4. In the first cell of the first row, key **Customary Units**. Press Tab and key **Metric Equivalent**. Format both headings as bold.
5. Key **1 ounce** in the first cell of the second row. Press Tab and key **23.3495 grams**. Key the data shown in Figure 13-20 for the remaining table cells.

Figure 13-20

1 pound	0.4536 kilogram
1 ton	0.907 metric ton
1 inch	2.54 centimeters
1 foot	30.48 centimeters
1 yard	0.9144 meter
1 mile	1.6093 kilometers

6. Select the first column, and click the **Table Tools Layout** tab on the Ribbon. Click the Insert Left button.
7. Select the first row, and click the Insert Above button on the Ribbon.
8. Position the insertion point in the first cell of the second row. Key **Weight** in bold. Position the insertion point in the first cell of the sixth row. Key **Length** and format the text as bold.
9. Select the table, and format all text as 12 points.
10. Select the cell containing "Weight" and the three blank cells below it. Click the **Table Tools Layout** tab, and click the Merge Cells button.
11. With the insertion point in the merged cell, click the Text Direction button on the Table Tools Layout tab to rotate "Weight" until it reads from top to bottom. Click the Text Direction button again so that "Weight" reads from bottom to top. Center the text horizontally and vertically by clicking the Align Center button.
12. Select the cells from the one containing "Length" to the last cell of the first column. Click the Merge Cells button on the Table Tools Layout tab.
13. With the merged cell selected, click the Text Direction button on the Table Tools Layout tab twice to rotate "Length" until it reads from bottom to top. Center the text horizontally and vertically.
14. Merge the cells in the first row, and key the title **Metric Conversion Table** in the merged row. Format the title as 16 points, bold, uppercase, and centered.
15. Select the entire table. Click the **Table Tools Layout** tab, and click the Properties button to open the Table Properties dialog box. Click the **Row** tab. Set the row height to exactly **0.5"**.
16. Click the **Table** tab. Click **Center** to horizontally center the table on the document page. Click **OK**.

17. With the table still selected, click the **Table Tools Layout** tab, click the AutoFit button, and then click **AutoFit Contents** to change all column widths to be as wide as the longest text in the column.

NOTE

When a table has a title, AutoFit changes the title's column to fit the length of the title. This might make the column much wider than is required for the widest text in the remaining columns. You can insert a line break to create a two-line title.

18. Select the cells from "1 ounce" to "1.6093" in the last row, and click the Align Center Left button to vertically center the text. Verify that the cells for the first two rows and the cells containing the text "Weight" and "Length" are centered horizontally and vertically.
19. Apply gray shading to the first row and to the cells that contain "Customary Units," "Metric Equivalent," "Weight," and "Length."
20. Select the table again. Using the Table Tools Design tab, change the Line Style to a double line, change the Line Weight 1 pt to **1½ point**, and change the Pen Color Pen Color to **Black**. Click the Borders button Borders to select **Outside Borders** to apply the double-line border to the outside of the table.
21. Click the Draw Table button to draw the same style border to separate the "Weight" and "Length" sections of the table. (Draw a horizontal bottom line under "Weight," "1 ton," and "0.907 metric ton.") Press Esc to turn off the Draw Table command.
22. Open the **Page Setup** dialog box. On the **Layout** tab, set the **Vertical alignment** to **Center** and click **OK**.
23. Save the document as ***[your initials]*13-17** in your Lesson 13 folder. Submit and close the document

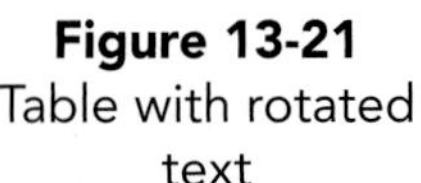

Figure 13-21
Table with rotated text

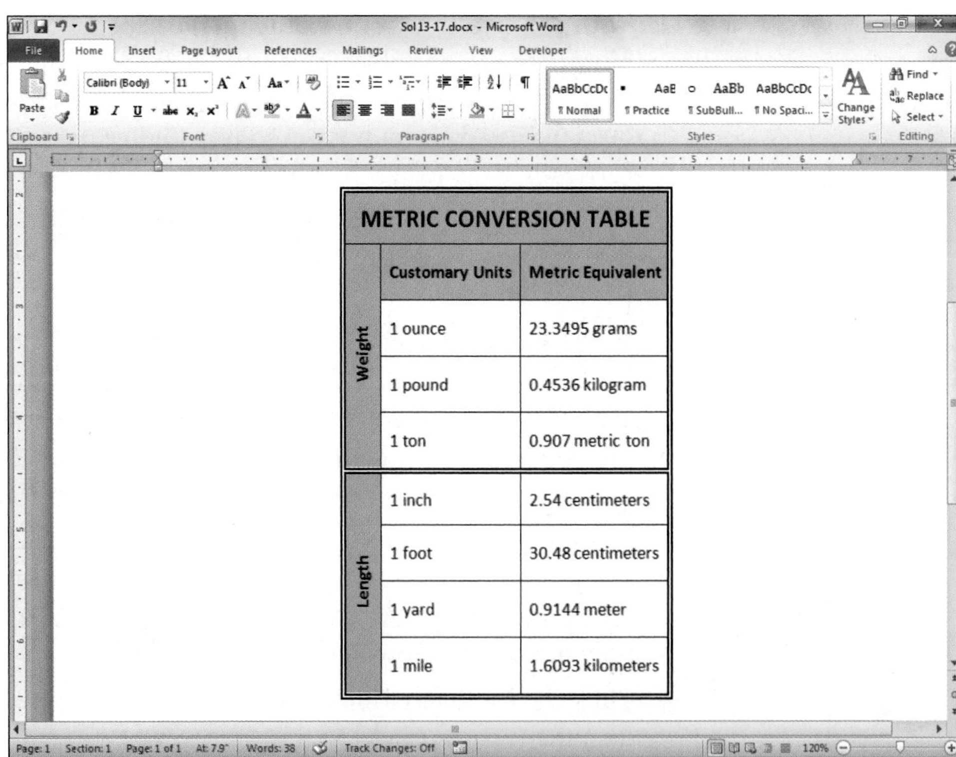

METRIC CONVERSION TABLE		
	Customary Units	Metric Equivalent
Weight	1 ounce	23.3495 grams
	1 pound	0.4536 kilogram
	1 ton	0.907 metric ton
Length	1 inch	2.54 centimeters
	1 foot	30.48 centimeters
	1 yard	0.9144 meter
	1 mile	1.6093 kilometers

Converting Tables and Text

You can convert existing tabbed text to a table, and doing so can be faster than keying text into an existing table. You can also convert an existing table to paragraphs of text, and you can choose to separate the converted text by paragraph marks, commas, or tabs. This might be useful when converting Word data for use in a database.

Exercise 13-18 CONVERT TEXT INTO TABLES

1. In a new document, key the text shown in Figure 13-22, with one tab character between each entry. Press Enter at the end of each line as usual. Use single spacing and 0 points spacing after. (Your text might line up differently from that in the figure. You will correct the document layout in the following steps.)

Figure 13-22

Quarters	2009	2010	2011
Q1	42.8	40.8	41.3
Q2	34.6	38.2	37.9
Q3	33.5	39.0	39.1
Q4	41.6	39.2	40.4

2. Select all the text. Click the **Insert** tab, and click the Table button. Click **Convert Text to Table**. The Convert Text to Table dialog box appears.
3. Make sure the **Number of columns** text entry is 4. In addition, check that **Tabs** is chosen under **Separate text at**. Click **OK**. The selected text appears in a 5 × 4 table.
4. Click the **Table Tools Design** tab, and click the **Light Shading – Accent 1** table style. Locate the **Table Style Options** group on the **Table Tools Design** tab, and verify that the **Header Row**, **Banded Rows**, and **First Column** check boxes are selected.
5. Select the table, and copy it to the Clipboard. You will need this table for the next exercise.
6. With the table still selected, click the **Table Tools Layout** tab, and locate the Table Row Height button. Change the row height to **0.3"**.
7. With the table still selected, click the Align Center button on the Table Tools Layout tab to vertically and horizontally center the text.
8. Use the Page Setup dialog box to center the table vertically on the page.
9. Insert a new row at the top of the table, and merge the cells in the row. In the first row, key the title **CAMPBELL'S CONFECTIONS' SALES** as 16-point bold type. Press Enter, and key **(in thousands)**. Format the second line as 11 points, no bold. Center each line of text in the first row.

10. Save the document as ***[your initials]*****13-18** in your Lesson 13 folder.
11. Submit and close the document.

Exercise 13-19 CONVERT TABLES TO TEXT

1. Start a new document. Paste the Clipboard contents that contain the copied table from step 5 of the previous exercise.
2. Select the table.
3. Click the **Table Tools Layout** tab, and locate the **Data** group on the Ribbon. Click the Convert to Text button. The Convert Table to Text dialog box opens.

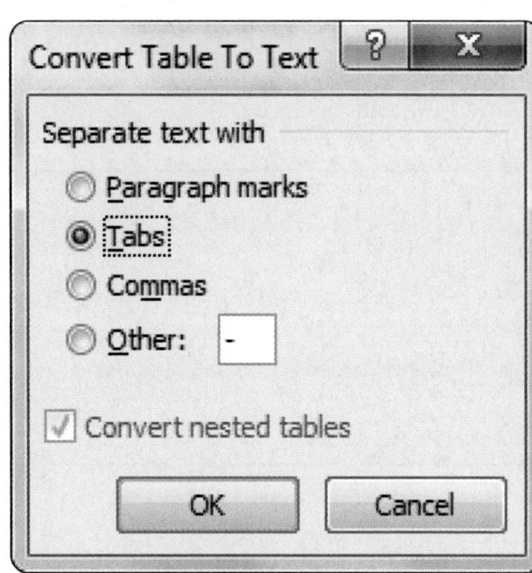

Figure 13-23 Convert Table to Text dialog box

4. Choose **Tabs**, if it is not already selected, to separate the contents of each cell with tabs.
5. Click **OK**. The text appears outside the table, with a tab replacing each end-of-cell marker and a paragraph mark replacing each end-of-row marker.
6. Close the document without saving it.

Lesson 13 Summary

- A table is a grid of rows and columns that intersect to form cells. The lines that mark the cell boundaries are called gridlines.
- There are several ways to create a table: Use the Insert Table menu, Insert Table command, table template; draw a table; or convert text to a table.
- Keying and editing text in tables is similar to working with text in paragraphs. But if you key text in a cell and press Enter, a new paragraph is created within the same cell.
- To move the insertion point to different cells in a table, use the mouse, the arrow keys, or keyboard shortcuts.
- Select cells by using the black right-pointing arrow or the shortcut keys or by dragging over text. With the cells selected, you can delete, copy, or move their contents or change the format.
- To help with selection, end-of-cell markers indicate the end of each cell. In addition, end-of-row markers to the right of the gridline of each row indicate the end of each row.

- Select rows by using the white right-pointing arrow, select columns by using the black column selector arrow, and select tables by using the table move handle. You can also use the Select command on the Table Tools Layout tab or drag to select.
- The header row is the first row of a table (or second row if the table has a title row), in which each cell contains a heading for the column of text beneath it.
- In addition to editing the contents of a table, you can edit a table's structure by adding, deleting, moving, and copying cells, rows, and columns. You can also merge and split cells or change a table's position or dimensions.
- In addition to using Ribbon commands and the shortcut menu, you can also use keyboard shortcuts to cut, copy, and paste.
- There are many ways to make a table more attractive and easier to read: Format table text, align text horizontally and vertically, apply borders and shading, use table styles, rotate the direction of text, and sort table text.
- You can convert existing tabbed text to a table, and doing so can be faster than keying text into an existing table. You can also convert an existing table to paragraphs of text, and you can choose to separate the converted text by paragraph marks, commas, or tabs.

LESSON 13 Command Summary

Feature	Button	Command	Keyboard
AutoFit		Table Tools Layout tab, Cell Size group	
Borders	Borders	Table Tools Design tab, Table Styles group	
Change column width		Table Tools Layout tab, Cell Size group	
Change row height		Table Tools Layout tab, Cell Size group	
Change text direction		Table Tools Layout tab, Alignment group	
Delete table		Table Tools Layout tab, Rows & Columns group	
Distribute columns		Table Tools Layout tab, Cell Size group	
Distribute rows		Table Tools Layout tab, Cell Size group	
Draw table		Insert tab, Tables group	

continues

LESSON 13		Command Summary *continued*	
Feature	**Button**	**Command**	**Keyboard**
Insert cells		Table Tools Layout tab, Rows & Columns group	
Insert columns to left		Table Tools Layout tab, Rows & Columns group	
Insert columns to right		Table Tools Layout tab, Rows & Columns group	
Insert rows above		Table Tools Layout tab, Rows & Columns group	
Insert rows below		Table Tools Layout tab, Rows & Columns group	
Insert table		Insert tab, Tables group	
Line Style		Table Tools Design tab, Draw Borders group	
Line Weight	1 pt	Table Tools Design tab, Draw Borders group	
Merge cells		Table Tools Layout tab, Merge group	
Select cells	Select	Table Tools Layout tab, Table group	
Select column	Select	Table Tools Layout tab, Table group	
Select row	Select	Table Tools Layout tab, Table group	
Select table	Select	Table Tools Layout tab, Table group	Alt+5 (Numeric keypad)
Shading	Shading	Table Tools Design tab, Table Styles group	
Sort text		Table Tools Layout tab, Data group	
Split cells		Table Tools Layout tab, Merge group	
Table Properties		Table Tools Layout tab, Table group	
Table Styles		Table Tools Design tab, Table Styles group	

Concepts Review

True/False Questions

Each of the following statements is either true or false. Indicate your choice by circling T or F.

T F 1. You can insert a table by using the Page Layout tab on the Ribbon.

T F 2. To move to the top cell in the current column, you press Alt+PageDown.

T F 3. You can use the Table Properties dialog box to center a table vertically.

T F 4. You press Alt+7 to select a table.

T F 5. Table templates insert tables with sample data.

T F 6. To split a merged cell, first delete all paragraph marks in the merged cell.

T F 7. By default, when you insert a table, it has borders that will be printed.

T F 8. You can apply shading by using the Table Tools Design tab.

Short Answer Questions

Write the correct answer in the space provided.

1. Which dialog box do you use to change column width?

____

2. Which keyboard shortcut moves the insertion point to the previous cell?

____

3. Which nonprinting character marks the end of a cell?

____

4. What are the nonprinting lines called that mark the boundaries of cells?

____

5. Which command is used to add a row above a selected row?

____

6. Which feature on the Table Tools Design tab do you use to remove a line?

____

7. Which table element can you select when the pointer appears as [icon]?

8. What would the button [icon] do to selected cells in a table?

Critical Thinking

Answer these questions on a separate page. There are no right or wrong answers. Support your answers with examples from your own experience, if possible.

1. You learned how to insert a table automatically and draw a table manually. What are the benefits of each method? Which do you prefer?
2. Review the table formats in the Table Styles gallery. Which table formats would you be most likely to use on a day-to-day basis? Are there any formats that are not particularly useful?

Skills Review

Exercise 13-20

Create a table. Key and edit text in the table.

1. Start a new document, and verify that you are using the Word 2010 Style Set.
2. Key the following text on three separate lines:

   Gift Certificates and Store Credits
   Location: ______________
   Month: ______________
3. Press Enter two times after the last line.
4. Position the insertion point at the last paragraph mark, and insert a table by following these steps:
   a. Click the **Insert** tab, and click the Table button [icon].
   b. Click **Insert Table** to open the Insert Table dialog box.
   c. Key **4** in the **Number of columns** text box, and key **32** in the **Number of rows** text box.
   d. Click **OK**.
5. Key text in the first row of the table by following these steps:
   a. With the insertion point in the first cell, key **Day**.
   b. Press Tab and key **Issued**.
   c. Press Tab and key **Redeemed**.
   d. Press Tab and key **Balance**.

6. Create a numbered list by following these steps:
   a. Select all cells in column 1 beginning with the cell below "Day."
   b. Click the **Home** tab, and click the down arrow beside the Numbering button.
   c. Select **Define New Number Format**. Select **01, 02, 03** for the **Number style**. In the **Define New Number format** text box, delete the period, but do not delete the number. Click **OK**.
   d. Open the **Paragraph** dialog box, and change the **Left** indent to **0** and the **Special** indent to **(none)**. Click **OK**.
7. Move around and edit text in the table, using keyboard shortcuts, by following these steps:
   a. With the insertion point in the last cell of column 1, press Alt+PageUp. Apply bold and small caps format to "Day."
   b. Press Tab, and apply bold and small caps to "Issued."
   c. Select "Redeemed" and "Balance," and apply bold and small caps format.
   d. Center "Issued," "Redeemed," and "Balance."
8. Select the three lines in the heading, and press Ctrl+E to center the lines.
9. Format the first line of the heading using 16-point bold and small caps. Format the second and third lines using 12-point bold and small caps.
10. Change the top margin to 1.5 inches.
11. Save the document as ***[your initials]*13-20** in your Lesson 13 folder.
12. Submit and close the document.

Exercise 13-21

Select, move, and copy cells, rows, and columns. Edit table structures.

1. Open the file **Rates**.
2. Cut the text in the table by following these steps:
   a. Make sure the Show/Hide ¶ button ¶ is turned on.
   b. Drag to select all the text in the table—but not the end-of-row markers.
   c. Cut the text.
3. Modify the table structure by inserting three columns by following these steps:
   a. Point to the top border of the first column, and click to select the column. Drag to the right to select the three empty columns.
   b. Click the **Table Tools Layout** tab.
   c. Click the Insert Right button on the Table Tools Layout tab to add three columns to the table.

4. Paste the text in the table by following these steps:
   a. Position the insertion point in the second cell of the first column.
   b. Paste the text.
5. Click in the second row of column 4, and key the text from Figure 13-24 in the new columns.

Figure 13-24

Column 4	Column 5
$25,000	$50,000
34.75	44.75
37.75	47.75
40.75	50.75
43.75	53.75
46.75	56.75
49.75	59.75
52.75	62.75
55.75	65.75

6. Delete column 6 by following these steps:
   a. Select the sixth column.
   b. Right-click and choose **Delete Columns** from the shortcut menu.
7. Change the column width and row height and center the table by following these steps:
   a. Select the entire table by clicking the table move handle.
   b. Click the **Table Tools Layout** tab, and click the Properties button.
   c. Click the **Column** tab, and set the **Preferred width** text box to **1"**.
   d. Click the **Row** tab. Select **Specify height**, and set the height to at least **0.3"**.
   e. Click the **Cell** tab. Select **Center** for the vertical alignment.
   f. Click the **Table** tab. Under **Alignment**, choose **Center**. Click **OK**.
8. Merge cells in the first row by following these steps:
   a. Select the second and third cells in the first row.
   b. Click the **Table Tools Layout** tab, and click the Merge Cells button. Key **Female—Nonsmoker** in the merged cell.
   c. Select the cells in the first row for columns 4 and 5, and merge the cells. Key **Male—Nonsmoker**.
9. Center the text in row 1, and format it as 14-point bold and small caps.
10. Select the text in rows 3 through 10, and press Ctrl+R to right-align the numbers. Right-align and bold the text in the second row.

11. Apply shading to the table by following these steps:
    a. Select the first row, and click the Table Tools Design tab. Click the arrow beside the Shading button, and click black in the palette.
    b. Select the second row, and apply a light shade of gray.
12. Format the document as a memo to "Store Managers" from Garland Miller. The subject is "Life Insurance." Use the current date. Add reference initials at the end of the document.
13. Use the Page Setup dialog box to change the top margin to 2 inches. Change the spacing after the Subject line to 24 points.
14. Save the document as ***[your initials]*****13-21** in your Lesson 13 folder.
15. Submit and close the document.

Exercise 13-22

Convert text to a table, and format the table.

1. Open the document **Nutrition - 1**.
2. Convert tabbed text to a table by following these steps:
    a. Select the tabbed text from "Nutritional Facts" to the end of the line beginning "Protein."
    b. Click the Insert tab, and click the Table button.
    c. Click Convert Text to Table in the Table menu.
    d. Key **5** in the Number of columns text box, and key **14** in the Number of rows if necessary. Verify that Tabs is selected under Separate text at. Click OK.
3. Click anywhere in the table, and click the Table Tools Design tab. Click the More arrow to display the Table Styles gallery. Select a style in the second row of the Built-In styles gallery.
4. Locate the Table Style Options group, and click the check box for Banded Columns.
5. Select the first row, click the Table Tools Layout tab, and click the Insert Above button to add a row to the top of the table. Merge the cells in the first row. Key **DARK CHOCOLATE SQUARES** in the new row. Center the text, and apply 14-point formatting.
6. Use the Table Properties dialog box to increase the height of every row in the table to at least **0.3"**.

7. Use the Table Properties dialog box **Cell** tab to vertically center the text in every cell of the table.
8. Select the text in columns 2 through 5, and right-align the text. Click the **Table Tools Layout** tab, and click the AutoFit button. Choose **AutoFit Contents**.
9. Center the table horizontally and vertically on the page.
10. Save the document as ***[your initials]*13-22** in your Lesson 13 folder.
11. Submit and close the document.

Exercise 13-23

Convert text to a table, and format the table.

1. Open the file **Trip**.
2. Select the text from "NAME:" to the end of the document. Convert the text to an 18-row by 1-column table, and define the **Fixed column width** as **2** inches. Click **OK**.
3. Select the first column, and insert a column to the right.
4. Change the row height for the entire table to exactly **0.4"**, and center the table horizontally. Vertically center the text in the cells.
5. Select the cells containing the text "Name," "Outbound Pickups," "Outbound Deliveries," and "Mileage." Apply bold formatting and light blue shading.
6. Select the "Name" cell and the empty cell in row 1, column 2. Merge the cells. Select the cell "Outbound Pickups" and the cell beside it. Merge the cells. Repeat this procedure for the "Outbound Deliveries" cell and the "Mileage" cell.
7. Center the two heading lines at the top of the document. Apply 24 points spacing after the "Trip Report" line.
8. Change the top margin to 1.5 inches.
9. Save the document as ***[your initials]*13-23** in your Lesson 13 folder.
10. Submit and close the document.

Lesson Applications

Exercise 13-24

Create a table, enter text in the table, and edit and format the table.

1. Start a new document. Change the line spacing to single, and change the spacing after to 0. Format the document as a memo to Robert Smith from Lynn Tanguay. Use today's date and the subject "Greek Alphabet."
2. Key the text in Figure 13-25 below the memo heading.

Figure 13-25

```
Listed below is a table containing the letters of the
Greek alphabet. Please post and file this table so that
everyone in production will have a reference for the
correct mold to use when embossing Greek letters on our
chocolate bars and chocolate squares.

Please let me know if you have any questions.
```

3. Press Enter two times. Create a table using the Table button and selecting the **Quick Tables** command. Select the **Greek Alphabet** table under the **Double Table** heading.
4. Select the title above the table, and apply 18-point bold and small caps formatting. Center the title. Change the spacing after to 18 points.
5. Select the table, and open the Table Properties dialog box. Center the table horizontally, change the row height to 0.3 inch, and center the text vertically within every cell.
6. Select the table, and click the **Table Tools Design** tab. Click the Line Style button, and choose the first line option. Click the arrow beside the Borders button Borders, and select **Inside Horizontal Border**.
7. Add a single-line bottom border to the subject line.
8. Select every other row beginning with "Beta," and apply light gray shading.
9. Save the document as ***[your initials]*****13-24** in your Lesson 13 folder.
10. Submit and close the document.

Exercise 13-25

Edit and format a table.

1. Open the file **WV Stores - 2**.
2. Select the table, and place a column to the left of the address information. Add a column to the right of the address information.

3. Select each of the rows containing an address, and change the row height to 1.5 inches.
4. Select the first column, and change the column width to 0.5 inch. Change the column width for the second and third columns to 2 inches.
5. Key **Manager** in the first cell of the third column. Key **Matthew Garrett** in the second cell of the third column. Key the following manager names in the appropriate cell of column 3: Fairmont store, **Marianne Bentley**; Morgantown store, **Ethan Myers**; and Wheeling store, **Jackson Sigmon**.
6. Key **Contact Information** in the first cell of the second column. Format the text in the first row using 16-point bold and small caps. Apply gray shading.
7. Click in the first cell of the second row, and key **Clarksburg**. Format the text using 16-point bold, small caps, and black shading. Center the text. Rotate the text so that it reads from the bottom of the cell to the top.
8. Key each city name in the first column, and apply the format used in step 7.
9. Add a row to the top of the table. Merge the cells, and key **WEST VIRGINIA STORES**. Format the text in the first row using 18-point bold, all caps, and center alignment. Place 12 points spacing before and 12 points spacing after the title.
10. Select the cells in the blank row below the Clarksburg store. Merge the cells, and apply gray shading. Merge the cells in the other three blank rows, and apply gray shading.
11. Select each of the cells containing the contact information, and center the text vertically within the cell. Select the text "Manager" and all the names below it, and center the text horizontally and vertically.
12. Center the table horizontally and vertically on the page.
13. Apply a 3-point double-line outside border to the table.
14. Save the document as ***[your initials]*****13-25** in your Lesson 13 folder.
15. Submit and close the document.

Exercise 13-26

Create a table, and edit and format the table.

1. Start a new document, and change the page to landscape orientation.
2. Insert a table with five rows and six columns, and key the text shown in Figure 13-26 in the table.

Figure 13-26

Monday	Tuesday	Wednesday	Thursday	Friday	sat./sun.
			1	2	3/4
5	~~5~~ 6	~~5~~ 7	~~5~~ 8	~~5~~ 9	10/11
12	13	14	15	16	17/18
91	20	21	22	23	2425

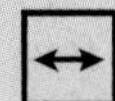

REVIEW

You might need to use the AutoCorrect Options button to undo the fraction ¾ after you key "3/4."

3. Add a sixth row to the table, and key **26**, **27**, **28**, **29**, and **30**, beginning with the first cell.
4. Change each column width to 1.2 inches.
5. Change the weekday headings in the top row to 14-point bold, italic, and centered. Change the top-row height to at least **0.4"**, and vertically center the text.
6. In the cell for day 6, key **Chamber of Commerce meeting** as a new paragraph below the date.
7. In the cell for day 1, key **Mail newsletter** as a new paragraph below the date.
8. In the cell for day 19, key **Meet with store managers** as a new paragraph below the date.
9. Key **Staff meeting** below the date in the cells for days 16 and 30.
10. Change the row height for rows 2 through 6 to exactly **0.9"**.
11. Insert a new first column, merge the cells in the column, and key **JUNE**.
12. Rotate the text "JUNE" until it reads from the bottom to the top of the column. Change the font size to 60 points and the column width to 1 inch. The text should be bold but not italic.
13. Center the text in column 1 vertically and horizontally within the column.
14. Change the zoom level to **Page Width** to view the entire table.
15. Apply a ½-point triple-line outside border to the table.
16. Apply a 3-point solid-line border between the first and second columns, and apply gray shading to the first column.
17. Draw a 2¼-point solid-line border at the bottom of row 1.
18. Center the table vertically and horizontally on the page.
19. Save the document as ***[your initials]*13-26** in your Lesson 13 folder.
20. Submit and close the document.

Exercise 13-27 ◆ Challenge Yourself

Convert text to a table, and then edit and format the table.

1. Open the file **Office Supplies**, and change the page orientation to landscape.
2. At the top of the document key the text in Figure 13-27.

Figure 13-27

```
Campbell's Confections
Internal Supply Requisition
Name:
Department:
```

3. Select the line that begins "Quantity," and convert the text to a table.
4. Insert 12 rows below the column headings.
5. Change the column width of the first column to 0.8 inch, the second column to 0.5 inch, and the "Description" column to 2 inches.
6. Select the header row, apply bold format, and center the text.
7. Apply a table style with header row and banded rows formatting.
8. Select the table, and apply a single-line, ½-point format to all borders.
9. Format the first line of the document title as 20-point bold, small caps, and centered. Format the second line of the title as 12-point, bold, small caps, and centered.
10. Format the "Name" and "Department" lines using bold, small caps, and a right-aligned, solid-leader tab at 7 inches. Press Tab at the end of each line to insert the leader line. Change the left and right indents to 2 inches. Change the spacing after the "Department" line to 24 points.
11. Change the row height for the table to 0.3 inch, and vertically center the text within the cells.
12. Horizontally center the table.
13. Preview the document. Save it as ***[your initials]*****13-27** in your Lesson 13 folder.
14. Submit and close the document.

On Your Own

In these exercises you work on your own, as you would in a real-life business environment. Use the skills you've learned to accomplish the task—and be creative.

Exercise 13-28

Create a table of monthly expenses. Include an expense name column, an average amount column, and a due date column. Adjust the row height and column width, and format the table so that it is readable and attractive. Spell- and grammar-check your document, and save it as ***[your initials]*****13-28**. Submit the document.

Exercise 13-29

Log on to the Internet, and find statistics on five stocks in which you are interested. Create a table showing the history of the stocks. (You might wish to copy and paste information into your document and then convert the text to a table.) Give the document a title, and spell- and grammar-check the document. Save the document as ***[your initials]*****13-29**, and submit it.

Exercise 13-30

Using the table feature, create a calendar for one of the months of the year, similar to the one you created in Exercise 13-26. Format the calendar attractively, and add information you want to remember for particular days. Save the document as ***[your initials]*****13-30**, and submit it.

Lesson 14

Advanced Tables

OBJECTIVES

After completing this lesson, you will be able to:

1. Work with long tables.
2. Use advanced table-formatting options.
3. Work with multiple tables.
4. Perform calculations in a table.
5. Work with Excel spreadsheets within Word documents.

Estimated Time: 1¾ hours

Tables can be an important part of any document. To make your tables readable, you need to know how to control page breaks, create header rows, and even split very long tables. Because tables add a graphical element to a document, Word provides formatting features to enhance them with special styles, spacing, margins, and captions. You can also size tables in a variety of ways to make sure they best fit their contents and the page. If a document includes multiple tables, you might even need to use more than one table on a single page. Word's capability to "nest" tables allows you to create tables within tables.

Word tables can do more than display text in rows and columns. You can use special sorting tools to arrange tabular information and perform calculations on the data in a table. If your needs are more complex, you can create an Excel spreadsheet and import the spreadsheet into a Word document.

Working with Long Tables

When a table spans more than one page, it can be difficult to read unless the column headings appear at the top of each page. Another problem can occur when rows contain multiple lines of text and a page break occurs in the middle of a row. Word provides options for controlling page breaks in a table and for repeating column headings at the top of each page in a multipage table.

Exercise 14-1 CONTROL PAGE BREAKS IN A TABLE

REVIEW
To select an entire table, click the table move handle in the upper left corner of the table.

1. Open the file **Order Form**. This document contains a long, unformatted table that spans three pages.
2. Select the entire table.
3. Click the Table Tools Layout tab, and click the Properties button. Click the Row tab.

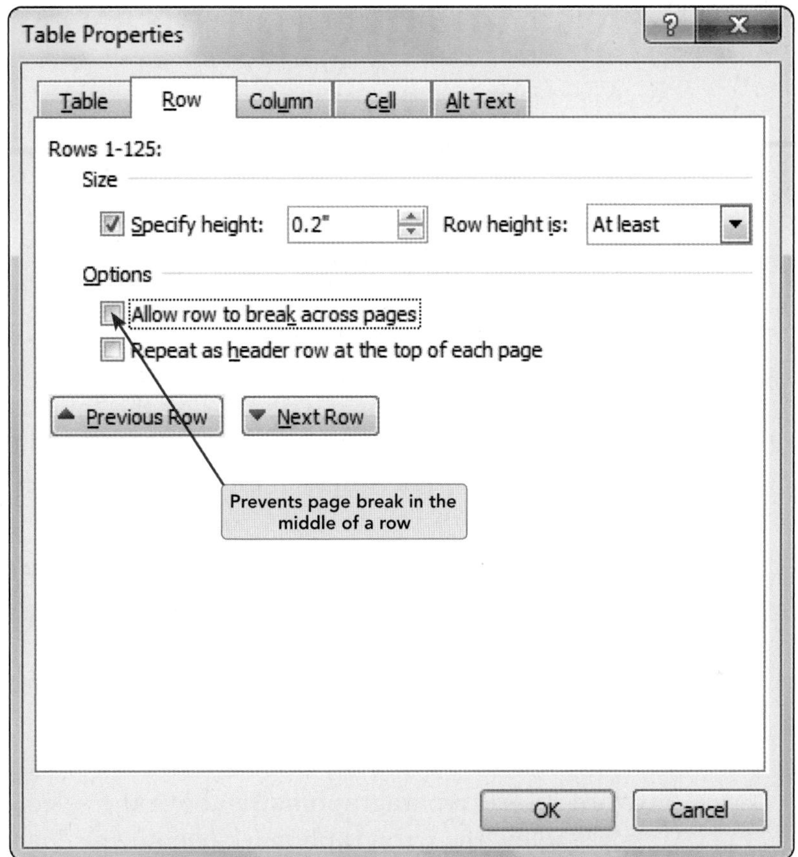

Figure 14-1 Table Properties dialog box with the Row tab displayed

4. Under Options, clear the Allow row to break across pages check box. Click OK. When this option is not checked, page breaks can occur before or after a row, but not in the middle of a row.
5. Click any cell to deselect the table.

Exercise 14-2 DEFINE A HEADER ROW FOR A TABLE

To create table header rows, you must first select the row or rows you want to appear at the top of each page. You can select one or more rows to serve as the table's header rows, but they must be at the beginning of the table.

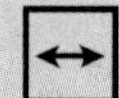

REVIEW

To select a row, position the mouse pointer to the left of the row and then click the mouse when you see the white right-pointing mouse pointer or drag the I-beam pointer across all the cells in the row.

1. Scroll to the top of the table, and select the first two rows of the table.
2. Click the **Table Tools Layout** tab, and click the Repeat Header Rows button.
3. Scroll to the top of page 2. The column headings now appear at the top of the page. They are also repeated at the top of page 3.

Exercise 14-3 TURN OFF THE REPEAT HEADER ROWS OPTION

1. With the first two rows still selected, locate the **Data group** of the Table Tools Layout tab. Notice that Repeat Header Rows is "on." Click **Repeat Header Rows** to turn off the header row feature.
2. Scroll to the top of page 2 to see that the header row no longer appears there. Click the Undo button to reset the header rows.
3. With the first two rows still selected, click the Properties button. Click the **Row** tab. Notice that the **Repeat as header row at the top of each page** check box is selected. Using the Table Properties dialog box is a second way to assign header rows to a table. Click **Cancel** to close the dialog box. Click anywhere in the table to deselect the rows.

Exercise 14-4 SPLIT A TABLE TO CREATE TWO SEPARATE TABLES

1. Near the top of page 3, click in the row containing the text "Chocolate Suckers." Check that the Show/Hide ¶ button ¶ is selected.
2. Click the **Table Tools Layout** tab, and click the Split Table button. Word inserts a paragraph mark above the selected row, and all the rows below the paragraph mark become a separate table. Notice that the new table does not contain the header row you defined previously.
3. Click in the row containing the text "Foil-Wrapped Chocolates," on page 2.
4. Click the Split Table button again to create another split.

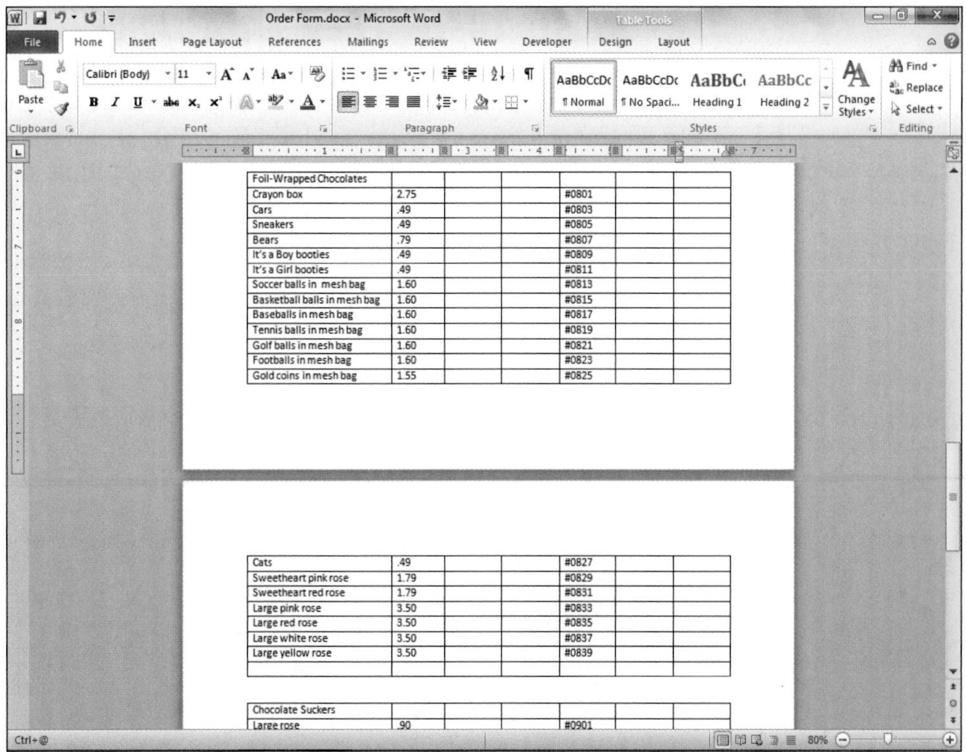

Figure 14-2 Second and third tables created by using the Split Table command

Exercise 14-5 INSERT TEXT ABOVE A TABLE

Sometimes a table is the very first object on a page. In this case, there is no paragraph mark before the table, indicating that there is no blank line above the table on which to key text. Use the Split Table command to insert a blank line above a table when needed.

1. Move to the top of the first page, and click in the table's first cell.
2. Click the **Table Tools Layout** tab, and click the Split Table button. A paragraph mark appears above the table.
3. Key the following text to create a title above the table. Use character and paragraph formatting to create your own design.

   Campbell's Confections
   Store Order Form
   For internal use only

4. With the following information, create a header that appears on all pages except page 1:

   Order Form **Page *[page number]***

5. Format the header text as 10-point Tahoma bold. "Order Form" should be left-aligned, and the page number should be right-aligned.

Exercise 14-6 PREVENT A TABLE FROM BREAKING ACROSS PAGES

In a previous exercise, you used the Row tab of the Table Properties dialog box to prevent page breaks from occurring in the middle of a row. To control page breaks between rows, use the Keep with next paragraph-formatting option.

1. Display nonprinting characters. Go to page 2, and scroll to see table 2, which begins with the row "Foil-Wrapped Chocolates." Notice that the table spans two pages.

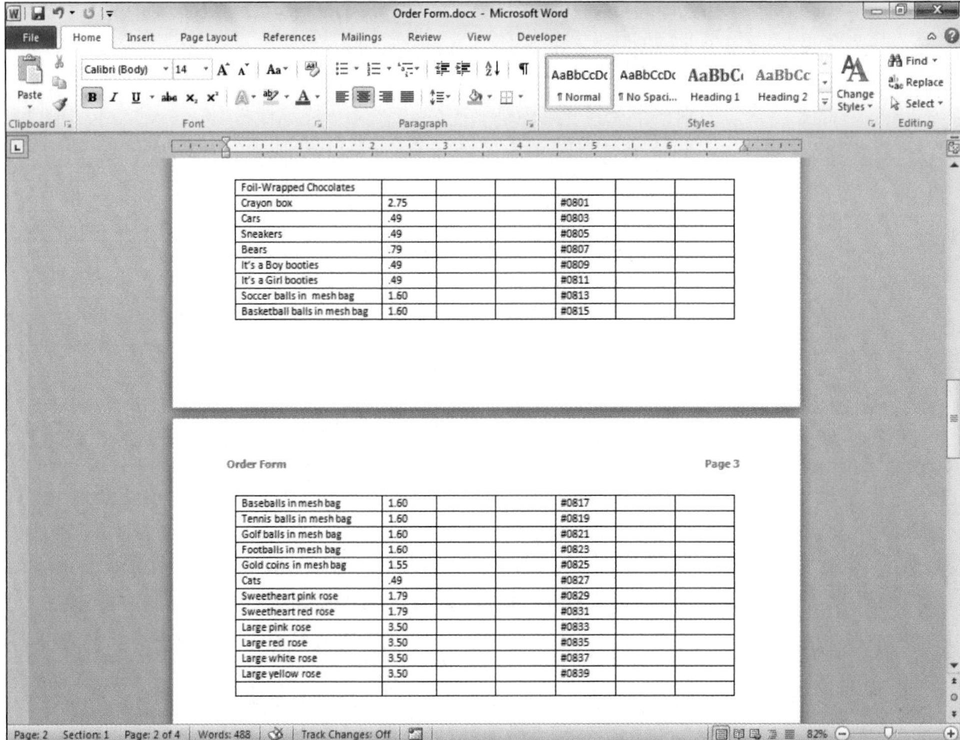

Figure 14-3
Table 2, with a page break between rows

2. Select all rows of the table that display on the bottom of page 2.
3. Open the **Paragraph** dialog box. On the **Line and Page Breaks** tab, select the **Keep with next** check box. Click **OK**. The entire table now appears on page 3.
4. Go to the bottom of page 1, and select the rows from "Almond bark" to the bottom of the page.
5. Apply the **Keep with next** paragraph-formatting option.
6. Go to page 3, and locate the table that begins with the text "Chocolate Suckers." Select all the lines of the table that appear on page 3, and apply the **Keep with next** option.

Using Advanced Table-Formatting Options

Advanced formatting features can enhance the appearance of a table. By changing cell margins, for example, you can add space between columns and rows. Or, if needed, you can decrease cell margins to fit more text within a cell. The Table Styles gallery formats a table by using a table style—a predesigned table format that includes fonts, colors, borders, and other formatting options. AutoFit enables you to automatically resize elements of a table or resize an entire table.

Exercise 14-7 CHANGE CELL MARGINS

Occasionally cells in a table appear crowded because the cell contents are too close to the cell borders; a little extra white space between the text and the borders gives the cells a cleaner appearance. You can control the amount of white space in cells by setting cell margins. You can set cell margins for an entire table using the Table Properties dialog box Table tab, or you can adjust the margins of individual cells using the Table Properties dialog box Cell tab.

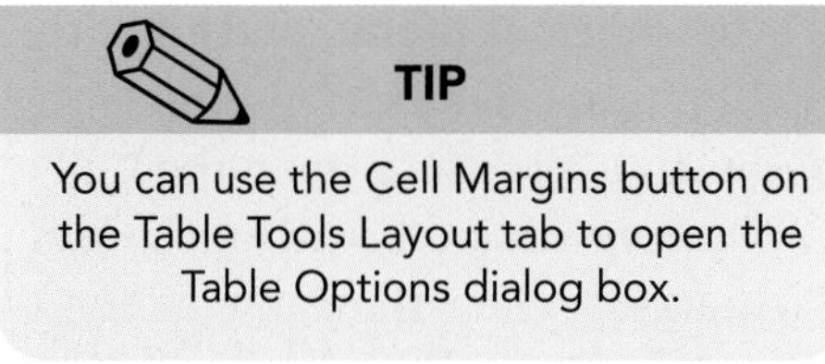

TIP

You can use the Cell Margins button on the Table Tools Layout tab to open the Table Options dialog box.

TIP

If nonprinting characters are displayed, your table's cells might look more crowded than they actually are. To get a better idea of the amount of space in your cells, click the Show/Hide ¶ button to hide these characters.

1. Go to the last table in the document, and select the entire table. Right-click the table, and choose **Table Properties** from the shortcut menu. Click the **Table** tab, and then click the Options button [Options...]. The Table Options dialog box opens.
2. Under **Default cell margins**, change the **Left** and **Right** margin settings to **0.1** inch. Click **OK** to close the Table Options dialog box; then click **OK** again to close the Table Properties dialog box. The slightly wider cell margins indent each cell's contents from the right and left borders. This change has no apparent effect in the table's top row or in the second column, where the text is already centered in the cells and surrounded by plenty of white space.

Figure 14-4
Changing left and right cell margins in the Table Options dialog box

Table Options
Default cell margins
Top: 0" Left: 0.1"
Bottom: 0" Right: 0.1"
Default cell spacing
Allow spacing between cells 0"
Options
Automatically resize to fit contents
OK Cancel

3. Select the first two rows of the first table (the header rows); then right-click to open the shortcut menu.
4. Choose **Table Properties** from the shortcut menu, and then click the **Cell** tab.
5. Click the Options button [Options...] to open the Cell Options dialog box.
6. Under **Cell margins**, clear the **Same as the whole table** check box. The Top, Bottom, Left, and Right text boxes become active.
7. Change the top and bottom margins to **0.08** inch. Click **OK**; then click **OK** again. The header row now has additional white space at the top and bottom. Use the Cell Options dialog box to format selected cells, and use the Table Options dialog box to format the entire table.

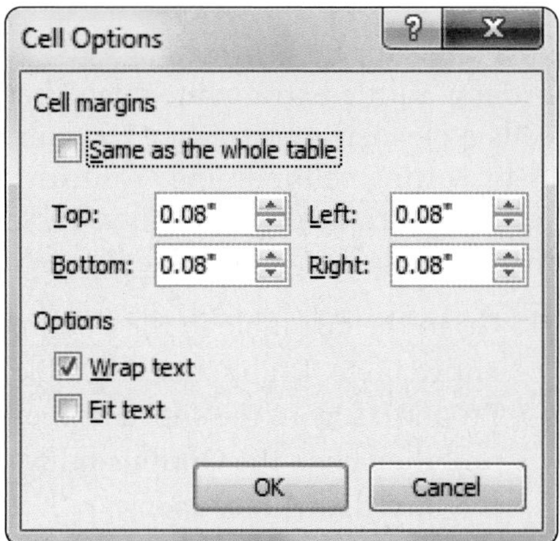

Figure 14-5
Setting top and bottom margins in the Cell Options dialog box

8. Go to the last table in the document, and select the first row of the table (the title row, containing the text "Chocolate Suckers"), and right-click to open the shortcut menu.
9. Choose **Table Properties** from the shortcut menu, and click the **Cell** tab. Click the Options button [Options...] to open the Cell Options dialog box. Under **Cell margins**, clear the **Same as the whole table** check box.
10. Change the top and bottom margins to **0.08** inch. Click **OK**; then click **OK** again. The title row now has additional white space at the top and bottom.

Exercise 14-8 CHANGE VERTICAL ALIGNMENT

TIP

The alignment buttons on the Table Tools Layout tab offer nine options, specifying both vertical and horizontal alignment. (If you right-click a selected table to open the shortcut menu, its Cell Alignment submenu will have the same nine options.) If you want to change the vertical alignment for an entire table but keep the existing horizontal alignments for various columns, use the options offered on the Cell tab of the Table Properties dialog box.

In addition to adjusting cell margins, you can change the vertical alignment of text relative to a cell's top and bottom borders.

1. Select the document's last table, and reopen the Table Properties dialog box.
2. Click the **Row** tab, and change the row height to **0.3** inch.
3. Click the **Cell** tab.
4. Under **Vertical alignment**, choose **Top**. Click **OK**, and then deselect the table. The cells' contents vertically align themselves at the top of each cell.

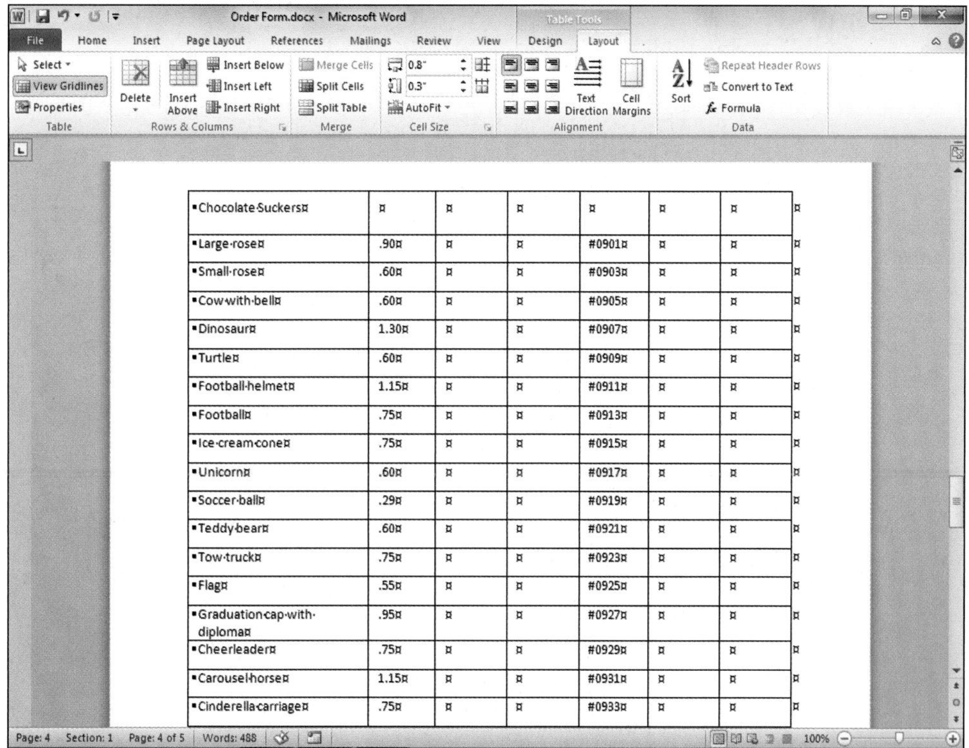

Figure 14-6
Table after changing cell margins and vertical alignment

5. Save the file as ***[your initials]*14-8** in a new folder for Lesson 14. Do not print the document, but leave it open for the next exercise.

Exercise 14-9 CREATE AND MODIFY CUSTOM TABLE STYLES

If you cannot find a table style in the gallery that suits your needs, you can create your own table style. You can even add the new style to Word's Table Styles gallery for use at a later time. When you save a style this way, Word adds it to the template used by the active document; the style will be available in any other document based on the same template.

1. Go to the second table in the document (with the title "Foil-Wrapped Chocolates"), and click in the first row.
2. Click the **Table Tools Design** tab, and locate the **Table Styles** group. Click the More arrow to open the Table Styles gallery. Click **New Table Style**.
3. Key *[your initials]***Table Special 1** in the Name box.
4. Verify that the **Style type** is **Table**.
5. Click the **Apply formatting to** drop-down arrow, and choose **Header row**. The formatting options you select next will apply only to the table's header row.
6. Using the font-formatting tools in the dialog box, set the font to 10-point Tahoma bold. Set the line style to **No Border**. Set the **Fill Color** to a medium blue.

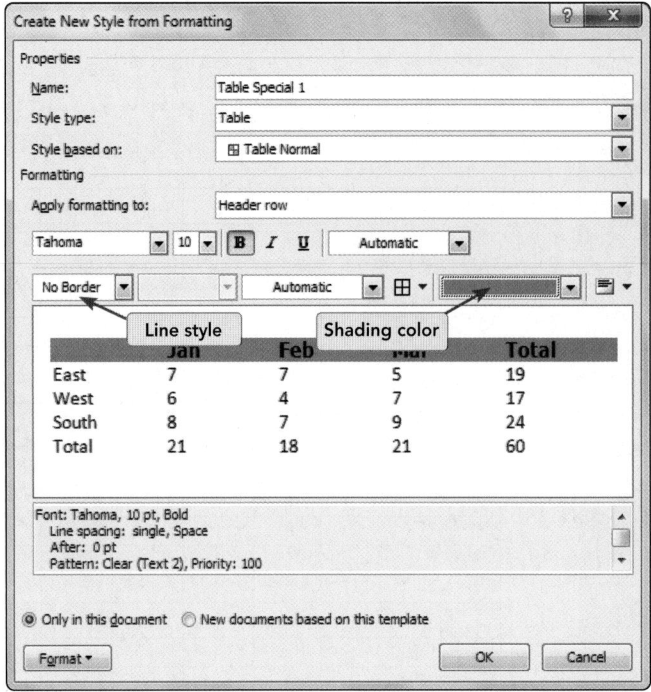

Figure 14-7
Creating a table style for the header row

7. Reopen the **Apply formatting to** drop-down list, and choose **Even banded rows**.
8. Set the **Fill Color** to light blue.
9. Select the **Only in this document** option, and then click **OK**. The new style is added to the list of styles in the Table Styles gallery.
10. Make sure that the insertion point is in the document's second table (with the title "Foil-Wrapped Chocolates"); then click the More arrow in the Table Styles group.
11. Locate the **Custom** heading in the Table Styles gallery. Point to the table style in the Custom section, and read the ScreenTip. Click the ***[your initials]*Table Special 1** style. The new table style is applied to the table.
12. Point to the first table style in the Table Styles group of the Design tab, and notice that the custom style appears on the Ribbon.
13. Click the More arrow, and click **Modify Table Style**. The Modify Style dialog box appears. It provides the same options as the New Style dialog box.
14. Open the **Apply formatting to** drop-down list, and choose **Whole table**. Change the line style from no border to the thin solid line. Set the line width to **¼ pt**. Click the Borders button arrow, and choose **Outside Borders**. Click the Borders button arrow again, and choose **Inside Horizontal Border**.
15. Select the **Only in this document** option; then click **OK**. The table now has an outside border and horizontal borders between all the rows.

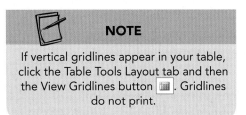

NOTE

If vertical gridlines appear in your table, click the Table Tools Layout tab and then the View Gridlines button. Gridlines do not print.

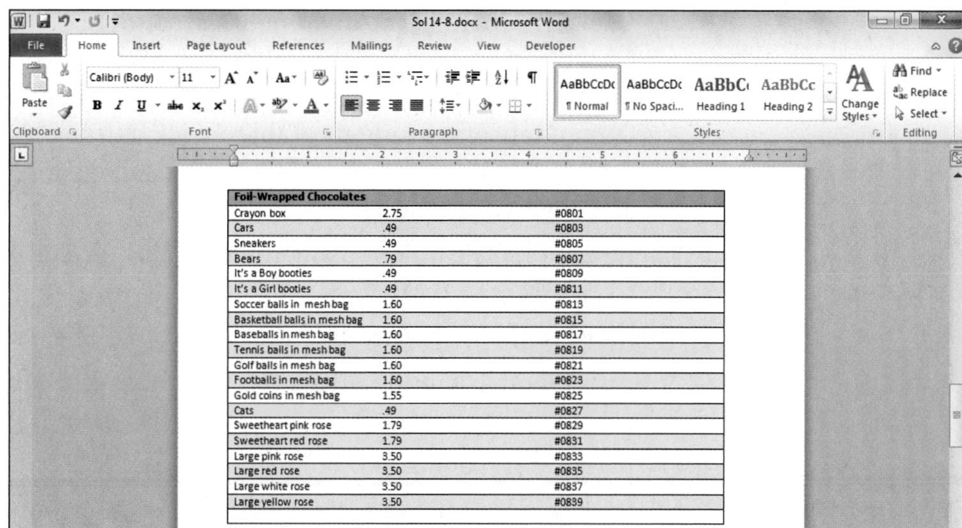

Foil-Wrapped Chocolates		
Crayon box	2.75	#0801
Cars	.49	#0803
Sneakers	.49	#0805
Bears	.79	#0807
It's a Boy booties	.49	#0809
It's a Girl booties	.49	#0811
Soccer balls in mesh bag	1.60	#0813
Basketball balls in mesh bag	1.60	#0815
Baseballs in mesh bag	1.60	#0817
Tennis balls in mesh bag	1.60	#0819
Golf balls in mesh bag	1.60	#0821
Footballs in mesh bag	1.60	#0823
Gold coins in mesh bag	1.55	#0825
Cats	.49	#0827
Sweetheart pink rose	1.79	#0829
Sweetheart red rose	1.79	#0831
Large pink rose	3.50	#0833
Large red rose	3.50	#0835
Large white rose	3.50	#0837
Large yellow rose	3.50	#0839

Figure 14-8
Table with a new custom style

16. Save the document as ***[your initials]*****14-9** in your Lesson 14 folder. Select just the styled table and print it.

Exercise 14-10 ADD TABLE CAPTIONS

A *caption* is a label that identifies a part of a document, usually with a number. A table caption, for example, might include a number for the table, followed by a short description, such as "Table 1: Delivery Schedule." In this exercise, you will add captions to all the tables in your document.

1. Go to the top of the document, and click anywhere in the first table's header row.
2. Click the **References** tab, and click the Insert Caption button. The Caption dialog box opens with the text "Table 1" displayed in the Caption text box.
3. After "Table 1" in the text box, insert a colon (:) and a space. Then key **Signature Chocolates** and click **OK**. The dialog box closes, and the new caption appears above the table.

Figure 14-9
Inserting a table caption

4. Click anywhere in the document's second table ("Foil-Wrapped Chocolates"). To make this table look more consistent with the third table, remove the table style you created earlier. Click the **Table Tools Design** tab, and locate the Table Styles buttons. Point to and click the **Table Grid** table style. The table returns to a simple format, with borders around all cells and no colors.
5. Insert a table caption, using the text **Table 2: Foil-Wrapped Chocolates**. Click **OK**.
6. Move to the table with the title "Chocolate Suckers."
7. Insert a table caption, using the text **Table 3: Chocolate Suckers**.
8. Display the Styles task pane, and modify the Caption style. Change the paragraph spacing to 6 points before and after.
9. Save the document as ***[your initials]*14-10** in your Lesson 14 folder.
10. Submit and close the document.

Working with Multiple Tables

When working with multiple tables on the same page, you can control the position of the tables in several ways. For example, you can do the following:

- Set a table's Text Wrapping property to Around, and then drag the table to any position on the page. If there is already text on the page, it will "flow" around the table.
- Create nested tables by placing tables inside the cells of another table.

Nested tables offer great ease and flexibility for arranging tables and text on a page. You control the position of objects (tables, graphics, and text) by changing the size, position, and margins of the table cells that contain those objects. You can draw a table directly in a cell of another table, or you can move and copy existing tables into another table's cells. A table that contains nested tables is often referred to as a *parent table*.

Exercise 14-11 DRAW A PARENT TABLE

You begin by drawing the parent table, which will contain two nested tables.

1. Open the file **Order Form - 2**.
2. Go to the end of the document. Create the table shown in Figure 14-10 by drawing the table approximately the same size as shown in the figure, but it does not need to be exact. Select the second row (both columns), and click the Distribute Columns button to size the columns equally.

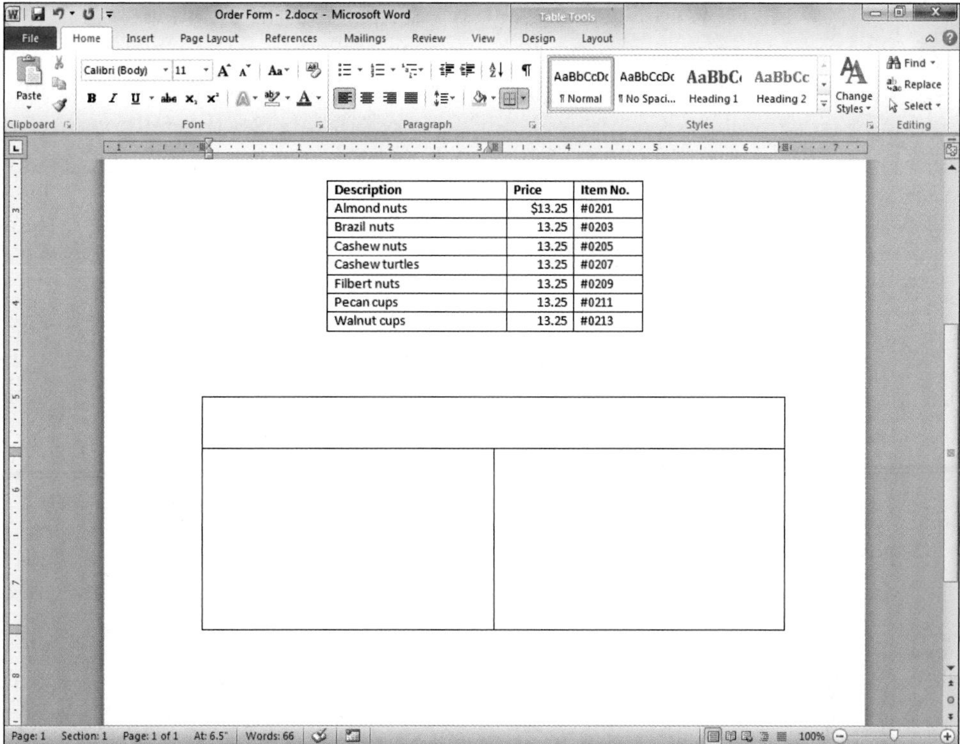

Figure 14-10 Drawing the parent table

3. Select the drawn table. Click the **Table Tools Layout** tab, and click the AutoFit button. Click **AutoFit Window**. Word adjusts the table's width to fill the space between the page margins.
4. Key the following text in the first cell of the drawn table. Apply the No Spacing style (Home tab, Styles gallery) to the paragraph.

   Three times a year, Campbell's Confections schedules a special promotional sale for its chocolate-covered nuts and chocolate melt-a-ways. The chocolate nuts and melt-a-ways are available in milk or dark chocolate. Dates for the promotional sale are listed on the company Web site.

Exercise 14-12 CREATE NESTED SIDE-BY-SIDE TABLES

1. Select the first table at the top of the document.
2. Cut the selected cells, and paste them into the left cell in the second row of the table you drew in the previous exercise.
3. Click anywhere in the nested table, click to select the **Table Tools Layout** tab, and click **AutoFit** and **AutoFit Contents**.
4. Select the table that begins "Almond nuts," cut it, and then paste the table into the right cell of the new table's second row.
5. Position the insertion point above the table, and key **Chocolate Promotional Sale** as a title for the document. Select the title, and apply 14-point bold and small caps formatting. Delete the extra paragraph marks above the title.

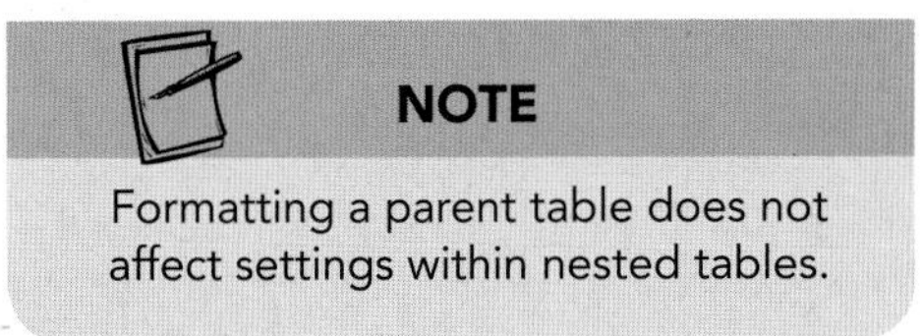

Formatting a parent table does not affect settings within nested tables.

6. Select the parent table (which now contains the two nested tables). Set all the cell margins to **0.05** inch by clicking the Cell Margins button on the Table Tools Layout tab. Set the cells' vertical alignment to **Top** by choosing the Cell tab in the Table Properties dialog box.

Exercise 14-13 ADJUST THE HEIGHT OF A TABLE

You can adjust the height of a table by adjusting the height of individual rows or by dragging the table resize handle up or down. However, to use the table resize handle, you need to first clear the Specify height option on the Row tab of the Table Properties dialog box. Otherwise, the rows will automatically readjust to the specified height when you release the table resize handle.

1. Select the melt-a-way table on the left within the parent table, and then open the Table Properties dialog box.
2. Click the **Row** tab, deselect the **Specify height** check box, and click **OK**.
3. Using steps 1 and 2 as a guide, clear the **Specify height** check box for the table on the right within the parent table.
4. Select the table on the left, and apply the **AutoFit Window** property. Then apply the **AutoFit Window** property to the table on the right. Now both of the nested tables should fill the space of the parent table's cells.

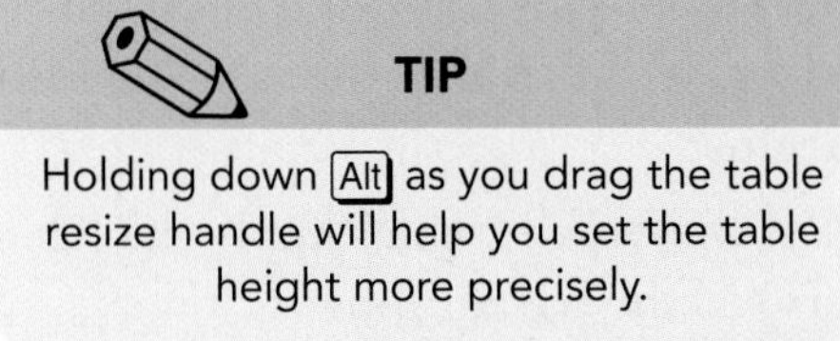

Holding down Alt as you drag the table resize handle will help you set the table height more precisely.

5. Click within the table on the left, and drag the resize handle downward to make the table the same height as the parent table cell height. Drag the resize handle for the table on the right downward to make the table equal to the size of the table on the left.
6. Select the entire parent table, and apply a light gray shading. Click in the first column in the table on the left (melt-a-ways), and click the Sort button. Sort the Description column in ascending order. Click **OK**.

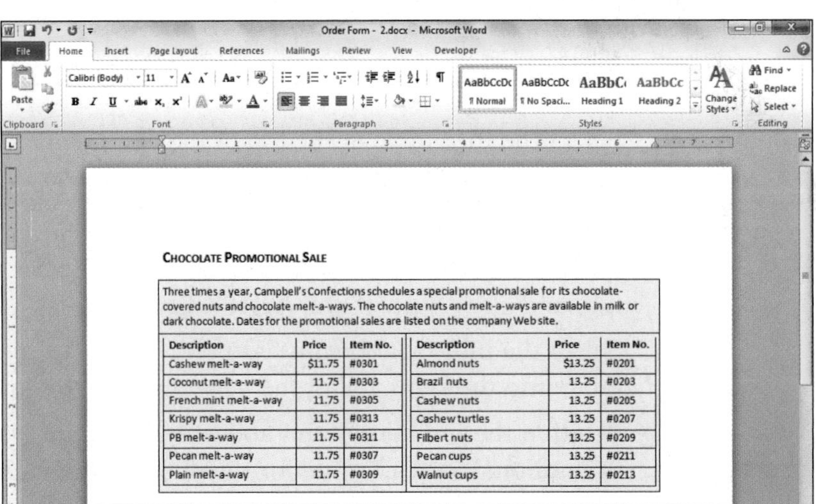

CHOCOLATE PROMOTIONAL SALE

Three times a year, Campbell's Confections schedules a special promotional sale for its chocolate-covered nuts and chocolate melt-a-ways. The chocolate nuts and melt-a-ways are available in milk or dark chocolate. Dates for the promotional sales are listed on the company Web site.

Description	Price	Item No.	Description	Price	Item No.
Cashew melt-a-way	$11.75	#0301	Almond nuts	$13.25	#0201
Coconut melt-a-way	11.75	#0303	Brazil nuts	13.25	#0203
French mint melt-a-way	11.75	#0305	Cashew nuts	13.25	#0205
Krispy melt-a-way	11.75	#0313	Cashew turtles	13.25	#0207
PB melt-a-way	11.75	#0311	Filbert nuts	13.25	#0209
Pecan melt-a-way	11.75	#0307	Pecan cups	13.25	#0211
Plain melt-a-way	11.75	#0309	Walnut cups	13.25	#0213

Figure 14-11
Nested tables

7. Save the document as ***[your initials]*14-13** in your Lesson 14 folder. Submit and close the document.

Performing Calculations in a Table

You can insert fields in any table to perform basic calculations.

To perform a calculation in a Word table, you insert a formula field within the cell that will display the result. The formula includes a *function,* which is a predefined mathematical operation. The function must also include a reference to the cells containing the numbers to be calculated. A function can use special built-in bookmarks that tell it to calculate all the cells above it or to its left. You can also tell the function which cells to include in the calculation by keying their cell addresses into the function.

Here is an example of a formula field that you might use in a Word table:

{=SUM(ABOVE)}

In this formula, =SUM() is the function, and ABOVE (placed inside the function's parentheses) is the bookmark, telling Word to add the values in the cells directly above the formula. The equals sign (=) indicates that the field is a formula field. Curly braces always surround fields.

TABLE 14-1 Common Functions for Tables

Function	Result
AVERAGE()	The average of a list of values
COUNT()	The number of items in a list
PRODUCT()	The result from multiplying a list of numbers
SUM()	The result from adding a list of numbers

TABLE 14-2 Special Bookmarks for Tables

Bookmark	Result
ABOVE	All the cells in the formula's column above the formula, from the formula to the first cell that does not contain a number.
LEFT	All the cells in the formula's row to the left of the formula, from the formula to the first cell that does not contain a number.

Exercise 14-14 CREATE A TABLE THAT PERFORMS CALCULATIONS

1. Start a new document. Key the following text as a document heading. Format it attractively, using character and paragraph formatting.

   Campbell's Confections
   State Totals
   Chocolate-Covered Nuts—2009 through 2011

TIP

Tables are made up of rows and columns. Each column is identified by a letter (A, B, C, and so on), and each row is identified by a number (1, 2, 3, and so on). Each cell has a unique address, which is determined by combining its column letter and its row number. The first cell in a table occurs where the first column (column A) intersects the first row (row 1), so the cell's address is A1. Likewise, the second cell in the first column is cell A2, the third cell in the fourth row is C4, and so on. Figure 14-12 includes headings to help you identify the columns, rows, and cell addresses.

2. Insert two or three blank lines after the heading, depending on the line spacing and spacing-after format applied to the last line of the heading.
3. With the insertion point on the last blank line below the heading, insert a new table with five columns and five rows. (Use the **Insert** tab and the **Table** command.)
4. Key the data shown in Figure 14-12, but do not key the column headings (A, B, C, and so on) or the row headings (1, 2, 3, and so on). Remember to key the commas.

Figure 14-12

	A	B	C	D	E
1		2009	2010	2011	Average
2	Pennsylvania	4,129	4,560	4,401	
3	Ohio	1,206	1,117	1,040	
4	West Virginia	3,588	4,264	4,502	
5	Total				

5. Position the insertion point within the table. Open the **Table Properties** dialog box, and click the **Table** tab. Set the table's preferred width to **5.5** inches, and center the table horizontally on the page. Format the table text as 10-point Arial, and apply a light aqua shading. Select columns 2 through 5, and center the text. Apply bold format to the text in the first row and the first column.

Exercise 14-15 FIND AVERAGE VALUES IN A TABLE

In the "Average" column of the table, you want to show the average number of sales of chocolate-covered nuts for each state during the past 3 years. You can do this by inserting a formula field into cells E2, E3, and E4. Each formula will calculate the average value of the three cells immediately to its left.

1. Click in cell E2 (the first cell below the "Average" column heading).

Figure 14-13
Formula dialog box

Formula
Formula:
=SUM(LEFT)
Number format:
Paste function:
Paste bookmark:
OK
Cancel

2. Click the **Table Tools Layout** tab, and click the Formula button to open the Formula dialog box.
3. Select all the text in the **Formula** text box except the equals sign (=), and press Delete. Only the equals sign should remain in the box.

4. Open the Paste function drop-down list, and choose AVERAGE. The function name AVERAGE appears in the Formula text box, followed by a set of empty parentheses. A blinking insertion point appears between the parentheses.
5. Key **LEFT** between the parentheses. This bookmark tells the function to calculate the values in all the cells immediately to the left that contain numbers.
6. Open the Number format drop-down list, choose the #,##0 option, and click OK. In cell E2, the number 4,363 appears; this is the average of the values in the three cells to the left of the formula.

> **NOTE**
>
> If you create a formula field in one cell and copy it into another cell, the copied formula will display the same results as the original. This is because Word's formulas are not relative; that is, they do not automatically adjust themselves when copied or moved to a new location. If you want to use the same formula in different cells, you should create a new formula each time to make sure it contains the correct cell references. If a bookmark is used in the formula, it may be possible to copy the formula, paste it, and update the field by pressing F9.

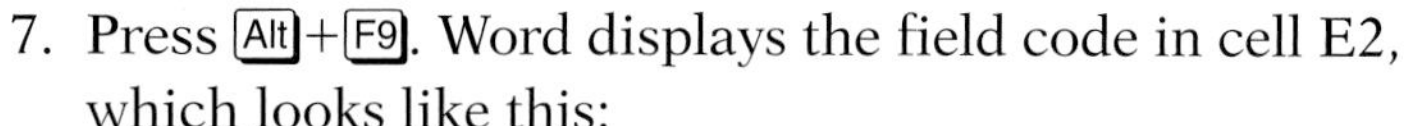

7. Press Alt+F9. Word displays the field code in cell E2, which looks like this:

   {=AVERAGE(LEFT) \# "#,##0"}

8. Press Alt+F9 again to hide the field code and to display normal values in the table.
9. Click in cell E3, and then click the Table Tools Layout tab. Click the Formula button. Delete the contents of the Formula box, and key **=AVERAGE(B3,C3,D3)**. Do not insert any blank spaces in the formula. Set the Number format to #,##0 and click OK. The value 1,121 appears in the cell. This time, instead of using a bookmark to identify the cells to be calculated, you identified them individually by keying each cell's address, separated from the next address by a comma.
10. Click in cell E4, and open the Formula dialog box. Delete the contents of the Formula text box and key **=AVERAGE(B4:D4)**. Do not insert any blank spaces in the formula. Set the Number format to #,##0 and click OK. The value 4,118 appears in the cell. This time, you identified the range of cells to be calculated by keying the range's first cell (B4) and last cell (D4), separated by a colon.

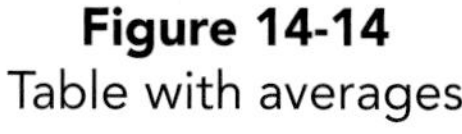

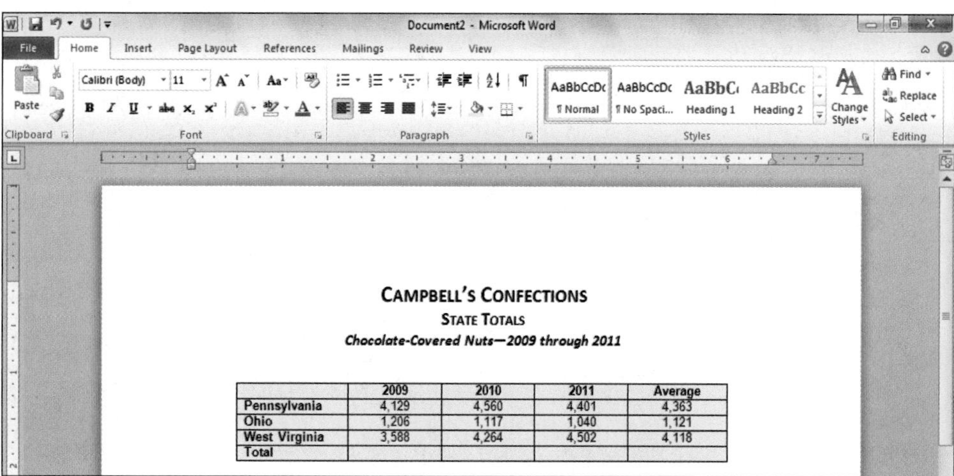

CAMPBELL'S CONFECTIONS
STATE TOTALS
Chocolate-Covered Nuts—2009 through 2011

	2009	2010	2011	Average
Pennsylvania	4,129	4,560	4,401	4,363
Ohio	1,206	1,117	1,040	1,121
West Virginia	3,588	4,264	4,502	4,118
Total				

Figure 14-14
Table with averages

11. Save the file as ***[your initials]*14-15** in your Lesson 14 folder. Leave it open for the next exercise.

Exercise 14-16 FIND TOTAL VALUES IN A TABLE

In the "Total" row of the table, you want to show the total number of sales of chocolate-covered nuts for each of the past 3 years. You can do this by inserting a formula field into cells B5, C5, and D5. Each formula will sum the values of the three cells immediately above it.

1. Click in cell B5 (the first cell to the right of the "Total" row heading), and open the Formula dialog box.
2. Look at the **Formula** text box; it should already contain the formula **=SUM(ABOVE)**. If so, go on to step 3. If not, select the **Formula** text box contents and key **=SUM(ABOVE)**.
3. Set the number format to **#,##0** and click **OK**. In cell B5, the number 10,932 appears. This total is too high. That is because the ABOVE bookmark told Word to total the values in all four cells above the formula, including the date. You don't want to include the date in the total, so you need to make a change.
4. Click in cell B5, and open the **Formula** dialog box. Delete the contents of the **Formula** text box and key **=SUM(B2,B3,B4)**. Do not insert any blank spaces in the formula. Set the number format to **#,##0** and click **OK**. The correct value (8,923) appears in the cell.
5. Click in cell C5, and open the Formula dialog box. Delete the contents of the **Formula** text box and key **=SUM(C2:C4)**. Do not insert any blank spaces in the formula. Set the number format to **#,##0** and click **OK**. The correct value (9,941) appears in the cell.
6. Click in cell D5, open the **Formula** dialog box, and create a formula that totals the values in cells D2, D3, and D4. Choose the same number format used in the preceding steps.

NOTE

The Paste function drop-down list in the Formula dialog box includes functions that range from simple (such as COUNT, which shows how many items are in a list) to complex (such as IF, which is a logical function that determines whether a criterion is true or false). By familiarizing yourself with these functions, you can add more power to your tables and avoid using Excel spreadsheets in your Word documents.

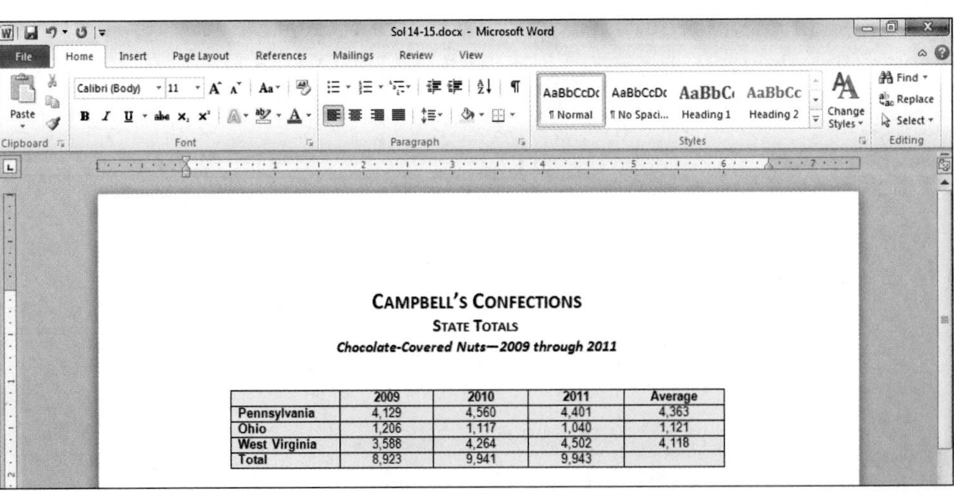

CAMPBELL'S CONFECTIONS

STATE TOTALS

Chocolate-Covered Nuts—2009 through 2011

	2009	2010	2011	Average
Pennsylvania	4,129	4,560	4,401	4,363
Ohio	1,206	1,117	1,040	1,121
West Virginia	3,588	4,264	4,502	4,118
Total	8,923	9,941	9,943	

Figure 14-15 Table with totals

7. Save the file as ***[your initials]*14-16** in your Lesson 14 folder. Submit and close the document.

Using Excel Spreadsheets in Word Documents

Word's advanced table features help you control many visual and structural effects in tables. Sometimes, however, you need the full strength of an Excel spreadsheet. You can easily insert an Excel spreadsheet into a Word document.

When you create a new Excel spreadsheet from within Word, it becomes an *embedded spreadsheet*. An embedded spreadsheet is completely contained in the Word document and does not have a corresponding Excel file. You can also create an embedded spreadsheet from an existing Excel file, but if you do this, changes you make in the embedded spreadsheet will be reflected only in the Word document and not in the original Excel file.

If you want an Excel file to be updated each time you make changes to its spreadsheet within a Word document, you must *link* the spreadsheet rather than embed it. When you work with a linked spreadsheet, all the spreadsheet's information is stored within the Excel file, and the Word document contains only a reference or pointer to the Excel file. None of the actual information is saved with the Word file.

Exercise 14-17 EMBED A NEW EXCEL SPREADSHEET IN A WORD DOCUMENT

1. Start a new document. Key the following text as a document heading. Format it attractively, using character and paragraph formatting or other effects.

   Campbell's Confections
   Cost Analysis
   Chocolate-Covered Nuts—2009 through 2011

2. Press Enter twice after the heading.
3. With the insertion point on the second blank line, click the **Insert** tab, click the Table button, and click **Excel Spreadsheet** in the table menu. An Excel spreadsheet is inserted into your document.
4. Notice that the Ribbon tabs contain Excel options and that the group commands have changed to Excel's commands.

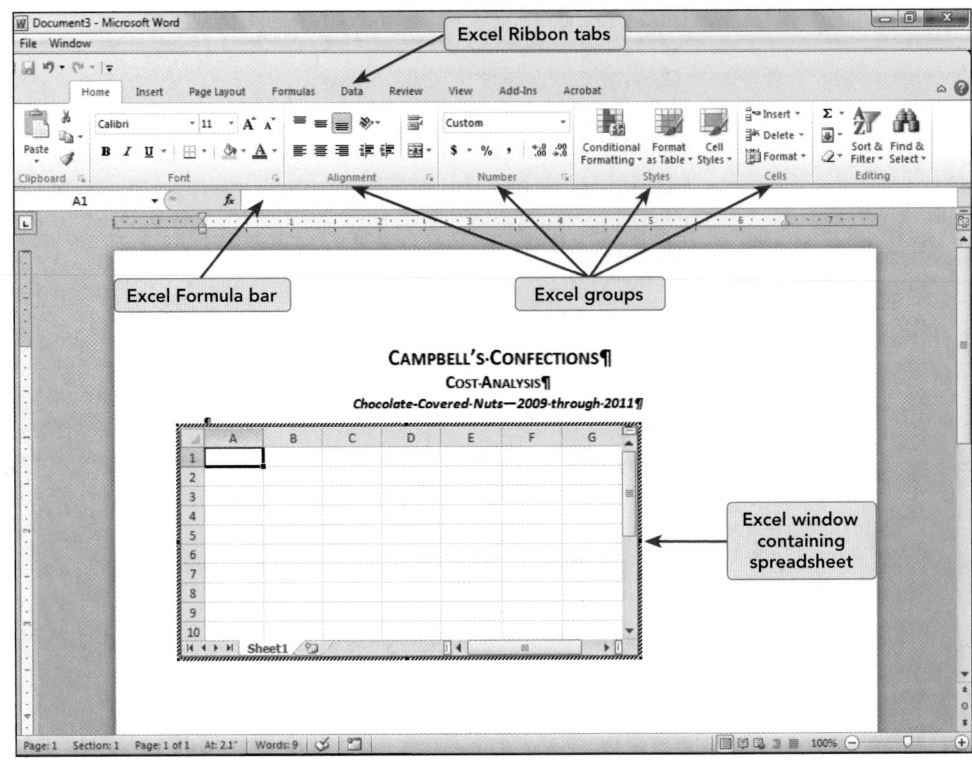

Figure 14-16 Excel spreadsheet inserted in a Word document

Exercise 14-18 ENTER AND FORMAT DATA

1. Key the data shown in Figure 14-17 into the cells of the Excel spreadsheet. Press the arrow keys to move between cells. In cell E2, key the formula as shown in the figure, including the punctuation. Do not include spaces before or after the formula. Press Enter after keying the formula.

Figure 14-17

	A	B	C	D	E
1		2009	2010	2011	Average
2	Pennsylvania	2200	2500	2800	=AVERAGE(B2:D2)
3	Ohio	1800	2200	2600	
4	West Virginia	3000	3300	3600	

2. Click anywhere outside the Excel window to view your spreadsheet in Word.
3. Double-click the spreadsheet to reopen the Excel window.
4. Working in the Excel window, move your mouse pointer over cell A1. When you see the white cross pointer, drag diagonally down and across to select all the cells from A1 to E4 in the Excel window.
5. Click the Increase Indent button on the **Home** tab, in the **Alignment** group. This button adds more space between the columns of text and numbers.

6. Right-click the selected cells, and choose **Format Cells** from the shortcut menu. The Format Cells dialog box opens.
7. Click the **Fill** tab, and choose a light aqua color under **Background Color**.
8. Click the **Font** tab. Verify that the font settings are 10-point Calibri. Click **OK**.
9. With the cells still selected, click the Format button on the **Home** tab, in the **Cells** group. Click **AutoFit Column Width** from the drop-down list. The cells are now wide enough for all the text and numbers.
10. Select cells B2 through E4, and click the Format button. Click **Format Cells.** Choose the **Number** tab, click the **Number** category, set Decimal places to **0**, and click the **Use 1000 Separator (,)** box to use commas in values that are greater than 999 Click **OK**.
11. Click cell E2 to make it active. (You previously keyed a formula in this cell.)
12. Move the white cross pointer from within the cell to the bottom right corner of the cell until it becomes a black cross pointer +.
13. Drag down to cell E4, and then release the mouse button. The formula in cell E2 is automatically copied into cells E3 and E4. This is Excel's AutoFill feature.

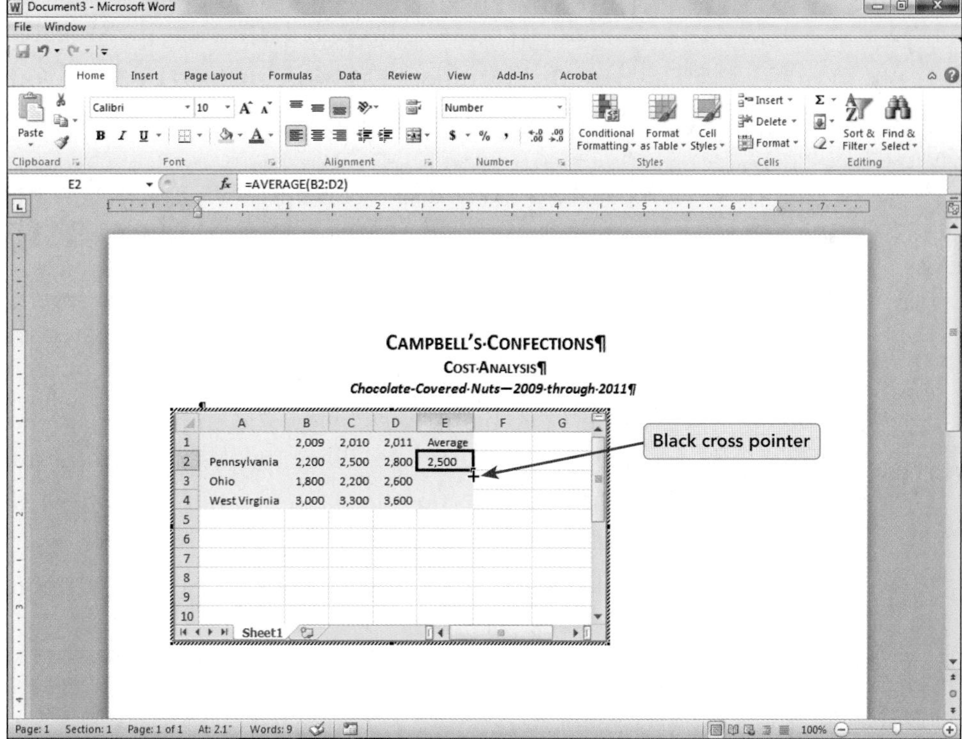

Figure 14-18 Using Excel's AutoFill feature

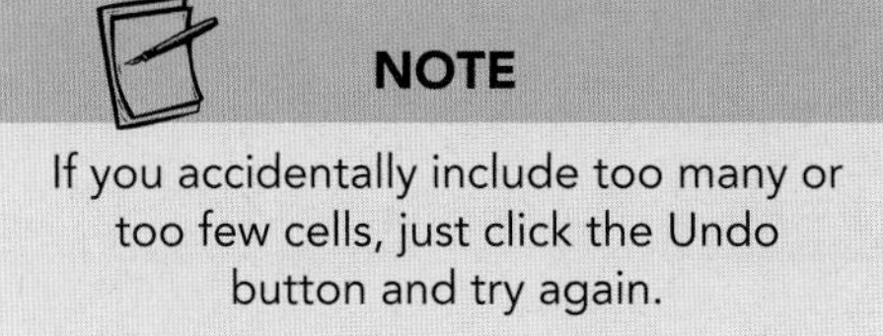

NOTE

If you accidentally include too many or too few cells, just click the Undo button and try again.

14. Click outside the spreadsheet to close Excel and return to the Word document.

Exercise 14-19 ADD A CAPTION TO AN EMBEDDED EXCEL SPREADSHEET

1. Click the embedded spreadsheet once to select it as a Word object. When selected, a spreadsheet is surrounded by a border and square sizing handles.
2. Click the **References** tab, and click the Insert Caption button. In the Caption dialog box, check that the **Label** list box is set to **Table**.
3. In the **Caption** text box, edit the caption to read **Table 1: Cost of Chocolate-Covered Nuts**. Click **OK**.
4. Select both the caption and the table, and press Ctrl+E. The table and its caption are now centered horizontally.
5. Select just the caption, and change it to 10-point Tahoma bold.
6. Double-click the spreadsheet to reopen the Excel window. Point to the small black square sizing handle in the middle of the right border of the spreadsheet. The mouse pointer changes to a two-headed arrow ↔. Drag the border to the left until the empty columns no longer display and you see columns A through E.
7. Drag the sizing handle of the bottom border (the black square in the middle of the border) up until the empty rows no longer display. You should see rows 1 through 4. Deselect the spreadsheet.
8. Save the document as ***[your initials]*14-19** in your Lesson 14 folder. Keep the document open for the next exercise.

Exercise 14-20 CREATE A WORD TABLE FROM AN EXCEL SPREADSHEET

You can easily copy information from an Excel spreadsheet and paste it into a Word document. When you do this, the pasted information becomes a Word table you can treat just as you would any other Word table.

1. Insert two blank lines below the embedded spreadsheet you created in the previous exercise. Place the insertion point on the second blank line.
2. While keeping the Word document open, start Excel. Open the Excel file **2011**.
3. Select cells A4 to D8, and copy them to the Clipboard.

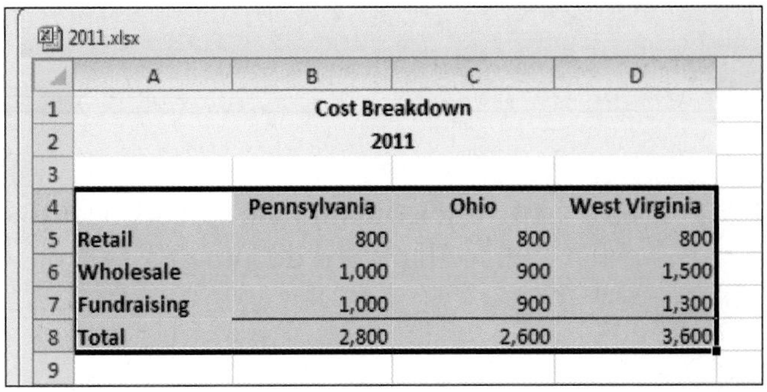

Figure 14-19 Selecting cells in the Excel spreadsheet

2011.xlsx

	A	B	C	D
1		Cost Breakdown		
2		2011		
3				
4		Pennsylvania	Ohio	West Virginia
5	Retail	800	800	800
6	Wholesale	1,000	900	1,500
7	Fundraising	1,000	900	1,300
8	Total	2,800	2,600	3,600
9				

REVIEW

The simplest way to switch to an open document or application is to click its button on the Windows taskbar.

4. Without closing the Excel spreadsheet, switch to ***[your initials]*****14-19** Word document.
5. With the insertion point on the second blank line below the table you created earlier, paste the Clipboard contents. The Excel spreadsheet cells appear in the Word document as a table.
6. Select the table and format it with the following attributes:
   - Using the Table Properties dialog box, **Table** tab, change the preferred width to **4.0** inches and center the table horizontally. Use the **Row** tab to format the row heights to at least **0.2** inch.
   - Text in the second, third, and fourth columns should be right-aligned. Text in the first column should be left-aligned.
   - Change the font in all cells to 10-point Calibri, with no bold or italic.
   - Change the cell shading to match Table 1.
   - Insert a caption with the text **Table 2: Cost Breakdown—2011**.
   - Change the caption font to 10-point Tahoma bold, centered.

NOTE

When you paste the table into the Word document, the Paste Options button appears. This button's options let you keep the source formatting, format the table to match the destination document's styles, create a link and keep the source formatting, create a link and use the destination document's styles, or keep text only. If you do not use this button to select any options, the pasted object maintains its original formatting by default.

Figure 14-20
Formatted table in the Word document

Table 2: Cost Breakdown—2011

	Pennsylvania	Ohio	West Virginia
Retail	800	800	800
Wholesale	1,000	900	1,500
Fundraising	1,000	900	1,300
Total	2,800	2,600	3,600

NOTE

Because pasting Excel information into Word creates a Word table, you can edit the information just as you would any Word table. You can also create a nested table by pasting the Excel information into a cell of an existing Word table.

7. Save the document as ***[your initials]*****14-20** in your Lesson 14 folder. Keep the document open for the next exercise.
8. Switch to Excel, and close the file **2011** without saving it (File tab, Close). Leave Excel open for the next exercise.

Exercise 14-21 EMBED AN EXISTING EXCEL SPREADSHEET

After you copy Excel spreadsheet cells to the Clipboard, you can use the Paste command to insert the cells into a Word document, creating a Word table. If you use the Paste Special command, however, you can insert the table in one of several different formats.

1. With your Word document still open, switch to Excel if necessary, and open the file **2010**.
2. Select cells A4 to D8, and copy them to the Clipboard.
3. Switch to your Word document. Insert two blank lines below Table 2, and position the insertion point on the second line.
4. Click the Home tab, and click the Paste button down arrow. Click Paste Special. The Paste Special dialog box opens.
5. Choose Microsoft Excel Worksheet Object from the list. Read the contents of the Result box at the bottom of the Paste Special dialog box.

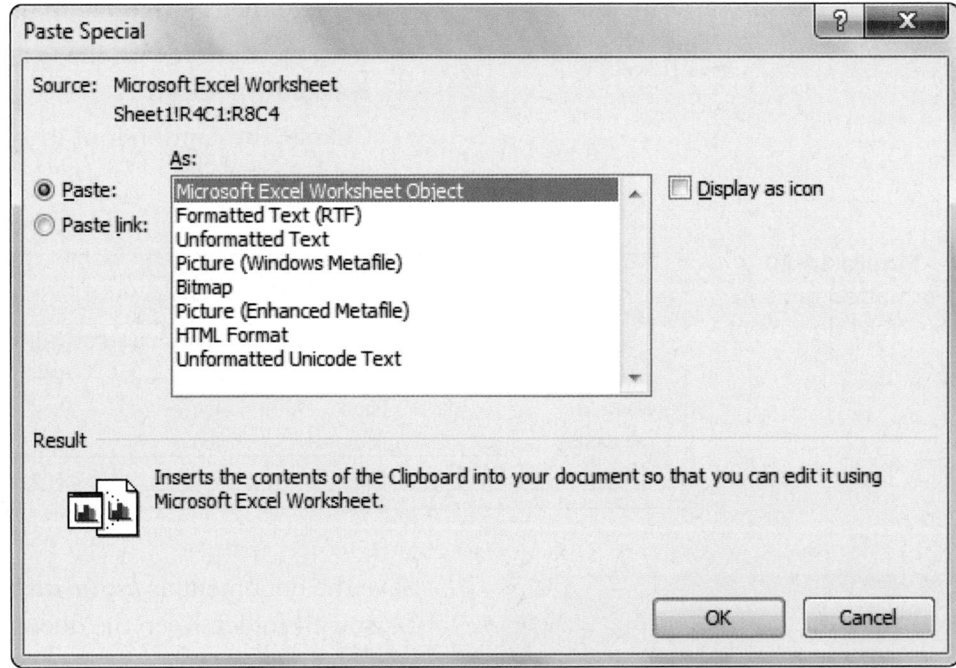

Figure 14-21
Paste Special dialog box

6. Make sure the Paste option is selected (not Paste link), and click OK. An embedded spreadsheet appears in the Word document. If you edit this spreadsheet, changes will be saved in Word. The original Excel spreadsheet will not be changed.

7. Right-click the embedded spreadsheet, and choose Format Object from the shortcut menu to open the Format Object dialog box.

TIP

If an object's wrapping style is set to In line with text, you can use the alignment buttons on the Ribbon for horizontal positioning. When the in-line option is not set, use the Format Object dialog box or the Table Properties dialog box to control the horizontal position.

8. Click the Layout tab, and set the wrapping style to In line with text if it is not already selected. Click the Size tab and change the Width to **4.0** inches. Click OK. If the table is not already center-aligned, press Ctrl+E. The spreadsheet is now aligned with the table above it and surrounded by a border and sizing handles.
9. Insert a caption for the embedded spreadsheet, using the text **Table 3: Cost Breakdown—2010**. Format the caption to match the other captions in the document.
10. Double-click the spreadsheet to open the Excel window. Change the font, font size, and cell shading to match the other tables in the document.
11. Save the document as ***[your initials]*14-21** in your Lesson 14 folder. Keep the document open for the next exercise.
12. Switch to Excel, and close **2010** without saving it. Leave Excel open for the next exercise.

Exercise 14-22 LINK AN EXCEL SPREADSHEET

If you link cells from an Excel spreadsheet, all changes you make—whether in Excel or in Word—are saved in the Excel spreadsheet and reflected in the Word document. When you are working with a linked spreadsheet inside a Word document, the spreadsheet file is called the *source document* and the Word document to which you link it is called the *destination document*.

1. Switch to your Word document. Insert two blank lines below Table 3 and position the insertion point on the second line.
2. Switch to Excel and open the file **2009**. Save the file as ***[your initials]*14-22** in your Lesson 14 folder.
3. Select cells A4 to D8, and copy them to the Clipboard.
4. Switch to your Word document, and click the Paste button down arrow. Click Paste Special. The Paste Special dialog box opens.
5. Select the Paste link option, and choose Microsoft Excel Worksheet Object from the list box. Click OK.
6. Use the Format Object dialog box to change the linked spreadsheet's width to **4.0** inches. Center the object horizontally between the page margins if it is not already centered.
7. Double-click the linked spreadsheet object to switch to Excel.

8. Press Esc to turn off the moving marquee border around cells A4:D8. (In Excel, this marquee border indicates that the selected cells have been copied to the Clipboard.) Click cell C6, which contains the number 999. Key **500** and press Enter. The number 500 appears in the cell.

NOTE

When you double-click a linked spreadsheet to make changes, the source document opens. After making the changes, you must save the source document. If you do not save it, the changes will not be reflected the next time you open the destination document (the Word document). This happens because when you open the Word document, it looks at the Excel spreadsheet to find the information that will be displayed.

9. Select cells A4 to D8, and change the cell shading, font size, and font effects to match the other tables in the Word document.
10. Resave the Excel spreadsheet; then close the spreadsheet and close Excel. Your Word document appears with the changes reflected in the last table. If the document does not reflect the changes, right-click the table and click **Update Link**.
11. Create a caption for the last table, using the text **Table 4: Cost Breakdown—2009**. Format the caption to match the other captions in the document.
12. Save the document as ***[your initials]*****14-22**.

Exercise 14-23 EDIT A LINK TO MAKE A DOCUMENT PORTABLE

A linked spreadsheet in a Word document exists within Word as a Link field. A Link field is similar to a Reference field, but it references a spreadsheet instead of a bookmark. When you link a spreadsheet, the Link field includes the source document's entire path as part of the link (for example, "C:\\StudentData\\Lesson14\\g114-22.xlsx"). If you move the source and data file to a different folder or a removable storage device, the link will be broken because the destination document (Word) will still look for the source document (Excel) in the C:\StudentData\Lesson14 folder.

You can edit the link to remove the path, leaving only the file name. Then Word will look for the source file in the same folder in which the Word document is saved. In this case, you can copy and move the source and destination files wherever you want, as long as you put them both in the same folder.

1. With Table 4 selected, press Alt+F9 to display the field codes. Notice that all the tables except the Word table (Table 2) change to field codes. Notice also that the captions contain a Seq field.
2. Locate the Link field at the bottom of the document. This field starts with the text "LINK."

Figure 14-22
Editing a Link field

```
{ LINK Excel.Sheet.12 "\\\\DELL\\Public\\Documents\\
Student Data Files\\Lesson 14\\

GL 14-22.xlsx" "Sheet1!R4C1:R8C4" \a \p \* MERGEFORMAT}

{ LINK Excel.Sheet.12 "GL 14-22.xlsx" "Sheet1!R4C1:R8C4"
\a \p \* MERGEFORMAT }
```

Path and file name before editing

File name after editing

3. Within the Link field, locate the path and file name. It might be similar to "C:\\Lesson14*[your initials]*14-22.xls."
4. Edit the path and file name so that it reads ***[your initials]*14-22.xlsx**, but be careful not to change any other part of the Link code.
5. Press Alt+F9 to hide the field codes and redisplay all the tables. Save the document as ***[your initials]*14-23** in your Lesson 14 folder, and then close it.

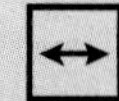

REVIEW

To print field codes, open the Word Options dialog box and click Advanced. Scroll to the Print group, and select the Print field codes instead of their values check box. After printing, reopen the Word Options dialog box, click Advanced, scroll to the Print group, and clear the Print field codes instead of their values check box.

6. If possible, copy the two files ***[your initials]*14-22** (the Excel file) and ***[your initials]*14-23** (the Word file) to a different folder or a removable storage device. Follow your instructor's directions.
7. Open the file ***[your initials]*14-23** from the new folder or removable storage device; then double-click Table 4. The linked Excel file appears. Close Excel.
8. Print the Word document with the field codes displayed. Then print it again without the field codes. Close the document.

Lesson 14 Summary

- You can prevent a page break from occurring in the middle of a table row. Open the Table Properties dialog box, click the Row tab, and clear the Allow row to break across pages check box. To prevent a page break from occurring between rows, use the Keep with next paragraph-formatting option.
- In tables that span multiple pages, you can assign column headings to repeat at the top of each page by using the Repeat Header Rows option.
- You can split a long table into two shorter tables by using the Split Table command.
- To insert text above a table when there is no paragraph mark above the table, click in the table's first cell and choose the Split Table command. Word inserts a blank paragraph mark above the table.
- To add white space between table text and cell borders, you can change cell margins in a table. You can set top, bottom, right, and left margins for individual cells or an entire table.
- You can change the vertical and horizontal alignment of text within table cells.
- Word's Table Styles gallery can quickly format a table by using one of many predefined styles. Word's AutoFit feature automatically adjusts the width of columns based on the amount of text they contain.
- You can use the Create New Style dialog box to create your own table styles. A table style can contain formatting for the entire table or for different parts of the table (such as the header row, the last row, or the right column).

- A caption is a numbered label, such as "Figure 1" or "Table 1: Year-End Revenue," that you can add to a table or some other object.
- Use the mouse pointer to resize table rows and columns by dragging their borders. Press Alt as you drag, and Word displays the precise row or column measurement on its rulers.
- Use the Table Properties dialog box to set precise row heights or column widths.
- To resize a table proportionally, adjusting its height or width, drag the table resize handle.
- To make sure multiple tables stay in position on the same page, nest them in the cells of a larger, parent table. Draw the parent table; then select and drag each of the other tables into its own cell.
- You can sort a table by any of its columns, in either ascending or descending order. You can also sort selected paragraphs or items in a list.
- Insert formula fields in a table to perform calculations on the table's data. Word's formulas can perform operations such as adding, averaging, and counting. See Table 14-1.
- To find the average of a row or column of values, insert the =AVERAGE() formula field. Between the parentheses, use the ABOVE or LEFT bookmark, key individual cell addresses, or key the cell range.
- To sum a row or column of values, insert the =SUM() formula field. Between the parentheses, use the ABOVE or LEFT bookmark, key individual cell addresses, or key the cell range.
- If you have data in an Excel spreadsheet, you can use that data in a Word document. You can embed the spreadsheet data in Word, making a table. If you link the spreadsheet, you can update the data either in Excel or in Word and the changes will appear in both files.
- You can embed a new Excel spreadsheet in a Word document. To enter data in an embedded Excel spreadsheet, double-click the table to display the Excel Ribbon in the Word window. Key data into cells, and format them as desired. Click outside the table to deactivate the Excel tools.
- To create a Word table from an Excel spreadsheet, select the data in Excel and use the Copy command. Switch to your Word document and use the Paste command.
- To embed an Excel spreadsheet into Word and keep it as an Excel object (rather than a Word table), copy the spreadsheet data, switch to Word, and use the Paste Special command (Microsoft Excel Worksheet Object option).
- To link an Excel Spreadsheet into Word, copy the spreadsheet data and use Word's Paste Special command (Paste link option).
- To maintain the connection between source and destination documents even if you move them, edit the object's Link field in the destination document. Remove all path information from the field so that it contains only the source document's name.

LESSON 14		Command Summary	
Feature	**Button**	**Command**	**Keyboard**
Cell margins		Table Tools Layout tab, Alignment group	
Embed/link copied spreadsheet		Home tab, Clipboard group	
Fit table to contents		Table Tools Layout tab, Cell Size group	
Fit table to window		Table Tools Layout tab, Cell Size group	
Insert Excel spreadsheet		Insert tab, Tables group	
Insert formula in table	*fx*	Table Tools Layout tab, Data group	
Insert table caption		References tab, Captions group	
Repeat header row		Table Tools Layout tab, Data group	
Sort	A Z	Table Tools Layout tab, Data group	
Split table		Table Tools Layout tab, Merge group	
Table properties		Table Tools Layout tab, Properties group	
Table styles		Table Tools Design tab, Table Styles group	

Concepts Review

True/False Questions

Each of the following statements is either true or false. Indicate your choice by circling T or F.

T F 1. You prevent page breaks in the middle of a row by applying the Keep with next paragraph-formatting option.

T F 2. Custom table styles cannot be added to the Table Style gallery.

T F 3. You can use the Split Table command to insert a blank line above a table.

T F 4. You can define a table's column headings so that they appear at the top of each page for a long table.

T F 5. When you embed an Excel spreadsheet, the changes you make to it are automatically saved in a new spreadsheet file.

T F 6. You can use the Table Properties dialog box or the Cell Margins button on the Table Tools Layout tab to open the Table Options dialog box.

T F 7. An Excel spreadsheet that you create in Word cannot be formatted.

T F 8. The Insert Caption command is located on the Insert tab.

Short Answer Questions

Write the correct answer in the space provided.

1. In the Table Properties dialog box, which tab contains the Options button you use to change the margins for all cells in the table?

 ____

2. Which button do you click to insert a new Excel spreadsheet in a Word document?

 ____

3. When an Excel spreadsheet is linked to a Word document, the workbook containing the spreadsheet is called the source document. What is the Word document called?

 ____

4. Which option in the Table Properties dialog box determines whether a page break will occur before or after a row?

 ____

5. Which command is used to divide a table into two tables?

 ____

6. Which command can you use to display column headings on each new page of a long table?

____

7. What is a nested table?

____

8. What do you call a table that contains another table?

____

Critical Thinking

Answer these questions on a separate page. There are no right or wrong answers. Support your answers with examples from your own experience, if possible.

1. With side-by-side nested tables, you can create an attractive page layout. What are some examples of documents you can create by using nested tables? What benefits and disadvantages do nested tables offer?
2. Embedding and linking Excel spreadsheets makes Word a more powerful tool for developing tables. When would it be more appropriate to embed a spreadsheet than to link it, and vice versa?

Skills Review

Exercise 14-24

Insert text above a table, define a table header row, use Table Styles and AutoFit, add a table caption, change cell margins and alignment, and control page breaks.

1. Open the file **Novelty**.
2. Insert a blank paragraph above the table by following these steps:
   a. Click in the first cell of the table.
   b. Click the Table Tools Layout tab, and click the Split Table button 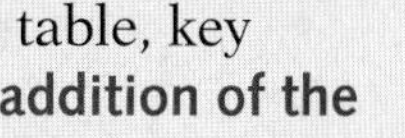.
   c. With the insertion point in the blank line above the table, key **Campbell's Confections is pleased to announce the addition of the following novelty chocolates, starting in February.**
   d. Change the spacing after to 0 points, and change the line spacing to single.
3. Style and autofit the table by following these steps:
   a. Select the table, and click the Table Tools Design tab. Click the More arrow to display the Table Styles gallery.
   b. Click a style in the third row of the Built-In styles. Locate the Table Style Options group on the Table Tools Design tab, and select the check boxes for Header Row, Banded Rows, and First Column.

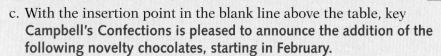

c. Select the table, and click the **Table Tools Layout** tab. Click the AutoFit button, and select **AutoFit Contents**.

4. Add a table caption by following these steps:
   a. Click anywhere in the table's header row.
   b. Click the **References** tab, and click the Insert Caption button.
   c. Edit the text in the **Caption** text box to read **Table 1: Novelty Chocolates**. Click **OK**.
   d. Format the caption as 10-point Arial bold, left-aligned.
5. Change cell margins and alignments by following these steps:
   a. Select the entire table. Click the **Table Tools Layout** tab, and click the Properties button.
   b. Click the **Table** tab and click **Options**.
   c. Change the **Top**, **Bottom**, **Left**, and **Right** cell margins to **0.15** inch. Click **OK** twice.
6. Define a header row for the table by following these steps:
   a. Select the table's first row. Format the header row's text as 12-point bold and small caps.
   b. Click the **Table Tools Layout** tab, and locate the **Data** group. Click the Repeat Header Rows button.
   c. Scroll to the second page to verify that the header row appears at the top of the page.
7. Prevent page breaks from occurring in the middle of a row by following these steps:
   a. Select the entire table.
   b. Open the **Table Properties** dialog box, and click the **Row** tab. Clear the **Allow row to break across pages** check box, and click **OK**.
8. Sort the table according to novelty name by following these steps:
   a. Select the entire table.
   b. Click the **Table Tools Layout** tab, and click the Sort button.
   c. Select **Name** in the **Sort by** box, **Text** in the **Type** box, and **Ascending** for the sort order. Verify that **Header Row** is selected. Click **OK**.
9. Create a memo heading at the top of the document. The memo is to "Store Managers" from Lynn Tanguay. The subject is "Novelty Chocolates." Key the current date. Position the insertion point in the first line of the memo heading, and change the spacing before to 72 points. Include your reference initials at the end of the paragraph you keyed in step 2. Place three blank lines between your reference initials and the table caption.
10. Add a right-aligned header to the second and third pages that contains **Page** followed by the page number.
11. Save the document as ***[your initials]*14-24** in your Lesson 14 folder. Submit and close the document.

Exercise 14-25

Split a table, create and modify a custom table style, and resize tables.

1. Open the file **Easter Candy**.
2. Use the Split Table command to insert a blank line above the table. Then key the following text and create an attractive title for the document using appropriate character and paragraph formatting:

   Campbell's Confections
   Easter Candy Molds

3. Split this long table into five shorter ones by following these steps:
   a. Scroll down to the row containing the text "Peanut Butter Molds," and click the Table Tools Layout tab. Click the Split Table button.
   b. Scroll down to the row containing the text "Dark Chocolate Molds," and click at the beginning of the cell. Click Split Table.
   c. Scroll down to the row containing the text "Sugar-Free Molds," and click at the beginning of the cell. Click Split Table.
   d. Scroll down to the row containing the text "Pink Molds," and click at the beginning of the cell. Click Split Table.

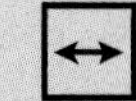

REVIEW

To merge cells, select the cells, right-click the selection, and choose Merge Cells from the shortcut menu.

4. Merge the cells in the first row of each table. Copy the second row in the first table (column headings), and paste the copied row as a new second row for the other tables.
5. Click anywhere inside the first table, and create a new custom table style by following these steps:
   a. Click the Table Tools Design tab, and click the More arrow in the Table Styles group.
   b. Click New Table Style.
   c. In the Name box, key **Table Special 2**. Verify that the Style type drop-down list displays Table.
   d. Open the Apply formatting to drop-down list, and choose Whole table. Use the font-formatting tools to set the table's font to 11-point Arial, with no effects.
   e. Click the Borders button arrow Borders, and choose No Border. Click the arrow again, and choose Inside Horizontal Border.
   f. Open the Apply formatting to drop-down list, and choose Header row. Use the font-formatting tools to change the font to 11-point Arial bold and italic. Set the shading color to a medium gray color (Darker 25%).
   g. From the Apply formatting to drop-down list, choose Even banded rows. Set the shading to a light gray color (Darker 5%).
   h. Select the Only in this document option, and click OK.
   i. Click the new style (Table Special 2) in the Table Styles group to apply the style to the table. Apply the Table Special 2 style to the other tables.

6. Modify the new table style by following these steps:
   a. Click anywhere in the first table, and right-click the Table Special 2 button in the Table Styles group.
   b. Click **Modify Table Style**.
   c. From the **Apply formatting to** list, choose **Whole Table**. Click the Align button, and change the alignment to Align Center Left.
   d. From the **Apply formatting to** list, choose **Header row**. Change the alignment to **Align Center**, and remove the italic formatting.
   e. Select the **Only in this document** option and click **OK**.
   f. Scroll through the document, and make sure the style has been updated for all five tables.
7. Change the column size for the first column of each table by following these steps:
   a. In the first table, point to the border of the first column (in any row but the header row). When the pointer becomes a resizing pointer, press Alt and drag the border to the right until the column's width is **2** inches.
   b. Go to the second table. Click in any cell in the first column (in any row but the header row). Right-click and click **Table Properties**. Click the **Column** tab.
   c. Click the **Preferred width** check box to activate it (so it is no longer dimmed). Then set the column width to **2** inches.
   d. Resize the first column for each of the remaining tables.
8. Resize a table proportionally by following these steps:
   a. Click the table resize handle of the last table, and drag the handle directly to the left. (Be careful not to drag downward.)
   b. Release the handle when it is even with the 6.75-inch marker on the horizontal ruler. Resize column 1 to 2 inches if necessary.
   c. Use the Table Properties dialog box, **Table** tab, to resize the other tables to 6.75 inches. Adjust the column width for column 1 to 2 inches if necessary.
9. Create header rows for the tables by following these steps:
   a. Select the first two rows of the first table. Click the **Table Tools Layout** tab, and click **Repeat Header Rows**.
   b. Go to the second table, and select the first two rows. Click the **Table Tools Layout** tab, and click **Repeat Header Rows**.
   c. Apply the **Repeat Header Rows** command to the other tables.
   d. Scroll through the document to make sure the header rows are present where a table breaks across pages.
10. Select each table, and use the Table Properties dialog box, **Row** tab, to specify a row height of at least **0.25** inch.
11. Go to the first table, and select the cells containing the "Price," "Ordered," and "Shipped" headings. Change the alignment to align center right. Repeat for the other tables.

12. Add a right-aligned header to page 2 that contains **Page** followed by the page number. Format the header as 10-point Arial, and add two blank lines below the header text.
13. Save the document as ***[your initials]*14-25** in your Lesson 14 folder. Submit and close the document.

Exercise 14-26

Create nested tables, use AutoFit and alignment features, change column sizes, and sort a table.

1. Open the file **Prices**.
2. Insert the current date in the "DATE" line of the memo heading.
3. Select the seven lines of columnar tabbed text below the heading "Retail Prices" (do not select the heading). Convert the selected text to a table.
4. Select the columnar tabbed text under the heading "Wholesale Prices." Convert the selected text to a table.

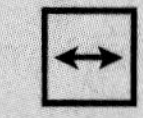

REVIEW

To convert text to a table, select the text, click the Insert tab, and then click Table and Convert Text to Table. Select the Tabs option under Separate text at.

5. Resize the table by following these steps:
   a. Click in the first table, and click the **Table Tools Layout** tab.
   b. Click **AutoFit** and **AutoFit Contents** to resize the table.
6. Use the table resize handle to change the overall size of a table by following these steps:
   a. Click anywhere in the second table. Move your mouse pointer over the table to display the table resize handle in the lower right corner.
   b. Drag the table resize handle to the left, making the table the same width as the table above it.
7. Insert a blank paragraph mark below the memo's opening paragraph of text, and insert a 1-row by 2-column table.
8. Create nested side-by-side tables by following these steps:
   a. Select the paragraph "Retail Prices" and the table following it; then drag them into the first cell of the new, blank table.
   b. Select the paragraph "Wholesale Prices" and the table following it; then drag them into the second cell of the new table.
9. Adjust the size and position of the parent table by following these steps:
   a. To select the parent table, click the table move handle for the parent table.
   b. Click the **Table Tools Layout** tab, **AutoFit**, and **AutoFit Contents**.
   c. With the parent table still selected, open the Table Properties dialog box.
   d. Click the **Table** tab, and click **Center**.
   e. On the **Table** tab, click the **Options** button. Change all cell margins to **0.1** inch. Click **OK** twice.

10. Adjust properties for the nested tables by following these steps:
    a. Select the entire "Retail Prices" table, and open the Table Properties dialog box.
    b. On the **Table** tab, under **Alignment**, choose **Center**. Make sure the text-wrapping option **None** is selected.
    c. Click the **Row** tab, and make sure the **Specify height** check box is not selected. Click **OK**.
    d. Repeat steps *a*, *b*, and *c* for the "Wholesale Prices" table.
    e. Use the resize handles of the nested tables to adjust the table heights to be equal.
11. Format the two nested tables by following these steps:
    a. Format both table titles ("Retail Prices" and "Wholesale Prices") as 10-point bold, small caps, and centered over the tables.
    b. In both tables, center and italicize the column headings.
    c. Select the entire "Wholesale Prices" table, and open the Table Properties dialog box. Click the **Cell** tab, click the **Center** option, and click **OK**.
    d. Select the entire "Retail Prices" table, and open the Table Properties dialog box. Click the **Cell** tab, click the **Center** option, and click **OK**.
    e. Verify that the bottom borders display for each table. If necessary, drag the bottom border of the parent table to display the borders for the nested tables.
12. Sort the "Retail Prices" table according to size, by following these steps:
    a. Select the "Retail Prices" table.
    b. Click the **Table Tools Layout** tab, and click the Sort button.
    c. In the Sort dialog box, select the **Header row** option.
    d. Under **Sort by**, click the drop-down arrow and choose **Size**.
    e. Click the **Type** drop-down arrow and choose **Text**.
    f. Click the **Descending** option to arrange the list from the highest value to the lowest Click **OK**.
    g. Repeat the sort steps for the Wholesale Prices table.
13. Save the document as ***[your initials]*14-26** in your Lesson 14 folder. Submit and close the document.

NOTE

You choose descending order because "8" is larger than "1." You could change 8 ounces to 0.5 pound for consistency in weight format.

Exercise 14-27

Perform calculations in a Word table, insert a blank Excel spreadsheet, and enter and format data in the spreadsheet.

1. Open the file **Novelty - 2**.
2. Insert a new, blank row at the bottom of the table. Then insert a new column to the right of the fourth column.

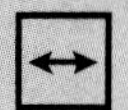

REVIEW

To add a new row to the bottom of a table, place the insertion point at the end of the table's last cell and then press Tab. To add a new column to the end of a table, select the end-of-row markers, right-click, and choose Insert Columns.

3. Click in the first cell of the new row (under "Greek letters"), and key **Total**. Click in the first cell of the new column (to the right of "Q3"), and key **Average**.
4. Add formula fields to the bottom row by following these steps:
   a. Click cell B4 and click the **Table Tools Layout** tab. Click the Formula button *fx*. In the **Formula** box, key **=SUM(B2,B3)**. Open the **Number format** drop-down list, and select **#,##0**. Click **OK**.
   b. Using the preceding step as a guide, add formula fields in cells C4 and D4.
5. Add formula fields to the last column, to average the dollar amounts in the cells to the left of them, by following these steps:
   a. Click cell E2 and open the **Formula** dialog box. In the **Formula** box, key **=AVERAGE(LEFT)**. Choose **#,##0** as the number format. Click **OK**.
   b. Using the preceding step as a guide, add formula fields in cells E3 and E4 that average the sales amounts in the cells to their left.
   c. Select the cells in the last column, and change the alignment to align center right.
6. Create a new Excel spreadsheet in the Word document by following these steps:
   a. Position the insertion point on the last line of the document. Press Enter twice.
   b. Click the **Insert** tab, and then click **Table** and **Excel Spreadsheet**.
   c. Point to the black square handle on the right side of the spreadsheet, and drag it to the left to display four columns (A–D). Drag the bottom center black handle up to display four rows.
7. In the new spreadsheet, key the data shown in Figure 14-23.

Figure 14-23

	A	B	C	D
1		2010	2011	2012
2	Mascots	8,600	9,150	9,590
3	Greek letters	6,300	6,850	6,190
4	Total	=SUM(B2,B3)		

8. Use Excel's AutoFill feature to copy formulas by following these steps:
   a. Select cell B4.
   b. Move the white cross pointer to the bottom right of cell B5 until it becomes a black cross pointer +.
   c. Drag the black cross pointer to the right to include cells C4 and D4.
   d. Release the mouse button.

9. Format the new Excel spreadsheet to match the other table by following these steps:
   a. Drag the white cross pointer from cell A1 to cell D4 to select all the cells.
   b. Right-click the spreadsheet, and choose **Format Cells** from the shortcut menu.
   c. Click the **Fill** tab, and select a light blue color.
   d. Click the **Font** tab, and set the font to 11-point Arial.
   e. Click the **Border** tab, click the Outline button, and then click the Inside button. Click **OK**.
   f. Format the spreadsheet's first row and first column as bold.
   g. Center the text in the first row. Center the spreadsheet.
   h. In the spreadsheet, select columns A, B, C, and D, and right click to display the shortcut menu. Choose **Column Width**, and key **15** for the column width. Click **OK** to close the Column Width dialog box.
   i. Click outside the spreadsheet window to return to the Word document.
10. Add a caption to the second table by following these steps:
    a. Click the second table to select it.
    b. Click the **References** tab, and click **Insert Caption**.
    c. In the **Label** list, make sure **Table** is selected.
    d. Edit the text in the **Caption** box to read **Table 2: Projected Sales: 2010—2012**.
    e. Format the caption to match the first table's caption.
11. Delete the blank paragraphs between the tables. Then format each of the captions with 12 points spacing before and 6 points spacing after.
12. Save the document as ***[your initials]*****14-27** in your Lesson 14 folder. Submit and close the document.

Lesson Applications

Exercise 14-28

Split a long table into multiple tables, set up header rows, resize tables and columns, insert text above a table, and use table styles.

1. Open the file **Chronology - 3**.
2. Convert the text to a table.
3. Sort the text in the table in ascending order by state and city.

TIP

Sort by state and then by city. Be sure to select Header Row.

4. Use the Split Table command to insert a blank line above the table. Then key the following document title as 14-point bold and small caps.

   Campbell's Confections
   Chronology of Stores by State

5. Change the spacing after the first line to 0, and change the spacing after the second line to 24 points. Change the line spacing for both lines to single.
6. Center the text in the first column.
7. Change the width of the second and third columns to 1.75 inches.
8. Insert a new first row at the top of the table.
9. Split the table at the row beginning "1962"—the first row for Pennsylvania" so that this cell is in the first row of the new table.
10. Scroll down a few lines, and split the table at the text "1982" so that Clarksburg is the first cell in the new table.
11. Merge the cells in the first row of the first table, and key **Ohio**.
12. Format the text as 12-point bold and small caps, with 12 points of spacing before and 6 points of spacing after. Center-align the text (you will center the table later).
13. Delete the last row of the second table ("Year, City, State").
14. Add a blank row at the top of the other tables, and key the appropriate state name for each table. Format the row to match the formatting of the first row in the first table.
15. Define each table's first row as a repeating header row for the table.
16. Select all the rows in the first table except the header row, and change the row height to 0.25 inch. Center the text vertically in the rows.
17. Change the row height for the rows below the header row for the second and third tables. Use 0.25 inch for the row height, and center the text vertically.

NOTE

After applying the table style, you might have to turn on the Repeat Header Rows option again.

18. Apply a table style to each table choosing a style from the first row of the Built-In styles in the Table Styles gallery.
19. Center the tables horizontally.
20. Change the bottom margin to 0.25 to keep the West Virginia text on page 1 of the document. If necessary, adjust the top margin.
21. Save the document as ***[your initials]*14-28** in your Lesson 14 folder. Submit and close the document.

Exercise 14-29

Create nested tables, sort tables, add formula fields to tables, and format tables.

1. Open the file **Trade**.
2. Change the letter's date to the current date.
3. On the second blank line below the paragraph beginning "The approximate cost of," insert a 1-row by 2-column table to be used as a parent table.
4. With your insertion point in the first cell, insert a blank table containing two columns and six rows.
5. Insert another 2-column by 6-row table in the second cell of the parent table.
6. Key the following information in the nested table on the left:

   All Candy Expo
   Registration 125.00
   Lodging 550.00
   Airfare 360.00
   Car Rental 315.00

7. Key the following information in the nested table on the right:

   Chocolate Show
   Registration 200.00
   Lodging 945.00
   Airfare 380.00
   Car Rental 320.00

   In both tables, leave the last row blank.

TIP

In the Sort dialog box, be sure to select the Header row option. Sort by the second column, in descending order. Make sure the type is set to Number.

8. Sort both tables in descending order according to the column that contains the dollar amounts.
9. In the bottom left cell of each nested table, key **Total**.
10. Insert table formulas in the appropriate cells to total the cost of each trip.
11. Format the parent table and the nested tables attractively, using all the following features:
    - Merge cells.
    - Align text in cells.
    - Apply text formatting.
    - Apply cell shading.
    - Insert dollar signs in front of the amounts in the first and last cells in the column.
    - Change cell margins to add space in the parent table surrounding the nested tables and to position aligned text and numbers within columns.

TIP

You can use the ABOVE bookmark with the formula's function, in both tables. Be sure to select the #,##0.00 number format.

12. Adjust the sizing and spacing of the tables as needed to fit the entire document on one page. You can also change the bottom margin to 0.5 inch.
13. Replace the text "xx" with your reference initials.
14. Save the document as ***[your initials]*****14-29** in your Lesson 14 folder. Submit and close the document.

Exercise 14-30

Create a table, add formula fields, and format the table.

1. Start a new document, and change the orientation to landscape.
2. Key **Deposit Report** at the top of the document, and format the text using 18-point bold and small caps, with center alignment and 18 points spacing after.
3. Insert a 12-column by 33-row table. Format all cells in the table using right alignment.
4. Key the text in Figure 14-24 across row 1.

Figure 14-24

Column 1	Day
Column 2	Cash
Column 3	Check
Column 4	Cash/Check Total
Column 5	Visa
Column 6	MasterCard
Column 7	Visa/MC Total
Column 8	Discover
Column 9	American Express
Column 10	Other Charge
Column 11	Total Charges
Column 12	Total Deposit

5. Format the first row using the Arial Narrow font in10-point bold. Vertically align the text in the row using the Bottom option. Center the text in row 1.
6. Key the numbers **1** through **31** in the first column, starting in row 2. In the last row of column 1, key **Total**.
7. Key **100.00** in row 2 for columns 2 ("Cash"), 3 ("Check"), 5 ("Visa"), 6 ("Mastercard"), 8 ("Discover"), 9 ("American Express"), and 10 ("Other Charge"). The amount 100.00 should appear in seven cells.
8. Click in the second row, fourth column ("Cash/Check Total"), and insert a formula to add the amounts in the second and third columns (columns B and C). Use appropriate number format.
9. Click in the second row, seventh column ("Visa/MC Total"), and insert a formula to add the amounts in the fifth and sixth columns (columns E and F). Use appropriate number format.
10. Click in the second row, eleventh column ("Total Charges"), and insert a formula to add the amounts in columns 5, 6, 8, 9, and 10 (columns E, F, H, I, and J). Use appropriate number format.
11. Click in the second row, last column ("Total Deposit"), and insert a formula to add the amounts in columns 4 and 11 (columns D and K). Use appropriate number format.
12. Click in the last row of column 1, and insert a formula to add the amounts in the first column. (Use the ABOVE function.)
13. Change the bottom margin to 0.25 to create a one-page document. Change the top margin if necessary.
14. Save the document as ***[your initials]*14-30** in your Lesson 14 folder. Submit and close the document.

Exercise 14-31 ◆ Challenge Yourself

Create side-by-side and nested tables, and embed Excel spreadsheets.

1. Open the file **Revenue**.
2. Draw a table below the last paragraph similar to the one shown in Figure 14-25.

Figure 14-25

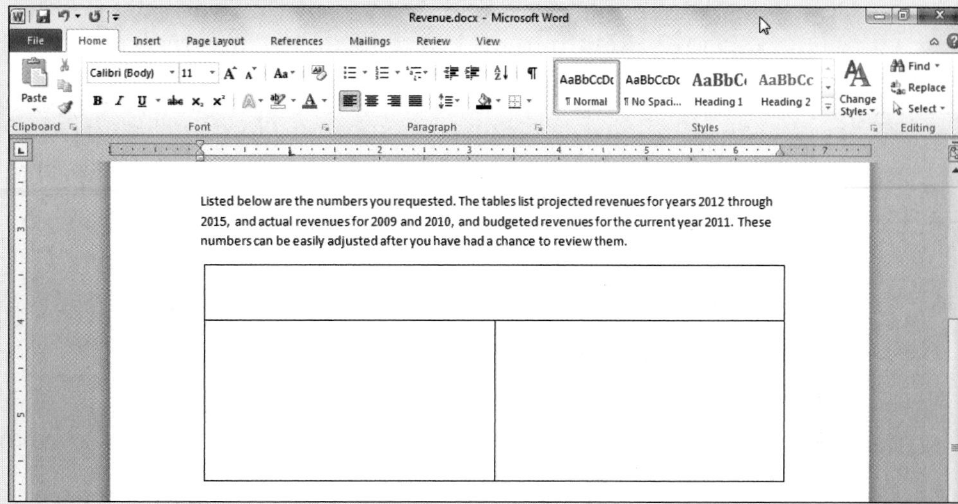

3. Start Excel, and open the Excel file **RevComp**.
4. Copy cells A1 to E8 to the Clipboard. Switch to Word, and paste the cells as an embedded spreadsheet into the first row of your Word table.
5. Switch to Excel. Press Esc to stop the copy-and-paste procedure (removing the marquee around the selected cells). Open the Excel file **Rev10**.
6. Copy cells A1 to C8 to the Clipboard, and then paste them as an embedded spreadsheet into the first cell in row 2 of the Word table.
7. Open the Excel file **Rev11**.
8. Copy cells A1 to B8 to the Clipboard, and then paste them as an embedded spreadsheet into the remaining cell of the Word table.
9. Select the entire parent table, and apply the **AutoFit Contents** setting. Remove all borders from the parent table.

TIP

To embed an Excel spreadsheet in Word, use the Paste Special command and paste (not paste link) as a Microsoft Excel Worksheet object.

10. Double-click the second spreadsheet in row 2 so that you can edit it. Select cell A2 (which contains the text "2011"). Change the text to read **2011 Budgeted Revenue**. Click in the document to deselect the spreadsheet.
11. Center the parent table, and then center the table in the first row of the parent table. Double-click the spreadsheet in the first row, select all cells, open the Format Cells dialog box, and apply an outline border to the spreadsheet. Repeat for the spreadsheets in the second row.
12. Return to the Word document, and insert today's date in the memo's date line.
13. Save the Word document as ***[your initials]*14-31** in your Lesson 14 folder. Submit and close the document. Close the Excel spreadsheet files, and close Excel.

On Your Own

In these exercises, you work on your own, as you would in a real-life business environment. Use the skills you have learned to accomplish the task—and be creative.

Exercise 14-32

Open the file **Activity Period**. Format the document attractively, and create a formula for the last row in the table. Consider changing the orientation to landscape, creating a table style, and changing the row height for improved readability. Apply shading where appropriate. Save the document as ***[your initials]*14-32** and submit it.

Exercise 14-33

Create a table to include a daily sales breakdown by category. Include categories for various types of chocolate (creams, nuts, clusters, etc.). Format the tables using landscape orientation, and apply a table style. Format the table using the Table, Row, Column and Cell tabs in the Table Properties dialog box. Include formulas in the table. Save the document as ***[your initials]*14-33** and submit it.

Exercise 14-34

Create a new document—a memo to the director of accounts receivable. Insert a table listing clients with past-due accounts. Insert a formula field to total the past-due amounts. Add text describing the status of these accounts, such as 30 days overdue, 60 days overdue, and 90 days overdue. Save the document as ***[your initials]*****14-34** and submit it.

Lesson 15
Columns

OBJECTIVES ***After completing this lesson, you will be able to:***

1. Create multiple-column layouts.
2. Key and edit text in columns.
3. Format columns and column text.
4. Control column breaks.
5. Use hyphenation.

Estimated Time: 1 hour

Word can arrange document text in multiple columns on a single page like those used in newspapers and magazines. The continuous flow of text from one column to another can make a document more attractive and easier to read.

Documents commonly have between one and three columns. A document can also use different column layouts. For example, a document might use a standard one-column layout in one section and a three-column layout in another section.

Creating Multiple-Column Layouts

There are two ways to create multiple-column layouts:

- Use the Columns button on the Ribbon, Page Layout tab.
- Use the Columns dialog box.

You can change the column format for the whole document, for the section containing the insertion point, or for selected text.

Exercise 15-1 USE THE RIBBON TO CREATE COLUMNS

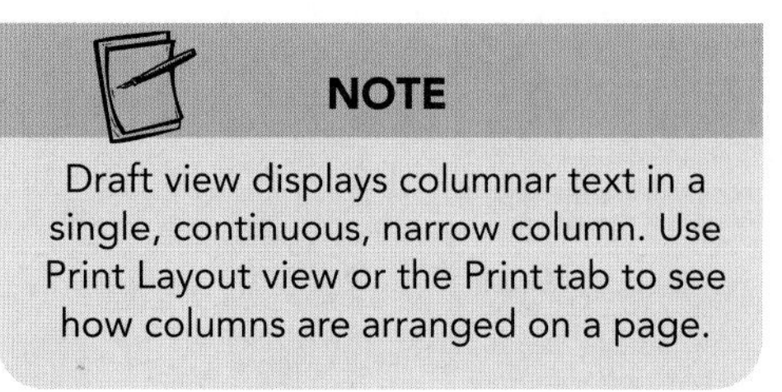

NOTE

Draft view displays columnar text in a single, continuous, narrow column. Use Print Layout view or the Print tab to see how columns are arranged on a page.

1. Open the file **Company - 3**. If nonprinting characters are not displayed, click the Show/Hide ¶ button ¶ to display them.
2. Position the insertion point at the beginning of the bold heading "Services" near the bottom of page 1 of the document.
3. Insert a continuous section break before the heading "Services" (Page Layout tab, Breaks).
4. Click the **Page Layout** tab, and locate the **Page Setup** group. Click the Columns button on the Ribbon. A menu appears below the button with options for the number of columns that will appear in your document.

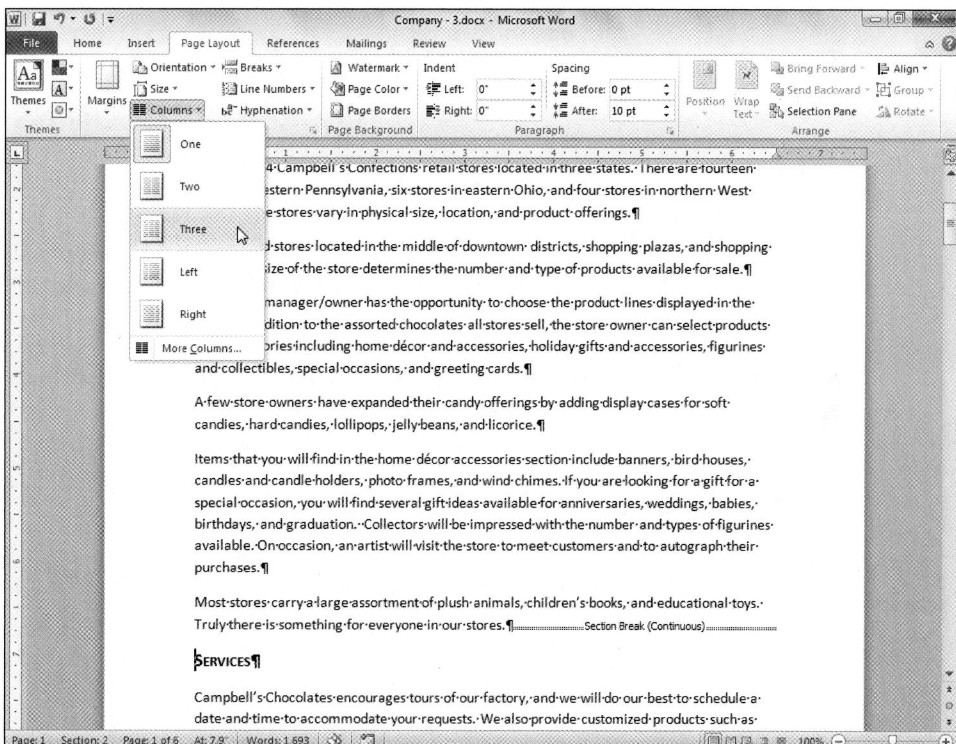

Figure 15-1
Choosing a column layout

5. Point to the menu option for **Three**, and click to choose the three-column layout. The new section is now in three columns.

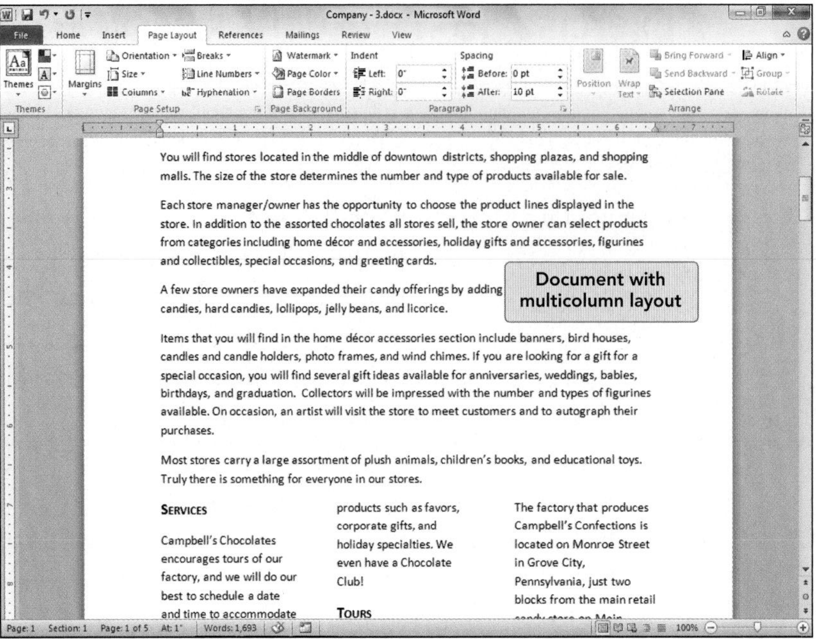

Figure 15-2 One- and three-column layouts in Print Layout view

Exercise 15-2 USE THE COLUMNS DIALOG BOX TO CREATE COLUMNS

When you choose an option from the Columns menu, Word applies default settings for column width and formats the section where the insertion point is located or formats the entire document if the document does not contain sections. You can change these settings in the Columns dialog box.

1. While still in Print Layout view, position the insertion point at the beginning of the paragraph that starts "Fundraising." (The paragraph is near the end of the document.)
2. Click the **Page Layout** tab, and click the Columns button to display the Columns menu. Click **More Columns** to open the Columns dialog box.

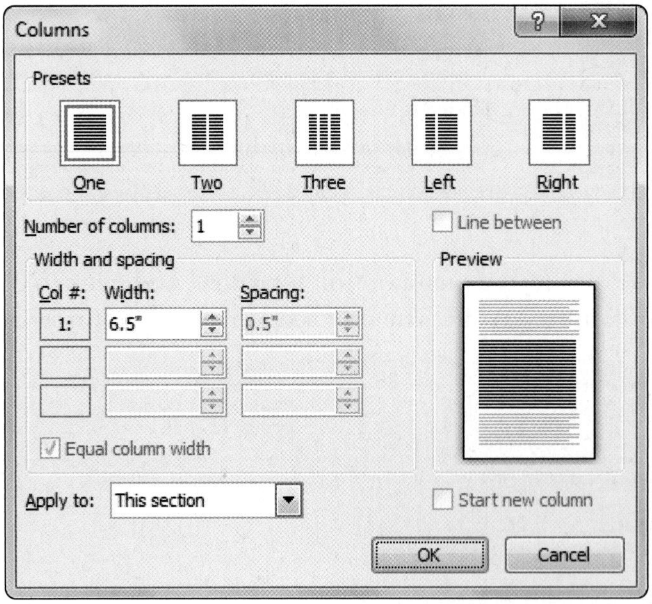

Figure 15-3 Columns dialog box

3. Key **1** in the Number of columns text box, or click One in the Presets section.
4. Choose This point forward from the Apply to drop-down list. The Preview box reflects the options you specify.
5. Click OK. A continuous section break is automatically inserted at the location of the insertion point, and the new section is formatted as one column. To see the section break, switch to Draft view 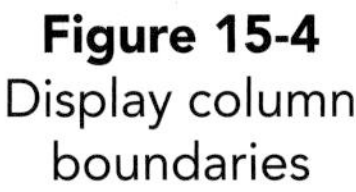. Remember that Draft view does not display multicolumn layouts. Switch to Print Layout view.
6. Press Enter to insert an extra blank line between the sections.
7. Position the insertion point at the beginning of the heading "Services" on the first page, and open the Columns dialog box.
8. Set the Spacing text box for Col #1 to **0.25"** to specify spacing between columns. Click the Equal column width check box to format all the columns as equal in width.
9. Choose This Section from the Apply to drop-down list to apply these settings to only this section; then click the Line between check box. Notice that the Preview box reflects these options.
10. Click OK. The columns in this section are spaced 0.25 inch apart with a line between them.
11. Open the Word Options dialog box, and click Advanced. Scroll to the Show document content group, and click Show text boundaries to select the option. Click OK. Single dotted lines display column boundaries and page margins.

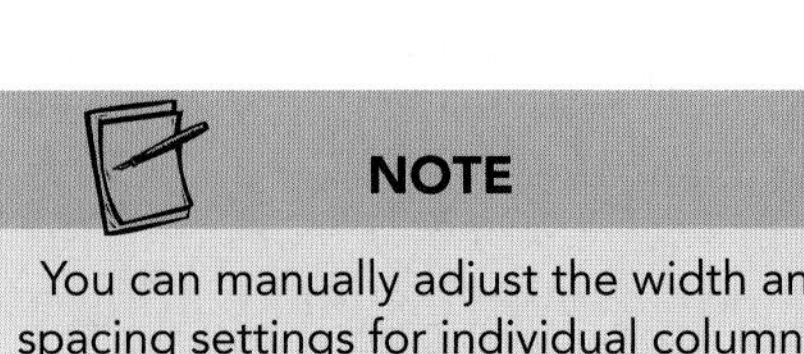

NOTE

You can manually adjust the width and spacing settings for individual columns if you clear the Equal column width check box. Then you can key a number in the appropriate Width and Spacing boxes or click the up and down arrows.

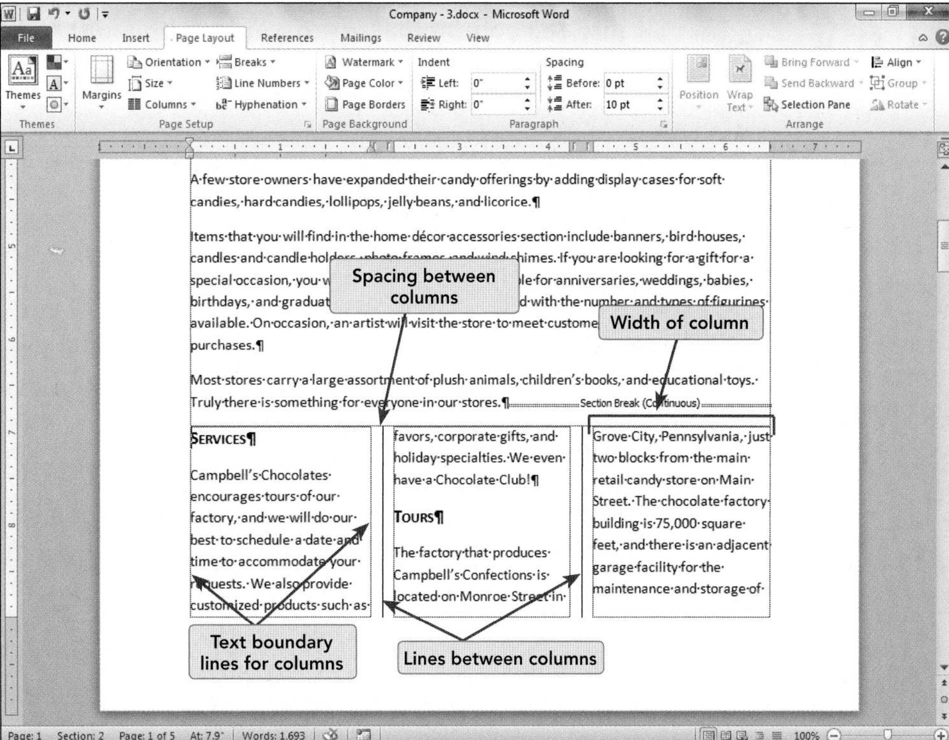

Figure 15-4
Display column boundaries

NOTE

Text boundary lines do not appear when a document is printed.

12. Scroll through the document and review all boundary lines.
13. Reopen the Word Options dialog box. Click **Advanced**, and scroll to Show document content. Click **Show text boundaries** to deselect this option.
14. Click **OK**. The boundary lines are hidden.

Keying and Editing Text in Columns

You can key and edit text in multiple-column layouts the same way you do in standard one-column layouts. Moving the insertion point around is a little different, however.

Exercise 15-3 KEY AND EDIT COLUMN TEXT

Keying and editing text in columns is very similar to keying and editing text in a standard document.

To move the insertion point from the bottom of a column to the top of the next column, you press →. You press ← to move from the top of a column to the bottom of the previous column. To move from the bottom line of a column to the first line of the same column on the next page, press ↓.

TIP

If a document has a page that contains blank lines between the end of the text in a column and the page break, press ↓ more than once to move to the top line of the column on the next page.

1. Scroll to the middle of page 3, to the paragraph that begins "Volume discounts" in the second column. Position the insertion point before the text "Volume."
2. Key the text shown in Figure 15-5. Notice that the text is inserted into the column paragraph just as it would be in a standard one-column document.

Figure 15-5

```
A luxurious, handmade chocolate gift is a great way to make
a sweet impression.
```

NOTE

When you use arrow keys to navigate in columns, you might need to press an arrow key twice to move past a space.

3. Position the insertion point at the end of the text in the third column on page 3, and press →. The insertion point moves to the first column at the top of the next page.
4. Press ← to return to the previous location.
5. Position the insertion point at the end of the first column on page 2, and press → again. The insertion point moves to the top of the second column.

6. Press [←] to return to the end of the first column. Position the insertion point anywhere in the middle of the last line of the first column.
7. Press [↓], and the insertion point moves to the same position in the same column at the top of the next page. If the first line is a blank line, you might have to press [↓] again.

Formatting Columns and Column Text

You can create and change font and paragraph formats for text in columns in the same way you create and change them for standard layouts.

There are two ways to change the width of a column and the amount of space between columns:

- Use the ruler.
- Use the Columns dialog box.

Exercise 15-4 FORMAT COLUMN TEXT

1. Just below the section break on the first page, select the text “Services.”
2. Format the text as 16-point bold and italic, with 18 points of spacing after the paragraph.
3. Press [Ctrl]+[A] to select the document.
4. Click the Justify button [≡] on the Home tab to justify the text. Notice the additional white space between words as a result of the justified text.
5. Click the Undo button [↶] to turn off the justification feature.

TIP

When you justify column text, it looks like text in a newspaper. Left-align column text to create more of a newsletter effect. It is rarely appropriate to center column material.

Exercise 15-5 CHANGE COLUMN WIDTH AND SPACING

1. Display the ruler if it is not displayed.
2. On page 2, position the insertion point in the first column. Notice that the column has its own indent markers and margin settings on the ruler.
3. Point to the column’s right margin on the ruler. When you see the ScreenTip “Right Margin” and the two-headed arrow [↔], drag the right margin 0.5 inch to the left. Hold down [Alt] while dragging to see the exact measurement.

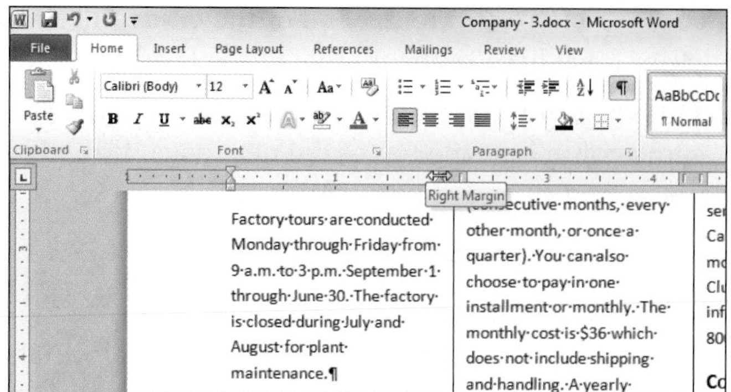

Figure 15-6
Using the ruler to adjust column width

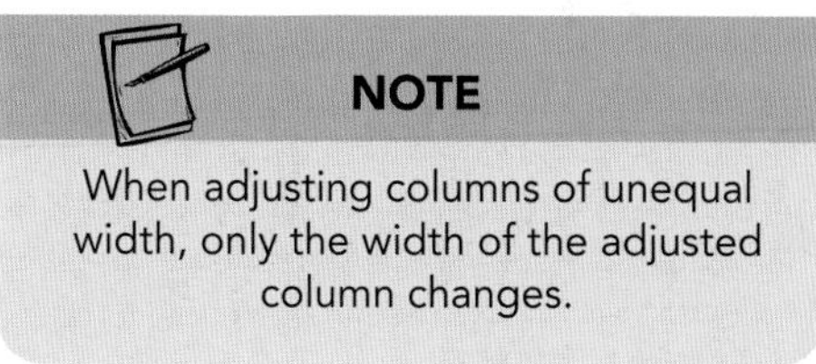

NOTE

When adjusting columns of unequal width, only the width of the adjusted column changes.

4. Release the mouse button. Because these columns were set to be of equal width, they all become narrower and the spacing between them increases. Notice that the page breaks change because the text reflows.
5. Open the **Columns** dialog box. Click **Equal column width** to deselect this option.
6. Click **OK**. The ruler now contains column markers in the shaded areas on the ruler. You can drag these markers to adjust the width of individual columns.
7. Position the pointer over the first column marker. A ScreenTip displays "Move Column."

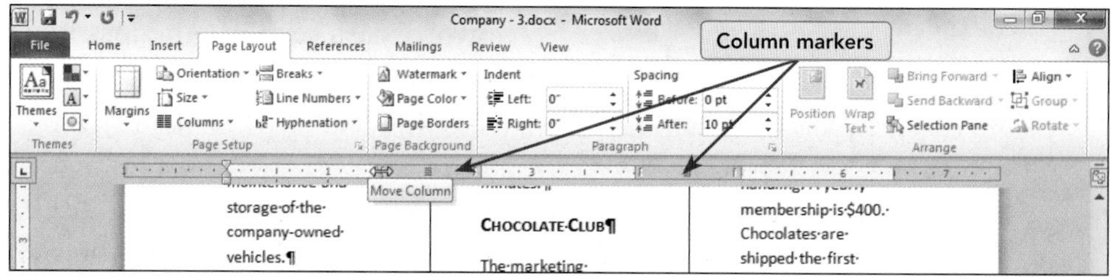

Figure 15-7
Dragging a column marker

8. Drag the column marker 0.5 inch to the right. The width of the first column increases as the second column becomes narrower.
9. Move the pointer to the left margin area of the second column. The ScreenTip "Left Margin" appears.

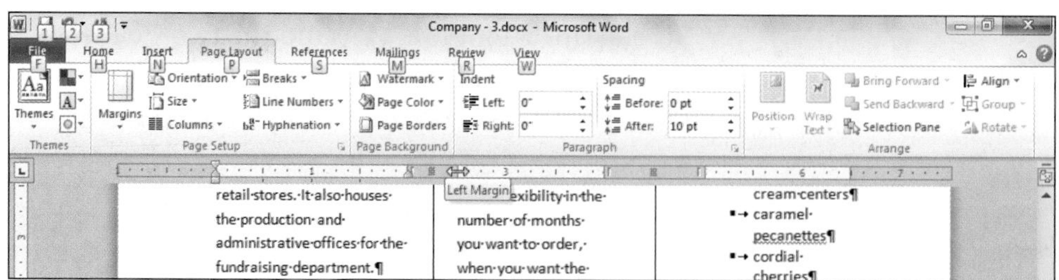

Figure 15-8
Adjusting the left margin of the second column

10. Drag the two-headed arrow pointer [↔] 0.5 inch to the left. This decreases the space between the first two columns.
11. Open the **Columns** dialog box. Notice the different settings for columns 1 and 2.
12. Set the spacing for column 1 to **0.4"**, and check **Equal column width**.
13. Click **OK**. Word changes the width for all three columns to 1.9 inches and the space between columns to 0.4 inch.

Controlling Column Breaks

Word automatically breaks columns at the end of the page or section, so column lengths are often uneven. However, you can insert a column break manually so that the columns end where you want them to end. You can also balance the columns by adjusting the column breaks to make them even.

Exercise 15-6 INSERT COLUMN BREAKS

There are three ways to insert column breaks:

- Use the Breaks dialog box.
- Press Ctrl+Shift+Enter.
- Use the Columns dialog box.

In this exercise you practice inserting column breaks by using each of the three methods.

1. On the fourth page of the document, position the insertion point before "Fundraising."
2. Click the **Page Layout** tab, and click **Breaks** to open the Breaks menu.
3. Click **Column**. A column break is inserted, and "Fundraising" appears at the top of the next page.
4. Press Backspace to delete the column break.
5. Press Ctrl+Shift+Enter to insert a column break again.
6. Press Backspace to remove it.
7. Open the Columns dialog box.
8. Choose **This point forward** from the **Apply to** drop-down list, click **Start new column**, and click **OK**. A new section is inserted. Notice that the section break has the same effect as the previous column breaks.
9. Click the Undo button [↶].

TIP

You can also use the Paragraph dialog box to control column breaks. For example, if a column break separates a paragraph from its heading, you can use the Keep with next pagination option.

Exercise 15-7 BALANCE THE LENGTH OF COLUMNS

You can balance the length of your columns on a partial page to add a professional appearance to a document.

1. At the end of the three-column section on page 4, position the insertion point to the immediate right of the paragraph mark after "Confection's catalog."
2. Press Delete. Section 2 becomes one column. (The formatting in the last paragraph mark now applies to section 2.)
3. Click within section 2, open the Columns dialog box, and reapply the formatting for this section: three columns with equal column width, spacing between the columns of 0.25 inch, and a vertical line between the columns.
4. Change the zoom level to 35%, and notice that the columns on the last page are not balanced.
5. Return the zoom level to 100%, and position the insertion point at the end of the three-column section on page 5, after "fundraising packet."
6. Insert a **Continuous** section break. Word creates columns of equal length on the last page.
7. Use the Zoom dialog box to display all pages of the document.

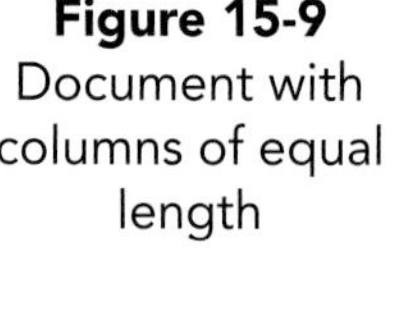

Figure 15-9 Document with columns of equal length

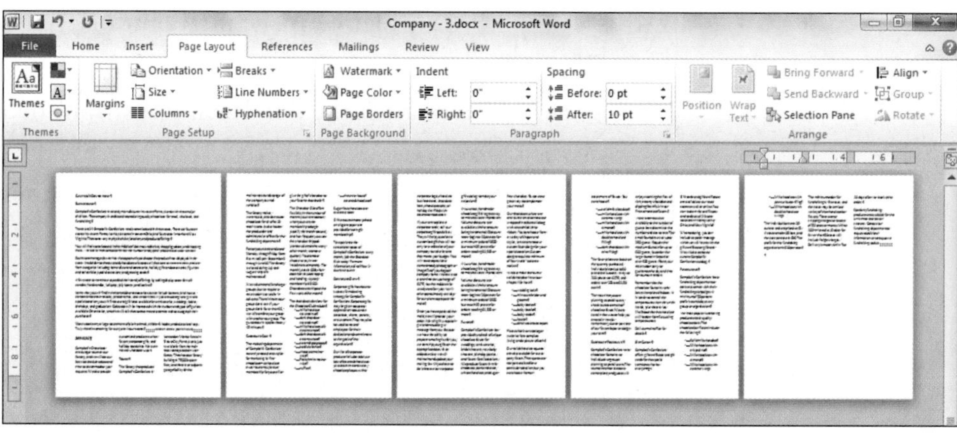

8. Return the zoom level to 100%.
9. Scroll to page 1, and position the insertion point in the first column below the Services heading. Open the Page Setup dialog box, and select the Layout tab. Change the continuous section break to a **New page** section break.
10. Scroll through section 2, and use the **Keep with next** option to prevent side headings from being separated from the paragraph that follows.
11. Apply page numbering, beginning in the second section, with numbers centered at the bottom of the page. Start numbering at 1, and make sure there is no page number in section 1.
12. Save the document as ***[your initials]*****15-7** in a new Lesson 15 folder.

Using Hyphenation

Hyphenation is used to divide words at the end of a line. You can hyphenate text manually, or Word can hyphenate text for you automatically. Word uses three types of hyphens:

- A normal hyphen is used for words that should always be hyphenated, such as "twenty-three" or "mother-in-law."
- A *nonbreaking hyphen* is used when a hyphenated word should not be divided at a line break. For example, you could use a nonbreaking hyphen in a hyphenated word, such as "self-employed." A nonbreaking hyphen is similar in purpose to a nonbreaking space, which was discussed in Lesson 1.
- An *optional hyphen* indicates where a word should be divided if the word falls at the end of a line. If the word does not fall at the end of a line, the optional hyphen disappears from the screen and is not printed.

Exercise 15-8 INSERT NORMAL, NONBREAKING, AND OPTIONAL HYPHENS

It is a good idea to use hyphenation when a document contains lines that seem to break very irregularly. You can also use hyphenation to potentially shorten a document's length.

1. In the current document, scroll to the top of page 3 and locate the telephone number in the first column. Delete the hyphen after "1," and insert a nonbreaking hyphen by pressing Ctrl+Shift+- (the Hyphen key). The nonbreaking hyphen will prevent the telephone number from being divided between two lines.
2. Go to page 2, and locate the paragraph that begins "The factory makes." Place the insertion point between the "e" and the "h" of "warehouses."
3. Insert an optional hyphen by pressing Ctrl+-. The optional hyphen indicates where "warehouses" should be divided.
4. In the same paragraph, locate "24," and delete the space that follows it. Insert a nonbreaking space by pressing Ctrl+Shift+Spacebar.
5. Locate the phrase "melt-a-ways" in the bulleted list in the third column on page 2. The phrase contains a normal hyphen. Notice the difference in shape and size among the three types of hyphens. All hyphens, however, have the same appearance when printed.

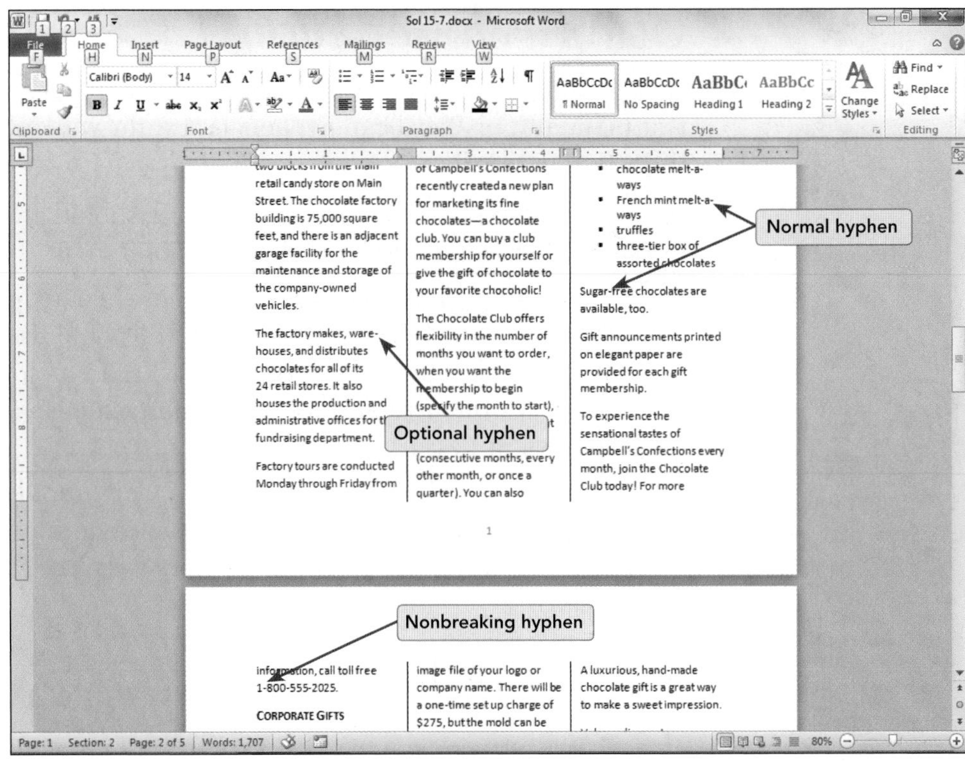

Figure 15-10 Normal, nonbreaking, and optional hyphens

Exercise 15-9 HYPHENATE A DOCUMENT

Word offers automatic hyphenation to control ragged edges at the ends of paragraph lines and to reduce the amount of space between words that Word inserts when text is justified. In the Hyphenation dialog box you can:

- Hyphenate the document automatically as you key text.
- Hyphenate words written in all-capital letters.
- Set a hyphenation zone measurement to control the amount of raggedness in the right margin. The default setting is 0.25 inch. A lower number reduces the raggedness, and a higher number reduces the amount of hyphenation.
- Limit the number of consecutive hyphens in lines of text by a number you enter.
- Manually hyphenate a document, which lets you confirm each hyphen.

Figure 15-11 Hyphenation dialog box

Hyphenation

Automatically hyphenate document

Hyphenate words in CAPS

Hyphenation zone: 0.25"

Limit consecutive hyphens to: No limit

Manual... OK Cancel

NOTE

You can also automatically hyphenate a document by clicking the Page Layout tab, clicking Hyphenation in the Page Setup group, and clicking Automatic. To remove automatic hyphenation, click the Page Layout tab, Page Setup group, Hyphenation, and None.

TIP

You can move the hyphenation point for a word in the Hyphenate at box by clicking another point in the word or by using 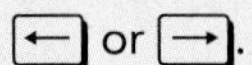.

1. Move the insertion point to the beginning of the document. Click the **Page Layout** tab, click the arrow beside the Hyphenation button, and then choose **Hyphenation Options**. The Hyphenation dialog box appears.
2. Set the **Limit consecutive hyphens** box to **2**, so no more than two consecutive lines end with hyphens.
3. Click **Manual**. Word begins the hyphenation process. The program asks for confirmation on each word to be hyphenated.
4. Click **Yes** to accept the hyphenation, but avoid hyphenating proper names or words containing fewer than six letters, such as "ha-ven."
5. When the dialog box appears to tell you hyphenation is complete, click **OK** to return to the document.
6. Save the document as ***[your initials]*15-9** in your Lesson 15 folder.
7. Submit and close the document.

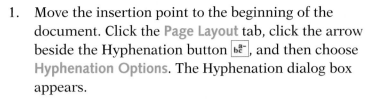

NOTE

The Gregg Reference Manual contains several guidelines for preferred hyphenation practices. For example, you should not hyphenate abbreviations or contractions (such as "shouldn't") or hyphenate a word that creates a one-letter syllable (such as "a-ware"). For more information about hyphenation, see Section 9, "Word Division," in *The Gregg Reference Manual*.

Lesson 15 Summary

- Word can arrange document text in columns like those used in newspapers and magazines. There are two ways to create multiple-column layouts: by using the Columns menu and by using the Columns dialog box.
- You can key and edit text in multiple-column layouts in the same way you do so in standard one-column layouts. Use the arrow keys to move between columns.
- You can create and change font and paragraph formats for text in columns in the same way you create and change them for standard layouts.
- Adjust column width and spacing by dragging column markers and column margins on the ruler or by using the Columns dialog box. Create equal column widths by clicking the Equal column width check box in the Columns dialog box.

- Word automatically breaks columns at the end of the page or section. However, you can insert a column break manually so that the columns end where you want them to end.
- Column lengths are often unequal at the ends of sections or pages. Insert a continuous section break after the unbalanced columns, and Word will balance the columns.
- Hyphenation is the division of words that cannot fit at the end of a line. A normal hyphen is used for words that should always be hyphenated. A nonbreaking hyphen is used when a hyphenated word should not be divided at a line break. An optional hyphen indicates where a word should be divided if the word falls at the end of a line.

LESSON 15		Command Summary	
Feature	**Button**	**Command**	**Keyboard**
Hyphenation		Page Layout tab, Page Setup group	
Insert column break		Page Layout tab, Page Setup group, Breaks	Ctrl+Shift+Enter
Insert columns		Page Layout tab, Page Setup group, Columns	
Nonbreaking hyphen			Ctrl+Shift+-
Optional hyphen			Ctrl+-

Concepts Review

True/False Questions

Each of the following statements is either true or false. Indicate your choice by circling T or F.

T F 1. You can open the Columns dialog box by using the Insert tab on the Ribbon.

T F 2. A continuous section break is used to balance columns.

T F 3. Formatting text in multiple columns is very different from formatting text in a typical document.

T F 4. Pressing [→] at the end of any column moves the insertion point to the top of the next column.

T F 5. Words containing nonbreaking hyphens cannot be divided across two lines.

T F 6. You can use the ruler to change column width.

T F 7. A single document can use different column layouts.

T F 8. When working with columns, use Draft view to see the columns as they are arranged on the page.

Short Answer Questions

Write the correct answer in the space provided.

1. What is the keyboard shortcut for inserting a column break?

___

2. Which dialog box do you use to add a vertical line between columns?

___

3. Which arrow do you press to move from the top of any column to the bottom of the previous column?

___

4. Which tab on the Ribbon includes the Columns button?

___

5. Which key do you press while adjusting column widths on the ruler to see an exact measurement display?

___

6. What shape is the pointer when you use the ruler to adjust column widths?

___

7. Which kind of hyphen do you use if you want to indicate where a word should be divided if the word falls at the end of a line?

---

8. What option in the Columns dialog box do you select to make all columns the same width?

Critical Thinking

Answer these questions on a separate page. There are no right or wrong answers. Support your answers with examples from your own experience, if possible.

1. Imagine a newspaper that doesn't use columns. Then imagine an 8½- by 11-inch newsletter, also without columns. What problems would these publications present to readers?
2. Find examples in magazines, newspapers, and newsletters of columns of different widths. Which width do you feel is most readable?

Skills Review

Exercise 15-10

Create multiple-column layouts.

1. Open the file **Current Events**. At the top of the document key the title **Corporate Connections** in 18-point, bold, small caps formatting. Center the text, and place 42 points spacing before and 24 points spacing after. Apply a thin, single-line bottom line border to the title.
2. Format the text from "Chocolate-Covered Cocoa Beans" to the end of the document into two equal-width columns with a vertical rule between the columns by following these steps:
   a. Position the insertion point at the beginning of the paragraph that begins "Chocolate-Covered Cocoa Beans."
   b. Click the **Page Layout** tab, and click the Columns button. Click **More Columns** to open the Columns dialog box.
   c. Specify **2** for **Number of columns** and **0.25"** for the **Spacing** of column 1.
   d. Choose **Equal column width**.
   e. Choose **This point forward** from the **Apply to** drop-down list, and check the **Line between** box.
   f. Click **OK**.

3. Select the paragraphs that follow each side heading, and change the paragraph format to 3 points spacing after and single spacing. Apply the same format to the bulleted lists.
4. Change the bottom margin to 0.5 inch.
5. Insert a footer with the date aligned at the right margin. Use the third date format.
6. Change the paragraph spacing for each side heading except the first side heading ("Chocolate-Covered Cocoa Beans") to 18 points spacing before and 6 points spacing after. Change the first side heading to 0 points spacing before and 6 points spacing after.
7. Save the document as ***[your initials]*****15-10** in your Lesson 15 folder.
8. Submit and close the document.

Exercise 15-11

Key and edit text in columns.

1. Open the file **Newsletter**. Change the top and bottom margins to 0.75 inch.
2. Position the insertion point at the beginning of the paragraph that begins "Chocolate Facts." Format the document from "Chocolate Facts" to the end of the document as two columns with 0.25-inch distance between the columns.
3. Insert column text by following these steps:
   a. Position the insertion point at the end of the bulleted paragraph that begins "Chocolate should not."
   b. Press Enter; then key the text shown in Figure 15-12.

Figure 15-12

```
• The center of the cacao bean is called a nib.
• The Ivory Coast is the world's largest producer of
  cacao pods.
```

4. Edit document text by following these steps:
   a. Select "detrimental" at the top of the second column, and key **harmful**.
   b. Edit the first bulleted paragraph under "Chocolate Facts" so that it is one sentence. Delete the period after "bean" and key **, and**; change "Each" to lowercase.
5. Select the text at the end of the second column from "Choc Talk" to the end of the document, and apply a thin-line box border with light gray shading.
6. Add a box page border, using a thin double-line style.
7. Save the document as ***[your initials]*****15-11** in your Lesson 15 folder.
8. Submit and close the document.

Exercise 15-12

Format columns, and adjust column width and spacing.

1. Open the file **Earth Day - 2**.
2. Create columns of unequal width by following these steps:
   a. Position the insertion point before the text "Earth Day will" in the first paragraph.
   b. Open the **Columns** dialog box.
   c. Choose the **Left** option in the **Presets** section, choose **Line between**, and choose **This point forward** from the Apply to list.
   d. Click **OK**.
3. Because this format is not appropriate for the document, use the ruler to change the column width and spacing by following these steps:
   a. Place the insertion point in column 1, and point to the column marker (a ScreenTip displays "Move Column").
   b. Hold down Alt and drag the marker to the right to change column 1 to 2 inches wide.
   c. Point to the left margin area on the ruler for column 2 (a ScreenTip displays "Left Margin").
   d. Drag the margin 0.5 inch to the right, making the second column 3 inches wide and increasing the space between columns to 1 inch.
4. Open the Columns dialog box. Select **Equal column width**. Change columns 1 and 2 to **2.75** inches wide with **0.5**-inch spacing.
5. Balance the columns by following these steps:
   a. Move the insertion point to the end of the document, after the Web site address.
   b. Click the Breaks button, and click **Continuous**.
6. Format the title of the document as 24-point bold, small caps, centered, with 72 points spacing before and 24 points spacing after.
7. Change the entire document font to Cambria.
8. Apply a double-line box page border to the document.
9. Save the document as ***[your initials]*15-12** in your Lesson 15 folder.
10. Submit and close the document.

Exercise 15-13

Balance columns, control column breaks, and hyphenate a document.

1. Open the file **Privacy Policy**.
2. Select the first line of the document, and apply 72 points spacing before and 12 points spacing after. Apply 16-point, bold, small caps formatting to the title. Add a bottom line border to the paragraph.

3. Format the document from "Campbell's Confections Privacy Policy" forward as two columns of equal width, with a line between columns.
4. Format the following headings using 14 points, bold, italic, small caps.

   Campbell's Confections Privacy Policy

   Information Collection and Use of Personal Information

   Shared Information

   Cookies and Beacons

   Personal Information Corrections

   Contact Campbell's Confections

   Private Policy Changes
5. Select the information under the paragraph that begins "Personal information collected," and format the text as a bulleted list. Apply the same bulleted list format to the text that begins "Internet Protocol" and ends "traffic patterns."
6. Balance the columns by following these steps:
   a. Move the insertion point to the end of the document, after "October 1, 20—."

   b. Click the Breaks button on the Page Layout tab, and choose **Continuous**.
7. Insert a column break by following these steps:
   a. Position the insertion point at the beginning of the heading on page 2 that begins "Contact Campbell's."

   b. Press Ctrl+Shift+Enter.
8. Apply a page border to the whole document. Add a footer to include a page number that will print on page 2 of the document. Include the word "Page" in front of the page number.
9. Hyphenate the document by following these steps:
   a. Move the insertion point to the beginning of the document.

   b. Click the **Page Layout** tab, and click **Hyphenation**.

   c. Select **Hyphenation Options**.

   d. Change the value in the **Limit consecutive hyphens to** box to **2**, and click **Manual**.

   e. Click **Yes** to confirm each hyphenation, but avoid hyphenating proper names.

   f. Click **OK** when hyphenation is complete.
10. Save the document as ***[your initials]*15-13** in your Lesson 15 folder.
11. Submit and close the document.

Lesson Applications

Exercise 15-14

Create a two-column layout, format text, and balance the columns.

1. Open the file **Guidelines**.
2. Position the insertion point at the beginning of the paragraph that begins "Business Structure." Use the Columns dialog box to create a two-column layout from this point forward, with 1 inch between the columns and no vertical lines.
3. Key the title **GUIDELINES** at the top of the document. Format the title in16 points, bold, all caps, with 24 points spacing after. Center the title.
4. Format each side heading using 14-point bold and small caps. Scroll through the document, and verify that side headings are not separated from the paragraph text that follows.
5. Balance the columns, and delete blank paragraph marks that may appear at the top of a column.
6. Change the top margin for section 1 to 2 inches. Add a page number that will print at the top right of pages 2 and 3 only. Include **Page** in front of the number.
7. Spell-check the document, and save it as ***[your initials]*15-14** in your Lesson 15 folder.
8. Submit and close the document.

Exercise 15-15

Create a three-column layout, change column spacing, and balance columns.

1. Open the files **Stores - 1** and **Intro**.
2. Select and copy the paragraphs in the **Intro** document.
3. Paste the selected text at the beginning of **Stores - 1**, and insert a blank line after the pasted text if necessary.
4. Insert a continuous section break before "Ohio Stores."
5. Create a three-column layout for the list of stores. Change the spacing between columns to 0.2 inch. Keep the columns equal in width (with no line between columns).
6. Key **Campbell's Confections** as a title at the top of the document. Change the spacing after to 24 points, and format the title as all caps, 16-point bold, italic, and centered.
7. Change the top margin of section 1 to 2 inches.

8. Format the three state headings as 12-point bold, italic, and small caps.
9. Insert a column break at the "West Virginia" state heading using Ctrl+Shift+Enter. Insert a column break in the first column at the beginning of the address for the Warren, Ohio, store. Press Enter twice to align the Ohio store names in the first and second column.
10. Insert a column break at the "Pennsylvania" state heading. Insert another column break at the beginning of the Erie, PA, store and the Monroeville, PA, store.
11. Create a footer for page 2 only that includes the centered text **Page** followed by the page number.
12. Save the document as ***[your initials]*15-15** in your Lesson 15 folder.
13. Submit the document. Close both documents.

Exercise 15-16

Create a two-column layout, key text in columns, and format and balance the columns.

1. Open the file **Staff**.
2. Change the page orientation to landscape.
3. Format the entire document as two columns.
4. At the top of the first column, key the heading **Campbell's Confections: Corporate Staff**.
5. Add 24 points spacing after the heading.
6. Format the heading as 24-point italic.
7. At the end of the document, key the new paragraph shown in Figure 15-13. Use the Format Painter to copy the format from one of the side headings in the document to the new heading.

Figure 15-13

```
Liz Hart, Advertising/Marketing
Liz has been with the company for 15 years. She started
working as a part-time employee when she was in high
school to save money for college. She joined the company
full-time after she graduated from college. She is married
with two sons. Her hobbies are cooking, collecting recipe
books, and spending time with her family.
```

8. Change the space between columns to 1 inch, and keep the columns equal in width.
9. At the beginning of the text under the heading (paragraph that begins "Campbell's Confections), insert a continuous section break. Change the bottom margin for section 2 to 0.5 inch.
10. Format the heading section as one column.

11. In the heading, delete the colon, and start the heading text beginning *"Corporate Staff"* on a new line.
12. Change the text in the new second line to small caps, and center both lines of the heading. Change the spacing after the second line to 24 points if necessary. Change the spacing after the first line of the heading to 0 points, and change the line spacing to single.
13. Delete the heading "Corporate Staff" in the middle of the first column.
14. Select all the text below the document heading, and change the font size to 11 points.
15. Balance the length of the columns in section 2.
16. Insert a page number that will print in the upper right corner of page 2 only. Adjust the tab setting to align with the right margin.
17. Save the document as ***[your initials]*15-16** in your Lesson 15 folder.
18. Submit and close the document.

Exercise 15-17 ◆ Challenge Yourself

Create a three-column layout, format columns and column text, balance columns, and hyphenate the document.

1. Open the file **Corporate Gifts**.
2. Key the title **Corporate Gifts** using 24-point bold and small caps format. Center the title, and add 24 points spacing after.
3. Insert a continuous section break at the first paragraph below the title.
4. Format the second section as three equal columns.
5. Balance the columns.
6. Change the font in section 2 to Cambria.
7. Format all the paragraphs in section 2 with a 0.25-inch first-line indent.
8. Change the space between the columns to 0.4 inch, and insert a line between the columns.
9. Change the document left and right margins to 1.25 inches. Center the whole document vertically on the page.
10. Hyphenate the document manually. Avoid hyphenating words that are six characters or less and any proper names.
11. Apply a 1½-point triple-line page border to the document.
12. Save the document as ***[your initials]*15-17** in your Lesson 15 folder.
13. Submit and close the document.

On Your Own

In these exercises you work on your own, as you would in a real-life business environment. Use the skills you've learned to accomplish the task—and be creative.

Exercise 15-18

Create a newsletter about a neighborhood event or activity. Apply a three-column layout. Format the newsletter attractively, and balance the columns. Give the newsletter a title, and spell- and grammar-check your document. Save the document as ***[your initials]*****15-18**. Submit the document.

Exercise 15-19

Create a newspaper article about a topic you would enjoy reporting. Use landscape orientation, and format the article with four columns and justified alignment. Apply very simple formatting that might appear in a newspaper. Balance the columns. Give the article a title, and spell- and grammar-check the document. Save the document as ***[your initials]*****15-19** and submit it.

Exercise 15-20

Log on to the Internet. Find Web sites about a health issue that interests you. Using the information, create a magazine article that is two columns and left aligned, with attractive formatting. Balance the columns. Give the article a title, and spell- and grammar-check the document. Save the document as ***[your initials]*****15-20** and submit it.

Unit 4 Applications

Unit Application 4-1

Create a memo that includes a table. Edit and format table structures and text.

1. Open the file **Fitness - 2**.
2. Insert a line above the table using the Split Table command.
3. Create a standard business memo format at the beginning of the document. The memo is to "Store Managers" from Garland Miller. Use the current date, and key **Fitness Centers** for the subject line. Format the subject line with 24 points spacing after.
4. For the body of the memo, key the text in Figure U4-1. Use single spacing and change the spacing after to 0. Include your reference initials at the end of the memo.

NOTE

Refer to Appendix B, "Standard Forms for Business Documents," if you need help with the memo layout.

Figure U4-1

```
We have compiled the survey responses from the area
fitness centers, and the results appear in the following
table. Please review the table information before our next
managers' meeting.
```

5. Insert a next page section break after the memo and before the table. Change the orientation for section 1 to portrait, and change the top margin to 2 inches.
6. Study the column headings above columns 2 and 3. Use the Split cells and Merge cells commands to apply similar formatting to the fourth and fifth columns and to the sixth and seventh columns. Edit the text for each column heading.

TIP

Try splitting the cells into one column and two rows before merging the cells.

7. Adjust the row height for the header rows, and center the text within the cells vertically and horizontally.
8. Select the seven rows below the header rows, change the row height to 0.4 inch, and center the text vertically within the cells.
9. Change the vertical alignment for section 2 to center. Center the table horizontally.
10. Right-align the dollar amounts, and change the right cell margin for the selected cells to 0.4 inch. (Use the Table Properties dialog box, Cell tab, Options command.)
11. Sort the seven rows below the heading rows in alphabetical order.

12. Apply gray shading to the header rows.
13. Key the title **Fitness Center Survey Results** at the top of section 2. Format the title using 20-point bold and small caps, with 24 points spacing after, and center it horizontally.
14. Key **$** in front of each of the numbers in the row beginning "Exercise and More."
15. Select the table, and apply a double-line outside border.
16. Save the document as ***[your initials]*u4-1** in a new Unit 4 Applications folder.
17. Submit and close the document.

Unit Application 4-2

Create column layouts, change column width and spacing, add a line between columns, and control column breaks.

1. Open the file **Rewards**.
2. Format the beginning of the document as a memo to "Store Managers" from Lynn Tanguay. Use the current date, and use "Rewards Club" for the subject.
3. Insert a next-page section break at the beginning of the line that begins "Campbell's Confections Rewards Club." Change the top margin for section 1 to 2 inches. Key your reference initials and an attachment notation at the end of the memo.
4. Beginning with the text "Rewards Club Benefits," format the document with two columns. Change the column spacing to 0.25 inch. Keep the column width equal, and add a vertical line between columns.
5. Format the title of section 2 using 18 points, bold, small caps; center the text, and add 24 points spacing after. Delete the blank paragraph that follows the heading.
6. Select the text "Rewards Club Benefits," and apply 12-point, bold, small caps formatting. Copy this formatting to the other side headings: "Eligibility," "How to Register," "Reward Certificates," and "Terms and Conditions."
7. Select the text below the heading "Rewards Club Benefits" from "Free piece" through "Electronic newsletter," and format the paragraphs as a bulleted list. Change the left indent to 0.
8. Apply the bulleted list format to the text under "Eligibility" beginning with "Must be 18" and ending with "phone number" and to the text under "Rewards Certificates" beginning with "Earn points" and ending with "gift certificates."
9. Select the paragraph that begins "*See," and apply 10-point formatting. Repeat the formatting to each of the paragraphs that begin "Note."

10. Insert a column break at the "Reward Certificates" side heading. Position the insertion point at the top of section 2, and apply a page border to the section. If necessary, change the bottom margin for section 2 to 0.5 inch.
11. Save the document as ***[your initials]*u4-2** in your Unit 4 Applications folder.
12. Submit and close the document.

Unit Application 4-3

Create a long table with nested tables.

1. Start a new document, and change the orientation to landscape.
2. Insert a parent table that is two columns wide by two rows.
3. In the first column, starting in the first row, key the following. Press Enter after each line.

   Repair Order No.
   Date:
   Notes:

4. In the second column, starting in the first row, key the following. Press Enter after each line.

   Vehicle No.
   License:
   VIN:
   Mileage:

5. Select the text in the first cell of the first column, and set a right-aligned solid leader tab at 4.25 inches. Position the insertion point after "Repair Order No.," and press Ctrl+Tab to insert the solid leader tab. Insert a solid leader tab for each line in the first cell of the first column.

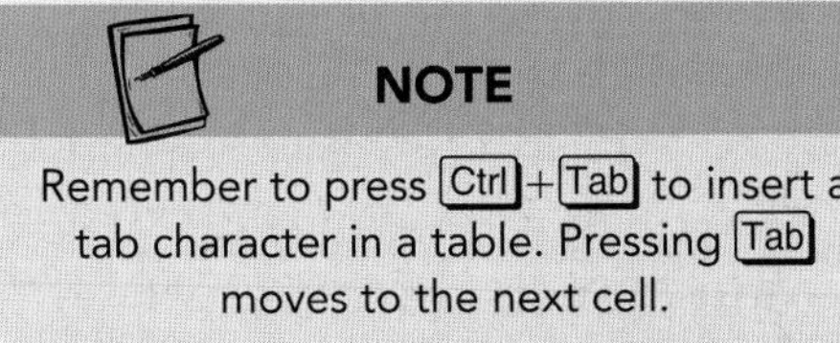

NOTE

Remember to press Ctrl+Tab to insert a tab character in a table. Pressing Tab moves to the next cell.

6. Set a right-aligned solid leader tab at 4.25 for the text in the first cell of the second column. Insert the solid leader tab after each line of text.
7. Select the text in the first row of the table, and apply 14-point bold, small caps, and 15 points spacing after.
8. Center the document vertically. Adjust the column width for each column to 4.5 inches.
9. Save the new document as ***[your initials]*u4-3** in your Unit 4 Applications folder.
10. Open the file **VM Form.**
11. Select the first table, and copy the table to the Clipboard.

12. Switch to the file ***[your initials]*u4-3**. Paste the Clipboard's contents in the first cell of the second row.
13. Switch to the file **VM Form**, and select the second table. Copy and paste the second table in the second row, second column.
14. Use the AutoFit Window feature for each of the nested tables.
15. Select the parent table, and change the cell margins for the top, bottom, left, and right to 0.1 inch. Apply a double-line outside border to the parent table.
16. Select each nested table, and change the row height to 0.25 inch.
17. Apply a 3-point, single-line border below the first row and between the columns of the first row of the parent table.
18. Use the Split Table command to insert a blank line above the parent table. Key **Campbell's Confections Vehicle Maintenance Form**. Format the title using character and paragraph formatting.
19. Apply a 1½-point, single-line outside border to each of the nested tables. Select the first row of the nested table on the left, and merge the cells. Merge the cells in the first row of the second nested table. Format the text in the first row of each nested table to 14-point bold, small caps, and centered. Apply gray shading to the first row in each nested table.
20. Select the text in the second row of the nested table on the left, and apply bold formatting. Repeat the format to the second row of the second nested table.
21. Select the nested table on the left, and center the text within the cells vertically. Repeat for the second nested table.
22. Resave, submit, and close the document. Close the VM Form document without saving.

Unit Application 4-4

Using the Internet, create a newsletter with tables and columns.

1. Start a new document, which will be a simple newsletter that is one to two pages in length.
2. Write a newsletter title. Use appropriate spacing and character formatting.
3. Develop four articles. Research the content of the articles online.
4. Each article should have a title.
5. All paragraphs within an article should be separated by appropriate paragraph spacing.

6. One of the articles should contain a bulleted list, using any bullet style.
7. Use column breaks, continuous section breaks, and page breaks to arrange the columns in a visually suitable layout.
8. Include one or two formatted tables with rotated text and shading.
9. Determine whether you need to horizontally center your table(s) within the boundaries of a column or the margins of the newsletter.
10. Each page should have a header and footer.
11. Include any other formatting to make the newsletter attractive.
12. On a new page in the document, create a bulleted list containing the references or Web sites you used. Save the document as ***[your initials]*****u4-4** in your Unit 4 Applications folder.

Unit 5

GRAPHICS AND CHARTS

Lesson 16

Graphics

OBJECTIVES ***After completing this lesson, you will be able to:***

1. Insert clip art.
2. Move and format clip art.
3. Create WordArt.
4. Work with shapes.
5. Modify shapes.
6. Control the order of, group, and align shapes.

Estimated Time: 1½ hours

This is the first of three lessons that teach graphics and desktop publishing using Word. This lesson focuses on clip art and shapes. You learn how to insert and modify clip art as well as create and format *drawing objects*—shapes such as squares, circles, stars, banners, and arrows. Special text effects can be added to a document using the WordArt feature.

Inserting Clip Art

Microsoft Office provides access to a wide variety of drawings, photographs, audio files, videos, and other media files, called *clips*.

When you want to insert clip art in a document, you can use one of two search methods:

- Open the Clip Art task pane, and search for pictures by keyword.
- Open the Microsoft Clip Organizer window, and view collections of clips organized by category (such as business, people, and transportation).

Exercise 16-1 FIND CLIPS BY USING KEYWORDS

Each clip in the Microsoft Office collection has keywords associated with it. Using a keyword is an easy way to narrow your search for an appropriate clip.

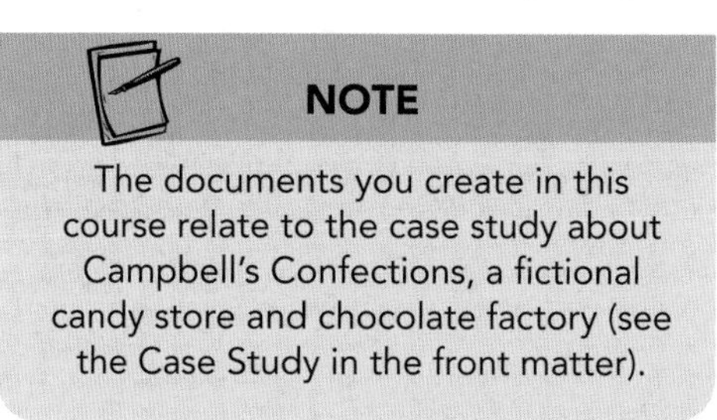

NOTE

The documents you create in this course relate to the case study about Campbell's Confections, a fictional candy store and chocolate factory (see the Case Study in the front matter).

1. Open the file **Chocolate Terms**.
2. Position the insertion point at the beginning of the first paragraph below the title.
3. Click the Insert tab, and click the Clip Art button. The Clip Art task pane displays.

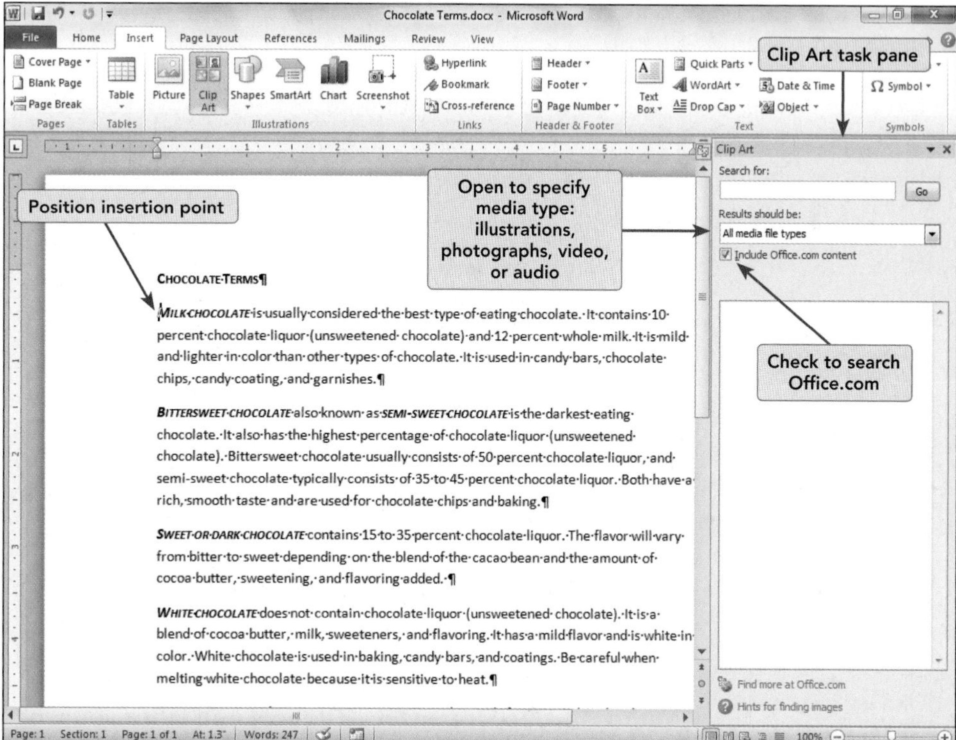

Figure 16-1
Using a keyword to find clips

4. Locate the Search for text box in the Clip Art task pane, and key **chocolate**. The Clip Art task pane has a search option box for searching specific collections of clips and an option to search for clips on Office.com. Use the Results should be drop-down list to narrow your search to specific collections.
5. Click the down arrow beside the Results should be text box, and select Illustrations and Photographs. Deselect Videos and Audio. Verify that the check box for Include Office.com content is checked.
6. Click the Go button Go. The task pane displays chocolate-related clips.
7. Scroll to locate a picture of chocolate candies. A ScreenTip displays the image size, file format (JPG), and keywords associated with the clip.

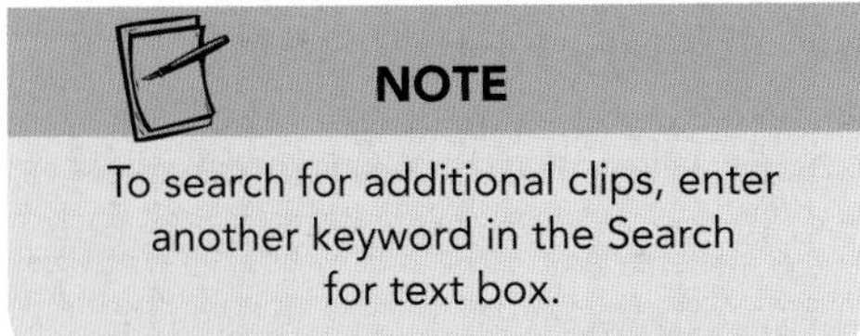

NOTE
To search for additional clips, enter another keyword in the Search for text box.

8. Click the clip to insert it into the document. The picture appears in the document at the insertion point position. It will be sized and positioned in a later exercise.

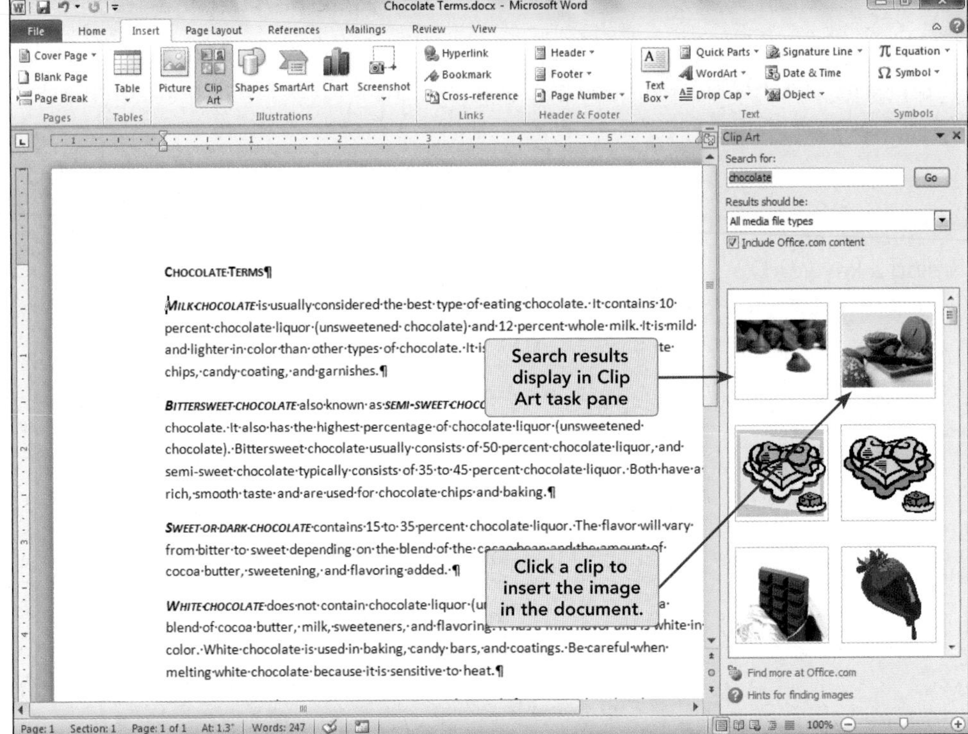

Figure 16-2
Inserting a clip from the Clip Art task pane

Exercise 16-2 FIND CLIPS BY BROWSING CATEGORIES

Microsoft Office clips are organized by category, and you can browse clips by category in the Microsoft Clip Organizer window. You can also use the Microsoft Clip Organizer to collect and store your media clips.

1. Click the Start button, and click **All Programs**. Click to select **Microsoft Office**, and then click **Microsoft Office 2010 Tools**. Choose **Microsoft Clip Organizer**.
2. Under **Collection List**, click the plus sign next to **Office Collections** to expand the list of categories.
3. Click various category names to display the available clips. Expand a category, if necessary, to display subcategories.
4. To locate a special-occasion picture, scroll to the **Special Occasions** category. Click the plus sign to expand the category, and then click **Special Occasions**.
5. Point to the heart picture selected in Figure 16-3. Click the down arrow that appears to the right of the picture. A drop-down list appears with several options. For example, you can copy the clip or preview a larger version of the clip.

Figure 16-3
Inserting a clip from the Microsoft Clip Organizer

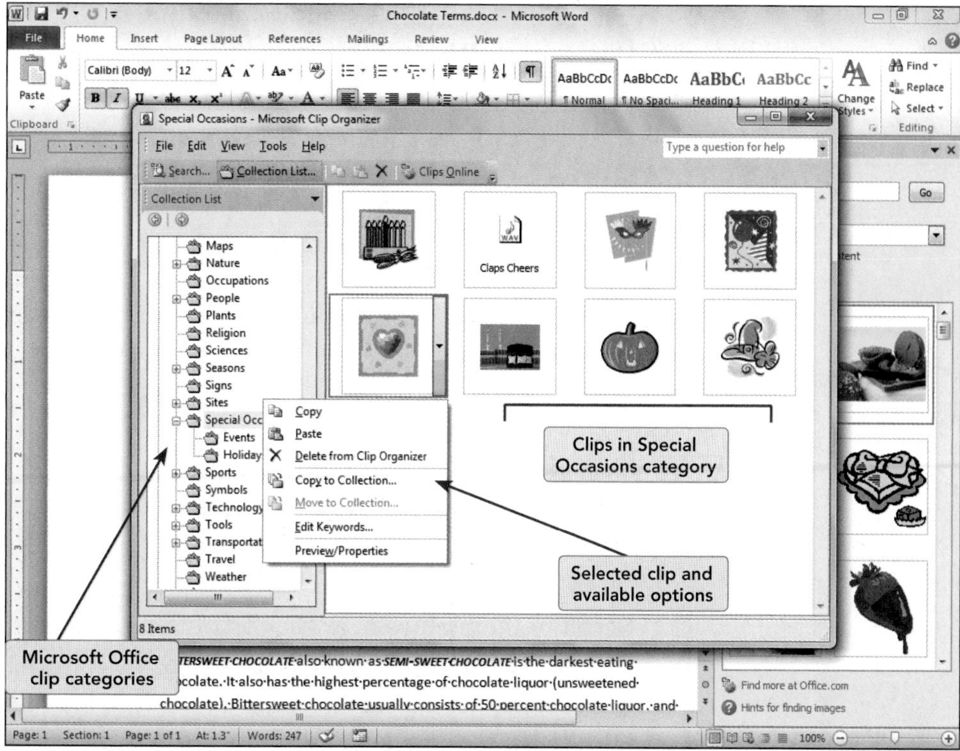

NOTE

You can also drag the picture to the document.

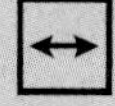

REVIEW

Right-click where you want to paste the clip, and then choose Paste from the shortcut menu, use the Paste button on the Ribbon, or press Ctrl+V.

6. Click **Copy** to copy the clip to the Clipboard.
7. Switch to the Word document, and scroll to the end of the document. Position the insertion point at the last paragraph mark, and paste the clip.
8. Save the document as ***[your initials]*16-2** in a new folder for Lesson 16.
9. Close the Clip Art task pane. Right-click the Microsoft Clip Organizer button on the Windows taskbar and close it. Click **No** when asked if you want the clip to remain on the Clipboard. Leave the document open for the next exercise.

Exercise 16-3 INSERT A PICTURE FROM A FILE

NOTE

The Insert button in the Insert Picture dialog box displays a drop-down list with options for inserting pictures. Choose Insert and Link to insert a copy of the picture and to maintain the link between the source (picture file) and the destination (Word document). Choose Link to File to create a link between the picture and the document that is automatically updated when a change is made to the picture.

In addition to the clip art images provided by Microsoft, you can insert pictures from a file. The pictures can be from the Clip Art gallery or can be digital pictures that you have saved. When you insert a picture, the default setting is to embed the picture, meaning the picture becomes a part of the document. Embedded pictures increase the size of the document.

1. Position the insertion point at the beginning of the paragraph that begins "White chocolate."
2. Click the **Insert** tab, and click the Picture button. The Insert Picture dialog box displays.

3. Locate the folder that contains the student data files, and double-click **Chocolate - P1**. A third picture is inserted in your document.
4. Press Ctrl+Z to undo the insertion.

Moving and Formatting Clip Art

After you insert a clip in a Word document, there are many ways to manipulate it. You can change its size, trim it, change its position, and apply formatting options. To manipulate any graphic, you must select it first.

Exercise 16-4 SELECT CLIP ART

To select clip art, you point to it and click. A selected graphic has a *selection rectangle* around it, formed by four small squares and four small circles at each side and corner of the object. These squares and circles are *sizing handles,* which you drag to resize the graphic.

1. Scroll to the picture near the top of the document.
2. Click the picture to select it. Notice the selection rectangle and the sizing handles. Also notice that the Picture Tools Format tab displays on the Ribbon.

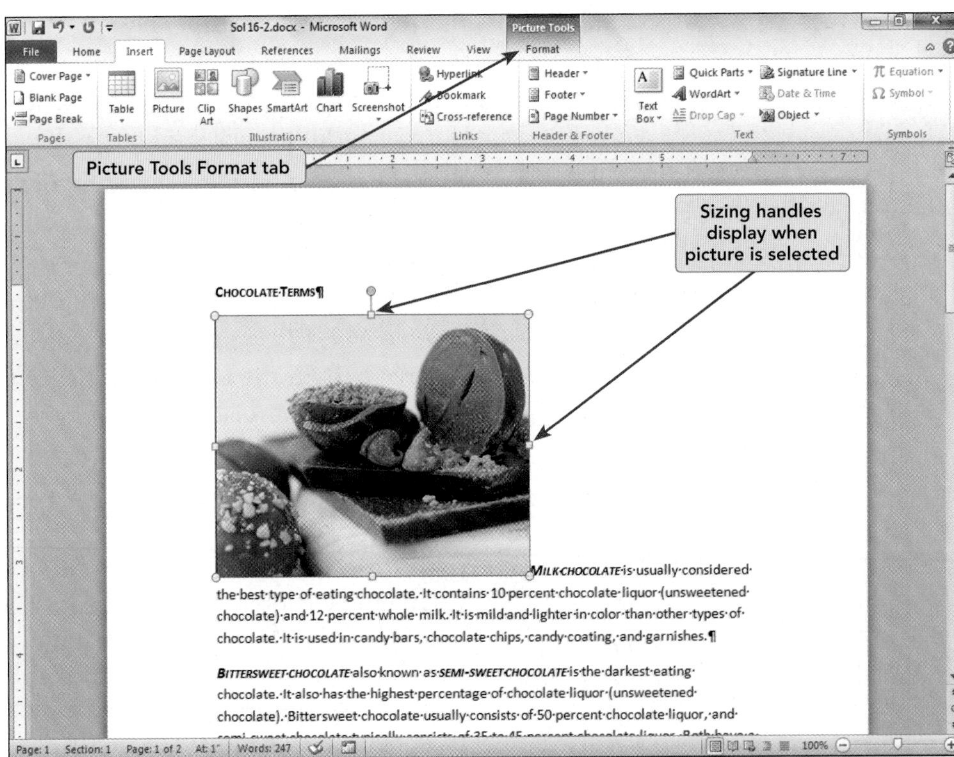

Figure 16-4
Clicking a picture to select it

3. Click outside the borders of the picture to deselect it. The Picture Tools Format tab is no longer displayed on the Ribbon.

Exercise 16-5 SIZE CLIP ART

When you *size* a picture, you reduce or enlarge the amount of space it occupies in the document. Point to and drag a sizing handle to change the size of the picture. You can *scale* a picture to be a percentage of its original size. For example, if a picture is 4 inches square and you choose to scale the picture by 50 percent, the scaled picture measures 2 inches. *Proportional sizing* resizes a picture while maintaining its relative height and width.

1. Click the chocolate picture to select it.
2. Move the pointer to the sizing handle in the top right corner until the pointer looks like this: ⤢.
3. Drag the sizing handle toward the center of the picture, and notice that a transparent box appears. The box represents the new size.

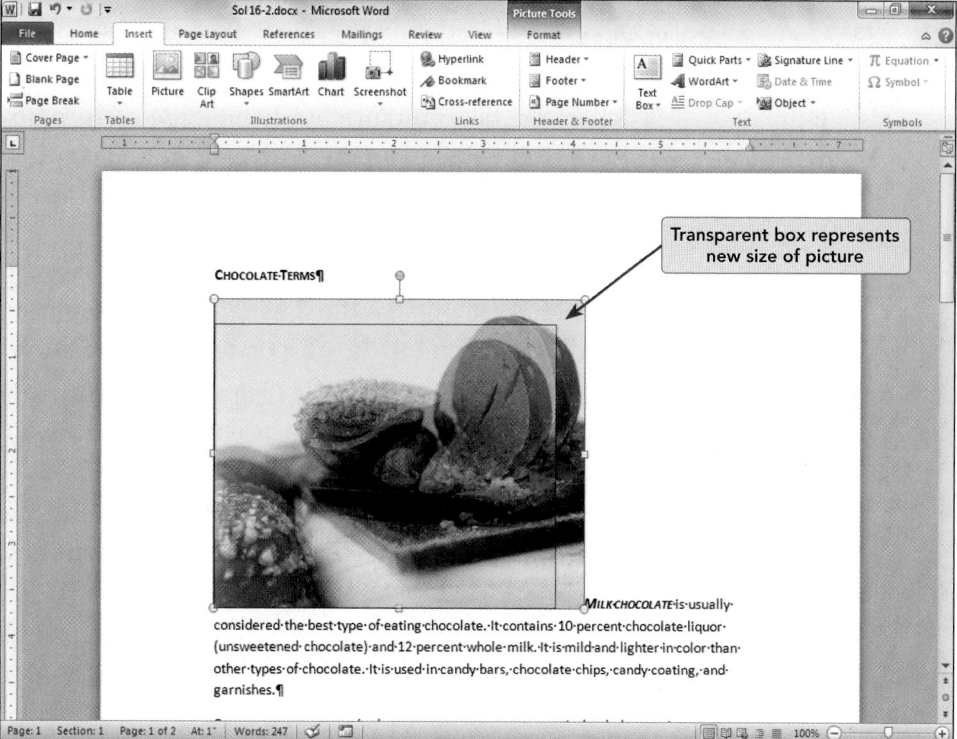

Figure 16-5
Sizing a picture

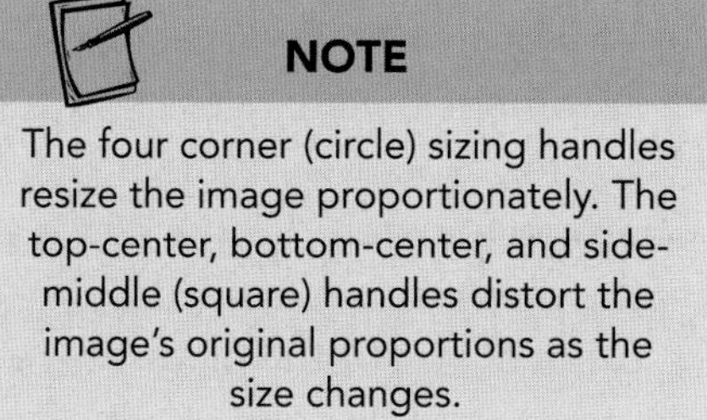

NOTE

The four corner (circle) sizing handles resize the image proportionately. The top-center, bottom-center, and side-middle (square) handles distort the image's original proportions as the size changes.

4. Release the mouse button, and notice that the picture size changes proportionately.
5. Drag the right-middle (square) sizing handle to the left, and release the mouse button. Notice that the picture size changes disproportionately. Dragging a middle, square sizing handle does not size an object proportionately.

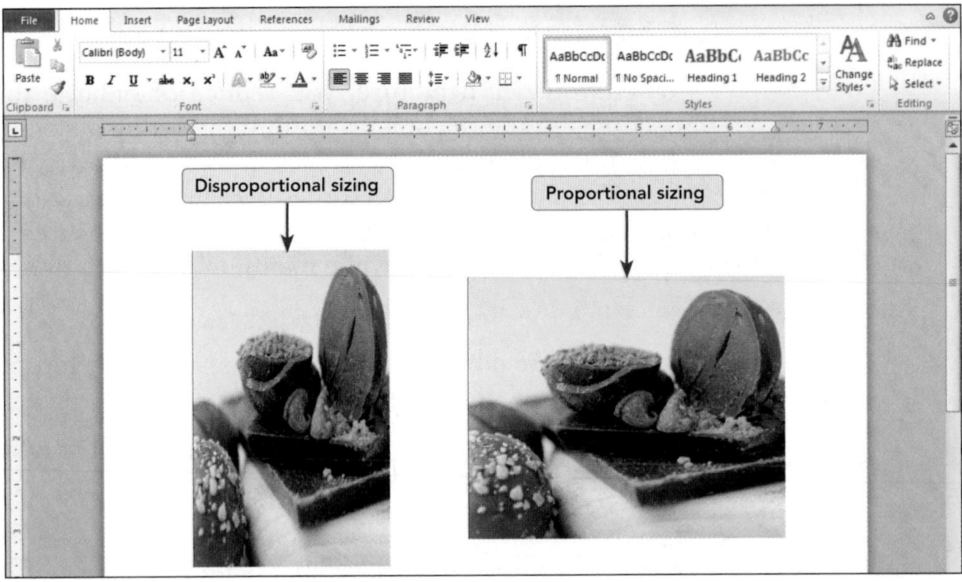

Figure 16-6 Picture sized disproportionately and proportionately

6. Click the Undo button to undo the disproportionate resizing.
7. Select the heart picture by clicking the picture. Press Ctrl and drag the lower-right sizing handle down and to the right. Release the mouse. Pressing Ctrl while dragging sizes the picture from the center of the shape rather than from the edge.
8. Select the heart picture again if necessary. Press Shift and drag the lower-right sizing handle down and to the right. Pressing Shift while you drag maintains the proportion of the picture.
9. Select the heart picture. Instead of using the sizing handles to size it, click the **Picture Tools Format** tab on the Ribbon.
10. Locate the **Size** group and the Shape Height button. Change the height to **2** inches by clicking the down arrow.
11. Select the chocolate picture, and click the Size Dialog Box Launcher to open the Layout dialog box. Click the Size tab.
12. Locate the **Scale** section, and change the **Height** to **50%**. Press Tab. The width measurement automatically changes to 50% because you are scaling proportionately. Locate and read the measurements for the original size of the picture. The picture will be scaled to one-half the height and width.

NOTE

When sizing or scaling a clip using the Size dialog box, be sure to read the original size measurements at the bottom of the dialog box. If the original size of the picture is large, avoid using the Reset button, which would return the picture to its original size.

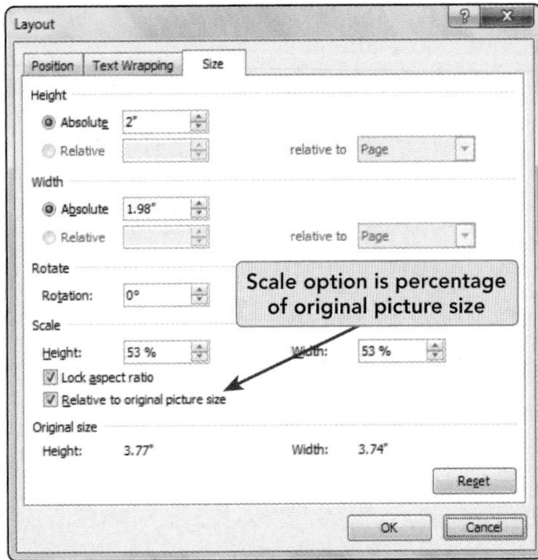

Figure 16-7 Size tab in the Layout dialog box

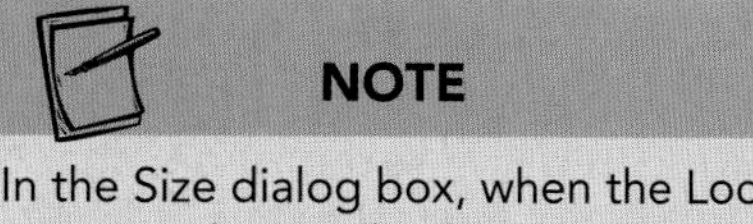

NOTE

In the Size dialog box, when the Lock aspect ratio box is checked, Word scales a picture proportionately, and when the Relative to original picture size box is checked, Word scales the picture from its original size.

TIP

Right-click the picture to display the shortcut menu and a Mini toolbar for objects. The Mini toolbar includes Shape Height, Shape Width, Bring Forward, Send Backward, Crop, and Rotate options.

13. Click **OK**. The chocolate picture is half its original size, but the picture is too big for the document. Click the Undo button to return the picture to its previous size.

Exercise 16-6 COMPRESS PICTURES

When a picture is inserted in a document, the file size of the document is increased. To save room on your storage medium (hard drive or removable storage device), you can compress pictures with little change in the quality of the image. It is important to note that not all pictures can be compressed and maintain good image quality. The file format determines whether image data are lost during compression.

1. Select the chocolate picture.
2. Locate the Adjust group on the Picture Tools Format tab. Click the Compress Pictures button to display the Compress Pictures dialog box.

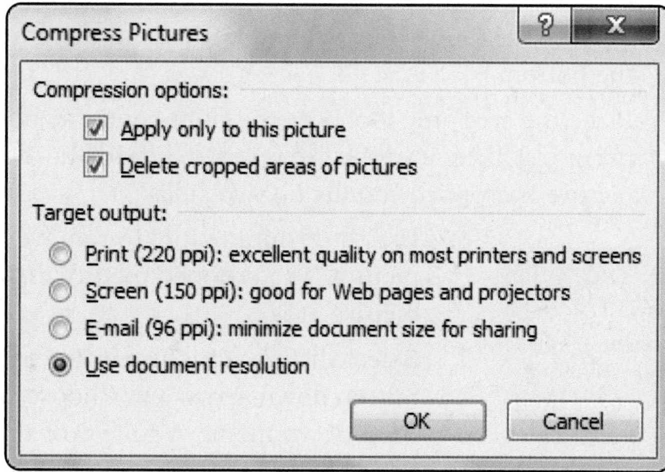

Figure 16-8
Compress Pictures dialog box

3. Click to select **Apply only to this picture** and **Delete cropped areas of pictures**. Under **Target output**, click **Use document resolution**. Click **OK**.

When a document includes multiple pictures, you may choose to compress all pictures in the document and change the output resolution. The default document resolution is 220 ppi. The ppi (pixels-per-inch) measure refers to the image display on a monitor. The higher the resolution,

NOTE

Another way to compress pictures is to open the Save As dialog box, click the Tools button [Tools] to the left of the Save button, and choose Compress Pictures.

the more pixels per inch. The Compress Pictures dialog box includes options for Print (220 ppi), Screen (150 ppi), and E-mail (96 ppi). You can change the default ppi by opening Word Options, clicking Advanced, and locating the Image Size and Quality section. In that section you can choose not to compress images, or you can set the default target output ppi.

Exercise 16-7 CROP CLIP ART

When you trim, or *crop,* a picture, you hide part of the picture. For example, if you have a picture of a person standing next to a computer, you can crop either the person or the computer out of the picture. What you crop is neither displayed on screen nor printed, but it remains part of the original image. You can also crop a picture to fit within a defined shape, resize the picture to fill the picture area, or fit the picture inside the picture area and maintain the original aspect ratio. When you compress a picture, you can choose to delete cropped areas. The crop button is a split button. Click the upper part of the button to crop a picture. Click the lower part of the crop button to select cropping options.

1. Select the heart picture.
2. Click the Crop button on the Picture Tools Format tab. The mouse pointer changes to the cropping tool pointer when you place it on a cropping handle.
3. Place the cropping tool pointer over the bottom-middle sizing handle, and drag it toward the top of the picture to remove the bottom border of the picture.
4. Release the mouse button, and notice that the graphic is cropped from the bottom.
5. Place the cropping tool over the right-center sizing handle, and press Ctrl. Drag it inward to remove the side border, and notice that the picture is cropped equally on two sides.
6. Use the cropping tool to remove the top border of the picture. The cropped picture displays within the picture area.
7. Select the heart picture if necessary, and click the Crop button down arrow. Choose **Crop to Shape** from the drop-down menu. A gallery of shapes appears. Locate the **Basic Shapes** category, and click the heart shape. The image is cropped to fill the heart shape.
8. Select the image if necessary, and click the Crop button. Position the cropped image within the frame by placing the mouse pointer in the middle of the heart and holding down the mouse button. When the four-headed arrow pointer appears, drag the graphic up, down, left, or right to adjust the position. Release the mouse and deselect the heart.

NOTE

The top, bottom, and side sizing handles crop those areas respectively. The four corner sizing handles crop a picture from each respective corner. Press Ctrl and drag a corner cropping handle to crop a picture on all four sides. To control picture position and crop position, right-click the picture and choose Format Picture. Change the width and height measurements as needed. Each change in measurement is reflected in the picture immediately. Notice that there is no Cancel button in the dialog box. Use the Undo command to reverse any change to the picture.

Exercise 16-8 RESTORE CLIP ART TO ITS ORIGINAL SIZE

1. Select the chocolate picture.
2. Click the **Picture Tools Format** tab, and locate the **Adjust** group. Click the arrow beside the Reset Picture button, and choose **Reset Picture & Size**. The picture changes back to its original size, as it appeared when you first inserted it. Change the height to **1.5"** using the **Shape Height** text box in the **Size** group of the Picture Tools Format tab.
3. Save the document as ***[your initials]*16-8** in your Lesson 16 folder.

Exercise 16-9 MOVE CLIP ART

You can move a picture by cutting and pasting or by dragging and dropping. When a picture is inserted, the default setting is to place the picture in-line with text; and the picture is treated like another character in the document. The easiest way to move an in-line graphic is to use the cut-and-paste method. In the next exercise you will learn how to change the wrapping style of a picture. Changing the wrapping style converts an in-line graphic to a free-floating graphic for quick and convenient positioning.

1. Select the heart picture and cut it, placing it on the Clipboard.
2. Paste the picture at the beginning of the paragraph that begins "Baking Chocolate."
3. Select the heart picture, point to it with the arrow pointer, hold down the left mouse button, and drag the picture back to the last paragraph mark of the document. The pointer changes to the drag-and-drop shape, the pointer you use for dragging and dropping text.

Figure 16-9
Dragging a picture

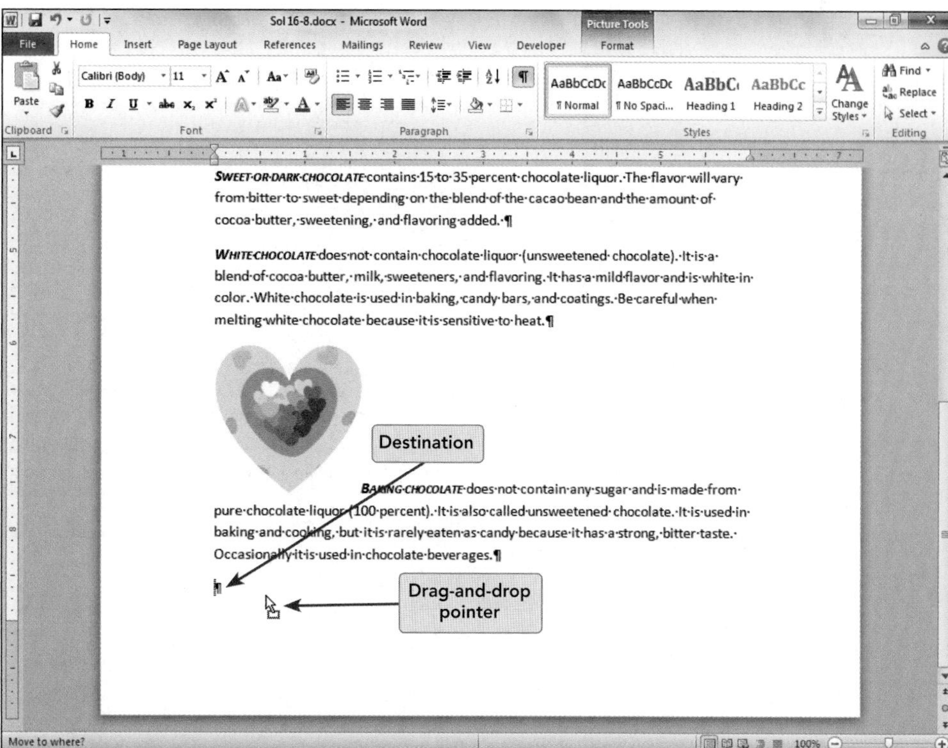

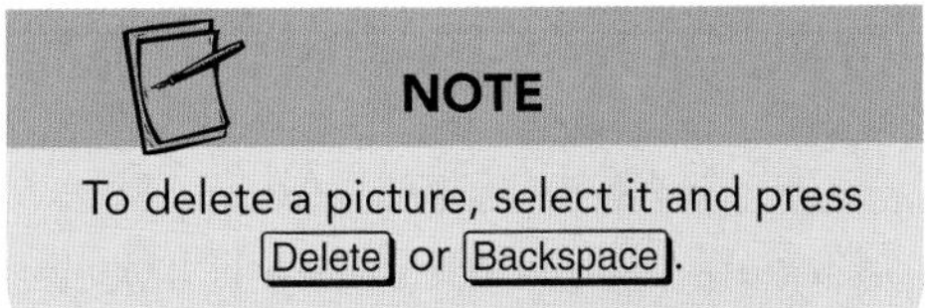

NOTE

To delete a picture, select it and press Delete or Backspace.

4. Release the mouse button. The picture is positioned at the last paragraph mark. If it is not, click the Undo button and drag it again.

Exercise 16-10 CHANGE WRAPPING STYLE

When you insert a graphic, it appears in the document as an *in-line graphic*, by default. An in-line graphic is treated like a character and aligns with the current paragraph. You can change an in-line graphic to a *floating graphic* by changing the text-wrapping option. A floating graphic is placed on the drawing layer of the Word document. You can move the floating graphic freely and layer it behind or in front of text or other objects, changing how text wraps around the graphic. This feature is called *text wrapping*.

1. Select the chocolate picture. The picture is an in-line graphic, treated by Word like any text object. It is left-aligned with its own paragraph mark.
2. Click the **Picture Tools Format** tab on the Ribbon, and click the Wrap Text button. Notice the wrapping options available.
3. Choose **Square**. Text now wraps around the picture. Notice the anchor symbol and the selection handles around the picture.

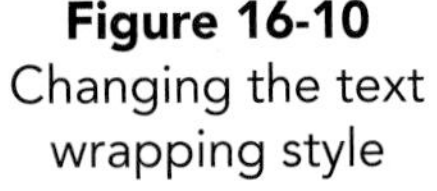

Figure 16-10
Changing the text wrapping style

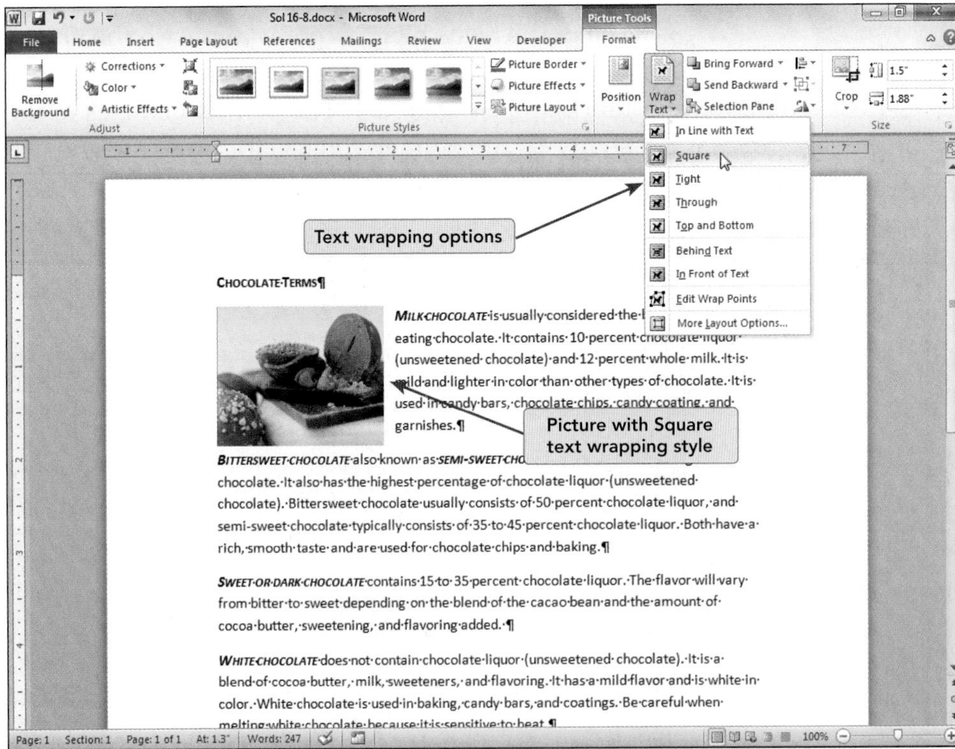

4. Move the pointer over the picture. The pointer is now a four-headed arrow [icon]. You use this pointer to drag the floating picture freely on the page. As you drag a floating picture, Word displays a transparent copy of the picture. You can use the top edge of the transparent picture as a positioning guide. Use the Shift key to control movement either horizontally or vertically.
5. Using the four-headed arrow, drag the picture to different locations in the document. Notice how the text wraps squarely around the picture. Drag the picture to the beginning of the first paragraph.
6. Change the picture back to an in-line graphic by choosing the **In-Line with Text** wrapping style. The picture returns to the area where it was first inserted. If it appears on the same line as the first paragraph, click before "Milk Chocolate" and press Enter, leaving a blank area below the picture.
7. Select the picture, and click the Position button [icon] on the Picture Tools Format tab of the Ribbon. Move the mouse over the gallery of options. Notice that there is one option for in-line graphics and there are nine options for floating graphics (graphics with a text-wrapping option selected). Deselect the menu.

TIP

To align an in-line picture, use the Alignment buttons on the Ribbon, in the Paragraph group. To align a floating picture, click the Position button and choose an option, or choose More Layout Options to open the Layout dialog box and select the Position tab.

8. Select the picture if necessary, and click the Center button [icon] on the Home tab of the Ribbon to center-align the picture.
9. Select the heart picture, and change the wrapping style to **Top and Bottom**.
10. Move the picture around. Notice how text wraps only around the top and bottom and not the sides of the picture.
11. Change the wrapping style to **Tight**. This style is like Square, but the text wraps more closely around the contours of the picture.
12. Position the picture to the left of the last paragraph.
13. Format the document title as 16 points with 36 points spacing before and 24 points spacing after the paragraph. Center-align the title.
14. Save the file as ***[your initials]*16-10** in your Lesson 16 folder, and print it. Leave it open for the next exercise.

TIP

To fine-tune the position of a floating graphic, use the arrow keys. To move a graphic by very small increments, hold down Ctrl while you press the arrow keys.

Figure 16-11
Preview of final document

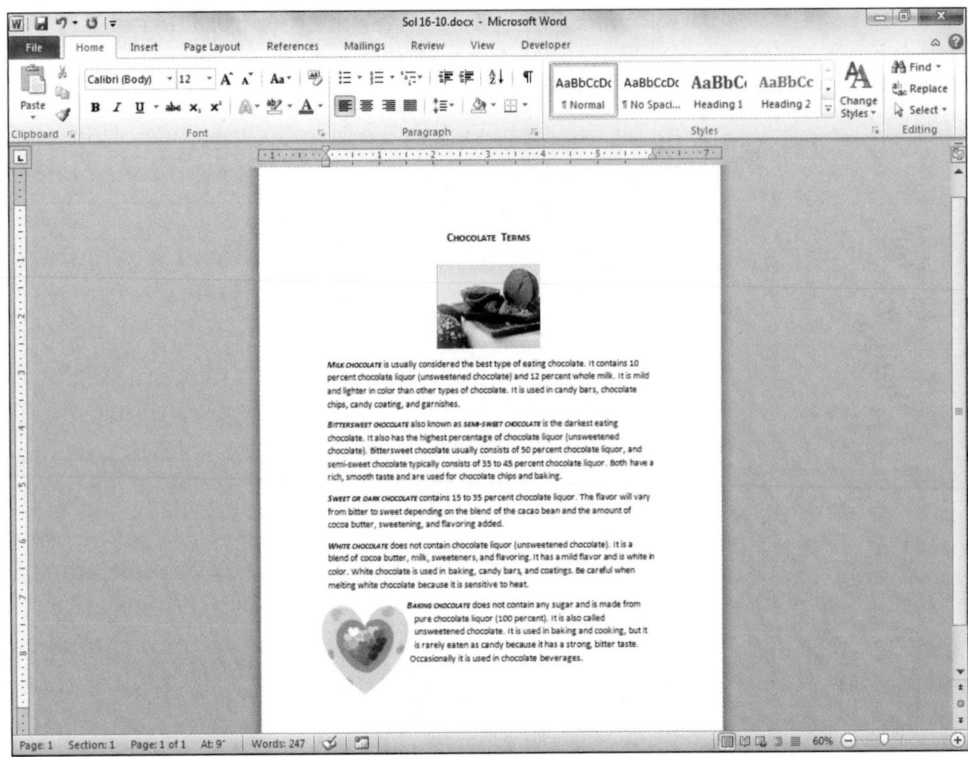

Exercise 16-11 ADJUST THE APPEARANCE OF A PICTURE

You can modify a picture by changing its brightness (how light or dark a color is), contrast (how dark and light an area is), or transparency (how much light can pass through). The Color feature enables you to recolor the picture, change the color tone, and change the color saturation. Special effects including shadow, reflection, glow, and soft edges are available to add a visual effect to the picture. Artistic effects are new to Word 2010 and include pencil grayscale, paint strokes, watercolor sponge, and photocopy. You can also apply a picture style to frame the selected image. When your document contains more than one picture or graphic object, you may want to display the Selection pane to assist you in selecting the correct graphic.

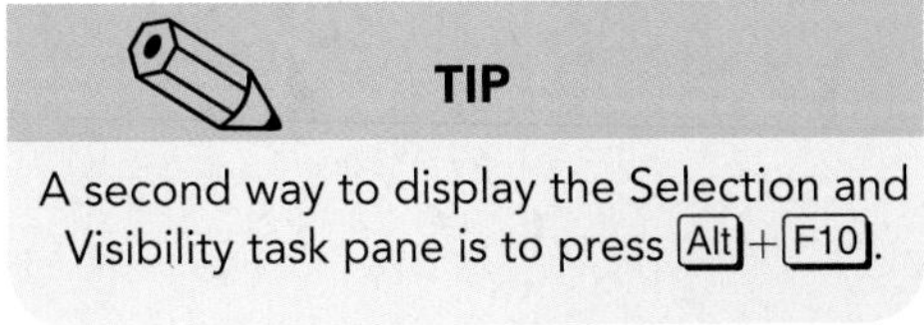

TIP

A second way to display the Selection and Visibility task pane is to press Alt+F10.

1. Select the chocolate picture if necessary, and display the Picture Tools Format tab. Locate the **Arrange** tab, and click the Selection Pane button. The Selection and Visibility task pane displays and lists two shapes for the page.
2. Select the heart picture by clicking the second picture label in the Selection and Visibility task pane. Scroll to the end of the document. Click the **Picture Tools Format** tab, locate the **Adjust** group, and click the Corrections button.
3. Drag the mouse over each of the brightness options in the gallery. As you move the mouse over the thumbnails in the gallery, Live Preview enables you to see the change in your picture. Click **Picture Correction Options**. The Format Picture dialog box displays.

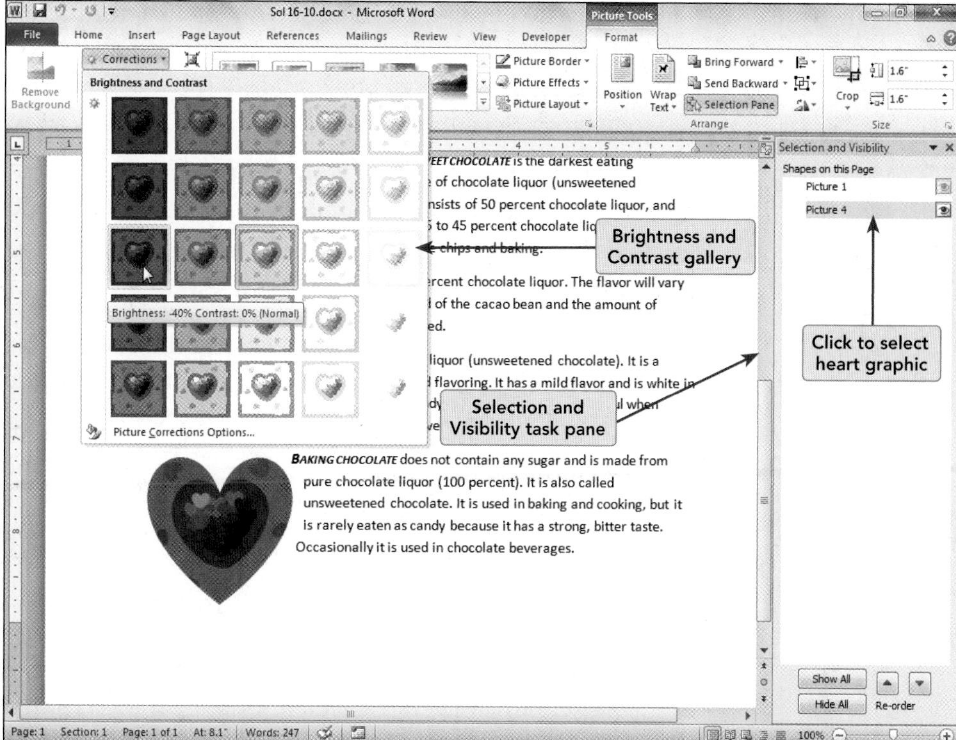

Figure 16-12 Adjusting the appearance of the picture

4. Click the **Picture Corrections** option in the left pane if necessary. Notice that the Format Picture dialog box includes the Brightness and Contrast gallery options as well as controls for manually adjusting Brightness and Contrast. Drag the **Brightness** slider to **-20%**, and change the **Contrast** value to **+35%**. Click **Close**.
5. Click the Color button, and click an option in the Recolor gallery.
6. Click the Color button, and click **Set Transparent Color**. The mouse pointer changes appearance.
7. Click one of the darker-colored, small hearts on the right side of the larger heart. Notice that the heart became the same color as the document background (white).

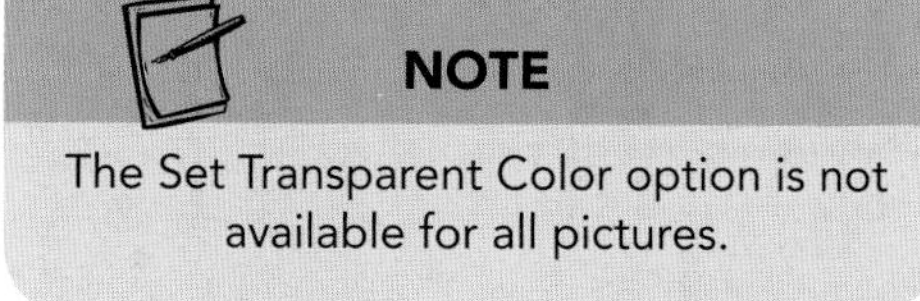

NOTE

The Set Transparent Color option is not available for all pictures.

8. Select the chocolate picture. Locate the **Picture Styles** group, and click the More arrow to display the Picture Styles gallery. Move the mouse over various styles, and observe the change in the frame around the selected picture. Click the **Thick Matte, Black** style. Change the picture height to 1.25 inches using the Shape Height button on the Picture Tools Format tab.
9. Select the heart picture, and click the Change Picture button (Adjust group of the Picture Tools Format tab). Locate the folder that contains the student data files, and double-click **Chocolate - P10**. The chocolate picture is inserted preserving the format and size of the heart picture. Change the height of the picture to 1.25 inches, and change the document bottom margin to 0.3 inch so that the document is one page.
10. Select the heart-shaped chocolate picture, and click the Picture Border button. Select a color from the Theme Colors palette. Click the Picture Border button again, and choose **Weight**. Choose **2¼** line weight.

11. Select the heart-shaped chocolate picture if necessary, and click the Picture Effects button. Point to the Shadow, Reflection, Glow, Soft Edges, and Bevel effects, and drag the mouse over the galleries for each category. Select an effect of your choice that is appropriate for the picture.
12. Save the document as ***[your initials]*16-11** in your Lesson 16 folder. Submit the document, and leave the document open for the next exercise.

Exercise 16-12 ROTATE AND FLIP CLIP ART

You can rotate and flip clip art by using the Rotate options on the Ribbon, or you can manually rotate the image by dragging the rotate handle. You can also reverse or flip an object.

1. Click the heart-shaped chocolate picture. Click the **Picture Tools Format** tab, and locate the **Arrange** group.
2. Click the arrow beside the Rotate button to display the Rotate drop-down list.
3. Move the mouse over each of the options, and observe the changes in the picture. Click **More Rotation Options** to open the Format Picture dialog box with the Size tab selected. Change the rotation to **15** degrees. Click **OK**.
4. Select the heart-shaped chocolate picture, and notice the green rotation handle at the top of the picture.
5. Place the mouse pointer on the green rotation handle, and drag the handle slightly to the left. Adjust the rotation if necessary.

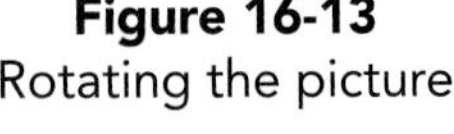

Figure 16-13
Rotating the picture

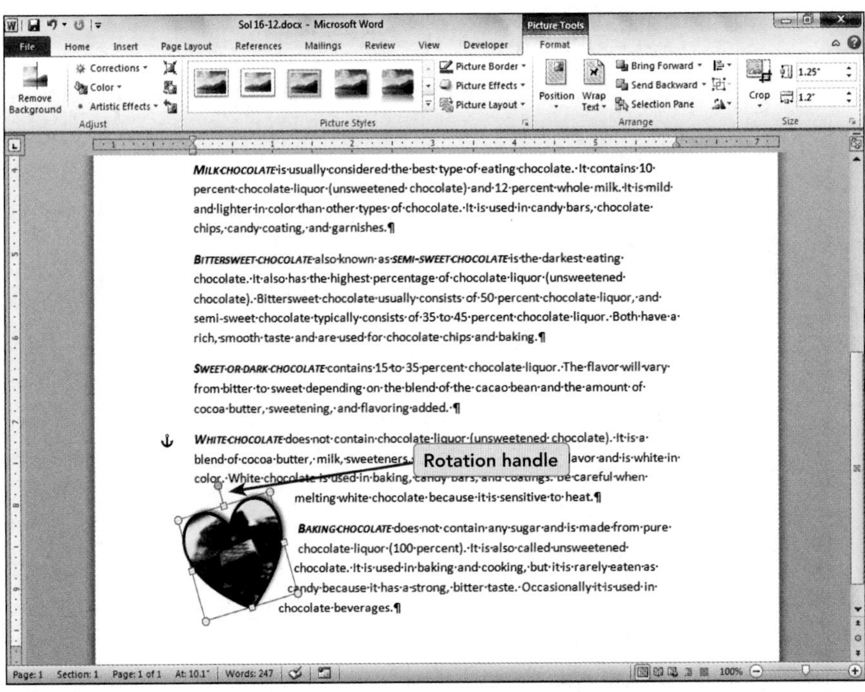

6. Save the document as ***[your initials]*16-12** in your Lesson 16 folder. Submit the document, and keep it open for the next exercise.
7. Close the Selection and Visibility pane.

Creating WordArt

WordArt is a drawing tool you can use to create special effects with text. Select text in a document, or key text to create the WordArt object. You can choose from a variety of WordArt styles and then modify the object by editing the text or changing the shape, wrapping style, size, color, or position.

Exercise 16-13 CREATE WORDART

1. Select the title text "Chocolate Terms" up to but not including the paragraph mark. (Because you will be creating WordArt from this text, not including the paragraph mark will retain the spacing before the title.)
2. Click the **Insert** tab, locate the **Text** group, and click the WordArt button . The WordArt gallery appears, displaying a number of WordArt styles.

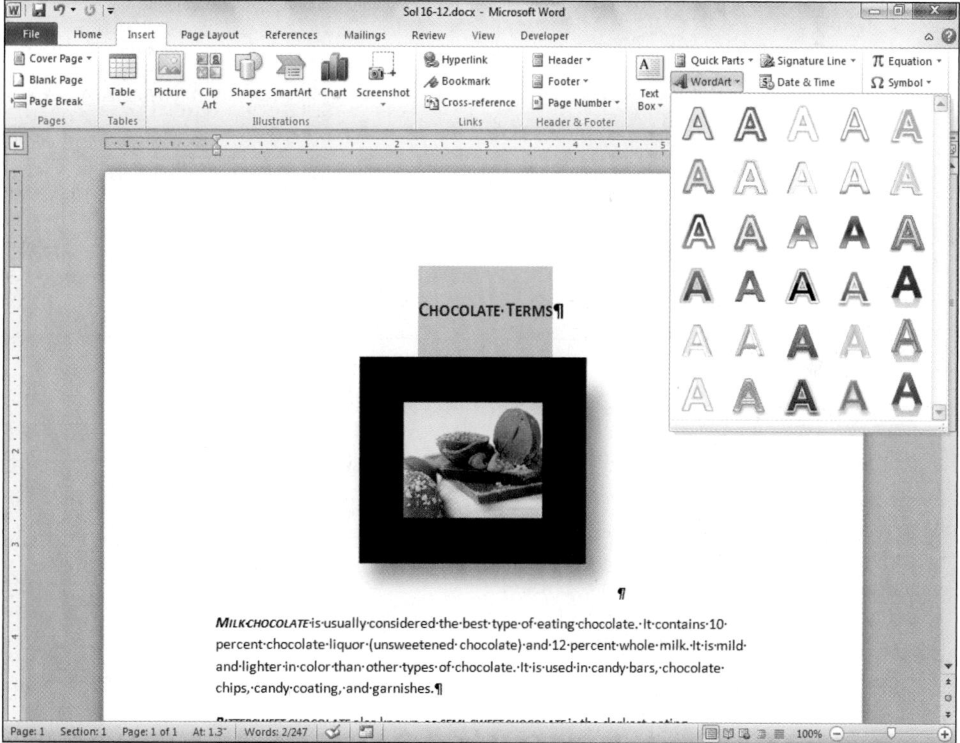

Figure 16-14
WordArt gallery

3. Choose one of the styles, and the document title is formatted with the WordArt style. The WordArt object is inserted in the document with square text wrapping. Drag the WordArt object above the chocolate picture at the top of the document.
4. Click the WordArt object to select it if necessary. The Drawing Tools Format tab appears. Locate the **WordArt Styles** group, and click the WordArt Quick Styles button to display the WordArt Styles gallery. Choose another style.

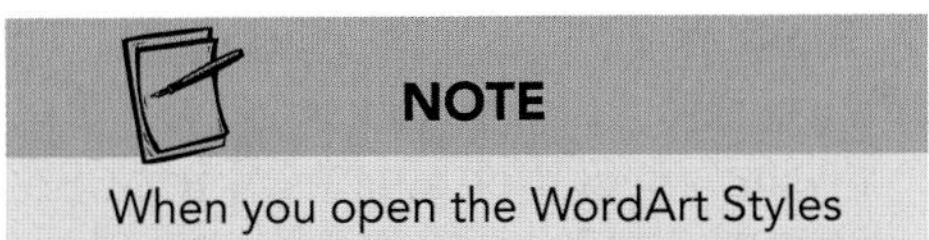

When you open the WordArt Styles gallery, move the mouse over each style to preview the change in your document.

5. Click the **Drawing Tools Format** tab on the Ribbon if necessary, and click the Text Effects button. Choose **Transform**, and select a shape in the fifth row of the Warp section. Click the Undo button if you do not like the results, and try another shape.

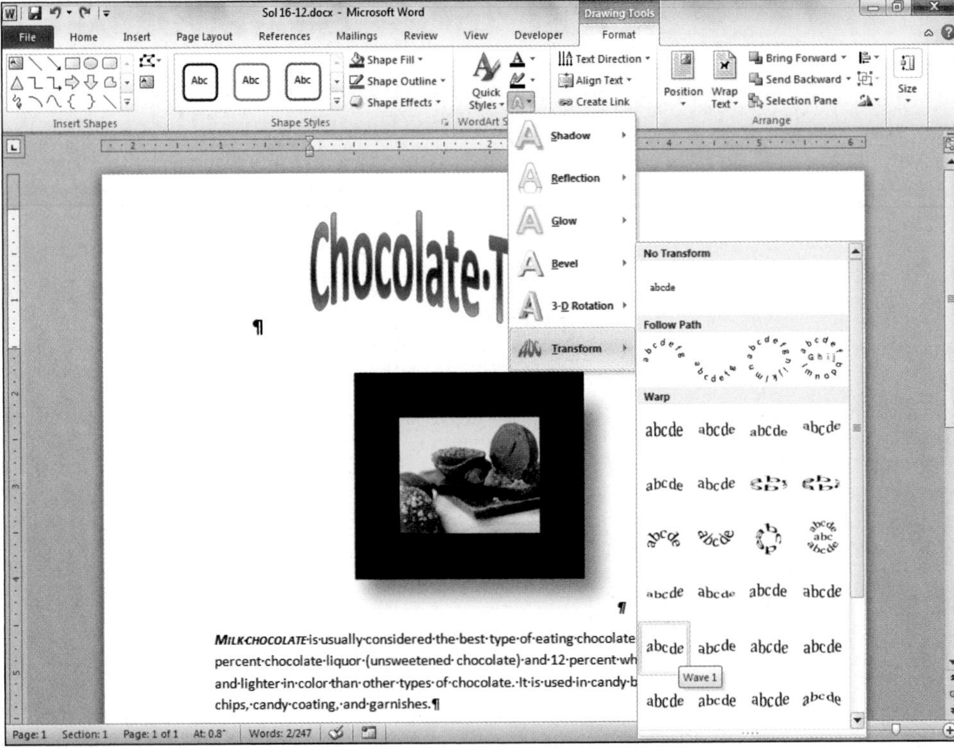

Figure 16-15
Transform gallery

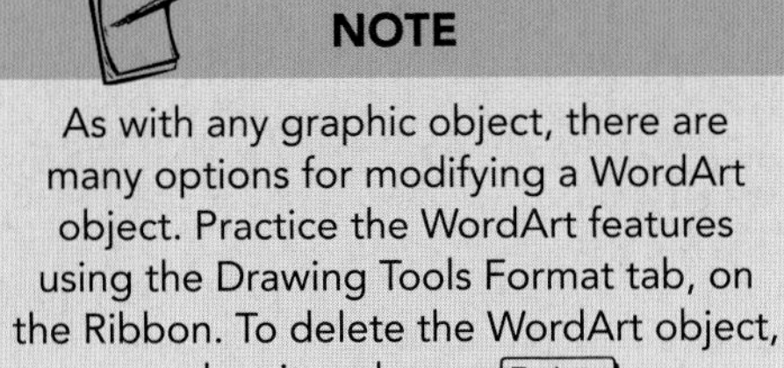

As with any graphic object, there are many options for modifying a WordArt object. Practice the WordArt features using the Drawing Tools Format tab, on the Ribbon. To delete the WordArt object, select it and press Delete.

6. Click the Position button, and click **More Layout Options**. Click the **Position** tab if necessary, and change the **Horizontal Alignment** to **Centered** relative to **Page**. Click **OK** to close the Layout dialog box. The WordArt object is centered horizontally on the page.

Exercise 16-14 FORMAT WORDART

You can change the appearance of WordArt objects by changing the text fill color, changing the text outline color, and adding special effects such as shadow and reflection.

1. Select the WordArt object, and locate the **WordArt Styles** group on the Ribbon. Click the arrow beside the Text Fill button. Point to **Gradient**, and choose **More Gradients** to open the Format Text Effects dialog box. Click the down arrow beside **Preset colors**, and choose the Mahogany option. Click **Close**.

2. Select the WordArt object, and click the arrow beside the Text Outline button in the WordArt Styles group. Select a color and weight for your WordArt object.
3. Select the WordArt object, and click the Text Effects button. Choose **Shadow**. Point to the various shadow styles, and choose one that is appropriate for your WordArt object. The Shadow gallery includes a listing for Shadow Options, which opens the Format Text Effects dialog box. Shadow settings include Transparency, Size, Blur, Angle, and Distance.
4. Display the Shadow gallery, and click **Shadow Options**. Move the Format Text Effects dialog box so that you can see the WordArt object. Experiment with the Shadow settings by dragging the slider or clicking the up and down arrows. Notice the effects on the WordArt Object. Click **Close** when finished.
5. Select the WordArt object if necessary, and point to the square sizing handle on the right. Drag the handle to increase the width to approximately 5.5 inches. Drag the top-middle sizing handle to size the object to approximately 1.5 inches. Drag the object to position it above the picture. Delete any blank paragraph marks between the WordArt object and the chocolate picture. Select the text in the document, and change the font size to 11 points. If necessary, change the bottom margin to 0.3 to keep text from flowing to a second page.

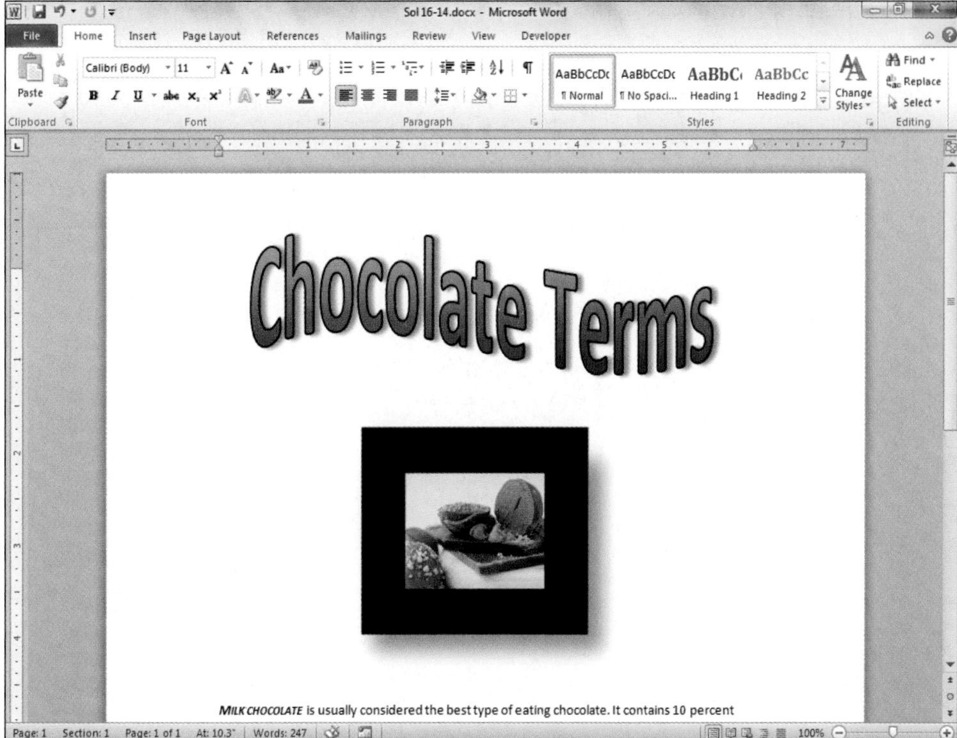

Figure 16-16
Title text with a WordArt style

6. Save the document as ***[your initials]*16-14** in your Lesson 16 folder.
7. Submit and close the document.

Working with Shapes and the Drawing Canvas

An easy way to add a graphic element to a document is to use the Insert tab, Illustrations group, to create a shape. You can draw simple geometric shapes or insert more complex predesigned shapes. There are eight categories for shapes including lines, basic shapes, block arrows, flowchart, callouts, and stars and banners. The Recently Used Shapes category appears at the top of the Shapes gallery to collect the shapes you have recently selected.

When you draw shapes, you can insert them directly into the document or place them in a *Drawing Canvas,* a bordered area in your document where you can size, move, and change the objects as a group. Use the Drawing Canvas when you plan to insert several shapes. The Drawing Canvas is an object you can modify. You can change its location and size as well as how text wraps around it.

Exercise 16-15 CREATE SHAPES

1. Start a new document. Open the **Page Setup** dialog box, and change the top, bottom, left, and right margins to 0.5 inch. Click the **Paper** tab, and choose **Executive** from the Paper size drop-down list. Click **OK**. In the following exercises you will practice inserting shapes and then you will create a letterhead for executive-size paper which measures 7.25 inches by 10.5 inches.

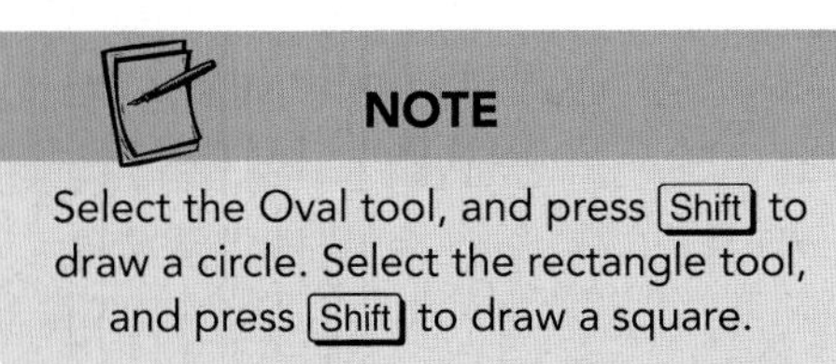

NOTE

Select the Oval tool, and press Shift to draw a circle. Select the rectangle tool, and press Shift to draw a square.

2. Display the rulers if necessary by clicking the View Ruler button on the vertical scroll bar.

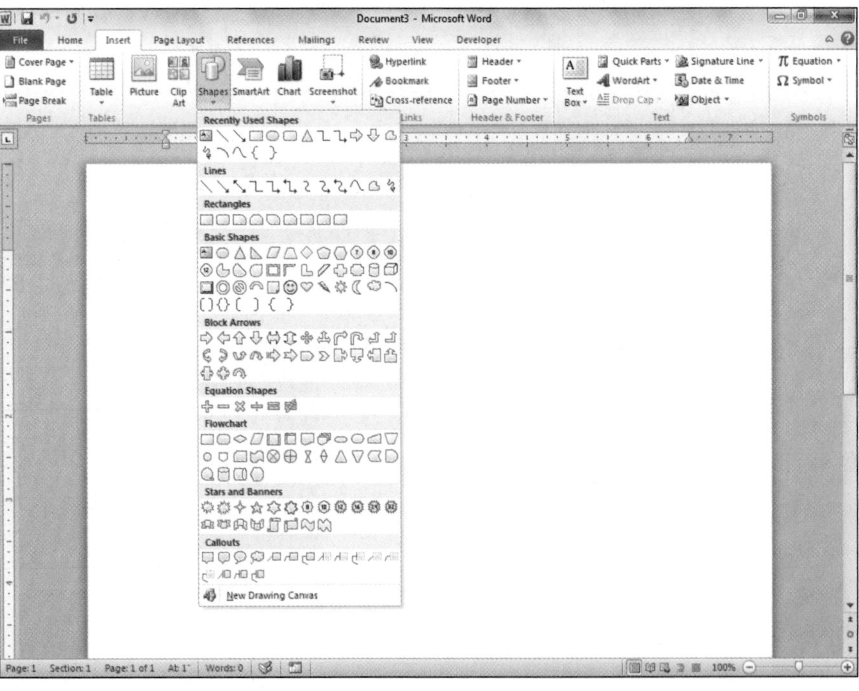

Figure 16-17
Shapes gallery

3. Click the **Insert** tab, and locate the **Illustrations** group. Click the Shapes button, and locate the **Basic Shapes** category. Click the

Oval shape on the first row. The mouse pointer changes to a crosshair pointer.

4. Position the crosshair pointer in the upper left corner of the document. Drag it down and to the right to draw an oval that extends across the page and is about ½ inch high. Release the mouse button.
5. A selected oval appears in the document window. Press Delete to remove the oval.
6. Display the **Insert** tab, and click the Shapes button again. Click the Oval shape. Press Shift and drag down and to the right to draw a circle approximately 2 inches in diameter. Press Delete to delete the circle.
7. Click the Shapes button on the Insert tab, and choose **New Drawing Canvas**. A Drawing Canvas appears in your document, and the Drawing Tools Format tab displays on the Ribbon. The Drawing Canvas will be used to arrange and format several shapes.
8. Locate the **Insert Shapes** group on the Drawing Tools Format tab, and click the Rectangle button.
9. Position the crosshair pointer in the upper left corner of the Drawing Canvas. Drag down and across to insert a rectangle that extends across the top of the Drawing Canvas and measures approximately ½ inch high.
10. Release the mouse button. The rectangle is displayed with eight sizing handles around its sides. An extra handle with a green circle extends from the top of the rectangle. You use this handle to rotate the object. When you see an object's sizing handles, the object is selected. Deselect the rectangle by clicking below the rectangle in the Drawing Canvas.

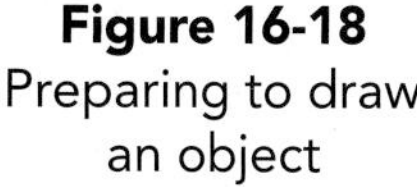

Figure 16-18
Preparing to draw an object

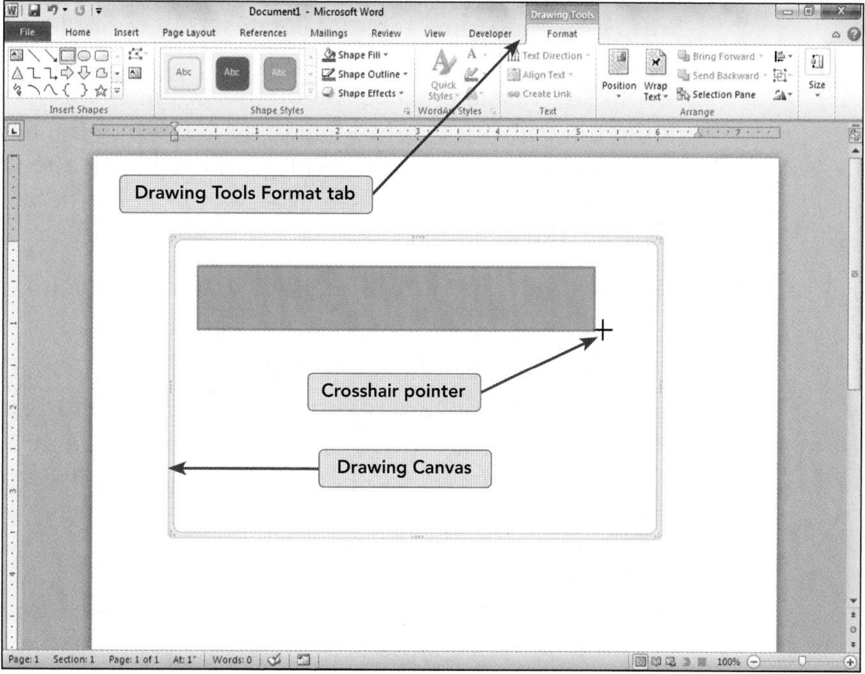

11. Click the Line button on the Drawing Tools Format tab, Insert Shapes group. Draw a horizontal line inside the Drawing Canvas ½ inch below the rectangle and the same length as the rectangle. Deselect the line.

NOTE

To insert a shape with a predefined size without dragging to draw it, click the Shape tool and click once in the document.

NOTE

Press Shift to maintain an object's width-to-height ratio as you draw. Press Ctrl to draw from the center point instead of from an edge.

12. Click the Oval button, and then click anywhere on the Drawing Canvas. A 1-inch circle appears on the Drawing Canvas. Deselect the circle.
13. Right-click the Rectangle button, and choose **Lock Drawing Mode**. Press Shift and draw a small square on the canvas. Draw a second square.
14. Press Esc to deactivate the tool. Use the Lock Drawing Mode to draw several shapes using the same tool rather than adding individual shapes.
15. Click the **Home** tab, locate the **Editing** group, and click the Select button. Choose **Select All**. All the shapes in the Drawing Canvas are selected. Press Delete to remove the objects from the Drawing Canvas. Select and delete the Drawing Canvas if necessary.

Modifying Shapes

Exercise 16-16 RESIZE AND MOVE SHAPES

You can resize, rotate, flip, color, combine, and add text to shapes. To modify a shape, you must first select it by clicking it. To select multiple objects, press Shift or Ctrl and click each object, or click the Select Objects button on the Home tab. A selected drawing object has sizing handles for reshaping.

To size a shape, place the mouse pointer on a sizing handle (the mouse pointer becomes a two-headed arrow) and drag the handle. To move a shape, click anywhere inside the shape and drag with the four-headed arrow. If a shape has a yellow diamond, you can change the contour of the shape by dragging the diamond.

1. Click the **Insert** tab, locate the **Illustrations** group, and click the Shapes button. Click **New Drawing Canvas**.
2. Right-click the Rectangle button, and choose **Lock Drawing Mode**. Draw a rectangle across the top of the Drawing Canvas. Draw another rectangle about 1 inch below and approximately 2 inches wide.
3. Press Esc to deactivate the drawing mode. Click to select the Drawing Canvas if necessary, and click the **Drawing Tools Format** tab on the Ribbon.
4. Locate the **Insert Shapes** group, and click the More arrow to display the gallery of shapes.

5. Locate the **Rectangles** group, and then click the Rounded Rectangle shape [ ].
6. Press [Shift], and draw a square with rounded corners on the left side of the Drawing Canvas, below the rectangles.

TIP

To insert a shape with a predefined size, click the desired shape button and then click in the document. To maintain a shape's width-to-height ratio, hold down [Shift] as you draw.

7. Right-click the Drawing Canvas border, and choose **Fit**. The height of the Drawing Canvas now fits the height of the objects you have drawn. There must be at least two objects in the Drawing Canvas to use the Fit command.
8. Right-click the Drawing Canvas border, and choose **Expand**. The Drawing Canvas expands slightly around the objects.

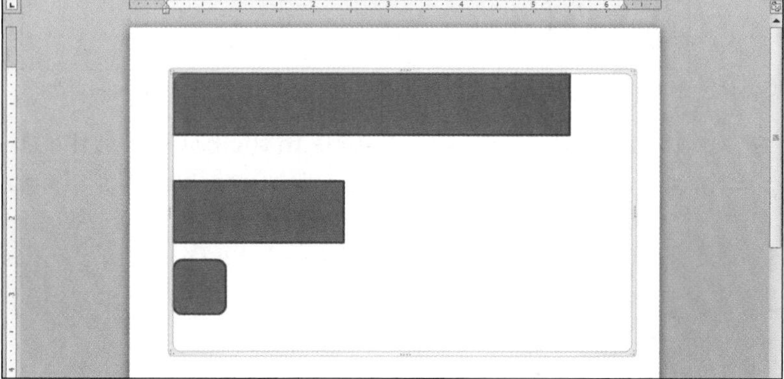

Figure 16-19
Adjusting the Drawing Canvas

9. Right-click the Drawing Canvas border, and click **Scale Drawing**. Move the mouse pointer to the bottom-right sizing handle of the Drawing Canvas. The mouse pointer turns to a diagonal two-headed arrow [ ].
10. Drag the handle diagonally up to change the size of the Drawing Canvas. The objects are scaled smaller.
11. Click the Undo button [ ]. Right-click the Drawing Canvas border, and deselect the Scale Drawing feature. The Drawing Canvas can be sized and formatted using the Drawing Tools Format tab.
12. Click within the Drawing Canvas. Click the **Drawing Tools Format** tab, and click the Wrap Text button [ ]. Click **Square**. Now you can move the Drawing Canvas and its contents freely on the page.
13. Move the pointer to the center of the square with rounded corners. Use the four-headed arrow [ ] to drag the shape to the center of the Drawing Canvas, positioned below the first rectangle.

NOTE

You might notice that when you drag an object to position it, the object moves in fixed increments. By default, objects align to an invisible grid that helps you position them evenly. If you want to precisely position an individual object, you can turn off the Snap to Grid feature or hold down [Alt] as you position the object. The Align button includes options to view gridlines and to change grid settings.

14. Point to the yellow diamond on the square with rounded corners. When the pointer turns into a small arrowhead, drag the yellow diamond into the center of the shape. The square now resembles a circle. Press Ctrl+Z to undo.

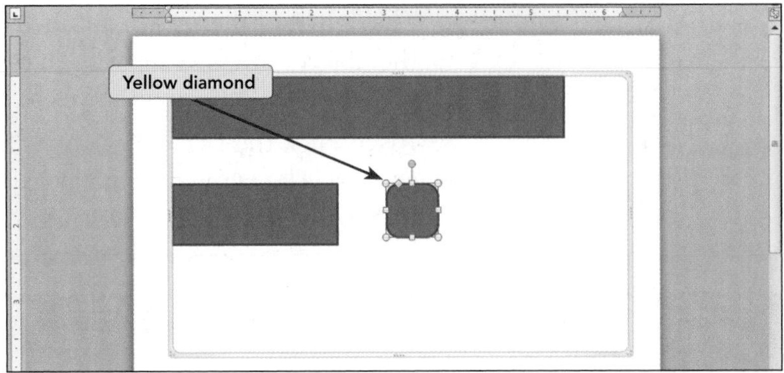

Figure 16-20
Changing the shape of an object

15. Drag the second rectangle to the bottom of the Drawing Canvas. Move the mouse pointer to the right-middle sizing handle of the second rectangle. The mouse pointer changes to a two-headed arrow ↔. Drag the handle to the right side of the Drawing Canvas. When you start to drag, the mouse pointer becomes a crosshair +.

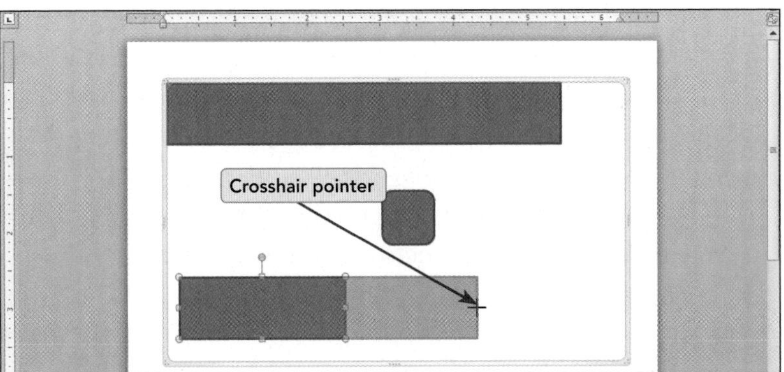

Figure 16-21
Resizing an object

16. The shape should should extend from the left side to the right side of the Drawing Canvas.

Exercise 16-17 ROTATE AND FLIP SHAPES

You can rotate an object left or right 90 degrees, flip it horizontally or vertically, or turn the rotate handle on an object. The rotate handle extends from an object and has a green circle.

1. Select the second rectangle, and click the **Drawing Tools Format** tab. Click the Rotate button, and click **Rotate Right 90°**. The rectangle shape rotates 90 degrees to the right.
2. Click outside the Drawing Canvas to deselect the shape and the canvas.

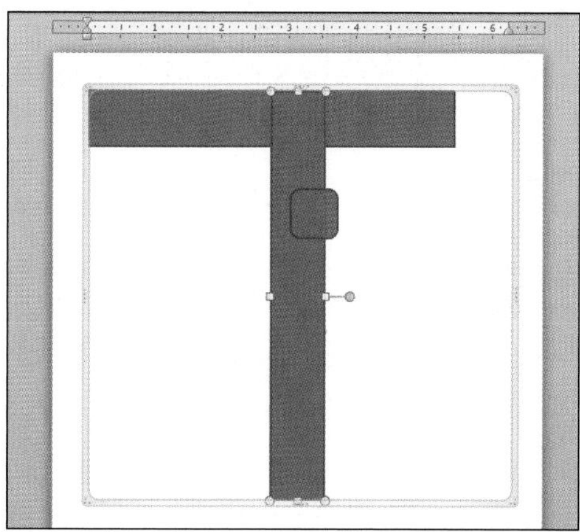

Figure 16-22
Rotated shape

3. Select the rotated shape.
4. Place the mouse pointer over the green circle on the rotate handle of the selected shape. Rotate the shape to the left, back to its original position.
5. Drag the bottom-middle sizing handle of the Drawing Canvas to reduce the size of the canvas. Drag the canvas back to the top of the document.

Exercise 16-18 FORMAT SHAPES

Document themes consist of colors, fonts, and effects and affect the overall appearance of a document. A *color set* in a theme includes four colors for text and background, six accent colors, and two colors reserved for hyperlinks. When you want to change the color of an object, the colors that display in the color gallery are determined by the document theme. When you change a document theme, the objects within the document are updated automatically.

Theme effects include three components: shape outline style, shape fill, and special effects including shadow and 3-D. Galleries display the shape outline and shape fill effects available. *Shape Styles* include various formatting options for objects and display as thumbnails in a gallery. When you move the mouse pointer over a thumbnail in the gallery, you can preview the color, shape outline, and shape fill effects for selected shapes.

1. Select the square object. Click the **Drawing Tools Format** tab, click the Shape Fill button, and choose **Gradient**. Click **More Gradients** to open the Format Shape dialog box.
2. Click the **Fill** option on the left pane, and click **Gradient fill**. Open the **Type** drop-down list, and choose **Radial**. Open the **Direction** drop-down list, and choose the third option, **From Center**. Locate **Gradient stops**, and click the first stop, labeled Stop 1. Click the Color button, and choose a dark blue. Click the last stop on the right, click the Color button, and choose a light blue. If there are any stops between the first stop on the left and the last stop on the right, click the stop then click the Remove Gradient Stop button for each stop. There should be only two stops on the slider. Click **Close**. The square is formatted with a gradient from dark blue to light blue.

NOTE

To format the Drawing Canvas (for example, to add a border or background color), select the Drawing Canvas and use buttons on the Ribbon. Or right-click the Drawing Canvas, open the Format Shape dialog box, and choose options.

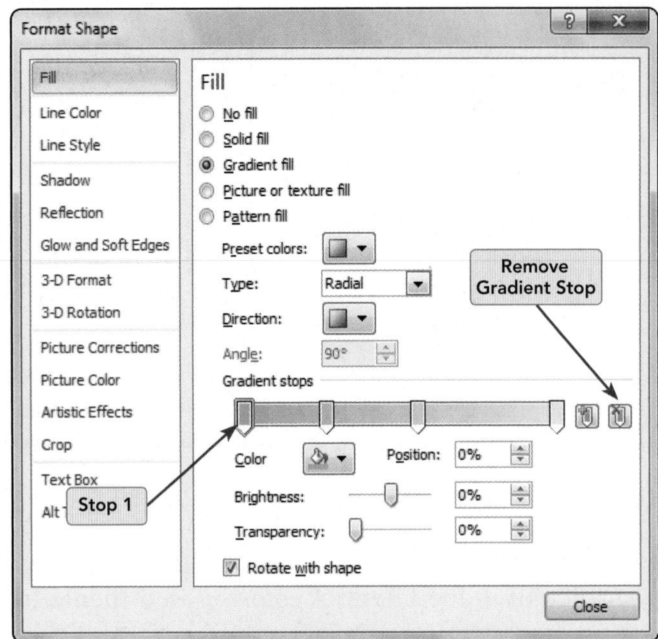

Figure 16-23
Format Shape dialog box

3. Select the square. Click the Shape Outline button, and click **More Outline Colors**. Click the **Standard** tab, and choose a color that coordinates with the gradient color. Click **OK**.

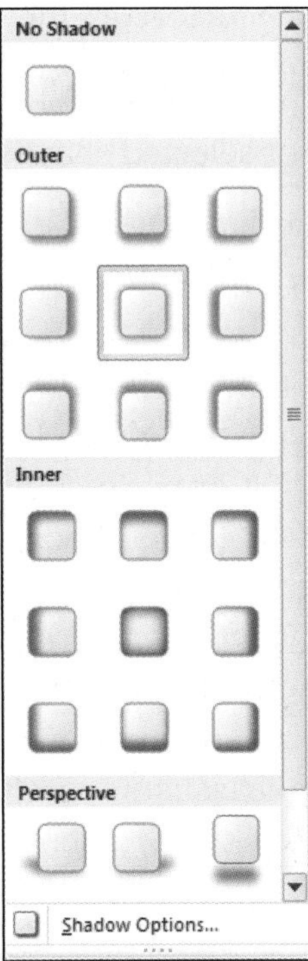

Figure 16-24
Shadow settings

4. Locate and click the Shape Effects button. Click **Shadow**, and experiment with the shadow styles to see the different effects; then apply a shadow effect from the Outer group.
5. Click the Shape Effects button, and display the Shadow gallery. Choose **Shadow Options**.
6. Click the Color button, and experiment with the Shadow colors. Choose the darkest blue color in the palette.
7. Study the current settings for Transparency, Size, Blur, Angle, and Distance. Drag each slider left and right to experiment with the special effects for shadows. Move the Format Shape dialog box if necessary to see the changes. Click **Close** when you have finished adjusting the shadow settings.
8. Click the second rectangle. Click the Shape Effects button, and choose 3-D Rotation. Choose an option from the **Perspective** group.

Figure 16-25
3-D settings

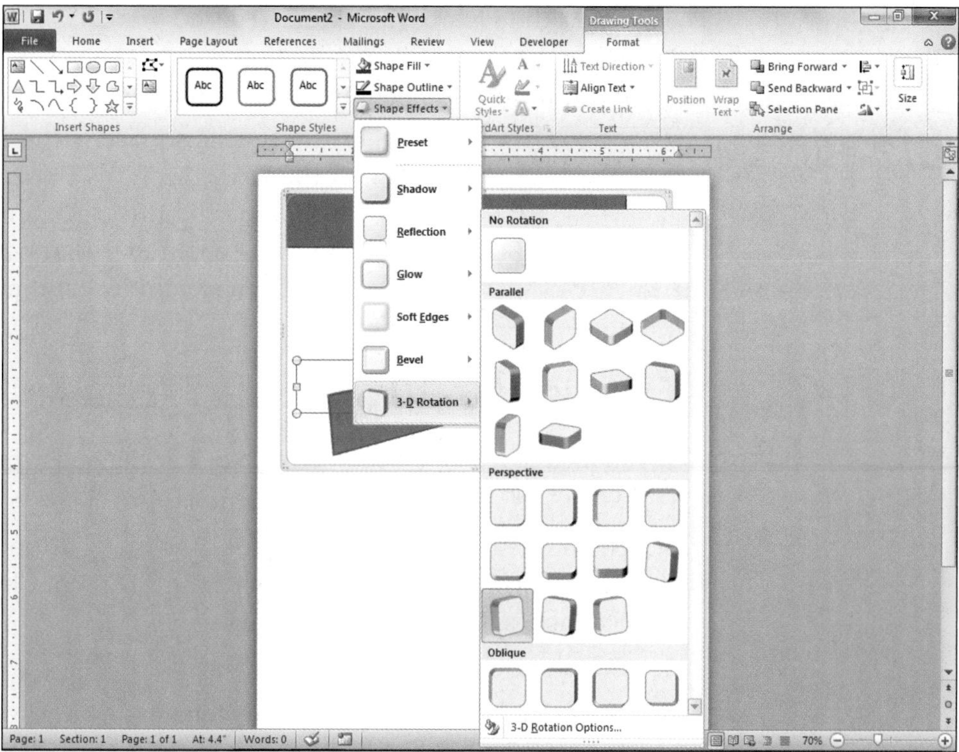

9. Click the Shape Effects button, and choose 3-D Rotation; then choose 3-D Rotation Options.
10. Drag the Format Shape dialog box to the side or bottom so that you can see the rectangle shape. Experiment with the Rotation settings, and apply a setting to the 3-D shape. Click Close.

Exercise 16-19 CHANGE SHAPES

After you insert a shape in a document, you can change it to another shape.

1. Click the second rectangle to select it.
2. Click the Drawing Tools Format tab, and locate the Insert Shapes group. Click the Edit Shape button, and click Change Shape.
3. Locate the Basic Shapes group, and choose Regular Pentagon.
4. Select the pentagon shape if necessary. Click the Shape Outline button, and choose black for the outline color. Click the Shape Outline button again, and change the Weight to 1½ points.
5. Select the pentagon shape if necessary, and click the Shape Fill button. Choose Texture, and then choose More Textures. Verify that Fill is selected on the left pane, and click the Pattern Fill option. Choose a pattern from the Pattern fill grid. Choose a Foreground Color from the drop-down color palette. Choose a Background Color, and click Close.

6. Select the square with rounded corners, and click the Home tab. Click to select the Format Painter button, and then click in the first rectangle to copy the formatting of the square shape to the rectangle shape.

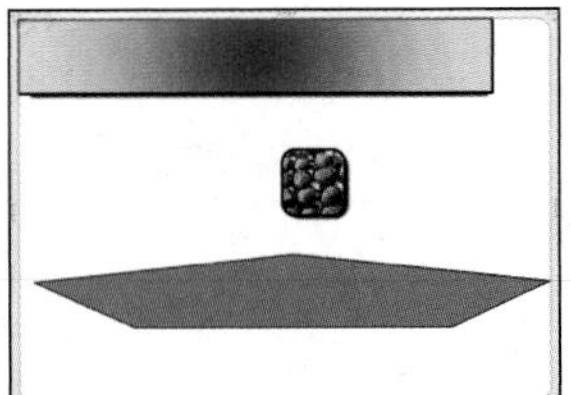

Figure 16-26
Modified shapes

7. Select the square with rounded corners. Click the Drawing Tools Format tab, and click the Shape Fill button, and choose **Picture**. Locate the folder that contains the student data files, and insert the file **Chocolate – P20**.

Exercise 16-20 ADD TEXT TO SHAPES

Text added to a shape becomes part of the shape. If you delete the shape, you also delete the text.

1. Select the top rectangle, and click the Size button on the Drawing Tools Format tab. Change the height to 1 inch. Change the width to 5.5 inches. Deselect the rectangle.
2. Select the chocolate square, and change the height and width to 0.75 inch.
3. Select and delete the pentagon-shaped object. Draw a rectangle below the chocolate square. Change the height to 0.75, and change the width to 2.5 inches.
4. Right-click in the second rectangle, and choose **Add Text**. Key **Campbell's**, press Enter, and key **Confections** on the second line.
5. Right-align the text, and apply 14-point bold formatting. Change the font to Cambria, change the font color to white, and add small caps with 2-point expanded character spacing. Change the line spacing to single and the spacing after to 0.
6. Deselect the text by clicking the shape. Right-click the shape, and choose **Format Shape** from the shortcut menu. Choose **Text Box** in the left pane. Verify the following settings, and click **Close**.

Vertical alignment:	Middle
Text direction:	Horizontal
Internal margins:	0.1 for Left, Right, Top, and Bottom

   Vertical alignment positions text at the top, middle, or bottom of the shape. Text direction options include rotated text and horizontal placement. Internal margins control the space between the text and the outside border of the shape.

Ordering, Grouping, and Aligning Shapes

A Word document is multilayered. When you insert a shape, the shape is placed on top of the text layer, which means it can obscure existing text. You can change the order of a shape by moving it to a different layer, such as

behind text. You can also change the order of shapes on a single layer so that one shape appears on top of or behind the others in the stack. You can group shapes into one object so that they can be manipulated as a whole. Aligning shapes involves positioning them in relation to each other or in relation to the Drawing Canvas.

NOTE

The Bring Forward drop-down list includes three options: Bring Forward, Bring to Front, and Bring in Front of Text. The Send Backward drop-down list includes options to Send Backward, Send to Back, and Send Behind Text. Use the Bring Forward and Send Backward options to move an object forward or backward one layer at a time. The Bring to Front option automatically places the object on top of the stack.

Exercise 16-21 CHANGE THE ORDER OF SHAPES

1. Select the chocolate square, and drag it on top of the first rectangle.
2. Click the **Drawing Tools Format** tab, and click the Send Backward button. Deselect the square. The chocolate-filled square disappears from view. Click the rectangle, click the arrow beside the Send Backward button, and choose **Send to Back** to place the rectangle on the bottom of the stack.

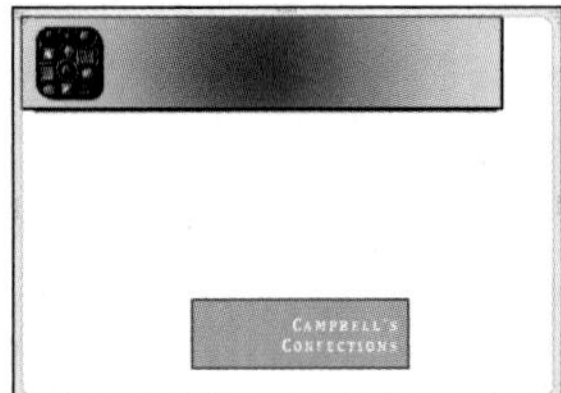

Figure 16-27
Changing the order and position of shapes

Exercise 16-22 GROUP SHAPES

1. Select the top rectangle, and drag it down and away from the Drawing Canvas borders. Select the chocolate square, and drag it to the left side of the rectangle, positioned between the top and bottom of the rectangle. Deselect the square.
2. Click the **Home** tab, and click the Select button located in the Editing group. Click **Select Objects**. Position the arrow pointer above and to the left of the top rectangle (keeping inside the Drawing Canvas). Then drag down to draw a selection box around the top rectangle and the chocolate square.

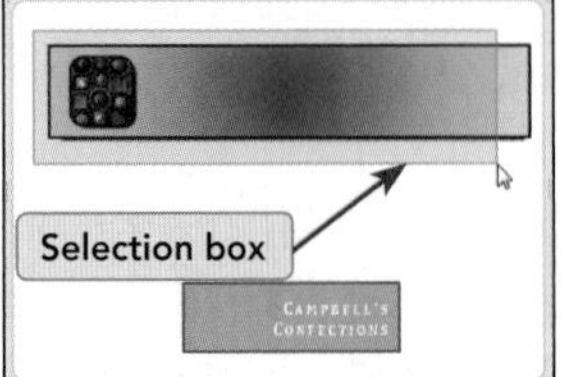

Figure 16-28
Drag to draw a selection box around the objects

3. Release the mouse button. Each object is selected and has its own sizing handles.
4. Click the **Drawing Tools Format** tab, and locate the Arrange group. Click the Group button, and click **Group**. The objects become a single object, with a single set of sizing handles.

5. Place the mouse pointer in the center of the grouped objects, and drag the group around on the Drawing Canvas. The grouped objects move as one object.
6. Click the Group button, and click **Ungroup**. The grouped object becomes individual objects again.

Exercise 16-23 ALIGN SHAPES

You can align shapes and distribute them evenly in a drawing by using the Align or Distribute options from the Arrange group on the Ribbon. You can align shapes in relation to each other or to the Drawing Canvas. For example, if you have three unevenly spaced shapes, you can align them to have equal space between shapes or align them to be equally spaced on the Drawing Canvas.

1. Select the rectangle tool and draw a rectangle approximately two inches wide and one-half inch high below the Drawing Canvas. Select the rectangle if necessary, and press Ctrl+D to duplicate the shape. Press Ctrl+D to create a third rectangle.
2. Drag each rectangle to position the shapes in a vertical column below the Drawing Canvas.
3. Press Shift and click to select each of the shapes below the Drawing Canvas. Click the Drawing Tools Format tab, and locate the Arrange group. Click the arrow beside the Align button, and click **Distribute Vertically**. The three objects are evenly spaced from each other.

Figure 16-29
Alignment options

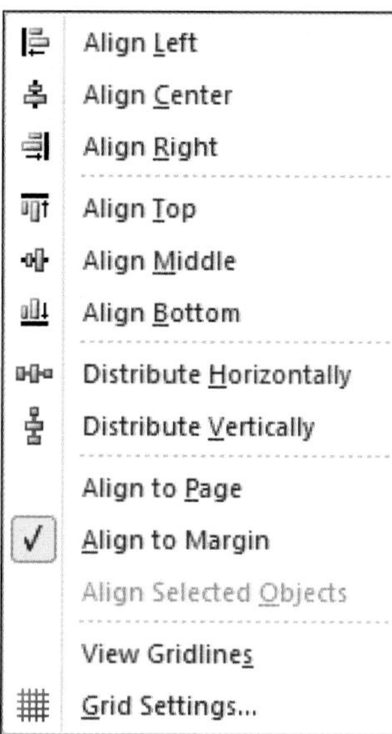

4. Select the three shapes below the Drawing Canvas if necessary, and then click the Align button. Choose **Align Left** to align the objects on the left margin.
5. With the objects still selected, press Delete.
6. Drag the chocolate square to the left side of the top rectangle, and position it between the top and bottom border if necessary. Group the square and the top rectangle.
7. Drag the rectangle containing the text "Campbell's Confections" to the right side of the top rectangle, centered between the top and bottom borders of the rectangle. Change the text fill color to black. Change the Shape Fill to **No Fill**, and change the Shape Outline to **No Outline**. Select the text rectangle, press Shift, and click the other rectangle. Group the objects.

8. Select the Drawing Canvas, and point to the middle-bottom sizing handle. Drag the bottom border toward the rectangle so that the Drawing Canvas surrounds the objects with a slight margin on all sides. Click the Drawing Canvas border, and click the Position button. Choose More Layout Options. Click Alignment under Horizontal, and choose Centered relative to Page. Click OK. The stationery now has a colorful letterhead centered at the top of the page.
9. Save the document as ***[your initials]*16-23** in your Lesson 16 folder.
10. Preview, submit, and close the document.

Using Online Help

Use Online Help to explore new features in Word 2010. Click the Help button or press F1 to open the Word Help window.

LEARN ABOUT SCREENSHOTS

1. Start Word.
2. Locate the Help button in the upper right corner of the screen. Click the Help button to open the Word Help window.
3. Key **screenshot** in the Search text box, and click Search. Click the link to insert a screenshot.
4. Read the article about inserting a screenshot. Close the Word Help window.
5. Practice inserting a screenshot by opening your Internet browser and keying www.candyusa.com.
6. Switch to Word. Click the Insert tab, and click the Screenshot button arrow. Click the Screen Clipping option. The Word screen minimizes and the Web page for the National Confectioners Association displays. The mouse pointer changes to a black plus.
7. Draw a selection box around the National Confectioners Association logo in the upper left corner of the Web page. After you release the mouse button, the captured logo displays as an inline graphic in the Word document.
8. Deselect the logo image, and press Enter two times.
9. Click the Insert tab, and click the Screenshot button. Click to select the National Confectioners Association Web page that displays under Available Windows. The screenshot for the National Confectioners Association displays below the logo. Each of the images can be formatted using the Picture Tools Format tab.
10. Close the document without saving.

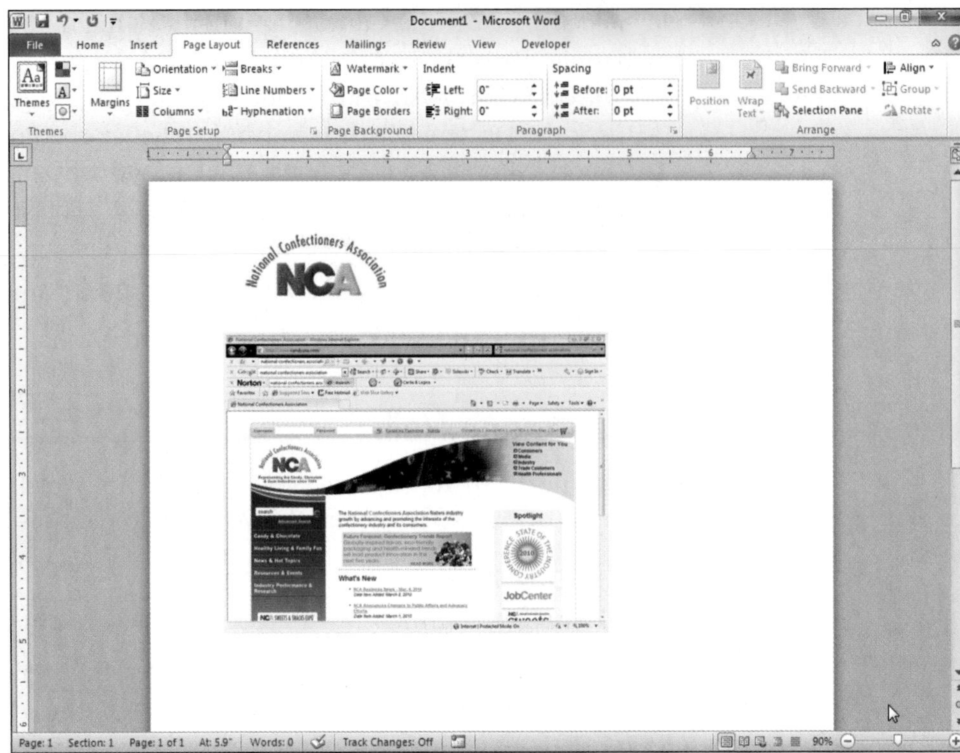

Figure 16-30
Sample screenshots

Lesson 16 Summary

- Add ready-to-use pictures to your document in the form of drawings (clip art) or photographs.
- Search for clips by keyword, using the Clip Art task pane, or view collections of clips by category from the Microsoft Clip Organizer.
- Click a clip to select it. You can copy, paste, resize, crop, and format a selected clip.
- A selected clip is surrounded by a selection rectangle with sizing handles at each side and corner. Drag a corner sizing handle to make a clip larger or smaller while keeping the original proportions of the clip. Use the Layout dialog box (Size tab) to resize a clip to exact measurements or a percentage of the original size (scale).
- Crop a clip to hide part of it from view. Click the Crop button on the Picture Tools Format tab, Size group. Position the crop tool on a sizing handle, and drag it until you have hidden the part of the picture you want cropped.
- You can undo any action applied to a clip. You can also restore a clip to its original size by clicking the Reset Picture button on the Picture Tools Format tab.

- By default, a clip is inserted in a document as an in-line graphic and treated like a character or word. To move a clip that is an in-line graphic, cut and paste the clip or drag and drop it. You can use the alignment buttons on the Home tab, Paragraph group, to change the horizontal alignment of a clip.
- To move a clip freely on the page, change it from an in-line graphic to a floating graphic by changing its wrapping style. Use the Wrap Text button on the Picture Tools Format tab. You can drag a floating graphic to position it anywhere on the page and have the document text wrap around the graphic. The square wrapping style wraps text around all sides of a graphic.
- Use the WordArt feature to create special effects with text. Choose from a variety of WordArt styles, and modify the WordArt object by using the Drawing Tools Format tab (to change shape, size, color, wrapping style, alignment, and so on).
- The Drawing Canvas is a bordered area in your document that contains objects you draw. You can size, move, and change the objects on the Drawing Canvas as a group.
- You can draw shapes such as rectangles, ovals, and lines by using the Insert tab, Shapes button. There are eight categories including lines, basic shapes, block arrows, flowchart, callouts, and stars and banners.
- Click a shape to select it. To select multiple objects, hold down Shift and click each object, or use the Select Objects button on the Home tab to draw a box around the objects.
- A selected shape has eight sizing handles. Drag a sizing handle to make a shape larger or smaller. Move a shape by dragging it with the four-headed arrow. Drag the yellow diamond in a shape to change its contour.
- Drag a shape's green rotation handle to manually rotate the object. You can also flip an object horizontally or vertically or rotate it 90 degrees left or right.
- Use the Format Shape dialog box or the Drawing Tools Format tab to apply formatting to shapes, including shape fill color, shape outline color, shadows, and 3-D effects.
- After a shape is inserted in a document, you can change it to another shape by using the Change Shape command.
- You can add text to a shape—the text you add becomes part of the shape.
- Shapes can be placed on different layers of a document, such as in front of another shape or behind text. You can also group shapes into one object so that they can be manipulated as a whole.
- You can align shapes and distribute them evenly in a drawing.

LESSON 16		Command Summary	
Feature	**Button**	**Command**	**Keyboard**
3-D effects		Drawing Tools Format tab, Shape Effects	
Align shapes		Drawing Tools Format tab, Arrange group	
Change order		Drawing tools Format tab, Arrange group	
Change shape		Drawing Tools Format tab, Insert Shapes group	
Change wrapping style for pictures		Picture Tools Format tab, Arrange group, Wrap Text	
Crop picture		Picture Tools Format tab, Size group	
Format picture		Picture Tools Format tab	
Group shapes		Drawing Tools Format tab, Arrange group	
Insert clip art		Insert tab, Illustration group, Clip Art	
Insert shapes		Insert tab, Illustration group	
Insert WordArt		Insert tab, Text group	
Position pictures or shapes		Drawing Tools or Picture Format tab, Arrange group	
Reset picture		Picture Tools Format tab, Adjust group	
Resize picture		Picture Tools Format tab, Size group	
Rotate or flip		Drawing Tools or Picture Format tab, Arrange group	
Select drawing objects		Home tab, Editing group	
Shadow effects		Drawing Tools Format tab, Shape Styles group	
Shape fill		Drawing Tools Format tab, Shape Styles group	
Shape outline		Drawing Tools Format tab, Shape Styles group	

Concepts Review

True/False Questions

Each of the following statements is either true or false. Indicate your choice by circling T or F.

T F 1. You can search for clip art by keyword in the Clip Art task pane.

T F 2. You can change an existing star shape to a block arrow shape.

T F 3. The terms "size" and "crop" are used interchangeably in Word.

T F 4. The Drawing Canvas appears when you click a drawing tool, such as the Rectangle button.

T F 5. To select a WordArt object, point to the object and click.

T F 6. If an object has a yellow diamond, you can change the contour of the object.

T F 7. Theme effects include shape fill, shape outline, and shape effects.

T F 8. You cannot apply a text-wrapping style to a picture.

Short Answer Questions

Write the correct answer in the space provided.

1. When you click the Dialog Box Launcher for the Shape Styles group on the Drawing Tools Format tab, which dialog box displays?

____

2. Which button on the Drawing Tools Format tab do you click to create a gradient color?

____

3. When you insert a picture, what is its default wrapping style?

____

4. What is the procedure for inserting WordArt?

____

5. Which button on the Drawing Tools Format tab is used to apply a 3-D effect?

____

6. Which group on the Ribbon is used to align, group, and rotate objects?

____

7. How do you apply the square text-wrapping option to an inserted picture?

____

8. How do you delete a shape you inserted in a document?

____

Critical Thinking

Answer these questions on a separate page. There are no right or wrong answers. Support your answers with examples from your own experience, if possible.

1. Find three examples of clip art in newsletters, advertisements, letters, or other publications. Explain how the clip art helps communicate the message of the text.
2. Locate examples of various shapes in magazines, newsletters, and advertisements. When or where are shapes most likely to be used in a document (footer graphic, page number graphic, etc.)?

Skills Review

Exercise 16-24

Insert, size, move, crop, align, rotate, and change the wrapping style of a picture.

1. Start a new document, and open the Page Setup dialog box. Click the **Paper** tab, and change the **Width** and **Height** measurements to **3** inches. Change all margins to **0.5** inch.
2. Key the text in Figure 16-31 using center alignment and single spacing. Format the text as shown in the figure.

Figure 16-31

Center Align

```
Strawberry Days — 12 pt Bold Small Caps, 0 points Spacing After
Arts & Music Festival — Bold
June 12-14 — Bold Italic
Enjoy our chocolate-covered strawberries!
Campbell's Confections — 12 pt Bold Small Caps
```

3. Insert a picture from a file at the top of the document by following these steps:
   a. Position the insertion point at the top of the document. Click the **Insert** tab, and click the Picture button.
   b. Locate the directory and folder for the student data files.
   c. Select **Chocolate - P16**, and click **Insert**.
4. Size and crop the picture by following these steps:
   a. Click the picture to select it, and display the Picture Tools Format tab.
   b. Locate the **Size** group. Click the Size Dialog Box Launcher to open the Layout dialog box.
   c. Change the **Height** to 0.75 inch, and verify that **Lock aspect ratio** is selected to maintain proportion. Click **OK**.
   d. Select the picture if necessary, and click the **Picture Tools Format** tab.
   e. Drag the Zoom slider to 200%.
   f. Click the Crop button.
   g. Place the crop handle over the middle-left handle, and drag to the center to crop the plate of strawberries from the picture. Crop the picture from the bottom to hide the strawberry in the lower right corner. The picture should display only one strawberry.
   h. Press Esc to turn off cropping. Return to 100% zoom.
5. Select the picture, and click the Wrap Text button. Click **Square**.
6. Drag the strawberry to the upper left corner of the document.
7. Select the picture, and press Ctrl+C to copy the picture. Deselect the picture, and press Ctrl+V to paste the picture. Drag the picture to the lower left corner of the document.
8. Paste the picture two more times, and place a strawberry in each corner of the document.
9. Align the pictures by following these steps:
   a. Click the picture in the upper left corner of the document. Press Shift, and click the picture in the upper right corner of the document.
   b. Click the Align button, and choose **Align Top**. Deselect the pictures.
   c. Click the picture in the upper left corner, and press Shift. Click the picture in the lower left corner, and choose **Align Left** from the Align menu. Deselect the pictures.
   d. Click the picture in the lower left corner, press Shift, and click the picture in the lower right corner. Choose **Align Bottom** from the Align menu. Deselect the pictures.
   e. Click the picture in the lower right corner, press Shift, and click the picture in the upper right corner. Choose **Align Right** from the Align menu. Deselect the pictures.
10. Open the Borders and Shading dialog box, and apply a red, thin, double-line page border.
11. Click the strawberry picture in the upper right corner, and display the Picture Tools Format tab if necessary. Point to and click the Rotate button, and click **Flip Horizontal**. Repeat for the strawberry in the lower right corner.

12. Add 12 points spacing before the line that begins "Enjoy," and add 18 points spacing before the last line of text.
13. Drag to position the strawberries if necessary.
14. Save the document as ***[your initials]*****16-24** in your Lesson 16 folder.
15. Submit and close the document.

Exercise 16-25

Insert, size, move, and change the wrapping style of clip art, and insert and format WordArt.

1. Open the file **Earth Day - 2**. Change the top margin to **2** inches.
2. Insert clip art by following these steps:
   a. Position the insertion point at the start of the paragraph that begins "In addition."
   b. Click the Insert tab, and click the Clip Art button. The Clip Art task pane displays.
   c. Key **earth** in the Search for text box. Click the drop-down arrow for Results should be:, and select Illustrations and Photographs. Verify that there is a check in the option Include Office.com content. Click Go.
   d. Select a clip showing a globe or a world map.

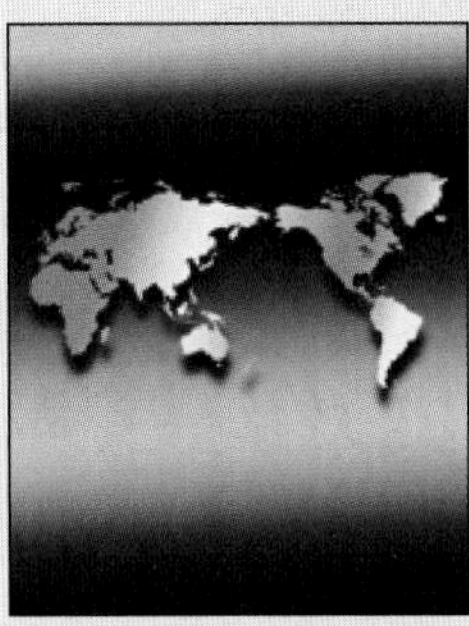

Figure 16-32
World map Clip Art

3. Resize the clip by following these steps:
   a. Click the clip to select it.
   b. Drag a corner handle slightly toward the middle of the clip to make the clip proportionately smaller.
   c. With the clip still selected, click the Picture Tools Format tab on the Ribbon. Locate the Size group.
   d. Change the height setting to **2** inches. The width should be automatically adjusted.
4. Move and align the clip by following these steps:
   a. With the clip selected, hold down the mouse button and drag the clip to the second paragraph. Release the mouse button.
   b. Click the Position button on the Picture Tools Format tab.
   c. Click the second option in the second row, Position in Middle Center with Square Text Wrapping.
5. Insert and format WordArt by following these steps:
   a. Position the insertion point at the top of the document.
   b. Click the Insert tab, and locate the Text group. Click the WordArt button.
   c. Choose an option in the second row.
   d. Key **Earth Day** in the WordArt text box.
   e. Locate the WordArt Styles group. Click the Text Fill button, and select a gradient color to coordinate with your clip art.

f. Click the Text Outline button, and select an outline color.

g. Click the Text Effects button, click Shadow, and select an option in the Outer group.

h. Display the Shadow gallery, and click Shadow Options. Click Shadow in the Format Text Effects dialog box. Select a color for the shadow that coordinates with your fill and line colors.

i. Change the value in the Distance text box to increase or decrease the depth of the shadow. Click Close.

6. Click the WordArt object, click the Position button, and click More Layout Options. Click the Text Wrapping tab. Click Top and Bottom. Click OK. Remove the shape outline.
7. Select the WordArt object if necessary, and click the Text Effects button. Choose Transform, and select a new shape for the WordArt object. Locate the Size button, and change the height to **1** inch and the width to **6** inches.
8. Drag to position the WordArt object if necessary.
9. Save the document as ***[your initials]*16-25** in your Lesson 16 folder.
10. Submit and close the document.

Exercise 16-26

Draw, move, format, and add text to a shape.

1. Open the file **Agenda - 3**.
2. Click the Page Layout tab, and click Themes. Choose the Concourse theme.
3. Insert a bevel shape by following these steps:

a. Place the insertion point at the top of the document, and click the Insert tab.

b. Click the Shapes button, and locate the Basic Shapes category.

c. Click the Bevel shape located in the third row, first icon.

d. Click the document to insert a square bevel.

4. Modify the bevel object by following these steps:

a. Right-click the shape, and choose Format Shape from the shortcut menu.

b. Click Fill on the left pane, and click the Gradient fill option. Change the Type option to Linear. Choose an option from the Direction drop-down list. Click the Stop 1 button, and choose a color from the Color drop-down list. Click the last stop on the Gradient stops slider, and choose a color. Remove any stops between the first and last stops by selecting the stop and clicking the Remove Gradient Stop button.

c. Click Line Style on the left of the Format Shape dialog box, and change the Width to 2 points. Click Line Color on the left of the Format Shape dialog box, and choose a color to coordinate with the gradient color. Click Close.

d. Locate the Size button, and click the Size Dialog Box Launcher. Click the **Size** tab if necessary. Change the **Height** to **Absolute 1** inch, and change the **Width** to **Absolute 6.5** inches.

e. Click the **Position** tab, and change the **Horizontal Alignment** to **Centered** relative to **Page**.

f. Click the **Text Wrapping** tab, and change the **Wrapping style** to **Top and Bottom**. Click **OK**.

5. Drag the box so that the top edge of the box aligns with the 0.5-inch mark on the vertical ruler.

6. Add text to the shape by following these steps:

   a. Right-click the bevel shape.

   b. Choose **Add Text** from the shortcut menu.

   c. Key **RISK MANAGEMENT** in the shape.

   d. Format the text using the Mini toolbar. Apply 14-point bold formatting, with center alignment. Change the font color if necessary.

   e. Place 15 points spacing before and 12 points spacing after the title "Risk Management." Change the line spacing to single.

7. Select the shape, and click the Drawing Tools Format tab. Open the Shape Styles gallery by clicking the More arrow. Click the first shape in the fourth row, **Subtle Effect – Black, Dark 1**.

8. Select the shape, and locate the yellow diamond handle. Drag the handle away from the shape to decrease the amount of bevel depth.

9. Draw a second bevel shape at the bottom of the document. Use Format Painter to format the shape to match the first shape. Change the height to **0.5** inch. Key **Sponsored by the Chamber of Commerce**. Center the text, and change the font size to 10 points. Change the spacing before and the spacing after to 0. Change line spacing to single. Add a page border to the document with a coordinating color. Drag the bevel shapes away from the border if necessary.

10. Save the document as ***[your initials]*16-26** in your Lesson 16 folder.

11. Submit and close the document.

Exercise 16-27

Insert, size, format, align, group, and add text to shapes.

1. Start a new document.

2. Insert a rectangle by following these steps:

   a. Click the **Insert** tab on the Ribbon, and click the Shapes button.

   b. Select the Rectangle shape.

   c. Drag the crosshair pointer down and across the top of the page, creating a rectangle approximately 0.5 inch tall and 6 inches wide.

3. Select the rectangle, and locate the Shape Styles group on the Drawing Tools Format tab. Click the More arrow to display the Shape Styles gallery. Click the blue color in the last row.

NOTE

The document theme determines the theme colors available.

4. Select the rectangle if necessary, and click the Shape Outline button. Click a color that coordinates with the shape style selected.
5. Change the Shape Height box to **0.5**, and change the Shape Width box to **6** inches.
6. Select the rectangle, and press Ctrl+C to copy the rectangle. Deselect the rectangle, and press Ctrl+V to paste it. Drag the pasted copy of the rectangle directly below the first rectangle.
7. Select the second rectangle, and open the Shape Styles gallery. Click the color red in the last row.

NOTE

Using Ctrl allows you to move selected objects in small increments.

8. Change the Shape Outline color to Red, Accent 2 (first row, sixth column).
9. Use the Ctrl key plus the arrow keys to position the second rectangle below the first rectangle with a thin line of white between the two rectangles.
10. Right-click the first rectangle, and click Add Text. Key **Campbell's Confections**. Format the text using 14-point bold and small caps, with a white font color and right alignment. Select the text, and open the Paragraph dialog box. Change the spacing before and after to 0, and change the line spacing to single if necessary.
11. Right-click the second rectangle, and click Add Text. Key the following text on two lines. Change the line spacing to single, and change the spacing before and after to 0.

    25 Main Street • Grove City, PA 16127
    Telephone: 724-555-2025 • Fax: 724-555-2050
12. Format the text in the second rectangle using bold, white font color, and right alignment.
13. Select the first rectangle, press Shift, and click the second rectangle. Click the Drawing Tools Format tab, and click the Align button. Click Align Left.
14. Group the rectangles as one object by following these steps:
    a. Click the first rectangle.
    b. Hold down Shift, and click the second rectangle.
    c. Click the Drawing Tools Format tab if necessary, and click the Group button. Click Group.
15. Save the document as ***[your initials]*16-27** in your Lesson 16 folder. Submit and close the document.

Lesson Applications

Exercise 16-28

Insert, position, and modify shapes.

1. Start a new document, and switch to landscape orientation. Verify that all margins are 1 inch.
2. Key the following text.

   Campbell's Confections
   Announces
   Chocolate Embossing for Greek Letters
3. Change the document theme to **Trek**.
4. Select the first line, and format it using the Mini toolbar or the Font dialog box. Apply 20-point bold, small caps, and a brown accent color (first row, sixth column). Format the second line using 14-point bold, italic, brown font color, and small caps. Format the third line using 16-point bold, small caps, and brown font color. Center the three lines of text.
5. Click the **Insert** tab, and click **Shapes**. Click the line shape, and draw a line below the last line of text from the left margin to the right margin.
6. Right-click the line, and click **Format Shape**. Apply the following format:
   - Change the **Line Color** to brown. Click **Line Style** in the left pane, and change the **Width** to 6 points. Locate the **Arrow settings** group, and click the drop-down arrow for **Begin type**. Click the second option in the second row. Click the down arrow for **End type**, and click the second option in the second row. Click **Close**.
   - Change the width of the line to 9 inches.
   - Select the line. Click the Position button, and click **More Layout Options**. Change the **Horizontal Alignment** to **Centered** relative to **Page**. Click **OK**.
7. Below the line draw a bevel shape approximately 2.5 inches square.
8. Select the shape, and apply the following format:
   - Expand the Shape Styles gallery, and click the third style in the second row (**Colored Fill – Brown, Accent 2**).
   - Drag the yellow contour handle outward to narrow the width of the outline and to resemble a chocolate candy square.
9. Right-click the shape, and click **Add Text**. Click the **Insert** tab, and click **Symbol** and then **More Symbols**. Change the font in the Symbol dialog box to **Symbol**. Scroll to locate the uppercase Greek letter sigma (Σ), click the symbol to select it, and click **Insert**. Close the dialog box.
10. Select the sigma symbol, and format the symbol using center alignment, bold, and 120 points (adjust the point size if necessary for your shape).

Figure 16-33
Chocolate square

11. Copy the chocolate square, and paste the object two times. Drag each of the pasted squares to the right to form a row of three chocolate squares.
12. Change the Greek letter in the second square to a capital epsilon (ϵ), and change the Greek letter in the third square to a capital delta (Δ). Verify that each letter is centered horizontally.
13. Click the **Home** tab, and click **Select**. Choose **Selection Pane**. Press Ctrl, and click each of the bevel shapes listed in the Selection and Visibility task pane.
14. Locate the **Arrange** group on the Ribbon, and click the Align button. Click **Align to Margin**, then click **Distribute Horizontally** to place an equal amount of space between the squares. Click **Align** again, and click **Align Bottom**. Close the Selection and Visibility task pane.
15. Add a page border to the document. Select a geometric design from the **Art** category that coordinates with the objects on the page. Change the color to brown, and adjust the width to 9 points.
16. Open the Page Setup dialog box, and change the vertical alignment to center.
17. Save the document as ***[your initials]*16-28** in your Lesson 16 folder. Submit and close the document.

Exercise 16-29

Insert and format pictures; insert and format WordArt.

1. Open the file **Favors - 4**.
2. Position the insertion point at the start of the first paragraph that begins “Campbell’s.” Format the text from the first paragraph to the end of the document as two columns with 0.4 inch spacing between columns.
3. Format the list beginning with “wedding bells” through “other assorted shapes” as a bulleted list using the small black square bullet (▪).
4. Apply the same bullet format to the list beginning with “solid milk chocolate” through “dark chocolate with mint filling.”
5. Select the title “Favors.” Click the **Insert** tab, and click the WordArt button. Select a style from the gallery. Change text wrapping to **Top and Bottom**.
6. Use the WordArt Styles group to change the text fill color and the text outline color. Change the size to an absolute width of 6.5 inches.

7. Keep the WordArt object selected, and open the Text Effect gallery. Click **Transform**, and select a style in the **Warp** gallery. Click **Text Effects**, click **Shadow**, and choose an option. Display the Shadow gallery, and choose **Shadow Options**. Select a color that coordinates with the fill and line colors. Experiment with the Distance and Angle options to create a shadow effect.
8. Click at the start of the paragraph that begins "Please check." Click the **Insert** tab, and click the Clip Art button. Key **baby rattle** in the Search for text box, and press Enter.
9. Click a clip to insert it in the document.
10. Select the clip, click the Corrections button, and choose an option in the gallery to create a special effect with your picture.
11. Change the text-wrapping option to **Top and Bottom**. Change the shape height to 1.25 inches.
12. Add a blank paragraph before the paragraph that begins "Please check." Drag the picture so that it follows the first bulleted list (drag to the blank paragraph).
13. Insert a column break at the paragraph beginning "Please check."
14. Click in front of the paragraph in the second column that begins "The favor prices."
15. Key **mascot** in the Clip Art Search for box, and press Enter. Click a mascot to insert in the document.
16. Select the mascot if necessary, and display the Picture Styles gallery. Select a picture style appropriate for your mascot.
17. Change the text-wrapping option to **Tight**, and change the shape height to 0.75 inch. Drag the picture to the middle of the paragraph that begins "In August." Use Ctrl and the arrow keys to move the picture in small increments. If necessary, move the picture to the left or right margin to improve text wrapping.
18. Apply a page border to the document. Insert a drop cap at the beginning of the first paragraph.
19. Save the document as ***[your initials]*****16-29** in your Lesson 16 folder.
20. Submit and close the document.

Exercise 16-30

Insert, size, position, format, and align clip art.

1. Start a new document, and open the Page Setup dialog box. Change the orientation to landscape, change all margins to 0.4 inch, and change the paper size to 4.5 inches wide and 3 inches high. Change the line spacing to single, and change the spacing before and after to 0.
2. Key the text in Figure 16-34.

Figure 16-34

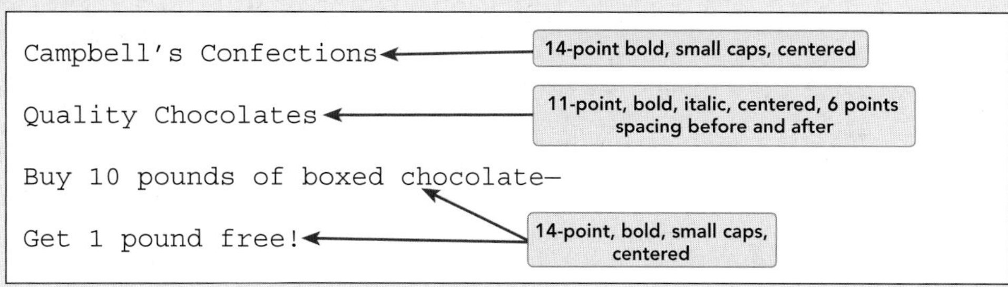

3. Draw a rectangle the width of the document and 0.25 inch high. Click **Shape Fill**, and apply a two-color gradient to the rectangle. Change the **Shape Outline** to coordinate with the fill color.
4. Copy and paste one copy of the rectangle.
5. Drag one rectangle to the top edge of the document, and drag one rectangle to the bottom edge of the document.
6. Open the Shapes gallery, and insert a diamond shape. Select the shape, and change the height and width to 0.5 inch. Change the text wrapping to square.
7. Select the diamond, and change the shape outline to a color that coordinates with the rectangles inserted at the top and bottom of the page.
8. Select the diamond, and change the shape fill to **Picture**. Insert **Chocolate - P18** from the student data files for Lesson 16.
9. Use the copy-and-paste feature to create two rows of pictures with each row containing five pictures.
10. Use the Align, Group, and Distribute options to position the pictures. Refer to Figure 16-35 for a sample document.

Figure 16-35
Sample document with two rows of pictures

11. Save the document as ***[your initials]*16-30** in your Lesson 16 folder.
12. Submit and close the document.

Exercise 16-31 ◆ Challenge Yourself

Insert and format shapes.

1. Open the file **WV Stores**. Change the top margin to 1.5 inches.
2. Beginning with the first address, format the document as two columns with 1 inch spacing between columns.
3. Select each of the cities (Clarksburg, Fairmont, Morgantown, and Wheeling), and apply 14-point bold, italic, and small caps formatting.
4. Insert a column break at the end of the document.
5. Position the insertion point at the top of the second column, and use the Clip Art task pane to locate a map of West Virginia.
6. Change the width of the map to 2.5 inches, and lock the aspect ratio to maintain proportion.
7. Change the text wrapping to square, and drag the picture to the middle of the second column.
8. Open the Shapes gallery, and click the Line Callout 1 shape (Callouts category, first row, fifth shape).
9. Point to the map of West Virginia, and draw a callout shape approximately 1.5 inches wide and 0.5 inch tall. Key **Clarksburg** in the callout. Draw three additional callout shapes for the map of West Virginia, and key a city name in each callout (Fairmont, Morgantown, and Wheeling).
10. Format the text in the callouts using appropriate character formatting. Size and format the callout shapes using an appropriate shape fill and shape line color. Apply shadow or 3-D effects if appropriate. Right-click the callouts, and choose **Format Shape – Line Style** if you want to add an arrow style to the callout lines.
11. Use an atlas or the Internet to determine the location of each of these cities in West Virginia, and drag the callout to its approximate location.
12. Format the title using a WordArt design.
13. Save the document as ***[your initials]*16-31** in your Lesson 16 folder. Submit and close the document.

On Your Own

In these exercises you work on your own, as you would in a real-life business environment. Use the skills you've learned to accomplish the task—and be creative.

Exercise 16-32

Search for a map of your home state using Word's Clip Art task pane or the Internet. Insert the map, and use callouts to identify five cities. Format the objects, and add a title to the document using WordArt. Save the document as ***[your initials]*16-32**. Submit the document.

Exercise 16-33

Create a design for a personal business card. Change margins, paper size, and orientation. Include shapes, pictures, or clip art. Apply special effects if desired. Choose character and paragraph formatting appropriate for the business card. Save the document as ***[your initials]*16-33**, and submit it.

Exercise 16-34

Write a report that includes three topics. The first topic should explain how to add digital photographs to the Microsoft Clip Organizer. Include the procedure for creating a new collection. The second topic should explain the advantages and disadvantages of using Artistic effects with photographs. The final section should discuss the Crop options available when you click the Crop button and the crop options available in the Format Picture dialog box. Include screenshots to demonstrate changes in picture position and crop position. Discuss the option that enables you to preserve the aspect ratio for pictures when cropping. Be sure to define aspect ratio and provide descriptions for 2:3, 3:2, and other formats. Include pictures in the report. Save the document as ***[your initials]*16-34**, and submit it.

Lesson 17

Text Boxes and Desktop Publishing

OBJECTIVES ***After completing this lesson, you will be able to:***

1. Apply page formatting.
2. Apply character and paragraph formatting.
3. Create and modify styles.
4. Create a newsletter-style column layout.
5. Insert text boxes.
6. Create a pull quote.
7. Link text boxes.
8. Work with a multisection layout.

Estimated Time: 1½ hours

In this lesson you use desktop publishing techniques to transform a document into a newsletter layout. You have already practiced many of the Word features presented in this lesson. However, you have not seen the relationship of the individual features in creating a desktop publishing document. You begin by changing the page background and applying paragraph and character formatting, specifying columns, inserting text boxes, and customizing clip art. Then you apply borders and shading and learn how to flow text between linked text boxes.

Applying Page Formatting

Page formatting consists of margins, orientation, columns, headers, footers, page numbers, and page breaks. Special effects can be applied to pages, including watermarks, color, and borders.

A *watermark* is a transparent graphic or text placed behind text. A watermark adds dimension to the printed page by creating a layered effect. Watermarks are often used on stationery.

Exercise 17-1 CREATE A TEXT WATERMARK

You can insert a watermark from the Watermark gallery, or you can create a custom watermark. To insert a watermark, use the Page Layout tab.

1. Start a new document.
2. Click the **Page Layout** tab, and locate the **Page Background** group. Click the Watermark button. A gallery of watermarks displays, as well as a link to watermarks available from Office.com.
3. Click the **Confidential 1** watermark. Notice the position and color of the watermark. Click Undo to remove the watermark.
4. Click the Watermark button, and click **Custom Watermark**.
5. Click the **Text watermark** option. Open the Text drop-down list to see the text options available. Close the list, and create your own watermark by keying **FOR REVIEW ONLY** in the text box. Notice that you can change the font, size, color, and layout (horizontal or diagonal) of the text watermark.

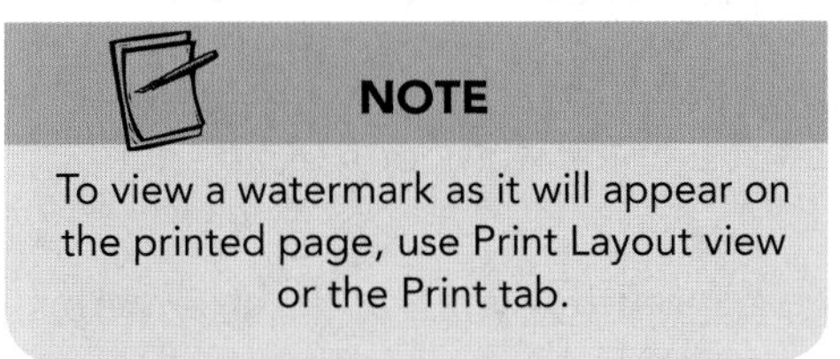

NOTE

To view a watermark as it will appear on the printed page, use Print Layout view or the Print tab.

Figure 17-1
Printed Watermark dialog box

6. Click **OK**. The text appears diagonally on the page.
7. Click the Watermark button, and click **Remove Watermark**.

Exercise 17-2 CREATE A PICTURE WATERMARK

You can create a picture watermark using the Printed Watermark dialog box, or you can manually create a picture watermark using the Corrections and Color controls to create a washout effect and changing the picture's wrapping style to Behind Text.

1. Open the Printed Watermark dialog box, and click the Picture watermark option.
2. Click Select Picture, and locate the directory and folder for the student data files. Click the file **Chocolate - P12**, and click Insert.
3. Verify that the Washout option is checked. Click OK.

Exercise 17-3 CHANGE THE BACKGROUND COLOR

The background of a document can be customized by changing the color and adding a gradient, texture, or pattern. Background color or fill effects are usually reserved for Web pages or documents viewed online.

1. Click the Page Layout tab, and click the Page Color button.
2. Point to several Theme Colors, and click a color that coordinates with the picture watermark.
3. Locate the Themes group on the Page Layout tab, and click the Themes button. Change the document theme to Median, and click the Page Color button on the Page Layout tab. Notice the change in theme colors. Select a different page color.
4. Click the Page Color button, and click Fill Effects. Click the Texture tab, and select the Brown marble texture. Click OK.
5. Close the document without saving.

Applying Character and Paragraph Formatting

Basic character formatting involves choosing a font, a font style, and a font size. The choice of font is an important design decision. Fonts, also called "typefaces," should be readable and appropriate to the document. The title font draws attention. The font for headings (often called "headlines" in newsletters) shows emphasis and breaks up the body text. Document themes include two fonts—one for headings and one for body text. The fonts may be the same font or two different fonts. When selecting a theme, you may want to review the font(s) defined by the theme.

Headings and titles are often *sans serif* fonts (with no decorative lines projecting from the characters), and body text is a *serif* font (with decorative lines) in printed documents. Online documents often use sans serif fonts for body text.

Sans serif: Arial, with bold italic font style, used for headings

Serif: Times New Roman, used for body text

Paragraph formatting includes indents, spacing, alignment, borders, and shading. In this lesson you also apply styles, which provide a combination of character and paragraph formatting.

Exercise 17-4 CHOOSE A CHARACTER FORMAT FOR A TITLE

The newsletter title, or *nameplate,* is the most noticeable element on the page. You can design a title by using a drawing program or create a WordArt shape. Or you can choose a font that is appropriate for the title or the business name. A large font provides contrast between the title and the body text. Avoid using uppercase text unless the text line is extremely short. In this exercise, you create the title using a unique bold font.

1. Open the file **Chocolate News**. Change the top, bottom, left, and right margins to 0.75 inch.
2. On a new line at the top of the page, key the title **Choc Talk**.
3. Start a new line under the title and key **Volume 1, Number 2**.
4. On the same line, insert two spaces, and key the current month and year.
5. Format the title in 60-point Arial Narrow, with bold and italic.
6. Format the line under the title as 10-point Arial.

Figure 17-2
Matching fonts with business names

Lucida Calligraphy	Magical Mystery Tour Co.
Impact Italic	North American School of Aviation
Tahoma	Vision Consultants of Freemont
Monotype Corsiva	Chez Pierre Catering
Century Schoolbook	Smithfield Savings and Loan
Comic Sans MS	Westport Design Studios
Bodoni MT Black	World Gym

Exercise 17-5 WORK WITH CHARACTER SPACING

Just as a typographer does, you can change character spacing to improve the look of your document text. Some character-spacing features also help you create character effects and control the size of the document.

Using the Font dialog box (Advanced tab), you can control character spacing in the following ways:

- Stretch or compress text horizontally by a percentage of its original size.
- Add or delete space between letters by a specific number of points.
- Raise or lower selected text in relation to the baseline.
- Adjust *kerning,* or the amount of space between certain combinations of characters, so that a word looks more evenly spaced.

1. Select the title text.
2. Open the **Font** dialog box, and display the **Advanced** tab.
3. Open the **Spacing** drop-down list, and choose **Condensed**. Notice the change in the Preview box. The text is condensed by 1 point.
4. Choose **Expanded** from the drop-down list, and click **OK**. The text is expanded by 1 point.
5. Notice the change in the space between individual letters of the words, particularly the space between the "T" and the "a" in "Talk." Select the title if necessary, and open the Font dialog box with the Advanced tab displayed. Click to select the check box **Kerning for fonts**. Verify that 60 appears in the **Points and above** text box. Click **OK**, and notice that the "T" and "a" are closer together.

Figure 17-3
Changing character spacing

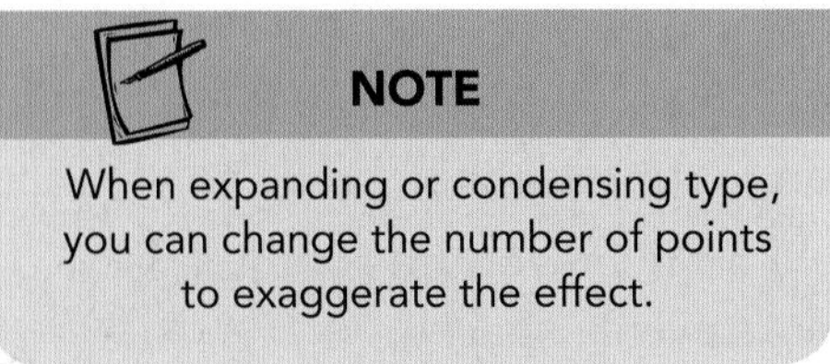

NOTE

When expanding or condensing type, you can change the number of points to exaggerate the effect.

6. Open the Font dialog box, and change the **Spacing** setting back to **Normal**. Open the **Scale** drop-down list, and choose **150%**. Click **OK**. This stretches each letter of text horizontally.
7. Reopen the **Font** dialog box, and key **130%** in the **Scale** text box. Click **OK**.
8. With the title selected, press Ctrl+Spacebar. All character formatting is removed.
9. Click the Undo button (or press Ctrl+Z) to restore the formatting.

Exercise 17-6 APPLY PARAGRAPH FORMATTING

In this exercise you apply basic paragraph formatting (align, indent, and spacing) to improve the text flow of the newsletter layout.

1. Center-align the title text, and right-align the line of text below the title.
2. Format the line below the title with 12 points spacing after paragraphs to provide additional white space below it.
3. Select the text from the first heading ("Chocolate Terms") to the end of the document.
4. On the Home tab, in the Paragraph group, click the Line Spacing button and choose **1.0**. The selected text now has single spacing.
5. Select the text from the paragraph beginning "Chocolate Terms" to the end of the document, and verify that the spacing after is 10 points.

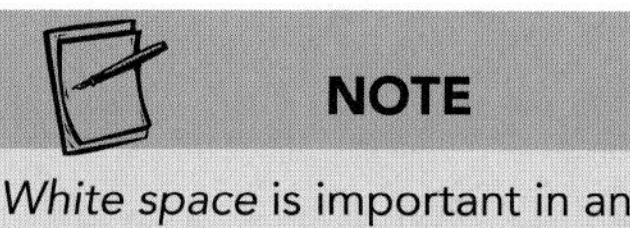

NOTE

White space is important in any layout and can be used as a design tool. It gives a newsletter "breathing room" and makes the content more readable. You can add white space before and after paragraphs, between columns, between letters and words, in the margins, around graphics, and so on.

Exercise 17-7 APPLY BORDERS AND SHADING

1. To change the title to white text against a black background (sometimes referred to as *reverse* or *drop-out* text), select the title, including its paragraph mark. Click the **Home** tab, and click the arrow beside the Shading button, and click the black square in the first row. Deselect the title.

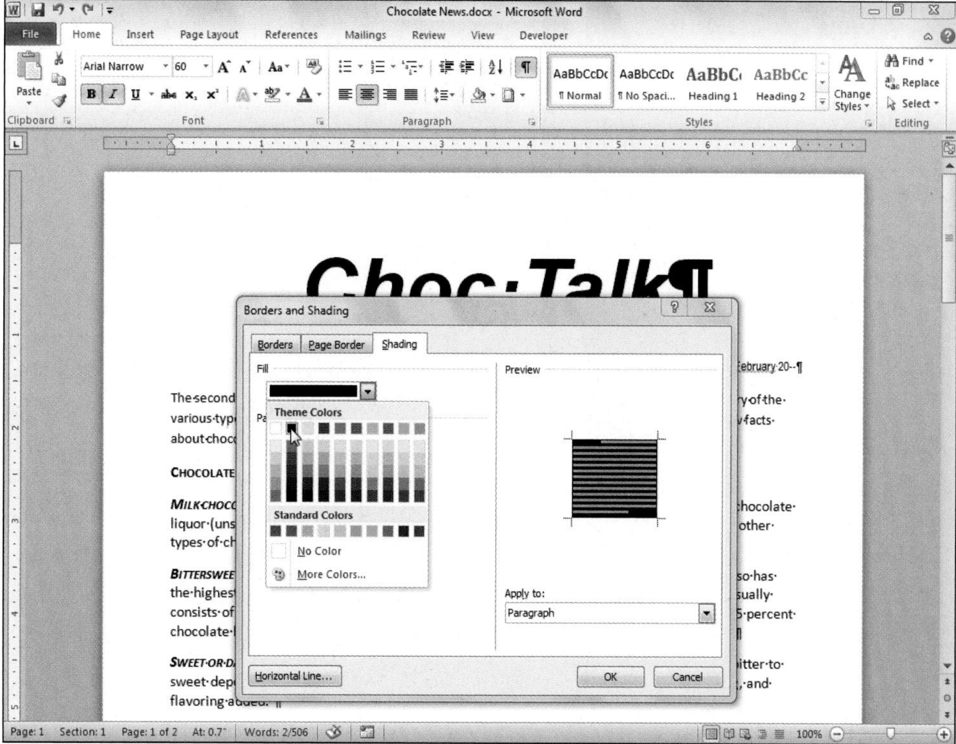

Figure 17-4
Applying shading to the title

2. Click the **Page Layout** tab, and click the Page Borders button. On the **Page Border** tab, choose the **Box** setting. Open the **Art** drop-down list, and choose an attractive (but not too busy) border. Make sure the width is no more than 12 points, or else the border will be too thick. Check that the **Apply to** box is set to **Whole document**.
3. Click the Options button Options... . The Borders and Shading Options dialog box shows you that the border will appear, by default, 24 points (1/3 inch) from the top, bottom, left, and right edges of the page. Click **OK**. Click **OK** again to apply the page border.

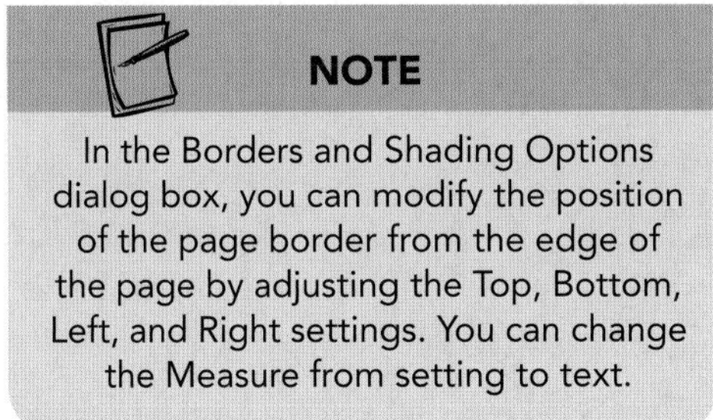

NOTE

In the Borders and Shading Options dialog box, you can modify the position of the page border from the edge of the page by adjusting the Top, Bottom, Left, and Right settings. You can change the Measure from setting to text.

Figure 17-5
Applying borders

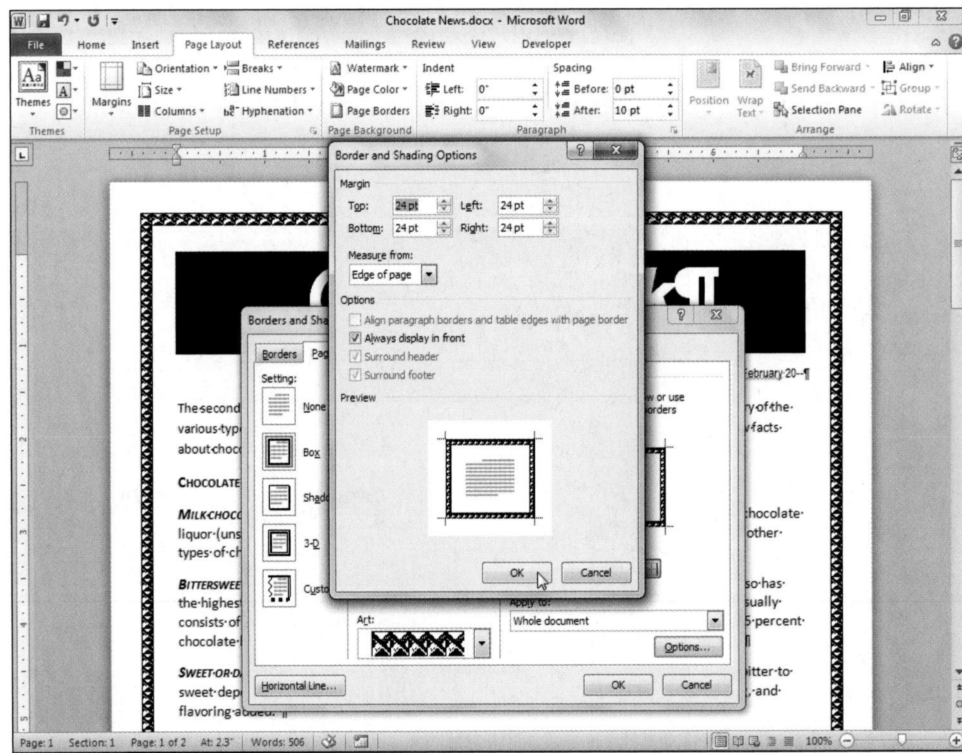

4. Save the document as ***[your initials]*17-7** in a new folder for Lesson 17 documents. Leave it open for the next exercise.

Creating and Modifying Styles

A *style* consists of formatting characteristics that you apply to paragraphs, characters, tables, or lists to give a document a consistent look. Word provides predefined styles you can apply to text, such as heading styles for document titles and body text styles for paragraphs. In this lesson, you create and name your own styles and then modify them.

Exercise 17-8 CREATE PARAGRAPH AND CHARACTER STYLES

Paragraph styles include formatting related to such characteristics as text alignment, tab stops, line spacing, borders, and fonts. Character formatting affects selected text within a paragraph and can include font, font size, and font style such as bold and italic formats.

1. Display the Styles task pane by clicking the **Styles Dialog Box Launcher** on the Home tab. At the bottom of the task pane, click **Options** to display the Style Pane Options dialog box. Click the drop-down arrow for the **Select styles to show** box, and click **Recommended**. Click **OK**. This option shows the styles you create and the styles in the Quick Styles gallery. The option *All Styles* lists all of Word's predefined styles. The option *In use* shows the formats currently used in the document.

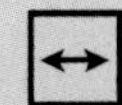

REVIEW

The Normal style always appears as formatting in use in a document. It is the default paragraph style on which other styles are based. It is 11-point Calibri, left-aligned, 1.15 line spacing, and 10 points spacing after.

2. Point to the Normal style in the Styles task pane to view its formatting instructions.
3. Click within the heading "Chocolate Terms." You are going to create a new paragraph style for the document headings. When formatting document headings, place more space before the heading than below it. Avoid separating headings from the related body text.
4. Click the New Style button at the bottom of the Styles task pane. In the Create New Style from Formatting dialog box, apply the following changes:

    - In the Name box, key the style name ***[your initials]*ParagraphHeading**. The Style type box should be set to **Paragraph**. The Style based on box should be set to **Normal**.
    - Under Formatting, change the font to Arial Narrow, 14-point bold.
    - Click the Format button, and choose **Paragraph**. In the Paragraph dialog box, set the spacing before to 12 points and the spacing after to 6 points. Click **OK** to close the Paragraph dialog box.

Figure 17-6
Creating a paragraph style

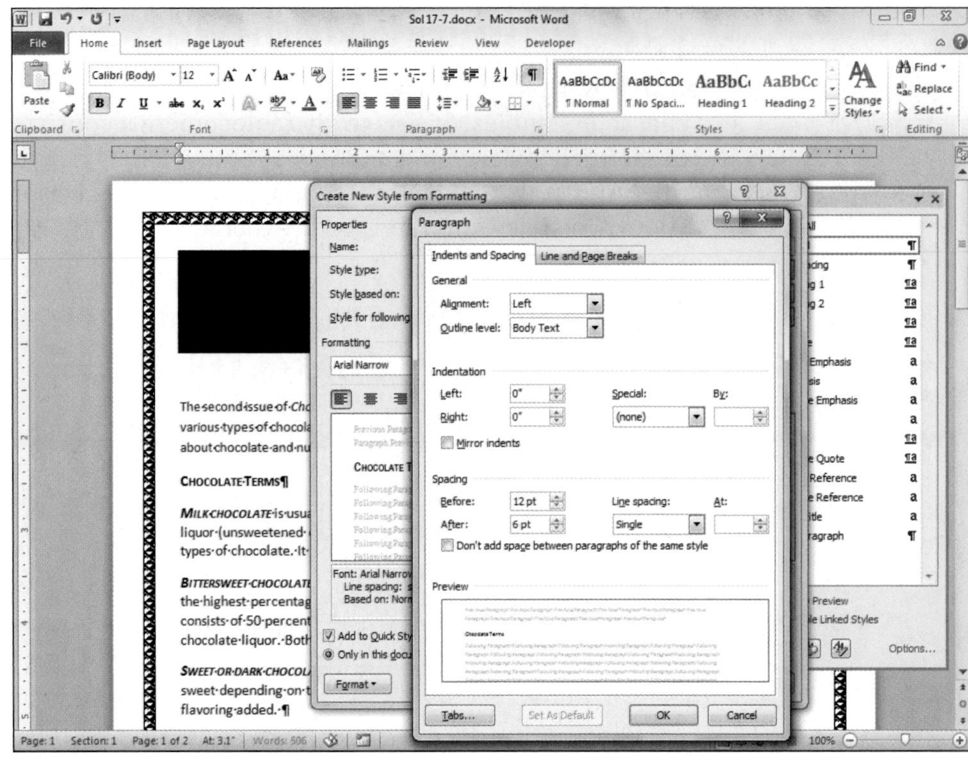

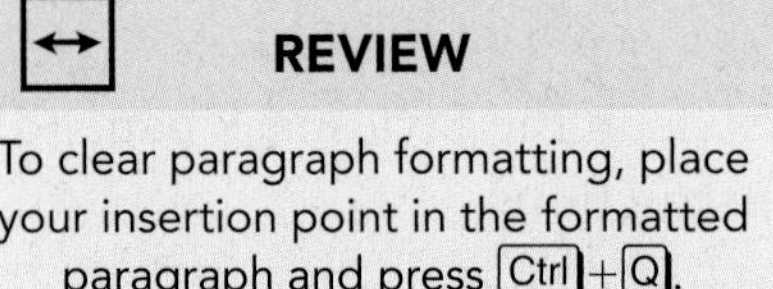

REVIEW

To clear paragraph formatting, place your insertion point in the formatted paragraph and press Ctrl+Q.

NOTE

You do not have to select text to apply a paragraph style; simply place the insertion point within the paragraph to which you are applying the style.

5. Click **OK** to close the Create New Style from Formatting dialog box. The new style appears in the Styles task pane.
6. With the insertion point still in the heading "Chocolate Terms," click the new style, *[your initials]* **ParagraphHeading**, in the task pane to apply the style.
7. Apply the *[your initials]*ParagraphHeading style to the following headings: "Chocolate Bloom" and "Storage."
8. In the paragraph beginning "Milk Chocolate," select the text "Milk Chocolate." You will create a character style for this text, and to do so you need to select the text.
9. Click the New Style button, and apply the following changes in the Create New Style from Formatting dialog box:
   - In the Name box, key the style name ***[your initials]*****Term**.
   - Set the Style type to **Character**.
   - Click the Format button Format and choose **Font**. Change the font to Impact, no bold, no italic, with 1.5-point expanded character spacing. Click **OK**, and then click **OK** again.
10. Apply the new character style to the selected text and to the terms "Bittersweet Chocolate," "Semi-sweet Chocolate," "Sweet or Dark Chocolate," "White Chocolate," "Baking Chocolate," and "Chocolate Bloom."

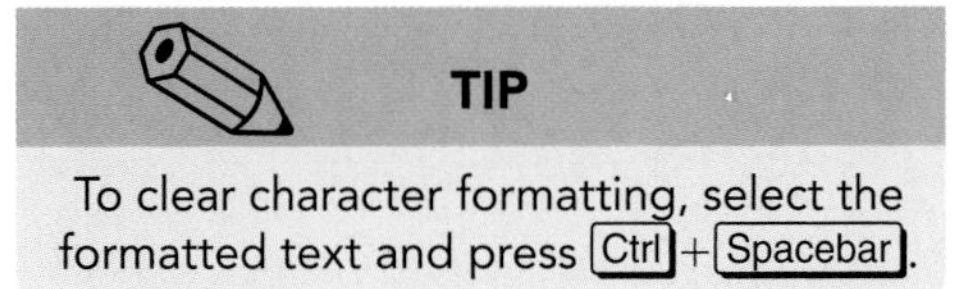

TIP

To clear character formatting, select the formatted text and press Ctrl+Spacebar.

11. Position the insertion point in the first paragraph of the document, which begins "The second issue." Create a new paragraph style called ***[your initials]* NewsletterBody** that is based on the Normal style. Use the font Book Antiqua, 12 points, single spacing, justified alignment, and 12 points spacing after.
12. Apply the new *[your initials]*NewsletterBody style to every paragraph except the three paragraphs formatted with the ParagraphHeading style. (Press F4 to repeat the style.) Notice that the applied paragraph style *[your initials]*NewsletterBody does not affect the character style.
13. Save the document as ***[your initials]*17-8** in your Lesson 17 folder.

Exercise 17-9 CREATE A STYLE FOR BULLET TEXT

You can create a style for a list of items and specify the numbering or bullet characters.

1. Position the insertion point at the end of the document.
2. Press Enter and key the following text. Press Enter after each sentence.

   Chocolate's flavonoids and antioxidants make it a "heart-healthy" food.

   Chocolate does not raise cholesterol because of a key ingredient, stearic acid. The darker the chocolate, the healthier it is for us because it has fewer calories but more antioxidants.
3. Click **Options** in the Styles task pane, and change the **Select styles to show** box to display **All styles**. Notice that the styles you created appear near the top of the list.
4. Position the insertion point in the line that begins "Chocolate's flavonoids." Open the Create New Style from Formatting dialog box, and create the following new style:
   - Name the style ***[your initials]*BulletedList**, and change the style type to **Paragraph**.
   - Click the Format button Format in the dialog box; then click **Numbering**. Click the **Bullets** tab.
   - Click **Define New Bullet** to choose a new symbol character, and click **Symbol** to open the Symbol dialog box.
   - Change the font to **Wingdings**, and choose a shadowed square symbol (❑). Click **OK** to close all open dialog boxes.

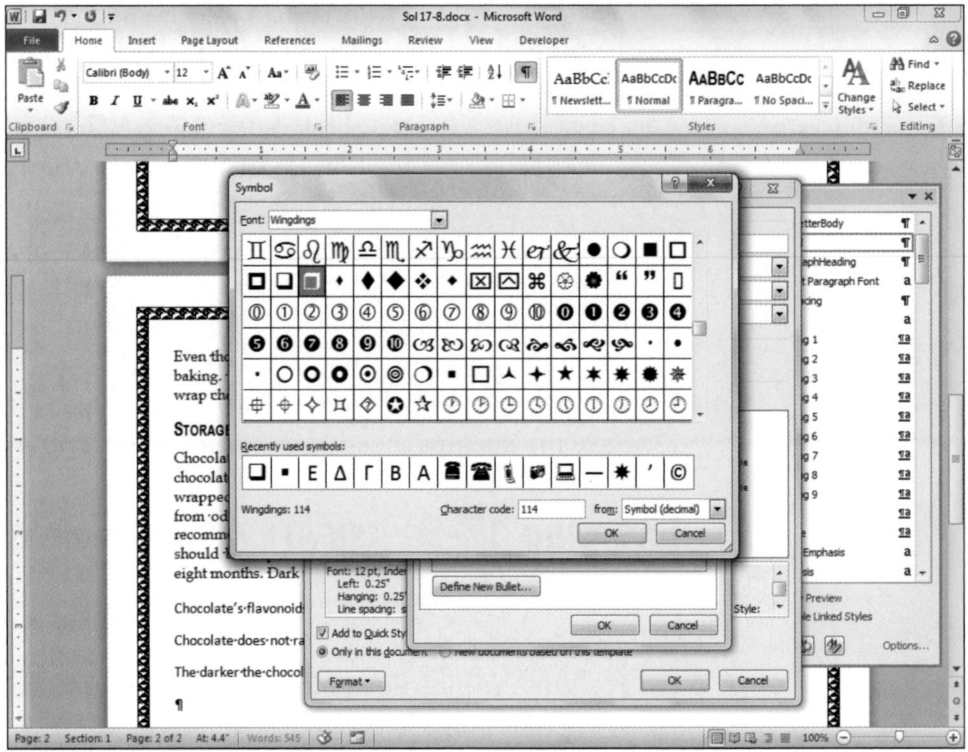

Figure 17-7
Choosing a symbol

5. Apply the *[your initials]*Bulleted List style to the three sentences that you keyed in step 2.

Exercise 17-10 MODIFY STYLES

After you create a style, you can modify it in a number of ways, such as renaming it or changing the formatting.

1. Right-click the style *[your initials]*NewsletterBody in the task pane, and choose Modify.
2. Change the font to Cambria, 11 points, left aligned, with 6 points spacing after paragraphs. Click OK to close the Modify Style dialog box. The changes appear throughout the document.
3. Position the insertion point in the "Chocolate Terms" heading. Point to the style named *[your initials]* ParagraphHeading in the task pane, click its down arrow, and choose Modify.
4. Open the drop-down list for the box labeled Style for following paragraph. Choose *[your initials]* NewsletterBody and click OK.
5. Position the insertion point at the end of the paragraph that begins "Chocolate products." Start a new paragraph and key **Chocolate and Nutrition**. Apply the *[your initials]* ParagraphHeading style to the text.

TIP

You can create or modify a style so that a different style is assigned to the paragraph that follows once you press the Enter key. This means you can have styles applied automatically as you key text. This is useful for heading styles. In the Create New Style from Formatting dialog box or the Modify Style dialog box, open the drop-down list beside Style for following paragraph and choose the style you want to follow.

6. Press Enter to start a new paragraph. Notice that the style *[your initials]* NewsletterBody is applied to the new paragraph. Key the following text:

   The following list includes several interesting observations about chocolate.

7. Click **Options** at the bottom of the Styles task pane, and change the **Select styles to show** box to **In use** so that you can see all the styles and formatting you have created for this document. Click to select the check boxes for **Paragraph level formatting**, **Font formatting**, and **Bullet and numbering** formatting. Selecting the check boxes allows you to see manual formatting applied to text in the document. Click **OK** to close the Style Pane Options dialog box.

Figure 17-8
Style Pane Options dialog box

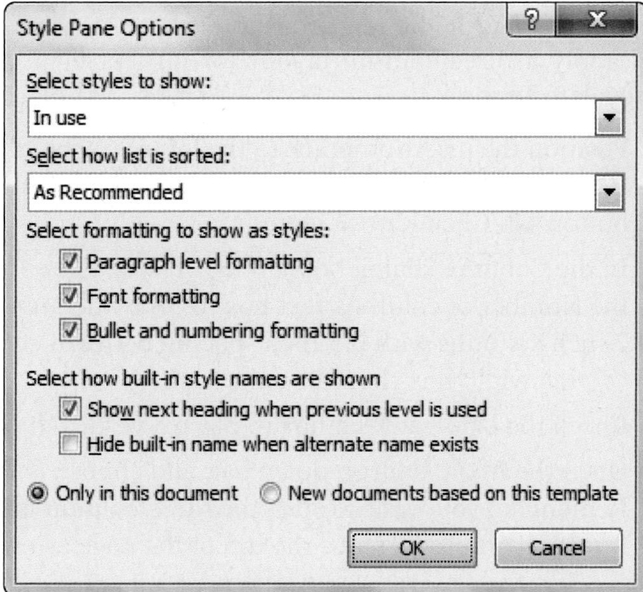

8. Click the first line in the document, the formatted newsletter title. Notice the format that is selected in the Styles task pane. Right-click the formatting description for the title in the Styles task pane, and choose **Modify Style**.
9. The selected format appears as the name of the style. Key the style name ***[your initials]*NewsletterTitle**. Click **OK**. Notice that the formatting now has a style name in the task pane.
10. Follow the same procedure to modify the formatting for the line below the title, giving it the style name ***[your initials]*Volume** and adding 6 points of spacing before the paragraph.
11. Change the Normal style font to Cambria.
12. Save the document as ***[your initials]*17-10** in your Lesson 17 folder. Leave it open for the next exercise.

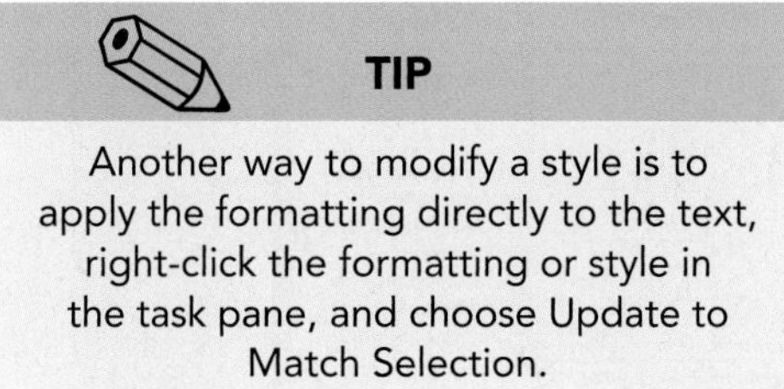

Another way to modify a style is to apply the formatting directly to the text, right-click the formatting or style in the task pane, and choose Update to Match Selection.

Creating a Newsletter-Style Column Layout

Newsletters typically use a column layout similar to that of a newspaper, in which text flows from the bottom of one column to the top of the next. When creating a newsletter, you need to determine the number, size, and placement of columns, all of which affect readability and the amount of white space on the page. The size and number of columns in the document influence the size and type of font used. Use a smaller font size when the columns are narrow. After your document is in column layout, you can use Word's many tools to control the flow of text.

Exercise 17-11 CREATE A MULTICOLUMN LAYOUT

In this exercise, you create a multicolumn layout. You keep the existing one-column format for the text from the title to the end of the first paragraph. You apply a three-column layout for all text beginning with the heading "Chocolate Terms."

1. Position the insertion point to the left of the bold paragraph heading "Chocolate Terms." Click the **Page Layout** tab, and click the Columns button . Click **More Columns**.
2. In the Columns dialog box, under Presets, click **Three**. (You can also set the Number of columns text box to **3**.) By default, this layout has three 2-inch columns with 0.5-inch spacing between columns. (The **Equal column width** box should be checked.)
3. Check the **Line between** box to place a vertical line between columns.
4. Open the **Apply to** drop-down list, and choose **This point forward**. Remember, you want to start the three-column layout from the insertion point and leave the top of the page as one column.

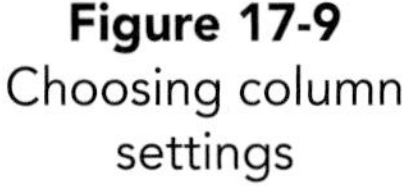

Figure 17-9 Choosing column settings

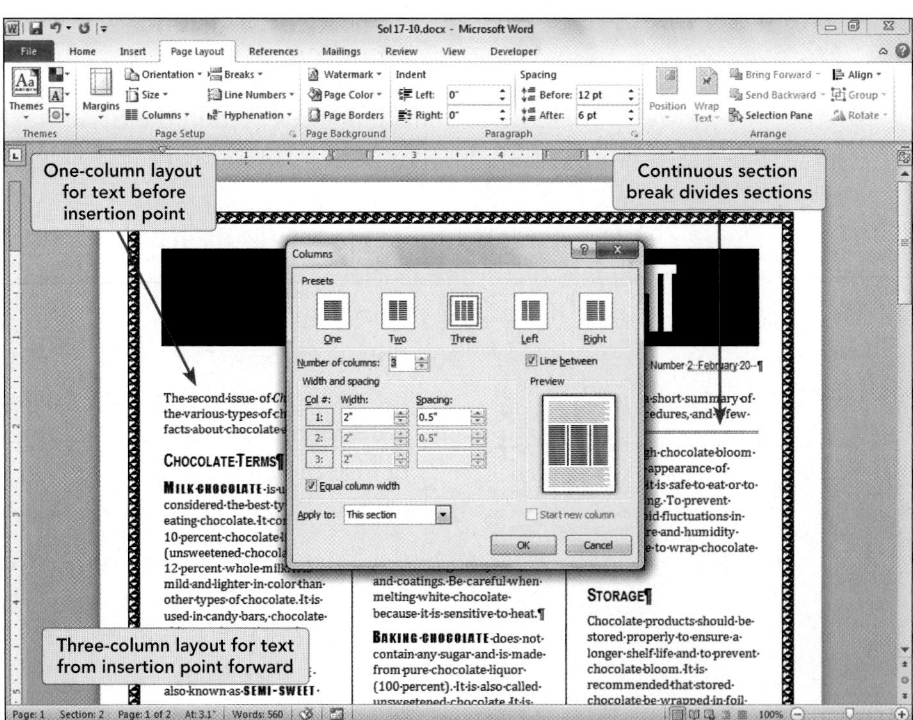

5. Notice the layout for the three-column format shown in the Preview box. This is the layout you will apply, but before doing so, click the other Presets (**Two**, **Left**, **Right**) and notice the layout changes.

NOTE

Column layouts do not have to be symmetrical. The Left and Right presets create two columns of unequal width.

6. Click **Three** again and click **OK**. The three-column text starts a new section. If necessary, click the Show/Hide ¶ button ¶ to see the continuous section break.
7. Position the insertion point at the end of the first section (to the right of "nutrition." and before the paragraph mark), and press Enter to add white space between the sections.
8. Format the heading "Chocolate Terms" with no spacing before the paragraph. This will align the heading with the text at the top of the second and third columns. (Do not modify the style; just change the formatting for that particular heading.)

NOTE

In newsletters, newspapers, and magazines, paragraphs following the first left-aligned paragraph are usually indented as they are here. This helps delineate new paragraphs.

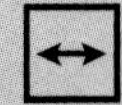

REVIEW

To insert a symbol, position the insertion point and click the Insert tab. Click the Symbol button. Click More Symbols, and click the Symbols tab. Choose a font, choose a symbol, and click Insert.

9. Locate the paragraph in the third column that begins "Even though," and format the paragraph with a 0.25-inch first-line indent. Use this formatting to create a new style called "NewsletterIndent." (Right-click the paragraph, and choose **Styles**. Click **Save Selection as a New Quick Style**. Key the style name ***[your initials]*****NewsletterIndent**, and click **OK**.)
10. At the end of the last paragraph in the document, insert a symbol of your choice from the font Wingdings or Webdings. This is often done in magazines to signify the end of an article.
11. Insert a symbol between "Number 2" and the month in the line after the title at the beginning of the document.

Exercise 17-12 BALANCE COLUMNS AND CONTROL TEXT FLOW

In a multicolumn layout, you can control how columns break. For example, you can insert a column break to force text to start at the next column, or you can insert a continuous section break to balance the length of columns.

For further control of how text flows in your layout, you can change text flow options in the Paragraph dialog box. For example:

- Make sure Word does not print the last line of a paragraph by itself at the top of a page (called a *widow*) or the first line of a paragraph by itself at the bottom of a page (called an *orphan*).
- Keep the lines of a paragraph together (preventing a page break within the paragraph).
- Keep one paragraph with another paragraph (preventing a page break between the paragraphs).
- Insert a page break before a paragraph.

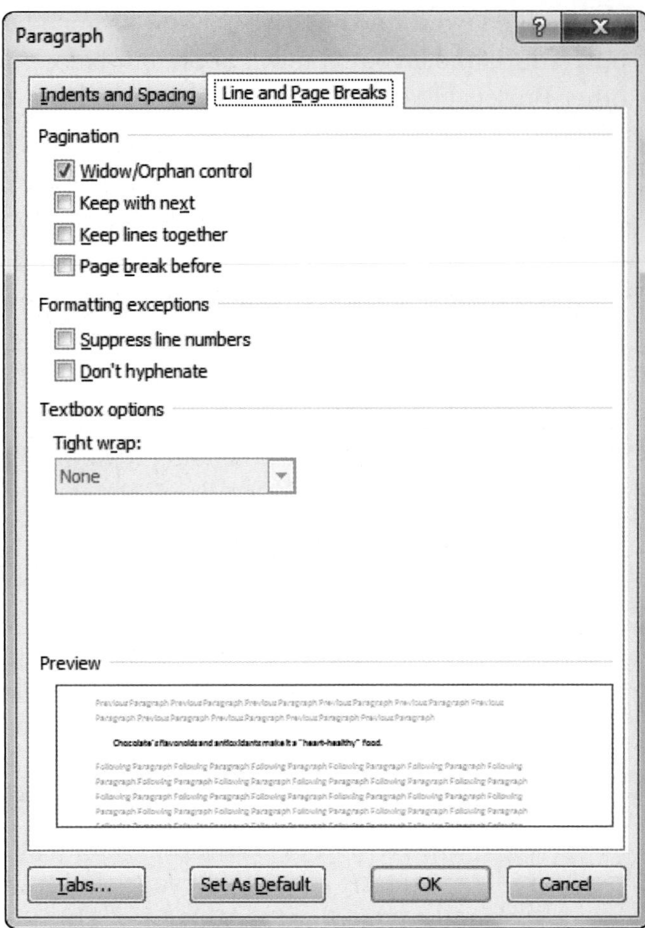

Figure 17-10 Choosing text flow options

1. Scroll to the end of the document.
2. To balance the length of the columns on page 2, position the insertion point at the end of the document (after the symbol).
3. Insert a continuous section break (**Page Layout** tab, **Breaks**). Word balances the length of the columns.

> **REVIEW**
>
> You can avoid a line break within text such as "2 a.m." by using a nonbreaking space. You can avoid a line break within text such as "3-hour" by using a nonbreaking hyphen. One method is to use the Symbol dialog box. You can also use the keyboard shortcuts (Ctrl+Shift+- for a nonbreaking hyphen and Ctrl+Shift+Spacebar for a nonbreaking space).

4. Scroll to the bottom of page 1, and change the zoom to **Text Width**. Select the heading "Chocolate and Nutrition," and open the Paragraph dialog box. On the **Line and Page Breaks** tab, check the **Keep with next** option. (The Keep lines together option is used for lines in the same paragraph.) Notice that the Widow/Orphan control option is turned on by default to prevent a paragraph's first line from appearing by itself at the bottom of a page and to prevent a paragraph's last line from appearing by itself at the top of a page. Click **OK**.
5. To change the line, column, and page breaks throughout the document, insert a Clip Art picture. Position the insertion point on page 1 at the beginning of the first paragraph ("The second issue"), and insert a Clip Art related to chocolate.

6. Select the clip art, and change the text wrapping to square. Crop the picture if appropriate. Change the height to 1 inch. Scroll through the document, and notice the change in text flow in the columns.
7. Delete the continuous section break at the end of the document (click before the break and press Delete). The columns are no longer balanced.
8. Place the insertion point in the third column of the first page at the beginning of the paragraph that begins "Even though," and insert a next page section break. Place the insertion point in the new section (page 2, section 3), open the Columns dialog box, and apply the following changes:
    - Change the column measurements to unequal widths. Set columns 1 and 2 to 2.3 inches wide with 0.25-inch space between them, and set column 3 to 1.9 inches.
    - Remove the line between columns for this section.
    - Click OK.
9. Click in the left column on page 1, reopen the Columns dialog box, and remove the line between columns for this section.
10. Save the document as ***[your initials]*17-12** in your Lesson 17 folder.
11. Submit the document. Leave it open for the next exercise.

Inserting Text Boxes

In this section, you add text to the layout. The easiest way to do this is by inserting a *text box*—a free-floating rectangular object. You can position a text box anywhere on a page and apply formatting to it.

Exercise 17-13 INSERT A TEXT BOX

You can create a text box from existing text or insert a blank text box and key text inside it (similar to drawing a shape and adding text to the shape).

1. Scroll to the bottom of page 2, and change the zoom level to 100%. Be sure you can see the lower right corner of the page. Click the Insert tab on the Ribbon, and locate the Text group. Click the Text Box button.
2. A gallery of text box designs displays. Click Draw Text Box.
3. The pointer changes to a crosshair. Draw a text box in the lower right corner of the page by dragging the crosshair down and to the right until the box measures approximately 2 inches wide and 3 inches tall.

NOTE

When you draw a text box, an anchor symbol appears on-screen, indicating that the text box is anchored to the nearest paragraph. This gives the text box a relationship to the surrounding document text.

Figure 17-11
Inserting text boxes

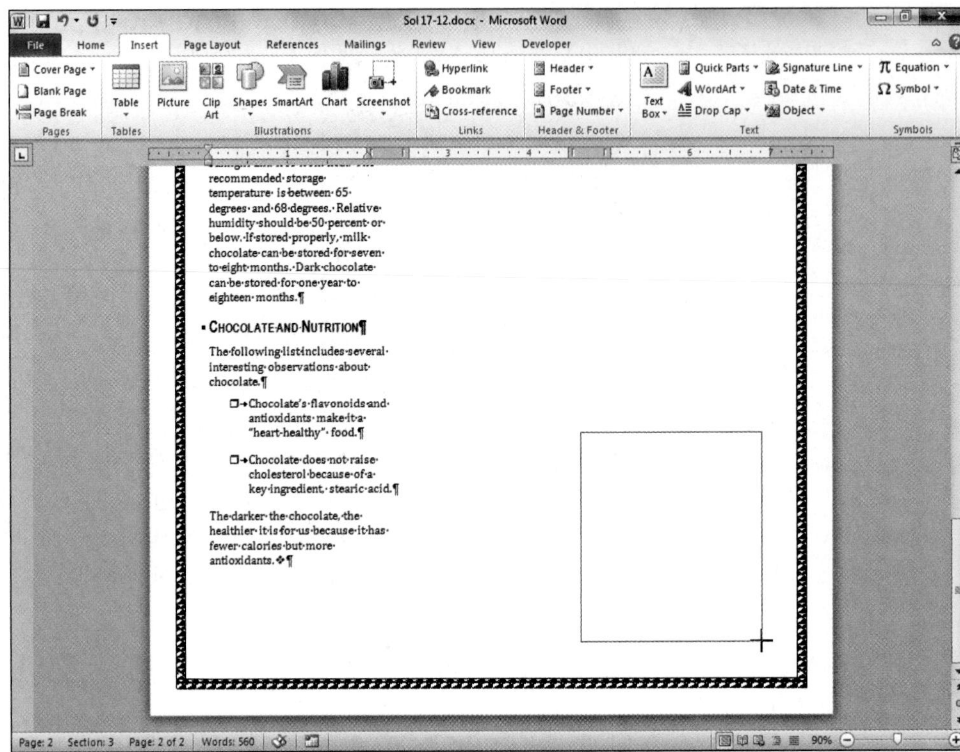

4. Select the paragraph mark in the text box, and open the Paragraph dialog box. Change the line spacing to single and the spacing after to 0 points. Key the text in Figure 17-12, and apply the appropriate format. Remove blank paragraph marks in the text box.

Figure 17-12

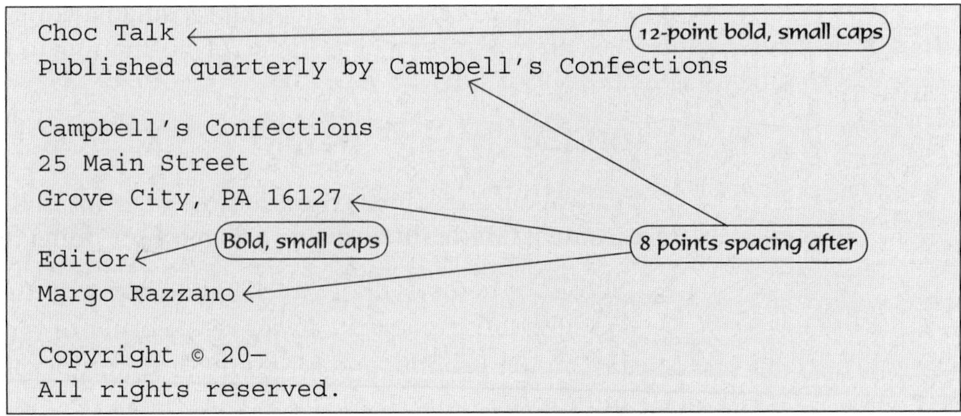
Choc Talk
Published quarterly by Campbell's Confections

Campbell's Confections
25 Main Street
Grove City, PA 16127

Editor
Margo Razzano

Copyright © 20–
All rights reserved.

Exercise 17-14 SELECT AND SIZE A TEXT BOX

When you click within a text box, you activate it. The text box is then in Text Edit mode—you can add, edit, delete, or format text.

When you click the text box border, you select the text box. You can then move or format the text box by changing the fill or line color. There is a subtle difference between the appearance of the text box border when it is in Text Edit mode (dotted line) and the appearance of the text box border when you click the border to select the object (solid line). An activated text box has its own ruler, which you can use to change margins, indents, and tab settings for text within the text box.

1. Click inside the text box containing text to activate it. Notice the border, made of dotted lines. You can add, edit, or format text in an activated text box.
2. Select the text "Published quarterly by." Apply italic formatting.
3. Point to the top-left resize handle of the text box. When you see the two-headed arrow pointer, drag the handle diagonally up and to the left approximately 0.25 inch.

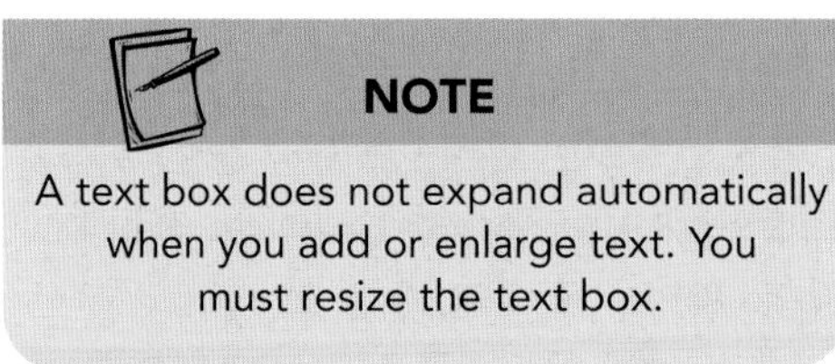

NOTE
A text box does not expand automatically when you add or enlarge text. You must resize the text box.

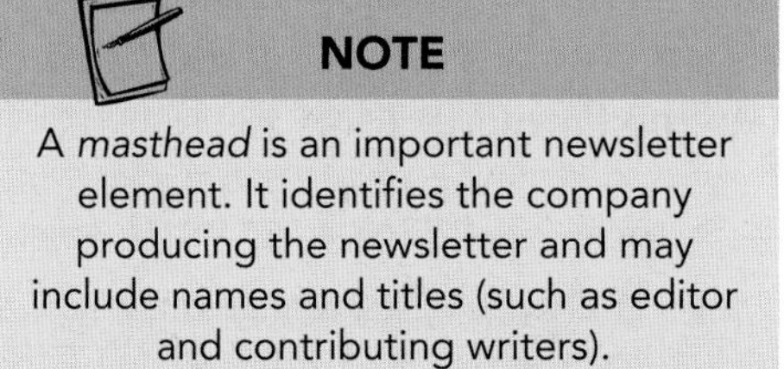

NOTE
A *masthead* is an important newsletter element. It identifies the company producing the newsletter and may include names and titles (such as editor and contributing writers).

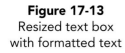

4. Use the middle-bottom handle to drag the bottom border up to fit the text. Notice that clicking on a text box border to resize it also selects the text box. The selected text box border has a solid line, rather than dotted lines.
5. Click the **Drawing Tools Format** tab. Locate the **Size** group, and click the Size button. Change the **Height** value to **2.5** inches, and change the **Width** value to **2** inches.
6. Drag the selected text box until it is positioned in the lower right corner of the page.
7. Resize and position the text box as needed to resemble the one shown in Figure 17-13.

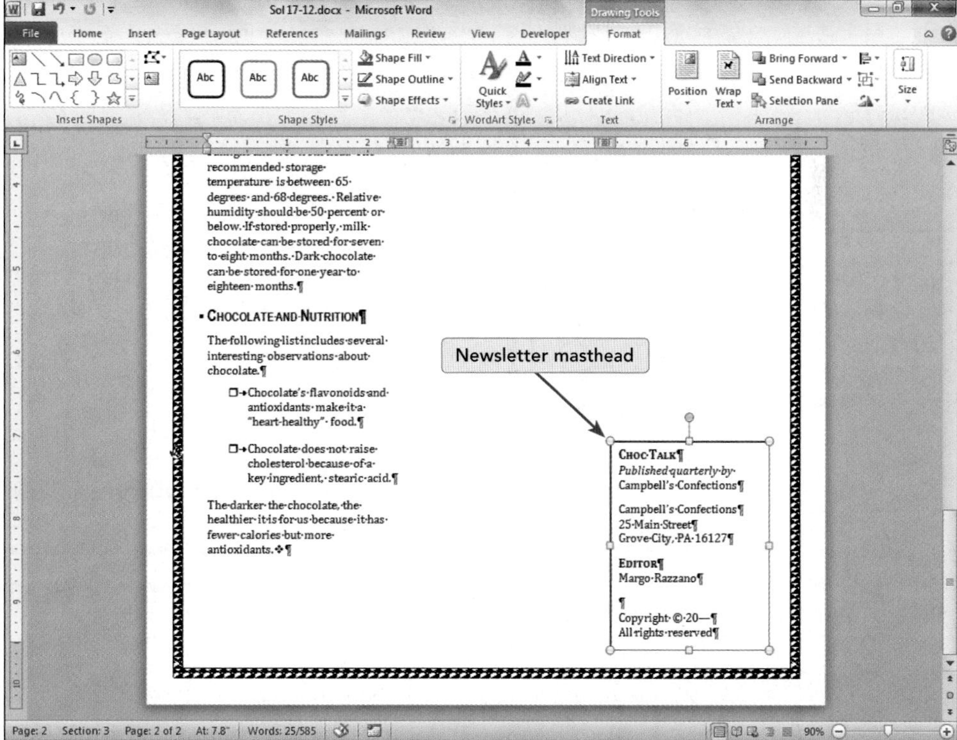

Figure 17-13
Resized text box with formatted text

Exercise 17-15 FORMAT A TEXT BOX

As with other drawing objects, you can change the border, fill, and alignment of a text box and size the box to exact measurements. You can also change the internal text box margins. You can use the Drawing Tools Format tab on the Ribbon or use the Format Shape dialog box.

1. Select the text box by clicking the text box border. Click the **Home** tab, and click the Center button ≡ to center-align the text.
2. With the text box still selected, click the **Drawing Tools Format** tab, and click the Shape Outline button. Click **Weight**, and choose **1½ pt**.
3. Click the Shape Effects button, and click the **Shadow** option. Click the first style in the first row under the Outer heading.
4. Right-click the text box, and choose **Format Shape**. Click the **Text Box** option, and click **Middle** under Vertical alignment. The text is centered vertically within the text box. Click **Close**. Another way to center the text vertically within the text box is to click the Drawing Tools Format tab and click the Align Text button.

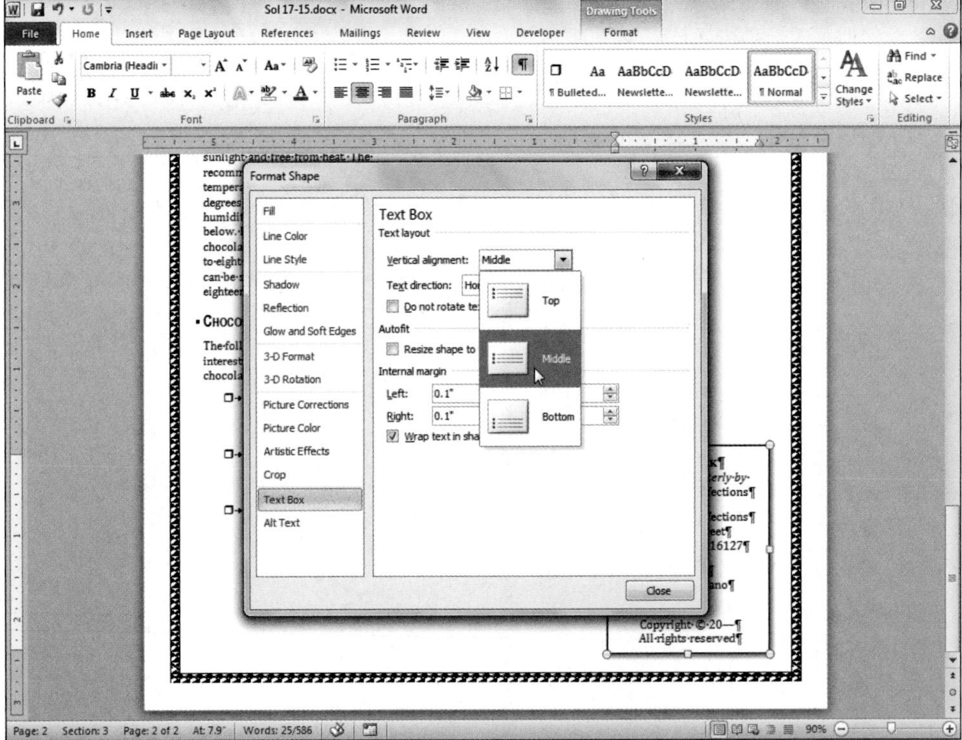

Figure 17-14
Choosing options in the Format Shape dialog box

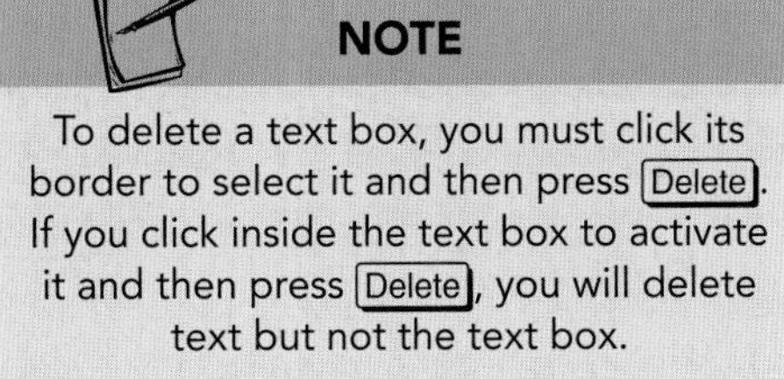

NOTE

To delete a text box, you must click its border to select it and then press Delete. If you click inside the text box to activate it and then press Delete, you will delete text but not the text box.

5. Preview the document.
6. Save the document as ***[your initials]*17-15** in your Lesson 17 folder, submit the document, and leave it open for the next exercise.

Exercise 17-16 USE ADVANCED LAYOUT SETTINGS TO POSITION OBJECTS

Instead of dragging to position a picture, text box, or shape, you can specify the exact position by using advanced layout settings. For example, you can position a picture or text box exactly on the page in relation to a particular margin.

1. Select the text box, and select the **Drawing Tools Format** tab. Click the Position button, and click **More Layout Options**. Select the **Position** tab.

NOTE

Because all the margins are 0.75 inch, using "relative to margin" settings enables you to easily align the objects on the page exactly 0.75 inch from the edge of the page. The Absolute position settings require you to enter an exact measurement in the text box. You can align or position an object in relation to the margin, page, column, or character. You can also choose Lock anchor if you do not want the object to move along with the paragraph to which the object is anchored.

2. On the **Position** tab in the Layout dialog box, apply the following changes:
   - Under Horizontal, click **Alignment** and set it to **Right relative to Margin**. This setting right-aligns the object with the right margin.
   - Under Vertical, click **Alignment** and set it to **Bottom relative to Margin**. This setting aligns the bottom of the object with the bottom margin. Click **OK**.

3. Save the document as ***[your initials]*****17-16** in your Lesson 17 folder. Submit the document, and leave it open for the next exercise.

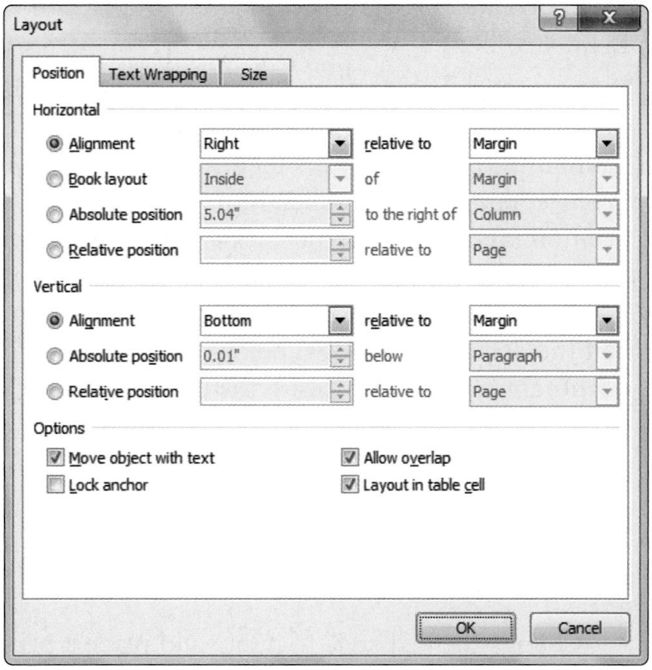

Figure 17-15 Choosing Layout options

Layout

Position | Text Wrapping | Size

Horizontal

- Alignment: Right, relative to Margin
- Book layout: Inside, of Margin
- Absolute position: 5.04", to the right of Column
- Relative position: relative to Page

Vertical

- Alignment: Bottom, relative to Margin
- Absolute position: 0.01", below Paragraph
- Relative position: relative to Page

Options

- [x] Move object with text
- [ ] Lock anchor
- [x] Allow overlap
- [x] Layout in table cell

OK | Cancel

Creating Pull Quotes

A *pull quote* is a sentence or quotation taken from a document and enlarged or set apart from the rest of the text for emphasis. When adding a pull quote, keep the following rules in mind:

- *Font, font style, and size:* Pull quotes should attract the reader's eye but not compete with headings or titles. The font should match other heading fonts.
- *Borders and shading:* Use these features to enhance the pull quote, but remember not to compete with headings or titles.
- *Position:* Pull quotes should be placed within a column or in the white space next to a column, but not between columns, which interrupts text flow.

Exercise 17-17 CREATE PULL QUOTES

To create a pull quote, you copy the text, convert it to a text box, and position the text box on the page. You can then format the pull quote for added emphasis by changing the font and adding borders.

1. Scroll to page 2. Click the **Insert** tab. Click the Text Box button [A]. Click **Draw Text Box**, and draw a text box approximately 1 inch high and 2 inches wide in the first column on page 2 above the heading "Chocolate and Nutrition." The text box is placed on top of the text in the column.
2. Scroll to the third bullet item on page 2, and locate the text "The darker the chocolate, the healthier it is for us." Copy the text, and paste the text in the text box.
3. Before moving the text box into position, select the text box and select the Drawing Tools Format tab. Locate the **Size** group, and change the width of the text box to **2.3** inches (the column width). Click the Position button, and click **More Layout Options**. Click to select the **Position** tab, and check the **Lock anchor** box. Make sure **Move object with text** is also checked. Click **OK**. With both these settings checked, the text box is "locked" to the paragraph at which it is inserted. If you edit the document, the text box will not jump to another part of the document but will move with the paragraph as text flow changes.
4. Select the text box if necessary, and change the text wrapping option to top and bottom. Use the [↓] to move the text box above the heading "Chocolate and Nutrition." After positioning the text box, you can move it closer to the heading by holding down [Ctrl] as you press an arrow key.
5. Apply the following changes to the text box:
   - Change the text style to italic, and place a period at the end of the sentence. Change the font size to 10 points.

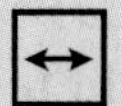

REVIEW

To apply a top and bottom border, click in the paragraph and open the drop-down list for Borders and Shading, or use the Borders and Shading dialog box. On the Borders tab, choose the solid line style, set the width to 1 point, and then click the Top Border button and the Bottom Border button.

- Change the spacing before and the spacing after to 3 points. Change the line spacing to single.
- Edit the text by starting the sentence with **Remember:**.
- Remove the line around the text box, and add a top and bottom 1-point border. Resize the height of the text box to fit the text and borders. To remove the line around the text box, select the text box, click the Shape Outline button on the Drawing Tools Format tab, and choose **No Outline**.

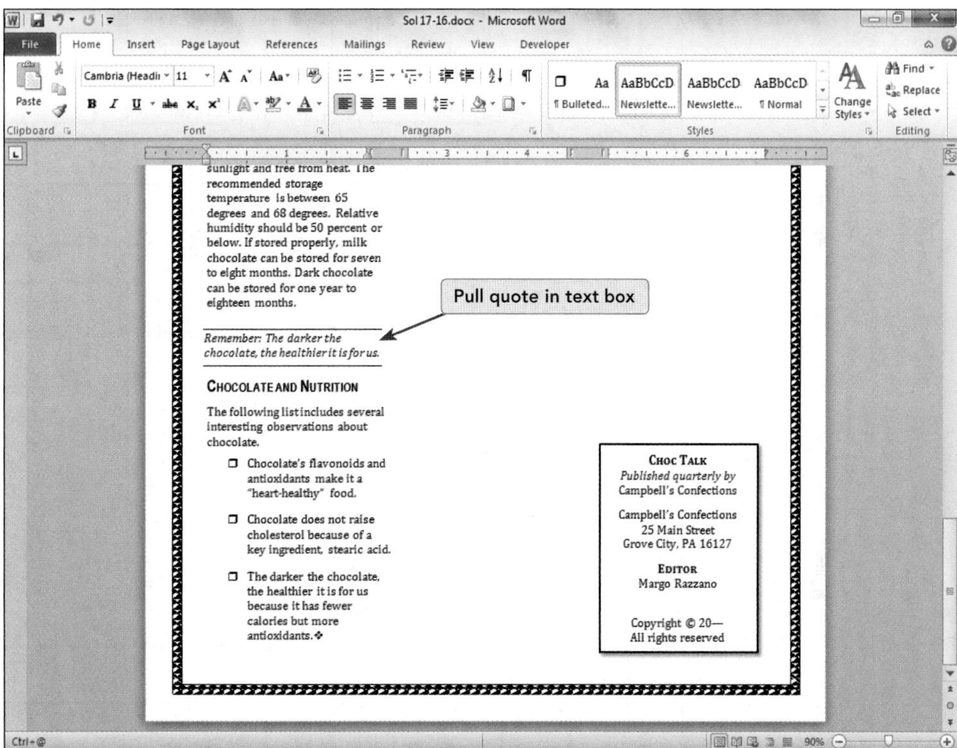

Figure 17-16
Using text boxes to create pull quotes

6. Save the document as ***[your initials]*17-17** in your Lesson 17 folder.
7. Leave it open for the next exercise.

Linking Text Boxes

Newsletters often use linked text boxes in one of two ways:

- *Flow an article from one text box into the other:* For example, you can have an article in a text box on page 1 that continues in a text box on page 3. You do this by linking the two text boxes.

- *Flow text in parallel text boxes from page to page:* For example, you create two side-by-side text boxes on two pages. You link the right text boxes to each other and the left text boxes to each other. This is useful for pairing two similar text blocks, such as an article in Spanish on the right and the English translation on the left.

Figure 17-17
Ways to link text boxes

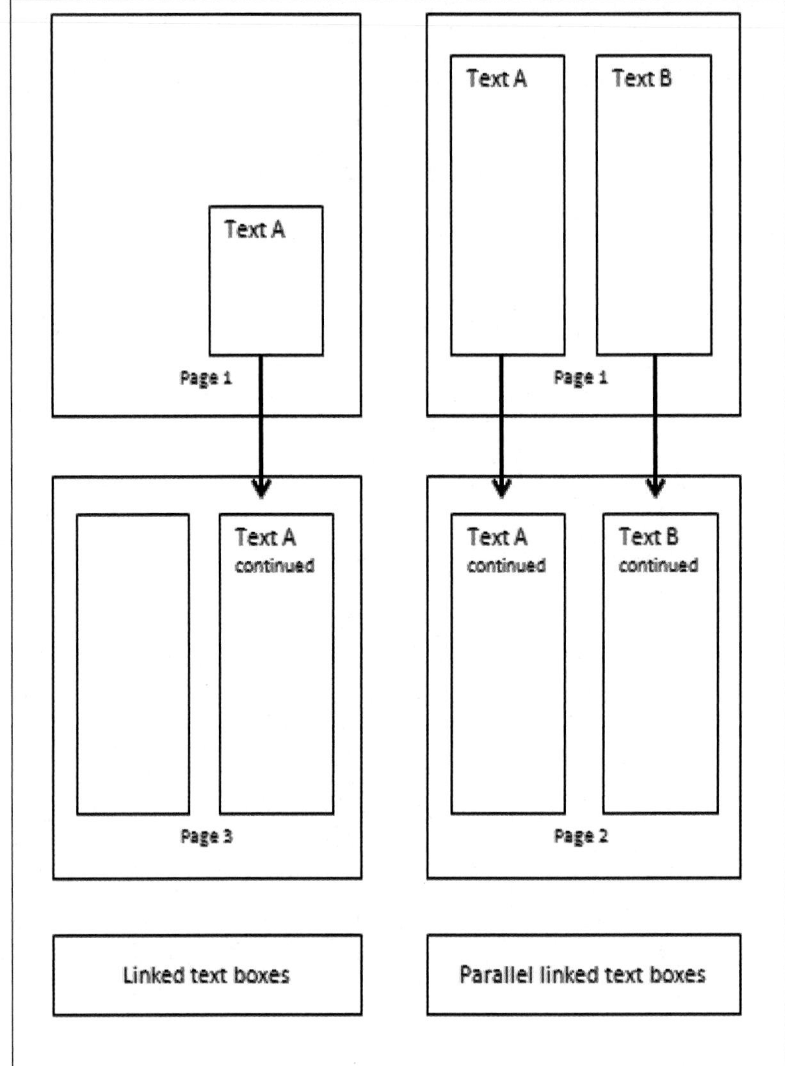

Exercise 17-18 INSERT AND LINK TEXT BOXES

In this exercise, you insert a text box in column 2 on page 2 and link it to a text box in column 3 on page 2 so that text flows from one to the other.

1. Change the zoom to **Whole Page**, display page 2, and click within the page. Click the **Insert** tab, and click the Text Box button. Click **Draw Text Box**; then draw a text box to cover the blank space in column 2.
2. Format the text box so that it is 1.9 inches wide and 7 inches high, with square text wrapping. Select the text box, and click the Position button. Select **More Layout Options**, and select the **Position** tab. Position the text box horizontally left relative to the column and vertically aligned at the bottom margin. Drag the text box to column 2 if necessary.

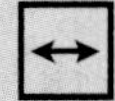

REVIEW

To insert a file, click the Insert tab and click the down arrow beside Object. Choose Text from File. Select the appropriate directory and folder for the student data files, and click Insert.

3. Draw another text box in column 3 that begins at the top of the column and extends to the existing text box. Format the text box so that it is 1.9 inches wide and 6.5 inches high. Apply square text wrapping, and use advanced layout settings to align the text box horizontally with the right margin and vertically with the top margin.
4. Change the zoom to Page Width; then click in the text box in column 2, and insert the document file **Special Events**. Scroll to the bottom of the text box. There is more text in this file than can fit in this text box.
5. To flow the overflow text into the text box in column 3, click in the column 2 text box. Click the Drawing Tools Format tab, and locate the Text group. Click the Create Link button. The mouse pointer changes to a pitcher.
6. Move the pitcher into the text box in column 3. The pointer changes to a pouring pitcher.
7. Click the column 3 text box. The text boxes are now linked. The text automatically flows from the first text box to the second text box.
8. Click the text box in the second column. Center the title, and apply 12 points spacing before and 24 points spacing after.
9. Select the store locations under each special event, and right-align the text.

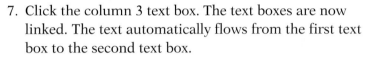

NOTE

To break text box links, select the text box that precedes the text box you want to unlink. Then click Break Link on the Ribbon, Drawing Tools Format tab, Text group.

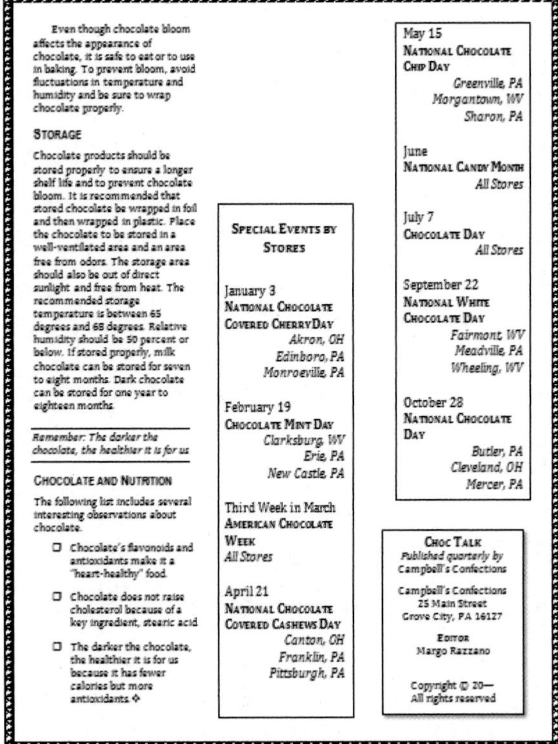

Even though chocolate bloom affects the appearance of chocolate, it is safe to eat or to use in baking. To prevent bloom, avoid fluctuations in temperature and humidity and be sure to wrap chocolate properly.

STORAGE

Chocolate products should be stored properly to ensure a longer shelf life and to prevent chocolate bloom. It is recommended that stored chocolate be wrapped in foil and then wrapped in plastic. Place the chocolate to be stored in a well-ventilated area and an area free from odors. The storage area should also be out of direct sunlight and free from heat. The recommended storage temperature is between 65 degrees and 68 degrees. Relative humidity should be 50 percent or below. If stored properly, milk chocolate can be stored for seven to eight months. Dark chocolate can be stored for one year to eighteen months.

Remember: The darker the chocolate, the healthier it is for us

CHOCOLATE AND NUTRITION

The following list includes several interesting observations about chocolate.

- Chocolate's flavonoids and antioxidants make it a "heart-healthy" food.
- Chocolate does not raise cholesterol because of a key ingredient, stearic acid.
- The darker the chocolate, the healthier it is for us because it has fewer calories but more antioxidants. ❖

SPECIAL EVENTS BY STORES

January 3
NATIONAL CHOCOLATE COVERED CHERRYDAY
Akron, OH
Edinboro, PA
Monroeville, PA

February 19
CHOCOLATE MINT DAY
Clarksburg, WV
Erie, PA
New Castle, PA

Third Week in March
AMERICAN CHOCOLATE WEEK
All Stores

April 21
NATIONAL CHOCOLATE COVERED CASHEWS DAY
Canton, OH
Franklin, PA
Pittsburgh, PA

May 15
NATIONAL CHOCOLATE CHIP DAY
Greenville, PA
Morgantown, WV
Sharon, PA

June
NATIONAL CANDY MONTH
All Stores

July 7
CHOCOLATE DAY
All Stores

September 22
NATIONAL WHITE CHOCOLATE DAY
Fairmont, WV
Meadville, PA
Wheeling, WV

October 28
NATIONAL CHOCOLATE DAY
Butler, PA
Cleveland, OH
Mercer, PA

CHOC TALK
Published quarterly by Campbell's Confections

Campbell's Confections
25 Main Street
Grove City, PA 16127

EDITOR
Margo Razzano

Copyright © 20—
All rights reserved

Figure 17-18
Linking text boxes

10. Change the zoom level to 60%, and adjust the text flow by resizing the height of the first text box. Drag the bottom-center sizing handle down to increase the height of the text box to accommodate all the text for the April 21 entry. If necessary, drag the text box slightly upward. The text "May 15" should appear at the top of the text box in the third column.
11. Insert a picture on page 2 in the middle column above the Special Events text box. Size and format the picture.
12. Move to page 1, and position the insertion point after the text "surface feels rough." Press Enter, and insert the file **Dogs**. Verify that the text below the "Chocolate and Dogs" heading is 10-point Cambria with single spacing and 0 points spacing after. Format the "Chocolate and Dogs" heading to 11 points, bold, small caps, single spacing, with 12 points spacing before and 6 points spacing after.
13. Insert the picture file **Chocolate - P14** in the third column. Change the text wrapping to square, crop the picture, and change the height to 0.75. Drag to position the picture in the middle of the third column, aligned on the right margin.
14. Select the Insert tab, and click the Shapes button. Choose the rounded rectangle tool, and draw a rectangle around the "Chocolate and Dogs" article in the third column on page 1 (the rectangle will cover the text below and should be large enough to include space between the text and the border). Change the fill color to a light color, and select a coordinating color for the shape outline. Change the order of the rectangle by choosing Send Behind Text from the Send Backward button on the Drawing Tools Format tab. If adjustments are necessary to the size of the rectangle, use the Select button Select on the Home tab to select the rectangle.
15. View the document in Print Preview. Make any adjustments, and then save as ***[your initials]*17-18** in your Lesson 17 folder.
16. Submit the document, and leave it open for the next exercise.

Creating a Multisection Layout

By creating a document with separate sections, you can format each section differently. For example, you can apply headers and footers to some but not all sections in a document, or you can change the vertical alignment of one section. In the following exercises, you add a new section to the newsletter to make it a self-mailer with one fold. You also add a page number to the second page and change the starting page number.

Exercise 17-19 ADD A NEW SECTION WITH A DIFFERENT LAYOUT

After inserting a section break to create a new section, you can apply different formatting to the section: You use the Columns dialog box to change the column layout and the Page Setup dialog box to change the margins.

1. Go to the end of the current document (Ctrl+End), and insert a next page section break. If necessary, apply the Normal style to the blank paragraph mark.
2. Format the new section as one column with no page border (verify that the Apply to box in the Borders and Shading dialog box is set to **This section**).
3. Open the **Page Setup** dialog box. Click the **Margins** tab, and change the left and right margins to 1 inch. Click **OK**.
4. At the paragraph mark in the new section, insert the picture file **Monogram**. Click the Size Dialog Box Launcher, and format the picture as follows:
   - Size: Scale height to 250%.
   - Text wrapping: Behind text.
   - Position: Centered horizontally relative to the page, positioned vertically 0.75 inch below the page.
   - Locate the Adjust group, Color button on the Picture Tools Format tab, and choose **Washout** from the Recolor gallery.
5. Draw a horizontal line across the middle of the page, dividing the page in half. Assume that the newsletter will be folded at this line. Format the line as:
   - Size: 7 inches wide.
   - Position: Centered horizontally and vertically relative to the page.
   - Color: Black.

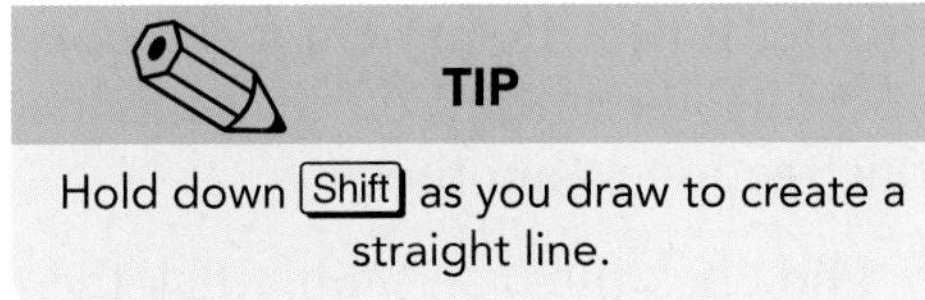

TIP

Hold down Shift as you draw to create a straight line.

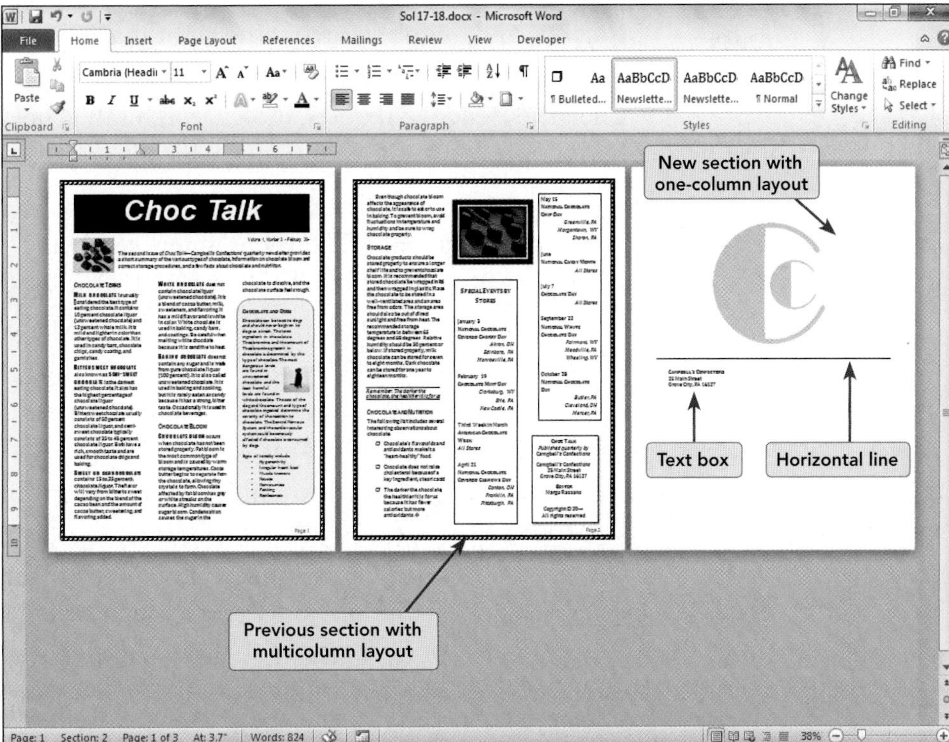

Figure 17-19 Creating and formatting a new section

6. Below the line, draw a text box as shown in Figure 17-19. Copy Campbell's Confections' name and address from the masthead, and paste it in the text box. Format the text box as follows:
   - Text: Left aligned, 10 points, with the company name in bold and small caps.
   - Text box: Right-click the text box, and open the **Format Shape** dialog box. Click the **Text Box** option, and click **Resize shape to fit text**.
   - Shape Outline: None (No outline).
   - Position: Below the line, as shown, and horizontally aligned left relative to the margin.

Exercise 17-20 UNLINK SECTION FOOTERS AND CHANGE STARTING PAGE NUMBERS

In this exercise you add page numbers in the footer area, but you do not want to number the last section. Remember that the default setting for the Link to Previous button is "on" when you work in the header or footer pane. As a result, the text you enter in the header or footer for the document is the same for every section. You can use the Link to Previous button to break the link between header and/or footer text from one section to another.

1. Go to the beginning of the document, and click the **Insert** tab. Click the Footer button, and click **Edit Footer**.
2. Notice that the pane is labeled "Footer–Section 1."
3. Press Tab twice to move to the right margin. Key the text **Page**, and key a space; then click the Page Number button, and choose **Current Position**. Choose **Plain Number**. Format the text as 11-point Arial Narrow, and align the text at the right margin by dragging the tab marker to the margin.
4. Click the **Header & Footer Tools Design** tab. Click the Show Next button to go to the next footer, which is on page 2. Notice the following:
   - This section is labeled "Section 3" because page 1 contains two sections and page 2 starts as a new section.
   - The Link to Previous button Link to Previous is turned on, which means this section is linked to the previous section, causing the same footer text to appear in this section.
5. Click the Show Next button to move to the next section, which is section 4, the last page. This part of the newsletter should not be numbered, so you need to unlink this section footer from the previous one.
6. Click the Link to Previous button Link to Previous to unlink the section 4 footer; then delete the footer text.
7. Go to the previous section footer to check that the page number is still there. Close the Header and Footer pane.

NOTE

Breaking the link for a section's footer does not break the link for the section's header. You must break that link separately.

8. Check the document footers to verify that pages 1 and 2 are numbered correctly.
9. Save the document as ***[your initials]*17-20** in your Lesson 17 folder. Submit and close the document.

Exercise 17-21 USE BUILDING BLOCKS TO FORMAT A DOCUMENT

Building blocks consist of AutoText entries, cover pages, headers, footers, page numbers, tables, text boxes, and watermarks. These items are reusable and are stored in galleries. You can insert building blocks through individual galleries such as footers and page numbers, or you can use the Building Blocks Organizer. One advantage of using built-in building blocks is the ability to create a document with a consistent design. In this exercise you create a framework for a document using built-in building blocks.

1. Start a new document.
2. Click the **Insert** tab, and click the Quick Parts button. Click **Building Blocks Organizer**. The Building Blocks Organizer displays.

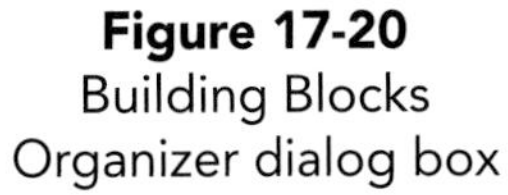

Figure 17-20
Building Blocks Organizer dialog box

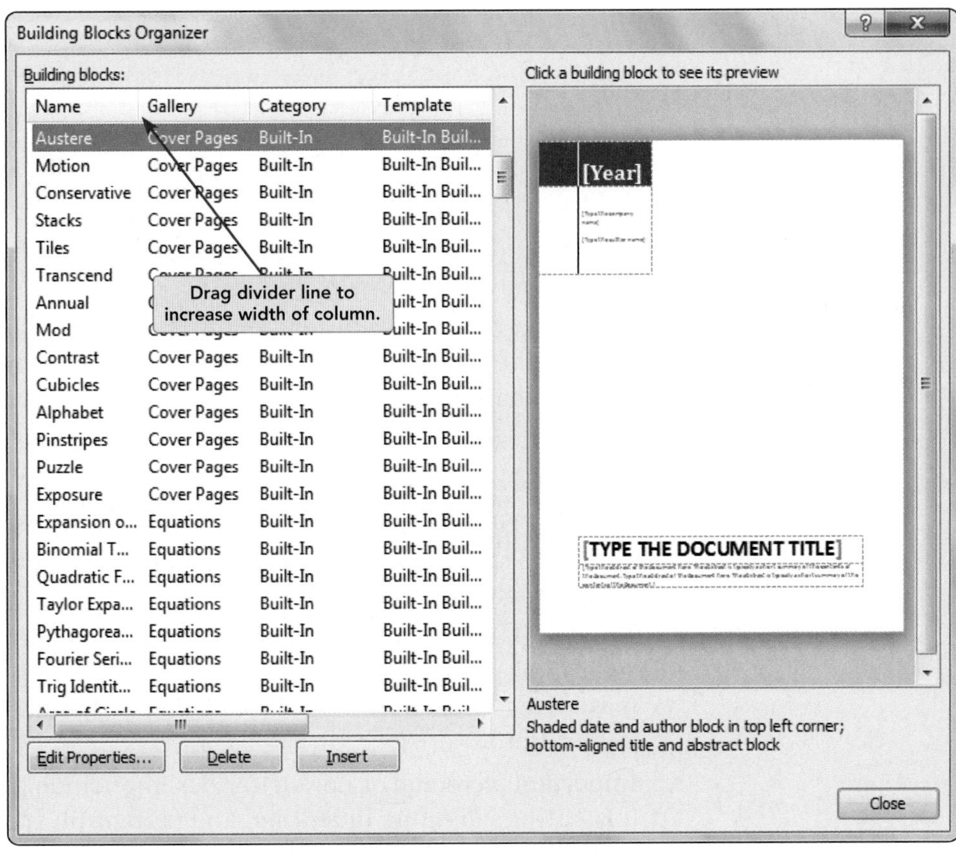

3. Click the **Gallery** column heading to sort the building block entries by category.
4. Scroll to view the Cover Pages category, and click **Cubicles**. The cover page appears in the preview box. Click **Insert**.
5. Click the company name placeholder, and key **Campbell's Confections**. Key your name in the author placeholder.
6. Scroll to page 2, and click to position the insertion point at the top of the page.

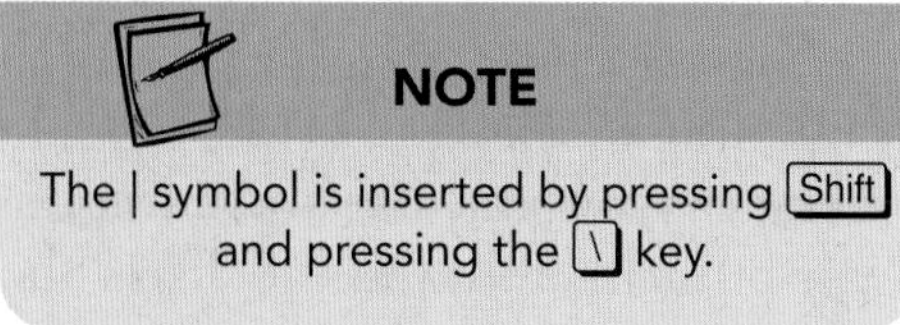

NOTE

The | symbol is inserted by pressing Shift and pressing the \ key.

7. Open the **Building Blocks Organizer** dialog box, and scroll to the Footers category. Locate the **Cubicles (Even Page)** entry, and click **Insert**. Click the company address placeholder, and key **25 Main Street | Grove City, PA 16127**. Close the Footer pane.

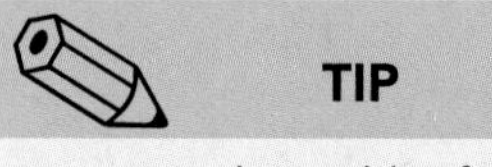

TIP

Increase the width of the Name column by dragging the vertical divider to the right.

8. Reopen the **Building Blocks Organizer** dialog box, and scroll to the Text Boxes category. Locate the **Cubicles Sidebar** entry, and click **Insert**. Read the information in the text box about the purpose of a side bar.
9. Save the document as ***[your initials]*17-21** in your Lesson 17 folder.

Lesson 17 Summary

- A text box is a free-floating rectangular object that you can format and position anywhere on a page.
- Size a text box by selecting it and dragging one of its sizing handles. Format a text box by changing its outline, fill, alignment, size, and internal margins.
- Change text direction in a text box by rotating the text 90 degrees to the left or right.
- Use advanced layout settings to position any object precisely, horizontally and vertically.
- A watermark is a transparent graphic or text placed behind text.
- A newsletter generally begins with a title, or nameplate, that uses a font style appropriate for the publication. A newsletter might also contain a masthead (which lists the company and people who produce the publication).
- Important elements of newsletter design include proper paragraph formatting (aligning, indenting, and paragraph spacing), use of borders and shading, and addition of white space in a document, all of which help make the content more readable.

- Clip art includes drawings that can be inserted from the Clip Art task pane.
- A clip is inserted as an in-line graphic until you apply a wrapping style. Then you can move the clip freely on the page. You can also apply advanced text-wrapping options to control the distance of clip art from text.
- Newsletters typically have a multicolumn layout and often contain multiple sections, each with a different layout. For example, a newsletter can begin with a one-column section and then continue with a three-column section.
- Newsletter columns can be of equal or unequal width and can have a vertical line separating them. You can alter the space between columns.
- To balance columns, insert a continuous section break at the end of the column layout. To control how columns break, insert a column break to force text to start at the next column.
- A pull quote is a sentence or quotation copied from a document and enlarged or set apart from the rest of the text for emphasis. Pull quotes are contained in text boxes.
- A sidebar is a text box that is usually aligned on the right or left side of a page. It typically contains text that is related to but separate from the main document text.
- Linked text boxes are used in newsletters to flow text from one page to another. You insert text into one text box and then link the text to another text box where the text flow continues.
- Use the Styles task pane to see and reapply the formatting you have created in a document and to apply styles. To see all of Word's predefined styles, change the Select styles to show box to All styles.
- When you create a style, you can base it on another style so that it will resemble that style's characteristics.
- After creating a style, you can modify it in many ways. For example, you can specify the style for the paragraph that follows the style and change the formatting (font, paragraph, tabs, borders, and so on).
- To control text flow, including line and page breaks, choose options from the Paragraph dialog box. For example, use the Keep lines together option to prevent a break between lines in the same paragraph, and use the Keep with next option to prevent a paragraph (such as a heading) from being separated from the paragraph following it.
- By using the Font dialog box, you can change character spacing to alter the appearance of text. For example, you can stretch or compress text horizontally by a percentage of its original size or add or delete space between letters by a specific number of points.
- Use the Building Blocks Organizer to insert text boxes stored in a gallery.

LESSON 17 Command Summary

Feature	Button	Command	Keyboard
Borders and shading		Home tab, Paragraph group,	
Building Blocks Organizer		Insert tab, Text group, Quick Parts command	
Character spacing		Home tab, Font group, Font dialog box, Advanced tab	
Columns		Page Layout tab, Page Setup group	
Create new style		Home tab, Styles group	
Insert text box		Insert tab, Text group	
Link text box		Drawing Tools Format tab, Text group	
Link/unlink section header or footer	Link to Previous	Header & Footer Tools Design tab	
Page color		Page Layout tab, Page Background group	
Paragraph formatting		Home tab, Paragraph group	
Remove character formatting		Home tab, Font group	Ctrl+Spacebar
Remove paragraph formatting		Home tab, Paragraph group	Ctrl+Q
Unlink text box		Drawing Tools Format tab, Text group	
Watermark		Page Layout tab, Page Background group	

Concepts Review

True/False Questions

Each of the following statements is either true or false. Indicate your choice by circling T or F.

T F 1. A newsletter title is sometimes called the nameplate.

T F 2. Times New Roman is an example of a sans serif font.

T F 3. You can create more white space on a page by decreasing the margins.

T F 4. A watermark is a transparent graphic or text placed behind text.

T F 5. "Condensed" is a paragraph spacing option.

T F 6. A pull quote is contained in a text box.

T F 7. By default, a two- or three-column layout has columns of equal width.

T F 8. Building blocks are inserted using the Page Layout tab.

Short Answer Questions

Write the correct answer in the space provided.

1. Which task pane do you use to create a new style?

____

2. What is the procedure for drawing a text box?

____

3. Which dialog box and tab contain options for controlling text flow?

____

4. Which button changes an in-line graphic to a floating graphic?

____

5. How do you insert vertical lines for separating columns in a three-column layout?

____

6. What is the name of the newsletter item that contains identifying information about the company (company name, editor, writers, and so on)?

____

7. What do you call text in a newsletter that is set apart for emphasis?

8. What is white space?

Critical Thinking

Answer these questions on a separate page. There are no right or wrong answers. Support your answers with examples from your own experience, if possible.

1. Choosing a font for a newsletter title is like designing a logo. Think of a title of a newsletter you might create. What type of font would be appropriate? Create a few versions of the title, using different fonts. Explain your choices.
2. What do you think are the most important ways to make a newsletter both attractive and readable? Which Word features would you incorporate to achieve that goal?

Skills Review

Exercise 17-22

Create a watermark, apply page formatting, and work with styles.

1. Open the file **Indiana**. Change the top margin to 2 inches, and create a memo heading. The memo is to "Store Managers" from Thomas Campbell. Use the current date and the subject "New Store."
2. Create a text watermark by following these steps:
   a. Click the **Page Layout** tab, and locate the **Page Background** group.
   b. Click the Watermark button, and click **Custom Watermark**.
   c. Click **Text watermark**, and choose **Confidential** from the Text drop-down list. Verify that the **Diagonal** and **Semitransparent** options are selected. Click **OK**.
3. Add a page border and a page texture by following these steps:
   a. Click the **Page Layout** tab, and locate the **Page Background** group.
   b. Click the Page Borders button. Select a double-line style and a dark blue color, and change the width to 1½ points. Click **OK**.
   c. Click the Page Color button, and click **Fill Effects**. Click the **Texture** tab, and choose **Parchment**. Click **OK**.

4. Change the document style set, and modify the Normal style by following these steps:
   a. Click the **Home** tab, and locate the **Styles** group.
   b. Click the Change Styles button, and click **Style Set**. Select **Distinctive**.
   c. Display the **Styles** task pane, and right-click **Normal** in the task pane. Click **Modify**. Change the font size to 11, and open the Paragraph dialog box. Change the spacing after to 0 points, and change the line spacing to single spacing. Click **OK** twice.
5. Save the document as ***[your initials]*17-22** in your Lesson 17 folder.
6. Submit and close the document.

Exercise 17-23

Create a newsletter-style column layout.

1. Start a new document, and change the left and right margins to 0.75 inch.
2. Create a newsletter format by following these steps:
   a. Click the **Insert** tab, and click the Quick Parts button. Click **Building Blocks Organizer**.
   b. Click the **Gallery** heading to sort the building blocks by type.
   c. Scroll to the Footers category. Locate and click **Alphabet**. Click **Insert**. Replace the placeholder text with **Campbell's Confections**. Apply italic formatting to the footer text. Close the Footer pane.
3. Draw a text box 2 inches wide and 6.5 inches tall. Position the text box on the right margin, centered vertically on the page. Insert the file **Bloom** (**Insert** tab, **Text** group, **Object** drop-down arrow command, **Text from File**), and change the spacing after to 6 points. Change line spacing to single spacing.
4. Key the heading **Bloom** at the beginning of the sidebar text. Format the heading using 14-point bold and small caps. Add 6 points spacing before and 18 points spacing after.
5. Select the heading if necessary, and open the Borders and Shading dialog box. Choose the **Custom** setting, and choose a double-line style similar to the line in the footer. Change the color to Red, Accent 2 (sixth column, last row). Select 3 points for the width, and click the button for a top border. Apply a bottom line border with the same format to the last paragraph in the sidebar. Select the text box, and click the **Drawing Tools Format** tab. Click the Shape Outline button, and choose **No Outline**.
6. Create a newsletter-style layout by following these steps:
   a. Go to the beginning of the document, and open the **Columns** dialog box.
   b. Change the **Number of columns** to **3**, and the **Spacing** to **0.25**. Click **OK**.

7. Insert the file **Chocolate Terms** at the beginning of the document. If the Bloom text box moves after inserting the Chocolate Terms text, drag it to the right margin.
8. Select the heading "Chocolate Terms," and format the heading as one column. Change the spacing after to 24 points. Change the font size to 16 points and small caps. Add a bottom border with the same format as that applied to the Bloom text.
9. Select the text from "Milk Chocolate" to the end of the last paragraph ("Baking Chocolate"), and change the line spacing to single.
10. Insert a column break at the paragraph beginning "White Chocolate." Add 12 points spacing before the following headings: "Bittersweet Chocolate," "Sweet or Dark Chocolate," and "Baking Chocolate."
11. Insert a picture of chocolate in the blank text area of the middle column. Size the picture if necessary.
12. Save the document as ***[your initials]*17-23** in your Lesson 17 folder.
13. Submit and close the document.

Exercise 17-24

Work with text boxes and advanced layout settings.

1. Start a new document.
2. Insert a photograph by following these steps:
   a. Click the **Insert** tab, and click the Picture button.
   b. Locate the directory and folder for the student data files, and select **Chocolate - P6**.
3. Change the text wrapping to square, and size the picture proportionally to 5.25 inches wide.
4. Center the picture 0.5 inch from the top of the page by following these steps:
   a. Select the picture, and click the Position button. Click **More Layout Options**, and click the **Position** tab.
   b. Click **Alignment** under Horizontal, and change the alignment to **Centered** relative to **Page**.
   c. Click **Absolute position** under Vertical, and change the value to **0.5"**. Change the below setting to **Page**. Click **OK**. Deselect the picture.
5. Create a text box by following these steps:
   a. Click the **Insert** tab, and click the Text Box button. Click **Draw Text Box**.
   b. Below the picture, draw a text box approximately 2 inches square by pressing Shift when you draw. Key **Chocolate Club** in the text box.
   c. Locate the **Text** group on the **Drawing Tools Format** tab, and click the Text Direction button. Click **Rotate all text 270 degrees**.

d. Select the text, and format the text as 26-point Candara bold and italic.

e. Center the text.

6. Size and position the text box by following these steps:
   a. Drag the text box over the bottom left corner of the picture.
   b. Drag the top resize handle of the text box to the top of the picture. Use the right resize square handle to size the text box wide enough to fit the text (approximately 0.75 inch). The text box should align with the left edge of the picture.
7. Remove the outline and fill colors of the text box by following these steps:
   a. Select the text box, and select the **Drawing Tools Format** tab. Click the Shape Outline button, and click **No Outline**.
   b. Click the Shape Fill button, and click **No Fill**.
8. Select the text in the text box, and change the font color to white.
9. Draw a text box below the picture, about the same size as the picture.
10. Place the insertion point inside the text box, and insert the file **Club - 3**. Press Ctrl+A to select the text, and change the font size to 10. Change the height of the text box to fit the text. Click the Drawing Tools Format tab, click the Align Text button, and choose **Middle**.
11. Drag the box that contains the text file so that it is about ¼ inch below the picture. Center the text box horizontally.
12. Select the text box, and change the shape outline weight to **4½** points, and select a color for the shape outline.
13. Save the document as ***[your initials]*17-24** in your Lesson 17 folder.
14. Submit and close the document.

Exercise 17-25

Apply character and paragraph formatting, and link text boxes.

1. Start a new blank document. Change the top margin to 0.75 inch. Set the bottom, left, and right margins to 1 inch.
2. At the top of the document, key the title **Campbell's Connections**, and press Enter two times.
3. Format the title using a 36-point font appropriate to a title that fits on one line. Apply black shading to the title (the text color should automatically change to white). Center the text, and apply bold formatting (unless the font is already bold).
4. At the second paragraph mark, insert a page break (Ctrl+Enter).
5. Change the zoom level to **Whole Page**.

6. Follow these steps to create side-by-side text boxes on both pages that you will use to flow parallel articles:
   a. On page 1, draw two text boxes to create two vertical columns. Size the text boxes **7"** high by **3"** wide.
   b. Position the left text box so that it is horizontally aligned with the left margin and vertically aligned with the bottom margin (Position button, More Layout Options).
   c. Position the right text box so that it is horizontally aligned with the right margin and vertically aligned with the bottom margin.
   d. Draw two text boxes on page 2, each **9"** high by **3"** wide. Use the same alignment you used for the text boxes on page 1.
7. On page 1, in the left text box, insert the file **News - 1**. Select the text in the left text box, and change the spacing after to 10 points. In the right text box, insert the file **News - 4**.
8. Link the two left text boxes and the two right text boxes by following these steps:
   a. Click the left text box on page 1. Click the **Drawing Tools Format** tab.
   b. Click the Create Link button on the Drawing Tools Format tab.
   c. Using the pouring-pitcher pointer, click the left text box on page 2.
   d. Use the same method to link the right text boxes.
9. Create a footer using a building block by following these steps:
   a. Click the **Insert** tab, and click **Footer**.
   b. Click **Edit Footer** in the Footer gallery.
   c. Click **Quick Parts** on the **Header & Footer Tools Design** tab.
   d. Click **Building Blocks Organizer**, and scroll to the Page Number gallery. Select **Bold Numbers 1**. Verify that the selection is a footer with the format "Page X of Y," and click **Insert**. Delete any blank paragraph marks that may appear in the Footer pane. Close the Footer pane.
10. Zoom to **100%**. On page 1, in the left text box, format the title "Employee Newsletter" using 14-point bold and small caps. Select the text beginning with the paragraph "Remember" and through the paragraph that begins "If your entry," and format it as a bulleted list.
11. Below the text in column 1 on page 2, insert the file **News - 2**. Select the text from "Name the" through the "Date" line, and apply a dotted-line box border to the text. Click the Options button Options... in the Borders and Shading dialog box, and change the Top and Bottom settings to 4 points.
12. On page 1, in the right text box, format the title "Recipe of the Month" using 14-point bold and small caps. Add 10 points spacing after to the title. Add 6 points spacing before to "Chocolate Fudge Cake." Select "Ingredients" and change the spacing after to 0 points. Select "Directions" and change the spacing after to 0 points. Select "Directions" on page 2, and change the spacing after to 0 points.

13. On page 2, two blank lines below the text in the right text box, create a masthead by keying the following text (include your name as editor):

    Campbell's Connections
    Edited by:
    [Your Name]
    Published Monthly by:
    Campbell's Confections
    25 Main Street
    Grove City, PA 16127
    Telephone: 724-555-2025
    www.campbellsconfections.biz

14. Increase the font size of "Campbell's Connections" in the masthead, and apply the font used for the newsletter title. Center all the masthead text, make it bold, and change it to white text against black shading. Add spacing before or after to improve the appearance and readability of the text.

15. On page 2, in the space at the bottom of the left text box, insert the file **News - 6.** If there is enough room after the "Health Fair" article, insert a health-related picture and format the picture height to 1 inch, with center alignment. Add a picture of a two-layer cake below the frosting recipe in the right column on page 2 if there is space.

16. If room permits, add a line of text below the title and preceding the parallel text boxes. Key and format the following text on one line:

    Volume 2, Number 10
    [Current Month and Year]

17. Make any other adjustments to improve the appearance of the document; then save it as ***[your initials]*17-25** in your Lesson 17 folder.

18. Submit and close the document.

Lesson Applications

Exercise 17-26

Insert and format text boxes.

1. Start a new document. Change to landscape orientation, change the top margin to 1.25 inches, and change the left and right margins to 0.75 inch.
2. Draw a text box at the top of the page measuring approximately 1.5 inches high and 9.5 inches wide.
3. Change the outline color to dark blue and the weight to 2¼ points. Adjust the height to 1.5 inches and the width to 9.5 inches. Change the horizontal alignment to left relative to the margin, and change the vertical alignment to top relative to the margin. Right-click to open the Format Shape dialog box, and click to select the Text Box option in the left pane. Change all internal margin settings to 0.1 inch, and select **Middle** for the vertical alignment. Change the text wrapping to square.
4. Key **Chocolate-Covered Creams** in the text box.
5. Format the text using 48-point Arial Narrow bold. Change the font color to white. Center the text.
6. Select the text box, and change the fill color to dark blue.
7. Draw a second box below the first text box and approximately the same size as the first text box. Format the text box as follows:
   - Change the outline color to dark blue, the weight to 2¼ points, and the fill color to dark blue.
   - Change the size to measure 1 inch high and 9.5 inches wide.
   - Change the horizontal alignment to left relative to margin.
   - Change the internal margin settings to 0.1 inch, and change the vertical alignment to middle.
   - Change the text wrapping to square, and drag the box approximately 3.5 inches below the first text box.
8. Key the following text in the second text box:

   Buy 10 pounds of chocolate, get 1 pound FREE!
9. Format the text using 24-point Arial Narrow bold, with small caps and center alignment. Change the font color to white.
10. Refer to Figure 17-22, and draw a third text box between the two existing text boxes that measures 3.5 inches high and approximately 4.7 inches wide. Format the text box as follows:
    - Change the line color to dark blue, the weight to 2¼ points, and the fill color to white.
    - Change the size to 3.5 inches high and 4.7 inches wide.
    - Change the horizontal alignment to right relative to margin.

- Change the internal margin settings to 0.1 inch, and change the vertical alignment to middle.
- Change the text wrapping to square, and drag the box directly below the first text box and aligning with the right border of the first text box.

11. Key the text shown in Figure 17-21 in the third text box. Use single spacing.

Figure 17-21

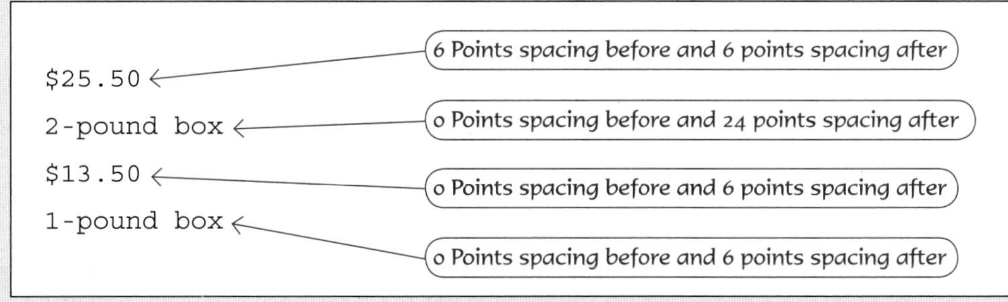

12. Format the text using 36-point Arial Narrow bold, with center alignment. Change the spacing before and the spacing after as indicated in Figure 17-21.
13. Draw a rectangle shape to the left of the middle text box. Size the rectangle to 3.5 inches high, and add a 2¼-point dark blue outline to the shape.
14. Select the rectangle, and change the shape fill to Picture. Insert **Chocolate - P8**.

Figure 17-22
Sample placement

15. Refer to Figure 17-22 for proper placement of the picture and text boxes.
16. Change the zoom to whole page to view the text boxes and picture placement.
17. Press Ctrl and the arrow keys to nudge the boxes into correct placement. Select each object, and apply the group command.
18. Save the document as ***[your initials]*17-26** in your Lesson 17 folder.
19. Submit and close the document.

Exercise 17-27

Create a newsletter-style layout, create and modify styles, insert text boxes, and create a pull quote.

1. Start a new document, and change the top, bottom, left, and right margins to 0.75. Save the document as ***[your initials]*17-27** in your Lesson 17 folder.

2. Select the paragraph mark, and modify the Normal style. Change the font to Cambria, change the line spacing to single, and change the spacing after paragraphs to 12.

3. Press Enter two times. Position the insertion point at the top of the document, and key **Choc Talk**. Select the text, change the font size to 60 points, and choose a font that will fit on one line and one that is appropriate for the title of a newsletter. Right-align the title, and change the spacing after to 0 points. Add a 6-point bottom border to the title.

4. Position the insertion point below the title, and set a center tab at 3.5. Set a right-aligned tab at the right margin. Key the following text on one line.

   Volume 3 Tab **Number 1** Tab **January 201-**

5. Format the second line of text using the same font at the title, and change the font size to 12. Add 12 points spacing before, and 18 points spacing after.

6. Position the insertion point at the end of the document, and open the Columns dialog box. Choose the Left preset, and apply the column format from this point forward.

7. Insert a column break to move to the top of the second column. Insert the student data file **Chocolate Tasting – 2**.

8. Select the heading "Chocolate Tasting," and create a style named ArticleHeading. Change the font to the same font used in the newsletter title (if appropriate), change the font size to 14, and change the left indent to −.25 (negative indent). Apply bold and small caps if the font is not too heavy. Change the spacing after to 3 points.

9. Insert the student data file **News – 10** below the Chocolate Tasting article. Read the text, and create a heading for the article. Select the heading, and apply the ArticleHeading style. Modify the ArticleHeading style to include 9 points spacing before.

10. Start a new page, and insert a column break to move to the top of the second column on page 2. Insert the student data file **Virtual Treats**. Apply the ArticleHeading style to the heading of the Virtual Treats article.

11. Insert the student data file **Chocolate Bars** following the Virtual Treats article. Apply the ArticleHeading style to the heading. Select the list of chocolate bars, and apply a bullet format.

12. Insert the student data file **Chocolate Rewards** below the Chocolate Bars article, and apply the ArticleHeading style.

13. Position the insertion point in the Chocolate Bars article, and open the Clip Art task pane. Locate and insert a picture of a chocolate bar. Change the text wrap to square, and change the size to one inch. Place the picture within the article.

14. Select the bulleted list in the Chocolate Rewards article, and click the arrow beside the Bullets button. Choose Define New Bullet, and click Picture. Click Import, and locate the student data files. Select the student data file Chocolate – P12, and click Add. Select the chocolate picture bullet, and click OK twice. Select the picture bullets, and change the font size to 14. Drag the hanging indent marker on the ruler to the right to increase the space between the bullet and the bullet text.

15. Add a footer to page 2 of the newsletter. At the right margin, key **Page** followed by the page number. Select the text, and apply black shading to the text (not the paragraph). Format the text.

16. Draw a text box at the bottom, left corner of page 2. Key and format the following text.

    Choc Talk, Published quarterly by, Campbell's Confections, 25 Main Street, Grove City, PA 16127, (724) 555-2025

17. Go to page 1, and insert a right triangle shape to the lower left corner of the page. Change the shape fill to black, and drag the shape to align with left and bottom edge of the page. The shape height should be approximately two inches, and the width should be approximately 2.5 inches.

18. Preview the document, and add a pull quote to page 2 using the text box feature. Remove the fill and outline from the text box. Format and position the text box.

19. Preview the document; and change formatting or placement of objects.

20. Save the document. Submit and close the document.

Exercise 17-28

Apply character and paragraph formatting, create styles, and link text boxes.

1. Start a new document, and change the left and right margins to 0.75 inch.

2. Key the title **Choc Talk** at the top of the document, and press Enter two times. Key the following line of text below the title: **Volume 2, Number 2 [Current Month and Year].**

3. Format the title as 72 points, using a font that fits on one line. Apply a dark shading color, and change the font color to white. Format the volume number text and the date using appropriate character and paragraph formatting.

4. At the blank paragraph insert a page break, and switch the zoom level to **Whole Page**.

5. Create a two-page layout to be used for linked text boxes. On page 1, draw two text boxes to create two vertical columns. Size the text boxes 7 inches high by 3.25 inches wide. Position the text boxes as follows:

    - *Left text box:* Horizontally aligned with the left margin, vertically aligned with the bottom margin.
    - *Right text box:* Horizontally aligned with the right margin, vertically aligned with the bottom margin.

6. Draw two text boxes on page 2. Each should measure 9 inches high by 3.25 inches wide. Use the same alignment you used for the text boxes on page 1.
7. On page 1, in the left box, insert the file **News - 8.**
8. Create a forward link from the left text box on page 1 to the left text box on page 2.
9. Change the zoom to Page Width, and verify that the text flows from the left text box on page 1 to the left text box on page 2.
10. On page 1, in the right box, insert the file **Current Events - 2**. Create a forward link from the right text box on page 1 to the right text box on page 2.
11. Go to page 1, and position the insertion point to the immediate left of the "Children's Candy-Making Session" heading, and press Enter to move the article to the top of the next page.
12. Insert the file **News - 9** below the left text box on page 2.
13. Insert the text file **News - 7** below the **News - 9** article on page 2 in the left column.
14. Apply dark shading (or the color used in the title) to the heading paragraph of the **News - 7** article, "Vote Today!!" Change the font color to white, and change the font size to 14.
15. Select the text "Candy-Making Classes" at the beginning of the first article on page 1. Create a paragraph style named ArticleHead and include the following font format: Cambria, 14-point bold, and small caps. Change the paragraph formatting to 15 points spacing before, 6 points spacing after, and single spacing.
16. Apply the ArticleHead style to the following headings: "Chocolate-Covered Cocoa Beans," "Open House," "Candy Making Corner," "Canvas Tote Bags," and Mobile Access."
17. Delete blank paragraphs that may appear as a result of the new style.
18. Go to the bottom of page 1, and draw a rectangle that slightly overlaps both text boxes at the bottom of the page. Add the text **Continued on page 2**. Format the text using 9-point Arial Narrow italic. Center the text. (See Figure 17-23.) Remove the shape fill color if necessary.

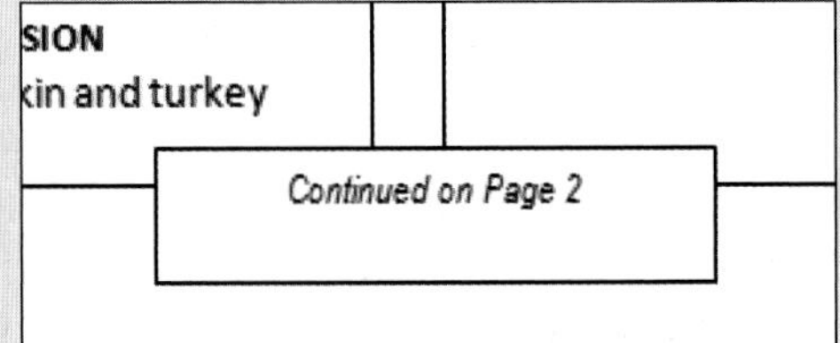

Figure 17-23
The continued line

19. Format the document with a page number positioned in the bottom right corner. The page number should not appear on page 1. Include the word "Page" in front of the number.

20. Review the newsletter, and add special effects such as borders, shading, or pictures.
21. Preview the document, and then save it as ***[your initials]*17-28** in your Lesson 17 folder.
22. Submit and close the document.

Exercise 17-29 ◆ Challenge Yourself

Insert text boxes and graphics to create a flyer.

1. Start a new document. Change all margin settings to 0.75 inch.
2. Draw a text box, and key **Campbell's**.
3. Draw a second text box, and key **Confections**.
4. Draw a third text box, and key the following text:

   Campbell's Confections Choice Assortment
   Milk or Dark Chocolate
   Chocolate-Covered Creams
   Chocolate-Covered Nuts
   Melt-a-ways

5. Draw a fourth text box, and key the following text:

   Campbell's Confections Assortment No. 1
   Milk or Dark Chocolate-Covered Nuts
   Almonds
   Brazils
   Cashews
   Filberts
   Pecans

6. Draw a fifth text box, and key the following text:

   Campbell's Confections Assortment No. 2
   Milk or Dark Chocolate Melt-a-ways
   Chocolate
   French Mint
   Crisped Rice
   Peanut Butter
   Pecans

7. Arrange the text boxes attractively on the page, and format the text within the text box. Consider font, font size, font color, and alignment.
8. Format the text boxes. Consider shape fill, shape outline, shape effects, height, and width.

9. Add a footer to the document. Include the following text. Center the text, and select an appropriate font, font size, and font color.

   25 Main Street ■ Grove City, PA 16127 ■ Telephone: 724-555-2025 ■ Fax: 724-555-2050 www.campbellsconfections.biz

10. Insert one or more of the following picture files.

    Chocolate - P6
    Chocolate - P8
    Chocolate - P10

11. Review the document in Print Preview.
12. Save the document as ***[your initials]*17-29** in your Lesson 17 folder.
13. Submit and close the document.

On Your Own

In these exercises you work on your own, as you would in a real-life business environment. Use the skills you've learned to accomplish the task—and be creative.

Exercise 17-30

Design the first page of a newsletter for an organization in which you are interested. Apply page and column formatting to the document. Create the nameplate and the general layout. Add headings with your own created style and text for the content. Add clip art and shapes if appropriate. Save the document as ***[your initials]*17-30** in your Lesson 17 folder, and submit it.

Exercise 17-31

Key a one-page report on newsletter design guidelines. Apply a three-column layout, and create two pull quotes. Format the pull quotes attractively. Size one of the pull quotes the width of a column and the other one the width of two columns. Save the document as ***[your initials]*17-31** in your Lesson 17 folder, and submit it.

Exercise 17-32

Draw four text boxes on one page to create two rows with two text boxes each. Link the first text box in the first column to the second text box in the first column, and link the first text box in the second column to the second text box in the second column. Create a document defining the following desktop publishing terms: "kicker," "side bar," "jumpline," and "sink." Insert the text in the first text box in the first column. Flow the text from the first text box to the second text box. Create a link from the second text box in the first column to the first text box in the second column. Flow the text. Continue flowing the text into the last text box. Format and position the boxes attractively on the page. Save the document as ***[your initials]*****17-32** in your Lesson 17 folder, and submit it.

Lesson 18

SmartArt and Charts

OBJECTIVES ***After completing this lesson, you will be able to:***

1. Create SmartArt.
2. Create charts.
3. Edit chart data.
4. Modify chart types.
5. Add and modify chart options.
6. Format charts and chart elements.

Estimated Time: 1¼ hours

Word provides two graphics tools to display information visually—SmartArt graphics and charts. SmartArt graphics are helpful when presenting conceptual ideas. Charts show numeric data in a graphical way. Word uses Microsoft Excel to create charts. Chart tools are used to modify and format charts.

After you create a chart, you can customize it. You can change the chart's type—for example, from a bar chart to a column chart. You can add information to a chart, such as titles and gridlines, and control the chart's appearance, including font, color, size, and shading.

Creating SmartArt

Using Word's SmartArt tools, you can insert eight types of SmartArt:

- *List* illustrates groups and subgroups of information or blocks of information in a vertical or horizontal format.
- *Process* illustrates a progression or sequential steps toward a goal.
- *Cycle* illustrates a process that has a continuous cycle.
- *Hierarchy,* sometimes called *org chart,* illustrates the top-down relationship of members of an organization.

- *Relationship* illustrates the relationship of objects to a main object.
- *Matrix* illustrates relationships of objects to a whole in quadrants.
- *Pyramid* illustrates foundation-based relationships.
- *Picture* uses pictures to accent descriptive text.

When you choose a layout for SmartArt graphics, consider the amount and type of text to include. Plan to include one shape for each main point, and determine the relationship between the shapes. There are several layouts available for each type of SmartArt, and it is easy to apply a new layout to an existing SmartArt graphic.

Exercise 18-1 CREATE A SMARTART GRAPHIC

To insert a SmartArt graphic, click the Insert tab and locate the Illustrations group. Click the SmartArt button and select a type (category) and layout.

1. Start a new document, and choose the Word 2010 Style Set. Key the title **Campbell's Confections—Ohio Stores**. Center the text and change it to 14-point Arial Black, with small caps. Change the spacing after to 24 points. Press Enter.
2. Click the **Insert** tab, and click the SmartArt button to open the Choose a SmartArt Graphic dialog box.

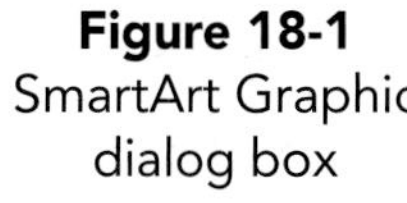

Figure 18-1
SmartArt Graphic dialog box

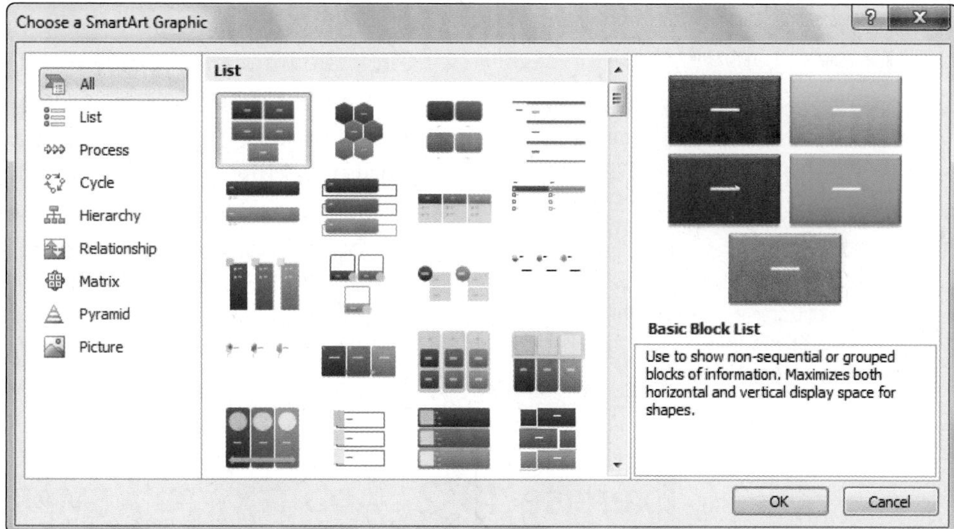

3. Click the **Cycle** type, and click the **Basic Radial** layout (third row, second graphic). Read the description of the Basic Radial SmartArt graphic. Click **OK**. The Basic Radial graphic is inserted in the document. The graphic displays with a drawing space and a nonprinting border. Inside the border are sizing handles. The left border displays a tab with arrows for displaying the text pane. Click the tab to display the text pane.
4. Select the innermost circle in the Basic Radial diagram if it is not already selected. To select a circle, point to the circle's edge and click when you see the four-headed arrow pointer. The selected circle has eight selection handles.

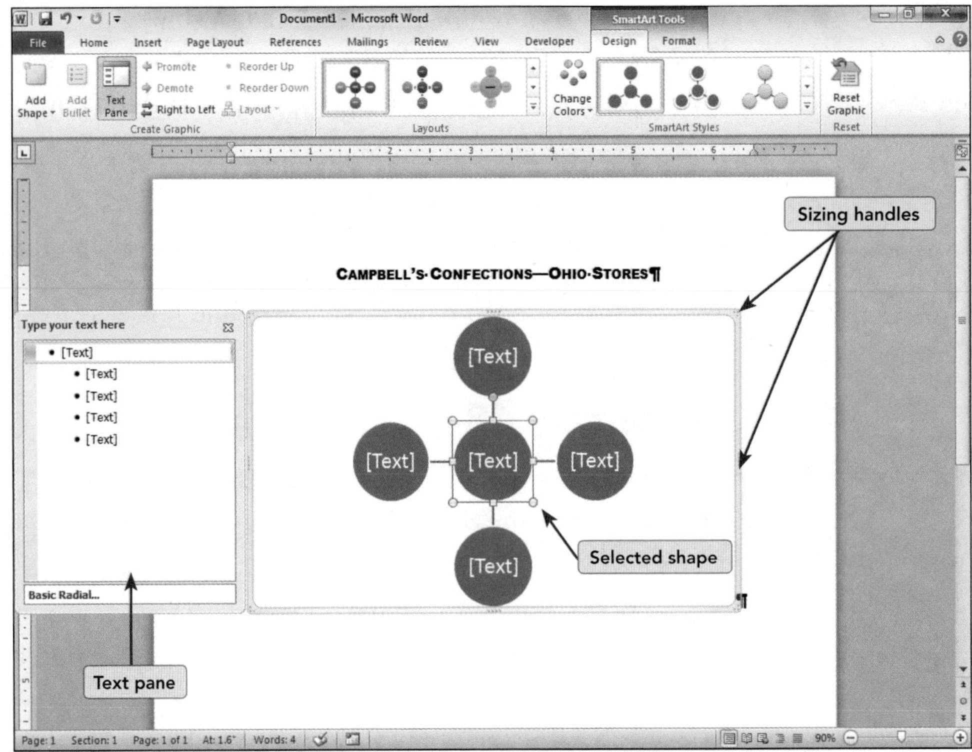

Figure 18-2 Inserting a Basic Radial SmartArt graphic

NOTE

Click the arrow beside the Add Shape button to display a list of options for inserting shapes. Choices include Add Shape After, Add Shape Before, Add Shape Above, Add Shape Below, and Add Assistant (available for organizational charts). The position of the insertion point in the text pane or the graphic object selected determines the placement of the new object.

5. Click the **SmartArt Tools Design** tab on the Ribbon. Click the innermost circle to select it if necessary, and locate the **Create Graphic** group. Point to the Add Shape button, and notice that the button changes color. Clicking the button automatically inserts a shape to the outer circle. Clicking the arrow beside the button displays a list of options for inserting a new shape. Click the Add Shape button. The Basic Radial diagram should now have five outer circles.

Exercise 18-2 ADD TEXT TO A SMARTART GRAPHIC

You can add text to a SmartArt graphic by clicking a shape and then keying the text, or you can click a [Text] placeholder in the text pane and key the text. The copy and paste commands can be used to add text to a SmartArt graphic.

TIP

To display the text pane, click the SmartArt Tools Design tab, and click the Text Pane button.

1. Click inside the center circle, and key **Ohio**. The text should automatically resize. Notice that the text pane displays "Ohio" at the top of the pane.

NOTE

To add a shape before an existing shape in a SmartArt graphic in the text pane, position the insertion point before the text where you want the new shape inserted. Key the text; then press Enter. To add a shape after an existing shape, place the insertion point at the end of the text where you want the new shape inserted, and press Enter. To indent the new shape, press Tab. Use the Promote and Demote buttons on the Ribbon to change the text level.

2. Click in the topmost circle to select it, and notice that [Text] is selected in the text pane. Key **Akron**.
3. Moving clockwise, key the following cities, one per circle, in each of the remaining circles: **Canton**, **Cleveland**, and **Massillon**.
4. Click the last bulleted item in the text pane, and key **Warren**. Press Enter to add a sixth circle to the SmartArt graphic. Key **Youngstown**.

Exercise 18-3 FORMAT A SMARTART GRAPHIC

There are two ways to change the appearance of a SmartArt graphic. One is to click the SmartArt Tools Design tab and change the layout, colors, or SmartArt style for the graphic. You can also click the SmartArt Tools Format tab, and change the shape fill, shape outline, shape effect, and other text effects. The colors and effects available are determined by the selected theme.

1. Click the SmartArt graphic border. Click the **SmartArt Tools Design** tab. Click the Change Colors button.

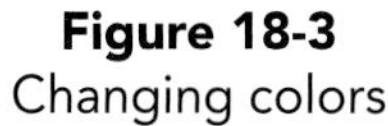

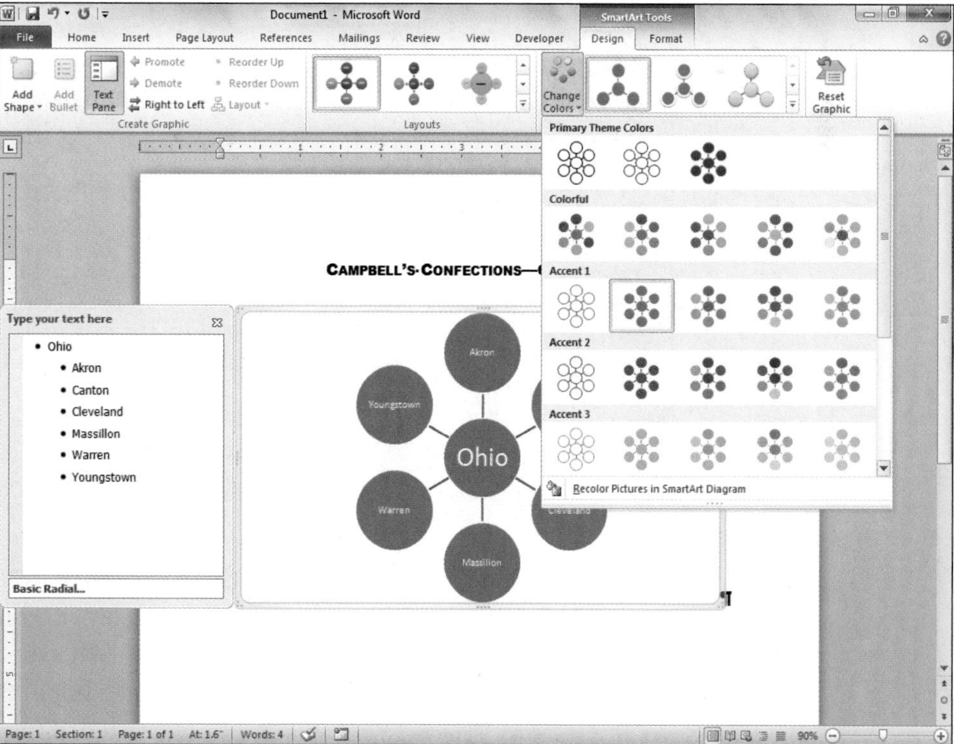

Figure 18-3
Changing colors

2. Select a **Gradient Range Accent** color. Remember that you can move the mouse over the various options to preview their effect on the SmartArt graphic.
3. Locate the **SmartArt Styles** group, and click the More arrow to display the SmartArt Styles gallery. Click the **3-D Flat Scene** style from the gallery.
4. Locate the **Layouts** group, and click the More arrow to expand the Layouts gallery. Click the **Diverging Radial** layout in the third row.

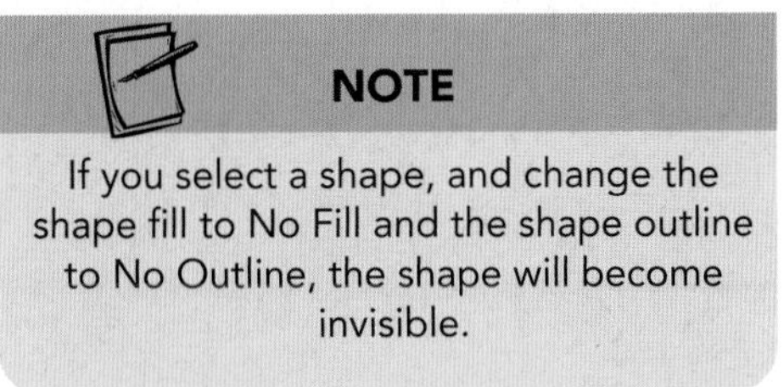

NOTE

If you select a shape, and change the shape fill to No Fill and the shape outline to No Outline, the shape will become invisible.

5. Click the **SmartArt Tools Format** tab. Click the Size button. Change the **Height** to **4** inches, and change the **Width** to **6** inches.
6. Click the Shape Fill button, and select an accent color for the background of the drawing canvas. Click the Shape Outline button, and select an appropriate color for the border.
7. Right-click one shape of the SmartArt graphic, and click **Format Shape** to open the Format Shape dialog box.
8. Click **Text Box**, and verify or change the following settings: Vertical alignment: **Middle**, Text direction: **Horizontal**, Internal margin: **0.01** inch for all sides. Click **Close**.

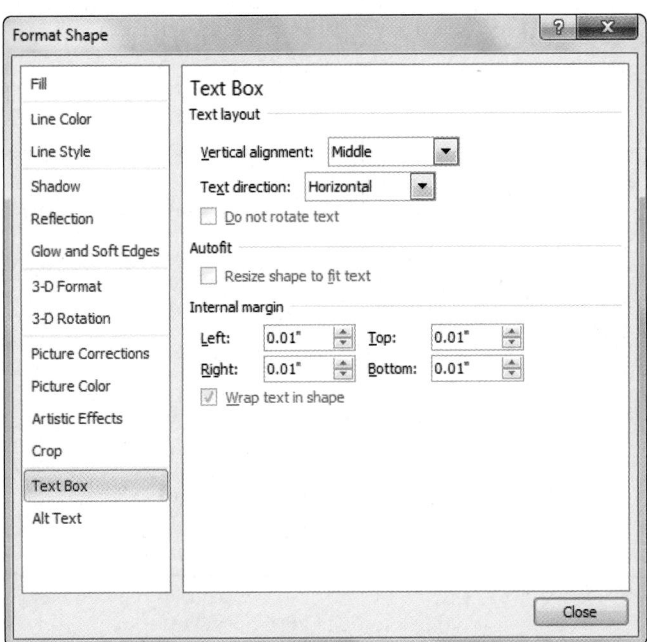

Figure 18-4
Format Shape dialog box

9. Click to select the Ohio shape. Click the **SmartArt Tools Format** tab, and click the Shape Fill button. Click **Picture**, and locate the directory and folder for the student data files. Click the file **Chocolate - P14,** and click **Insert**. Notice the picture within the shape. Press Ctrl+Z to undo.
10. Center the document vertically on the page (Page Setup, Layout tab).
11. Save the file as ***[your initials]*18-3** in your Lesson 18 folder.
12. Submit and close the document.

Creating Charts

A chart is a visual representation of numeric data. Charts often make values in a table easier to understand. You can usually look at a chart and quickly grasp the meaning of the numbers.

You create a chart in a Word document by inserting a generic chart as an embedded object. The chart data are stored in an Excel spreadsheet. When you first create the chart, the spreadsheet contains sample data and the chart is displayed in a column graph format. You replace the sample data with your own numbers and column labels.

Exercise 18-4 INSERT A CHART IN A DOCUMENT

1. Open the file **Mills**. Add the current date. The letter is from Lynn Tanguay, vice president. Include your reference initials and an enclosure notation.
2. Position the insertion point in the blank line below the paragraph that begins "As you requested."
3. Click the **Insert** tab, and locate the **Illustrations** group. Click the Chart button. The Insert Chart dialog box displays.
4. Click **Column**, and click the first chart in the first row. Click **OK** to insert the column chart. A sample chart is inserted in the document between the second and third paragraphs, and the Word document window and the Excel spreadsheet window appear side by side. The chart is based on the sample data in the Excel spreadsheet. You will replace this data with your own labels and numbers in the next exercise.

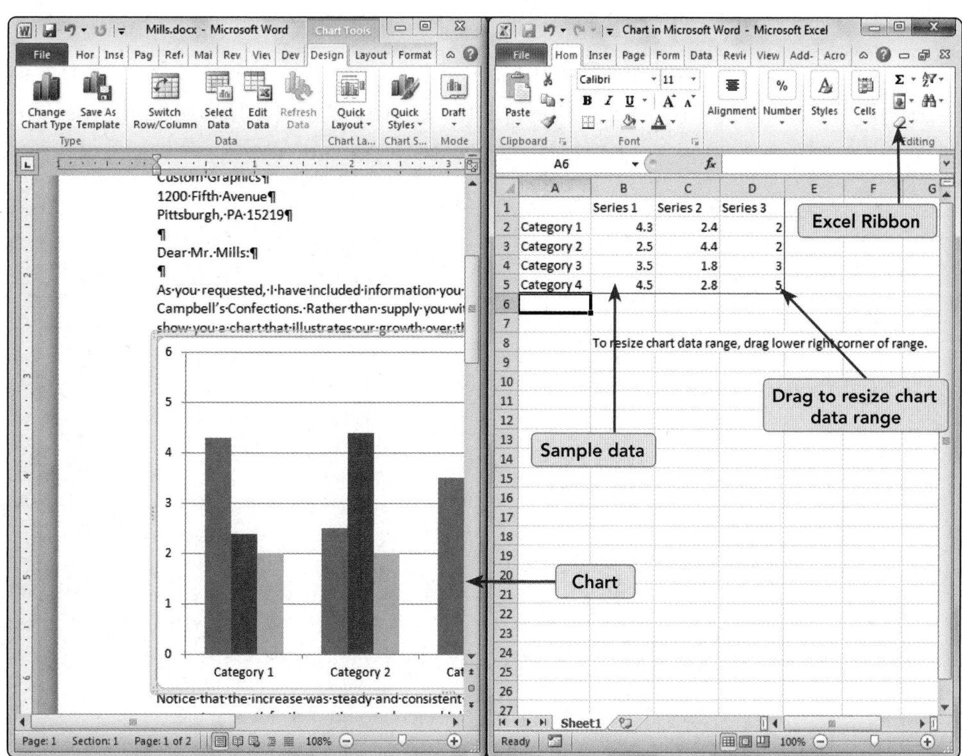

Figure 18-5
Inserting a chart

5. Drag the lower right corner of the data range to column F, row 4. Notice the change in the chart.
6. Click anywhere in the Word document, and maximize the document window.

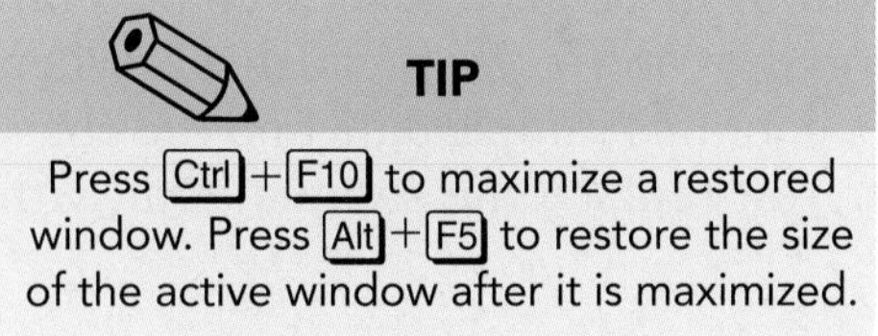

TIP

Press Ctrl+F10 to maximize a restored window. Press Alt+F5 to restore the size of the active window after it is maximized.

7. Click the chart border to select the chart. The Word Ribbon displays the Chart Tools Design, Layout, and Format tabs. Notice the chart selection handles. Word treats the chart as an in-line graphic object. You can move or resize it. To edit the chart, you can click the Edit data button on the Chart Tools Design tab or click the Microsoft Excel button on the Windows taskbar.

Exercise 18-5 KEY DATA IN THE SPREADSHEET

1. Click the **Chart Tools Design** tab, and click the Edit Data button . The spreadsheet displays.
2. Verify that the data range is A1 through F4.
3. Click the upper left box of the spreadsheet (to the left of column A) to select the entire spreadsheet (or press Ctrl+A).
4. Press Delete. This deletes the sample data. The entire spreadsheet is now blank and ready for you to key new data. Notice the change in the chart when you erase the sample data.
5. Key the data and headings shown in Figure 18-6. The chart grows as you key the data. Notice that you cannot see the entire row 1 label "Total Revenues" after you enter the value in the adjacent column—this does not affect how the label is displayed on the chart.
6. Press Enter after keying the last figure to make sure it is entered in the chart. Data are not entered until you move to another cell.

TIP

You can change the width of spreadsheet columns to display text that might be hidden. Move the pointer to the divider line between the columns until the two-headed arrow appears; then hold down the mouse button and drag to the desired width (or double-click the divider line). If the spreadsheet is too small to show all the data, point to the side or bottom border of the datasheet window and then use the two-headed arrow pointer to drag to a larger size.

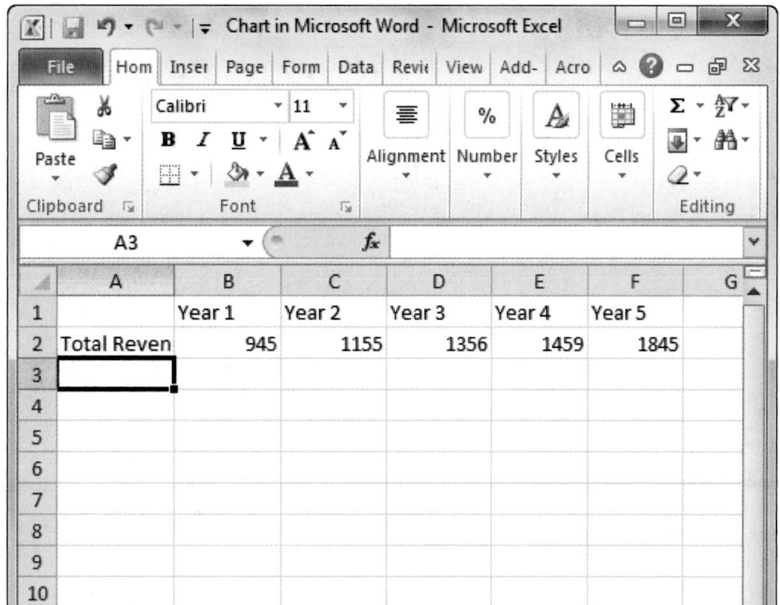

Figure 18-6
Spreadsheet with new data

7. Click anywhere in the document to redisplay the Word Ribbon. Notice the change in the appearance of the groups and buttons on the Ribbon when Word and Excel are both open.
8. Save the document as ***[your initials]*18-5** in your Lesson 18 folder. Leave it open for the next exercise.

Editing Chart Data

After you create a chart, you might need to edit the data. Numbers in a chart can be changed only on the spreadsheet.

Exercise 18-6 EDIT CHART DATA

1. In the document ***[your initials]*18-5**, select the chart. Select the **Chart Tools Design** tab, and click the Edit Data button.
2. Change the Year 5 total revenue to **2155** (press Enter after keying the text to enter the value). Notice that the chart changes with the new value.
3. Add two new rows of data to the datasheet for "New Business" and "Repeat Business," as shown in Figure 18-7. Adjust the width of the first column to accommodate "Repeat Business."

Figure 18-7
Spreadsheet with two new rows

	A	B	C	D	E	F
1		Year 1	Year 2	Year 3	Year 4	Year 5
2	Total Revenues	945	1155	1356	1459	2155
3	New Business	661	742	762	808	816
4	Repeat Business	284	413	594	651	1339

Exercise 18-7 SWITCH DATA SERIES FROM ROWS TO COLUMNS

Data are plotted in a chart in groups of *data series,* which are collections of related data points. These values are usually found within the same column or row in the spreadsheet. Each data series is distinguished by a unique color. Sometimes it is hard to know in advance if it is better to arrange your data in rows or in columns on the datasheet. You can enter it either way and switch back and forth.

TIP

Depending on the type of data in your chart, switching data series between row and column orientations is often a good idea. Sometimes a different view can emphasize and improve chart data in a way you didn't anticipate.

NOTE

Charts are inserted in-line with text by default. Change the text-wrapping option to move a chart freely on the page, or use the Align button.

1. Maximize the Word window. Select the chart, and click the **Chart Tools Design** tab.
2. Click the Switch Row/Column button. The graph displays three data series, and each row heading in the data sheet appears in the legend. The category labels along the x-axis represent the column headings in the data sheet.
3. Click the Switch Row/Column button to change the data series groupings back to a column orientation.
4. Click the chart to select it if necessary. Click the **Chart Tools Format** tab, and click the Wrap Text button. Click **Top and Bottom**.
5. Locate the **Arrange** group, click the Position button, and click **More Layout Options** to open the Layout dialog box. Click the **Position** tab, and change the **Horizontal Alignment** to **Centered** relative to **Page**. Click **OK**.
6. Create a letterhead for the document by keying the following information in the header pane, formatted as 10-point Calibri, right aligned.

   CAMPBELL'S CONFECTIONS
   25 Main Street
   Grove City, PA 16127
   724-555-2025
   www.campbellsconfections.biz
7. Change the top margin to 1.5 inches and the bottom margin to 0.5 inch. Size the chart to 3.25 inches if necessary to fit the letter on one page. To add white space between the first paragraph and the chart, change the spacing after to 6 points.
8. Preview the document; then save it as ***[your initials]*****18-7** in your Lesson 18 folder.

Figure 18-8 Document with modified chart and letterhead

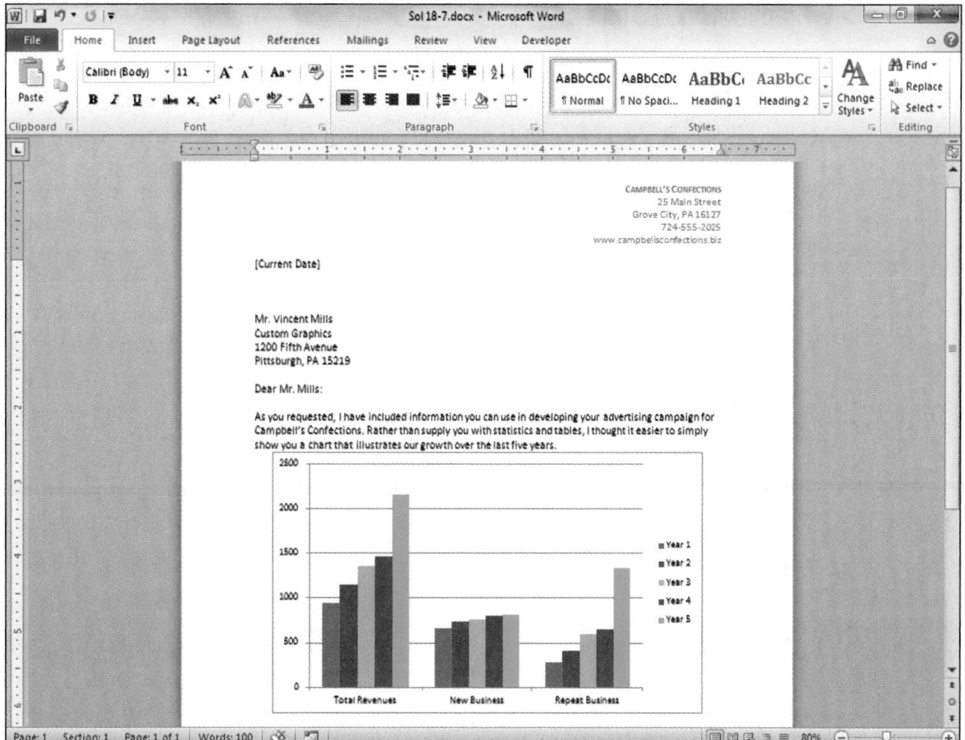

9. Submit the document.

Modifying Chart Types

After creating a chart, you might want to change the way the data are displayed. Microsoft Excel offers a wide variety of chart types, each designed for a specific purpose.

Many charts can be displayed with a 3-D visual effect, and you can combine different types within a single chart, such as column and line. Table 18-1 summarizes the available chart types.

TABLE 18-1 Chart Types

Type	Definition
Area	Shows the relationship of parts to a whole and emphasizes the magnitude of change (includes 3-D effects).
Bar	Illustrates comparisons among items or shows individual figures at a specific time (includes 3-D effects).
Bubble	Compares sets of three values. Bubble charts are like scatter charts, with the third value displayed as the size of the bubble marker (includes 3-D effects).
Column	Shows variation over a period of time or demonstrates a comparison among items (includes 3-D effects).
Doughnut	Compares the sizes of parts of a whole. Each chart can show more than one data series.

continues

TABLE 18-1 Chart Types *continued*

Type	Definition
Line	Shows trends in data over a period of time at the same intervals, emphasizing the rate of change over time (includes 3-D effects).
Pie	Compares the sizes of parts of a whole. Each chart shows only one data series (includes 3-D effects).
Radar	Shows changes or frequencies of data relative to a center point and to other data points. Each category has its own value axis radiating from the center point. Lines connect all values in the same series (includes 3-D effects).
Stock	Requires three series of values in high, low, and close order. Stock charts are frequently used to illustrate stock prices. Also known as "high-low-close charts."
Surface	Displays optimum combinations between two sets of data. It can show relationships between large amounts of data that would otherwise be difficult to see (includes 3-D effects).
XY (Scatter)	Compares trends over uneven time or measurement intervals plotted on the category axis. Scatter charts also display patterns from discrete *x* and *y* data measurements.

Exercise 18-8 CHANGE A CHART TYPE

1. In the Word document ***[your initials]*18-7**, select the chart to activate the graph-editing tools. Verify that the years display on the *x*-axis. If not, click the Switch Row/Column button.
2. Click the **Chart Tools Design** tab.
3. Click the Change Chart Type button. Choose **Line**, and click the fourth option. Click **OK**. The chart changes, and each of the data series ("Total Revenues," "New Business," and "Repeat Business") is represented as a line. Along each line, a marker indicates the series' value for each of the 5 years.

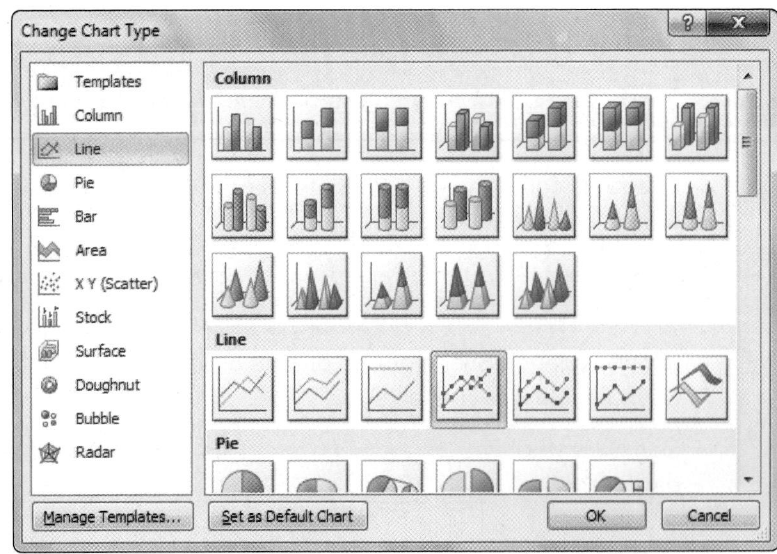

Figure 18-9
Change Chart Type dialog box

4. Click the Change Chart Type button again, click **Area**, and click the first option in the first row. Click **OK**. Notice that this chart type shows the trend over time of each of the three series combined together, or "stacked." Although the area chart creates a dramatic effect, determining the individual values of each series at any given time is difficult.
5. Open the **Change Chart Type** dialog box, and click **Line**. Seven subtypes are available for line charts.
6. Click the last subtype, which is the **3-D Line** chart (or "ribbon" chart). Click **OK**. The dialog box closes, and the chart changes to the new type. Like the stacked area chart, the 3-D line chart provides an interesting effect. It also allows readers to see the upward trend in all the data categories. But some of the data are hidden because of the 3-D effect. This chart type might work better with data categories that have more widely varying values.

TIP

If you accidentally apply the wrong chart type to the chart, you can use the Undo command to restore the chart to its previous state. Or reopen the Chart Type dialog box, and choose another chart type.

7. Reopen the **Change Chart Type** dialog box. Click **Column** from the Chart type list.
8. Choose the second subtype on the first row, **Stacked Column**. Click **OK**. Notice that this subtype shows the contribution of each value to a total across 5 years.
9. Reopen the **Change Chart Type** dialog box, and click **Column**. Click **Clustered Column**, the first subtype, and click **OK**. The chart type is changed to a simple two-dimensional column chart.
10. Click anywhere in the document to return to Word. Notice that removing the 3-D effect has made the chart easier to read.
11. Leave the document open for the next exercise.

Exercise 18-9 COMBINE CHART TYPES

Microsoft Excel enables you to combine certain chart types in a single chart. Each data series can be assigned its own chart type.

1. Select the chart, and change the row-column display so that "Total Revenues," "New Business," and "Repeat Business" appear in the legend if necessary.
2. Click one of the "New Business" columns. The "New Business" data series is selected.
3. Click the Change Chart Type button .
4. Click the **Line** type. Click the fourth subtype, which is the **Line with Markers** at each data value. Click **OK**. The "New Business" data series now appears as a line.

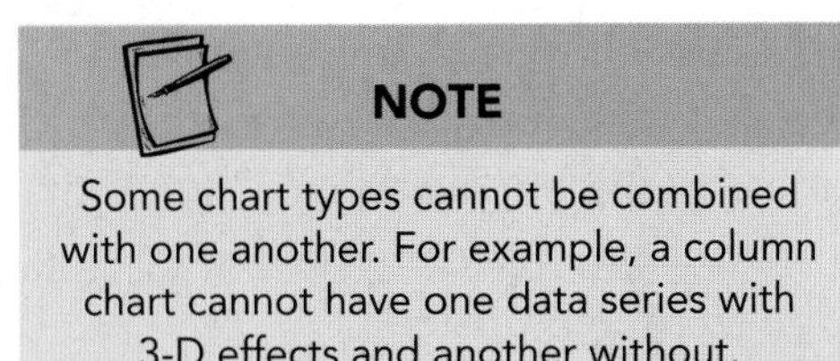

NOTE

Some chart types cannot be combined with one another. For example, a column chart cannot have one data series with 3-D effects and another without.

5. Select the "Repeat Business" data series by clicking one of the green columns.
6. Reopen the **Change Chart Type** dialog box, and click the **Area** chart type.
7. Select the first subtype and click **OK**. The "Repeat Business" data series appears as an area chart.
8. Click anywhere in the document to redisplay the Word document.

Figure 18-10
Combined chart types

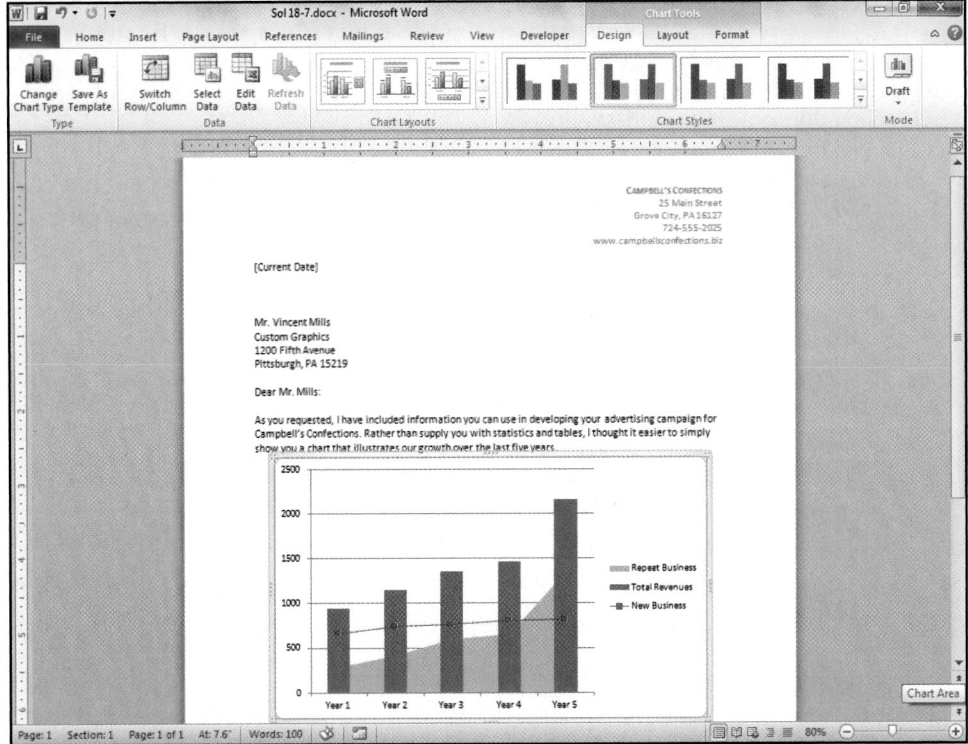

9. Save the document as ***[your initials]*18-9** in your Lesson 18 folder. Submit the document and leave it open.

Adding and Modifying Chart Options

After you create a chart, you can add and modify various options in the chart. Besides showing the numeric data from the datasheet, charts can include other elements that you can select and modify individually:

- The *category axis* is the horizontal (or *x*) axis along the bottom of most charts; it frequently refers to time series.
- The *value axis* is the vertical (or *y*) axis against which data points are measured.
- The *plot area* is the rectangular area bounded by the two axes; it includes all axes and data points.
- A *data marker* is an object that represents an individual data point. It can be a bar, area, dot, or picture, or some other symbol, that marks a single data point or value.

- A *legend* is a guide that explains the symbols, patterns, or colors used to differentiate data series.
- A *tick mark* is a division mark along the category (x) and/or value (y) axis.
- A *data point* is a single piece of data.
- A *data series* is a collection of related data points. These values are usually found within the same column or row in the datasheet.
- The *chart title* is the name of the chart. Titles can also be assigned to the axes.

Figure 18-11
Chart elements

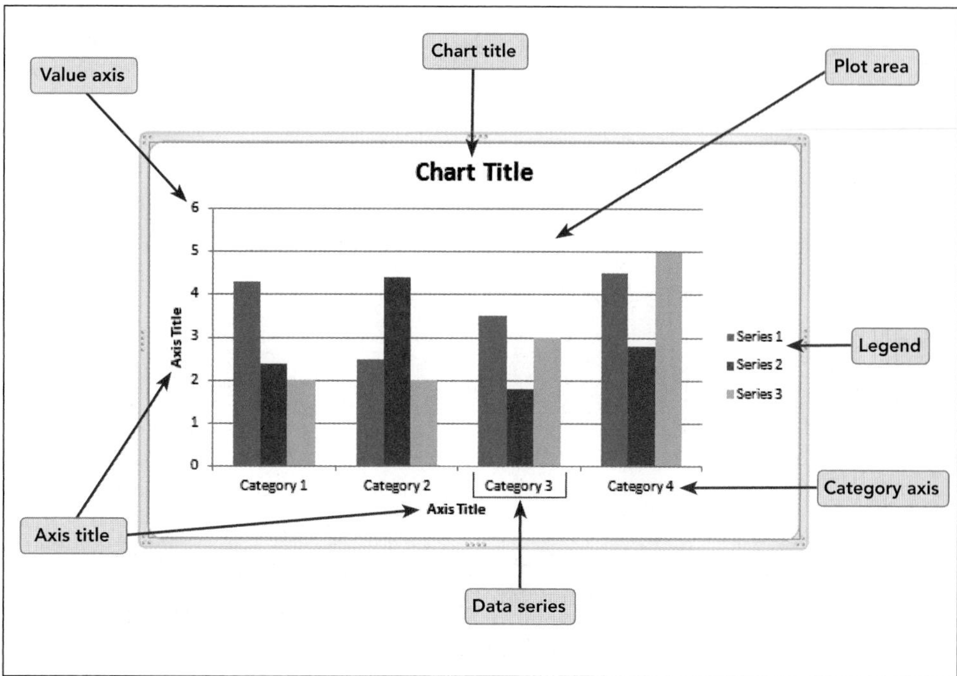

Exercise 18-10 ADD CHART TITLES AND GRIDLINES

1. Select the chart to activate the chart-editing tools. Maximize the Word document window.
2. Position the pointer over the legend, and notice that a ScreenTip appears. Move the pointer to the white area above the legend, and notice that this is identified as the chart area. Move the pointer around the different areas of the chart, and notice the ScreenTips.
3. Click the Chart Tools Layout tab, locate the Labels group, and click the Chart Title button.
4. Click Above Chart. Drag to select the text in the Chart Title text box, and key **Growth at Campbell's Confections**. Deselect the chart title text box.
5. Click the Chart Tools Layout tab, and click the Axis Titles button. Click Primary Vertical Axis Title, and click Rotated Title. Drag to select the text in the Vertical Axis Title text box, and key **(Thousands)**. Deselect the title.

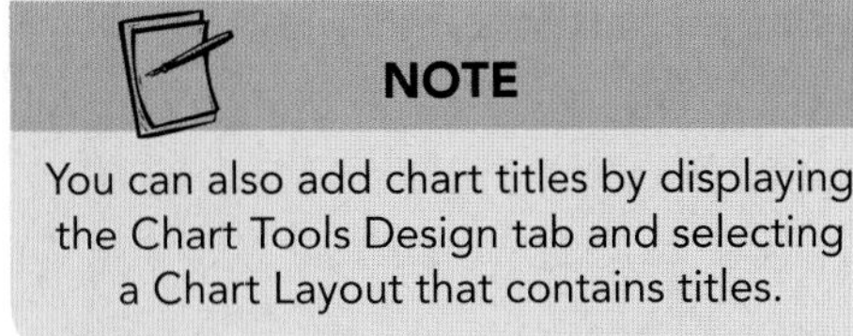

NOTE

You can also add chart titles by displaying the Chart Tools Design tab and selecting a Chart Layout that contains titles.

6. Select the chart if necessary. Click the Gridlines button. Click **Primary Vertical Gridlines**, and click **Major Gridlines**. The gridlines are added to the chart. Notice that the plot area has been compressed to compensate for the additional text. You will resize the chart later in the lesson.

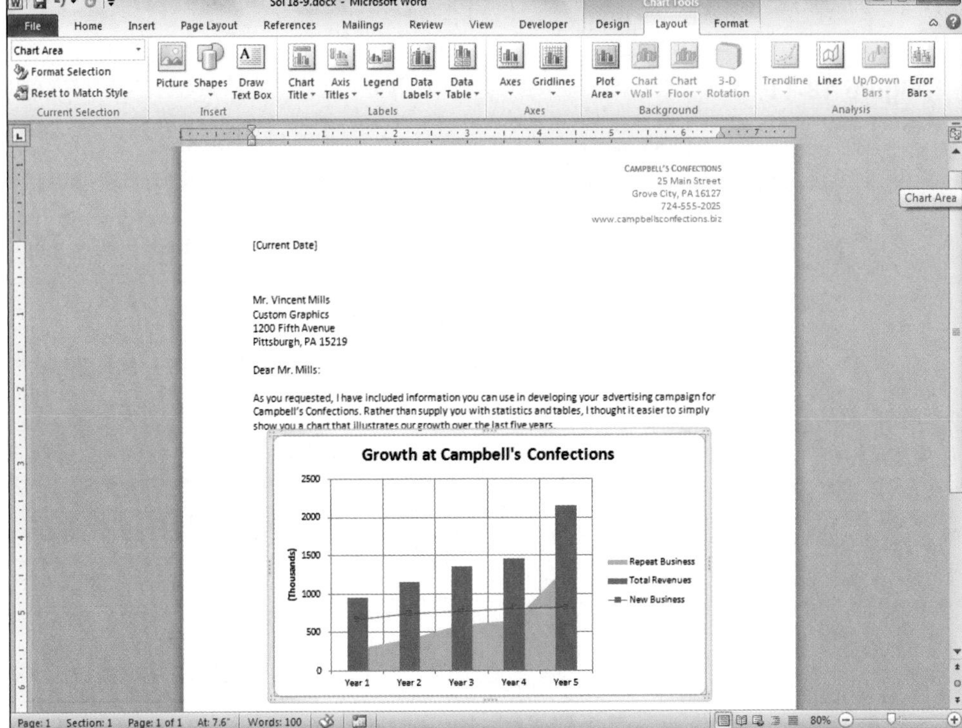

Figure 18-12
Adding chart titles and gridlines

Exercise 18-11 ADD A SECONDARY AXIS

The addition of a secondary value axis can enhance a chart when there are data series representing widely different numeric values.

1. Select the chart; then select the "Repeat Business" data series.
2. Click the **Chart Tools Format** tab. Click the Format Selection button, and click **Series Options**. Click **Secondary Axis**. Click **Close**. A secondary value axis appears in the chart. This axis will represent the "New Business" and "Repeat Business" values. You will need to add an axis label to reflect this change.
3. Select the chart if necessary. Add a secondary vertical axis title by clicking the Axis Titles button on the Chart Tools Layout tab, and clicking **Secondary Vertical Axis Title** and **Rotated Title**. Drag to select the text. Key **New and Repeat Business**. Press Enter and key **(Thousands)**. A second value axis appears in the chart. Because "New Business" and "Repeat Business" refer to the same axis, the chart would be clearer if both data series used the same chart type.

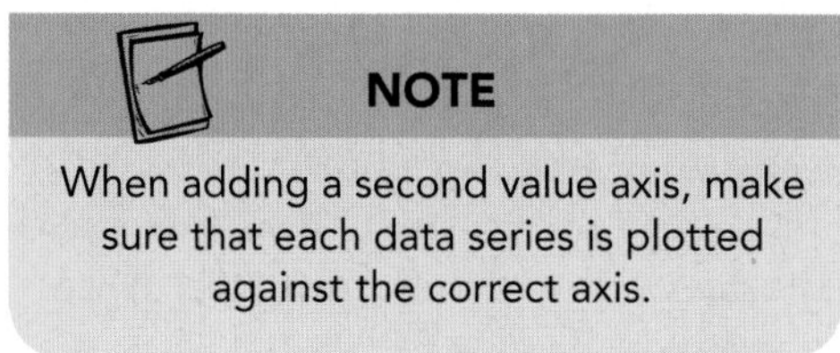

NOTE

When adding a second value axis, make sure that each data series is plotted against the correct axis.

4. Right-click anywhere in the "Repeat Business" data series, and choose **Change Series Chart Type** from the shortcut menu.
5. Click the **Line** type, and click the fourth subtype. Click **OK**. The "New Business" and "Repeat Business" data series are both line charts.
6. Right-click the "New Business" data series, and choose **Format Data Series** from the shortcut menu.
7. In the Format Data Series dialog box, click **Series Options**, and click **Secondary Axis**. Click **Close**. The "New Business" data series is now plotted on the correct axis. Check to make sure the "Repeat Business" data series is also plotted on the secondary value axis.
8. Click anywhere in the document to return to Word.
9. Resize the chart, making it wider.

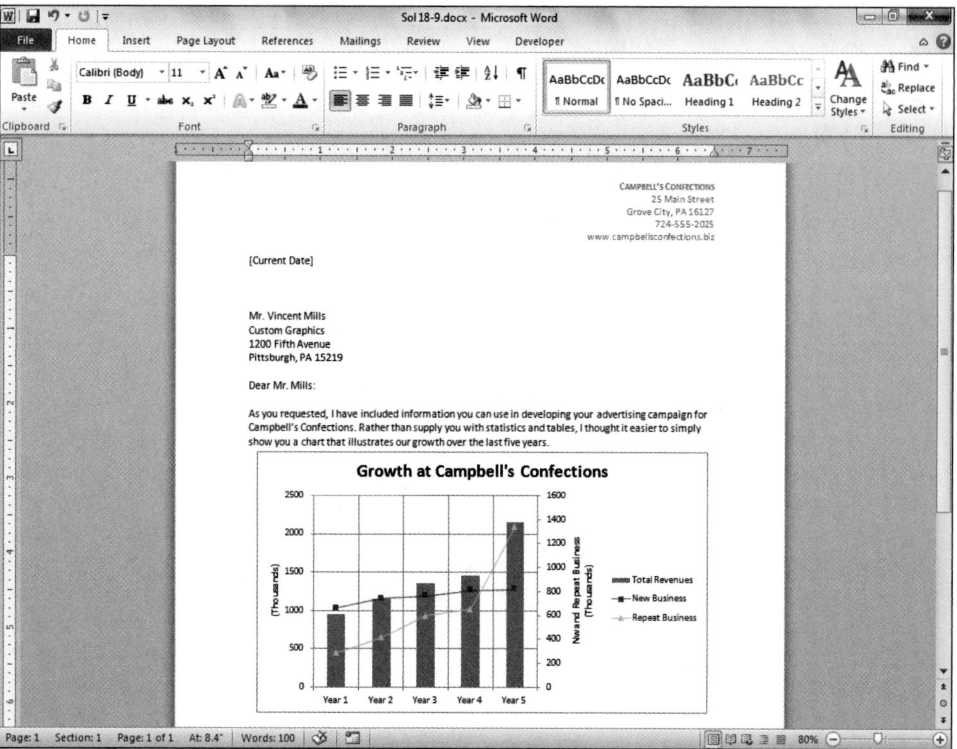

Figure 18-13
Chart with second value axis added

10. Save the document as ***[your initials]*18-11** in your Lesson 18 folder.
11. Submit the document. Leave it open for the next exercise.

Formatting Charts and Chart Elements

Charts have a wide variety of formatting options. You can change the colors and patterns of the data markers, for instance, and control the fonts used throughout a chart. You can reposition the legend or even eliminate it. You can also format the numbers on the value axis.

NOTE

You can select a chart element by using the Chart Tools Layout tab, Current Selection group. Click the arrow next to the Chart Elements box, and click the appropriate chart element. When you select a chart element, the label on the button changes to reflect the last selection. For instance, when you select the chart, the label changes to "Chart Area."

Exercise 18-12 CHANGE COLORS AND PATTERNS

Colors and patterns add interest to your chart. You can change the color of individual columns or an entire group of columns. Even the background color can be changed to achieve a special effect.

1. Select the chart.
2. Right-click one of the "Total Revenue" columns, and click **Format Data Series** from the shortcut menu. The Format Data Series dialog box appears.

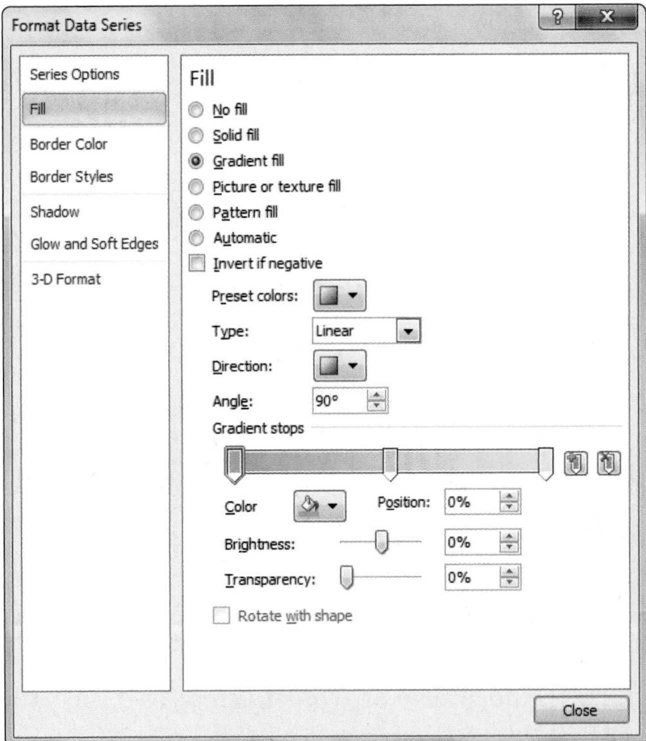

Figure 18-14 Format Data Series dialog box

3. Click **Fill**. Click **Gradient fill**. Click **Close** to accept the default settings.
4. Right-click the plot area, and choose **Format Plot Area** from the shortcut menu. The Format Plot Area dialog box appears.

NOTE

To change an individual column, first select the entire data series and then click the individual column whose color you wish to change. This selects only that column in the data series. When you right-click, you will display the Format Data Point dialog box, which is similar to the Format Data Series dialog box.

5. Click **Fill**, and select a coordinating color for your chart. Adjust the **Transparency** level if desired. Click **Close**.
6. Right-click the "Repeat Business" data series, and choose **Format Data Series** from the shortcut menu.
7. Click **Line Color**, and click **Solid line**. Select a line color. Click **Marker Fill**, and click **Solid fill**. Click **Close**.

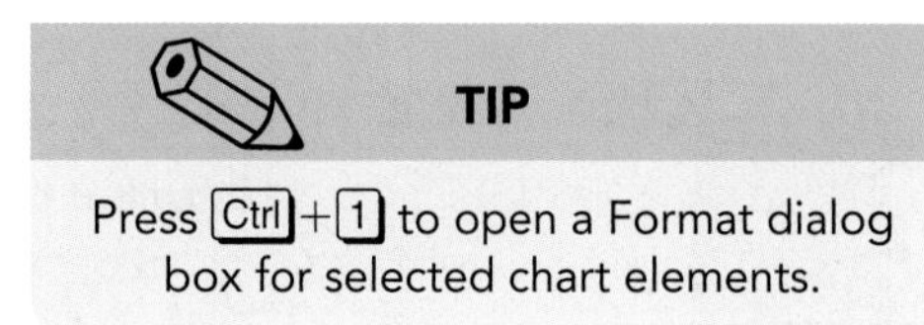

TIP

Press Ctrl+1 to open a Format dialog box for selected chart elements.

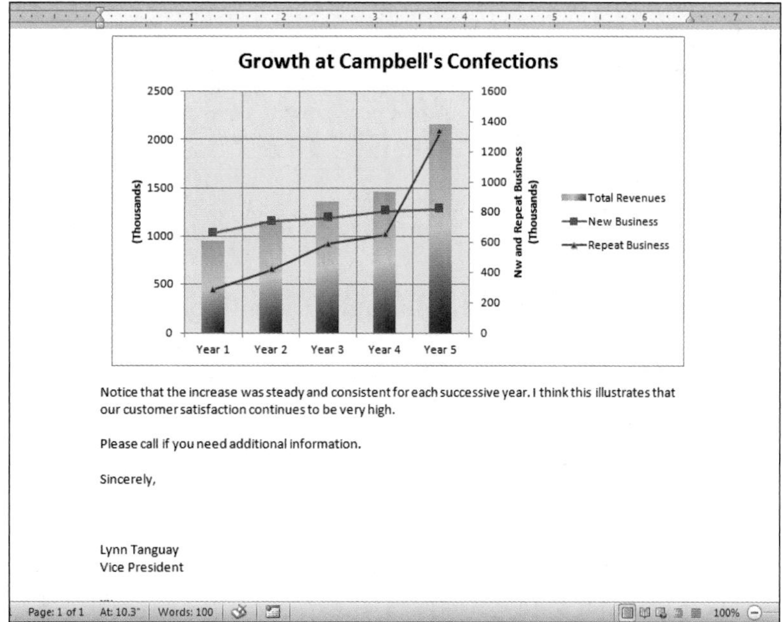

Figure 18-15
Chart with new colors for the data series and plot area

Exercise 18-13 FORMAT THE LEGEND

You can change the placement, font, and appearance of a chart's legend.

1. Right-click the legend. Choose **Format Legend** from the shortcut menu. The Format Legend dialog box appears.
2. Click **Legend Options**, and choose **Bottom**. This moves the legend under the chart.
3. Click **Border Color**. Click **No line**. This removes the box around the legend. Notice that you can use the Fill options to change the background color and patterns of the legend box. For now, leave these unchanged. Click **Close**.

4. Select the legend, and use the Mini toolbar to make sure the font size is 10 points. The legend is reformatted, and the chart area adjusts to accommodate the additional space now available on the right.
5. Use the left and right sizing handles to expand the legend box width. This provides more space between the items and makes them easier to read.

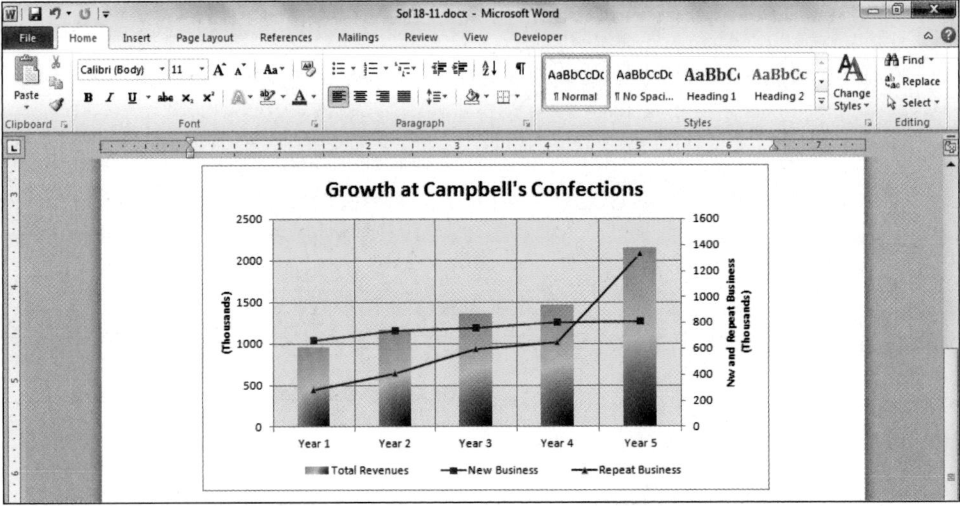

Figure 18-16 Chart with reformatted legend

Exercise 18-14 FORMAT THE AXES

1. Right-click the value axis (the numbers along the left edge of the chart), and select **Font**. The Font dialog box appears.
2. Click the **Font** tab, and change the font to 9-point bold. Close the Font dialog box.
3. Right-click the secondary value axis (the numbers along the chart's right edge). Change the font to 9-point bold.
4. Right-click the category axis (the row of years along the chart's bottom), and change the font to 9-point bold. With a smaller font for the three axes, the legend now appears too large. Change the legend font to 9 points.

Exercise 18-15 FORMAT CHART TITLES

You can format titles by using dialog boxes, or you can edit them directly in the chart.

1. Select the primary value axis title "(Thousands)" by clicking it once.
2. Move the pointer inside the selected title. The pointer changes to an insertion point. Drag over the word "(Thousands)."
3. Change the font size to 8 points, and apply bold italic formatting. Click **OK**.
4. Click anywhere in the chart area.
5. Right-click the secondary value axis title, and change the font size to 8 points.

6. Right-click the secondary value axis, and click **Format Axis Title**. Click **Alignment**. Click the drop-down arrow beside **Text direction**, and click **Rotate all text 90°**. This reverses the orientation of the text.
7. Click **Close**. Notice that you cannot edit text or format individual parts of the text in the dialog box. To italicize the "(Thousands)" portion of the axis title, you will need to edit it directly.
8. Select the secondary axis title.
9. Apply italic formatting to "(Thousands)," and then click anywhere in the chart area. The "(Thousands)" portion of the title appears in italic.
10. Click anywhere outside the chart to return to Word.

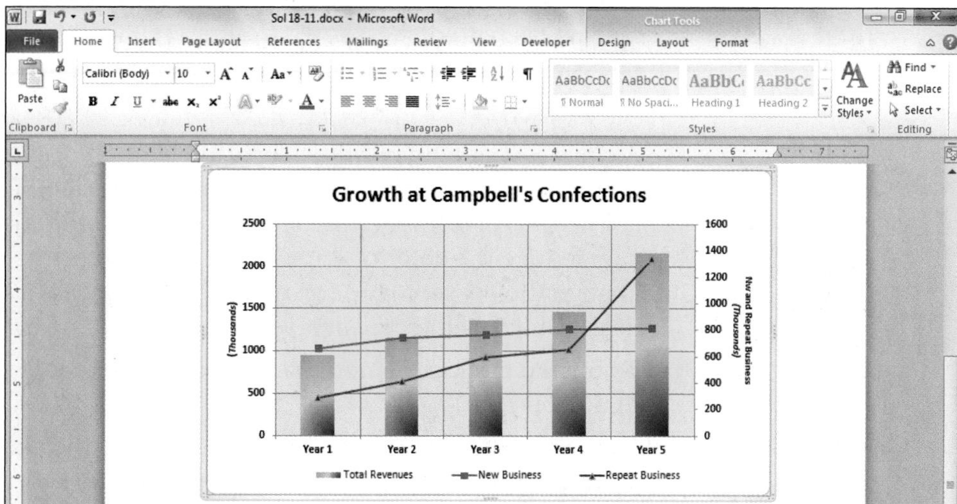

Figure 18-17
Chart with reformatted titles

11. Save the document as ***[your initials]*18-15** in your Lesson 18 folder.

Exercise 18-16 CHANGE THE LAYOUT OR STYLE OF A CHART

You can format a chart very easily by using the predefined styles and layouts provided. Once a style or layout is selected, you can customize it by manually changing the format.

1. Select the chart.
2. Click the **Chart Tools Design** tab, and locate the **Chart Layouts** group. Click the More arrow to see the Chart Layout gallery. Click **Layout 1**, and notice the changes in the position of the chart and chart elements.
3. Open the **Chart Layout** gallery, and click **Layout 3**.
4. Select the chart if necessary, and click the **Chart Tools Design** tab. Locate the **Chart Styles** group.
5. Click the More arrow to open the Chart Quick Styles gallery.
6. Select a style.
7. Save the document as ***[your initials]*18-16** in your Lesson 18 folder.
8. Submit and close the document.

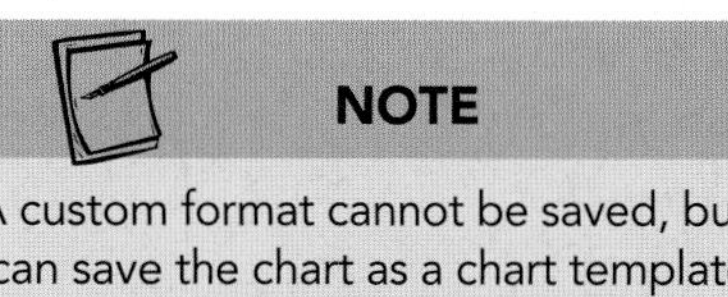

NOTE

A custom format cannot be saved, but you can save the chart as a chart template. To save a chart as a chart template, click the Chart Tools Design tab, and click the Save As Template button.

Lesson 18 Summary

- Use Word's SmartArt feature to insert different types of SmartArt graphics. Add text to a SmartArt graphic by clicking a shape or clicking a text placeholder in the text pane.
- Format SmartArt graphics by using the SmartArt Tools Design tab or the SmartArt Tools Format tab on the Ribbon. You can change the layout, colors, style, fill, outline, and effects of the graphic.
- Use the Insert tab, Illustration group, to insert a chart.
- Microsoft Excel offers 11 types of charts. (See Table 18-1.) Each chart type has multiple subtypes available. You can modify the chart type after a chart is created.
- If a chart uses multiple data series, you can apply a different chart type to each series.
- A chart is made up of many separate elements, such as axes, data markers, gridlines, legend, and more. Each element's attributes (its size, color, font, placement, and so on) can be modified. For example, you can change the color of data series columns or the plot area. You can change the position and formatting of the legend. You can also add or delete chart elements, such as a chart title or a secondary axis title.
- To format a chart element, right-click the element and open the Format dialog box.
- To format a text element of a chart, such as the chart title, click the title and then select the text. Use any of Word's text-formatting tools to change the text's font, size, alignment, and other options. Click outside the title when you have finished editing.

LESSON 18		Command Summary	
Feature	**Button**	**Command**	**Keyboard**
Chart type		Chart Tools Design tab, Type group	
Create a chart		Insert tab, Illustrations group	
Create SmartArt graphics		Insert tab, Illustrations group	
Format selected chart object		Chart Tools Design, Layout, or Format tab	Ctrl+1
Format SmartArt		SmartArt Tools, Design or Format tab	

Concepts Review

True/False Questions

Each of the following statements is either true or false. Indicate your choice by circling T or F.

T F 1. SmartArt graphics are best used to present numeric data.

T F 2. Right-click a chart area to display a shortcut menu with format options.

T F 3. You can add or delete shapes from a SmartArt graphic.

T F 4. Pie charts can show only one data series.

T F 5. Every chart type has a corresponding 3-D version.

T F 6. Every chart type can be combined with every other chart type.

T F 7. The sample data of a chart display in a Word table.

T F 8. You cannot change the color of an individual column in a chart.

Short Answer Questions

Write the correct answer in the space provided.

1. When a chart is inserted in Word, where are the sample data located?

____

2. Which chart axis is the vertical (or *y*) axis?

____

3. Which chart axis is the horizontal (or *x*) axis?

____

4. Each chart type has several different versions. What are these versions called?

____

5. What shortcut menu command would you choose to change the color of a selected data series?

____

6. What is the procedure for changing a chart type?

____

7. What is the name of the guide in a chart that explains the symbols, patterns, or colors used to differentiate data series?

____

8. What type of SmartArt graphic illustrates the top-down relationship of members in an organization?

____

Critical Thinking

Answer these questions on a separate page. There are no right or wrong answers. Support your answers with examples from your own experience, if possible.

1. How would you decide if a chart would be a useful addition to your document? When would you use a chart instead of a simple table? Explain your answer.
2. You have seen the number of details and elements that can be added to a chart. Is there a point at which you can have too much detail in a chart? Explain how you would decide what amount of detail is appropriate for the message you want to communicate.

Skills Review

Exercise 18-17

Insert and format a SmartArt graphic.

1. Start a new document.
2. Change the document orientation to landscape.
3. Key **Campbell's Confections—Holiday Favorites**. Press Enter. Format the title by centering it and using 18-point bold, small caps.
4. Create a SmartArt graphic by following these steps:
   a. Position the insertion point below the title. Click the **Insert** tab, and locate the **Illustrations** group.
   b. Click the SmartArt button.
   c. Click the **List** type, and click the **Picture Accent List** style (third row, third style).
   d. Click **OK**.
5. Click the rotated [Text] placeholder for the left rectangle, and key **Halloween**. Click the rotated [Text] placeholder for the middle rectangle, and key **Valentines**. Key **Easter** in the third rotated [Text] placeholder.
6. Key the following text as bulleted text in each of the rectangles:

Halloween rectangle	Valentine rectangle	Easter rectangle
Chocolate Bars	Gift Box Chocolates	Solid-Chocolate Rabbits
Chocolate Suckers	Novelty Chocolates	Chocolate Eggs

7. Format the SmartArt graphic by following these steps:
   a. Select the SmartArt graphic border.
   b. Click the SmartArt Tools Design tab. Click the Change Colors button, and select a color from the Change Colors gallery.
   c. Select the SmartArt graphic border. Click the SmartArt Tools Format tab, click the Shape Fill button, and select a color for the background. Click the Shape Outline button, and select a color and weight for the line border.
   d. Click the Arrange button if the Arrange group commands do not display. Click the Position button, and click the Position in Middle Center with Square Text wrapping option.
   e. Click the Size button, and change the Width to 8 inches.
8. Insert a picture by following these steps:
   a. Click the picture placeholder for "Halloween," and click the Shape Fill button. Click Picture, and locate the picture file **Chocolate - P7**.
   b. Click the picture placeholder for "Valentines," and insert the picture file **Chocolate - P2**.
   c. Click the picture placeholder for "Easter," and insert the picture file **Chocolate - P3**.
9. Add a page border using a 3-point double-line format.
10. Save the document as ***[your initials]*18-17** in your Lesson 18 folder.
11. Submit and close the document.

Exercise 18-18

Create a chart, and edit chart data.

1. Open the file **Memo - 5**. Key the current date in the memo heading.
2. Insert a chart by following these steps:
   a. Position the insertion point at the end of the document. Click the Insert tab, and locate the Illustrations group.
   b. Click the Chart button.
   c. Click the Pie type, and click the second style, Pie in 3-D. Click OK.
3. Key the following data in the Excel spreadsheet:

Cell	Data
A2	Chocolate Nuts
A3	Chocolate Creams
A4	Chocolate Melt-a-ways
A5	Other
B2	38
B3	34
B4	26
B5	2

4. Click in the Word document, and maximize the document window to view the chart.

5. Edit the chart data by following these steps:
   a. Select the chart in the Word document, and click the **Chart Tools Design** tab.
   b. Click the Edit Data button.
   c. Change the value "38" to **36**, change the value "26" to **24**, and change the value "2" to **6**.
6. Return to Word, and maximize the Word window. Center the chart by pressing Ctrl+E.
7. Key your reference initials at the end of the document.
8. Save the document as ***[your initials]*18-18** in your Lesson 18 folder.
9. Submit and close the document.

Exercise 18-19

Add chart titles, gridlines, and a secondary axis.

1. Open the file **Gift Sales**. Set the top margin to 2 inches.
2. Key your name in the "From" line.
3. Insert a properly formatted Date field to show the current date.
4. Select the chart.
5. Add a chart title and gridlines by following these steps:
   a. Click the **Chart Tools Layout** tab.
   b. Click the Chart Title button, and click **Above Chart**. Key **Gift Sales** in the Chart Title box.
   c. Select the chart if necessary, and click the Gridlines button on the Chart Tools Layout tab. Click **Primary Vertical Gridlines**, and click **Major Gridlines**.
6. Add a secondary value axis by following these steps:
   a. Select the chart, and select the "Figurines/Collectibles" data series.
   b. Click the **Chart Tools Layout** tab, and click the Format Selection button. Click **Series Options**, and click the **Secondary Axis** option. Click **Close**.
7. Center the chart horizontally, and add a border to the chart using the Shape Outline button. Click outside the chart to deselect it.
8. Save the document as ***[your initials]*18-19** in your Lesson 18 folder.
9. Submit and close the document.

Exercise 18-20

Add and format chart titles, change chart colors, format the legend, and format axes.

1. Open the file **Market - 1**. Select the chart by clicking it once.
2. Resize the chart, dragging the right sizing handle until it is even with the right margin.

3. Select the chart.
4. Change the chart type by following these steps:
   a. Click the **Chart Tools Design** tab, and click the Change Chart Type button.
   b. Click **Column** for the chart type, and click **Clustered Column** for the layout.
5. Add a chart title positioned above the chart. Key the chart title **Specialty Chocolate Sales**.
6. Change the chart area color by following these steps:
   a. Move the pointer into the chart area.
   b. Right-click, and choose **Format Chart Area** from the shortcut menu.
   c. Click **Fill**, and select a color. Click **Close**.
7. Format and resize the legend by following these steps:
   a. Right-click the legend, and choose **Format Legend** from the shortcut menu.
   b. Click **Legend Options**, and click **Top Right**. Click **Close**.
   c. Change the format of the legend text to 9-point bold and italic.
8. Format the value axis by following these steps:
   a. Right-click the value axis, and choose **Format Axis** from the shortcut menu.
   b. Click **Number**. In the Category list, click **Number**. Set **Decimal places** to **0**, and select the **Use 1000 Separator** check box.
   c. Click **Axis Options**. Change the value in the **Maximum** box to **Fixed** and **250**. Click **Close**.
   d. Format the text using 9-point bold and italic.
   e. Add minor gridlines to the value axis (with the **Chart Tools Layout** tab).
9. Format the chart title by following these steps:
   a. Select the chart title.
   b. Format the title using 14-point bold and italic.
10. Change the color of a data series by following these steps:
    a. Right-click one of the green columns.
    b. Choose **Format Data Series** from the shortcut menu.
    c. Click **Fill**. Click **Gradient fill**. Select a color, type of gradient, and direction.
11. Click outside the chart to deselect it. Key your initials at the bottom of the document.
12. Select the chart. Click the **Chart Tools Format** tab, and change the **Height** to 3.25 inches. Change the bottom margin to 0.5 inch.
13. Make any final adjustments to improve the layout if needed, and then save the document as ***[your initials]*****18-20** in your Lesson 18 folder.
14. Submit and close the document.

Lesson Applications

Exercise 18-21

Create a chart, change the chart type, and add and modify chart elements.

1. Create a new document, and change the orientation to landscape.
2. Insert a chart using the bar type, and the 100% Stacked Bar in 3-D layout.
3. Key the text from Figure 18-18 in the Excel spreadsheet. (Drag to resize the chart range to include only the column and row data.)

Figure 18-18

	A	B	C	D	E	F
1		Chocolate Bars	Gift Box	Novelty	Dark	Sugar-Free
2	Retail	540.4	953.3	347.8	168.6	69.5
3	Wholesale	216.7	383.7	124.6	134.6	74.4

4. Change the chart type to Column, and change the layout to Clustered Column.
5. Change the color of the plot area to light blue, and change the color of the "Novelty" data series to yellow.
6. Format the legend box, removing its border and moving it to the bottom of the chart. Change the font to 9-point regular. After repositioning the box, manually widen it so that its width is the same as the plot area.
7. Key a chart title with the text **Chocolate Sales by Division**.
8. Change the height of the chart to **6** inches and the width to **8** inches. Click the Chart Tools Layout tab, click Data Labels, and click Center.
9. Apply a 3-point dark blue outline to the chart.
10. Change the font for both the category and value axes to 9-point bold.
11. Center the chart vertically and horizontally on the page.
12. Add a primary vertical axis title using the Rotated Title option. Key **(Thousands)** in the title box.
13. Format the value axis using the following settings: Minimum: Fixed **0**; Maximum: Fixed **1000**; Major unit: **200**.
14. Make any final adjustments to improve the layout if needed, and then save the document as ***[your initials]*****18-21** in your Lesson 18 folder.
15. Submit and close the document.

Exercise 18-22

Edit chart data; modify the chart type; and add, modify, and format chart elements.

1. Open the file **Revenue - 2**, and select the chart.
2. Switch to the spreadsheet, and change the number "645" to **625**.

3. Change the chart type to Stacked Column.
4. Key the chart title **Revenue Comparison**. Format the title as 16-point bold and italic.
5. Format the value axis as 10-point bold and italic, with a currency number format and no decimal places. Format the category axis as 10-point bold and italic.
6. Format the legend as 9-point bold and italic, and place it at the bottom of the chart. Manually widen the legend box, adding more space between the text and the symbols.
7. Resize the chart by using the bottom sizing handle.
8. Change the "2011" data series color.
9. Change the color of the plot area.
10. Apply a coordinating border color to each data series.
11. Add a border to the chart.
12. Save the document as ***[your initials]*18-22** in your Lesson 18 folder. Submit the document.
13. Select the chart, and change the chart type to Clustered Column.
14. Save the document as ***[your initials]*18-22b** in your Lesson 18 folder.
15. Submit and close the document.

Exercise 18-23

Insert and modify a SmartArt graphic.

1. Start a new document and create a memo heading. The memo is to "Store Managers" from Lynn Tanguay. Use today's date and the subject "Setting Goals."
2. Key the following text below the memo heading:

   The following diagram illustrates our new approach to improving sales and productivity at Campbell's Confections. Please use this model to create your goals and objectives for the new fiscal year. We will meet next Thursday to discuss company goals and individual store goals.

3. Insert a SmartArt graphic using the Cycle type and the Nondirectional Cycle style (first row, fourth style).
4. Key **Customer** in the first shape. Move in a clockwise direction, and key the following terms in the shapes:

   New Products
   Technology Innovations
   Marketing and Sales
   Leadership Skills

5. Select the SmartArt graphic, and apply a 3-D SmartArt style. Change the color of the graphic.

6. Apply a fill and an outline color to the graphic.
7. Change the height of the graphic to 4 inches, and center the SmartArt graphic horizontally.
8. Key your reference initials at the end of the document.
9. Save it as ***[your initials]*****18-23** in your Lesson 18 folder.
10. Submit and close the document.

Exercise 18-24 ◆ Challenge Yourself

Change a chart's type, and add and modify chart elements.

1. Open the file **WV Sales**.
2. Select the chart, and switch the row and column data to change the data series groupings. (There should be four groups of two columns.)
3. Change the chart width to 6.5 inches.
4. Change the color of the plot area to light blue. Change the colors of both the "2011" and "2012" data series to complementing shades of blue using a solid fill color.
5. Format the scaling in the value axis so that the major unit is 10,000. Change the font to 9-point bold and italic.
6. Key the chart title **WV Sales**. Format the title as 14-point bold.
7. Adjust the sizing and placement of the chart so that it is balanced and centered horizontally on the page. Apply an outline color and shadow effect to the chart.
8. Save the document as ***[your initials]*****18-24** in your Lesson 18 folder.
9. Submit and close the document.

TIP

To change the data's grouping, click the Chart Tools Design tab and click the Switch Row/Column button. If the Switch Row/Column button is not active, click the Select Data button, verify the data range, and click OK.

On Your Own

In these exercises you work on your own, as you would in a real-life business environment. Use the skills you've learned to accomplish the task—and be creative.

Exercise 18-25

Visit the Web sites of three popular computer manufacturers. Check the price that each one charges for a PC that is "perfect" for you. Create a Word document that uses a chart to show the different prices. Include a SmartArt graphic in the document to display the list of manufacturers and contact information. Save your document as ***[your initials]*****18-25**, and submit it.

Exercise 18-26

Create a Word document that summarizes your personal expenses. Use a pie chart to show what percentages of your total expenses go toward clothing, food, and other expenses. Save your document as ***[your initials]*18-26**, and submit it.

Exercise 18-27

Create a Word document, and change the bottom margin to 0.5 inch. Key **Campbell's Confections** at the top of the document. Press Enter and key **Organization Chart** for the second line of the document title. Format and center the two-line title. Below the second line of the title, insert a SmartArt graphic. Select the Hierarchy category, and choose Organization Chart.

Figure 18-19

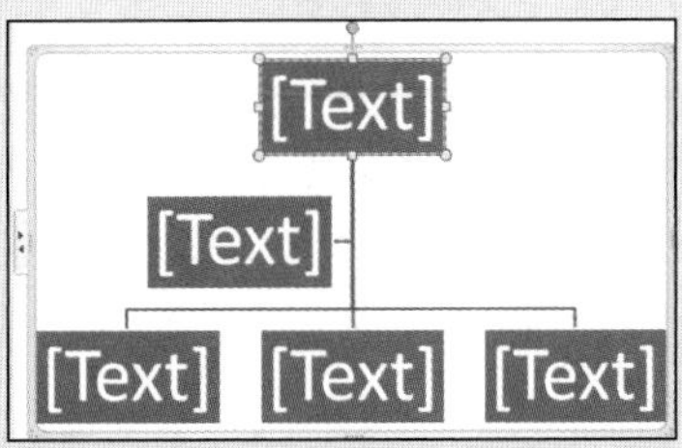

Add and delete shapes to the chart to create the organization chart shown in Figure 18-20. Format the shapes and the chart by changing the shape fill, shape outline, and shape effects. Size the shapes and the chart to fit on one page. Adjust line spacing, paragraph spacing, font, size, and color for the shapes. Save your document as ***[your initials]*18-27**, and submit it.

Figure 18-20

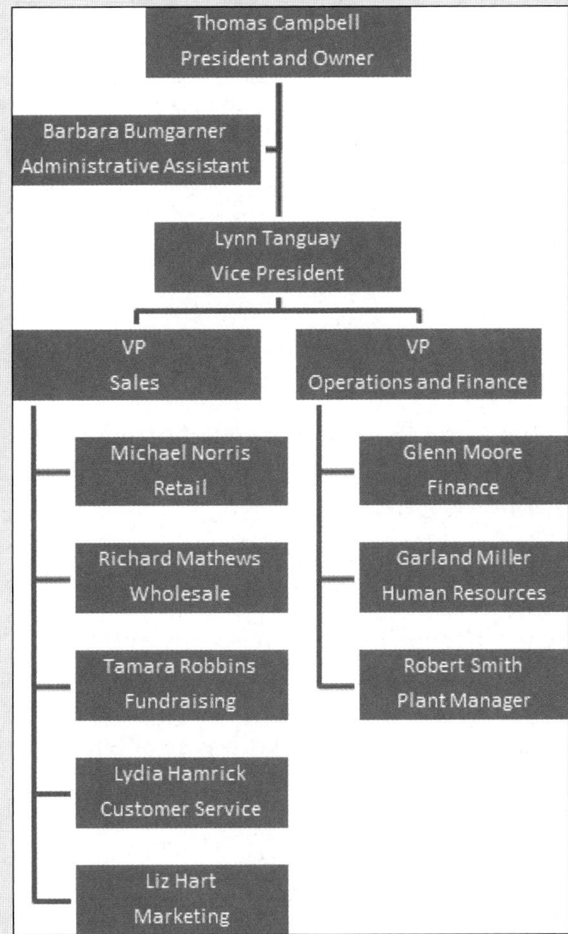

Unit 5 Applications

Unit Application 5-1

Create a flyer using clip art, pictures, and WordArt.

1. Start a new document, and change the orientation to landscape.
2. Key the text shown in Figure U5-1.

Figure U5-1

```
Introduction to Candy Making
Saturday, September 21
9 a.m. to 4 p.m.
Campbell's Confections—Auditorium
Instructor: Patricia Hoover
Registration: $25
Topics:
Temper, dip, mold, and decorate chocolate.
Acquire an understanding of taste factors—flavor and texture.
Master the techniques for making cream centers.
Learn where to buy chocolate-making ingredients, supplies,
and equipment.
```

3. Center the text, and apply appropriate formatting for emphasis.
4. Add a page border to the document, and change the color of the border to a chocolate-brown. Enhance the page with a light fill color or a light texture.
5. Move to the top of the document, and insert a table with one row and nine columns.
6. Placing one letter in each cell, key **Chocolate** in the table. Format the text using 48-point bold, with either small caps or all caps. Select a display font for the text.
7. Change the row height for the table to 0.5 inch, and center the table horizontally. Center the text in the cells vertically and horizontally.
8. Delete the letter "o" from the two cells in the table, and replace the letters with a circle shape. Change the text wrapping of the shape to in-line with text, and size the clip to fit in the cell. Change the shape fill to a picture, and insert a clip art image of chocolate. Refer to Figure U5-2 for an example.

Figure U5-2

CHOCOLATE

9. Preview the document, and make adjustments to the format or placement of the text.
10. Save the document as ***[your initials]*****u5-1a** in a new folder for Unit 5 Applications.
11. Delete the table at the top of the document, and replace the table with a WordArt object. Format and size the WordArt object.
12. Save the document as ***[your initials]*****u5-1b** in your Unit 5 folder.
13. Submit and close the document.

Unit Application 5-2

Create a one-page newsletter using clip art, pictures, and text boxes.

1. Start a new document. Change the top margin to 0.75 inch.
2. Click the Insert tab on the Ribbon, and open the Text Box gallery. Click the Mod Sidebar style.
3. Key **Campbell's Connections** in the sidebar. Rotate the text 270 degrees. Size the box to 1.5 inches wide and 9.25 inches high.
4. Format the title in a 48-point (or larger) font. The title should fill the text box but not wrap to a new line. Center the text horizontally and vertically, and apply bold formatting if the font is not already bold. Select the text box, and apply a dark blue fill color. Change the font color of the title to white. Align the text box so that it is 0.5 inch from the left edge of the page.
5. Position the insertion point at the paragraph mark at the top of the document, and format the document from this point forward with three columns of unequal width. The first column is reserved for the sidebar, and the second and third columns are for the newsletter articles. Choose appropriate widths for the columns.
6. Insert the file **New Products** at the beginning of the second column. (If necessary, insert a column break to place the insertion point at the beginning of the second column.)
7. Format the title of the article. Select the text in the New Products file, and change the line spacing to single spacing. Select the last two paragraphs of the article, and format the paragraphs with a 0.25-inch first-line indent.
8. Insert a column break at the end of the second column, and insert the file **Volunteers**. Select the text in the third column, and change the line spacing to single.

9. Format the title of the article using the same format applied to the first article. Select the last paragraph, and format it with a 0.25-inch first-line indent.
10. At the beginning of the last paragraph of the second article, insert a clip art image of a chocolate heart. Change the text wrapping to tight, and change the height to 0.75 inch. Drag the heart into the first paragraph.
11. Draw a text box at the bottom of the second column measuring 2.25 inches wide and 3.75 inches high.
12. Draw a second text box at the bottom of the third column measuring 2.25 inches wide and 5 inches high. Change the shape outline to rounded rectangle, and add a light blue fill.
13. Select the text boxes and add a shape outline. Choose a 2.25-point dark blue color to coordinate with the text box on the left margin. Align the boxes using the Align Bottom option.
14. Insert the file **Survey Results** in the text box in the third column. Format the title to match the other articles. Select the column headings for the tabbed text, and format the headings.
15. Position the insertion point in the text box at the bottom of the second column. Key the title **Chocolate Resources**. Format the title. Apply a shadow effect to the text box.
16. Use the Internet or a local library to list the names of two or three resources related to chocolate. For books, include the title, author, publication date, cost, and ISBN number. For magazines or periodicals, include subscription information.
17. Add a page border to the document. Preview the document, and make final adjustments.
18. Save the document as ***[your initials]*u5-2** in your Unit 5 folder.
19. Submit and close the document.

Unit Application 5-3

Create and format a chart.

1. Start a new document.
2. Set a 2-inch top margin, and add a memo heading to the document. The memo is to "Store Managers" from Glenn Moore. Use the current date and the subject "Chocolate Sales."
3. Key the following text below the memo heading:

   The following chart reflects the change in consumer preferences for chocolate. As a result of the increase in dark chocolate sales, we will modify our dark chocolate production schedules. Please use the new point-of-sale software to continue tracking chocolate preferences for the next six weeks.

4. Create a column chart using the information in Figure U5-3.

Figure U5-3

	A	B	C	D	E
1		Q1	Q2	Q3	Q4
2	Milk Chocolate	299	350	385	418
3	Dark Chocolate	60	73	96	128

5. Switch the row and column format if necessary to place the quarters along the *x*-axis.
6. Edit the chart data. Change the text in B3 to **58**.
7. Key the chart title **Chocolate Sales**.
8. Format the legend text using 10-point bold and italic.
9. Center the chart horizontally.
10. Add vertical gridlines, and format the chart area using a gradient fill.
11. Save the document as ***[your initials]*****u5-3** in your Unit 5 folder.
12. Submit and close the document.

Unit Application 5-4

Design and create a newsletter with a multisection layout.

1. Use the Internet to research information about the steps in manufacturing chocolate. Begin with harvesting the pods, fermentation, drying, and roasting. After the drying and roasting process, beans are shipped to chocolate factories, where they are stored, blended, and roasted. After the shell is separated from the inside of the bean (nib), the beans go through the next steps—grinding and mixing. Blending, conching, tempering, and cooling are the final steps in the production cycle. Write a minimum of four articles related to the manufacture of chocolate. You may choose to include the different types of beans and where they are grown. Locate clip art related to the production of chocolate. You may want to include pictures of the pods, beans, and final molded product. Add a SmartArt graphic to show the steps in the cycle.
2. Create a two-page newsletter.
3. Include the following elements in your newsletter:

   Nameplate

   Masthead

   Multicolumn format

   Pull quote using copied text from one of your articles
4. Create a style for the body text and a style for the article headings.

5. Include the following additions or modifications to the newsletter:
    - Change the document theme.
    - Change the font of the body text and headings.
    - Add horizontal lines.
    - Add bullets.
    - Insert clip art images.
6. Adjust text flow (line breaks, column breaks, page breaks), paragraph spacing, and character spacing as needed.
7. Add page numbers.
8. Save the document as ***[your initials]*****u5-4** in your Unit 5 folder.
9. Submit and close the document.

Unit 6

ADVANCED TOPICS

Lesson 19
Mail Merge

OBJECTIVES ***After completing this lesson, you will be able to:***

1. Create a main document.
2. Create a data source.
3. Insert merge fields into a main document.
4. Perform a mail merge.
5. Use data from other applications.
6. Edit an existing main document.
7. Sort and filter a data source.
8. Create mailing labels.

Estimated Time: 1½ hours

Businesses and organizations often want to send the same letter to several people or other businesses and organizations. *Mail merging* combines a document, such as a form letter, with a list of names and addresses to produce individualized documents. Using this process, you can create hundreds of personalized letters from just two documents:

- The *main document*, which contains special merge fields that act as placeholders for the recipient's name and address.
- The *data source*, which lists the specific recipient information (including the name, the address, and any additional data such as the phone number) to be inserted in the merge fields.

You can also create mailing labels or envelopes by using Word's mail merge feature.

Creating a Main Document

The mail merge process involves the following steps for completing a mail merge:

1. Create or identify the main document.
2. Create or identify the data source.
3. Refine the list of recipients through sorting and filtering.
4. Insert merge fields (placeholders) in the main document.
5. Merge the data source with the main document.

You can create the main document and data source during the mail merge, or you can use existing files. The first step is to identify the main document.

Exercise 19-1 SELECT A STARTING DOCUMENT

You can mail-merge different types of documents, including letters, e-mail, envelopes, and labels. In this exercise, your main document will be a business letter.

NOTE

The documents you create in this course relate to the case study about Campbell's Confections, a fictional candy store and chocolate factory (see the Case Study in the front matter).

1. Start a new document. Select the paragraph mark at the beginning of the document, and apply the No Spacing style which changes the line spacing to single and the spacing after to 0 points. Change the font to Cambria.
2. Format the current document as a business letter. Set a 2-inch top margin. Insert a date field at the top of the document, using the third format in the Date and Time dialog box. Make sure **Update automatically** is checked. Press Enter four times.
3. Click the **Insert** tab, click the Header button, and choose **Edit Header**. Create a letterhead for Campbell's Confections within the header by keying the following text. Center the text, and apply bold and small caps to the first line. To separate the phone and fax numbers, insert a symbol, such as the bullet character shown. Format the last line of the letterhead with a single-line bottom border. Close the Header & Footer pane.

   Campbell's Confections
   25 Main Street
   Grove City, PA 16127
   Telephone: 724-555-2025 ■ Fax: 724-555-2050
   www.campbellsconfections.biz

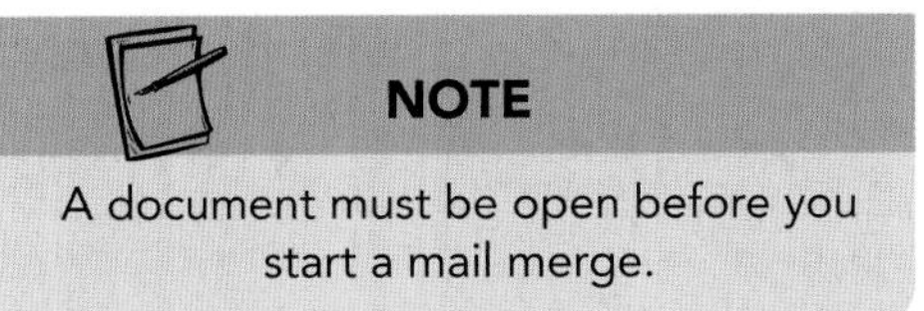

NOTE

A document must be open before you start a mail merge.

4. Click the **Mailings** tab on the Ribbon. Notice the five groups associated with mail merge: **Start Mail Merge**, **Write and Insert Fields**, **Preview Results**, **Finish**, and **Acrobat**.
5. The first step in mail merge is to select the document type. Click the Start Mail Merge button, and click **Letters**.

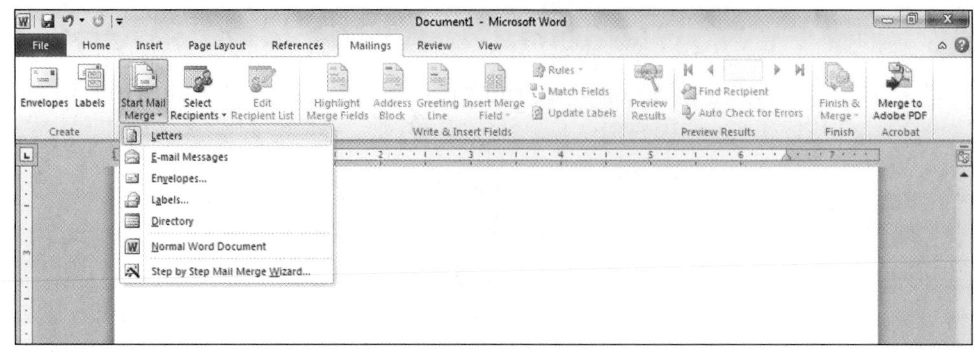

Figure 19-1 Mailings tab on the Ribbon

6. Save the document as ***[your initials]*19-1main** in a new folder for Lesson 19.

Creating a Data Source

A data source is a file that contains information, such as names and addresses, and the information is organized in a table. Each column of the table represents a category of information, such as last name. The column heading of each category is called a *field name.* Each row of the table represents a *record,* which is usually a person's name and his or her contact information. Each piece of information in a record is a *field.*

To perform a mail merge, you can use a preexisting data source in the form of a Word table, an Excel spreadsheet, an Access table, or an Outlook contact list. Or you can create your own data source during the mail merge process, which creates an Access database file. To do this, you first define the data (fields) you need for each record (person), such as title, name, and address, and then you enter each item of information.

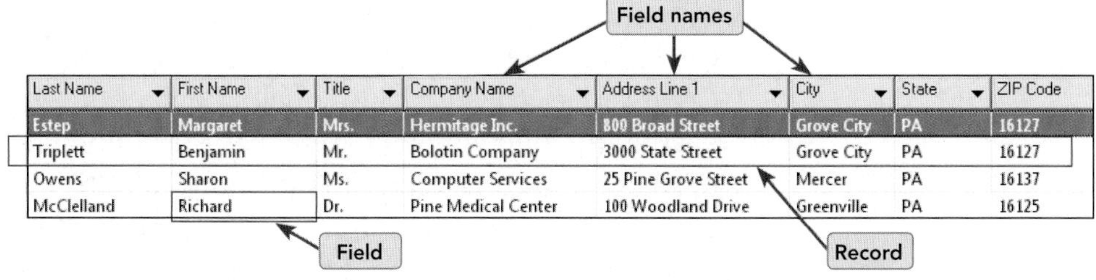

Last Name	First Name	Title	Company Name	Address Line 1	City	State	ZIP Code
Estep	Margaret	Mrs.	Hermitage Inc.	800 Broad Street	Grove City	PA	16127
Triplett	Benjamin	Mr.	Bolotin Company	3000 State Street	Grove City	PA	16127
Owens	Sharon	Ms.	Computer Services	25 Pine Grove Street	Mercer	PA	16137
McClelland	Richard	Dr.	Pine Medical Center	100 Woodland Drive	Greenville	PA	16125

Figure 19-2 Sample data source table

Exercise 19-2 CREATE A DATA SOURCE

When you click the Select Recipients button, you have three choices: You can use an existing list, such as an Excel or Access data file; you can select from contacts you might have entered in Outlook; or you can type a new list.

1. Click the Select Recipients button, and click **Type New List**. Word opens the New Address List dialog box. You will create your own data source by entering the data needed for this mail merge.

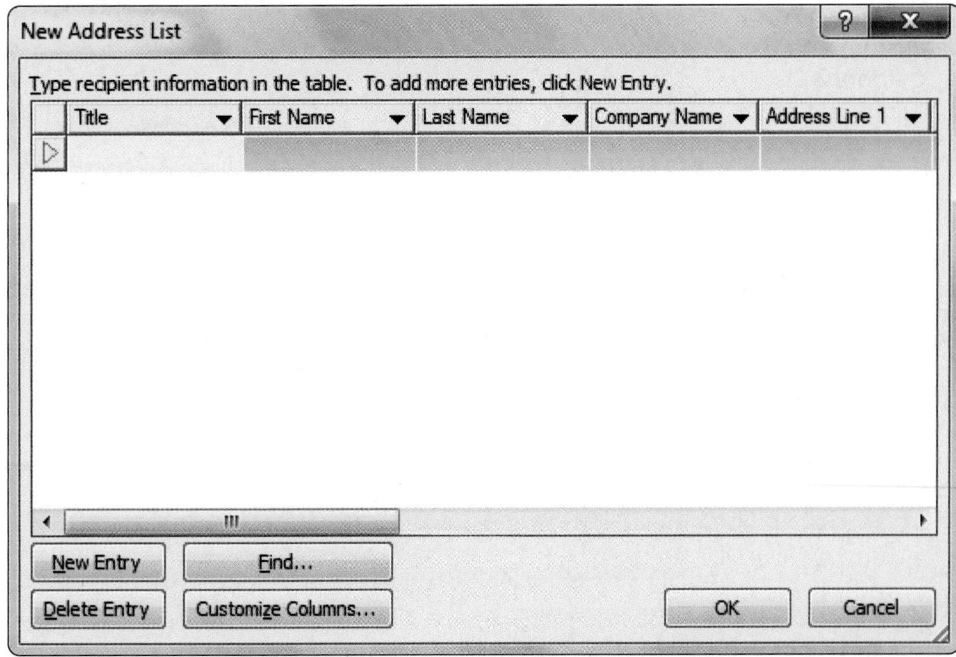

Figure 19-3 New Address List dialog box

2. Use the horizontal scroll bar in the dialog box to see a list of commonly used field names. You will customize this address list to include only the fields you need.
3. Click the Customize Columns button Customize Columns... in the New Address List dialog box to open the Customize Address List dialog box, where you can delete, add, or rename field names and change their order.

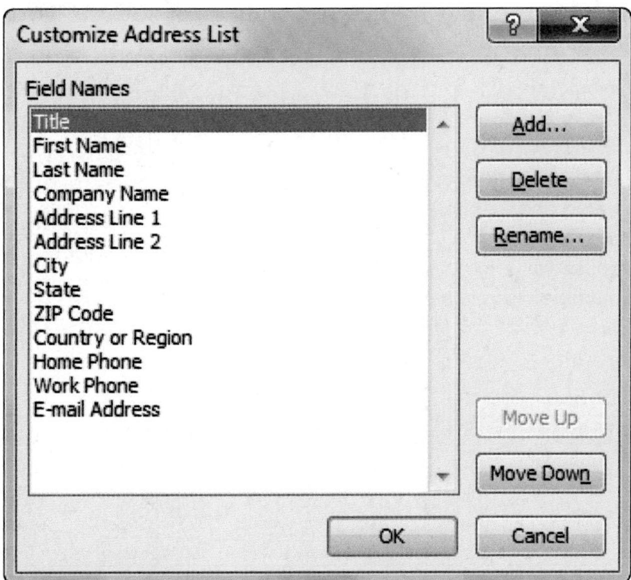

Figure 19-4 Customize Address List dialog box

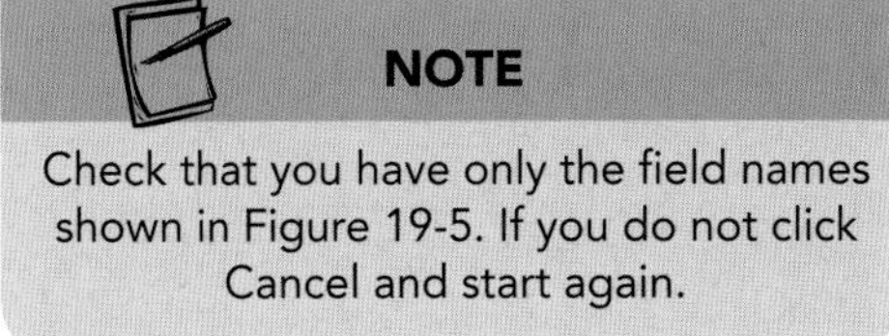

NOTE

Check that you have only the field names shown in Figure 19-5. If you do not click Cancel and start again.

4. Select **Address Line 2**. Click **Delete**. Click **Yes** when Word asks if you are sure you want to delete the field. The field name is removed from the list.
5. Using the same technique, remove the following fields from the list: "Country or Region" and "Home Phone."

Figure 19-5 Customizing the Address List information

NOTE

When preparing to enter data, it is best to customize the address list so that you can quickly key each line of data and move from record to record without worrying about a missed or blank field.

6. Click **OK** to close the Customize Address List dialog box. The New Address List dialog box lists only the fields you will need for your mail merge letters. You are now ready to enter data.

Exercise 19-3 ENTER RECORDS IN A DATA SOURCE

After defining field names for your data source, you can create records for mail merging.

TIP

To move from field to field within a record, press Tab to move to the next field and press Shift+Tab to move to the previous field. You can also click the mouse to position the insertion point in a field.

1. In the New Address List dialog box, key **Mrs.** in the Title field and press Tab.
2. Key the information shown in Figure 19-6 in the appropriate text boxes, pressing Tab after each field entry. After you key the ZIP Code, you will need to press Tab three times to move to the next record, or you can click the New Entry button New Entry.

Click to sort by last name.

Title	First Name	Last Name	Company Name	Address Line 1	City	State	ZIP Code
Mrs.	Margaret	Estep	Hermitage Inc.	800 Broad Street	Grove City	PA	16127
Mr.	Benjamin	Triplett	Bolotin Company	3000 State Street	Grove City	PA	16127
Ms.	Sharon	Owens	Computer Services	25 Pine Street	Mercer	PA	16137
Dr.	Richard	McClelland	Pine Medical Center	100 Woodland Drive	Greenville	PA	16125

Figure 19-6 Entering data

NOTE

You can add or remove a recipient to include in your mail merge by selecting or clearing the check box next to the recipient's last name.

3. Click the **Last Name** column heading (not the down arrow to the right of the column heading) to sort the list alphabetically by last name.
4. Click **OK** to close the New Address List dialog box.

5. In the Save Address List dialog box, open your Lesson 19 folder, key ***[your initials]*19-3data** as the file name, and click **Save**.

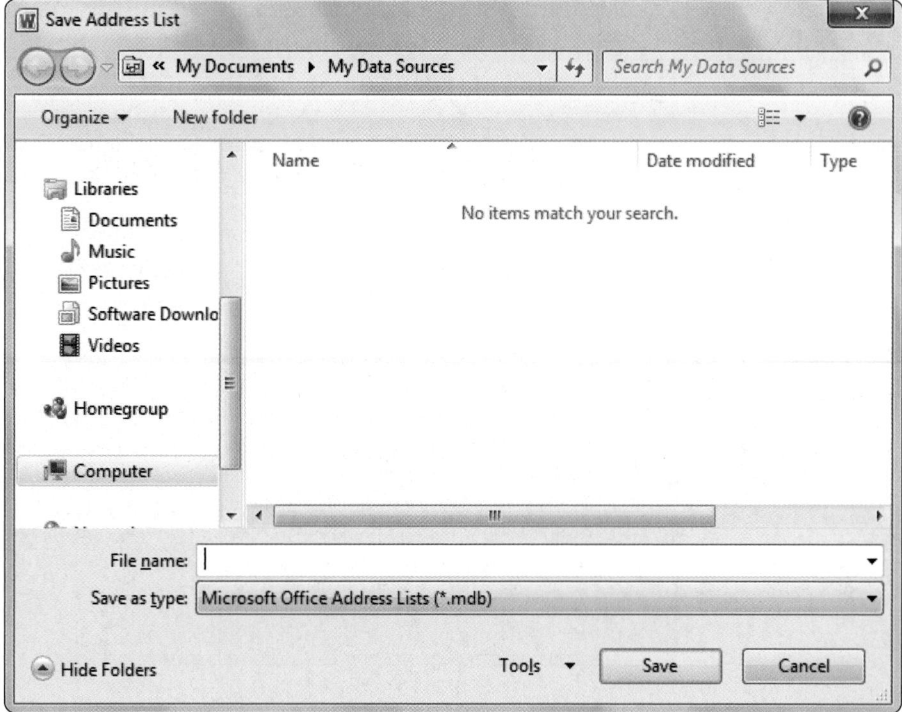

Figure 19-7
Save Address List dialog box

Inserting Merge Fields into a Main Document

Now that you have created a data source, you can complete the main document by keying text and inserting placeholders for data called *merge fields*. Merge fields appear in the main document as *field codes*, which show the field name, such as «Title». Mail merging replaces these fields with information from your data source, changing «Title» to "Mr.," for example.

When a field name such as "Last Name" has a space in its title, Word displays the merge field in the document as «Last_Name», with an underscore for the space.

Exercise 19-4 INSERT MERGE FIELDS INTO THE MAIN DOCUMENT

When you return to your main document, you are ready to key the body of the letter and add field placeholders. Word provides two mail merge fields—address block and greeting—that insert fields automatically. You can also insert individual fields.

1. Position the insertion point four lines below the date. Click the Address Block button. The Insert Address Block dialog box opens.
2. The Preview box shows the field elements for the address block: title, first and last names, company, street address, city, state, and ZIP Code. Click **OK**. The address block is inserted in the document and contains the recipient's name and address.

Figure 19-8
Insert Address Block dialog box

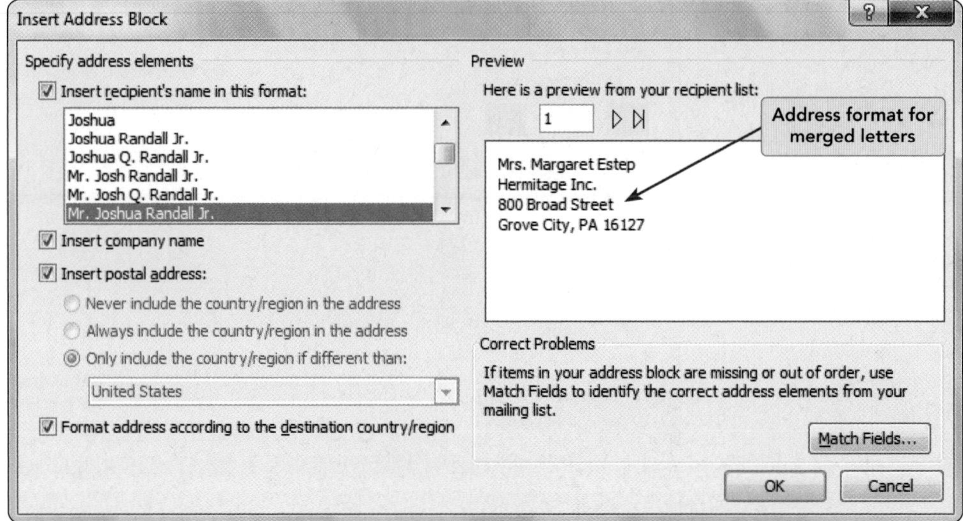

3. Position the insertion point two lines below the address block, and then click the Greeting Line button. The Insert Greeting Line dialog box opens.
4. Change the comma in the greeting line format to a colon. The Preview box shows how the greeting will appear in your letters. The greeting includes "Dear," followed by the title field, the last name, and a colon. Click **OK**.

Figure 19-9
Insert Greeting Line dialog box

Insert Greeting Line
Greeting line format:
Dear
Mr. Randall
,
:
(none)
Change to colon
Greeting line for invalid recipient names:
Dear Sir or Madam,
Preview
Here is a preview from your recipient list:
1
Dear Mrs. Estep,
Correct Problems
If items in your greeting line are missing or out of order, use Match Fields to identify the correct address elements from your mailing list.
Match Fields...
OK
Cancel

NOTE

When you point to the Insert Merge Field button, the button displays two colors. Click the lower part of the button (the darker color) to display a list of the fields in the data source. Click the upper part of the button to open the Insert Merge Field dialog box.

5. Position the insertion point two lines below the greeting line, and key **Thank you,** followed by a space.
6. Click the top half of the Insert Merge Field button, and click the "First Name" field. Click **Insert** then click **Close**. Key a comma, press Spacebar, and key the following opening paragraph:

   for agreeing to serve on the Western Pennsylvania Charity Foundation Steering Committee. We are looking forward to an exciting year, and we have high expectations for our annual fund-raising campaign.

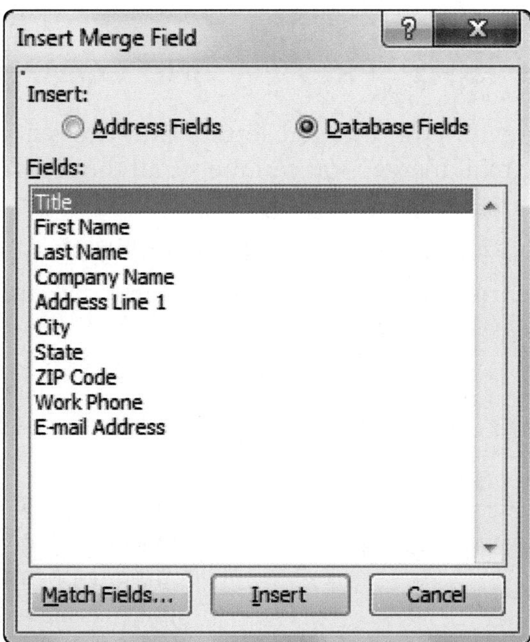

Figure 19-10
Insert Merge Field dialog box

TIP

When you insert fields in a main document, make sure to include the correct spacing and punctuation.

7. Press Enter twice to start a new paragraph.
8. Key the following closing paragraph:

   An agenda for our first planning meeting is enclosed. Please let me know if you cannot attend. Once again, thank you for your support.

9. Press Enter twice and key **Sincerely,**.
10. Press Enter four times and key **Thomas Campbell**. Key **President** on the next line. Add your reference initials, followed by an enclosure notation.

NOTE

To create the most attractive letters, *The Gregg Reference Manual* recommends adjusting margins to suit the length of a letter and positioning the date either 2 inches from the top of the page or, as in this case, 0.5 inch from the bottom of the letterhead.

11. Click the Preview Results button. The fields in the letter are replaced by the information from the first record.
12. Change the left and right margins to **1.25** inches, and change the header distance from the page to **1** inch. Add three blank lines before the date.
13. Click the Save button to save these changes to the main document.

Performing a Mail Merge

Now that you have created both the main document and the data source, you can begin the mail merge. The mail merge will create one copy of the main document customized for each record. In each copy, the merge fields will be replaced by data from one record in the data source.

The simplest way to perform the mail merge is to:

- Preview the merged letters on-screen to see how they look with the merged data.
- Complete the merge by merging directly to the printer or merging to a new document that you can save and print later.

Exercise 19-5 PREVIEW AND COMPLETE THE MERGE

After you preview the merged letters and are satisfied with the results, complete the mail merge. You can merge all the records or a certain range of records, such as records 2 through 4.

1. Locate the **Preview Results** group on the **Mailings** tab, and click the Next Record button. The fields display the information from the second record.

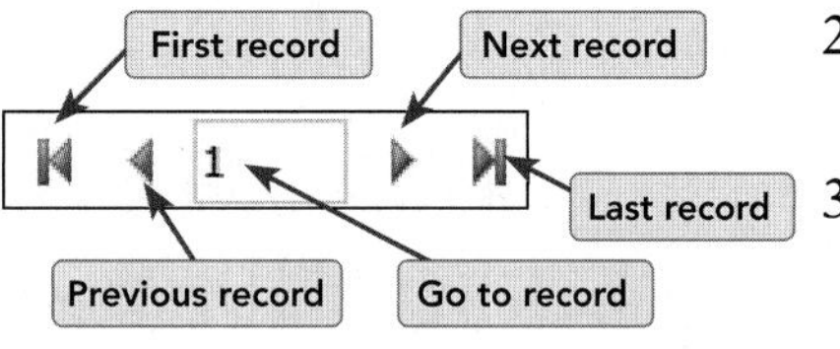

Figure 19-11 Moving in a merged document

2. Continue to click the Next Record button to review each merged letter.
3. Click the Finish & Merge button. You can choose to edit individual documents, print documents, or send e-mail messages.
4. Click **Print Documents**. The Merge to Printer dialog box displays. In the Merge to Printer dialog box, you can choose to print all merged letters or specific records.

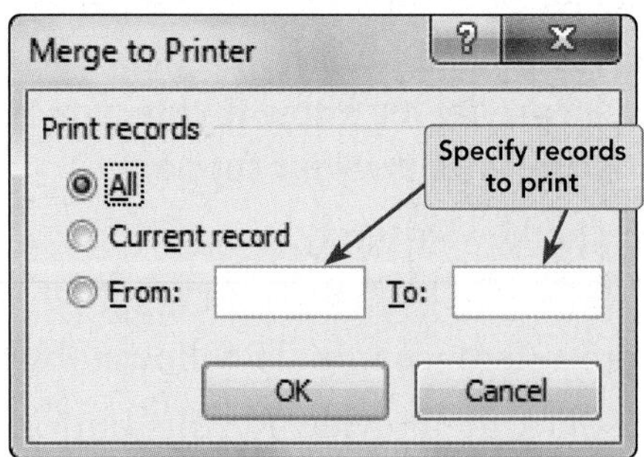

Figure 19-12 Merge to Printer dialog box

5. Key **1** in the **From** box and key **2** in the **To** box to print just the first two merged letters. Click **OK**.
6. Click **OK** in the Print dialog box. Word prints records 1 and 2 as merged letters.
7. Click the Finish & Merge button, and click **Edit Individual Documents**.
8. In the Merge to New Document dialog box, choose **All** and click **OK**. Word creates a new document, temporarily called Letters1, containing four merged letters. Scroll through the document to check the letters. Each letter appears as a separate section.

9. Save the merged document as ***[your initials]*****19-5merged** in your Lesson 19 folder.
10. Print pages 3–4 so you have a complete printout of all four letters.
11. Close the merged document and the main document, saving changes.

Using Data from Other Applications

A data source can be a different file type, such as a Word table, an Excel spreadsheet, or an Outlook contact list. When you create a data source using the Mailings tab on the Ribbon, you create a database file automatically.

Exercise 19-6 USE DATA FROM A WORD DOCUMENT

1. Open the file **Tour Names**. This is a Word table that will be used as a data source in a mail merge.

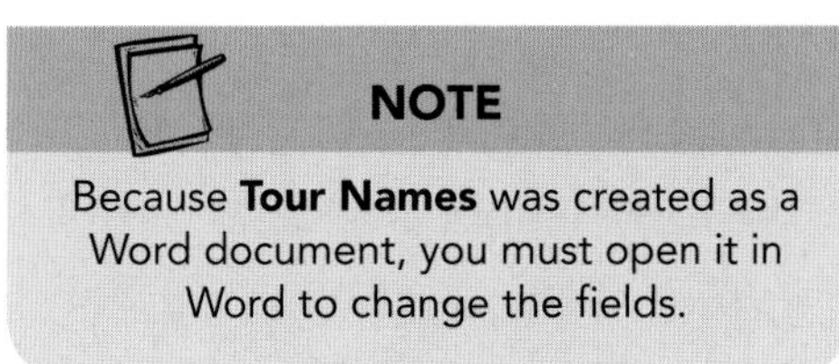

NOTE

Because **Tour Names** was created as a Word document, you must open it in Word to change the fields.

2. Insert a column on the far left of the table. In the top cell of the new column, key **Title**. This is a new field name you are adding to the data source file **Tour Names**.
3. Key **Mr.** as the title for the first record, **Mrs.** for the second record, and **Ms.** as the title for the last record. (Remember to press ↓, not Enter, when going to the next cell in the column.)

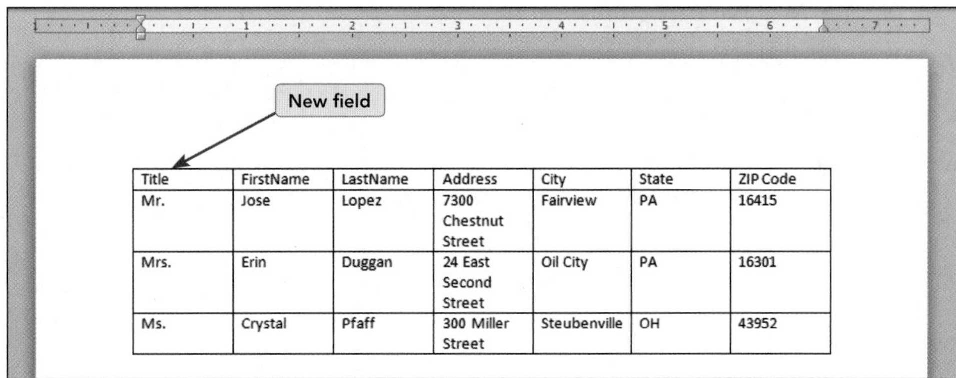

Title	FirstName	LastName	Address	City	State	ZIP Code
Mr.	Jose	Lopez	7300 Chestnut Street	Fairview	PA	16415
Mrs.	Erin	Duggan	24 East Second Street	Oil City	PA	16301
Ms.	Crystal	Pfaff	300 Miller Street	Steubenville	OH	43952

Figure 19-13 Using and editing a Word data source file

4. Save the revised data source as ***[your initials]*****19-6data** in your Lesson 19 folder. Close the document.
5. Open the file **Tour Info**. This is a document that will serve as the main document in a mail merge, but it is missing merge fields.
6. Replace “*<xx>*” with your reference initials.
7. Click the Mailings tab, and click the Start Mail Merge button. Click Letters. Save the document as ***[your initials]19*****-6main** in your Lesson 19 folder.

8. Click the Select Recipients button, and click **Use Existing List**. The Select Data Source dialog box opens.
9. Locate the directory and folder for ***[your initials]*****19-6data** file. Click **Open**. The file is now open for use with the **Tour Info** main document, but it is not visible.
10. Position the insertion point on the fourth blank line below the date. Click the Address Block button. Click **OK**.
11. Press Enter twice, and click the Greeting Line button. Change the comma (,) to a colon (:). Click **OK**.
12. Check that there is one blank line above and below the Greeting Line merge field and three blank lines between the date and the Address Block merge field.
13. Click the Preview Results button to view the first record of the mail merge.
14. Click the Finish & Merge button. Click **Edit Individual Documents** to open a new document.
15. Click **OK** to close the Merge to New Document dialog box.
16. Scroll through the document to view the three letters.
17. Save the merged document as ***[your initials]*****19-6merged** in your Lesson 19 folder. Display the Print tab, and change the **Pages per sheet** option to **4**. Click **Print**, and close the merged document.

TABLE 19-1 Mail Merge Buttons

Button	Description	Function
	Start Mail Merge	Formats a main document for a specific type of mail merge, such as letters or labels, or restores the document to a normal Word document.
	Select Recipients	Attaches an existing data source to the active document, or creates a new list. The active document becomes a mail merge main document if it is not one already.
	Edit Recipient List	Displays a dialog box where you can sort, search, filter, add, and validate mail merge recipients.
	Highlight Merge Fields	Applies background shading to mail merge fields in a main document to make them more visible.
	Address Block	Provides different address formats (including title, name, and address) to insert into a main document for a mail merge.
	Greeting Line	Provides different greeting line formats (including salutation, name, and punctuation) to insert into a main document for a mail merge.
	Insert Merge Field	Inserts merge fields from your data source or from a list of standard address fields into the main document.

continues

TABLE 19-1 Mail Merge Buttons *continued*

Button	Description	Function
	Rules	Inserts into the main document Word fields, such as Ask and Fill, to control how Word merges data.
	Match Fields	Displays a dialog box where you can match fields from a data source to fields in a main document that have different field names.
	Update Labels	Copies the field codes for one label into the rest of the labels in a mail merge main document.
	Preview Results	Displays the main document merged with information from the associated data source.
	First Record	Displays the main document merged with information from the first record in the data source, if the View Merged Data button is clicked.
	Previous Record	Displays the main document merged with information from the previous record in the data source, if the View Merged Data button is clicked.
1	Go to Record	Shows the currently merged record number. To display the main document merged with a specific record, key the record number and press Enter.
	Next Record	Displays the main document merged with information from the next record in the data source, if the View Merged Data button is clicked.
	Last Record	Displays the main document merged with information from the last record in the data source, if the View Merged Data button is clicked.
	Find Recipient	Searches the database for text contained in a specified mail merge field.
	Auto Check for Errors	Reports errors in the main document or data source that prevent merging.
	Finish and Merge	Completes the mail merge.
	Merge to Adobe PDF	Merges document to PDF files.

Exercise 19-7 USE AN EXCEL SPREADSHEET AS A DATA SOURCE

1. With ***[your initials]*****19-6main** still open, click the Select Recipients button, and click **Use Existing List**. The Select Data Source dialog box opens.
2. Locate the folder for lesson 19 student data files, and open the Excel file **Group Names**. This is an Excel workbook that contains fields necessary for use with **Tour Info**. Click **Open**.

3. In the Select Table dialog box, click **OK** to use data from the first spreadsheet in the Excel workbook. The file is now open for use with **Tour Info**.
4. Click the Edit Recipient List button. The Mail Merge Recipients dialog box displays, and the data from the Excel spreadsheet appears in the data source.
5. Locate the **Data Source** section, and click **Group Names.xlsx** to activate the file name. Click **Edit** to open the Edit Data Source dialog box. Click **New Entry** to add a name to the data source.
6. Key the following information in the new record.

Title	Mr.
FirstName	Brent
LastName	Bohmueller
Address	560 Clark Street
City	Hollidaysburg
State	PA
ZIP Code	16648

NOTE

The field names in this letter match the field names in the data source. If you tried to merge this main document with a data source that had different field names, you would get errors. You could correct these errors through a matching fields process, but it is best to match a main document with the correct data source. Naming fields consistently is also a good idea.

7. Click **OK** to close the Edit Data Source dialog box, and click **Yes** to update the recipient list. Click **OK** to close the Mail Merge Recipients dialog box.
8. Click the Finish & Merge button. Click **Edit Individual Documents**, and click **OK** to merge all records.
9. Preview the merged document.
10. Save the merged document as ***[your initials]* 19-7merged** in your Lesson 19 folder. Submit and close the document.
11. Close the ***[your initials]*19-6main** document and save the changes.

Editing an Existing Main Document

After you have created a main document, you can edit and reuse it. In the main document, you might want to change the text or add a new field from the data source. When you open a main document that is associated with a data source, the following dialog box may appear. Click Yes to continue. If the associated data source is not located, it may be necessary to browse to locate the file.

Figure 19-14
Alert message

Microsoft Word

Opening this document will run the following SQL command:

SELECT * FROM \\DELL2006\Public\Documents\2010 Microsoft Word\Student Data Files\Lesson 19\Tour Names - 2.docx WHERE ((LastName = 'Steele') AND (ZIP_Code > 15500)) ORDER BY LastName, FirstName

Data from your database will be placed in the document. Do you want to continue?

Show Help >>

Yes No Help

Exercise 19-8 EDIT AN EXISTING MAIN DOCUMENT

1. Reopen *[your initials]***19-6main**.
2. Click Yes to continue.
3. Position the insertion point in the first paragraph after the first sentence (after "tours.").
4. Key the following sentence.

   The factory is located on Monroe Street in Grove City, just two blocks from the retail candy store on Main Street.
5. Save the document as *[your initials]***19-8main** in your Lesson 19 folder. Submit and close the document.

NOTE

If you discover an error in the merged document during a preview of the completed merge, edit the main document so that the changes will appear in all the merged documents.

Sorting and Filtering a Data Source

At times you might want to sort your data source before merging with your main document. You can also filter the data so that only records with certain characteristics are merged.

Exercise 19-9 SORT A DATA SOURCE

1. Open **Tour Info**. Start a mail merge for letters.
2. Click the Select Recipients button, and click Use Existing List. Locate and open the file **Tour Names - 2**.
3. Insert the Address Block and Greeting Line fields after the date. Remember to change the comma to a colon in the Insert Greeting Line dialog box. Verify spacing between the parts of the letter.
4. Click the Edit Recipient List button.
5. Click the LastName column heading (not the down arrow to the left of the column heading) to sort the list alphabetically by last name. When you click the field name once, the names are sorted in alphabetical order. If you click the field name a second time, the names are sorted in reverse order.
6. Click the Sort link to open the Query Options dialog box.
7. In the Then by drop-down list, choose FirstName. Notice that the default order is Ascending.
8. Click OK. The records are sorted by last name and then by first name.

NOTE

You can click the down arrow next to any of the field names and click (Advanced) to access the Query Options dialog box. Also, you can click the down arrow next to a field name and choose one of the fields listed. This filters the data based on the field you choose.

Exercise 19-10 FILTER A DATA SOURCE

1. Click the Filter link to open the Query Options dialog box with the Filter Records tab selected.
2. In the first Field text box, choose LastName from the drop-down list.

3. Make sure the **Comparison** drop-down list box is set to **Equal to**.
4. In the **Compare to** text box, key **Steele**.
5. In the text box below and to the left of **LastName**, choose **And** from the drop-down list if it is not selected. (See Figure 19-15.)
6. In the **Field** text box to the right of **And**, choose **ZIP_Code** from the drop-down list.
7. In the **Comparison** text box, choose **Greater than**.
8. In the **Compare to** text box, key **15500**.

Figure 19-15
Filtering data by using comparisons

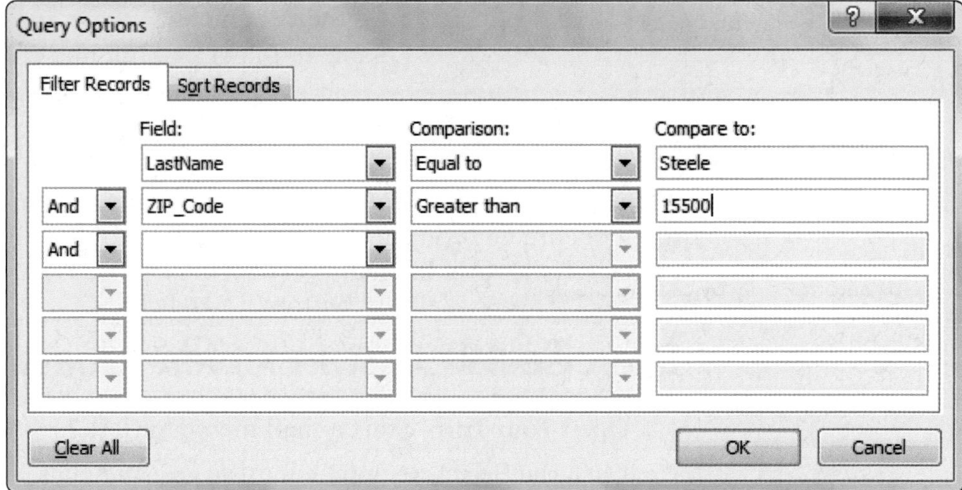

9. Click **OK** to filter the data—Word looks for records with the last name "Steele" and a postal code greater than "15500" and finds one record. Click **OK** again to accept the filtered data.
10. Add your reference initials to the letter, and change "Enclosure" to plural (more than one item will accompany the letter).
11. Save the document as ***[your initials]*****19-10main** in your Lesson 19 folder.
12. Click the Finish & Merge button. Click **Edit Individual Documents**, and click **OK** to merge to a new document. The record for "Raymond Steele" is merged with the main document to create a new document.
13. Save the document as ***[your initials]*****19-10merged** in your Lesson 19 folder.
14. Submit the letter and close all open documents, saving changes if prompted.

Creating Lists and Mailing Labels

You can merge data from a data source to create a list or a directory. You can also create mailing labels from a merge document to address envelopes and packages. Word enables you to designate the style of the label and insert the merge fields for the addresses.

Exercise 19-11 CREATE A LIST FROM A DATA SOURCE

To create a list from a data source, you use the Mailings tab on the Ribbon.

1. Start a blank document, and click the Mailings tab on the Ribbon.
2. Click the Start Mail Merge button.
3. Choose Directory from the list.
4. Click the Select Recipients button, and click Use Existing List. Locate and open **Tour Names - 2** as a data source. Save the document as ***[your initials]*19-11main** in your Lesson 19 folder.
5. Open the Mail Merge Recipients dialog box by clicking the Edit Recipient List, and sort the data source alphabetically by last name by clicking the column heading LastName. Click OK.

NOTE

If you click the lower part of the Insert Merge Field button, you can insert the fields automatically by clicking the field name. Click the upper part of the Insert Merge Field button to open the Insert Merge Field dialog box.

NOTE

You must insert a paragraph mark after the ZIP_Code field or the last field in the paragraph. Otherwise, each record will be listed one after the other in one paragraph.

6. Click the lower half of the Insert Merge Field button, and choose LastName from the list of fields. The field is inserted in the document.
7. Press Tab, and click the lower half of the Insert Merge field button, and choose ZIP_Code from the list.
8. Set a left tab at the 1.5-inch mark on the ruler. Insert a new paragraph mark after the ZIP_Code field.
9. Click the Finish & Merge button, click Edit Individual Documents, and click OK to allow all the records to be merged.
10. Save the merged list as ***[your initials]*19-11merged** in your Lesson 19 folder and submit it.
11. Close only the merged document. Save the document ***[your initials]*19-11main**.

Exercise 19-12 CREATE A CATALOG-TYPE MAIN DOCUMENT

Not only can you merge data to create a list, but you can also create more extensive catalog-type documents or directories.

1. With your insertion point directly after the «LastName» field, click the lower part of the Insert Merge Field button.
2. Choose FirstName from the list.
3. Insert the field State after the «FirstName» field by clicking the lower part of the Insert Merge Field button.

Exercise 19-13 ADD FORMATTING TO A CATALOG-TYPE MAIN DOCUMENT

1. Insert tab characters before each of the fields except the first field.
2. Select the paragraph containing the fields, clear the 1.5-inch tab, and set 1.75-inch, 3.75-inch, and 5.0-inch left tabs.
3. Select the «LastName» field and apply bold formatting.
4. Apply numbering to the paragraph containing the fields by clicking the Numbering button on the Home tab.
5. Apply double-line spacing to the paragraph containing the fields, and change the spacing after to 0 points.
6. Set a 2-inch top margin, and apply a single-line page border to the document.
7. Save the document as ***[your initials]*****19-13main** in your Lesson 19 folder.
8. Click the Finish & Merge button on the Mailings tab, click Edit Individual Documents, and click OK to allow all the records to be merged.
9. Key a title at the top of the catalog directory: **Catalog Directory of Customer Requests**. Format it as 14-point bold, with small caps and centered.
10. Change the spacing after the title to 12 points.
11. Save the merged catalog directory as ***[your initials]*****19-13merged** in your Lesson 19 folder and submit it.
12. Close all open documents, saving changes if prompted.

Exercise 19-14 CREATE MAILING LABELS

Creating labels follows the same process as creating form letters. Identify the main document, and select recipients.

The process of creating mailing labels requires that you:

- Create a mailing label main document.
- Choose a data source.
- Specify label size and type.
- Insert merge fields.
- Merge the main document and the data source.

1. Start a blank document.
2. Click the Mailings tab.
3. Click the Start Mail Merge button, and click Labels. The Label Options dialog box displays.
4. Select Avery US Letter in the Label vendors box.
5. Scroll the Product number list and choose 5160. Click OK. The document is now formatted for labels.

TIP

To create envelopes instead of labels, choose Envelopes as the document type and then follow the mail merge steps.

6. Click the Select Recipients button, and click Use Existing List.
7. In the Select Data Source dialog box, locate and open **Tour Names - 2**. Word adds the merge field «Next Record» to your labels.
8. Click the Edit Recipient List button, and display the last column. Click the column heading, ZIP_Code. The records are now sorted by ZIP Code.
9. Click OK.
10. Click the Address Block button, and click OK. Word adds the «Address Block» field to the first label.

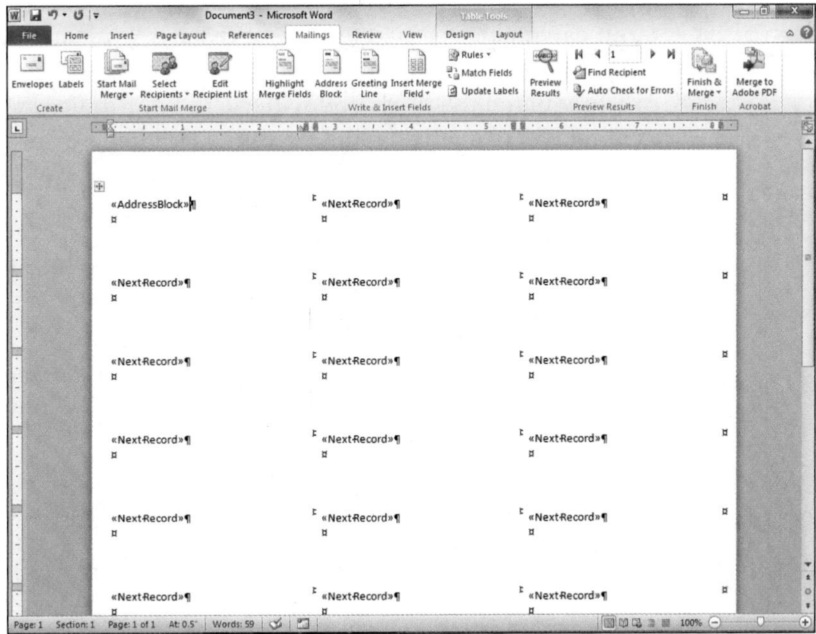

Figure 19-16 Adding the Address Block field

11. Click the Update Labels button. Word automatically adds the «Address Block» field to each label.
12. Click the Preview Results button. Word merges the data from **Tour Name - 2** with your label document. Show table gridlines by clicking the Table Tools Layout tab and clicking the View Gridlines button if they do not already appear.
13. Click the Mailings tab. Click the Finish & Merge button, and click Edit Individual Documents. Click OK to merge to a new document.
14. Save the merged labels as ***[your initials]*19-14labels** in your Lesson 19 folder.
15. Prepare your printer with the correct label sheet or a blank sheet of paper, and print the document. (Check with your instructor for special instructions for printing labels.)
16. Close and save the document. Do not save the main document.

Lesson 19 Summary

- Mail merging combines a main document (such as a form letter) with a data source (such as a list of names and addresses) to produce individualized documents. The main document contains merge fields. The data source is a table—column headings are field names and rows are records. Each cell of a record is a field that appears in the matching merge field of the main document.
- The main document is a Word document; the data source can be a Word table, an Excel spreadsheet, an Access table, or an Outlook contact list.
- Use the Mailings tab to create mail merge documents.
- You can create a new data source by keying records into a data form called the New Address List dialog box. You can customize the fields in this dialog box to match the fields you will use in your main document. A data source created by using the New Address List dialog box produces a database file.
- You insert merge fields in a main document individually or as field blocks, such as Word's built-in Address block.
- You can preview the data merged into your main document before performing the merge. Complete the merge by merging directly to a printer (or merging to e-mail addresses) or to a new document.
- At any point before or after merging, you can edit mail merge documents. Edit the main document or the data source file (if it is a Word table) as you would any Word document.
- You can sort and filter data source files to produce only the merged files you want. Use more than one field for advanced sorting capability.
- You can merge data from a data source to create a list or a catalog-type document or directory.
- You can create mail merge envelopes or mailing labels. Choose envelopes or labels as the main document type, choose or create a data source, choose envelope or label options, insert merge fields into the main document, and then perform the merge.

LESSON 19		Command Summary	
Feature	**Button**	**Command**	**Keyboard**
Create or select data source		Mailings tab, Start Mail Merge group	
Identify main document		Mailings tab, Start Mail Merge group	
Insert merge fields		Mailings tab, Write & Insert Fields group	
Merge data		Mailings tab, Finish group	
Preview merge		Mailings tab, Preview Results group	
Sort or filter data source		Mailings tab, Start Mail Merge group	

Concepts Review

True/False Questions

Each of the following statements is either true or false. Indicate your choice by circling T or F.

T F 1. Field names are the column headings in a data source table.

T F 2. A field contains several pieces of unrelated information.

T F 3. Mail merging inserts the information from the merged document into copies of the data source.

T F 4. Each record in a data source table must contain the same number of fields.

T F 5. A row in a data source table is called a record.

T F 6. You cannot edit an existing main document.

T F 7. When you create a data source by using the Mailings tab, you create a database.

T F 8. Data source files can only be Word documents.

Short Answer Questions

Write the correct answer in the space provided.

1. What serves as a placeholder in the main document for information found in the data source?

____

2. List an example of a document type for a mail merge main document.

____

3. What are the two major documents used in mail merging?

____

4. What does a record contain?

____

5. Which button in the New Address List dialog box is used to add or delete field name columns in the New Address List dialog box?

____

6. What is the procedure for sorting a list of names in the New Address List dialog box?

____

7. What is the mail merge field called that contains a salutation, a name, and punctuation for letters?

---

8. Which button on the Mailings tab do you click to create a new document containing all merged letters?

Critical Thinking

Answer these questions on a separate page. There are no right or wrong answers. Support your answers with examples from your own experience, if possible.

1. Businesses use a mail merge process to send personalized letters for fundraising or sales promotions. For a business, what are the advantages and disadvantages of sending personalized mail of this type?
2. Have you or a member of your family ever received a personalized mailing from a business? Describe the reaction you had to receiving it.

Skills Review

Exercise 19-15

Create a main document and a data source, insert merge fields, and perform a mail merge.

1. Create a memo main document by following these steps:
   a. Create a new blank document, and change the top margin to 2 inches, and set a 1-inch left tab. Click the No Spacing button [AaBbCcDc ¶ No Spaci...] in the Styles group of the Home tab to change line spacing to single and to change the spacing after to 0 points.
   b. Click the **Mailings** tab.
   c. Click the Start Mail Merge button, and choose **Letters**.
2. Key the memo heading shown in Figure 19-17. Press Enter after keying the subject line.

Figure 19-17

```
MEMO TO:
FROM:      Lynn Tanguay
DATE:      [Current Date]
SUBJECT:   Visitation Schedule
```

3. Create a data source by following these steps:
   a. Click the Select Recipients button.
   b. Click Type New List.
   c. Click Customize Columns.
   d. With the first field name selected (Title), click Delete and click Yes to verify the deletion.
   e. Select the third field name (Company Name), click Rename, and key **Quarter**. Click OK.
   f. Delete the following fields: Address Line 1, Address Line 2, City, ZIP Code, Country or Region, Home Phone, Work Phone, and E-mail Address.
   g. Click to select the State field, and click Move Up to place the State field above the Quarter field.
   h. Click OK.
   i. Key the data shown in Figure 19-18.

Figure 19-18

FirstName	LastName	State	Quarter
Elizabeth	Veritz	Pennsylvania	First
Jackson	Sigmon	Ohio	Second
Patrick	Donaldson	Ohio	Second
Vince	Teague	West Virginia	Third

   j. Click OK to save the data source and to return to the main document.
4. Save the data source as ***[your initials]*****19-15data** in your Lesson 19 folder.
5. Key the body of the memo as shown in Figure 19-19. Use correct spacing after the subject line and between paragraphs. Insert merge fields in place of field names by clicking the lower half of the Insert Merge Field button. Include spaces around merge fields where needed.

Figure 19-19

The quarterly visitation schedule for the retail stores has been completed. Your store is scheduled for a visit during the second week of the «quarter» quarter. Our plan is to visit all stores in Pennsylvania during the first quarter, Ohio stores in the second quarter, and West Virginia stores in the third quarter.

Please let me know if you are aware of any conflicts with this schedule.

6. Add your reference initials to the end of the document.

7. After the heading "MEMO TO:" insert the FirstName and the LastName merge fields by following these steps:
   a. Position the insertion point. Click the lower half of the Insert Merge Field button, and click **First_Name**.
   b. Press Spacebar, and click the Insert Merge field button, and click **Last_Name**.
8. Save the main document as ***[your initials]*19-15main** in your Lesson 19 folder.
9. Preview the merged data by following these steps:
   a. Click the Preview Results button.
   b. Click the Next Record button to see the next record.
   c. Make any corrections to the main document that might be needed, and save the document.
10. Complete the merge by following these steps:
   a. Click the Finish & Merge button.
   b. Click **Edit Individual Documents** to merge the data to a new document.
   c. In the Merge to New Document dialog box, choose **All** and click **OK**.
11. Save the merged document as ***[your initials]*19-15merged** in your Lesson 19 folder and print 4 pages per sheet.
12. Close all open documents, saving changes if prompted.

Exercise 19-16

Use and edit a data source from Word, edit an existing main document, sort and filter data, and merge the documents.

1. Edit an existing Word data source and add a new record by following these steps:
   a. Open the file **Contributors**. This is a Word table that will be used as a data source.
   b. Change the abbreviation "Rd." to **Road**, "St." to **Street**, and "Dr." to **Drive**.
   c. Change the "City" of Ms. Merita Loy-Jones to **Mercer**.
   d. Insert a new row at the bottom of the table.
   e. Key the data shown in Figure 19-20.

Figure 19-20

Title:	Ms.
FirstName:	Linda
LastName:	Del-Reo
Address:	12 East Main Street
City:	Harrisville
State:	PA
PostalCode:	16038

2. Add a new field by following these steps:
   a. Insert a new column before the "Address" column. Key the column heading **Company** at the top of the new column.
   b. Key the company names shown in Figure 19-21 directly into the table.

Figure 19-21

LastName	Company
Little	Liberty Cable Works
Loy-Jones	Millcreek Consultants
Abadini	Oakwood Planning Association
Del-Reo	B & G Enterprise

3. Center the table horizontally on the page. Save the file as ***[your initials]*****19-16data** in your Lesson 19 folder. Submit and close the document.
4. Open the file **Gala**.
5. Insert the date field at the top of the document, with three blank lines below it. Set a 2-inch top margin and 1.5-inch left and right margins.
6. Click the **Mailings** tab, and click the Start Mail Merge button, and click **Letters**.
7. Open an existing data source by following these steps:
   a. Click the Select Recipients button, and click **Use Existing List**.
   b. Locate and choose ***[your initials]*****19-16data** as the data source file.
8. Modify the main document by following these steps:
   a. Position the insertion point at the beginning of the first paragraph, and click the Address Block button. Click **OK**, and press Enter two times.
   b. Position the insertion point at the beginning of the first paragraph, click the Greeting Line button, and change the punctuation from a comma to a colon. Click **OK**. Press Enter two times.
   c. Add your reference initials to the main document, and add an enclosure notation.
9. Save the document as ***[your initials]*****19-16main** in your Lesson 19 folder.
10. Sort and filter data by following these steps:
    a. Click the Mailings tab, and click the Edit Recipient List button.
    b. Click the **LastName** column heading to sort by last name.
    c. Click the down arrow to the right of **LastName** and choose **(Advanced)**.
    d. Click the **Sort Records** tab and click **Descending**. Make sure the **Then by** text box is empty. Click **OK**.
    e. Click the **Filter** link at the bottom of the dialog box.
    f. In the first **Field** text box, choose **City** from the drop-down list.
    g. In the **Comparison** text box, choose **Equal to** if it is not selected.
    h. In the **Compare to** text box, key **Grove City**.
    i. In the text box below and to the left of the **City** field, choose **Or** from the drop-down list.

j. In the **Field** text box next to **Or**, choose **Zip_Code** from the drop-down list.

k. In the **Comparison** text box, choose **Less than**.

l. In the **Compare to** text box, key **16100**.

m. Click **OK** twice.

11. Preview and complete the merge by following these steps:

a. Click the Preview Results button to see the data merged with the main document.

b. Click the button again to see the fields.

c. Click the Finish & Merge button, and click **Edit Individual Documents**.

d. With **All** selected, click **OK** to merge the record.

12. Save the merged document as ***[your initials]*19-16merged** in your Lesson 19 folder.

13. Submit the letter and close all open documents, saving changes if prompted.

Exercise 19-17

Create and format a directory-type main document.

1. Create a catalog-type main document by following these steps:

a. Start a blank document.

b. Click the Start Mail Merge button.

c. Choose **Directory** from the list.

d. Locate and select the data file **Managers** as a data source.

e. Click the Edit Recipient List button, and click the **LastName** field to sort alphabetically. Click **OK**.

f. Click the lower half of the Insert Merge Field button, choose **LastName**.

g. Choose **FirstName**.

h. Choose **City**.

i. Press Enter to insert a blank paragraph mark after the last field.

2. Format the document by following these steps:

a. Set 2.75-inch and 5-inch left tabs in the fields line.

b. Insert a tab before the «FirstName» and «City» fields.

c. Apply numbering to the field paragraph.

d. Apply 1.5-line spacing to the field paragraph.

e. Format the «City» field using small caps.

3. Save the document as ***[your initials]*19-17main** in your Lesson 19 folder.

4. Click the Finish & Merge button, click **Edit Individual Documents**, and allow all the records to be merged.

5. Key a title at the top of the catalog directory: **Pennsylvania Store Managers**. Format the title using 14-point bold, with small caps and centered. Change the spacing after to 18 points.
6. Press Enter after the title, and change to left alignment, 12 points spacing after. Change the font size to 12 points. Key the following column headings:

   Last Name
   First Name
   Location
7. Set three left tabs to position the column headings above the columns.
8. Set a 1.5-inch top margin.
9. Save the merged catalog directory as ***[your initials]*19-17merged** in your Lesson 19 folder and submit it.
10. Close all open documents, saving changes if prompted.

Exercise 19-18

Create labels.

1. Create a main document for labels that will be used as a name tag by following these steps:
   a. Start a new document.
   b. Start the mail merge by clicking the **Mailings** tab and choosing **Labels** as the starting document.
   c. Choose **Avery US letter** from the **Label vendors** drop-down box.
   d. Choose **5383 - Name Tag Kit** from the **Product number** drop-down list, and click **OK**.
   e. Click the **Table Tools Layout** tab, and click the View Gridlines button to display label gridlines.
2. Locate and select the data source **Managers**.
3. Insert merge fields for a name tag by following these steps:
   a. Scroll in the main document to the top left label, and click to position the insertion point.
   b. Insert the fields FirstName and LastName. (Be sure to place a space between the fields.)
   c. Click the Update Labels button.
4. Preview the merge.
5. Select the table, and format the text as 24-point bold, with small caps. Use the table align option to center the text vertically and horizontally in the cell. Apply the **All Borders** option from the Borders drop-down list.
6. Complete the merge by merging all records to a new document.
7. Save the merged document as ***[your initials]*19-18merged** in your Lesson 19 folder.
8. Submit the document. Close all open documents without saving.

Lesson Applications

Exercise 19-19

Create a main document and a data source, and merge the documents.

1. Create a new form letter main document with a 2-inch top margin. Change the left and right margins to 1.25 inches.
2. Create a data source with the following field names: **SalesRep**, **Date**, **Contact**, **Hotel**, and **Comment**.
3. Key the two records shown in Figure 19-22. In the "Date" row, key today's date for both records.

Figure 19-22

Field name	**Record 1**	**Record 2**
SalesRep	Doris Simms	Korey Walters
Date	*[Current date]*	*[Current date]*
Contact	Ethel Lewis	Mark Hunter
Hotel	Plaza Hotel	Premium Hotels
Comment	Dark chocolate sales are increasing.	Seasonal chocolates are very popular.

4. Save the data source as ***[your initials]*19-19data** in your Lesson 19 folder.
5. Key the following heading in the main document followed by three blank lines:

   Campbell's Confections
   25 Main Street
   Grove City, PA 16127
6. Format the heading as 14-point bold, centered, small caps, and 6 points spacing after the last line. Add a 1-point shadow paragraph border and light gray shading to all lines of the heading.
7. Key **CALL REPORT** as uppercase, bold, and centered below the document heading.
8. Change the paragraph spacing for "CALL REPORT" to 18 points spacing before and 18 points spacing after.
9. Position the insertion point at the paragraph mark below "Call Report," and set a 2.25-inch hanging indent. Change the alignment to left alignment. Turn off bold formatting.
10. Key the text, press Tab, and insert the merge field codes shown in Figure 19-23. Apply small caps to the headings on the left margin. The merge field codes should align at the 2.25-inch indent.

Figure 19-23

Sales Representative:	«SalesRep»
Date of Contact:	«Date»
Name of Contact:	«Contact»
Hotel:	«Hotel»
Comment:	«Comment»

11. Select the text below "CALL REPORT," and apply 12 points spacing after and 0 points spacing before.
12. Save the main document as ***[your initials]*****19-19main** in your Lesson 19 folder.
13. Add a new entry to the data source by clicking the Edit Recipient List button. In the Mail Merge Recipients dialog box, locate Data Source in the lower left corner, and click to select the data source for Exercise 19-19. Click the Edit button, and key the following information. Update the recipient list when prompted.

Sales Representative:	Steven Godfrey
Date of Contact:	*[Current Date]*
Name of Contact:	Mary Jane Daniels
Hotel:	Harmony Ridge Hotel
Comment:	Most popular selections are Melt-a-ways and Caramel pecanettes.

14. Preview the merged data. Correct the main document and data source, if necessary, and save any changes.
15. Complete the merge by merging all records to a new document.
16. Save the new document as ***[your initials]*****19-19merged** in your Lesson 19 folder.
17. Print 4 pages per sheet. Close all open documents, saving changes if prompted.

Exercise 19-20

Create a directory-type document.

1. Create a new document, and change the top margin to 1.5 inches. Change the left and right margins to 2 inches.
2. Click the Mailings tab, and start a mail merge by choosing Directory as the main document type.
3. Locate and open the file **Directory - 3** as the data source.
4. Sort the data source alphabetically by department.

5. Set left tabs at 2 inches and 4 inches. Insert the following fields in the document: **Name**, **Department**, and **Extension**. Place a tab character between the fields, and press Enter at the end of the line. (The Extension field code may wrap to the next line.)
6. Save the document as ***[your initials]*19-20main** in your Lesson 19 folder and submit it.
7. Finish the merge by merging to a new document and selecting all records.
8. Key the title **Corporate Telephone Extensions by Department** at the top of the document. Apply 14-point bold, with small caps and center alignment. Change the spacing after to 18 points. Add column headings to the document, and align the headings using tabs. Apply 12-point bold, small caps, and 12 points spacing after. Select the text below the title, and change the line spacing to 1.5 lines, and change the spacing after to 0 points.
9. Save the document as ***[your initials]*19-20merged** in your Lesson 19 folder. Submit the directory.
10. Close all documents, saving any changes.

Exercise 19-21

Edit existing mail merge documents, filter data, and perform a mail merge.

1. Open the file **Invoice**.
2. Format the first six lines (the heading) as bold and centered. Change the spacing after to 4 points, and verify that the line spacing is single. Under the heading, change the word "Invoice" to 14-point uppercase and centered with 18 points spacing before and after.
3. Edit the rest of the document as follows:
   - Replace each colon (:) with a tab character.
   - Convert the paragraphs from "Date" to "Total Due" (including the tabs) into a two-column table by selecting the text and clicking the Table button on the Insert tab.
   - Format the first column to be 1.75 inches wide and the second column 2.5 inches wide.
   - Change the row height for all rows to at least 0.4 inch.
   - Center the table horizontally on the page, and center the cell contents vertically.
   - Apply bold and small caps formatting to the first column.
   - Apply 1-point gridlines inside the table and a 3-point double-line (one thick, one thin) outside border to the table.
   - In the first row, second column, insert the date as an automatically updating field, using the December 25, 20—, format.
4. Save the document as ***[your initials]*19-21main** in your Lesson 19 folder.

5. Open the file **Accounts**. This file will be the data source for the main document. Edit the table as shown in Figure 19-24. Change the page orientation to landscape to make space for the extra columns created by reorganizing the data in the Address2 field. (Hint: To avoid rekeying data, create the new columns and drag and drop data to the new cells).

Figure 19-24

AcctNo	InvNo	Name	Address1	Address2	Total
2037L	797411	Nicole R. Sanchez	798 Armden Drive	Manchester, OH 45144	$598~~.00~~
2943L	1856429	Emery Ellis	2720 Summer ~~Dr.~~ Street	Chillicothe, OH 45601	$875~~.00~~
1243S	617831	Sara O'Neill	83 Morris Boulevard	Sunbury, OH 43074	$458~~.00~~

Add two columns to the table. Separate the Address2 column information into three columns—City, State, and ZIP_Code. Change the column headings.

6. Use the AutoFit Contents option to set the width of the columns.
7. Save the data source as ***[your initials]*19-21data** in your Lesson 19 folder and submit it. Close the document.
8. Switch to your main document, and choose ***[your initials]*19-21data** as its data source.
9. Edit the main document to insert the appropriate merge fields from the data document into the second column of the table. Use the Address1 field code for the Street label in the first column.

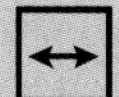

REVIEW

You do not have to use the Query Options dialog box to filter the data. You can simply choose the city name from the list of fields under "City."

10. Save changes to the main document and submit it.
11. Filter the data source to define "Sunbury" as the city.
12. Merge to create a new document. Save the new document as ***[your initials]*19-21merged** in your Lesson 19 folder and submit it.
13. Close all open documents, saving changes.

Exercise 19-22 ◆ Challenge Yourself

Use an Excel spreadsheet as a data source, sort the data, create and edit the main document, merge the documents, and create mailing labels.

1. Open the file **Campaign**. This file will be the main document of a mail merge.
2. Use the Excel file **Campaign Data** (Sheet1$) as the data source.
3. Create a two-level sort of the recipients by last name and then by first name.

4. Make the following changes to the main document to format it as a letter:
   - Set a 2-inch top margin.
   - Insert the date as an updating field, using the correct date format.
   - Insert the address block.
   - Insert the greeting line. Make sure to change the greeting line punctuation to a colon.
   - Insert your reference initials.
5. In the last sentence of the first paragraph, edit the text at the beginning of the sentence as follows: Insert the SalesRep merge field at the beginning of the sentence followed by a comma. Change "One of our" to "one of our."
6. Save the main document as ***[your initials]*19-22main** in your Lesson 19 folder.
7. Preview the merged data; then merge to a new document.
8. Save the new document as ***[your initials]*19-22merged** in your Lesson 19 folder, and print 4 pages per sheet.
9. Close the merged document and main document, saving changes.
10. Create mailing labels. Use the 5160 product number and the **Campaign Data** data source you used earlier for this exercise. Use the Address Block field in the labels.
11. Merge the labels to a new document. Format the label text as 14-point Arial Narrow bold.
12. Save the labels as ***[your initials]*19-22labels** in your Lesson 19 folder.
13. Submit the labels and close the file. Close the main label document without saving.

On Your Own

In these exercises you work on your own, as you would in a real-life business environment. Use the skills you've learned to accomplish the task—and be creative.

Exercise 19-23

Create a form letter for Campbell's Confections. The purpose of the letter is to notify customers of a past due balance and to request payment. Create a data source containing six records including address information, account number, account balance, and the number of days overdue. Include at least three merge fields in the body of the form letter. Save the main document and the data source with appropriate file names. Merge the documents to a new file called ***[your initials]*19-23merged** and submit it.

Exercise 19-24

Create a Word table to be identified as a data source that contains 10 records. Include first name, last name, street address, city, state, ZIP Code, telephone number, cell number, and e-mail address for each contact. Create name tag labels that contain just the first and last name, formatted attractively. Save the merged labels as ***[your initials]*19-24** and submit it.

Exercise 19-25

Use Help to research the following mail merge topics: Highlight Merge Fields, Match Fields, Find Recipient, Auto Check for Errors, and Merge to Adobe PDF. Create a form letter main document, and include a paragraph describing each of the mail merge features you researched. Create a data source to include five records and the following fields: Title, First Name, Last Name, Street, City, State, and Zip Code. E-mail and telephone numbers are optional. Save the main document and the data source with appropriate file names. Merge the documents to a new file called ***[your initials]*19-25** and submit it.

Lesson 20
Fields and Forms

OBJECTIVES *After completing this lesson, you will be able to:*

1. Insert fields.
2. View, edit, and update field codes.
3. Understand bookmarks.
4. Create a template to use as a form.
5. Insert content controls.
6. Protect and save a form.
7. Use and edit a form.

Estimated Time: 1 hour

A *field* is a placeholder for information that can change in a document. You can insert most fields into a document by using familiar Ribbon commands and buttons, such as inserting a page number in a header or footer or inserting a date in a letter. Other examples of fields that are automatically inserted are those for creating tables of contents and indexes.

This lesson explains how to insert fields and how to modify those fields by adding options to change the way the fields are displayed. You will also learn how to create electronic forms, which can be used over and over. Electronic forms are based on a custom template.

Inserting Fields

You can use many different types of fields in a Word document. Fields are used to insert basic document information, such as a date, page number, document file name, or document author. Special fields can be used with mail merge operations or content controls to gather information on an electronic form. Fields are inserted automatically through built-in commands or inserted manually.

When you choose a field, the *field code syntax* is displayed in the Field dialog box along with a text box that displays the actual characters in the field and a description of the selected field's purpose. The field code's syntax is shown in a format similar to a diagram, indicating optional and required information and the required order for inserting that information.

Exercise 20-1 SET FIELD CODE VIEW OPTIONS

Field codes might be displayed differently on different computers, depending on the selected options. To begin this lesson, you verify the display options for field codes.

1. Open the file **Promotion**.
2. Open the Word Options dialog box, click Advanced, and display the Show document content group.
3. Locate the option Show field codes instead of their values, and make sure the check box is clear. This will keep the codes from displaying in your document—the field results will show instead.
4. Locate the Field shading option. Open the Field shading: list box and choose Always. This will highlight fields with light gray shading. The shading will display on your screen but will not print.

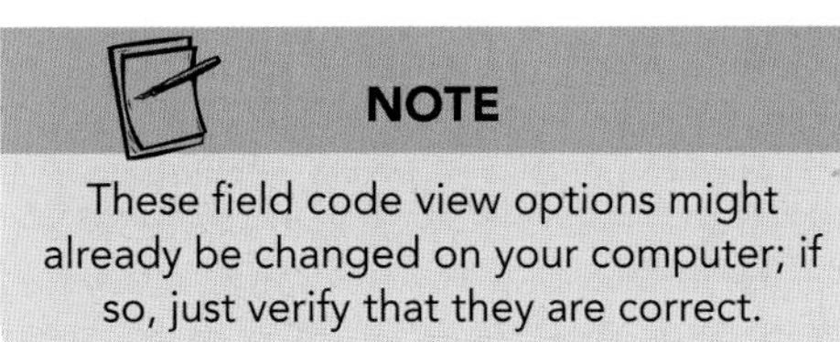

NOTE

These field code view options might already be changed on your computer; if so, just verify that they are correct.

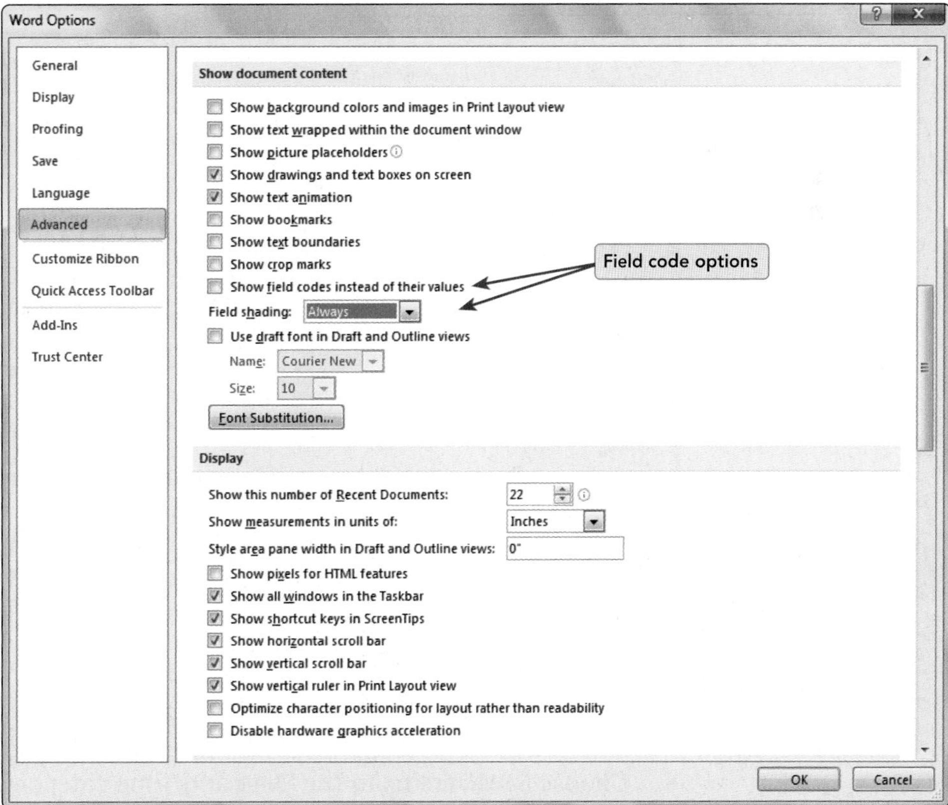

Figure 20-1
Setting view options for field codes

5. Click OK to close the Word Options dialog box.

Exercise 20-2 USE VARIOUS DATE FIELDS

When you insert a date field by using the Date and Time command on the Insert tab, you insert the current date in text form. If you choose the Update automatically option, a date field is inserted and updated to reflect the current date each time you open the document. Other date and time fields are available that display the date the document was created, the date it was last printed, or the date it was last saved.

1. Place the insertion point to the right of the text "Date Created:" and press Tab.
2. Click the **Insert** tab, click the Quick Parts button, and click **Field** to open the Field dialog box.
3. Open the **Categories** drop-down list and choose **Date and Time**. From the **Field names** list, choose **CreateDate** if it is not already highlighted.
4. Click the Field Codes button Field Codes at the bottom of the dialog box. Notice the field code syntax under the Field codes text box.
5. Make sure the **Preserve formatting during updates** option in the lower portion of the dialog box is checked. This option ensures that any formatting you apply to the field—such as bold or underline—will be preserved if the field's result or value changes.

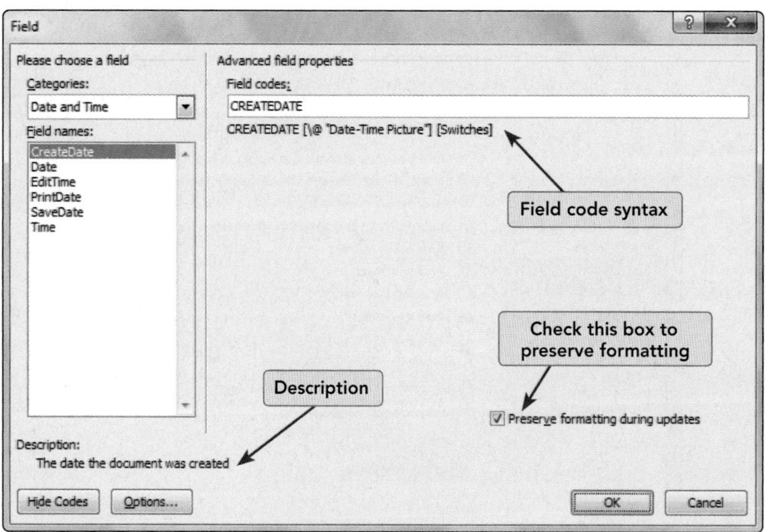

Figure 20-2 Field dialog box

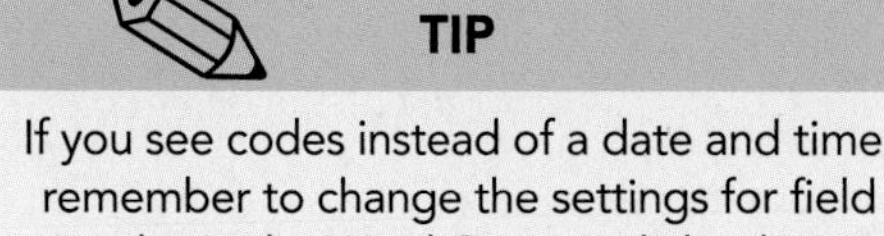

TIP

If you see codes instead of a date and time, remember to change the settings for field codes in the Word Options dialog box.

6. Click **OK**. The date and time when the document was first created appear. It is shaded, indicating that it is a field rather than text. Remember that the shading will not print.
7. Insert a tab character after the text "Date Last Revised:" and then reopen the Field dialog box.
8. Choose **SaveDate** from the **Date and Time** category, and then click **OK**. The date and time when the document was last saved appear.
9. Insert the **PrintDate** field on the line with the text "Date Last Printed." Remember to press Tab before inserting the field.

Exercise 20-3 EXPLORE OTHER TYPES OF FIELDS

1. Insert a tab character after the words "Number of Pages:" and then reopen the Field dialog box.
2. Choose the **Numbering** category. The field names for the numbering category include AutoNum and Page.

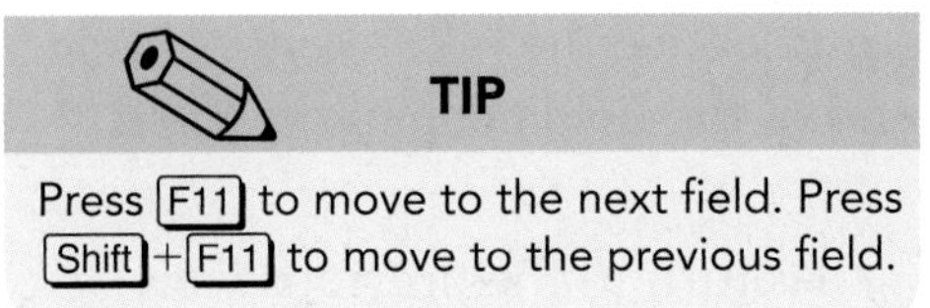

TIP

Press F11 to move to the next field. Press Shift+F11 to move to the previous field.

3. Choose another category and examine its list of field names.
4. Choose the **Document Information** category, choose **NumPages**, and then click **OK**. The number of pages contained in the document displays.

Viewing, Editing, and Updating Field Codes

While editing your document, it is sometimes convenient to see which options you have added to a field and to edit them directly in the document. You can easily toggle between the field code and the field result when necessary.

The date codes you inserted display the date and time in the default date format. You can choose other field properties in the Field dialog box to change the field format. The field code options available depend on the field code you choose. Some field codes enable you to choose more than one option at a time. When you choose one or more options, they are added to the Field codes text box, preceded by a backslash (\). These added options are called *switches*.

Exercise 20-4 CHANGE FIELD PROPERTIES

Use the Field properties section of the Field dialog box to change formatting and other features of the fields in your document. For example, you can change a date from a short format to a long format, and you can change case and number formats if appropriate for that field.

1. Drag the I-beam over the date on the "Date Created" line, but do not select the paragraph mark. The entire date is selected.

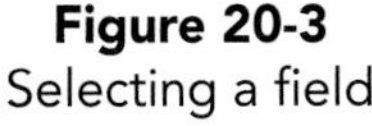

Figure 20-3
Selecting a field

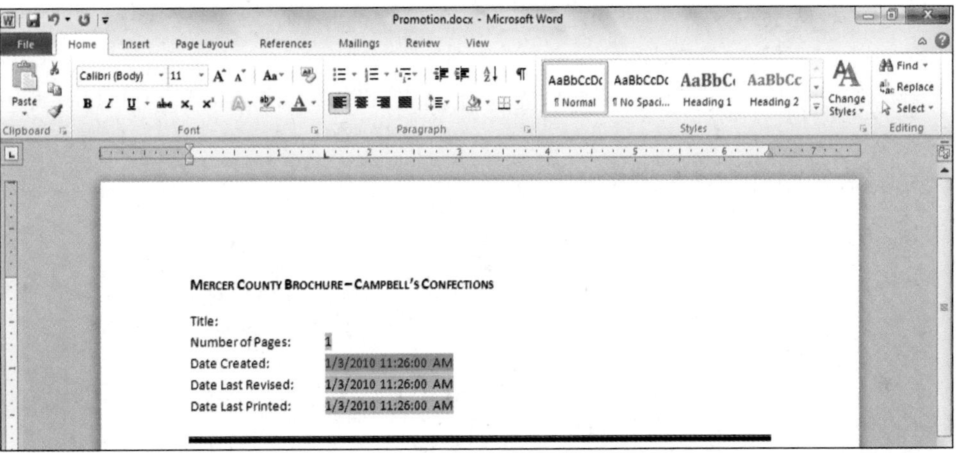

2. Click the **Insert** tab, click the Quick Parts button, and click **Field** to open the Field dialog box.
3. Choose **CreateDate** from the **Date and Time** category.
4. From the **Date formats** list, choose the fifth date format. The text "yyyy-MM-dd" appears in the Date formats text box. This format is for a four-digit year, two-digit month, and two-digit day. It does not display the time.
5. Click the **Field Codes** button [Field Codes] and notice the "**\@ "yyyy-MM-dd"** switch (option) that is added to the end of the field code in the Field codes text box.
6. Click the Hide Codes button [Hide Codes] to return to the previous view of the dialog box.
7. Click **OK** to insert the changed field in your document.
8. Using steps 1–7, change the formatting of the other date fields to match. (Use the SaveDate field for "Date Last Revised" and the PrintDate field for "Date Last Printed.") Another method to open the Field dialog box to edit a field is to right-click the field, and choose **Edit Field** from the shortcut menu.

TABLE 20-1 Useful Field Code Options

Field Result	Option	Switch	Result Example
Date or time	M/d/yy	\@ "M/d/yy"	1/9/12
	MM/dd/yyyy	\@ "MM/dd/yyyy"	01/09/2012
	MMMM d, yyyy	\@ "MMMM d, yyyy"	January 9, 2012
	dddd,MMMM d, yyyy	\@ "dddd,MMMM d, yyyy"	Sunday, January 9, 2012
	h:mm am/pm	\@ "h:mm am/pm"	11:30 PM
Numbering	1, 2, 3, . . .	* Arabic (default)	21
	I, II, III, . . .	* Roman	XXI
	One, Two, Three . . .	* CardText	twenty-one
	First, Second, Third . . .	* OrdText	twenty-first
	Dollar Text	* DollarText	twenty-one and 00/100
	0.00	\# "0.00"	21.00
	0%	\# "0%"	21%
	$#,##0.00;($#,##0.00)	\# "$#,##0.00;($#,##0.00)"	$21.00
Text	Uppercase	* Upper	CAMPBELL
	Lowercase	* Lower	campbell
	Title case	* Caps	Campbell
	First capital	* FirstCap	Campbell conf.

Exercise 20-5 APPLY MULTIPLE OPTIONS TO A FIELD CODE

1. Select the field to the right of "Number of Pages" (now displaying the numeral "1").
2. Open the **Field** dialog box. Choose **NumPages** from the Document Information category and choose **One, Two, Three** from the Format list.

3. Click the Field Codes button [Field Codes]. Notice the switch * CardText appears in the Field codes text box, indicating that cardinal numbers will be displayed as text.
4. Click the Options button [Options...] to open the Field Options dialog box.
5. Under the Formatting options list, scroll to the bottom and choose Uppercase; then click the Add to field button [Add to Field]. Notice the switch *Upper is added to the field code in the Field codes text box. Now there are two options (switches).
6. Click OK twice to return to your document. The text "ONE" is displayed.
7. On a new line under the "Date Last Printed" line, key **File name:** and press Tab. Create a hanging indent that aligns with the tab.
8. Open the Field dialog box. From the Document Information category, choose FileName.
9. Click the Field Codes button [Field Codes] and then click the Options button [Options...].
10. Click the Field Specific Switches tab. With \p highlighted, click the Add to Field button [Add to Field].
11. Click OK twice. The file name along with the file path is now included in the document.

Exercise 20-6 VIEW AND EDIT FIELD CODES IN A DOCUMENT

When you display a field code in a document, the field code name and the options you selected are enclosed in curly braces. If you selected the Preserve formatting during updates option, the option (or switch) "* MERGEFORMAT" appears as part of the code. Also, field codes will not print automatically. You must set print options to print field codes.

Figure 20-4 Anatomy of a field code

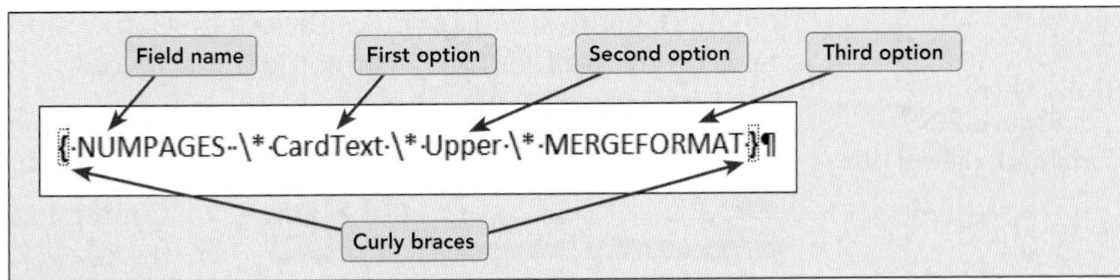

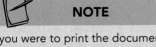

NOTE

If you were to print the document now, the field result would print instead of the field code. You must set print options to print field codes.

1. Right-click the NumPages field (displayed as "ONE"), and choose Toggle Field Codes from the shortcut menu. (Or click the field and press Shift+F9. Press Alt+F9 to display or hide all field codes in the document.) The field code appears.
2. Select the text "Upper" within the code and replace it with **FirstCap**.

NOTE

When you edit field codes directly within a document, you must be absolutely sure you have the correct syntax. It is usually best to make changes by using the dialog boxes.

3. Right-click the field code again, and choose **Toggle Field Codes** from the shortcut menu. The field result is once again displayed, but the text is still uppercase. You must manually update the field code to see the new result. Field codes are automatically updated when you first open a document, but changes that you make while editing a field are not displayed in the current document until you manually update it.

Exercise 20-7 UPDATE FIELD CODES

1. Right-click the field containing "ONE," and choose **Update Field** from the shortcut menu. (Or click the field and press F9.) The capitalization is changed to "One."
2. Format the six lines below the title "Mercer County Brochure" (beginning with the "Title" line) in 10-point type.
3. Save the document as ***[your initials]*20-7** in a new folder for Lesson 20.
4. Press Ctrl+A to select the entire document.
5. Right-click anywhere in the document, and choose **Update Field**. Now all the fields contain the most current information.
6. Save the document.

Understanding Bookmarks

A *bookmark* is a named location in a document. It can be a group of characters or words, a graphic or other object, or simply an insertion point position. You can use bookmarks to jump to a place you designate in a document.

Exercise 20-8 INSERT A BOOKMARK

Bookmark names can include all letters of the alphabet and many other characters as well, but they cannot include spaces.

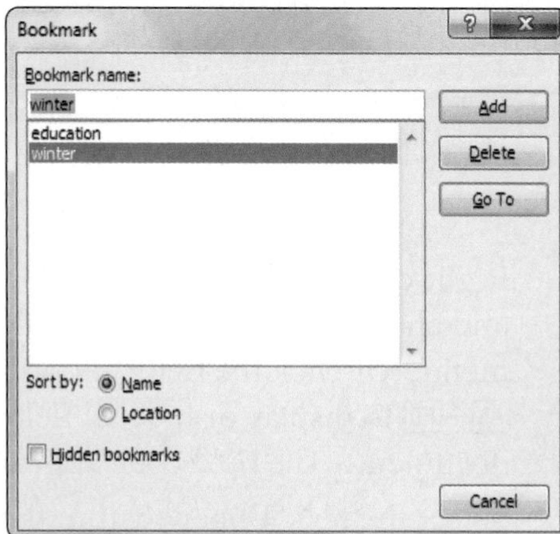

Figure 20-5
Bookmark dialog box

1. Select the heading below the horizontal line "Campbell's Confections" (do not include the paragraph mark in the selection).
2. Click the **Insert** tab, and locate the **Links** group. Click the Bookmark button to open the Bookmark dialog box. Two bookmarks have already been inserted in this document.

3. Under **Bookmark name**, key **BrochureTitle**. Do not key a space between the words.
4. Click **Add**. The bookmark is inserted, but the document might not indicate that anything has changed.
5. Open the **Word Options** dialog box. Click **Advanced**, and scroll to **Show document content**.
6. Click to select the **Show bookmarks** option.
7. Click **OK**. Deselect the bookmarked text, which is now contained in brackets. The brackets will not print, but they will help you see what you have bookmarked in the document.

Exercise 20-9 GO TO A BOOKMARK

Bookmarks provide a convenient way to navigate through a long document. Insert bookmarks at the beginning of important sections or chapters. Then use the Go To command to move quickly to the bookmarked locations.

1. Press Ctrl+G. The Find and Replace dialog box opens, with the Go To tab selected.
2. Under **Go to what**, choose **Bookmark**.
3. Under **Enter bookmark name**, click the down arrow to see a list of bookmarks in this document.
4. Choose **winter** and then click **Go To**. The dialog box remains open, but the area of the document that includes "winter" is displayed. (The "winter" bookmark was inserted in the document previously.)
5. Open the bookmark name list again, and choose **BrochureTitle**.
6. Click **Go To**. Now the bookmark you created is selected. (You might need to drag the Find and Replace dialog box out of the way to see it.)
7. Click **Close** to close the Find and Replace dialog box.

Exercise 20-10 USE A BOOKMARK IN A FIELD

Another use for a bookmark is to insert it as part of a field. For example, the Ref field syntax requires a bookmark. The bookmark's text will appear where you insert the Ref field.

1. Insert a tab character after the text "Title:" at the top of the document.
2. Click the **Insert** tab, click the Quick Parts button, and click **Field** to open the Field dialog box.
3. Choose **Links and References** from the Categories list, and then choose the field name **Ref**. Read the field description.
4. Click the Field Codes button Field Codes. Notice the field code syntax "REF Bookmark [Switches]." The name of the field is "Ref," and the bookmark name must follow the field name. "Switches" is enclosed in brackets to indicate that switches are not required, but if you use them, they must appear after the bookmark.
5. Make sure the **Preserve formatting during updates** check box is checked.

6. Click the Options button [Options...]. The Field Options dialog box has three tabs.
7. Click the **Bookmarks** tab. All the bookmarks contained in the document are listed.
8. Choose **BrochureTitle** and then click the Add to Field button [Add to Field]. The bookmark name is inserted after the field name Ref in the Field codes text box.
9. Click the **General Switches** tab. Under Formatting, choose **Title case**. Click the Add to Field button [Add to Field]. The text "*Caps" is added to the field code.

Figure 20-6
Inserting a bookmark in a field

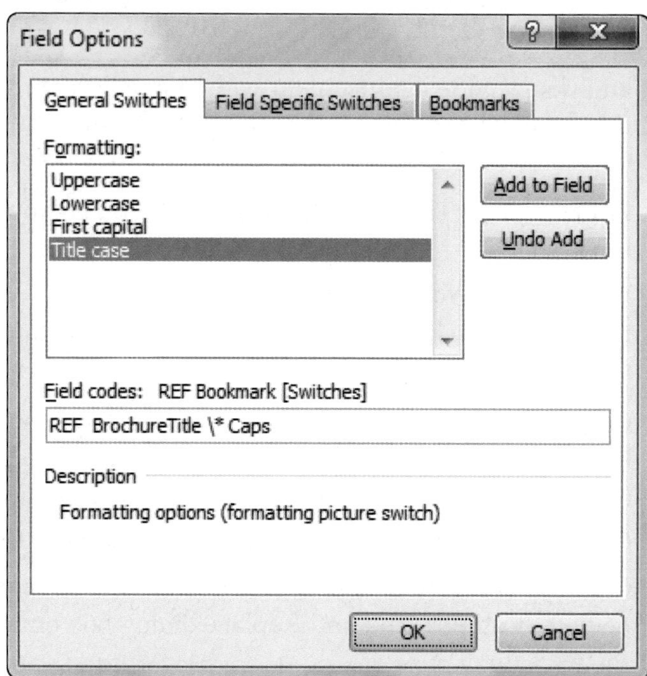

10. Click **OK** twice to close the dialog boxes and insert the field into the document. The text "Campbell's Confections" now appears in two places in the document—in the bookmarked text and in the Ref field you just created.
11. Right-click the **Ref** field, and choose **Toggle Field Codes** from the shortcut menu.

Figure 20-7
Completed Ref field code

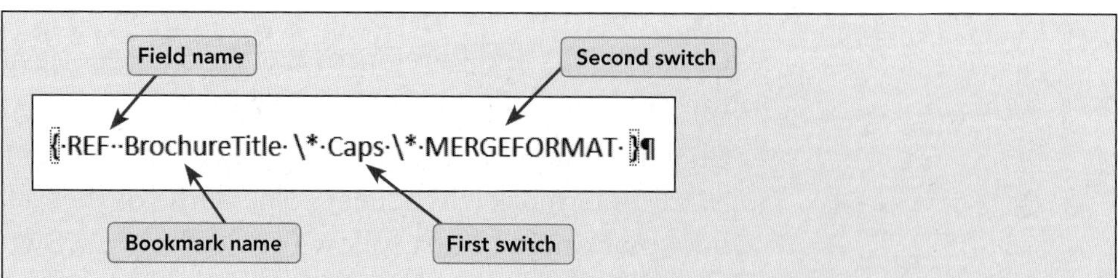

NOTE

The type size of the text "Campbell's Confections" in the Ref field is 12 points even though the type size for the field code when you toggle it is 10 points. The field result takes on the type size of the bookmark text. A little later you will change the field result type size to match the field code type size.

12. Verify that the field code is the same as Figure 20-7. If not, you can either edit it directly or delete the code and re-create it.
13. Toggle the field code again to display the field result.

Exercise 20-11 MAKE CHANGES TO BOOKMARK TEXT

You can change the text inside a bookmark if you do not delete all the characters between the brackets. Always leave at least one space or one other character. If all the characters are deleted between the brackets, the bookmark will be deleted and you will need to create a new one in its place. (Remember, if you do not see the brackets, open the Word Options dialog box to turn them on.)

1. Position the insertion point in the bookmark below the horizontal line, between the words "Campbell's" and "Confections."
2. Key **Chocolate** and add a space where necessary. Notice that the Ref field you created at the top of the document still contains the text "Campbell's Confections."
3. Right-click the **Ref** field containing the text "Campbell's Confections," and then choose **Update Field** from the shortcut menu. The text in the field changes to reflect the change you made to the bookmark.
4. Select the Ref field result "Campbell's Chocolate Confections," and change the font size to 10 points.

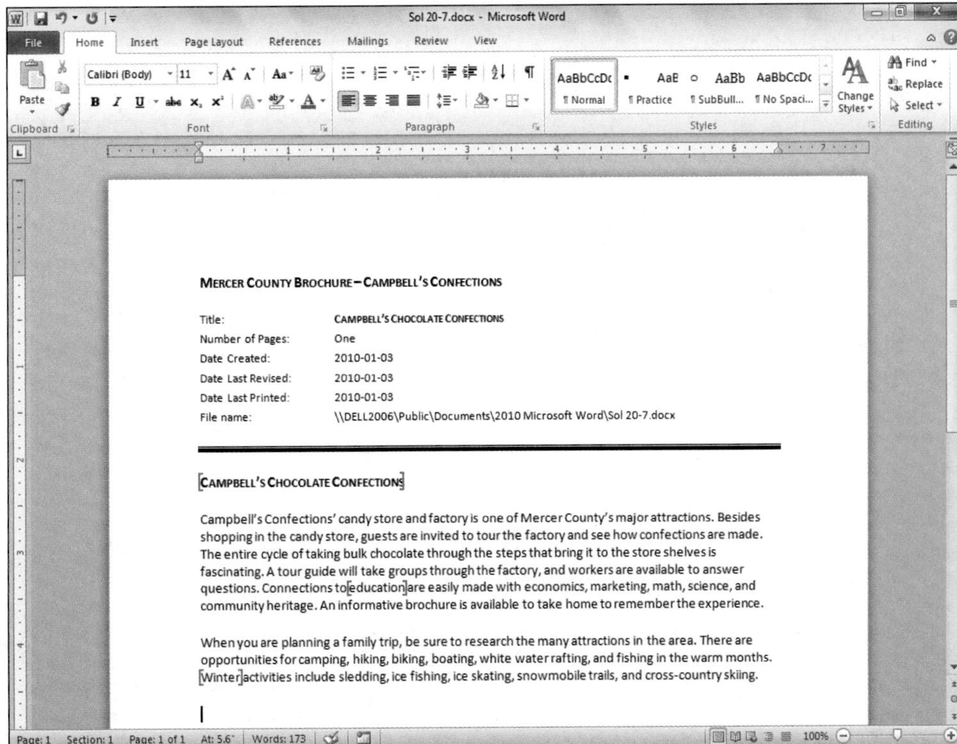

Figure 20-8 Completed document with field results displayed

Exercise 20-12 USE PRINT OPTIONS FOR FIELD CODES

You can set print options to print field codes or to update fields automatically each time you print a document. If you set the option to print field codes, be sure to clear that option before printing the final document with the field results. When a document contains several fields, you may want a hard copy of the field codes and the field code options for future reference.

1. Save the document as ***[your initials]*20-12** in your Lesson 20 folder.
2. At the top of the document, update the file name field.
3. Open the **Word Options** dialog box, and click **Advanced**.
4. Scroll to the **Print** group.
5. Click to select the option **Print field codes instead of their values**. Click **OK**.
6. Print the document.
7. Open the **Word Options** dialog box, and click **Advanced**.
8. Scroll to the **Print** group.
9. Click to deselect the option **Print field codes instead of their values**. Click **OK**.
10. Open the **Print** tab, and print the document.
11. Save the document again, and then close it.

Creating a Template to Use as a Form

When creating an electronic form, you start with a template. The person filling out the form creates a new document based on your template form. When you base your form on a template, the template form remains unchanged and is available for use the next time the form needs to be completed.

Exercise 20-13 CREATE A TEMPLATE TO USE AS A FORM

1. Click the **File** tab, and click **New** to display the available templates.
2. Click **My templates** to open the New dialog box. Click the **Blank Document** icon.

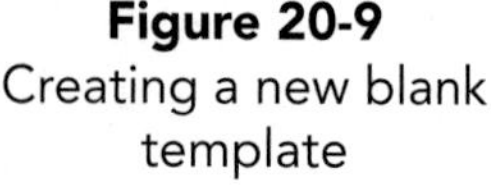

Figure 20-9
Creating a new blank template

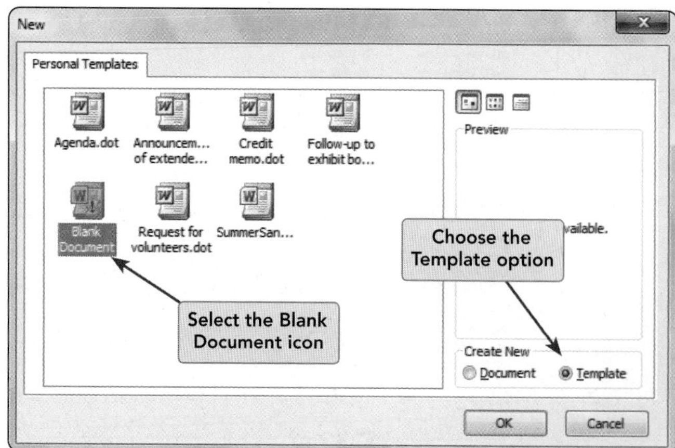

NOTE

When you or someone in your workgroup chooses New from the File tab, two factors determine which templates are available: the location of the template and your file location settings for User templates and Workgroup templates. To check your template file location settings, open the Word Options dialog box, click Advanced, and scroll to the General group. Click File Locations. *Workgroup templates* are templates that are stored centrally on a network server. To specify a default file location for Workgroup templates, click Workgroup templates from the File types list, click Modify, choose the folder you want to use, and click OK. To keep custom templates from being inadvertently altered by others, the files should be protected (which you will learn about later in this lesson) or marked as read only. Click Close and Cancel to close the dialog boxes.

3. Under Create New, choose Template (in the lower right corner). Click OK. A new template, based on the Normal template, appears on your screen. Its temporary file name is **Template1** (or another number).
4. Open the Font dialog box. Display the Font tab and choose +Body, Regular, 12 points.
5. Click Set as Default in the lower left corner; then click the option All documents based on the Template1 document to change the default font for this template and future documents based on this template. Click OK. The Normal template's default font remains unchanged.

Exercise 20-14 KEY TEXT IN A FORM

When you create a form, a good idea is to create a rough draft or layout sketch first, including the text and the fields the form will contain. As you create the form, you key the standardized text and insert regular fields and content controls where needed. Keep the following in mind to decide the kind of field to use:

- Use a content control wherever you want the person using the form to key information.
- Use document information fields and other fields discussed previously if you want the form to insert the information automatically.

TIP

CreateDate is usually the best date field to use on a form. It inserts the date that is current when a new document based on the template form is created. It does not update if the document is opened or printed at a later date.

1. Key the text shown in Figure 20-10. Format the first line as 16-point bold, with small caps. Apply bold and small caps to the second line. Center the first two lines. Apply bold formatting to lines 3 through 6, and set a left tab at 1.75 inches. Change the paragraph spacing and line spacing as indicated in the figure. Set a left tab at 1.75 inches for the seventh line.

Figure 20-10

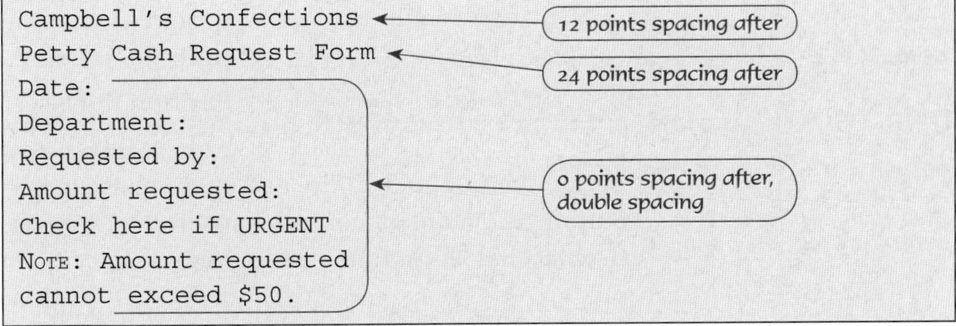

2. Position the insertion point after the text "Date:" and press Tab. Then click the Insert tab, click the Quick Parts button, and click Field.
3. Choose CreateDate from the Date and Time category, and then choose the third Date format option. Close the Field dialog box.

Insert Content Controls

Content controls enable users to key information in forms and allow you to control the type of entry the user can make. Content controls are found on the Developer tab. Table 20-2 shows the eight content controls.

TABLE 20-2 Content Controls

Button	Description	Purpose
Aa	Rich Text Content Control	Short paragraphs. Formatting can be saved.
Aa	Plain Text Content Control	Plain text paragraph.
	Picture Content Control	Drawing, shape, chart, table, clip art, or SmartArt.
	Building Block Gallery Content Control	Gallery options.
	Combo Box Content Control	List that can be edited.
	Drop-Down List Content Control	List of restricted choices.
	Date Picker Content Control	Calendar control for entering date.
	Check Box Content Control	Check box.

Exercise 20-15 INSERT A CONTENT CONTROL

1. Open the **Word Options** dialog box, and click **Customize Ribbon**. Locate the **Customize The Ribbon** section, and verify that Main Tabs is selected. Click to select the **Developer** option in the list under Main Tabs. Click **OK**.

Figure 20-11
Controls group

2. Click the **Developer** tab, and click the Design Mode button. Use Design Mode to insert and edit controls.
3. Position the insertion point after the text "Requested by:" and press Tab.
4. Locate the **Controls** group, and click the Rich Text Content Control button Aa. A content control is inserted at the insertion point. Notice the placeholder and the instructional text.
5. Position the insertion point after the text "Amount requested:" and press Tab. Insert another Rich Text content control.

Exercise 20-16 WORK WITH CONTENT CONTROL PROPERTIES

You can set or change properties for content controls. For example, you can change the style of the content control to format the contents.

To help users understand the kind of information you expect them to enter in your form, you can edit the instructions and add a title.

1. Click within the **Requested by** content control. The field is highlighted, indicating that it is selected.

Figure 20-12 Setting Content Control Properties

2. Edit the placeholder text to read **Key first and last name.**
3. Click within the **Amount requested** content control, and change the instruction to read **Key amount in currency format ($0.00).**
4. Right-click the content control for **Requested by**, and click **Properties**. Key **Name** in the Title text box. Click **OK**. Right-click the content control for **Amount requested**, and click **Properties**. Key **Amount** in the Title text box. Click **OK**.

Exercise 20-17 INSERT A CHECK BOX CONTENT CONTROL

A Check Box content control works just like the check boxes you often use in dialog boxes. The person filling out your form can click to put an X in the box, or click again to remove the X.

1. Position the insertion point at the end of the line "Check here if URGENT." Press Tab.
2. Click the Check Box Content Control button to insert a check box.
3. Right-click the **Check Box Content Control**, and choose **Properties**. Locate Check Box Properties, and notice that you can change the symbol for the checked and unchecked status of the content control. Click **Cancel**.

Exercise 20-18 INSERT A DROP-DOWN LIST CONTENT CONTROL

1. Click at the end of the line with the text "Department:" and press Tab.
2. Click the Drop-Down List Content Control button . A Drop-Down List content control is inserted.

3. Click the Properties button in the Control group on the Ribbon to open the Content Control Properties dialog box.
4. Key **Department** in the Title text box.
5. Click the Add button Add... .
6. Key **Retail Sales** in the Display Name text box, and click **OK**. Key each of the following entries for the Drop-Down List content control. Click **Add** (or press Enter) for each, key the name, and click **OK** or press Enter.

   Wholesale Sales
   Fundraising
   Customer Service
   Accounting
   Human Resources

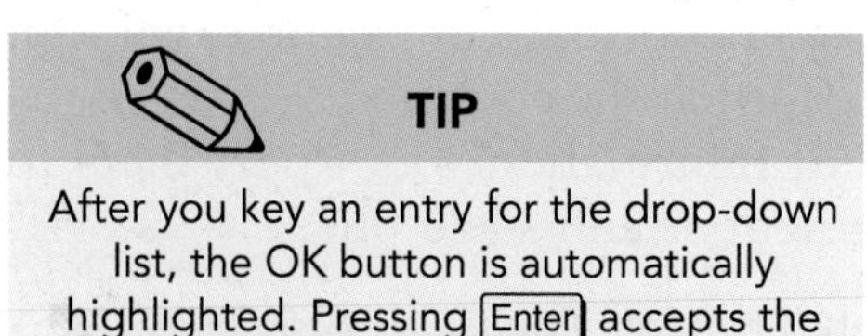

After you key an entry for the drop-down list, the OK button is automatically highlighted. Pressing Enter accepts the entry and returns you to the Content Control Properties dialog box with the Add button automatically selected. Press Enter to add a second entry. Consequently, it is not necessary to click the Add button and OK button.

7. In the list of drop-down items, click **Accounting**, and then click the Move Up button Move Up four times. "Accounting" is now the first entry in the list.
8. Use the Move Up button or the Move Down button to alphabetize the list of departments. Click **OK** to close the dialog box. You will see the entire list with a drop-down arrow when a document based on this form is created a little later in this lesson.

Figure 20-13
Adding items to a drop-down list Content Control

Protecting and Saving a Form

Before saving a form, you should protect it by locking it. When you *lock* a form, the person filling out the form has access only to the content control fields. The other text, regular fields, and elements such as graphics are locked and cannot be changed by the user. This ensures that all documents created from the form will be uniform in layout and content.

Because a form is actually a special-purpose template, you save it in the same way you save a template.

Exercise 20-19 PROTECT A FORM

1. Click the Design Mode button to turn off Design Mode.
2. Click the Restrict Editing button. The Restrict Formatting and Editing task pane displays.
3. Locate the Editing restrictions section. Click the check box to **Allow only this type of editing in the document**. Click the drop-down arrow and choose **Filling in forms**. This option locks everything on the form except the content controls.

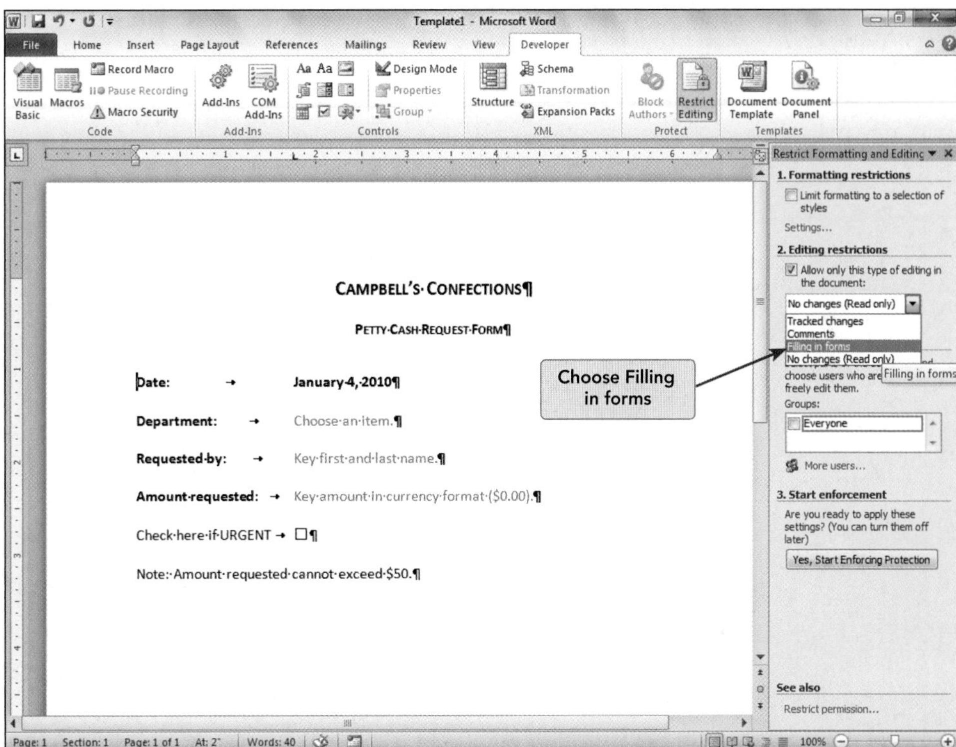

Figure 20-14
Protecting a form

TIP

A password would prevent a user from unprotecting a document based on your form. Avoid passwords if you can, but if one is necessary, keep a duplicate copy of your form without a password in a safe place out of circulation. If you forget the password you used for the template and need to make changes later, you are out of luck unless you have an unprotected backup copy.

4. Click **Yes, Start Enforcing Protection** in the Restrict Formatting and Editing task pane. Click **OK** to close the Start Enforcing Protection dialog box. Do not enter a password. Notice that the Restrict Editing button on the Ribbon displays a lock symbol, indicating that the form is now protected. Also notice the change in the Restrict Formatting and Editing task pane. Close the task pane.
5. Double-click the text "Campbell's" on the first line of the form. Notice that you cannot select it, because the form is protected.
6. Click the field to the right of "Department:" containing the text "Choose an item." A drop-down arrow and list appear.
7. Choose **Customer Service**. Notice that the text box expands to accommodate all the characters.

NOTE

By default, Word saves a new template (or form template) in the Templates folder on your hard disk. Before proceeding, ask your instructor where you should save your forms. If you use the default location (or a subfolder below it) or the Workgroup Templates file location (if one is specified), you can create new documents based on your form template by using the Templates dialog box. If you save your form in your Lesson 20 folder, you will use Computer or Windows Explorer to create a new document.

Exercise 20-20 SAVE A FORM

1. Check to make sure the form is protected.
2. Open the Save As dialog box. Change the Save as type drop-down list to **Word Template**.
3. Save your form as a Word template named ***[your initials]*****Form20-20** in your Lesson 20 folder (unless your instructor advises you to save in the default Templates folder).
4. Submit the form, and close the template.

Using and Editing a Form

A form is a special type of template. You use a form by starting a new document based on the form template. Depending on where you saved the template, you start the new document in one of the following ways:

- If you saved the form template in the Templates folder, in a subfolder under the Templates folder, or in the Workgroup Templates folder, use the New tab to access the template you created.
- If you saved the form template in your Lesson 20 folder, right-click the Windows Start button and use Windows Explorer to find and use your form template.

NOTE

To create a new document based on your form, you can also right-click the template file and choose New from the shortcut menu. If you choose Open from the shortcut menu, the form template will open. To create a new document based on your form using the Templates dialog box, be sure to click the Document option under Create New.

Exercise 20-21 CREATE A DOCUMENT BASED ON A FORM

1. Right-click the Windows Start button, and choose **Open Windows Explorer** from the shortcut menu.
2. In the Folders list, navigate to your Lesson 20 folder and click to open it.
3. Locate the form template ***[your initials]*****Form20-20**.
4. Double-click the file to start Word and a new document based on the form template.

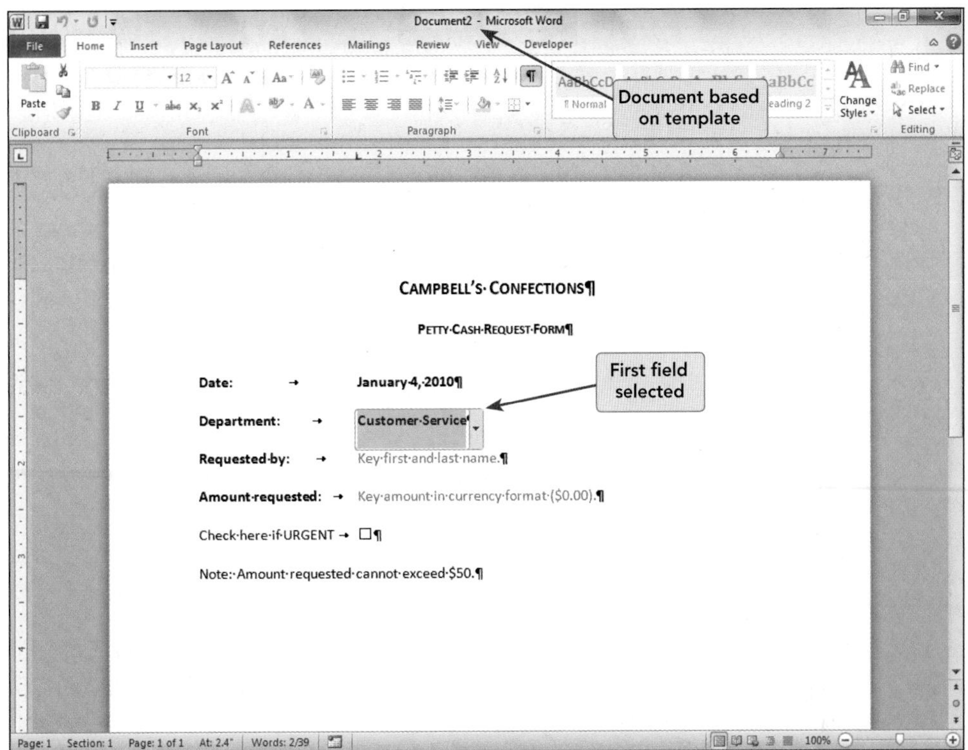

Figure 20-15 Creating a new document based on the form template

Exercise 20-22 ENTER INFORMATION IN THE FORM DOCUMENT

When you create a document based on a form that has been protected, the first content control is automatically selected and ready for you to enter information. You can navigate around a form document by clicking a content control.

1. Click the content control next to "Department:" and choose **Accounting** from the drop-down list.
2. Click the "Requested by:" content control. Key **Glenn Moore**.
3. Click the **Amount requested** content control.
4. Key **$40.00**.
5. Click the check box on the next line to place an "X" in the box, or press Spacebar to toggle the check box on.
6. Save the document as ***[your initials]*20-22** in your Lesson 20 folder.
7. Submit the document and close it.

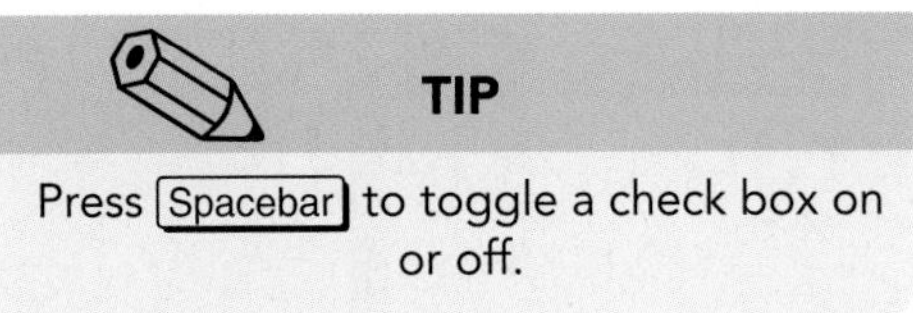

TIP

Press Spacebar to toggle a check box on or off.

Exercise 20-23 CREATE A NEW FORM BASED ON AN EXISTING FORM

When you want to make changes to a form or create a new form based on an existing one, you open the form and edit it in the same way as a document file, but with the following additional steps:

- You must change the Files of type setting in the Open dialog box to either Document Templates or All Files. If the setting is different, you will not see your form in the list of files.
- You must unprotect the document before you can edit it.

After opening an existing form, a good idea is to save it with a new name before making any changes. That way, you won't accidentally save to the existing form the changes intended for a new form.

1. Display the Open dialog box, and choose **All Word Templates** from the Files of type drop-down list.
2. Navigate to your Lesson 20 folder (or follow your instructor's directions).
3. Choose the form template ***[your initials]*Form20-20**, and then click **Open**.
4. Save the form as a template with the new name ***[your initials]* Form20-23**.
5. Click the **Developer** tab, and click the Restrict Editing button. Click **Stop Protection**.
6. Refer to Figure 20-16, and make the following changes to the form.
   - Delete the text "Petty Cash Request Form," and key in its place **Office Supply Requisition Form**. Verify that the text is bold and small caps.
   - Delete the line containing the text "Amount requested:" (including the content control.
   - Delete the last line that begins "Note."
   - Apply small caps formatting to "Date," "Department," and "Requested by."

Figure 20-16
Edited form

CAMPBELL'S CONFECTIONS

OFFICE SUPPLY REQUISITION FORM

DATE:	January 4, 2010
DEPARTMENT:	Customer Service
REQUESTED BY:	Key first and last name.
Check here if URGENT	☐

7. Insert a table at the end of the document measuring 4 columns by 12 rows. Refer to Figure 20-17 for content and column width. Select a table style that includes banded rows. Center the table horizontally, change the row height to 0.4 inch, and center the cell text vertically. Change the line spacing to single.

Figure 20-17
Sample table format

QTY.	ITEM NO.	DESCRIPTION	UNIT PRICE
[1" wide]	[1.25" wide]	[2" wide]	[1" wide]

8. Save the form. Submit and close the document.

Lesson 20 Summary

- A field is a placeholder for information that can change in a document. You can insert most fields into a document by using familiar Ribbon commands, such as inserting a page number in a header or footer or inserting a date in a letter.
- Every field contains a field code—text and instructions that will produce the field result.
- You can change field properties, such as changing the date format for a date code. You can also apply one or more field code options to selected fields. These options are added to the field code text, preceded by a backslash (\) or switch. See Table 20-1.
- You can edit field codes directly in the document. To do this you toggle between the field result and the field code.
- When you display a field code in a document, the field code name and the options you selected are enclosed in curly braces. If you selected the Preserve formatting during updates option, the option (or switch) "* MERGEFORMAT" appears as part of the code.
- Field codes are automatically updated when you first open a document, but changes you make while editing a field are not displayed in the current document until you manually update the fields.
- A bookmark is a named location in a document. It can be a group of characters or words, a graphic or other object, or simply an insertion point position. Insert bookmarks at the beginning of important sections or chapters; then use the Go To command to move quickly to the bookmarked locations.
- You can change the text inside a bookmark if you do not delete all the characters between the brackets. Always leave at least one space or other character. If all the characters are deleted between the brackets, the bookmark will be deleted and you will need to create a new one in its place.

- If you have dollar amounts or other numerical values in a document, you can perform calculations on them by using the formula field and bookmarks.
- You can set print options to print field codes. If you set the option to print field codes, be sure to clear that option before printing the final document with the field results.
- There are two basic types of forms: (1) a paper form that you create by using normal editing tools and then print for someone to fill in by hand and (2) an electronic form, such as one based on a custom template that a user completes in Word.
- When creating a Word electronic form, you start with a template. The person filling out the form starts a new document based on the template form.
- Before creating a form, create a rough layout sketch, including the text and the fields the form will contain. When you create the form in Word, you key the standardized text and insert regular fields and content controls where needed.
- Use a text content control wherever you want the person using the form to key information. Use document information fields and other fields when you want the form to insert the information automatically.
- You can set content control options to control the formatting and the type of entry the user can make. To help people understand the kind of information you expect to be entered in your form, you can edit the instructional text that appears with the content control.
- Before saving a form, you should protect it by locking it. When a form is locked, the person filling out the form only has access to the content controls. The user cannot change the other form elements.
- You use a form by starting a new document based on the form template. Depending on where you saved the template, you create the new document by using the New tab or Windows Explorer.
- When you create a document based on a protected form, the first form field is automatically selected and ready for you to enter information. You can navigate around a form document by clicking a content control or by pressing Tab.

LESSON 20		Command Summary	
Feature	**Button**	**Command**	**Keyboard**
Insert a bookmark		Insert tab, Links group, Bookmark	
Insert a field		Insert tab, Text group, Quick Parts, Field	Ctrl+F9 (empty field)
Protect/unprotect a form		Developer tab, Protect tab	
Toggle field codes		Shortcut menu, Toggle Field Codes	Shift+F9
Update selected field(s)		Shortcut menu, Update Field	F9

Concepts Review

True/False Questions

Each of the following statements is either true or false. Indicate your choice by circling T or F.

T F 1. Fields can be inserted only by using the Field dialog box.

T F 2. If you toggle field codes to see the code rather than the result, the codes will always print.

T F 3. A field's syntax is the set of rules that describes how to construct the field.

T F 4. When you add an option to a field, it must be preceded by a backslash.

T F 5. Forms must always be saved in the Templates folder.

T F 6. Bookmark names cannot contain a space.

T F 7. Use the Plain Text content control when formatting must be saved.

T F 8. When you protect a form, you must assign a password.

Short Answer Questions

Write the correct answer in the space provided.

1. What is a placeholder for information that can change in a document?

____

2. What dialog box do you need to open to change the shading of a field code?

____

3. How do the switches * CardText * Upper" format a numerical field?

____

4. What must you do to update a field code?

____

5. If you open a protected form template, what must you do before you can edit the form?

____

6. How do you insert a bookmark?

____

7. How do you jump to a bookmark in a document?

---

8. What is the result of the SaveDate field?

Critical Thinking

Answer these questions on a separate page. There are no right or wrong answers. Support your answers with examples from your own experience, if possible.

1. The CreateDate field inserts the date a document was first created (or saved with a new name). The Date field displays the current date each time you open the document. When is the Date field appropriate to use in a document, and when should you instead use the CreateDate field?
2. When creating a report, are bookmarks something you would consider helpful? When might you use bookmarks in either a long or short document?

Skills Review

Exercise 20-24

Insert fields, change field properties, toggle the field code view, apply field options, and update fields.

1. Open the file **Inventory**.
2. Position the insertion point three lines below the table in the document. Key **Revision date:** and press Spacebar.
3. Insert the date the document was last saved by following these steps:
   a. Click the **Insert** tab, click the Quick Parts button, and click **Field**.
   b. Open the **Categories** list and choose **Date and Time**. Choose **SaveDate** from the **Field names** list.
   c. Choose the third date format from the **Date formats** list. **MMMM d, yyyy** should appear in the Date formats text box. Click **OK**.
4. Toggle to view the date's field code by following these steps:
   a. Right-click the date field.
   b. Choose **Toggle Field Codes** from the shortcut menu. Review the field code.
   c. Right-click the date field again.
   d. Choose **Toggle Field Codes** from the shortcut menu.
5. On a new line below "Revision date" line, key **File name:** and press Spacebar.

6. Insert the File name field with the path option by following these steps:
   a. Click the Insert tab, click the Quick Parts button, and click Field.
   b. Click the Document Information category, and then click FileName from the Field names list.
   c. Click the Field Codes button and then click Options.
   d. Click the General Switches tab if it is not active, and then choose Lowercase.
   e. Click Add to Field.
   f. Click the Field Specific Switches tab.
   g. With the \p switch highlighted, click Add to Field.
   h. Click OK twice to close both dialog boxes.
7. Save the document as ***[your initials]*20-24** in your Lesson 20 folder.
8. Update the fields by following these steps:
   a. Select the last two lines (which contain the fields).
   b. Right-click the selection, and choose Update Field from the shortcut menu.
9. Format the two lines containing fields as 10-point italic.
10. Add a right-aligned footer to the document. Key **Page** and a space, and then add the page number field.
11. Save the document again, submit the document, and close it.

Exercise 20-25

Change field display options; view, edit, and update field codes.

1. Open the file **Class**.
2. The date at the top of the letter is a field. If it is not shaded, follow these steps to display shaded fields:
   a. Open the Word Options dialog box.
   b. Click Advanced and scroll to the Show document content group.
   c. Locate Field shading:, and choose Always. Click OK.
3. Toggle to view the date's field code.
4. Modify the date format to eliminate the name of the day by following these steps:
   a. Select "dddd" within the field code and press Delete.
   b. Delete the comma and space that followed "dddd."
   c. Examine the resulting code, and make any necessary editing changes so it matches the following:
   {CREATEDATE\@ "MMMM dd, yyyy"*MERGEFORMAT}
   d. Use the shortcut menu to update the field.

5. Change the field name from "CREATEDATE" to "SAVEDATE" by following these steps:
   a. Display the date's field code.
   b. Double-click CREATEDATE within the field code to select it.
   c. Key **SAVEDATE**.
6. Insert your reference initials at the end of the document; then save the document as ***[your initials]*20-25** in your Lesson 20 folder.
7. Update the field once more. Then save, submit, and close the document.

Exercise 20-26

Insert and go to bookmarks.

1. Open the file **Community - 2**.
2. Create a bookmark by following these steps:
   a. Select the text "Community Involvement" at the top of page 1. Be careful not to select the paragraph mark at the end of the line.
   b. Click the Insert tab, and click the Bookmark button.
   c. In the Bookmark name text box, key **DocTitle**. Be sure not to key a space between the words.
   d. Click Add.
3. Display the brackets surrounding the bookmark by following these steps:
   a. Open the Word Options dialog box.
   b. Click Advanced and scroll to Show document content. Click to select Show Bookmarks. Click OK.
4. Create bookmarks for the following terms, and name them appropriately. Remember not to key a space between words.

   United Way
   March of Dimes
   Humane Society
   Susan G. Komen Foundation
   Grove City Charitable League
5. Go to a bookmark by following these steps:
   a. Press Ctrl+G.
   b. Under Go to what, choose Bookmark.
   c. Under Enter bookmark name, click the down arrow to see a list of bookmarks in this document.
   d. Choose DocTitle and then click Go To. Close the Find and Replace dialog box.
6. Change the title to 18-point bold and italic.
7. Save the document as ***[your initials]*20-26** in your Lesson 20 folder.

8. Add a right-aligned footer to every page. Key **Page** and a space, and then add the page number field.
9. Submit and close the document.

Exercise 20-27

Create a form template, insert content controls, and protect and save the form.

1. Create a template form by following these steps:
   a. Open the file **Telephone Order**.
   b. Open the Save As dialog box, and change the Save as type to Word Template.
   c. Save the document as ***[your initials]*****Form20-27** in your Lesson 20 folder.
2. Insert content controls by following these steps:
   a. Display the Developer tab by opening the Word Options dialog box, and clicking Customize Ribbon. Locate the Customize The Ribbon section on the right side. Verify that Main Tabs is selected in the Customize the Ribbon drop-down list. Click to select Developer, and click OK.
   b. Click the Developer tab, and click the Design Mode button.
   c. Position the insertion point to the right of "Date:" and press Spacebar two times.
   d. Click the Date Picker Content Control button.
   e. Change the instructional text to read **Enter today's date**.
3. Click to the right of "Sold by:" and press Spacebar two times. Click the Rich Text Content Control button Aa. Change the instructional text to read **Sales Associate**.
4. Insert a Rich Text content control to the right of each heading item under "Billing Information" and to the right of each heading item under "Shipping Information." Place two spaces between the heading and the Rich Text content control.

NOTE

When you insert the content controls for the city, state, and ZIP Code, the content control text may wrap to the next line.

5. Add a title to the content controls by following these steps:
   a. Select the Date Picker content control, and click the Properties button on the Developer tab.
   b. Key **Date** in the Title text box, and select the third date format. Click OK.
6. Select each control in the Billing Information section and the Shipping Information section, and change the title for each. Use the shortcut menu or click the Properties button on the Ribbon.

7. Insert a Drop-Down List Content Control by following these steps:
   a. Click to the right of "Type of chocolate," and press Spacebar two times.
   b. Click the Drop-Down List Content Control button.
   c. Click the Properties button on the Developer tab.
   d. Click the Add button Add..., and key **Milk Chocolate** in the Display Name text box. Click **OK**.
   e. Add **Dark Chocolate** and **White Chocolate** to the Drop-Down List Properties.
   f. Click **OK** to close the dialog box.
8. Insert a Drop-Down List Content Control to the right of "Chocolate." Add the following items to the control properties. After keying the items, use the Move buttons to arrange the list in alphabetical order.

   Nuts

   Creams

   Melt-a-ways

   Assorted
9. Insert Rich Text content controls to the right of "Quantity," "Account No.," and "Expiration Date." Add a title to each control.
10. Insert a Check Box content control by following these steps:
    a. Click to the right of "Check," and press Spacebar twice.
    b. Click the Check Box Content Control button.
11. Insert a Drop-Down List Content Control to the right of "Credit Card." Add the following items to the control properties:

    Visa

    MasterCard

    Discover

    American Express
12. Protect the form by following these steps:
    a. Click the Design Mode button to turn off the design feature.
    b. Click the Restrict Editing button.
    c. Click to select the check box to **Allow only this type of editing in the document**.
    d. Click the drop-down arrow and click **Filling in forms**.
    e. Click **Yes, Start Enforcing Protection**. Click **OK**.
13. Save the template.
14. Submit and close the document.

Lesson Applications

Exercise 20-28

Create a form and insert content controls.

1. Open the file **Health Fair - 2**.
2. Save the document as a template and name it ***[your initials]*****Form20-28** in your Lesson 20 folder. Turn on Design Mode.
3. Select the headings "Last Name" through "Maiden Name" and set a left tab at 2 inches. Press Tab after each heading, and insert a Rich Text content control. Key a title for each content control.
4. Delete the text under the heading "Store Location," and insert a Drop-Down List Content Control on the same line as the "Store Location" heading. Set a 2-inch left tab stop, and insert a tab character before the content control. Key **State** for the content control title. Add **Pennsylvania**, **Ohio**, and **West Virginia** to the Drop-Down List Properties.
5. Select the three lines that follow the heading "Preferred Sessions," and open the Tabs dialog box. Clear the tab setting, and add a left tab at 2 inches. Insert a Drop-Down List Content Control for each choice. Add a title for each content control, and include the following items. Alphabetize the list. (Hint: Use copy and paste.)

   CPR
   First Aid
   Lifting techniques
   Preventive techniques for carpal tunnel syndrome
   Massage therapy
   Pain management
   Fatigue

6. Delete the lines preceding "Yes" and "No" at the bottom of the page, and replace the lines with a Check Box content control.
7. Insert a footer to the document, and key the text: **Revision Date:**. Insert the SaveDate field, using a date format of your choice.
8. Turn off Design Mode, and protect the form. Save the template. Submit and close the template.
9. Create a new document based on the Form 20-28 template. Complete the form, and save the document as ***[your initials]*****20-28**. Submit and close the document.

Exercise 20-29

Create a bookmark, insert fields, change field properties, view and edit fields, go to a bookmark, and update fields.

1. Open the document **Glossary**.
2. Save the document as ***[your initials]*20-29** in your Lesson 20 folder.
3. Create a bookmark named **Date** for the date in the date line of the letter.
4. Format the document for a different first page for headers and footers, and change the header margin to 1 inch from the edge.
5. On page 2, create a continuation page header:
   - Key **Mrs. Doris Forman** as the first line of the header.
   - On a new second line, key the word **Page** and press Spacebar. Then insert the page number field.
   - On a new third line of the header, insert the first type of date format for the CreateDate field.
   - Insert two blank lines after the CreateDate field.
6. Display the field code for the CreateDate field in the header. Then change the date format to

   {CREATEDATE \@ "MMMM d, yyyy"* MERGEFORMAT}
7. Update the field code, and then close the header pane.
8. Go to the "Date" bookmark, and replace the entire bookmark with a CreateDate field which has the same date style as the header.
9. Add your reference initials and an enclosure notation to the end of the letter. Save, submit, and close the document.

Exercise 20-30

Insert, view, edit, and update fields; insert and update formula fields that use bookmarks; and print field codes.

1. Open the file **Mercer.**
2. Replace the date with a CreateDate field, using the fourth date format.
3. Toggle the field code view for the date field.
4. Edit the date field switch to **\@ "MMMM d, yyyy"**.
5. Update the field.

6. Create the following bookmarks for the dollar amounts in the first paragraph:

Amount	Bookmark name
$480	Deposit
$720	Total

7. Open the Word Options dialog box, and click the Advanced tab. Scroll to the Show document content group, and click to select the option to **Show bookmarks**.
8. Key the following sentence at the end of the first paragraph: **Please send your final payment in the amount of.**
9. Press Spacebar and open the Field dialog box. Display the **Equations and Formula** category, click the Field name **=(Formula)**. Click **Formula** to open the Formula dialog box. Click the **Paste bookmark** down arrow, and click **Total**. Type a minus (-), and click the Paste bookmark down arrow, and click **Deposit**. Select the third format in the **Number format** drop-down list. Click **OK**.
10. Key the following text after "$240": **30 days after the date of your invoice.**
11. Change the total amount from "720" to **840**. (Do not delete the bookmark brackets.)
12. Update the formula field.
13. Add your reference initials at the end of the document.
14. Save the document as ***[your initials]*20-30** in your Lesson 20 folder.
15. Update the date field again.
16. Submit the document, showing the field codes.
17. Submit the document again without displaying the field codes, save, and close it.

Exercise 20-31 ◆ Challenge Yourself

Create a form template that includes fields and content controls, and protect and save the form.

1. Open a new blank template; then key the heading text in Figure 20-18. Format the heading, choosing an appropriate font and aligning text to make an attractive arrangement.

Figure 20-18

Mid-Atlantic Confections Association

Annual Conference

Sponsored by

The Nut and Fruit Plantation

Conference Evaluation Form

1. Who was your group leader? <Insert a drop-down list>
2. Please rate the registration process:

The registration process was:	❑ Smooth ❑ OK ❑ Tedious
The registration personnel were:	❑ Helpful and efficient ❑ OK ❑ Not helpful

3. Please rate the information presented: ❑ Very useful ❑ Somewhat useful ❑ Not at all useful
4. Please state briefly what you enjoyed the most (or least) about the conference:

____

____

5. Your name (optional): ________________________

2. Key the text for question 1. Insert a Drop-Down List Content Control at the end of question 1 where indicated on the figure. Include the following names in the drop-down list and alphabetize the names:

   Eddie Martin
   Jodie Berger
   Melissa Alvarez
   Jon McGill

3. Insert nine Check Box Content Controls before each option for questions 2 and 3.
4. Insert a Rich Text Content Control in place of the line below question 4 and another Rich Text Content Control to the right of question 5.
5. Protect the form, and then save it as a template named ***[your initials]*** **Form20-31** in your Lesson 20 folder (or follow your instructor's directions). Print the form and close it.
6. Open a new document based on the form, choosing **Melissa Alvarez** as your group leader and choosing whichever check boxes you want.

7. In the text form field for question 4, key the following: **Ms. Alvarez was knowledgeable, presented her material clearly, and was very patient with all my questions.**
8. In the text form field for question 5, key **Your name**.
9. Save the document as ***[your initials]*20-31** in your Lesson 20 folder; then submit and close it.

On Your Own

In these exercises you work on your own, as you would in a real-life business environment. Use the skills you've learned to accomplish the task—and be creative.

Exercise 20-32

You are a volunteer at an animal shelter and have been asked to create a form template for possible adopters. Include a section for personal information (future adopter) and a section for pet preferences. Use Date Picker, Rich Text, and Drop-Down List Content Controls to complete the task. Format the form appropriately, save the template as ***[your initials]* Form20-32**, and submit it. Open a new document based on the form, and fill-in the form. Save the document as ***[your initials]*20-32**, and submit it.

Exercise 20-33

Use the Microsoft Word Help Index to research and explore other types of fields. Locate information on two fields that can be used in a mail merge. One is the Ask field, and the other is the Fill-in field. Write a summary about each and how to incorporate the fields into a document. Prepare a sample document using the fields. Save the document as ***[your initials]*20-33** and submit it.

Exercise 20-34

Use the Internet to research three automobiles that interest you. Create a table with Rich Text, Drop-Down List, and Check Box Content Controls to compare the features of each car. Record information on class of car, interior and exterior features, price, reliability and safety records, and other features that you want to include. Save the table as a template with the name ***[your initials]*Form20-34** and submit it. Open the template as a new document and record your findings. Save the document as ***[your initials]*20-34** and submit it.

Lesson 21

Macros

OBJECTIVES

After completing this lesson, you will be able to:

1. Create a macro.
2. Run a macro.
3. Edit a macro.
4. Copy, rename, and delete macros.
5. Customize the Quick Access Toolbar.

Estimated Time: 1½ hours

A Word *macro* enables you to quickly perform repetitive tasks involving command sequences and keystrokes. With a macro, you can save a sequence of tasks in a single command. Then you can execute one command to perform the entire sequence automatically. A macro can include Ribbon commands, formatting options, keystrokes, and dialog box selections. For example, you can create a macro that automatically inserts a header or footer.

Creating a Macro

When you create macros, you store them in either a document or a template. By default, Word stores macros in the Normal template; however, it is usually best to store special-purpose macros in a special-purpose template. You can attach the template to a document when you need to use its stored macros, AutoText, or styles. Store macros that you use on a regular basis in the Normal template.

Sometimes it is better to use styles or AutoText instead of a macro. Here are some guidelines for deciding:

- Use AutoText to save standard text paragraphs, sometimes called *boilerplate* text. Use a macro to automate the insertion of AutoText.
- Use paragraph or character styles to save special formatting.

- Use AutoText to save specific text that is formatted in a special way.
- Use a macro to combine several Ribbon and dialog box choices that you use regularly—for example, inserting a sequence of AutoText entries or applying special formatting to a table.

Exercise 21-1 CREATE AN AUTOTEXT ENTRY TO USE WITH A MACRO

1. Press Ctrl+O to display the Open dialog box. Change the type of file box to Word Macro-Enabled Templates. Open the template **Campbell - Letter 1** from the student data files. This template contains a letterhead and a date field. Two AutoText entries are also stored in the template.

REVIEW

To create the AutoText entry, select all the lines, starting with "Sincerely" and ending with your reference initials. Click the Insert tab, and click the Quick Parts button. Click AutoText; then click Save Selection to AutoText gallery. Key Signature in the Name text box. Select AutoText in the gallery drop-down list. Select Campbell Letter - 1 in the Save in drop-down list. Click OK.

2. On the last line of the template, create a signature block using **Sincerely**, as the closing, **Tamara Robbins, Fundraising Department** as the author, and your reference initials.
3. Create an AutoText entry from the signature block. Name it **Signature** and store it in the **Campbell Letter - 1** template.
4. Delete the signature block you just created. (Remember that it is now an AutoText entry.)
5. Save the template as ***[your initials]*****LetterTemplate1** in a new folder for Lesson 21.

Exercise 21-2 PREPARE TO RECORD A MACRO

NOTE

When naming a macro, be careful not to use names of built-in Word macros. If you do, your macro actions will replace the built-in Word macro actions. To see a complete list of built-in macro names, click the Developer tab on the Ribbon, and locate the Code group. Click the Macros button, and select Word Commands in the Macros in list box.

Before beginning a macro recording, you should plan the steps you want the macro to perform, choose a name for it, and decide where it will be stored.

The macro created in this exercise will be stored in the currently open template. It will insert a boilerplate closing paragraph and the signature block AutoText entry you created in the previous exercise.

1. Display the Developer tab on the Ribbon by clicking the File tab and clicking Options. Click Customize Ribbon, and click to select Developer under Main Tabs in the Customize the Ribbon section. Click OK.

NOTE

If you attempt to record a macro by using an invalid macro name, you will get an error message stating "Invalid procedure name." If this happens, click OK and start with step 1 again, remembering to key a macro name that does not contain spaces.

2. Click the Record Macro button. In the Macro name text box, key **LetterClosing1**. Like merge field names, macro names must not contain spaces and must begin with an alphabetic character.
3. Under Store macro in, choose Documents Based On ***[your initials]*LetterTemplate1**.
4. In the Description box, key **Inserts closing paragraph 1 and the signature block for Tamara Robbins.**

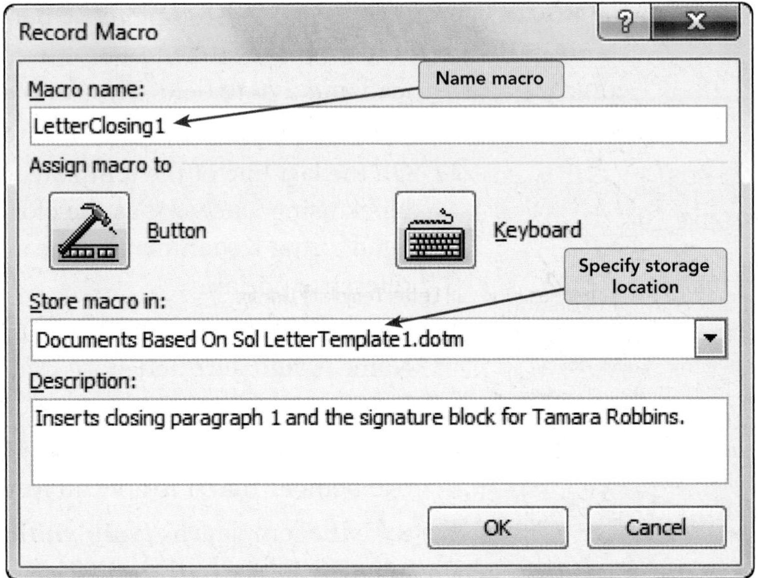

Figure 21-1
Record Macro dialog box

5. Click the Keyboard button. This opens the Customize Keyboard dialog box, where you can assign a keyboard shortcut to your macro.

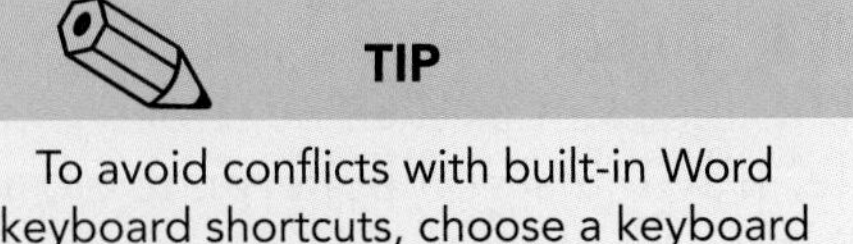

TIP

To avoid conflicts with built-in Word keyboard shortcuts, choose a keyboard combination that uses Alt plus a letter or number character.

6. With the insertion point in the **Press new shortcut key** text box, press Alt+1. The message "Currently assigned to: [unassigned]" appears under the Current keys text box. If you choose a key combination that is already assigned to a Word command, delete your choice and try a different key combination.
7. Locate the Save changes in drop-down list, and choose ***[your initials]* LetterTemplate1**, if it is not active.

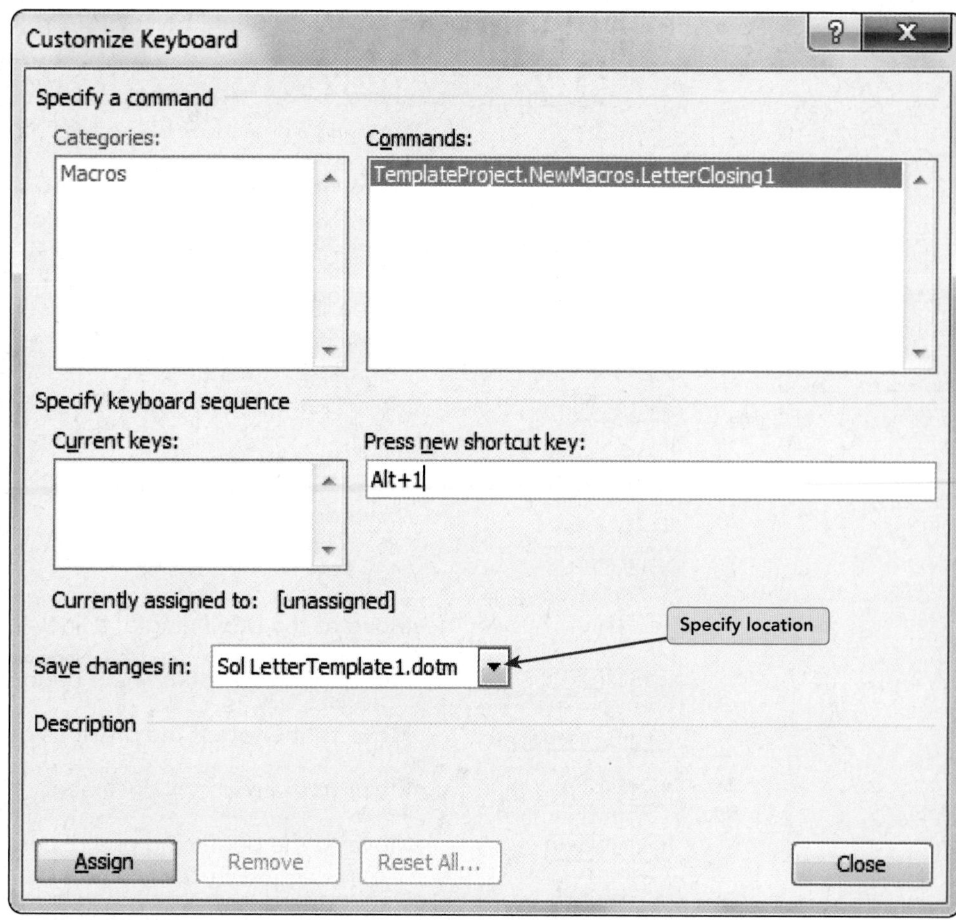

Figure 21-2 Customize Keyboard dialog box

8. Click **Assign** to assign the shortcut keys. The key combination "Alt+1" now appears in the Current keys list.
9. Click **Close**. The Stop Recording button appears on the Developer tab, and the mouse pointer changes to the recording pointer.

Exercise 21-3 RECORD A MACRO

When you see the recording pointer, every action you take with the mouse or the keyboard is being recorded in your macro.

You cannot use the macro pointer to select text or move the insertion point. It is not possible to record mouse movements in a macro. Use the macro pointer to select Ribbon commands and to move within a dialog box. Use keyboard equivalents for selecting text or repositioning the insertion point.

TABLE 21-1 Shortcut Keys for Navigating, Selecting, and Deleting in a Document

Keystroke	Result
←	Move one character to the left.
→	Move one character to the right.
Ctrl+←	Move one word to the left.
Ctrl+→	Move one word to the right.
Ctrl+↑	Move up one paragraph.
Ctrl+↓	Move down one paragraph.
↑	Move up one line.
↓	Move down one line.
End	Move to the end of a line.
Home	Move to the beginning of a line.
Ctrl+Page Down	Move to the top of the next page.
Ctrl+Page Up	Move to the top of the previous page.
Ctrl+End	Move to the end of a document.
Ctrl+Home	Move to the beginning of a document.
Backspace	Delete one character to the left.
Ctrl+Backspace	Delete one word to the left.
Delete	Delete one character to the right or delete selected text.
Ctrl+Delete	Delete one word to the right.
Shift+→	Select one character to the right.
Shift+←	Select one character to the left.
Ctrl+Shift+→	Select to the end of a word.
Ctrl+Shift+←	Select to the beginning of a word.
Shift+End	Select to the end of a line.
Shift+Home	Select to the beginning of a line.
Shift+↓	Select one line down.
Shift+↑	Select one line up.
Ctrl+Shift+↓	Select to the end of a paragraph.
Ctrl+Shift+↑	Select to the beginning of a paragraph.
Ctrl+Shift+Home	Select to the beginning of a document.
Ctrl+Shift+End	Select to the end of a document.
Ctrl+A	Select the entire document.

1. Using the recording pointer, click the **Insert** tab, and click the Quick Parts button. Click **Building Blocks Organizer**, and click the AutoText entry for **ClosingPara1**. Click **Insert**. The paragraph is inserted into the template.

TIP

You can record a macro even if you do not have any documents open on the screen. This enables you to record in a macro the steps to open a document.

2. Click the Quick Parts button. Click **Building Blocks Organizer**, and click the AutoText entry for **Signature**. Click **Insert**. The signature block is now inserted below the closing paragraph.
3. Click the **Developer** tab, and click the Stop Recording button on the Ribbon. The mouse pointer returns to its normal shape, indicating that the recording is completed.
4. Delete the paragraph and signature block you inserted while recording the macro. Your template should have a letterhead, date, and four blank lines below the date.
5. Save the template.

Running a Macro

If you assigned a shortcut key to a macro when you recorded it, the easiest way to run the macro is to press the shortcut key combination. You can also run a macro from the Macros dialog box, which lists all the macros in the current template, the Normal template, or the Word built-in macros.

Exercise 21-4 SET MACRO SECURITY

Security settings for macros are located in the Trust Center. To view or change settings, open the Word Options dialog box and either click Trust Center and then Trust Center Settings or click the Macro Security button in the Code group of the Developer tab. There are four settings for macros:

- Disable all macros without notification.
- Disable all macros with notification (default).
- Disable all macros except digitally signed macros.
- Enable all macros (not recommended; potentially dangerous code can run).

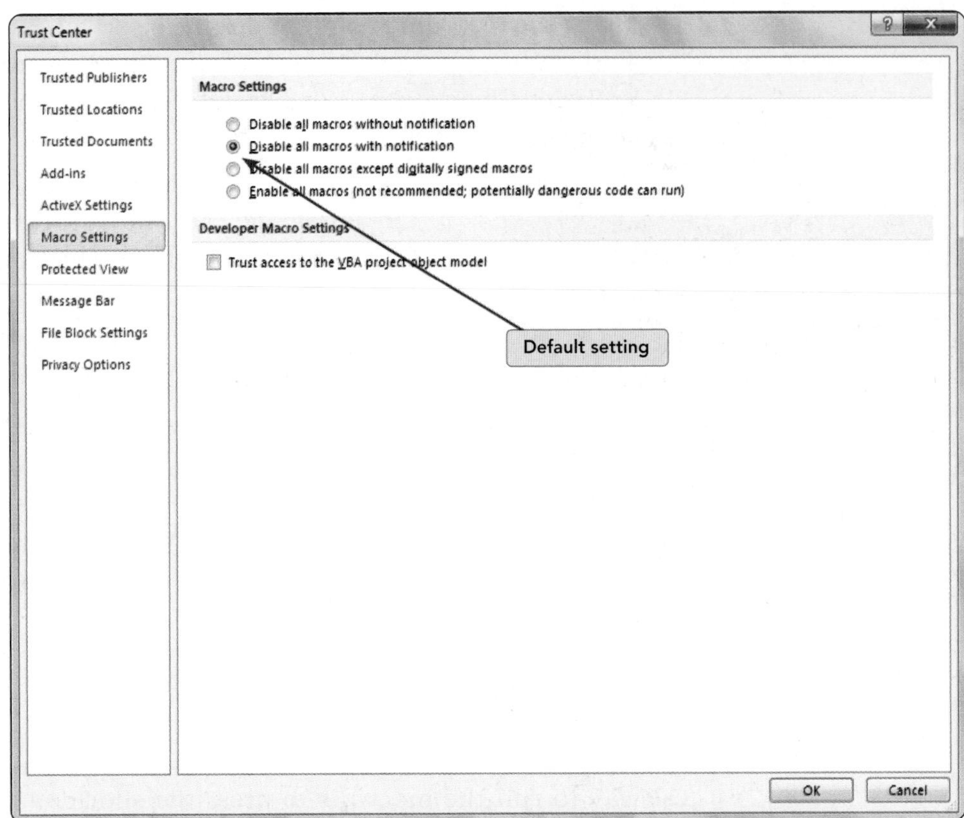

Figure 21-3 Trust Center dialog box

You may have occasion to work with documents containing macros that were created by another user. Since macros can threaten the security of your computer and contribute to the spread of a virus, you should exercise caution when running macros. The Trust Center settings determine what happens on your machine when you run a macro. A security dialog box may appear with options to enable the macro or to leave it disabled. Do not enable the macro unless you know it is from a trustworthy source.

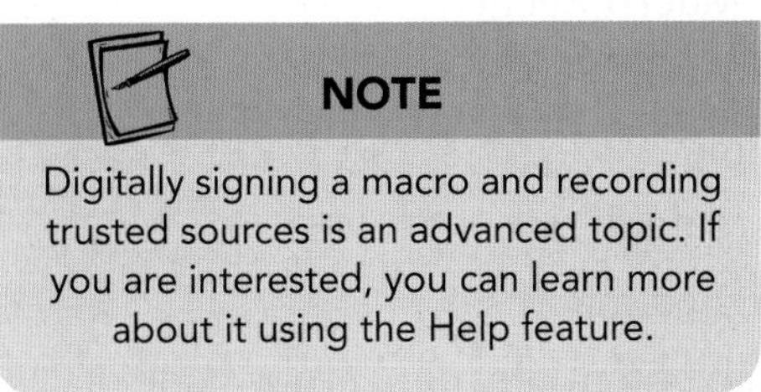

NOTE

Digitally signing a macro and recording trusted sources is an advanced topic. If you are interested, you can learn more about it using the Help feature.

Macros may include a digital signature, which is an encrypted stamp of authentication. The signature ensures that the macro originated from the signer and has not been altered. Digital signatures are issued by a commercial organization. When macros are not signed, the identity of the macro publisher cannot be verified by the Trust Center.

1. Display the **Developer** tab, and click the Macro Security button.
2. Click **Macro Settings**.
3. View the Macro Settings, and verify that **Disable all macros with notification** is selected. Click **OK**.
4. Close the template, saving it if necessary. Before the new security level can take effect, it is necessary to close the template and reopen it.

Exercise 21-5 RUN A MACRO

1. Reopen the template you just created. Be sure to open the template and not a new document based on the template. Position the insertion point below the date.

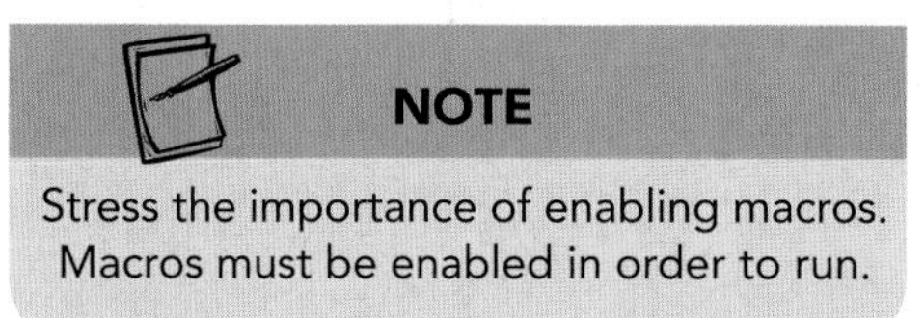

NOTE
Stress the importance of enabling macros. Macros must be enabled in order to run.

2. Notice the security warning that appears below the Ribbon indicating that macros have been disabled.
3. Click the Enable Content button [Enable Content] to enable the macros. Click **Yes** if the Security Warning dialog box displays.

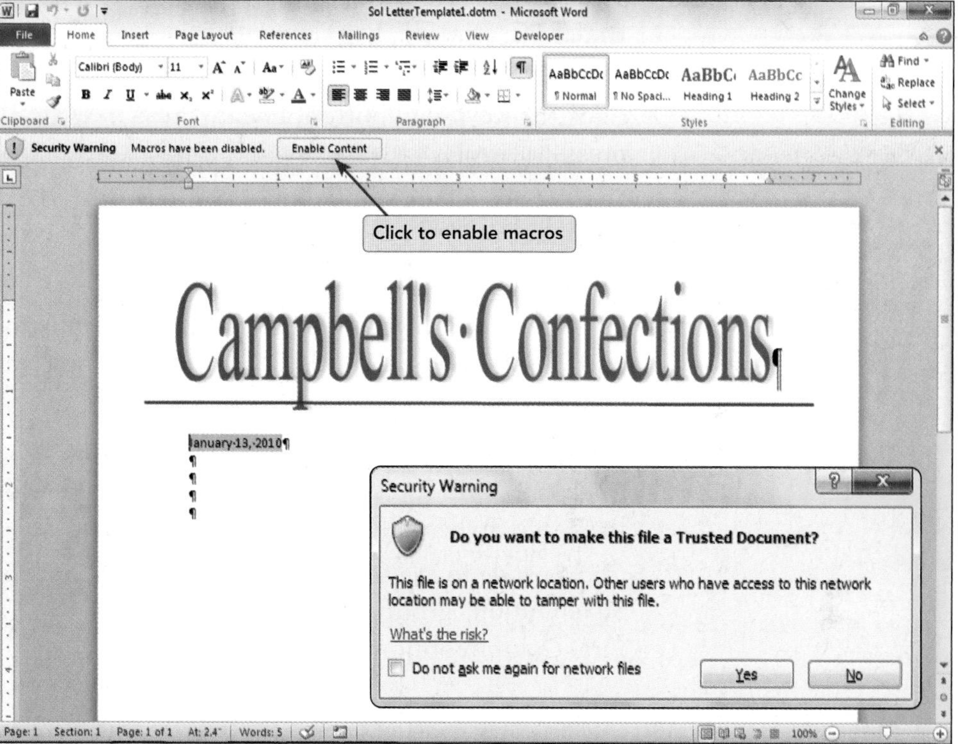

Figure 21-4
Enable macros

4. Move the insertion point to the end of the template.
5. Click the **Developer** tab, and click the Macros button. Verify that ***[your initials]*LetterTemplate1** is selected from the Macros in list box. LetterClosing1 is the only macro listed.
6. Select **LetterClosing1** and click **Run**. The closing paragraph and the signature block are inserted at the insertion point.
7. Click the Undo button twice to remove the signature block and closing paragraph from the template.
8. Press Alt+1, the shortcut key combination for the macro. The closing paragraph and signature block are inserted again.
9. Press Ctrl+Z twice to remove the text inserted by the macro.

Exercise 21-6 CREATE A MACRO THAT CONVERTS TEXT TO A TABLE

1. With the insertion point four lines below the date, insert the file **AddrText**. A tab-delimited address list is inserted.
2. Select all the text in the address list.
3. Click the **Developer** tab, and click the Record Macro button. The Record Macro dialog box opens.
4. Key **MakeTable** in the Macro name text box,
5. Under Store macro in, choose Documents Based On ***[your initials]*****LetterTemplate1**.
6. Under Description, key **Converts selected tab-delimited text to a formatted table.**
7. Click the **Keyboard** button. Locate **Press new shortcut key:**, press Ctrl+Alt+Shift+T.
8. Under Save changes in, choose ***[your initials]*****LetterTemplate1**, if it is not active.
9. Click **Assign** and then click **Close**.
10. With the recording pointer, click the **Insert** tab, and click the Table button. Choose **Convert Text to Table**. The Convert Text to Table dialog box opens.
11. Under Separate text at, make sure **Tabs** is chosen. Click **OK**.
12. Click the **Table Tools Design** tab, and click the More arrow to display the Table Styles gallery.
13. Click a style in the second row of the Built-In styles. Locate the **Table Style Options** group on the Table Tools Design tab, and verify that the First Column option is not checked.

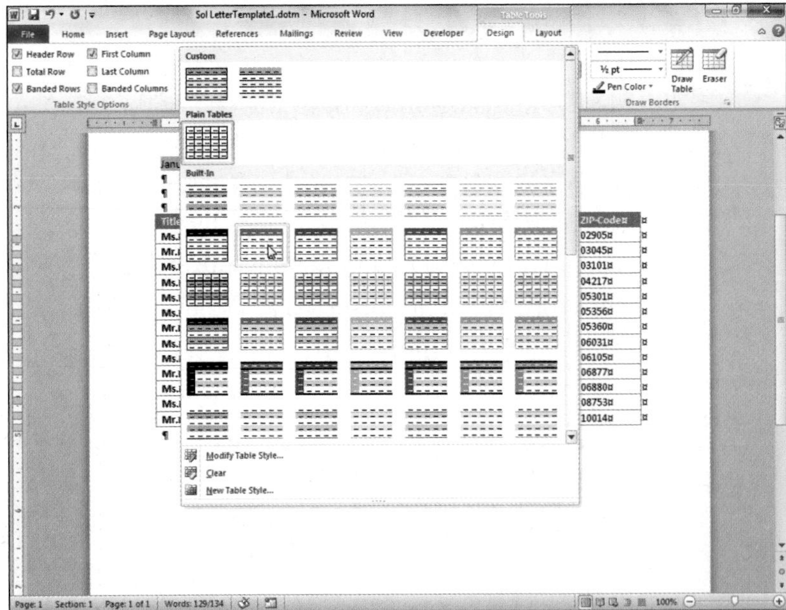

Figure 21-5
Choosing a table style

14. Click the Table Tools Layout tab, and click the AutoFit button. Click AutoFit Contents.
15. Click the Properties button and click the Table tab.
16. Under Alignment, choose Center and click OK. The table is now horizontally centered on the page.
17. Press ↓ once to deselect the table.
18. Click the Developer tab, and click the Stop Recording button. The address list is now a formatted table.
19. Click the Undo button five times to change the table back to a tab-delimited list. (Pressing Undo will not remove the macro.)
20. Make sure all the text in the list is selected, and then press Ctrl+Shift+Alt+T (the keyboard shortcut you assigned) to run the MakeTable macro.

Editing a Macro

When you record a Word macro, a computer program is created that uses Visual Basic for Applications. Even if you do not understand Visual Basic programming, you can do simple editing to change your macro—if you are careful.

The Visual Basic Editor is made up of several windows that you can display or hide, depending on the task you are performing. When you edit a recorded macro, the Code window displays. *Code* is a programmer term for the text written in the Visual Basic language (or other programming languages) that makes up a macro or program.

The MakeTable macro will be successful only for tables that are six columns wide. The number of columns and the number of rows are *hard-coded*, meaning that the exact number of rows and columns is written into the program. You can safely delete the part of the program that specifies the number of columns and the number of rows to make the macro work for any number of rows and columns.

Exercise 21-7 EDIT A MACRO

1. Click the Macros button or press Alt+F8 to open the Macros dialog box.
2. In the Macros in text box, choose ***[your initials]*****LetterTemplate1 (template)**, choose MakeTable, and then click Edit. The Microsoft Visual Basic for Applications window opens.

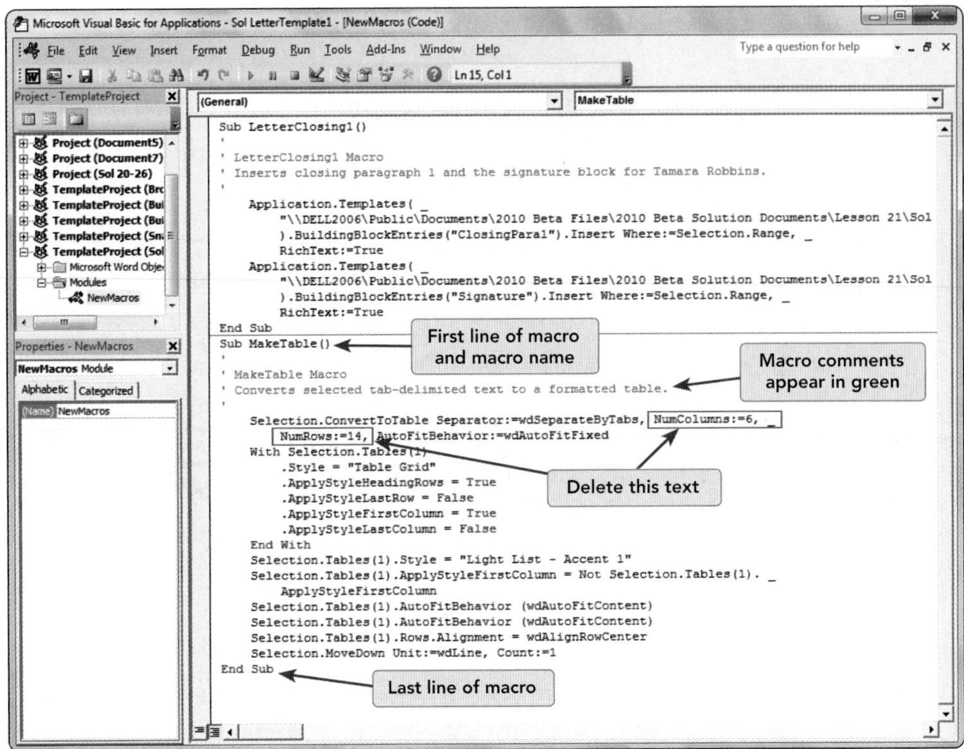

Figure 21-6 Microsoft Visual Basic window

NOTE

Your screen might look slightly different from the figure.

NOTE

Comments are not part of the actual macro program. A comment can contain any text that identifies the macro or makes it easier to understand. Each comment line must begin with an apostrophe.

TIP

If a line of code turns red while you are editing, there is an error in the code. If you cannot figure out how to repair it, press Ctrl+Z to undo the editing and try again.

3. If necessary, maximize the Code window and drag its left edge to make it wide enough to display the entire width of the code.
4. Using Figure 21-6, locate the various parts of the MakeTable macro: the first line and macro name, "Sub MakeTable()"; the last line, "End Sub"; and the comments, which are the green lines beginning with an apostrophe.
5. In the MakeTable macro, locate the text "Selection. ConvertToTable." ConvertToTable is a Word built-in macro. When working in a document, if you choose Table, Convert Text to Table, Word automatically runs the ConvertToTable macro. The code that follows on the next several lines of the macro specifies various table settings.
6. Notice that many lines end with a space and an underscore (_). The underscore is a symbol that represents a line continuation. In other words, the complete command with all its settings is too long to fit on one line. When editing, make sure you do not delete an underscore and the space before it.

NOTE

When you record a macro that inserts AutoText, the default is to insert the AutoText as unformatted text. This will not be apparent until you actually run a macro that inserts AutoText that has special formatting. To force your macro to insert the AutoText with its formatting intact, add the text "Richtext:=True" to the end of the line that inserts an AutoText entry.

7. In the MakeTable macro, select the text "NumColumns:=6," (including the space before and the comma after) and delete it. Use Figure 21-6 to help you locate the text. (Press Shift+→ to control text selection in the macro.) This part of the code tells Word to make the table six columns wide. If the number of columns is not specified, Word will adjust the number of columns to the number of tabs in a row of selected text.
8. Select the text "NumRows:=14," and delete it.

Figure 21-7
MakeTable macro after editing

```
Sub MakeTable()
'
' MakeTable Macro
' Converts selected tab-delimited text to a formatted table.
'
    Selection.ConvertToTable Separator:=wdSeparateByTabs, _
        AutoFitBehavior:=wdAutoFitFixed
    With Selection.Tables(1)
        .Style = "Table Grid"
        .ApplyStyleHeadingRows = True
        .ApplyStyleLastRow = False
        .ApplyStyleFirstColumn = True
        .ApplyStyleLastColumn = False
    End With
    Selection.Tables(1).Style = "Light List - Accent 1"
    Selection.Tables(1).ApplyStyleFirstColumn = Not Selection.Tables(1). _
        ApplyStyleFirstColumn
    Selection.Tables(1).AutoFitBehavior (wdAutoFitContent)
    Selection.Tables(1).AutoFitBehavior (wdAutoFitContent)
    Selection.Tables(1).Rows.Alignment = wdAlignRowCenter
    Selection.MoveDown Unit:=wdLine, Count:=1
End Sub
```

9. Click the Save button on the Visual Basic Editor's toolbar; then choose **File** and **Close and Return to Microsoft Word** (or press Alt+Q) to close the Visual Basic Editor window.

Exercise 21-8 TEST CHANGES MADE TO A MACRO

To test the MakeTable macro, try it on a tab-delimited list that requires a number of columns other than six.

1. Move to the bottom of the template, below the table, and insert two blank lines.
2. Insert the file **Fund 3** at the insertion point.
3. Select all lines of the inserted text.
4. Press Ctrl+Shift+Alt+T to run the MakeTable macro. A formatted table appears.
5. Delete both tables from the template, and make sure there are only four blank lines below the date. Save the template. It should now contain a letterhead, a date, and four blank lines below the date.
6. Display the **Print** tab. Under Settings, open the drop-down list for Print All Pages. Scroll to locate **Key Assignments**. Click to select the Key Assignments option. Print the key assignments, and then close the template.

Exercise 21-9 CREATE A LETTER BY USING MACROS

1. Start a new document based on ***[your initials]*LetterTemplate1**.
2. Click Enable Content in the Security Warning area if prompted. A new document based on your template opens.
3. Key the text in Figure 21-8, formatting it as a standard business letter.

Figure 21-8

```
Mr. Robert Briggs
543 Hermitage Road
Transfer, PA 16154

Dear Mr. Briggs:

Thank you for your recent letter regarding Campbell's
Confections Fundraising Program. The following table lists
several order options including cost and profit.
```

REVIEW

To open a document based on a template saved in your Lesson 21 folder, use Windows Explorer or Computer to navigate to the folder. Locate the file ***[your initials]*LetterTemplate1**, and double-click it (or right-click it and choose New from the shortcut menu).

4. On the second line below the paragraph you keyed, insert the file **Fund 3**.
5. Select all the tabbed text, and press Ctrl+Shift+Alt+T to run the MakeTable macro.
6. Position the insertion point two lines below the table, and then press Alt+1 to run the LetterClosing1 macro.
7. Select and center the numbers in the first column. Select and right-align the numbers in the second and third columns.
8. Save the document as ***[your initials]*21-9** in your Lesson 21 folder. Submit and close the document, saving changes.

Copying, Renaming, and Deleting Macros

You can edit, rename, or delete macros by using the Macros dialog box. Simply select the macro and click the appropriate button. To copy macros from one document or template to another, use the Organizer. You might already be familiar with using the Organizer for moving or copying styles from one template to another. In the same way, you can move and copy macros from one template to another.

Exercise 21-10 COPY MACROS

When you record a macro, it is stored in a *module*. In Word, a module is a container attached to a document or template, where macros and other program code are stored. All recorded macros are stored in a module named *NewMacros*. If you want to copy macros from one template to another, you copy the NewMacros module. All macros contained in the module are copied to the new template.

1. Open the template file **Letterhead3**. This template contains three AutoText entries, but it contains no macros.
2. Press Alt+F8 to open the Macros dialog box. Notice that there are no macros listed.
3. Click the Organizer button Organizer... to open the Organizer dialog box.
4. Click the **Macro Project Items** tab. The left side of the dialog box lists modules in the current template or document—in this case, **Letterhead3.** The right side lists the document or template you will use to copy modules to or from, currently the Normal template.
5. On the right side of the dialog box, click the Close File button Close File. The Normal template closes, and the Close File button changes to Open File.
6. Click the Open File button Open File... on the right side of the dialog box, and navigate to the Lesson 21 folder for student data files.
7. Choose **FormatTemplate** and click **Open**. The module NewMacros appears in the list on the right.

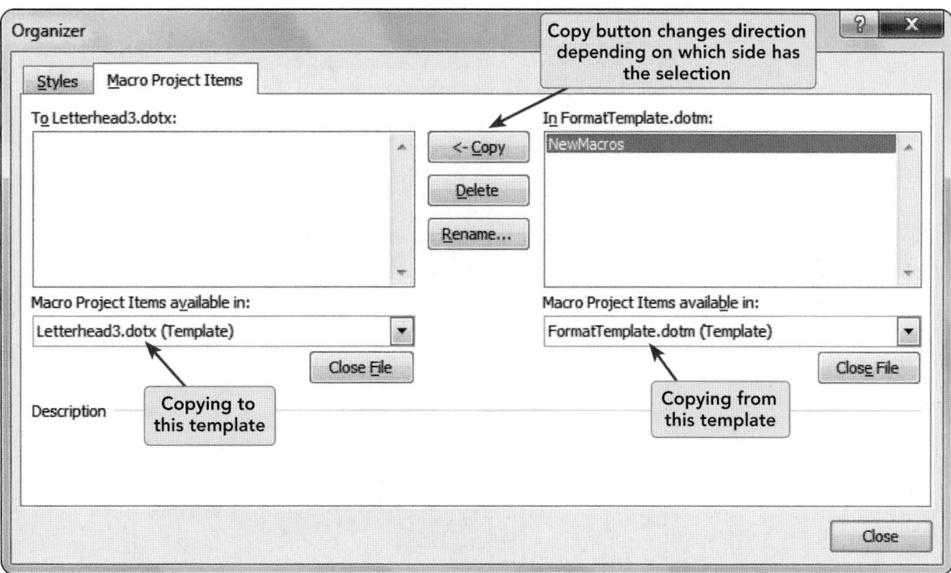

Figure 21-9
Copying the NewMacros module

8. Make sure **NewMacros** is selected in the list on the right side, and then click **Copy** to copy all the macros in the NewMacros module to the list on the left side. Click **Close**.
9. Save the template as ***[your initials]*LetterTemplate2** in your Lesson 21 folder. Be sure to choose **Word Macro-Enabled Template** from the Save as type list box.
10. Press Alt+F8 to reopen the Macros dialog box. Two macros now appear in the list.

Exercise 21-11 COPY AN INDIVIDUAL MACRO

You can copy and paste a macro within a module. This can be convenient if you have a useful macro that can serve a different purpose with a few changes.

To copy a macro, select the macro name in the Macros dialog box and then click Edit. In the Visual Basic Editor window, select all of the macro's text and then click Copy. Place the insertion point at the beginning of the first line of an existing macro, or place it on a new line at the end of the module; then click the Paste button.

1. If necessary, reopen the Macros dialog box.
2. Select **TitleFormat** and click **Edit**. The Visual Basic Editor opens, with the TitleFormat macro displayed at the top of the code window.
3. Select all the text in the macro, beginning with "Sub TitleFormat()" and ending with "End Sub," as shown in Figure 21-10.
4. Click the Copy button on the Visual Basic toolbar.

Figure 21-10 Copying an individual macro

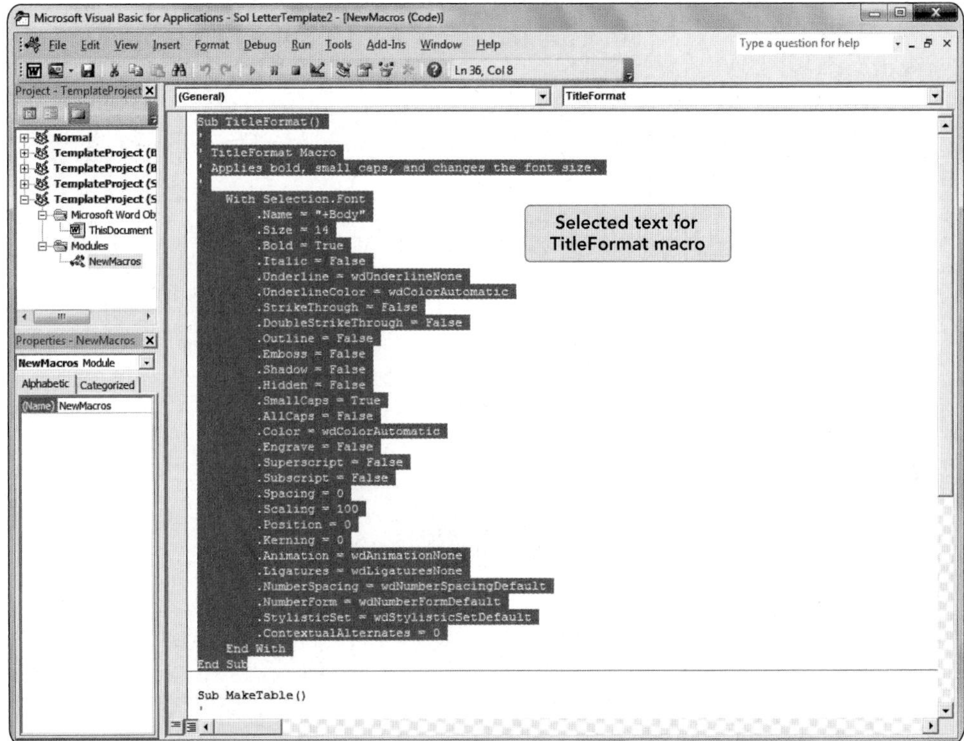

5. Scroll to the bottom of the code window, and position the insertion point on a blank line below the MakeTable macro.
6. Click the Paste button on the Visual Basic Standard toolbar. A copy of the TitleFormat macro appears.

Exercise 21-12 RENAME A MACRO

Because a module cannot contain two macros with the same name, you must rename the copy of TitleFormat. To do that, you edit the text after the word "Sub" on the first line of the macro.

1. On the first line of the pasted macro, change the text "Sub TitleFormat()" to **Sub HeadingFormat()**.
2. In the green comment text, change "TitleFormat Macro" to **HeadingFormat Macro**. Change "Applies bold, small caps, and changes the font size" to Applies bold, italic, small caps, and changes the font and font size.
3. Change Name = +Body to Name = Tahoma. Change Size = 14 to Size = 16. Change Italic = False to Italic = True.

Be sure to include the parentheses, quotation marks, period, space, and underscore. The renamed and edited macro should agree with Figure 21-11.

Figure 21-11
Copied and renamed macro after editing

```
Sub HeadingFormat()
'
' HeadingFormat Macro
' Applies bold, italic, small caps, and changes the font and font size.
'
    With Selection.Font
        .Name = "Tahoma"
        .Size = 16
        .Bold = True
        .Italic = True
        .Underline = wdUnderlineNone
        .UnderlineColor = wdColorAutomatic
        .StrikeThrough = False
        .DoubleStrikeThrough = False
        .Outline = False
        .Emboss = False
        .Shadow = False
        .Hidden = False
        .SmallCaps = True
        .AllCaps = False
        .Color = wdColorAutomatic
        .Engrave = False
        .Superscript = False
        .Subscript = False
        .Spacing = 0
        .Scaling = 100
        .Position = 0
        .Kerning = 0
        .Animation = wdAnimationNone
        .Ligatures = wdLigaturesNone
        .NumberSpacing = wdNumberSpacingDefault
        .NumberForm = wdNumberFormDefault
        .StylisticSet = wdStylisticSetDefault
        .ContextualAlternates = 0
    End With
End Sub
```

4. Click the Save button on the Visual Basic toolbar to save the template.
5. Choose **Print** from the Visual Basic **File** menu, and then click **OK** to print a copy of your macro code. Close the Visual Basic window and return to Word.

6. Press Alt+F8 to open the Macros dialog box. Notice that three macros are now listed.
7. Select HeadingFormat. In the Description box, key **Applies bold, italic, small caps, and changes the font and font size**. Do not close the Macros dialog box.

Exercise 21-13 DELETE A MACRO

The easiest way to delete a macro is in the Macros dialog box.

TIP

You can also delete a macro in the Visual Basic Editor. Be careful to select the entire macro and nothing else. Then press Delete.

1. Reopen the Macros dialog box if it is not already open.
2. Select TitleFormat.
3. Click Delete and then click Yes.
4. Click Close to close the Macros dialog box.

Exercise 21-14 ASSIGN A KEYBOARD SHORTCUT TO A COPIED MACRO

1. Open the Word Options dialog box, and click Customize Ribbon. Near the bottom of the dialog box, locate the section Keyboard shortcuts.
2. Click the Customize button Customize... at the bottom of the dialog box. The Customize Keyboard dialog box opens.
3. Under Categories, scroll to the bottom of the list and choose Macros.
4. Make sure ***[your initials]*****LetterTemplate2** is selected from the Save changes in list box.
5. Under Macros, choose HeadingFormat, if it is not active.
6. In the Press new shortcut key box, press Alt+2.
7. Click Assign and then click Close.
8. Click OK to close the Word Options dialog box.
9. Key your name at the end of the document, and select the text. Test the macro by pressing Alt+2. Delete your name.
10. Save the letter template and close it.

Customizing the Quick Access Toolbar and the Ribbon

By now you have probably found several Ribbon commands that you use over and over again. To save time when creating documents, you can customize the Quick Access Toolbar by adding frequently used Ribbon commands. You can also assign a macro to the Quick Access Toolbar and change the position of the Quick Access Toolbar.

Exercise 21-15 ADD A COMMAND TO THE QUICK ACCESS TOOLBAR

The Quick Access Toolbar displays three commands by default. You can add additional commands, by customizing the Quick Access Toolbar. Use the Word Options dialog box or click the Customize Quick Access Toolbar button to add commands to the Quick Access Toolbar. You can also right-click selected buttons on the Ribbon to open the Word Options dialog box.

1. Create a new document.
2. Click the Customize Quick Access Toolbar button, located on the right side of the Quick Access Toolbar. A list of commands displays.

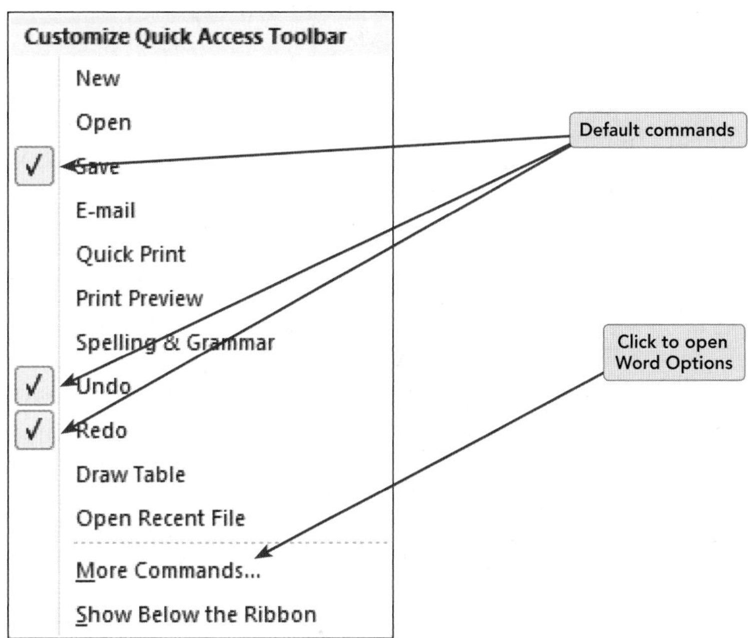

Figure 21-12 Quick Access Toolbar command list

3. Notice that the three default commands are selected as indicated by the checkmarks.
4. Click **Print Preview and Print**. The Print Preview button appears on the Quick Access Toolbar.

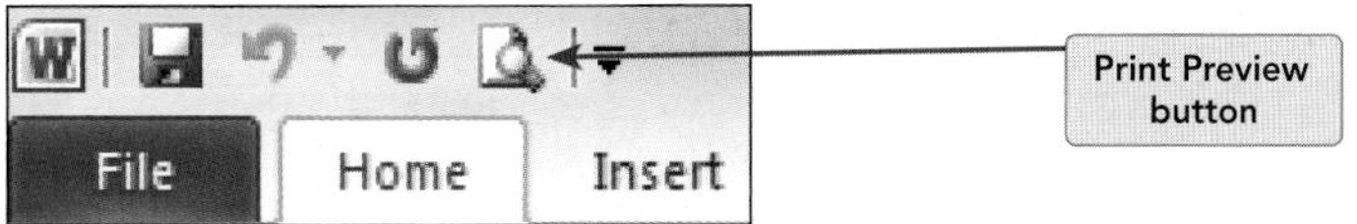

Figure 21-13 Customized Quick Access Toolbar

5. Click the Customize Quick Access Toolbar button, and click **More Commands**. The Word Options dialog box opens with the Quick Access Toolbar selected.

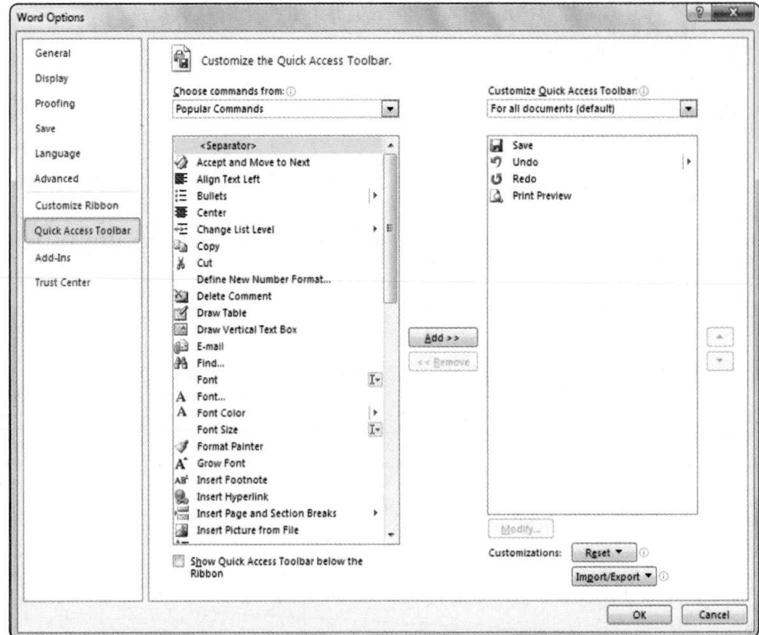

Figure 21-14 Word Options: Quick Access Toolbar

6. Click the down arrow to open the drop-down list box for **Choose commands from**. Select the **Popular Commands** category. Drag the scroll box in the list of commands to locate the **Spelling & Grammar** command. Click the command to select it, and click **Add**. The Spelling and Grammar command is added to the Quick Access Toolbar. Click **OK**.
7. Notice the appearance of the Quick Access Toolbar with the additional button.
8. Click the **Page Layout** tab, and right-click the Margins button. Click **Add to Quick Access Toolbar**. The Margins command is added to the Quick Access Toolbar.

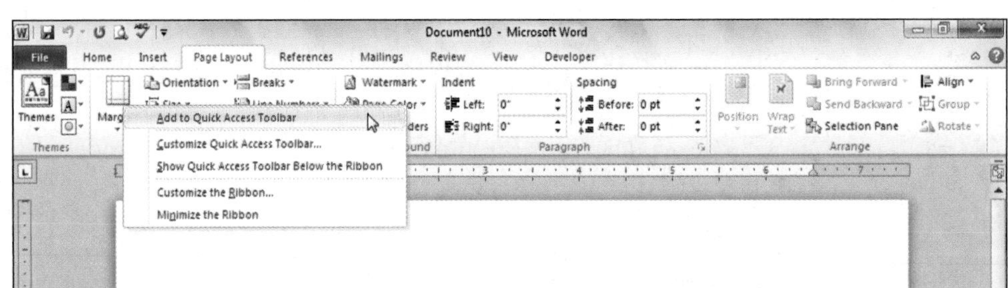

Figure 21-15 Shortcut menu to customize the Quick Access Toolbar

Exercise 21-16 MOVE THE QUICK ACCESS TOOLBAR

The default location for the Quick Access Toolbar is above the Ribbon You can change its position by placing it below the Ribbon.

1. Click the Customize Quick Access Toolbar button, and click **Show Below the Ribbon**.
2. Click the Customize Quick Access Toolbar button again, and click **Show Above the Ribbon**. The position of the Quick Access Toolbar is a personal preference. If you customize the Quick Access Toolbar by adding several buttons, you may prefer to display the toolbar below the Ribbon.

Exercise 21-17 ASSIGN A MACRO TO THE QUICK ACCESS TOOLBAR

When you record a macro, you can assign the macro to appear on the Quick Access Toolbar.

1. Click the **Developer** tab, and click the Record Macro button.
2. Key **InsertPageNumber** in the Macro name box. Remember not to insert spaces between the words. Click the down arrow for the Store macro in box, and click **Document1 (document)**. (Your document number may differ from Document1.)
3. Click Button.
4. Locate the heading Choose commands from in the Word Options dialog box. Click **Project.NewMacros.InsertPageNumber**.
5. Locate the heading for the **Customize Quick Access Toolbar** drop-down list on the right side of the Word Options dialog box. Select **For Document1** (or the document number that appears).
6. Click **Add**. Click **OK**.
7. Record the macro by following these steps:
8. Click the **Insert** tab, and click the **Footer** button. Click **Edit Footer**, and press Tab twice to move to the right margin. Key **Page**, press the Spacebar, and insert the Page numbering field. Click **Close** to close the Header and Footer pane. Click the **Developer** tab, and click the Stop Recording button. Notice the macro button on the Quick Access Toolbar.

Exercise 21-18 RESET THE QUICK ACCESS TOOLBAR

1. Open the Word Options dialog box, and click **Quick Access Toolbar**.
2. Click the Reset button Reset ▾. Click **Reset all customizations**, and click **Yes** to restore the Quick Access Toolbar. Click **OK**.
3. Close the document without saving.

Lesson 21 Summary

- A Word macro enables you to quickly perform repetitive tasks involving command sequences and keystrokes. With a macro, you can save a sequence of tasks as a single command.
- When you create macros, you store them in either a document or a template. By default, Word stores macros in the Normal template, but it is best to store special-purpose macros in a special-purpose template.
- Before beginning a macro recording, plan the steps you want the macro to perform, choose a name for it, and decide where it will be stored.
- When you see the recording pointer, every action you take with the mouse or the keyboard is being recorded in your macro.
- You can assign a macro to a button, the Quick Access Toolbar, or to a keyboard shortcut key, which you can then use to run the macro. You can also run a macro from the Macros dialog box.
- When you record a Word macro, a computer program is created that uses Visual Basic for Applications. You can change the macro by carefully editing the Visual Basic code.
- You can use the Macros dialog box to edit, rename, or delete macros.
- You use the Organizer to copy macros from one document or template to another.
- You can customize the Quick Access Toolbar by adding and deleting commands. The Quick Access Toolbar can also be moved to display below the Ribbon.

LESSON 21		Command Summary	
Feature	**Button**	**Command**	**Keyboard**
Close the Visual Basic Editor		File menu, Close and Return to Microsoft Word	Alt+Q
Customize the Quick Access Toolbar		Quick Access Toolbar, Customize Quick Access Toolbar	
Edit a macro		Developer tab, Code group	Alt+F8
Open the Macros dialog box		Developer tab, Code group	Alt+F8
Record macros		Developer tab, Code group	
Set macro security		Developer tab, Code group	
Stop recording		Developer tab, Code group	

Concepts Review

True/False Questions

Each of the following statements is either true or false. Indicate your choice by circling T or F.

T F 1. The pointer [pointer icon] indicates that a macro is being recorded.

T F 2. When a macro is being recorded, you can use the special mouse pointer to select text.

T F 3. You should never use the Shift key when assigning shortcuts to macros.

T F 4. Unless you are an advanced programmer, you should never delete the underscore (_) at the end of a line when editing a macro.

T F 5. The code for a macro always ends with the words "End Sub."

T F 6. By default, macros are saved in a separate file named NewMacros.

T F 7. You can key anything you want in comments, as long as each line begins with an apostrophe.

T F 8. You can use the Word Options dialog box to customize the Quick Access Toolbar.

Short Answer Questions

Write the correct answer in the space provided.

1. Which dialog box do you use to copy a macro module from one template to another?

____

2. What do you do to tell Word you have finished recording a macro?

____

3. What color are macro comment lines?

____

4. If a line in a macro you are editing turns red, what does it mean?

____

5. What do you call the container where macros are stored?

____

6. On what line of a macro do you find the macro's name?

____

7. Which dialog box is used to remove a command from the Quick Access Toolbar?

8. How do you rename a macro?

Critical Thinking

Answer these questions on a separate page. There are no right or wrong answers. Support your answers with examples from your own experience, if possible.

1. Describe briefly three word processing tasks you think a macro could simplify.
2. Which buttons would you include on a customized Quick Access Toolbar and why?

Skills Review

Exercise 21-19

Create and run macros.

1. Start a new template.
2. Save the template as ***[your initials]*****LetterTemplate3** in your Lesson 21 folder. Select Word Macro-Enabled Template in the Save as type box.
3. Start a macro recording by following these steps:
   a. Click the Developer tab, and click the Record Macro button.
   b. In the Record Macro dialog box, under Macro name, key **InsertLogo**.
   c. Under Store macro in, select Documents Based On ***[your initials]*****LetterTemplate3**.
   d. Under Description, key the description **Inserts letterhead logo**.
   e. Click the Keyboard button to open the Customize Keyboard dialog box.
   f. Under Press new shortcut key, press Ctrl+Alt+Shift+L.
   g. Under Save changes in, make sure ***[your initials]*****LetterTemplate3** is selected.
   h. Click Assign and then click Close. The recording pointer appears.
4. Record the steps to insert the logo, as follows:
   a. Click the Insert tab, and click the Picture button.
   b. Locate the folder for the student data files, and click the file **Letterhead Logo**.

c. Click **Insert**, and click the Stop Recording button on the Developer tab.

d. Delete the logo.

e. Press Ctrl+Alt+Shift+L to test-run the macro. Delete the logo.

5. Create a macro to insert a watermark by following these steps:

a. Click the **Developer** tab, and click the Record Macro button.

b. In the Record Macro dialog box, under Macro name, key **InsertWatermark**.

c. Under Store macro in, select **Documents Based On *[your initials]*LetterTemplate3.**

d. Under Description, key the description **Inserts corporate watermark**.

e. Click the **Keyboard** button to open the Customize Keyboard dialog box.

f. Under Press new shortcut key, press Ctrl+Alt+Shift+W.

g. Under Save changes in, make sure ***[your initials]*LetterTemplate3** is selected.

h. Click **Assign** and then click **Close**. The recording pointer appears.

6. Record the steps to insert the watermark, as follows:

a. Click the **Page Layout** tab, and click the Watermark button.

b. Click **Custom Watermark**, click **Picture watermark**, and click **Select Picture**. Locate the folder for the student files, and click the file **Monogram.** Click **Insert**. Verify that **Washout** is checked, and click **OK**.

c. Click the Stop Recording button on the Developer tab.

d. Undo the watermark.

e. Press Ctrl+Alt+Shift+W to test-run the macro.

f. Undo the watermark.

7. Save the letter template, and print the key assignments by following these steps:

a. Display the **Print** tab.

b. Click the down arrow beside **Print All Pages**. Scroll to and click **Key assignments**. Click **Print**.

8. Close the template.

9. Start a new document based on ***[your initials]*LetterTemplate3**. Enable the macros by clicking **Enable Content**.

10. Press Ctrl+Alt+Shift+L to run the InsertLogo macro.

11. Insert a CreateDate field below the logo with appropriate format.

12. Save the document as ***[your initials]*21-19** in your Lesson 21 folder. Submit and close the document, saving changes.

Exercise 21-20

Create an AutoText entry and create a macro that uses the AutoText entry.

1. Start a new template. Insert the Letterhead Logo picture file located in the folder storing the student data files.
2. On a blank line below the logo, select the paragraph mark and apply the No Spacing style. Create a signature block keying **Sincerely**, and press Enter four times.
3. Key **Lynn Tanguay**, press Enter, and key **Vice President**. Press Enter two times, and key your reference initials.
4. Save the template as a Word Macro-Enabled Template named ***[your initials]*****CampbellLetterhead** in your Lesson 21 folder, but do not close it.
5. Select the entire signature block, including your reference initials.
6. Create an AutoText entry for the signature block, and name it **SignatureBlock**. (Be sure to select AutoText for the Gallery and ***[your initials]*****CampbellLetterhead** as the location for storing the AutoText entry.)

TIP

To create an AutoText entry, click the Insert tab, click Quick Parts, click AutoText, and click Save Selection to AutoText Gallery.

7. Delete the signature block from the template.
8. Start a macro recording named **SignatureBlock** that is stored in ***[your initials]*****Campbell Letterhead**. Enter an appropriate description for inserting a signature block. Assign the keyboard shortcut Ctrl+Shift+Alt+S.
9. Record the macro by following these steps:
   a. Click the Insert tab, and click Quick Parts. Click Building Blocks Organizer.
   b. Choose SignatureBlock.
   c. Click Insert.
   d. Click the Developer tab, and click the Stop Recording button.
10. Delete the signature block; then resave the template and close it.
11. Start a new document based on the ***[your initials]*** **CampbellLetterhead** template. Enable macros. Select the paragraph mark below the letterhead logo, and apply the No Spacing style. Key the current date. Press Enter four times.
12. Use the following information for an inside address and a salutation:

    Ms. Elizabeth Craemer
    Harold James Keller Group
    182 South Street
    Ganister, PA 16693

13. For the body of the letter, insert the file **Craemer**.
14. Run the SignatureBlock macro.

15. Add an enclosure notation, and change the bottom margin to 0.5 inch.
16. Save the document as ***[your initials]*21-20** in your Lesson 21 folder. Submit and close the document, saving changes.

Exercise 21-21

Create macros, copy a macro, rename a macro, and delete a macro.

1. Start a new document and save the document as a Word Macro-Enabled Template named ***[your initials]*OhioLogos** in your Lesson 21 folder.
2. Record a macro to insert the Akron Logo picture file. Name the macro AkronLogo, and store the macro in ***[your initials]*OhioLogos.** Key a brief description, and click OK to start recording. Click the Insert tab, click the Picture button, and locate the folder for the student data files. Click to select the **Akron Logo** file, and click Insert. Stop recording the macro and delete the picture.
3. Rename a macro by following these steps:
   a. Press Alt+F8 to open the Macros dialog box.
   b. Select **AkronLogo** and click Edit.
   c. Locate the text "Sub AkronLogo()" and change it to **Sub AkronLetterhead()**.
   d. Click Save, and leave the Visual Basic Editor window open.
4. Select and copy the AkronLetterhead ( ) macro code. Paste the copied macro below the existing macro. Change the four references to Akron in the copied macro to Cleveland. Click Save. Click File, and click Close and Return to Microsoft Word.
5. Assign keyboard shortcuts to both macros by following these steps:
   a. Open the Word Options dialog box, and click Customize Ribbon.
   b. Click the Customize button to open the Customize Keyboard dialog box.
   c. Under Categories, choose Macros (at the bottom of the list).
   d. Make sure ***[your initials]*OhioLogos** is selected in the Save changes in list box.
   e. From the Macros list, select AkronLetterhead.
   f. In the Press new shortcut key box, press Ctrl+Alt+Shift+A.
   g. Click Assign, but do not close the dialog box.
   h. Assign an appropriate keyboard shortcut for the ClevelandLetterhead macro.
   i. Click Close to close the Customize Keyboard dialog box. Then click OK to close the Word Options dialog box.
6. Delete a macro by following these steps:
   a. Press Alt+F8 to open the Macros dialog box.
   b. Select AkronLetterhead from the list of macros.
   c. Press Delete. Click Yes.
   d. Click Close.

7. Save and close the template.
8. Start a new document based on the template ***[your initials]*OhioLogos**. Enable macros.
9. Using the key assignment you created for the Cleveland letterhead, run the macro.
10. Imagine you work for Campbell's Confections. Create a business letter to include a date, an inside address, salutation, and one or two paragraphs announcing a new chocolate product.
11. Include a closing, and use your name as the writer.
12. Save the document as ***[your initials]*21-21** in your Lesson 21 folder. Submit and close the document, saving changes.

Exercise 21-22

Copy a macro, edit a macro, print macro code, and customize the Quick Access Toolbar.

1. Open the template file **Candy Classes**. This template contains three special styles: CompanyName, ClassName, and Quarter.
2. Key the following text on three lines:

   Campbell's Confections
   Candy Making Classes
   Fall Schedule

3. Save the template as ***[your initials]*CandyClasses** in your Lesson 21 folder.
4. Start recording a new macro named **ClassHeading** with the description **Formats the first three lines of a document as a centered heading**. Assign the keyboard shortcut Ctrl+Shift+Alt+H. Make sure the macro will be stored in the ***[your initials]*CandyClasses** template.
5. Record the steps to apply styles to each heading line, as follows:
   a. Press Ctrl+Home to move the insertion point to the top of the document.
   b. Apply the style **CompanyName** to the first line.
   c. Press ↓ once to move to the second line, and then apply the style **ClassName**.
   d. Press ↓ once again to move to the third line, and then apply the style **Quarter**.
   e. Stop recording.
6. Customize the Quick Access Toolbar by following these steps:
   a. Click the Customize Quick Access Toolbar button, and click **More Commands**.
   b. Click the down arrow for the Choose Commands from box, and click **Commands Not in the Ribbon**.

c. Scroll to locate Small Caps. Click to select **Small Caps**, and click **Add**. Scroll to Quick Print, and click to select the command **Quick Print**. Click **Add**.

d. Click **OK**. The Quick Access Toolbar displays two new buttons.

7. Create three new styles for the three lines of text. Name them **Favorite1**, **Favorite2**, and **Favorite3**. Choose appropriate font and paragraph formatting for each style. You may want to select the three lines of text and apply the Normal style before creating the new styles.

8. Remove the new commands from the Quick Access Toolbar by following these steps:

   a. Open the Word Options dialog box.

   b. Click **Quick Access Toolbar**.

   c. Click the **Reset** button. Choose **Reset only Quick AccessToolbar**. Click **Yes** when the Reset Customizations message box displays.

   d. Click **OK** to close the Word Options dialog box.

9. Save the template.

10. Copy an individual macro by following these steps:

    a. Press Alt+F8 to open the Macros dialog box.

    b. Make sure ***[your initials]*****CandyClasses** (template) is selected in the Macros in list box and **ClassHeading** is selected in the Macro name list box.

    c. Click **Edit**.

    d. Select all the macro code in the code window, and copy it to the Clipboard.

    e. Press ↓ to move to the last line in the code window.

    f. Click the Paste button.

11. Edit the copied macro by following these steps:

    a. Change the macro name from "ClassHeading" to **FavoriteHeading**. Remember to change the comment lines as well.

    b. Locate the three style names "CompanyName," "ClassName," and "Quarter." Change the style names to **Favorite1**, **Favorite2**, and **Favorite3**.

TIP

Be careful to make sure each style has the correct punctuation. Example: ActiveDocument.Styles("Favorite1").

12. Save the macro code and then print it. Close the Visual Basic window to return to Word.

13. Assign the keyboard shortcut Ctrl+Shift+Alt+F to the FavoriteHeading macro and Ctrl+Shift+Alt+C to the ClassHeading macro.

14. To test the macro, press Ctrl+Shift+Alt+C to apply the ClassHeading macro. Then press Ctrl+Shift+Alt+F to apply the FavoriteHeading macro.

15. Delete all the text in the template, and then apply the Normal style to the remaining paragraph mark.

16. Resave the template, print the key assignments, and then close the template.

17. Start a new document based on the ***[your initials]*CandyClasses** template. Enable macros.
18. Key the following text on three separate lines:

    Campbell's Confections
    Chocolate Tempering
    Winter Schedule

19. Save the document as ***[your initials]*21-22** in your Lesson 21 folder.
20. Run the ClassHeading macro, and save and submit the document.
21. Run the FavoriteHeading macro, and save the document as ***[your initials]*21-22b** in your Lesson 21 folder.
22. Submit and close the document.

Lesson Applications

Exercise 21-23

Create a macro that changes page orientation to landscape and another macro that changes a page to a two-column format.

1. Start a new template.
2. Create a letterhead of your own design, using the following information:

   Campbell's Confections
   25 Main Street
   Grove City, PA 16127
   Telephone: 724-555-2025
   www.campbellsconfections.biz

3. Insert four blank lines below the letterhead.
4. On the third line below the letterhead, key **Chocolates**.
5. Select "Chocolates," center it, and format it as 14-point Calibri, with bold, italic, and small caps.
6. Save the template as a macro-enabled template named ***[your initials]*** **Chocolates** in your Lesson 21 folder.
7. Record a macro named **Landscape**, and store it in the ***[your initials]*** **Chocolates** template. Enter appropriate descriptive text in the description box. Assign the keyboard shortcut Ctrl+Shift+Alt+L. In this order, change the orientation to landscape, set 0.5-inch top and bottom margins, and set 1-inch left and right margins. Stop recording.
8. When the macro is completed, change the page orientation back to portrait with 1-inch top and bottom margins and 1-inch left and right margins. Save the template.
9. Record a second macro named **TwoColumns**, and store it in ***[your initials]*****Chocolates** with an appropriate description. Assign the keyboard shortcut Shift+Ctrl+Alt+C. This macro should create a two-column layout with 0.5-inch between columns that is applied from the insertion point to the end of the document. Stop recording.
10. When the macro is completed, click the Undo button to change the number of columns back to one. Then save the template.
11. Print the template's key assignments, and close the template.
12. Create a new document based on ***[your initials]*****Chocolates**. Enable macros.
13. Position the insertion point three lines below "Chocolates," and insert the file **Chocolate Terms**.

14. Position the insertion point at the beginning of the first line of inserted text ("Milk Chocolate").

15. Run the Landscape macro and the TwoColumns macro. (Press Ctrl+Shift+Alt+L and then Ctrl+Shift+Alt+C, but remember to run the TwoColumns macro from the beginning of the inserted text.)

16. Insert a column break at the beginning of the line with the text "White Chocolate." Select the column text, and apply 12 points spacing after.

17. Save the document as ***[your initials]*****21-23** in your Lesson 21 folder. Submit and close the document, saving changes.

Exercise 21-24

Create a macro that inserts an AutoText picture; copy the macro, rename it, and edit it to insert a different AutoText picture.

1. Open the file **ChocPic**. This template contains a letterhead and a picture that has been formatted to be behind the text and to allow overlapping.

2. Select the picture, and then click the Picture Tools Format tab. Click the Color button, and click the Washout option in the first row, fourth option under Recolor.

3. Save the macro-enabled template as ***[your initials]*****ChocPic** in your Lesson 21 folder.

4. With the background picture selected, create an AutoText entry named **ColorBackground** in the template ***[your initials]*****ChocPic**.

5. Select the background picture if necessary. Click the Artistic Effects button on the Picture Tools Format tab, and change the background picture to Pencil Grayscale.

6. With the background picture selected, create an AutoText entry named **GrayscaleBackground** in ***[your initials]*****ChocPic**.

7. Delete the background picture so only the letterhead is displayed.

8. Record a macro named **ColorPicture** in ***[your initials]*****ChocPic** that inserts the ColorBackground AutoText entry. Add an appropriate description.

9. When you finish recording the macro, delete the background picture.

10. Open the Visual Basic Editor by selecting the ColorPicture macro in the Macros dialog box and clicking Edit.

11. Copy the entire macro and then paste a copy below it.

12. Change the name of the copied macro to **GrayscalePicture**, editing the comments where necessary.

13. In the macro code, change the text "("ColorBackground")" to **("GrayscaleBackground")**, the name of the other AutoText entry.

14. Save and print the macro code. Close the Visual Basic Editor.

TIP

Key the text before running the background picture macro. Keying text on top of a graphic can be difficult.

15. Assign the keyboard shortcut Ctrl+Shift+Alt+G to the GrayscalePicture macro and Ctrl+Shift+Alt+C to the ColorPicture macro.
16. Resave the template, print the key assignments, and then close the template.
17. Create a new document based on the ChocPic template; then key the text shown in Figure 21-16, formatting and arranging it attractively on the page. Adjust line breaks if needed to enhance your design.

Figure 21-16

```
You are cordially invited to attend
A presentation and lecture
"Chocolate Enrobing"
Presented in our auditorium
By world-renowned chocolatier
Jenna Bergen
8 p.m. on Thursday, October 12, 20–
```

18. Run the GrayscalePicture macro by pressing Ctrl+Shift+Alt+G. Save the document as ***[your initials]*21-24gray** and then submit the document.
19. Delete the background picture, and then run the ColorPicture macro by pressing Ctrl+Shift+Alt+C.
20. Save the document as ***[your initials]*21-24color** in your Lesson 21 folder. Close the document, saving changes.

Exercise 21-25

Create macros to change page orientation and to format a table. Copy the table macro, and edit the macro to create a second table format.

1. Start a new template.
2. Save the new template as macro-enabled template ***[your initials]*Tables** in your Lesson 21 folder.
3. Record a macro that changes page orientation to portrait with 1-inch margins for the top, bottom, left and right. Name it **PortraitPage**, and assign the keyboard shortcut Ctrl+Shift+Alt+P. Store the macro in the ***[your initials]*Tables** template.
4. Create another macro that changes page orientation to landscape with 1-inch top and bottom margins and 1.25-inch left and right margins. Name it **LandscapePage** and assign the keyboard shortcut Ctrl+Shift+Alt+L. Store it in ***[your initials]*Tables** and insert an appropriate description.

5. With the page orientation set to landscape, insert the file **Event Schedule**.
6. Select the table.

TIP

When you copy a macro, shortcut keys you have assigned are sometimes lost. Assign shortcut keys after copying and editing a macro.

7. Start recording a macro named **TableStyleGrid**. Store it in the ***[your initials]*****Tables** template with an appropriate description for applying the Light Grid style. Do not assign a keyboard shortcut at this time.
8. With the recording pointer, choose AutoFit from the Table Tools Layout tab; then choose AutoFit Contents.
9. Click the Table Tools Design tab, and expand the Table Styles gallery. Then choose a Light Grid style from the third row of built-in styles. Deselect the First Column option in the Table Styles Options group.
10. Click the Properties button from the Table Tools Layout tab. On the Table tab, click the Options button. In the Table Options dialog box, change the Top and Bottom default cell margins to **0.05** inch. Make sure the Automatically resize to fit contents box is checked. Click OK.
11. In the Table Properties dialog box, make sure Preferred width is unchecked. Choose Center alignment.
12. Click the Cell tab of the Table Properties dialog box, and click Center.
13. Click OK to close the dialog box, press ↓ once to deselect the table, and then stop recording.
14. Press Ctrl+Shift+Alt+P to change the page orientation to portrait.

NOTE

The number of your Accent color may vary based on the color you selected for the Light Grid style.

15. Copy the macro code for the TableStyleGrid macro, and paste it at the end of the macro code. Name the copy **TableStyleShading**. Edit the copied macro so it applies a different table style—**Medium Shading 1 - Accent 1**. Be sure to edit the comments as well. (Hint: Locate the text "Style = "Light Grid - Accent 1""; change it to **Style = "Medium Shading 1 - Accent 1"**.)
16. Save and print the macro code. Close the Visual Basic window, and return to Word.
17. Assign the keyboard shortcut Ctrl+Shift+Alt+S to the TableStyleShading macro. Assign the keyboard shortcut Ctrl+Shift+Alt+G to the TableStyleGrid macro.
18. Delete the table from the template, and save the template.
19. Print the key assignments for the template. Close the template.
20. Start a new document based on the Tables template. Enable macros.
21. Insert the file **Event Schedule**. If there are extra blank lines at the bottom of the table, delete them.
22. Apply the LandscapePage macro; then select the table and run the TableStyleShading macro. Center the table vertically on the page. Key and format a title for the table.

23. Save the document as ***[your initials]*21-25a** in your Lesson 21 folder, and then submit it.
24. Apply the PortraitPage macro; then select the table and run the TableStyleGrid macro. Center the table vertically on the page.
25. Save the document as ***[your initials]*21-25b** in your Lesson 21 folder. Submit and close the document.

Exercise 21-26 ◆ Challenge Yourself

Create a template with a customized Quick Access Toolbar, create AutoText entries and macros to insert the AutoText entries, and compose letters using the AutoText entries.

1. Start a new template. Save it as a macro-enabled template named ***[your initials]*PittLetter** in your Lesson 21 folder.
2. Customize the Quick Access Toolbar to include Print Preview and Print, Spelling and Grammar, and Quick Print buttons.
3. Design a letterhead using character and paragraph formatting. The letterhead should read as follows:

   Campbell's Confections
   40 Station Square
   Pittsburgh, PA 15219
   Telephone: 412-555-2025
   Fax: 412-555-2050
   www.campbellsconfections.pitt.biz

4. Create an AutoText entry for the letterhead. Store it in ***[your initials]*PittLetter**, and name it **LetterheadSimple**.
5. Delete the letterhead, and design a second letterhead for the Pittsburgh store using WordArt, clip art, text boxes, or other graphic elements. Group graphic elements, and set appropriate word wrap and overlap properties. (Consider using the Drawing Canvas to group the elements.)
6. Create an AutoText entry for the new letterhead. Name it **LetterheadFancy**.
7. Delete the letterhead and resave the template.
8. Compose a generic closing paragraph that thanks the customer for doing business with Campbell's Confections. Create an AutoText entry for it, naming it **ThanksForBusiness**. Be sure to store it in ***[your initials]*PittLetter**.
9. Compose a second generic closing paragraph that asks the customer to contact the company if he or she wants to know more about ordering gourmet chocolate or custom gift boxes. Create an AutoText entry for the second paragraph, naming it **Request**.

10. Create another AutoText entry for a signature block, using your name and reference initials **sm**. Name it **Signature**.

11. Record a macro that inserts the LetterheadSimple AutoText entry. Name it **SimpleLetter**. Be sure to store it in ***[your initials]*****PittLetter**.

TIP

Use Word Options, Customize, to assign keyboard shortcuts to macros.

12. Open the Visual Basic window. Copy and paste the SimpleLetter macro. Edit the pasted macro so it inserts the LetterheadFancy AutoText entry instead. Name the macro **FancyLetter** and save it.

13. Assign Ctrl+Shift+Alt+S for the SimpleLetter macro and Ctrl+Shift+Alt+F for the FancyLetter macro.

14. Record a macro named **RequestClose** that inserts the Request and Signature AutoText entries. Store it in ***[your initials]*****PittLetter**.

15. Open the Visual Basic window. Copy and paste the RequestClose macro. Name the pasted macro **ThankYouClose**, and edit it so it inserts the ThanksForBusiness AutoText entry instead of the Request AutoText entry. Save the new macro.

16. Assign the keyboard shortcut Ctrl+Shift+Alt+R for the RequestClose macro and Ctrl+Shift+Alt+T for the ThankYouClose macro.

17. Delete all the text and graphics from the template, and then resave it.

18. Print the key assignments, and then close the template.

19. Create a new document based on the template you just created. Enable macros. Run the macro to insert the simple letterhead. Create a business letter addressed to anyone you choose. Compose a first paragraph that tells your customer you have a new line of gourmet chocolate and custom gift boxes.

20. As a second and closing paragraph, run the RequestClose macro.

21. Save the document as ***[your initials]*****21-26a** in your Lesson 21 folder; then print and close it.

22. Create a second letter based on the same template. For the second document, use the macro that inserts the fancy letterhead. Address the letter to the same person as the first letter. Compose a paragraph confirming a recent order for one of the products you mentioned in the first letter. Run the ThankYouClose macro.

23. Save the document as ***[your initials]*****21-26b** in your Lesson 21 folder. Submit and close the document.

On Your Own

In these exercises you work on your own, as you would in a real-life business environment. Use the skills you've learned to accomplish the task—and be creative.

Exercise 21-27

Create a letter template to send to co-workers announcing a seminar on advanced topics for Microsoft Word. Include macros that insert AutoText entries for the body of the letter and the closing. Save the template as ***[your initials]*21-27a**. Open a new document based on the letter, and create a letter for a co-worker. Save the document as ***[your initials]*21-27b** and submit it.

Exercise 21-28

In this exercise you are asked to design a birthday party announcement. Before you create the announcement, customize the Quick Access Toolbar by adding formatting buttons that do not appear on the Ribbon, and then use the customized toolbar to apply formatting to the announcement. Save the document as ***[your initials]*21-28** and submit it. Reset the Quick Access Toolbar.

Exercise 21-29

Research the Internet for great prices on three electronic devices that interest you. Create a three-column tabbed list to include name, model, and cost. Create a macro to convert the three-column tabbed list to a table. In the macro include a table style. Save the document as a template file named ***[your initials]*21-29a**. Create a document based on the template ***[your initials]*21-29a**. Save the new document as ***[your initials]*21-29b** and submit it.

Unit 6 Applications

Unit Application 6-1

Create a main document and a data source, edit the data source, and merge the documents.

1. Start a new document based on the Metro theme.
2. Create a letterhead design using the company address listed below.

   Campbell's Confections
   25 Main Street
   Grove City, PA 16127
   724-555-2025
   www.campbellsconfections.biz
3. Display the Styles task pane, and modify the Normal style to font size 12 points, 0 points spacing before, and 0 points spacing after, and apply single spacing.

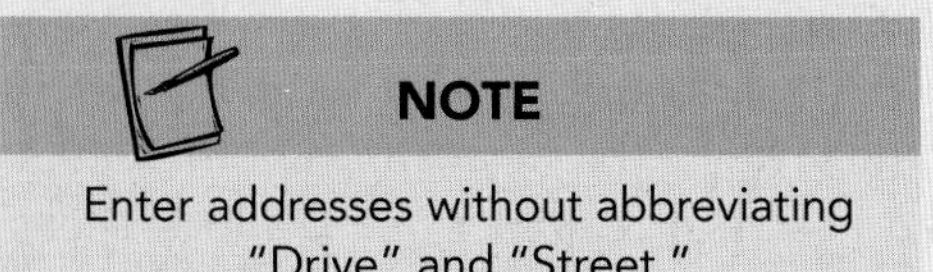

Enter addresses without abbreviating "Drive" and "Street."

4. Insert the date as an automatically updated field using business letter format, and identify the letter as a main document for a mail merge.
5. For the data source, key the data in Figure U6-1. Customize the list of field names as needed.

Figure U6-1

Title	First Name	Last Name	High School	Address	City	State	ZIP
Mr.	Gary	Hines	Elk High School	1115 Sunset Drive	Arden	NY	10910
Ms.	Donna	Albert	Armstrong High School	12 Avon Lane	Nichols	NY	13812
Mr.	Paul	Green	Somerset High School	55 Elm Street	Newbury	NH	03255
Ms.	Lucy	Chin	Clearfield High School	154 Fourth Avenue	Highland Park	NH	08904
Ms.	Gina	Saxion	Clinton High School	55 Lincoln Avenue	Camden	NJ	08105
Mr.	Raymond	Steele	Greene High School	667 Washington Boulevard	Glenwood	NJ	07418

6. Save the data source as ***[your initials]*****u6-1data** in a new folder for Unit 6 Applications.
7. Check the recipient list against Figure U6-1 for errors, and then sort the list by ZIP Code.
8. Three blank lines below the date, insert the Address Block followed by the Greeting Line block. Specify a colon in the Greeting Line dialog box rather than a comma. Verify correct spacing between the parts of the letter.
9. For the body of the letter, key the text shown in Figure U6-2.

TIP

It may be necessary to match fields in the Insert Address Block dialog box. Match the High School field with Company.

Figure U6-2

```
Enclosed is the fundraising information you requested. You
will notice from the enclosed brochure that we have five
quality chocolate bars.

The chocolate bar flavors include:

Solid milk chocolate

Milk chocolate with almonds

Milk chocolate with caramel filling

Milk chocolate with peanut butter filling

Milk chocolate with double chocolate filling

The individual bars are 2.5 ounces and are priced at $1.
A case contains 36 bars, and the cost per case is $36.
Your profit is 50 percent, or $18 per case.

Please let us know if you would like one of our sales
representatives to meet with you or your students to
discuss fund-raising strategies.
```

10. Key an appropriate complimentary closing. The letter is from Tamara Robbins, Fundraising Department. Add your reference initials and an enclosure notation.
11. Edit the last paragraph that begins "Please" to read as follows:

    Please let us know if you would like one of our sales representatives to visit «High School» to meet with you or your students. . . .
12. Preview the letter with the merged data, making sure the letter fits on one page.
13. Sort alphabetically the list of chocolate bars, and format it as a bulleted list.
14. Save the main document as ***[your initials]*****u6-1main** in your Unit 6 Applications folder and print it.

15. Edit the data source to change Mr. Raymond Steele to Mr. **Harold** Steele and add a new record for **Mr. Allen Jones, 34 Sky Road, Allegheny High School, Park Ridge, NJ 07656**. Sort the list by ZIP Code. (To edit the data source and to add the new record, click Edit Recipient List on the Mailings tab, and click the name of your file under Data Source. Click Edit to open the Edit Source dialog box.)
16. Complete the merge, merging all data to a new document.
17. Save the new document as ***[your initials]*****u6-1merged** in your Unit 6 Applications folder.
18. Print the document, four pages per sheet.
19. Use the data source created in this application to create mailing labels. Use the **5160–Address** product number. Alphabetize the data source by last name. Save the merged labels to a new document.
20. Format the label text as 11 points with 0 points spacing after. Save as ***[your initials]*****u6-1labels**. Submit the labels.
21. Close all documents, saving changes when prompted.

Unit Application 6-2

Create an electronic form with content controls.

1. Start a new template to use as an electronic form. Save the template as ***[your initials]*****FieldForm** in your Unit 6 Applications folder.
2. Create a form that Campbell's Confections employees can use to schedule field trips to the factory. The form should include the following information:

Figure U6-3

```
                Campbell's Confections
             Field Trip Planning Worksheet
                 (For internal use only)

Group Name:

Type:

Contact:

Telephone:

E-mail:

Anticipated number in group:

Requested date:

Time of arrival:
```

3. Format the document as follows:
   - Format the first three lines as a document heading. You may include clip art, shapes, borders, or a company logo.
   - Insert Rich Text Content Controls for the following headings: Group Name, Contact, Telephone, E-mail, Requested date, and Time of arrival.
   - Add titles for the Rich Text Content Controls, and edit the instructions.
   - Set a tab to align the Rich Text Content Controls.
   - Insert a Drop-Down List Content Control for "Type." The list should include:

     School
     Civic
     Tourists
     Other
   - Insert a Drop-Down List Content Control for "Anticipated number in group." The list should include:

     10–15
     16–20
     >20
4. Format the form headings.
5. Save the form.
6. Protect and resave the form. Submit and close the form.
7. Create a document based on the form inserting text for each Rich Text Content Control and selecting an item from each of the drop-down lists. Save the document as ***[your initials]*u6-2** in your Unit 6 Applications folder and submit it. Close the document.

Unit Application 6-3

Create a template, record document format macros, and customize the Quick Access Toolbar.

1. Start a new template. Save the macro-enabled template as ***[your initials]*BusinessDocuments** in your Unit 6 folder.
2. Create a business letter format macro using the following guidelines:
   a. Insert the picture file **LetterheadLogo**, and format the picture as follows: top and bottom text wrapping, horizontally centered on the page, and positioned vertically 0.5 inch from the top of the page. Select the picture, create an AutoText entry named **Logo**, and store it in your ***[your initials]*BusinessDocuments** template. Delete the picture.

b. Record a new macro named **LetterFormat**, and store it in your ***[your initials]*** **BusinessDocuments** template.

- Create a header, and insert the Logo AutoText entry.
- Change the top margin to 2 inches. Change the font to Cambria, and the font size to 12 points, change the spacing after to 0 points, and apply single spacing.
- Insert an automatically updated date field, and select the third date format.
- Press Enter four times, and stop recording the macro.

c. Delete all text in the template including the logo in the header.

3. Create a memo format macro using the following guidelines:
   - Record a new macro named **MemoFormat**, and store it in your ***[your initials]*****BusinessDocuments** template.
   - Change the top margin to 2 inches.
   - Set a 1-inch left tab. Change the spacing after to 0 points, and apply single spacing.
   - Turn on Caps Lock, and key the following:

     MEMO TO: Tab Enter Enter
     FROM: Tab Enter Enter
     DATE: Tab **«Date field»** Enter Enter
     SUBJECT: Tab Enter Enter Enter
   - Stop recording the macro.
   - Delete all text in the template.
4. Open the **Word Options** dialog box, and click **Quick Access Toolbar**. Select **Macros** in the Choose commands drop-down list. Select your ***[your initials]*****BusinessDocuments** template in the Customize Quick Access Toolbar drop-down list.
5. Select each of the macros, and click **Add**. Click **OK** to close the Word Options dialog box.
6. Save and close the template.
7. Create a new document based on the ***[your initials]*****BusinessDocuments** template. Enable macros.
8. Run the macro to create a business letter format by clicking the Letter Format button on the Quick Access Toolbar.
9. Save the document as ***[your initials]*****u6-3a.** Submit and close the document.
10. Create a new document based on the ***[your initials]*****BusinessDocuments** template. Enable macros.
11. Run the macro to create a memo format by clicking the Memo Format button on the Quick Access Toolbar.
12. Save the document as ***[your initials]*****u6-3b.** Submit and close the document.

Unit Application 6-4

Using the Internet, design a template that includes AutoText and creates a form.

1. Use the Internet to locate a graphic or graphic elements you will use in creating a letterhead template and form for a business or school organization. Save each graphic as a file in your Unit 6 Applications folder. Search for free fonts, and locate a font for the letterhead template.

2. Create a new template, and save it as ***[your initials]*****u6-4LetterA** in your Unit 6 Applications folder. Perform the following actions in relation to the new template:

   - Create a letterhead that includes the following information: name of business or school organization, complete address, phone and fax numbers, and Web address.
   - Format the letterhead text by applying character and paragraph attributes.
   - Create an AutoText entry for the letterhead text, and store the entry in the template.
   - Save and submit the template.

3. Perform these additional actions with the template:

   - Add a graphic to the letterhead. Position the graphic and text to create an attractive design.
   - Create an AutoText entry for the graphic, and store the entry in your ***[your initials]*****U6-4LetterA** template.
   - Save the letterhead and graphic as a new template named ***[your initials]*****u6-4LetterB** in your Unit 6 Applications folder.
   - Submit and close the template.

4. Design and create a form to be used by your company or school organization, using one of the AutoText entries for the letterhead. Save the template as ***[your initials]*****u6-4Form** in your Unit 6 Applications folder.

   - Record a macro to insert one of the AutoText entries.
   - Assign a shortcut key for the macro, and then save the template. Print the key assignments.
   - Include Rich Text, Drop-Down List, and Check Box Content Controls and appropriate options.

   Protect and resave the form. Print the form with field codes displayed. Close the form.

5. Create a new document based on the Form template, and complete the form. Save, submit, and close the document.

Unit 7

LONG DOCUMENTS AND DOCUMENT SHARING

Lesson 22

Footnotes and Endnotes

OBJECTIVES ***After completing this lesson, you will be able to:***

1. Add footnotes and endnotes.
2. View footnotes and endnotes.
3. Edit and format footnotes and endnotes.
4. Move, copy, and delete footnotes and endnotes.
5. Change the placement of footnotes and endnotes.
6. Change the numbering of footnotes and endnotes.
7. Create a bibliography.

Estimated Time: 1 hour

Text references that appear at the bottom of the page in a report, a book, or some other document are called *footnotes*. They are used for two purposes: to credit the source of information or to offer additional explanation. Text references assembled at the end of a document are called *endnotes*.

Adding Footnotes or Endnotes

Adding a footnote or endnote to a document is a two-part process. First, you insert a *reference mark* within the document text; the mark can appear as a number or a character (such as an asterisk). You then enter the corresponding footnote or endnote text in a separate pane.

Begin by working with footnotes. By default, Word automatically numbers footnotes and provides space for them at the bottom of the page by adjusting page breaks.

Exercise 22-1 ADD FOOTNOTES TO A DOCUMENT

NOTE

The documents you create in this course relate to the case study about Campbell's Confections, a fictional candy store and chocolate factory (see the Case Study in the front matter).

NOTE

By default, footnote and endnote text appears as 10-point Calibri.

Use Print Layout view to insert footnotes. You can add a footnote by clicking the Insert Footnote button or by launching the Footnote and Endnote dialog box.

1. Open the file **Ordering**.
2. On page 1, in the paragraph that begins "The goal," place the insertion point immediately after the period at the end of the paragraph (after "areas.").
3. Click the **References** tab, and locate the **Footnotes** group. Click the Insert Footnote button AB[1]. A superscript reference mark appears above the document text, and a separator line is inserted at the bottom of the page with a superscript reference mark.

Figure 22-1
Inserted footnote

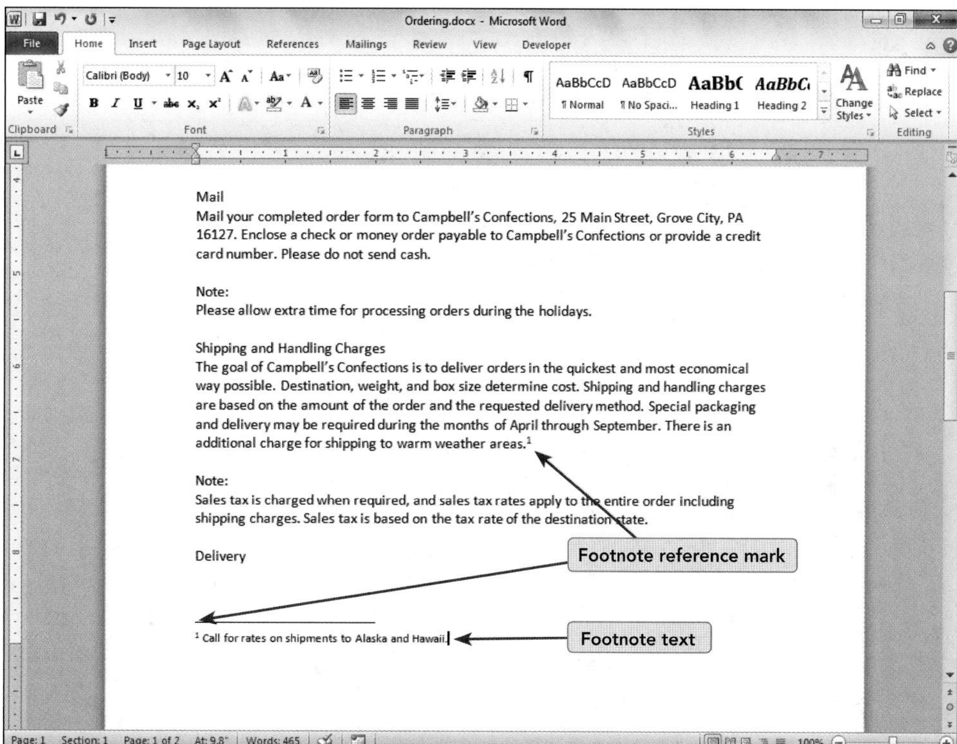

4. Key **Call for rates on shipments to Alaska and Hawaii.**
5. Double-click the reference mark (the number 1) in the Footnotes pane to return to the reference mark in the document.
6. Click the Show/Hide ¶ button ¶ to hide nonprinting characters if they are showing. This makes the reference mark easier to see.
7. Locate the sales tax paragraph, and position the insertion point at the end of the paragraph following "destination state."

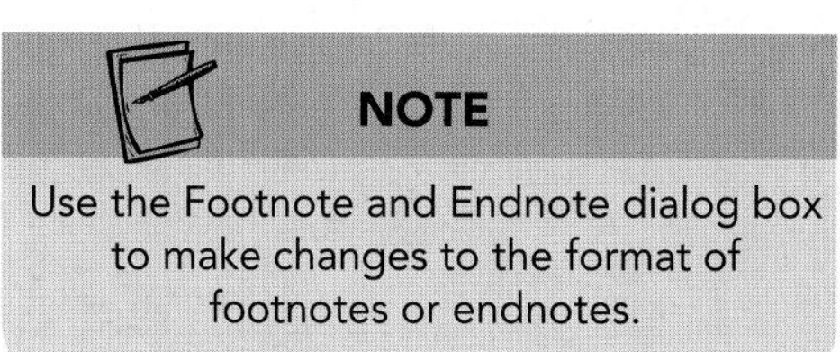

NOTE

Use the Footnote and Endnote dialog box to make changes to the format of footnotes or endnotes.

8. Click the **References** tab. Click the Footnote and Endnote Dialog Box Launcher. The Footnote and Endnote dialog box opens.

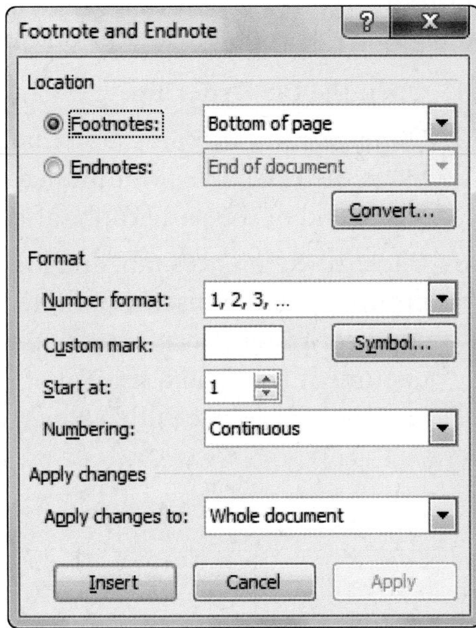

Figure 22-2
Footnote and Endnote dialog box

TIP

The keyboard shortcut for inserting a footnote is Ctrl+Alt+F.

9. Make sure **Footnotes** is selected. Under Format, note that the default numbering of footnotes is 1, 2, 3.
10. Click **Insert**. Notice that Word automatically numbered the footnote with a superscript 2.
11. Key the following footnote text: **Candy sales are subject to sales tax.**
12. Double-click the reference mark (the number 2) to return to the reference mark in the document.

NOTE

It is important to use the correct form for footnotes or endnotes that refer to published material. For magazine articles, include author, article title, magazine name, date, and page number(s). For books, include author, book title, publisher, place of publication, year of publication, and page number(s).

You have inserted two consecutively numbered footnotes in the document. To create endnotes, you follow similar steps: After placing the insertion point in the desired position, open the Footnote and Endnote dialog box, choose Endnotes (or press Alt+Ctrl+D), and key the note text in the Endnotes pane. You can also use the Insert Endnote button.

You can format footnotes and endnotes in many different styles. For example, the American Language Association (ALA) style differs from *The Gregg Reference Manual* style, and both differ from Word's default style. Figure 22-3 compares *Gregg* and Word styles. This book uses Word's default style—its automatic formatting is easy to use and ensures consistency.

NOTE

Your instructor might prefer a style other than the Word default and direct you to modify footnotes and endnotes accordingly.

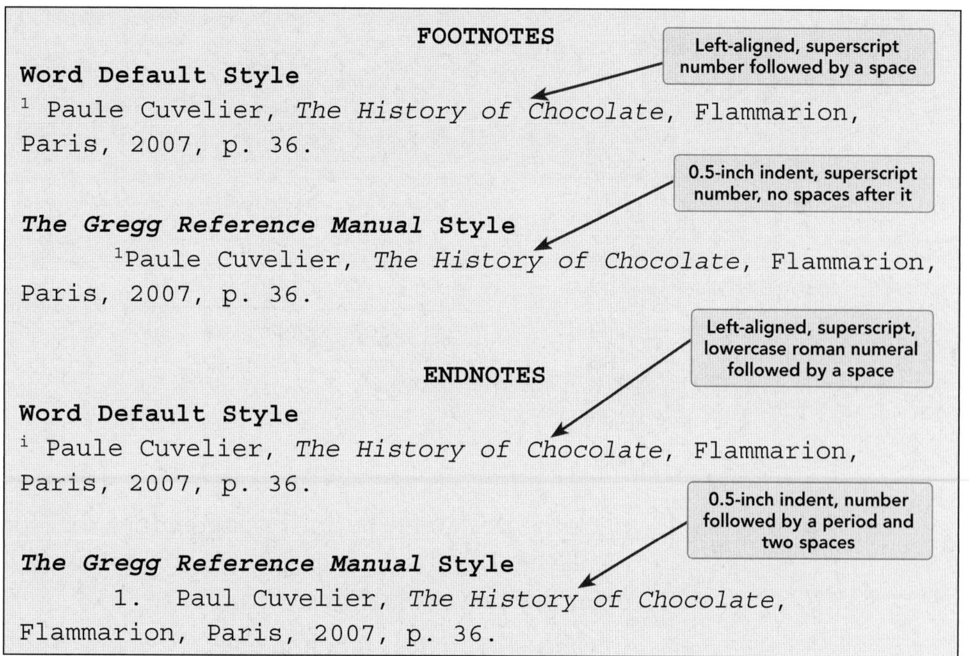

Figure 22-3 Two common footnote and endnote styles

Viewing Footnotes or Endnotes

You can view footnotes or endnotes in a document in three ways:

- Point to the reference mark to display a ScreenTip containing the note text.
- Switch to Draft view, and click the Show Notes button in the Footnotes group.
- Use the Print tab or Print Layout view to see how footnotes and endnotes will appear on the printed page.

To locate footnotes or endnotes in a document, use the Next Footnote button. You can also use the Go To command or set the Select Browse Object button to browse by footnotes or endnotes.

Exercise 22-2 VIEW FOOTNOTES

1. Point to the superscript reference mark for footnote 1. A ScreenTip displays the footnote text.
2. Double-click the reference mark in the document. The insertion point moves to the footnote.
3. Scroll to the bottom of page 1. Word reduced the number of text lines on the page and placed the two footnotes above the 1-inch bottom margin. Separating the footnotes from the document text is a 2-inch horizontal *note separator*.

Figure 22-4
Footnotes in Print Layout view

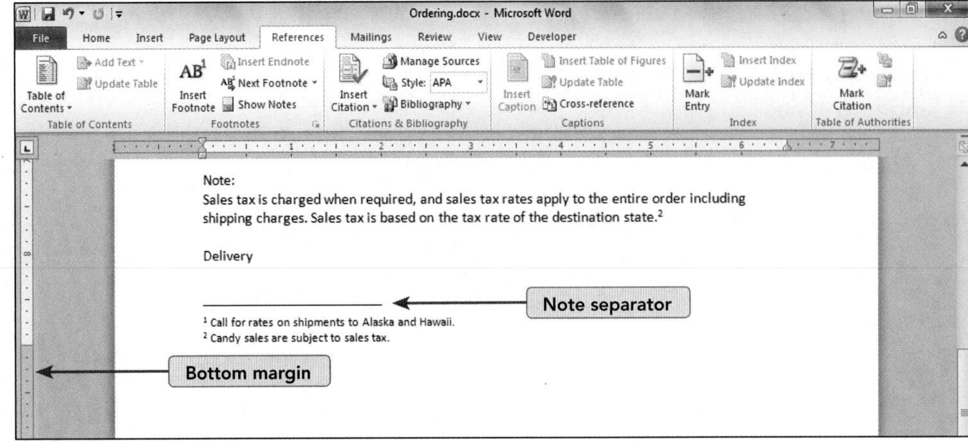

4. Click the Draft view button, and notice that footnotes are not displayed. Draft view does not display footnotes, headers, columns, and other page layout features.
5. Click the **References** tab, and click the Show Notes button. The Footnotes pane appears at the bottom of the page.
6. Click within the footnote 1 text in the Footnotes pane. Notice that the text in the document window scrolls to display the corresponding reference number.

Figure 22-5
Footnotes Pane in Draft view

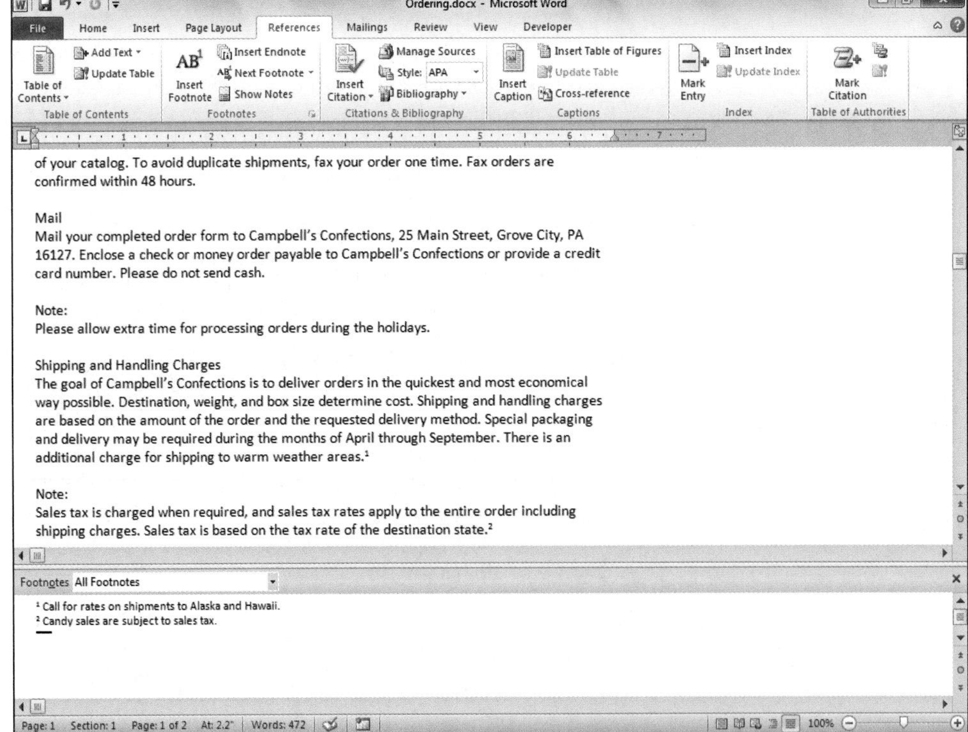

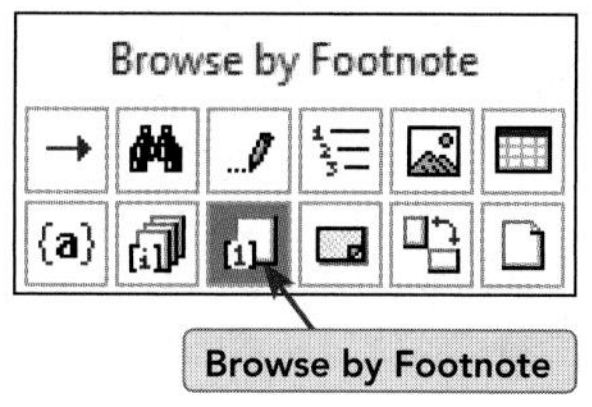

Figure 22-6
Setting the Select Browse Object button

7. Click the Close button [×] to close the Footnotes pane.
8. Click the Select Browse Object button [○], and set it to browse by footnote by clicking the Browse by Footnote button.
9. Click the drop-down arrow beside the Next Footnote button, and choose **Previous Footnote**. Use the Previous Footnote and Next Footnote commands to scroll from footnote to footnote. In a long document, this is an easy way to scroll between footnotes.

TIP

To locate a specific footnote, use the Go To command. Double-click the page number on the status bar or press F5 to open the Find and Replace dialog box. Choose Footnote from the Go to what list box, and enter the footnote number (or click the Next or Previous button to scroll from note to note).

Editing and Formatting Notes

You edit and format footnotes and endnotes just as you do any other text. For example, you can cut, copy, and paste note text. You can also change fonts, font sizes, styles, and paragraph formatting. You can make these changes in the footnotes area, on the endnotes page, or in Print Layout view.

Exercise 22-3 EDIT AND FORMAT FOOTNOTES

1. Move the insertion point to the end of the paragraph heading "Fax." Press Alt+Ctrl+F to insert a footnote.
2. Key the following text for the footnote: **Please do not fax your order a second time or duplicate your order by phone or mail. We are not responsible for duplicate orders.**
3. Place the insertion point in the text for footnote 2, and edit the text as follows: **Call for rates on shipments to Alaska, Hawaii, and Canada.**
4. Edit footnote 3 to read **Candy sales are subject to sales tax in most states.**
5. Select all the text in the Footnotes pane, and change the font size to 9 points.

NOTE

You can apply character or paragraph formatting to footnote or endnote text just as you do to other text in a document. Simply select the text and open the Font dialog box or the Paragraph dialog box.

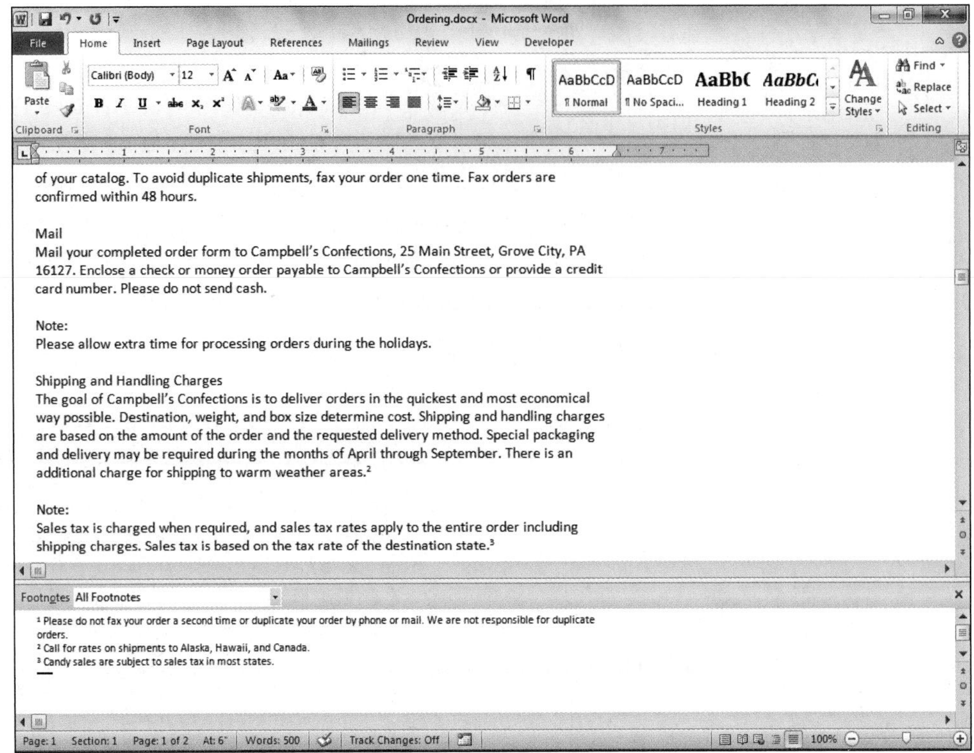

Figure 22-7 Edited footnotes

Moving, Copying, and Deleting Notes

You can move, copy, or delete footnotes or endnotes. To do so, you work with the reference mark, not the actual footnote or endnote text. For example, you move a footnote by selecting the reference number and cutting and pasting it (or dragging it) to another location in the document. When you move, copy, or delete a note, Word automatically renumbers the remaining notes.

Exercise 22-4 MOVE FOOTNOTES

1. Click the Show/Hide ¶ button ¶ to display nonprinting characters.
2. Select the reference mark for footnote 1 (after "Fax").
3. Click the Cut button to cut the number. Notice that the note text disappears.
4. Move to the end of the paragraph under the "Fax" heading (after "48 hours"), and paste the reference number. The footnote text appears in the footnote area of the document.
5. Select reference number 2 in the document. Use the arrow pointer to drag it to the end of the "Shipping and Handling Charges" heading.

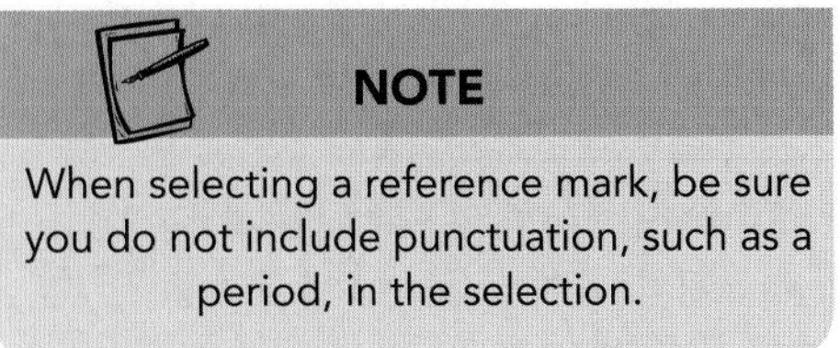

NOTE

When selecting a reference mark, be sure you do not include punctuation, such as a period, in the selection.

Exercise 22-5 COPY AND DELETE FOOTNOTES

1. Select and copy reference number 2 in the document.

TIP

Another way to copy footnotes is to use the Ctrl method: Select the reference mark, hold down Ctrl, and drag the mark to the new location.

2. Scroll to page 2, and paste the reference mark after "toll-free number." You copied the footnote, and Word automatically assigns the next value to the footnote.
3. Select the copied reference mark (number 4) in the document.
4. Press Delete or Backspace to delete the reference mark and the footnote text.
5. Save the document as ***[your initials]*****22-5** in a new folder for Lesson 22.
6. Submit the document. Leave it open for the next exercise.

Changing the Placement of Notes

You can insert footnotes in a document at either of two locations:

- The bottom of the page (the default setting)
- Immediately below the last line of text on the page

Likewise, you can place endnotes at either of two locations:

- The end of the document (the default setting)
- The end of a section

Another way to change the placement of note text is to convert footnotes to endnotes or endnotes to footnotes.

Exercise 22-6 CHANGE THE PLACEMENT OF FOOTNOTES

1. Scroll to the footnotes at the bottom of page 1. Click within the footnote text for the third note, and notice the position of the text on the status bar (approximately 9.8 inches from the top of the page).

TIP

If the position 9.8 inches does not appear in the status bar, right-click the status bar and click Vertical Page Position. Verify that the document view is Print Layout.

2. Scroll to the paragraph that begins "Note:" followed by the "Sales tax" paragraph at the bottom of page 1, and insert a hard page break at the beginning of the "Note" paragraph. Notice that footnote 3 moved to the bottom of page 2.
3. On page 2, at the end of the paragraph that ends "toll-free number," insert a new footnote by clicking the Footnotes Dialog Box Launcher.
4. Open the Footnotes drop-down list and change the location from Bottom of page to **Below text**. Check that the Apply changes to option is set to **Whole document**.

5. Click **Insert**. Notice that the existing footnote on page 2 is now positioned just below the last paragraph on the page. Scroll to see how much space is now available on the page.
6. Next to the number 4, key the new footnote text: **Web site: www.campbellsconfections.biz or call 800-555-2025.**
7. Format the new footnote as 9 points.
8. Click the **References** tab if necessary. Click the arrow beside the Next Footnote button, and click **Previous Footnote** to look at the footnotes on page 1. The change you made in footnote placement applies to all footnotes in the document.

Exercise 22-7 CONVERT ALL FOOTNOTES TO ENDNOTES

1. Before converting all footnotes to endnotes, insert one endnote. Position the insertion point on page 2 at the end of the last paragraph, and click the Insert Endnote button.
2. Key the endnote text: ***Policies and Procedures Manual* (Campbell's Confections, 2011) 25**. (Remember to key the period at the end of the note.) Notice that endnotes are numbered in lowercase roman numerals by default. Turn off nonprinting characters to see the numbers better.
3. Format the endnote as 9 points.
4. Switch to Draft view, and click the Show Notes button if you do not see the Footnotes or Endnotes pane. Choose the option **View endnote area**, and click **OK**. When a document contains footnotes and endnotes, the Show Notes dialog box displays after you click the Show Notes button.
5. In the Endnotes pane, open the **Endnotes** drop-down list and choose **All Footnotes**. Use the scroll bar, if necessary, to see the footnotes.
6. Select all the footnote text in the Footnotes pane.
7. Click the right mouse button, and choose **Convert to Endnote** from the shortcut menu.

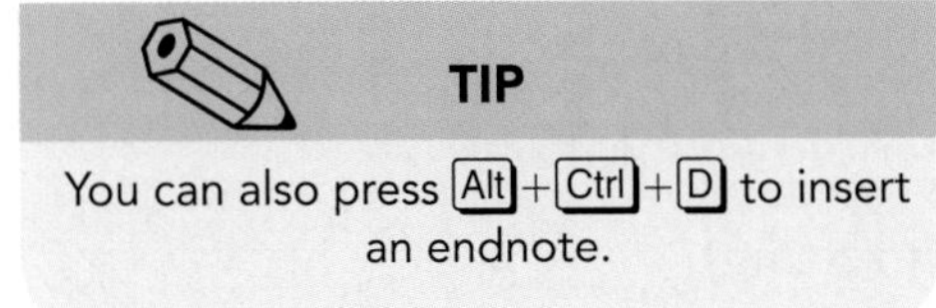

TIP

You can also press Alt+Ctrl+D to insert an endnote.

TIP

Use the selection area to select note text. Position the pointer to the left of the note. When the arrow is pointing to the text, press Ctrl and click to select all the text in the pane.

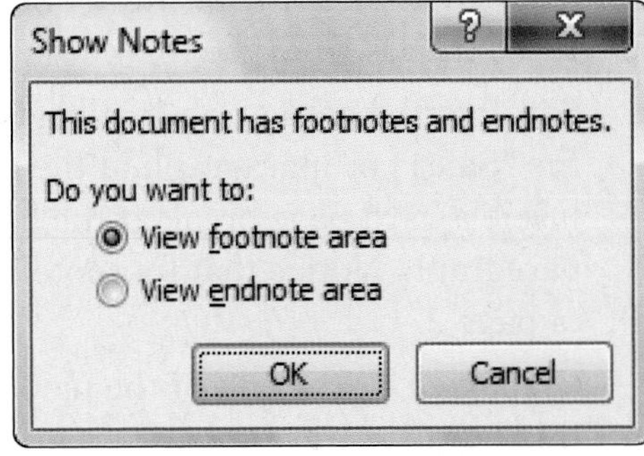

Figure 22-8 Show Notes dialog box

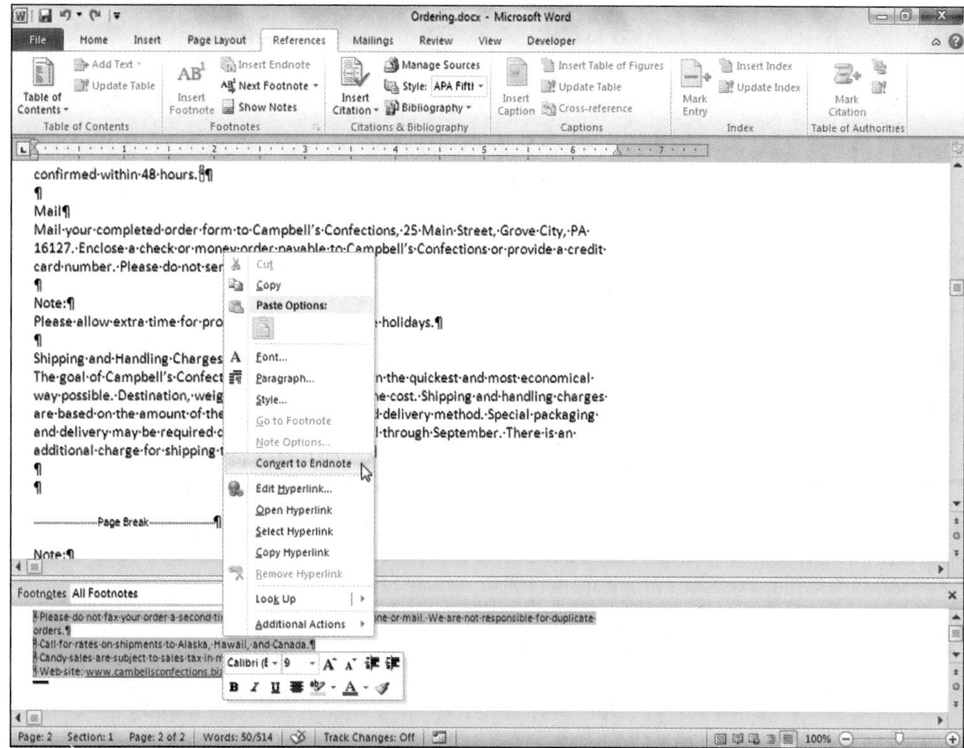

Figure 22-9
Converting footnotes to endnotes

8. Scroll through the Endnotes pane. All the footnotes are now endnotes, numbered in the order they are referenced in the document.
9. Close the Endnotes pane, and look at the last page of the document in Print Layout view. Insert a blank line after each note, and check that all note text is 9 points.

Exercise 22-8 CONVERT INDIVIDUAL ENDNOTES TO FOOTNOTES

You can convert individual footnotes to endnotes, or endnotes to footnotes, by using the same method. In this document, you will keep the source note (the note that refers to a specific publication) as an endnote and change the remaining notes to footnotes.

1. Still in Print Layout view, scroll to page 2 to display the endnotes. Right-click endnote i. Choose Convert to Footnote from the shortcut menu. This moves the endnote from the pane and renumbers the remaining notes.
2. Repeat step 1 for the next three endnotes. There should be only one endnote.
3. Scroll toward the beginning of the document. The document now has footnotes and endnotes. The four endnotes you converted to footnotes are numbered 1 through 4, using the default footnote-numbering style.

Exercise 22-9 PLACE ENDNOTES ON A SEPARATE PAGE

Endnotes are usually placed with a centered title on a separate page at the end of the document. The title begins 2 inches from the top of the page, and two blank lines separate the title and the notes. The separator can be formatted so that a title and spacing are inserted automatically.

1. Switch to Draft view. Open the Endnotes pane by clicking the Show Notes button, and click **View endnote area** in the Show Notes dialog box. Click **OK**.
2. Choose **Endnote Separator** from the drop-down list in the Endnotes pane. Now you can edit, delete, or format the separator.
3. Display nonprinting characters if they are not showing.
4. With the insertion point at the beginning of the separator line in the pane, press Enter four times.
5. Select the separator line and press Delete.
6. Key **NOTES** in bold uppercase, and click the Center button on the Home tab to center-align the text.
7. Press Enter twice. Four paragraph marks should appear above the title and two below it.
8. Close the Endnotes pane.
9. Press Ctrl+End to go to the end of the document, and insert a page break.
10. Change to Print Layout view to see the new endnotes page.

TIP

You can also edit, delete, or format the footnote separator. For example, you can center the separator so that it is not left-aligned, or you can delete it and insert a double-line bottom border in its place.

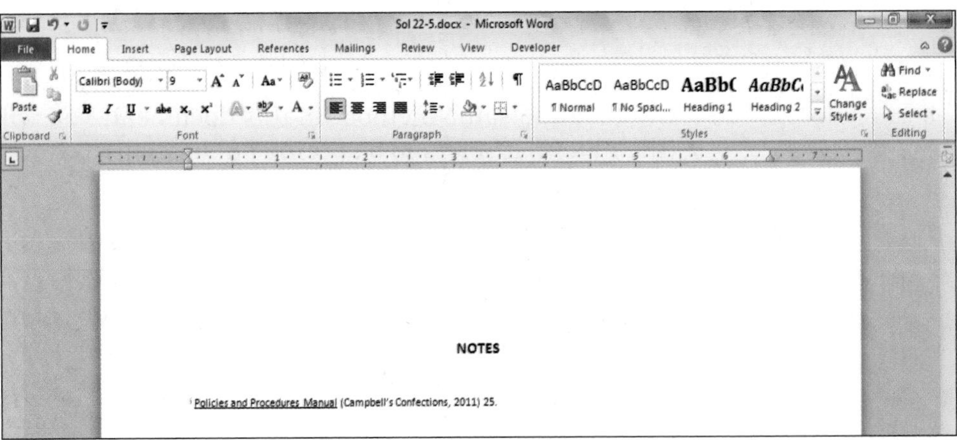

Figure 22-10
Endnotes page

11. Save the document as ***[your initials]*22-9** in your Lesson 22 folder. Submit the document.

Changing Numbering of Reference Marks

Instead of using cardinal numbers for footnotes and lowercase roman numerals for endnotes, you can choose a different type of number formatting. Another option is to choose your own custom reference mark. For example, you can use any symbol key on the keyboard or choose one from the Symbol font. For a more graphical symbol, you can choose an image from the Wingdings font.

In the current document, you change the footnotes to asterisks and the endnotes to cardinal numbers.

Exercise 22-10 CHANGE FOOTNOTE REFERENCE MARKS TO SYMBOLS

1. Still in Print Layout view, use the Go To feature to locate the second footnote. (Press F5, choose **Footnote**, enter the number **2**, click **Go To**, and close the dialog box.)
2. Right-click the footnote text, and choose **Note Options** from the shortcut menu to open the Footnote and Endnote dialog box.
3. Open the **Number format** drop-down list, and choose the last format (the one that begins with an asterisk). This format starts by applying the asterisk, applies the next symbol to the next footnote, and so on.
4. Open the **Numbering** drop-down list, and choose **Restart each page**. This option will start numbering each page of footnotes with the asterisk.

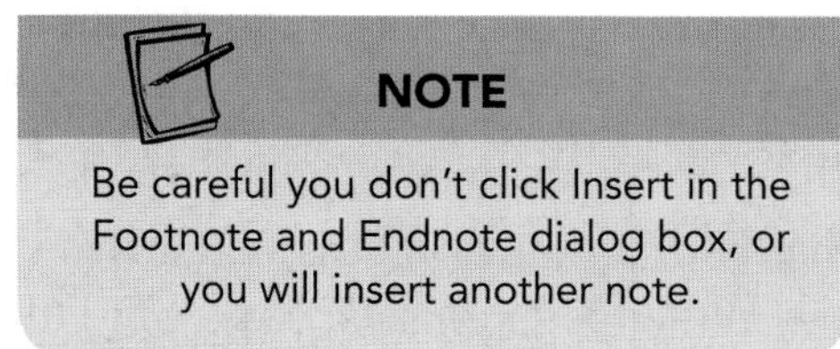

NOTE

Be careful you don't click Insert in the Footnote and Endnote dialog box, or you will insert another note.

Figure 22-11 Choosing footnote options

5. Click **Apply**. The footnotes are now marked with asterisks.

Exercise 22-11 CHANGE THE NUMBER FORMAT FOR ENDNOTES

1. In Print Layout view, display page 3 (the endnote).
2. Right-click the endnote number, and choose **Note Options** from the shortcut menu.
3. In the Footnote and Endnote dialog box, change the number format to **1, 2, 3**, and click **Apply**. The new numbering format appears in the document.
4. Add page numbers to the bottom right of the document. Do not number the first page.
5. Format the title on page 1 ("How to Place an Order") with 72 points of space before the paragraph and 24 points spacing after. Center the title, and apply 16-point bold, small caps. Apply the Heading 2 style to the document side headings (do not style the "Note" headings).
6. Apply italic and 6 points spacing before to the "Note" paragraphs. Delete the blank paragraph marks in the document, and review the document page breaks. Delete the page break on page 2, and verify that there is a page break before the NOTES page.
7. Position the insertion point at the end of the paragraph on page 2 that begins "Our customer service," and press Enter.
8. Key the following paragraph below the "Customer Service" paragraph.

   Campbell's Confections guarantees that your orders and gifts will arrive in perfect condition when using our recommended method of shipping. If you are not satisfied with your order, we will be glad to replace or exchange the products or issue a refund.

NOTE

Format long quotations (four or more lines) using single spacing, and indent the text a half inch from the left and right margins. A blank line should precede the text, and do not use quotation marks to enclose the text.

9. Select the paragraph, and open the Paragraph dialog box. Change the left and right indents to 0.5. Change the spacing before to 12 points, and change the line spacing to single if necessary.
10. Save the document as ***[your initials]*22-11** in your Lesson 22 folder.
11. Submit and close the document.

Create a Bibliography

A *bibliography* is a list of sources that identifies references consulted or cited in a report or manuscript. A bibliography usually appears at the end of a formal report.

Word generates a bibliography automatically using document citations, and it formats the bibliography according to the style you select.

Exercise 22-12 ADD A CITATION

1. Open the file **Books**.
2. Click the References tab, and click the arrow beside the Style button. Click MLA.

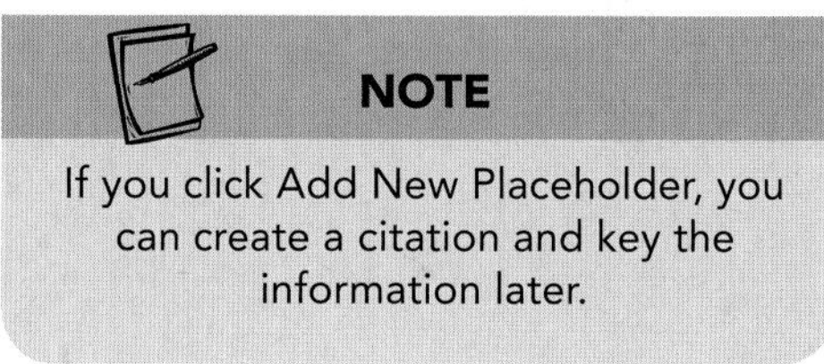

NOTE

If you click Add New Placeholder, you can create a citation and key the information later.

3. Locate the list of books at the end of the memo, and position the insertion point at the end of the title of the first book *(Chocolate: History, Culture, and Heritage)*.
4. Click the Insert Citation button, and click Add New Source. The Create Source dialog box appears. Verify that "Book" is listed in the Type of Source drop-down list box.

Figure 22-12
Create Source dialog box

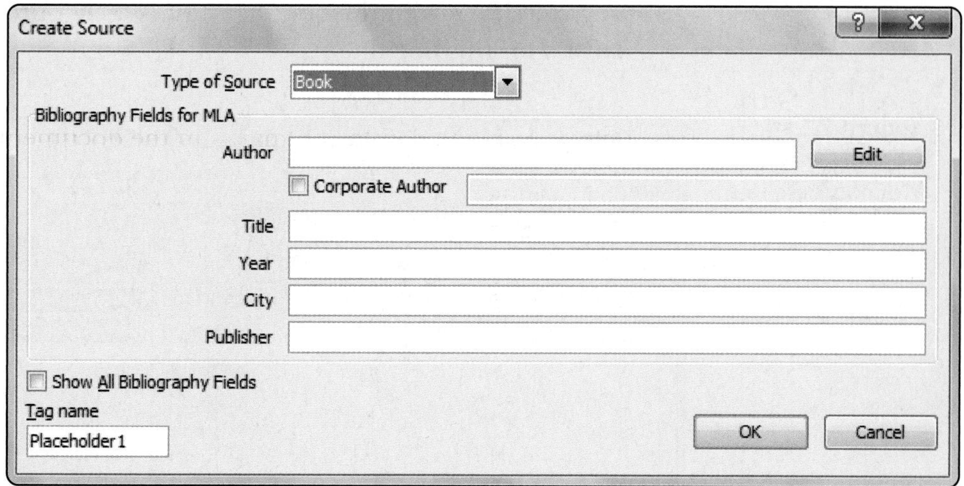

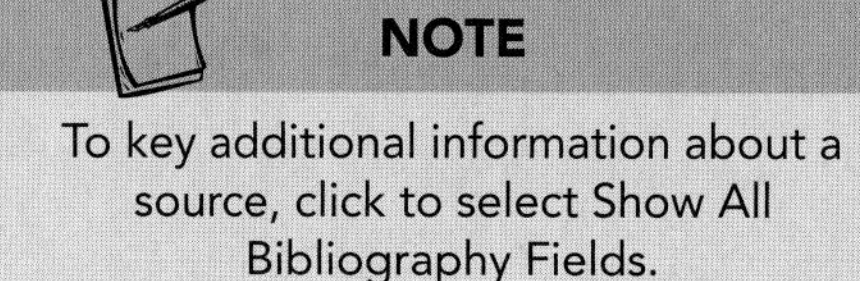

NOTE

To key additional information about a source, click to select Show All Bibliography Fields.

5. Key the following information in the dialog box:

   Author: **Louis E. Grivetti**
   Title: **Chocolate: History, Culture, and Heritage**
   Year: **2009**
   Publisher: **John Wiley & Sons, Incorporated**

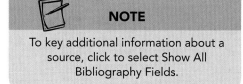

6. Click the Edit button Edit beside the Author text box. Key the following text for the name of the second author:

   Last Name: **Shapiro**
   First Name: **Howard-Yana**

7. Click Add, and click OK to close the Edit Name dialog box. Click OK to close the Create Source dialog box.
8. Create three citations for the other books listed using the information in Figure 22-13. Remember to position the insertion point at the end of each book title. Notice that each time you add a citation, the citation text displays when you point to the Insert Citation button.

Figure 22-13

Author	Chloe Doutre-Roussel	Maricel Presilla	Beth Kimmerle
Title	The Chocolate Connoisseur	The New Taste of Chocolate: A Cultural and Natural History of Cacao with Recipes	Chocolate: The Sweet History
Year	2006	2009	2005
Publisher	Tarcher	Ten Speed Press	DIANE Publishing Company

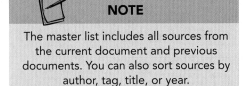

9. Click the Manage Sources button to open the Source Manager dialog box. The Master List on the left is a comprehensive list of available sources. The Current List on the right is a list of recently created sources for this document.

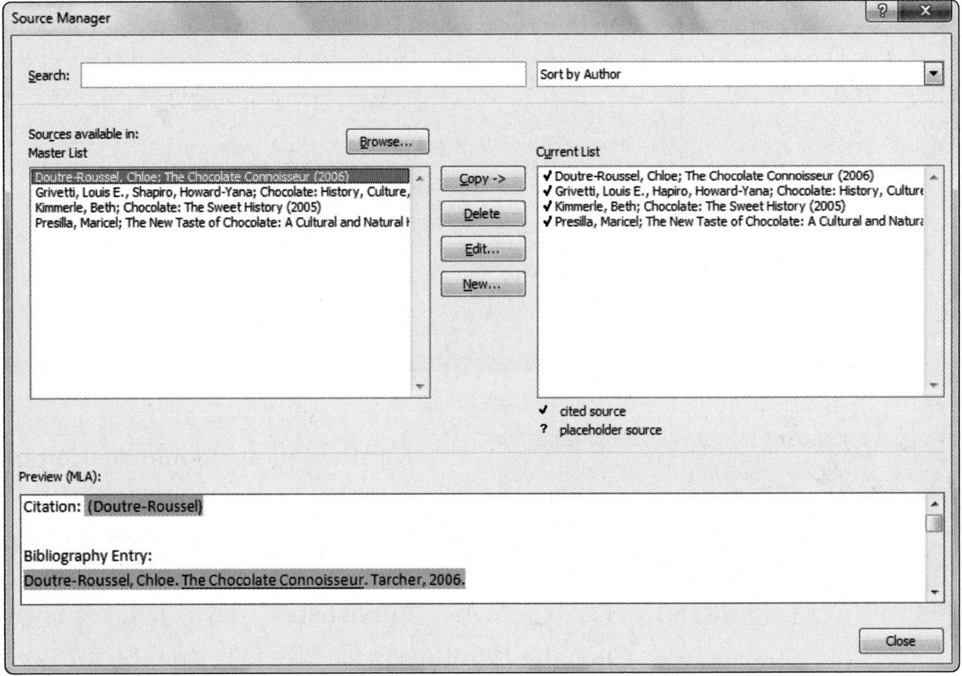

Figure 22-14 Source Manager dialog box

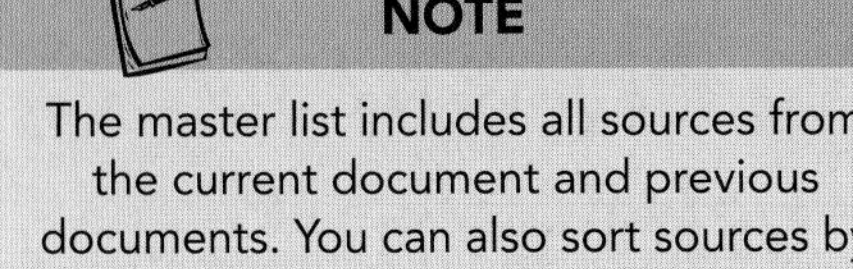

NOTE

The master list includes all sources from the current document and previous documents. You can also sort sources by author, tag, title, or year.

10. Click to select the entry for Beth Kimmerle, and click Edit. Change the year to **2009**. Click OK; click Yes to update the master list, then click Close.
11. Go to the end of the document, and insert a page break. Key **BIBLIOGRAPHY** and press Enter twice. Format the title using 12-point bold and uppercase letters. Center the title.

12. Position the insertion point below the title, click the Bibliography button on the References tab, and click **Insert Bibliography**. A bibliography is created automatically. To turn off the field shading, open Word Options, click the **Advanced** option, and locate the Show document section. Change the field shading option.
13. Save the new document as ***[your initials]*22-12** in your Lesson 22 folder.
14. Save, submit, and close the document.

Lesson 22 Summary

- Text references can appear at the bottom of the page as footnotes or at the end of a document as endnotes. By default, footnotes and endnotes are preceded by a 2-inch horizontal note separator.
- To insert a footnote or endnote, first insert a reference mark in the document text and second key the note text in a separate pane. Word automatically numbers footnotes and endnotes.
- To view footnotes or endnotes, point to the reference mark in the document to display a ScreenTip containing the text or open the Footnotes or Endnotes pane. You can also see footnotes and endnotes in Print Layout view or Print Preview on the Print tab.
- You can edit and format note text just as you do any other text. By default, note text is 10-point Calibri, single-spaced.
- To move, copy, or delete footnotes or endnotes, work with the reference mark in the document, not the actual note text.
- Footnotes can be placed at the bottom of the page or below the last line of text on the page. Endnotes can be placed at the end of the document or section.
- You can convert existing footnotes to endnotes or endnotes to footnotes. You can convert all notes or individual notes.
- By default, footnotes are numbered with cardinal numbers (1, 2, 3) and endnotes are numbered with roman numerals (i, ii, iii). You can change either footnotes or endnotes to cardinal numbers, roman numerals, letters, or symbols.
- Change note options (for example, location and format) in the Footnote and Endnote dialog box. A quick way to open the dialog box is to right-click the note text and choose Note Options from the shortcut menu.
- To insert a citation, select a format style, and key the bibliography field information. Use Manage Sources to edit or locate a source.
- To create a bibliography, position the insertion point at the end of the document, and click the Bibliography button. Select a format for the bibliography.

LESSON 22		Command Summary	
Feature	**Button**	**Command**	**Keyboard**
Insert bibliography		References tab, Citations & Bibliography group	
Insert citation		References tab, Citations & Bibliography group	
Insert endnote		References tab, Footnotes group	Alt+Ctrl+D
Insert footnote	AB[1]	References tab, Footnotes group	Alt+Ctrl+F
Manage sources		References tab, Citations & Bibliography group	
Open Footnotes or Endnotes pane		Draft view, References tab, Footnotes group, Show Notes	
Select browse object		Vertical scroll bar	

Concepts Review

True/False Questions

Each of the following statements is either true or false. Indicate your choice by circling T or F.

T F 1. Every footnote corresponds to a reference mark.

T F 2. A reference mark must be either a number or a letter.

T F 3. You can insert a footnote by pressing Alt+Ctrl+F.

T F 4. Footnotes display by default in either Draft or Print Layout view.

T F 5. Book titles and magazine names should be italicized in footnotes or endnotes.

T F 6. The note separator is a 2-inch vertical line that divides note text from document text.

T F 7. The footnote separator line is 3 inches in length.

T F 8. You can add a placeholder to insert a citation at a later time.

Short Answer Questions

Write the correct answer in the space provided.

1. What is the default placement for footnotes?

____

2. When you point to a footnote reference mark in a document, what does Word display?

____

3. What is the default numbering format for endnotes?

____

4. With a document in Draft view, which button do you use to display the Footnotes pane?

____

5. By default, footnotes are placed immediately above what part of a page?

____

6. What would you insert at the end of a document to make endnotes print on a separate page?

____

7. What setting for footnotes is the alternative to the default placement?

8. What feature is used to create a list of sources?

Critical Thinking

Answer these questions on a separate page. There are no right or wrong answers. Support your answers with examples from your own experience, if possible.

1. Do you prefer using footnotes or endnotes? Why? Which is the most popular method?
2. In this lesson you learned that there are different styles for footnotes and endnotes. Compare the differences in the footnote and/or endnote styles of three professional associations. Which style do you prefer? Why? How close are these styles to the Word default style?

Skills Review

Exercise 22-13

Add and view footnotes.

1. Open the file **Community - 2**.
2. Add the footnotes shown in Figure 22-15 by following these steps:
   a. Position the insertion point after "United Way" in the second paragraph below the heading.
   b. Click the **References** tab on the Ribbon.
   c. Click the Insert Footnote button AB1.
   d. Key the first footnote shown in the figure. Do not press Enter after the text—you will single-space these footnotes.
   e. Position the insertion point after "March of Dimes."
   f. Press Alt+Ctrl+F, and key the second footnote.
   g. Add the third footnote after "Humane Society," and add the fourth footnote after "Foundation."

Figure 22-15

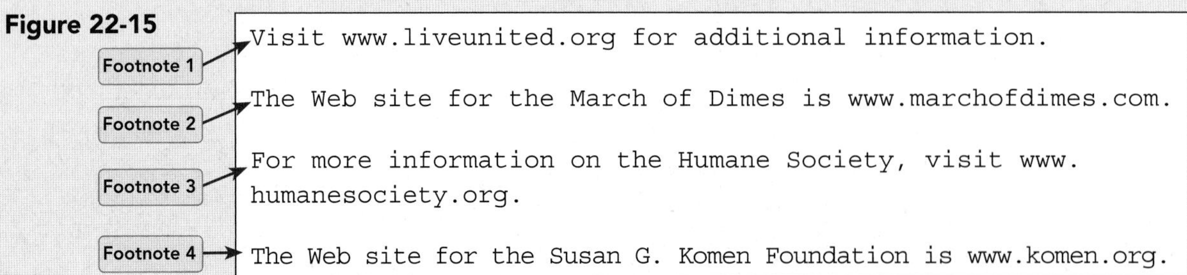

Footnote 1
Visit www.liveunited.org for additional information.
Footnote 2
The Web site for the March of Dimes is www.marchofdimes.com.
Footnote 3
For more information on the Humane Society, visit www.
humanesociety.org.
Footnote 4
The Web site for the Susan G. Komen Foundation is www.komen.org.

3. Display the Print tab to preview the footnotes.

4. Save the document as ***[your initials]*22-13** in your Lesson 22 folder. Submit and close the document.

Exercise 22-14

Edit footnotes in a document.

1. Open the file **Tax Update**.

2. Position the insertion point in the first line of the memo heading and add 72 points spacing before. Select all text in the memo, and change the font to Cambria.

3. Double-click the reference mark (the superscript 1) in the second paragraph of the memo.

4. Edit the footnote in the Footnotes pane by following these steps:
   a. Delete the text "Publication 15."
   b. Italicize the text "(Circular E), Employer's Tax Guide."
   c. Change the font for the footnote text to Cambria.

5. Add a new footnote by following these steps:
   a. Position the insertion point after "W-3" at the end of the first paragraph.
   b. Press Alt+Ctrl+F.
   c. Key **You must provide registration information to file electronically.**
   d. Insert a blank line between the footnotes. Change the font for the first footnote text to Cambria.

6. Save the document as ***[your initials]*22-14** in your Lesson 22 folder. Submit and close the document.

Exercise 22-15

Move, copy, and delete footnotes.

1. Open the file **Promote**.

2. Move a footnote by following these steps:
   a. Scroll to the paragraph that begins "Most stores carry."
   b. Select the reference mark for footnote 3. Cut the reference mark, placing it on the Clipboard.
   c. Move the insertion point to the end of the paragraph that begins "Campbell's Confections encourages," and paste the Clipboard contents. Delete the space character that is inserted to the left of the reference mark.

3. Copy a footnote by following these steps:
   a. Double-click the second footnote in the Footnotes pane to locate the reference mark in the Document pane.

b. Select the reference mark for the second footnote in the Document pane, copy it, and paste it at the end of the last paragraph. Delete the space character that Word inserts preceding the reference mark.

4. In the Footnotes pane, edit footnote 4 by changing "Eva Robinette" to **Kim Abbington**, "A Chocolate Wonder" to **Candy-Making**, "April" to **October**, and "40" to **4**.
5. Delete footnote 1 by selecting the reference mark (the number 1) in the Document pane and pressing Delete.
6. Change the top margin to 1.5 inches.
7. Save the document as ***[your initials]*22-15** in your Lesson 22 folder. Submit and close the document.

Exercise 22-16

Insert citations and create a bibliography.

1. Open the file **Email**.
2. Go to the end of the document (blank line below your reference initials), and insert three citations by following these steps:

a. Click the **References** tab, and click the Insert Citation button.

b. Click **Add New Source**.

c. Refer to Figure 22-16, and key the text for the first entry in the appropriate text boxes. Click **OK**.

d. Press Enter, and insert the second citation. Repeat the procedure to insert a citation for the third book.

Figure 22-16

Brian Halligan, *Inbound Marketing: Get Found Using Google, Social Media, and Blogs*, John Wiley & Sons, Inc., 2009.

Eric Groves, *The Constant Contact Guide to E-mail Marketing*, John Wiley & Sons, Inc., 2009.

David Meerman Scott, *The New Rules of Marketing and PR: How to Use News Releases, Blogs, Podcasting, Viral Marketing, and Online Media to Reach Buyers Directly*, John Wiley & Sons, Inc., 2008.

3. Create a bibliography by following these steps:

a. Insert a page break at the end of the document.

b. Key **BIBLIOGRAPHY**, and press Enter. Format the heading using 14-point bold and all caps. Center the heading, and apply 24 points spacing after.

c. Position the insertion point on the blank line below the title. Select the **References tab**, and select **MLA** from the Style drop-down list.

d. Click the Bibliography button, and click **Insert Bibliography**.

4. Save the document as ***[your initials]*22-16** in your Lesson 22 folder. Submit and close the document.

Lesson Applications

Exercise 22-17

Add, view, and edit footnotes.

1. Open the file **OH Stores**.
2. Format the title with the Heading 1 style, and apply 36 points spacing before.
3. Format each of the store names with the Heading 2 style.
4. Indent all the document text so that it is centered horizontally on the page.
5. Delete the blank paragraph marks.
6. Add the footnote text in Figure 22-17 to the document, and place the reference mark to the right of the appropriate store name. Use default autonumbering and placement. Include the corrections and formatting shown in the figure.

Figure 22-17

Double space between footnotes.

The akron store will host National Chocolate-Covered Cherry Day ~~in~~ on January 3.

The Canton store will host National Chocolate Covered Cashews Day on April 12.

The Youngstown store will host Chocolate Day on July 7.

7. Change the footnote font size to 9 points.
8. Save the document as ***[your initials]*22-17** in your Lesson 22 folder. Submit and close the document.

Exercise 22-18

Locate, format, move, and delete endnotes.

1. Open the file **College**.
2. Apply the following formatting changes to the document:
   - Change the top margin to 2 inches.
   - Apply the Heading 2 style to all the names of colleges and universities on page 2.

3. Use the Go To command to locate the reference number for endnote 1. Move the reference number to the end of the previous sentence, and delete the extra space Word inserts to the left of the number.
4. Switch to Draft view, and click the Show Notes button on the References tab.
5. Click endnote iv in the Endnotes pane to locate the text reference, and delete the note.
6. Display the endnote separator by clicking the down arrow beside the Endnotes drop-down list in the Endnotes pane and clicking Endnote Separator. Add four blank lines before the separator.
7. Close the pane, and switch to Print Layout view.
8. To all endnote text, apply paragraph spacing of 6 points after and increase the font size by 1 point.
9. Save the document as ***[your initials]*22-18** in your Lesson 22 folder. Submit and close the document.

Exercise 22-19

Add, move, and format footnotes; convert footnotes to endnotes; and change the endnote numbering format.

1. Open the file **Candy Making - 2**.
2. Add 72 points spacing before the title on page 1.
3. Convert footnote 2 to an endnote by using the shortcut menu.
4. Right-click the endnote, and open the Note Options dialog box. Change the endnote numbering format to A, B, C.
5. Switch to Draft view, and display the Endnotes pane. Replace the endnote separator line with the word **NOTES**. Format the "NOTES" heading as 12-point bold, uppercase, and centered. Insert four blank lines before the word and two blank lines after it. Switch to Page Layout view.
6. Insert a page break at the end of the document to place the endnotes on a new page.
7. On page 2, locate the paragraph that begins "Centers." Insert the following endnote: **Norma Crawford, "Perfect Centers,"** ***Food Today,*** **February 2010: 47.**
8. Locate footnote 3, and move it to the end of the line beginning "Pour out."
9. Format all the footnote text as 9 points.
10. Format all the endnote text as 10 points with one blank line between notes.

11. Create a header on pages 2 and 3 only, to print the page number in the upper right corner with the text **Page** immediately preceding the number.

12. Save the document as ***[your initials]*****22-19** in your Lesson 22 folder. Submit and close the document.

Exercise 22-20

Add and format footnotes, convert footnotes to endnotes, and change the endnote numbering format.

1. Open the file **Document Management**.

2. Go to page 2, and locate the bulleted text that begins "The average office worker." Position the insertion point at the end of the paragraph, and click the References tab.

3. Key the following footnote text.

   Paper Recycling **(2008, September 30). Retrieved January 20, 2010, from the U.S. Environmental Protection Agency: www.epa.gov.**

4. Position the insertion point after the second bulleted item, and insert a new footnote with the text **Dan Costa, "Three Steps to the Paperless Office,"** ***PC Magazine,*** **March 27, 2008.**

5. Go to the end of the third bulleted item, and insert a footnote using the text: **MSW is an acronym for Municipal Solid Waste.**

6. Locate the "Level One" heading, and position the insertion point after the paragraph that begins "Switch to." Insert this footnote: **Investigate vendors of electronic forms software.**

7. Locate the "Level Three" heading, and place the insertion point after the first paragraph that begins "Implement." Insert the following footnote text: **Contact three companies specializing in document management, and schedule a presentation.**

8. Insert a footnote after the fourth bullet on page 2. Key the following footnote text: **K. J. McCorry, "Becoming the Paperless Office,"** ***informIT,*** **April 17, 2009, <www.informit.com>.**

9. Insert a footnote after the last bulleted item, and key the following text: **Shannon Zipoy, "January is a Great Time to Clean Out Files and Destroy Sensitive Information,"** ***NAPO,*** **January 18, 2010, <www.napo.net>.**

10. Create a footer as follows:

    - Include the text **Campbell's Confections** aligned at the left margin; include the page number (and the word **Page**) aligned at the right margin.
    - Format the footer text as 10-point italic.
    - The footer should appear on every page except the first.

11. Switch to Draft view, display the Footnotes pane, and format all the footnote text as 9 points. Switch to Print Layout view.
12. Adjust page breaks that separate paragraphs from headings or that make paragraphs look unattractive.
13. Save the document as ***[your initials]*****22-20a** in your Lesson 22 folder.
14. Submit the document.
15. Convert all the footnotes that refer to a publication to endnotes.
16. Place the endnotes on a separate page. Format the endnote separator by replacing the line with the word **NOTES** in bold uppercase letters, and center it. Add 72 points spacing before and 24 points spacing after the text.
17. Change the numbering format for the endnotes to 1, 2, 3.
18. Format the endnotes with 12-points spacing after, and increase the font size to 11 points.
19. Adjust page breaks if necessary.
20. Save the document as ***[your initials]*****22-20b** in your Lesson 22 folder.
21. Submit and close the document.

On Your Own

In these exercises you work on your own, as you would in a real-life business environment. Use the skills you have learned to accomplish the task—and be creative.

Exercise 22-21

Research using the Internet or *The Gregg Reference Manual* to learn about the use of footnote or endnote abbreviations such as "ibid." and "op. cit." Write a short document describing their use, and create some examples. Save the document as ***[your initials]*****22-21**, and submit it.

Exercise 22-22

Key at least six lines of poetry from a famous author. Add footnotes to at least three of the lines, giving your interpretation or insight into the poem's meaning. Change the placement of the footnotes so that they appear below the text. Format the document attractively, save it as ***[your initials]*****22-22**, and submit it.

Exercise 22-23

Using a report (in the form of a Word document) you created for another class, add at least three footnotes that relate to the report content and at least three endnotes that cite your information sources. Place the endnotes on a separate page at the end of the document, under the bold heading "NOTES." Change the endnote numbering format to uppercase letters. Add an appropriate header to the document. Insert citations and create a bibliography. Save it as ***[your initials]*22-23**, and submit it.

Lesson 23

Outlines, Indexes, and Tables of Contents

OBJECTIVES

After completing this lesson, you will be able to:

1. Create an outline
2. Identify index entries.
3. Format and compile an index.
4. Edit and update an index.
5. Create a table of contents.
6. Format a table of contents.
7. Edit and update a table of contents.

Estimated Time: 1½ hours

Outlining is a powerful way to organize ideas. Writers typically use an outline to help them decide what to say and in what order to say it. With a good outline, it is easier to develop a document that is orderly and logical. In Word, you can build a document by creating an outline and assigning various levels to headings and body text. You can also outline an existing document. After a document is outlined, you can use Word's outline features to review and reorganize the document quickly and easily.

An *index,* typically found at the back of a book or the end of a document, directs readers to the pages where specific words, phrases, or topics are located. You create an index in Word by using field codes to identify the text you want to include in the index. After you identify all the entries, you compile the index. If you change your document by adding or removing pages, you can update the index to include the new page numbers. A *table of contents (TOC)* is usually found at the beginning of a book or document. It is a list of topics with their page numbers, arranged in the order in which they appear in the document.

Creating an Outline

The process of creating an outline involves determining the content and order of the final document. An outline generally consists of the following:

- *Headings:* The major points.
- *Subheadings:* The topics under the headings (and under other subheadings).
- *Body text:* The text under a heading or subheading.

You create an outline in Outline view, where you can assign different levels to text as you key it. For example, you can *promote* a heading (raise it to a higher outline level) or *demote* a heading (move it to a lower outline level). Word allows as many as nine levels in an outline. You can also apply heading styles to text in Draft view or Print Layout view to create an outline or to outline an existing document. You can then use Outline view to reorganize the outline.

Exercise 23-1 CREATE AN OUTLINE

1. Start a new document, and click the Outline view button on the status bar. The Outlining tab displays on the Ribbon.

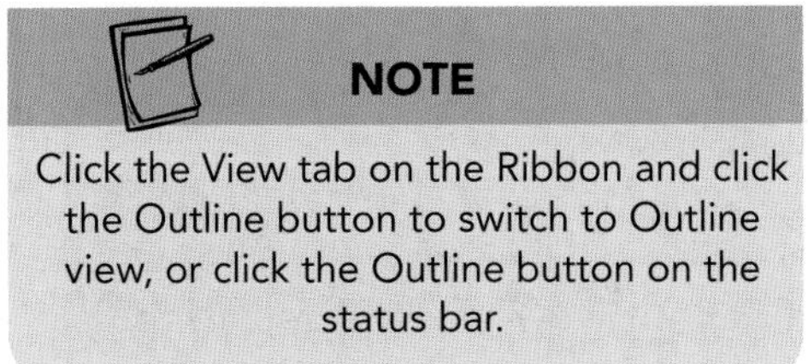

NOTE

Click the View tab on the Ribbon and click the Outline button to switch to Outline view, or click the Outline button on the status bar.

2. Key the heading **Theobroma tree**. It is automatically assigned the Heading 1 style (14-point Cambria, bold). A selection symbol shaped like a large minus sign in a circle appears to the left of the text. It indicates that no *subtext* (any lower-level heading or body text) appears below the heading.

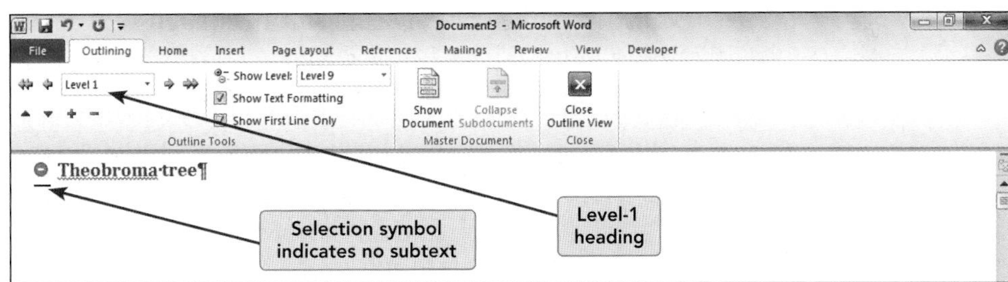

Figure 23-1
Level-1 heading in Outline view

3. Press Enter and click the Demote button. This demotes the new blank paragraph one level, so it becomes a level-2 heading. Notice that the first heading now has a selection symbol shaped like a plus sign, indicating that subtext follows.
4. Key the subheading **Varieties**, and press Enter. Notice that the subheading is assigned the Heading 2 style (13-point Cambria, bold). Press Tab to demote the subheading.

5. Key **Criollo**. The Heading 3 style is applied. Press Enter.
6. With the insertion point on the blank line, click the Demote to Body Text button. Locate the **Show First Line Only** check box and deselect if checked. Key the text shown in Figure 23-2.

Figure 23-2

```
The Criollo variety has a smaller yield per tree, but
provides 10 percent of the world crop. It is used for
premier chocolate.
```

7. Press Enter. Your outline now includes first-, second-, and third-level headings and body text. Body text is assigned the Normal style and is indicated in the outline by a small circle to the left of the paragraph.

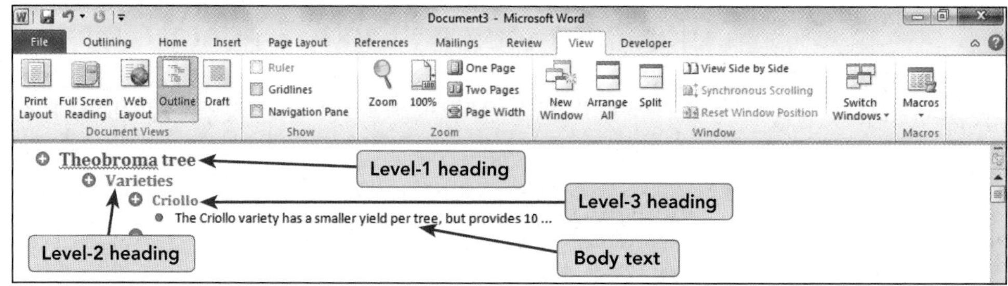

Figure 23-3
Outline with Level-1, -2, and -3 headings and body text

8. Switch to Print Layout view. In Print Layout view you can see all the style characteristics, including paragraph formatting. Notice that the text is not indented in the actual document—indents appear in Outline view only to make viewing the outline structure easier.
9. Switch back to Outline view to continue your outline. With the insertion point still on the last blank line of the document, click the Promote button to create a level-3 heading, and key **Forastero**.
10. Press Enter, click the Demote to Body Text button, and key **This variety provides 80 percent of the world crop.**
11. Press Enter and click the Promote button. Key **Trinitario.**
12. Press Enter, click the Demote to Body Text button, and key **This variety is the easiest to cultivate, and it provides 10 percent of the world crop.**

NOTE

Always be sure you are on a new line before demoting or promoting a heading so that you do not change the level of an existing heading by accident.

TABLE 23-1 Outlining Tab Buttons and Keyboard Shortcuts

Button	Function	Keyboard
Promote to Heading 1	Promotes any text to a level-1 heading	
Promote	Promotes one heading level	Alt+Shift+← or Shift+Tab
Level 1 Outline Level	Assigns an outline level to text	
Demote	Demotes one heading level	Alt+Shift+→ or Tab
Demote to Body Text	Demotes any heading to body text	Ctrl+Shift+N
Move Up	Moves heading up in document	Alt+Shift+↑
Move Down	Moves heading down in document	Alt+Shift+↓
Expand	Displays subheadings and body text	Alt+Shift++
Collapse	Hides subheadings and body text	Alt+Shift+−
Show Level: Show Level	Displays selected heading levels	
Show First Line Only Show First Line Only	Displays first line only of body text	Alt+Shift+L
Show Text Formatting Show Formatting	Displays character formatting in Outline view	/ (on numeric keypad)

Exercise 23-2 COLLAPSE AND EXPAND AN OUTLINE

You can *collapse* an outline so that only the main headings appear, and you can *expand* it again to display your subtext. You can also collapse an outline to display headings and only the first line of text paragraphs. When you collapse an outline, you can see the "main points" of the document, which makes it easier to rearrange the text in a logical sequence.

1. To collapse the outline, open the **Show Level** drop-down list on the **Outlining** tab and choose **Level 3**. This tells Word to display only headings that are level 3 or higher; all other text is hidden, or "collapsed." A gray line appears under all headings that have collapsed text.

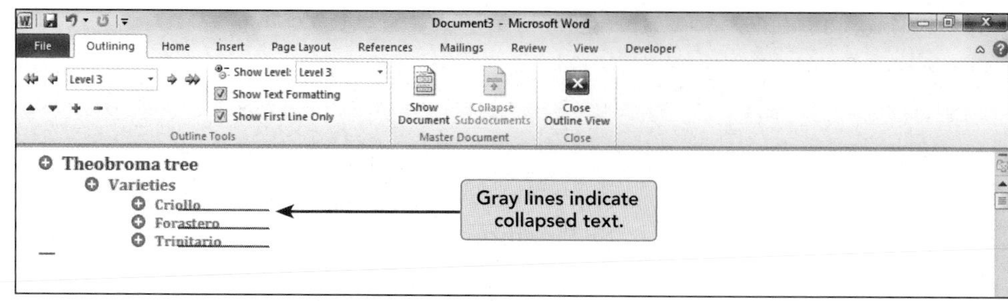

Figure 23-4 Outline with body text collapsed

2. Open the **Show Level** drop-down list and choose **Level 2**. Word displays only level-1 and level-2 headings and collapses level-3 headings.
3. Choose **Level 3** from the drop-down list again. All three heading levels are displayed again.
4. Position the insertion point in the level-2 heading, "Varieties." Click the Collapse button to collapse the subheadings for that heading. Click the Expand button to display the subheadings once again.
5. Position the pointer on the selection symbol for the first heading, "Theobroma tree." When the pointer changes to a four-headed arrow, double-click to collapse all the text below the heading.

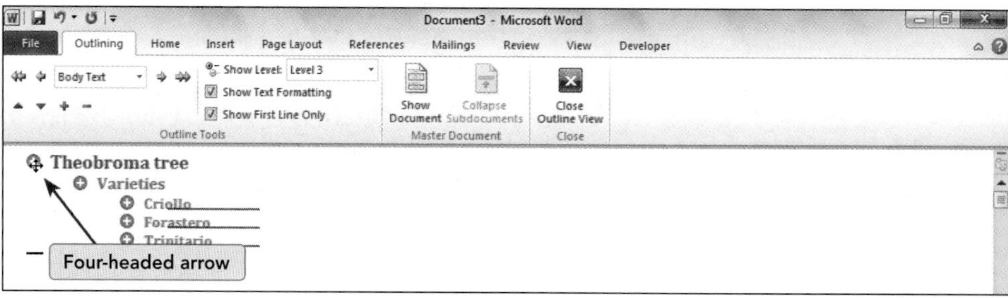

Figure 23-5 Double-click selection symbol to collapse text

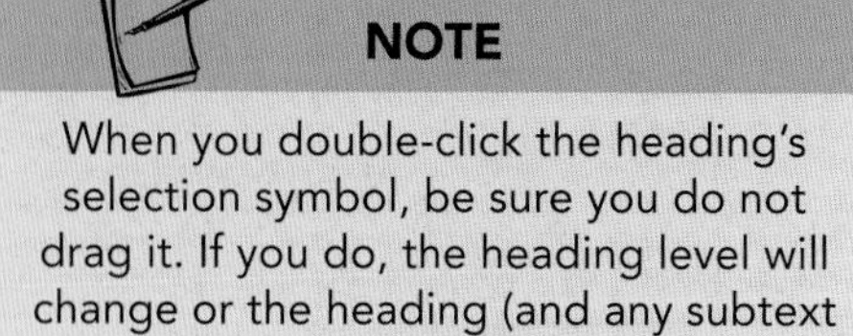

NOTE

When you double-click the heading's selection symbol, be sure you do not drag it. If you do, the heading level will change or the heading (and any subtext beneath it) will be repositioned.

6. Double-click the selection symbol to expand the outline completely. Notice that double-clicking a selection symbol selects both the heading and all its subtext.
7. With the entire outline expanded and selected, click the Show First Line Only check box Show First Line Only. Now only the first line of each text paragraph is displayed.
8. Click to deselect the Show First Line Only check box Show First Line Only and expand all the body text. Click within the outline to deselect it.
9. Save the document as ***[your initials]*****23-2** in a new folder for Lesson 23.
10. Submit the document.

Exercise 23-3 NAVIGATING IN AN OUTLINE

When you modify an outline, you need an efficient way to move around if the outline extends beyond the length of your screen. You can collapse the outline, find a certain heading or section, and then expand it, but this is cumbersome when the outline is large or when you have several changes to make. Instead, you can set the Select Browse Object button to move the insertion point from heading to heading. Or you can use a feature called the *Navigation Pane*—a separate pane on the left side of the screen that shows the headings of your document. The Navigation Pane check box appears on the View tab, in the Show group.

TIP

You do not have to be working on an outline to use the Navigation Pane. This feature is useful for navigating in any document with headings. Note, however, that your headings must have a heading style applied before they will appear in the Navigation Pane.

NOTE

The Next and Previous buttons "remember" which object you last selected with the Select Browse Object button.

1. Click in the first heading, "Theobroma tree." Click the Select Browse Object button near the bottom of the vertical scroll bar.
2. Click the Browse by Heading button. The insertion point moves to the beginning of the next heading, "Varieties."
3. Click the Next Heading button just below the Select Browse Object button. The insertion point moves to the next heading, "Criollo."
4. Click the Previous Heading button two times to move back to the first heading, "Theobroma tree."
5. Click the **View** tab on the Ribbon. Click to select the **Navigation Pane** check box. A new pane opens on the left side of your screen, displaying each heading in your outline.

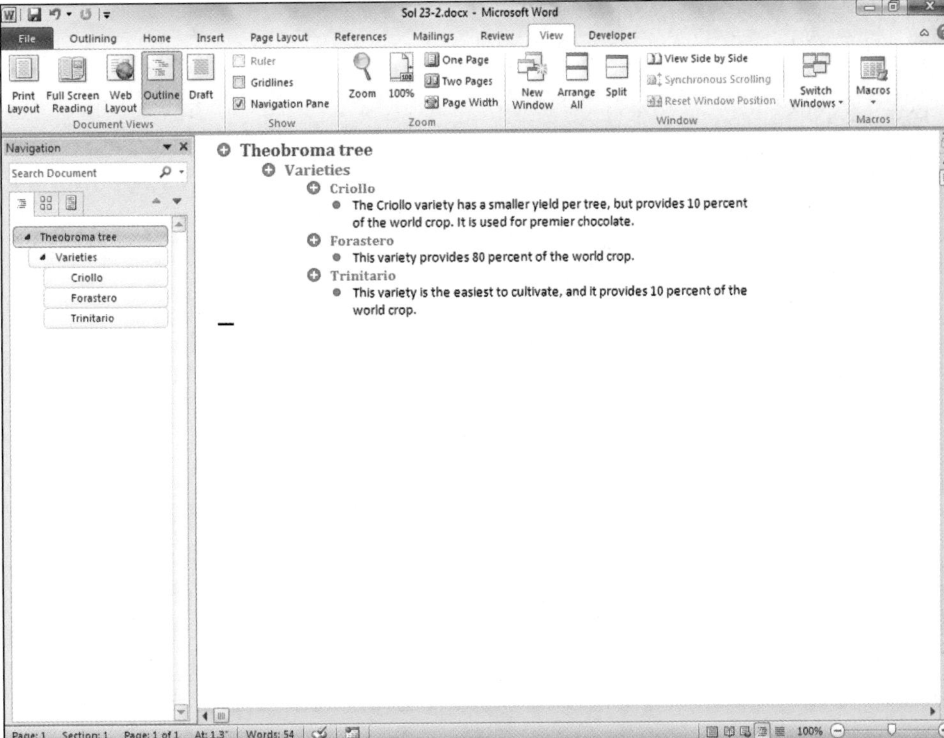

Figure 23-6
Navigation Pane in Outline view

NOTE

You can expand and collapse the headings in the Navigation Pane by clicking the arrow symbols to the left of each heading.

6. Click the heading "Trinitario" in the Navigation Pane. The heading scrolls to the top of the Document pane, and the insertion point moves to the beginning of the heading.
7. Click the heading "Theobroma tree" in the Navigation Pane to return to the beginning of the outline.
8. Click the **View** tab on the Ribbon if necessary. Click to deselect the **Navigation Pane** check box. (You can also click the Navigation Pane Close button.)
9. Close the document.

Identifying Index Entries

The first step in creating an index is to identify (or mark) the text you want indexed and—at the same time—indicate how you want the entries to be worded in the index itself. An index entry can be an individual word, phrase, symbol, or range of text. Word gives you three ways to identify an entry for inclusion in an index:

- Mark the text by selecting it; then open the Mark Index Entry dialog box.
- Place the insertion point where you want the entry to be; then key the entry into the Mark Index Entry dialog box.
- Create a concordance file, and use the AutoMark command in the Index and Tables dialog box. This method marks many entries at once.

Exercise 23-4 MARK TEXT TO IDENTIFY INDEX ENTRIES

NOTE

Always create an index *after* you make all changes and revisions in your document. This approach ensures accuracy in the index page-number references.

1. Open the file **Ordering - 2**. The file has been formatted using Word's built-in styles.
2. Select the heading "Online."
3. Click the **References** tab on the Ribbon, and locate the **Index** group.

Figure 23-7
Index group

NOTE

You can key or edit text in the Main entry text box.

4. Click the Mark Entry button. The Mark Index Entry dialog box appears with "Online" displayed in the Main entry text box. Click **Mark** to mark "Online" for the index. The index entry appears in the document as a field, enclosed in braces and quotation marks. In the field, "XE" stands for index entry. Do not close the Mark Index Entry dialog box.

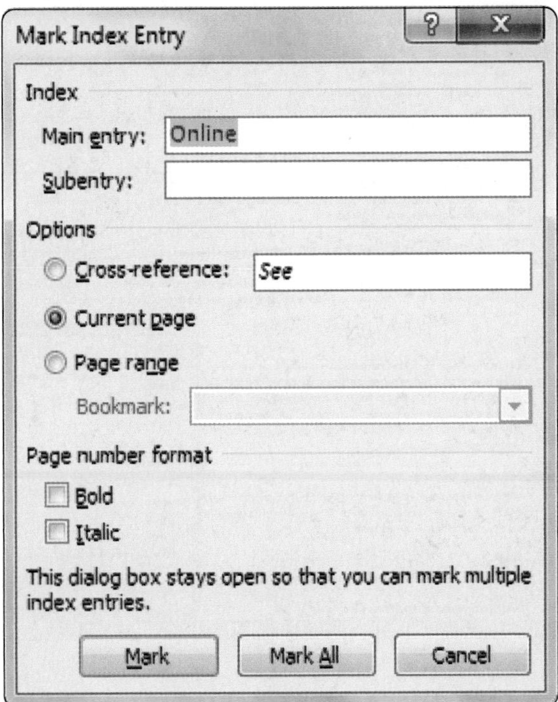

Figure 23-8
Mark Index Entry dialog box

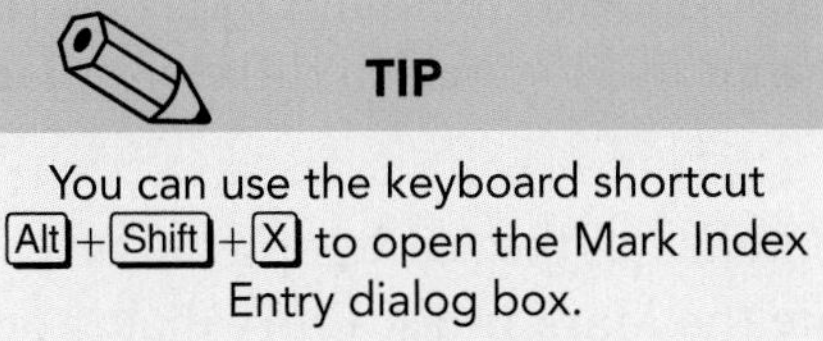

TIP

You can use the keyboard shortcut Alt+Shift+X to open the Mark Index Entry dialog box.

NOTE

The Mark Index Entry dialog box remains open while you mark index entries in your document. You can even use the Find and Replace commands to locate and index other topics while the dialog box remains open.

5. Drag the Mark Index Entry dialog box to the lower right portion of the document window so that you have space to view your document.
6. Select the heading "Telephone." Click the title bar of the Mark Index Entry dialog box. The selection appears in the **Main entry** text box.
7. With "Telephone" displayed in the Main entry text box, click **Mark**.
8. Select "E-mail" in the last sentence of the first paragraph.
9. Activate the Mark Index Entry dialog box by clicking its title bar. Then click **Mark** to mark this selection as an index entry (see Figure 23-9).

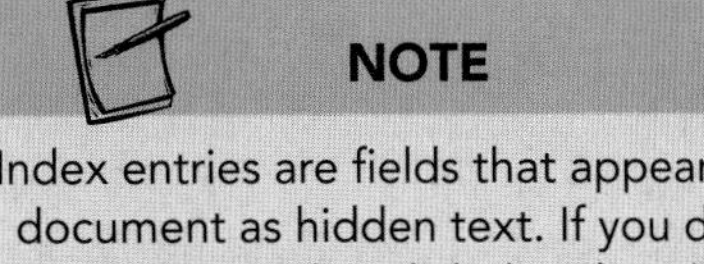

NOTE

Index entries are fields that appear in the document as hidden text. If you do not see {XE "E-mail"}, click the Show/Hide ¶ button to display the fields.

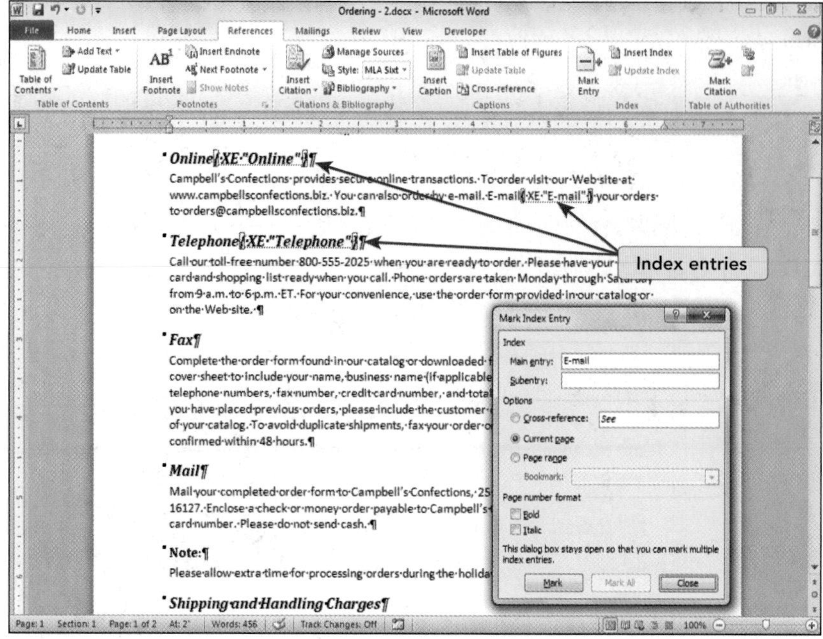

Figure 23-9
Index entry

Exercise 23-5 MARK MULTIPLE-LEVEL INDEX ENTRIES

You can also create *subentries* that are subordinate to the main index entries. This is useful when a topic has subtopics that are located in different places in the document.

1. Select "Rush delivery" in the second sentence of the paragraph under "Delivery." Press Alt+Shift+X to activate the Mark Index Entry dialog box.
2. Edit the Main entry to read **Delivery**. Click in the Subentry text box and key **Rush delivery** as the subentry.
3. Click Mark. Word inserts a new index field. This index field has the main entry ("Delivery") followed by a colon and the subentry ("Rush delivery").

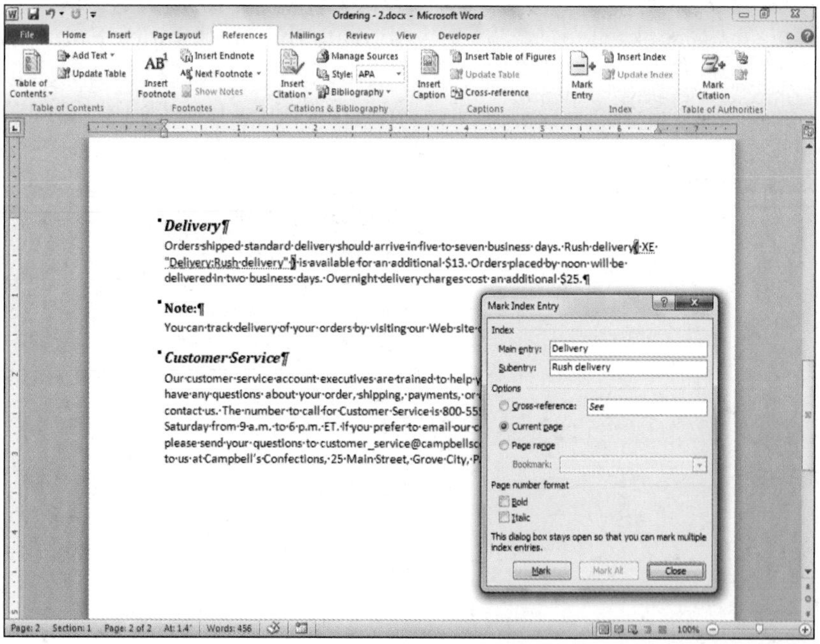

Figure 23-10
Creating a subentry

TIP

You can select and reformat the text contained within the field code braces of your document and edit or delete your index entries with the Mark Index Entry dialog box closed, much as you would edit ordinary text. Any changes you make to index entries will be included in your index the next time it is updated.

4. Select "Overnight delivery" in the paragraph below the "Delivery" heading, and activate the Mark Index Entry dialog box. Key **Delivery** in the Main entry text box, and key **Overnight delivery** in the Subentry text box. Click **Mark**. Now two headings are in your index under "Delivery" ("Rush delivery" and "Overnight delivery"), with page numbers for each one.
5. Close the Mark Index Entry dialog box.

Exercise 23-6 MARK A RANGE OF PAGES AS AN INDEX ENTRY

Sometimes an index refers readers to a range of pages (rather than to just one page) if the topic extends beyond one page. To do this, you need to create a bookmark for the text to be indexed and then use the bookmark to mark the text for the index.

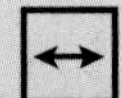

REVIEW

To bookmark selected text, click the Insert tab, and click the Bookmark button. Key the bookmark's name in the Bookmark name text box, and click Add. Remember that bookmark names cannot contain spaces.

1. Select all the text from the heading "Shipping and Handling Charges" to "our toll-free number" (the end of the "Note" paragraph following the "Delivery" paragraph).
2. Create a bookmark named **ShippingandHandling**. The selected paragraphs are now marked as a bookmark.
3. Place the insertion point at the end of the section you just bookmarked (after "toll-free number").
4. Press Alt+Shift+X to open the Mark Index Entry dialog box. Key **Shipping** in the Main entry text box. This will be the entry that appears in the index you create.

Figure 23-11
Using a bookmark to mark an index entry

Mark Index Entry
Index
Main entry: Shipping
Subentry:
Options
Cross-reference: See
Current page
Page range
Bookmark: ShippingandHandling
Page number format
Bold
Italic
This dialog box stays open so that you can mark multiple index entries.
Mark | Mark All | Cancel

5. Click **Page range**. Click the down arrow next to the Bookmark text box to display the list of bookmarks. Choose the bookmark you created in step 2 (ShippingandHandling).
6. Click **Mark**. The field code for the index entry is inserted at the end of the bookmarked section. Now when you create the index, the page number for this entry will be "1–2" instead of just "1."

Exercise 23-7 ADD A CROSS-REFERENCE

You use a cross-reference when you want readers who look up one entry in the index to be referred to another entry. There is an option for creating a cross-reference in the Mark Index Entry dialog box.

1. With the Mark Index Entry dialog box still open, scroll to the bottom of page 1. Select the words "sales tax" in the middle of the first sentence under the heading "Note." Click the Mark Index Entry dialog box title bar. Capitalize the "s" in "sales tax."

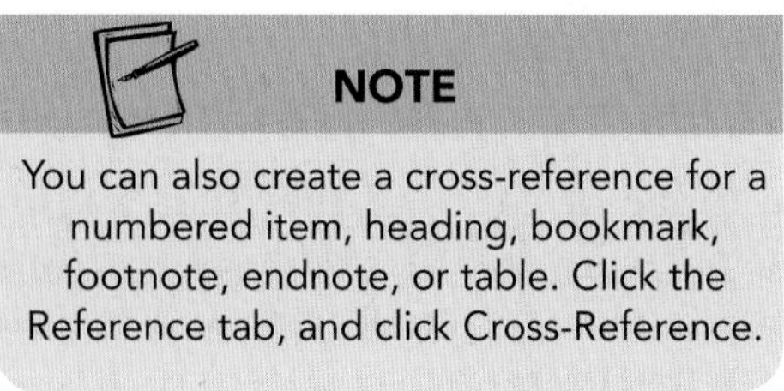

NOTE

You can also create a cross-reference for a numbered item, heading, bookmark, footnote, endnote, or table. Click the Reference tab, and click Cross-Reference.

2. Click the **Cross-reference** option in the Mark Index Entry dialog box. The selected text appears in the Main entry text box, and the insertion point is in the Cross-reference text box, one space after "*See*."
3. Key **Shipping and Handling Charges** and click **Mark**. The cross-reference appears in your index entry in the document. "*See* Shipping and Handling Charges" will now appear under "Sales tax" in your index.

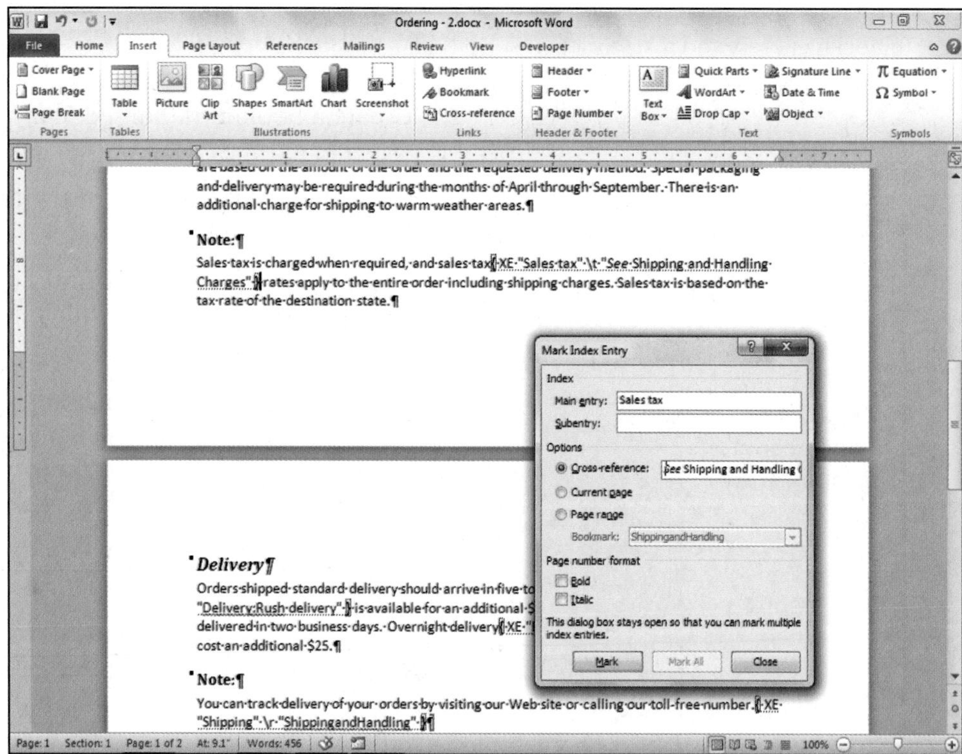

Figure 23-12
Creating a cross-reference

4. Close the Mark Index Entry dialog box.

Formatting and Compiling an Index

After you mark all the index entries in your document, you are ready to create the index. Generally, an index is placed at the end of a document, on a separate page.

You can control the basic layout of the index. For example, you can choose the number of columns and specify one of several styles with which to format the index text.

Exercise 23-8 FORMAT AND COMPILE AN INDEX

1. Position the insertion point at the end of the document. Press Enter twice and click the **References** tab. Locate the **Index** group, and click the Insert Index button. The Index dialog box appears.
2. On the **Index** tab, click the **Run-in** option to the right of **Type**. Notice the change in the Print Preview area of the Index dialog box. Click the **Indented** option, and notice the difference.
3. Open the **Formats** drop-down list box, and click each index format, examining each style in the Print Preview window.
4. Choose the **From template** format, which uses styles from the default template attached to the document. Notice that the index is set for two columns.
5. Click the **Right align page numbers** check box. Notice the change in the Print Preview window. Click the check box again to clear it.
6. Click **Modify**. The Style dialog box appears.
7. Click the various styles (**Index 1** through **Index 9**) in the Styles list, noticing the effect in the Preview box. Instead of using one of these preset choices, you can modify each style.
8. Choose the **Index 1** style and click **Modify**. The Modify Style dialog box appears.

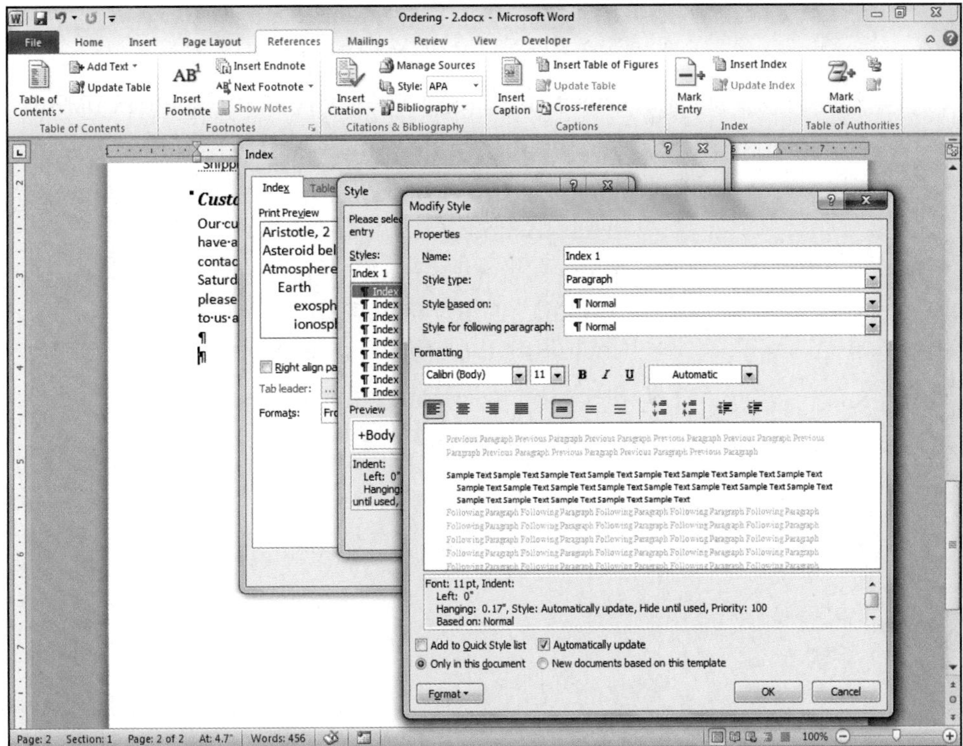

Figure 23-13
Modify Style dialog box

NOTE

By default, the index begins and ends with a continuous section break. Switch to Draft view to see the continuous section breaks.

9. Change the font size to 11 points. Click **OK** to close the Modify Style dialog box.
10. Click **OK** to close the Style dialog box; then click **OK** to compile the index. The index is inserted at the bottom of the document.

Editing and Updating Indexes

To edit your index, change the text contained in the index entry (XE) fields of the document and then update the index.

NOTE

If you make changes to the index itself, your changes will be lost the next time your index is updated unless you make the same changes to the index entries in the text.

After editing the index entry, you have three ways to update the index:

- Click the Update index button on the Ribbon.
- Press F9.
- Use the shortcut menu.

Exercise 23-9 EDIT AND UPDATE AN INDEX

1. Locate the bold index entry "Online" in the first heading of your document (*not* in the index). In the index entry field (the text in brackets—not the heading itself), change the uppercase "O" to lowercase.
2. Place the insertion point in the index.
3. Click the Update Index button. Word recompiles and replaces your old index with a new one.
4. Check the index, and verify that the index listing "online" is lowercase.
5. Change the "online" index entry to uppercase.
6. Place the insertion point in the index, and press F9. The index is instantly updated.
7. In the first paragraph of the document, locate the index entry for "E-mail." Drag the pointer over the entire index entry to select it (including the brackets), and press Delete.
8. Place the insertion point in the index, and right-click. Click **Update Field** from the shortcut menu.

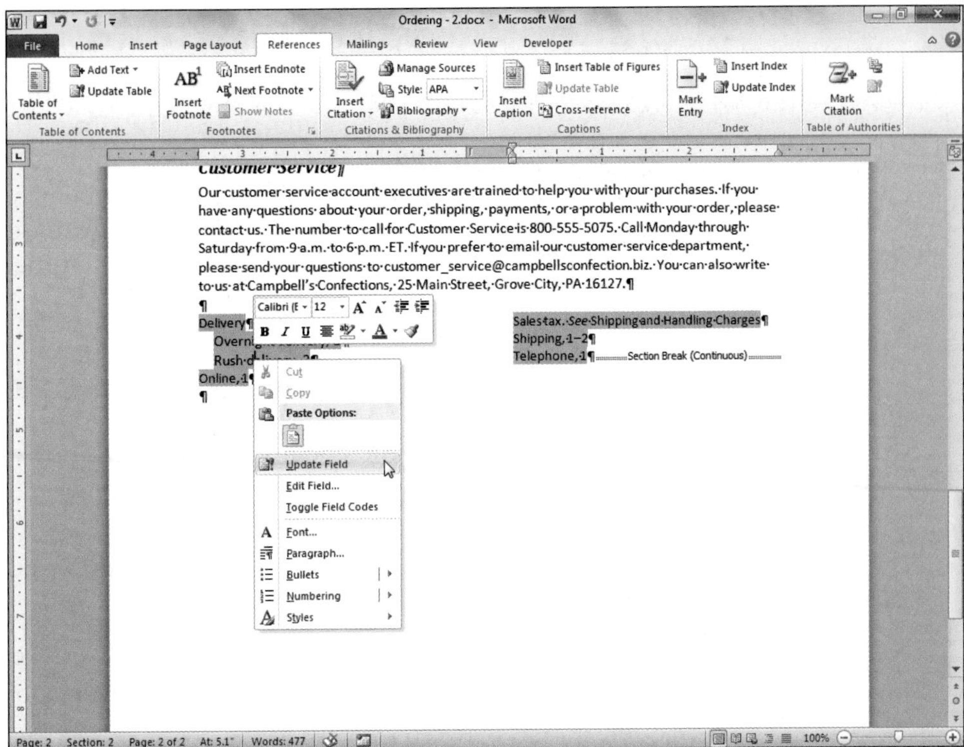

Figure 23-14
Using the shortcut menu to update an index

9. Switch to Draft view. Place the insertion point just above the index, at the end of the previous section. Insert a page break to start the index on a new page.

10. On the new page, on a blank line above the index, key **INDEX** and press Enter. Apply the Heading 1 style to the word and center it. Switch to Print Layout view.

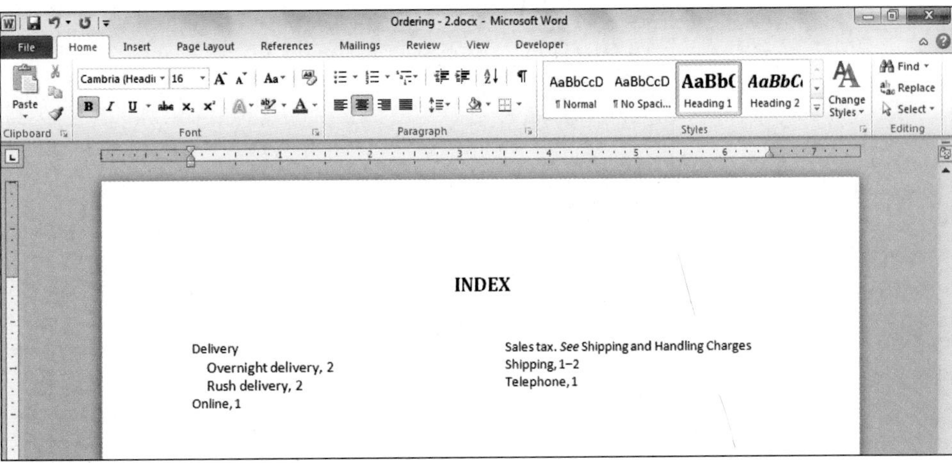

Figure 23-15
Index in Print Layout view

11. Save the document as ***[your initials]*23-9** in your Lesson 23 folder.

Creating a Table of Contents

TIP

Create the index before you create a table of contents, and format the index title with a heading style that will appear in the table of contents. In this way, your index will be listed in your table of contents.

The easiest way to generate a table of contents is to use Word's heading styles (Headings 1–9) for your document headings. Word can then search for the heading styles, record the associated page numbers, and create the table. After the table of contents is created, you can update it periodically to reflect changes in the document.

Exercise 23-10 CREATE A TABLE OF CONTENTS

1. Move to the top of the document, and click the Styles Dialog Box Launcher to display the Styles task pane. Notice that the title of the document is formatted using the Heading 1 style.
2. Click in the "Online" heading, and notice that it is formatted using the Heading 2 style.
3. Position the insertion point in one of the "Note" paragraphs, and modify the Heading 3 style. Change the font size to 12 points.
4. Position the insertion point at the beginning of the document, and insert a page break. (The table of contents usually appears at the front of a document, on a separate page.)

NOTE

You can click one of the built-in table of contents styles listed in the drop-down list, or you can click Insert Table of Contents for more options.

5. Move to page 1, and click the **References** tab on the Ribbon. Click the Table of Contents button. Click **Insert Table of Contents**. The Table of Contents dialog box appears. Click **OK** to accept the default settings. The table of contents is inserted at the beginning of the document on the new page.

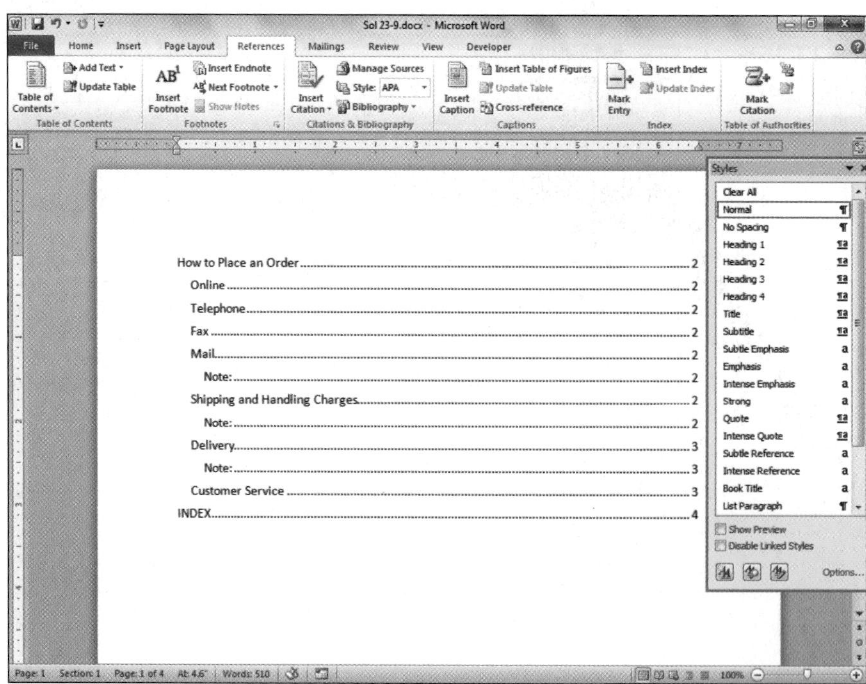

Figure 23-16
Table of Contents

Formatting a Table of Contents

To format the table of contents, you can choose from several styles and formatting options in the Table of Contents dialog box.

Exercise 23-11 FORMAT A TABLE OF CONTENTS

1. Click once anywhere in the table of contents to select it. Notice that the selected text is highlighted in gray.

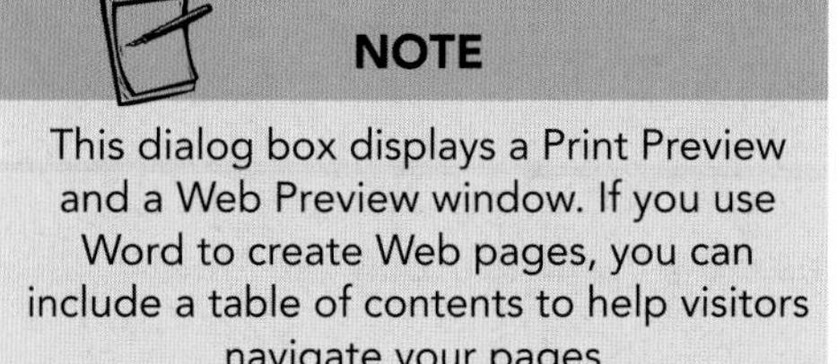

NOTE
This dialog box displays a Print Preview and a Web Preview window. If you use Word to create Web pages, you can include a table of contents to help visitors navigate your pages.

2. Click the Table of Contents button, and click **Insert Table of Contents**. The Table of Contents dialog box displays.
3. Open the **Formats** list box. Click each choice to see how the format looks in the Print Preview window.
4. Choose the **Classic** format.
5. Open the **Tab leader** list, and choose the solid line leader.

Figure 23-17
Formatting the Table of Contents

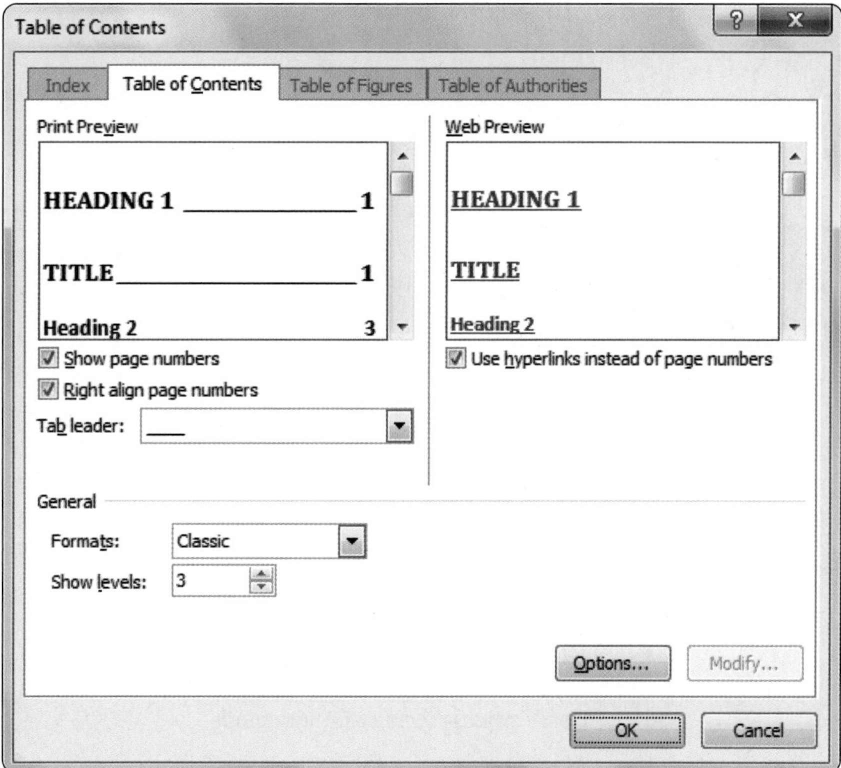

6. Locate **Show levels** in the General section. Change the setting to **2**. This feature determines how many heading levels appear in the table of contents.
7. Click **OK**. When you are prompted to replace the selected table of contents, click **Yes**.

Editing and Updating a Table of Contents

NOTE

If you make changes to the table of contents itself, your changes will be lost the next time you update it unless you make the same changes to the headings in the document.

To edit the table of contents, change the headings in the document and then update the table of contents.

After you edit the document's headings, you can update the table of contents by using the Update Table button, pressing F9, or using the shortcut menu.

Exercise 23-12 EDIT AND UPDATE A TABLE OF CONTENTS

1. Press Ctrl and click the text "Shipping and Handling Charges" in the table of contents. Word moves the insertion point directly to that heading in the document.
2. Position the insertion point at the end of the "Note" paragraph that follows "Shipping and Handling," and press Enter.
3. Key the following text:

   Payment
   We accept checks, money orders, and Visa, MasterCard, Discover, and American Express credit cards.

4. Select "Payment" and click the Add Text button. Click **Level 2**, which corresponds to a Heading 2 style. Verify that the paragraph text below the "Payment" heading is the Normal style.
5. Press Ctrl+Home and press F9. When you are prompted to update the table of contents, click **Update entire table** and click **OK**.

NOTE

You can update the table by clicking the Update Table button or displaying the shortcut menu.

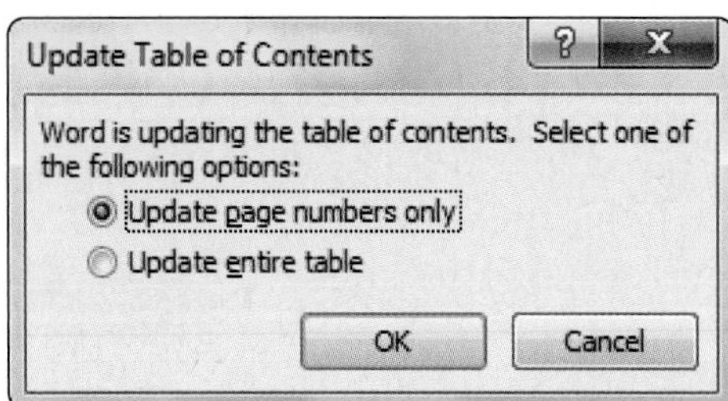

Figure 23-18 Update Table of Contents dialog box

6. Click the Show/Hide ¶ button ¶ to hide the field codes.

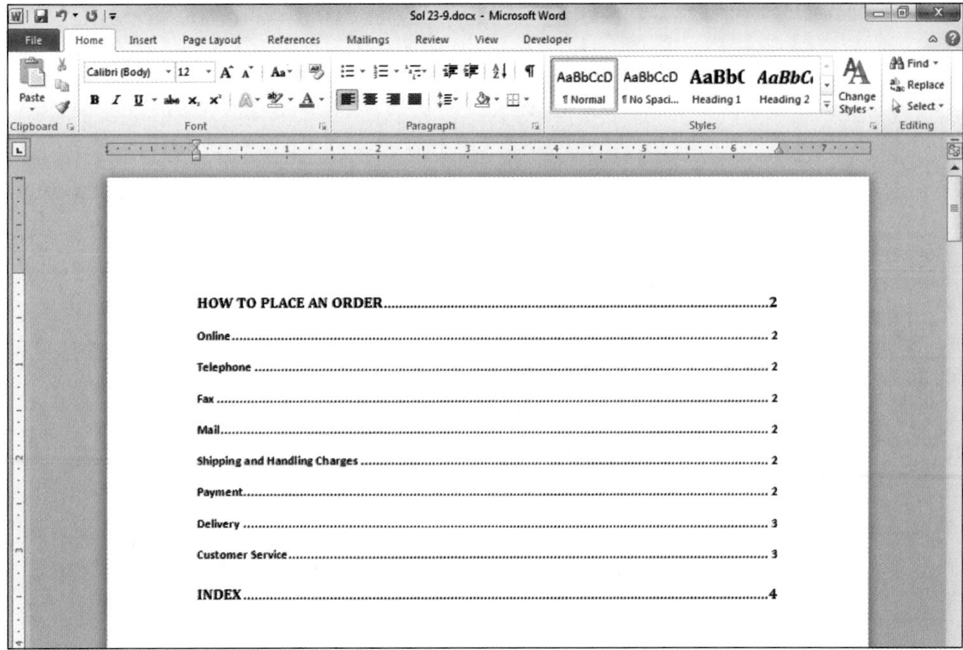

Figure 23-19 Completed table of contents

7. Click below the table of contents to deselect it.
8. Apply page numbers to the lower right corner of every page of the document.
9. Update the index because page references have changed since you added the table of contents (and hide the index field codes).
10. Save the document as ***[your initials]*****23-12** in your Lesson 23 folder.
11. Submit and close the document.

Exercise 23-13 CREATE, MODIFY, AND UPDATE A TABLE OF FIGURES

A table of figures is used to create a list of captions within a document. Captions can be added to figures, tables, equations, or other objects. The Table of Figures dialog box contains many of the same options found in the Table of Contents dialog box. You can choose to show page numbers, select a tab leader option, and select a format for the table. You can also select a caption label.

Caption
Caption: Table 1
Options
Label: Table
Position: Above selected item
Exclude label from caption
New Label... Delete Label Numbering...
AutoCaption... OK Cancel

Figure 23-20 Caption dialog box

1. Open the file **Figures**, and click the References tab.
2. Position the insertion point in the first row of the first table, and click the Insert Caption button to open the Caption dialog box.
3. Click OK to accept the default settings. The caption appears above the table and is formatted with the Caption style.

4. Insert a caption for each table in the document, accepting default settings for each. Verify that you have five captions in the document.
5. Go to the end of the document, and insert a page break.
6. Key **TABLE OF FIGURES** at the top of the new page, and press Enter.
7. Click the Insert Table of Figures button to display the Table of Figures dialog box.

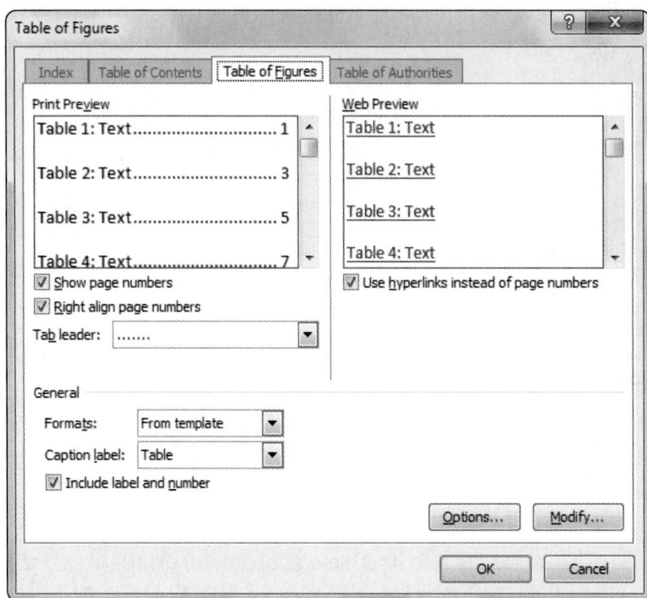

Figure 23-21
Table of Figures dialog box

8. Click the down arrow for **Formats**, and click **Formal**. Select the dotted leader format for the tab leader. Click **OK**.
9. Format the heading for the table of figures using 14-point bold, with all caps and 24 points spacing after, and center it. Delete blank paragraph marks after the heading.
10. Select the caption, all rows of the third table, and the blank line following the table. Press Ctrl+X to cut the table.
11. Position the insertion point at the top of the document, to the left of the caption for Table 1.
12. Press Ctrl+V to paste the table.
13. Select the caption for the first table in the document, and right-click to display the shortcut menu. Click **Update Field** to renumber the caption.
14. Select and update each of the remaining captions.
15. Go to the table of figures, and right-click it. Click **Update Field**. Click **OK**.
16. Select the caption and all rows of the third table. Apply the **Keep with next** paragraph formatting option.
17. Select the caption and all rows of the fifth table, and apply the **Keep with next** option.

18. Update the entire table of figures.
19. Save the document as ***[your initials]*23-13** in your Lesson 23 folder.
20. Submit and close the document.

Exercise 23-14 CREATE, MODIFY, AND UPDATE A TABLE OF AUTHORITIES

A table of authorities is used to cite references to cases, statutes, and other legal documents. To create a table of authorities, you mark citations and then insert the table of authorities. The procedure is very similar to creating an index or a table of contents.

1. Open the file **Email - 2**, and click the References tab.
2. Go to page 2, and select the text "§ 7661."
3. Click the Mark Citation button to open the Mark Citation dialog box.

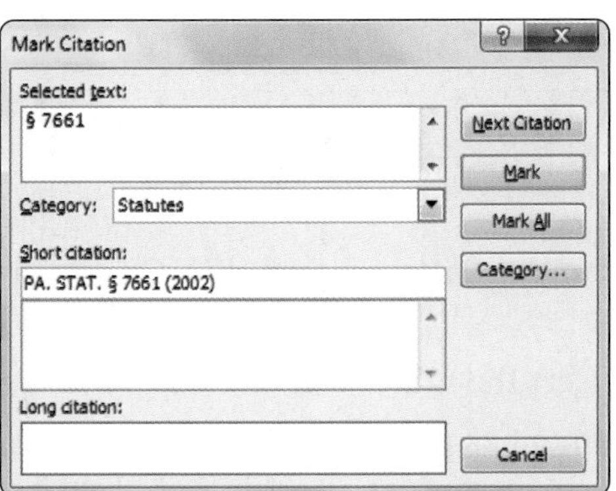

Figure 23-22 Mark Citation dialog box

4. Change the Category to Statutes, and edit the Short citation text box to read **PA. STAT. § 7661 (2002)**.
5. Click Mark and Close the dialog box. A {TA} field code is inserted in the document.
6. Select the text "§ 2250.1" in the second legal reference, and press Shift+Alt+I. Edit the Short citation to read **PA. STAT. § 2250.1 (2002)**. Click Mark.
7. Click Next Citation in the Mark Citation dialog box to move to the next section mark. Click in the document and select "§ 7702." Click in the Selected text section of the Mark Citation dialog box to update the selection.
8. Edit the Short citation to read **15 U.S.C. § 7702**, and click Mark.
9. Click Next Citation, and expand the selection to "§ 7703." Click in the Mark Citation dialog box, and edit the Short citation to **15 U.S.C. § 7703**. Click Mark.

NOTE

To insert the symbol for a section, click the Insert tab. Click Symbol and click More Symbols. Click the drop-down arrow for the Font box, and click (normal text). Scroll to locate the symbol for a section. Click Insert, and close the dialog box.

10. Click Next Citation, and expand the selection to "§ 2701." Click in the Mark Citation dialog box, and edit the Short citation to **18 U.S.C. § 2701**. Click Mark.
11. Click Next Citation, and expand the selection to "§ 1030." Click in the Mark Citation dialog box, and edit the Short citation to **18 U.S.C. § 1030**. Click Mark, and click Close.
12. Insert a page break at the end of the document, and key **TABLE OF AUTHORITIES**. Press Enter, and format the title using 14-point bold, with center alignment. Change the spacing before to 72 points and the spacing after to 24 points. Position the insertion point below the title.

13. Click the Insert Table of Authorities button on the References tab to open the Table of Authorities dialog box.

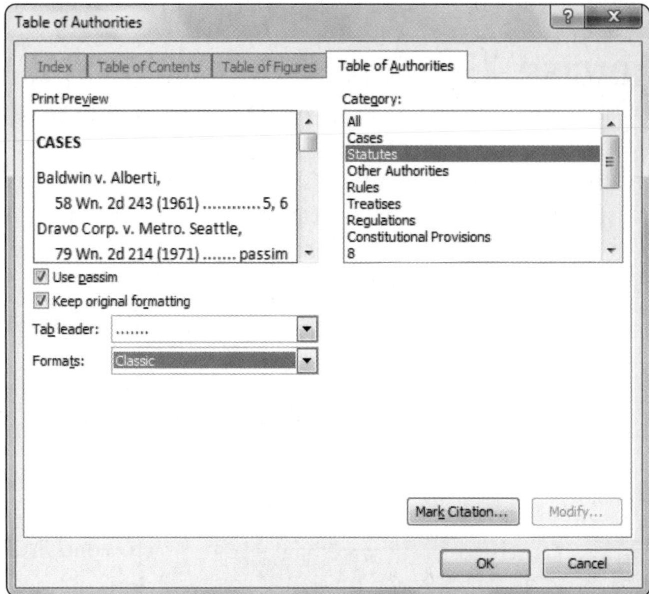

Figure 23-23
Table of Authorities dialog box

14. Click **Statutes** under Category, and click **Classic** in the Formats drop-down list.
15. Click **OK** to insert the table.
16. Save the document as ***[your initials]*****23-14** in your Lesson 23 folder.
17. Submit and close the document.

Lesson 23 Summary

- You create an outline to determine the content and order of a final document. An outline consists of styled headings, subheadings, and body text. To create an outline, switch to Outline view. Then key headings, and apply the appropriate styles by using the Outlining toolbar's buttons. See Table 23-1.
- You assign different levels to your outline text. For example, you can promote a heading (raise it to a higher outline level) or demote a heading (move it to a lower outline level). Word allows as many as nine levels in an outline.
- The easiest way to rearrange text in an outline is to first collapse the outline to show only the headings and body text you want. After rearranging the outline text, you can expand the outline to display all subtext. To collapse or expand an outline so that only the desired heading levels are visible, use the Show Level drop-down list.
- To navigate an outline by jumping from one heading to another, set the Select Browse Object to browse by heading; then click Next Heading or Previous Heading on the vertical scroll bar.

- Another navigation tool for outlines is the Navigation Pane: a separate pane on the left side of the screen that shows the headings of your document. Click a heading in the Navigation Pane, and Word jumps to that heading in the Document pane.
- To move text in an outline, collapse the outline to show the heading levels you want. Select a heading; then click the Move Up button or the Move Down button to move the heading and its subtext to a new location. You can also move a selected heading by dragging it up or down in the outline.
- To move text by using the Clipboard, select the heading you want to move, copy it, place the insertion point where you want the text to appear, and paste it. Then delete the original heading and its subtext.
- To delete a heading and its subtext in an outline, select the heading and press Delete.
- Indexes and tables of contents are common features in long documents. An index usually appears at the end of the document and lists the pages where specific words, phrases, or topics can be found. The table of contents usually appears at the beginning of the document and lists topics and their page numbers in the order in which they appear in the document.
- To create an index, you first identify, or mark, the text you want indexed. You use the Mark Index Entry dialog box to mark text. Marking the text inserts field codes in the document.
- When a topic has subtopics that are located in different parts of a document, you can create subentries that are subordinate to the main index entry. You do this in the Mark Index Entry dialog box.
- To mark several entries automatically, you can create a concordance file—a list of words, in the form of a two-column Word table, to be located and indexed in a document. Column 1 contains the words you want to locate in the document; column 2 contains the words as they should appear in the index. You use the AutoMark command in the Index dialog box (Index tab) to mark the document with your concordance file.
- When a topic extends beyond one page and you want the index to refer readers to a range of pages, you create a bookmark for the text to be indexed and then use the bookmark to mark the text.
- When you want readers who look up one entry in the index to be referred to another entry, you use the cross-reference option in the Mark Index Entry dialog box.
- After you mark all the index entries in a document, you use the Index dialog box (Index tab) to compile the entries and create the index. The dialog box also contains formatting options.
- To edit an index, make changes to any of the index entry fields in the document. After editing index entries, update the index by clicking within the index and then pressing F9.
- To create a table of contents, apply heading styles to the document headings. Word can then search for the heading styles, record the associated page numbers, and create the table. Use the Table of Contents dialog box (References tab). The dialog box also contains formatting options.
- If you make changes to the document that affect headings or pagination, update the table of contents by selecting it and then pressing F9.

- To create a table of figures, insert captions in your document and use the Table of Figures dialog box to format and number the table of figures.
- To create a table of authorities, mark citations in the document, and use the Table of Authorities dialog box to insert the table in the document.

LESSON 23	Command Summary		
Feature	**Button**	**Command**	**Keyboard**
Demote a heading		Outlining tab, Outline Tools group	Alt+Shift+→ or Tab
Demote a heading to body text		Outlining tab, Outline Tools group	Ctrl+Shift+N
Navigation Pane	Navigation Pane	View tab, Show group	
Insert a caption		References tab, Captions group	
Insert index		References tab, Index group	
Insert table of authorities		References tab, Table of Authorities group	
Insert table of contents		References tab, Table of Contents group	
Insert table of figures		References tab, Captions group	
Mark a citation		References tab, Table of Authorities group	Alt+Shift+I
Mark index entry		Insert, Reference, Index and Tables group	Alt+Shift+X
Outline view		View tab, Document Views group	Alt+Ctrl+O
Promote a heading		Outlining tab, Outline Tools group	Alt+Shift+← or Shift+Tab
Show only first line of body text	Show First Line Only	Outlining tab, Outline Tools group	Alt+Shift+L
Show selected heading levels	Show Level:	Outlining tab, Outline Tools group	
Update index		References tab, Index group	F9
Update table of contents		References tab, Table of Contents group	F9

Concepts Review

True/False Questions

Each of the following statements is either true or false. Indicate your choice by circling T or F.

T F 1. An index can contain subentries.

T F 2. The plus sign symbol in outline view indicates a heading with subtext.

T F 3. When you mark index entries, Word marks each occurrence of an index entry in each paragraph.

T F 4. You can use the F9 key to update an index.

T F 5. You need to create a bookmark before you can mark index entries.

T F 6. The most reliable way to add an entry to an index is to key it into the index list and then add a page number.

T F 7. The easiest way to create a table of contents is to create your own heading styles.

T F 8. A selected table of contents is shaded gray.

Short Answer Questions

Write the correct answer in the space provided.

1. What is the name of an index entry that is subordinate to a main entry?

____

2. Which selection symbol in Outline view indicates a heading with no subtext?

____

3. What is the keyboard shortcut for marking an index entry?

____

4. If index entry fields are not visible in a document, which button should you click to display them?

____

5. Within the braces of an index entry field, which two letters appear first?

____

6. Which key should you press when you click a heading in a table of contents if you want to jump to that section of the document?

____

7. Which command can you choose from the shortcut menu to update your index or table of contents?

---

8. Which dialog box displays a preview of the table of contents formats?

Critical Thinking

Answer these questions on a separate page. There are no right or wrong answers. Support your answers with examples from your own experience, if possible.

1. Some people find Outline view useful for building reports, term papers, and other business or school documents. Others write these documents using Print Layout view. Which do you prefer? Why?
2. Some people prefer to use an index to locate subject matter, and others prefer to find topics by using the table of contents and then skimming the topic to locate specific subject matter. Which do you prefer? Why?

Skills Review

Exercise 23-15

Create an outline.

1. Start a new document, and switch to Outline view.
2. Key the heading **CAMPBELL'S CONFECTIONS FALL RETREAT AGENDA**.
3. Create a level-2 heading by following these steps:
   a. Press Enter, and click the Demote button ➔.
   b. Key **Objectives**.
4. Create three level-3 headings by following these steps:
   a. Press Enter, and click the Demote button ➔.
   b. Key **Year-to-Date Performance Analysis**. Press Enter.
   c. Key **Strategy for Next Year**. Press Enter, and key **Five-Year Plan**.
5. Press Enter, click the Promote button ⬅, and key the following level-2 headings.

   Staff to Attend
   Dates and Location
   Activities Planned
6. Key the following lines as level-3 headings under "Activities Planned."

   Business
   Leisure

7. Add body text to the level-1 heading by following these steps:
   a. Position the insertion point at the end of the first line, and press Enter. Deselect the check box for **Show First Line Only**.
   b. Click the Demote to Body Text button, and key **This fall, we will refresh our spirits and plan for the future at our favorite resort in western Pennsylvania.**
8. Switch to Print Layout view to view the document.
9. Save the document as ***[your initials]*23-15** in your Lesson 23 folder.
10. Submit and close the document.

Exercise 23-16

Identify single and multiple index entries, and compile an index.

1. Open the file **Computer Use Policy**. Make sure the Show/Hide ¶ button ¶ is turned on.
2. Mark computer terms as index entries by following these steps:
   a. Select "Computer theft" in the first indented line of the first paragraph.
   b. Click the **References** tab, and click the Mark Entry button.
   c. Click **Mark** in the Mark Index Entry dialog box. Drag the dialog box to the lower right corner of the window so that you can see the document area.
   d. Select the next computer term, "Computer trespass." Click **Mark** in the Mark Index Entry dialog box.
   e. Mark index entries for each of the following terms in the document.

      Computer invasion of privacy
      Password
      Pirated software
3. Mark a main entry with two subentries by following these steps:
   a. Select the text "disruption of computers" in the paragraph that begins "State and federal."
   b. Activate the Mark Index Entry dialog box, and make sure "Disruption of computers" is in the Main entry text box. In the Subentry text box, key **Invasion of privacy** and click **Mark**.
   c. Place the insertion point after the text "steal computer services." In the Main entry text box, key **Disruption of computers**, and in the Subentry text box, key **Steal computer services**. Click **Mark**.
   d. Place the insertion point after the text "commit fraud." In the Main entry text box, key **Disruption of computers**, and in the Subentry text box, key **Commit fraud**. Click **Mark**.
   e. Close the Mark Index Entry dialog box.
4. Add 72 points spacing before the title "Computer Use Policy."

5. Compile the index, using the default index format settings, by following these steps:
   a. Click the Show/Hide ¶ button [¶] to hide the field codes.
   b. Place the insertion point at the end of the document.
   c. Press Enter and insert a page break.
   d. Key **INDEX** and press Enter twice. Format the word "INDEX" as 14-point bold and centered.
   e. Move the insertion point to the second blank line after the title "Index."
   f. Click the References tab, and click the Insert Index button. Click OK.
6. Save the document as ***[your initials]*23-16** in your Lesson 23 folder. Submit and close the document.

Exercise 23-17

Mark index entries by using a concordance file; mark a range of pages; and compile, edit, and update an index.

NOTE

A concordance file is used to generate several index entries at one time. The file contains a list of words to be located in the document and is formatted as a two-column table. The first column contains the words you want to locate in your document. The second column contains the words as they should appear in the index.

1. Open the file **Health Events**.
2. Create a concordance file for health topics by following these steps:
   a. Start a new document, and insert a 2-column by 1-row table.
   b. Key the text shown in Figure 23-24, pressing Tab after keying each item.
   c. Save the concordance file as ***[your initials]*23-17a** in your Lesson 23 folder. Submit and close the file.

Figure 23-24

Height and weight	Height and weight
BMI	Body mass index
Body composition analysis	Body composition analysis
Obesity and weight loss	Obesity and weight loss
Blood pressure	Hypertension monitoring
Blood typing	Blood typing
Diabetes screening	Diabetes screening
Cholesterol ratios	Cholesterol ratios
Glaucoma screening	Glaucoma screening
Allergy screening	Allergy screening
Asthma screening	Asthma screening

3. Use the concordance file to mark index entries automatically by following these steps:
   a. Click the Show/Hide ¶ button ¶ to display nonprinting characters if they are not already showing in the "Health Events" document.
   b. Click the **References** tab on the Ribbon, and click the Insert Index button.
   c. On the **Index** tab, click **AutoMark**.
   d. Choose the file ***[your initials]*23-17a**, which you created in step 2. (If necessary change the type of file to **All Files**.)
   e. Click **Open**. The index entries appear in the document.
4. Use a bookmark to mark a range of text by following these steps:
   a. Select the sessions on page 2 beginning with "Board Room No. 1" and ending with "Fatigue."
   b. Click the **Insert** tab; click the Bookmark button; key **Seminars** in the Bookmark name text box; and click **Add**.
   c. Place the insertion point at the end of the document, and press Alt+Shift+X to open the Mark Index Entry dialog box.
   d. Key **Seminars** in the Main entry text box. Click **Page Range**, and click the **Bookmark** drop-down arrow. Click **Seminars**. Click **Mark**.
   e. Close the Mark Index Entry dialog box.
5. Insert centered page numbers at the bottom of the page, and number page 1.
6. Format and compile the index by following these steps:
   a. Move to the end of the document, and insert a page break.
   b. Key **INDEX TO HEALTH EVENTS**. Apply the Heading 1 style, center the text, and add 24 points spacing after. Press Enter.
   c. Click the **References** tab, click the Insert Index button, and choose **Modern** from the Formats list.
   d. Select the **Right align page numbers** check box.
   e. Choose leader dots from the Tab leader list, and click **OK**.
7. Edit an index entry and update the index by following these steps:
   a. On page 1, locate the index entry for "Cholesterol ratios."
   b. Insert the words **and triglycerides** after "ratios" in the index entry field.
   c. Click the Show/Hide ¶ button ¶ to hide the field codes.
   d. Right-click anywhere within the index, and choose **Update Field** from the shortcut menu.
8. Save the indexed document as ***[your initials]*23-17b** in your Lesson 23 folder. Submit and close the document.

Exercise 23-18

Create, format, edit, and update a table of contents.

1. Open the file **Guidelines - 3**.
2. Insert page numbers aligned at the bottom right margin.
3. Create and format a table of contents by following these steps:
   a. Place the insertion point at the top of the document, insert a page break, and click within the page break.
   b. Click the **References** tab, and click the Table of Contents button. Click **Insert Table of Contents**.
   c. Open the **Formats** drop-down list, and choose the **Distinctive** format. (This format right-aligns page numbers and includes an underline tab leader.) Click **OK**.
4. Change the left and right margins for the document to 1.25 inches.
5. Locate the heading "Corporations" by pressing Ctrl and pointing to and clicking the heading in the table of contents. Change the style to Heading 3.
6. Update the table of contents by right-clicking it and then choosing **Update Fields** from the shortcut menu. Update the entire table.
7. On a new line above the table of contents, key the heading **TABLE OF CONTENTS**. Apply the Normal style to the heading, and change the formatting to 14-point bold, centered, with 72 points spacing before and 24 points spacing after.
8. Save your document as ***[your initials]*23-18** in your Lesson 23 folder. Submit and close the document.

Lesson Applications

Exercise 23-19

Outline a document.

1. Open the file **Marketing Plan**, and switch to Outline view.
2. Apply the level-1 heading style to the first line.
3. Apply the level-2 heading style to the following lines:

   Purpose/Mission
   Analysis
   Marketing Strategy/Objectives
   Promotion
   Budget & Implementation
4. Apply the level-3 heading style to the following lines:

   Analyze Product
   Analyze Target Market
   Analyze Competitors
   Financial Analysis
   Market Growth
   Financial Objectives
   Market Share
   Advertising
   Sales Promotion
   Personal Selling
   Public Relations
   Performance Analysis
   Timelines
   Spending by Product/Segment
5. Apply the level-4 heading style to the remaining lines in the document.
6. Delete blank lines in the document.
7. Switch to Print Layout view.
8. Save the document as ***[your initials]*23-19** in your Lesson 23 folder. Submit and close the document.

Exercise 23-20

Mark index entries, mark a range of text, and compile an index.

1. Open the file **Leave Policy**.
2. Change the left and right margins to 1.25 inches, and add 72 points spacing before the title.

3. Mark an index entry for each heading in the document beginning with the "Eligibility" paragraph and ending with the "Leave without Pay" paragraph.
4. Find the text "medical leave of absence" in the second paragraph below the heading "Family & Medical Leave," and mark an index entry.
5. Select the table on page 1, and create a bookmark for this text, naming it "AnnualLeave." Mark the text as an index entry, using "Annual Leave" as the main entry. Select the Page range option, and select the AnnualLeave bookmark. Close the Mark Index Entry dialog box.
6. Insert page numbers on all pages, centering the numbers at the bottom of the page.
7. Turn off the display of hidden text.
8. Add a page break at the end of the document.
9. Key **INDEX** below the page break, and press Enter. Format "INDEX" as 14-point bold and centered. Change the spacing before to 72 points and the spacing after to 24 points.
10. Position the insertion point below "INDEX," and insert the index. Use the default format (**From template**) with right-aligned page numbers and dotted leaders.
11. Edit the index entry "medical leave of absence" by capitalizing "Medical."
12. Update the index.
13. Save the document as ***[your initials]*****23-20** in your Lesson 23 folder. Submit and close the document.

Exercise 23-21

Create and format an index and a table of contents.

1. Open the file **History - 4**.
2. Apply the Heading 1 style to the first line of the document. Modify the Heading 1 style to 18 points with 24 points spacing before and 3 points spacing after.
3. Add a footer that starts on page 2. Use the text **Campbell's Confections**, aligned at the left margin, and **Page** plus the page number, aligned at the right margin. Change the footer text to 10 points.
4. Go to page 1, and locate the paragraph under the heading "Background." Mark an index entry for "retail," "wholesale," and "fundraising."
5. Mark as index entries the text listed in Figure 23-25.

Figure 23-25

```
Tours
Chocolate Club
Corporate Gifts
Favors
Fountains
Gift Cards
Fundraising
E-commerce
Gourmet Chocolate
```

6. Select "Internet" in the E-commerce paragraph. Click in the Mark Index Entry dialog box, and create a cross-reference. Key **E-commerce** after "*See*."
7. Insert the index on a separate page at the end of the document, under the heading **INDEX** (apply the Heading 1 style to the index heading, and center the heading). Use the Formal style with right-aligned numbers and a dotted tab leader, and change the number of columns to 1.
8. Go to the top of the document, and insert a page break. At the top of the document, before the page break, key the heading **TABLE OF CONTENTS**. Apply the Normal style to the heading to separate it from the table of contents. Format the heading as 14-point bold, all caps, with 24 points of spacing after, and center it.
9. Turn off the display of hidden characters; then insert the table of contents below the heading you just created. Use the Formal style, and show three levels.
10. Delete the index entry "fundraising" on page 1. Edit the index entries "retail" and "wholesale" on page 1 so that each entry is capitalized. Update the index.
11. Save the document as ***[your initials]*****23-21** in your Lesson 23 folder. Submit and close the document.

Exercise 23-22 ◆ Challenge Yourself

Insert, edit, and update an index and a table of contents.

1. Open the file **Confidential Documents**.
2. Mark as index entries the text listed in Figure 23-26. Capitalize the first letter of each index entry.

Figure 23-26

```
Confidential documents (located in the paragraph below the
Definition heading)
Proprietary information
Data creation
Compliance
Staff development
Code of Conduct
Disposal and Destruction
Environmental factors
Mobile shredding services
Password protection
Encrypt (Change entry to read "Encryption")
Confidentiality agreement
```

3. Create a main index entry for "Office Procedures," and create two subentries for "Office procedures." The subentries are "Electronic files" and "Hard copies."
4. On a new page at the end of the document, key the index heading **Index to Confidential Documents**. Apply the Heading 1 style to the index heading, apply all caps, and center the heading. Apply 24 points spacing after the heading.
5. Insert the index below the index heading. Use a format of your choice.
6. Mark one additional index entry, and update the index.
7. At the beginning of the document, insert a new page, key **Table of Contents**, and apply the Normal style. Insert a table of contents below the heading. Use an appropriate format.
8. Format the table of contents heading as 16-point bold, all caps, with 24 points spacing after, and center it.
9. Turn off the display of hidden characters, and adjust page breaks as needed.
10. Update the table of contents and the index.
11. On every page of the document, add a footer that includes **Campbell's Confections** aligned at the left margin and the page number aligned at the right margin. Use the format "Page 1" for the page numbering. Format the footer as 10 points.
12. Save the document as ***[your initials]*23-22** in your Lesson 23 folder. Submit and close the document.

On Your Own

In these exercises you work on your own, as you would in a real-life business environment. Use the skills you have learned to accomplish the task—and be creative.

Exercise 23-23

Create a detailed outline for a document that describes a hobby or one of your interests. Use headings to introduce categories of information, and include a minimum of three heading levels and one occurrence of body text. Remember to apply heading styles throughout the document. Save the file as ***[your initials]*23-23**, and submit it.

Exercise 23-24

Using a report you created for another class, add a table of contents and an index. Format the table of contents and the index so that they match and are consistent in style with the rest of the document. Save the file as ***[your initials]*23-24**, and submit it.

Exercise 23-25

Use the Internet to research three popular tourist destinations in the United States. Look up facts such as population, most popular tourist attractions, restaurants, and other information. Write a three-page report on these destinations, using headings to indicate various levels of information. Add a table of contents and an index of the most frequently used terms in the document. Save the file as ***[your initials]*23-25**, and submit it.

Lesson 24

Sharing Your Work and Hyperlinks

OBJECTIVES ***After completing this lesson, you will be able to:***

1. Create comments.
2. Use the Track Changes feature.
3. Compare and merge documents.
4. Review a document and secure document content.
5. Insert hyperlinks.

Estimated Time: 1½ hours

In most offices, more than one person works on a document. A document might have a primary author and several editors. Word provides tools that make it easy to collaborate with others—on your computer instead of on paper—to produce a finished document. After you have a finished document, you might take it one step further—sharing it with others on the World Wide Web. You will also learn to work with hypertext to link documents.

Creating Comments

Comments are notes or annotations you add to a document. Each person who adds a comment is called a *reviewer*. Comments are color-coded by reviewer. Word refers to comments and any other type of document revision marks as *markup*. You can display, hide, or print markup.

In Print Layout view, you insert, edit, and view comments in the *Reviewing pane*—a narrow horizontal or vertical pane that opens at the bottom or left side of the screen, or you can enter, edit, and view comments in *markup balloons* that appear in the document margin with a line leading to the position where the comment was inserted.

Exercise 24-1 ADD COMMENTS TO A DOCUMENT

The easiest way to add a comment to a document is to use the Review tab on the Ribbon. You can also use the keyboard shortcut Alt+Ctrl+M.

1. Open the file **CruiseFAQs**.
2. Click the **Review** tab, and locate the **Comments** group.
3. Open the Word Options dialog box, and click **General**. Review the information in the **Personalize your copy of Microsoft Office** section.
4. Enter your name and initials in the appropriate data fields. Click **OK**.

TIP

If you review a document using another person's computer, your comments will be attributed to the person whose name appears in the User Information section. Make sure to change the User Information to your name when you insert comments, and then change back to the original user's name when you are finished.

5. Position the insertion point at the beginning of page 2.
6. Click the New Comment button on the Ribbon. A balloon appears in the margin, displaying your reference initials and an insertion point. A line leads from the balloon to the position of the comment insertion.
7. Key the following text in the balloon: **Verify the number of employees and family members planning to attend the sales conference.**

Figure 24-1
Inserting a comment

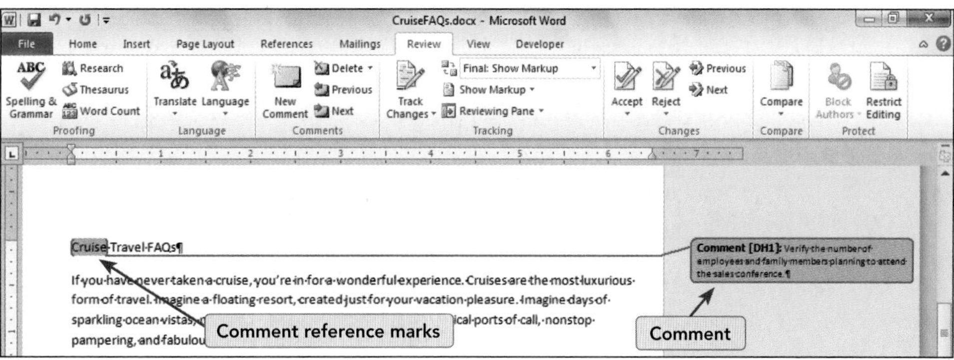

8. Click the arrow beside the Reviewing Pane button. Click **Reviewing Pane Horizontal**. The Reviewing Pane displays at the bottom of the screen, showing your name, followed by the date and time you inserted the comment. The entry in the Reviewing Pane is color-coded to the reviewer. *Comment reference marks* also appear in the document where you insert the comment. The reference marks are color-coded to the reviewer.

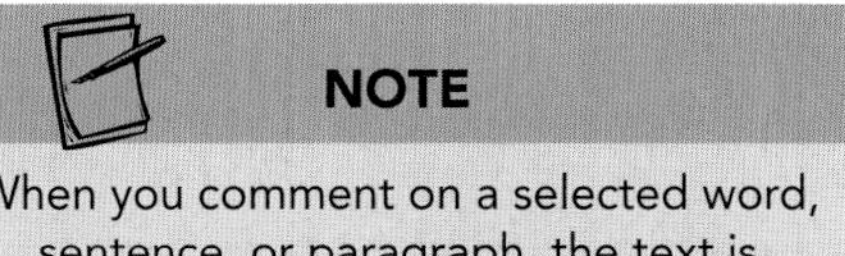

NOTE

When you comment on a selected word, sentence, or paragraph, the text is enclosed by two comment reference marks. You can also position the insertion point at a particular location and insert a comment.

9. Scroll within the document to the paragraph below *"Is a cruise good for families with kids?"* Select "programs" in the first line, and click the New Comment button to insert another comment. A second balloon displays with an insertion point for keying the new text.

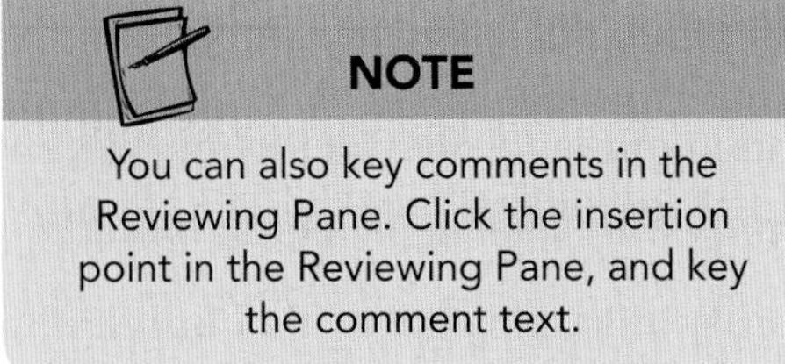

NOTE

You can also key comments in the Reviewing Pane. Click the insertion point in the Reviewing Pane, and key the comment text.

10. Key **Request a copy of the activities planned for children during our cruise.** Notice the comment reference marks around "programs" in the document.
11. Move the insertion point over a balloon. A ScreenTip displays the name of the reviewer and the time and date that the reviewer entered the comment.

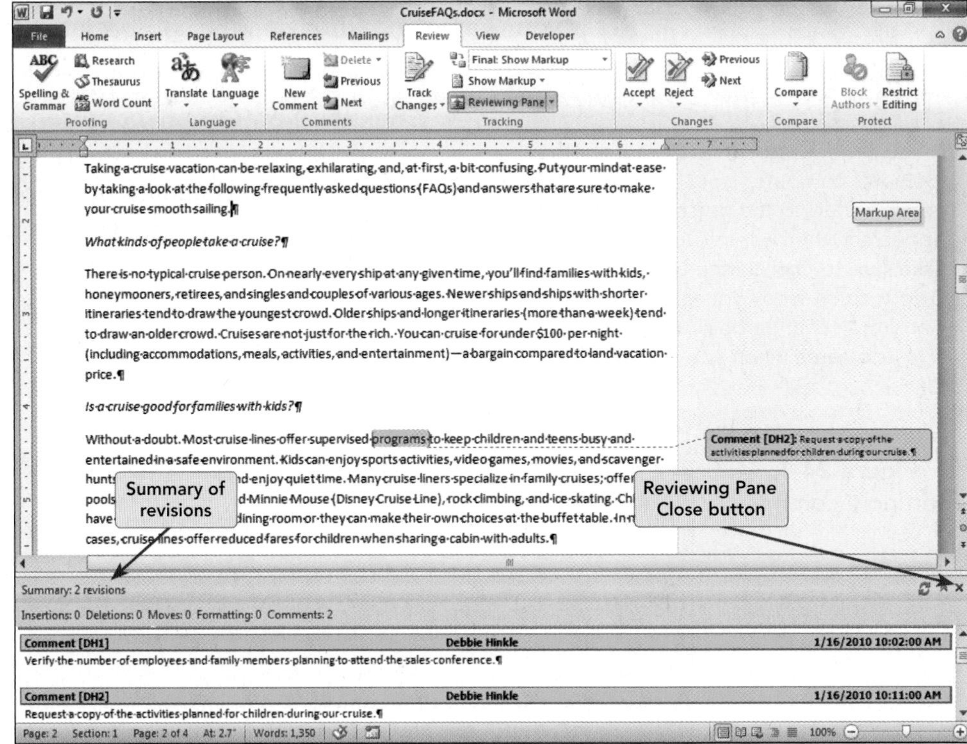

Figure 24-2
Comments displayed in the Reviewing Pane

12. Click the Reviewing Pane Close button [×] to close the Reviewing Pane.
13. Locate the paragraph below the text *"What documentation is needed?"* Select the entire paragraph (which starts "This depends").
14. Press Alt+Ctrl+M to insert a new comment. Word inserts a balloon in the right margin area.
15. Key the comment **Verify the documentation that we will need.** The document now has three comments.

Exercise 24-2 EDIT AND DELETE COMMENTS

You can edit and delete comments by working directly with the balloon text in Print Layout view or by using the Reviewing Pane.

TIP

The Next and Previous buttons are helpful for jumping from one comment to another, particularly in a long document. The insertion point moves to the next or previous comment.

NOTE

You can also delete a comment by right-clicking the comment balloon and choosing Delete Comment from the shortcut menu. To delete all comments, click the down arrow on the Delete button and choose Delete All Comments in Document.

1. Click the comment in the first balloon. The comment appears highlighted (the balloon's background color darkens and the dotted connector line becomes solid).
2. Key **total** before "number." Increase the zoom level if necessary to key the text.
3. Click the Next button on the Review tab. The second comment mark is highlighted. Click the button again to move to the third comment.
4. Click the Delete button on the Ribbon. The comment is removed from the document.
5. Display the Reviewing Pane, and use the Reviewing Pane scroll bar to display the two remaining comments.
6. Edit the first comment to read: **Verify the total number of adults and children planning to attend the sales meeting.**

Figure 24-3
Edited text of two remaining comments

NOTE

You can insert a comment in an existing comment balloon. Click in the balloon, click the New Comment button, and key the text.

7. Close the Reviewing Pane.
8. Save the document as ***[your initials]*24-2** in a new folder for Lesson 24.

Exercise 24-3 PRINT COMMENTS

You can print a document with its balloon comments, as they appear in Print Layout view, or you can print just a list of a document's comments. You can also print a document without comments.

TIP

You can set the Select Browse Object button on the vertical scroll bar to browse by comments. Then the double-arrow scroll buttons become the Previous Comment and Next Comment buttons.

1. Verify that the document displays in Print Layout view.
2. Display the Print tab. Notice that the document preview displays the comments in the right margin. If you choose to print the document, the comments would print. The default print setting is to print markup. Click the Home tab to return to Print Layout view.
3. Switch to Draft view. Notice that the balloon comments are not displayed.
4. Display the Print tab.

NOTE

Word sets the zoom level and page orientation to best display the comment balloons in your printed document.

TIP

From the Print All Pages list, deselect the Print Markup option to print a document without comments, or choose List of Markup to print the document's comments only.

5. Click the drop-down arrow beside the Print All Pages option, and choose **List of Markup**. Click **Print**. Word prints your comments as a list, similar to the way comments appear in the Reviewing Pane.
6. Close the document, saving changes.

Using the Track Changes Feature

When the job of revising a document is shared by more than one person, you can use the Track Changes feature to mark each person's changes. When this feature is turned on, Word tracks changes as you edit the document. These *tracked changes,* also called *markup,* are revision marks that show where deletions, insertions, and formatting changes were made. When you review the document, you can either accept the changes or return to the original wording.

Word displays tracked changes in the following way:

- *Underline:* New text is underlined.
- *Strikethrough:* Deleted text has a horizontal line through it.
- *Revision bar:* A vertical bar appears in the margin next to revised text.

To show tracked changes in the text and also in *markup balloons* in the document margin, change the balloons setting by clicking the Show Markup button, clicking Balloons, and clicking Show Revisions in Balloons. Balloons make it easy to see and respond to document changes, additions, deletions, and comments.

Exercise 24-4 USE THE TRACK CHANGES FEATURE TO ENTER REVISIONS

To track changes in a document, turn on Track Changes by clicking the Track Changes button. When you point to the Track Changes button, you see a divider line. Click the upper part of the button to turn on and to turn off Track Changes. Click the lower portion of the button to display options for Track Changes.

Figure 24-4 Track Changes button

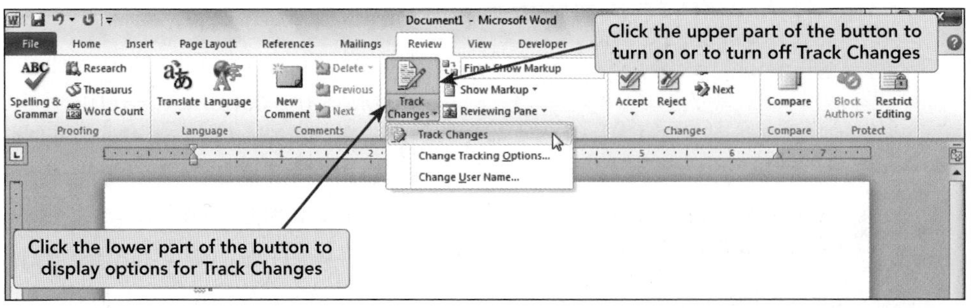

1. Open the file **Wholesale - 2**. Tracked changes already appear in the document, indicating that another reviewer has edited the document. You are going to make additional revisions to the document.
2. Make sure the Show/Hide ¶ button ¶ is turned on (Home tab, Paragraph group).
3. Right-click the status bar, and click **Track Changes**. The status bar shows the status of Track Changes. Click the Review tab, click the Show Markup button, and click **Balloons**. Click **Show Revisions in Balloons**.
4. In the first paragraph, change the beginning of the second sentence to read **Contracts were negotiated with two large hotel chains**. The new words appear underlined and in another color, and the deleted word appears in a balloon in the margin.
5. Select the heading "Wholesale," and change the font size to 14 points. A balloon displays the formatting change.

NOTE

Word can display as many as eight different colors for tracked changes. The first eight reviewers of a document are automatically assigned different colors.

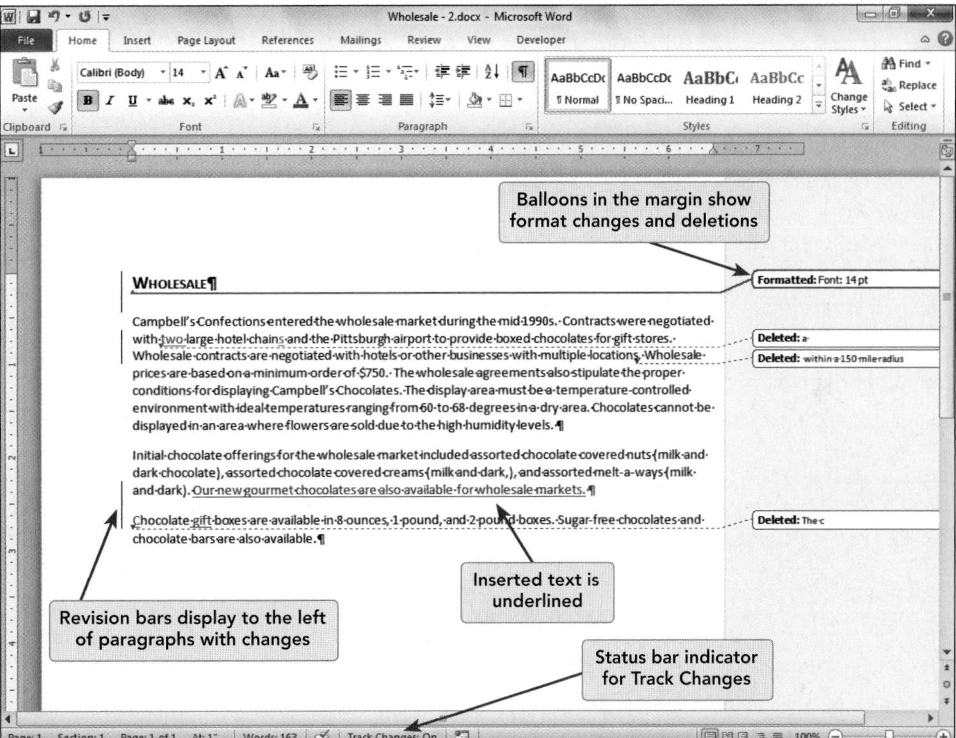

Figure 24-5
Tracked changes in Print Layout view

NOTE

To see tracked changes for formatting revisions, you must be in Print Layout view. When you change the Balloons setting to Show All Revisions Inline, you will not see formatting revisions.

6. Select "$750" in the first paragraph, and apply italics.
7. Select the last sentence in the first paragraph, and press Delete to remove it. The sentence appears in a balloon.
8. Select the last paragraph, and cut the selection.

REVIEW

When you are making changes to a document that will be reviewed by others, a good idea is to insert comments to explain why you made specific changes. To add a comment, click the New Comment button. You can also use the keyboard shortcut Alt+Ctrl+M.

9. Position the insertion point before the sentence that begins "Our new gourmet," and paste the cut text. Vertical bars appear to the left of the paragraphs to show they were changed.

10. Click the lower part of the Track Changes button to display Track Changes options. Click **Change Tracking Options**. The Track Changes Options dialog box displays.

Figure 24-6
Track Changes Options dialog box

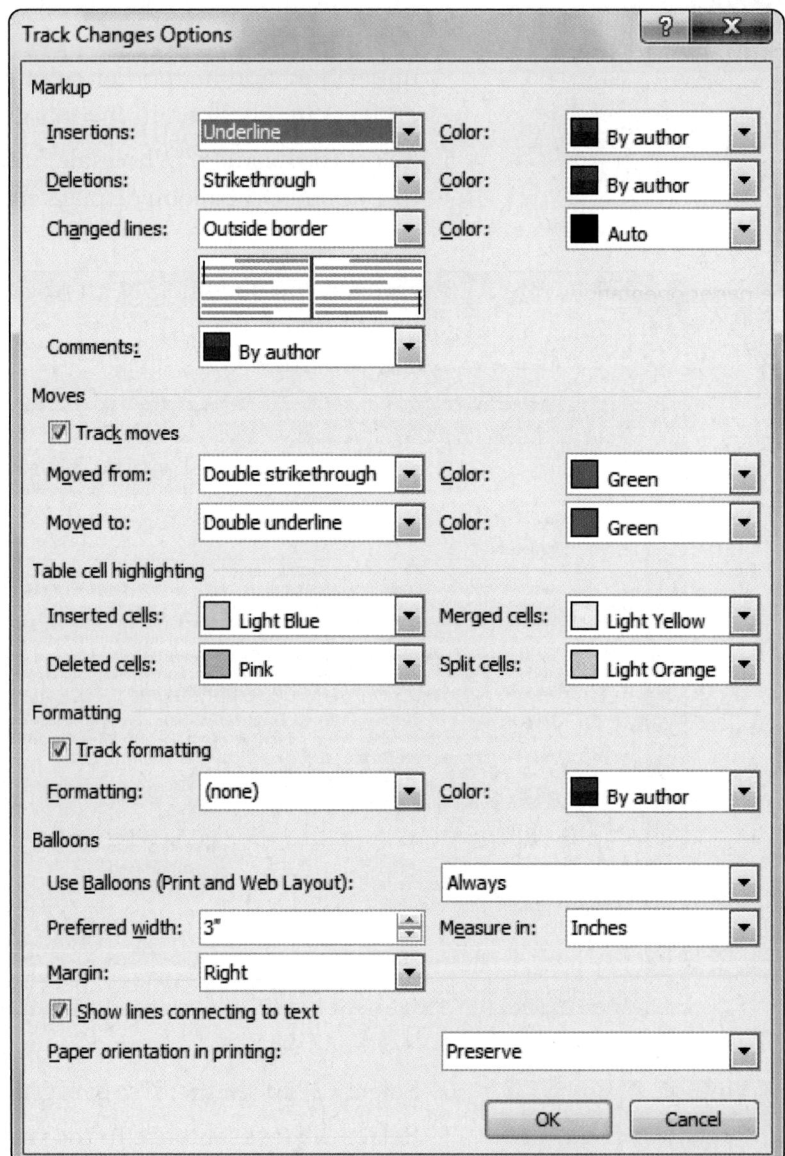

11. Locate the **Markup** section of the Track Changes Options dialog box. The default settings for Insertions, Deletions, and Changed lines are displayed. Locate the **Balloons** section. Notice the default settings for Preferred width, Margin, and Show lines connecting to text. Locate the section for **Moves**. Study the default settings.

NOTE

Not only can you track changes made to the main body of a Word document, but you can also track changes made to headers and footers and to footnotes and endnotes.

TIP

You can also click the Track Changes button on the Ribbon to turn off Track Changes.

NOTE

Switch the page orientation to landscape when printing tracked changes and balloon text to improve readability. You can change the paper orientation in printing tracked changes by opening the Track Changes Options dialog box and opening the Paper orientation in printing drop-down list. Change the Preserve default setting to Force Landscape. The Preserve setting prints the orientation specified in the Page Layout dialog box.

12. Click the down arrow for the Color drop-down list for Insertions. Notice the colors available for reviewers.
13. Click Cancel to close the dialog box without making changes.
14. Display the Reviewing Pane below the document.
15. Scroll through the list of revisions. The Reviewing Pane lists the total number of revisions, number of insertions, deletions, moves, and comments.
16. Click the Track Changes indicator Track Changes: On on the status bar to turn off Track Changes mode. When you turn off Track Changes, any new changes you make to the document will not appear as tracked changes. The existing track changes are not removed from the document.
17. Save the document as ***[your initials]*****24-4** in your Lesson 24 folder.
18. To print the document with tracked changes, open the Print tab. Make sure Print Markup is selected in the Print All Pages drop-down list. Click Print. Tracked changes appear on the printed page just as they do in Print Layout view.
19. Leave the document open for the next exercise.

Exercise 24-5 ACCEPT AND REJECT REVISIONS

You can review a document after it is edited and decide if you want to accept or reject the revisions. You can review changes by the type of change made or review only changes made by a particular reviewer. If you accept the revisions, Word deletes the strikethrough text, removes the underlining from the new text, and removes the revision bars. If you do not want to make the revisions, you can reject them and restore the original document. You can accept or reject changes individually or all at once.

To accept or reject revisions, you can do one of the following:

- Use the Ribbon.
- Use the Reviewing Pane.
- Right-click the revision, and use the shortcut menu.

You can also merge revised files from other reviewers into the same document. Then you can protect the document from revisions and allow only the author to turn off the tracking or accept or reject revisions.

1. Click the Reviewing Pane button to display the Reviewing Pane.
2. Review the summary information, and notice the total number of revisions and the breakdown by insertions, deletions, and formatting.

3. Point to the Accept and Move to Next button. Notice that this button has a divider line. When you point to the upper half of the button, the revision is accepted and you move to the next change. If you click the lower half of the button, a list of options appears.

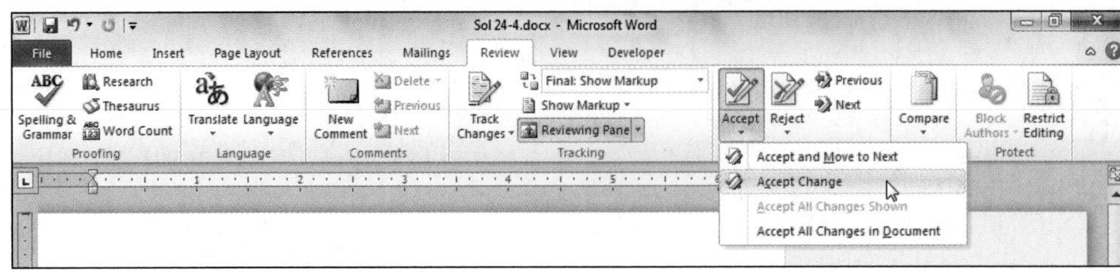

Figure 24-7
Accept button

NOTE

You can leave the Comments option turned on because there are no comments in the document. The Markup Area Highlight option shades the markup area.

4. Select the title at the beginning of the document. Click the Accept and Move to Next button on the Ribbon to accept the change. The text in the next balloon is highlighted.
5. Click the Show Markup button, and deselect the **Insertions and Deletions** option, leaving the **Formatting** option checked. Now only the changes to formatting appear in the document.

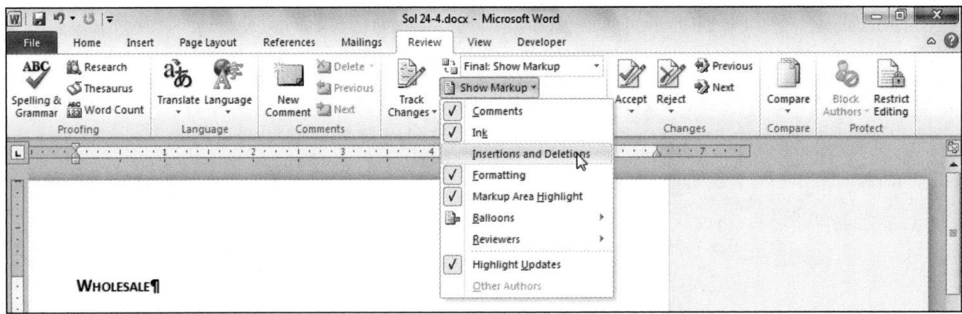

Figure 24-8
Show Markup options

6. Click the Next button, if necessary, to move to the next formatting change in the document.
7. Click the Reject and Move to Next button on the Ribbon to reject the formatting change. Click **Cancel** if a Word question box displays. Notice the change in the Summary information in the Reviewing Pane.
8. Click the Show Markup button, and choose **Insertions and Deletions**. Now the other changes you made to the document appear.
9. Click the inserted word "two" in the first paragraph. Click the Accept and Move to Next button. The change is accepted.
10. Right-click the balloon that contains the deleted text that begins "Chocolates cannot." Click **Reject Deletion**, and the sentence appears at the end of the paragraph.
11. Click the Next button to select the next revision. Click the Accept and Move to Next button to accept the change.

NOTE

To review only the changes made by a particular reviewer, click the Show Markup button and choose Reviewers. Deselect each reviewer name except the one whose changes you want to review. To display all reviewer changes again, click the Show Markup button, choose Reviewers, and then choose All Reviewers.

12. Repeat this process to accept the remaining revisions. When you reach the end of the document, click **Yes** to continue searching from the beginning of the document. Accept all remaining changes, and click **OK** when a message box appears stating, "The document contains no comments or tracked changes." Review the Summary section of the Reviewing Pane, which indicates there are no revisions.
13. Close the document without saving it, and then reopen ***[your initials]*24-4**.

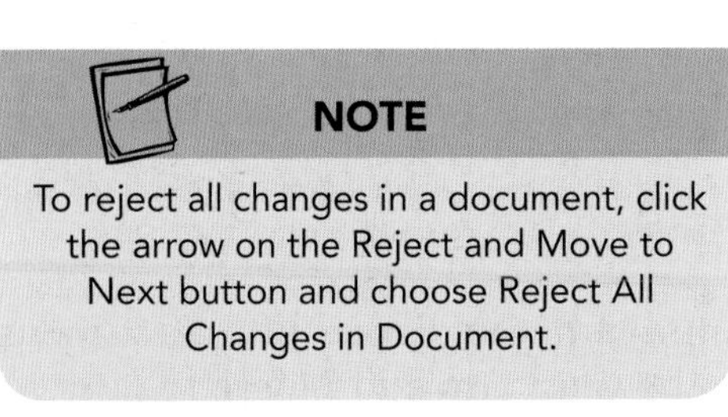

NOTE

To reject all changes in a document, click the arrow on the Reject and Move to Next button and choose Reject All Changes in Document.

14. Click the **Review** tab, and click the drop-down arrow beside the Final: Show Markup button. Choose **Final** to see the document with all changes accepted. Choose **Original** to see the original document without changes. Choose **Final: Show Markup** to display deleted text and inserted or formatted text in the paragraph.
15. Click the down arrow on the Accept and Move to Next button. Choose **Accept All Changes in Document**.

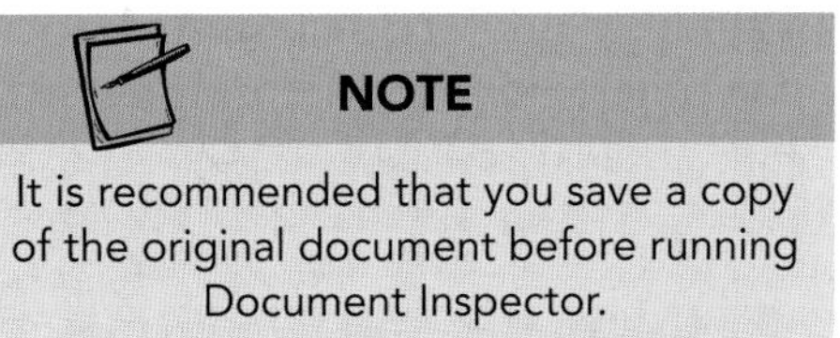

NOTE

It is recommended that you save a copy of the original document before running Document Inspector.

16. Save the document as ***[your initials]*24-5** in your Lesson 24 folder.
17. Open the **File** tab, and click the **Check for Issues** button. Click **Inspect Document**. The Document Inspector dialog box opens and is used to check documents for comments, revisions, hidden text, and other content.

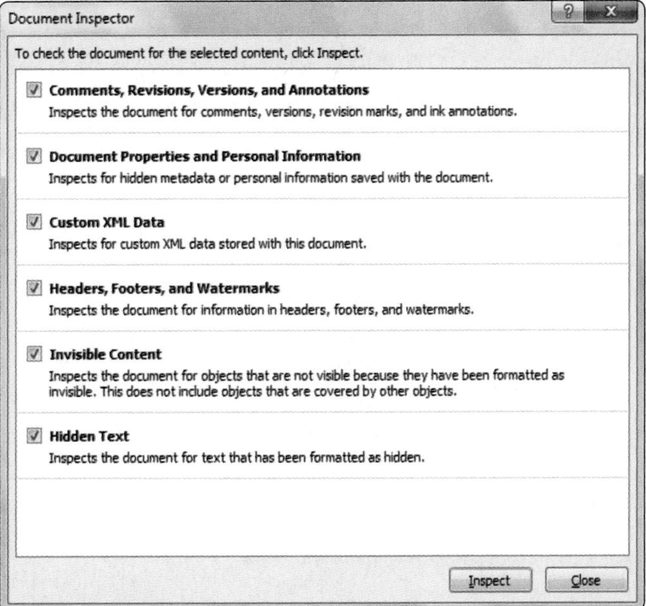

Figure 24-9
Document Inspector dialog box

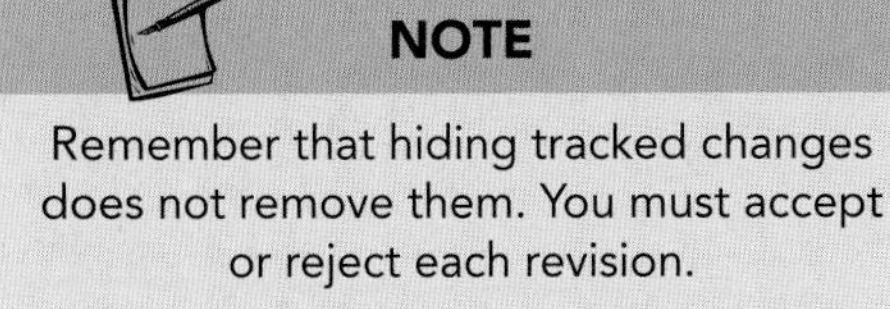

NOTE

Remember that hiding tracked changes does not remove them. You must accept or reject each revision.

18. Verify that **Comments, Revisions, Versions, and Annotations** is checked. Deselect all other options. Click **Inspect**. Review the results. If necessary, remove all tracked changes. Click **Close**.

19. Click the **File** tab if necessary, and locate the Permissions section. Click **Protect Document**, and then click the **Mark as Final** option.

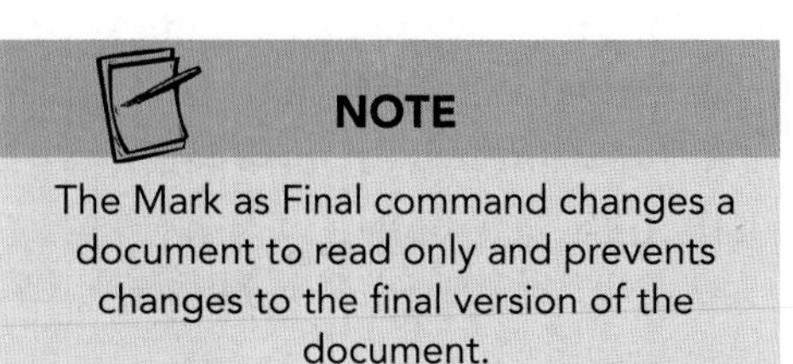

NOTE

The Mark as Final command changes a document to read only and prevents changes to the final version of the document.

20. Click **OK** to mark the document as final and to save it. Click **OK** to close the information box.
21. Click the Home tab to return to the document, and notice the Information section at the top of the document. Examine the document title bar to see that the document is now identified as a read-only document.
22. Submit and close the document.

Comparing and Merging Documents

Suppose you have two similar documents—an edited copy of a document and the original document. You can use the Compare and Merge feature to compare the edited document with the original. Word will show the differences as tracked changes. When comparing two documents, use the *legal blackline* feature, which compares the documents and creates a third document that shows the changes. Law firms use this feature to maintain records of all document revisions and versions.

NOTE

The legal blackline feature compares the two documents and opens a new document to display the changes. When comparing more than two documents, choose Combine.

Exercise 24-6 COMPARE AND MERGE DOCUMENTS

1. Start a new document. Click the **Review** tab on the Ribbon. Click the Compare button, and click **Compare** to open the Compare Documents dialog box.
2. Click **More** to expand the dialog box.

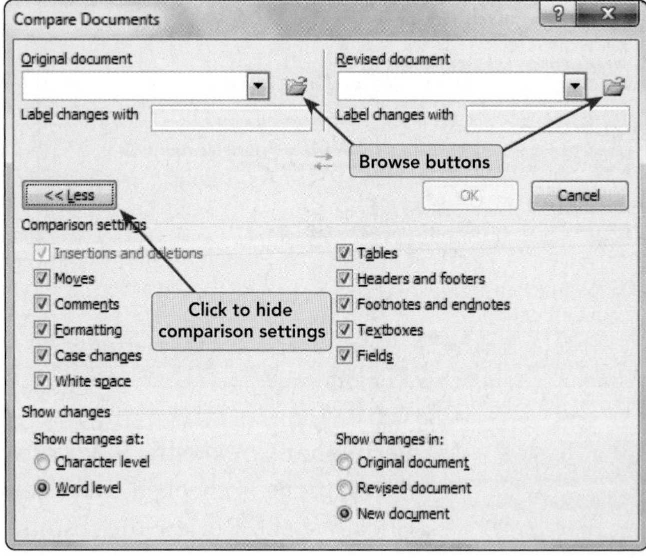

Figure 24-10 Expanded Compare Documents dialog box

NOTE

Changes made in the Comparison settings section and the Show changes section will be the selected options for the next comparison.

NOTE

Click the Compare button, and choose the Show Source Documents option to specify which document(s) to view. You can hide the source documents, show both source documents, show the original, or show the revised document. If the Reviewing Pane does not display, click the Reviewing Pane button and click Reviewing Pane Vertical.

3. Click the Browse button for the Original document text box, and select the student data file **Club - 2**. Click Open. Click the Browse button for the Revised document text box, and double click **Club - 3**.
4. Verify that Word level is selected in the Show changes section and that New document is selected in the Show changes in section.
5. Click OK to create a new document. Word opens a new document that compares the edited file **Club - 3** with the original file **Club - 2** in the Compared Document pane. All changes appear as revision marks. Deleted text appears as strikethrough text; new text is underlined. Revisions are color-coded by reviewer. A revision bar appears to the left of each line with a revision. The Reviewing Pane displays the number and type of revisions. The Original Document pane displays the **Club - 2** file, and the Revised Document pane displays the **Club - 3** file.

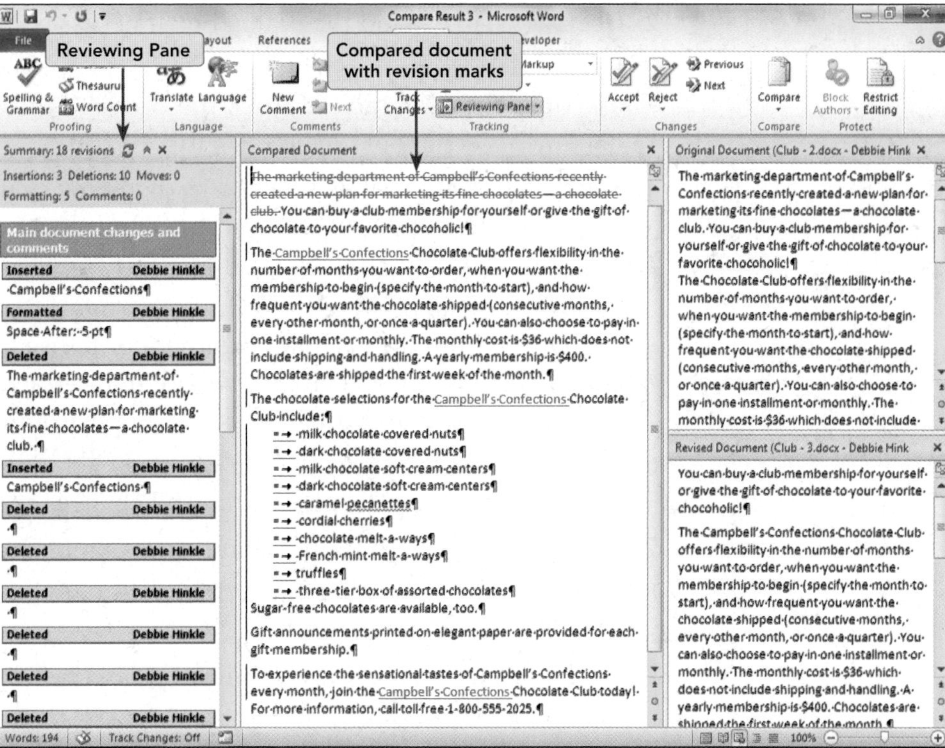

Figure 24-11
Merged documents showing revision marks

TIP

Use the View Side by Side button on the View tab, Window group, to display two documents side by side to compare content and not merge changes.

NOTE

Printing a document with revision marks is a good way to keep a record of changes made to a document.

6. Drag the scroll box in the Compared Document pane, and notice that the text in both the Original Document pane and the Revised Document pane scrolls too.
7. Click the Compare button, click the Show Source Documents option, and click Hide Source Documents. Close the Reviewing Pane.
8. Save the document as ***[your initials]*24-6** in your Lesson 24 folder.
9. Submit, print, and close the document. Word prints the document with the revisions, changing the zoom level to best display the revision balloons.

Exercise 24-7 COMBINE REVISIONS FROM MULTIPLE USERS

1. Start a new document. Click the Review tab on the Ribbon. Click the Compare button, and click Combine to open the Combine Document dialog box.
2. Click More to expand the dialog box if necessary.
3. Click the Browse button in the Original document section. Locate and open the file **Club - 2**. Click the Browse button in the Revised document section and open the **Club - 3** file.
4. Verify that Word level is selected in the Show changes section and that Original document is selected in the Show changes in section.
5. Click OK to combine the documents. Only one set of formatting instructions can be stored at a time. You may be prompted to choose formatting from the original document or to use formatting from the edited document. You can also choose not to track formatting changes by clearing the Formatting check box in the Comparison settings section.
6. Click The other document (Club - 3) and click Continue with Merge. Word combines the documents, and all changes appear as revision marks.
7. Click the Compare button, and click Combine.
8. Click the down arrow for the Original document text box, and open the file **Club - 2**.
9. Click the Browse for Revised button in the Revised document section, and open the **Club - 4** file.
10. Click Original document. Click OK to combine the documents.
11. Click The other document (Club - 4) and click Continue with Merge. Word combines the documents and all changes appear as revision marks.
13. Click the Compare button, and click Combine.
14. Click the down arrow for the Original document text box, and open the file **Club - 2**.
15. Click the Browse button in the Revised document section, and open the **Club - 5** file. Click Open.

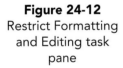

16. Verify that **Original document** is selected in the Show changes in section. Click **OK** to combine the documents.
17. Click the Accept and Move to Next button and click **Accept All Changes in Document**.
18. Key **Chocolate Club** at the top of the document, and apply character and paragraph formatting to the title. Delete extra paragraph marks if necessary.
19. Save the document as ***[your initials]*24-7** in your Lesson 24 folder.
20. Submit and close the document. Close any open documents without saving.

Exercise 24-8 PROTECT A DOCUMENT FROM REVISIONS

You can protect a document from changes in several ways. One is to require a password to open or modify the document. Another way is to designate the document as a read-only file. *Read only* allows a user to open or copy a file but not to change or save the file. Another way is to allow users to insert comments, or you can specify that any changes appear only as tracked changes.

1. Open the file **Club - 3**.
2. Click the **Review** tab.
3. Save the document as ***[your initials]*24-8** in your Lesson 24 folder.
4. Turn on Track Changes, and verify that you are in Print Layout view.
5. Click the Restrict Editing button. The Restrict Formatting and Editing task pane displays.

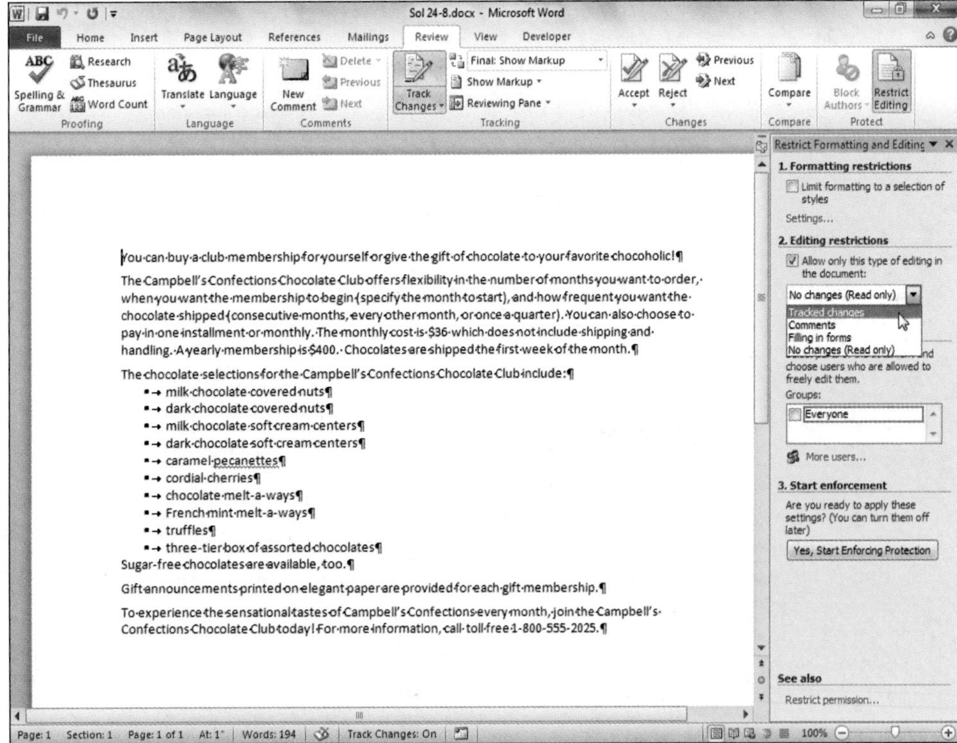

Figure 24-12
Restrict Formatting and Editing task pane

6. Click the check box under **Editing Restrictions**, and choose **Tracked changes** from the drop-down list.
7. Click the **Yes, Start Enforcing Protection** command. Do not enter a password, but click **OK** to apply the editing restrictions.

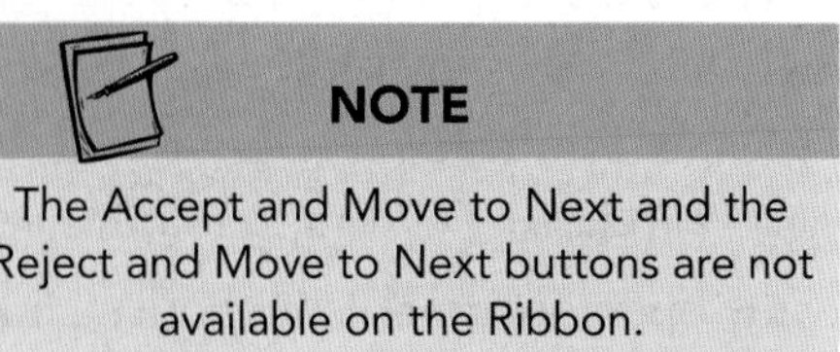

NOTE

The Accept and Move to Next and the Reject and Move to Next buttons are not available on the Ribbon.

8. Locate and select the text "caramel pecanettes" in the bulleted list, and delete the text. The deletion appears as a tracked change.
9. Right-click the markup balloon. Notice that the **Accept Deletion** and **Reject Deletion** options are not available. As long as the protection is turned on, revisions cannot be accepted or rejected.

Figure 24-13
Revision attempt with protection enabled

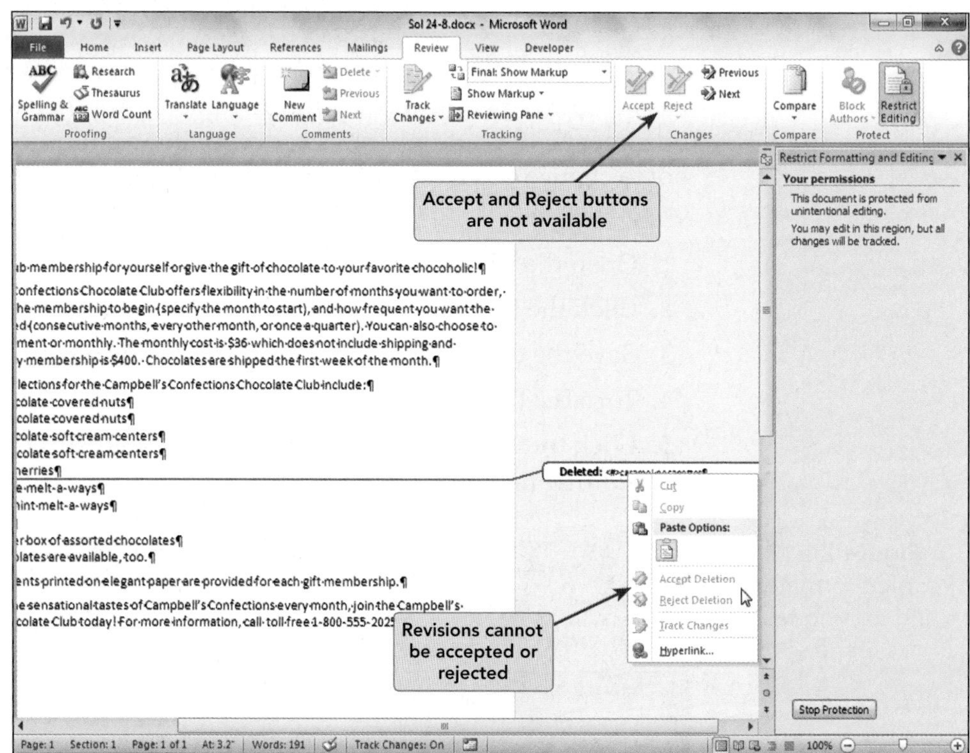

10. Click the **Stop Protection** command in the Restrict Formatting and Editing task pane.

NOTE

Words, sentences, or paragraphs in a document can be designated as unrestricted for editing. You can also specify which individuals have permission to modify the unrestricted areas of the document. Click the More users link to enter the names of the users who have permission to edit the document.

11. Click the down arrow in the Editing restrictions section of the Restrict Formatting and Editing task pane, and choose **Comments**.
12. Select the first and second paragraphs of the document, and select the **Everyone** check box in the Groups section. The first and second paragraphs can be edited by any user.
13. Click **Yes, Start Enforcing Protection**. Do not enter a password, and click **OK**. The unrestricted area of the document is highlighted.

14. Delete the text "You can" in the first paragraph. Capitalize "buy."
15. Select the last paragraph of the document. Press Delete. The status bar displays a message indicating that you cannot modify this paragraph. Click **Stop Protection**.
16. Close the document without saving.
17. Reopen ***[your initials]*24-8**.
18. Click the **Review tab**, and click the Restrict Editing button.
19. Click the check box under **Editing Restrictions**, and choose **No changes (Read only)**. Click **Yes, Start Enforcing Protection**. Click **OK**.
20. Save, close, and reopen the document. Click the **Review tab**, and click the Restrict Editing button. Word displays a message in the Restrict Formatting and Editing task pane indicating the document is protected.
21. Open the **File** tab and click **Save As**. The Save As dialog box appears. Locate and click the **Tools** down arrow Tools. Click **General Options**. The General Options dialog box appears. Use the General Options dialog box to set a password, to open or modify a document, or to apply the Read-only option.

Figure 24-14
General Options dialog box

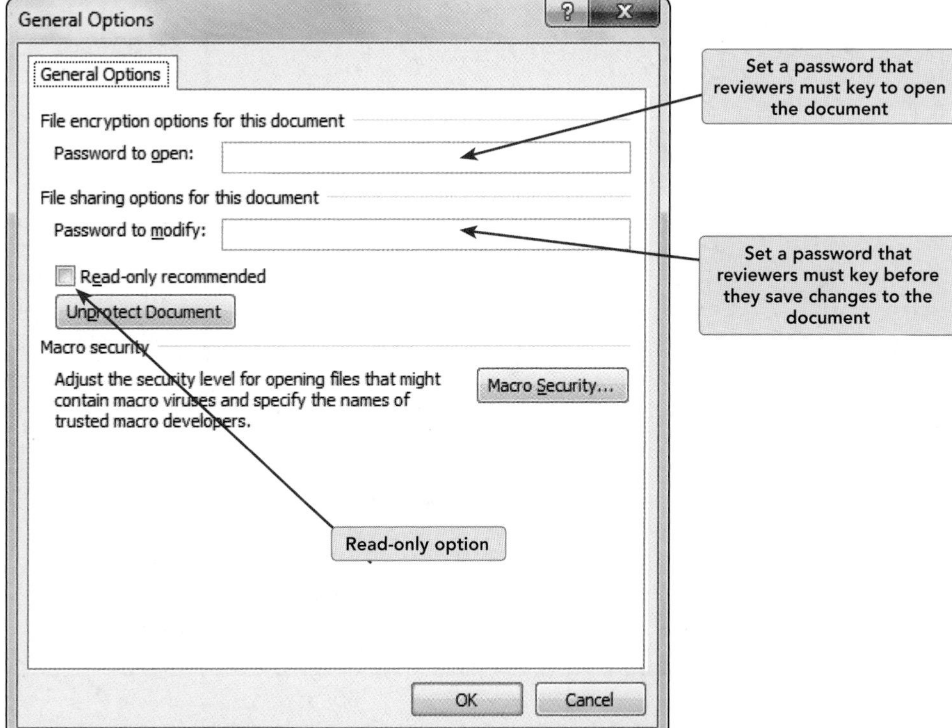

22. Click the **Read-only recommended** option and click **OK**. Save, close, and reopen the document. Word displays a prompt to open the file as read only. Click **Yes**. Notice the change in the document name in the title bar. Close the document.

Review a Document

When a document has been revised and reviewed several times, you can choose Full Screen Reading view to read the document and to verify its accuracy and content. Full Screen Reading view hides the Ribbon and displays the Navigation Pane.

There are two ways to switch to Full Screen Reading view:

- Click the View tab, Document Views group.
- Click the Full Screen Reading view button on the status bar.

Exercise 24-9 REVIEW A DOCUMENT

1. Open the file **History – 5**, and save the document as ***[your initials]*24-9**.
2. Click the **View** tab, and click to select **Navigation Pane**. The Navigation Pane displays with a listing of the document headings.
3. Click the Full Screen Reading button.

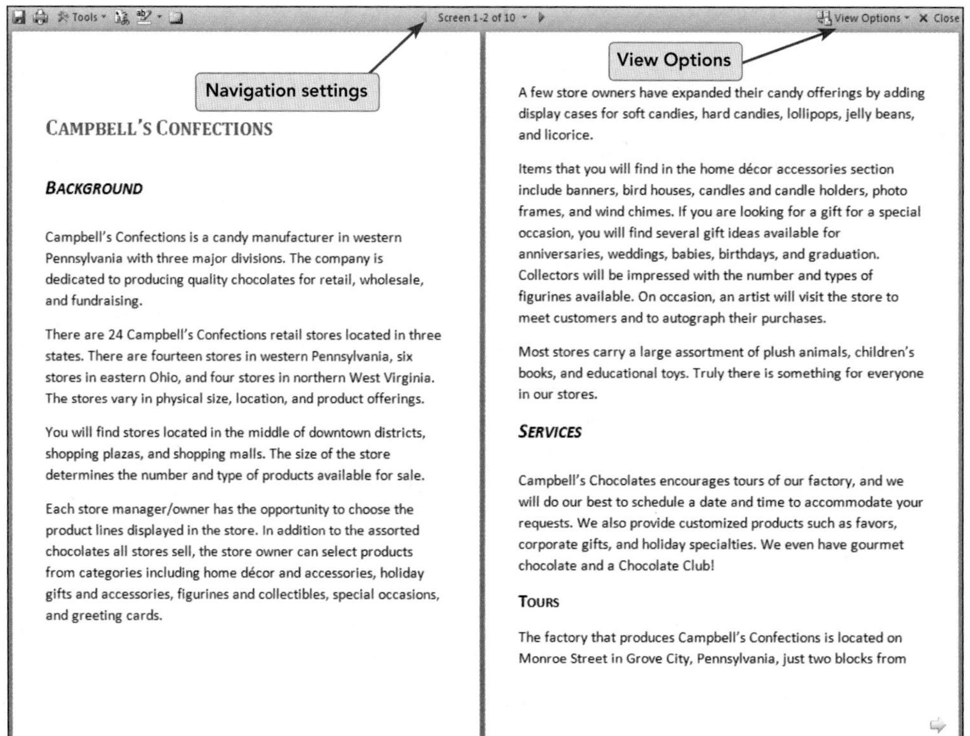

CAMPBELL'S CONFECTIONS

BACKGROUND

Campbell's Confections is a candy manufacturer in western Pennsylvania with three major divisions. The company is dedicated to producing quality chocolates for retail, wholesale, and fundraising.

There are 24 Campbell's Confections retail stores located in three states. There are fourteen stores in western Pennsylvania, six stores in eastern Ohio, and four stores in northern West Virginia. The stores vary in physical size, location, and product offerings.

You will find stores located in the middle of downtown districts, shopping plazas, and shopping malls. The size of the store determines the number and type of products available for sale.

Each store manager/owner has the opportunity to choose the product lines displayed in the store. In addition to the assorted chocolates all stores sell, the store owner can select products from categories including home décor and accessories, holiday gifts and accessories, figurines and collectibles, special occasions, and greeting cards.

A few store owners have expanded their candy offerings by adding display cases for soft candies, hard candies, lollipops, jelly beans, and licorice.

Items that you will find in the home décor accessories section include banners, bird houses, candles and candle holders, photo frames, and wind chimes. If you are looking for a gift for a special occasion, you will find several gift ideas available for anniversaries, weddings, babies, birthdays, and graduation. Collectors will be impressed with the number and types of figurines available. On occasion, an artist will visit the store to meet customers and to autograph their purchases.

Most stores carry a large assortment of plush animals, children's books, and educational toys. Truly there is something for everyone in our stores.

SERVICES

Campbell's Chocolates encourages tours of our factory, and we will do our best to schedule a date and time to accommodate your requests. We also provide customized products such as favors, corporate gifts, and holiday specialties. We even have gourmet chocolate and a Chocolate Club!

TOURS

The factory that produces Campbell's Confections is located on Monroe Street in Grove City, Pennsylvania, just two blocks from

Figure 24-15 Full Screen Reading view

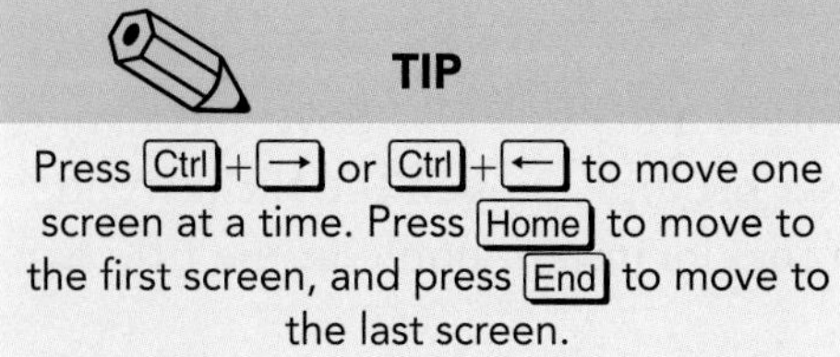

TIP

Press Ctrl+→ or Ctrl+← to move one screen at a time. Press Home to move to the first screen, and press End to move to the last screen.

4. To navigate in the document by page, click the Next arrow or the Previous arrow in the lower corner of the page, press PageUp or PageDown, or click the navigation arrows at the top of the screen Screen 3-4 of 10.

5. To control the appearance of the screen, click the arrow beside the View Options button View Options. Click **Show One Page** to read one page at a time, or click **Show Two Pages** to read two pages at a time. Click the **Increase Text Size** option to display text in a larger size.

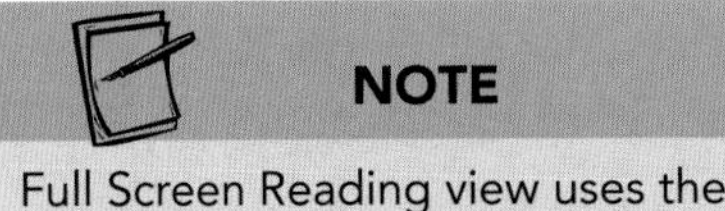

NOTE

Full Screen Reading view uses the term "screen" rather than pages because the screens do not display an entire page of text. The document does not display as it would in Print Layout view.

6. Click the down arrow beside the navigation arrows Screen 3-4 of 10 at the top of the screen, and click **Navigation Pane**. The Navigation Pane displays on the left of the screen. Click the Browse the pages in your document button to display the document pages as thumbnails. *Thumbnails* are miniature representations of each page.
7. Scroll through the thumbnails, and click on screen 4. The thumbnail is highlighted and displays in an enlarged view.
8. Click the Browse the headings in your document button beside the Browse the pages in your document button in the Navigation Pane. The Navigation Pane displays headings in the document. Click a heading to move to that part of the document. Click the "Gourmet Chocolate" heading to move to the end of the document. Click the "Campbell's Confections" heading to return to the top of the document.
9. Click the arrow beside the Tools button Tools (located in the title bar), and notice that you can insert comments, highlight text, or find text in Full Screen Reading view. You can also display the Research task pane. Close the list.
10. Click the arrow beside the View Options button View Options, and notice that you can track changes and show comments in Full Screen Reading view.
11. Click the Close button Close in the Full Screen Reading view title bar to return to Print Layout view. Click the **View** tab, and deselect **Navigation Pane**.

Exercise 24-10 ATTACH DIGITAL SIGNATURES

An Office document can be digitally signed to ensure that the signer of the document is who he or she claims to be, to ensure that the content has not been altered since it was digitally signed, and to verify the origin of the signed content. A *digital signature* is used to authenticate documents, e-mail messages, and macros. The digital signature must be valid and current and must be signed by a trusted person or organization. You can purchase a digital signature from a Microsoft Partner, or you can create your own digital signature. You will need a digital certificate from an authorized third party if your documents need to be verified for authenticity. There are two ways to use a digital signature:

- Add a visible signature line to the document.
- Add an invisible digital signature to the document.

A visible signature line resembles a signature line in a business letter and includes information about the signer of the document. Once a document is digitally signed, it becomes read only. An invisible signature provides authenticity but is not visible within the document. A document with an invisible signature displays a Signatures button on the status bar. In the following exercise you will add a visible and an invisible digital signature to the document.

1. Go to the end of the document.
2. Click the **Insert** tab, and locate the **Text** group. Click the arrow beside the Signature Line button, and click **Microsoft Office Signature Line**. Click **OK** in the message box.

Figure 24-16 Signature Setup dialog box

3. Key ***[your name]*** in the Suggested signer text box. Key **Customer Service Representative** in the Suggested signer's title text box. Click **OK** to insert the signature line in the document.

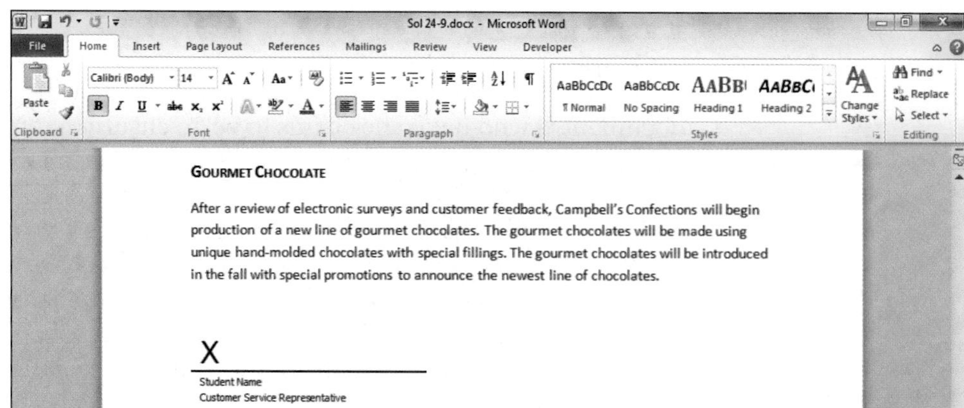

Figure 24-17 Signature line

4. Save and close the document; then reopen the ***[your initials]*24-9** document.
5. Notice the Signatures Information Bar at the top of the document. Click **View Signatures**. (See figure 24-18 on the next page.)

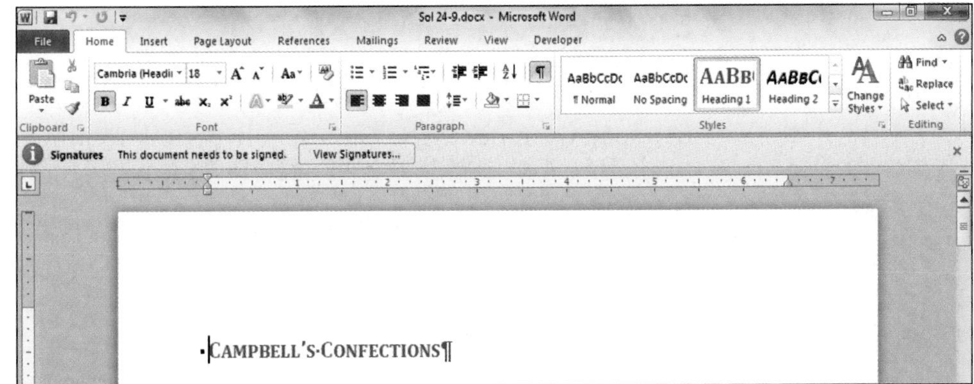

Figure 24-18
View Signatures Information Bar

6. The Signatures task pane displays and indicates that the document is not signed.
7. Point to the down arrow beside your name in the Signatures task pane, and choose **Sign**. Click **OK**. Key ***[your name]*** in the Sign dialog box, and click **Sign**. Click **OK** when the Signature Confirmation dialog box displays. The status bar displays a Signature icon indicating the document contains a signature.
8. Right-click the signature line, and choose **Remove Signature**. Click **Yes** to confirm removal of the signature. Click **OK** to close the Signature Removed dialog box. Close the Signatures task pane, and delete the signature graphic object. The visible signature has been removed from the document.
9. Click the **File** tab, and click **Info**. Locate the **Permissions** section, and click **Protect Document**. Click to select **Add a Digital Signature**. Click **OK**.
10. Click **Sign**, then click **OK** to close the Signature Confirmation dialog box. Notice the changes displayed on the Info tab. The Signed Document section indicates that the document has been signed and should not be edited. The Permissions section states that the document has been marked as final.
11. Click the Home tab, and notice that the Ribbon has been replaced with a Marked as Final Information Bar.
12. Click the **File** tab, and click **Info**. Click View Signatures. The Signatures task pane displays. Click the down arrow beside your signature name. Choose **Remove Signature**, and click **Yes** to close the Remove Signature dialog box. Click **OK**.
13. Close the Signatures task pane, and close the document.

Creating Hyperlinks

A hypertext link, called a *hyperlink*, is text you click to move to another location. The location to which you move can be within the same document, in another document, or somewhere on the World Wide Web or your company's intranet. Readers use hyperlinks to jump to related information. You can create a series of hyperlinks, thereby creating your own "web" of locations.

In a document, hypertext links can be a word or phrase. Hypertext links are usually blue and underlined.

Exercise 24-11 CREATE A HYPERLINK WITHIN THE SAME DOCUMENT

In a long document, you can use a hyperlink to jump quickly from one page to another. You can do this in one of two ways:

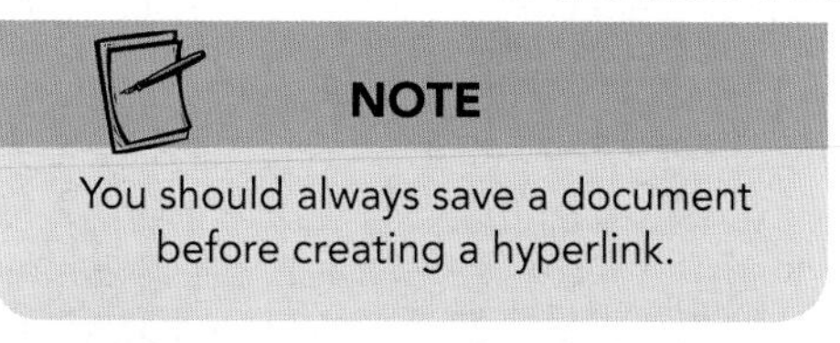

NOTE

You should always save a document before creating a hyperlink.

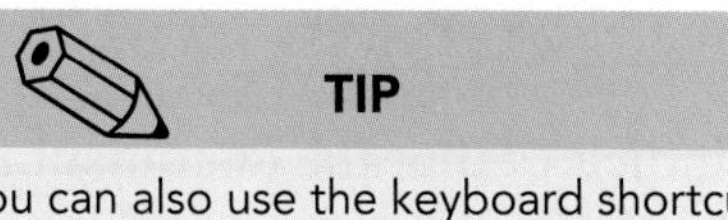

TIP

You can also use the keyboard shortcut Ctrl+K to open this dialog box.

- Create a bookmark at a particular location in the document, and then insert a hypertext link to the bookmark.
- Apply a heading style to text in the document, and then insert a hypertext link to the styled text.

1. Open the file **History - 4**.
2. Save the document as ***[your initials]*24-11** in your Lesson 24 folder.
3. Using a bookmark, you will create a hyperlink from the text "corporate gifts" on page 1 to the description of corporate gifts on page 3. Scroll to the top of page 3. Position the insertion point to the left of the heading "Corporate Gifts," and insert a bookmark named **CorporateGifts**. (Click the **Insert** tab and **Bookmark**. Remember, bookmark names cannot contain spaces.)
4. Below the heading "Services" on page 1, select the text "corporate gifts."
5. Click the **Insert** tab, and click the Hyperlink button to open the Insert Hyperlink dialog box.

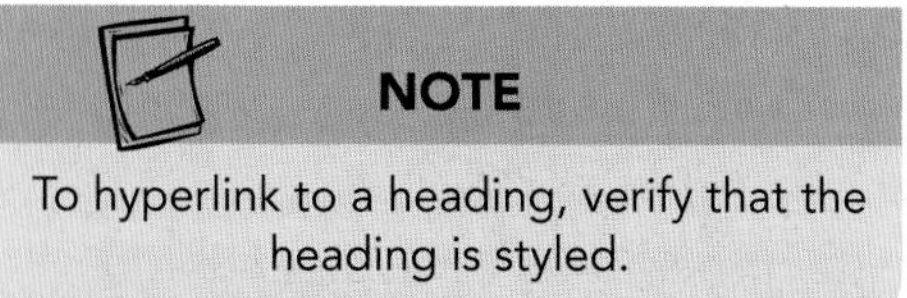

NOTE

To hyperlink to a heading, verify that the heading is styled.

6. Under Link to, click **Place in This Document**. Scroll to view the Bookmarks section.
7. Click **CorporateGifts** under Bookmarks to choose this bookmark as the "jump to" location.

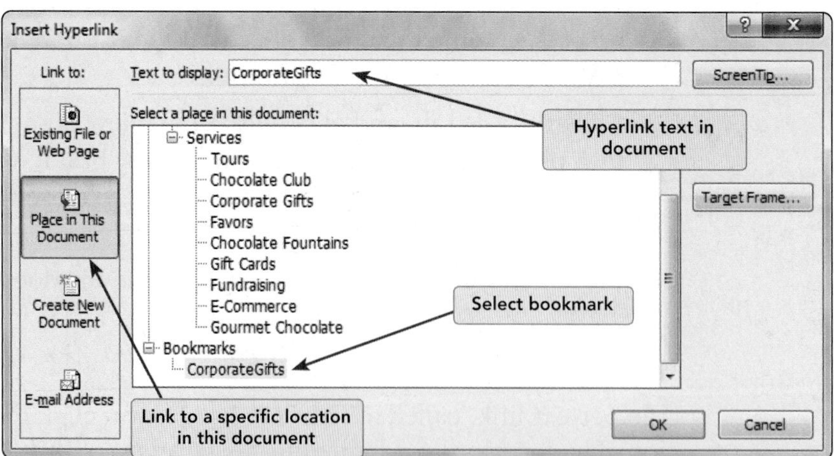

Figure 24-19
Creating a hyperlink to a bookmark

TIP

Instead of scrolling back and forth to create hyperlinks within a document, you can split the document and display the appropriate text within each pane. Click the View tab, and click Split (or double-click the split bar on the vertical scroll bar).

NOTE

After creating a hyperlink, you can change the blue hyperlink text as well as the link destination. To change the text, right-click the hyperlink, click Select Hyperlink from the shortcut menu, and then key different text. To change the hyperlink destination, right-click the hyperlink, choose Edit Hyperlink, and then choose a different heading or bookmark in the document to which you want to link. To remove a hyperlink, right-click the hypertext and choose Remove Hyperlink.

8. Click **OK** to close the Insert Hyperlink dialog box. The words "corporate gifts" are blue and underlined, indicating you have created a hyperlink.
9. Point to the blue hyperlink text. A ScreenTip displays the bookmark name with the instructions "CTRL + click to follow link." Press Ctrl, and the pointer changes to a pointing hand.
10. Test the hyperlink by clicking it. The insertion point jumps to the description of corporate gifts on page 3.
11. Scroll to the hyperlink text on page 1. Notice the change in color, indicating you have used the hyperlink.
12. On page 1, below the "Services" heading, select the text "Chocolate Club" at the end of the paragraph.
13. Open the Insert Hyperlink dialog box. If necessary, click **Place in This Document**. Click the heading **Chocolate Club**, and then click **OK**.

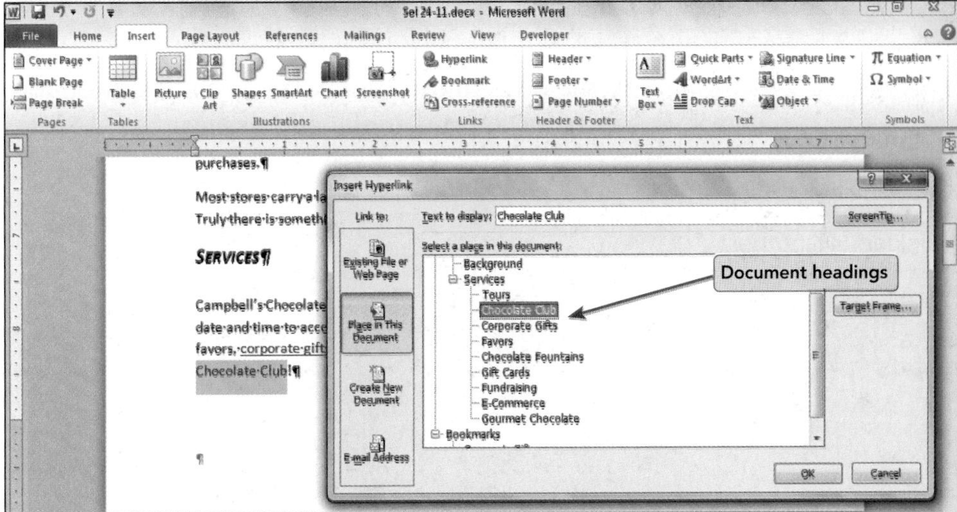

Figure 24-20
Creating a hyperlink to a heading

14. Press Ctrl, and click the hyperlink to test it. The insertion point jumps to the heading "Chocolate Club" on page 2.
15. Save, submit, and close the document.

Exercise 24-12 CREATE A HYPERLINK TO ANOTHER DOCUMENT

You can create hyperlinks to another Word document or to Office documents such as an Excel worksheet or a PowerPoint presentation.

1. Start a new document. Create a memo to **Store Managers** from **Lynn Tanguay**. Key **January 10** for the date. The subject is **Risk Management Seminar**. For the body of the memo, key the text shown in Figure 24-21.

Figure 24-21

```
The agenda for the Risk Management Seminar has been
finalized.

Participants should receive their materials by Friday.
```

NOTE

To jump to a specific area of the linked document, you would click Bookmark and use the Select Place in Document dialog box. In this case, however, because the linked document is short, you do not need to select a more specific location.

2. Add your reference initials to the memo, and save it as ***[your initials]*24-12** in your Lesson 24 folder.
3. Select "agenda" in the first paragraph.
4. Click the Insert Hyperlink button, or press Ctrl+K.
5. In the Insert Hyperlink dialog box, under Link to, click **Existing File or Web Page**.
6. Click **Current Folder** if it is not active.
7. In the Look in text box, locate and click the student data file **Risk**. The file name appears in the Address text box.

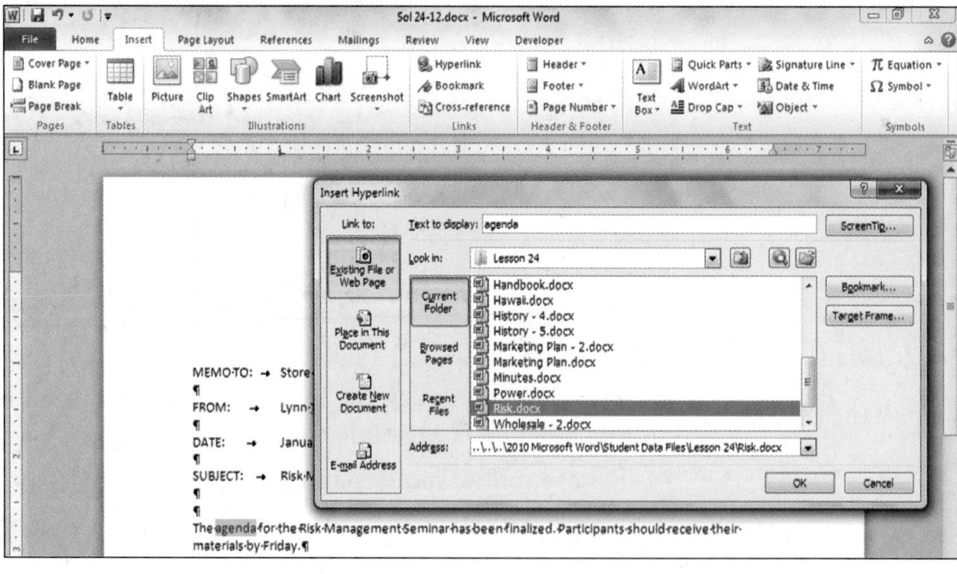

Figure 24-22 Linking to another document

NOTE

After inserting a hyperlink to another document, you can select the hyperlink text and modify it. You can also change the document or location to which you want to link. Right-click the hyperlink, choose Edit Hyperlink, and choose a different location. If documents are stored on a network drive, users must have appropriate permissions to access folders.

8. Click **OK** in the Insert Hyperlink dialog box. The text "agenda" is blue and underlined, indicating you have created a hyperlink.
9. Press Ctrl, and click the hyperlink to test it. Word opens the linked document. Close **Risk**.
10. Save the document and close it.

Exercise 24-13 CREATE A HYPERLINK TO A WEB SITE

In addition to creating hyperlinks between documents, you can create a link to a location on the World Wide Web. For example, suppose you are sending an e-mail memo to the store managers about upgrading software and hardware. You can include a hyperlink to a Web site that lists up-to-date information on features and pricing.

NOTE

You cannot link to the Web without an Internet connection. Your computer must be equipped with appropriate hardware and software for navigating the Internet.

To link to a Web site, you need to know the site's address, or *URL* (Uniform Resource Locator). A URL is a combination of characters that is recognized by the Internet. For example, the Web address for Microsoft is http://www.microsoft.com. The prefix "http://" (which stands for hypertext transfer protocol) is used for Web addresses but is understood and is no longer necessary when keying a Web address.

1. Start a new document. Create the memo shown in Figure 24-23. When you key the Web address www.microsoft.com, Word will automatically apply the hyperlink character formatting.

Figure 24-23
Creating automatic hypertext

```
MEMO TO:          Store Managers

FROM:             Lynn Tanguay

DATE:             [Current Date]

SUBJECT:          Upgrades

Please check the Microsoft Web site, www.microsoft.com,
periodically to learn the projected release date for the
operating system update. We are planning to implement a two-
year replacement schedule for our computers and software.
```

NOTE

If you receive an error message, ask your instructor how to proceed.

TIP

Instead of using a Web address as a hyperlink in a document, you can use any word or phrase in the document. Simply select the document text, open the Insert Hyperlink dialog box, and enter the URL in the Address text box (just as you entered the path to link a document).

2. Add your reference initials to the memo, and save it as ***[your initials]*24-13** in your Lesson 24 folder.
3. Press Ctrl, and click the new hyperlink to test it. Word jumps to the Microsoft home page on the Web if your Internet connection is activated. If it is not, you might be asked to sign on.
4. Scroll to the bottom of the Web page. Notice that the Web page contains both text and graphics. Scroll back to the top of the Web page.
5. Try two or three links on the Web page.
6. Close the Internet connection.
7. Use the taskbar to return to the document. Submit and close the document.

Lesson 24 Summary

- Use comments to insert notes in a document. Comments are color-coded by reviewer. Make sure your name and initials appear in the text boxes in the General section in the Word Options dialog box before inserting your comments.
- Comments appear in the Reviewing Pane or as balloons in the margins.
- Edit comment text in either the comment balloon or the Reviewing Pane. Use the Next button and the Previous button on the Ribbon to move from comment to comment.
- To delete a comment, click within the comment text and click the Delete button, or right-click the comment text and choose Delete Comment from the shortcut menu.
- To print comments with a document, use the Print tab. Word scales the document text of the printed document to make room for the comment balloons.
- To print comments separately from a document, open the Print tab and choose List of Markup from the Print All Pages drop-down list.
- Use the Track Changes feature to collaborate with others when revising documents.
- Tracked changes appear as revision marks that show where deletions, insertions, and formatting changes were made. In Draft view, inserted text appears underlined, deleted text has a horizontal line through it, and a revision bar appears to the left of every revised paragraph. In Print Layout view, tracked changes appear in the text and also in balloons in the right margin. Formatting changes appear only in Print Layout view. Changes also appear in the Reviewing Pane.

- You can review a document after it is edited and decide whether you want to accept or reject the revisions. Use the Ribbon to accept or reject revisions, or right-click a revision mark and use the shortcut menu.
- You can review changes by the type of change made. You can also review only the changes made by a particular reviewer.
- To accept all revisions at once, click the arrow on the Accept and Move to Next button and choose Accept All Changes in Document.
- When several people have reviewed a copy of a document, you can use the Compare feature to consolidate revisions into one file.
- You can compare two documents, such as an edited copy of a document and the original document. Open the Compare Documents dialog box, browse for the original document, and browse for the revised document. Select appropriate comparison settings and options for showing changes, and click New document under Show changes in. Click OK. Word opens a new document that shows the differences as color-coded revision marks.
- When you compare more than two documents, select Combine from the Compare drop-down list. Word combines the documents and displays the differences as color-coded revision marks.
- To review the content of a document, switch to Full Screen Reading view. The document appears as a series of screens for easier readability. You can change the view of the document and navigate through the screens.
- You can protect a document from changes by requiring a password to open or modify the document. You can also designate the document as a read-only file.
- Use digital signatures to authenticate documents, e-mail messages, or macros. You can add a visible signature line or an invisible digital signature to a document.
- A hypertext link, called a hyperlink, is text you click to move to another location. The location to which you move can be within the same document, in another document, or somewhere on the World Wide Web or your company's intranet.
- In a long document, you can use a hyperlink to jump quickly from one page to another. You can do this by creating a bookmark in a document and inserting a hypertext link to the bookmark or by inserting a hypertext link to a heading.
- You can create hyperlinks to another Word document or to Office documents such as an Excel spreadsheet or a PowerPoint presentation.
- In addition to creating hyperlinks between documents, you can create a link to a location on the World Wide Web. To link to a Web site, you need to know the site's address, or URL (Uniform Resource Locator). A URL is a combination of characters that is recognized by the Internet.

LESSON 24		Command Summary	
Feature	**Button**	**Command**	**Keyboard**
Accept change		Review tab, Changes group	
Comments		Review tab, Comments group	Alt+Ctrl+M
Compare and combine documents		Review tab, Compare group	
Full Screen Reading view		View tab, Document Views group	
Insert a hyperlink		Insert tab, Links group	Ctrl+K
Navigation Pane	Navigation Pane	View tab, Show group	
Print comments		File tab, Print	
Protect a document		Review tab, Protect group	
Reject change		Review tab, Changes group	
Signature line		Insert tab, Text group	
Track changes		Review tab, Tracking group	Ctrl+Shift+E

Concepts Review

True/False Questions

Each of the following statements is either true or false. Indicate your choice by circling T or F.

T F 1. In Draft view, comments appear in balloons.

T F 2. You can access the Reviewing Pane from the View tab.

T F 3. You can print a document with or without revision marks.

T F 4. Both comments and revision marks appear in Print Preview.

T F 5. A hypertext link is usually blue and underlined.

T F 6. Use the legal blackline feature to compare two documents.

T F 7. When you protect a document from revisions, no one can add a revision to the document without entering a password.

T F 8. You can turn off tracked changes by clicking Track Changes on the status bar.

Short Answer Questions

Write the correct answer in the space provided.

1. When you are checking revisions, which command is used when you do not want to accept the changes?

____

2. Which feature is used to authenticate documents and e-mail messages?

____

3. When you point to a comment balloon in Print Layout view, what does the ScreenTip display?

____

4. Where are comments displayed if you want to view them in Draft view?

____

5. How do you use the shortcut menu to delete a comment in Print Layout view?

____

6. Which view displays document pages as a series of screens?

____

7. Which Ribbon tab do you use for comments and tracked changes?

---

8. What does the mouse pointer change to when you point to a hyperlink and press Ctrl?

Critical Thinking

Answer these questions on a separate page. There are no right or wrong answers. Support your answers with examples from your own experience, if possible.

1. Think of a scenario in which three of the new features introduced in this lesson could be helpful. Discuss the Comments, Track Changes, and Compare Documents features. Include advantages and disadvantages of using each feature.
2. What are the advantages of attaching digital signatures to a document?

Skills Review

Exercise 24-14

Insert, delete, edit, and print comments.

1. Open the file **Email - 3**.
2. Prepare the document for the insertion of comments by following these steps:
   a. Open the Word Options dialog box, and click **General**.
   b. Make sure your name and initials are in the appropriate data fields.
   c. Click **OK**.
   d. Click the **Review** tab on the Ribbon. Click the lower part of the Track Changes button. Click **Change Tracking Options**. Locate the Comments box in the Markup section, and click the down arrow to display the list of colors. Select **Blue**.
   e. Verify the balloon options. The preferred width should be 3 inches, and balloons should display on the right margin.
   f. Click **OK** to close the Track Changes Options dialog box.
3. Add comments by following these steps:
   a. Select "e-mail marketing" in the first bulleted item.
   b. Click the New Comment button on the Review tab.
   c. Key **Purpose could be to advertise, improve customer service, and/or send an e-mail newsletter.** in the Comment balloon.
   d. Select "Tracking" in the third bulleted item, and click the New Comment button. In the balloon, key the comment **Tracking includes analyzing bounces, delivered e-mail, click rates, and open rates.**

e. Create a comment for "Risks" in the last bulleted item, keying the text **Investigate breach of confidentiality, legal liability, and damage to the IT system.**

4. Delete the "e-mail marketing" comment by clicking within the balloon and clicking the Delete button on the Review tab, Comments group.
5. Edit the comment text for "Risks" by clicking within the balloon and typing **potential** before "damage."
6. Save the document as ***[your initials]*24-14** in your Lesson 24 folder.
7. Print the comments as balloons with the document text and as a separate list by following these steps:
   a. Display the Print tab.
   b. Verify that the Print All Pages drop-down list box is set to Print Markup. Click Print.
   c. Open the Print tab again.
   d. Change the Print All Pages drop-down list box to List of Markup. Click Print.
8. Submit and save the document.

Exercise 24-15

Track changes in a document.

1. Open the file **Hawaii**.
2. Click the Review tab, and click the Track Changes button to turn on Track Changes.
3. Position the insertion point to the immediate left of "macadamia" in the first sentence of the first paragraph, and key **three**.
4. Locate the text "instead of using" in the first paragraph. Key **our** before "present."
5. Add the following paragraph after the first paragraph:

   Since this nut is one of the hardest nuts to crack, I am somewhat dubious of these claims. It would certainly be a most profound development if the process works.
6. Delete the sentence that begins "Good luck" in the last paragraph.
7. Go to the top of the document, and click the Next button in the Changes group.
8. Click the Accept and Move to Next button to accept the insertion of "three." Accept the insertion of "our."
9. Move to the next change, and reject the addition of the paragraph.
10. Accept the deletion of the sentence in the last paragraph. Click OK.
11. Save the document as ***[your initials]*24-15** in your Lesson 24 folder.
12. Submit and close the document.

Exercise 24-16

Merge three revisions of the same document, and protect a document.

1. Start a new document.
2. Compare the **Email Marketing - 2** file with the original by following these steps:
   a. Click the Review tab.
   b. Click the Compare button, and click Combine. In the Combine Documents dialog box, click the Browse for original button to locate and select the original file **Email Marketing**. In the Revised document box, locate and select the file **Email Marketing - 2**.
   c. Click More to display the Comparison settings. Locate the Show changes in section, and click Original document.
   d. Click OK.
   e. Click the Compare button, and click Combine.
   f. Locate and select the file **Email Marketing** for the Original document box. Locate and select the file **Email Marketing - 3** for the Revised document box.
   g. Verify that Original document is selected under Show Changes in, and click OK.
   h. Click the Compare button, and click Show Source Documents. Click Hide Source Documents. Close the Reviewing Pane if necessary.
3. Click the Show Markup button, and click the Balloons option. Choose Show Revisions in Balloons. Right-click each balloon, and click Reject Deletion.
4. Click the Display for Review button, and click Final.
5. Protect the document from further revisions by following these steps:
   a. Click the Review tab. Click the Restrict Editing button.
   b. In the Restrict Formatting and Editing task pane, click the check box below Editing Restrictions to select it. Choose Tracked changes from the drop-down list, and click Yes, Start Enforcing Protection.
   c. Click OK in the Start Enforcing Protection dialog box. Close the Restrict Formatting and Editing task pane.
   d. In the last paragraph, delete the word "filtering." Check the document protection by attempting to accept the revision. Undo the deletion.
6. Save the document as ***[your initials]*****24-16** in your Lesson 24 folder.
7. Submit the document with revision marks; then close the document.

Exercise 24-17

Create hyperlinks within a document, to another document, and to a Web site.

1. Open the file **Community - 2**.
2. Save the document as ***[your initials]*****24-17** in your Lesson 24 folder.

3. Create a link between the word "schools" on page 1 and a paragraph on page 2 by following these steps:
   a. Go to the paragraph that begins "Last year." Select the text "Campbell's Confections Educational Foundation."
   b. Click the **Insert** tab, and click the Bookmark button. Key **Foundation** for the bookmark name. Click **Add**.
   c. Go to page 1, and select "schools" in the second line of the paragraph that begins "Another way."
   d. Click the **Insert** tab, and click the Hyperlink button.
   e. Click **Place in This Document** if it is not active. Locate and select the bookmark **Foundation**, and click **OK**.
   f. Press Ctrl, and click the hyperlink to test it.
4. Create a hyperlink to the file **Power** by following these steps:
   a. Select the word "communities" in the last sentence of the first paragraph. Press Ctrl+K to open the Insert Hyperlink dialog box.
   b. Click **Existing File or Web Page**.
   c. Click **Current Folder** if it is not active.
   d. In the Look in text box, locate the student data file **Power**, and click **OK**.
   e. Test the hyperlink.
   f. Close **Power**.
5. Create a hyperlink to a Web site by following these steps:
   a. Locate and select the text "Humane Society" in the paragraph that begins "It is not just."
   b. Open the Insert Hyperlink dialog box. In the Address text box, key the URL **www.humanesociety.org**. Click **OK**.
   c. Make sure your Internet connection is active, and click the hyperlink to test it.
   d. Close the Web page.
6. To all pages in the document, add a footer that contains the file name, left-aligned, and "Page" followed by the page number, right-aligned. Update the file name field.
7. Review the document in Full Screen Reading view by following these steps:
   a. Click the Full Screen Reading view button on the status bar.
   b. At the top middle of the screen, click the down arrow, and choose **Navigation Pane**. Change the Navigation Pane view by clicking the Browse the pages in your document button. Review the first screen, and click the thumbnail for the second screen.
   c. Close Full Screen Reading view by clicking the Close button.
8. Save the document.
9. Submit and close the document.

Lesson Applications

Exercise 24-18

Create comments, track changes, and accept revisions.

1. Open the file **Minutes**.
2. Turn on Track Changes.
3. Select the first line of the document, and change the font size to 14 points.
4. Position the insertion point at the end of the "Attendance" paragraph (after "1:30 p.m."), and key the following comment: **Bryson Clark from the Sharon store was not present.**
5. At the end of the "Old Business" paragraph, key the following text: **The official date for shipping the gourmet chocolates is April 10.**
6. Change February "20" to February **16**.
7. Change "Internet and e-mail policy" to **computer use policy**.
8. Edit the "Attendance" paragraph to include the comment text.
9. Accept all revisions.
10. Save the document as ***[your initials]*24-18** in your Lesson 24 folder.
11. Submit and close the document.

Exercise 24-19

Create a hyperlink from one document to another.

1. Open the file **Chamber**.
2. Verify that the top margin is 2 inches, and key your reference initials at the end of the document.
3. Spell-check the document, and save it as ***[your initials]*24-19** in your Lesson 24 folder.
4. Create a hyperlink between the text "PowerPoint presentation" and the file **Power**.
5. Test the hyperlink. Close the Power document.
6. Save, submit, and close ***[your initials]*24-19**.

Exercise 24-20

Review a document, and protect a document from revisions.

1. Open the file **Handbook**.
2. Save the document as ***[your initials]*24-20** in your Lesson 24 folder.

3. Click the Review tab, and protect the document from any changes (read only). Enforce the protection, and do not assign a password.
4. Save and close the document. Reopen the document.
5. Switch to Full Screen Reading view, and click the View Options button to display two pages. Close the Navigation Pane if necessary.
6. Click the Tools button [Tools], and click Find. Key **leave** in the Find what text box. Click Find Next, and close the Find and Replace dialog box.
7. Return to Print Layout view.
8. Close the document.

Exercise 24-21

Merge two revisions of the same document, track revisions, and accept revisions.

1. Open the file **Marketing Plan**.
2. Save the document as ***[your initials]*24-21** in your Lesson 24 folder. Close the document.
3. Start a new document.
4. Compare the document ***[your initials]*24-21** (original document) with **Marketing Plan - 2** (revised document) using the Show changes at the Word level and Show changes in the original document comparison settings.
5. Accept all revisions in the document.
6. Switch to Outline view, and turn on Track Changes mode.
7. Change "Purpose/Mission" to **Purpose and Mission**.
8. Change the entries under "Analysis" to the following:

   Product Analysis
   Target Market Analysis
   Competitor Analysis

9. Turn off Track Changes mode, and accept all revisions in the document.
10. Switch to Print Layout view.
11. Modify the Heading 2 style to a left indent of 0.25 inch, modify the Heading 3 style to a left indent of 0.5 inch, and modify the Heading 4 style to a left indent of 0.75 inch.
12. Save the document.
13. Submit and close the document.

On Your Own

In these exercises you work on your own, as you would in a real-life business environment. Use the skills you have learned to accomplish the task—and be creative.

Exercise 24-22

Use Help to create a document comparing and contrasting the View Side By Side feature located on the View tab with the Compare feature located on the Review tab. Insert at least three comments. The comments could be reminders to research additional Help topics to further develop your report, or they could be comments regarding formatting. Practice editing, deleting, and navigating through the comments. Save the document as ***[your initials]*24-22** in your Lesson 24 folder. Submit the document with comments displayed.

Exercise 24-23

Create a one-page rough draft report on a current electronic device. Save the document, and edit the document to create a final copy. Save the final copy using a different file name. Compare the two documents. Insert a comment describing your results. Save the new document as ***[your initials]*24-23** in your Lesson 24 folder, and submit it with revision marks displayed.

Exercise 24-24

Go to the Internet, and research digital certificates and the procedure for obtaining a digital certificate. Write a report (at least one full page, double-spaced) about the topic. Insert hyperlinks to locations within the document and to Web sites. Test the hyperlinks. Use the Full Screen Reading view to review the content. Save the document as ***[your initials]*24-24** in your Lesson 24 folder, and submit it.

Unit 7 Applications

Unit Application 7-1

Compare two documents, track changes, and insert comments.

1. Compare the **Summary** file and the **Summary 2** file, merging both documents into a new document.
2. Review the tracked changes, and accept the formatting changes. Reject the chart deletion.
3. Save the revised document as ***[your initials]*****u7-1** in your Unit 7 folder.
4. Insert a comment at the end of the document. Key the text **Add a concluding paragraph.**
5. Insert a comment on page 1 after the first paragraph, which ends "strongest gain." Key the text **Add a chart for net income.**
6. Add a three-line header to page 2 only that includes the following text:

   Year-End Summary
   Page *[Insert page number]*
   January 7, 20--

7. Save the document.
8. Submit and close the document.

Unit Application 7-2

Insert footnotes, and create an index and a table of contents.

1. Open the file **Catalog**.
2. Save the document as ***[your initials]*****u7-2** in your Unit 7 folder.
3. Use the Find command to locate the first occurrence of "MAW."
4. Insert a footnote, and key the text **MAW is the abbreviation for melt-a-way.**
5. Position the insertion point after "Product Catalog" at the top of the document, and insert a footnote. Key this text: **This is a partial listing. It does not include specialty candies or sugar-free candies.**

6. Mark index entries for the following, using the first occurrence of each under "Boxed Chocolate":

   Choice Assorted
   Nut Assorted
   Cream Assorted
   Light & Dark Assorted
   Light & Dark Creams
   Light & Dark Nut
   Dark Assorted
   Dark Nut Assorted
   Dark Cream Assorted
   Bark
   Candy Bar

7. Mark index entries for the following using the first occurrence of each under "Bulk Chocolate."

   Creams
   Nuts
   Turtles
   Break Up
   Clusters

8. Create an index entry for "MAW" with a subentry for "Boxed Chocolate" and a subentry for "Bulk Chocolate."
9. Create an index on a separate page at the end of the document. Select an appropriate format, and key the heading **INDEX**.
10. Add page numbers to the bottom margin, aligned at the right. Number each page, and format the text using 10-point italic.
11. Go to the top of the document, insert a page break, and create a table of contents with an appropriate format and the heading **TABLE OF CONTENTS**.
12. Save the document and submit it. Close the document.

Unit Application 7-3

Using the Internet, work with footnotes and create a table of contents and an index.

1. This is a group exercise. The class as a whole chooses a specific theme, such as:

   - A current event
   - A popular movie
   - A book

Each class member will create a short document that discusses one aspect of the selected theme. For example, if the class selects a movie as the major topic, one student could write a document about the film's plot, another student could write about the director, and others could write about the actors. Students should look for interesting topics to cover. For example, if the movie was based on a book or another movie, someone could discuss this. Was the film based on a real-life event? Did reviewers give the movie favorable or unfavorable reviews, and was attendance affected by their comments? If so, there's another interesting topic to discuss.

2. Log on to the Internet to research your specific topic. Find as much detailed information as you can in the time allotted by your instructor.
3. When you finish your research, create your document in Word. The document should have a Heading 1–style heading, body text, and lower-level headings as appropriate. Include footnotes and endnotes for reference sources. The document should also include a footnote attached to the main heading, containing your name and identifying you as the document's author. Save your document as ***[your initials]*****u7-3** in a location your instructor specifies.
4. Copy your document and your classmates' documents into your Unit 7 Applications folder. Open your document, and insert all of your classmates' documents into a single document.

NOTE

Ask your instructor where to save the file so that it is available to all students in the class. You will insert your classmates' files to create a long document.

5. Format the document attractively, using consistent styles. Change the font and font size of the footnotes. You might also include clip art or other graphics (avoid altering your heading styles).
6. Create an index and a table of contents for the document. Format them appropriately. Create a title page for the document.
7. Save and submit the document.

APPENDIXES

APPENDIX A

Proofreaders' Marks

Proofreaders' Mark		Draft	Final Copy
¶	Start a new paragraph.	ridiculous!¶If that is so	ridiculous! If that is so
⁀	Delete space.	to gether	together
#	Insert space.	Itmay be	It may not be
⌒	Move as shown.	it is (not) true	it is true
∩∪	Transpose.	beleivable	believable
		is it so	it is so
◯	Spell out.	(2) years ago	two years ago
		16 Elm (St.)	16 Elm Street
^	Insert a word.	How much ^is it?	How much is it?
⌐ OR —	Delete a word.	it may ~~not~~ be true	it may be true
^ OR ⅄	Insert a letter.	temperture	temperature
∂ OR ∂	Delete a letter and close up.	committment to buny	commitment to buy
⌐ OR —	Change a word.	~~and~~ but if you ~~won't~~ can't	but if you can't
....	Stet (don't delete).	I was ~~very~~ glad	I was very glad
/	Make letter lowercase.	Federal Government	federal government
≡	Capitalize.	Janet L. greyston	Janet L. Greyston
∨	Raise above the line.	in her new book*	in her new book*
^	Drop below the line.	H2SO4	H_2SO_4
⊙	Insert a period.	Mr Henry Grenada	Mr. Henry Grenada
↑	Insert a comma.	a large old house	a large, old house
∨	Insert an apostrophe.	my childrens car	my children's car
∨∨	Insert quotation marks.	he wants a loan	he wants a "loan"
= OR ⩮	Insert a hyphen.	a first=rate job	a first-rate job
		ask the coowner	ask the co-owner
M	Insert an em dash.	Here it is cash!	Here it is—cash!
N	Insert an en dash.	Pages 1 5	Pages 1–5
—	Insert underscore.	an issue of Time	an issue of Time
(ital)	Set in italic.	(ital) The New York Times	*The New York Times*

Proofreaders' Mark		Draft	Final Copy
bf	Set in boldface.	bf the Enter key	the **Enter** key
rom	Set in roman.	rom the *most* likely	the most likely
( )	Insert parentheses.	left today May 3	left today (May 3)
⊐	Move to the right.	$38,367,000 ⊐	$38,367,000
⊏	Move to the left.	⊏ Anyone can win!	Anyone can win!
ss [	Single-space.	ss I have heard he is leaving	I have heard he is leaving
ds [	Double-space.	ds When will you have a decision?	When will you have a decision?
+ 1 line	Insert 1 line space.	Percent of Change + 1 line 16.25	Percent of Change 16.25
− 1 line	Delete (remove) 1 line space.	Northeastern − 1 line regional sales	Northeastern regional sales

APPENDIX B

Standard Forms for Business Documents

Reference manuals, such as *The Gregg Reference Manual*, provide a variety of letter and memorandum styles, as well as styles for reports and other documents. Many businesses also have their own styles for documents. This appendix includes two basic styles—a business letter and a memorandum. It also shows the most common format for a continuation page (used for either letters or memos).

TABLE B-1 Parts of a Letter

Part of Letter	Location/Description
Heading	
Letterhead or return address	Often appears on preprinted stationery; can also be created in Word. Includes the company name, address, and other contact information.
Date line	Two inches from the top of the page on letterhead stationery or 0.5 inch below the letterhead. Use the date format shown in Figure B-1.
Opening	
Inside address	Starts three blank lines below the date; consists of name and address (and possibly company name and job title) of person to whom you are writing.
Salutation	One blank line below the inside address; typically includes a courtesy title (Mr., Mrs., Ms., Miss) and ends with a colon.
Body	
Message	Content of the letter, single-spaced with one blank line between paragraphs.
Closing	
Complimentary closing	One blank line below the last line of the body of the letter. Common closings are "Sincerely" or "Sincerely yours" followed by a comma.
Writer's signature block	Three blank lines below the closing, to leave space for a signature; includes the writer's name and job title (and sometimes the department).
Reference initials	One blank line below the writer's name and title; consists of the typist's initials in small letters.
Enclosure notation	On a new line below the reference initials if letter has an enclosure. Specify the number of enclosures. Can also use "Attachment" if the material is attached.
Optional features	File name notation—indicates document name for reference purposes; delivery notation—method of delivery (other than regular mail); copy notation—people who will receive copies of the letter (usually begins with "c:" or "cc:")

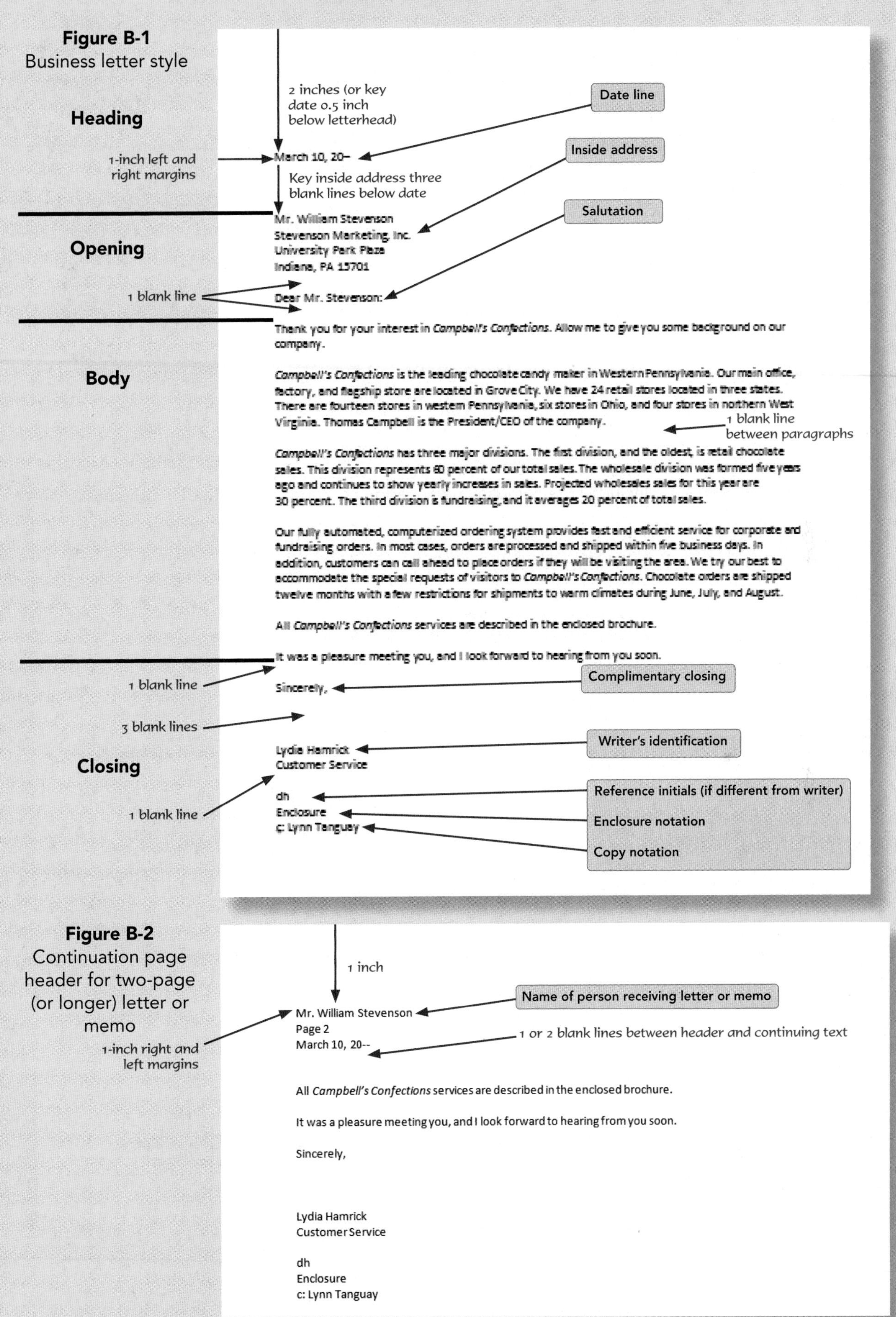

Figure B-1
Business letter style

March 10, 20–

Mr. William Stevenson
Stevenson Marketing, Inc.
University Park Plaza
Indiana, PA 15701

Dear Mr. Stevenson:

Thank you for your interest in *Campbell's Confections*. Allow me to give you some background on our company.

Campbell's Confections is the leading chocolate candy maker in Western Pennsylvania. Our main office, factory, and flagship store are located in Grove City. We have 24 retail stores located in three states. There are fourteen stores in western Pennsylvania, six stores in Ohio, and four stores in northern West Virginia. Thomas Campbell is the President/CEO of the company.

Campbell's Confections has three major divisions. The first division, and the oldest, is retail chocolate sales. This division represents 50 percent of our total sales. The wholesale division was formed five years ago and continues to show yearly increases in sales. Projected wholesales sales for this year are 30 percent. The third division is fundraising, and it averages 20 percent of total sales.

Our fully automated, computerized ordering system provides fast and efficient service for corporate and fundraising orders. In most cases, orders are processed and shipped within five business days. In addition, customers can call ahead to place orders if they will be visiting the area. We try our best to accommodate the special requests of visitors to *Campbell's Confections*. Chocolate orders are shipped twelve months with a few restrictions for shipments to warm climates during June, July, and August.

All *Campbell's Confections* services are described in the enclosed brochure.

It was a pleasure meeting you, and I look forward to hearing from you soon.

Sincerely,

Lydia Hamrick
Customer Service

dh
Enclosure
c: Lynn Tanguay

Figure B-2
Continuation page header for two-page (or longer) letter or memo

Mr. William Stevenson
Page 2
March 10, 20--

All *Campbell's Confections* services are described in the enclosed brochure.

It was a pleasure meeting you, and I look forward to hearing from you soon.

Sincerely,

Lydia Hamrick
Customer Service

dh
Enclosure
c: Lynn Tanguay

TABLE B-2 Parts of a Memo

Part of Memo	Location/Description
Heading	Starts 2 inches from top of page using plain paper or letterhead stationery or on 0.5 inch below memo letterhead. Consists of guide words ("MEMO TO," "FROM," "DATE," and "SUBJECT") in capital letters followed by a colon. Entries after guide words align at a 1-inch left tab setting. Use the date format shown in Figure B-3.
Body	Starts two blank lines below the memo heading; contains the message, single-spaced with one blank line between paragraphs.
Closing	One blank line below the last paragraph; includes reference initials (the typist's initials in small letters). Might also include an enclosure notation, a file name notation, and a copy notation or distribution list.

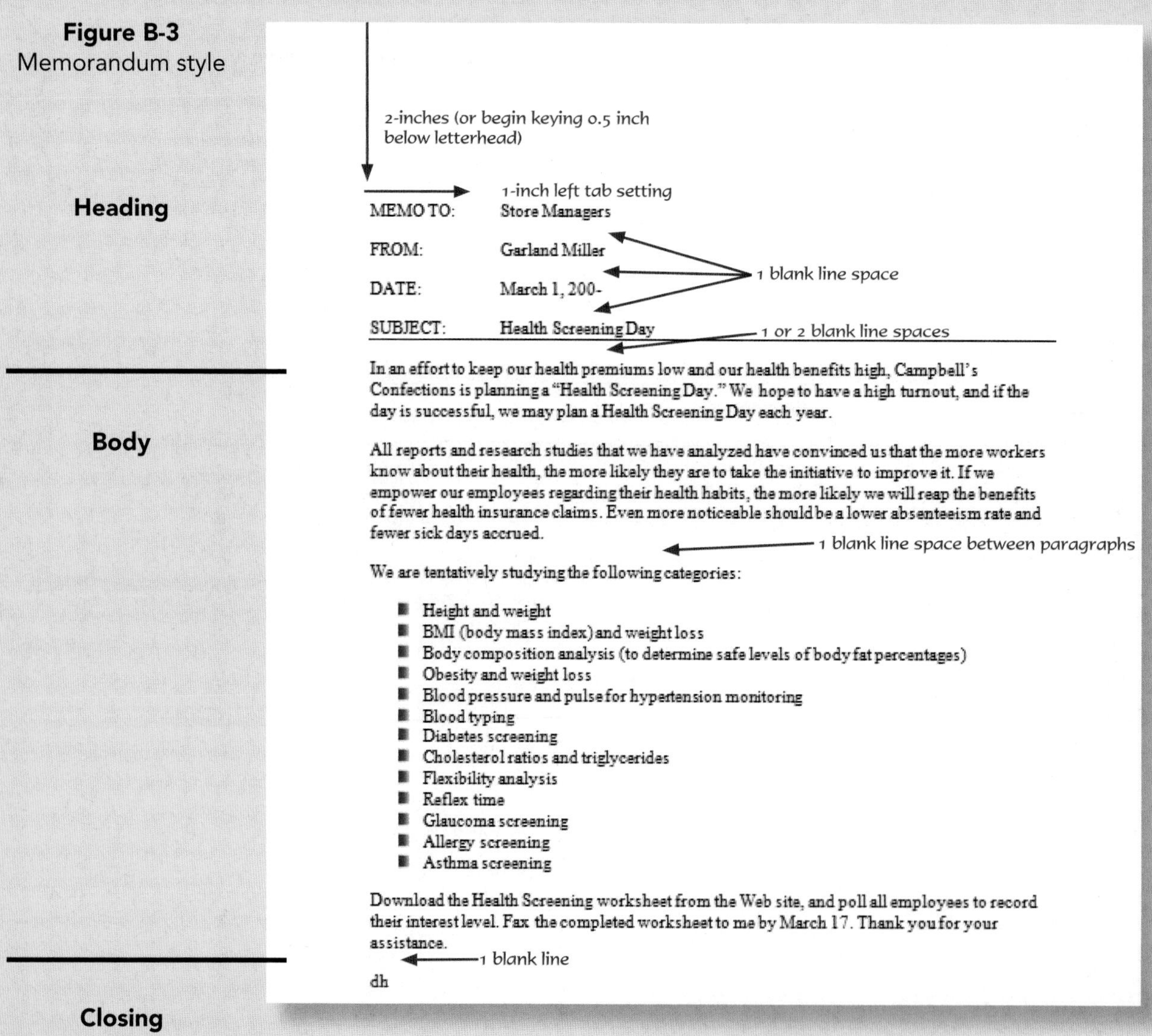

MEMO TO: Store Managers

FROM: Garland Miller

DATE: March 1, 200-

SUBJECT: Health Screening Day

In an effort to keep our health premiums low and our health benefits high, Campbell's Confections is planning a "Health Screening Day." We hope to have a high turnout, and if the day is successful, we may plan a Health Screening Day each year.

All reports and research studies that we have analyzed have convinced us that the more workers know about their health, the more likely they are to take the initiative to improve it. If we empower our employees regarding their health habits, the more likely we will reap the benefits of fewer health insurance claims. Even more noticeable should be a lower absenteeism rate and fewer sick days accrued.

We are tentatively studying the following categories:

- Height and weight
- BMI (body mass index) and weight loss
- Body composition analysis (to determine safe levels of body fat percentages)
- Obesity and weight loss
- Blood pressure and pulse for hypertension monitoring
- Blood typing
- Diabetes screening
- Cholesterol ratios and triglycerides
- Flexibility analysis
- Reflex time
- Glaucoma screening
- Allergy screening
- Asthma screening

Download the Health Screening worksheet from the Web site, and poll all employees to record their interest level. Fax the completed worksheet to me by March 17. Thank you for your assistance.

dh

Figure B-3
Memorandum style

GLOSSARY

() denotes Lesson number where term can be found.

Active window Window in which you are currently working that shows the title bar and taskbar button highlighted. (6)

Antonym Word that is opposite in meaning to another word. (3)

Ascending sort order Arrangement that places items in first-to-last or lowest-to-highest order, such as from A to Z or 0 to 9. (5) (14)

Attribute Setting, such as boldface or italics, that affects the appearance of text. (2) (11)

AutoComplete Automatic Word feature that suggests the completed word when you key the first four or more letters of a day, month, or date. (3)

AutoCorrect Automatic Word feature that corrects commonly misspelled words as you key text. (3)

AutoFormat Word feature that automatically changes formatting as you key text or numbers. (2)

AutoRecover Word feature that automatically saves open documents in the background. The backup version of the document can be recovered in case the original is lost or damaged in a power failure or because of a system problem. (1)

AutoText Word feature you can use to insert text automatically. (3)

Background pagination Automatic process of updating page breaks and page numbers that occurs while you are creating or editing a document. (10)

Bar tabs Used to make tabbed columns look more like a table with gridlines. A bar tab inserts a vertical line at a fixed position, creating a border between columns. (5)

Bibliography List of sources that identifies references consulted or cited in a report or manuscript. (22)

Boilerplate Standardized text used in business documents. (21)

Bookmark Item or location in a document that you name so you can refer to it later. (20)

Border Line, box, or pattern placed around text, a graphic, or a page. (4)

Building Blocks AutoText entries, cover pages, headers, footers, page numbers, tables, text boxes, and watermarks that are stored in galleries to be inserted in documents. (3) (10) (17)

Bulleted list List of items, each preceded by a bullet (•). Each item is a paragraph with a hanging indent. (4)

Caption Label that identifies a part of a document, such as a figure or table. A caption can include a number and usually includes text that describes the object, such as "Table 1. Delivery Schedule." (14)

Category axis Horizontal (or *x*) axis along the bottom of most charts; frequently refers to time series. (18)

Cell Portion of a table that is formed by the intersection of rows and columns. (13)

Character style Formatting applied to selected text within a paragraph; includes font, font size, and font style. (11)

Chart title Label that appears at the top of a chart and identifies the chart. (18)

Check Box Content Control A field that can be selected or cleared. (20)

Click and type Insert text or graphics in any blank area of a document. Position the insertion point anywhere in a document, click, and then key text. Word automatically inserts paragraph marks before that point and also inserts tabs, depending on the location of the insertion point. (4)

Clip art Ready-to-use drawings that can be inserted into a document. (16)

Clipboard Temporary storage area in the computer's memory used to hold text or other information that is cut or copied. (6)

Clips Multimedia files that can be clip art, photographs, movies, or sound files. (16)

Code Text written in a programming language to create a macro or other computer program. (21)

Collapse To hide body text and subheadings under a heading in Outline view. (23)

Color set Feature for applying color. It includes four colors for text and background, six accent colors, and two colors reserved for hyperlinks. (11) (16)

Comment Electronic note that you add to a document. In Visual Basic and other programming languages, text that is not part of the macro or program and identifies the macro or makes it easier to understand. In Visual Basic, comment lines must always begin with an apostrophe. (21) (24)

Comment reference mark Vertical line that appears where a reviewer has inserted a comment; the mark is color-coded to reviewer. (24)

Concordance file Two-column table of words to be located and indexed in a document. (23)

Contiguous text Any group of characters, words, sentences, or paragraphs that follow one another. (1)

Copy Method for copying text or other information, storing it on the Clipboard, and then placing it in a new location. (6)

Crop Trim a picture so that only a portion of the original shows. (16)

Cut and paste Method for moving text or other information by removing it from a document, storing it on the Clipboard, and then placing it in a new location. (6)

Cycle SmartArt graphic Illustrate a process that has a continuous cycle. (18)

Data marker Object that represents individual data points in a chart. (18)

Data point Single piece of datum in a chart. (18)

Data series Group of related data points plotted in a chart, originating from the datasheet rows or columns. Each data series is distinguished by a unique color. (18)

Data source Variable information in a mail merge, such as names and addresses, to use in personalizing the main document. (19)

Demote To move a heading to a lower level in Outline view. (23)

Descending sort order Arrangement that places items in last-to-first or highest-to-lowest order, such as from Z to A or 9 to 0. (5) (14)

Destination document File that displays information stored in a different file. For example, a Word document that displays a linked Excel worksheet. (14)

Digital signature An encrypted stamp of authentication. (24)

Document theme Feature that includes colors, fonts, and effects which affect the overall appearance of a document. (11)

Drag and drop Method for moving or copying text or other objects short distances by dragging them. (6)

Drawing canvas Rectangle graphic object in which you can draw multiple shapes and then size and format them as a group. (16)

Drawing objects Shapes, such as squares, circles, stars, banners, arrows, that you can draw and modify in Word. (16)

Drop cap Large letter that appears below the text baseline, usually applied to the first letter in the word of a paragraph. (2)

Drop-Down List Content Control A field that controls the choices that can be selected. (20)

Em dash Dash twice as wide as an en dash and used in sentences where you would normally insert two hyphens. (4)

Embedded worksheet Worksheet that exists only in the Word document or other file in which it is embedded. There is no corresponding Excel file. (14)

En dash Dash slightly wider than a hyphen. (4)

Endnote Text reference at the end of a document to credit the source of information or to offer additional explanation. (22)

End-of-cell marker Character that indicates the end of the content of each cell in a table. (13)

End-of-row marker Character to the right of the gridline of each row in a table; indicates the end of the row. (13)

Expand To display body text and subheadings under a heading in Outline view. (23)

Facing pages Document with a two-page spread. Right-hand pages are odd-numbered pages, and left-handed pages are even-numbered pages. (8)

Field Hidden code that tells Word to insert specific information, such as a date or page number. In a data source table, each item of information contained in a record. (3) (8) (19) (20)

Field code Merge field that appears in the main document as a placeholder for data from a data source. (19)

Field code syntax Field code text shown in a diagramlike format, indicating optional and required information and the required order for inserting that information. (20)

Field name In a data source table, the column heading of each category of information. (19)

File name Unique name given to a document saved in Word. (1)

File tab Tab that displays the Backstage View which lists the commands to create, open, save, and print a document. (1)

Find Command used to locate text and formatting in a document. (7)

First-line indent Indent for the first line of a paragraph. (4)

First-line indent marker Top triangle on the left side of the ruler. Drag the indent marker to indent or extend the first line of a paragraph. (4)

Floating graphic Graphic inserted on the drawing layer of a document so it can be positioned freely on the page, in front of or behind text and other objects. (16)

Font The design applied to an entire set of characters, including all letters of the alphabet, numerals, punctuation marks, and symbols. (2)

Footer Text that appears in the bottom margin of a page throughout a section or document. (10)

Footnote Text reference that appears at the bottom of a page to credit the source of information or to offer additional explanation. (22)

Form Standardized document used to request specific information. (20)

Formatting mark Symbol for a tab, paragraph, space, or another special character that appears on the screen, but not in the printed document. (1)

Function Predefined mathematical operation that can be used within a formula to process numerical data in a table. (14)

Gallery List of design options for modifying elements of a page. (10)

Gridlines Lines that mark the boundaries of cells in a table. (13)

Gutter margins Extra space added to the inside or top margins to allow for binding. (8)

Hanging indent Indentation of the second and subsequent lines of a paragraph. (4)

Hanging indent marker Bottom triangle on the left side of the ruler. Drag the marker to indent the second and subsequent lines in a paragraph. (4)

Hard-coded Number, color, font, or other property that is specified exactly in a computer program. (21)

Hard page break Page break inserted manually. Does not move, regardless of changes in the document. (9)

Header Text that appears in the top margin of a page throughout a section or document. (10)

Header row First or second row (if the table has a title row) of a table, in which each cell contains a heading for the column of text beneath it. (13)

Hierarchy SmartArt graphic Graphic that illustrates the top-down relationship of members of an organization. (18)

Hyperlink Text or graphic you click to move to another location. (24)

Hyphenation The process of dividing a word that cannot fit at the end of a line or of joining two words. (15)

I-beam Shape of the mouse pointer when it is positioned in the text area. (1)

Indent Increase the distance between the sides of a paragraph and the two side margins (left and right). (4)

Indent marker On Word's horizontal ruler, small box or triangle that you drag to control a paragraph's indents. (4)

Index Lists the page numbers where specific words, phrases, or subjects occur in a printed document. (23)

Inline graphic Graphic inserted in a line of text, on the same layer as the text. (16)

Insert mode Mode of text entry that inserts text without overwriting existing text. (1)

Insertion point Vertical blinking bar on the Word screen that indicates where an action will begin. (1)

Kerning Adjusting the amount of space between certain combinations of characters so a word looks evenly spaced. (17)

Key Tips Letters that appear over commands after you press the Alt key. Press the letter of the command you want to activate. The Key Tips may also be called *badges*. To turn off the Key Tips, press Alt again. (1)

Landscape Page orientation setting in which the page is wider than it is tall. (8)

Leader characters Patterns of dots or dashes that lead the reader's eye from one tabbed column to the next. (5)

Left and right indent Indent left and right sides of paragraph (often used for quotes beyond three lines). (4)

Left indent Indent paragraph from left margin. (4)

Left indent marker Small rectangle on the left side of the ruler. Drag the marker to indent all lines in a paragraph simultaneously. (4)

Legal blackline Word feature that lets you compare and merge two documents. The differences between the two documents appear in a new document as revision marks. (24)

Legend In a chart, guide that explains the symbols, patterns, or colors used to differentiate data series. (18)

Line break character Character that starts a new line within the same paragraph. Insert by pressing Shift+Enter. (1)

Line space Amount of vertical space between lines of text in a paragraph. (4)

Link Relationship between the data in a destination file and its source file, so that when the data are changed in one file, the other file is updated automatically to reflect the change. (14)

Linked style Paragraph formatting applied to selected text. (11)

List SmartArt graphic Graphic that illustrates groups and subgroups of information or blocks of information in a vertical or horizontal format. (18)

List style Formatting instructions applied to a list, such as numbering or bullet characters, alignment, and fonts. (11)

Lock To protect a form document, so the person filling out the form can have access only to the form fields. (20)

Macro Automated procedure consisting of a sequence of word processing tasks. You can create a macro by recording mouse commands and keystrokes or you can write one by using Visual Basic editor. (21)

Mail merge Process of using information from two documents (a main document and a data source) to produce a set of personalized documents, such as form letters or mailing labels and envelopes. (19)

Main document Document in a mail merge to be merged with a data source and sent to many people or printed on envelopes or labels. The main document is information that is constant (it does not change). (19)

Margins Spaces at the top, bottom, left, and right of the document between the edges of text and the edges of the paper. (8)

Markup Comments and tracked changes, such as insertions, deletions, and formatting changes. (24)

Markup balloon Comment or tracked change in the margin of a document in Print Layout view. (24)

Masthead Part of a newsletter that contains publication information, such as the address, telephone number, editorial staff names, frequency of publication, and so on. (17)

Matrix SmartArt graphic Graphic that illustrates relationships of objects to a whole in quadrants. (18)

Merge fields In a mail merge, placeholders inserted in a main document that indicate where to insert information from the data source. (19)

Mirror margins Inside and outside margins on facing pages that mirror one another. (8)

Module In Word, a container attached to a document or template and containing macro code. (21)

Multilevel list Numbering sequence used primarily for legal and technical documents. (4)

Nameplate Publication title with a distinctive typeface and graphic design. (17)

Navigation Pane Separate pane that displays a list of headings in a document; used to quickly navigate through the document and keep track of your location. (23) (24)

Negative indent Extends a paragraph into the left or right margin areas. (4)

Nested table Table that is contained within a single cell of another table. (14)

Nonbreaking hyphen Hyphen used in a hyphenated word or phrase that should not be divided at a line break. (15)

Nonbreaking space Space between words, defined by a special character, that prevents Word from separating two words. Insert by pressing Ctrl+Shift+Spacebar. (1)

Noncontiguous text Text items (characters, words, sentences, or paragraphs) that do not follow one another, but each appears in a different part of a document. (1)

Nonprinting character Symbol for a tab, paragraph, space, or another special character that appears on the screen, but not in the printed document. (1)

Normal style Default paragraph style with the formatting specifications 11-point Calibri, English language, left-aligned, 1.15 line spacing, 10 points spacing after, and widow/orphan control. (11)

Note separator Short horizontal line that separates text from footnotes. (22)

Numbered list List of items preceded by sequential numbers or letters. Each item is a paragraph with a hanging indent. (4)

Optional hyphen Indication where a word should be divided if the word falls at the end of a line. (15)

Organizer Feature that lets you copy styles from one document or template to another or copy macros from one template to another. (12)

Orientation Setting to format a document with a tall, vertical format or a wide, horizontal format. (8)

Orphan First line of a paragraph that remains at the bottom of a page. (9)

Outline Summary of a document based on heading levels. (23)

Overtype mode Mode of text entry that lets you key over existing text. (1)

Pagination Process of determining how and when text flows from the bottom of one page to the top of the next page in a document. (9)

Pane Section of a window that is formed when the window is split. A split window contains two panes. (6)

Paragraph Unique block of text or data that is always followed by a paragraph mark. (4)

Paragraph alignment Determines how the edges of a paragraph appear. (4)

Paragraph mark On-screen symbol (¶) that marks the end of a paragraph and stores all formatting for the paragraph. (1) (4)

Paragraph space Amount of space (measured in points) before and after a paragraph; replaces pressing Enter to add space between paragraphs. (4)

Paragraph style Formatting instructions applied to a paragraph; includes alignment, line and paragraph spacing, indents, tab settings, borders and shading, and character formatting. (11)

Parent table Table containing one or more nested tables. (14)

Placeholder text In a template (or a new document based on a template), text containing the correct formatting, which you replace with your own information. (12)

Plot area Rectangular area bounded by two axes in a chart; includes all axes and data points. (18)

Point Measure of type size; 72 points equals 1 inch. (2)

Portrait Page orientation setting in which the page is taller than it is wide. (8)

Positive indent Indentation between the left and right margins. (4)

Process SmartArt graphic Graphic that illustrates a progression or sequential steps toward a goal. (18)

Promote To move a heading or body text to a higher level in Outline view. (23)

Proofreaders' marks Handwritten corrections to text, often using specialized symbols. (1) (Appendix A)

Property Any information, such as the filename, date created, or file size, that describes a document. (1)

Proportional sizing Resizing an image while maintaining its relative height and width. (16)

Pull quote Sentence or quotation that is taken from a document and enlarged or set apart from the rest of the text for emphasis. (17)

Pyramid SmartArt graphic Graphic that illustrates foundation-based relationships. (18)

Quick Access Toolbar Toolbar containing frequently used commands and which is easily customized. (1)

Quick styles Various formatting options for text and objects that display as thumbnails in a gallery. (11)

Record In a data source table, a row of related information (such as name, address, city, state, and ZIP Code) for one person or business. (19)

Reference mark Number or other symbol marking text that is accompanied by a footnote or endnote. (22)

Relationship SmartArt graphic Graphic that illustrates the relationship of objects to a main object. (18)

Replace Command used to replace text and formatting automatically with specified alternatives. (7)

Reverse text White text on a colored background. (13) (17)

Reviewer Person who adds a comment or tracked change to a document. (24)

Reviewing pane Narrow horizontal or vertical pane that opens at the bottom or side of the screen to display revisions and comments. (24)

Revision bar Black vertical line that appears to the left of each line containing a revision. (24)

Revision mark Mark that Word applies to text that has been changed while the Track Changes feature is turned on. (24)

Ribbon Seven default tabs, each tab containing a group of related commands. (1)

Rich Text Content Control A field where users can enter information. (21)

Right indent Indent paragraph from right margin. (4)

Right indent marker Triangle on the right side of the ruler; drag the marker to indent the right side of a paragraph. (4)

Ruler Part of the Word window that shows placement of indents, margins, and tabs. (1)

Sans serif Font characteristic in which the font has no decorative lines, or serifs, projecting from its characters, such as Arial. (2) (17)

Scale Change the size of an image as a percentage of its original size. (16)

ScreenTip Brief explanation or identification of an on-screen item such as a Ribbon command. (1)

Scroll bar Bar used with the mouse to move right or left and up or down within a document to view text not currently visible on screen. (1)

Section Portion of a document that has its own formatting. (8)

Section breaks Double-dotted lines that appear on screen to indicate the beginning and end of a section. (8)

Selection Area of a document that appears as a highlighted block of text. Selections can be formatted, moved, copied, deleted, or printed. (1)

Selection rectangle Box formed by the sizing handles of a selected object. (16)

Serif Font characteristic in which the font has decorative lines projecting from its characters, such as Times New Roman. (2) (17)

Shading Applying shades of gray, a pattern, or color to the background of a paragraph. (4)

Shapes Ready-made shapes that are grouped by category: lines, basic shapes, block arrows, flow chart symbols, callouts, and stars and banners. (16)

Shortcut menu Menu that opens and shows a list of commands relevant to a particular item that you right-click. (2)

Sidebar Text box that is usually aligned on the right or left side of a page. It typically contains text that is related to but separate from the main document text. (17)

Size Change the size of an object. (16)

Sizing handles Squares or circles that appear around the border of a selected object and are used for resizing the object. (16)

Smart quotes Quotation marks that curl in one direction (“) to open a quote and curl in the opposite direction (”) to close a quote. (4)

SmartArt graphic Visual representation of ideas. (17)

Soft page break Page break automatically inserted by Word and continually adjusted to reflect changes in the document. (9)

Sort To arrange items in a particular order, such as alphabetical or numerical order. Sorting is often done on tables and lists but can also be performed on text paragraphs within a document. (5) (13) (14)

Source document File containing information to be linked to another file. For example, an Excel worksheet that contains information to be displayed in a Word document. (14)

Special characters Characters such as the trademark symbol™ or those used in foreign languages. (4)

Split bar Horizontal line that divides a document into panes. (6)

Split box Small gray rectangle located just above the vertical scroll bar. You can drag it down to split a document into two panes. (6)

Status bar Bar located at the bottom of the Word window that displays information about the task you are performing, shows the position of the insertion point, and shows the current mode of operation. (1)

Style Set of formatting instructions that you apply to text. (11) (17)

Style set List of style names and their formatting specifications. (11)

Subentries Index entries that are subordinate to the main index entries. (23)

Subtext Any heading or body text beneath a heading. (23)

Switches Parameter that controls the field display. Switches (or options) are inserted at the end of the field code and preceded by a back slash (\). (20)

Symbol Special character, such as the copyright symbol ©. (4)

Synonym Word that is similar in meaning to another word. (3)

Tab Paragraph-formatting feature used to align text. (5)

Tab characters Nonprinting characters used to indent text. (1)

Tab marker Symbol on the horizontal ruler that indicates a custom tab setting. (5)

Tab stop Position of a tab setting. (5)

Table Grid of rows and columns that intersect to form cells. (13)

Table of authorities List of cases, statutes, and other references that appear in a legal document. (23)

Table of contents List of topics contained in a document, arranged numerically by the page numbers where the topics appear. (23)

Table of figures List of captions and the pages where they appear in a document. (23)

Table style Formatting instructions applied to a table, such as borders, shading, alignment, and fonts. (11)

Table template Table based on a gallery of preformatted table designs. Usually contains sample data. (13)

Task pane Pane to the right or left of the text area that provides access to a variety of functions. (3) (6) (11) (16)

Template File that contains formatting information, styles, and text for a particular type of document. (12)

Text box Free-floating rectangle that contains text. (17)

Text wrapping Graphic option that lets text flow around an object or that positions the object behind or in front of text. (16)

Theme Set of formatting instructions for the entire document. (2) (11)

Thesaurus Tool you can use to look up synonyms for a selected word. (3)

Thumbnail Miniature representation of a page in Reading Layout view. (24)

Tick mark Division mark in a chart along the category (x) and value (y) axes. (18)

Title bar Bar that displays the name of the current document at the top of the Word window. (1)

Tracked changes Revision marks that show where an insertion, deletion, or other editing change occurred. (24)

Value axis Vertical (or y) axis in a chart, against which data points are measured. (18)

Watermark Transparent graphic or text placed behind text, adding dimension to the printed page by creating a layered effect. Often used on stationery. (17)

White space Unused space in a page layout that provides the necessary contrast for text and graphics. (17)

Widow Last line of a paragraph that remains at the top of a page. (9) (17)

Wildcard Symbol that stands for missing or unknown text. (7)

Wingdings Font that includes special characters, such as arrows. (4)

Workgroup templates Templates that are stored centrally on a network server. (20)

INDEX

D

E

F

L

M

Q

R

S

T

U

V

W

X

Y

Z

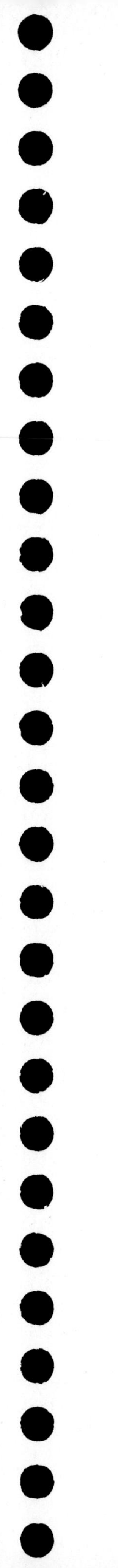